THE OFFICIAL HISTORY
of
ELBERT COUNTY
1790-1935

BY
JOHN H. McINTOSH

SUPPLEMENT
1935-1939

BY
STEPHEN HEARD CHAPTER
DAUGHTERS OF THE AMERICAN REVOLUTION
ELBERTON, GEORGIA

Southern Historical Press, Inc.
Greenville, South Carolina

This volume was reproduced from
A personal copy located in the
Publisher's private Library

All rights reserved. No part of this publication may be reproduced,
stored in a retrieval system, transmitted in any form, posted
on to the web in any form or by any means without
the prior written permission of the publisher.

Please direct all correspondence and orders to:
www.southernhistoricalpress.com
or
SOUTHERN HISTORICAL PRESS, Inc.
PO Box 1267
375 West Broad Street
Greenville, SC   29601
southernhistoricalpress@gmail.com

Originally published: 1940
ISBN #0-89308-871-4
All rights Reserved.
Printed in the United States of America

To My Daughters
Mary Louise and Elizabeth Arnold McIntosh
and to all children of Elbert County with the
sincere hope that they will preserve and transmit to their descendants the needs of
their worthy ancestry

"Those who do not cherish the memory of their ancestors do not deserve to be remembered by posterity"

—Edmund Burke

INDEX

	PAGE
MEMBERS OF STEPHEN HEARD CHAPTER, D. A. R.	v
PREFACE	vii
CHAPTER I	1

(General Samuel Elbert—Water Courses—Soil—Climate—Natural Resources—Local Acts of General Assembly Relative to Elbert County Prior to 1851—Congressional and Senatorial Districts—Superior Court Transfers.)

CHAPTER II 10

(Indians of Elbert County—Text of Deed Cancelling Indian Debts to Traders—Building of Heard's Fort—Early Settlements—Fort James and Dartmouth—Lord Gordon's Settlement.)

CHAPTER III 13

(The American Revolution—Attitude of Colonies—Tory Activity—Battle of Kettle Creek—Stephen Heard Wounded—Daniel McGirth—Nancy Hart—Mammy Kate—Heard Elected Governor—John and Thomas Cook—Major Land Grants of Elbert County.)

CHAPTER IV 32

(Conditions in Georgia—General George Mathews—Early Settlers — Petersburg — Settlement of Heardmont — Daniel Tucker—Text of Act Creating Elbert County—Militia Districts—First Officers of County—Minutes of First Superior Court.)

CHAPTER V 51

(Dozier Thornton—Van's Creek Baptist Church—Thomas Maxwell—Dove's Creek Church—Falling Creek and Bethel Churches—First Georgia Methodist Conference—Dr. Richard Banks—Beaverdam Preaching House.)

CHAPTER VI 70

(Alexandria—Beverly Allen Kills Forsythe—Voter's List, 1795—Elbert County Duels—Judge Jones—James Osgood Andrews—Text of Act Regulating Elberton—General Wiley Thompson—Bethlehem Church—War of 1812—Wiley Barron—Jonas Harrison.)

CHAPTER VII 91

(Elberton and Eliam Methodist Churches—Elberton First Baptist Church—Tamar Tyner—William Suttles—John Murrell—Ruckersville—Joseph Rucker—Acts of the Legislature Regarding Ruckersville—Philomathia Academy—Allen Daniel—Meteoric Shower of 1850—Blue-Eyed Negroes—Ante-Bellum Banjo Songs.)

CHAPTER VIII 108

(Outbreak of War Between the States—Elbert County Resolutions—Organization of Elbert County Commands—Colonel William M. McIntosh—Report of Actions in Virginia—Lieutenant Colonel R. P. Eberhardt—Reconstruction—Colonel Thomas W. Thomas—Samuel Snellings and "Betsy.")

INDEX—*(Continued)*

PAGE

CHAPTER IX 132
    (Retrospective—Organization William M. McIntosh Camp U. C. V.—Spanish-American War—George Hailey Fortson—Unveiling of Confederate Monument—Faculties of Elberton Institute and Elberton Seminary—Water Works Bond Election—Granite City Carnival—Organization Stephen Heard Chapter D. A. R.—Elbert County Schools—First Commercial Club Organized—Hawkes Library Established—First Selective Draft—John H. Jones Memorial Church—Organization E. B. Tate Post American Legion—Dead in World War—Business Progress.)

PART II—STATISTICAL SECTION 164
    List of early Elbert County residents whose name do not appear elsewhere 164
    National law makers of Elbert County 166
    State officers of Elbert County.. 166
    County officials of Elbert County... 168
    Election returns, 1902-1932 172
    Elberton Postmasters 176
    Lawyers of Elbert County 176
    Abstract of eighty early deeds from original instruments............ 177
    List of original land warrants on file in Clerk's office..................... 183
    Census of Elbert County 185
    Aggregate taxable value of Elbert County property—1894-1928 185
    Elbert County Revolutionary soldiers and their widows (partial list) 185
    Revolutionary officers of Elbert County 186
    Partial muster roll of Confederate soldiers from Elbert County 186
    Confederate soldiers commands partially unknown 197
    Dead in the War Between the States from Elbert County........... 198
    Soldiers of the War of 1812 who participated in Gold Lottery of 1832 202
    Old graves in Elbert County 202
    Justices of the Peace of Elbert County 205
    Judges of City Court of Elberton... 205
    Solicitors of the City Court of Elberton 205
    Mayors, Councilmen and Clerks of Elberton 206
    Members of Elberton Light Infantry, August 7, 1917..................... 208
    Early Ferries of Elbert County 209
    Abstracts of early wills and administrations 209
    Land lotteries of 1806, 1821, 1827, 1832 211
    Marriage records of Elbert County 226

SUPPLEMENT OF GENERAL INFORMATION 299

    Elberton rests on acres of diamonds 300
    Elberton—"The Granite Center of the South" 301
    Congressman Paul Brown 302
    Judge Clark Edwards, Jr. 302
    John Judson Brown 302
    City officials of Elberton 303
    Elbert County Schools 305
    Elberton Chamber of Commerce 305
    Elbert County Junior Chamber of Commerce 306
    Southern Marble and Granite Credit Service 306
    Wholesale Granite Manufacturers and Quarries 307
    Elberton Coca-Cola Plant 308

INDEX—(Continued)

PAGE

Elberton Oil Mills	308
The American Legion	308
The American Legion Auxiliary	309
The Service Star Legion	309
Jefferson Davis Chapter, U. D. C.	310
Elberton W. C. T. U.	311
Elberton Rotary Club	312
Elberton Kiwanis Club	313
Elberton Pilot Club	314
Elberton Garden Club	315
Georgia Sorosis Club	315
Civic League of Elberton	316
Markers placed by Stephen Heard Chapter, D. A. R.	316
A few of the graves marked by Stephen Heard Chapter, D. A. R.	317
Home site of Nancy Hart	318
The Elberton Star	318
Elberton Air Line Railway	319

GENEALOGICAL SECTION 321

Families of:

Adams	322
Allen	329
Allgood	342
Alston	345
Arnold	352
Banks	359
Barnett	364
Blackwell	368
Brewer	371
Brown	375
Butler	377
Cade	379
Carpenter	381
Carter and Family	383
Carter	384
Christian	388
Clark or Clarke	392
Joseph Clark and Larkin Clark	398
Cleveland	401
Crawford	407
George Barnett Conwell	408
Darden	412
Joseph Deadwyler	419
DuBose	420
Eberhardt	422
Eavenson	426
Fortson	427
Goolsby	432
Hailey or Haley	433
Carlton and Hall	437
Hammond	439
Hansard	440
Haynes	442
Heard	443
Henry	457
Herndon	458
Higginbotham	461

INDEX—(Continued)

	PAGE
Hudson	462
Hunt	468
Jones	473
Key	474
Lanier	481
LeGrand	485
Marks	486
Mathews	486
Maxwell	491
McIntosh or Mackintosh	508
McMillan	513
Middleton	514
Oliver	516
Rice	518
Stark	524
Swift	527
Thornton	529
Wall	540
Walthall	542
Webb	546
Wilhite	547
Willis	549
Woolridge	551
Worley	552
Wyche	554

HISTORY OF ELBERT COUNTY

To each member of the Publication Committee and to every one who assisted in this splendid work, I extend my sincere thanks.

EDNA ARNOLD COPELAND (Mrs. Z. W.)
Chairman, Publication Committee

Members of the Stephen Heard Chapter who made possible the publication of the Elbert County History by serving on the Publication Committee.

ARNOLD, MARY HILL (Mrs. C. A.) ....Regent
GROGAN, ADELINE STARKE (Mrs. G. C.) ....Vice-Regent
RICE, ELIZABETH HASLETT (Mrs. J. N.) ....Secretary
BELL, PAULINE EDWARDS (Mrs. H. S.) ....Treasurer
EDWARDS, JEWETTE WEBB (Mrs. Clarke) ....Auditor
HAYES, ELIZABETH FORTSON (Mrs. Z. C.) ....Registrar
IRVIN, LULA VERNER (Mrs. W. H.) ....Chaplain
COPELAND, EDNA ARNOLD (Mrs. Z. W.) ....Librarian
HANSARD, MARY (Miss) ....Historian
REEVES, ROSA WILLIS (Mrs. J. F.) ....Curator
BREWER, LULA TREADWELL (Mrs. S. S.) ⎫
ROGERS, EDNA (Miss)   ⎬ ....Chapter Representatives
TABOR, ZELMA ALLEN (Mrs. T. O., Jr.) ⎭

    BOWERS, LUCILLE BAKER (Mrs. W. M.)
    BROWN, FRANCES ARNOLD (Mrs. Paul)
    BYNUM, WILLIE SUE ADAMS (Mrs. H. R.)
    DENNIS, ROBERTA HEARD (Mrs. J. T.)
    DOHME, MARGARET HEARD (Mrs. C. L.)
    DICKINSON, MARGARET MARSH (Mrs. G. W.)
    DUNCAN, ANNA AULD (Mrs.)
    FORTSON, ELLIE (Miss)
    FORTSON, ETHEL WILKINSON (Mrs. F. S.)
    FORTSON, ADDIE BOWIE (Mrs. W. E.)
    HASLETT, SUE WORLEY (Mrs. George)
    HAWES, JULIA CADE (Mrs. A. S.)
    LEE, MARY CARITHERS (Mrs. Lester)
    MAXWELL, JANIE HULME (Mrs. T. M.)
    MINTER, BERNICE IVEY (Mrs. W. B.)
    MOORE, ANNIE LEE CADE (Mrs. R. F.)
    PAINE, NELLA SANBORN (Mrs. W. H.)
    PAYNE, THELMA WRIGHT (Mrs. H. B.)
    PATTERSON, MARION REEVES (Mrs. F. M.)
    PEEK, LULA (Miss)
    REID, SARA GOOLSBY (Mrs. I. D.)
    RICE, LEILA VICKERY (Mrs. R. L.)

ROGER, ALPHA (Miss)
ROGERS, SARA LEE (Mrs. Z. B.)
RUCKER, WILLIE VICKERY (Mrs. K. E.)
SEYMOUR, RUTH BROWN (Mrs.)
SMITH, NELL WILSON (Mrs. F. A.)
SNELLINGS, IRENE HEARN (Miss)
SNELLINGS, REBECCA (Miss)
STAPLETON, VERA BOND (Mrs. Raymonde)
TABOR, FANNIE HERNDON (Mrs. T. O., Sr.)
TATE, CARRIE HUDSON (Mrs. O. E.)
THORNTON, CLYDE ARNOLD (Mrs. D. J.)
THORNTON, ARNOLDINA (Miss)
TUTT, ELIZABETH SWIFT (Mrs. W. D.)
VICKERY, SALLIE THORNTON (Mrs.)
WARLICK, FRANCES RICE (Mrs. T. H.)
WATSON, LUCILLE TURNER (Mrs. H. H.)
WEBB, OLA JACKSON (Mrs. J. E.)
WRIGHT, MARY LIZZIE (Miss)

PAST REGENTS

Mrs. A. O. Harper, Mrs. H. K. Gairdner, Mrs. F. L. Bartow, Mrs. Z. W. Copeland, Mrs. George Grogan, Mrs. A. S. Hawes, Mrs. H. S. Jaudon, Mrs. S. P. Rampley, Miss Nora Jones, Miss Edna Rogers, Mrs. W. H. Paine, Miss Mary Lizzie Wright, Mrs. T. O. Tabor, Jr., Mrs. W. H. Irvin, Mrs. Z. W. Copeland.

Organized June 6, 1901.

PREFACE

In accepting the appointment as Official Historian of Elbert County, the author realized that a vast amount of research work would be necessary, and that many interesting incidents learned of would, of necessity, be eliminated. After, however, minutely examining many records, attempting always to deal with unbiased fairness, the author feels that the greater portion of essential matter is herein incorporated.

Elbert County is one of the older divisions of Georgia, and as such, is naturally rich not only in history, but legend and tradition as well. Many of America's most noted families have in the past had, and still have, descendants residing within its limits. Therefore, this history dealing with events having occurred in an old county, with a distinguished citizenry, must in the natural course be somewhat exhaustive.

The compilation of this work has not been an easy task, but every hour spent in its formation has given pleasure and satisfaction to the compiler. Its purposes are many. It has been written for those who have failed to secure valuable information from their forebears and, in consequence, know little of their ancestors. It has been written for the purpose of refreshing the memories of those of us prone to forget, but the primary purpose in view has been to preserve for future generations the history of a great county and an unexcelled people.

Many persons have rallied to the support of this important undertaking; but others, for reasons best known to themselves, have shown a spirit of indifference. The author feels that the latter class will be the first to criticise and complain of omissions.

To those who have so freely given access to family papers, documents and information they have gleaned from varied sources much credit is due, for without all this little success could attend this effort.

Special acknowledgment is made to the following persons: Hon. Peter Brannon, Montgomery, Alabama; Mrs. Annie McIntosh Wall, North Augusta, South Carolina; Professor Albert W. Matthews, Carlton, Georgia; Miss Ruth Blair, Atlanta, Georgia; Mr. John Frank Harper, Anderson, South Carolina; Mrs. Margaret Heard Dohme, Atlantic Beach, Florida; Mrs. Edgar L. Smith, Washington, Georgia; Mr. Silas Wright Heard, St. Louis, Missouri; Mrs. Janna Wilhite Bowden, Hampton, South Carolina; Mr. Guy E. Wood, Atlanta, Georgia; Miss Bunice Adams, Dyersburg, Tennessee; Mrs. F. C. Fox, Carnack, Texas; Mr. Hugh Middleton, Augusta, Georgia; Miss Annie Lou Maxwell, New York, New York; Mrs. Samuel Fortson, Augusta, Georgia; Dr. W. I. Hailey, Hartwell,

Georgia; Miss A. B. Lyons, Montgomery, Alabama; Dr. and Mrs. B. C. Teasley, Hartwell, Georgia; Mr. B. B. Poole, Washington, Georgia; Mrs. Edna Arnold Copeland, Mrs. Sarah Louise Arnold Jaudon, Mrs. Susan Fortson Wester, Mrs. Vesta Fortson Turnell, Mrs. Lucia H. Rucker, Mr. Guy G. Rucker, Mrs. Virginia Cleveland Wall, Miss Julia Webb, Mrs. Minor Carpenter Smith, Mrs. Mary Clark Fortson, Miss Edna Rogers, Mrs. Minnie Fortson Anderson, Mrs. Susan Worley Haslett, Mrs. Adeline Stark Grogan, Mrs. Zelma Allen Tabor, Ben H. Willis, Mrs. Julia Cade Hawes, Mrs. Mary Jane Arnold McIntosh, Mr. James McIntosh, Mrs. Annie Lee Cade Moore, Mrs. James Farmer, Mrs. Cora Thomas Tate, Mrs. Addie Harper Worley, Mrs. Thelma Wright Payne, Mrs. Norma Wright Hawes, Colonel William Fitzpatrick Jones, Mrs. Harry Herndon, Dr. Amos Smith, Mrs. Julia Wilson Smith, Mr. Parker B. Smith, Mrs. Kathleen Carroll Heard, Mrs. Roberta Heard Dennis, Mrs. George W. Dye, Miss Mary Elizabeth Wright, Mrs. Mary Tate Mattox, Miss Lenora Jones, Mrs. James F. Reeves, Mr. Alexander S. Lunsford, Miss Sally Henry, Miss Fanny Henry, Mr. J. E. Tate, Mrs. Mildred Henry Elliott, Mr. Thomas H. Verdell, Mr. William A. Rucker, Mr. Clark Edwards Jr., Mr. Paul Brown, Mr. C. L. Smith, Mrs. Elizabeth Swift Tutt, Mrs. Raymonde Stapleton, Col. Z. B. Rogers, Mr. L. H. Hunt, and Mrs. Poppy Dye Hammond, all of Elbert County.

J. H. M.

Elberton, Georgia
1935.

The Author

John Hawes McIntosh was born in Elbert County on November 26, 1895, the son of James and Mary Jane (Arnold) McIntosh. He was a member of a family which had distinguished itself early in the history of Georgia and which traces its lineage to the McIntosh or Mackintosh clan of Scotland.

An attorney by profession, he served variously as Secretary of the Tax Board of Elbert County, as County Attorney, and as Assistant Secretary of the Georgia Senate. He was a veteran of World War I.

Upon recommendation by the Grand Jury in 1929, he was appointed to the position of County Historian and authorized to "prepare a complete history of the formation, development and progress of said county from its creation up to February 12, 1933, together with the accounts of such persons, families and public events as have given character and fame to said county, the state and the nation." Through the cooperation of the Stephen Heard Chapter, Daughters of the American Revolution, the completed history was published in 1940.

Mr. McIntosh died at Elberton on June 7, 1956. By his marriage on June 19, 1918 to the former Fay Ann White, he was the father of two daughters, Mrs. J. W. Cook and Mrs. Leslie Baker, to whom he had dedicated his book, and both of whom survived him.

CHAPTER I

GENERAL SAMUEL ELBERT—WATER COURSES—SOIL—CLIMATE—NATURAL RESOURCES—LOCAL ACTS OF GENERAL ASSEMBLY RELATIVE TO ELBERT COUNTY PRIOR TO 1851—CONGRESSIONAL AND SENATORIAL DISTRICTS—SUPERIOR COURT TRANSFERS.

"Samuel Elbert was born in South Carolina in the year 1740. When quite young, becoming an orphan, he went to Savannah seeking employment. There he was engaged in mercantile pursuits until the beginning of the American Revolution. He became a member of the Council of Safety which was organized in 1775. In February, 1776, he was made a Lieutenant Colonel of a body of troops that was raised by the General Assembly of Georgia.

"In September of the same year, he was promoted to the rank of Colonel. In May, 1777, he commanded an expedition intended by Governor Button Gwinnett for the reduction of Florida.

"In April, 1778, Colonel Elbert performed an exploit that deserves special attention. Darien is situated on one of the channels of the Altamaha River, about 12 miles above its entrance into the Altamaha Sound, just north of St. Simon's Island. In the northern part of this island was the town Fredrica, founded by James Oglethorpe, and incidentally the only place in America where he lived in a house. Between the island and mainland there is a channel called Fredrica River. Colonel Elbert, who was situated with his force at Fort Howe, learned that three British vessels were anchored in the Fredrica River, near the town of the same name. This trio was composed of a brigatine, a sloop and a brig. On April 18th, he selected about three hundred men from the troops under his command and put them on board three galleys—the Washington, the Lee and the Bulloch. He placed a detachment of artillery with two field pieces on board one of the boats. With this little force, Colonel Elbert dropped down the river, across Altamaha Sound into Fredrica River. A landing was effected that evening about one mile below Fredrica on a bluff. About one hundred men went into the town where they were successful in capturing a few British sailors and marines before returning to the landing. The next morning the three little men-of-war boldly attacked the three larger vessels, which had spread terror along the American coasts, and were drawn up in line of battle. The weight of the American metal soon dampened the courage of the enemy, who took to their boats and abandoned their vessels, leaving everything on board. The Americans immediately took possession. It is interesting to note that not one of Elbert's men were killed or wounded during the hostilities.

"Later, in the month of December, 1778, after Samuel Elbert had received his commission as General, he was serving under General Howe in the defense of Savannah. The ritish found a route through a large swamp to the rear of the Americans. General Howe was amazed and dumbfounded when he found his forces attacked both front and rear. General Elbert, and his command, fought bravely, but the entire army was driven from the field and Savannah was occupied by the British.

"General Howe immediately retreated into South Carolina where he was disposed from his command to be succeeded by the intrepid General Lincoln.

"The patriot victory at Kettle Creek, in Wilkes County, on February 14, 1779, so alarmed Colonel Campbell that he hastily evacuated Augusta and retreated to a point below the mouth of Brier Creek. General Ashe was then ordered by General Lincoln to cross the Savannah River into Georgia. He took up a very strong position at the mouth of Brier Creek, in what is now Screven County, and straightway proceeded to weaken his forces by sending out reconnoitering expeditions. Colonel Campbell, with his large force of British, suddenly made a surprise attack on the Americans. The greater part of the raw militia was panic stricken and many fled without firing a gun. The left wing, composed of 60 regulars, under Colonel John McIntosh and about 150 Georgia militia under General Elbert, was an honorable exception and made a most determined and desperate resistance until nearly every man was killed, wounded, or captured. General Elbert, during the heat of the battle, fell into the hands of the British and was made captive.

"When General Elbert was finally exchanged he learned that Charleston had fallen, and that the South was almost completely over-run. He went northward to offer his services to General Washington who gladly accepted them. At the seige of Yorktown to which place Cornwallis had retreated, General Elbert was honored with the command of the 'Grand Deposit of Arms and Military Stores.'

"After the close of the Revolutionary War, General Elbert was made Major General of Georgia troops. He was elected Sheriff of Chatham County, and in 1785 was named Governor of Georgia by an almost unanimous vote. He had advanced marvelously indeed since the time when as a homeless, friendless, and penniless little boy, he had cast his lot with the infant State of Georgia. As a boy and a man he was always true and loyal. When success was possible he unfailingly achieved it. When reverses came he was always the more determined to succeed.

"After the British captured Savannah, James Wright, who had been the Royal Governor, returned and established a Tory Government. On July 6, 1780, he caused a disqualifying act to be passed rendering 150 persons named therein incapable of holding any office of trust, honor, or profit and commanded them all and singular, to bring in, his or their arms, swords, pistols and other warlike instruments for the use of his Majesty King George III and also rendered them subject to arrest.

"General Elbert was honored by having his name placed on this roll as, 'Sam'l Elbert, a rebel General.' As none of the patriots named in the aforesaid act aspired to office under King George III, they were not in the least disturbed and as all of them needed the weapons there was no rush to deliver them for the use of his high and mighty majesty.

"Samuel Elbert died November 2, 1788, loved and honored by the people he had helped to make free."

The author is indebted to Professor Albert W. Matthews, of Carlton, Georgia, for the use of the foregoing sketch. It first appeared in *The Elberton Star* during the year 1916.

The public spirited citizens erected some years since, on the south side of the Elberton Public Square, a modern hotel designed after the English style and in patriotic manner named the structure in honor of General Samuel Elbert. Elbert County can well be proud that she bears the name of so distinguished a patriot.

Elbert County lies between two rivers of importance—the Savannah and the Broad. Both of these streams are capable of developing tremendous power for the purposes of manufacturing. There are also many other streams flowing throughout the county. Among the more important are: Beaverdam Creek, Big Coldwater Creek, Little Coldwater Creek, Van's Creek, Falling Creek, Dove's Creek, Carter's Creek, Warhatchie Creek, Cedar Creek, and Deep Creek. Both the municipal water and power plants, owned by the City of Elberton, are situated on Beaverdam Creek a few miles from the city limits. These city owned enterprises have always been financially successfully and are largely responsible for the excellent city school system and exceedingly low municipal tax rate.

Elbert County, as a whole, is of a rolling and somewhat hilly nature. Near the various streams, however, there are **many fine** bodies of fertile bottom lands or savannas. The soil varies in different sections of the county. The United States Bureau of Chemistry and Soils in their survey of Elbert County in 1928, says in part in their report of some 50 pages:

> "The soils of Elbert County are typical of those in the southern Piedmont plateau. There are large areas having light gray or yellowish-gray sandy loam surface soils which are underlaid by red, yellow, or yellowish-red clay subsoils. The soils are very mellow and friable and are extremely easy to cultivate. On them crops mature earlier than on the heavy soils of the county and they are well suited to the production of cotton, peanuts, bright tobacco and garden vegetables, also for corn if

a sufficient amount of organic matter is available. In the southeastern part of the county is an extensive area of so-called flatwoods, and here the surface soil is loam and the subsoil is a plastic impervious clay. This soil, when properly handled, is fairly productive. Throughout the county are areas of dark red and red clay subsoils. These are the heavy soils of the county and are well suited to the production of alfalfa, clovers, and small grains. Small areas of second-bottom terrace land and extensive strips of first-bottom soils are developed along the rivers and larger creeks. These are excellent soils for the production of hay and corn crops.

"Good opportunities are offered settlers, especially on some of the clay-loam soils. The price of farming land depends on the character of the soil, the location and improvements thereon. Much good land can be purchased at a very low price."

This territory is fortunate in having abundant rainfall and moderate winters. The summers are mild and even during the hottest months the nights are rarely uncomfortable.

Elbert County is rich in natural resources although exploitation has been exceedingly slow. The huge granite deposits, which are of the highest grade, have of late been developed in a businesslike manner. Mica, graphite and gold are found, but have never received serious consideration.

The area of the county is 338 square miles and there are approximately 950 miles of public highways within its boundaries. Twenty-four miles of paving have been laid from the Madison County line to the line of South Carolina. Elbert County is bounded on the north by Hart; on the northwest by Franklin; on the east and southeast by South Carolina; on the south by Wilkes and Lincoln; on the west by Madison; and on the southwest by Oglethorpe.

Elberton is served by two railroads: the main line of the Seaboard Air Line and the Elberton-Toccoa Branch of the Southern. Excellent passenger and freight service are furnished by these corporations.

Before the granite deposits became of importance, the county was almost entirely populated by descendants of early Georgia settlers. Within the last 10 years natives of Italy, Scotland, Sweden and Spain have come in ever increasing numbers to engage in the rock industry. These people have proven themselves to be hard working and thrifty and take great interest in the civic improvement of the community. Practically all of them have become American citizens.

The following article written by Mrs. Edna Arnold Copeland dealing with the granite deposits, states:

"It is impossible to determine the nature and age of the original rock formations in the Elberton-Oglesby granite areas.

"In some sections of the area, due to several intrusions, the rock varies in color, texture, structure and mineral composition. The intruded origin of these masses is evident in many of the quarries, for the outline of the top of the intrusion and the jointing near the surface is curved. Often disintegration has gone so far that the boulders are left on the surface or are embedded in the residual soil. These, on account of their great size, are mistaken for small intrusions and are worked until their true nature is shown by quarrying.

"The rock in this area is primarily granite. The granite contains quartz, feldspar and biotite, with a heterregenous arrangement of those minerals. The gneisses contain the same minerals, but the various minerals tend to occur in individual groups of bands giving the stone the appearance of being formed in layers.

"The rock is biotite granite and gneisses. The most abundant mineral present is arthoclose feldspar, followed by quartz, microline feldspar, the piagioclase feldspar, albite and oligoclose and the mica biotite. The feldspars are white to dark gray in color, smooth and bright. The quartz is a colorless type of translucent dark color, glassy and with little luster. Biotite is a black, sparkling flat, micaceous mineral which gives the name biotite granite to the stone.

"Rock suitable for many purposes is found in this area. It grades from the finest memorial stone to rock well adapted to any purpose to which crushed rock is put. The stone is massive and unusually uniform in texture and mineral composition. The chief variation is in its color. It ranges from a very light grey to an unusually dark bluish grey. There are a few areas where the stone has a pinkish tinge.

"There is some variation in the hardness. Its ratio of obsorption is extremely low, varying from .06 to .10. Its specific gravity varies from 2.66 to 2.84 and the crushing strength averages 28,000 pounds to the square inch. The average weight of a cubic foot of this rock is about 167 pounds. Some of the darker varieties run as high as 177 pounds. The better grades of stone take a handsome polish.

"There is an adequate contrast between the hammered and polished surfaces. The various quarry faces show little effect of weathering, even on surfaces that have been exposed for many years. Its hardness and toughness makes it an ideal stone for road material and concrete work.

"The amount of stone in this area is inexhaustible. The quarries already opened have made no appreciable inroads upon the supply in sight. Several large deposits contain millions of tons that have not been touched.

"The cutting sheds in Elberton are equipped to do the finest work, and it is worth a trip here to see the stone in process of manufacture. Yet the granite industry in Elberton is young. The work done here is no more than a scratch on the tremendous amount of this stone. Twenty quarries could be operated where one is operated today.

"The stone is easy to get at, often being on the surface with little or no overburden. The weather allows constant working. Shipping points are numerous, freight rates are favorable, and labor cheap.

"Elberton ships her granite to every state in the Union and much to foreign lands."

The pioneers of the granite industry were Dr. N. G. Long, Thomas M. Swift, Sr., Peter Bartoni. Herbert L. Wiggs, and John Comolli. Jose Canales, Omer Bond, C. M. Mattox, Felix Salino, D. D. Mercer, D. H. Mercer, Parker Hunt, Cleve Allen, Coogler Brothers, J. F. Bailey, J. J. McLanahan, and Jack Fleming are among the leading quarriers and manufacturers at the present time (1935).

Note: More complete data found elsewhere in History. (See Supplement).

There are 24 sheds in the City of 'Elberton and approximately as many quarries in operation throughout the county.

Until a few years ago a number of Indian Mounds could be seen in several sections of the county. The majority of these have been entirely destroyed by the high waters of the Savannah and Broad rivers or by collectors in search of relics. The major portion of these mounds were found along the shores of the two principal rivers near the intersection at the point on lands owned at the present time by Mr. J. E. Tate. Mr. Tate is making laudable efforts to obtain and preserve all information concerning these mounds. Recently he has constructed a beautiful country home overlooking the former site of the largest of these mounds on the Savannah River. He is contemplating placing bronze tablets above the huge living room fire place relating the history of these words.

One of the mounds, a small portion of which can be seen, stood three miles above old Petersburg on the waters of the Savannah and was described by Bartram, the celebrated traveler and historian, who visited the spot in the latter part of the Eighteenth century:

"These wonderful labours of the ancients stand in a level plain, near the banks of the river, some 20 or 30 yards from it. They consist of conical mounts of earth and four square terraces. The great mount is in the form of a cone, 40 or 50 feet high and the circumference at its base some 200 or 300 yards, entirely composed of the loamy, rich earth of the low grounds; the top or apex is flat; a spiral path or track, leading from the ground to the top, is still visible, where now grows a large, beautiful spreading red cedar. There appear four niches excavated out of the side of this hill, at different heights from the base, fronting the four cardinal points. The niches or sentry boxes, are entered into from the winding path and seem to have been meant for resting places or look-outs. The circumjacent level grounds are cleared and planted with Indian corn at present; and I think the proprietor of these lands, who accompanied us to this place, said the mount itself yielded above 100 bushels in one season."

The local acts of the General Assembly of Georgia applying to Elbert County prior to the year 1851, as compiled by Thomas R. R. Cobb, follow:

Laid out from Wilkes County 1790, Vol. I, 163—Line between Elbert and Franklin established, 1803, Vol. II, 175; 1806, Vol. II, 304—Part set off to Madison, 1811, Vol. III, 181; 1819, Vol. III, 240.

Public Site and Buildings, 1790, Vol. I, 164; 1808, Vol. II, 493; 1809, Vol. II, 522—Authorized to build new court-house, 1816, Vol. III, 121.

ACADEMIES

Philomathia Academy incorporated, 1823, Vol. IV, 14—County Academy incorporated, 1823, Vol. IV, 20—Eudisco Academy incorporated, 1823, Vol. IV, 15—Elberton Female Academy incorporated, 1826, Vol. IV, 33—Act incorporating Philomathia Academy amended, 1827, Vol. IV, 45—Acts concerning County Academy consolidated, and more trustees appointed, 1828, Vol. IV, 52.

CHURCHES AND CAMP GROUNDS

Van's Creek Baptist Church incorporated, 1804, Vol. II, 179—Act repealing, 1806, Vol. II, 315—Methodist Camp Ground incorporated, 1833, Pam. 44.

ELECTION DISTRICTS AND ELECTIONS

Elections to be held in Major Allen's Battalion at Simeon Henderson's, or the future batallion muster ground; at Dobb's in Dobb's Batallion, or at future muster ground; and at Big Holly Springs and at the court-house for Major Richardson's Batallion, 1825, Vol. IV, 165; at Ruckersville, 1827, Vol. IV, 173—Compensation for carrying up precinct returns, 1834, Pam. 111—Elections at the store of Asa Dobbs, 1835.

POOR

1808, Vol. II, 490—Tax for their benefit, 1826, Vol. IV, 294—Inferior Court authorized to establish an asylum, 1828, Vol. IV, 139; 1834, Pam. 42.

ROAD LAWS

Amended as to Elbert, and several other counties, 1816, Vol. III, 777—Penalty on defaulting commissioners, who are to be presented by the grand jury, 1826, Vol. IV, 392—Justices of the inferior court empowered to lay a road tax, and let out the roads to be repaired by contract, 1836, Pam. 245.

SHERIFFS

1811, Vol. III, 190—Allowed to advertise in Milledgeville, 1827, Vol. IV, 406—Sheriff's compensation for summoning jurors, 1836, Pam. 252.

FISH

In Savannah River, 1812, Vol. III, 488; Vol. III, 506.

FERRIES

Allen's Ferry at Tucker's Landing, on the Savannah, 1831, Pam. 55—Deadwyler's Ferry, at the junction of the N. and S. forks of Broad River, 1831, Pam. 55—Nelms' across Broad River, 1836, Pam. 127—Oliver's (formerly Webb's) across the same river, 1836, Pam. 131—Denny's Ferry across Broad River, 1822, Vol. IV, 375.

EXTRA TAXES

1807, Vol. II, 423; 1815, Vol. III, 904; 1826, Vol. IV, 294; 1834, Pam. 234.

ELBERTON

Acts for its regulation, 1803, Vol. II, 144—Limits and jurisdiction enlarged, 1808, Vol. II, 500—Acts more fully regulating it, 1824, Vol. IV, 454—Act amended, 1828, Vol. IV, 479.

PETERSBURG

Commissioners appointed, 1802, Vol. II, 92—Act amended, 1804, Vol. II, 182—Flour inspection, 1814, Vol. III, 329—Commissioners appointed for the better regulation, 1828, Vol. IV, 478—To open the streets, 1831, Pam. 231.

RUCKERSVILLE

Commissioners appointed for its better regulation, 1822, Vol. IV, 442.

LOCAL ACTS, 1836-1850

ACADEMIES

Farmer's Academy incorporated, 1841, Pam. 5.

ELECTIONS

Precinct established at Mt. Pleasant Academy, 1837, Pam. 108—At Centerville, 1839, Pam. 180—At N. Duncan's, 1843, Pam. 53—Changed from B. Thornton's to B. Barrow's, 1840, Pam. 164—From academy to factory at Anthony Shoales, 1850, Pam. 164.

CAVALRY COMPANY

Incorporated in Ruckersville, 1837, Pam. 171.

LINES

Part added to Madison, 1837, Pam. 69.

JURORS

Grand and petit compensated, 1837, Pam. 162—Act amended as to appropriate the fees collected by the clerks, 1838, Pam. 112—Amended 1841, Pam. 151—Amended 1850, Pam. 291.

TAX

Extra to build court-house, 1850, Pam. 380.

TOWNS

Ruckersville charter amended, 1839, Pam. 84; 1845, Pam. 112; 1847, Pam. 43.

ROAD LAWS

Amended as to Elbert, 1837, Pam. 235—John D. Watkins authorized to build turnpike around Anthony's Shoales, 1850, Pam. 366

Ebert County, since its creation, has been placed in the following Congressional Districts, Senatorial Districts, and Superior Court Circuits:

CONGRESSIONAL DISTRICTS

3rd.	December 22, 1825—December 18, 1826.[1]
6th.	December 23, 1843—February 22, 1850.[2]
8th.	February 22, 1850—March 23, 1861.[3]
6th.	March 23, 1861—October 26, 1865.[4]
5th.	October 26, 1865—July 30, 1872.[5]
8th.	July 30, 1872—August 25, 1931.[6]
10th.	August 25, 1931—to date.[7]

[1] Dawson, pp. 161, 168. [2] Acts 1843, p. 54. [3] Acts 1849-1850, p. 115. [4] Confederate Records, I, p. 732 and Code of Georgia, 1860, p. 12. [5] Confederate Records IV, p. 146. [6] Acts 1872, p. 12. [7] Acts 1931, p. 46.

SENATORIAL DISTRICTS

36th.	December 23, 1843—January 21, 1850.[1]
37th.	January 21, 1850—January 19, 1852.[2]
30th.	July 2, 1861—to date.[3]

[1] Acts 1843, pp. 15, 17. [2] Acts 1849, 1850, p. 367. [3] Acts 1851, 1852, p. 48.

SUPERIOR COURT CIRCUITS

Western Circuit, December 10, 1790—December 19, 1818.[1]
Northwestern Circuit, December 19, 1818—to date.[2]

[1] Watkins, pp. 429, 480. [2] Lamar, p. 361.

The Legislature of Georgia has been generous in honoring the memory of citizens of Elbert County. Four counties of the state bear the names of Elbert County celebrities: Heard, created in 1830, named in honor of Governor Stephen Heard; Bibb, created in 1822, named in honor of Dr. William Wyatt Bibb; Hart, created in 1853, named in honor of the intrepid Nancy (Morgan) Hart; and Banks, created in 1858, named in honor of Dr. Richard Banks. Alabama, too, honored Dr. William Wyatt Bibb by naming a county in his honor.

CHAPTER II

INDIANS OF ELBERT COUNTY—TEXT OF DEED CANCELLING INDIAN DEBTS TO TRADERS—BUILDING OF HEARD'S FORT—EARLY SETTLEMENTS—FORT JAMES AND DARTMOUTH—LORD GORDON'S SETTLEMENT.

The Indian, whose origin is lost in antiquity, held unmolested sway over all the territory lying between the Savannah and Broad rivers until the Eigtheenth century was well advanced.

The territory from which Elbert County was created was a portion of the hunting and burial grounds of the Cherokee and Creek Indians. There is room for considerable doubt regarding a large number of Indian villages which were supposed to have flourished in what is not Elbert County, but in that portion which now composes Hart County, it may be reasonably assumed that such villages existed there. Physical evidence, such as mounds, beads, arrow-heads, and bits of pottery found within territory now embraced in Elbert County proves beyond doubt that the Indians hunted, fought battles and buried their dead throughout this area.

There is an island in the Savannah River, just off the Elbert County shore, now known as McCalla's Island, but formerly known as Heard's Island. It was a portion of one of the land grants to Governor Stephen Heard for his patriotic activities during the period of the American Revolution. This body of land, comprising several hundred acres, has furnished ample proof of Indian interments. Many old residents recall having seen skeletons, beads, pottery, stone axes and tomahawks brought from this island after the high waters, which often inundate it, had receded.

In the year 1773, the Indians of upper Georgia had become indebted to the traders of Augusta and Savannah in a sum far exceeding $100,000.

King George III, after many petitions directed to him for some means of redress, purchased in that year, through Sir James Wright, a large tract of land for approximately $200,000 from the Creeks and Cherokees. This tract included the present counties of Elbert, Wilkes, Hart, Oglethorpe, Lincoln, and portions of Greene, Talliaferro, and Madison. The treaty of purchase was made at Augusta July 1, 1773, and this territory became known as the "Ceded Lands." Enough of the purchase price was withheld to pay the Indian's obligations to the traders.

In the year 1777, all of the Ceded Lands were, by the State Constitution, created into Wilkes County. This county bears the name of John Wilkes, a member of the English Parliament, who bitterly opposed the measures directly responsible for the outbreak of the Revolution. So staunch was his opposition to the burdensome taxation placed on the colonies that he became a martyr to the right of a Free Press.

Towards the close of the year 1773, Stephen Heard, a Colonial Captain, formerly under the command of Colonel George Washington, and his brother, Barnard Heard, led a band of Virginians to a site on which the town of Washington, Georgia, now stands. At this place, on the first day of January, 1774, this band of cavalier adventurers broke earth for the erection of a stockade fort, called Heard's Fort in honor of their leader. Heard's Fort was destined to play a prominent role in the history of Georgia.

Shortly after this time a band of North Carolinians settled in this section. The families of Mercer, Dooly, and Murray were of this company.

A spirit of rivalry soon became evident and the strife between the two became almost feudal in character. The Virginians were cavaliers; the North Carolinians unpretentious and democratic.

The direct outcome of this feud, between these early settlers, was the establishment of two separate and distinct political factions in Georgia. The feud grew so rapidly and became so widespread in nature that the entire state was finally involved. For several decades it remained the one real issue in Georgia politics.

These settlements, due to the sturdy and frugal nature of the North Carolinians and the dare-devil spirit of the pleasure loving Virginians, were successful from their inception. They, of course, met with many hardships, disappointments and even calamities, but were, on every occasion, able to withstand the storm.

The living conditions were, at first, of necessity crude, but as time passed and more Virginians came, the customs to which they had been used were resumed and what might well be termed a small Virginia was firmly established in the wilds of Georgia.

While comparatively few Virginians settled in the territory now composing Elbert County most of the North Carolinians did and it was but a short time until the Virginians followed them.

The first real settlement to be made upon Elbert County soil was that of Dartmouth which stood on the site which was in after years occupied by the important town of Petersburg. The number of inhabitants is unknown, but it was of sufficient importance to command the erection of a stockade, called Fort James, for its protection. A land court was held at Dartmouth from September, 1773, through June, 1775, for the purpose of disposing of the Ceded Lands.

Fort James, in the spring of 1776, according to William Bartram, was manned by 50 well mounted and equipped rangers. The accoutrements of each ranger consisted of a rifle, two pistols, a hanger, a powder horn, a shot pouch, and a tomahawk.

This four square stockade, for such it was, stood at what is now known as "The Point." Here the Broad and Savannah Rivers unite forming a neck of land roughly resembling an arrow point. A number of swivel guns were placed at strategic intervals for its defense. The erection of this fort is ample proof that although a treaty of peace had been made with the Indians in 1761, and also a treaty of cession had been consummated in 1773, the settlers feared that the Indians might still attempt to drive them out.

In all probability Fort James stood for a number of years after the visit of Bartram and rendered valued service to the town of Petersburg. All physical signs of the location of the stockade have, for years, been obliterated.

While there is no actual proof to substantiate the belief, it is unquestionably reasonable to assume that Fort James was manned by Scots who came to the Dartmouth territory with Lord George Gordon. Several years previous to the visit of Bartram, Lord Godon brought a colony of Scots to America and settled on lands now embraced within the boundaries of Elbert County. These thrifty commoners gave their indentures for a period of five years to pay for their passage and supplies. Gordon had pictured the new country, to which they had so trustingly embarked, as Utopian.

For some time all went well. Lands were cleared, cabins built, crops planted and a number of wives and sweethearts came from Scotland to join them. These frugal people were well content in their new surroundings.

At the outbreak of the Revolution, Lord Gordon immediately sold the indentures to whatever purchaser he could find, collected his money, and fled to England. This was, of course, virtually selling the Scots into slavery.

These people appalled by such treatment at the hands of a British lord at once joined their destinies with the colony of Georgia and many of them served with distinction throughout the Revolution.

Among these colonists were the families of McKee, McKay, McDowell, McKiver, McKluskey, Cameron, and Fergus. Some of them later returned to Scotland, but not until they had, with the honesty native to the Scots, paid in full all monies still owing on their unfortunately made indentures. It is strange to note that not one of these families have descendants living in Elbert County today.

CHAPTER III

THE AMERICAN REVOLUTION—ATTITUDE OF COLONIES—TORY ACTIVITY—BATTLE OF KETTLE CREEK—STEPHEN HEARD WOUNDED—DANIEL McGIRTH—NANCY HART—MAMMY KATE—HEARD ELECTED GOVERNOR—JOHN AND THOMAS COOK—MAJOR LAND GRANTS OF ELBERT COUNTY.

At the beginning of the Revolution there were three distinct classes of people living in colonial territory. One class believed that the British Government, under which their ancestors had so long lived, should be supported with loyalty and fidelity. This class had benefited materially from royal favor and desired to take no chances on their future prosperity. Many of them became active Tories and were guilty of many of the worst depredations of the struggle. The second class recognized and openly admitted that there were certain wrongs which should be righted, but insisted that this could be accomplished by arbitration and without an open break. The third class was composed of such men as Samuel Adams, James Otis, Lachland McIntosh, George Washington, Charles Carroll, and John Hancock. They believed that if the rights of the colonies were consistently ignored after they had, time after time, been pointed out, the only manner in which relief could be obtained was by openly fighting for it. As time passed and the pleas of the colonies went unheard this third class became open agitators. In this manner they became more compactly organized and thus secured the upper hand.

It is great error to suppose that the people of America were at any time unanimously in favor of independence, or even favored the least resistance. In New England the Revolution was born (as was later the War Between the States), and yet approximately one-fourth of its population opposed any action whatsoever. In the Central States the proportion was, perhaps, one-half and in the South it was even greater. This ratio held true even during the major portion of the second year of the war.

Georgia, as a whole, at the inception of the Revolution, might have been said to have been slightly pro-British in sentiment. It was the youngest of all the colonies and had received from King George III, in consequence, the greatest consideration. Sir James Wright, the Royal Governor and Superintendent, despite many partisan historians, who have attempted to picture him in a false light, was a wise and excellent official rendering conscientious allegiance to his royal patron and benefactor. His influence was undeniably great and it was felt throughout the whole colony, even in the uppermost parts of Wilkes County which is now Elbert, and then the last outpost of Georgia civilization.

Wilkes County, at the outset, was no exception to the rule and was divided in opinion. The Virginians, many of them being descendants of younger sons of English, Scotish and Irish noblemen, though living under new conditions on the very edge of the wilderess, still clung to Great Britain as their mother nation.

The North Carolinians, most of whom were of excellent yoeman birth, felt far less sentiment and expressed themselves in most instances as being heartily in favor of a speedy, and if need be, bloody separation.

It is not unreasonable to assume that had the Tories been less active in Wilkes County, in all likelihood, the up-country would have taken scant interest in the ultimate outcome of the Revolution. "The Hornet's Nest," as Wilkes County was later designated by the Tories, would have remained inactive, but such was not destined to be the case.

The Tories in Georgia were very active even before the transfer of major hostilities to the South. The settlements in Wilkes County were forced to suffer daily harassments from them and their Indain allies. What is now Elbert County territory, being situated near the Indian country, suffered many wanton acts of barbarism. Dwellings were burned, crops destroyed, cattle spirited away, fathers murdered and mothers and protectless children driven from their homes, and, in many instances slain and scalped. In truth, it was war to the axe, to the torch, and to the knife in the territory lying between the Savannah and Broad Rivers.

Stephen Heard, one of the most ardent patriots, while living in Wilkes County, returned to his home from a military conference in Augusta to find that his wife and their young adopted daughter, a child of Mrs. Heard's deceased sister, had been driven from his home. It was during the middle of a severe winter and both the wife and their young adopted daughter, subsequently died from the exposure. Such acts of unnecessary cruelty caused the crystallization of sentiment, which, in truth, made Wilkes County a veritable "Hornet's Nest" for the British troops and Tories.

Major Barnard Heard, a brother of Stephen Heard, and their father, John Heard Junior, were captured by the Tories and taken to Augusta. A drumhead court martial sentenced them to be hanged as rebels. Although they requested the death of honorable' soldiers, by shooting, they were insultingly refused. Fortunately, on the eve of the seige, they made their escape and were thus able to continue their prominent part in the crusade for independence.

Major Heard was actively engaged in many battles and survived the war to become a leading citizen and office holder of Wilkes County.

The victory of the Patriots at Kettle Creek, in Wilkes County, on February 17, 1779, unquestionably turned the tide of warfare in the South. When the glad news reached the other colonies new determination was the result. Although this action has never received its proper place among the battles of the Revolution it was one of the major engagements and will, in time, be recognized as such.

In February, 1779, Colonel Boyd crossed the Savannah River at the Cherokee ford, the place of crossing between South Carolina and Elbert County, with a command exceeding more than 800 able and well equipped men. Here he encountered a vastly inferior force of Americans and a heated skirmish took place with the result that he lost in killed and wounded approximately 100 men. This was not his only loss for 25 of his men deserted to the Patriots. The fighting was of short duration and when the Americans had retired Boyd continued his march towards the present town of Washington. On the morning of St. Valentine's Day he halted at a farm near Kettle Creek.

In the meantime, February 12th, Pickens, Dooley, Clark, and Heard learning of his whereabouts from, it is said, the redoubtable Nancy Hart, cautiously pursued him and camped the following night within four miles of the enemy.

Early on the morning of the 14th, Boyd, with astounding carelessness, allowed his men to disperse in various directions for the purposes of gathering food supplies and fire wood. It was the universal practice of the Tories to forage the country through which they passed and confiscate all food supplies and live stock in the area. Order was exceedingly lax and few, if any, sentries had been posted. The Tory army, realizing their greater numerical strength, and foolishly discounting the determination and bravery of the Americans, had no inkling of the fact that they were closely pursued.

Colonel Pickens, in command of the Americans, ordered the position of the enemy quietly reconnoitered. This having been successfully accomplished the Patriots advanced in three divisions: the right wing under Colonel Dooley; the left under Colonel Clark, and the center led by Pickens. Strict orders were given not to fire a gun until within 25 paces of the enemy.

Boyd, by this time, having learned of the impending attack, took command of all the available men and met with bravery the center under Pickens. His line was partially protected by a fence of fallen rails which gave him no small advantage over the Americans entirely in the open.

Colonel Pickens, at once recognizing this disadvantage, drew off at double-quick to a small hill on his right and in this manner flanked the troops of Boyd.

On the first sustained fire by the Americans, Colonel Boyd fell mortally wounded and his men fled in disorder across the creek.

Major Spurgen, who now assumed command of the British forces, gallantly rallied them and the battle again became fierce.

After Spurgen had assumed command it appeared that the British, so superior in numbers, were destined to force the Americans to retire, but such was not the case for the invincible Clark rallied his men showing superb military genius.

Seeing the Patriots were about to be overcome he followed a path leading to a ford across the creek and under a sustained fire from the enemy gained a hill in the rear of the Tories. The troops under his command at this time numbered about 60 and all of them were Georgians. Among this number were: Major Barnard Heard, Captain Drury Cade, Benjamin Hart, Austin Dabney, William Bailey, William Harper, Ambrose Beasley, and Thomas A. Carter.

During the greater part of the engagement Colonel Boyd, suffering acutely from his wounds, lay within the line of fire watching the outcome.

The enemy were now between two balling fires and were forced to flee in great disorder.

At the close of the action, and when order had to some measure been restored, Colonel Pickens went to Boyd and offered to serve him in any possible manner.

Colonel Boyd thanked him and raising himself slightly from the ground said, "Had I not fallen your victory would have been defeat."

According to Captain Hugh McCall, who was actively engaged in the battle, Boyd said, "I marched from my rendezvous with 800 men of which number 100 were killed and wounded or deserted at the Savannah River; and on the morning of this action I had 700 men under my command. Colonel Campbell had promised that McGirth would join me with 500 men at Little River, but this he failed to do."

After talking to Captain McCall for a few moments he requested that someone be left to give him water and bury him in a decent manner after his death. He then turned to Colonel Pickens, who stood looking down at him, and requested that he write a letter to Mrs. Boyd and send her certain articles about his person. He died early in the night and all of his request were complied with.

Many men who resided in what is now Elbert County were engaged in this battle. The following named undoubtedly were actively engaged and, perhaps, many others of which this is no record: Colonel Stephen Heard, Major Barnard Heard, Benjamin Hart, Austin Dabney, Dionysius Oliver, William Bailey, William Harper, William Allen, Robert Harper, Captain Drury Cade, Thomas A. Carter, Mr. Easter, Ambrose Beasley, Mr. Arnold, and Mr. Cosby. The M. Cosby mentioned in all likelihood was Richmond T. Cosby who in after years served in the Georgia Legislature from Elbert County.

During this period the famous Nancy Hart performed her magnificent deeds of bravery. Due to many conflicting stories, regarding her many exploits, it is doubtless well to allow the reader to consider her career somewhat at length and from the viewpoints of several historians. In this manner one may be able to arrive at an unbiased conclusion.

Mr. Snead, a connection of the Hart family, said of her:

"On one evening she was at home with the children, sitting around the log fire, with a large pot of soap boiling over the fire. Nancy was busy stirring the soap and entertaining her family with the latest news of war.

"The houses in those days were all built of logs, as well as the chimneys. While they were thus employed, one of the family discovered someone from the outside peeping through the crevices of the chimney and gave a silent intimation to Nancy. She rattled away with more and more spirit, now giving exaggerated accounts of the discomfortures of the Tories, and again stirring the boiling soap, and watching the place indicated for the reappearance of the spy. Suddenly, with the quickness of lightning, she dashed the ladle of boiling soap through the crevice full in the face of the eavesdropper, who, taken by surprise, and blinded by the soap, screamed and roared at a tremendous rate, whilst the indominitable Nancy went out, amused herself at his expense, and with gibes and taunts, bound him fast as her prisoner."

White, in his "History of Georgia," says:

"Soon after the close of the Revolution she removed with her family to Brunswick, then a frontier place. She was the mother of six sons, Morgan, John, Benjamin, Thomas, Mark, Lemuel, and two daughters, Sallie and Reziah. Her oldest daughter Sallie, married a man by the name of Thompson, who took largely of the qualities of Nancy. Sallie and Mr. Thompson followed Mrs. Hart to Brunswick several years later. Upon their journey a most unfortunate affair occurred. In passing through Burke County, they camped for the night on the roadside. Next morning a white man was employed as a wagoner and on being ordered by Thompson, in a preemptory manner, to do some particular thing, he returned an insolent answer, and refused. Thompson, enraged, seized a sword, and with a single blow severed his head from his body. He then with apparent unconcern mounted the team, and drove on himself until he came to the first house, where he stopped and told the inmates, "I just cut off a fellow's head at the camp and you best go down and bury him!" He then drove on, but was pursued and taken back to Waynesborough, and confined in jail. This brought the heroic Nancy to the up-country again. She went to Waynesborough several times and a few days after her appearance thereabouts Thompson's prison was found open, and he gone!''

"Mrs. Hart, speaking of this occurrence, said rather exhaultingly, 'That the way with them all. Drat 'em, when they get in trouble they always send for me!'

"Not long after their removal Nancy lost her husband. But after paying suitable respect to his memory, she consoled herself, like most other good wives who have the luck, by marrying a young man, with whom she lifted up her stakes and set out among the early pioneers for the wilds of the West.''

The Yorkville (S. C.) Pioneer, in a sketch published about the middle of the year 1850, gives the following:

"Nancy Hart and her husband settled before the Revolutionary War a few miles above the ford on Broad River in Elbert County, Georgia. An apple orchard still remains to mark the spot.

"In altitude, Mrs. Hart was a patagonian, and remarkably well limbed and muscular. She was a sharpshooter, nothing was more common than to see her in full pursuit of the bounding stag. The huge antlers that hung around her cabin, or upheld her trusty gun, gave proof of her skill in gunnery, and the white comb, drained of its honey and hung up for ornament, testified of her hours spent in bee-finding.

"Many can testify to her magical art in the maze of cookery —being able to get up a pumpkin in as many forms as there are days in the week. She was extensively known and employed for her professional knowledge in the management of all ailments.

"But she was most remarkable for her military feats. She professed high toned ideas of liberty.

"The clouds of war gathered, and burst with a dreadful explosion in this state. Nancy's spirit rose with the tempest. She declared and proved herself a friend to her country, ready to do or die.

"All accused of Whigism had to hide or swing. They kept up a prowling, skulking kind of life, occasionally sallying forth in a sort of predatory style. The Tories at length, however, gave Mrs. Hart a call and in true soldier manner ordered a repast. Nancy soon had the necessary materials for a good feast spread before them. The smoking venison, the hasty hoecake, and the fresh honeycomb was sufficient to have provoked the appetite of a gorged epicure! They simultaneously staked their guns and seated themselves, when, quick as thought, the dauntless Nancy seized one of the guns, cocked it, and declared that she would blow out the brains of the first mortal that offered to rise, or taste a mouthful! They all knew her character too well to imagine that she would say one thing and do another.

" 'Go,' said she to one of her sons, 'nd tell the Whigs that I have taxen six base Tories.' They sat still, each expecting to be offered up, with doggedly mean countenances, bearing the marks of disappointed revenge, shame and unappearsed hunger. They were soon relieved and dealt with according to the rules of the times.

"This heroine lived to see her country free."

Mrs. Ellet, in her "Women of the Revolution," says:

"In this county is a stream, formerly known as 'War Woman's Creek.' Its name was derived from the character of an individual who lived near the entrance of the stream into the river. This person was Nancy Hart, a zealous lover of liberty and the 'liberty boys' as she called the Whigs. She was well known to the Tories, who stood in fear of her revenge for any grievance or aggressive act, though they let pass no opportunity of worrying and annoying her when they could do so with impunity.

"On the occasion of an excursion of the British camp at Augusta, a party of Tories penetrated into the interior, and having savagely murdered Colonel Dooley in bed and in his own house, they proceeded up the country for the purpose of perpetrating further atrocities. On their way, a detachment of five of the party diverged to the east, and crossed Broad River to make discoveries about the neighborhood, and pay a visit to their old acquaintance, Nancy Hart. On reaching her cabin, they entered it unceremoniously, received no welcome from her but a scowl, and informed her that they had come to know the truth of a story current respecting her, that she had secreted a noted rebel from a company of King's men who were pursuing him. Nancy undauntedly avowed her agency in the fugitive's escape. She told them that she had at first heard the tramp of a horse rapidly approaching, and had then seen a horseman coming towards her cabin. As he came nearer she knew him to be a Whig, and flying from pursuit. She let down the bars a few steps from her cabin, and motioned him to enter, to pass through both doors, front and rear of her single-roomed house; to take to the swamp and secure himself as best he could. She then threw up the bars, entered her cabin, closed the door and went about her business. Presently some Tories rode up to the bars and called out boisterously to her, she muffled her head and face and opened the door, inquiring why they disturbed a sick, lone woman. They said they had traced a man they wanted to catch, and asked if anyone had passed that way. She answered no, but said she saw somebody on a sorrel horse turn off of the path into the woods some two or three hundred yards back. 'That must be the fellow,' said the Tories; and asking her direction of the way he took they turned about and went off.

" 'Well fooled,' said Nancy, 'In the opposite course to that of my Whig boy; when if they not been so lofty minded, but had looked on the ground inside the bars, they would have seen the horse's tracks up to that door as plain as you can see the tracks on this here floor, and out t'other door down the path to the swamp.'

"This bold story did not much please the Tory party, but they could not wreck their vengence upon the woman who thus unscrupously avowed her daring aid to a rebel, and the cheat she had put upon the pursuers, otherwise than by ordering her to aid and comfort them by giving them something to eat. She replied, 'I never feed King's men if I can help it; the vilians have put it out of my power to feed my own family and friends, by killing and stealing all of my poultry and pigs, except that one old gobbler you see in the yard.'

" 'Well, you shall cook that for us,' said one who appeared to be the head of the party; and raising his musket, he shot down the turkey, while another of the men brought it into the house and handed it to Mrs. Hart to cook without delay. She stormed and swore a while—for Nancy occasionally swore—but seemingly at last to make a merit of necessity, began with alacrity the arrangements for cooking, assisted by her daughter, some 10 or 12 years old.

"The spring, of which every settlement had one near at hand, was just at the edge of the swamp, and a short distance within reach of it was a high, snag-toothed stump, on which was placed a conch shell. This rude trumpet was used by the family to give information by means of a variation of notes, to Mr. Hart and his neighbors who might be working in a field just beyond the swamp, that the 'Britishers' or Tories were about; that the master was wanted at his cabin, or that he was to keep close or make tracks for another swamp. Pending the operations of cooking, Mrs. Hart had sent her daughter Sukey to the spring for water, with directions to blow the conch in such a manner as would inform Mr. Hart that the Tories were in the cabin, and that he should keep close with the three neighbors who were with him, 'till he heard the conch again.

"The party had become merry over their jug, and sat down to feast upon the slaughtered gobbler. They had cautiously stacked their arms where they were in view, and within reach, and Mrs. Hart assidious in her attention upon the table, and to her guest, occasionally passed between them and their muskets. Water was called for, and as there was none in the cabin—Mrs. Hart so contrived that Sukey was again sent to the spring, instructed by her mother to blow the conch so as to call up Mr.

Hart and his neighbors immediately. While Mrs. Hart had slipped out one of the pieces of pine which constituted a chinking between the logs of the cabin, and dexterously put out of the house, through the space, two of the five guns. She was detected in the act of putting out a third. The party sprang to their feet. Quick as thought, Mrs. Hart brought the piece that she held to her shoulder and declared that she would kill the first man who approached her. At length, one of them made a motion to advance upon her. True to her threat, she fired. He fell dead upon the floor! Instantly seizing another musket she brought it to position to fire again. By this time, Sukey had returned from the springa nd taking up the remaining gun, carried it out of the house, saying to her mother, 'Daddy and them will soon be here.' They proposed a general rush. No time was to be lost; she fired again and brought down another Tory. Sukey had another musket in readiness, which her mother took, and posting herself in the doorway, called upon the party to surrender 'the carcasses to a Whig Woman.' They agreed to surrender and proposed to shake hands upon it, but the conqueror kept them in their places a few moments, until her husband and neighbors came up to the door. They were about to shoot down the Tories, but Mrs. Hart stopped them, saying they had surrendered to her, and her spirit being up to the boiling point, she swore, 'Shooting was too good for them.' This hint was enough. The dead men were dragged out of the house, the wounded Tory and the others were bound, taking out beyond the bars and hung. The tree upon which they were hung, was pointed out in 1838, by one who lived in those bloody times, and who also showed the spot once occupied by Mrs. Hart's cabin.''

White, in his ''Historical Collection of Georgia,'' says in part:

''On one occasion when information as to what transpired on the Carolina side of the river was anxiously desired by the troops on the Georgia side, no one could be induced to cross the river to obtain it. Nancy promptly offered to discharge the perilous duty alone, the dauntless heroine made her way to the Savannah River, but finding no mode of transport across, she procured a few logs, tying them with a grape vine, constructed a raft upon which she crossed, obtained the desired intelligence, returned and communicated it to the Georgia troops.

''On another occasion having met a Tory on the road, and entering into conversation with him, so as to divert his attention, she seized his gun, and declared that unless he immediately took up the line of march to a fort not far distant, she would shoot him. The dastard was so intimidated, that he actually walked before the brave woman, who delivered him to the Commander of the American Fort.

''Once more, when Augusta was in the possession of the British, the American troops in Wilkes County, then under the command of Colonel Elijah Clarke, were very anxious to know something of the intentions of the British. Nancy assumed the garments of a man, pushed on to Augusta, went boldly into the British camp, pretending to be crazy, and by this means was enabled to obtain much useful information, which she hastened to lay before the Commander, Colonel Elijah Clarke."

A story appearing in the *Atlanta Constitution* on December 22, 1912, seems not only to substantiate the story of Nancy Hart, but also fixes beyond question the location of her home. The articles written by Z. B. Rogers Sr., reads:

"Skeletons of six Tories captured at her dinner table, and afterwards hung to trees near her home by Nancy Hart more than a century ago was unearthed last week by a squad of hands at work grading the Elberton and Eastern Railrod. They were buried about three feet under ground in what is known as the Heard field, near the mouth of Warhatchie Creek, some half a mile from where it empties into Broad River. The bones are all there, in a splendid state of preservation, all the bones of the heads and under jaws, are especially well preserved, and the teeth are perfect. The place where the skeletons were unearthed, together with the fact that they were so close together, near the surface, with no sign of anything like a coffin anywhere around, makes the evidence convincing that these are the bones of the Tories captured by the Revolutionary heroine, Nancy Hart. The house in which Nancy Hart lived was located on Warhatchie Creek, near a spring, some half or three-quarters of a mile from where the skeletons were found. The place is now owned by the Daughters of the American Revolution. This place is about 13 miles from Elberton."

Had Nancy been a member of the opposite sex her genius in warfare, her cool bravery, her unprecedented nerve, and her strength of character would have led her to high positions in the councils of her country.

Another incident demonstrating the bravery of womankind is worthy of mention:

Mammy Kate, a house slave belonging to Governor Stephen Heard, was a giantess, more than six feet tall. In an old letter, written in 1820, she was referred to as, "The biggest, the tallest, the most imposing Negress I have ever seen and she has proven herslf to be a strong, a kindly, a never failing friend to Colonel Heard and his family." Kate was of pure African blood and declared herself to be the daughter of a great king. She was entirely fearless and when she learned that her master had been captured and sentenced to death by the Tories, followed him to his prison for the ostensible purpose of caring for his wants.

One morning, carrying on her head a large covered basket, she presented herself at the fort and asked the sentry on duty for the privilege of securing her master's soiled linen. The request was carelessly granted and the guard offered the information that, "The damned Rebel would soon be hung."

She entered the cell, secreted her master, who was of small statue, in the basket, covered him with clothing, and conveyed him from the place of incarceration on her head, calmly sauntering past the sentry, and several British and Tory officers, who stood idly about the quadrangle.

The night previous to this remarkable rescue she had brought two of Stephen Heard's fine Arabian horses, Lightfoot and Silverheels, to the outskirts of Augusta and left them in keeping of a trusted friend of her master. She leisurely made her way to the place of concealment where they mounted the horses and galloped away.

While they were traveling homeward her master turned to her and said, "Kate, you have this day saved my life and I shall set you free."

"Na, Marse Stephen," she answered, "You may set me free, but I ain't 'gwiner set you free!"

Mammy Kate was given her freedom, a deed to a small tract of land and a comfortable four-roomed house, but she faithfully remained with the Heard family until her death.

On her death bed she gave each of Governor Heard's children one of her own. She lies buried in the corner of the Heard, Allen, McIntosh, Mattox burial ground at Heardmont. No marker shows the resting place of this heroine.

Mammy Kate has a number of descendants living in Elbert County today and all of them are respected members of the Negro race. Among them are Andy Clark, Moon Clark, Mary Clark, Lucinda Clark, and Georgia Clark.

When Colonel Boyd fell at the Battle of Kettle Creek his army, at once began to disintegrate. Some of his men joined the Georgia troops, some formed an alliance with the Indians hostile to the American cause and a large number of them returned to their homes in the Carolinas fully convinced that Georgia, at least, would soon be free. The Battle of Kettle Creek was a deciding factor in the warfare of upper Georgia. Colonel Campbell, unable to retain his force in any semblance of military order, evacuated his strong position at Augusta and retreated to Savannah. In the latter part of 1779, he bet his hasty retreat and left in his wake many stores and much ammunition which was immediately appropriated by the Georgia forces. These stores and ammunition aided the cause of independence to a great degree.

Although the Patriots had met with surprisingly good fortune, from a militaristic standpoint, the State of Georgia, as a whole, was in a deplorable condition. Smallpox had devastated every settlement, no taxes were levied or collected, salt could scarcely be had and the lower counties were entirely under British and Tory domination.

On the 5th day of February, 1780, the seat of government was, for the better protection of the records, removed to Heard's Fort in Wilkes County. Governor Howley resigned to take his seat in the Continental Congress. George Wells, elected to succeed him, was shortly killed in a duel. Stephen Heard was then elected Governor. At this period the State of Georgia could claim the allegiance of but two counties, Richmond and Wilkes.

The *Royal Gazette,* published in Charleston, South Carolina, carried the following item:

"We hear the Rebel Junto are endeavoring to outdo each other in every species of rapine and villany. Even Howley and his associates were gentlemen when compared to this set. When such murdering villians as Dunn, Inman, and McCay are colonels, councillers, and assemblymen, it is easy to guess what must be the result of their counsels.

"This period was the darkest that Georgia experienced during the entire Revolution, but Governor Heard and his associates on the Council were able, by almost superhuman effort, to hold the long suffering Patriots together.

"In the latter part of 1781, Augusta again became the capitol of Georgia. The proceedings of the Executive Council of January 2, 1782, follow:

"Augusta, Wednesday 2nd. January 1782.

The Executive Council of the State of Georgia met

Present

His Honor the Governor
Stephen Heard	Thomas Lewis
Charles O'dignail	Jenkins Davis
Holman Freeman	Benjamin Andrews
Abraham Ravot	William Glascock
James Maxwell	Andrew Burns

Jonathan Bryan

"The Board proceeded to ballot for a President. When on casting up the poll it appeared that Stephen Heard Esq., was duly elected."
(Minutes Executive Council, 1778-1785).

Shortly after the above mentioned date indications became apparent that Georgia was to be freed from the hated British and Tory rule.

Many veterans of the American Revolution settled in Elbert County shortly after the close of hostilities. Among this number was Captain Thomas Cook who came from North Carolina in 1784. He was born in Hanover County, Virginia, May 15, 1752, and died in Henry County, Georgia, March 5, 1841.

In his application for a Federal pension he tells most interestingly of his activities during the Revolution. His second affidavit in support of his second pension claim is herewith set out in full:

"GEORGIA, HENRY COUNTY.

"Personally appeared before me the undersigned, a Justice of the Peace, Thomas Cook, who being duly sworn, deposeth and saith, that by reason of old age and the consequence loss of memory he cannot swear positively and exactly as to the precise time of his service, but according to his best recollection, he served not less than the periods below and in the following grades:

"On July tenth, Seventeen hundred and seventy six (1776), I entered the service as a private soldier in Captain John Leek's Company (Guilford Militia), Colonel James Martin's regiment, Griffith Rutherford, General; marched to the Cherokee Nation to suppress the Indians; burnt their town and killed destroyed as many Indians as we could get hold of; remained in the Nation as long as we could get provisions, and were compelled to return back again. On the 25th of November, landed at our starting point, being out four months and 15 days—4 months and ½. This was known as the 'Cherokee Expedition.' This service was in an embodied corps, called out by competent authority by the State of North Carolina.

"On the first day of September, Seventeen hundred and seventy-seven (1777), I was elected First Lieutenant of a company of Martin's regiment, company commanded by John Leek and attached to the said brigade commanded by the same General (Griffith Rutherford). The intention of this company was to scout the country throughout, for the Tories were very mischevious, indeed, in the lower part of the State along the seaboard. We were raised as protectors of our State; McCloud was the Tory General who headed the Tories in the Scotch settlements, as aforesaid. In this service I was out three months, when we returned back to our country and homes. This was known as the 'Scotch Expedition.'

"About Christmas or the 1st of January (1778), we were ordered out as before, to the lower part of the State, to hunt for the same Tory (Commander) McCloud, for the Tories, as soon as we had left their particular section, commenced their mischief. Sometime in the winter we came upon McCloud in the Scotch settlement at a bridge (name of bridge not recollected), but near a swamp called Drowning Swamp, where we had a fight and killed several of the Tories and caused McCloud to flee with the balance. Colonel Paisley commanded our Regiment at that time—Colonel Martin, with some of the men, remained in the upper part of the State. We consumed the whole of this year as we did the latter part of the former, backward and forward continually. This was likewise known as the 'Scotch Expedition,' making in the whole of this kind of service fifteen (15) months. I was commissioned by Governor Caswell.

"Early in January, Seventy-nine (1779), I was elected Captain of a company in Colonel Martin's regiment composed of Guilford Militia, and was commissioned by Governor Caswell of North Carolina. Joined the regiment at Guilford Court House: marched immediately for South Carolina, General Rutherford still commanding. Went through South Carolina directly to the Savannah River; Joined General Lincoln at a place called 'Smoking Camp,' about seventy miles below Augusta. From the 'Smoking Camp' marched up the river to a place known as the 'Sister Ferry.' From the latter place a detachment was sent under General Ashe into Georgia, where they had a fight with the British and got defeated. This is known as the 'Brier Creek Battle,' or 'Ashe's Defeat.' During this expedition I remained with the army under General Lincoln, and upon guard at the time and could hear the guns. Immediately after the above fight General Lincoln and General Moultrie marched the main army up the river to a place called 'Turkey Hill,' General Lincoln had a road cut from the hill directly into the country for about six miles. This was done in sight of the British army, and, as I thought, for a *feint*, but I now know the intentions of our General in cutting said road, for the day they quit the road we directly marched up the river to the 'Black Ewamp.' Staid a few days. General Lincoln took the whole body of the regulars from the main army and marched for Stono. The balance of the army, consisting of North Carolina and South Carolina militia, was left under care of General Moultrie at 'Black Swamp,' at which place I remained until the relief from North Carolina, which was about the first of June in said year. This was a six months expedition with no particular designation but that of the 'United States Expedition against the British.' At this time I received a written discharge from General Moultrie to march my company home, and in our proper county be discharged. During our travel we had, from the hands of our General, orders to draw provisions for my company at the various commissaries as we passed on. This was about the middle of June 1779.

"After our return home, we were instructed by our General to hold ourselves in readiness to meet any emergency that might arise.

"From June 1779, until September 1780, I was not in any embodied corps doing service, but was frequently called out by our Colonel, who at this time was Paisley, to suppress large bodies of Tories. During this interval of time it is impossible to relate fully the kind of service performed, for it was of a very unsettled nature. We did not remain at home at any one time longer than about two weeks before we would receive orders to scout the country and restore peace and quiet for a while.

"In September 1780 (Seventeen hundred and eighty), I was ordered to raise a Horse Company containing of about thirty (30), or as many as I might think necessary for the occasion—known as 'Rangers.' I marched out and met Davie and Brisbane in Mecklenburg County, North Carolina. From this county, we marched in a body to join General Davidson on the Catawba River, where we remained scouting the country and harrassing the British until Davidson was killed. He was killed by fire of a cannon across the river from the British side and by the British. After the death of Davidson we dispersed and fled over the Yadkin. We were in a very distracted state after the death of our General, until Greene came to take charge of us. All this service was confined to the State of North Carolina. As General Greene passed through our State with regulars for the South, we were required to join him and march with him to the South until he could or should intercept Cornwallis. We marched from Guilford towards Camden in South Carolina, where we supposed the British to be. We met him about the Catawba, and General Greene's forces being too feeble, he retreated before him into Virginia. Now I received orders from General Greene to go back to my State and county and raise more men and meet him as soon as possible, which I did, and met him at High Rock Ford on Haw River and continued marching and counter-marching through the country, until we met the British at Guilford. In the Battle of Guilford, I bore a part under General Greene, but our forces being too weak, we were forced to flee and give ground. The British did not follow us one yard—just took our cannon and fired it upon us. I rode off with Greene from the battlefield. According to our agreement (if it should be necessary to give them ground), we would flee to the Iron Works—7 miles—which we did. The second day, including the battle day, Cornwallis sent to the General to come and bury his dead, which he did. From Guilford Court House, we pursued Cornwallis to Ramsey's Mill, on Deep River, where we came in sight of them, but the river being high and rising, General Greene considered it not safe to cross, for the British were on the opposite bank. I think the British had about two thousand rails in a formation on a floating raft to pass over upon, and after they had passed over destroyed, as much as was in their power, the means they had used in crossing. General Greene considered it safest and best for our common country to retrace his steps and push for Eutaw Springs. Upon our arrival near the place we discovered the British. We halted and prepared for battle. I think this battle was in September 1781, but will not say certainly. General Greene gave Lord Rowden a fight and compelled him to retreat with his British subjects and flee the country. During the battle, I and my commander and several others were reserved by the orders of the Commander-in-Chief to cover his retreat, should he deem it necessary for the safety of his country to make one. From the above place I was sent back with my company and several others to our proper county and State to protect it and defend it and our women and children from the plunderings of the Tories and the British; for they scattered over the whole country, and distress and dismay covered our land. I was, by General Greene, ordered to disband my company upon our return home, but to be ever vigilant and scout the whole upper country of our State until he should require our assistance, and if he should we would be immediately informed of it and ordered to march. I did as ordered, until I received instructions from Headquarters that peace was made and there was no more use for us. Upon which news I was discharged from the service and ordered to discharge my company. I did so, which ended my labors. I think it was in the Spring of (1783) that we were discharged as stated above."

On September 18, 1832, while a resident of Elbert County, John Cook applied for a pension as a Revolutionary soldier which was granted.

The following is a copy of his statement of record in the Bureau of Pensions, Washington, D. C., where it is listed as "Survivor's File No. 16,343."

"Elbert County Superior Court, September Term, 1832.

"On the eighteenth day of September, personally appeared in open Court, before William H. Crawford, Judge of the Superior Courts of the Northern Circuit of said State, now sitting for the County of Elbert, John Cook, aged seventy years and about ten months, (was born the ninth of December, Seventeen hundred and sixty-one, according to the register kept by his father, which is now in his possession), who being first duly sworn according to Law doth make his oath to the following in order to obtain the benefits of an Act of Congress passed June the seventh, 1832 . . . .

"That he entered the service of the United States under the following named officer and served as herein stated to-wit,

"The nineteenth day of July, 1776, I entered the service of the United States as a volunteer under Capt. John Leeks, Lieut. John Davies; Thos. Owens was our Major; General Rutherford Commander. I started from Guilford, North Carolina. We went through Salisbury and up to the head of the Catawba near a fort called Cahtey's Fort; from that fort we crossed the mountain and went down the Swananoa River; thence to the Indian towns upon the Tennessee and its waters and destroyed sixteen of their towns. I remained three months in that tower and returned home.

"2nd Tower. I volunteered for three months, Richard Vernon was my Captain; Robert Vernon my Lieutenant, and joined General Davidson in the State of North Carolina near the line of South Carolina but do not recollect the county or the name of the place, it was called Head Quarters, not far distant from where Cornwallis and his army were stationed. I continued with General Davidson. During the time there was a little scrimmage in Charlotte, North Carolina—the army sometimes advanced and often retreated, being unable to come in contact with Cornwallis. General Davidson discharged me when the time of service had expired, on the other side of the Yadkin River and I went home.

"3rd Tower. In a short time after I returned home after the last tower I volunteered under Captain Thomas Cook—a Mr. O'Neal was our Major, and John Pacely our Colonel. We marched down upon Deep River and dispersed a large body of Tories said to be under command of Colonel Fanning. I volunteered for three months but did not stay the whole time in service. The whole company was sent home until called for but held ourselves in readiness (as ordered) when called upon.

"4th Tower. I volunteered again (being unwilling to be drafted) for another tower of three months under Captain Richard Vernon—was rendezvoused at Guilford Court House, North Carolina, equipped and prepared for the service—but was ordered home to hold ourselves in readiness when called upon, we were not called upon in this Tower any further—my residence during the whole War of the Revolution, in Guilford Court House in the State of North Carolina. I was born in the State of Virginia. I now reside in the State of Georgia, Elbert County.

"The year of the Treaty of Shoulderbone, I removed to the State of Georgia, and have resided in said County and State ever since."

The Executive Council was not slow in rewarding the active patriots who had served their country with such faith and fidelity. The following grants were made to citizens who resided in territory now within the bounds of Elbert County:

STEPHEN HEARD:
    January 28, 1784—1,965 acres in Wilkes County.
    January 28, 1784—658 acres in Wilkes County.
    January 28, 1784—300 acres in Wilkes County.
    February 27, 1784—2,340 acres in Wilkes County.
    October 22, 1784—500 acres in Wilkes County.
    October 26, 1784—800 acres in Wilkes County.
    October 26, 1784—287½ acres in Washington County.

DYONISIUS OLIVER:
    July 14, 1784—850 acres in Wilkes County.
    July 21, 1784—1,800 acres in Wilkes County.
    July 23, 1784—425 acres in Wilkes County.

GEORGE MATHEWS:
    September 22, 1784—1,700 acres in Wilkes County.

EVAN RAGLAND:
    February 12, 1784—500 acres in Wilkes County.
    September 21, 1784—450 acres in Wilkes County.
    September 22, 1784—600 acres in Wilkes County.

JAMES EASTER:
    September 21, 1784—600 acres in Wilkes County.
    September 28, 1784—450 acres in Wilkes County.

GEORGE DARDEN:
   July 28, 1784—200 acres in Wilkes County.
THOMAS GREGG:
   September 29, 1784—850 acres in Wilkes County.
   September 30, 1784—575 acres in Franklin County.
RICHARD TYNER:
   September 21, 1784—200 acres in Wilkes County.
JOHN WHITE:
   September 21, 1784—200 acres in Wilkes County.
SAMUEL TYNER:
   September 21, 1784—200 acres in Wilkes County.
MARK THORNTON:
   September 21, 1784—200 acres in Wilkes County.
RICHARD AYCOCK, JR.:
   September 18, 1784—200 acres in Wilkes County.
JEREMIAH WALKER:
   September 24, 1784—264 acres in Wilkes County.
JOHN BANKS:
   September 23, 1784—100 acres in Wilkes County.
JAMES AYCOCK:
   September 23, 1784—200 acres in Wilkes County.
JOHN WOODALL:
   December 9, 1784—200 acres in Wilkes County.
NATHANIEL SMITH:
   September 23, 1784—287½ acres in Washington County.
JACOB HIGGINBOTHAM:
   September 23, 1784—287½ acres in Washington County.
JOSIAH CARTER:
   September 30, 1784—400 acres in Wilkes County.
JOHN BLACK:
   September 21, 1784—250 acres in Wilkes County.
JOSEPH WILLIAMS:
   May 12, 1784—1,750 acres in Wilkes County.
   May 23, 1784—50 acres in Wilkes County.
   January 4, 1785—287½ acres in Washington County
NATHAN BARNETT:
   January 4, 1785—576 acres in Franklin County.
JOHN DUDLEY:
   January 3, 1785—100 acres in Wilkes County.
JOHN WINGFIELD:
   January 3, 1785—200 acres in Wilkes County.

WILLIAM WEBB:
  September 21, 1784—400 acres in Wilkes County.

NATHANIEL HUDSON:
  September 24, 1784—287½ acres in Washington County.

HOLMAN FREEMAN:
  February 27, 1784—600 acres in Wilkes County.
  September 20, 1784—1,900 acres in Wilkes County.
  September 29, 1784—690 acres in Washington County.
  September 30, 1784—1,150 acres in Wilkes County.

WILLIAM WALKER:
  September 25, 1784—200 acres in Wilkes County.

WILLIAM MOSS:
  September 21, 1784—600 acres in Wilkes County.

George Wyche, who served with distinction throughout the period of the Revolution, also received land grants in what is now Elbert County.

Upward of 30,000 acres of land were granted veterans who lived in Elbert County within the period embraced between January 28, 1784, and January 3, 1785.

It is interesting to note that only 10 of the Revolutionary soldiers listed above have descendants now (1935), residing in Elbert County. They are Stephen Heard, George Mathews, George Darden, Richard Tyner, Mark Thornton, Jacob Higginbotham, John Black, William Moss, and George Wyche.

CHAPTER IV

CONDITIONS IN GEORGIA—GENERAL GEORGE MATHEWS — EARLY SETTLERS — PETERSBURG — SETTLEMENT OF HEARDMONT—DANIEL TUCKER—TEXT OF ACT CREATING ELBERT COUNTY—MILITIA DISTRICTS—FIRST OFFICERS OF COUNTY—MINUTES OF FIRST SUPERIOR COURT.

When the War of the Revolution finally came to a close, Georgia was in a deplorable state of disorganization. Suffering upon every hand had been intense. The prosperous planter as well as the backwoodsman had been forced to feed his family on meal made from a mixture of weevil infested corn and peas supplemented by such game and fish as the surrounding territory afforded. The Angel of Death had been busy at his appointed work. Contagious disease and bloody warfare had taken a mighty toll. Sorrow had entered thousands of homes and poverty stricken widows and orphans were to be found on every hand.

An acute feeling of hatred was still in evidence between the Whigs and Tories. In the Savannah Valley it, at times, narrowly missed causing fresh outbreaks of intensive belligerency. In some cases the Tories were so greatly despised that their Whig neighbors drove them from their homes, forcing them to abandon the country.

A rumor, which became widespread, to the effect that the older colonies were to enter into a compromise treaty of peace with Great Britian, excluding Georgia and South Carolina from participation in independence, struck fear into the hearts of the long suffering Georgians. This rumor, coupled with the many acts of barbaric warfare practiced by the Tories and British, tended to further embitter the citizens of the new commonwealth who had fought for independence at such appalling cost. The aftermath left wounds as slow in healing as did the actual conflict.

The Indians were still close at hand, in an unsettled state, and the fact that Florida, in the possession of hostile Spain, might at any time attempt invasion caused an earnest desire among the people of Georgia for a hasty and permanent arrangement looking towards a strong central government.

From 1783, until the ratification of the Constitution of the United States on January 2, 1788, Georgia, the fourth to ratify, remained in a perilous condition. The consummation of the long awaited ratification was the signal for great rejoicing within the new-born state. Salutes were fired, celebration after celebration, was held as the welcomed news spread throughout the settlements. New vigor at once became evident and as each year passed Georgia grew in power and prosperity. Many new settlers came, mainly from Virginia and the Carolinas, but even the then distant New England States, notably Connecticut and New Hampshire, were largely represented. New Jersey and Delaware furnished a number of citizens to the town of Petersburg. The firm establishment of the Federal Union had caused the dawning of an era of great prosperity throughout Georgia.

Lands lying within the confines of the present Elbert County were quickly cleared and large plantations were established for the cultivation of tobacco and flax. The production of cotton was looked upon with something of disfavor.

In the year 1784, General George Mathews, who later became Governor, brought a large number of Virginians and North Carolinians to the Broad and Savannah River country and they established themselves in the territory around the site of what was soon to become the thriving and commercially important town of Petersburg.

In the eyes of these adventurers, as they made their way westward, shone the light of interest; of fearlessness, and of conquest. Some afoot with their long squirrel rifles nestled securely beneath their arms—some driving lumbering ox carts along faint trails and across unbridged streams—young mothers with suckling babes at their breasts—aged men and calm eyed grandmothers—an occasional horseman with his sword and sash, knee breeches and silver buckled shoes —the aristocrat and the yoeman—side by side—wending their way onward—with one accord, seeking new worlds to conquer.

Governor Mathews was a man of high principles and a great soldier. He it was who saved the Americans from rout at the famous Battle of the Brandywine. While Governor of Georgia he approved the Yazoo Act which brought down upon him a veritable storm of criticism, but there was nothing of chicanery or deceit in his official actions. He was merely the unconscious tool of grasping politicians. George Mathews is buried in St. Paul's churchyard, in the City of Augusta, having died August 30, 1812.

Many interesting stories have been told with Mathews of the central figure. It has been related that while John Adams was President of the United States, he recommended Mathews to the Senate to be Governor of the Mississippi Territory, but finally withdrew his name from consideration for the reason that active opposition developed due to his part in the so-called Yazoo Fraud. Learning of the President's action Mathews, at once, set out for Philadelphia to interview him.

After many days of hard travel, on horseback, he reached his destination and went directly to the "President's Palace." He hitched his horse, mounted the steps and gave a loud knock at the door. His three-cornered hat was on his head and his Revolutionary sword swinging at his side. When the servant appeared he asked to see the President. He was rather curtly informed that the President was engaged, to which he replied, "I presume that it is your business to carry messages to Mr. Adams. Now, if you do not, at once, inform him that a gentleman from Georgia wishes to see him, your head will answer the consequences!" This obtained speedy admittance.

When he was ushered into the room where the President sat, he asked, "Are you John Adams, President of these United States?"

The President arose and formally bowed.

Mathews continued, "My name is Mathews, Governor Mathews, sometimes known as the hero of Germantown and the Brandywine. Now sir, I understand that you nominated me to be Governor of the Mississippi Territory and then took it back. If you had known me you would not have taken back your nomination and if you didn't you should not have nominated me in the first place. Unless you can satisfy me your position as President shall not shield you from my vengence!"

The dumbfounded, and perchance frightened, Mr. Adams, with right good will, set about satisfying him. This was somewhat easily accomplished when they found each other to be Federalist in politics. To clinch the matter, however, the President suggested that he tender General Mathews' son, John, the appointment of Supervisor of the Public Revenue in Georgia. Upon hearing this the old soldier beamed. "My son, John," he said, "is a man about my inches, possessed of good education and for his honesty and integrity I pledge you, sir, my head."

Mathews always spoke very proudly of his military accomplishments as being unsurpassed by any man who ever lived and equalled only by those of General Washington. His ordinary apparel was a three-cornered hat, fairtop boots, velvet breeches and a full ruffled shirt. He was seldom seen in public without his long sword at his side. George Mathews was provoking and boastful. He was impatient, obstinate, intolerant of criticism and yet, with all this, he was generous, capable and wholly lovable. His make-up contained traits of a Napoleon, a St. Peter and a Mr. Micawber all interwoven into a single character.

George Mathews was one of the delegates from Wilkes County who signed the ratification of the Federal Constitution.

One of the daughters of Governor Mathews married General Samuel Blackburn who at one time lived in Elbert County, but moved away after the Yazoo Fraud incident. Blackburn was both a lawyer and teacher of distinction. He represented Elbert County in the Georgia Senate in 1791 and 1792.

To arbitrarily list all the names of settlers who accompanied General Mathews to Georgia is patently impossible, but the following were the earlier settlers throughout the entire county and one may well assume that many came with him:

Thomas Akin, Beverly Allen, William Allen, William Alston, Benjamin Ashworth, Mr. Allgood, Mr. Arnold, W. W. Bibb, William Bowen, A. Brown, William Barnett, James Bell, John Boyd, William Brown, Thomas Burton, Joseph Blackwell, Edmund Brewer, Samuel Blackburn, Jacob Bugg, Drury Cade, Richmond T. Cosby, William Caines, J. P. Crow, James Christian, John Cason, David Cosby, Christopher Clark, Robert Crook, Thomas A. Carter, P. Duncan, George Darden, John Darden, Joseph Deadwyler, Larkin Gatewood, William Gaines, John Gill, William Hailey, Benjamin Head, Stephen Heard, John Heard, John Hightower, Robert Huddleston, John Henderson, William Higginbotham, J. Higginbotham, John Hulme, David Hudson, Richardson Hunt, Mr. Highsmith, John King, William Key, Thomas Key, Aaron Johnson, Reuben Lindsey, John LeGrande, Benjamin Mattox, Robert Middleton, Samuel McGee, William Moss, John Millican, James F. Nunnelee, Reni Napier, Thomas Oliver, Dyonius Oliver, Drudy Oglesby, Jacob Odom, Robert Peyton, Frank Powell, Leroy Pope, James Rogers, L. Rice, William Rucker, Evan Ragland, Thomas P. Scott, Absolom Stinchcomb, Edmund Shackleford, Ethreal Tucker, Charles Tait, Dozier Thornton, Mark Thornton, Thomas Thornton, Joel Thomas, Richard Tyner, Isham Thompson, Joseph Underwood, David Vineyard, Edward Walthall, Gerrard Walthall, James S. Walker, William Ward, Rev. Mr. White, P. M. Wyche, George Wyche, Mr. Wall, Jeremiah Walker, John Watkins, Middleton Wood, and James Wood.

In this connection, it is interesting to note, that the Second Charter of Virginia, granted in 1609, carries many names of persons whose descedants later settled in Elbert County, among them are:

Thomas Davis, Robert Johnson, Dr. Turner, Captain Clark, Richard Lindsay, Captain Thomas Wood, Thomas Walker, Esquire; Thomas Webb, Esquire; Charles Anthony, John Banks, Williams Evans, John Harper, Thomas Carpenter, George Holman, Edward Allen, George Pretty, Thomas Hammond, Martin Bond, Daniel Tucker, Robert Middleton, Lewis Tate, James Swifte, Thomas Hunt, William Taylor, William Gibbs, James Campbell, Miles Banks, Richard Webb, William Carpenter, Randolph Carter, Alexander Chiles, John Gairdner, and Mr. Brown.

Petersburg was established upon the site formerly occupied by the trading settlement of Dartmouth, which, as we have seen, was of comparative short duration.

On February 3, 1786, the General Assembly of the State of Georgia, while in session at Augusta, passed an act authorizing Dyonysius Oliver to erect upon his lands a warehouse for the storage and inspection of tobacco. The complete text of the act reads as follows:

"An Act to authorize Zachariah Lamar, Esquire, to lay out a town at the mouth of Broad River, and to establish inspection in the County of Wilkes.

"Whereas it is necessary, and will be greatly conducive to the general convenience of the citizens in the upper part of the State, that a town be laid out, and a tobacco inspection established at the mouth of Broad River in the County of Wilkes, *BE IT enacted by the representatives of the freemen of the State of Georgia assembled met, and by the authority of the same,* that Zachariah Lamar of the aforesaid county, be and he is hereby fully authorized and empowered to lay out a town on his own lands, situated on the south side of the mouth of Broad River, in to any and such number of half acre lots as he may think proper, and to dispose of and make title to the same; according to the usual manner of conveyances; which said town shall be called and known by the name of *Lincoln;* and the said Zachariah Lamar is hereby fully authorized and empowered to erect a public warehouse for the reception and inspection of tobacco in the said town of Lincoln, subject always to the laws that have been made or may hereafter be provided for the inspection of tobacco.

"II. *And Whereas* Dionysius Oliver, of the aforesaid county of Wilkes, hath petitioned the legislature to authorize him to erect a tobacco warehouse on his own land, in the aforesaid county of Wilkes, in the forks between the aforesaid Broad River and the river Savannah, for the reception and inspection of tobacco; *And Whereas,* the same is likewise thought necessary for the convenience of the upper settlers; *Be it further enacted,* that the said Dionysius Oliver is hereby authorized and empowered to erect said warehouse, and the said inspection is hereby established, subject always to such laws as have been, or may hereafter be made regulating the inspection of tobacco as aforesaid.

Augusta, February 2, 1786.

WILLIAM GIBBONS, Speaker.''

The Oliver warehouse was at once erected on Lot Number 1, according to the plan of Petersburg. On March 9, 1788, it was sold by Dionysius Oliver to John Oliver for the sum of One Thousand Pounds.

Section One of the foregoing act, although not applying to territory which is now a part of Elbert County, but of Lincoln, tends to show the rapidity of development of the surrounding territory directly after the close of the Revolution. The town, Lincoln, did not become of any importance due to the proximity of Petersburg.

Since the settlers were mainly from Virginia and North Carolina they were keenly interested in tobacco from a commercial standpoint and found the soil of the Petersburg area well suited to its culture. It soon became the money crop of the planters and as there was a law prohibiting the exportation of tobacco without inspection it was necessary to erect warehouses at convenient terminals.

Tobacco was cultivated in every section of Elbert County and a large portion of each year's crop was rolled to Petersburg in huge hogsheads. Some of the up country planters, however, sent their tobacco to Edinburg, a small village in upper Elbert County, adjacent to Gregg Shoals. Produce carried to Edinburg was later sent to Petersburg on large flat boats. Gregg Shoals were so-called due to the fact that John Gregg, who owned large acreage adjoining them, was the first real settlers there.

Petersburg after the establishment of the first warehouse was not long in becoming a thriving town of more than 2,000 permanent inhabitants. Stores, shops and two taverns were erected and it soon become second in importance to Augusta in upper Georgia. The taverns were generally filled to capacity with people who came from further north in Georgia to purchase goods and dispose of their produce. During the summer months numbers of persons from Savannah, Waynesborough, Darien and other points in the lower country visited Petersburg for the gay social life and for the purpose of drinking the water of a famous lithia spring in the vicinity. Even people from distant New Jersey made summer pilgrimages to this spa.

More tobacco warehouses were soon erected and the local citizenry enjoyed an era of great prosperity. A few years before this territory had been virgin wilderness peopled only by roving bands of Indians.

In September, 1795, the following deed was filed for record in Elbert County and is recorded in Deed Book "C," Page 41, demonstrating that the gentlemen of Petersburg enjoyed their pastimes as do they of the present day:

> "This Indenture witnesseth that we have for and in consideration of the sum of two thousand dollars, the receipt whereof do we hereby acknowledge, sold to John R. Ragland one-half of a lot in the town of Petersburg in the forks of the Savannah and Broad Rivers Marked No. Twenty on the west side of Point Street agreeable to a plan laid off and exhibited to the purchasers containing half an acre, forty four yards on the street and fifty five yards extending outward, also half of all the improvements on said lot, Together with the billiard tables, balls and all that appertains thereto and we do hereby oblige ourselves, our heirs, executors and administrators to warrant and defend the said half lot with improvements. In witness whereof we have hereunto set our hands and seals this 23rd day of September One Thousand Seven Hundred and Ninety Five.
>
>   Henry G. Walker (Seal)
>   James Coleman (Seal)"

Witnessed
John Oliver
Robert Thompson
Asa Thompson

Several social clubs were organized in Petersburg and the Masonic Lodge was said to have been the second established in Georgia. It was antedated by Solomon Lodge of Savannah.

The people were highly intelligent and progressive looking always to the further upbuliding of their community. In the year 1802, a number of the more prominent men formed an organization for the purpose of educating the illiterate of the community and for the additional purpose of alleviating want. The membership of this union was: Shaler Hillyer, John William Walker, Memorable Walker, Oliver White, James Sanders, John A. Casey, Thomas Casey, Robert Watkins, William Jones, Albert Bruxe, Robert H. Watkins, Rignual Groves, Nicholas Pope, Andrew Green Semmes, James Coulter, William Wyatt Bibb, Thomas Bibb, and Garland T. Watkins.

The town was governed by a commission form of government and in the year 1802, Robert Thompson, Leroy Pope, Richard Easter, Samuel Watkins, and John Ragland were the commissioners. Clayton's Digest of Georgia Laws, Page 92, states that these men were appointed for the purpose of securing better regulations and government for the town.

Dr. William Wyatt Bibb, for whom Bibb County, Georgia, was named, served in the United States Senate while a resident of Petersburg. He later became the first territorial Governor of Alabama and when statehood was assumed he became its first Governor.

Dr. Bibb was born in Amelia County, Virginia, October 2, 1781. In his early years he came to Petersburg and engaged in the practice of medicine. His chosen profession did not, however, long claim him for at the age of 24 years he was elected to a seat in the United States House of Representatives where he served with distinction until the year 1813, when he was elevated to a seat in the United States Senate. In 1816, he resigned the toga because of a storm of protest throughout the nation occasioned by the passage of an act increasing the salaries of the congressional members. He, as a vast majority, voted for the measure.

President Monroe, who recognized his unusual ability, refused to allow him to leave the public service and immediately appointed him Governor of the Alabama Territory. He was the only man ever to hold this position.

Governor Bibb met his death in a tragic manner. During the summer of 1820, while riding a spirited horse, during a severe thunder storm, the animal became frightened at the noise and threw his rider. Injuries received from the fall caused his death. This unfortunate incident took place in Ortanga County, Alabama.

William Wyatt Bibb was five feet 10 inches in height, dark haired and brown eyed. His wife was Mary Freeman, a daughter of Colonel Holman Freeman, a noted Revolutionary patriot, who resided, at one time, in Elbert County.

Petersburg also furnished another national lawmaker in the person of Judge Charles Tait. While residing there he served in both houses of the United States Congress. His colleague in the Senate was Dr. Bibb and this is the only instance in the history of the United States when two men served from the same town simultaneously.

Even after Eli Whitney had perfected his cotton gin, and it had become widely used, Petersburg still clung to the culture of tobacco. As cotton gained the ascendency the once thriving town ceased to grow.

A disaster in the form of a veritable scourge of yellow fever visited the town and it was almost depopulated in a single year. The fever was caused by the two rivers overflowing their banks and flooding cellars of the houses and stores. The few people who did not move away at the outbreak of the fever and survived its ravages, immediately left the vicinity upon recuperation.

Dionysius Oliver, Sr., may well be termed the real founder of Petersburg. One of his land grants included the site whereon the town was subsequently built and it was through his efforts that the first settlement was made. He surveyed and laid out streets, marked off and numbered lots, each containing one-half an acre, and found ready market for them at prices ranging from three to 15 Pounds.

The names of the streets running east and west were: Front, Broad, Point, and Back. Those running north and south were: First, Second, Third and Cross. There were approximately 700 lots forming the town. There were, no doubt, other streets, but unfortunately the plat of the town of Petersburg, which for a number of years was on file in the Elbert County court house, has been lost.

Among the early purchasers of lots were: John Oliver, William Hatcher, Jeremiah Walker, W. W. Bibb, Charles Tait, Leroy Pope, Matthew J. Williams, William Allen, James Tate, Evan Ragland, Stephen Heard, John Darden, Drury Cade, and Richardson Hunt.

The only visible evidence of this once populous town is a dilapidated cemetery with broken headstones overrun by a tangled growth of vines and Cherokee roses.

Mrs. Mary Clark Fortson, who died in 1933, was authority for the statement that the mercantile establishments of Petersburg, of which there were at one time 35, during its highest peak of prosperity, carried the finest merchandise procurable. She tells of her mother, a lady of ample fortune, buying her wedding garments there and some of the laces used in making them cost in excess of $10 a yard. Chipman & Weston, Pope & Oliver, Littleberry & Whitfield Wilson, and James Holliday conducted the leading mercantile establishments.

The post office at Petersburg was established January 1, 1795, and the following postmasters served:
> William I. Hobby, appointed January 1, 1795.
> Oliver White, appointed July 1, 1795.
> James S. Walker, appointed October 1, 1803.
> Leroy Pope, appointed January 1, 1804.

Alexander Pope, appointed October 1, 1810.
John Watkins, appointed April 1, 1814.
Henry M. Watkins, appointed February 17, 1824.
James M. Hester, appointed October 8, 1834.
Archibald M. Sayer, appointed January 11, 1842.
Felix G. Edwards, appointed February 4, 1842.
Archibald M. Sayer, appointed March 18, 1843.

The name of the office changed to Lisbon, Lincoln County, July 2, 1844.

Mark L. Anthony, appointed July 2, 1844.

Name changed to Petersburg, November 24, 1844.

Archibald Stokes, appointed November 21, 1844.

Office discontinued June 22, 1855.

When one considers such historic spots as Petersburg, hallowed by the resting places and memories of pioneer heroes and heroines, he can but feel as did the poet Goldsmith when he sang:

> *"But now the sounds of population fail,*
> *No cheerful murmurs fluctuate in the gale,*
> *No busy steps the grass-grown footway tread,*
> *But all the bloomy flush of life is fled."*

In the latter part of the 18th Century Stephen Heard removed from Wilkes County into what is now Elbert County. He settled about 12 miles below the present city of Elberton, near the Savannah River, and constructed the first lathed and plastered house in the county. While the building was under construction people for many miles around came to see it. Many of them had never seen so handsome a building. The house was of imposing appearance. Huge columns supported the double verandas and the rooms were more than 30 feet square. The furniture was of solid mahogany, having been imported from Europe.

The house was destroyed more than half a century ago, but the site is well known and can be pointed out by any child of the community. The dining room was moved to Rose Hill by Thomas Jefferson Heard, youngest son of Stephen Heard, and is still in use. The other portions of the house were used to construct a Negro school, a church building and several tenant houses by Captain William H. Mattox, who purchased the property shortly after the War Between the States.

A little hamlet grew up around this house and it became known as Heardmont.

A short distance to the rear of the Heard home is the cemetery of the families of Heard, Allen, McIntosh, Darden, Mattox, and others allied by ties of blood and marriage. A few acres of land lying just without the walled portion of the burial ground is owned by the Stephen Heard Chapter of the Daughters of the American Revolution. The cemetery proper, known as "God's Acre," is the property forever of the descendants of Governor Heard. Buried within the enclosure are Stephen Heard and Elizabeth Darden, his wife; Dr. George Washington Heard, John Adams Heard, Singleton Walthall Allen and Jane Heard, his wife; Colonel William McPherson McIntosh and Maria Louisa Allen, his wife; Singleton Allen McIntosh and Eliza Cade, his wife; Budd Clay Wall, husband of Anna Cassandra McIntosh; John Darden, George Allen, Theodore Allen, and many others.

The inscriptions on the tombs of Governor Heard and his wife follow:

> Sacred to the memory of Colonel Stephen Heard. He was a soldier of the American Revolution, and fought with the great Washington for the liberties of his country. He died on the 15th of November, 1815, in the 75th year of his age, beloved by all who knew him.
>
> *"An honest man is the noblest work of God."*
>
> Sacred to the memory of Mrs. Elizabeth Heard. She was born in the United States of America. At an early age she came with her father, Mr. George Darden, to Georgia where she married Colonel Stephen Heard and after living a useful and exemplary life died on the fifth of June, 1848, in the 83rd year of her age.
>
> *"Daughters have done virtuously, but thou exceedeth them all."*

Between the home site and the cemetery there is still standing an ancient and towering oak under which, it is said, a band of hostile Indians captured and murdered the beautiful daughter of one of Governor Heard's overseers. She had dreamed the night before of an Indian attack and had so informed her mother who dismissed her fears with a smile. The child was left alone and her dream was realized. This band of murderers were never apprehended.

A short distance eastward stands another oak where a Tory, by the name of Ballard, attempted to murder Colonel Heard. The country around had suffered greatly from the lack of the necessities of life and Heard, a man of wealth, had fed families of Whigs and Tories alike. Among the number so aided was Ballard and his large family.

Colonel Heard has just dismounted from his horse when Ballard stepped from his concealment in a thicket of elder bushes and threw up his rifle to shoot down the benefactor of his family. Heard, who was unarmed, called out, "Ballard, would you do that? Would you shoot a man who has saved your children from starvation?"

Ballard hesitated. As he lowered his gun it was, in some manner, discharged, killing Stephen Heard's mount, the famous "Light Foot." The animal, in falling, overthrew Heard and fell partially across his body and fracturing his leg. Ballard fled the country, taking his family with him. He was never again heard of in Elbert County.

This period marked the beginning of a neighborhood, which from the standpoint of wealth, culture and refinement was unsurpassed within the boundaries of all Georgia. From this beginning later grew the famous village of Ruckersville, named not for Joseph Rucker the banker, but for a family which settled in Elbert County while he was but a child. Within a radius of 15 miles of Heardmont lived the families of Tate, Alston, Walthall, Heard, Allen, Brewer, Wall, Remberts, Ragland, Blackwell, Walker, Clark, Middleton, Carter, Cade, Oliver, Cleveland, Pope, Nunnelee, Edwards, and Williams. A short time later came the Ruckers, Carpenters, Harpers, Martins, Underwoods, and a host of other families of note. Just across the Savannah River, in South Carolina, lived the Tuckers, the McCallas, the Allans, and the Calhouns.

A famous member of the Tucker family was the Reverend Daniel Tucker, the subject of the song, "Old Dan Tucker."

He lies buried in Elbert County, on a high bluff, overlooking the waters of the Savannah River. Although the song regarding him would lead to the belief that he was accustomed to drinking far too much; such was not, in reality, the case. He was a highly respected minister, of excellent family, and a man of wealth. Such songs were often sung about the time of Daniel Tucker's ministry regarding men of prominence and almost without exception the sentiments expressed were totally without foudation. The marker of soapstone which stands at the head of Daniel Tucker's grave bears this inscription:

> Sakred to the memory of
> Rev. Daniel Tucker, Born Feb. 14, 1740.
> Dp. this life April the 7, 1818. Age 78.

The bluff on which Daniel Tucker lies buried is located on Point Lookout, so named for the reason that a watchman was often stationed there, it being the highest point in the surorunding territory, to advise the people of the vicinity, by loud blasts on a conch shell, of the approach of the supply boats from Augusta. Mrs. Annie C. McIntosh Wall recalls, as a young woman, directly after the War Between the States, gathering fresh water mussels at its base in company with her brother, William M. McIntosh Junior.

Another citizen of note, who resided in the Heardmont area, was Lieutenant-Colonel William Alston. In December, 1774, he was a member of the Council of Safety for Halifax County, North Carolina, and a short time later he became a member from Tyron, now Lincoln County, of the Provincial Congress which met at Hillsboro, August 21, 1775. He was also a delegate to the Constitution Convention held at Halifax, November 12, 1776. An earlier Provincial Congress, held at Halifax in April, 1776, appointed him Lieutenant-Colonel of a regiment of Continental troops, with Jethro Sumner as Colonel, and Samuel Lockhart as Major. In the capacity of Lieutenant-Colonel he served until late in 1777 when he resigned.

William Alston was born on Christmas Day, 1736, and in the year 1774, he married Charity, his cousin, a daughter of James Alston and Christian Lillington. His wife was a lady of great personal beauty and charm and during the trying days of the Revolution proved herself an ardent patriot.

Directly following the close of the Revolution he removed with his family to Elbert County where he acquired large holdings on the Savannah River and Beaverdam Creek. There is a spring of crystal clear water, near Heardmont, which is still known as the "Alston Spring."

William Alston died in the year 1810, universally loved and respected in his adopted county. His children were: James, George, Mary, Elizabeth, William Hinton, Phillip H. (who was one of the commissioners appointed by Governor Forsyth, Wednesday, December 26, 1827, to lay out the town of Columbus, Georgia), Solomon, Christian, Nancy, and Sally. (In South Carolina can be seen lovely old mahogany furniture and rare pieces of silver once owned by the William Alston family which was imported from England.)

By legislative action in December of the year 1790, Elbert County was created. The text of the act, taken from Watkin's Digest of the Laws of Georgia, page 429, is as follows:

"An Act for dividing the County of Wilkes; and for other purposes;

I. *Be it enacted by the Senate and House of Representatives of the State of Georgia in general assembly met,* That all that part or parcel of the County of Wilkes, lying on the north side of Broad River, from the mouth thereof to the main fork, thence up the south main fork to where it intersects the line dividing the County of Wilkes from Franklin, shall be one county; to be called and known by the name of Elbert, and all that part of the said County of Wilkes, lying on the couth side of Broad River shall retain the name of Wilkes; and the court house and gaol thereof shall be and continue at the town of Washington, to place formerly appointed by law for holding courts in said county.

II. *And be it further enacted by the authority aforesaid,* that the justices of the inferior court of the County of Elbert, be and they (or any three of them) are hereby authorized and empowered to fix on the most convenient place for building a court house gaol in the said County of Elbert, and until such court house gaol shall be completed, the superior and inferior courts of the said county shall be held at some place to be agreed on by the said justices.

III. *And be it further enacted,* that the justices of the inferior court of the said County of Elbert, are hereby authorized and empowered to contract with such person or persons to undertake, carry on and completely finish the aforesaid public buildings on such plan and in such manner and from as the said justices or any three of them shall direct; and when such buildings shall be completed, to raise by tax on said county to be by them assessed, such sum or sums of money as shall be sufficient for the above purposes, provided that the same does not exceed Two Hundred and Fifty Pounds.

IV. *And be it further enacted,* That the aforesaid County of Elbert shall be entitled to elect one member to represent them in the House of Representatives out of the number allowed by the Constitution to the County of Wilkes.

V. *And be it enacted,* That the time for holding the superior and inferior courts of the County of Elbert, be on the Thursday in the week for holding superior and inferior courts in the County of Franklin.

JOSEPH HABERSHAM, Speaker of
the House of Representatives.

NATHAN BROWNSON, President of
the Senate.

EDWARD TELFAIR, Governor
December 10, 1790.

On June 21st, 1791, the following militia districts were established for the new county:

"State House, Augusta
Tuesday 21st, June, 1791.

"A letter dated the 20th instant from James Meriwether, Esquire, with its enclosures, being a report in conformity to the order of the 13th instant, were received and read,

"Whereupon,

Government House, Augusta.
21st June, 1791.

"The County of Elbert is divided into the following districts until otherwise directed:

"First District—Beginning at the mouth of Broad River, thence to Butram's Creek, thence up said creek to the Allen's road, thence along said road to the Beaverdam, thence down Beaverdam to the Savannah River, thence to the beginning.

"Second District—Beginning at the mouth of Butram's Creek thence up Broad River to the mouth of Falling Creek, thence up the middle fork of said creek to the source; thence to Carter's plantation on the Beaverdam, thence down the Beaverdam to the line of the First District.

"Third District—Beginning at the mouth of Butram's Creek, thence up Broad River to the mouth of Cedar Creek, thence up the said creek to the source, thence in a direct line to the head of Falling Creek, thence down the said creek to the beginning.

"Fourth District—Beginning at the mouth of Cedar Creek,

thence up the north fork of Broad River to Big Creek, thence up the said creek to Peter Brown's, thence to Thomas Burke's, thence to the head of Cedar Creek, thence down the said creek to the beginning.

"Fifth District—Beginning at the confluence of the north and south forks of Broad River, running thence up the said south fork to Skule Shoal Creek, thence in a direct line to the north fork of Broad River, thence to the beginning.

"Sixth District—Beginning at Skule Creek (The upper line of District Number 5 and running up the south fork of Broad River to the line of Franklin County, thence along the said line of the north fork of Broad River, thence down the said river until it intersects the upper line of District Number 5).

"Seventh District—Beginning at the mouth of Big Creek, thence up the north fork of Broad River to the line of Franklin County, thence along the said line to the north fork of the Beaverdam, thence down the Beaverdam to William Higginbotham's, thence in a direct line to the upper boundary of District Number 4.

"Eighth District—Beginning at William Higginbotham's on the Beaverdam, thence down the Beaverdam to the line of District Number 2 at Carter's plantation, thence along the said line until it intersects the line of District Number 3, thence along the said line to Thomas Burke's, thence to the beginning.

"Ninth District—Beginning at the north corner of District Number 7 on the north fork of the Beaverdam, thence along the line of Franklin County to Coldwater Creek, thence down the said creek to Cunningham's road, thence along the said road to the Beaverdam, thence up the Beaverdam to the beginning.

"Tenth District—Beginning at the north corner of District Number 9, thence down the said river to Cedar Creek, thence up the said creek to Cunningham's road, thence along the said road to Coldwater Creek, thence up the said creek to the beginning.

"Eleventh District—Beginning on Savannah River at the mouth of Cedar Creek, thence down the said river to the mouth of Coldwater Creek, thence up the said creek to Cunningham's road, thence along the said road to Cedar Creek, thence down the said creek to the beginning.

"Twelfth District—Beginning at the mouth of Coldwater Creek, being the lower corner of District Number 11, running thence down the Savannah River to the corner of District Number 1 at the mouth of the Beaverdam, thence up the said Beaverdam to Cunningham's road, thence along the said road to Coldwater Creek, thence down the said creek to the beginning.

"The rank and arrangement of the Militia of Elbert County are established this day in the following order:

John Cunningham, Esquire, Colonel.
Evan Ragland, Esquire, Lieut. Colonel.
Samuel Neilson, Esquire, Major.

FIRST COMPANY
William Hatcher, Esquire, Captain.
William Thompson, Gent., 1st. Lieut.
James Coleman, Gent., 2nd. Lieut.

SECOND COMPANY
Archibald Burton, Esquire, Captain.
Thomas Burton, Gent., 1st. Lieut.
William Hightower, Gent., 2nd. Lieut.

THIRD COMPANY
James McClusky, Esquire, Captain.   June 18, 1791.
John Brauner, Gent., 1st. Lieut.
Joshua Sewill, Gent., 2nd. Lieut.

FOURTH COMPANY
Thomas Scott, Esquire, Captain.
John Dupriest, Gent., 1st. Lieut.
Joseph Dred Wildred, Gent., 2nd. Lieut.

FIFTH COMPANY
John Hodge, Esquire, Captain.
William Patton, Gent., 1st. Lieut.
Montfort Stokes, Gent., 2nd. Lieut.

SIXTH COMPANY
David McCluskey, Esquire, Captain.   June 16, 1791.
John Vainyard, Gent., 1st. Lieut.
Henry Stricklin, Gent., 2nd. Lieut.

SEVENTH COMPANY
John Collins, Esquire, Captain.
James Dudley, Gent., 1st. Lieut.
James Cook, Gent., 2nd. Lieut.

EIGHTH COMPANY
Benjamin Higginbotham, Esquire, Captain.
Thomas Penn, Gent., 1st. Lieut.
John Grinnell, Gent., 2nd. Lieut.

NINTH COMPANY
John Blackwell, Esquire, Captain.
John Rucker, Gent., 1st. Lieut.
William Hansford, Gent., 2nd. Lieut.

TENTH COMPANY
Hugh McDonald, Esquire, Captain.
Archibald Walker, Esquire, 1st. Lieut.
Joel Thomas, Gent., 2nd. Lieut.

ELEVENTH COMPANY
Hezekiah Bailey, Esquire, Captain.
Robert Means, Gent., 1st. Lieut.
William Means, Gent., 2nd. Lieut.

TWELFTH COMPANY
William Allen, Esquire, Captain.
Richard Colbert, Gent., 1st. Lieut.
Thomas Colbert, Gent., 2nd. Lieut.

State House Augusta
21st June, 1791.

"Ordered that the Secretary of State prepare commissions bearing date this 21st day of June for the several officers agreeable to the foregoing arrangement."

On January 20, 1791, the first session of Elbert County Superior Court was held at the home of Thomas A. Carter, on Beaverdam Creek, some four miles northwest of the present city of Elberton. George Walton, signer of the Declaration of Independence, was the presiding judge.

On December 31, 1790, the following entry was made in Minute Book "A" of the Elbert County Superior Court:

"Chambers Augusta, 31st December, 1790.
Present the Honorable George Walton.

"The Clerk of the Superior Court attending with the names of the residents of Elbert County selected as well as could be for the present from the present residents of Wilkes County they being separated for the grand and petit jury boxes. The Judge proceeded to have the juries drawn for the ensuing term as follows:

"For the Grand Jury: (1) Thomas Burton, (2) Isham Thompson, (3) Robert Cosby, (4) Samuel Baker, (5) John Crosby, (6) Avington Muckelroy, (7) Jeremiah Walker, (8) Samuel Nelson, (9) Benjamin Baker, (10) Benjamin Hart, (11) James Easter, (12) Charles Cosbey, (13) Robert Pullman, (14) William Tate, (15) William Moon, (16) William Higginbotham, (17) Julius Howard, (18) Evans Ragland, (19) John F. Thompson, (20) Henry Caldwell, (21) William Morse, (22) Drury Thompson, (23) Robert Burton.

For the ePtit Jury: (1) John Teasley, (2) George Claudus, (3) Benjamin Brown, (4) Robert Crouder, (5) James Vineyard, (6) John Lamb Sr., (7) Nathaniel Smith, (8) Thomas Lovelady, (9) James Patton, (10) Franklin Manline, (11) Patrick Murdock, (12) John Greenwood, (13) John McDaniel, (14) Martin Turman, (15) Joseph M. Russell, (16) Thomas Turman, (17) Thomas Martin, (18) Hardy Hinton, (19) William Strong, (20) John Brown, (21) George Alexander, (22) James Ready, (23) John Westbrook, (24) Noah Cloud, (25) John Hogg, (26) Joseph Nail, (27) John Barnett, (28) Edward McGary, (29) David Adams, (30) Nathan Barnett, (31) John M. Key, (32) David Cullen, (33) Robert Turman, (34) John Kilgore, (35) Nathan Evins, (36) Austin Webb.

Tuesday, January 21, 1791.

Court met according to adjournment—Present the Honorable Judge Walton.

"The Attorney General stated to the Court that there were several Indictments for Petty offences found in the County of Wilkes before the division committed in that part now Constituting the County of Elbert and Prayed the Judgment of the Court in that regard and it is thereupon adjudged that all such Indictments should be quashed and the Attorney General is at Liberty to *Proiced Denovo* in this County.

"The Grand Jury returned the following bills:

"State Vs. John Smith. Rape.

"The following Jury was sworn:

(1) Francis Cook, (2) Joseph Moore, (3) Ruben Cook, (4) William Hightower, (5) Thomas Lovelady, (6) Edward McGary, (7) Thomas Aikins, (8) Benjamin Head, (9) Lewis Gaar, (10) James Baker, (11) James Bell, (12) James Tuttle.

"State's Evidence

"Richardson Hunt, Elizabeth Fulgum, Sarah Collins, M. Sperlock and William Hansford.

"Prisoner's Evidence

"Delila Williams, John Smith, Peter Brown, John Greenwood and Ruben Allen.

"We the Jury find the defendant not guilty.

James Bell, Foreman."

It was during this first term of Elbert County Superior Court that one James Meredith was indicted, tried and convicted of the offense of murder. On the 22nd day of February, 1791, he was hanged on the Thomas A. Carter plantation. Thus it happened that the first legal execution in Elbert County took place less than three months after its formation.

At a Superior Court continued from January, 1791, until July of the same year, and held at the home of Thomas A. Carter. Henry Osburn served as judge due to the illness of George Walton.

The following named persons attended and were sworn as Grand Jurors:

Walker Richardson, James F. Nunnelee, James McClusky, Jacob Bugg, John Oliver, David Hudson, Robert Pulliam, Francis Satterwhite, William Allen, Joseph Rucker, John Henderson, John Templeton, Benjamin Higginbotham, Barnabas Pace, James Tait, and Benjamin Allen.

The following named Petit Jury served for the same term:

John Johnston, George Turman, Christopher Deadwilder, Edward Walthall, Jonathan Russell, William George, William Litch, Leonard Barnett, George Watts, James Tuttle Jr., Thomas Wilkins, John Brawner, John Palmer, Charles Hutchins, John Morris, Francis Brown, James Cook, Henry Cosby, John Keys, William Wolridge, Alexander Thompson, John Moore, Thomas Akins, Thomas Helly, Richard Easter, Samuel Hunter, William Chapman, John Vineyard, John Boyd, William Thomas, Jacob Hamman, James Cook, Robert Ross, James Walthall, William Willen, and William Daniel.

During this term of court J. Walker, W. Barnett, Jas. Tait, Evan Ragland, R. Hunt, Thos. B. Scott, Reuben Allen, Jno. Banks, Jno. Cunningham, Wm. Higginbotham, Harry Caldwell, Francis Cook, and John Fergus were sworn in as Justices of the Peace for the new County of Elbert.

Certain recommendations of the Grand Jury were put in effect, among them being:

The appointment of John Oliver and William Thompson as Commissioners over the road from Petersburg to McElroy's Ferry.

John Fergus and John Pettigrew as Commissioners from McElroy's Ferry to Franklin County.

James Tait and Walter Nunnelee as Commissioners to the Beaverdam Creek at William Allen's, from said Allen's, William Allen, Joseph Blackwell, and Hezekiah Bailey were named Commissioners.

The fact that tobacco was not accepted at Petersburg in payment of the general tax was presented as a grievance.

George Walker, Thomas Carter, and Josiah Walton were presented for profane swearing.

Elieu Post was presented for selling spirits.

For the January term, 1793, the following Grand Jurors served:

John P. Harper, Zachariah Collins, Thomas Gregg, Daniel White, Thomas Burton, Joseph Rucker, Laughlin Fannin, Daniel White, Barnabas Pace, Moses Haynes, F. Higginbotham, Isham Thompson, Thomas Cook, Walter Nunnelee, William Hightower, Francis Saterwhite, and Thomas Napier.

Grand Jurors for the February term, 1794, were:

William Hightower, William Dudley, Charles Hudson, Ralph Banks, Robert Griffth, John Wilkins, Benjamin Cook, Samuel Montgomery, John Hudson Sr., George Watts, Joseph Underwood, John Crowder, Moses Fleming, William Moon, Caleb Higginbotham, A. Alexander, Richard Tyner, Moses Davis, William Hodge, Joseph Nail, William Barker, John Statham, and William Patten.

The Superior Court of the new county did not convene with reguarity. The first term was held January, 1791, with Thomas Burton as Foreman of the Grand Jury; the second term, July, 1791, with William Richardson, Foreman; the third, August 14, 1792, William Booker, Foreman; the fourth, January 29, 1793, John P. Harper, Foreman; and the fifth term, February 4, 1794, with William Booker again acting Foreman.

On June 5, 1792, the Commissioners of Elbert County, Richardson Hunt, William Barnett, Evan Ragland, and James Tait purchased from John Baker 40 acres of land, "All that dividend parcel of land lying and being in said County of Elbert on a branch of Falling Creek beginning at Mary Cook's corner pine, thence off a new line North Seventy degrees West eleven chains and thirty-six lengths to a corner stake thence off South twenty degrees West to the old Trading Path seven chains and twenty-five links to said branch of Falling Creek running out ten chains and fifty links to a corner stake twenty-two chains and thirty-six lengths, thence off South Seventy degrees East to a corner pine Twenty-two chains and thirty-six lengths, thence off North twenty degrees East to the said old Trading Path ten chains and fifty links to a corner stake on said Mary Cook's line Twenty-two chains and thirty-six links, thence along said Cook's line to the beginning corner Eleven chains which said boundaries comprehend fifty acres of land and the Court House and Gaol for the County aforesaid and is part of a survey of Nine Hundred and Fifty acres granted to the said John Baker on the ninth day of April in the year of our Lord One Thousand Seven Hundred and Ninety-two by his Excellency Edward Telfair . . .''

The branch of Falling Creek referred to is the "Public Springs Branch" and the Old Trading Path ran in the neighborhood of the present McIntosh Street.

A large portion of the 50 acres conveyed was divided into town lots and sold by the Commissioners. Among the early purchasers were:

William Cook—Lot No. 10, purchased January 29, 1793.
Eli Eavenson—Lots Nos. 17, 18, 19, 20, purchased December 19, 1793.
Thomas A. Carter—Lot No. 2, purchased January 29, 1793.
Womack Blankingship—Lot No. 12, purchased January 29, 1793.
Richard Coulter—Lot. No. 32, purchased April 14, 1794.
James Flood—Lot No. 29, purchased April 1, 1794.

It is evident from the text of the foregoing deed that a court house and jail, though probably built of logs and temporary in character, was constructed during the year 1791.

A study of activities in Elbert County during the administration of Richard Hunt, William Barnett, Evan Ragland, and James Tait reveals the facts that these men were active, progressive and proficient. The records show that they were always in sympathy with any movement to better the conditions of the people as a whole.

CHAPTER V

DOZIER THORNTON—VAN'S CREEK BAPTIST CHURCH—
THOMAS MAXWELL—DOVE'S CREEK CHURCH—FALLING
CREEK AND BETHEL CHURCHES—FIRST GEORGIA METH-
ODIST CONFERENCE—DR. RICHARD BANKS—BEAVER-
DAM PREACHING HOUSE.

While Petersburg and the Savannah River section were fast developing the remainder of the territory comprising the new County of Elbert also began to flourish. Settlements sprang up almost over night, and with this mecurial activity horse racing, cock fighting, turkey shoots, gaming and fox hunting became the order of the day. Briefly, and very briefly indeed, did such a state of affairs continue unchallenged, for in 1784, when General George Mathews came to Georgia he was accompanied by the Reverend Dozier Thornton.

Perhaps in all the annals of Georgia Baptist history there has never been a more interesting character than Dozier Thornton. In a degree he was, perhaps, fanatical, but his sincerity cannot be questioned. He was born in Virginia in the year 1765, the son of Mark Thornton and Susannah Dozier (daughter of Leonard Dozier, born 1710, will probated in Lunnenburg County, Virginia, 1787).

His father was a staunch member of the Church of England, or as it became known in America, the High Church. His mother was an early convert to the Anabaptist Society.

While still a young man he left his home in Virginia to seek his fortune in the newer colony of North Carolina. Shortly after his arrival there he was converted to the Baptist faith by a preacher named Lunsford.

For a time, wavering between his conscience and the teachings of a stern father, he declined baptism, but immediately began preaching, a minister without a pulpit, to anyone who would listen.

In a few weeks, however, his conscience proved victorious over the training of his father and he was immersed by Lunsford to enter the ministry of the Baptist Church in which he spent the remainder of a long life. He established several churches in North Carolina and they grew with startling rapidity. Shortly after the close of the Revolution, in which he fought with bravery, he migrated to Georgia. He married Miss Lucy (Elizabeth) Hill who accompanied him on his perilous journey. Throughout the entire trip he preached in every settlement through which he passed and made many converts.

Before the act of the Georgia Legislature was passed creating the County of Elbert, Dozier Thornton was busily engaged in preaching throughout the entire area of Wilkes County.

For a time he and Middleton Meeks served as missionaries to the Cherokee Indians. Neither Thornton nor Meeks evidenced the least fear upon entering the most hostile Indian town and never once were they molested. It was during this period that David Van, the famous Chief of the Cherokees, was converted by the preaching of Thornton and they became fast friends.

The first important act of Dozier Thornton, in Georgia, was the establishment of Vans Creek Baptist Church, named in honor of his Indian friend. This event took place early in 1785, and Van's Creek became the sixth church of the Baptist faith to be established in all Georgia. It was antedated by Kiokee in Columbia County, established by David Marshall in 1772; New Savannah, established 1773; Little Brier Creek, established 1777; Fishing Creek, in Wilkes County, established 1783, and Upton's Creek, established 1784. In point of continuous service Van's Creek is the oldest church of the Baptist denomination in Georgia.

The original members of Van's Creek were: Dozier Thornton Sr., Lucy (Elizabeth) Thornton, Elizabeth Thornton Jr., William ffirnold, first deacon and clerk; Susan Arnold, Nathan Morgan, Elizabeth Morgan, Thomas Gilbert, John White, and Milly White. John White was a licensed Baptist preacher, but had not been formally ordained at this period.

In October, 1788, Thornton established Dove's Creek Baptist Church, four miles west of Elberton, and in the same year Thomas Maxwell was the moving spirit in the raising of Falling Creek Baptist Church which is still flourishing three miles south of Elberton.

Thomas Maxwell, while a resident of Virginia, was a number of times imprisoned for preaching the doctrines of the Baptist faith, but he was dauntless in his determination. On one occasion while in prison, after the manner of St. Paul, he converted the keeper of his jail together with his entire family. Maxwell not only fought the army of the devil with fiery zeal, but played a conspicuous part in the American Revolution. It is a family tradition that he rubbed away a portion of his prominent nose by preaching through the bars of his cell. Reverend Thomas Maxwell was born September 8, 1742, and died December 12, 1837.

On February 27, 1802, a separate constitution was granted to the following named members of Van's Creek Church:

Frederick Crowder Sr. and wife, Frederick Crowder Jr., Minnie Hales, Winny Hales, William Arnold Jr., Thomas Head and wife, Fanny Head, Elizabeth Head, John Dingler and wife, Sally Woldridge, Zachariah Smith, Mrs. Zachariah Smith, Prudence Richardson, Susan Hubbard, Cassy Childers, Haley Childs, Peggy Childs, Nancy Childs, Nathan Childs and wife, Hannah Walker, Elizabeth Swilevant, Patsy Swilevant, Sally Colber, and Elizabeth Nix. This church was constituted in the home of Nathan Childs. There is some doubt as to just what church this may be, but considering the names of the members it is possibly one of the churches now located in that portion of Hart County which was taken from Elbert in 1853.

Beaverdam Church, now Bethel Church in Longstreet District, was granted a separate existence by Van's Creek on August 15, 1829, with Biddy C. Henderson, Frances Colson, Jane Heard, Lucy Carter Brewer, Thomas Colbert, Nancy Burton, Solomon Jones, Holman Childers, Jordan Jones, Joseph Bell Sr., Lewis I. Jones, and 33 slaves, belonging to Singleton W. Allen and Edmund Brewer, as charter members.

From this church Dr. Spaulding entered the ministry. He was ordained the Friday before the first Sunday in July, 1832. He served churches in Greenwood, South Carolina, and Gainesville, Georgia. His son, Albert Theodore, born in Elbert County October 20, 1831, also became a Baptist minister. He graduated at Mercer University and at the age of 22 supplied the First Baptist Church of Augusta, Georgia. His subsequent charges were Aiken, South Carolina; Madison, Georgia; Berean in Philadelphia; Selma, Alabama, and St. Francis at Mobile, Alabama. He married Miss Constance Schaffner of Charleston, South Carolina.

Antioch, an arm of Dove's Creek Church, was established separately during the month of September, 1846.

Rock Branch Church, in Gaines District, an arm of Van's Creek, was granted separate existence on October 18, 1845, with the following memebrs:

George Gaines, Mary Gaines, William Terrell, Martha Terrell, John Hulme, Elizabeth Hulme, James M. Cleveland, Mary Cleveland, Lewis Powell, William Alexander, Anne Alexander, Nancy Alexander, Mary Alexander, Robert Alexander, Sarah L. Alexander, Nancy M. Crawford, Manda Ann Taylor, Martha Taylor, John Terry, Susan Terry, Joseph Strickland, Richard Stowers, Levi Galloway, Mary Haley, William R. Galloway, Wiley Abney, Eleanor Abney, David Daniel, Francis Daniel, Mary Daniel, Elizabeth Means, Diadem Gaines, Ann Gaines, John Hinton, Eliza Hinton, Martha Hinton, Elizabeth L. Gaines, Benjamin Brown, Milly Brown, Matilda Crawford, William Alexander, Elizabeth Alexander, Thomas Steedman, Elizabeth Steadman, Sarah Wilson, Henry Stamps, Asa Rice, B. C. Thornton, Fleming Thornton, Harriet Adams Thornton, George H. Cornwell, Nancy Adams, John Thomason, John Cunningham, and Jane Cunningham.

In 1931 this church erected a new and modern brick house of worship and were able to dedicate it without a single outstanding obligation.

The membership of Dove's Creek Church at this period was:

Joseph Deadwyler, William Marvin, Martin Deadwyler, Sherid Morris, Henry P. Brawner, James Almond, James McLanahan, James Kerlin, Prudence Webb, Otis Deadwyler, Elizabeth Vaughan, Elizabeth Almond, Mary McLanahan, Lina Webb, Lucy Pressley, Elizabeth Tucker, Lucy Kerlin, Alexander Vaughan, William Oglesby, John Booth, James M. Brawner, John B. Webb, M. J. Almond, William Vaughan, John Moore, Sarah Johnson, Ann Almond, Miley Willis, Elizabeth Brawner, Martha Moore, Ann Johnson,

Judy Moore, Sarah Stephens, Perlina Webb, Jacob W. Davis, Isaac Almond, Fortunatus Webb, Haston Upshaw, John F. Oglesby, George Wylie, Jacob Kerlin, Rody Upshaw, Matthew J. Black, Elizabeth Oglesby, Margaret David, Sarah Bray, Letty Webb, Adeline Ann Arnold, Mary Oglesby, Elizabeth Kerlin, Mary Manning, Mily Vaughan, Ann Booth, Elizabeth Anderson, Cherry Brawner, Abner Webb, Thomas B. Oglesby, Lucinda Oglesby, Susan Montegue, Elizabeth McClain Wilhite Arnold, Davis Arnold, William M. Almond, Terry Wilhite, Priscilla Barnes, John E. Bentley, Mary Barnes, Henry Cabiness, Thomas Oglesby Sr., John Almond, and Mary Goss.

Three independent churches with an aggregate membership of almost 200 persons were taken from Van's Creek Church within a period of 40 years and all of them are flourishing today.

The Georgia Baptist Convention was held at Van's Creek Church in 1837. During this convocation Edward A. Stevens, of the Sunbury Church, was ordained as a foreign missionary to the East. He was the first native born Georgian to labor among the people of the eastern world.

Reverend Dozier Thornton served Van's Creek Church for 43 years, 1785-1828. He was succeeded by Francis Calloway, 1829-1832; Asa Chandler, 1833-1869-1872-1873, a minister of great power and a staunch advocate of an everlasting and burning hell. He delivered the main sermon at the Georgia Baptist Convention held at Penfield in 1840. Asa Duncan succeeded Chandler, April, 1869, to January, 1870; G. M. Campbell, 1870-1871. Among the other ministers to serve this charge are: L. W. Stephens, G. J. Christian, P. B. Butler, J. B. Saylor, Thomas A. Thornton, George W. Hulme, T. J. Rucker, J. C. West, and C. J. Hampton.

During the ministries of Dozier Thornton and Asa Chandler the following ministers were ordained: Joseph Chipman, July 12, 1806; William B. Jones, October 25, 1832; Benjamin Thornton Jr., October 13, 1837; Isham H. Goss, August 15, 1840; William R. Goss, October 19, 1845; C. C. White, January, 1849, and Benjamin Goss in 1854.

Isham H. Goss, William R. Goss, Benjamin Goss, and Horatio J. Goss Jr., were all Baptist ministers and the sons of Horatio J. Goss Sr. Little is known of the father save that he was a deacon and clerk of Sardis Church for more than 20 years and died in the year 1851. Benjamin, the eldest son, was born in Elbert County, 1810. He joined Van's Creek Church in 1838, and was ordained in 1854. Immediately after his ordination he was called to the pastorates of Rock Branch and Bethel. His ministerial career was of short duration for he died in 1865.

Another Baptist minister of note, William Mosely, the son of Reverend Elijah Mosely, was born in Elbert County October 21, 1796. The family removed to Putnam County where he was baptized in 1821. His activities were confined mainly to Putnam and Henry counties, in Georgia. He died in Alabama in the latter part of 1865.

After his resignation as pastor of Van's Creek Church, Thornton made numerous trips into the wilds of Kentucky where he established several churches which are today in a thriving condition. These trips were invariably made alone, on horse back, through the unpopulated wilderness.

He died in Franklin County, Georgia, in 1843, almost 90 years of age.

The first constitution and covenant of Van's Creek Baptist Church, together with the minutes from 1785 through July, 1797, were lost or destroyed and the following constitution and covenant were drawn up by Dozier Thornton and adopted by the church in January, 1798:

CONSTITUTION OF THE BAPTIST CHURCH OF CHRIST AT VAN'S CREEK BAPTIST CHURCH

Whereas, a considerable portion of the records of this church, together with the Articles of Faith and Church Covenant have been lost or mislaid so that we are unable to find them: The Baptist Church at Van's Creek in conference do make the following declaration of faith; and do enter into the following Church Covenant, to be placed on record:

1st. Declaration of Faith, the Scriptures. We believe that the Holy Bible was written by men divinely inspired and is a perfect treasure of Heavenly instruction, and that it has God for its author, salvation for its end, and truth without any mixture of error for its matter; that it records the principles by which God will judge us; and therefore is, and shall remain to the end of the world the true center of Christian Union, and the supreme standard by which all human conduct, creeds and opinions shall be tried.

2nd. Of the True God. We believe that there is one and only one true and loving God; the Maker and Supreme Ruler of Heaven and Earth; inexpressably glorious in holiness and worthy of all possible honor, confidence and love revealed under the personal and relative distinctions of the Father, Son and Holy Ghost, equal in every Divine perfection and executing distinct and harmonious offices, in the great work of redemption.

3rd. Of the Fall of Man. That man was created in a state of holiness under the law of his Maker, but by voluntary transgressions fell from that holy and happy state in consequence of which, all mankind are now sinners, not by constraint, but by choice being by nature utterly void of the holiness required by the law of God; wholly given to the gratification of their own sinful passion, and, therefore under the just condemnation to eternal sin without defense or excuse.

4th. On the Way to Salvation. That the salvation of sinners is wholly of grace through the meritorious offices of the Son of God; who took upon him our nature, yet without sin, honored by the laws by his personal obedience, and made atonement for our sins by his death; and is now entered into Heaven; and uniting in his wonderful person the tenderest sympathies, with Divine perfections, in every way qualified to be a suitable, a compassionate and all suffering Savior.

5th. Of Justification. That justification consists in the pardon of sin, and the promise of eternal life, on principles of righteousness that it is bestowed, not in consideration of any works of righteousness which we have done, but solely through the righteousness of Christ.

6th. Of the Freeness of Salvation. That the blessings of salvation are made free to all by the Gospel; that nothing prevents the salvation of the greatest sinner on earth except his own voluntary refusal to submit it to the Lord Jesus Christ; which refusal will subject him to an aggravated condemnation.

7th. Of Regeneration. That in order to be saved we must be regenerated or born again—that regeneration consists in giving a holy disposition to the mind and is effected in manner above—comprehension or calculation by the power of the Holy Ghost so as to secure our voluntary obedience to the Gospel, that its proper evidence is found in the holy fruit which we bring forth to the glory of God.

8th. Of God's Purpose of Grace. That election is the gracious purpose of God, according to which he regenerates, sanctifies, and saves sinners; that being perfectly consistent with the duties and obligations of men, it comprehends all the means connected with the end; that it is a most glorious display of God's sovereign goodness, being infinitely wise, holy and unchangeable; that it utterly excludes boasting and promotes humility, prayer, praise, trust in God and is active indication of his mercy; that it encourages the use of means to the highest degree, that it is ascertained by its effects in all who believe the Gospel; it is a foundation of Christian assurance, and that to ascertain it with regard to ourselves, demands and deserves our utmost diligence.

9th. Of the Perseverence of the Saints. That such only and real believers as endure unto the end; that the persevering attachment to Christ is the grand mark which distinguishes them from superficial professors; that a special providence watches their welfare, and they are kept by the power of God through faith unto salvation.

10th. Of a Gospel Church. That a visible Church of Christ is a congregation of baptized believers, associated by covenant in the faith and fellowship of the Gospel; observing the ordinances of Christ; governed by His laws and exercising the gifts, rights and privileges invected in them by His word; that its only proper officers are bishops or pastors and deacons whose qualifications, claims and duties are defined in the Epistles of Timothy to Titus.

11th. Of baptism and the Lord's Supper. That Christian baptism is the immersion of a believer in water in the name of the Father, Son and Spirit; to show forth in solemn and beautiful emblem our faith in a crucified, buried and risen Savior, with its purifying power; that it is a prerequisite to the privileges of a church relation and to the Lord's Supper in which the members of the church, by the use of bread and wine and to commemorate together the dying love of Christ, proceeded always by a solemn self examination.

12th. Of Civil Government That Civil Government is of Divine appointment for the interest and good order of human society; that magistrates are to be prayed for continually, honored and obeyed, except in things opposed to the will of our Lord Jesus Christ who is the only Lord of the conscience and the Prince of the kings of the earth.

13th. Of Future Government. That the end of the world is approaching, that at the last day Christ will descend from Heaven and raise the dead from the grave to the final judgment; that a solemn separation will then take place; that the wicked will be adjudged to endless punishment, and the righteous to endless joy and that this judgment will fix forever the final state of men in Heaven or Hell upon principles of righteousness.

TELOS.

CHURCH COVENANT

Having been, as we trust, brought by Divine grace to embrace the Lord Jesus Christ and given ourselves wholly to Him; we do now solemny and joyously covenant with each other, to walk together in brotherly love, to His glory as our common Lord. We do, therefore, in His strength, engage that we will exercise a mutual care, as members, one to another, to promote that growth of the whole body in Christian knowledge, holiness and comfort, to the end that we may stand perfect and complete in all the will of God. That to promote and secure this object, we will uphold the public worship of God, and the ordinances of His house; and hold communion with each other therein; that we cheerfully contribute of our property for the support of the poor and maintenance of a faithful minister of the Gospel among us.

That we will not omit closet and family religion at home or allow ourselves in the too common neglect of the great duty of religiously training up our children, and those under our care, with a view to the service of Christ and the enjoyment of Heaven. That we will walk circumspectly in the world, that we may win souls, remembering that God hath not given us the spirit of fear, but of power, of love and a sound mind; that we are the light of the world, and the salt of the earth, and that a city set on a hill cannot be hid.

That we will frequently exhort and if occasion shall require, admonish one another according to 18th Matthew in the spirit of meekness concerning ourselves lest we be tempted, and that as in baptism we have been buried with Christ and risen again so then it is on us a special obligation, henceforth to walk in.....................of life.

The minutes taken from the original record for the period ending from August 12, 1797, through June 12, 1802, are given in full below:

THE CHURCH OF CHRIST AT VAN'S CREEK

August 12, 1797 . Met in conference and proceeded to business as follows: 1st. Inquired into the fellowship of the church. Sister Mary White came forward with an acknowledgment for talking in anger and saying that which was not lawful. Dismissed.

Sept. 7th, 1797. Met in conference and proceeded as follows: 1st. Inquired into the fellowship. 2nd. Opened a door for the reception of members. Received by experience a black woman by the name of Hannah belonging to Mr. Thos. White. 3rd. Appointed Brothers Thornton and White delegates to the Association. Dismissed.

Oct. 7th, 1797. Met in conference and proceeded to business as follows: 1st. Inquired into fellowship, found in peace. 2nd. Opened a door for the reception of members. Received by experience a black woman by the name of Fanny and a black man by the name of George belonging to Mr. John Jones. 3rd. A black man by the name of Tom belonging to Mr. Wm. Banks came with a repentance, after some consultation referred his case till next meeting and directed Bro. Joshua Underwood to write Mr. Banks relative to his conduct that he would send us a note stating it. 4th. Bro. Burke presented a query to the church. Is it a duty to support our minister? Answer: It is. Dismissed.

Dec. 9th, 1797. Met in conference and proceeded as follows: 1st. Inquired into the fellowship, Brother Mark Thornton came forward with a complaint against himself for drinking too much. Made acknowledgment satisfactory to the church and was retained in fellowship. 2nd. Took up the case of Tom belonging to Mr. William Banks, a reference of last meeting, and after some inquiry relative to the case received him into the church. 3rd. John Patterson came to the church with a satisfactory repentance and was received into fellowship. Dismissed.

Jan. 17th, 1798. Met in conference and proceeded to business as follows: A complaint brought against Brother Thomas Thornton for drinking to excess and wanting to fight, he not being present a committee was appointed to cite him. Dismissed.

Feb. 10th, 1798. Met in conference and proceeded as follows: 1st. Inquired for fellowship. Bro. John Patterson brought a charge against himself for getting angry—made satisfactory acknowledgment and was retained in fellowship. 2nd. Took up Brother Thomas Thornton's case, a reference of last meeting, and upon finding him guilty he was excluded. 3rd. A complaint brought against Bro. Carroll for the sin of drunkenness, he being absent appointed Bro. Mark Thornton and Kidd to cite him to the next conference to answer the charge. 4th. Opened a door for the reception of members. 5th. A complaint brought against Sister Mary White for getting mad and using words unbecoming and unlawful, she made satisfactory acknowledgment and was retained in fellowship. 6th. Sister Car and Brother James Maxwell applied for letter of dismission which was granted. Dismissed.

March 10th, 1798. Met in conference and proceeded to business as follows: 1st. Inquired for fellowship. A report saying that Brother Reuben White was guilty of getting drunk, he made it appear that the report was false and was retained in fellowship. Dismissed.

April 7th, 1798. Met in conference and proceeded to business as follows: 1st. Inquired for fellowship. Brother Carroll came before the church and made satisfactory acknowledgment and was retained in fellowship. 2nd. Received a petition from Holly Springs Church for Bro. Thornton and Bro. White to attend their meeting in June, which was granted. Dismissed.

May 11th, 1798. Met in conference and proceeded to business as follows: 1st. Inquired for fellowship. Brother Jacob Prewit brought a complaint against himself. Made satisfactory acknowledgment to the church and was retained in fellowship. May 12th. William Arnold, once a member, came forward, made satisfactory acknowledgment to the church for his transgression and was received into fellowship. 2nd. Received by experience Marthy Bennet. Dismissed.

June 9th, 1798. Met in conference and proceeded to business as follows: Opened a door and received by experience a black man by the name of Frank belonging to Mr. Clark. Dismissed.

Met the 4th Lord's Day in June, 1798. Inquired and found the church in peace. Dismissed.

July 7th, 1798. Met in conference and proceeded to busidness as follows: Received by experience Ann Douglas, Thomas Head and Littleton Johnson, formerly of Jeremiah Walker's church. Dismissed.

August 11th, 1798. Met in conference and proceeded to busidness as follows: 1st. Inquired for fellowship, Brother Littleton Johnston brought a complaint against himself for getting angry and quarreling, made satisfactory acknowledgment and was retained in fellowship. Bro. Thornton brought a complaint against a black brother by the name of Frank belonging to Mr. Clarke for the sin of fornication, and being found guilty was excommunicated. 2nd. Opened door for the reception of members, and received by experience Elizabeth Williams, Henry Shackleford, Hannah belonging to Bro. John White, Biddy belonging to Mr. Benj. Head, and John Dingler. Dismissed.

At a meeting held at Nathan Childs', 15th July, 1798. Opened a door for the reception of members. Sister Elizabeth Head came forward with a recommendation and received into fellowship; Sister Nancy Head came forward and was received into membership. Received by experience John Head and Fanny Head. Dismissed.

At a meeting held at Bro. Arnold's, 22 July, 1798. Opened a door for the reception of members and received by experience John Mann, a black man, Bowman, belonging to Mr. Middleton. Dismissed.

At a meeting August 26th, 1798. Proceeded as follows: 1st. Inquired into the fellowship, a complaint was brought forward against a black brother by the name of Lace, belonging to Mr. Pullom. In laboring with him he became angry, would not hear the church, and was excommunicated. 2nd. Brother Carroll brought a complaint against himself for wanting to fight, made satisfactory acknowledgment and was retained in fellowship. Dismissed.

At a meeting held at Bro. Childs', 29th August, 1798. Opened a door for the reception of members, and received into fellowship a black woman by the name of Lucy, belonging to Mr. Hudson, and a free black woman by the name of Peggy, formerly of Jeremiah Walker's church. Dismissed.

Sept. 8th, 1798. Met in conference and proceeded to business as follows: 1st. Inquired into fellowship, brought up the case of Brother Prewit, a reference of August conference, he made satisfactory acknowledgment for his transgression and was retained in fellowship. 2nd. Restored Bro. William Arnold to the Deaconship. 3rd. Appointed Bro. D. Thornton, Bro. White and Bro. William Arnold delegates to the Association. Dismissed. D. Thornton, Moderator.

Oct. 13, 1789. Met in conference and proceeded to business as follows: Inquired for fellowship. Bro. Dozier Thornton brought a complaint against Bro. Jeremiah Thompson for unlawful proceeding, he being absent the charge was referred till next meeting. Appointed Bro. Thornton and Bever to cite him to attend. 2nd. Bro. D. Thornton brought a query of the Association before the church: Is it the duty for the head of every Christian family to hold divine worship in his or her home? Answer: It is. 3rd. Opened a door for the reception of members and received by letter Wm. Gibbs. Dismissed. D. Thornton, Moderator.

Met on the 14th. Opened a door and received by experience Judith Mann. Dismissed.

Nov. 10th, 1798. Met in conference and proceeded to business as follows: 1st. Inquired into the fellowship of the church. Brother Prewit brought a complaint against himself, made satisfactory acknowledgment and was retained in fellowship. 2nd. The letter to the Association was read and approved. Dismissed. D. Thornton, Moderator.

October Conference, after some consideration referred it till next meeting. 3rd. Opened a door for the reception of members and received by letter Bro. Frederick Crouder from Clouds Creek. Dismissed. D. Thornton, Moderator. (The above is evidently a portion of the December, 1798, or January, 1799, record, since the minutes for the above named months are torn from the original minute book).

Feb. 9th, 1799. Met in conference and proceeded to business as follows: 1st. Inquired into the fellowship of the church. 2nd. The case of Bro. Jeremiah Thompson took up and laid over till next meeting. Received by letter Sister Jane Underwood from Cabin Creek. 3rd. Lace, belonging to Mr. Pullom, once a member, came before the church with a repentance and made satisfactory acknowledgment, and was again received into fellowship. 4th. Catherine Legs came before the church, told her condition, wanted to join the church, and after due examination and strict inquiry, we received her into fellowship. Dismissed. D. Thornton, Moderator.

March 9th, 1799. Met in conference and proceeded as follows: 1st. Took up the case of Bro. Jeremiah Thompson, he neglected to hear the church and was excommunicated. 2nd. Sister Elizabeth Brown applied for dismission, which was granted. 3rd. Opened a door for the reception of members and received by experience Nancy Prewit. 4th. Sister Susannah Housey asked for a letter of dismission, which was granted. D. Thornton, Moderator.

April 13th, 1799. Met in conference and proceeded to business as follows: 1st. Inquired into the fellowship of the church. James Arnold . . . . 3rd. Bro. D. Thornton brought a complaint against Sister Catherine Rucker for unlawful proceeding. She being absent the case was referred until next conference and appointed Brehtren John Cason and Reuben White to cite her to attend. 4th. Sister Elizabeth Williams applied for a letter of dismission, which was granted. Dismissed. D. Thornton, Moderator.

May 11th, 1799. Met in conference and procedeed to business as follows: 1st. Inquired into the fellowship of the church. Took up the case of Sister Catherine Rucker, a reference of last meeting; she being absent, it was referred till next meeting. 2nd. Brothr Arnold brought a complaint against Bro. Thomas Woldridge for using unbecoming language to his mother. From the acknowledgment he made to Bro. Arnold the church received satisfaction and retained him in fellowship. 3rd. Brother Arnold brought a complaint against himself for unlawful proceeding. Made satisfactory acknowledgment and was retained. 4th. Opened a door for the reception of members, and received by letter Bro. Robert Moor and Sister Moor, his wife. 5th. Appointed delegates to serve in conference, viz., Brethren D. Thornton, White and Crouder. Dismissed. D. Thornton, Moderator.

June 8th, 1799. Met in conference and proceeded to business as follows: 1st. Inquired into the fellowship of the church. 2nd. Took up the case of Catherine Rucker, laid over till next meeting. 3rd. Bro. D. Thornton brought a query: Is it right for black members to trade on the Lord's Day? Answer: No. 4th. Opened a door for the reception of members. Dismissed. D. Thornton, Moderator.

July 13th, 1799. Met in conference and proceeded to business as follows: 1st. Inquired into the fellowship of the church. Bro. Benjamin Mallen brought a complaint against himself for unlawful proceeding and playing cards. Made satisfactory acknowledgment and was retained in fellowship. 2nd. Bro. John White brought a complaint against Bro. John Carroll for getting drunk. He being absent the charge was referred till the next meeting. Appointed Brethren John White and Henry Shackleford to cite him to attend. 3rd. Opened a door for the reception of members and received by letter Sister Herndon, by experience Barbry Head. Dismissed. D. Thornton, Moderator.

Aug. 10th, 1799. Met in conference and proceeded as follows: 1st. Inquired into the fellowship of the church. Took up the case of Sister Catherine Rucker; she neglected to hear the church and was excommunicated. 2nd. Took up the case of Bro. Carroll, a reference of last meeting; he made satisfactory acknowledgment and was retained in fellowship. 4th. Brother John Head brought a complaint against himself for being too familiar with a woman, confessed his fault, made satisfactory acknowledgment and was retained in fellowship. 5th. A complaint brought against Sister Barbry Head for getting angry; she made satisfactory acknowledgment and was retained in fellowship. D. Thornton, Moderator.

Sept. 17th, 1799. Met in conference and proceeded to business as follows: 1st. Inquired into the fellowship of the church. 2nd. Appointed delegates to the Association, viz.: Bro. John White, Bro. Robert Moor, and Bro. Littleton Johnston. Dismissed. D. Thornton, Moderator.

Oct. 13th, 1799. Met in conference and proceeded to business as follows: 1st. Inquired into the fellowship of the church; found in peace. 2nd. Bro. D. Thornton brought a query before the church: Is there any Divine authority for yearly Associations to be conducted as they have been lately? Dismissed. D. Thornton, Moderator.

Nov. 9th, 1799. Met in conference and proceeded to business as follows: 1st. Inquired into the fellowship of the church; found in peace. 2nd. Took up the query laid at last meeting by Bro. Thornton, threw it under the table and was dismissed. D. Thornton, Moderator.

Dec. 7th, 1799. Met in conference and proceeded to business as follows: 1st. Inquired idnto the fellowship of the church and found in peace. 2nd. Opened a door for the reception of members and received by letter Sister

Milly Crouder. 3rd. Bro. Joshua Underwood brought a query before the church: Is there any Divine authority for yearly Associations to be conducted as they lately have been? After some debate it was answered there is none, and was dismissed. D. Thornton, Moderator.

Jan. 11th, 1800. Met in conference and proceeded to business as follows: 1st. Inquired into the fellowship of the church. Bro. John Patterson brought a complaint against himself for drinking too much, made satisfactory acknowledgment and was retained in fellowship. 2nd. Bro. Thornton, a complaint against Jeffrey for dishonest acting. He being absent it was referred till next meeting. Brethren Reuben White and Kidd brought a complaint against Bro. Benjamin Allen for the sin of fornication and he was excommunicated. 4th. Bro. Joseph Deadwyler brought a complaint against Bro. John White for going to law before unbelievers; he being absent the case was referred till next meeting. Appointed Bro. John Cason to cite him to attend. 5th. Bro. oJhn Cason brought a complaint against Bro. Carroll for drinking too much. He being absent, appointed Brethren William Arnold and John Mann to cite him to attend. 6th. Opened a door for the reception of members. Received by letter Bro. Robert Burk and Sister Sarah Burk. Dismissed.

Feb. 8th, 1800. Met in conference and proceeded to business as follows: 1st. Inquired into the fellowship of the church. Took up the case of Bro. John White, a reference of last meeting; he made satisfactory acknowledgment and was retained in fellowship. 2nd. HTook up the case of Bro. Carroll, a reference of last meeting; he made satisfactory acknowledgment and was retained in fellowship. 3rd. Took up the case of Jeffrey and upon inquiry he was found not guilty and accordingly retained in fellowship Dismissed. D. Thornton, Moderator.

(The pages in the original minute book containing the minutes from February 8th, 1800, to May 10th, 1800, are missing).

May 10th, 1800. Met in conference and proceeded to business as follows: 1st. Inquired into the fellowship of the church. Bro. John Carroll brought a complaint against himself for quarreling. He made satisfactory acknowledgment and was retained. 2nd. Opened a door for the reception of members and received by letter Bro. Charles Witt, Bro. John Ford, and Sister Ford, his wife. Dismissed. D. Thornton, Moderator.

June 6th, 1800. Met in conference and proceeded to business as follows: 1st. Inquired into the fellowship of the church and found in peace. 2nd. Opened a door for the reception of members. Received by letter Sister Sarah Wheeler. Dismissed. D. Thornton, Moderator.

July 12th, 1800. Met in conference and proceeded to business as follows: 1st. Inquired into the fellowship of the church; found in peace. 2nd. Opened a door for the reception of members. Received by experience Susannah Hubbard, a black woman by the name of Nancy, belonging to Mr. William Pullom, and a black man by the name of Robert, belonging to Mr. Jas Brown Received by letter a black woman named Edy, belonging to Mr. James Alston, Sister Peggy Anderson by the name of . . . . belonging to Mr. B. . . . . . D. Thornton, Moderator.

Aug. 9th, 1800. Met in conference and proceeded to business as follows: 1st. Inquired into the fellowship of the church. Bro. John Carroll brought a complaint against himself for making use of unlawful language; made satisfactory acknowledgment and was retained in fellowship. Dismissed.

Sept. 13th, 1800. Met in conference and proceeded to business as follows: 1st. Inquired into the fellowship of the church; found in peace. 2nd. Appointed Bro. D. Thornton, Bro. F. Crouder and Bro. John White delegates to the Association. 3rd. Opened a door for the reception of members and received by experience a black man by the name of Cato, belonging to Mr. Thos. Fortson. Dismissed.

Oct. 6th, 1800. Met in conference and proceeded to business as follows: 1st. Inquired into the fellowship of the church; found in peace. Dismissed. D. Thornton, Moderator.

Nov. 8th, 1800. Met in conference and proceeded to business as follows: 1st. Inquired into the fellowship of the church. Bro. John Patterson brought a complaint against himself for getting drunk, made satisfactory acknowledgment and was retained in fellowship. Dismissed.

Dec. 11th, 1800. Met in conference and proceeded to business as follows: 1st. Inquired into the fellowship of the church. Found in peace. Dismissed. D. Thornton, Moderator.

Jan. 10th, 1801. Met in conference and proceeded to business as follows: 1st. Inquired into the fellowship of the church. Took up a report against Bro. John Patterson, saying he had been drunk; he made it appear that the report was false. Bro. Dozier Thornton brought a complaint against Bro. John Carroll for getting drunk; he being absent it was referred till next meeting. Bro. John White and Bro. Henry Shackleford to cite him to attend. Dismissed. D. Thornton.

Feb. 7th, 1801. Met in conference and proceeded to business as follows: 1st. Inquired into the fellowship of the church. Took up the case of Bro. John Carroll, a reference of last meeting, continued until next meeting. 2nd. Another charge against Bro. Carroll laid over till next meeting. 3rd. Bro. Mark Thornton brought a complaint against Bro. John Patterson for wanting to fight. He being absent it was referred till next meeting. Brethren Reuben White and John White to cite him to attend. Sister Henry applied for a letter of dismission, which was granted. 5th. Received Bro. James Jones by experience. Dismissed. John White, Moderator.

Mar. 7th, 1801. Met in conference and proceeded to business as follows: 1st. Inquired into the fellowship of the church. Took up the case of Bro. John Carroll; he made satisfactory acknowledgment and was retained in fellowship. 2nd. Took up the case of Bro. John Patterson, a reference of last meeting; he being found guilty was excommunicated. 3rd. By request granted letters of dismission to Bro. Wm. Gibbs, Sister Cersy, Sister Glover and Sister Huff. D. Thornton.

April 11th, 1801. Met in conference and proceeded as follows: 1st. Inquired into the fellowship of the church. Bro. John White brought a complaint against Bro. John Cason. Referred to a committee and it was settled to the satisfaction of the church. 2nd. Bro. John Head came before the church and made recantation for his going disorderly, to the satisfaction of the church, and was retained in fellowship. 3rd. Sister Elizabeth Thornton brought a complaint against Sister Rucker and she neglected to hear the church and was excommunicated. 4th. Received Bro. John Johnston by letter. D. Thornton, Moderator.

May 9th, 1801. Met in conference and proceeded to business as follows: 1st. Inquired into the fellowship of the church. Found in peace. Dismissed.

June 13th, 1801. Met in conference and proceeded to business as follows: 1st. Inquired into the fellowship of the church. Bro. D. Thornton brought a complaint against a black sister by the name of Peg, belonging to Joseph Davis. She was excommunicated. 2nd. Bro. D. Thornton brought a complaint against Bro. Carroll, a report saying he had been drunk. He being absent it was referred till the next meeting the 4th Saturday in this month. Bro. John Mann to cite him to attend. 4th. A grievance between Sister Cleveland and Bro. Kid and Sister Kid, his wife, referred to a committee, viz.: Bro. J. White, Bro. Wm. Arnold, Bro. Crouder, Bro. John Ford, Bro. John Cason and Bro. Littleton Johnston. Bro. D. Thornton laid a query: Is it good order when brethren have a dispute, for them not to be faithful in dealing with each other for it? Answer: It is not good order. Dismissed. D. Thornton, Moderator.

June 29th, 1801. Met in conference and proceeded to business as follows: 1st. Took up the case of Bro. Carroll; he failed to hear the church and was excommunicated. 2nd. Took up the case of Bro. Kid and Sister Kid; they refused to hear the church and were excommunicated. 3rd. Bro. John Underwood laid a query before the church: Is it right to sue for slander? Answer: Let every one use their own pleasure. 4th. Took up the case of Lydda, a reference from last meeting, was taken up. She mad satisfactory acknowledgment and was retained in fellowship. Dismissed. D. Thornton, Moderator.

July 10th, 1801. Met in conference and proceeded to busidness as follows: 1st. A decorum presented, read and accepted. 2nd. Inquired into the fellowship of the church. Took up a report against Sister Milly Cleveland, saying she was guilty of telling lies. She made it appear that the report was groundless, and false, to the satisfaction of the church and was retained in fellowship. Dismissed. D. Thornton, Moderator.

August 22nd, 1801. Met in conference and proceeded to business as follows: 1st. Opened a door for the reception of members and received by experience Jeremiah Thornton, Aeuben Thornton, Amy Childs, Benjamin Fortson and William, a black man belonging to Jim Thornton. 2nd. Inquired into the fellowship of the church. Bro. Jacob Prewit came with a charge against himself for drinking too much, and being too familiar with a woman; made satisfactory acknowledgment and was retained in fellowship. Dismissed. D. Thornton, Moderator.

Sept. 12th, 1801. Met in conference and proceeded to business as follows: 1st. Opened a door for the reception of members and received by experience Jane Arnold, Peggy Thornton, Sarah Underwood, Edy, a black woman belonging to Mr. Benjamin Fortson; Barber, a black man belonging to Webb Kid; Tamor, a black woman belonging to Joseph Henderson; Wiggin, a black man belonging to N. Allen; Martin Kid, Benjamin Herndon, Nanct Davis, John Jones and John Childs. Dismissed.

Sept. 13th, 1801. Met and opened a door for the reception of members and received by experience William Gye; Rachel, a black woman belonging to Thomas Pery. 2nd. John Carroll came forward with satisfactory repentance for his crime and was restored to fellowship. 3rd. Brother Yet came forward and made satisfactory repentance and acknowledgment for his crime and was restored to fellowship. Dismissed.

Oct. 9th, 1801. Met in conference and proceeded to business as follows: 1st. Appointed Bro. Dozier Thornton, Bro. Frederick Crouder, Bro. John White and Bro. William Arnold delegates to the Association. 2nd. Inquired into the fellowship of the church. Bro. John White brought a complaint against a black sister by the name of Lydda, belonging to Benajmin Head, for turning away her husband and she was excluded. 3rd. Opened a door for the reception of members and received by experience Sarah Thornton, Winey Hales, Ann McOpin, Mary Thornton, Elizabeth Johnston, Lucy Childs, Prudence Richardson, Milly Hales, Con Moss, Ann Allen, Sussannah Herndon, Joseph Allen, Lucy Cash and William Arnold, Jr. Night meeting at James Browns' opened a door for the reception of members, and received by experience Polly Mann, Joseph Rucker and Milly Rucker. Dismissed.

Oct. 10th, 1801. Met at the meeting house; opened a door for the reception of members and received by experienc Jincy Fanning, Lucy Nix, John Willis, Nancy Gaar, Darcas Ford, Caty Head, Nancy Childers, Elizabeth Sharp, Elizabeth Head, Polly Arnold, Ann Brown, Jane Head, Nancy Head, Violetta Morrison, Margaret Hulme, Elizabeth Fortson, John Lyon, Phillip Johnston, Zachariah Smith, Sally Jones, John Hulme, Patsy Hulme, James Childers, Charles Fanning; Jane, a black woman belonging to Thomas Fortson; Rachel, a black woman belonging to John Craft; and Patty, a black woman belonging to William Kid. Dismissed.

Oct. 11th, 1801. Met and opened a door and received by experience

Thomas Blare, Letty Blare, and Betty, a black woman belonging to Thomas Carter. Dismissed.

Oct. 13th, 1801. Met at Bro. John Childs'; opened a door for the reception of members and received by experience Clary G. Morrison, Polly Hopkins, Charity Woodall, Paschal Cole, Wiley Childers; James, a black man belonging to Bro. Thomas Head; John Childs, Catey Childs; Judy, a black woman belonging to Thomas White; Jacob, a black man belonging to Bro. John Childs; Ambrose, a black man belonging to Sister Viletty Moroson; and Patsy Smith. Dismissed.

Oct. 31st, 1801. At a meeting at Bro. Nathan Childs', opened a door and received by experience Nancy Childs, Peggy Childs, Benjamin Childs, Eunity Head, and Haley Jones. Dismissed.

Nov. 7th, 1801. Met in conference and proceeded to business as follows: 1st. Opened a door for the reception of members and received by experience Elizabeth Ford, Patsy McOpin, Susannah Childs, Drucilla Allen, Elizabeth Nix, Rebecca Shepherd, Rhoda Davis, Sally Arnold, James Arnold, Jane Mann, Jane Hubbard, Reuben White, Benjamin Davis, William Patterson, Ann Oliver; Lewis, a black man belonging to Joseph Henderson; Hezziah, a black woman belonging to Bro. Underwood; Henry, a black man belonging to Joseph Rucker; Sally, a black woman belonging to Thomas Burton; Betty, a black woman belonging to Peter Wich; Becky, a black woman belonging to Phillip Lewis; Briester, a black man belonging to Mr. Fortson; and Isbell, a black woman belonging to Barnett Jeter. Dismissed.

Nov. 11th, 1801. At a meeting at Bro. John Childs', opened a door and received by experience Peggy Rucker, Joseph Chipman, Molly Hutson, Fanny Woodall, George Nix, and Martin, a black man belonging to John Beck.

Dec. 10th, 1801. Met and proceeded to business as follows: 1st. Bro. D. Thornton proposed that a fund be raised for the use of the church, which was agreed to. 2nd. Bro. D. Thornton moved for a church meeting at Bro. Nathan Childs'; agreed to. 3rd. Opened a door for the reception of members and received by experience James Mann, Lizzie Mann, Polly Roebuck, Frederick Crouder, Lewis Easter, Zachariah Skelton, Mary Skales, Jesse Patterson; Franky, a black woman belonging to Bro. R. Moore; and Jacob, a black man belonging to Bro. R. Moore. Dismissed.

Dec. 11th. At a night meeting at Bro. John Cason's, opened a door and received by experience Sally Nix, Milly Roebuck, and Bridget, a black woman belonging to William Ward. Dismissed.

Jan. 8th, 1802. Met in conference and proceeded to business as follows: 1st. Granted Sister Sartain a letter of dismission. 2nd. Gave letter of dismission to a black brother by the name of Jack and a black sister by the name of Sukey, belonging to Bro. Bell. 3rd. Granted letter of dismission to Bro. Hamshire. 4th. Granted letter of dismission to a black sister by the name of Betty, belonging to Frank Cook. 5th. Opened a door for the reception of members and received by experience Molly Craft. Dismissed.

Jan. 9th, 1802. Met, opened a door for the reception of members, and received by experience Wm. Kidd, Jonathan Thornton, Henry Mann, Rhoda Cleveland, Henry Gaines; John, a black man belonging to Bro. John Jones; and Savey, a black woman belonging to John Moore. 2nd. Chose and appointed two deacons, viz.: Bro. John Dingler and Bro. Littleton Johnston. 4th. Dismissed Bro. Mark Thornton from the deaconship. Dismissed.

Jan. 12th, 1802. At a meeting at Bro. John Hanes', opened a door, and received by experience Castleton Lyons, Patsy Lyons, Nancy Chipman, Sally Shakelford, Molly Dobbs; and Joe, belonging to Bro. Reuben White.

Jan. 13th, 1802. At a meeting at Bro. Nathan Childs', opened a door and received by experience Patsy Swilevant; and Joe, a black man belonging to Bro. Nathan Childs. Dismissed.

Jan. 23rd, 1802. Met at Bro. Nathan Childs'; opened a door for the reception of members and received by experience Elizabeth Nix, Matthew Brewer, and John Childs, a son of Nathan Childs. Dismissed.

Jan. 24th, 1802. Met at Bro. Childs'; opened a door and received by experience Charlet, a black woman of Nathan Childs'. Dismissed.

Feb. 6th, 1802. Met at Bro. Joseph Chipmans'; opened a door and received by experience Polly Jones, John Moore, Vicey Moore, and Sally Colbert. Dismissed.

Feb. 12th, 1802. Met in conference and proceeded to business as follows: 1st. Bro. Wm. Arnold came forward to answer a report against him, said he had been too fond of a woman; the report being proved, was excommunicated. 2nd. A petition for a constitution at Bro. Nathan Childs', the request was granted. 3rd. At the request of the Brethren appointed Bro. Dozier Thornton and Bro. John White to form a Presbytery for the purpose of forming a Constitution at Bro. Nathan Childs'. 4th. Opened a door for the reception of members and received by experience Amy, a black woman belonging to Bro. John White; Chany, a black woman belonging to Sister Cleveland; Jacob Cleveland, Rhody Cleveland, wife of Jacob Cleveland, Patsy Jones, Nancy Jones, daughters of Bro. James Jones; and Sam, a black man belonging to Bro. John White. Dismissed.

Feb. 13th, 1802. Met at the meeting house, opened a door for the reception of members, and received by experince Patson White, Patsy Lyons, Fanny Harris, Franky Kidd, Patsy Gaines, Daniel Thornton, Elizabeth Wanslow, George Alexander, Patsy Wanslow, Polly Alexander; Sukey, a black woman belonging to Mr. Roebuck; Elizabeth Kidd, Thomas White, and Calop Oliver. The ordination of Bro. John Dingler till the Constitution at Bro. Childs'.

Feb. 27th, 1802. Met at Bro. Nathan Childs' and proceeded to business as follows: 1st. Agreeable to a petition presented at Van's Creek Church for a Constitution at this place, which was granted, those appointed attended, formed a Presbytery and after examination having found them ripe for Constitution, the business acceded to, and constituted Frederick Crouder, Sr., and wife, Frederick Crouder, Jr., Milly Hales, Winey Hales, Wm. Arnold, Jr., Thomas Head and wife, Fanny Head, Elizabeth Head, John Head and wife Elizabeth Head, Caty Head, Jane Head, Nancy Head, Unity Head, Elizabeth Sharp, John Dingler and wife, Sally Woldridge, Zachariah Smith and wife, Prudence Richardson, Susan Hubbard, Cassy Childs, Hailey Jones, James Childers and wife, Sally Jones, John Childs and wife, Benjamin Childs, Peggy Childs, Nancy Childs, Nathan Childs and wife, Matthew Brewer, John Childs, son of Nathan Childs, Hanah Walker, Elizabeth Swilevant, Sally Colbert and Elizabeth Nix, and sat them to work as a church. Dismissed.

March 13th, 1802. Met in conference and proceeded to business as follows: 1st. Inquired into tht fellowship of the church. Bro. John Willis brought forth a complaint against himself for getting angry, made satisfactory acknowledgment and was retained in fellowship. 2nd. Took up the charge against a black sister by the name of Patty, belonging to Web Kid, for swearing and lying, for which she was excommunicated. 3rd. A complaint brought against a black brother by the name of Joe, belonging to Nathan Childs. Appointed Brethren Daniel Thornton and Littleton Johnston to cite him to attend our next meeting to answer the charge. 4th. Opened a door and received by letter Mary Woodall. 5th. William Arnold came forward with satisfactory repentance and acknowledgment and was restored to fellowship again. 6th. Appointed Bro. John Mann deacon and to be ordained at our next meeting. 7th. Granted letters of dismission to Charlot, belonging to Nathan Childs; Jack, Lucy, Phobe and Rachel, belonging to Sister Woldridge; Peggy, belonging to Mr. Hutson; Phillis, belonging to R. Middleton; Edgecomb, belonging to James Alston; James, belonging to Bro. Thomas Head; Ambrose, belonging to Sister Moroson; Tabby, belonging to Thomas Burton; Betty, belonging to Peter Wiche; Phillis, belonging to Thos. Colbert; and Rachel, belonging to Walter Richison. 8th. Made a settlemtnt with William Arnold by Bro. John Cason and Bro. Thomas Woldridge on behalf of the church. This account was $8.80/¾ which balanced against to $8.80/¾ placed in his hands Dec. 11th, 1801, for the use of the church. Dismissed.

April 10th, 1802. Met and proceeded to business as follows: 1st. Opened a door for the reception of members and received by experience Martha Shepherd. 2nd. Zidy Colbert came forward with a satisfactory repentance and acknowledgment, justified the church in her exclusion, and was restored to fellowship. 4th. Ordained Bro. John Mann to the deaconship. 5th. George Nix came forward and confessed his fault in drinking too much, made satisfactory acknowledgment and restored to fellowship and granted a letter of recommendation to the church to which he has moved. 6th. Took up the case of Joe, belonging to Nathan Childs, a reference of last meeting, and excommunicated him for lying and stealing. 7th. Granted letters of dismission to Bro. Wiley Childers, Sister Childers, his wife, and Zachariah Skelton. 8th. Ordered that Bro. Reuben White, Jr., Bro. Martin Kid and Bro. Jeremiah Thornton have liberty to exercise their gifts in the bounds of the church. Dismissed.

Sunday, the 11th, opened a door and received by experience John Pikens and Lemuel Underwood.

May 8th, 1802. Met in conference and proceeded to business as follows: 1st. Opened a door for the reception of members and received by experience Sibrey Pollard; received by letter Standley Jones and Nancy Jones, his wife. 2nd. Inquired into the fellowship of the church. Bro. Jesse Patterson came forward with a complaint against himself for swearing and dancing, and crave to be excluded and accordingly was. 3rd. Brought a complaint against Bro. Robert Crook for telling lies, for which he was excommunicated. 4th. Bro. John Willis brought a complaint against himself for getting angry, made satisfactory acknowledgment and retained in fellowship. 5th. Brought a charge against a black sister by the name of Lucy, belonging to John Rucker, for stealing a handkerchief; it appeared from plain circumstances that she was guilty. She was excommunicated for the same. 6th. Granted a letter of dismissal to Bro. Paschal Cole. 7th. Ordered Bro. John Cason and Bro. Joseph Chipman have liberty to exercise their gifts within the bounds of the church.

May 30th, 1802. Met at Bro. John Jones', opened a door for the reception of members, and received by experience Sally Shakelford, Milly Wanslow, Patsy Moore, Hannah McGovern, and Charity, a black woman belonging to Thomas Greeg. Dismissed.

June. 12th, 1802. Met in conference and proceeded to business as follows: 1st. Opened a door for the reception of members and received by experience Wiley Thornton. 2nd. Inquired into the fellowship of the church. Bro. Thomas Blare came forward with a complaint against himself for drinking too much, made satisfactory acknowledgment and was retained in fellowship. Bro. Joseph Chipman brought a complaint against Bro. Lewis Easter for keeping bad company and riding a race on the Sabbath Day. Bro. Chipman and Bro. James Shackleford appointed to cite him to attend our next meeting.

One member of Van's Creek Church held the unusual distinction of being ex-communicated and restored to fellowship three times during a period of less than six years. This individual was one John Carroll. On June 29th, 1801, he was ex-communicated for drinking to excess and restored September 13th, 1801. On January 11th, 1806, he suffered expulsion for the same offense and was restored on February 8th of the same year. On July 11th, 1806, he met with the same fate and was again restored May 9th, 1807.

The following list comprises all white persons who joined Van's Creek Church during the periods extending from 1803 through 1831 and from 1844 through 1867, which is available.

Adams, Samuel—Dec. 8, 1810.
Adams, Ritta—June 9, 1827.
Adams, Samuel—Aug. 21, 1831.
Adams, Nancy—Aug. 21, 1831.
Adams, Elizabeth—June 19, 1857.
Adams, Ann—Oct. 23, 1853.
Adams, F. C., Mrs.—Aug. 17, 1867.
Alexander, Judy—June 9, 1822.
Alexander, James—Sept. 13, 1823.
Allen, Jane Heard—Dec. 27, 1828.
Bell, Joseph, Jr.—Jan. 24, 1829.
Brown, Dozier—July 16, 1831.
Brown, Mary—July 16, 1831.
Brown, Benjamin, Jr.—July 16, 1831.
Brown, George W.—July 16, 1831.
Brown, Dillard—Aug. 22, 1831.
Brown, J. A.—Sept., 1848.
Brown, J. A., Mrs.—Sept., 1848.
Brown, Sarah M. F.—Sept., 1848.
Brown, John S.—Sept., 1848.
Brown, Nancy—Sept. 15, 1860.
Brown, Russell D.—April 9, 1867.
Brown, Sarah F.—April 19, 1867.
Buffington, W. M.—July, 1848.
Buffington, Nancy—Sept., 1848.
Buffington, William—Sept. 1, 1860.
Burton, Nancy—Dec. 27, 1828.
Cash, Patsy—July 10, 1813.
Chandler, Asa—March 18, 1831.
Chandler, Asa, Mrs.—March 18, 1831.
Childers, Sarah—June 12, 1824.
Childers, Holman, Aug. 18, 1828.
Christian, Thomas—Aug. 10, 1855.
Christian, Luther M.—Sept. 17, 1859.
Cleveland, Mary—July 19, 1853.
Cleveland, Peter—July 16, 1831.
Colbert, Thomas—Sept. 6, 1804.
Colbert, Thomas—Aug. 7, 1824.
Colson, Frances—Dec. 27, 1828.
Conwell, Susan—Nov. 12, 1826.
Conwell, Daniel—Dec. 9, 1826.
Craft, Pleasant—July 4, 1813.
Darden, David—Aug. 13, 1803.
Davis, Peggy—Nov. 11, 1820.
Dutton, Nancy—Sept. 6, 1804.
Evans, J. E. B., Mrs.—May 16, 1853.
Evans, Willis, Sr.—Dec. 9, 1826.
Evans, Milton—May 15, 1853.
Evans, Mary J.—May 15, 1853.
Evans, J. E. B.—May 16, 1853.
Faulkner, A. E.—June 20, 1856.
Ferrell, Tabitha—Nov. 13, 1802.
Ford, Jinsey—May 7, 1812.
Ford, John—April 8,, 1821.
Ford, Mary—May 10, 1827.
Green, Rebecca—April 19, 1804.
Greenway, Sally—Nov. 12, 1826.
Greenway, Lucy—Nov. 12, 1826.
Goss, Mary—Sept. ,1848.
Haley, William—July, 1847.
Harris, John—Dec. 9, 1820.
Harris, Mary—April 7, 1821.
Harris, John—March 8, 1823.
Harris, Mary—March 8, 1823.
Head, Francis—Jan. 13, 1821.
Henry, Alexander—Aug. 13, 1803.
Herndon, Fanny—July 10, 1813.
Herndon, Rachel—Nov. 12, 1826.
Herndon, Biddy—Jan. 24, 1829.
Herndon, Edward—Sept., 1831.
Herndon, Dillard—Aug., 1831.
Herndon, Nancy—Aug. 22, 1831.
Higginbotham, Nancy—July, 1806.
Higginbotham, Tabitha—July, 1812.
Hill, Rachel—Feb. 6, 1816.
Hilly, Francis—Jan. 13, 1827.
Hilly, Mary—Jan. 13, 1827.
Hulme, Milly—Dec. 6, 1826.
Hulme, Nancy—Aug. 8, 1831.
Hulme, John H.—March 17, 1860.
Hulme, Frances—Aug. 17, 1861.
Hulme, J. D.—May 20, 1865.
Johnston, Larkin—April 18, 1821.
Johnston, Thomas—Sept., 1848.
Jones, James—Sept. 12, 1812.
Jones, Garland—June 9, 1827.
Jones, Winny—June 9, 1827.
Jones, Lewis I.—July 26, 1829.
Jones, William, Jr.—July 16, 1831.
Kelly, G. W.—Sept. 19, 1857.
Keys, Agatha—March 13, 1824.
King, Thomas—Aug. 11, 1827.
Langston, Patsy—Nov. 11, 1820.
Langston, Jesse—Aug. 12, 1826.
Lewis, Elenor—Sept. 11, 1802.
Lewis, Hattie—Oct. 2, 1802.
Lewis, Catherine—Oct. 2, 1802.
Lewis, Catey—Feb. 10, 1816.
McGowen, James—Aug. 13, 1803.
McLanahan, James—Nov. 12, 1826.
McLanahan, James, Mrs.—Nov. 12, 1826.
McDaniel, Mary—Aug. 6, 1859.
Mann, Holman—Aug. 18, 1828.
Mann, Robert—July 16, 1831.
Mann, Elizabeth—Aug. 7, 1831.
Maley, Elizabeth—July 16, 1831.
Maxfield, Clary—May 12, 1827.
Mills, Moses—Feb. 11, 1815.
Mills, Keppinhappuck—Feb. 11, 1815.
Nuccles, Nathaniel—Aug. 18, 1828.
Oliver, Henry S.—Dec. 9, 1826.

Page, Polly—Dec. 9, 1822.
Patterson, Elizabeth—Nov. 12, 1826.
Pollard, Daby—May 9, 1807.
Richerson, Prudence—Aug. 13, 1803.
Rouzee, Frank—Dec. 8, 1810.
Rouzee, Louisa—May 19, 1865.
Ryan, Betty—Sept. 12, 1812.
Ryan, Elizabeth—June 10, 1815.
Ryan, Barry—Feb. 10, 1816.
Smith, Frances—Jan. 6, 1804.
Terry, Polly—Aug. 7, 1824.
Thornton, Martha—Aug. 9, 1823.
Thornton, Benj., Sr.—Dec. 9, 1826.
Thornton, Sally—Nov. 10, 1805.
Thornton, Elizabeth—July 4, 1812.
Thornton, Elijah—March 9, 1806.
Thornton, Mourning—Sept. 13, 1823.
Thornton, Daniel—Dec. 9, 1826.
Thornton, Benj.—June 13, 1827.
Thornton, Sarah—March 15, 1828.
Thornton, Benj. C.—Feb. 15, 1857.
Tibbs, Thomas—Sept. 6, 1804.
Tibbs, Thomas—Feb. 11, 1809.
Tibbetts, Rachel—April 7, 1827.
Tomason, Elizabeth—March 7, 1818.
Wall, Burgess—Feb. 10, 1816.
Warren, Wm. H.—May 17, 1856.
Warren, John M.—May 17, 1856.
Warren, T. J.—Sept. 1, 1860.
Warren, Elizabeth—May 17, 1862.
White, Rachel—Feb., 1814.
White, Mary—July 16, 1831.
White, Henry—Sept., 1831.
White, Elizabeth—Sept., 1831.
White, John H.—June 18, 1846.
White, Jonas H.—July 17, 1843.
Whipple, Ann E.—March 15, 1856.
Willis, David C.—May, 1848.
Wheeler, Pamima—Jan., 1827.

Reverend Benjamin Thornton Jr., who was ordained a minister at Van's Creek on October 13, 1837, was the ancestor of 469 descendants. He was thrice married, but his first wife, Nancy Payne, was the mother of all his children.

He was unusual in that he was not only a strong and popular minister, but served in the Georgia Legislature and accumulated a fortune as a dealer in live stock.

When selling an animal he would never fix a price, but would take whatever sum that might be offered. It was his proud boast that never once was he the loser. If asked the age of an animal he would spread his huge fingers above the animal's back and reply, "Under 10, Sir. Yes Sir. Under 10." He lived to a ripe old age and is buried in Hart County, Georgia.

Still another Baptist minister who resided in Elbert County should be mentioned here.

William Davis was a native of Orange County, Virginia, where he was born January 7th, 1765.

At the age of 15 he joined a Baptist Church in Orange County, known as "Blue Run." When he was 16 he became a soldier of the American Revolution under the command of Marquise Lafayette. He was wounded in the head, but recovered and was present at the surrender of Lord Cornwallis.

In 1788 he was licensed to preach in Virginia and in 1793 in Elbert County. He was ordained by Dozier Thornton and Thomas Maxwell.

His children, of which there were 12, followed in his footsteps for three of them, Jonathan, James, and Jesse, became Baptist ministers, and two others, Jepthan and William Jr., were deacons.

William Davis served the church in the fork of Broad River 23 years and Beaverdam Baptist Church for 12 years. Under his ministry E. Shackleford, Isaac Suttles, Elijah Mosely, and Sylvanus Gibson entered the ministry. He died October 31, 1831.

David Cook, a Baptist minister, was born in Elbert County during the year 1803, but his activities were centered in Newton County, where he died in 1876. He is buried at Macedonia Church near the town of Oxford.

Thomas A. Carter, during the Spring of 1788, deeded Nathaniel Allen, Richardson Hunt, John Tallet, John Harkleford, Robert Brown, William Hanson, and Peter Stubbs, as trustees, one acre of land including a church building, known as "Beaverdam Preaching House," for the sum of five shillings. The deed provided that, "They permit only such persons as are appointed by the conference of the people called Methodist, and no other, for the purpose of preaching and expounding God's word, and that the said persons preach no other doctrines than is contained in Mr. Wesley's notes on the New Testament and his four volumes of sermons and the Minutes of the Conference."

This church was the second Methodist Church to be built in Georgia, having been antedated by Grant's Meeting House in Wilkes County.

During the Winter of 1788, Bishop Asbury determined to organize a Methodist Conference in Georgia. Previous to this time he had spent several months in the territory which now comprises Elbert County and had made many staunch converts. It was, therefore, a natural desire on his part to hold the first Georgia Conference in a section that reacted favorably to his doctrines.

On the day set for the meeting the weather was extremely unpleasant and when Asbury, and those making up his party, reached the home of Judge Charles Tait, near the town of Petersburg, it was decided to meet there rather than continue several miles distant to the first designated place of assemblage known as "Thompson's Meeting House." (now known as Bethlehem Methodist Church.)

The hospitable Judge, a warm friend of the Bishop, made the party heartily welcomed and thus, in his home, the first conference of the Methodist Episcopal Church of Georgia was held. (A handsome boulder of granite marks this spot.)

The members of this conference were: Bishop Asbury, who presided; Richard Ivey, Thomas Humphries, Moses Parks, Hope Hull, James Conner, Bennet Maxey, Isaac Smith, Mathew Harris, Reuben Ellis, and John Moses.

Shortly after this important event there was born near the site of the future Ruckersville one Richard Banks, who became a famous physician and surgeon. Dr. Banks, the son of a wealthy and cultured family, received a liberal education at the University of Georgia and the University of Pennsylvania. He was employed by the United States Government to visit the Cherokee Indians and gained a national reputation by virtue of performing 60 lithotomy operations with but two even partially unsuccessful. Dr. Banks was also an expert in the delicate operation of removing cataracts. He died in Gainesville, Georgia, in the year 1832. Banks County, Georgia, is named in his honor.

CHAPTER VI

ALEXANDRIA—BEVERLY ALLEN KILLS FORSYTHE—VOTER'S LIST, 1795—ELBERT COUNTY DUELS—JUDGE JONES—JAMES OSGOOD ANDREWS—TEXT OF ACT REGULATING ELBERTON—GENERAL WILEY THOMPSON—BETHLEHEM CHURCH—WAR OF 1812—WILEY BARRON—JONAS HARRISON.

Petersburg and Eberton were not the only towns within the confines of Elbert County that were laid out in lots previous to the year 1800. A deed recorded in Book "D," page 92, in the office of the Clerk of the Superior Court recites in part, the following:

"For and in consideration of the sum of ten pounds to me the said John McGowen in hand paid at and before the sealing and delivering of these presents the receipt whereof is hereby acknowledged have bargained and sold Remised released conveyed and confirmed unto the said Lewis Gaar his heirs and assigns one Lot No. 5 and one Lot No. 6 in the said Town of Alexandria in the State and County aforesaid which said Town lots—————."

This instrument was recorded on the 16th day of September, 1797.

Another deed for lots Numbered 13 and 14, in the town of Alexandria, is of record in Book "D," page 113, from John and Hannah McGowen to Henry Harper. This instrument bears the recording date of November 14, 1797.

The exact location of Alexandria is unknown and few persons have heretofore known even of its existence. Judging, however, from the names of the grantors, grantees and witnesses to the above mentiond instruments, John McGowen, Lewis Gaar, Henry Harper, and John Cunningham, and the locality in which they were known to have lived, it is reasonable to assume that this forgotten village was situated on or near the Savannah River a few miles below where Ruckersville was later founded.

A fact of interest, tending to show that Alexandria was probably of more importance than Elberton, is the purchase price paid for the lots, five pounds each, while lots in Elberton were selling, at the same period, for considerably lower prices.

Danville, another village of Elbert County on Broad River and in what is now Webbsboro District, was laid out in lots about 1798, by Clairborne Webb, but failed to survive. Lots were sold as late as 1801.

Several miles above Petersburg, on Beaverdam Creek, at what is now known as "Pearl Mills" or more properly, Beverly, an incorporated town site, two wealthy and cultured brothers from Virginia, settled and engaged in an extensive mercantile business. Their names were Beverly and William Allen. They not only engaged in business in Georgia, but had two establishments in South Carolina as well. In the readjustments occasioned by the rise of cotton, they became heavily indebted to wholesalers in Augusta and in consequence several suits were filed against them.

During the early part of June, 1794, the brothers made a trip to Augusta for the purpose of making settlements. Just as they entered the town, and before they had been able to interview their creditors, one Robert Forsythe, then United States Marshal for Georgia, and father of John Forsythe who later became Governor of Georgia, arrested Beverly Allen. When placed in jail high words ensued between Allen and Forsythe. In defense of his person Beverly Allen shot and killed the Marshal. William Allen, with the assistance of some of the creditors, with whom he had reached satisfactory settlements, released his brother and they made their way to Elbert County unmolested.

Beverly Allen, a few years later, removed to Kentucky, where he lived to be 90 years of age.

Soon after reaching his new home Allen entered the ministry and was highly esteemed by all who knew him. He left no descendants in Elbert County, but a number in Kentucky and Tennessee. He was a splendid specimen of physical manhood, more than six feet in heighth, courtly in manner and gifted in speech.

His brother, William, remained in Elbert County, and has a large number of descendants. His son, by his second wife Nancy Walthall, Singleton Walthall Allen married Jane Lanier Heard, daughter of Governor Stephen Heard and Elizabeth Darden. He was the only child, his mother dying a few months after his birth.

The following interesting letter written to Governor George Mathews by William Barnett sheds the true light upon an incident that has heretofore been written of in a misleading manner:

"Elbert County, 28th June, 1794.

"Dear Sir:

"On the 15th instant the sheriff of this County with myself an several others went to the house of Mr. William Allen where we had reason to believe that Beverly Allen who had escaped from Richmond County Goal, was conceiled. We accordingly found him very ingeniousley secreted in the garratt of the house of Wm. Allen. We carried him from thence to our goal. In about two hours after our arrival we were suprised by an armed force to the amount of some thirty odd, headed by Wm. Allen whose intentions he said were to protect Beverly Allen from Insults and from being carried to Augusta, though for some cause best known to themselves, theay Retreated without any further molestation. Our guard at that time was some 7 or 8 armed men. I emmediately advised the sheriff to call for assistance from the Militia officers some of which had not timely notice others being the particular friends of Allen, we were suplied with men who were our enemies. The 17th instant about 40 or 50 armed men came (from the best information) who were disguised with their faced blacked. The officer of the guard seeing their number ordered his men not to fire, as he had but ten guns and theay in Poor order. The mob advanced and rescued the prisoner. We have on slight testimony apprehended four of the party to of which were Militia Captains. It is extroordinary to think of the influence this man has had on the minds of the citizens of this County. I think theay are a majority in his favor. I have thought proper to mention these facts as they all came to my knowledge that should your excellency think it worthy of an Executive interference we should be happy to receive any assistance you might think proper to give (I mean the Proclamation being made which would call more emmediately the attention of the officer.)

    I am very Respectfully your Excellency's very
        Humble Servant, Wm. Barnett.
His Excellency,
George Mathews, Esq., Augusta.''

 The writer of the foregoing letter was born March 4, 1761, and died October 2, 1834. He married Mary Meriwether, born 1766, died 1850. He was Tax Collector of Richmond County, Georgia, from January 1, 1783, until June 23, 1784, and also served in the same capacity 1786 to April, 1789. Prior to 1784, he served as Sheriff of Richmond County and on August 7, 1790, he was a first lieutenant in the Richmond County Milita.

 In the latter part of 1790, he removed to the new County of Elbert and was one of the first five Justices of the Peace. He was also elected a delegate to the Constitution Convention of 1795, and again served with Richardson Hunt and Benjamin Moseley as delegate to the Constitution Convention of 1798. Barnett served as a member of the Georgia Senate from 1796 through 1811, and presided over that body in the year 1801. He was a representative in the lower branch of the United States Congress, 1811-1815. Barnett, by profession, was a physician, but gave little time to the practice.

 One can readily see where the sympathy of the people of Elbert County lay, after reading the above letter, and even the Governor, himself, knowing both Allen and Barnett personally, showed no disposition to interfere. The "Tempest in the tea pot" seemed to have been entirely of Barnett's brewing.

 There is little question that Barnett was prejudiced against Beverly Allen. He had, for many years, been closely associated with

Robert Forsythe and, in consequence, a warm personal friendship had grown up between them.

In the election for delegate to the Constitutional Convention of 1795, William Barnett defeated a Mr. Allen by some 30 votes. It is generally assumed that the Mr. Allen in question was Beverly. A list of the participants in this election as they appear on the original list, now on file in the Georgia Department of Archives and History, follows:

Charles Cosby
Jas. Lowery
Thos. Carter
Thos. Wilkins
— — Hudson
Edw. Clark
Jas. Brady
Wm. Forkner
Benj. Brown
Henry Moseley
Frar. Cook
Richards Hunt
James Sutton
Wm. Sewell
Reuben Lindsey
J. H. Morrison
Wm. Suttles
Isacc Davis
— — Morrison
Benj. Brawner
Chas. Webb
Thos. Aiken
Jno. Wingfield
Wm. Morris
Geo. Cook
Anthony Beverly
Elisha Lowry
Nat. Hudson
Larkin Hickerson
Lenard Rice
Thomas B. Scott
Peter Wyche
Jno. McKay
John McKee
Hez'h Chandler
Robert Moseley, Jr.
— — Merit
Endosius Cook
Wm. McKee
Laughlin Fannin
William Hansford
Peter Stubs
Robt. Huddleston
Daniel Thornton
Reuben Thornton
Richard Bond
Reuben Thornton
Charnel Hightower
Geo. Wych

Samuel Clark
Pleasant Webb
Abel Howell
San'd Higginbotham
Reuben Cook
Edmund Shackleford
Thos. McDowell
Jas. Tait
Allen Jones
Wm. Aiken
Jno. Greenwood
Benjamin Fannin
Gilbert Border
David Martin
William Daniel
Isacc Suttles
Thomas Foster
Thomas Burton
Edward Ware
William Dudly
Benjamin Goss
Henry Browner
Zack Collins
Samuel Wood
Leonard Turman
William Oliver
J. P. Harper
Jesse Ross
Joseph Turman
John Gill
Jos. Deadwyler
Wm. Prewit
John Cook
James Colbert
Jacob Higginbotham
John Baker
Josiah Cook
Jacob Prewit
Lewis Mosely
William Means
Henry Shackleford
James Freeman
Joseph Terry
Samuel Wood
Val. Smith
J. L. Huff
Thomas Jones
Robert Moseley
Zack Clark

John Wilkins
Nelson Barnett
Jesse Hendrick
John Shackleford
James Glover
Jeremiah Blackwell
William Brown
William Hall
Barnabas Pace
Dudly Cook
Moses Bailey
John McKiver
George Henderson
Nat. Smith
Hez'h Gray
Richmond Cosby
William Blake Sr.
Jesse White
Benjamin Cook
William Abbit
James Brown
Jacob Odom
James McClusky
Thomas Cook
Richmond Hubbard
Caleb Higginbotham
Joseph Crow
Robert Cosby
John Rucker
Abram Colson
John Rousey
Larkin Gatewood
David Clark
Wm. H. Tate
William Hightower
William Cook
Samuel Mogin
Christopher Clark
William Higginbotham
Archibald Burdin
Ambros Ham
John A. Baker
Joseph Huddleston
Edmund Rousy
J. L. Bell
Samuel Blackburn
J. P. Almond
J. Kidd
Jesse Statom

John Hathcock	Beverly Allen	Joshua Clark
Joseph Miller	John Chiles	J. L. Almond
Arthur Tobs	William Allen	Benj. Cook Jr.
William Spears	William Ware	Henry Hunt
Luke White	John Cook	Womack Blankingship
Webb Kidd	Smith Cook	Lembard King
Benj. Higginbotham	William Blake Jr.	D. Brady
William Forson	Benj. Glover	John Browner
Thomas Carter Jr.	Isacc Coker	David Porterfield
John Staom Sr.	Middleton Wood	John Brown
Henry Gatewood	John Lowery	Absolom Stinchcomb
Thomas Penn	Nathaniel Barnett	William Burch
Ezakiel Bailey	William Collins	J. L. Lowery
Thomas Napper	Eli Eavenson	John Heard
Burket Green	John DePriest	Sharles Goss
Ezekiel King	James Certain	Charter Harper
Jos. Higginbotham	Francis Higginbotham	David Vineyard
John Satterwhite	James Dudley	Jacob Cleveland
William Aycock	Daniel White	Robert Paxton
Moses Wilcox	Andrew McIver	William Abbot
Joshua Sewell	Jos. Tuttle	Jesse Brawner
John Hubbard	Jason Wilson	John Cleveland
John Blacke	Samuel Higginbotham	John Gatewood
Benj. Forson	Frank Satterwhite	John Higginbotham
John Martin	Samuel Dailey	D. Cosby
Joseph Williams	John Cotter	C. Hutson
John Millican	Geo. Ivins	Lewis Moore
L. W. Curry	Andrew Eliot	Samuel Tolbert
Isacc Ford	William Barnett	Adam Gar
William Brawner	Thomas Lovelady	John Casey
Chas. Hendrick	Robert Hathorn	M. Sewell
Whitehead Hendrick	James Camron	Joseph Blackwell
	John Spears	

During the early part of the last century Peter Lawrence Van Alan, a near kinsman of Mrs. Martin Van Buren, settled in Elbert County, having come from his native New York. He was a lawyer of marked ability, and very soon allied himself with the Clark faction. Van Alan was unquestionably politically ambitious and it is probable that he felt that his opportunities would be greater as a partisan of Clark. If such was the case his surmise was correct. He was, within a very short time, elected Solicitor General of the Western Circuit of Georgia of which Elbert County was then a part.

The election of the New Yorker did not by any means please the Crawfordites and in consequence the bitterness between the factions reached still greater heights. The "Code Duelo" soon became the order of the day.

Judge Charles Tait, a noted lawyer, living in the vicinity of Petersburg, was the associate in the practice of law with Mr. Crawford. He was made a defendant in a cause, entirely without merit, brought by Solicitor General Van Alan in Elbert County Superior Court. During the trial of the issue Van Alan assailed the character of Judge Tait in a most merciless and undignified manner. In fact, his remarks to the jury were slanderous and insulting. This was done with the deliberate hope that Tait would challenge Van Alan to a duel and thus bring Crawford into an open quarrel.

When the case finally came to its hectic close, the verdict of the jury being favorable to Tait, the judgment of the Clarkites proved correct. The aristocratic, wooden-legged Tait immediately challenged Van Alan, naming Crawford as his second.

General Clark and his followers were jubilant.

Van Alan declined to meet Judge Tait on the grounds that the renowned jurist was not a gentleman. This refusal was, of course, another deliberate insult. Val Alan expected that Crawford, as second to Tait, would step into the breach and take up the challenge. With his usual quick wittedness Crawford refused to spring the trap so cleverly and painstakingly baited.

Some two or three months later, while court was in session at Washington, Mr. Crawford unexpectedly encountered Van Alan in one of the corridors of the old Willis Hotel. Van Alan, angered at the sight of his enemy who had no neatly defeated and humiliated him, began to curse and abuse Crawford. The result of this meeting was naturally the arrangements for the long sought duel.

The place of meeting was set at old Fort Charlotte, a famous dueling ground, about 10 miles below Petersburg on the South Carolina side of the Savannah River. The hour of meeting was a few moments before sunrise.

On the first fire neither combatant was hit. On the second, just as the sun rose, with Val Alan facing the east, he fell mortally wounded. Mr. Crawford was untouched.

There is somewhere in Holy Writ the admonition that he who lives by the sword shall so die. Circumstances placed Van Alan towards the east; the sun rise, perhaps blinding him, and ruined his aim. At any rate the followers of Crawford looked upon the incident as an Act of God.

Judge Tait figured prominently in another challenge and acceptance to a duel which terminated in a most unforseen and humorous manner. This incident took place while he was United States Senator from Georgia.

John M. Dooley, a widely known wit and son of Colonel Dooley, succeeded Charles Tait as Judge of the Superior Court of the Western Circuit of Georgia. The Crawford and Clark controversy was still very much in evidence and Dooley owed his elevation, to a great extent, to General Clark and his cohorts.

During the trial of a case, Dooley from the bench, and Tait from the counsel table, engaged in a heated debate regarding certain legal points at issue. Tait finally lost his none too placid temper and challenged Dooley to a duel. The challenge was immediatey accepted and Dooley named General Clark as his second while Tait, of course, called upon his bosom friend, William H. Crawford, to act for him.

At the hour appointed Tait and Crawford arrived at the rendezvous to find Judge Dooley calmly seated on a stump chewing pine needles. Mr. Crawford inquired the whereabouts of General Clark, to which Dooley replied:

"General Clark is looking for a big bee-gum."

"May I ask," inquired Mr. Crawford, "What earthly use he intends to make of a bee-gum in a duel with pistols?"

"Certainly," replied the Judge, "I want to put one of my legs in it!"

"Put your leg in it?" asked Crawford, "In God's name, why?"

"Do you suppose that I am going to risk my two good legs against that wooden stump of Tait's? If I should shoot low and hit his stump one of his niggers could whittle him out another by tomorrow night, but if he hit mine I might be killed, and certainly I would lose a leg. To be on the same footing with him, I demand a bee-gum for protection. Then we can fight evenly."

"Does this mean you do not intend to fight, Tait?" roared the outraged Crawford.

"Well," calmly answered Dooley, "I thought every one knew that."

"Perhaps so," said Mr. Crawford, "but you will be posted a coward and a craven in 20 taverns for such dastardly action!"

"So it may be," answered Dooley, "I had rather be posted in five hundred taverns as a craven than to have my obituary posted in one!"

Needless to say Judge Tait and Mr. Crawford left the scene in disgust and it is probably true that no other public man in Georgia could have evaded a duel in such an unusual manner.

Another scheduled duel, which never took place, was an affair between William M. McIntosh and Amos T. Ackerman. McIntosh challenged Ackerman who accepted, but later retracted remarks made regarding political differences between the parties. This incident took place in 1860.

In the year 1859 politics were particularly heated. Llewellyn Nelms, a lawyer of Elberton, caused Dr. Holmes to be burned in effigy. A duel was arranged which took place near Savannah. Mr. Nelms was desperately wounded, but recovered. Dr. Holmes and Mr. Nelms became friends and both gave their lives to the Southern Confederacy.

A contemporary of such men as Judge Tait, Judge Dooley, and William H. Crawford was Obediah Jones. He was born in Burke County, North Carolina, in 1763, and became an orphan by the time he had reached the age of 16.

The law, at that time, compelled the courts to take orphans, who were under age, and bind them out to a trade or profession. This did not appeal to the youthful Obediah so he quietly left the neighborhood in which he lived with such worldly goods as he possessed tied up in a large bundle, and walked more than 20 miles to the nearest town.

Upon his arrival he sat down outside a tavern, or ordinary, to rest. A gentleman rode up and asked him to hold his horse while he went inside. When the man returned he gave the boy a shilling and inquired pleasantly who he was. Upon being told he said, "I knew your father well." Then he inquired of young Jones just what he intended to do. The lad replied, "Anything I can find to make an honest living."

The gentleman was Judge Knight, a prominent North Carolina jurist. After the conversation with the boy, he went back into the ordinary and asked the owner to give the boy shelter and something to do. This was done.

The tavern keeper gave such good reports of the youth that in three months Judge Knight took him into his own home. He at once became an accredited member of the family and read law under his benefactor. He remained with the Judge for several years, but as the tide of emigration was pouring into eastern Georgia he decided to seek new fields.

Judge Knight, wishing to give him a present, requested him to make his own selection. He decided upon a Negro slave, named Gratton. Thereafter, until Judge Jones died, Gratton was his faithful and devoted body servant.

Judge Jones settled in Elbert County and entered upon the practice of his profession. About 1803, he returned to North Carolina and married Miss Elizabeth Cowden, a daughter of Captain James Cowden of Revolutionary fame.

In 1802, Judge Jones was elected to the Georgia Senate from Elbert County and on March 3, 1805, he was commissioned Judge of the Mississippi Territory which, evidently, he failed to accept for we find him still in Elbert County in 1810. However, on March 6, 1810, he was again commissioned and at this time he removed to what is now Limestone County, Alabama. He died May 24, 1825, while holding the office of Judge of the Superior Court of Alabama. He was universally known as "Honest Obediah."

Ten years, almost to the day, after the arrival of the Reverend Dozier Thornton in Elbert County, there was born near Bethlehem Church, on Beaverdam Creek, a child that was destined to become equally as great a representative of the Methodist denomination as Dozier Thornton was of the Baptist. This child was James Osgood Andrew, the son of a struggling and woefully unsuccessful pedagogue. George Smith in his "History of Methodism" located the birth place of Andrew on Cedar Creek, near Jones' Ferry on Broad River, but Mr. Smith, though he did much to preserve early Georgia history, was prone in this instance, as in many others, to take the casual word of some uninformed person without personal investigation of records. The exact date of James Osgood Andrew's birth was May 3, 1794.

The late Reverend James N. Wall, for may years a leading Methodist preacher and educator of Elbert County and at one time a member of the Georgia House of Representatives, said of him: "The mark of the proverbial circuit rider, then, was grit, grace and poverty. While young Andrew could scarcely read, by close application, hard study and a devout life he rose to the highest office in the gift of his church, which he filled with great ability and to the entire satisfaction of his brethren. Notwithstanding his final success he was advised, after preaching for some time, to try something else, as he did not promise enough in the pulpit to authorize the belief that he would ever amount to much as a preacher."

By virtue of his determined spirit this little noticed circuit rider became Bishop of the Methodist Episcopal Church before he had reached his middle years, and he was universally recognized as a great scholar as well as a consecrated Christian.

The Methodist schism of 1854, was more or less caused by his second marriage to Mrs. Leonara Greenwood, of Greensboro, Georgia.

The marriage was a happy one for the Bishop. His wife was attractive in manner and an excellent home maker. As soon as the marriage was consummated Bishop Andrew relinquished, in due form of law, all rights that he had under the existing laws of Georgia to her property. Mrs. Andrew died in the year 1854, and her husband inherited from her estate certain propeties among which were several slaves. The good Bishop, however, did not retain ownership, but generously dispossessed himself a second time in favor of her children by her former marriage.

The news that a Bishop of the Methodist Church owned slaves was soon noised abroad and a great excitement was caused in the councils of Methodism within the boundaries of the Free States. The Bishop was unaware of any criticism until he reached the City of Baltimore in the year 1854, enroute to the General Conference to be held in New York City during the month of May. He learned, to his great surprise and consternation, after his arrival at the Conference, that a most serious discussion had arisen.

Dr. George Smith says:

"He resolved to resign, and so expressed himself, both in Baltimore and New York. This resolution, however, he did not execute, for the reason that the Southern delegates demurred in formal resolutions and urged him not to do so, on the grounds that it would inflict an incurable wound upon the whole South, and inevitably lead to division.

"Resignation now became almost an impossibility, and when it was intimated that he had broken faith or must resign or be disposed, then resignation was entirely out of the question. The issue had come. The mass of the Northern preachers were opposed to slavery, but they were not abolitionist. They found themselves hard put to defend themselves; and when it became known that a Bishop was a slave holder they felt that they were in a sad predictiment. Accordingly, Alfred Griffith and John Davis, two members of the Baltimore Conference, were put forward to lead the attack. Andrew was nominated by the slave holding states to the Conference because he was not a slave holder; and that having become one 'Therefore be it resolved, That James O. Andrew be affectionately requested to resign.'

"This precipitated the issue, the discussion was Christian in spirit and courteous in language, to which, however, there were some exceptions. To ask him to resign was so painful to many who did not wish a slave holder in office that Mr. Finley, of Ohio, introduced the famous substitute, declaring that it was the sense of the General Conference that he desist from the exercise of the office of Bishop as long as the impediment remained. Mr. Finley was Bishop Andrew's personal friend and offered the substitute believing it to be less offensive to the Southern delegates, than the original resolution. But it was really more offensive, because since it could not be consistently remove the impediment, it amounted to permanent disposition."

Some days later, after long and heated debate, a vote was taken on the substitute which was carried 111 to 69. Bishop Andrew at once returned to Georgia. The question of division was in this manner settled. In May, the following year, the first General Conference of the Methodist Episcopal Church, South, was held in Petersburg, Virginia, and James Osgood Andrew became the first Bishop.

It may be said that Bishop Andrew did, at the time of the New York meeting, hold a female slave in trust. This girl had been devised to him by a lady of Augusta who specified in her will that he was to retain her until she reached her majority and then send her to Liberia, where she was to be free. The slave, however, was given the option in the will, of remaining in America as the chattel of Bishop Andrew; and she asserted her right to the latter course. Since the Bishop had accepted the trust he was far too honorable to break it.

James Osgood Andrew died March 2, 1871, and is buried in the town cemetery at Oxford, Georgia. He was a great power for good not only in his native Georgia, but throughout the entire South and West. He was generally recognized as one of the foremost divines of his time.

In 1795, when Georgia's boundaries extended from the Savannah

River to the Mississippi, and from Crow Town to the St. Marys, with Natchez as its westernmost settlement, Elberton was situated on a high bluff between Waynesborough and Savannah. This town, long since a memory, had a population in excess of 400 people. The reason for its decadence is unknown, but probably like many other villages situated on the banks of water courses, river fogs and poor sanitary conditions caused its abandonment.

A hundred miles or more to the northward, in the new County of Elbert, stood the tiny hamlet of Elbertville. So unimportant it was, that the maps of Georgia did not show its location until after the year 1800. It was, however, mentioned in the statistics of several gazetters as being a small hamlet in Elbert County near the towns of Petersburg and Washington.

This village, after the original Elberton ceased to exist, changed its name, by common consent of the inhabitants, to Elberton. No legal action was taken to formally change the name, and this fact, is cumulative evidence, at least, proving that Elberton, Elbert County, was not incorporated by the Georgia Legislature until the year 1803.

"Park's Annotated Code of Georgia" indexes Elberton as being incorporated in the year 1793, but the acts of the General Assembly of Georgia for that year show no statute enacted regarding the present Elberton. The Elberton referred to was unquestionably the village between Waynesborough and Savannah.

The first act concerning Elbertton, Elbert County, was passed by the General Assembly of Georgia on December 10th, 1803:

"AN ACT

To appoint Commissioners for the better regulation and government of the town of Elberton.

"WHEREAS, the town of Elberton requires regulation :-

SEC. I. *Be it therefore enacted by the Senate and House of Representatives in General Assembly met,* That the following persons to wit: Middleton Woods, Reuben Lindsey, Doctor John T. Gilmer, Beckman Dye, and James Alston, be and they hereby are appointed Commissioners of the town of Elberton, and that they, or a majority of them, shall immediately upon the passage of this Act, convene and proceed to the appointment of a clerk and such other (sic) officers, as they may deem necessary to carry this Act into execution.

SEC. 2. *And be it further enacted,* That the said Commissioners shall hold their respective appointments given them, until the first Monday in January, 1805, at which time, and on every subsequent first Monday in January, thereafter, the citizens of Elberton entitled to vote for members of the General Assembly, shall choose by ballot five persons to succeed them as Commissioners of said town, and they shall have and they are hereby vested with full power and authority to make such by-laws and regulations, and inflict and imposed such pains, penalties and forfeitures, as in their judgment shall be conducive to the good order and government of said town of Elberton; Provided that such by-laws and regulations be not repugnant to the laws and Constitution of this State.

SEC. 3. *And be it further enacted that any* two or more Justices of the Peace for said County of Elbert, are hereby authorized and required to preside at such elections for Commissioners aforesaid: Provided always nevertheless, That nothing contained herein, shall be construed so as to prevent the election of the Commissioners hereinbefore named, and any person or persons who may hereafter be elected Commissioners of said town shall be re-eligible at the next, or any subsequent election after the expiration of the time for which he or they may be elected Commissioners under this Act.

ABRAHAM JACKSON, *Speaker of House of Representatives.*

DAVID EMANUEL, *President of the Senate.*

Assented to December 10, 1803.

JOHN MILLEDGE, GOVERNOR.

The foregoing was introduced in the House of Representatives by the Elbert County delegation, composed of Richmond T. Cosby, Dr. W. W. Bibb, and Allen Daniel.

There were several reasons why the site on which Elberton now stands was selected by the early settlers for their county seat. It was located near the center of the territory forming Elbert County, on a naural water shed, well elevated and with a bold spring of ice like water, still flowing freely to this day, in its center.

Thomas Jones, one of the earlier settlers and one time sheriff of the county, was quick to recognize the advantages of good water and in consequence built his home on an eminence, within a stones throw and overlooking the spring site. At the present time his granddaughter, Miss Lenora Jones, lives on the exact spot where the first house stood. The original house was replaced in the late sixties by a large two storied frame dwelling.

In the early days houses were few in Elberton. They were mainly built on the present Elbert Street, between Oliver and McIntosh, and on the present North Oliver Street between College Avenue and Railroad Street. A few scattered dwellings stood on the South Public Square with the courthouse occupying the center. Near the corner of South Oliver Street stood a large two storied house. The person responsible for its construction is unknown, but it is believed to have been built between 1799 and 1803. At any rate, it was occupied and owned successively by John A. Heard, Young L. G. Harris, founder of Young Harris College and donor of the Harris-Allen Library, and Colonel William M. McIntosh. The rooms were more than 25 feet square with extremely high ceilings and portions of the interior woodwork were of solid mahogany, in all likelihood, brought to Savannah on sailing vessels and then to Elberton overland. This landmark, some years after the War Between the States, was completely destroyed by fire. On the corner of South McIntosh Street stood the one storied building used by William M. McIntosh as a law office and adjoining it was the shoe shop of Nathan Harris, a slave, belonging to Judge Thomas W. Thomas.

On the site of the present courthouse stood Elberton's first commercial hotel, known as the Globe. This building was two and a half stories in height and was surrounded by a high picket fence. It, too, was eventually destroyed by fire.

Heard Street, of the present day, was known as Main Street for the reason that most of the travel leading to and from the more important town of Petersburg traversed it. Near the present intersection of Heard and Thomas Streets lived the famous Wiley Thompson, State Senator, United States Representative, and General of the United States Army.

The first building to be constructed of Elbert County's most valuable asset, granite, was the old jail that stood on the southwest corner of Oliver Street and College Avenue.

Few taverns were in operation during the early portion of the last century and it was the custom for some outstanding citizen of each community to furnish accommodations to travelers.

On February 23, 1803, he following license was granted Beverly Allen, nephew and namesake of the Beverly Allen who slew Marshall Forsythe:

"INFERIOR COURT FEBRUARY TERM 1803.

"Ordered that the following rates be observed by those who obtain license to keep a Tavern for the present year to-wit:

For Dinner	$0.31½
For Supper	.25
For Breakfast	.25
For Lodging	.12½
For Stableage	.12½
For Corn and Oats, per gallon	.12½
For Fodder, per bundle	.03
For Jamacia Rum, per gallon	3.43
For West India, per gallon	3.00
For Northward, per gallon	2.00

For Brandy, per gallon 3.00
For Whiskey, per gallon 2.00
For Gin, per gallon 3.00
For Cider, per gallon.. .50
For Porter, per gallon 2.00
For Wine, per gallon 3.00
Extracts from the Minutes.

M. WOODS, Clerk.

"GEORGIA, Elbert County: Inferior Court February Term, 1803.

"By the Honorable Justices of the said Court for the County aforesaid.

To Beverley Allen Greetings,

"Whereas the application to use has been made, the license money paid, bond and security given according to law, and we Reposing confidence in you, the said Beverly Allen, do therefore permit you to keep a tavern to your own Dwelling-house for and during the term of twelve months beginning from the date of these presents and from thence until the next Inferior Court.

"Witness the Honorable William Barnett one of the Justices of said Court this 23rd day of February 1803.

M. WOODS, Clerk."

At the same time John Oliver was granted a license. The Allen tavern was situated at what is now known as Pearl Mills and that of Oliver in the vicinity of Petersburg. Inns of this type were free rendezvous to all decent travelers and one can visualize the hale and hearty old squires sitting about the huge fire places with tankard and pipe discussing the election of Thomas Jefferson as President of the United States and the future of the infant nation.

Elberton after its incorporation, in 1803, gained rapidly in population. In 1808 the General Assembly of Georgia, by House Bill 528, allotted Elbert County three representatives as against two for the older County of Richmond. This fact unquestionably proves that Petersburg was rapidly gaining ascendency and bade fair to surpass the town of Augusta.

In either the year 1803 or 1804, Bethlehem Church was organized. Mrs. Adeline Stark (George C.) Grogan, for many years a member of this church, gives the following sketch of its interesting history:

"This church is located in the southeastern part of Elbert County, 10 miles from old Petersburg where the Savannah and Broad Rivers unite.

"It is a great pity that the records of the early history of this church are so meager, and, in a way, obscure. The work of the early church was in making history, not recording it. Except for facts, recorded in George G. Smith's 'History of Methodism,' a carefully compiled book published in 1912, there are no records. The old people who knew about Bethelhem, have all passed on. Through all the years of its history, Bethehem has stood for all that is highest and best. Many able ministers have preached in its pulpit, and has been the spiritual center of one of the best communities in all our Southland. Bethlehem is probably the oldest Methodist Church in Georgia, but we have no records to prove it.

"There was a church, in the Little River Circuit in Wilkes County, known as Grant's Meeting House, that claims to be the oldest, and has a marker to prove this claim, however, many believe that Bethlehem is entitled to this distinction.

"Originally, this Methodist house of worship was known as 'Thompson's Meeting House.' A family of that name lived in this section of Elbert County. Probably some members were active in organizing and building the church.

"General Wiley Thompson, who was killed by Osceola, Chief of the Seminole Indians, during the Seminole War in Florida and whose grave is in the garden of Mrs. Peyton M. Hawes, was of this Thompson family, also a daughter married James Easter of this section, from this union the Brewer family of Elbert County are descendants.

"Thompson's Meeting House was located on lands, now owned by Mr. James Hall, about two miles from the present church of Bethlehem, between there and the store of Mr. Joseph Balchin. The place can be located now by the four rock pillars on which the house rested. Most probably the structure was of logs, built in crude fashion, covered with boards riven from trees, as at this time there were no saw mills. The few nails used were hand wrought. The boards for covering, were fastened with hand-made pegs.

"No one living knows when Thompson's Meeting House was moved to its present site, and the name changed to Bethlehem. It was probably between the years 1830 and 1835. Two houses have stood on the present site. A few years ago the second building was considerably changed and enlarged into the present structure.

"With the most efficient aid of Mr. Thomas H. Verdell, I have thoroughly searched the records contained in the old deed books and the only recorded information concerning the purchase or gift of land to Bethlehem Church is found in Deed Book 'N,' page 88, the date July 25, 1804, where David and Ann Graham, his wife, sell to Andrew Walker, James Walker, and James Gilman, Trustees, for the Methodist Church, two acres of land, for the consideration of $6.00. This deed was recorded December 22, 1810. Evidently this was land on which Thompson's Meeting House was located. In the year 1877, in Deed Book 'EE,' page 642, land, the acreage not mentioned, was given to Bethlehem Church by Jane Nelms. Tradition says that land was given this church by Mrs. Agnes Hunter, but no record is found.

"The land owned by the church is estimated around five acres. There is a large and interesting cemetery. The dates of some of the tombs are very old. Doubtless many of the charter members sleep in this sacred old church-yard.

"Reverend Z. C. Hayes Jr., has done exhaustive research work concerning early Bethlehem. To him I am indebted for a list of names of pastors and presiding elders of Bethlehem for the past 60 years. Before that period, the status of the church is obscure, changes constantly made and nothing recorded.

"I have heard old people speak of great meetings held at Bethlehem, and of noted revivalist, who must have been missionary-evangelist. Among them, Lorenzo Dow, Uncle Jimmy Danley, Brother Dudley Jones and many others. Camp meetings were most numerous in those days, and people would go miles, with their families, and enjoy great spiritual refreshment at camp meetings.

"Lorenzo Dow in his journal speaks of having preached at Petersburg, February 2, 1803, and at Thompson's Meeting House the same year.

"In the year 1857, Reverend J. W. Knight was assigned to the territory of Elbert County; Reverend J. W. Talley of Athens District, as Presiding Elder. In 1859, Bishop G. F. Pierce sent Reverend Tyre B. Harbin and Reverend Lake R. McNamor, preachers, to the territory of Elbert County; J. O. A. Clark, Athens District, Presiding Elder. In 1860, Bishop Kavanaugh sent Tyre B. Harden and William C. Perry to Elbert County. Bethlehem was one of the churches served by these preachers.

"The church during the years embracing the War Between the States seemed to have been disorganized and irregular.

"The year 1867 was the first year of the Elberton District of the Methodist Episcopal Church. Reverend D. J. Myrick was Presidin Elder. He served one year and was folowed by Reverend John Henry Grogan, who served the district for a period of three years."

The following named pastors have served Bethlehem Church since 1872:

Year	Pastor	Year	Pastor
1872	John Henry Grogan	1899-1900	W. H. Cooper
1873	Joshua M. Parker	1901	A. D. Echols
1874	A. W. Williams	1902	G. W. Pharr
1875	John Henry Grogan	1903-1904-1905	A. A. Tilly
1876	W. F. Lewis	1906-1907	H. C. Emory
1877-1878	J. W. G. Watkins	1908	J. R. Lewis
1880-1881-1882	A. G. Worley	1909	F. M. McLeskey
1883	H. J. Ellis	1910	B. H. Greene
1884	B. E. L. Timmons	1911	J. W. Stipe
1885	N. T. Glenn	1912	J. S. Abercrombie
1886	W. Dunbar	1913-1914	J. W. Brinsfield
1887-1888	Eli Smith	1915-1916-1917-1918	W. T. Watkins
1889	L. P. Winter and Supply	1919	J. B. Gresham
1890-1891	B. P. Allen	1920-1921	R. E. Silvey
1892	L. W. Lyle	1922	W. B. Mills
1893	L. G. Johnson	1923-1924	O. E. Smith
1894	W. F. Colley	1925-1926	J. A. Griffes
1895	J. F. Tyson	1927-1928	G. G. Ramsey
1896	W. F. Colley	1929-1930-1931	L. G. Cowart
1897-1898	G. D. Stone		

Among the tombs in Bethlehem Churchyard the following inscriptions are to be found:

Sacred to the memory of
JAMES C. NELMS

Who was born June 10, 1810, and departed this life December 15, 1876.

> Rest, husband, in the silent tomb!
> Rest, for the shadows and the gloom of death is passed.
> Rest from the grief thy path beset!
> Rest, dear one, till we have met in Heaven at last.

Sacred to the memory of
CAP. DUNSTAN BLACKWELL

Who was born April 7, 1775, and died November 5, 1873.

Sacred to the memory of
REV. THOMAS HEARN, M.D.

Who departed this life January 25th, 1857, aged 71 years and 10 months.

He was a minister of the Gospel in the communion of the M. E. Church 51 years and died as he believed, a churchman.

JAS. F. NUNNELEE

Born Jan. 2, 1760; died Jan., 1838.

U. O. TATE

Born Feb. 17, 1810; died Nov. 4, 1884. Aged 74 years.

REBECCA CLARK

Wife of U. O. Tate, 1824-1923

Little of historic significance took place in Elbert County during the interim from 1804 to 1812. The population increased somewhat rapidly, lands were cleared and a few roads constructed. It was a new county hewn from the virgin wilderness and almost completely surrounded by uncertain, if not openly hostile, Indians.

War was formally declared against Great Britain, for the second time, on June 18th, 1812.

John C. Calhoun together with Henry Clay, and other high spirited young men, forced the careful Madison to agree to war, threatening him, should he refuse, with a loss of a second term as President.

Elbert County, being far removed from the scene of hostilities and being virtually uneffected by the embargoes laid down by Great Britain, took far less interest than might be supposed. Nevertheless, she furnished as always, more than her quota of men. Few of the volunteers, however, saw active service.

The land lottery list of 1821, gives the following men as soldiers of the War of 1812 from Elbert County:

Rhoda Evans (widow of soldier), Samuel Karr, Thomas Haynes, Obedience Jordan (widow of soldier), William Burden, Eppy White, William M. Smith, Haley Butler, Rollin Lunsford, William B. Campbell, Thomas Oliver, Isaac Almand, Levi Stinchcomb, James Oliver, Thomas Phelps, Elijah J. Christian, John Booth, John S. Colvard, John Edwards, Robert Booth Sr., Joseph Y. Wilhite, Gabriel Booth, John M. Tucker, Robert Denny, Janitius Dudley, Edward A. Denny, Whitehead Hendricks, Samuel Bentley, David Denny, Dabney Raines, and William Nelms.

A number of men who served did not, for unknown reasons, participate in the lottery. General Wiley Thompson, Captain Gaines Thompson, 4th Regular Georgia Militia; James Lunsford, who subsequently drew land near Springfield, Illinois; Captain William Allen (Elbert County Militia 1790), Allen Daniel, William Allgood Sr., and Wiliam Allgood Jr., the last two named serving in Captain Gaines Thompson's Company at Fort Hawkins from May 6, 1813, until November 21, 1814.

A study of the foregoing lists of names reveals that the majority of these men lived in that section of Elbert County known today as Webbsboro, Pike and Goshen Districts.

Of all the volunteers from the county Thomas Haynes probably saw the most active service. He was with the redoubtable Andrew Jackson in his famous campaign and fought with distinctive bravery under him at the Battle of New Orleans. It is said that Haynes was an authority on the happenings of the campaign and that he could relate many incidents in an unusually interesting manner. Haynes served for a number of years in the capacity of Justice of the Peace.

When war finally ended under the terms of the Treaty of Ghent, which was signed December 24, 1814, Elbert County had sustained few, if any, casualties.

General Wiley Thompson, above referred to, born 1781, and son of Isham Thompson, was a prominent figure in the affairs of Georgia during the early part of the last century. He served as a member of the upper branch of the Georgia Legislature 1817, 1818, 1819, and in the lower branch of the United States Congress 1821 through 1833. He was a resident of Elbert County when elected to both legislative bodies. During his service in Washington he displayed great interest in military affairs and thus gained the favorable notice of Andrew Jackson, then President of the United States. In the year 1834, President Jackson appointed him Indian agent for Florida.

In 1835, a pow-wow was held at Payne's Landing between the Seminoles, General Thompson and his associates which resulted in the famous, and subsequent fatal, treaty bearing the name of that place. The provisions of the treaty called for the gradual removal of the Indians to lands ceded them by the United States. Most of the chiefs readily agreed to the conditions, but a minority party, led by the Mico-Mico or Chief-Chief, was bitterly opposed, and, in consequence, refused to sign the treaty.

The brothers Omatla (who were sub-chiefs), especially Charles, favored removal and for this reason General Thompson determined to depose the reigning king, or Mico-Mico, and elevate Charles to his place.

The king's family tribe, known as the "Red Sticks," became exceptionally bitter against Thompson upon learning his intentions and not one of them would sign. General Thompson, possessed of a fiery and determined spirit on his own account, immediately deposed the king, the chiefs, the sub-chiefs and head men who had allied themselves with the "Red Sticks." A number of them were arrested and placed in temporary confinement.

Osceola, a chief, when called upon to place his signature on the document advanced with great deliberation to the table whereupon it lay, looked Thompson, and his aides, who were seated in a semicircle about the table, squarely in the faces, and with a gesture of supreme contempt drove his hunting knife to the hilt through the signature of Charles Omatla. This rash and wholly unexpected act caused the conference to end in confusion.

General Thompson, now thoroughly angered, ordered General Clynch to arrest Osceola, hoping in this manner to so intimidate him that his strong influence over deposed King Onopo would be lost and so bring about the complete signing of the much desired treaty.

After his arrest Osceola was chained to the floor of his cell in the fort for a period of six days. On the morning of the seventh, resorting to craftiness since open defiance had patently failed, he sent word to Thompson that he had considered the matter well and had at last decided to sign. The General, jubilant over what he considered a distinct moral victory, hastened to the cell with the treaty. Osceola calmly placed his signature on it and was immediately given his release. So pleased with his supposed victory General Thompson presented Osceola with a silver mounted gun. When the chains were stricken off Osceola stalked straight into the surrounding forest uttering the Seminole war cry, "Yoho-ee! Yoho-ee!"

The released prisoner acted swiftly. The followers of Onopo, who had camped in the neighborhood during his incarceration, joined him and under his leadership surprised the chiefs, who had voluntarily signed and openly advocated the treaty, on the road from Tallahassee and completely annihilated them. With his own hands Osceola killed Charles Omatla, using for the deed the very knife with which he had spurned the treaty.

After this massacre the band, lusting for more blood, fell upon several unprotected white settlements and ruthlessly killed every person found in them. The torch was applied to the houses and all live stock driven into the Everglades and hidden

When news of these autrocities reached General Thompson he at once dispatched scouts to Fort Brooks for additional forces. A relief column composed of 106 men, under the command of Major Dade, was caught unawares by Osceola, and his banditti, on their way to Fort King and all were killed and scalped with the exception of three privates, two of whom later died from wounds.

A few hours after the slaughter of the relief expedition, on December 28, 1835, an attack was made upon Fort King. General Thompson and five other gentlemen were dining at the home of Mr. Rogers. Osceola and several members of his band entered the house and killed General Thompson, Lieutenant Constantine Smith, Mr. Suggs, Mr. Hitler, and Erastus Rogers. Scarcely waiting for the breath to leave the body of the General, Osceola took his scalp with the same knife that had slain Charles Omatla. When the bloody deed had been accomplished he again uttered the war cry, "Yoho-ee! Yoho-ee!"

Many reasons have been advanced for the slaughter of Thompson by Osceola, but Gordon, Kingston, and many other historians agree that it was done in a spirit of revenge for placing him in irons. Mrs. Thompson was authority for the statement that her husband was killed with the gun that he had presented Osceola upon his release.

The body of Wiley Thompson was interred in Florida, but the widow was so concerned about the care of his grave that she employed Mr. Edward Roberts, a contractor of Elbetron, to make a trip to Florida and return the remains to Elberton for a second burial.

In due time Roberts returned with the bones of the General packed in a long wooden box. It had taken him more than three months to make the hazardous journey.

Mrs. Thompson removed the bones, one by one, and measured them to make sure, as she often stated, that they were in reality the bones of her husband. Having fully satisfied herself on this score and having been greatly attached to the General she refused for more than a year to inter the bones, but kept them beneath the bed in which she slept. Finally, however, her husband's nephew, Captain Gaines Thompson, prevailed upon her to bury them. The grave can today be seen in the garden of Peyton M. Hawes of Elberton.

The estate of General Thompson, which was large, finally came into the hands of his nephew, Gaines Thompson, since he had no children.

Osceola was born in 1804, on the banks of the Chattahoochee River, in Georgia. He was the son of William Power, a trader, and an Indian Princess. He married the daughter of a runaway

Georgia slave and during 1835, she was seized by the Whites and carried into slavery. His Indian name, of which Osceola is a corruption, was Asseheholar, meaning in the Seminole tongue, "Black Drink." His grave, in a beautiful grove near Fort Moultrie, bears the following inscription:

OSCEOLA, PATRIOT AND WARRIOR

Died at Fort Moultrie

January 30, 1838.

A few years previous to the outbreak of the War of 1812, Wylie Barron was born in the hamlet of Elberton. In early young manhood he removed to Augusta where he soon became the proprietor of a sporting club which was known as, "The Monte Carlo of the South." His establishment was famous throughout the whole country and Barron was highly esteemed for the reasons that he possessed high ideals and perfect manners. He was what was then known as a "Gentleman Gambler." When anyone lost more than could be afforded he would, without exception, return it. He would never allow bank employees or minors to play at his tables. Barron amassed a great fortune but finally died almost in want. Before his losses, however, he caused his tomb to be erected in the old Augusta Cemetery which bears the following quaint and unusual inscription:

> *"Farewell, vain world, I have enough of thee*
> *And now am careless of what thou sayest of me;*
> *My cares are past, my head lies quiet here.*
> *What faults you knew in me take care to shun*
> *And look at home, anough there's to be done."*

Judge Richard Clark said of him, "He was among the most distinguished looking men in his prime that I have ever seen. Tall and slender he appeared to be more than six feet and carried himself like a prince. His hair was black, his complexion of the typical brunette kind, which suggested Spanish or Italian blood."

Jonas Harrison who became one of the greatest Texas Titans in the revolution against Mexico lived in Elbert County during 1819 and 1820. He was born in Woodbridge, New Jersey, in 1777, but little is known of him until the year 1807 when he appeared before the Supreme Court of the Michigan Territory as counsel in the Dennison case, one of the most celebrated of all cases dealing with the slavery question. From 1808 until 1819 he lived in western New York and was one of the founders of the City of Buffalo. He was, in fact, the first truly great lawyer of that section. Harrison removed to Texas in 1820, where he died in the month of August, 1836.

CHAPTER VII

ELBERTON AND ELIAM METHODIST CHURCHES—ELBERTON FIRST BAPTIST CHURCH—TAMAR TYNER—WILLIAM SUTTLES — JOHN MURRELL — RUCKERSVILLE — JOSEPH RUCKER—ACTS OF THE LEGISLATURE REGARDING RUCKERSVILLE—PHILOMATHIA ACADEMY—ALLEN DANIEL—METEORIC SHOWER OF 1850—BLUE-EYED NEGROES—ANTE-BELLUM BANJO SONGS.

On October 18th, 1815, Archalus Jarrett, Gabriel Christian, Thomas Oliver, Absolom Stinchcomb, and James Banks purchased, as trustees, from Thomas Jones, and for the use of the Broad River Circuit of the Methodist Episcopal Church, for the consideration of $500.00, "One certain lot or parcel of land situate in said county and in the town of Elberton, bounded by and joining James Murry lot on the East, William Fortson's land on the North, David S. Booth lot on the West and the public road or street on the South, containing three-fourths of an acre of land, more or less." This instrument was witnessed by James Wood, D. S. Booth, and William Patterson. The land described is the same on which the Elberton Central School, at the corner of College and Forest Avenues, now stands.

About a quarter of a century later Dr. Henry Bourne, a prominent physician, donated two and one-half acres to the Elberton Methodist Church and this is the site of the present First Methodist Church, at the southeast corner of Church and Thomas Streets. The title was vested in Alfred Hammond, Amos Vail, William A. Swift, Robert Hester, and Mr. Nelms, as trustees.

In the year 1886, the present building of the First Methodist Church was constructed under the able pastorate of J. B. Robbins.

A pipe organ was installed in the new building, but was not used for some time due to the opposition of some of the older members. They felt that the use of organ music was not the proper manner in which to worship what they believed to be a stern and jealous God. The local newspaper, of that time, devoted considerable space to the controversy.

The following named ministers have served this church since 1820: David Garrison, Thomas Smith, Robert L. Edwards, J. B. Chappell, William J. Parks, Wiley Warwick, Joel Townsend, John B. Chappell, Richard Moseley, John Oliver, George W. Carter, Smith Crandall, Thomas Capers, George W. Persons, Samuel Hardwick, H. P. Pickford, James Jones, Wesley P. Arnold, Robert Stribbling, William C Crumley, Robert Lane, L. G. R. Wiggins, J. E. Cook, Robert Conner, John C. Carter, William A. Florence, George Bright, M.

M. Hibbard, H. H. Parks, William C. Cone, J. W. Knight, T. B. Harbin, John Henry Grogan, James Austin, John Henry Grogan, A. G. Worley, F. G. Hughes, W. P. Rivers, J. M. Dickey, W. J. Cotter, A. G. Worley, J. H. Baxter, A. M. Thigpen, J. R. Parker, J W. Roberts, George H. Pattillo, J. B. Robbins, H. J. Adams, A. C. Thomas, W. L. Wooten, John H. Mashburn, B. F. Frazier, S. R. Belk, Ford McRee, J. T. Daves, R. J. Bigham, John Tilly, B. P. Allen, W. B. Dillard, R. F. Eakes, R. C. Cleckler, S. A. Harris, John G. Logan, W. H. Cooper, L. Wilkie Collins, A. G. Shankle, J. T. Robbins, Fred W. Glisson, W. T. Hunnicut, J. W. O. McKibben, John F. Yarborough, H. L. Byrd, and B. Frank Pim.

Perhaps of all the ministers who have faithfully served this great church, John H. Mashburn was the most beloved. "Uncle Johnny," as he was known by members of all denominations, saints as well as sinners, lived in Elberton after his retirement. His wife was also universally loved.

Hanging in the belfry of this church is the sweetest toned bell in the country. It was purchased the year 1881, when J. H. Baxter was pastor, and when the Board of Stewards was composed of J. H. Jones, Robert M. Heard, James J. Burch, Robert Hester, Thos. M. Swift, James A. Andrew and Josiah F. Auld. The bell was purchased 58 years ago, the church building completed 50 years ago. The date, name of pastor and names of Stewards are inscribed on the bell. The present church edifice was built of brick burned by the late Luther Turner, Sunday School Superintendent and member of the Board of Stewards for many years, at a kiln on Falling Creek, of the finest brick clay in this section. Homer C. Mickel, popular contractor and member of the church, superintended its construction.

The site of the second oldest Methodist Church in this state is southwest of Beaverdam Creek and was known as Beaverdam Meeting House. This land was deeded by Thos. A. Carter.

Archibald Burton and his wife, Elizabeth, deeded to Peter Oliver, McCarty Oliver, David Clark, and David Hudson, as Trustees of the Methodist Eliam Society, for the sum of $10.00, "A certain parcel of land situate, lying and being in the State and County aforesaid, on the waters of Warhatchee Creek, contigious and convenient to a spring of said Archibald which he does hereby grant the free use of to said Society on all public days of worship forever. Said lot of land bounded by the said Archibald's land, beginning at a parsley haw near Hillyer's road on said Archibald's line adjoining Thomas Bell, thence southwardly 50 steps along said line to a hickory, thence Eastwardly to a persimmon in the old field, thence Northwardly to a pine, thence to the beginning corner by estimation one acre be the same, more or less." This instrument bearing date of August 25, 1817, is of record in the office of the Clerk of the Superior Court of Elbert County in Deed Book 2, page 68, and is witnessed by Bins Burton, Sanson Burton, and Joseph Bell, Justices of the Peace.

While many Baptist churches were flourishing throughout Elbert County at this period Elberton had none until the year 1860.

Mrs. George I. Barr, *nee* Rachel Willis, together with her son, began an agitation for the organization of a church and their efforts were soon marked with notable success. Reverend L. W. Stephens, who had married one of the daughters of Mrs. Barr, aided materially. Funds were raised and a building was constructed near the corner of what is now Thomas and Elbert Streets. Joseph Y. Arnold was the contractor.

The charter members of the Elberton First Baptist Church were: Mrs. George I. Barr, Thomas J. Heard, Mrs. Thomas J. Heard, Joseph Y. Arnold, Mrs. Joseph Y. Arnold, William H. Edwards, Dr. M. P. Deadwyler, Mrs. M. P. Deadwyler (who died in 1934, in her 101st year), Mrs. Roebuck, Mr. Eaves, and probably others, but no further records are available.

The present modern house of worship owes its existence, to a great measure, to the generosity of Dr. and Mrs. M. P. Deadwyler. They gave large sums of money towards its construction and worked untiringly for its completion.

The following named pastors have served this church since its establishment:

L. W. Stephens, Asa Chandler, Isham Goss, Gibson Campbell, J. A. Munday, C. A. Stakely, E. R. Carswell, J. J. Farmer, William S. Rogers, H. W. Williams, Brewer G. Boardman, J. T. B. Anderson, Samuel C. Dean, William H. Rich, W. A. Wray (the minister, while serving at Sandersville, who shot a jay bird for disturbing the congregation during services), Henry T. Brookshire, and Hoke Shirley.

Several ministers have gone out from this church, among them being, Reverend Vandiver Herndon and Reverend John Webb, pastor of the First Baptist Church of Columbia, South Carolina.

Both the First Baptist Church and the First Methodist Church maintains missions in the cotton mill district.

For two decades and more, 1817-1843, the Indians of Georgia harrassed the people sorely. Raids on isolated settlements frequently took place and many lives were lost.

William S. Burch, a prominent citizen, owned many slaves, some of whom possessed one-half Indian blood. He lived about two and one-half miles below Elberton and on January 12, 1822, was found foully murdered a short distance from his home. A coroner's jury was quickly summoned and a verdict returned to the effect that he had met his death at the hands of three of his own slaves: Jesse, Joe, and Sam, all of whom were of Indian extraction. They were duly tried, convicted and sentenced to be hanged. The executions took place simultaneously on three gallows erected near the corner of Heard and Thomas Streets where the home of Colonel William F. Jones now stands.

Living in that section of Elbert County now known as Gaines was the Tyner family.

Early one morning in the late fall, Richard Tyner left his home on a hunting expedition leaving his wife, two sons, the younger bearing the name of Noah, three daughters Mary, Tamar, and an infant whose name is lost to us. A few hours after his departure a band of hostile Cherokees made an attack upon the house and although the mother and older children fought fearlessly with an old musket left for defense they were soon overpowered, but not until two Indians had been slain and a third severly wounded. Mrs. Tyner and her infant daughter were immediately slain and scalped. Little Noah secreted himself in a hollow tree and thus evaded capture. The eldest son escaped by flight and the two daughters, both in their 'teens, were made captives and carried away.

As soon as the alarm was spread the stern pioneers formed a posse, but after days of fruitless pursuit they were forced to abandon the chase. The family and friends gave the girls up for lost for few captives ever returned when taken by the hostile Indians of that period.

About three years later the attention of one John Monack, an Indian trader, was attracted to two beautiful girls and he quickly recognized that they were not of Indian blood. He knew of the abduction of the Tyner girls and realized that he had located them. Monack after much bargaining reached an agreement whereby he was able to purchase Mary, but by no means of pursuasion could he induce the Indians to part with Tamar. The Indians calmly stated that she was quick to obey, of good disposition, tireless in work, and hence necessary to them.

Finally, realizing that his efforts were of no avail, he and Mary set out for Elbert County and shortly afterwards were married. Neither Mary nor her husband were fully content for the knowledge that Tamar still remained a captive haunted them continuously.

In a few weeks Monack again set out for the Indian towns with the determination to either purchase or abduct his sister-in-law. Upon reaching his destination he alternately begged and threatened, but once again to no avail. His every movement was spied upon and he was finally forced to return home, frankly admitting defeat.

A day of two after his departure from the village the Indians seemed very suspicious of Tamar and she was informed by an old squaw, whom she had befriended, that the headmen believed that she was soon to be rescued by a body of troops and rather than give her up they were to burn her at the stake on the next ceremonial day.

Tamar prevailed upon the squaw to furnish her a canoe and provisions. One night, with the aid of her faithful Indian friend, she successfully made her escape.

Down the turbid waters of the Chattahoochee she paddled. All night she would make the best time possible and during the day would hide along the river bank, sleeping no more than was absolutely necessary. Several times she barely escaped recapture, but finally with all her provisions exhausted, she reached the waters of Appalachicola Bay were she was sighted by a passing merchantman and conveyed in safety to Savannah. The good people of that city, upon hearing her strange story, received her as a heroine, as indeed she was, and furnished her with the necessary means of travel to Elbert County. The news of her coming preceeded her and she was welcomed at Petersburg with great rejoicing.

A short time after her arrival home she was married to a gentleman by the name of Hunt. Today many of her descendants reside in Elbert and Hart Counties. She lived to be quite an old lady and thrilled her numerous grandchildren with tales of the Indian towns. It is said that she delighted to point out the hollow oak in which her young brother Noah had hidden. This tree, which stood for many decades, was known throughout the whole countryside as "Noah's Ark."

Shortly after the Tyner incident a band of roving Cherokees made an attack upon the inhabitants a short distance above the spot where Edinburg once stood and several persons were scalped and murdered.

A beautiful 14 year old girl, whose name has long since been forgotten, was spared in the massacre and taken captive.

William Suttles, a gunsmith and lay preacher of Edinburg, heard of the raid and determined to rescue the child. Arming himself with an excellent rifle he at once set out alone on his dangerous mission.

About midnight he came in sight of the Indian camp fire. In true frontier fashion he made his way to within 30 yards of the encampment and saw the terror stricken little girl being forcibly held upon the lap of a stalwart brave. In a few moments this brave arose and began talking in a loud voice with the accompaniment of many gestures.

Suttles from his ambush, raised his rifle and, with coolest deliberation, shot the gesturing brave through the body.

Instantly the entire camp was in turmoil, in consequence, no doubt, of what they supposed to be a surprise attack by a large force of angry and determined whites.

The child, with rare presence of mind, rushed to the spot from which the gun had been fired and Suttles taking her in his arms, ran to the place where his horse was concealed and safely carried her to his home.

About the year 1822, John Murrell, the outlaw minister, made his first trip through Elbert County. He, together with his band, established a rendezvous near where the present Concord Church stands. The site of his camping place was well known as recently as 40 years ago.

It was the practice of this unusual bandit to steal slaves in Virginia and North Carolina and bring them South for sale. When the people of Georgia finally learned of his illegal practices they refused to traffic with him and he sought new markets in Mississippi and Louisiana.

Murrell continued to pass through Elbert County until 1826, and would sally forth from his camp to preach to any gathering that he could find. It is said, that in 1825, when the veterans of the American Revolution held a celebration at Ruckersville, on the fourth of July, he was among the many persons present and made a spectacular appearance in his gudy costume.

There is no record of any specific depredations on the part of Murrell and his banditti having occurred in Elbert County, but months after his passage every minor offense against law and order, when the offender was unknown, was charged to him and his followers. It is true, perhaps, that many slaves thought to have run away were sold down the Mississippi by him.

Perhaps Ruckersville of all the early settlements of Elbert County has received the greatest publicity notwithstanding the fact that in its era of greatest prosperity it could boast of no more han 200 inhabitants and a great number of these were slaves. This state of affairs has been brought about, no doubt, by the outstanding achievements of a number of its citizens.

Ruckersville's most noted citizen was Joseph Rucker. This unusual man was the descendant of Peetr Rucker of Orange County, Virginia, and the son of John Rucker and Elizabeth Tinsley. He was born January 12, 1788. His wife Margaret Houston Speer, whom he married in January 1812, was a daughter of William Speer.

In his young manhood he evidenced a decided genius for business and without having inherited property of any great value soon accumulated large holdings in land and slaves. When banking was in its infancy he established the Bank of Ruckersville in a wooden store building and conducted this institution with marked success. He was the only stockholder, the president and cashier. Bills of this bank were honored in every section of the United States without the least question. This institution has been said to have been the first of its kind established in Georgia.

Perhaps a portion of the graphic account given by his son-in-law, Reverend James S. Lamar, will present a true insight to his character:

"Squire Rucker's judgment was never known to fail. Violently opposed to secession, when the final act came at Milledgeville, he said, pointing to one of his slaves, 'See that fellow. A year ago he was worth $1,500, today he isn't worth a thrip.' But he accepted the situation—helped to equip a company—took $30,000 of the first issue of Confederate bonds, at par. These bonds were lying in the old Bank of Athens, in the care of the late Albin Dearing, when the war was over, not a coupon had ever been clipped.

"He was always called Squire Rucker. I well remember the first time that I saw him. It was in the summer of 1856. He was dressed in an old-fashioned suit of broadcloth, a vest also of cloth, and a coat of the same material in the style called shad-belly—somewhat like the cutaways of the present day. He wore it unbuttoned—a watch chain with a heavy seal hanging from a fob, or watch pocket. His neck cloth was then as always white. It was not a simple tie but a sort of folded handkerchief, put on by laying the middle against the throat leading the ends back and crossing them, then bringing them to the throat to be tied together. The knot was plain. I am not sure it was even a bow.

"He was polite, but very reserved. He seemed to be studying me, his conversation was mainly questions—chiefly about men and women and things in Augusta—Mrs. Tubman, the Cummings, the Claytons, the Gairdners, and Mr. Metcalf—then about cotton and business prospects, but no human being could have told by any expression on his face what effect my answers had upon him or what inference as to me he drew from them."

Joseph Rucker was sadly effected by the results of the War Between the States and in 1865, he followed his wife to the grave within a month. He was truly a remarkable character and many of his descendants, Joseph Rucker Lamar, Associate Justice of the United States Supreme Court; Elbert Rucker, Tinsley W. Rucker, United States Congressman and noted lawyer and wit; and Jeptha Rucker, postmaster of Athens for many years, were all born in Ruckersville, and took first rank among Georgians.

Joseph Rucker Lamar was appointed to the United States Supreme Court by the affable William H. Taft. His choice was excellent for Justice Lamar served the nation with unwavering faith, ability and fidelity. Lamar's father was Reverend James S. Lamar who married Mary Rucker; his grandfather, Phillip Lamar Jr. married Margaret Anthony; his greatgrandfather Phillip Sr., married Ruth Davis, and his great-greatgrandfather, Robert, married Sarah Wilson. Mrs. Joseph Rucker Lamar, prominent in Georgia society and club work, was Clarinda Huntington Pendleton, daughter of Dr. William K. Pendleton once President of Bethany College.

In the year 1822, the date of Ruckersville's incorporation, it had become a small trading center and was, it then seemed, destined to become a town of major importance. In 1827, according to Sherwood's Gazetter, the village contained 10 houses, six stores, an academy and a Baptist church. In the year 1849, there were 200 inhabitants and this was undoubtedly its greatest era of prosperity.

The citizenship of Ruckersville was of the highest type and a number of characters of note were born there. Among these were: Nathaniel J. Hammond, Major Peter W. Alexander, Joseph R. Lamar, Mrs. Corra White Harris, James Lofton, Dr. Richard Banks, Elbert M. Rucker, Tinsley White Rucker, and William H. H. Underwood. The Adams, Taylors, Banks, Clevelands, Loftons, and Wansleys live there. Descendants of the illustrious families still reside in the locality.

With the outbreak of the War Between the States Rukersville began to wane, and at its close when chaos and confusion, poverty and sadness reigned, its death knell as a town of importance was sounded. The most vivid reminders of Ruckerville's importance today are the remains of the Joseph Rucker home, now owned by Earl W. Rucker, one of his descendants, and Van's Creek Baptist churchyard, where many of the early inhabitants sleep.

The act of the General Assembly of Georgia incorporating Ruckersville is set out below:

"AN ACT

To appoint Commissioners for the better regulation and government of the village of Ruckersville, in the County of Elbert.

Be it enacted by the Senate and House of Representatives of the State of Georgia in General Assembly met, and it is hereby enacted by the authority of the same.

That the following named persons, to-wit: John Banks, Henry Bourne, John S. Wilson, William White, and William H. Underwood, be and they are hereby appointed Commissioners of Ruckersville, in the County of Elbert, and that they or a majority of them shall immediately after the passage of this Act, convene and proceed to the appointment of a Clerk and such other officers as they may deem necessary to carry this Act into execution.

"Sec. 2. *And be it further enacted by the authority aforesaid,*

"That the said Commissioners shall hold their respective appointments hereby given them, until the first Monday in February, eighteen hundred and twenty-four, at which time, and on every subsequent first Monday in February thereafter, the citizens of Ruckersville entitled to vote for members of the General Assembly shall choose by ballot five persons to succeed them as Commissioners of said village. And they shall have and are hereby vested with full authority to make such by laws and regulations, and inflict and impose such pains, penalties and forfeitures as in their judgment shall be most conducive to the good order and government of said village: *Provided*, such by-laws and regulations be not repugnant to the laws and constitution of this State.

"Sec. 3. *And be it further enacted by the authority aforesaid,* That any two or more justices of the peace for the said County of Elbert, are hereby authorized and required to preside at said election for Commissioners aforesaid: *Provided nevertheless,* that nothing contained shall be so construed as to prevent the election of the Commissioners hereinbefore named. And any person or persons who may hereafter be elected Commissioners of said village, shall be re-eligible at the next or any subsequent election after the expiration of the time for which he or they may be elected Commissioners under this Act.

ALLEN DANIEL,
Speaker of the House of Representatives.

MATHEW TALBOT,
President of the Senate.
Assented to December 9, 1822.
JOHN CLARK, GOVERNOR.''

The foregoing was introduced in the House of Representatives by Barnard C. Heard, Charles W. Christian, and William Moore, the Elbert County delegation, and was sponsored in the Senate by Beverly Allen, of the County of Elbert.

Had the village of Ruckersville continued to thrive a subsequent Act would, perhaps, have been necessary for the text of the Act does not mention the important matter of boundary lines.

Rukersville, considering its population, led all Georgia in educational facilities. There were two seminaries, one male and one female. Young people, not only from Georgia, but South Carolina as well attended these excellent institutions.

Eudisco Academy, situated at Ruckersville, was incorporated by the General Assembly in 1823, and John Banks, Bedford Heard, William H. Underwood, Asa Thompson, and Joseph Rucker were named trustees.

One year after Eudisco Academy was incorporated the following Act was passed and assented to by Governor Troup:

"AN ACT

"To incorporate Philomathia Academy in the County of Elbert and to appoint Commissioners therein named.

"*Be it enacted by the Senate and House of Representatives of the State of Georgia, In General Assembly met, and it is hereby enacted by the authority of the same,* That from and after the passage of this Act the Academy in the County of Elbert known by the name of Philomathia Academy, shall be called and known by that name; and that Beverly Allen, Henry White, Asa Thompson, Bedford Harper, and Richard Banks, the present

Trustees of the said Academy and their successors in office, be and in the same are hereby declared to be a body politic and corporate, by the name and style of the Trustees of Philomathia Academy ....

"Sec. 2. ....
"Sec. 3. ....
"Sec. 4. ....
"Sec. 5. *And be it further enacted*, That Wiley Thompson, Jeptha V. Harris, Archelus Jarret, John A. Heard, and Thomas Jones be and are hereby appointed Trustees of the Elbert County Academy. . . . .

DAVID ADAMS,
Speaker of the House of Representatives.

THOMAS STOCKS,
President of the Senate.

Assented to December 19, 1823.

G. M. TROUP, GOVERNOR."

Section five (5) of the foregoing act refers to the academy which was located in the town of Elberton. This school proved of great benefit to the surrounding country and continued to thrive for more than half a century.

Until the public school system was established in Elberton there were two institutions known as the "Elberton Male Academy" and "Elberton Female Academy."

Allen Daniel, who was Speaker of the House of Representatives in 1822, when Ruckersville was incorporated, was for many years a citizen of Elbert County. He was born in Virginia in 1772, and married Mary Jones, born 1774 and died 1814, the daughter of James and Elizabeth Jones. The father of Allen Daniel was also named Allen. He was born in Virginia in 1738, and died 1814. During the American Revolution he was Captain in the 8th Virginia Line Regiment.

In 1804, and a portion of 1805, Allen Daniel Jr., served as a member of the Georgia House of Representatives from Elbert County. He resigned in 1805, and was succeeded by his kinsman, Captain William Allen. In 1807, 1808, 1809, 1810, and 1811 he returned to the House.

While a member of the House in 1811, he was mainly instrumental in passing the Act creating Madison County and when successful, donated the lands on which the court house and jail were built. He was the moving factor in organizing the first Superior Court in the new county and for his patriotic activities the people named the county seat Danielsville in his honor.

In the year 1807, he was Brigadier-General of the First Brigade of the Fourth Division of Georgia Militia, and from 1812 to 1817, inclusive, he served as Major-General of the Fourth Division of Georgia Militia.

Allen Daniel was the first State Senator elected from Madison County, serving 1812, 1813, 1814, and 1815. He also represented Madison County in the House, 1821, 1822, and 1823.

Allen Daniel Candler, one of Georgia's governors, was named for him.

There has been much confusion regarding Allen Daniel for the reason that his uncle, John O. Daniel, brother of Allen Daniel Sr., was the father of a son who also bore the name of Allen. This Allen was the father of a son named Allen. Since all of them resided in Elbert County and Allen, son of John, was near the same age as Allen, son of Allen, it can readily be understood why confusion has so often arisen.

John O. Daniel served in the Revolution with distinction and came to Elbert County in 1785 with General George Mathews.

Allen Daniel, grandson of John O. Daniel, married Mary Cash and they were the parents of Fleming, Lindsey, Raphel, and Marion Daniel.

In the year 1832, Ruckersville Methodist Church was chartered by an Act of the Georgia Legislature.

The trustees named were Richard C. Adams, Alfred Hammond, Peter Alexander, John Jones, and William Bailey. They, and their successors, in office, were empowered to employ a marshal whose authority, within a three mile limit of the church building, was the same as the county high sheriff. This provision has never been repealed. The muster ground of the militia was within the prescribed limit and on one occasion two young militia officers, having drunk too freely of the plentiful spirits of the day, were chained to trees for a period of three hours. The trees were used in lieu of a house in which to confine them.

This church is closely interwoven with the history of the families of Alexander, Adams, Bailey, Banks, Burch, Cleveland, Hammond, Jones, Blackwell, and others.

In 1932, the centennial celebration of the church was held and a large number of persons attended from every section of Georgia. Reverend O. A. Vickery was pastor at that time.

When the famous meteoric shower of 1833 took place, the vast majority of people believed that the end of time had come and that the universe was to be destroyed by fire. Some at once began to pray, some sat quietly in their homes, calmly awaiting the end, some fled to storm cellars, while the more practical minded began to seek means by which they might save their worldly possessions.

John Watkins, of Petersburg, when the shower first begun, caused his slaves to lower his family into wells about his large plantation where they were forced to stand for several hours in water almost to their necks. Mr. James M. Tate rushed his wife and children out of doors, into the barn yard, and caused all of his female slaves to be placed beside them. He then ordered his male slaves to draw bucket after bucket of water to throw upon them in the event their clothing should begin to ignite. It is a matter of conjecture just what his intentions were in the event that the men's clothing began to burn. At any rate, it demonstrated the fact that not only at sea did women and children come first.

It is, of course, a matter of history that no damage was done by the falling particles since they became extinguished before reaching the earth. The occurrence of the phenomena, however, caused many persons to believe that the final reckoning was indeed near and another wave of religious fervor literally swept the country. Cult after cult sprang up. There were Grahamites, Millerites, and even those who refused to wear buttons on their clothing. Poison toad stools sprouting overnight in the hot, teeming soil of superstition and fear. Fanatical ministers, confidently prophecying that the end was at hand, went about the country, somewhat after the manner of John preaching in the wilderness, shouting "Repent Ye! Repent Ye!" And indeed their harvest was exceedingly great.

It was the year following the meteoric shower that Elberton's first Jewish merchant arrived. This man's name was Rosenbaum and he soon became very popular with the people. His wife, a quaint little Jewess, soon endeared herself to the ladies of the town by her good naturedness and desire to please. The actions of Mrs. Rosenbaum, upon the approach of a thunder storm, were unusual and demonstrated a magnificent religious faith. At the first signs of an approaching cloud, which promised anything like a thunder storm, she would rush about her house throwing up windows and opening wide the doors. The other ladies, of course, were busily engaged in closing both doors and windows. On one occasion she was asked just why she reversed the custom which was so universally practiced in Elberton. She replied, "I am always expecting Jesus. He will come in a cloud so I open both doors and windows so that he may come into my home."

It is said that Rosenbaum served in the Confederate Army and after the close of the war he did not return to Elberton. All traces of this interesting family have been lost.

According to the Census of the United States for the year 1850, the population of Elbert County was 12,959. Of this number there were 3,374 white males; 3,302 white females; six free colored males; 12 free colored females, and 6,267 slaves. There were 1,177 dwellings; 804 plantations, and 20 manufacturing establishments.

In the year 1851, according to the Elbert County tax returns, there were 5,993 slaves. Joseph Rucker returned 215; Singleton W.

Allen, 213; U. O. Tate, 122; Thomas J. Heard, 104; Gerrard W. Allen, son of Singleton W. Allen, 99; Elizabeth Burch, 90; E. H. Brewer, 82; Bedford Harper, 66; Alfred Hammond, 65; B. C. Wall Sr., 54; R. D. Durrett, 50; William Dooley, 49; William Bowen, 48; Peter Alexander, 43; John A. Carey, 42; E. B. Norman, 40; H. P. Mattox, 40; Guilford Cade, 35; William B. White, 34; Felix G. Edwards, 33. The above named persons were the 20 largest slave holders of the county for that year. Their combined holdings being 1,502.

Major Oliver, who owned a great body of land on Broad River, was the proprietor of a number of slaves and was known throughout the section as a most humane master.

Around some of the huge oak trees in his yard he caused to be fashioned circular tables and here the little Negroes were fed each day when the weather permitted. Each child had its own plate and spoon and was charged with the responsibility of keeping them clean.

Among the adult slaves the Major owned was an African Voodoo doctor by the name of Jim. This man was physically grotesque. His arms were extremely long, reaching almost to his knees; his head was unusually large and his eyes seemed to literally stand out from their sockets. His gorilla-like appearance did not deter him from falling in love with Amy, a Negress more than six feet tall, belonging to William M. McIntosh. They were soon married. Mr. McIntosh at once purchased Jim, since it was his belief, that husband and wife should not be owned by different masters.

Jim was by no means a field worker so the usual domestic process was reversed. Jim kept house and looked after the children while Amy went to the fields.

In due time 12 children made their appearance and among them was "Monkey Bill" McIntosh, a well known character throughout the county for a number of years. He it was who would catch a fish from a stream and devour it while yet alive and struggling.

Jim was an excellent Voodooist as he claimed to be able to "unconjure" anyone and set at naught the work of others of his cult, but possessed no power to "conjure." When the slaves were freed Jim and Amy continued to live and work in the neighborhood of Heardmont until their deaths.

Mrs. Annie C. McIntosh Wall in speaking of slaves owned by her father, William M. McIntosh, and maternal grandfather, Singleton W. Allen, gives a rare and unusual picture of some of these Negroes and, incidentally, clears up something of a mystery, she says:

"Once I was puzzled in regard to the old Virginia Negroes, and their kinship to the Indians. But when looking over some old Walthall papers, I found something of importance in an old will. In this will, the testator instructs his executors to buy 'one Indian girl' for his daughter.

"So it develops that Indian children were sold into slavery. Especially orphans and dependents.

"Proving the Indians to have been good business men with the ability to take every available opportunity of mending their broken fortunes.

"My grandfather, Singleton Walthall Allen, gave to each of his daughters on their marriage—a coachman, a carriage and horses, a maid and a cook.

"Richmond, our cochman, proved to be all that could be desired in a faithful servant. Tall and though darker than an Indian, he carried himself with the dignity charcteristic of that race, he being of an old Virginia Negro family. His strength and ability for managing horses saved his owners from accidents, and relieved them from anxiety when he held the lines.

"In the case of the maid, my mother was not so fortunate. The day after her arrival, she was found rolling on the floor of my mother's room in a deep state of intoxication. Fascinated by the fragrance of the cologne, which she had found on the dressing table, it seems that she went a little farther, by drinking it and so came to grief.

"The cook also proved to be a failure, and the two women were sent back to the cotton fields.

"My father making efforts to alleviate the situation, found two Negro girls in the market and bought them. One was a large, fine looking young woman with one blue eye and one black eye.

"The mismatched eye gave her rather an odd expression. But her countenance was so pleasing that one soon forgot to notice her eyes. This was Jane.

"The slender girl, Jane's sister, has well matched black eyes, with the light of intelligence beaming from them. This was Julia. Of course, Jane's pleasing appearance suggested the promise of a good cook. But being more timid than her sister, she did not hasten to step forward.

"Julia stepped out, took her sister's hand and led her to her mistress, 'Speak to your new mistress, Jane,' she said.

"Then the embarrassment was over. 'Take Julia for the cook,' said my father. Julia, our wonderful cook, was perhaps the finest in Georgia. "Richmond and Jane were married that winter. When the War Between the States came on, 'Big Jane,' as Richmond's wife was called, took charge of the weaving—for cloth had to be woven on the plantation to clothe the Negroes.

"Richmond and Jane raised a large family and half of their children had blue eyes. George, who was named for his mother's grandfather, had blue eyes. Jane and Julia were granddaughters of 'Blue-eyed Indian George.'

"Not long ago, in my sister's kitchen, I met Alice. Alice was the cook.

"'This is Alice,' said my sister, 'One of Uncle Richmond's grandchildren. She is the daughter of De De (Mary), their youngest child.' And she had one blue eye.

"Sometimes I seem to hear the refrains coming from the old plantation, sweet and low.

"The spirituals were very good, but we will never hear the banjo songs again.

"One of the choruses:

>"My mammy was a wild cat;
>My daddy was a tiger,
>And I am what you call,
>The old Virginny Nigger."

"I asked a friend the other day if she had ever heard of blue-eyed Indians.

"'Yes, indeed,' she replied, 'I have seen plenty of them on the North Carolina Reservation'."

The statements in the foregoing article seem to demonstrate the fact that Indians and Negroes intermarried and that the latter inherited their blue eyes from the former.

The banjo songs of the Elbert County Negroes were all composed by the slaves and many of them are pregnant with wit and logic. For example:

>"Beef steak when I'se hungry,
>Licker when I'se dry—
>Greenbacks when I'se hard up;
>And 'ligion when I die!"

>"Bill Mattox is yo' marster—
>Bill Mattox is yo' frin,
>Bill Mattox toes de long cowhide,
>An' nebber fail to len'."

>"Miss Beck 'vite yo' in 'de parlor—
>'Dey fan yo' wid' 'de fan;
>Oh, mudder, oh, dear mudder,
>I lubs dat gamblin' man."

And still another:

>"I'se got a sweetheart in de town,
>She wear er yaller striped gown;
>An' when she strut dem streets er roun'—
>De hollow of her foot cut er hole in de groun'."

An amusing story is connected with the "Bill Mattox" song. William H. Mattox, large slave owner and prosperous planter. He would order certain work done by a given time, and if it were not finished no excuse would save the slacker from punishment.

The song had been sung not only by his slaves, but those of many other planters. In fact, it became well known throughout Georgia, but Mr. Mattox had never heard it. The Negroes feared him far too much to sing it within his hearing.

On one occasion, while in Augusta, he chanced to be walking down Broad Street when to his surprise he heard Negro workmen singing, "Bill Mattox is yo' marster."

He stopped and listened for a moment. Then walking over to the Negroes he inquired where they learned that song.

"Marster," one of them replied, "ain't you nebber heard of ole Bill Mattox 'Dats 'de meanest man dey is!"

Immediately losing his uncertain temper Mr. Mattox rushed towards his informant and Broad Street witnessed a veritable marathon. The Nego won the ace.

Colonel Mattox, in after years, delighted in telling this story. He became a power in politics during the Reconstruction period, but unfortunately lost his fortune and was killed in a gun battle with one of his sons-in-law.

During this period of crinoline, lavender, and old lace—this period of chivalry, and true honor—the aristocrats of Georgia sang quaint songs to the accompaniment of the spinet and the square piano. Among them were "Johnny Sands," and "There Was a Jolly Blade."

"Johnny Sands," tells the story of a youth, bearing that name, who married Betsy Haig:

> *"There was a man named Johnny Sands,*
> *He married Betsy Haig—*
> *And though she brought him land and gold,*
> *She proved a terrible plague—*
> *She proved a terrible plague."*
>
> *"Said he to her, 'I'll drown myself,*
> *The river runs below.'*
> *'Pray do,' said she, 'You silly elf,*
> *I've wished it long ago—*
> *I've wished it long ago.'*
>
> *' "Now tie my hands behind my back,'*
> *And when securely done—*
> *'Now stand upon the brink,' said she*
> *'While I prepare to run—*
> *While I prepare to run.'*
>
> *"Now down the hill his loving wife,*
> *She sped with all her force—*
> *And Johnny Sands, he stepped aside;*
> *And she fell in, of course—*
> *And she fell in, of course.*
>
> *"Now splashing, dashing, like a fish;*
> *'Oh save me, Johnny Sands'*
> *'I would, my dear, yes, much I wish,*
> *But you have tied my hands!*
> *But you have tied my hands!' "*

"There was a Jolly Blade," recites:

> "There was a jolly blade
> Married to a country maid,
> She was neat and she was smart,
> And she pleased him to his heart,
> But alas and alack.
> She was dumb, dumb, dumb."

He then takes his wife to a physician who tells him that it is only the work of a moment to set his wife's tongue at liberty and straightway the miracle is accomplished.

> "To scolding she began
> About the house and things,
> Till it rattled in his ears
> Like a drum, drum, drum.
>
> To the doctor again he goes,
> With his heart all full of woes—
> 'Oh, doctor, oh doctor, you have me—
>   undone—
> My wife has proved a scold and
>   her tongue she will not hold,
> Can you not again
> Make her dumb, dumb, dumb?'
>
> "'When first I did undertake
> For to make your wife to speak,
> I told you 'twas easily done—
> But it's past the art of man
> Let him do what e'er he can,
> To make a scolding woman
> Hold her tongue, tongue, tongue!'"

During the War Between the States, "A Nigger Will Be a Nigger Till He Dies," was popular:

> "It's been the way of some,
> Ever since the war begun,
> To worry the head about the nigger;
> When secession came to view,
> And the abolition, too,
> The fight was all about the nigger.
> Now he may wash and may scrub,
> He may paint and he may rub,
> But a nigger will be a nigger till he dies!"

CHAPTER VIII

OUTBREAK OF WAR BETWEEN THE STATES—ELBERT COUNTY RESOLUTIONS — ORGANIZATION OF ELBERT COUNTY COMMANDS—COLONEL WILLIAM M. McINTOSH—REPORT OF ACTIONS IN VIRGINIA—LIEUTENANT COLONEL R. P. EBERHARDT—RECONSTRUCTION—COLONEL THOMAS W. THOMAS—SAMUEL SNELLINGS AND "BETSY."

Douglas and Johnson, Bell and Everette, Beckenridge and Lane had all been strongly supported throughout Georgia. William M. McIntosh was chosen as one of the electors at large from Georgia as a supporter of Beckenridge and Lane. The Charleston convention was a *fiasco* and Baltimore proved to be little better. With three kindred tickets in the field the final result could easily be surmised. It was, in truth, a case of a house divided against itself.

Eventually came news of the result of the election with Lincoln and Hamlin victorious. The effect, though not unforeseen, was to the average man a calamity and to the unionist truly appalling.

The Georgia General Assembly, the personnel being the same as 1859, met and called a convention of the citizens of the State to consider the question of union or secession. This body met at Milledgeville Janury 16, 1861.

Several weeks prior to the assembling of the secession convention the people of Elbert County held a meeting and drw up the following resolutions:

"The election of Lincoln as President and Hanibal Hamlin as Vice-President of these United States, by a large and decided majority in the abolition States, and by a vote and party purely sectional and hostile to the interests, rights, honor and safety of the State of Georgia, speaks a voice of warning and defiance which a prudent people will not fail to hear, and a brave people will not fail to act upon. This hostile party has come into power with principles avowed, which being fairly summed up, amount to this: That the Negro by nature is the equal of the white man and ought by law enjoy equal civil, political and social rights. Our duty to ourselves and our posterity demand that we should meet such a party and a government pledged to such principles with a firm, determined and effectual resistence. To fail to do so would disgrace us in the eyes of mankind; would disgrace the ancestry from which we sprung and would go far to justify the fate which our enemies hold impending over us. We, as have always been, are willing to abide the union which our fathers made, so long as it is compatible with our honor and safety, and no longer. We are able to defend ourselves and we are not willing to have our political, religious and social rights destroyed and crushed. In the issue which the abolition States have forced upon us, we cannot see where in the least we have been unjust. They have refused to give up fugatives from justice, who have been guilty of the most autrocious crimes in relation to our slave population—they have refused to give up fugitive slaves, and both are plainly commanded in the Constitution which all their officers are sworn to support. They have it a penitentiary offense if our citizens assert their rights to fugativev slaves, peaceably in the courts according to the form of law, an act of actrocious bad faith not paralleled in the government of any country, civilized or savage. They have insultingly asserted their power to rule over us by the votes of a majority, and which votes they swell by the Negroes they have stolen from us. They have shot down and murdered citizens in the pursuit of their rights, peaceably according to law. Under all these multiplied wrongs, we have been patient and hopeful—have not revenged ourselves, have instituted or counternanced no scheme or plan to disturb the peace of the abolition States or injure their people or property. Longer forbearance would not be a virtue without immediate preparation for redress and protection.

"Therefore, RESOLVED. 1. That the crisis we are in the midst of and the dangers which hang over us, compel us to obtain ample indemnity for the past and security for the future.

"2. That if we remain in the Union, we ought to obtain speedy and sure guarantee for our rights, safety and honor; and failing this we ought to resume our soverignty as a State, and declare our separation and independence of the Federal Union.

"3. That for the purpose of uniting all our people, we are willing that sufficient time (to be judged by the State Convention), be allowed to try any means that may seem just, wise and proper to secure our rights in the Union.

"4. That if this time be extended longer than the fourth of March next, we hereby declare it to be our will, and so instruct our delegates in convention, that from and after the fourth of March next, the Federal Government should not be allowed to exercise any of its functions, nor execute any Federal laws within the jurisdictional limits of the State of Georgia until we obtain indemnity for the past and security for the future from the abolition States and the Federal Government; and we hereby instruct our delegates in convention to vote for and obtain, if possible, such laws and ordinances in said convention as will secure us from all exercise of Federal power, and the operation of Federal law, until such indemnity and security are obtained.

"5. To carry out these principles we hereby nominate Luther H. O. Martin and John C. Burch to represent us in convention."

The Elbert County resolutions, together with those of several other counties, were presented to the state convention and incorporated in the proceedings of that body.

According to schedule the convention assembled with former Governor George W. Crawford presiding and A. R. Lamar, of Columbus, acting as secretary. The men composing this body were the flower of Georgia manhood and many of them were destined to prove themselves fearless and able soldiers. Not a few sacrificed their lives with willingness and even reckless abandon for a cause that they knew was just.

After many long debates, and much serious consideration, the decision was eventually reached to withdraw from the Union. The Stars and Stripes were lowered from the flag pole of the building where the meeting was in session to be supplanted by the colonial flag of Georgia.

The committee appointed by Chairman Crawford was not long in drawing up the Georgia Ordinance of Secession.

On the roll call, the vote was found to be more than two to one in favor of disunion, the Elbert County delegation voting with the majority, and thus on January 19, 1861, Georgia joined her destinies with South Carolina, Alabama, and Mississippi.

When the news reached the village of Elberton that Georgia had seceeded a scene of excited celebration took place. Torch light processions were formed; bonfires lighted, guns fired and speeches made on the public square by Emory P. Edwards, Robert Hester, Thomas J Heard, and others. Elberton and Elbert County expressed in no uncertain terms their hearty approval of the convention's action.

With the withdrawal of other states quickly following that of Georgia, a need for a compact confederation was soon recognized, and in consequence a convention of all seceeding states was called to meet in Montgomery, Alabama, and there the Confederate States of America was born. Jefferson Davis, of Mississippi, was elected President, and Alexander H. Stephens, of Georgia, became Vice-President.

Immediately following the firing on Sumter came war. Elbert County, due to its close proximity to South Carolina and its determined type of citizenry, at once began active preparations for war. Elections for militia officers were held throughout the county with every district participating.

In Elberton, the 189th Georgia Militia District, Madison A. Marcus received 24 votes for captain; Emory P. Edwards received 23 votes for first lieutenant, and J. T. McCarty received 23 votes for second lieutenant. Robert P. Eberhardt received 84 votes for lieutenant-colonel of the 42nd Batallion; B. C. Henry received 65, and William A. Brown received four. For major of the 41st Batallion, David E. Harris received 98 votes, and William I. Hollingsworth received 49. This organization incuded Longstreet, Petersburg, Ruckersville, Moss, Gaines, and Centerville districts.

In the 202nd Georgia Militia District (Webbsboro), Henry P. Deadwyler was elected captain, Benjamin Colvard first lieutenant, and George M. Gaines second lieutenant.

The Fireside Guards was organized with Luther H. O. Martin Sr., as captain, Robert M. Heard as first lieutenant, F. B. Bowman as second lieutenant, and J. H. Lofton as third lieutenant.

The Bowman Volunteers was officered by John C. Burch, captain; Larkin L. Clark, first lieutenant, and J. W. Craft, second lieutenant. This company took its name from Thomas Jefferson Bowman who completely equipped it at his own expense. He was, in after years, known as "Colonel" Bowman, but in reality saw no military service.

The McIntosh Volunteers: William M. McIntosh, captain; Joseph T. Smith, first lieutenant; Peter J. Shannon, second lieutenant, and W. J. Clark, ensign. The following letter is on file in the Georgia Department of Archives and History:

"Elberton, Georgia.

"General Henry C. Wayne,

Milledgeville, Ga.

Sir:

"We the undersigned, having received our Commissions as Captain, 1st and 2nd Lieutenants and Ensign of the McIntosh Volunteers, accept our Commissions and have taken and subscribed the oaths attached to the Commissions.
"May 21, 1861.

Very respectfully,

Wm. M. McINTOSH
JOS. T. SMITH
P. J. SHANNON
W. J. CLARK."

A drill master was secured in the person of one Colonel Sharpe, a West Point graduate, who divided his time between the several companies.

Another Elbert County company was organized which was known as the Goshen Blues. This company was attached to the 38th Georgia Regiment of Infantry Volunteers.

On either the 26th or the 27th day of May, 1861, the Bowman Volunteers, the Fireside Guards, the Goshen Blues and the McIntosh

Volunteers left their temporary camp, at Poplar Spring, on the northern outskirts of Elberton, for Atlanta. As they marched through the streets of Elberton they were led by James McIntosh, afterwards Sheriff of Elbert County for ten years and County Commissioner for 12, the youngest son of William M. McIntosh, a barefoot child of four years, dressed in the uniform of a Zouave, proudly and desperately beating upon one of the drums belonging to his father's command. From the sidewalks and atop buildings the entire populance of the county, save the bedridden, cheered these soldiers as they mounted the vehicles that were to convey them to the railroad. A picturesque array of slaves followed the troops, some shouting, some singing spirituals, and some praying aloud. Several of them, who were to accompany their masters as body servants, led their fellows. There was little doubt in the minds of the fair women that their men were merely going upon a holiday excursion for the women of the South believed in the poweress of their men.

Upon their arrival in Atlanta, the McIntosh Volunteers, Bowman Volunteers, and the Fireside Guards were inducted into the 15th Georgia Regiment of Infantry Volunteers. Howell Cobb was colonel; Linton Stephens, lieutenant-colonel, and William M. McIntosh was at once elevated to a majorship. This regiment upon formation at once entrained for Virginia and arrived in the midst of the famous rout at the first Manassas.

The first soldier of Elbert County to lose his life was Dilliard Adams. There were, at first, no special duties required of the raw recruits so the boys engaged in exciting and dangerous sports. In one of their games Adams ran against a bayonet and died from the wound after several days of horrible suffering.

Within a few days after the arrival of the 15th Georgia in the zone of war, Howell Cobb resigned his commission as colonel to become a brigadier general; Judge Thomas W. Thomas, of Elbert County, succeeded him. Linton Stephens also resigned and McIntosh became lieutenant-colonel.

Early in 1862, Colonel Thomas, due to illness, relinquished his position and William M. McIntosh succeeded to the command. William T. Millican, of Franklin County, became lieutenant-colonel.

The following letter is in the possession of one of the descendants of Colonel McIntosh:

"EXECUTIVE DEPARTMENT
"ADJUTANT'S GENERAL'S OFFICE

"Milledgeville, Ga.
April 7th, 1862.

"Colonel Wm. M. McIntosh,
  Orange C. H., Va.,

"Sir:

"Herewith you have the Commission of yourself as Colonel of the 15th Regiment of Georgia Volunteers.

"You will please state in writing directed to this office immediately whether you accept this Commission, and if so, you have taken and subscribed the oath thereto attached.

>Very respectfully,
>H. C. WAYNE,
>Adjutant General.
>Per L. H. Brisco."

"31st March, 1862.

Conditions at the front during the latter part of 1861 are vividly portrayed by the following letter written by Colonel William M. McIntosh to Young L. G. Harris, his brother-in-law:

>"Camp Pine Creek,
>September 26th, 1861.

"Dear Harris,-

"I received, a few days ago, your very kind letter. Amid my camp duties, I assure you, I think of you often, and certainly, would have written to you before this if I could have found anything of interest to communicate.

"Although we are almost in the very face of the enemy we actually know less of what is transpiring around us than you do at home. We get almost all of our reliable information from the newspapers and you have better means of access to them than we have. We are expecting a fight shortly. Indeed, we have been looking for it for some time. We know nothing with certainty about our future movements. We are left to inference from facts which our commanding officers are forced to communicate to us. They have issued orders to all of the Brigades to keep constantly on hand three days cooked rations, and are, also moving all the sick to the rear. From these things we conclude that an advance movement is intended, but when it will be put into operation, we can form no definite opinion. I suppose it will be, in the line of truth, if I say between this and the time winter sets in. If our Generals do fail, to make a demonstration, before cold weather, the people will have a heavy account to settle with them for we are now on the border of enemy's country with an army of between 50,000 and 100,000 effective men anxious to be led even across the Potomac, if the cowardly Yankees will not meet them on this side. These men have to be fed and the expenditures for that purpose are enormous. Death and disease are likewise making rapid inroads upon them daily, striking down many.

"I cannot understand this inaction, which, so far, as I can see, weakens our strength, and destroys our means. Toombs, is getting very impatient at the delay, and has given Johnson some very plain talk. Our Regiment has suffered very much on account of the measles. It has been our greatest scourge. There are not now more than 450 of our men fit for duty. Thomas, our Colonel, is stretched on his back with measles; and Linton Stephens from the same disease has been away from camp more than six weeks and is not yet recovered. So far as I am concerned I have no reason to complain. I have stood camp life very well, even better than I expected. But, during the next five days I am to experience a new phase of it: the Regiment is under orders to march tomorrow morning at 7 o'clock, to Munson, a distance of 12 or 15 miles; there to do duty for the period mentioned above. We carry no tents, but go with our blankets only, and are to sleep on the ground in the open air. I feel no fear about the experiment.

"Bill Mattox has not held up as well as I have. He is, even now, under the weather not confined to his bed, but complaining. I got him into a house not far from the camp, where he is doing very well, and I hope, will soon be able to return to duty. My friend, the greatest trouble I have had to encounter since I embarked in the defense of my country is the great distress of my wife. But, I am not disposed to complain. Thousands of others have gone through the same ordeal. I speak of this to show you place me under great obligations by expressing a willingness and desire to serve not only me, but those I have left behind. Yourself and Sister Susan, I have no doubt, can do much to reconcile Lou, and she, as well as myself, will appreciate your kindness. She came to Virginia and remained for some three weeks. But I found that her stay here would prove of no satisfaction, either to herself or me, and I advised her to return home. She reached home, as you have learned, doubtless, before this reaches you.

"Monday the 16th inst.,

"I have given myself to the cause of my country. If we are to be enslaved I hope never to live to see it. If we are to achieve our independence, of course, I wish to live and enjoy the fruits. But many perils beset the soldier and if I never return, I know without asking it that both you and Sister Susan would interest yourselves for those left behind who are dearer to me than life itself. I feel deeply indebted to you for many past favors, as well as your late kind promises, and the only return I can make is the assurance of continued warm friendship. Give my very best and kindest regards to Sister Susan.

"Truly your friend.

W. M. McINTOSH."

The 15th Georgia engaged in many skirmishes and minor battles throughout 1861, and during the first three months of 1862, always acquiring themselves with honor.

On June 27th, 1862, the engagement at Garnett's Farm, in reality Malvern Hill, was fought. The 2nd and 15th Georgia being mainly engaged.

As the 15th, led by Colonel McIntosh, went to the support of the 2nd, under Colonel Butts, the usually brusk and profane Brigidier-General Toombs was seen by Captain Snyder, one of the surgeons of the 15th, weeping unrestrainedly. Snyder stopped and inquired why he wept. General Toombs replied, "Snyder, I have been forced, by order of that damned McGruder, to send McIntosh, one of the best men God ever made, to his certain death." His words were indeed prophetic for not only was Colonel McIntosh mortally wounded, but Captain John C. Burch (Elbert County delegate to the Secession Convention), Lieutenants Tilly and Ivey were instantly killed as were many officers of lower grades and privates. General Toombs and Colonel McIntosh had been associated in the practice of law at Washington.

The ensuing official report speaks eloquently of the demeanor of the 2nd and 15th Georgia Regiments:

"NUMBER 274

"Report of General Toombs, C. S. Army, Commanding First Brigade, of the action at Garnett's Farm and Battle of Malvern Hill.

"Headquarters First Brigade, First Division Right Wing, Army of the Potomac in the field July 7, 1862.

"I then ordered forward, the Fifteenth Georgia, Colonel (W. M.) McIntosh to Colonel Butts support in the ravine, and ordered the Seventeenth Georgia, Colonel Henry L. Benning, on the left flank and Colonel J. B. Cummings, of the Twentieth Georgia, on the right flank. The action now raged with great violence for an hour and a half, the enemy exhibiting a determined purpose to drive us out of the position in the ravine; but finding themselves incapable of wrenching it from the heroic grasp of the Second and Fifteenth Georgia Volunteers, were driven back and repulsed after two hours and fierce and determined conflict. Nothing could exceed the courage and good conduct of the two regiments mainly engaged. The Second lost, in killed and wounded, about one-half of the men carried into action; the Fifteenth went to their support under a severe and galling fire within eighty yards of their front and gallantly sustained the action until the enemy was repulsed, losing seventy-one men out of three hundred carried into action, including their chivalous Colonel McIntosh, mortally wounded, Captain Burch and Lieutenant Tilly killed in action.

"I am not able at this time, from the circumstances under which this report is made, to refer particularly to minute events of individual instances of good conduct, of which there were many, but I can say with the utmost candor that the conduct of the whole brigade, without an individual exception as far as I know was excellent, and that of the Second and Fifteenth more actively engaged, was brilliantly heroic.

R. TOOMBS
Brig. Gen. First Brig., First Div.,
Army of the Potomac.

"CAPT. A. COWARD,
"A. A. G. First Division,
Army of the Potomac."

A portion of the report of Colonel William T. Millican, who succeeded Colonel McIntosh, and who was himself killed in the Battle of Sharpesburg, follows:

"NO. 276

"HEADQUARTERS FIFTEENTH GEORGIA VOLUNTEERS

"Camp McIntosh, July 26, 1862.

"On June 26 the Regiment (Col. William M. McIntosh in command) by order of Brigadier-General Toombs, occupied the entrenchments of the north side of the nine mile road, near Price's house, and remained in the position until about 6 P. M. on June 27, when by order of General Toombs the Regiment moved to the front near three-quarters of a mile; took a position at the edge of a field some 200 yards to the left of a brick house known as James Garnett's house; sent two companies (Captain John C. Burch Company F and Captain Stephen Z. Hernsberger Company G) as skirmishers to support the pickets of the Second Georgia and feel the enemy. In a few moments the firing on both sides became brisk. Soon the enemy's line was re-enforced and General Toombs ordered Colonel McIntosh with the balance of this command to the support of the skirmishers . . . . The engagement now became general and intensely fierce along the line and raged until after dark. when the enemy retired and the firing ceased.

"Colonel McIntosh, who was at the front, and on the most exposed part of the line, gallantly cheering the men on, fell mortally wounded early in the conflict and was borne from the field."

General D. R. Jones in his official report said:

"The Fifteenth Georgia Regiment led by the intrepid, but now lamented McIntosh, rushed promptly to the support, and the fight was maintained with energy until the enemy's advance was checked and driven back and his firing had entirely ceased."

Colonel McIntosh, after receiving the wound which proved fatal, died a few days later in the Exchange Hotel in Richmond. His wife was in Virginia at the time and was with him two days before his death. He survived long enough to receive his commission as brigadier general for gallantry in action.

After his death his remains were brought to Elberton and interred in the family cemetery at Heardmont.

A pathetic incident portraying the character of the faithful slave took place a few hours after Colonel McIntosh had been wounded.

Cuffy, a slave who had been his property, went to Virginia with him at the outbreak of the war as his body servant, he was an excellent servant, but lacked the quality of bravery, and as he expressed it. "When 'dem Yankees 'gun to shoot I banished over 'de hill 'till 'dey stopped."

On the night of June 27th, when the firing had finally ceased, Cuffy made his way to a point where he believed the Fifteenth Georgia was bivouaced, but soon lost his way and could not find the Regiment in the confusion.

He went from campfire to campfire asking everyone he met, "Massa, is you saw Marse William? Wha' am Marse William?"

At length he found a soldier from Elbert County whom he knew and was told of his wounded master. Disregarding picket lines he made his way to Richmond and was able to see his beloved master before he died.

Less than a month before his death Colonel McIntosh wrote the following letter to his son, Singleton, who was then a student in the Georgia Military Institute at Marietta. This leter demonstrates the loyalty and deep patriotism of the Southern youth.

"Camp near Richmond.
30th May, 1862.

"My dear Son:

"I am glad to learn, through reliable sources, that you have behaved yourself well during your connection with the Institute at Marietta. But, Maj. Jones writes me word that both you and Tom are becoming anxious to join the Army.

"This is very natural, considering your age, and, I must say, patriotic. But I have no idea that it is best for yourselves, or, for your country. You and Tom are both young, ardent; and you are inclined to view things through a false medium. You have not the remotest idea of the trials, hardships, and difficulties which camp life would expose you to, but you could endure all these things if you should keep your health. Your lot would be a hard one, even then. Yet, you can, by no means, count on that here. You are young and your constitution is not yet formed and strengthened; and, the chances are, that you will fall a victim to disease in some phase.

"It is estimated that there are now sick in Richmond more than 20,000 soldiers. This estimate, may be, probably, too small.

"I do not wish you to understand that this, or any kind of hardship or risk, ought to deter us from doing our duty. But, in my judgment, it does not lie in the line of your duty to leave your studies, at your time of life, and go into the Army. You will benefit, both yourself and your country, most, to remain where you are, at present, and improve your physical self.

"If you expect pleasure, by coming into the Army, you will be greatly deceived. Thousands have gone out with that expectation and are now disappointed. This thing of soldiering looks better at a distance than it does close by. Hard and bitter reality takes the patriotism out of many a bosom. This should not be so. I hope it would not be so were you to embark in the Cause. So far, as I am concerned, I did not enter the service, with the expectation of deriving pleasure; on the contrary, I was making a great sacrifice. I have not been disappointed, but this is in line of my duty and, if it had been a hundred times greater I would not have hesitated. If I were situated, as you are, with my knowledge of men and things, I should not hesitate doing as I advised you to do—that is, remain where you are, and complete your education.

"If after all I have said you still conclude to go to the war you must come to my regiment. I can make your situation, at least, less disagreeable. But, there are great uncertainties in war; and, by the time this reaches you, I may not be in command of the regiment, for an engagement is now impending here; and even now, even while I write, I hear away down on the line, to my right, the continuous roar of artillery and the rattle of musketry. Tomorrow, it is expected, the fight will be general all along the line. We have near 100,000 men. The Yankees outnumber us some, but we think we shall conquer them. If you remain, to complete your education, you will be much better qualified to serve your country.

"Write to me and give me your views and conclusions. Let Tom Jones read this and tell him the advice contained in it is equally applicable to him.

Your affectionate father,
W. M. McINTOSH.''

Both Singleton McIntosh and Thomas A. Jones (son of Major J. H. Jones), soon entered the service of the Confederate States and served throughout the remainder of the conflict.

From June 26th through June 30th, 1862, the Fifteenth Georgia lost, in killed and wounded, 105 men, four of whom were commissioned officers. The great majority of the 101 privates were natives of Elbert County.

One father of Elbert County, Sion Hunt, surpassing the famed Mrs. Bixby of Massachusetts, gave four sons on the altar of patriotism: Harrison Hunt died in Richmond from wounds July 7, 1862; Benjamin died at the same place and from the same cause on July 31, 1862; James died from wounds at Winchester, Virginia, on July 25, 1863, and Dozier died at Richmond October 14, 1864. Perhaps no other father in the entire Confederate States suffered the loss of so many sons.

The losses of the Thirty-eighth Georgia, from June 26th through June 30th, 1862, was also 105 men in killed and wounded. Many of these, too, were Elbert County citizens. At the Battle of Gaines Mill this regiment continued to face the enemy, notwithstanding the fact that all ammunition had been exhausted. They advanced with stones, bayonets, clubbed rifles and fence rails as their only weapons. Captain Lawton in command on this occasion, all superior officers having been either killed or wounded, led his men in a charge of a strongly fortified hill and actually took it in the face of a withering fire.

One of the Elbert County units, attached to the 38th Georgia Infantry Regiment, was the Goshen Blues commanded by Robert P. Eberhardt, who, at the cessation of hostilities, held a commission as lieutenant-colonel. This company saw active service at Malvern Hill, Second Manassas, Cold Harbor, Sharpesburg, Winchester, Gettysburg, Mine's Run, Frederick City, Shepherd's Town, Fort Hare, and Appomattox.

Upon the induction of the Goshen Blues into the service of the Confederate States they were attached to Wright's Legion, formed and commanded by Augustus R. Wright. and were stationed at a place called Camp Kilpatrick, on the Georgia Railroad, near Atlanta. R. P. Eberhardt was elected captain of this company. At this time he was 27 years of age.

The Legion was armed with Enfield rifles of the latest pattern and they were instructed in the use of them in the City of Savannah, a short distance to the rear of Forest Park.

Upon reaching Virginia the Goshen Blues were transferred to the 38th Georgia, in the Army of Northern Virginia. This regiment was first under the command of General A. R. Lawton in the corps of Stonewall Jackson and still later assigned to the famous Gordon Brigade which was at one time commanded by General Clement A. Evans.

R. P. Eberhardt was no neophyte in the art of warfare. When William Walker, "The Unsmiling Usurper," invaded Nicorogua, Eberhardt was one of the adventurers led by this lawyer-doctor-journalist, possessed of repellant manner, but a military genius of Alexandrian statue.

One of the prized possessions of Miss Gussie L. Eberhardt, daughter of R. P. Eberhardt, is the following:

"Headquarters of the Army Adjutant General's Office, Rivau, Dec. 27th, 1856.

"SPECIAL ORDER NO. 132

"(Extract) 2. R. P. Eberhardt, Co. 'F' 1st Rifles, is honorably discharged from the Army.
Enlisted Dec. 25th, 1855.

By Command of William Walker, General Commanding in Chief, Ph. R. Thompson, Adjutant General N. A."

After his return to Elbert County he talked so incessantly of Walker and Nicaragua that he was given the sobriquet of "Nick." As he prospered a small hamlet grew up around his home and it was given the name of Nickville in his honor.

R. P. Eberhardt was born in territory now included in Madison County and removed, when 10 years of age, with his parents into territory now within the confines of Elbert County. In later years he lived in Atlanta where he became a prosperous and influential business man.

Joseph T. Smith, who entered the service in 1861, as an officer of the McIntosh Volunteers, became major of the Ninth Georgia Batallion in 1862, in the Department of Tennessee, under General E. Kirby Smith.

In 1863, after the famous Battle of the Chickamauga, General William B. Bates said in his official report of the engagement:

"I cannot close this report without noticing the distinguished services rendered by my field officers, Cols. Tyler, Smith, Rudder, and Jones."

At this time Joseph T. Smith held the rank of lieutenant-colonel. Colonel Smith, after the War Between the States, removed to Augusta where he legally changed his name from Smith to Armand, the latter being his mother's maiden name. He was engaged in business in Augusta for a number of years.

John T. Lofton, a native son of Elbert County and the son of the cultured James Lofton, distinguished himself as Colonel of the

6th Georgia Regiment of Infantry Regulars. He was killed in action during the campaign of 1864.

Luther H. O. Martin Sr., served for a time as a Colonel on the staff of General Robert Toombs. When Robert Toombs was fleeing from the Northern troops, sent to capture him, after the close of the war, he took the name of Colonel Martin and used passports bearing it.

When the Southern arms were at length overcome by sheer numbers and gold, Elbert County was well represented at Appomattox. The following named officers and men of the 15th Georgia Regiment made their way homeward, from Virginia, as best they could. Some walked with shoeless feet, some rode mules and horses found running at large, and others in pairs aiding each other, arm in arm, along the tortuous way:

Peter J. Shannon, Major.
Lovic Pierce Jr., First Lieutenant and Adjutant.
John D. Duppy, Surgeon.
William F. Robinson, Chaplain.

COMPANY I.

A. J. Teasley, Second Lieutenant.
R. W. Cleveland, First Sergeant.
J. L. Deadwyler, Second Sergeant.
W. E. Fortson, Third Sergeant.
J. D. Adams, Second Corporal.
J. L. Gaines, Third Corporal.

PRIVATES

W. G. Anderson, A. W. Brown, M. R. Bond, E. K. Fortson, J. B. Fortson, M. E. Fortson, D. A. Fortson, J. N. Faulkner, P. Gaines, F. Gaines, E. Higginbotham, W. T. Hollingsworth, A. A. Jones, H. B. Mattox, A. Mason, E. B. Norman, S. L. Pledger, W. C. Faust, T. R. White, A. J. Webb, and M. Webb.

COMPANY C.

David Hudson, Captain.
L. H. Alexander, Ensign.
J. M. Hudson, Second Sergeant.
W. T. Clark, Second Corporal.
J. S. Tate, Fourth Corporal.

PRIVATES

J. L. Anderson, W. H. Bullard, N. B. Cosby, J. H. Cosby, J. C. Cosby, A. W. Caldwell, Henry Colvard, Edmond Colvard, S. R. Cash, J. R. Dye, Manuel Franklin, M. L. Heard, E. C. Holbrook, W. D. Hudson, J. W. Lovingood, J. W. McLanahan, J. M. Moon, J. L. Norman, Martin Ruff, J. W. Smith, and W. T. Smith.

COMPANY F.

James J. Burch, Captain.
L. H. Gainies, First Lieutenant.
F. O. Bailey, First Sergeant.
F. F. Rouzee, Fourth Sergeant.
J. W. Jones, Fifth Sergeant.

PRIVATES

D. B. Alexander, D. W. Bradford, W. A. Craft, B. S. Crawford, J. M. Gulley, R. B. Galloway, N. R. Higginbotham, J. D. Hulme, C. Hadden, Ben Murrah, Z. B. Taylor, and William Walseman.

Major Peter J. Shannon was the ranking officer of the Fifteenth Georgia Regiment at the time of General Lee's surrender and had distinguished himself on many hard fought fields.

When the Battle of the Chickamauga was fought, October 19th and 20th, 1863, General Henry L. Benning said, in part, in his report of the engagement:

"Colonel Waddell of the Twentieth, Major Shannon of the Fifteenth, and Major Charlton of the Second, the only field officers left, proved a shining example to their men."

No less than 23 Confederate field officers were slain in this battle. More than twice that number were maimed and wounded.

Major Shannon, during the entire four years of the conflict, remained with the 15th Georgia Regiment and his military genius should have been rewarded with nothing less than a Generalship. Due, however, to the confusion that was everywhere in evidence during the latter part of the struggle, Major Shannon, as many other deserving officers, failed to secure their merited promotions. Had the fortunes of war been reversed such men as Shannon, because of their honorable conduct and unsurpassed bravery, would have risen to the highest offices, within the gift of their country, both military and political.

It is said that Major Shannon attended the United States Military Academy at West Point, and his bravery as well as his brilliancy as a statistician seem to fully bear out this assertion.

While the men, both middle aged and beardless, fought with arms as no other army has ever fought, the women of Elbert County and the entire Confederacy fought equally as well and suffered as heart-rending hardships as did their husbands and sweethearts.

At the close of hostilities there was hardly a silk dress in all of Elbert County. All had been sent to Richmond for use in making the historic observation balloon. Silver services and jewelry, many of wheih were heirlooms and wedding gifts, were freely given to the cause.

Narcotics could scarcely be had in the South. Many ladies planted fields of opium poppies and tended them with their own hands to furnish the sorely needed drug.

In the Heardmont neighborhood Mrs. Jane Heard Allen planted some 10 acres in opium poppies and one could see little Negro boys, wearing nothing save long homespun shirts rushing about the fields catching Spanish flies to be used in making poultices for the soldiers.

The shortage of salt was so acute that smokehouse floors were dug up and such salt as could be found was carefully recovered. Sugar was not to be had under any conditions and home-made sorghum was used as a substitute. Coffee was nothing more than a pleasant memory and parched wheat used in its place.

When hostilities ceased the fortunes of war had sadly depleted the young manhood of Elbert County. Federal guns and contagious disease had reaped an appalling harvest. The Confederate Soldier reached his home to find money totally lacking, and even food, in hundreds of instances, scarcely to be had. The problems, of the freed slaves and Carpet Baggers, the greatest and most alarming that have yet faced any nation of the earth, were met with determination, and often, with stern force. With strength of character native to the deep South broken threads of government and social welfare, that had taken almost a century to spin, were taken up and the building of a new social order came into being.

Frances Letcher Mitcher, in her "Georgia Land and People" says:

"During the dark days of lawlessness and misrule, a party of Radicals and Rebel soldiers were sent to Elbert County to establish a Freedman's Bureau. The first night after their arrival, their camp was surrounded, and though no one was visible, the welking rang with shouts, hoots, yells, and the snapping of guns and pistols until it seemed that pandimonium was turned loose. This deafening noise was kept up, hour after hour, so that sleep fled from the eyes of the intruders. Before the break of day the sounds gradually grew fainter until they melted away in the woods.

"The next day the Radicals left without accomplishing their purpose, saying they would return with a regiment of Federal soldiers and burn every house in the county; by nothing was ever heard of them.

"Elberton was the banner county of Georgia during the Reconstruction period. No Freedman's Bureau was ever established there, nor was a single Radical vote cast while Georgia was in the power of the Federal Congress.

"The reason of this happy state of affairs was that Elbert County was far removed from the railroad, and was inhabited by people of pure Southern blood whose land was not for sale. Their beautiful plantations descended from father to son for generations—in some instances from the Colonial period—so there was no alien blood to cause a division of the people and Elbert County was a unit against Radicalism."

The *Elberton Gazette* of Friday, November 6, 1868, carried an editorial by its capable editor, S. N. Carpenter, which throws an interesting light upon the sentiments of the citizens during this period.

"THE BANNER COUNTY

"In all the bright annals of old Elbert the election Tuesday was the most illustrious—the victory was complete and more glorious, because of the subtle foe we had to deal with, who had his subtle campaign well planned and his dusky columns well organized for the onset. Precautions were taken to have a gallant Yankee Captain with his Company to report here to the Sheriff (This Captain with his whiskers shall appear in another part of the scene), for what purpose nobody known and nobody cares, for the Sheriff plainly told him that he had not sent for him and had no aprehensions that his services would be called into requisition, for he, being a white man, free born, with no fear of dark deeds, well knew that his people always carried their points by moral force and not by brute force. Early in the morning the polls were open as usual on such occasions, the sun rose, clear and beautiful, throwing his auspicious beams about us with more than ordinary loveliness, gilding all nature with heavenly beauty; everything was as quiet as flocks grazing on the green sward; and the voting was going on with no noise but the calling of the names by the Managers; but presently a noise was heard around the corner about the stables, and it was natural that such a thing should attract attention. Lo and Behold! It was the little Radical for the State at Large, AMOS T. ACKERMAN, assembled with a crowd of Negroes in front of the Yankee quarters harranging them with great vehemence. This he kept up for two hours or more with much effort to influence the minds of his dusky audience, no doubt, with intention of provoking, 'A fat outrage.'

"At the close of his harangue, he distributed his tickets and formed a column in two ranks and marched at its head to the polls. On entering the Square the ranks began to dissolve; one by one, and two by two, the Negroes fell out and went to white men and got tickets and went up and voted like honest men. So when the redoubtable scalawag, Colonel Amos arrived at the polls, he was more chagrined that the mink that lost his chicken by the stratagem of the fox, when he looked around with the air of triumph, to find his magnificent column had vanished, and he left like a dog, 'With no tail at all.' With ill concealed rage and pretended fear, he called to the Sheriff to protect him while he voted. No one had taken any especial notice of him, hence there were no grounds for fear, but Sheriff Adams, moved with pity, gratified his demand, 'Do thyself no harm, I am with thee.'

"Then he went and entered a protest against the further proceedings of the election, on the grounds of violence in the streets and inability to reach the polls. These grounds were false and so entered by E. P. Edwards Esq., for there had been nothing but a very small difficulty between two men, such as occur on all such occasions, and was soon over with. No doubt Amos T., will make bloody reports, but near unto a thousand men will swear that no violence was offered him. But after he made himself ridiculous, mirth was irrepressable, and the boys had to have a monkey show. How could they help it? Boys will be boys with such animals about.

"Now we come to where we must give a few touches to the brave, the handsome, the gallant Yankee Captain. Captain Dougherty is his name. He wears upon his graceful brow wreaths of heroic deeds. As we well remember this is the name of the Captain that made that gallant charge on Mrs. Booth, the soldier's widow of this county, a few months since and beat her so that she has not yet recovered, and for whom there was a subscription gotten up to relieve her of her grievous distress, having lost all her earthly possessions at the hands of Captain Dougherty and his banditti. And reports reach us now of his having committeed similar outrages on his return and advance to this place. Since his arrival we have lost the services of one of our most skilled mechanics by the assault of some of his men. We know nothing of the circumstances of this affray. Mr. Broadwell may not have been in his right place, neither were these soldiers. At all events we can see nothing to justify the unmerciful beating of this man—long indulgence of their brutish propensities could have actuated them to it. Of course, we do not implicate the Captain in this, but it shows the discipline his men are under, and these men are sent here to protect citizens! Still with all this, we have treated this band with nothing but courtesy, offered them no unkindness. And it is in but a spirit of kindness now that we warn them to keep their ranks in future, for there is a point where the most cowed will turn upon their oppressors and sting."

The same issue of *The Gazette* carried the following election returns:

	Democratic	Radical
Elberton	798	21
Ruckersville	102	0
Fishdam	14	0
Goshen	101	12
	1,015	33

In the election held December 20, 1870, Emory P. Edwards, a renowned lawyer of Elbert County, was the Democratic candidate for representative. He was opposed by Nathaniel Blackwell, Negro *protogee* of Amos T. Ackerman. When the ballots were counted it was found that Mr. Edwards had received 904 votes as against 256 for Blackwell.

Mr. Ackerman was so greatly interested in the candidacy of Blackwell, according to the *Elberton Gazette*, that he made a special trip from Washington, D. C., to cast his ballot for him.

Amos T. Ackerman came to Elbert County and entered the practice of law about 10 years before the outbreak of the War Between the States. During the war he served in the Confederate Army as a wagon master and at its close became a rabid Radical and was finally rewarded for his activities by appointment to the position of Attorney General of the United States in the Cabinet of President Grant.

The Elberton Gazette of January 3, 1871, carried this notice:

"DEPARTED:

ATTORNEY-GENERAL ACKERMAN left this place (perhaps forever), on Wednesday last, apparently disappointed and disgusted with the result of the elections. We care not how long he may live, nor how far he may go. He carried his family with him."

S. N. Carpenter, editor of *The Gazette,* was a gifted journalist. He was entirely fearless and openly wrote and spoke his convictions of every subject he thought worthy of comment. At one time he was nominated Clerk of the Superior Court of Elbert County.

The Negro population of Elbert County, as a whole, after the Emancipation remained with their old masters and disregarded the efforts of Carpet Baggers to arouse them against their late owners. There were, of course, isolated instances where drastic measures were necessary to retain complete white supremacy, but they were the exception rather than the rule.

In the latter part of May, 1866, about 9 o'clock at night, in the neighborhood of Heardmont the people were surprised to hear the beating of drums. The drumming was mingled with wierd cries and moans and seemed to come from the vicinity of the Savannah River bottoms.

Several men of the community quietly set about to investigate. After traveling some little distance towards the place from which the noise issued they sighted a great bonfire around which a number of Negroes, both men and women, were dancing and singing to the accompaniment of the drums. In the center of the group stood a buxom woman. She was Susan Allen, ex-slave of Mrs. Jane Heard Allen. She was only partially clothed. She stood erect and would at intervals proclaim herself a princess in a loud and high pitched voice. The Negroes dancing about would occasionally bend their knees and bow to her. This state of affairs continued until well past midnight. The same thing took place the following night. The farm workers failed to report on time in the mornings and showed a spirit of extreme indifference. The white men of the community held a meeting on the fifth night and as the semi-barbaric ceremony reached its heighth some 20 armed gentlemen appeared, almost without sound, before the fire.

There was a tense moment. But one of the party stepped quickly up to Susan and jerked her from her place. The Negroes were ordered home and lost little time in obeying the command. Thus ended what might have been a serious outbreak of voodooism throughout Elbert and adjoining counties. Had it been allowed to continue lives and property would have been destroyed. Susan lost little time in changing her mind regarding her royal status and afterwards became an excellent domestic servant.

Although the period of Reconstruction continued well into the Seventies and conditions remained chaotic, the younger soldiers of the Confederacy, undismayed by conditions, did much to dispel the gloom by holding a tournament and coronation party.

On December 18, 1869, notwithstanding extremely cold weather, a huge concourse of people crowded the streets of the village of Elberton. The occasion was the long awaited tournament—the first since the beginning of the War Between the States.

E. G. Roan, Knight of Tallulah; William Henry Heard, Knight of the Soil; L. L. Blackwell, Knight of the Red Cross; Harry K. Gairdner, Knight of the Tin Medal; Joseph E. Deadwyler, Knight of Elberton; W. M. Thornton, Knight of the County; Thomas J. Blackwell, Knight of the Lost Cause; A. Bangus, Knight of the Wandering Jew; Matthew Blackwell, Knight of the Ex-Rebel; E. B Starke, Knight of Navarre; A. H. Roebuck, Knight of the White Plume; John P. Shannon, Knight of the Golden Circle; William M. McIntosh Jr., Knight of Scotia's Highlands; Thomas J. Hester, Knight of the Mohicans; McAlpin A. Arnold, Knight of the Savannah; A. O. Thomas, Knight of the Lone Star, and Samuel L. Carter, Knight of the Palmetto State, participated.

The knights were formed into two ranks by Marshal Robert M. Heard and led to a field fronting the home then occupied by Robert Glenn. They presented a truly spectacular appearance arrayed in all the trappings of former times.

After drawing for numbers, they mounted, and John P. Shannon, soon to become Grand Master of Georgia Masons and brilliant lawyer, rendered an appropriate oration.

Three rides were allowed and at the conclusion the winners were:
First, J. L. Deadwyler; second, L. L. Blackwell; third, T. J. Hester; fourth, William M. McIntosh Jr., A. H. Roebuck, Thomas J. Blackwell, and S. L. Carter. McIntosh, Roebuck, and Blackwell relinquished their claims and the Knight of the Palmetto State was awarded the prize.

The knights chose Miss Lula Vail, Queen of Love and Beauty, and Misses Julia Foster, Sallie Statham, and Miss Ida Jones (who became the wife of Captain James J. Burch), Maids of Honor and Companions of the Queen. The Coronation Party was held on Monday evening, December 20th.

The excitement caused by the tournament was responsible for an amusing incident.

A certain Mr. Parker Slay and his wife, Martha Ann, attended the celebration and Mrs. Slay, inspired by the beautiful gowns worn by the ladies who participated, spent the afternoon in shopping. Mr. Slay did not accompany her on her rounds. One may only surmise what transpired after their arrival home, but the following notice was posted on the court house door, in Elberton, about a week later:

"NOTICE

"I do hereby notify and forewarn all persons trading with my wife, Martha Ann Slay, with the expectation of collecting the money from me, as I am determined not to pay any contract made by her.

PARKER SLAY."

Six days later the following notice appeared by the side of the first:

"NOTICE

"My credit was much better before I married Mr. Slay than it has been since, but it may be good again if I am relieved from supporting him. But I fear that I shall suffer from HIS contracts; so I caution and forewarn all persons from buying any property from him until they are satisfied that it is not mine he is trading off.

MARTHA ANN SLAY."

On October 15, 1865, a little band of Christian men and women gathered in the Elberton Methodist Church and organized the Presbyterian Church of Elberton.

The organization was perfected by Reverend Robert W. Milner, of Hopewell Presbytery; Reverend J. D. Buckner, and Elder A. Walker, of the South Carolina Presbytery. The charter members were: C. W. Fenton, John T. McCarty, Amos T. Ackerman, Sophia G. Bruce, and Rachel A. Auld. J. D. Buckner was elected pastor.

Although situated in a section where the Baptist and Methodist denominations vastly outnumbered all others combined, this church has grown until the present membership exceeds 200.

A number of prominent ministers have served this charge: F. P. Mulally, C. H. Turner, E. W. Green, John O. Lindsey, F. Jacobs, P. C. Morton, R. W. Milner, W. G. F. Wallace, J. F. Pharr, J. D. Buckner, T. P. Cleveland, 1867-1872; J. B. Morton, 1875-1876; H. F. Hoyt, 1891-1895; A. R. Fowler, 1896; S. L. Wilson, 1896-1897; L. A. Simpson, 1897-1898; F. D. Thomas, 1899-1903; J. E. Stephenson, 1904 until his death in June, 1905; C. I. Stacy, 1905-1914; W. W. Morton, 1914-1918; H. W. Koeling, 1919-1927; H. R. Boswell, 1927. Edd Rampage, Mark Wursing.

From the membership of this church several ministers have been ordained, George W. Wilcox (elected head of the Synod of Georgia,

1932), and William Frierson are of this number. Miss Marion Wilcox, a member of this church, is serving as a missionary in China.

The history of the Elberton Presbyterian Church has been closely allied with the families of: Auld, Wilcox, Frierson, Irvin, Stillwell, Bruce, Payne, Clark, Hunter, Sheppard, Wyche, Turner, and Huie.

A modern house of worship was erected a few years ago during the pastorate of C. I. Stacy. It was largely through his progressive efforts that the funds were secured for its construction. A number of Elbert County citizens not affiliated with this church give financial aid towards its construction. The building is free from encumbrance.

The Synod of Georgia held its annual session at this church during the year 1932.

Forty years previous to the establishment of the Elberton Church, there had flourished in Gaines District a church of the same faith. The exact date of its establishment is unknown, but is was abandoned in 1830, and for several years afterwards was used as a school building. This house was constructed of hand hewn logs and chincwed with mud.

Among the membership of this church were the families of Cash and Fowler. These families left Elbert County for the Alabama and Mississippi territories and their departure, no doubt, caused the abandonment of the earliest Presbyterian meeting house in this section.

There is little doubt that this church was under the jurisdiction of the South Carolina Presbytery and was served by ministers from that State.

An amusing incident took place about this time with Sam Harrison, an ex-slave, who had belonged to Judge Thomas W. Thomas, as the central figure.

A certain lady of Elberton, who had known Sam many years previous to emancipation, met him on the street. He had just returned home from service as the member of the legislature. Sam, upon seeing the lady, very politely removed his high crowned hat and in a humble manner inquired:

"How is Miss 'Riah and all 'de Chilluns, Miss Annie?"

"They are all well, Sam," she answered. "I understand that you have come up in the world since you were freed. What did you do in the Legislature?"

"Miss Annie," he replied, "I sho' had a mighty fine time. I 'tens to 'de do' and blacked the white gemmen's shoes!"

Just previous to this period Elbert County sustained a great loss in the untimely death of Judge Thomas W. Thomas, a brave soldier and a learned judge. Dr. B. C. Smith, a gallant Confederate soldier, in writing of him, said:

"Davidson Maley, son of Sidney Maley, who resided about the place now known as Hardcash, was an overseer on a farm below Elberton, where a burly Negro overpowered him and wounded him so severely that there was little hope of recovery—consequently he did not join the early volunteers. The Negro was promptly jailed. This event recalls memories of one of Elberton's most noted citizens. A few men who feigned familiarity spoke of him as 'Tom,' but his name was Thomas W. Thomas. As a lawyer and a person he was considered domineering. He had a rather austere bearing, but in a heart to heart acquaintance he was a most genial mn. Some reasons why he was considered rash, inconsistent and a self-constituted autocrat are in order. In his early years of public life he shot Postmaster Smyth, of Augusta, with intent to kill.

"Thomas was wont to inquire of country people about crop conditions. Once there was a common wail of 'No rain'—crops being cut off, he rambled through Pike, Goshen, and Dogsboro Districts, *en route* to Hartwell, and found crops in a fairly flourishing condition; he declared that if he were the Almighty he'd send drought until people would gladly acknowledge a shower of rain. Extreme comparisons are often used to emphasize an idea.

"In the case of shooting with intent to kill, he gave Smyth an equal chance by going through the formalities, and meeting him on an island in the Savannah River beyond the jurisdiction of state law, and settling the question of honor according to the code duello.

"Thomas had a kind feeling for the poor—his pets were the unfortunate poor.

"When Thomas was elected Judge of the Superior Court there was a prevailing apprehension that he would exercise all the powers vested in him in ways calculated to goad the people into obedience of law, according to his construction. Probably the most extreme thought of the judge, 'Who neither regarded man nor feared God.' His first court was at Hartwell and was watched with vigilant interest and some apprehension. But it was an amazing revelation to find that he was the very embodiment of 'Wisdom, Justice and Moderation.' Probably a more erudite had not, or has, filled the office in many years. He was a man of rare resources in emergencies.

"This episode turns me back to the episode in Judge Thomas' career which I was about to relate in connection with the supposed murder of Maley, which kindled a spirit of vengence in the people generally.

"A mass meeting seemed to take place without call or expressed object. There was no boisterous talk, but enough was known to prove that an open lynching was imminent. Judge Thomas had a call from the balcony for all the people to assemble in the court room, which was soon full of men anxious in expectation. The Judge stood up and talked in the regular conversational tone as calmly as on an ordinary occasion. He had knowledge of human nature to understand that prating about the majesty of the law would intensify the rage of a mob. Knowing the absorbing interest which the masses of the people felt about the impending war, he talked seriously and entertainingly on the subject until he captured the attention of his audience. Then proceeding to say that the eyes of all civilized nations were on the Southern States—particularly respecting the institution of slavery, and treatment accorded the Negroes—the importance of favorable recognition of foreign powers—that the murder of the Negro in question might turn the tide of foreign power against the South. Meanwhile, a growing company engaged in undertones of conversation outside at the foot of the stairway. The issue seemed to be critical when a leader remarked openly, 'No use listening to that man talk—come on, men.' And moved towards the jail. There was a faltering following for a few paces, and then a halt. Most of the men returned to the court room. Judge Thomas' tact had averted the otherwise inevitable lynching in open day and without disguise. This was the chief *d'auvre* of his eventful career."

During the period extending from the establishment of Elbert County through the early Eighties game of many kinds was abundant. It is said of Samuel Snellings that on one occasion he purchased at the store of William A. Swift one pound of black powder. This purchase, as the story goes, was accounted for in the following manner:

    January 13, 1868—Fired one shot and killed 13 wild turkeys.
    February 4, 1868—Fired one shot and killed 60 crows.
    February 10, 1868—Fired one shot and killed 200 blackbirds.
    February 25, 1868—Fired one shot and killed 92 doves.

His gun was an old flint and steel, single barrel, which stood in the stock six and one-half feet long. He would use tremendous loads and was frequently rendered unconscious by the force of the recoil. Mr. Snellings always called his unweilding weapon "Betsy."

He was considered a truthful gentleman and Reverend J. N. Wall, writing of him in 1908, said that no one doubted, for a single instant, that his report of game killed was entirely accurate. It is, of course, true that the fields were baited with grain several days before he made each kill.

CHAPTER IX

RETROSPECTIVE—ORGANIZATION WILLIAM M. McINTOSH CAMP U. C. V. — SPANISH-AMERICAN WAR — GEORGE HAILEY FORTSON—UNVEILING OF CONFEDERATE MONUMENT—FACULTIES OF ELBERTON INSTITUTE AND ELBERTON SEMINARY—WATER WORKS BOND ELECTION—GRANITE CITY CARNIVAL — ORGANIZATION STEPHEN HEARD CHAPTER D. A. R.—ELBERT COUNTY SCHOOLS—FIRST COMMERCIAL CLUB ORGANIZED—HAWKES LIBRARY ESTABLISHED—FIRST SELECTIVE DRAFT—JOHN H. JONES MEMORIAL CHURCH—ORGANIZATION E. B. TATE POST AMERICAN LEGION—DEAD IN WORLD WAR—BUSINESS PROGRESS.

To those who remember the town of Elberton during the latter part of the last century, and the first decade of the present one. the first portion of this chapter will, perhaps, awake memories of both joy and sorrow.

Which of you, if one there be, who does not remember the "Tribune" building where the Piedmont Hotel now stands; the wooden store building of Jones & Company basking with seeming content beneath the gnarled mulberry trees; the cotton warehouse, belonging to Colonel Thomas M. Swift, on the corner of Oliver and Elbert Streets; the red brick school building; the burial of the "Dutchman," pulled from his pedestal in the center of the Square; Gairdner & Arnold, Elberton's leading store—Allen Cason, Miss Lou Haslett, Ben Kay, Jim Wilhite, Lonnie Black, W. T. Arnold; Brewer's ice plant and public baths; first electric lights; water works and the constructoin of the tank; pavement; the First Methodist Church without its coat of stucco; the Episcopal Church, which the wind carried away; the cotton wagons on the Square; the Hotel Roberts and its genial hostess; the old Southern Depot; Auld's Shop, a beehive of industry in the manufacturing of sturdy wagons and buggies; Moore's Drug Store, where the First National Bank Building now stands; James' Grove and the bicycle track; the home of Judge and Miss Mary Roebuck on North Oliver Street; Pressley's harness shop; Brewer's stables; Clark and Adams Shop; the public well; the fire bell; the wagon yard on the John James property at Oliver and Elbert Streets; the Tate Block fire; the dynamite explosion; the building of the Maxwell House; Willis Vaughan's Barber Shop; one night stand shows at the "Opera House;" Black Patti; balloon ascensions—puffed sleeves, roached hair, trailing dresses, church picnics, tandems, mustaches; the crimes of William Branch and Henry Jones and the cool and collected manner in which James McIntosh, then Sheriff, prevented mob violence, and the subsequent legal and public executions?

How well do you recall the canine, "Three Muskateers"—Trip, Snider and Friday; the three-legged Shepherd dog, "Devil," the constant companion of Sam Olive; Joe, the Maxwell House carriage driver, who met all trains, and Dock, the trusted pilot of the Hotel Roberts bus; Uncle "Dirty Head," 120 years old and his cotton sack; Blind Jack and "Monkey Bill" McIntosh; Brewer Swearengin driving Jerry, his educated horse; Mrs. Mamie Brown, expertly handling the spirited Mack; Captain Willis Adams, leading the Militia Company; the school children marching in a body to Memorial Day services; trips to Franklin Springs; "Aunt" Nancy Swift, whose love and interest encompassed every child; Mrs. Adeline Deadwyler, in the front pew of the First Baptist Church; Judge P. P. Profit; McAlphin Arnold, walking from his business to his home; "Aunt" Sarah Arnold and her constant companion, Mrs. Sue Wilhite McAllister; E. B. Tate, slowly strolling thoughtfully to town eating an apple; Mrs. Robert Heard, working unceasingly in the interest of the Confederate Veterans; Mrs. J. F. Stillwell and Mrs. Allie Stevens, on their way to school; John Langston, as school superintendent; Mrs. John Brown, and her primary class at the First Baptist Church; Zeke Harris, and his drays; Mrs. H. P. Hunter, singing at public gatherings; Mrs. L. Y. A. Blackwell, at Harris-Allen Library; Faust Rouzee and his eternal "Na Na;" election day fights; the first motion picture show, "A Trip to Mars;" the "Talking Pony;" the old Baptist Church turned into a flour mill and presided over by John Brewer; "Uncle" Lem, driving D. P. Oglesby's cows to pasture and his efforts to frighten school children by barking like a dog; "Aunt" Mary Burden, the only Negro member of the First Baptist Church; Arnold's old mill, John Robinson's Circus, the yearly carnival, Captain Jim Burch, Fred W. Auld, Dun Alexander, Abda Oglesby, Major J. H. Jones, Policeman Ham, Policeman Joe Deadwyler, W. H. Irvin Sr., H. W. Williams, S. R. Belk, Robert F. Wright, Brewer G. Boardman, J. T. B. Anderson, Judge H. A. Roebuck, Clarence Harris, Ira C. Vanduzer, Marcus Bell, I. G. Swift, Robert M. Heard, George C. Grogan, Reverend John Henry Grogan, E. B. Stark, S. S. Brewer, Thomas M Swift Sr., Billy Anderson, Dr. Bell, Bynum Grimes, John C. Carr, W. J. Matthews, "Uncle" Lee Stevens, Dr. Tom Bond, John R. Mattox, Captain Clark Mattox, John Hudgens, William H. Mattox, Billy Parks Clark, D. P. Oglesby, T. O. Tabor Sr., Thomas Jones, Matt Willis, J. H. Turnell, Jim Whitesides, J. H. Duncan, L. H. Turner, Max Silverman, Harry Rose, Jake Silverman, Mrs. E. B. Tate, "Tiny" Roebuck and sister, Sam Carter, Charlie Taylor, Dr. L. P. Eberhardt, Dr. B. F. Smith, Dr. Bishop, Dr. Terrell, Dr. R. F. Moore, Dr. S. B. Adair, J. N. Wall, Dr. N. G. Long, Tom Hester and his dogs, John C. and Dilliard Brown, Sing McIntosh, "Uncle" Billy McIntosh, Captain W. B. Henry, J. L. Heard, Reverend A. G. Worley, Mart Webb, Jim Stephenson, Dave Arnold, H. A. Norrell, Reverend E. L. Sisk, Asbury Tate, "Babe" Tate, "Uncle"

Johnny Nelms, W. L. Skelton, M. J. Thornton, Benson Higginbotham, J. Hop Brewer, William Thornton, Will Heard, "Uncle" Nap Cosby, W. D. Tutt Sr., E. P. Bailey, John James, and Perry Bruce. All familiar figures seen daily on the streets of Elberton.

Can one forget seeing the red, brass trimmed fire wagon making its initial run; the baseball games; Jim LaFitte, Ed LaFitte, Hugh Arnold, Parks Heard, "Bear" Alford, "Chick" Vickery, "Uncle" Andrew Cleveland, the official scorer; "Uncle" Lev Bailey and L. C. Edwards, rooting for the home team; the Elberta Club, the first X-ray machine in the county owned by Dr. L. P. Eberhardt; the ice shaving contraption at Terrell's; Early Adams and his famous barbecues; the "Hop Joint" in West End (still "A 'hopping"); Cleveland's ice cream sodas; round dances held in the basement of the Maxwell House where lived: Mr. and Mrs. John C. Brown, Miss Emma McKnight, Mr. and Mrs. James McIntosh, Mr. and Mrs. "Coon" Black, Mr. and Mrs. Jim Whitesides, Dr. and Mrs. R. F. Moore, Dr. and Mrs. A. S. Hawes, Mr. and Mrs. R. E. Hudgens, Miss Mary Hansard, Jack McIntosh, Miss Grace Short, Miss Sarah Powers, Harry Black, "Grits" Rice, Miss Bessie Haslett, Miss Willingham, Nick Salios, Ed Cobb, Mr. Cozene, in charge of the first brick paving; Tom Verdel, Foster Simpson, Laura Lee Simpson, Sidney Gaines, Luke Deadwyler, Mr. and Mrs. John Oglesby, and the Vaughan's; Halley's Comet, with the attending prophecies concerning the end of time; protracted meetings; Hoke Smith and Joe Brown; Baptist Missionary Society suppers, Mrs. Dilliard Brown's cake, Mrs. H. J. Brewer's salads, Mrs. James McIntosh's coffee; Richard Pierson Hobson, speaking at the court house; Willie Upshaw and his "I thought I could" train; home talent minstrels, sponsored by the Elks; three hour long music recitals given by the pupils of Mrs. Agnes Eberhardt, Mrs. John Brown and Mrs. H. P. Hunter; ladies at church services slyly taking cloves from their gloves and daintily nibbling them; Dr. Judd Matthews, and his rustling cuffs?

All this has past, but in passing there is left to us happy memories mingled with regrets, and being trite may we not say, "A rose for every thorn?"

March 1st, 1898, saw the organization of the William M. McIntosh Camp of the United Confederate Veterans. E. B. Tate was elected President; Robert M. Heard, Vice-President; R. M. Willis, Secretary; A. J. Matthews, Surgeon, and W. D. Tutt Sr., Historian. The following named constituted the charter members: John M. Brewer, Company C, 15th Georgia; Abda Oglesby, Company H, 38th Georgia; John B. Almond, Company F, 38th Georgia; E. B. Higginbotham, Company F, 38th Georgia; Thomas S. Davis, Company C, 7th Georgia Cavalry; R. M. Willis, Company C, 15th Georgia; Peter C. Gaines, Company C, 37th Georgia; William G. Sanders, Company A, 1st Georgia; Henry P. Norman, Company A, 3rd Texas Cavalry; E. N. Kennebrew, Company C, 15th Georgia; R.

C. Adams, Company G, 37th Georgia; John D. James, Company K, 6th Georgia; A. J. Matthews, Company A, 37th Georgia; W. T. Moore, Durham's Batallion; J. W. Booth, Company H, 38th Georgia; S. D. Colson, Company C, 15th Georgia; A. W. Vaughan, Company H, 38th Georgia; J. H. Brewer, Toomb's Brigade; W. M. Thornton, Company F, 38th Georgia; J. F. Stillwell, 32nd Band; J. A. Burden, Company G, 37th Georgia; H. H. Colvard, Company H, 29th North Carolina; N. B. Cosby, Company C, 15th Georgia; W. J. Eavenson, 15th Georgia; W. H. Bond, Company I, 15th Georgia; J. W. Tibbetts, Company I, 5th Arkansas; E. B. Norman, Holcomb's Legion; A. J. Bond, Company C, 38th Georgia; T. A. Jones, Company C, 7th Georgia Cavalry; E. B. Tate, Company C, 15th Georgia; W. D. Tutt, Company A, 15th Georgia; John D. Hulme, Company I, 15th Georgia; John A. Gentry, 24th South Carolina; J. H. Jones, 15th Georgia; M. D. Webb, Company C, 15th Georgia; T. F. Rousey, Company F, 15th Georgia; D. J. Maxwell, Toomb's Brigade; J. H. Stovall, Company C, 15th Georgia; B. D. Brown, Company C, 7th Georgia Cavalry; D. A. Fortson, Company F, 38th Georgia; W. J. Sizemore, Company E, 37th Georgia; L. B. Partain, Company F, 38th Georgia; L. M. Heard, Company C, 15th Georgia; T. B. Dye, Toomb's Brigade; M. B. Adams, Company G, 37th Georgia; William Seymour, Company I, 15th Georgia; D. V. Locklin, Company K, 3rd Georgia; D. E. Cleveland, Company I, 15th Georgia; A. M. Shumate, Company C, 7th South Carolina; John M. Eavenson, Company F, 38th Georgia; J. R. Brown, Company B, 24th Georgia; James M. Braswell, Company F, 2nd Georgia; James C. Townsend, Company H, 2nd Georgia; James J. Burch, Company F, 15th Georgia; John H. Cosby, Company C, 15th Georgia; Mallory J. Thornton, Company I, 15th Georgia; I. D. Gloer, Company F, 15th Georgia; M. E. Pulliam, Company I, 15th Georgia; S. W. Saxon, Company D, 10th Georgia; T. D. Thornton, Company F, 38th Georgia; F. O. Bailey, Company F, 15th Georgia; T. L. Gray, Company D, 37th Georgia; D. M. Wheelis, Company C, 15th Georgia; T. S. Gaines, Company I, 15th Georgia; J. H. Fleming, Company H, 3rd Georgia; J. W. Bullard, Company D, 7th Georgia Cavalry; E. P. Bailey, Company G, 37th Georgia, and W. L. Charping, Company H, 30th Georgia.

During the year 1898, Mrs. Sally Harper (E. B.) Heard, in whose home the first chartered Woman's Club of Georgia was organized (Sorocis), conceived the novel and helpful idea of the Traveling Library. She was successful in interesting the officials of the Seaboard Air Line Railway Company in her project and with their financial assistance, organized and perfected the Seaboard Air Line Traveling Library. Thousands upon thousands of books have been made available to country schools and individuals that could never have had access to them in any other manner. The library has proved a marked success and continues, year after year, to be of untold benefit to the general public. This idea and its perfection will stand a lasting monument to the memory of Mrs. Heard. After her death, Mrs. Sue Heard (J. Y.) Swift, the daughter of the founder, carried on the work in a most capable manner until 1934, the year in which she died, following her father to the grave by precisely one week. The library still functions under the management of Mr. J. Y. Swift.

On April 21, 1898, war was formally declared against the Spanish power. Although scarcely 30 years had elapsed since Appomattox, Elbert County, as did all Georgia, rallied to the support of the Federal Government. Among the volunteers were: Lientenant W. P. ("Billy Park") Clark, Company A; Sergeant W. A. Shumate, Company A; Corporal James T. Burden, Company A; Corporal Isiah T. Irvin, Company A; Privates Robert E. Almond, Company A; Elbert O. Bailey, Company A; James Bynum Bell, Company A; William F. Carlton, Company A; Eugene D. Carter, Company A; James L. Clark, Company A; John W. Clemons, Company A; Jesse P. Cleveland, Company A; William T. Cook, Company A; John G. Ellis, Company A; Lindsey A. Gray, Company A; Marion E. Hambrick, Company A; Joseph E. Haralson, Company A; Guy E. Harper, Company A; Duval E. Hutto, Company A; Ben D. Maxwell, Company A; William T. Maxwell, Company A; Bohler Moon, Company A; James O. Phelps, Company A; Calvin P. Rampey, Company A; John D. Sayer, Company A; James A. Smith, Company A; Robert B. Tribble, Company A; Carl Deadwyler, Company E; Richard E. Hall, Company K; Gaines Wansley, Company K; Charles H. Power, Company F; B. F. Burnett, Company A; Quince L. Arnold, Company A; M. W. Glenn, Company A; Lonze E. Esco, Company E; William A. Cooper, Company B; Williard S. Johnson, Company A; Arnold Worley, Thomas H. Verdel, Andrew Gaines, Paul Gaines, and George Beasley.

A native son of Elbert County, although a citizen of Seattle, Washington, at the time, won undying fame during this struggle. George Hailey Fortson, the son of George Green Fortson and Louisa Wall, was Captain of a Militia Company from the State of Washington. At the outbreak of hostilities he at once volunteered for active service, in the zone of war, and was sent at the head of Company B of Washington troops to the Phillipines.

Captain Fortson, while gallantly leading his troops up a sharp incline, was mortally wounded and died March 27, 1899. In recognition of his heroic and intrepid conduct he was cited for bravery on the field.

George Hailey Fortson was born October 19, 1860, in Elbert County, and studied law under the well remembered Judge William Reese in Washington, Georgia. At the age of 22 years he was admitted to the Bar, and in 1885, practiced law in Palatka, Florida.

In 1886, he removed to Seattle where by virtue of industry coupled with unusual native ability he was soon elected City Attorney.

On March 4, 1896, he married Miss Minnie Fry, a daughter of George Fry one of the pioneers of the State of Washington.

Too little credit has been given the soldiers of the Spanish-American War. While it is true that many of the men saw no active service they were forced to undergo hardships unsurpassed by any experienced in the other wars in which the United States has engaged. Malaria was rampant. Food unfit for eating was forced upon them by grafting politicians, and Tampa, where many of them were stationed throughout the war, was rank with horrible disease and poisonous mosquitos. These men who gladly suffered hardships, forced upon them in so needless a manner deserve eternal appreciation for their unselfish heroism.

The morning of July 15, 1898, presented a colorful scene in Elberton. Carriages, buggies, wagons, carts and horseback riders blocked the streets. Pedestrians and horsemen thronged into the town from every quarter. The reason for such widespread interest was the unveiling of the monument to the soldiers of the Southern Confederacy.

The line of march was formed at the court house with the colorful band of the Third Regiment leading the procession. To the strains of "Dixie," the Confederate survivors, the local militia, and the Masons in full regalia, joined the parade.

Upon reaching the Harris-Allen Library the marchers were met by the ladies of the Memorial Association and Miss Roberta Heard (Mrs. John T. Dennis) with her maids of honor and the flower girls.

Miss Sarah Louise McIntosh (Mrs. A. F. Archer), the granddaughter of Colonel William M. McIntosh, who was selected to present the Flag to the veterans, said, "As the granddaughter of William M. McIntosh, whose memory you have so highly honored as to give your Camp his name, I have been selected by my aunts, Mrs. John C. Brown and Mrs. Peyton M. Hawes, and my father, James McIntosh, to present to you, loyal and brave Confederate veterans, whom their father loved, this battle Flag to show their high appreciation of your constancy to his memory and as evidence of their love to the Cause for which he died and for which you so gallantly fought and suffered."

Captain Robert M. Heard, a wounded Confederate veteran, accepted the Flag with the following remarks: "Cousin Louise, I accept this beautiful Flag, the emblem of our government, and though meteoric in its existence, gave to the nation the most noble, heroic and patriotic men, the most beautiful, modest and self-sacrificing women the world has ever known. No, no, there is no country like our dear Southland and no people like those who dwell in Dixie. We prize this Flag not only because of its beauty; not only because it was once the pride of the Southern Army, but it carries us back to the time when we followed Lee, Jackson, Longstreet, Gordon, Evans, and our own beloved William M. McIntosh. We promise you this Flag shall never trail in the dust, never dishonor, and when this band of Confederates shall have been disbanded by death we will bequeath it to our children as a priceless legacy."

At the conclusion of the ceremonies at the Library the line of march was again formed and proceeded to the Monument on the Public Square.

After the unveiling, Captain James J. Burch introduced the speaker of the day, General Clement A. Evans, whos address was profoundly interesting and pregnant with gems of oratory.

Those participating in the ceremonies were John P. Shannon, Past Grand Master of Georgia Masons; Thomas A. Jones, Deputy Grand Master; William Parks Clark, Senior Warden; William O. Jones, Marshal; B. F. Frazier, Chaplain; John T. Heard, Secretary; I. G. Swift, Treasurer; Andrew J. Cleveland, Senior Deacon; L. H. O. Martin, Junior Deacon; Dr. N. G. Long, Architect; George Leohr, Bearer of the Three Great Lights; S. O. Hawes and E. H Turner, Stewards, all of Philomatha Lodge No. 25 of Free and Accepted Masons; Mrs. Robert M. Heard, President of the Ladies Memorial Association; Mrs. James McIntosh, Mrs. John C. Brown, Mrs. Peyton M. Hawes, Mrs. L. Y. A. Blackwell, and Mrs. William M. Wilcox.

The young ladies assisting Miss Roberta Heard in unveiling the monument were: Misses Sarah Louise McIntosh (Mrs. A. F. Archer), Annie McCalla (Mrs. John Purdue), Hammond Burch (Mrs. Jack Fleming), Edna Arnold (Mrs. Z. W. Copeland), Jessie Roberts (Mrs. Parks), and Mary Jim Cason (Mrs. Thurmond).

The flower girls in attendance were Emma Tate (Mrs. John Horton), Bernice Blackwell, Ethel Willis (Mrs. Weyman Mashburn), Jennie Rae Auld (Mrs. Worley Nall), Florence Brown (Mrs. D. N. Thompson), Maud Brown (Mrs. Will Adams), Irene Stillwell (Mrs. Herbert Wilcox), Mattie Carrie Heard, Camilla Pharr (Mrs. G. D. Barnett), Marguerite Brewer (Mrs. Horace H. Manley), Zelma Allen (Mrs. T. O. Tabor Jr.), and Mary Alexander.

The present First Baptist Church Building was formally dedicated on August 28, 1898. The sermon was delivered by the pastor, H. W. Williams, who used the following text: "How amiable are Thy tabernacles, O Lord of Hosts! My soul longeth, yea, ever fainteth for the courts of the Lord." Psalms 84:1. 2.

The Granite City Carnival, held in Elberton during the month of August, 1899, brought many prominent visitors. Joseph Rucker Lamar, James M. Smith, Benjamin R. Tillman, Colonel A. E. Thornton, William M. Howard, A. S. Clay, and Mrs. Rebecca Lamar Felton were among them.

A colorful parade was held on the first day of the celebration. The Elberton Cotton and Compress Company, S. S. Brewer, J. J. Stephenson, J. F. Auld's Sons, J. A. Champion, J. M. Wester, Elberton Oil Mills, Nelson, Morris & Company, and Uncle "Dirty Head" Mattox entered floats.

Miss Jessie Robert was selected Queen and her Maids of Honor were Miss Lizzie Willis, Miss Corinne Smith, Miss Dorothy Shannon and Miss Aileen Harper. The Out Riders were W. N. "Sweet" Auld, M. H. Pressley, R. E. Oglesby, and Harry L. Cleveland. Miss Elise Oglesby was selected Floral Queen and appointed the following named attendants: Miss Fanny Hawes (Mrs. J. A. Champion), Miss Julia Hines (Mrs. Whitaker), and Miss Azalee Herndon (Mrs. R. E. Oglesby).

The faculty of the Elberton Institute for the term beginning Septerber, 1898, was: William F. Jones Sr., Collegiate Department; William H. Gorman, High School and Commercial Department; Mrs. M. T. Payne, Intermediate Department; Miss Edna Peacock, Primary Department; Dr. A. S. J. Stovall, Anatomy and Hygiene; Mrs. Alice M. Hester and Mrs. Ruth Toole Robinson, Music Department, and Mrs. Annie Burney Smith, Art Department. The Board of Education was composed of John P. Shannon, S. M. Pickens, James C. Swearengin, and others.

For the same period W. C. Sams, Mrs. L. Y. A. Blackwell and Mrs. J. F. Stillwell made up the faculty for the Elberton Female Seminary.

On May 2nd and 3rd, 1899, the Grand Council of Royal Arcanum met in Elberton with an attendance of more than 100 delegates. H. J. Brewer was elected Grand Chaplain and Peyton M. Hawes was named Grand Trustee, both of Elberton.

During the early morning hours of May 10, 1899, a calamity in the form of a disastrous fire destroyed a large portion of the business section of Elberton. The Elberton Furniture Company, Tate & Oliver, the United States Post Office, W. C. Smith & Brother, and L. H. Turner lost their buildings and contents.

The Stephen Heard Chapter of the Daughters of the American Revolution was organized in Elberton on June 6, 1901. The charter members were: Mrs. Eugenia Long Harper (Mrs. A. O.), Miss Hattie Allen (Mrs. Charles Whitmire), Miss Roberta Heard (Mrs. John T. Dennis), Mrs. Georgia Heard Johnson (Mrs. J. E. Sr.), Mrs. Vohammie Heard Pharr (Mrs. Marcus), Mrs. Susan McCalla Adams (Mrs. W. B.), Mrs. Florence Long Bartow, Mrs. Susan Heard Swift (Mrs. J. Y.), Mrs. Lavonia Jones Gairdner (Mrs. Harry K.), Mrs. Mattie Wright Tate, Miss Lenora Jones, Miss Annie McCalla (Mrs. John Purdue), Mrs. Emma Heard Long (Mrs. N. G. Long), and Mrs. Bessie Thurmond Swift (Mrs. I. G.).

The Chapter has had only three treasurers since its inception: Mrs. Bessie Thurmond Swift, Mrs. Minnie Tunison Murray, Mrs. Minnie Fortson Anderson.

The membership of the Chapter in 1925 was: Anderson, Mrs. Minnie Fortson; Archer, Louise McIntosh; Asbury, Nora Carter; Bradford, Rose West; Brown, Mary McIntosh; Brock, Ruby Conwell; Burriss, Nona Herndon; Copeland, Edna Arnold; Davis, Nancy Heard; Dennis, Roberta Heard; Fortson, Mary Clark; Fortson, Ellie; Gairdner, Lavonia Jones; Grogan, Sarah Pope; Grogan, Adeline Stark; Haslett, Susan Worley; Hawes, Julia Cade; Hawes, Norma Wright; Hayes, Elizabeth Fortson; Jaudon, Sarah Louise Arnold; Johnson, Georgia Heard; Jones, Lenora; McCurry, May Lillie Teasley; Miles, Mary Stuart; Moore, Annie Lee Cade; Murray, Minnie Tunison; Oliver, Eleanor; Paine, Nella Sanborn; Payne, Thelma Wright; Rampley, Georgia Herndon; Ransome, Lilly Gray; Rogers, Sarah Lee; Rogers, Alpha; Rogers, Edna; Simmons, Marion Brewer; Smith, Martha Sparks, Snellings, Rebecca; Snowden, Martha King; Stapleton, Vera Bond; Swift, Bessie Thurmond; Swift, Susan Heard; Tabor, Fannie Herndon; Wright, Janie Tate; Wright, Mary Lizzie. A more complete list elsewhere added by D. A. R. Chapter. A number of other persons have joined the Chapter since the above mentioned date.

Previous to the War Between the States there were few schools in Elbert County. In Elberton, Pike, Petersburg, and Ruckersville there were Academies, but in most instances the wealthier planters of the small communities would employ tutors, generally young Northern men of good family and college education, for their children, and classes were held in the homes. When the war had ended and poverty supplanted plenty it became necessary to establish the community school. These schools for the most part were taught by young gentlemen who had served in the Confederate Army. The buildings were generally about 30 to 40 feet square, built of rough hewn logs. A doorway was cut out of the logs, and a rude door swung on leather hinges. The chimneys were also made of logs and daubed with the red mud of the section. The teachers' station was on an elevated platform facing the pupils, and the children occupied rude benches made of rough pine lumber.

As the South battled gallantly through the period of Reconstruction and conditions gradually grew better, more buildings were erected of an improved type and schools flourished throughout the entire county.

In 1852, Dewey Rose School was in operation. The teachers who served this institution were: 1852-1854, Charles Andrews; 1854-1858, Thomas Bowers; 1859, J. D. Brown; 1860, 1861, 1862, the school, due to the confusion occasioned by war, failed to operate; 1864-1865, Ella Anderson; 1866, E. B. Norman; 1867-1870, F. M. Taylor; 1871-1873, Cone Bond; 1874-1877, J. T. Osburn; 1878-1879, Joseph Fowler; 1880, Dr. McCurry; 1881-1882, L. Brown; 1883-1884, Stephen White; 1886, John Hulme; 1887, William Vickery; 1888-1892, L. C. Edwards; 1893, Leila Norman; 1894, Mary Carlton; 1895-1896, Mrs. Martha Jones; 1897, Bessie Adams; 1898, Minnie Clark; 1899, Henry Banks; 1900, Mae Montgomery; 1901-1902, Eugenia Haslett; 1903, Sula Hudson; 1904, George Adams; 1905-1906, J. W. Denny; 1907-1909, Sarah Wall; 1910-1912, W. P. Addison; 1913, F. M. Gaines; 1914, W. R. Barnett; 1915, R. S. Crawford.

Antioch School, near Nickville, was established in 1858. The roster of teachers there includes: John Cooper, Bud Booth, Henry Alexander, John L. Mize, R. R. Glenn, Marcus A. Bell, Mary Campbell, Lee Payne, Dr. John Christian, Thomas D. Biggs, Mrs. Turner Payne, Peter V. Rice Jr., Ollie Christian, Early Vickery, J. P. Booth, Del Ray Adams, Mrs. Nellie Wilson, Mrs. Leona Haynes, John Andy Smith, and Era Pitts.

Flatwoods Academy, established 1868, had as its first trustees Reverend John Henry Grogan and Jeptha B. Jones. The teachers, many of whom became prominent in the field of education, were: John P. Shannon, Marion Taylor, George Quillian, Theodore Monroe, Matthew H. Wyche, Mr. Elliot, Lollie White, Maggie Knox, John C. Langston, Kate Little, Julia McGraw, Edna Brewer, Kathleen Mitchell, Sarah Louise Stark, Darlina Bell, Julia Stark, Rebecca Snellings, Mrs. Mattie Jones, and Irene Snellings.

Cold Water was established in 1870, Deep Creek in 1874, Hulmeville in 1887, Longstreet in 1894, Adams Academy in 1878, Locust Treet, 1888; Savannah, 1898; Goss, 1858; Bell in 1902, Stella in 1905, and Johnson Town in 1909.

Oak Hill, established 1878, had among its teachers John Frank Harper, Captain Samuel Barnett, Thomas Chandler, Vandiver Brown, Darlina Bell, Norvelle Lyle, Annie McLanahan, Howard Thornton, Harold Thornton, and Sue Bell.

Indian Hill, established 1882, had among its instructors the following: Darlina Bell, Cassie Wall, Lucy Willis, Nell Proffit, Mrs. Stephen Fortson, Mrs. T. E. Brown, Sarah Black, Sue Watson, Allie Wyche, Annie McLanahan, M. C. Turner, J. C. Asbury, Doc Hudgens, Ella Powell, Annie Wolf, Glenn Cleveland, Bertha Hudson, Gladys Ham, and Gussie Moore.

Hardaman's Academy, established 1887, had as its teachers: Ida Calloway, Clara Parks, Jesse Deadwyler, Carrie Rogers, Welina Harper, Nell Stovall, Nellie Wilson, and Grace Spears.

Thirteen Forks, established 1887, had as its first trustees: A. S. Lunsford, M. G. Fleming, F. L. M. Gaines, and J. B. Burden

Evergreen, founded 1890, in Moss, had the following named teachers: 1890, B. R. Cordell; 1891, Mr. David; 1892, Llewyllen Hulme; 1893-1895, George Haley; 1896, Hettie Scott; 1897-1898, Mary Hansard; 1899, Mary Alexander; 1900, Lucy Goss; 1901-1902, A. L.

Adams; 1903, H. S. Crawford; 1904, C. P. Ward and Eliza Hansard; 1905, Ada Parks; 1906, Blanche Gaines; 1907-1909, Aurelia Greenway; 1910, Ola Eavenson; 1911-1912, Lillie McCurry; 1913, Cora Warren and Hassie Shiflett; 1914, Mary Hansard and Hassie Shiflett; 1915, Mary Hansard and Hattie Wansley; 1916, Blanche Gaines and Tommye Haley; 1917, Blanche Gaines and Icie Eavenson.

Farmer's Academy was incorporated by the Georgia Legislature in 1841.

Centerville was created in 1904, and had R. E. Ward, H. K. Ertzberger, Marcua A. Bell, H. S. Crawford, Bertha Hudson, Darlina Bell, Ella Rucker, and Willie Vickery as instructors.

The majority of these schools, together with others, have been consolidated. At the present time Elbert County has Nancy Hart, Middleton, Rock Branch, Bowman, Centerville, and Consolidated Number One. All of these are consolidated schools and recognized as standard. Miss Mary Hansard is, at the present time, head of the County School System.

The consolidation of the schools of the county will stand as a lasting monument to Z. B. Rogers and Thomas J. Cleveland. Through their untiring efforts this progressive step was realized. Their task was by no means easy of accomplishment. Opposition was met with on every hand and almost unsurmountable difficulties overcome. Mr. Rogers is co-author of the Rogers-Barrett school law, and Mr. Cleveland, for many years, served as the head of the Elbert County school system.

The public school system of Elberton was inaugurated in the year 1901. On December 24, 1900, an election was called for the purpose of deciding whether or not such a system should be adopted. The result of the election showed that public schools carried 274 to 5.

The faculty of the new system for 1901 was: John C. Langston, head of the system; Peter Zellars, W. D. Reid, Miss Mildred Thompson, Miss Addie Hill, Miss Kate Carswell, Miss Sarah Black, Miss Mary Louise McIntosh, and Mrs. J. F. Stillwell. In 1902, two new members were added to the faculty: J. P. B. Allen and A. F. Archer. Among the superintendents who have since served the school are: P. B. Winn, Wilbur Colvin, Professor Stephenson, W. A. Anderson, C. E. Dryden, Paul Spence, L. M. Spruell, Theodore Rumble, Boyce M. Grier, at present head of the Athens, Georgia, school system; Thomas N. Gaines, who died in office during 1934; John H. Green. Paul Blackwell, an Elberton Negro, is at present the capable head of the colored school.

During the administration of Boyce M. Grier two modern grammar schools were constructed. These schools were named in honor of two veteran and beloved teachers, Mrs. Allie Tate (Lee) Stephens and Mrs. J. F. Stillwell. The present Central School Building was erected during the administration of P. B. Winn.

On February 9, 1902, fire again destroyed the major portion of the business section of Elberton. Four blocks of buildings were consumed. This property was situated on McIntosh Street and known as the Tate and Swift blocks. The firms whose stock of goods were destroyed were: John R. Mattox, Tabor & Almond, S. O. Hawes, M. E. Maxwell, J. F. Stillwell, Joe Cohen, and E. B. Tate & Sons. The total loss was in excess of $125,000.

During this year there were many deaths in Elbert County. Among them were J. H. Stovall, aged 72; Frank Gaines, Mrs. J. B. Childs, Mrs. Albert M. Brown, W. T. Kinnebrew, Mrs. Carrie Brock, W. H. Carpenter, Miss Adeline Verdel, Mrs. Eliza Bristol, aged 82; Thomas J. Bond Sr., Mrs. E. V. Clark, L. S. Childs, and John P. Shannon, Past Master of Georgia Masons.

On Tuesday, September 22, 1903, the 104th annual session of the Georgia Baptist Sarepta Assocaition met with the First Baptist Church of Elberton. There were more than 150 delegates in attendance.

The first commercial organization to be founded in Elberton was organized July 19, 1905. It bore the name of the Commercial Club. McAlpin Arnold was named president; H. E. Hawes, secretary, and L. Cleveland treasurer. The committee on location, named by the president, was composed of Sam L. Olive, T. O. Tabor, Ed C. Williams, H. L. Cleveland, and J. E. Asbury. The finance committee was composed of Harry L. Cleveland, Clarence P. Harris, and Paul A Cleveland. The committee on by-laws was made up of W. O. Jones, Perry H. Smith, and C. P. Harris.

During September of this year, through the efforts of the Commercial Club, the district meeting of the Odd Fellows came to Elberton with an attendance of more than 250 delegates.

Previous to the year 1908, Elberton had three banks and in this year the fourth was organized under the name of the First National Bank. The officers elected were: J. F. Holder, President; M. E. Maxwell, Vice-President; R. L. Cauthen, R. F. Moore, S. S. Brewer, Thomas T. Thornton, Robert P. Ward, George H. McLanahan, J. A. Cauthen, E. B. Stark, George P. Allen, and John R. Mattox to the Board of Directors. M. E. Maxwell, a short time later became President and retained this post until the institution was reorganized after the bank holiday declared by President Franklin D. Roosevelt. (Capt. H. P. Hunter, President of the State Bankers Association, was Cashier for many years.)

During the same year John R. Mattox was elected President of the League of Municipalities of Georgia at their annual meeting held at Albany during the early part of October.

On July 15 and 16, 1908, the Hebron Baptist Association met in its 25th annual convention at Bowman. John P. Cash, of Elbert County, was named as its head.

The second commercial organization to be formed in Elberton was perfected January 25, 1909. This body was known as the Elberton Chamber of Commerce. William O. Jones was named President; T. O. Tabor Sr., Vice-President; Zack W. Copeland, Secretary and Treasurer. A committee on enrollment was composed of W. L. Skelton, J. E. Tabor, and Z. W. Copeland. This organization proved effective for several years and was instrumental in bringing to Elberton several new enterprises.

While Elbert County has always been strongly partisan in politics, never once failing to vote for the Democratic nominee for President of the United States, the Elberton Chamber of Commerce raised funds by public subscription to send the local Militia Company to the inauguration of William Howard Taft. The following named members of the Elberton Light Infantry marched in the inaugural parade: Captain John C. Reese, Lieutenant George W. Leohr, Lieutenant J. E. Kelly, First Sergeant John Henry Hulme, Corporals George A. Wyche, Oliver R. Walker, Privates S. J. Adams, Herbert Kay, J. Cliff Swearengin, J. H. Sayer, Dr. D. N. Thompson, F. H. Walker, Foster Simpson, G. Burden, J. O. Roberts, O. F. Mattox, Jim Rice, Otis Clark, T. S. Jones Jr., G. M. Hulme, George W. Attaway, J. F. Beasley, R. L. Cosby, J. W. Hall, A. G. Vaughan, Sidney Isreal, R. G. Cosby, A. N. Drake, R. B. Robert, W. H. Roberts, W. C Kennebrew, Claud Barnwell, and J. Bynum Bell.

During the early part of August, 1909, Willis B. Adams was notified that he had been appointed the head of the Census for the Eighth Congressional District of Georgia. This important position came to him virtually unsought, in fact, he had been endorsed by 18 banks in the District before he made formal application. The manner in which he handled the position proved his ability as an executive.

On September 2, 1909, the cornerstone of the present Central School of Elberton was laid with Masonic ceremonies. Thomas H. Jeffries, Grand Master of Georgia Masons, was present and presided. The building was constructed at a cost of $35,000. Bonds had been voted in the early part of the year in this amount. Since its erection there have been many improvements made and it ranks well with any building for its size within the State.

Perhaps in all the history of the county the meeting of the Georgia Federation of Womens Clubs held in Elberton November 17, 18, 19, 1909, was its most outstanding social event. The sessions were held in the newly decorated First Methodist Church and receptions were given by the local lodge of the Elks, Mrs Eugene B. Heard, at her home "Rose Hill," near Middleton, and the Research Club. There were more than 200 delegates in attendance. The officers elected were: Mrs. Hugh Willett, President; Mrs. A. C. White, of Athens, First Vice-President; Mrs. J. M. Wester, of

Elberton, Second Vice-President, and Mrs. Florence Long Bartow, as General Secretary for Georgia.

The year 1910 saw Elberton in the midst of a building program. Brown Brothers constructed a large cotton warehouse. a block of buildings was constructed on the East side of North Oliver Street, the Seaboard Air Line Railway Company built the present passenger station and a number of private residences were constructed.

Although the convention of the Georgia Federation of Womens Clubs was brilliant from a social standpoint it could not equal in numbers the Georgia Baptist Convention, which convened at the First Baptist Church November 15, 1910. There were 600 delegates present and the homes and hotels of Elberton were taxed to the utmost to care for them.

The opening prayer of the convention was offered by Reverend J. T. B. Anderson, pastor of the First Baptist Church of Elberton. Mayor J. M. Wester, on behalf of the city; Reverend J. F. Eakes, on behalf of the other denominations of Elberton, and Honorable Samuel L. Oliver made addresses of welcome. These were responded to by Reverend J. M. Long of Fort Valley.

The election of officers was then held which resulted in naming S. Y. Jamison, of Macon, as President; Judge A. W. Fite, of Cartersville, as Vice-President; Z. B. Rogers, of Elberton, as Vice-President; B. D. Ragsdale, of Mercer University, as Secretary, and E. J. Forrester, of Mercer University, as Treasurer.

At this period in the history of the Elberton First Bapitst Church D. P. Oglesby, Peyton M. Hawes, D. B. Maxwell, Z. W. Copeland, S. O. Hawes, M. J. Brown, Dilliard H. Brown, George W. Deadwyler, G. L. A. Almond, and H. J. Brewer composed the Board of Deacons. Z. W. Copeland was secretary of the church, and G. L. A. Almond treasurer.

The convention was a great success and was so made largely by the efforts on the part of the Board of Deacons and the Chamber of Commerce.

An agitation which for some years had been in evidence, both in Elbert and Wilkes counties, for the construction of a railroad, eventually to terminate in Augusta, came to a head in 1911. A charter was granted for the Elberton and Eastern Railroad Company at a meeting held in Elberton July 27, 1911, the following officers were named: President, William O. Jones; Vice-President, Thomas W. Skelton; Secretary and Treasurer, J. H. Blackwell; General Counsel, Z. B. Rogers; W. O. Jones, Thomas W. Skelton, J. C. Kerr, J. S. Rogers, J. A. Moss, J. J. Wilkinson, W. J. Adams, L. M. Heard, J. H. Blackwell, W. F. Anderson, R. L. Cauthen, and John T. Dennis, Directors.

Bonds were voted in the sum of $300,000, and the contract was let during the month of December to Ira L. McCord of New York City.

The road was completed in 1913, from Elberton to Tignall, a distance of 20 miles, giving rail facilities to a rich and beautiful farming area. The road was later extended to Washington.

In 1932, a receiver was appointed for the road, but it was continued in operation until 1934, when it was sold and scrapped.

During this period Dr. A. S. J. Stovall was serving with rare ability and force the County of Elbert in the Georgia Legislature. In 1908, he was elected to the House of Representatives and began his service in the year 1909. From the outset he became a determined leader and commanded the respect and attention of all members. His service in the House extended over a period of four years and he also served for two terms in the Senate. During his unselfish service he sponsored many progressive measures with marked success and was the main factor in making Georgia "A Bone Dry State." Always a "Dry," he was a still greater Democrat. During the presidential campaign of 1924, he threw his influence solidly behind Alfred E. Smith, notwithstanding this candidate's avowed wetness, and was instrumental, together with such leaders as P. M. Hawes, James McIntosh, A. S. Hawes, A. S. Lunsford, and James Beasley Sr., in carrying Elbert County for Alfred E. Smith. The vote was exceedingly close, the Democratic candidate winning by only 93 votes. The battle was fierce with every minister in the county openy allied with Hoover. Such leaders as Joseph N. Worley, J. E. Asbury, Mrs. Sue Worley Haslett, and Mrs. Dudley Sheppard, together with the Woman's Christian Temperance Union, were staunch fighters in the Hoover camp. They claimed to be, what was, of course a total impossibility, "Hoover Democrats."

Doctor Stovall, if not the most influential member of the House of Representatives from Northeast Georgia during the last century, was undoubtedly among the leaders. Born 1861 in Elbert County, near Ruckersville. Was a graduate of University of Georgia; the Georgia Medical College in Augusta with first honor, also post graduate of the Polytechnic in New York City. Married Miss Vesta Pearce Mathews, daughter of Dr. Albert Clark Mathews, in 1888. He was selected by the citizens of Elbert County to represent them in the House of Representatives and in the Senate for 25 years. During the World War he served on the Georgia Medical Advisory Board during the Wilson administration. His death in the early summer of 1934 caused widespread regret, and removed from Elbert County one of its leading citizens.

The great Sunday School Convention met in Elberton on April 22, 23, and 24, 1913, with an attendance of 500 delegates. Dr. Joseph Broughton was elected President, and W. M. Wilcox and S. O. Hawes, of Elberton, became members of the Executive Committee. The singing was under the direction of E. O. Excell. The sessions were held at the First Baptist Church and the First Methodist Church.

Although Middleton was incorporated by the Georgia Legislature in the year 1911, it was not laid out until May, 1913. Its limits, under the act of incorporation, were prescribed as one mile in every direction from the center of the village. The first Mayor was W. J. Hammond and was inducted into office with Dr. J. E. Cole, W. S. Harrison, Grady Hutcherson, G. V. Hammond, and W. M. Grogan, as Councilmen. While this village has a population of only about 100 it numbers among its citizens men prominent in the life of the county. Here live W. J. Hammond, E. C. Rhodes, J. E. Tate, A. B. Crisp, and George Alford.

During the summer of 1913, a school census was taken of the entire county. The results showed 1,649 white males, 1,562 white females, 1,635 colored males, and 1,692 colored females. The previous census taken in 1908, showed a total of 5,710 children of both races of school age as against 6,539 for 1913.

On June 28th, of that year, the first train over the newly constructed Elberton & Eastern Railway ran from Elberton to Tignall. Leaving the former place at 9:43 A. M. and reaching the latter at 1:30 P. M. A large number of prominent citizens of both Elbert and Wilkes Counties made the trip. A great celebration was held upon the arrival in Tignall dubbed by the enthusiastic citizens of that place as "Little Atlanta." Carrol M. "Dutch" Heard acted as conductor. Data on earlier railroads (Southern and S. A. L.) found elsewhere in history.

Elberton entertained two other important gatherings in 1913. The Eighth Congressional District Medical Association met August 20, and Dr. W. J. Matthews, of Elberton, was chosen to head it for the ensuing year. The North Georgia Conference of the Methodist Episcopal Church, South, convened November 20, and remained in session for a period of four days. Bishop Collins Denny, of Richmond, Virginia, presided. The delegates were welcomed by Reverend R. C. Cleckler, pastor of the Elberton Church; Mayor J. M. Wester and Judge George C. Grogan. The responses were made by Bishop Denny and Reverend W. J. Cotter, of Newnan.

About this period Mrs. Corra White (Lundy) Harris became internationally famous as a novelist. Her "Recording Angel," "A Circuit Rider's Wife," "Eve's Second Husband," and "My Book and Heart" rank among the better novels of the present time. Especially was "My Book and Heart" appealing to Elbert County for many of the characters were easily recognized as local citizens of years past and most of the scenes were laid around Elberton and Farm Hill. Her clear style and sparkling wit makes all of her works charmingly readable. Mrs. Harris was born in Elbert County in the village of Ruckersville, but spent the greater portion of her girlhood at Farm Hill, her father's farm, near Middleton. Her husband, a Methodist minister, was often unable, due to a delicate constitution and the small pittance paid ministers of the Gospel, to provide all of the comforts of life for his wife and daughter,

Faith. Mrs. Harris, to aid in securing these, began her career which made her a celebrity of letters. The daily articles which appeared in *The Atlanta Journal* for several years previous to her death, early in 1935, were gems of clear thought and philosophy. Corra White Harris was the daughter of Tinsley White by his first marriage to Miss Matthews, and was a lineal descendant of Joseph Rucker, of Ruckersville. Some of her works, it must be admitted, scandalized the more straight laced members of the Methodist denomination by their utter frankness, but the open minded and unbiased reader finds them rich not only in style and expression, but pregnant with real and frank truths as well. Mrs. Harris was one of Elbert County's most famous personages and her passing was mourned sincerely in the county of her birth as well as throughout a great portion of the United States.

The year 1914, with Europe in turmoil, brought to Elbert County the business stagnation that prevailed throughout the nation. Cotton reached a low ebb in price and only after hard campaigning could the price be forced to even 10 cents a pound. Money was very scarce and a decided feeling of depression and gloom was everywhere in evidence. Just two years before one of Elbert County's leading business men and advisers died. This was McAlpin Arnold and his loss was sorely felt during this period. The years 1915 and 1916 brought about changing conditions for the better and the pall to a greater extent was lifted.

The year 1917, will, perhaps, be remembered as one of the most memorable in the history of the United States. War was declared on the Central Powers; the Draft Act passed after heated discussion and much opposition; men enlisted; army camps sprang up almost overnight; sums of money so large as to almost, at that time, appear fantastic appropriated by Congress for war activities and for the various organizations.

When the day for registration under the Draft Act came there were no less than 1,585 men of Elbert County who appeared in compliance with its provisions.

Although the patriotism of the people reached great heights, they were saddened by the thought of many youths going into foreign lands never to return, and, too, the deaths of outstanding citizens of Elbert County reached almost unprecedented total. Within this year E. B. Tate, Confederate officer, at one time Ordinary and Clerk of the County; Mrs. J. N. Hall, William Oglesby, Confederate soldier, 91 years of age; Mrs. T. H. Powell, Allen Miles, Jim Payne, Charles H. Fortson, Mrs. Mark Rouzee, L. M. Heard, President of Citizens Bank; D. W. King, a Mason for 50 years; Mrs. Fanny Ginn, Mrs. W. I. Gaines, John C. Brown, former Mayor of Elberton and leading merchant; Miss Margaret Jones, Mrs. W. A. Carrington, E. P. Seymour, 86 years of age; J. J. Warren, Andrew J. Webb, Confederate soldier; G. W. Ginn, Confederate soldier; Omer Seymour, Mrs. Martha Smith, 87 years of age; Mrs. Pearl Brewer (T. V.) Bagwell, Dr. N. G. Long, father of Elbert County granite industry and former Mayor and State Senator; J. H. Maxwell, Mrs. Rebecca Bell, S. M. Downer, Confederate soldier; Howell W. Carithers, T. J. Cordell, Mrs. T. C. Harper, Ham Moss, W. Arch Moss, Confederate soldier; Mrs. T. Jesse Maxwell, H. A. Barnwell, Mrs. Nancy J. Swift, 99 years of age; Thomas B. Crawford, one time County Commissioner and road expert; Calloway Thornton, Confederate soldier; James L. Clark, R. W. Ayers, Confederate soldier; Miss Nellie Tunison, and Charles Oglesby, died.

From January 22nd through the 26th, the seventh annual meeting of the Women's Missionary Society of the North Georgia Methodist Conference met in Elberton. There were present 250 delegates. Mrs. Harry K. Gairdner, of Elberton, was elected Honorary President; Mrs. W. B. Higginbotham, of West Point, was named President.

On February 14th, the Odd Fellows of the Fourteenth Division of Georgia met in Elberton. The city also entertained the Eighth Congressional District High School Meet.

From a political standpoint Elbert County received marked recognition. Tinsley W. Rucker was sworn in as a member of the United States House of Representatives, for the short term, to succeed the late Samuel J. Tribble. John J. Brown, of Bowman, was appointed to the position of Commissioner of Agriculture for the State of Georgia. Subsequently he was elected by the people to this office.

The City of Elberton was notified during January of 1917, that the philanthropist, A. K. Hawkes, of Atlanta, had devised to the municipality the sum of $7,000 to be used in the construction of a building to be known as "Hawkes Library for Children." The funds so devised were shortly afterwards received and a substantial brick building constructed on the Central School grounds. The Library has continued to function, and today, under the able direction of Mrs. Vesta Fortson (J. H.) Turnell, ranks well with any library of its type within Georgia.

Elbert County was indeed prosperous during 1917; farmers who had lived all their lives "from hand to mouth," became landed proprietors; small merchants became large merchants, struggling lawyers, doctors and other professional men collected substantial fees, and dealers in automobiles and other luxuries became plutocratic. Such conditions, inflated and unnatural as they were, continued for an hysterical period of three years.

The War Registration Board was convened on June 5, 1917. It was composed of James C. Thornton Jr., William A. Rucker, L. C. Edwards, Dr. W. J. Matthews, and H. B. Payne. The registrars in the various districts throughout the county were: Elberton, Z. P. Rogers; Eliam, Frank B. Fortson Sr.; Petersburg, Zimri A. Tate; Longstreet, William Cole; Wyche, H. G. Thornton; Moss, W. A.

Shumate; Pike, L. G. Brown; Gaines, H. A. Adams; Goshen, Benjamin R. Cordell; Webbsboro, W. Manley Grogan; Centerville, Dr. Thomas W. Bond.

The local Board of Examiners was composed of J. C. Thornton Jr., William A. Rucker, Dr. J. E. Johnson. These men were ably assisted by Dr. L. P. Eberhardt, Dr. D. V. Bailey, W. A. Nall, J. N. Rice, and R. L. Rice. The first serial number, 258, chanced to fall to a young Negro, Lumpkin Huff, and hence he was the first to be examined.

While the vast majority of the citizens of Elbert County approved in no uncertain terms, the views of President Wilson and the majority of the members of Congress there were isolated instances of real opposition.

The issue of the *Elberton Star* appearing August 17, 1917, carried the following:

"ANTI-DRAFT MEETING REACTS BACKWARDS
SECOND MEETING CALLED AND DELEGATES
NAMED TO GO TO STATE CONVENTION AT MACON.

"Strong resolutions endorsing the War policies of President Wilson and the selective draft in particular, were passed at a mass meeting of the people of Elbert County held at the court house Thursday afternoon. Dr. A. S. Hawes, chairman of the meeting, announced to vote as 390 to 1.

"The meeting was first organized by electing Mr. S. G. Childs as chairman, and Mr. Earl Mason as secretary. Mr. W. C. Christian stated the object of the meeting to be to inquire into the constitutionality of the conscript laws and to petition senators and congressmen to repeal it and closed his talk by nominating a delegate to a meeting to be held in Macon.

"Several motions were then made asking that the meeting be given resolutions in writing for consideration. The chair favored the suggestion, and there was some desultory discussion of the proposition, with little being done for some time. Finally, Mr. W. C. Christian offered verbal resolutions condemning the conscript law and asking that delegates be sent from Elbert County to Macon to protest against the law, test its constitutionality and to lay foundation for its repeal. Written resolutions adopted later, and referred to in the opening paragraph hereof, were introduced by Judge George C. Grogan. Discussion of the two resolutions finally percipated the resignation of the chairman and secretary, the chairman remarking that the town people had come out and taken charge of the meeting. Mr. W. L. Fowler, a countryman, feelingly retorted from the audience, 'that more country people present were standing by the President and the country than there were town people present.' The meeting adjourned and anti-conscriptionists left the building.

"Shortly afterwards with the same chairman and secretary, 78 of them met in the court house yard and selected the following delegates to the Macon meeting: J. W. Moore, C. L. Seymour, and D. W. Davis.

"The delegates were empowered to select their own alternates. The expenses of the delegates will be paid by popular subscription."

The following named white men of Elbert County were subject to the first selective draft:

ELBERTON—189TH DISTRICT

Allen, Louis Eugene
Alexander, Clifton, L.
Adams, McDowell W.
Allen, Fred Walton
Attaway, Jesse
Anderson, William N.
Bullard, Thomas H.
Brewer, Samuel Stark
Brown, Clois Clifton
Brown, Julian Thomas
Berman, Moses Aaron
Brewer, Albert Thomas
Brown, Edgar Chandler
Boswell, Clifton
Bailey, Harris Zodock
Bell, Harry Sanders
Bailey, Carl L.
Bynum, Henry R.
Bell, George N.
Brown, Herman J.
Brady, Henry Lee
Barnwell, Claud Humon
Craft, Raymond Roy
Cleveland, Hastings L.
Cline, Francis Xavier
Christian, William H.
Cordell, Actor
Carlton, Keifer A.
Cleveland, William G.
Cheek, John Bynum
Colvard, Howard H.
Christian, Robert
Clerici, Giovanni
Cleveland, Grover F.
Duchini, Petro
Deadwyler, Womack C.
Davis, George Bynum
Evans, Fred Wilborn
Ennis, Leonard J.
Eavenson, Roscoe L.
Fortson, Lee Anderson
Farmer, James R.

Fagan, Eulis Littleton
Fleming, Julian D.
Fambrough, Karl T.
Fagleson, George
Freeman, Luther Lee
Gilby, John H.
Gaines, Seth Milton
Gantt, Fred H.
Grady, James Lamar
Ginn, Lonnie C.
Green, George William
Galloway, Gip Robert
Harris, Compton Pierce
Hawes, Guilford M.
Hulme, Dillard Marion
Heard, James Lawrence
Herndon, Fred
Hall, Frank Dupree
Haslett, Ambrose W.
Hulme, John Henry
Hondros, Louis B.
Haley, George Marion
Hornsby, Marvin J.
Hutto, Lon L.
Hulme, Guy Carswell
Haley, Jack
Jenkins, J. P.
Jones, Thomas Solomon
Jenkins, Clinton
Jones, Drukell
Johnson, William E.
Jones, Brewer B.
Johnson, Albert Sidney
Jones, Luther Thomas
Jones, W. F. Jr.
Kay, Benjamin Herbert
Kennebrew, Thomas L.
Lanti, Enrico
Mewborn, Lloyd R.
Mabry, James Walton
Mattox, George William
Maxwell, Herbert Elmer

Manley, Julian B.
Maxwell, P. C.
Maxwell, James A.
Maxwell, Asmond L.
Moss, Omer Goss
Moss, Holcomb Harper
Manley, Horace H.
Mattox, Robert Tate
Mattox, Benjamin Bibb
Martin, Aaron
Myers, Robert Lonnie
McLanahan, Walter
McLanahan, John W.
McRae, Oscar Brents
McCurry, William B.
McLanahan, Thomas J.
McIntosh, John Hawes
McMullan, William O.
Nall, Worley A.
Oliver, Stanley M.
Orrison, E. K.
Pierce, Ralph E.
Plonk, Thomas M.
Palma, Filiberton D.
Quillian, Guyton R.
Rudder, Luther Verdel
Redd William J.
Roberts, James Griggs
Roberts, Jasper
Richardson, James M.
Royston, Arthur W.
Ray, James William
Rampley, Woodfin
Robertson, Thomas
Royston, J. Leo
Rammage, Tillman
Roberts, William H.
Stapleton, Raymond
Snellings, Will J. Jr.
Smith, General Dorsey
Smith, John Kennard
Smith, Cyrus

Stone, William Perry
Smith, Olin Parks
Stark, Thomas R.
Smith, Henry P.
Smith, Henry Thomas
Swift, Samuel T.
Strickland, Lacy M.
Sheppard, Vergil
Smith, Burt Moody
Swearengin, L. H.
Shivers, Herbert M.
Smith, Victor Emory
Stiglis, John
Thornton, Ira A.
Turner, J. M.
Thornton, Wade A.
Thornton, Willie T.
Tabor, T. O. Jr.
Taylor, John C.
Tate, Edmund Brewer
Thomason, John Henry
Thomason, Grover G.
Thompson, Dallas M.
Turner, Neil
Vaughan, W. C.
Wester, John Winder
Wallace, Lewis E.
Webb, John H.
Webb, J. R. O.
Wansley, T. Q.
Whiteside, Charles C.
Wallace, Lloyd
Walker, Curtis E.
Walker, William J.
Welborn, Joseph
Ward, Grover Ben
Whitaker, C. B.
Wilcox, C. R.
Willis, Onie H.
Wilcox, H. H.
Wright, Robert
Wickliffe, Thomas R.
Watt, Mack
Yong, Tong

LONGSTREET—190TH DISTRICT

Atchison, Henry V.
Brough, Whit O.
Boles, Allen
Bowman, Luther W.
Bonds, Worley
Bellew, John
Beasley, Ben F.
Bobo, Isom
Chandler, Raymond E.
Christian, James C.
Crittenden, Henry
Cowart, Oscar J.
Crisp, Ben
Dye, Obe D.
Dye, Carey C.
Davis, Jefferson
Fleming, William S.
Foster, Henry E.
Hammond, Zackery B.
Harris, William A.
Hagood, Robert H.
Hill, James William
Hammond, Benjamin F.
Hilley, William B.
Harbert, Michael C.
Hall, Hugh Hamilton
Johnson, James W.
Jordan, Wilton
Jones, Ossie Thompson
Jones, Ora Hollins
Jones, Grady
Lovingood, W. L.
Moss, Elmer B.
Moss, Oscar J.
Mewborn, Grady
Mauldin, J. W.
McLanahan, T. B.
Norton, Robert L.
Rosser, W. A.
Rosser, George T.
Rice, William C.
Smith, Marion D.
Saxon, Oscar
Smith, Leonard L.
Smith, Clay
Smith, Dewitte T.
Threlkeld, Jesse
Threlkeld, Arthur Paul
Thomason, Willis E.
Taylor, J. R.
Wall, Paul Walton
Watkins, W. T.

ELIAM—191ST DISTRICT

Alexander, Hugh H.
Bell, Thomas J.
Bell, Henry A.
Bell, Guy T.
Bond, Thomas C.
Broadwell, W. C.
Burden, L. L.
Clamp, J. J.
Chastine, Geo. Guy
Chastine, Thomas N.
Chastine, Boyd C.
Durham, W. E.
Dye, Clarence L.
Davis, George A.
Dye, Herbert J.
Durham, James Oscar
Dye, Edgar C.
Durham, T. P.
Freeman, B. F.
Ginn, John Gordon
Greeson, H. C.
Gentry, B. T. H.
Gentry, O. O.
Grogan, J. Henry
Gentry, Ed.
Henderson, C. S.
Henderson, L. P.
Hudson, L. P.
Harper, John Frank
Harper, Leonard A.
Hilley, W. A.
Howard, Rufus T.
Jones, Carrol W.
Jones, William B.
Moon, Isaac Lee
Mills, William R.
Moon, George Henry
Mercer, Will Tom
Mauldin, Henry H.
Mashburn, John H.
Martin, Jacob B.
Mills, Joseph E.
Norman, England K.
Nash, Elbert Bell
Nash, Homer D.
Nash, William E.
Peyton, John Henry
Peppers, Lester H.
Peppers, Clifton W.
Richardson, L. E.
Rhodes, Henry C.
Rhodes, Enoch C.
Scarborough, J. B.
Smith, John Duncan
Smith, Tom Will
Smith, Charlie Howard
Slay, Lonnie G.
Stark, John Allen
Scarborough, M. F.
Sudsbury, J. W.
Smith, Carl B.
Smith, Ora
Smith, Jackson S.

Snellings, Thomas W.
Snellings, Duncan H.
Smith, Henry Frank
Todd, George
Wheelis, Grady W.
Willis, James Carswell
Wheelis, Hugh F.
Wheelis, Reuben D.

PETERSBURG—192ND DISTRICT

Crittenden, L. L.
Childs, Ben Tillman
Childs, John Frank
Childs, Hugh
Childs, Willis
Dixon, Robert H.
Edwards, Walter W.
Guest, Walker Davis
Hall, James William
Hall, John Spruell
Johnson, Mark E.
Johnson, Obie B.
Johnson, Clarence L.
McCall, H. C.
McGee, Dillard Elzie
Mathews, Willie
Owens, John Shannon
Pressley, Thomas H.
Partain, Charles S.
Rhodes, William Leon
Richardson, William M.
Rucker, Guy Pressley
Rice, Lester Richard
Saxon, Ollie Lofton
Saxon, Mac Mattox
Sizemore, DeGilcie
Smith, W. R.
Saxon, Walter Boyd
Smith, Julian J.
Terrell, James Olin
Trippe, Albert L.
Wansley, Walter S.
Wansley, Paul R.

WYCHE—193RD DISTRICT

Bell, T. K.
Bradshaw, H. D.
Brown, B. D.
Bradshaw, Kenny
Carlan, B. B.
Caldwell, W. R.
Davis, C. A.
Dunbar, C. A.
Dixon, J. F.
Fortson, P. E.
Fortson, C. S.
Fortson, H. C.
Glenn, P. M.
Johnson, C. F.
Johnson, W. T.
Mattox, G. W. R.
Maxwell, R. M.
Peppers, C. S.
Rice, J. H.
Smith, Leverette H.
Smith, Taylor B.
Smith, J. C.
Slay, Roy
Thornton, J. F.
Thornton, Dan J.
Thornton, O. J.
Thornton, L. J.
Thornton, L. M.
Thornton, C. W.

RUCKERSVILLE—195TH DISTRICT

Barksdale, T. F.
Brown, William N.
Brown, John Hilliard
Burton, E. Walter
Burriss, William Dean
Brown, Brooks
Barksdale, John H.
Brown, Arthur Barton
Boles, John Beard
Cleveland, Woodfin A.
Chandler, Ezekiel
Davis, Obe Walker
Dove, William S.
Dunn, Waco
Fain, E. W.
Frierson, William C.
Fleming, A. M.
Fowler, Paul Silas
Gulley, Thomas M.
Hill, Mack
Hill, Willis L.
Jones, Henry Martin
Jones, H. P. M.
Lovingood, Lester
Mize, Carl H.
Mercer, Samuel W.
Mundy, John B.
Mize, Robert W.
McMullan, Guy F.
Mundy, James Elmer
Prince, Hugo W.
Prince, Henry
Powell, George M.
Rucker, Harley W.
Rucker, K. Earl
Rucker, James H.
Simmons, Willie
Taylor, Frank G.
Thornton, Jamie
Wall, Longstreet
Wall, Thomas
Wells, Jim
Wall, Harry Ambrose

MOSS—196TH DISTRICT

Anderson, Sanford G.
Anderson, Thomas L.
Anderson, Walton L.
Craft, Clark Howell
Clark, John Andrew
Clark, Ora Frank
Daniel, Henry Willie
Gaines, Claud Ralph
Hammond, Jack
Higginbotham, M. T.
Hulme, J. Guy
Higginbotham, L. B.
Hulme, Jesse Clay
Higginbotham, Carl P.
Hammond, James E.
Jones, Willie
Morrow, Gaines W.
Outz, F. M.
Outz, Lloyd H.
Rhodes, Claud H.
Stratton, T. Julian
Stratton, H. C.
Wansley, Fred Cole
Ward, Albert Marion
Warren, Charles A.
Warren, Coy Tinsley
Yeargin, Thomas H.

PIKE—197TH DISTRICT

Adams, Louis Paul
Andrews, Dorsey
Ayers, Joseph G.
Adams, Harvey N.
Ayers, Hansel O.
Adams, Wylie W.
Bates, John W.
Brooks, Leo
Brown, Roy J.
Booth, Arthur L.
Bates, Claud
Booth, Elmer Hoyt
Brown, Thomas Clyde
Burden, Grover C.
Booth, Asa Grady
Butler, Sam Jones
Borders, Thomas W.
Bell, Arthur Roy
Conwell, James Guy
Carithers, James P.
Dickerson, John Early
Dickerson, William A.
Dickerson, John Henry
Dickerson, Willie T.
Dickerson, Tommie
Dickerson, Onnie B.
Denny, Robert T.
Fields, John Sam
Franklin, Peter
Guest, Jesse James
Hewell, Asa G.
Hewell, Guy Crawford
Hall, Raymond G.
Hammond, Arch J.
Hammond, S. T.
Hammond, George E.
Hall, Horace Carlton
Hall, Patrick H.
Hall, Thomas C.
Heard, George E. Jr.
Hewell, Ora Goss
Hewell, Lester David
Jones, William H.
Kelly, John Thomas
Kelly, Robert Walton
Lunsford, Carswell J.
Mann, Thomas Floyd
Motes, Wade Hampton
Mann, John A.
Maxwell, Doc James
Moore, Coyle
Moore, Clifton
Maxwell, Mark McCoil
Maxwell, Gordon
Nelms, Alex Gaines
Nelms, Arthur C.
Nelms, George W.
Pulliam, Joe J.
Pulliam, Henry Grady
Pulliam, DeWitt
Phelps, Lonnie William
Pierce, Luther Clayton
Phelps, Amos Lester
Phelps, John A. B.
Phelps, John Gairdner
Parham, Joe Griff
Rousey, Abraham
Roberts, John William
Sayer, Charlie David
Sanders, William H.
Sanders, Ernest
Smith, Omer
Taylor, John Leo
Thornton, Ollie Benj.
Teasley, Erwin Clifton
Vaughan, James Homer
Wansley, Pierce Ashby
Webb, Roy
Yeargin, John Benj.

GAINES—199TH DISTRICT

Adams, Howell Parker
Atkins, William H.
Alexander, Worley
Adams, Harper Wesley
Anderson, W. Frank
Atkins, James Verdel
Bennett, H. C.
Bond, Holcombe B.
Brown, James W.
Brown, George
Brewer, LeRoy C.
Charping, Augustus O.
Crawford, George C.
Cash, J. Clarence
Crawford, Hilliard O.
Charping, J. O.
Cleveland, James Roy
Conwell, George S.
Conwell, Pierce
Crawford, Gipson Grady
Cleveland, Robert C.
Cleveland, Doctor Mell
Cheek, A. M. Jr.
Cleveland, Paul J.
Craft, Ralph R.
Cooley, Thomas Hayes
Dixon, Andrew C.
Dickerson, Floyd T.
Drennon, S. A.
Drennon, D. G.
Daniel, John O.
Evans, E. A.
Fields, J. C.
Fleming, W. G.
Gulley, C. E.
Gaines, O. B.
Gaines, R. A.
Gulley, B. A.
Gingles, S. H.
Gaines, W. F.
Gaines, I. M.
Greenway, Coy
Greenway, Grover
Greenway, Willie L.
Gaines, L. A.
Gaines, I. A.
Gaines, Otis
Greenway, Hugh A.
Greenway, Lindsey A.
Gaines, Fred
Hill, Peyton Barney
Haley, Frederick P.
Herring, James Marion
Haynes, Lake W.
Johnson, Henry T.
Lee, L. O. C.
Lawrence, Lewis Irvin
McMullan, Frank Alex
McMullan, T. C.
Mullinax, George H.
McCurley, W. H.
Mann, P. O.
Moss, Luther Adams
Mann, Paul Grady
Newton, Frederick F.
Partain, A. R.
Powell, W. L.
Partain, J. F.
Partain, W. E.
Partain, Dillard K.
Partain, Bartow Butler
Richardson, Inman S.
Roberts, Milton
Skelton, James Mallory
Sanders, John Elias
Sanders, C. H.
Stowers, F. C.
Smith, G. L.
Smith, W. M.
Stowers, W. A.
Stowers, L. S.
Sanders, Clarence E.
Stratton, Omer Grady
Stowers, S. A.

Stovall, Olin James
Smith, David Curlin
Stratton, Ira Wall
Smith, T. O.
Shiflett, S. E.
Sanders, James E.

Thomason, William Ira
Turner, Clifford Lee
Teasley, Omer Gip
Turner, A. A.
Taylor, A. C.
Thrift, Calloway

Ward, George Henry
Ward, Robert Martin
Ward, Ike Swift
Whitman, Verman
Whitman, Clifton Gary

GOSHEN—201ST DISTRICT

Almond, Gholston Long
Adams, Charles Emory
Ashworth, Thomas N.
Adams, Robert England
Adams, James Belton
Butler, Jasper C.
Bowen, Charles Benson
Booth, Toombs Jones
Borders, Alvin Orin
Butler, Weston A.
Bryant, Morrison M.
Butler, James Albert
Booth, James E. T.
Brown, Sylvester
Brown, John William
Berryman, Fayette
Bone, James Willie
Brown, Isom G. G.
Bragg, Charles W.
Burden, James Hoyt
Brown, James Polk
Burton, Jasper Homer
Busby, J. P.
Cochran, George Hugh
Carter, Thomas C.
Craft, Thomas G. C.
Cordell, Thurmond R.
Colvard, Gibson C.
Cornell, Henry G.
Carithers, Harold G.
Carithers, Claud W.
Cornell, Lewis Thomas
Denny, James Elijah
Duncan, Marcus G.
Dickerson, Alvin
Duncan, John Martin
Denny, Judge Haley
Denny, Ivey
Dickerson, T. Gaines
Duncan, William Asa
Dickerson, Llewllyn T.
Duncan, Lacey Jones
Eaves, Alfred R.
Eaves, Arthur C.
Eaton, Grover C.
Eaton, William P.

Eberhardt, Lonnie
Fitzpatrick, Dock
Franklin, James Benj.
Fleeman, William O.
Fleeman, James Ezra
Fleeman, Evan Lonnie
Free, Oscar
Fleming, Oscar L.
Gloer, Joseph A.
Ginn, Pope Bently
Ginn, Sat White
Haynes, Clifford
Hendrick, John A.
Harris, James Gordon
Hilliard, Thomas H.
Hairston, Julius C.
Hall, Coleman
Hilliard, Clayton S.
Herring, W. Luther
Harris, Lawrence D.
Hall, John
Herndrick, Martin S.
Hall, Boston
Herndon, Isom L.
Harris, William DuB.
Hewell, Wilton Harper
Hilliard, Frank A.
Hulme, Albert Woodfin
Jones, Lonnie Daniel
Jordan, Clyde C.
Jordan, Leman
Johnson, Walton A.
Johnson, Lyndon Pope
Johnson, Charles A.
King, Claud Johnson
Kellum, Gip
King, Willie S.
Maxwell, Charles P.
Masch, Early V. Lee
Moore, Herbert Thomas
Moon, Sanford N.
Moon, Joseph Worley
Moseley, Edgar A.
Maxwell, Robert B.
Moon, C. H.
Mason, Charlie

Moon, Omer F.
Moon, William David
Maxwell, Boyce L.
McGuire, James Alonzo
Nelms, Gordon T.
Nash, Henry A.
Phillips, Sam Jones
Parker, Earl Rogers
Patterson, George W.
Pulliam, Eff J.
Parham, Jasper E.
Patterson, Arthur S.
Parham, Lester G.
Rousey, William E.
Rossar, Zera M.
Rice, Claud
Ray, Claud
Rhyne, Clarence Little
Rice, Morgan
Seymour, Holcomb G.
Sanders, Clifton
Smith, John William
Smith, George W.
Seymour, Robert Boyd
Sanders, Henry Walter
Scoggins, John Daniel
Seymour, Emory J.
Seymour, Early Gibson
Seymour, William L.
Seymour, Rufus Albert
Seymour, Lonnie O.
Seymour, Grady G. R.
Shaw, John William
Seymour, James Clark
Taylor, Frazier Brown
Vaughan, Charles B.
Vaughan, Albert J.
Wallace, Tracey
Wilson, Milford Lonnie
Walker, Lloyd Z.
Wells, Jesse Lee
Winn, Guy Earl
Webb, Lester Austin
Whitmire, William B.
Wood, Charlie M.
Young, Willie P.

WEBBSBORO—202ND DISTRICT

Almond, George Milton
Anderson, Joseph P.
Bowers, Lucius Edwin
Brown, Frank Stark
Compton, J. Douglas
Cleveland, Grady
Fortson, Jefferson H.
Fortson, Henry A. Jr.
Guest, Sidney J.
Hall, E. Everett
Hall, John W.
Moore, W. Stark
Moore, Toliver P.
Moore, Hoyt
Moore, Ezra
Moore, Luke W.
Moore, George S.
Oglesby, Clarence T.
Oglesby, J. Charles
Oglesby, Drue Gibson
Oglesby, Nathaniel W.
Parham, Omer S.
Partet, Carl A.
Rogers, Ezekiel Q.
Sanders, Alonzo Eppie
Thornton, Lee
Willis, James Milton
Webb, Lincoln Morrison
Webb, William P.
Webb, Hoyt
Webb, George W. Jr.
Webb, Grover C.
Willis, E. Paul
Wilson, Samuel C.
Yeargin, John Thomas

CENTERVILLE—315TH DISTRICT

Aderhold, David W.
Adams, Carl Turner
Adams, Clarence D.
Bond, Benjamin E.
Black, Hester T.
Bond, Charlie Walker
Bone, William Andrew
Brewer, Charles H.
Burdette, William H.
Bates, Milton
Collins, Lewis
Carter, James Martin
Craft, Ezra Boyd
Cordell, Moses F.
Clark, I. B.
Collins, Fred
Carter, McAlpin Calvin
Craft, Arthur Lee
Carter, Raymond C.
Cleveland, Hugh
Driver, John Hilliard
Daniel, Enos Roscoe
Driver, Alexander
Eavenson, Julian W.
Eavenson, Paul Pascal
Eavenson, Croley C.
Fleming, Guy Isom
Gaines, Isom S.
Greenway, Barney
Gunter, Thomas G.
Gaines, Benj. Franklin
Harris, Grady Cantrell
Hunt, Charlie W.
Hulme, Doctor Mel
Harris, James C. Jr.
Hulme, John E.
Hulme, Ezra Bowers
Hulme, John
Kesler, Deenis H.
Lunsford, Thomas S.
Lunsford, Henry Grady
Lunsford, Holcomb B
Moore, A. Coleman
Maxwell, Leonard V
Matthews, Lee Walton
Maxwell, Artimus
Maxwell, Simeon
Norman, Ango Wesley
Norman, Jeptha P.
Poole, Charlie B.
Pulliam, Homer H.
Shiflette, Lonnie James
Skelton, John
Sanders, Leonard G.
Teasley, Early C.
Thornton, Pelham W.
Teasley, Martin T.
Wansley, William H.
Ward, Thomas Marion

Shortly after the close of the World War, Colonel William Fitzpatrick Jones Sr., began the laborious task of securing a short sketch of every soldier who served from Elbert County in the struggle. This laudable undertaking has been completed and will stand as a monument to him in the years to come. The work was done as an act of unselfish patriotism and its worth cannot be measured by the present generation. It is a distinct benefaction to the generations that are to come.

At the annual dinner given the soldiers of the Confederacy, on April 26, 1917, there were 50 of these heroes present. The average age of those attending was 76½ years. Captain William B. Henry was the oldest being 92, and J. A. Holliday the youngest, aged 68. Only one of these soldiers of the Sixties was living in 1935.

The harvest taken by death in 1918, was equally as appalling as that of the previous year. Among those who died were J. E. Tunison, 72; Thomas J. Hewell Sr., 82; R. A. Gaines, 89; J. B. Vaughan, the composer of sacred songs; E. W. Bell, Sam C. Stark, F. M. Crawford, Confederate soldier; Mrs. Alice Oglesby (H. J.) Brewer, George T. Fortson, Mrs. T. M. Hulme, 84; Parks Norman, 80; David W. Meadow, once Judge of the Superior Courts of the Northern Circuit; A B. Andrews, J. W. Holman, Major in the United States Army and President of Gibson-Mercer Institute at Bowman; Corporal Rice, Company C, 121st Infantry, died March 6th, the first soldier of Elbert County to die in the service during the World War; Alvin Gillispie, Thomas J. Brown, former Solicitor General of the Northern Circuit; John F. Thornton, Confederate soldier; G. H. McLanahan, Mrs. John P. Shannon, Captain William B. Henry, 93, Confederate soldier, and oldest living graduate of Emory College; James L Leohr, soldier of the World War; C. C. Whiteside Sr., and W. W. Reese, Confederate soldier.

It was during this year that the John Henry Jones Memorial Church was formally dedicated in Lienze, China. The building, seating 350 persons, was the gift of his youngest daughter, Miss Lenora Jones. Since its dedication this church has continued to thrive and will stand as a fitting memorial to the donor and to the memory of John Henry Jones, for many years a leading citizen of Elbert County.

While the soldiers of Elbert County were in hand to hand conflict with the Central Powers, the Red Cross organization of the county was busy raising money for their care. The knitting section, under the able leadership of Mrs. Charles W. Parker, did yoeman service.

Peyton M. Hawes served in a most capable manner as Food Administrator, and J. Gordon Ginn, as Fuel Administrator, proved himself a worthy official.

With the close of the World War, Elbert County entered upon its most prosperous era. The people of the county voted 1,623, as against 29, for bonds totalling $200,000 for road improvements. A commission was appointed, composed of James Y. Swift, C. P. Hairston, Thomas H. Gaines, John A. Stark, and E. L. Adams. The funds so voted were mainly used in soiling and grading the road from Elberton to Bowman.

Elberton also voted bonds to the extent of $50,000 for the purpose of enlarging educational facilities and sewer extension. These bonds carried by a vote of 292 for and 6 against.

On April 8, 1919, Group Two of the Georgia State Bankers' Association convened in Elberton. There were 200 delegates present. Orville A. Park, of Macon; Professor C. M. Strahan, of the University of Georgia, and H. B. Payne, of Elberton, were the speakers.

During this time Elbert County had five banks within its limits. The First National of Elberton with resources of $1,200,000; Elberton Loan and Savings Bank with $600,000; Bank of Elberton with $610,000; Bank of Bowman $465,000, and the Farmer's Bank of Bowman with $300,000. A charter was granted the Elbert County Bank in November of 1919. Peyton M. Hawes was named President and H. B. Bynum named Cashier. This institution continued in successful operation for several years and was eventually absorbed by the Bank of Elberton. All stockholders were paid full value for their shares and the latter institution purchased all notes held by the former at face value.

The Edmund Brewer Tate Post of the American Legion was organized at a meeting held in the Elbert County court house on September 26, 1919. Howard B. Payne was elected Commander; J. E. Kelly, Vice-Commander, and Robert F. Wright Jr., Adjutant. Edmund Brewer Tate, for who mthe Post was named, met his death in action during the latter part of the war. Lientenant Tate was in command of a machine gun outfit and was in the midst of heavy fighting when he was killed. The Major of his batallion, in a letter to his parents, Mr. and Mrs. Ora E. Tate, spoke in glowing terms of his intrepid bravery in the face of a withering fire from the enemy. Lieutenant Tate, at the time of his death, was only 23 years of age and was a young man of great promise.

During the summer of 1919, Colonel Thomas M. Swift was named as head of the United States Census for the Eighth Congressional District of Georgia. Despite his age, 72 years, he made an efficient official and was ably assisted by Mr. Thomas H. Verdel.

During the early morning hours of Decembber 23, 1919, the First National Bank Building was totally destroyed by fire. The second floor was occupied by Grogan & Payne, attorneys; E. K. Orrison, osteopath; R. E. Cunningham, dentist; Dr. Harding, dentist; John H. McIntosh, attorney; W. J. Matthews, physician; and W. E. Snowden, insurance; the lower floor housed the bank and a motion picture theatre. The loss was estimated upward of $300,000.

Through the efforts of Colonel William Fitzpatrick Jones a complete list of World War soldiers, from Elbert County, who were killed or died from disease, was procured from Washington during January, 1920. This list follows: Captain James V. Holman, Lieutenant Edmund Brewer Jones, Alvin Gillespie, Hascal C. Smith, John William Smith, John D. Lock, John Webb Smith, Marvin Rice, Fred Wansley, Walter McLanahan, James Leohr, Lieutenant George W. Mattox, Patrick Hansard Hall, James T. Rayle, and George B. Conwell. The foregoing list constitutes the white soldiers only. The Negroes who died in service were: Henry Clayton Bone, Tinsley Rucker, Emerson Tate, Arthur Sturghill, Nathaniel G. Burden, and Joseph Wall.

Much interest was shown in the presidential primary held in Elbert County during April, 1920. Mitchell Palmer received 677 votes, Thomas E. Watson received 676, and Hoke Smith 568 votes. Watson carried Goshen, Eliam, Pike, Petersburg, and Wyche Districts. Palmer carried Elberton, Webbsboro, Gaines, Moss and tied Watson in Centerville. Hoke Smith carried Ruckersville and Longstreet Districts.

During the first six months of 1920 approximately $1,000,000 was expended in construction work throughout the county—$200,000 good road bonds; $42,000 school and sewer extensions; $15,000 for Negro school; $15,000 electric light improvements; $170,000 First National Bank Building; Carhartt Cotton Mills improvement $40,000; cotton warehouse, $25,000; overall factory, $25,000; Bank of Elberton (now 1937 Granite City Bank) structure, $30,000, and numerous private residences.

In the municipal election of Elberton held December 23, 1920, the first woman of Elbert County to cast a ballot was Mrs. H. E. (Norma Wright) Hawes. Her ballot number was 3. Mrs. Z. W. (Edna Arnold) Copeland was a close second.

The population of incorporated towns and villages in Elbert County, exclusive of Elberton, were: Bowman, 730; Middleton, 152; Beverly, 132, and Ruckersville, 111.

The years 1921 through 1929 wrought many changes in Elbert County. The price of cotton reached an all-time high since the War Between the States and there was every indication that conditions would make the United States a nation of millionaires. Lands that had brought $10.00 an acre soared to 20 and 30 times that figures; carpenters and brick layers received $15.00 for eight hours work for the asking; every tenant farmer, previously satisfied with a mule and buggy, demanded and secured rapid transit in the form of a high priced automobile and jeans and calico gave place to broadcloth and satin.

In the Fall of 1921 cotton took a downward trend falling from more than 40 cents a pound to 22 cents and in the Summer of 1922 cotton fell still lower and the dreaded boll weevil began work in earnest. The thinking business man began to retrench but many continued in the belief that a mere temporary lull had come and times would again reach that unprecedented level theretofore unknown. The natural consequences was that money became almost non-existent and many farms and automobiles were of necessity returned to the original owners at a staggering loss to both parties concerned.

However, Elbert County with its industries weathered the storm and in 1927 was recognized throughout the South as the most prosperous and less hard hit county within its boundaries. In fact, in the Fall of 1927 not a single storeroom was vacant in Elberton and the rock sheds and quarries were working full six days each week. The trojan work of the Chamber of Commerce was largely responsible for keeping up the morale of all the citizens.

During this period Elberton had its bank failures but it is interesting to note that practically 100 cents in the dollar was repaid to all depositors.

The primary election held in Elbert County on September 10,

1930, disclosed most unusual facts. Peyton S. Hawes, 27 years old, was elected to the Georgia House of Representatives. His father, Dr. A. S. Hawes, served in the same body 1927-1928; his paternal uncle, Peyton M. Hawes, was a member of the House 1900, 1901, 1902, 1903 and of the Senate 1907, 1908. Hawes was the youngest representative to serve Elbert County over a period of 104 years.

During the year 1932 Elberton and Elbert County suffered from the world-wide depression as did all Georgia but to a lesser degree. With the liberal payrolls of the rock and silk industries money remained to a reasonable extent in a liquid state. True, the price of farm products were at a low ebb and the cotton farmer found it virtually impossible to make net profits but little actual suffering was in evidence. The Chamber of Commerce, the American Legion, the Rotary and Kiwanis Clubs, together with other organizations and liberal individuals saw to it that all needy persons were amply provided for.

Under the able leadership of the veteran Chief of Police W. H. Irvin, work was provided for the unemployed on various public projects. Those so employed were given script exchangeable for the necessities of life. Clothing was provided for needy school children, largely through the untiring efforts of Miss Janie Parsons, the able school nurse. To commend too highly this "Good Samaritan" is impossible. Indeed, it may be said, "Daughters have done virtuously, but thou exceedeth them all."

Elbert County owes a debt of gratitude to such professional men as Dr. A. S. Johnson, Dr. D. N. Thompson, Dr. Walton Johnson, Dr. J. E. Johnson Sr., Dr. D. V. Bailey, Dr. A. S. J. Stovall, Dr. A. C. Smith, Dr. Fletcher Smith, Dr. Q. G. Logan, Dr. John Jenkins, and Dr. Charles Johnson, who gave so freely of their time and skill without compensation, to the indigent.

The Elbert County Hospital, under the management of Mrs. W. H. Paines, Joe Allen and Miss Lula Peek, proved a God send to the territory. R. H. Johnson, who succeeded the former in December, 1932, proved capable, industrious and generous.

The Chamber of Commerce under the leadership of John T. Heard and such co-workers as Z. W. Copeland, F. D. Smith, P. V. Price, J. S. Asbury, Fred Herndon, John H. Cook, R. H. Johnson, R. E. Hudgens, Raymond Stapleton, T. O. Tabor Jr., W. D. Tutt, C. F. Herndon, T. T. Thornton, Henry T. Brookshire, Carter A. Arnold, Jule M. Cleveland, Harry G. Thornton, H. P. Hunter, Z. B. Rogers, John T. Dennis Jr., Thomas N. Gaines, Parks E. Heard, O. H. Smith, J. E. Asbury, Webb Tatum, Paul Brown, Fred Auld, Sam Patz, Joe Allen, Frank Fortson, Clark Edwards Jr., G. T. Christian, and a host of others by unstinted efforts placed Elberton well in the forefront of Georgia cities.

Another citizen, perhaps the most valuable from the standpoint of securing justice for the unfortunate, was Clark Edwards Jr.,

Ordinary of Elbert County and service office of the Edmund Brewer Tate Post of the American Legion. He gave freely of both time and means to aid disabled soldiers of the World War to secure their just compensation from the Federal Government. With him labored three lieutenants, William F. Jones Jr., Guy M. Sanders, and David C. Auld, adjutant of the Edmund Brewer Tate Post Number 14.

During 1932 Elberton royally entertained the Georgia Conclave of DeMolay (Edna May Copeland was sponsor for Elberton DeMolay), the Presbyterian Synod of Georgia, the Georgia Building and Loan Association of which Fred Herndon was president, and the Tenth Congressional District High School Meet.

During the years 1931 and 1932 four distinguished Elbertonians were taken by death: W. O. Jones, ex-Mayor, banker, merchant, and many years member of the school board; Thomas M. Swift Sr., banker, merchant, and legislator; John T. Heard, ex-postmaster, banker, merchant, and perhaps Elberton's most beloved citizen; W. L. Skelton, editor of *The Elberton Star*, a man laboring under physical handicap but an outstanding, progressive citizen and a loyal friend. Several persons past their 80th birthdays died during this period: Thomas M. Swift Sr., Mrs. Thomas M. Swift Sr., Mrs. S. N. Carpenter and Mrs. James J. Burch.

Elbert County, regardless of economic conditions, entered the year 1933 without outstanding obligations. O. H. Smith, County Commissioner, kept the county free from debt and maintained a good surplus in the treasury notwithstanding the fact that he reduced the tax rates to the lowest in all Georgia and the land valuations to the lowest in the Tenth Congressional District. In the reduction of land valuations he had the complete cooperation of the Elbert County Board of Tax Equalizers composed of D. J. Thornton, C. P. Hairston and James E. Hammond. The roads, public buildings and bridges were of the first rank.

The city of Elberton opened the year 1933 in a better financial condition than in which it had been for years. The City Council, composed of R. E. Hudgens, T. O. Tabor Jr., Dr. D. V. Bailey, J. S Asbury, and Dr. A. S. Johnson, reduced taxes and yet made many needed improvements. They were ably assisted by their competent Clerk and Treasurer, Miss L. Stillwell and her able assistant, Mrs. Ethel Mashburn. (Later data found elsewhere in the History.)

Elbert County's part in the Georgia Bi-centennial celebration began auspiciously with the appointment of Z. B. Rogers as Chairman. During the early part of January, 1933, he named the following committees:

Executive Committee: Z. B. Rogers, chairman; Z. C. Hayes, Mrs. Z. W. Copeland, Clark Edwards Jr., Miss Edna Rogers, Mrs. S. S Brewer, A. W. Bussey, Miss May Tate, Mrs. W. C. Allen, Mrs. Homer Brock, Harry G. Thornton, Fred Herndon, Carter A. Arnold,

C. P. Hairston, Miss Lula Peek, Webb Tatum, O. H. Smith, Paul Brown, H. B. Payne, and Fred Auld.

General Committee: Z. B. Rogers, chairman; W. F. Jones Sr., O. H. Smith, P. V. Rice Jr., Mrs. S. S. Brewer, Miss Delray Adams, Clark Tate, John H. McIntosh, Mrs. Z. W. Copeland, A. W. Bussey, Z C. Hayes, Miss Edna Rogers, Mrs. James Y. Swift, Miss Mary Lizzie Wright, Mrs. W. H. Paine, Miss Mary Hansard, Miss Sarah Wall, Silas G. Booth, Miss Lula Peek, F. M. Young, W. H. Simpson, Mrs. George A. Gaines, Webb Tatum, Mrs. Carter A. Arnold, Edzel Snowden, Mrs. F. L. Adams, and others.

Historical Markers Committee: John H. McIntosh, chairman; W. F. Jones Sr., Mrs. Z. W. Copeland, Miss Edna Rogers, Miss Mary Lizzie Wright, A. T. Hinds, Edzel Snowden, Mrs. Sue Heard Swift, Miss Delray Adams, Mrs. James Carpenter, Mrs. Mary Clark Fortson, Frank S. Fortson Sr., Henry Bell, Joe Hill, Mrs. Lucia H. Rucker, Mrs. Howard B. Payne, Mrs. T. O. Tabor Jr., Mrs. Lloyd Outz, Guy G. Rucker, Mrs. Virginia Wall, Miss May Tate, C. B. Elkins, Mrs. W. C. Allen, Miss Mary Hansard, O. H. Smith, W. H. Simpson, Mrs. Reid Caldwell, Miss Sarah Wall, Mrs. Homer Brock, Mrs. L. W. Hendricks, B. I. Thornton, T. J. Cleveland, J. J. Blachin, and W. G. B. Jones.

General Plans Committee: Thomas N. Gaines, chairman; Z. C. Hayes, Clark Edwards Jr., Mrs. Z. W. Copeland, Miss Edna Rogers, Miss Lula Peek, G. T. Christian, G. W. Dickerson, F. M. Young, E. C. Young, Mrs. C. S. Allen, Miss Delray Adams, Joel Allen, Mrs. W. H. Paine, Mrs. W. C. Allen, W. H. Simpson, Dr. C. A. Johnson, C. P. Hairston, W. A. Teasley, Mrs. Homer Brock, Miss Mary Lizzie Wright, Mrs. W. D. Tutt, Miss Mary Hansard, Ben I. Sutton, and Raymonde Stapleton.

Church Committee: Z. C. Hayes, chairman; Miss Mae Tate, Miss Mary Lizzie Wright, J. C. West, Miss Mary Hansard, A. W. Bussey, A. T. Hinds, Mrs. Homer Brock and Mrs. F. L. Adams.

Pageants Committee: Miss Edna May Copeland, chairman; Mrs. W. H. Paine, vice-chairman; Miss Mary Thomas Maxwell, Edzel Snowden, Mrs. Emmie De Robinson, Mrs. George A. Gaines, Mrs. Harris Bailey, Mrs. W. T. Thornton, Mrs. John H. McIntosh, Mrs. R. L. Rice, Miss Mary Teasley, Mrs. F. M. Young, Miss Inez Balchin, Miss Myrtle Carpenter, Mrs. Jim Ridgeway, Mrs. C. S. Allen, Mrs. Jim T. Maxwell, Mrs. J. T. Dennis Jr., Mrs. Marie S. Hosher, J. T. Dennis Jr., A. S. Simmons, G. C. Robinson, Peyton S. Hawes, W. P. Huie, E. C. Young, F. M. Young, Miss Sarah Wall, Miss Mary L. Wright, Miss Gladys Sheppard, Webb Tatum, Mrs. C. A. Arnold, and Mrs. Hewell Mann.

Flower and Music Festival Committee: Mrs. Sue Heard Swift, chairman; Mrs. J. E. Johnson, Mrs. L. W. Hendricks, Mrs. A. F. Archer, Mrs. W. E. Hall, Mrs. Earl McCalla, Mrs. Jim Deadwyler, Mrs. Tom Maxwell, Mrs. C. A. Arnold, Mrs. Z. W. Copeland, Mrs. T. D. Seymour, Mrs. D. N. Thompson, Mrs. H. H. Manley, Mrs.

Thomas Hayes, Mrs. W. A. Johnson, S. B. Seymour, J. D. DuBose, P. V. Rice Jr., Miss Evelyn Bussey, A. A. Seymour, Floyd Christian and Quartette, Homer Burton Sr., Mrs. E. E. Bailey, Mrs. Vail Deadwyler, Dillard H. Brown, Mrs. C. J. Almond, Mrs. Robert Bass, Miss Virginia Smith, Mrs. J. E. Asbury, Mrs. Clyde Teasley, Mrs. Fred Auld, Stuart Asbury, Buford Maxwell, W. T. Thornton, George Lee White, Parker Smith, W. H. Paine, Fred Auld, Mrs. Paul Brown, Mrs. W. E. Snowden, Jack Fleming, Mrs. Jule M. Cleveland, Mrs. Vernon Bailey, Mrs. Fred Herndon, Miss Nora Jones, Mrs. Tom Colley, Mrs. O. H. Smith, Mrs. George L. Herndon, Mrs. C. L. Smith, Mrs. H. P. Hunter, Mrs. John H. Cook, August Korten, and Mrs. August Korten.

Exhibit Committee: Mrs. Z. W. Copeland, chairman; John H. McIntosh, Mrs. S. S. Brewer, Mrs. A. S. Simmons, W. F. Jones Sr., Z. B. Rogers, Miss Edna Rogers, Mrs. Pauline Brewer Brown, Mrs. Lucia H. Rucker, and others.

The Bi-centennial Celebration proper was held on Wednesday, February 10, 1933, with out-of-town visitors exceeding 5,000 present. At noon a mammoth parade was led by Miss Elizabeth Brown portraying "Lady Oglethorpe." Many clubs and business houses entered unique floats many of which depicted historical events native to Elbert County. In the afternoon and evening a number of historic pageants were given and during the morning and afternoon a striking flower show was open to the public.

One of the most unique and interesting features of the celebration was the historic collection of articles secured and shown by the Exhibit Committee. There were ancient army uniforms, hoop skirts, tin types, guns, sabers, spinning wheels, jewelry, silverware, pottery, cooking utensils, books, swords, samplers, Indian relics from Elbert County mounds and numerous other articles of historic significance.

March 10, 1935, brought to a close the remarkable career of R. W. Cleveland. He was born in 1844 and was among the first to enlist for service in the War Between the States. He saw service in the Fourteenth Georgia Regiment of Infantry Volunteers from its organization until Appomattox. He was twice wounded and when the war closed he held the rank of First Sergeant. He was elected surveyor of Elbert County in 1877, which office he held continuously until his death. The length of his service, 57 years, is perhaps a record for an elective office in Georgia. Mr. Cleveland was twice married and a large number of his descendants survived him.

Elbert County with a background of almost a century and a half, a background peopled with great statesmen, soldiers, lawyers, ministers, planters and physicians, a retrospective holding four major wars and many panics looks forwards with confidence to the early restoration of normal conditions—looks forward with the faith with which its founders demonstrated in hewing a great county from the virgin wilderness—and looks forward with its faith firmly fixed upon the unwavering belief in the power of a gracious and all understanding Diety to restore order from chaos and confusion.

PART II.

Statistical Section

REVOLUTIONARY SOLDIERS—SOLDIERS OF WAR OF 1812—SOLDIERS OF WAR BETWEEN THE STATES—SOLDIERS OF SPANISH-AMERICAN WAR—SOLDIERS OF WORLD WAR—ABSTRACT OF EARLY WILLS AND DEEDS—LAND LOTTERY—MARRIAGE RECORDS—POSTMASTERS OF ELBERT COUNTY — CEMETERY INSCRIPTIONS — ELECTION RETURNS—OFFICIALS OF ELBERT COUNTY—LAW MAKERS OF ELBERT COUNTY—MAYORS AND CITY COUNCILMEN OF ELBERTON.

LIST OF EARLY ELBERT COUNTY RESIDENTS WHOSE NAMES DO NOT APPEAR ELSEWHERE IN THIS VOLUME—THE DATE AFTER EACH NAME INDICATES ITS FIRST APPEARANCE OF RECORD.

Name	Date	Name	Date
Ashley, James	1800	Calvert, John	1796
Alexander, William	1796	Cloud, John	1798
Allen, Josiah	1796	Christian, James	1798
Allen, Asa	1796	Conway, Phillip	1792
Arrington, Henry	1801	Carrol, Peter	1796
Atchison, Nathaniel	1800	Connely, Charles	1799
Appleby, William	1800	Cleghorn, George	1800
Alexander, Isacc	1794	Cocke, Nathaniel	1801
Black, Wm., Capt.	1802	Chapman, William	1800
Booth, George	1801	Carrington, Tim	1801
Butler, Zachariah	1801	Crouder, Robert	1790
Bryant, Stinson	1800	Campbell, Duncan	1794
Brooks, Dudley	1801	Dye, Prettyman	1801
Bradley, William	1799	Dye, Martin	1802
Bradley, Drury	1799	Dale, William	1801
Brown, Bedford	1796	Duncan, Henry	1799
Beasley, Ephriam	1797	Dixon, Outerbridge	1797
Baker, Elias	1796	DePriest, Randolph	1797
Barton, Benjamin	1797	Duncan, John	1799
Brawner, John	1795	David, Peter	1800
Bond, Joseph	1799	Donihoo, Cornelius	1799
Blackwell, George	1799	Dollar, Ambrose	1799
Baker, Samuel	1800	Douglas, Thomas	1799
Ball, Isacc	1799	Easton, Richard	1794
Bowen, Horatio	1799	Ellis, John	1799
Bennett, Jessee	1799	Evins, George	1799
Bryant, T.	1798	Edwards, Peter	1799
Brady, Joseph	1798	Edwards, Augustine	1796
Brady, James	1798	Fleming, Robert	1792
Cearrey, Stephen	1799	Ford, Isacc	1793
Chislom, William	1793	Floyd, William	1801
Cochran, William	1794	Fulghum, Stephen	1802
Colbert, Nichodemus	1798	Forbes, John	1801
Cook, Smith	1800	Franklin, John	1799
Creagh, Thos. B.	1798	Fleming, Moses	1796
Caldwell, Alexander	1800	Flood, James	1798

Name	Year	Name	Year
Fain, Charles	1799	Mathews, Lewis	1801
Foote, Justin	1799	Morris, John	1797
Guttery, William	1799	Moon, William	1797
Guy, William	1800	Morrow, Joseph	1798
Gray, William	1799	Morrison, Peter	1799
Goss, Charles	1800	Mann, James	1798
Gadis, John	1797	Moon, Francis	1800
Giles, John M.	1797	McGuire, Alleghaney	1800
Garrett, John	1796	McDougle, Alexander	1795
Graham, William	1796	McEver, Andrew	1798
Gaines, Hiram	1797	McKee, Thomas	1791
Greenlaw, David	1800	Newton, William	1800
Gaddy, David	1800	Norris, Roy	1796
Gantt, Benjamin	1795	Nash, Henry	1798
Gibbs, Herod	1792	Nix, Joseph	1798
Gillelan, Jacob	1792	Nelloms, David	1799
Grimes, William	1793	Nelms, David	1797
Haney, Bridger	1798	Owens, Thomas	1801
Hawthorne, John Sr.	1794	Oglesby, Garratt	1801
Holliday, James	1798	Pace, Patrick	1800
Hawthorne, James	1799	Prior, Joseph	1794
Hawthorne, John Jr.	1799	Payton, William	1800
Ham, John	1799	Perry, Thomas	1802
Hodge, Alexander	1800	Patterson, William	1801
Hooper, Obediah	1798	Phipps, Lewis	1798
Howard, Benjamin	1800	Price, Thomas	1797
Horton, Thomas	1799	Patton, Samuel	1797
Hulm, William	1800	Penn, Thomas	1798
Holmes, Gideon	1798	Penn, Phillip	1798
Hunt, Nathaniel	1797	Post, William	1799
Howard, Nehemiah	1798	Park, Robert	1794
Hobby, Winsley	1796	Park, James	1794
Hendricks, Elias	1796	Reylee, James	1796
Harris, Christopher	1795	Ray, Samuel	1798
Hammond, Dudley	1797	Riley, John	1798
Hopkins, Josiah	1801	Rose, Drury	1798
Hall, Natianiel	1802	Ridgway, James	1799
Jennings, Joseph	1799	Rucker, George Sr.	1800
Jackson, Henry	1799	Roberts, Abraham Isacc	1801
Jones, Aaron	1800	Riddle, Archibald	1801
Jones, Allen	1797	Ross, Drury	1792
Jordan, River	1795	Sheperd, Peter	1792
Jordan, John	1795	Strong, William	1790
James, Joseph	1796	Stokes, Sylvanus	1800
Jones, Arthur	1797	Stowe, Warren	1797
King, John	1794	Starr, Christopher	1797
Kerr, Samuel	1797	Shoemaker, Lindsey	1793
Kidd, James	1796	Shannon, Quinton	1797
Kettler, John	1800	Smith, Alexander	1797
Kelley, Martin	1800	Stephens, Thomas	1798
Lawson, Jesse	1798	Stinchcomb, Alexander	1800
Lawson, Robert	1798	Skelton, Robert	1800
Long, Joseph	1800	Skinner, Archibald	1799
Luckie, John	1798	Snellings, George	1800
Lyon, Edward	1799	Shockley, Thomas	1800
Lowrey, Meshack	1798	Sigman, John	1800
Landrum, Burton	1801	Sanders, Richard	1798
Maline, Franklin	1790	Terrell, Jeremiah	1799
Murrah, John	1800	Thomas, William	1794
Martin, John	1800	Taylor, Roland	1800

Thurmond, Phillip	1795	Wilmoth, William	1799
Turman, Garrett	1797	White, Thomas	1797
Turner, James	1797	Waller, Daniel	1800
Turnodett, Daniel	1797	Walthall, Gerrard	1799
Thomason, John	1800	Wilson, Little	1800
Taylor, Charles	1801	Wyler, D.	1798
Vickery, William	1802	Woodward, Thomas	1797
Vaughan, William	1800	Wilkie, William	1800
VanHook, Samuel	1793	Wingfield, John	1800
Vinson, Isacc	1800	Wallace, John	1794
Vinson, Jesse	1800	Wells, Jeremiah T.	1796

NATIONAL LAW MAKERS OF ELBERT COUNTY

UNITED STATES SENATORS
Dr. W. W. Bibb, 1813-1816.
Charles Tait, 1899-1819.

UNITED STATES REPRESENTATIVTS
*George Matthews, 1787-1791.
W. W. Bibb, 1805-1813.
William Barnett, 1811-1815.
Wiley Thompson, 1821-1833
N. J. Hammond, 1879-1881.
Paul Brown, July 1933-Dec. 1936-1939-

GOVERNORS OF GEORGIA
Stephen Heard, 1781.
*George Matthews, 1782-1788.

ATTORNEY GENERAL OF GEORGIA
N. J. Hammond.

PRESIDENTS OF GEORGIA SENATE
William Barnett
Allen Daniel

PRESIDENT OF EXECUTIVE COUNCIL
Stephen Heard, 1782.

GOVERNORS OF ALABAMA FROM ELBERT COUNTY
W. W. Bibb,
Thomas Bibb

MEMBERS OF THE GEORGIA HOUSE OF REPRESENTATIVES

1799 —Reuben Easter, James Banks, Christopher Clark.
1800 —Reuben Easter, Richmond T. Cosby, Christopher Clark.
1801-02—Reuben Easter, Richmond T. Cosby, Allen Daniel.
1803-04—Richmond T. Cosby, Allen Daniel, W. W. Bibb.
1805 —W. W. Bibb, David Hudson, Allen Daniel (resigned), Capt. William Allen.
1806 —Barnett Jeter, David Hudson, John Johnston.
1807 —Barnett Jeter, John B. Posey, Allen Daniel.
1808-09—Barnett Jeter, Allen Daniel, John Johnston.
1810 —Allen Daniel, David Hudson, Archalus Jarratt.

---

*While it is generally considered that George Matthews was a resident of Oglethorpe County, official records show that he resided for a time in territory embraced in Elbert County.

1811 —Allen Daniel, Jeptha V. Harris, David Hudson.
1812 —James Hatcher, Jeptha V. Harris.
1813 —William Fortson, Thomas Oliver, Robert Roebuck.
1814 —Robert Roebuck, James Wood, William Foster.
1815 —James M. Tait, James Wood, John Johnston.
1816 —John Carroll, James Morrison, Robert Kennedy.
1817 —Beverly Allen, John A. Heard, John Ashley.
1818-19—Beverly Allen, John A. Heard, James Morrison.
1820-21—James Morrison, James M. Tait, James Alston (resigned), Charles W. Christian.
1822 —Barnard C. Heard, William Moore, Charles W. Christian.
1823 —Barnard C. Heard, Charles W. Christian, John Banks.
1824-25—Simeon Oliver, Joshua Clark, James M. Tait, George W. Heard.
1826 —George W. Heard, James M. Tait.
1827 —George W. Heard, James M. Tait, Isacc N. Davis.
1828-29—Singleton W. Allen, Simeon Oliver, William A. Herring.
1830 —Simeon Oliver, Joseph Blackwell, Alexander P. Houston.
1831 —Singleton W. Allen, Simeon Oliver, Joseph Blackwell.
1832-33—Thomas J. Heard, William Herndon, William A. Beck.
1835 —Anderson Craft, Isaac N. Davis, Duncan McCurry.
1836 —David S. White, Isaac N. Davis, Thomas Johnston.
1837-38—Thomas F. Gibbs, Charles W. Christian, Anderson Craft.
1839 —Anderson Craft, Jeremiah S. Warren, William Jones.
1840 —Jeremiah S. Warren, Anderson Craft, Abram Parks.
1841 —Tinsley W. Rucker, Young L. G. Harris, J. S. Patterson.
1842 —Anderson Craft, J. H. M. Barrett, William H. Adams.
1843-44—Anderson Craft, William A. Black, William D. Adams.
1845 —Thomas F. Willis, J. H. M. Barrett.
1846-47—William M. McIntosh, McAlpin A. Arnold.
1848 —No data.
1849-50—Henry R. Deadwyler, Henry M. Barrett.
1851-52—Rev. Benjamin Thornton Jr., Henry R. Deadwyler.
1853-54—Luther H. O. Martin, E. L. Rucker.
1855-56—T. Johnson.
1857-58—Willis Craft.
1859-60—Larkin J. Clark.
1861-62—Robert Hester.
1863-64—Robert Hester (unseated), Samuel Stark. The unseating of Hester was due to the fact that the votes of the absent Confederate soldiers were late in arriving and on the face of the local returns it appeared that Hester had defeated Stark, but such was not the case when the soldier vote was counted.
1865-66—William H. Mattox.
1867 —No data. Elbert County probably was not represented due to the "Carpet Bag Rule."
1868-69—U. O. Tate.
1871-72—Emory P. Edwards.
1873-74—Henry P. Mattox.
1875-76—No data.
1877 —James Burch.
1878-79—Robert Tate.
1880-81—James Hopkins Brewer.
1882-83—Jeptha B. Jones.
1884-85—Robert M. Heard.
1886-87—Richard E. Adams.
1888-89—Phillip W. Davis.
1890-91—William Henry Heard.
1892-93—Dr. David P. Bell.
1894-95—Joseph N. Worley.
1896-99—Thomas M. Swift.

1900-01—Peyton M. Hawes.
1902-03—Peyton M. Hawes, L. H. O. Martin Jr.
1904-08—L. H. O. Martin Jr., Willis B. Adams.
1909-12—A. S. J. Stovall, Benjamin R. Cordell.
1913-14—A. S. J. Stovall, James N. Wall.
1915-16—Tinsley W. McLanahan, Dr. W. J. Matthews.
1917-18—William F. Jones Sr., Dr. F. L. Adams (resigned), A. F. Westmoreland.
1919-20—Z. B. Rogers, A. B. Deadwyler (died), Thomas M. Swift Sr.
1921-22—W. T. Brownlee, Thomas M. Swift Sr.
1923-24—T. J. Hulme, A. S. J. Stovall.
1925-26—
1927-28—Dr. A. S. Hawes, Thomas J. Hewell Jr.
1929-30—Thomas J. Hewell Jr., H. A. Adams.
1931-32—Peyton S. Hawes, T. J. Sisk.
1933-34—T. F. Kelly.
1935-36—T. F. Kelly.

GEORGIA STATE SENATORS FROM ELBERT COUNTY

1791-92—General Samuel Blackburn.
1793-98—No data.
1799-1801—William Barnett.
1802   —Obediah Jones.
1803-07—No data.
1808   —Captain Patrick Jack.
1809-11—William Barnett.
1812-13—Robert H. Watkins.
1814-15—David Hudson.
1816   —Robert Burke.
1817-19—Wiley Thompson.
1820-21—William Woods.
1822-24—Beverly Allen.
1825   —Jeptha V. Harris.
1826-27—Beverly Allen.
1828-29—James M. Tait.
1830-31—Beverly Allen.
1832   —Simeon Oliver.
1833   —Benajah Houston.
1834   —Beverly Allen.
1835-36—Thomas J. Heard.
1837   —William A. Beck.
1838   —Singleton W. Allen.
1839-40—Charles W. Christian.
1841   —Thomas Johnston.
1842   —Joseph Blackwell.
1843-44—William Johnston.
1845-46—Singleton W. Allen.
1851-52—Robert Little.
1849-50—Thomas Johnston.
1851-52—Robert Liittle.
1853-54—William B. White.
1855-56—William M. McIntosh.
1857-58—William H. Adams.
1859-60—James M. Carter.
1861-72—Data missing.
1873-76—Robert Hester.
1880-81—William H. Mattox.
1882-83—Phillip W. Davis.
1883-93—Data missing.
1894-95—Dr. N. G. Long.
1900-01—Thomas M. Swift Sr.
1907-08—Peyton M. Hawes.
1914-15—A. S. J. Stovall.
1921-22—Charles Bond.
1928-29—A. S. J. Stovall.
1933-34—J. T. Sisk.

COUNTY OFFICIALS OF ELBERT COUNTY

CLERKS OF THE SUPERIOR COURT

1790-1806—Middleton Woods.
1807-10—William Woods.
1811-12—D. S. Booth.
1813-16—William Woods.
1817-18—D. S. Booth.
1819   —Gaines Thompson.
1820-22—William Bowen.
1823-33—Benajah Houston.
1834-57—Benjamin Smith.
1858-61—Moses Mills.
1862-65—James A. Andrews.
1866-68—E. B. Tate Jr.
1869-70—J. L. Deadwyler.
1871-72—Dr. B. A. Henry.
1873   —Johnson Brown.
1874   —James A. Andrews. Ordinary acting.
1875-82—T. A. Chandler.
1883-1900—R. M. Willis.
1901-36—W. A. Rucker, elected for term Jan. 31, 1937, to Jan. 1, 1940.

ORDINARIES OF ELBERT COUNTY

1790-1806—William Higginbotham.
1807-12—A. Pope.
1813-14—William Woods (serving in capacity of both Clerk and Ordinary).
1815-32—Job Weston.
1833-58—W. B. Nelms.
1859-68—William H. Edwards.
1869-72—E. B. Tate Jr.
1873-96—G. L. Almond.
1897-1908—James J. Burch.
1908   —H. A. Roebuck, acting.
1909-20—L. C. Edwards Sr.
1921-36—L. C. Edwards Jr., elected for term Jan. 1, 1937, to Jan. 1, 1940.

SHERIFFS OF ELBERT COUNTY

1790-99—Robert Middleton.
1800-01—Robert Cosby.
1802-03—Robert Middleton.
1804-05—Robert Cosby.
1806-09—James Woods.
1810-13—Thomas Jones.
1814-15—James Woods.
1816-20—Benjamin Cook.
1821-22—John Willis.
1823-24—Pressley Christian.
1825   —David Dobbs.
1826-29—Leroy Upshaw.
1830-31—Martin Deadwyler.
1832-36—William Johnston.
1837-38—William Downer.
1839-43—William Johnston.
1844-45—Henry R. Deadwyler.
1846-49—Eppy W. Roebuck.
1850-53—No data.
1854-55—Martin Bond.
1856-59—No data.
1860-68—T. M. Turner.
1869-78—W. H. H. Adams.
1879-90—D. B. Alexander.
1891-94—J. I. Chandler.
1895-98—John M. Brewer.
1899-1908—James McIntosh.
1909-16—S. N. Haley.
1917-18—J. C. Thornton Jr.
1919-26—Jack Haley.
1927-36—S. B. Seymour.
Elected for unexpired term of S. B. Seymour and for term ending Jan. 1, 1940—J. A. Stark.

TAX COMMISSIONERS OF ELBERT COUNTY

1929-32—A. F. Westmoreland.
1933-36—A. F. Westmoreland, died in office, 1935
1935-36—John Frank Harper.
Elected for term ending Jan. 1, 1940 John Frank Harper.

TAX COLLECTORS OF ELBERT COUNTY
(Incomplete)

1871-72—R. M. Willis.
1899-1900—T. S. Gaines.
1901-14—George Haslett.
1915-21—J. L. Strickland.
1922-24—Mel Strickland (died in office).
1924   —Sam Clark.
1925-28—James E. Brewer.
Office abolished, 1929.

TAX RECEIVERS OF ELBERT COUNTY
(Incomplete)

1812   —James O. Cosby.
1816   —William Haynes.
1871-72—Joseph Anderson.
1899-1904—H. A. Fortson.
1905-06—M. F. Adams.
1907-10—James E. Brewer.
1911-12—J. L. Strickland.
1913-28—W. J. Smith.
Office abolished, 1929.

SURVEYORS OF ELBERT COUNTY
(Incomplete)

1818-19—Adam Garr.
1822-23—Benjamin Cook.
1826-26—Robert Kennedy.
1832-45—David R. James.
1851-52—William C. Davis.
1855-56—Robert Dickerson.
1861-77—Washington Christian.
1878-1936—R W. Cleveland (died).
1935   —
1936   —A. W. Bussey.

COUNTY COMMISSIONERS OF ELBERT COUNTY

The first Commissioners, who served for a period of 11 years, were Richardson Hunt, Evan Ragland, James Tait and William Barnett. William Higginbotham also served with this body for a short period. No records are available showing the membership of this body from 1802 through 1895.

1896 —Thomas M. Swift Sr., Francis Gaines, J. C. Hudgens, J. W. McCalla, Thomas B. Crawford.
1897-98—J. W. McCalla, J. C. Hudgens, Francis Gaines, T. B. Crawford, T. O. Tabor Sr.
1899-1901—T. O. Tabor Sr., R. E. Adams, Z. A. Tate, D. J. Winn, I. H. Thornton
1902-06—E. B. Tate, W. M. Denny, A. P. Deadwyler.
1907-10—Zan Blackwell, Jesse Thomas, Thomas B. Crawford.
1911-12—James McIntosh, A. A. Seymour, J. E. Hammond.
1913-18—James McIntosh.
1919-20—E. Lucas Adams.
1921-22—L. H. Smith.
1923-24—James McIntosh.
1925-36—O. H. Smith.
Elected term ending 1940—S. B. Seymour.

COUNTY ATTORNEYS OF ELBERT COUNTY
(Incomplete)

1911-12—Z. B. Rogers.
1913-18—Z. B. Rogers.
1919-20—S. B. Swilling; John S. Haley succeeded by Clark Edwards Jr.
1921 John H. McIntosh.
1922 —Howard B. Payne.
1923-24—Z. B. Rogers.
1925-36—W. D. Tutt and Paul Brown. Tate Conyers.

CLERKS OF COUNTY COMMISSIONERS
(Incomplete)

1911-12—E A. Cason.
1913-18—E. A. Cason.
1919-20—Clark Edwards Jr.
1921-22—W. O. Smith.
1923-24—L. L. Stovall.
1925-36—R. L. Rice (resigned); Dozier J. Thornton.

JUSTICES OF THE PEACE, 1790-1805

Allen, William
Allen, Reuben
Alexander, John B.
Alston, James
Bell, James
Barnett, William
Banks, Ralph
Banks, James
Cook, Thomas
Cook, Francis
Carroll, John
Coleman, John
Caldwell, Harry
Cameron, James
Christian, Elijah
Cunningham, John
Daniel, Allen
Fortson, Thomas
Fergus, John
Goode, Edward

Gray, Hezekiah
Hodge, William
Haynes, Moses
Harper, John P.
Hightower, William
Hudson, J. O. A.
Hudson, Nathaniel
Hudson, David
Hunt, Richardson
Higginbotham, Samuel
Higginbotham, William
Jarrett, Archalus
Jeter, Barnett
Jones, Thomas
Lindsey, Reuben
Lewis, John
Leeper, Allen
Martin, James
McCleskey, James
McCune, William
McDonald, Hugh

McDonld, James
Moss, William
Nelson, Samuel
Pope, Leroy
Pace, Barnabas
Ragland, Evan
Rogers, James
Rucker, Joseph
Shields, Samuel
Scott, Thomas B.
Smith, B.
Staples, John
Stinchcomb, Absolom
Tait, James
Walker, Jeremiah
Woods, Middleton
Woods, Samuel
Wooten, Thomas
Worsham, Robert
Watkins, Robert

JUSTICES OF THE INFERIOR COURT
(Serving during good behavior)

Jeremiah Walker—December 15, 1790-February 18, 1791 (resigned).
William Barnett—December 15, 1790-October 21, 1797.
James Tait—December 15, 1790-October 21, 1797.
Evan Ragland—December 15, 1790-October 21, 1797.
Richardson Hunt—December 15, 1790-October 21, 1797.
Harry Caldwell—February 18, 1791-December 24, 1793.
Samuel Higginbotham—December 16, 1793-October 21, 1797.
William Barnett—October 21, 1797-February 14, 1799.
Richardson Hunt—October 21, 1797-February 14, 1799.
Ralph Banks—October 21, 1797-February 14, 1799.
Reuben Allen—October 21, 1797-February 14, 1799.
Reuben Higginbotham—February 14, 1799-1803 (died).
David Hudson—May 2, 1803-1804 (resigned).
John Johnson—December 4, 1804-1810 (resigned).
Barnett Jeter—December 4, 1804-1805 (resigned).
Walter Nunnelee—December 4, 1804-1811 (resigned).
Leroy Pope—December 3, 1804-1809 (resigned).
Hezekiah Gray—December 13, 1805-1806.
Archelus Jarrett—June 25, 1806-1812.
William Barnett—February 13, 1809-1811 (resigned).
William Fortson—December 7, 1810-October 28, 1813.
James Banks—December 13, 1811-October 28, 1813.
John Wilson—December 14, 1811-1812 (resigned).
William Woods—April 21, 1812-November 30, 1812; (elected November 30, 1812, declined to serve).
John Rucker—November 30, 1812-October 28, 1813.
John Upshaw Jr.—November 30, 1812-October 28, 1813.
John Johnston—June 8, 1813-October 28, 1813.
John Upshaw Jr.—October 28, 1813-November 1, 1817.
James Banks—October 28, 1813-1816; (resigned).
John Carroll—October 28, 1813-November 1, 1817-1820; (resigned).
Littleton Johnson—October 28, 1813-November 1, 1817; 1818-1820; (resigned).
James Woods—November 1, 1817-1821; (resigned).
Shelton White—April 6, 1818-1820; (resigned).
William Woods—August 26, 1818-October 26, 1821.
Robert Kennedy—July 12, 1820-October 26, 1821.
Archelus Jarrett—October 5, 1820-October 26, 1821.
Benjamin Brown—October 5, 1820-October 26, 1821.
Beverly Allen—March 22, 1821-October 26, 1821.
Beverly Allen—October 26, 1821-January 25, 1825.
Beverly Allen—January 25, 1825-1828.
William Woods—1821-1824; (died in office).
Joseph Blackwell—October 26, 1821-January 25, 1825.
Henry White—October 26, 1821-January 25, 1825.
Jeremiah Thornton—October 26, 1821-January 25, 1825.
James Morrison—January 20, 1825-1827; (died in office).
Henry White—January 15, 1825-January 13, 1829.
Benjamin Smith—January 23, 1827-January 13, 1829.
George Cook—March 28, 1828-1830; (removed from county).
Benjamin Smith—January 13, 1829-January 15, 1833.
Dionysius Oliver—January 13, 1829-January 15, 1833.
James Upshaw—1829-1830.
Gardner McGarity—1829-1831.
James Oliver—1830-1833.
Dillard Herndon—November 9, 1830-January 13, 1833.
William A. Beck—December, 1831-January, 1833.
Robert B. Christian—January 15, 1833-1836.

Isaac Almond—January 15, 1833-1835.
Thomas J. Heard—April 15, 1833-January 12, 1849-1861-1865.
Thomas Johnston—1836-1842.
Charles W. Christian—1837-1841.
William Jones—1837-1841.
Jeremiah S. Warren—1837-1841-1842-1845.
Robert Hester—1841-1843.
William J. Roebuck—1841-1845.
William Mills—1842-1845.
William H. Edwards—1843-1845.
Joseph Sewell—1845-1849.
William Mills—1845-1849.
Martin Deadwyler—1845-1846.
William M. Almond—1845-1847.
Samuel D. Blackwell—1846-1849.
George I. Barr—1847-1849.
Beverly Allen—1833-1837.
Joseph Sewell—1849-1853.
Eppy W. Bond—1849-1853.
Thomas R. Alexander—1849-1853.
Pressley B. Roberts—1849-1853.
Thomas F. Willis—1849-1853.
William J. Clark—1853-1857.
James Lofton—1853-1857.
James M. Willis—1853-1857.
Elijah H. Harper—1853.
William B. Bowen—1853-1855.
John Henry Jones—1853-1857.
Joseph T. Smith—1855-1857.
Joseph T. Smith—January 12, 1857-January 10, 1861; (entered Confederate service).
Anderson Craft—1857-1859.
John G. Deadwyler—1857-January, 1861.
Jasper Kennebrew—1857-1861.
Phillip A. Wilhite—1857-1861.
Peter Cleveland—March 14, 1859-January 10, 1861.
Samuel Ham—1861-1864.
Samuel D. Blackwell—1861-1865.
John A. Trenchard—1861-1865; (removed to Texas).
John T. Hulme—1861-1865.
Solomon Marcus—1864-1865; (removed from county).
Dozier Thornton—1865-1868.
Joseph T. Smith—January 23, 1865; (resigned and moved to Augusta; assumed after removal mother's maiden name of Armand),
John T. Hulme—1865-68.
James C. Harper—June 27, 1866-1868.

ELECTION RETURNS, 1902-1932
ELECTION OF JANUARY 5, 1902

Governor—J. M. Terrell, 1,067; DuPont Guerry, 605; J. M. Estill, 66.
State School Commissioner—W. D. Merritt, 873; Mark Johnson, 415; G. R. Glenn, 309.
Commissioner of Agriculture—O. B. Stevens, 1,569; R. T. Nesbit, 158.
Prison Commissioner—Thomas Eason, 1,270; Wiley Williams, 399.
Representatives (2)—L. H. O. Martin Jr., 1,187; Peyton M. Hawes, 1,125; W. B. Adams, 723; J. T. Colvard, 398.
Clerk of Superior Court—W. A. Rucker, **1,781.**
Sheriff—James McIntosh, 1,775.

Tax Receiver—H. A. Fortson, 744; M. F. Adams, 715; J. E. Snellings, 301.
Tax Collector—A. J. Mewborn, 345; John L. Wilhite, 339; T. R. Adams, 132; T. B. F. Willis, 75; J. W. Bond Sr., 57; B. B. Hutto, 57; J. E. Anderson, 25.
County Surveyor—R. W. Cleveland, 1,760.
Coroner—E. D. Clark, 987; W. T. Smith, 727.
County Commissioners (3)—E. B. Tate, 1,108; W. M. Denny, 1,061; A. P. Deadwyler, 865; J. C. Thomas, 845; E. W Bell, 458; I. H. Thornton, 451; R. E. Adams, 431.

DEMOCRATIC PRIMARY, APRIL 1904

Solicitor General Northern Circuit—I. C. Vanduzer, 1,091; David W. Meadow (elected), 478.
Representatives (2)—W. B. Adams, 1,483; L. H. O. Martin Jr., 1,479.
Ordinary—James J. Burch, 1,569.
Clerk of Superior Court—W. A. Rucker, 1,581.
Sheriff—James McIntosh, 1,576.
Tax Receiver—M. F. Adams, 588; J. E. Brewer, 435; W. N. Dye, 421; D. H. Warren, 114.
Tax Collector—George Haslett, 617; T. J. Carithers, 571; George M. Ward, 376.
County Surveyor—R. W. Cleveland, 795; Marcus A. Bell, 752.

DEMOCRATIC PRIMARY, MAY 6, 1906

State Senator—Peyton M. Hawes, 1,696.
Representatives (2)—L. H. O. Martin Jr., 1,169; W. B. Adamas, 1,120; Peter V. Rice Jr., 933.
Sheriff—James McIntosh, 1,753.
Clerk of Superior Court—W. A. Rucker, 1,753.
Tax Receiver—J. E. Brewer, 987; M. F. Adams, 739.
Tax Collector—George Haslett, 835; T. J. Carithers, 574; J. S. Tate, 329.
Treasurer—E. D. Clark, 1,750.
County Commissioners (3)—T. B. Crawford, Zan Blackwell, Jesse Thomas.

DEMOCRATIC PRIMARY, JUNE 4, 1908

Representatives (2)—A. S. J. Stovall, 1,485; Benjamin R. Cordell, 1,330; E. B. Stark, 1,034.
Sheriff—S. N. Haley, 964; Henry H. Brown, 959.
Tax Receiver—J. E. Brewer, 1,048; D. H. Warren, 858.
Tax Collector—George Haslett, 847; T. J. Carithers, 703; G. M. Ward, 362.
Treasurer—A. E. Hammond.

DEMOCRATIC PRIMARY, MAY 5, 1910

Clerk of Superior Court—W. A. Rucker, 2,003.
Sheriff—S. N. Haley, 929; Henry H. Brown, 746; George T. Maxwell, 218; A. P. Smith, 88.
Tax Receiver—J. L. Strickland, 640; W. J. Smith, 464; J. E. Brewer, 248; D. H. Warren, 303; M. A. Bell, 179; J. S. Tate, 63; J. L. Bryan, 46.
Tax Collector—George Haslett, 1,009; T. J. Carithers, 978.
County Commissioners (3)—A. A. Seymour, 1,182; James McIntosh, 1,077; J. E. Hammond, 995; T. B. Crawford, 940; E. B. Tate, 524; Jesse Thomas, 643; E. W. Bell, 370; J. E. Foster, 191.
County School Commissioner—Thomas J. Cleveland, 1,227; Peter V. Rice Jr., 764.
Treasurer—J. A. Teasley.
Coroner—George B. Mize.

DEMOCRATIC PRIMARY, 1912

Ordinary—L. C. Edwards, 1,773.
Clerk of Superior Court—W. A. Rucker, 1,775.
Sheriff—S. N. Haley, 1,103; W. W. Vaughan, 658.
Tax Receiver—W. J. Smith, 919; J. L. Strickland, 436; J. E. Brewer, 415.
Tax Collector—George Haslett, 947; T. J. Carithers, 818.
Coroner—George B. Mize, 829; S. Parham, 547; J. L. Clark, 375.

DEMOCRATIC PRIMARY, 1914

Sheriff—S. N. Haley, 1,391; W. W. Vaughan, 575.
Clerk of Superior Court—W. A. Rucker, 1,977.
Tax Receiver—W. J. Smith, 1,400; Vaughan, 205; Teasley, 364.
Tax Collector—George Haslett, 613; W. G. B. Jones, 498; T. J. Carithers, 397; G. M. Ward, 270.
County Commissioner (1)—James McIntosh, 716; Thomas M. Swift Sr., 679; T. B. Crawford, 569.
Treasurer—H. A. Denny.
County Surveyor—R. W. Cleveland.
Coroner—S. B. Seymour.

DEMOCRATIC PRIMARY, MAY 3, 1916

Ordinary—L. C. Edwards, 2,203.
Clerk of Superior Court—W. A. Rucker, 1,820; C. E. Earl, 383.
Sheriff—S. N. Haley, 1,337; W. H. Irvin, 870.
County Commissioner (two highest run over)—Thomas M. Swift Sr., 1,085; James McIntosh, 991; J. E. Hammond, 105.
County Commissioner (run over)—James McIntosh, 1,158; Thomas M. Swift, 1,142.
Tax Receiver—W. J. Smith, 1,149; W. M. Grogan, 577; John Mann, 284; L. A. Harper, 184.
Tax Collector (two highest run over)—J. L. Strickland, 550; W. G. B. Jones, 369; E. H. Ward, 351; W. H. Heard, 309; R. F. Moore, 215; T. J. Carithers, 211; George Haslett, 113; T. J. McLanahan, 75.
Tax Collector (run over)—J. L. Strickland, 1,313; W. G. B. Jones, 1,000.
Treasurer—T. E. Fleming.
Coroner—J. Luther Seymour.

DEMOCRATIC PRIMARY, SEPTEMBER 11, 1918

Representatives (2)—Z. B. Rogers, 781; W. J. Jones Sr., 613; M. P. Deadwyler, 659; Dr. T. W. Bond, 644; W. T. Brownlee, 536.
County Commissioner—E. L. Adams, 904; J. Tom Ginn, 734.

DEMOCRATIC PRIMARY, APRIL 20, 1920

Representatives—W. T. Brownlee, Thomas M. Swift Sr.
County Commissioner—Leverette H. Smith, 791; J. J. Adams, 623; Claud Crawford, 551.
Tax Collector—J. L. Strickland, 773; W. G. B. Jones, 436. (Strickland died in office and was succeeded by his son, Mel Strickland, who likewise died in office); Tinsley J. Hulme, 746.
Tax Receiver—W. J. Smith, 1,456; J. L. Seymour, 484.
Treasurer—B. B. Bell, 1,069; W. J. Christian, 861.

DEMOCRATIC PRIMARY, SEPTEMBER 13, 1922

Representatives (2)—T. J. Hulme, 1,799; A. S. J. Stovall, 1,134; J. T. Sisk, 901; W. T. Brownlee, 760.
County Commissioner—James McIntosh, 1,160; Leverette H. Smith, 1,139.

DEMOCRATIC PRIMARY, MARCH 19, 1924

County Commissioner—O. H. Smith, 1,615; James McIntosh, 1,135.
Clerk of Superior Court—W. A. Rucker.
Ordinary—Clark Edwards Jr.
Coroner—E. V. Clark.
County School Commissioner—Miss Mary Hansard, 1,378; T. J. Cleveland, 1,352.
Tax Collector (Long Term)—J. E. Brewer, 2,514 (unopposed).
Tax Collector (Short Term to succeed Mel Strickland, deceased)—Sam Clark, 771; Rachel Strickland, 597; J. Harry Grogan, 437; W. G. B. Jones, 353; Claud Stovall, 197; Guy M. Sanders, 84; K. E. Rucker, 116.

DEMOCRATIC PRIMARY, SEPTEMBER 8, 1926

State Senator—A. S. J. Stovall, 867; Z. B. Rogers, 550; J. T. Sisk, 786.
Representatives—A. S. Hawes, 1,392; T. J. Hewell, 1,154; W. T. Brownlee, 892; J. E. Hammond, 790.
County Commissioner—O. H. Smith, 2,252 (unopposed).

DEMOCRATIC PRIMARY, MARCH 7, 1928

Ordinary—Clark Edwards (unopposed).
Clerk of Superior Court—W. A. Rucker (unopposed).
County Commissioner—O. H. Smith (unopposed).
County School Commissioner—T. J. Cleveland, 1,183; Miss Mary Hansard, 1,160.
Tax Commissioner—A. F. Westmoreland, 871; E. J. Ward, 637; J. E. Brewer, 393; Harold Thornton, 352.
Sheriff—S. B. Seymour, 1,552; D. C. Downer, 799.
Treasurer—M. A. Bell (unopposed), 2,344.
Coroner—E. V. Clark, 1,079; T. J. Hill, 870; D. Davis, 154.
County Surveyor—R. W. Cleveland (unopposed), 2,352.

DEMOCRATIC PRIMARY, SEPTEMBER 12, 1928

Representatives (2)—H. A. Adams, 1,093; T. J. Hewell, 1,049; A. S. Hawes, 1,002.

DEMOCRATIC PRIMARY, SEPTEMBER 10, 1930

United States Senator—W. J. Harris, 1,400; John M. Slaton, 499.
Governor—R. B. Russell Jr., 1,022; John N. Holder, 433; George Carswell, 187; E. D. Rivers, 119; James A. Perry, 54.
Secretary of State—Nat. H. Ballard, 380; D. T. Bowers, 381; J. J. Flynt, 227; C. N. Guess, 180; A. H. Henslee, 46; Louis Moore, 73; J. M. Pitner, 362; John Wilson, 148.
Attorney General—Dorsey Davis, 808; George M. Napier, 1,054.
State Treasurer—W. J. Speer, 1,358; L. P. Patillo, 486.
Comptroller General—B. M. Bullard, 511; E. T. Gentry, 92; W. B. Harrison, 556; Homer C. Parker, 674.
Commissioner of Agriculture—J. J. Brown, 1,105; Eugene Talmadge, 791.
Commissioner of Labor—Hal M. Stanley, 1,313; F. M. Morgan, 534.
State Superintendent of Schools—M. L. Duggan, 1,030; M. D. Collins, 849.
Pension Commissioner—John J. Hunt, 1,462; R. deT. Lawrence, 379.
Prison Commissioner—Hill C. Tuggle, 1,013; G. A. Johns, 841.
Public Service Commissioner—Calvin W. Parker, 1,323; Guy O. Stone, 528.
Supreme Court Justice—S. C. Atkinson, 1,264; Robert B. Blackburn, 574.
Judge Court of Appeals—Nash R. Broyles, 1,070; Joe Quillian, 781.
State Senator—J. O. M. Smith, 1,043; G. P. Whitworth, 787.
Representatives (2)—J. T. Sisk, 1,056; Peyton S. Hawes, 902; A. S. J. Stovall, 698; T. J. Hewell, 451.
County Commissioner—O. H. Smith, 1,874; E. J. Ward, 1,477.

County School Superintendent—Mary Hansard, 890; A. W. Bussey, 839; Clark Tate, 604.
Tax Commissioner—A. F. Westmoreland, 2,656; J. G. Ginn, 669.
Clerk of the Superior Court—W. A. Rucker, 2,279; Charles N. Bond, 1,004.
Treasurer—Alex Webb, 1,040; R. M. Dickerson, 502; James H. Gaines, 420; Mrs. Mary Smith, 404; Mrs. M. A. Bell, 283; J. W. Anderson, 253; J. B. Adams, 177; S. C. Dowdy, 103.

ELBERTON POSTMASTERS

Middleton Woods—Oct. 1, 1795.
James Alston—Oct. 1, 1801.
William Woods—Jan. 1, 1805.
George Inskeep—Oct. 24, 1820.
Benajah Houston—Aug. 20, 1829.
J. W. Carter—March 13, 1830.
Zachariah Smith—March 16, 1835.
James Brawner—Dec. 21, 1848.
J. M. Wyche—Jan. 26, 1852.
William Teasley—July 30, 1852.
J. M. Wyche—July 3, 1854.
M. E. Mills—Jan. 31, 1857.
A. L. Vail—Dec. 8, 1865.
Thomas M. Swift—April 17, 1871.
A. E. Hunter—March 12, 1873.
J. H. Duncan—April 17, 1876.
D. M. Burnes—Nov. 15, 1881.
Harry K. Gairdner—July 13, 1885.
Ella M. Henry—June 12, 1889.
John T. Heard—May 27, 1893.
Ella M. Henry—July 27, 1897.
Carroll M. Heard—April 4, 1902.
Thomas A. Jones—Aug. 16, 1904.
Charles W. Parker—Oct. 23, 1906.
L. C. Brown—Feb. 24, 1914.
Nick Oglesby
J. S. Lunsford
Mrs. Norma Wright Hawes—1934-39.

LAWYERS OF ELBERT COUNTY

1790-1800—Stephen Heard, Samuel Blackburn, William I. Hobby, Fortunatus Cosby, Peter Lawrence Van Alan, Robert Walker, Charles Tait, George Mathews, Thomas Griffin, Matthew McAllister.

1801-1810—Shaler Hillyer, Jones, Martin, Shackelford, Frank, Naylor.

1811-1820—John D. Bibb, George Cook, Jeptha V. Harris, Archibald Pope, James Smith, Stephen W. Harris, James Cook, John A. Heard, William H. Underwood, R. W. Cook, John Watkins, Nunnelee, Campbell, Brewer, Posey.

1821-1830—Jesse M. Davis, Thomas J. Heards, Wilhite, Alston, Groves, Burch.

1831-1840—Young L. G. Harris (removed to Athens), Hammond, Robert McMillan (removed to Clarkesville).

1841-1850—William M. McIntosh, Robert Hester.

1851-1860—J. M. Hutcherson, L. A. Nelms, L. M. Pegg, T. J. Bowers, Robert M. Heard, Amos T. Ackerman, McAlpin A. Arnold, B. H. Lofton.

1861-1870—John C. Burch, Emory P. Edwards, James Lofton, Colonel Davant, W. T. Vanduzer, H. A. Roebuck, Marcus A. Knight (removed to Texas), John A. Trenchard, James J. Burch.

1871-1880—William M. McIntosh Jr., John P. Shannon, Tinsley W. Rucker (removed to Athens), Joseph N. Worley, George C. Grogan, W. D. Tutt Sr.

1881-1890—Thomas Carlton (removed to Oklahoma), Phillip W. Davis Sr., (removed to Lexington, Ga.).

1891-1900—Thomas J. Brown, H. J. Brewer, C. P. Harris, P. P. Proffit, Z. B. Rogers, I. C. Vanduzer, Samuel L. Olive (removed to Atlanta), W. D. Tutt Jr.

1901-1910—Worley A. Nall (removed to Florida), J. T. Sisk.

1911-1920—H. B. Payne, R. J. Ward (removed to Atlanta), T. D. Bennett (removed to Atlanta), George Lowery Seymour, John Andy Smith (removed to Talbotton), Raymonde Stapleton, Sam B. Swilling, John S. Haley (removed to Daytona, Fla.), John H. McIntosh, Clark Edwards Jr., Scott Berryman (removed to Florida).

1921-1930—Worley E. Hall, Paul Brown, Comers G. Moore (removed to South Carolina), Peyton S. Hawes, Joseph McGinty, Charles Emory Smith (returned to Metter, Ga.), Charles McLanahan.
1931-1936—Tate Conyers.
The foregoing dates indicate the first appearance of record of the persons listed thereunder. In many instances certain of the lawyers have practiced in other localities before settling in Elbert County: Paul Brown in Lexington, Sam B. Swilling in Royston, Comers G. Moore in Danielsville, John S. Haley in Canon, Charles Emory Smith in Athens, W. D. Tutt in Augusta and Thomson.

PARTIAL LIST OF NATIVE BORN MINISTERS OF ELBERT COUNTY

Baptist—Benjamin Thornton Jr., John Webb, Vandiver Herndon, George Hulme, Benjamin Goss, Isham H. Goss, William R. Goss, Horatio J. Goss Jr., E. Shackleford, James Hales, Isaac Suttles, James Theodore Spaulding, John D. Adams, Joe Deadwyler, Tinsley, Thomas J. Rucker.
Methodist—James O. Andrew, Osgood Grogan, O. E. Smith, J. N. Wall, Tinsley R. Adams, Z. C. Hayes Jr.
Presbyterian—George Wilcox.

SECTION OF GENEALOGY

KEY

B.—Born.
D.—Died.
M.—Married.
R.S.—Revolutionary Soldier.
C.S.—Confederate Soldier.
S.W.W.—Soldier World War.

ABSTRACT OF EIGHTY EARLY DEEDS FROM ORIGINAL INSTRUMENTS

Nov. 7, 1787—John Liddell Dixon of town of Augusta, Georgia, to John Simpson, 468 acres of land on waters of Cedar Creek. Consideration: 100 pounds lawful money of Georgia. Witnesses: T. McCall, John King. Recorded in Book "B," Folio 99, April 15, 1794.

Jan. 15, 1790—David McCleskey and Mary, his wife, to James McCleskey, 300 acres on Falling Creek, being an original grant to David McCleskey made Feb. 1, 1788. Consideration: 20 pounds sterling. Witness: John Fergus, Justice of the Peace. Recorded in Book "D," Folio 37, Feb. 24, 1797.

Nov. 16, 1790—Thomas Wilmot to Abenezer Buckhanan, 200 acres on Savannah River, including one island. Consideration: 5 pounds sterling. Witness: John Gilleylen. Recorded in Book "D," Folio 35, Feb. 14, 1797.

Feb. 7, 1791—Horatio Marbury of Columbia County, to Peter Carnes of Richmond County, 800 acres on south fork of Cold Water Creek, adjoining Middleton Woods, Hugh McDonald, Mark Thornton and Teasley. Consideration: 200 pounds specie. Witnesses: B. Porter and Elihu Lymon. Recorded in Book "D," Folio 27, Jan. 16, 1797.

Dec. 6, 1792—Thomas Hightower and Sarah, his wife, to Robert Huddleston, all of Elbert County, part of a 550 acre tract of land containing 275 acres, more or less, along the banks of Broad River. Granted to said Hightower, Jar. 20, 1786. Consideration: 125 pounds sterling. Witnesses: James Bell, J. P., Thomas Oliver. Recorded in Book "A," Folio 153, May 29, 1793.

Jan. 29, 1793—William Barnett, James Tait, Evan Ragland and R. Hunt, Commissioners, to Thomas Carter of Elbert County, Lot No. 3 at the court house (Elberton). Consideration: 8 pounds and 5 shillings. Witnesses: John Fergus, J. P., J. M. Coleman. Recorded in Book "D," Folio 71, June 24, 1797.

April 25, 1793—John Herndon to John Calhoun, both of 96th District, South Carolina, 1,000 acres on Pickens Creek, granted to Absolom Jackson, on Feb. 25, 1786. Consideration: 500 pounds sterling. Witnesses: James Spivey, Patrick Forbes and John Calhoun. Recorded in Book "B," Folio 16, July 18, 1793.

Sept. 29, 1794—William Allen of Elbert County, to John Waller of Hancock County, Georgia, Lot No. 30 in the town of Petersburg. Consideration. 60 pounds lawful Georgia money. Witnesses: Stephen Heard, Thomas Thornton, William Moss, J. P. Recorded in Book "D," Folio 135, Dec. 30, 1797.

Sept. 15, 1794—Samuel Porter of Abbeville County, South Carolina, to Stephen Heard of Elbert County, Georgia, 200 acres, bounded north by Thomas Colbert and on waters of Beaverdam Creek. Consideration: 50 pounds lawful money of South Carolina. Witnesses: Samuel Wimbish, Wm. Spear, Joseph Turnbull. Recorded in Book "D," Folio 134, Deec. 30, 1797.

Oct. 8, 1794—Thomas Colbert and Ann, his wife, to Philpot Colbert, all of Elbert County, 100 acres on Van's Creek, beginning at the original line of Moses Trimble and adjoining Roland Ware. Consideration: 60 pounds. Witnesses: Nicodemus Colbert, Thomas Wooten, J. P. Recorded in Book "D," Folio 117, Dec. 16, 1797.

Jan. 4, 1794—William Johnson Offutt of Columbia County, to Thomas Keys of Elbert County, 500 acres adjoining Reuben Allen on northeast and vacant land on all other sides. Consideration: 60 pounds. Witnesses: Wm. Goode, J. P., Wm. I. Hobby, Edw. Goode. Recorded in Book "D," Folio 125, Dec. 20, 1797.

Jan. 1, 1794—John Darden of Wilkes County, to Basil Human of Elbert County, 370 acres on Holly Creek waters of Broad River. Consideration: 50 pounds. Witnesses: Edw. Goode, J. P., Ezekiel Wells, Basil Human. Recorded in Book "D," Folio 65, May 27, 1797.

March 4, 1794—Absolom Jorden to John Jorden, bill of sale to six slaves, carrying a consideration of 200 pounds, and witnessed by River Jorden, Jean Jorden, Wm. Spears. Recorded in Book "D," Folio 29, Jan. 21, 1797.

Feb. 25, 1795—John Griffith and Ann, his wife, of Oglethorpe County, to Hardin Evins of Elbert County, 17 acres on Fork Creek adjoining James Griffith. Consideration: 100 pounds sterling. Witnesses: James Griffith, Wm. Head, J. P. Recorded in Book "D," Folio ?, Dec. 20, 1797.

Oct. 22, 1795—Gerrard Walthall Sr., to John J. Creigh, a negro boy named Daniel. Consideration: love and affection. John J. Creigh mentioned as grandson. Witnesses: Edward Walthall, Aaron Jones. Recorded in Book "D," Folio (?), Dec. 20, 1799.

Nov. 3, 1795—Joseph Bell and Elizabeth, his wife, to Henry Mosley, all of Elbert County, 279 acres of land on Falling Creek, being a part of a 579 acre tract granted to George Martin, July 20, 1786. Consideration: 200 pounds sterling. Witnesses: James Bell, J. P., David Porterfield. Recorded in Book "D," Folio 79, July 19, 1797.

May 4, 1795—H. Heard, Tax Collector of Greene County, Georgia, to Ruth and Rosannah Kain of Elbert County, 250 acres on Broad River, adjoining B. Pace and others. Consideration: 2 pounds and 10 shillings. Witnesses: Richard Kain, John Coffee. Recorded in Book "D," Folio 42, March 18, 1797. (In reality a tax deed to the property of William Kain).

April 6, 1795—Isham Thompson and Elizabeth Williams, his wife, to Robert L. Tait, all of Elbert County, 44 acres on Coodies Creek, adjoining the property of Edward Walthall and Zimri Tait. Consideration: 30 pounds. Witnesses: L. B. Thompson, Evan Ragland. Recorded in Book "D," Folio 51, April 5, 1797.

Aug. 20, 1795—Thomas Burk to Michael Saylors, both of Elbert County, 200 acres on Dove's Creek. Consideration: 50 pounds. Witnesses: Thomas B. Scott, J. P., Charles S. Cosby. Recorded in Book "D," Folio 43, March 11, 1797.

June 22, 1795—John Walton and Nancy, his wife, to Edward Clark, all of Elbert County, 100 acres. Consideration: 100 pounds sterling. Witnesses:

Robert Mosley, M. Walker. Recorded in Book "D," Folio 57, April 18, 1797.

June 17, 1796—Samuel Sewell, Attorney-in-Fact for David Wells, to Andrew Brown, both of Elbert County, a tract of land granted to David Wells, Feb. 24, 1785, on waters of Cedar Creek. Consideration: $200. Witnesses: Elias Baker, Benjamin Baker, Henry Sewell. Recorded in Book "D," Folio 102, Oct. 18, 1797.

Dec. 27, 1796—Edward Walthall and Nancy, his wife, to Zimri Tait, all of Elbert County, 106 acres on Coodies Creek, adjoining Zimri Tait, Hutson Tait and James Tait. Consideration: 90 pounds. Witnesses: Benjamin Cook, Evans Ragland, J. P. Recorded in Book "D," Folio 78, July 19, 1797.

May 23, 1796—William Alexander to John McGowen, both of Elbert County, tract of land on Cold Water Creek. Consideration: 50 pounds. Witness: J. Cunningham, J. P. Recorded in Book "D," Folio 59, April 19, 1797.

Aug. 29, 1796—Thomas Commander Russell of Lincoln County, to Wells Thompson of Elbert County, Lot No. 22 in the town of Petersburg, bounded east by Front Street, west by Commons or Broad Street, south by Cross Street, North by Lot No. 24. Consideration: $125.00. Witnesses: John Oliver, William Moore. Recorded in Book "D," Folio 48, April 4, 1797.

Jan. 10, 1796—John Heard Jr., and Elizabeth, his wife, of Wilkes County, to George Darden of Elbert County, 150 acres on south side of Beaverdam Creek, adjoining George Darden's land. Consideration: 150 pounds sterling. Witnesses: Buckner Darden, Robert L. Tait, Jesse Heard, J. P. (Wilkes County). Recorded in Book 'D," Folio 49, April 5, 1797.

May 13, 1796—Jincey Brown of Richmond County, to Joseph Glenn of Elbert County, 400 acres on Brown River, known as William Brown survey. Consideration: 85 pounds sterling. Witnesses: Anthony Hanie, Edwin Glenn. Recorded in Book "D," Folio 52, April 18, 1797.

April 5, 1796—Evan Ragland to James Coleman, both of Elbert County. Lot No. 18 on Front Street in the town of Petersburg. Consideration: 11 pounds sterling. Witnesses: Joseph Groves, J. M. Coleman. Recorded in Book "C," Folio 125, July 19, 1796.

Aug. 3, 1796—Richard Easter and Mary, his wife, to John Oliver, all of Elbert County, 300 acres on Savannah River and being part of tract granted to Julious Howard. Consideration: 85 pounds. Witnesses: Evan Ragland Jr., Charles Scott Cosby, Asa Thompson. Recorded in Book "D," Folio 45, April 4, 1797.

Dec. 3, 1796—Elizabeth Cunningham of Elbert County, to Thomas Oglesby of Buckingham County, Virginia, 250 acres on Pennington's Fork of Dove's Creek, originally granted to Joshua Perkins, April 8, 1785. Consideration: 190 pounds sterling. Witnesses: R. Hunt, J.P., Allen Jones. Recorded in Book "D," Folio 16, Dec. 4, 1796.

Oct. 17, 1797—Sally S. Bibb, Adm. of estate of William Bibb, to Richardson Hunt, all of Elbert County, 500 acres on north fork of Beaverdam Creek. Consideration: 50 pounds sterling. Witnesses: Thos. B. Scott, J. P., James Scott. Recorded in Book "D," Folio 138, Jan. 5, 1798.

Dec. 27, 1797—Robert Crockett, Adm. of the estate of Samuel Crockett of York County, South Carolina, to Stephen Heard of Elbert County, 200 acres on Savannah River, bounded north by Bud's Island and east by river. Consideration: 200 pounds sterling. Witnesses: William Sharp, Thomas Thornton, William Allen, J. P. Recorded in Book "D," Folio 127, Dec. 30, 1797.

Sept. 6, 1797—Benjamin Fannin and Arbuler, his wife, to William S. Burch, all of Elbert County, 70 acres adjoining William Brown, William S. Burch, and the courthouse road. Consideration: 30 pounds sterling. Witnesses: M. Woods, Rn. Lindsey, J. P. Recorded in Book "D," Folio 87, Sept. 6, 1797.

June 17, 1797—Ezekiel Cloud to Daniel Orr, both of Elbert County, 105 acres on the waters of South River. Consideration: $100. Witnesses: James Walker, William Preston Elliott. Acknowledged before Samuel Nelson, J. P. Recorded in Book "D," Folio 86, Sept. 4, 1797.

July 10, 1797—Thomas Thornton and Molly, his wife, to William Arnold, all of Elbert County, 123 acres on Beaverdam Creek, adjoining Reuben Allen. Consideration: 71 pounds, 10 shillings. Witness: William Allen, J. P. Recorded in Book "D," Folio 84, August 26, 1797.

Aug. 14, 1797—Joseph Wilson of Elbert County, to Ferdinand Phinizy of Oglethorpe County, Georgia, 272 acres, bounded by Human, Lovingood, George Watts, Archelus Walker and Patrick Mitchell: Consideration: $15. Witness: John Cunningham, J. P. Recorded in Book "D," Folio 76, August 15, 1797.

May 29, 1797—John M. Whitney and Bridget, his wife, to Joseph Long, all of Elbert County, 50 acres adjoining Burch. Consideration: $20. Witness: M. Woods, J. P. Recorded in Book "D," Folio 66, May 29, 1797.

May 10, 1797—David Nelms and Unity, his wife, to Thomas Price, all of Elbert County, 100 acres on the south side of the north fork of Beaverdam Creek, adjoining Clabourne Sandridge, Nicholass Tuttle and John Greenwood. Consideration: 100 pounds. Witness: Wm. Higginbotham, J. P. Recorded in Book "D," Folio 83, August 12, 1797.

May 7, 1797—Mark Thornton and Mary, his wife, of Elbert County, to Hiram Gaines Jr., of Fluvana County, Virginia, a parcel of land on Coldwater Creek, bounded west by Mark Thornton, south by Charles McDonald, east by William Gaines, north by John Teasley. Consideration: 50 pounds. Witnesses: Wm. Gaines, John Cunningham, J. P. Recorded in Book "D," Folio 63, May 27, 1797.

Jan. 14, 1797—Richard Easter and Mary, his wife, to Littleberry and Whitfield Wilson, all of Elbert County, Lot No. 34 on the west side of Front Street in the town of Petersburg. Consideration: $100. Witnesses: James Bell, J. P., Jos. Bukley. Recorded in Book "D," Folio 31, Jan. 27, 1797.

March 1, 1797—Christopher Starr and Mary, his wife, to Thomas Connolley, all of Elbert County, 250 acres on Broad River. Consideration: 75 pounds. Witnesses: Wm. Brawner, M. Woods, J. P. Recorded in Book "D," Folio 42, March 1, 1797.

Jan. 30, 1797—John Heard and Elizabeth, his wife, of Wilkes County, Georgia, to James Alston Sr., of Elbert County, 300 acres of land granted to Barnard Heard, Oct. 26, 1784, on Beaverdam Creek. Consideration: $2,000. Witnesses: Ledfind Parrott, Nathl. Alson, Jno. Abernathee. Recorded in Book "D," Folio 55, April 18, 1797.

March 17, 1797—Thomas B. Scott and Betsy, his wife, to William Hall, all of Elbert County, 200 acres on Dove's Creek adjoining Elijah Strong and Lindsey Shoemaker. Consideration: 50 pounds. Witness: John Andrew. Recorded in Book "O," Folio 112, Nov. 6, 1797.

Oct. 12, 1797—Jeremiah Cleveland to Jacob Cleveland, both of Elbert County, all right, title and interest in the estate of Jacob Cleveland Sr. Consideration: $37. Witnesses: Edmond Harper, William Kidd. Recorded in Book "D," Folio 112, Nov. 6, 1797.

March 13, 1798—Jeptha Ruch of Franklin County, Georgia, to James Highsmith of Elbert County, 33 acres on both sides of Big Sedar Creek, bounded by Thomas Hookar and James Freeman. Consideration: $50. Witnesses: James Terrell, John Swift. Recorded in Book "N," Folio 210, October 21, 1811.

March 3, 1798—John Oliver and Frances, his wife, to Robert Martin Jr., all of the town of Petersburg, Elbert County, Lot No. 68 on west side of Broad Street in said town. Consideration: $130. Witnesses: Jn. Coleman, J. P., Thos. Douglass. Recorded in Book "E," Folio 18, March 5, 1798.

April 18, 1798—Archibald Burton and James Adams, Admrs. of estate of David Adams, to Thomas Burton, all of the County of Elbert, 270 acres on Warhatch Creek. Consideration: $600. Witness: Wm. Higginbotham, J. P. Recorded in Book "E," Folio 33, April 18, 1798.

Jan. 3, 1798—Middleton Woods and Martha, his wife, to James Mann, all of Elbert County, 327 acres on Van's Creek, bounded by John White, Colson, Patterson and McKeen. Consideration: $500. Witness: John P. Harper, J. P. Recorded in Book "E," Folio 12, Feb. 8, 1798.

Nov. 6, 1798—Howell Jarrett, Sheriff of Wilkes County, Georgia, to Stephen Heard of Elbert County, 150 acres. Consideration: $405. Witnesses: Hubbard Harris, M. Lipham. Recorded Jan. 5, 1801, in Book "E," Folio 26.

May 25, 1798—Thomas Cook and Elizabeth, his wife, to Peter Wyche, all of Elbert County, 250 acres on Falling and Warhatch Creeks. Consideration: 50 pounds sterling. Witnesses: Rn. Lindsay, J. P., Elisha Cook. Recorded in Book "E," Folio 57, June 29, 1798.

April 17, 1798—William Arnold and Susannah, his wife, to Henry Gaines, all of Elbert County, 100 acres on Van's Creek. Consideration: 50 pounds sterling. Witnesses: William Akin, Reuben Allen, J. P. Recorded in Book "E," Folio 38, April 18, 1798.

May 29, 1799—Edward Woolridge and Sally, his wife, of Greenville County, South Carolina, to Sarah Woolridge of Elbert County, 100 acres bounded northwest by Arnold's land, northeast by Hudson's land. Consideration: $70. Witness: Nathl. Hudson, J. P. Recorded in Book "E," Folio 97, July 26, 1801.

Dec. 31, 1799—John McGowen and Hannah, his wife, to Thomas Jones, all of Elbert County, two lots of one-half acre each on the east side of Main Street in the town of Alexandria. Consideration: $70. Witnesses: Joseph Chipman, John Cunningham, J. P. Recorded in Book "E," Folio 21, Jan. 28, 1801.

Nov. 15, 1799—John S. Head and Barbary, his wife, to John Ford, all of Elbert County, 100 acres on Beaverdam Creek, adjoining Beverly and Tate. Consideration: $20. Witnesses: Dozier Thornton, Elizabeth Thornton. Recorded in Book "E," Folio 33, Feb. 3, 1801.

Jan. 2, 1800—Thomas Coleman and Edna, his wife, to John Coleman and Memorable Walker, all of Elbert County, 380 acres bounded south by George Turman, west by William Hatcher, north by Robert Turman and east by Julius Howard. Consideration: $2,000. Witnesses: Dudley Brooks, Lewis Mathews, Leroy Pope, J. P. Recorded in Book "E," Folio 11, Jan. 11, 1801.

Feb. 7, 1800—William Sharp and Arberrilar, his wife, of Oglethorpe County, Georgia, to Jacob Strickland of Elbert County, 200 acres on south fork of Broad River. Consideration: $342. Witness: Alex Gordon, J. P. Recorded in Book "F," Folio 37, Feb. 7, 1801.

May 23, 1800—Ambrose Gordon, U. S. Marshall for the District of Georgia, to James Holliday of Petersburg, in Elbert County, Lot No. 34 as the property of Littleberry & Whitfield Wilson. Consideration: $1,050. Witnesses: Geo. Watkins, Newel Walton, Isaac Herbert, City Counselor of Augusta. Recorded in Book "F," Folio 24, Feb. 5, 1801.

Nov. 12, 1800—William T. Cook and Frances, his wife, to William Whaley, all of Elbert County, 10 acres on Dove's Creek. Consideration: $20. Witnesses: R. Hunt, J. P. Stinson Bryant. Recorded in Book "E," Folio 15, Jan 5, 1801.

Dec. 18, 1800—Reuben Allen and Elizabeth, his wife, of Elbert County, to Joseph Clarke of Orange County, Virginia, 450 acres adjoining John Pollard, John Beck, William Arnold and Sally S. Bibb. Consideration: $3,000. Witnesses: R. Hunt, J. I. C., Nathaniel Allen, John Beck. Recorded in Book "E," Folio 7, Dec. 20, 1800.

Dec. 29, 1800—George Rucker and Catherine, his wife, of Elbert County, to James Freeman of Elbert County, 200 acres originally granted to John Cunningham on Cold Water Creek. Consideration: $2,000. Witnesses: John Martin, Saml. Hollingsworth. Recorded in Book "F," Folio 35, Feb. 3, 1801.

Jan. 24, 1801—James Butler and Sally, his wife, to John Rich, all of Elbert County, 69 acres. Consideration: $160. Witness: Wm. Hightower, J. P. Recorded in Book "F," Folio 39, Feb. 9, 1801.

Jan. 30, 1801—John Andrew of Elbert County, to George Ward of the State of Deleware, 300 acres originally granted to Joel Chandler, bounded by lands of Jesse White, Joe Brawner and William Robins and on the waters of Falling Creek, and also 300 acres originally granted to Bazil

Brawner and bounded by lands of Archy Jarrett, Henry Brawner and William Suttles. Consideration: $3,730. Witnesses: Nathl. Cooke, Wm. Pope. Recorded in Book "F," Folio 34, Feb. 19, 1801.

Jan. 21, 1801—William Arnold to Littleton Johnston, both of Elbert County, 18 acres on Beaverdam Creek adjoining Thomas Thornton on the west. Consideration: $36. Witnesses: John S. Head, Leroy Pope, J. P. Recorded in Book "F," Folio 39, Feb. 9, 1801.

Dec. 2, 1802—Mallichi Culpepper and Elizabeth, his wife, to Jos. Pulliam, 100 acres on Beaverdam Creek, adjoining Burkit Green, Blackwell, Darden and Larkin Higgason. Consideration: $300. Witnesses: William Lane. Thomas Lane. Recorded in Book "H," Folio 68, Dec. 15, 1802.

Dec. 2, 1802—Silvanus Stokes to Thomas Allen, both of Elbert County, 118 acres on Beaverdam Creek, originally granted Thomas Carter. Consideration: $590. Witnesses: B. Fortson, Thos. Fortson, J. P. Recorded in Book "H," Folio 96, Feb. 21, 1803.

July 18, 1803—Martin Turman and Nancy, his wife, to William Cross, all of Elbert County, 400 acres bounded by Briggs Hall and Lawson. Consideration: None given. Witnesses: R. T. Cosby, J. P., Joel Butler. Recorded in Book "I," Folio 123, Feb. 19, 1805.

Feb. 18, 1804—Nathaniel P. Beach and William Watkins Jr., to Joseph Watkins, all of Elbert County, one-half of Lot No. 40 and house in Petersburg. Consideration: $600. Witnesses: Ro. H. Watkins, Leroy Pope, J. P. Recorded in Book "I," Folio 37, Feb. 21, 1804.

Jan. 1, 1805—Robert Cosby, Sheriff of Elbert County, to Robert Moore of Elbert County, 200 acres on the Savannah River, levied on as the property of John F. Gerrald, adjoining Abner McGarity. Consideration: $140. Witnesses: Thomas Cook, J. P., Benj Head. Recorded in Book "I," Folio 169, Oct. 22, 1805.

May 4, 1806—Robert Middleton, Sheriff of Elbert County, to James Hamilton of Columbia County, Georgia, Lot 34 in town of Petersburg, levied and sold as the property of Ebazer Early. Witnesses: Geo. Clark, R. Lindsay, J. P. Recorded in Book "K," Folio 43, Sept. 2, 1806.

Jan. 15, 1806—Duke Hamilton of Elbert County, Attorney-in-Fact for Thomas Gordon of Petersburg, Virginia, to John Willowford of Elbert County, 330 acres on Broad River. Consideration: $413.75. Witnesses: T. Hamilton, Geo. Hamilton, William Willowford. Recorded in Book "L," Folio 113, April 20, 1809.

Jan. 14, 1806—Reuben Jones and Patty, his wife, to William Ganes, all of Elbert County, 53 acres on Cold Water Creek. Consideration $150. Witnesses: W. Woods, (?) Brewer, Rn. Lindsay, J. P. Recorded in Book "I," Folio (?), Jan. 31, 1806. (Page partially destroyed):

Feb. 17, 1807—Middleton Woods to James Christian, both of Elbert County, 300 acres bounded by Larrimore, Shepherd and Oliver. Consideration: $550. Witnesses: W. Woods, Rn. Lindsay, J. P. Recorded in Book "K," Folio 234, Dec. 29, 1807.

April 2, 1808—Reuben Jones and Patsy, his wife, to Robert Jones, all of Elbert County, 110 acres on Cold Water Creek. Consideration: $100. Witnesses: John Hulme, J. Johnston, J. I. C. Recorded in Book "K," Folio 251, April 5, 1808.

Sept. 7, 1809—Christopher David and Joshua Clark, executors of the estate of Christopher Clark Sr., to Andrew Woodly, all of Elbert County, 50 acres on Warhacha Creek. Consideration: $50. Witnesses: David Hudson, Wm. Hightower, J. P. Recorded in Book "M," Folio 113, Feb. 7, 1810.

Feb. 7, 1810—Thomas Jones, Sheriff, to William Hightower, 322 acres on Warhatch Creek, levied on and sold as the property of Samuel Clark. Consideration: $151. Witnesses: James Wood, Thos. Cook, Edward Brown. Recorded in Book "M," Folio 113, Feb. 7, 1810.

July 31, 1810—Robert Thompson and Sally, his wife, of Elbert County, to Raphal Wheeler of Wilkes County, Georgia, Lot. No. 23 on the east side of Front Street in the town of Petersburg. Consideration: $1,000. Witnesses: Leroy Pope, Jesse Thompson, Wm. Barnett, J. I. C. Recorded in Book "P," Folio 184, March 6, 1816.

Dec. 5, 1810—Wiley Thompson to Gaines Thompson, both of Elbert County, power of attorney. Witnesses: Richard I. Easter, Wm. Woods. Recorded in Book "O," Folio 129, May 15, 1813.

June 29, 1811—Joseph Rucker Jr., to John Beck, both of Elbert County, 200 acres on Van's Creek adjoining Larkin Clark on the north, Henry Gaines on the west, Zachariah Smith on the south, and John Beck on the east. Consideration: $1,000. Witnesses: Thos. Jones, B. Allen, B. Jeter, J. P. Recorded in Book "O," Folio 149, May 27, 1811.

LIST OF ORIGINAL LAND WARRANTS ON FILE IN OFFICE OF CLERK OF ELBERT COUNTY SUPERIOR COURT

	Acres	Date Granted	Reason
Allen, Nathaniel	309	Deec. 3, 1787	Head Right
Allen, Nathaniel	1027	June 3, 1787	Lieu Old Warrant
Aderhold, Conrad	200	Sept. 5, 1791	Head Right
Allen, Reuben	——	Jan. 2, 1792	Head Right
Brady, John	200	June 6, 1791	Head Right of Thomas Aiken
Brazel, Frederick	76	Apr. 5, 1791	Head Right
Bray, John	381	Sept. 5, 1791	Head Right and Old Warrant of Hillery Hendricks
Bates, Francis	——	Feb. 6, 1792	Head Right
Beck, John	——	Oct. 2, 1797	Head Right
Brawner, Bazel	150	May 26, 1790	Part Head Right
Burch, William S.	——	Mar. —, 1798	Head Right
Cain, Rosannah	200	Nov. 22, 1791	Head Right
Cain, Ruth	200	Nov. 22, 1791	Head Right
Coleman, John	——	Sept. 5, 1791	Head Right
Collins, John	200	Sept. 5, 1791	Head Right
Collins, Zachariah	100	Aug. 7, 1789	Head Right
Davis, Gideon	120	Jan. 2, 1792	Old Warrant of Julian Naile
Davis, Wiley	50	Sept. 3, 1787	Head Right
Davis, Absolom	100	Sept. 3, 1787	In lieu of Old Warrant
Elliott, William	550	Apr. 1, 1791	Head Right
Forbes, Atkins	800	Apr. 4, 1794	Own Head Right and that of John Hawthorne
Fleming, Robert	550	May 2, 1792	Own Head Right and that of family
Franklin, David	100	June 7, 1790	Head Right of Hezekiah Bailey
Green, Jesse	——	Oct. 6, 1795	Head Right
Greenwood, Fleming	200	Sept. 5, 1791	Head Right
Gurthie, Robert	400	July 7, 1794	Own Head Right and that of John Williams
Gilmer, Thomas	——	Sept. 5, 1791	Head Right
Gill, John	600	Apr. 5, 1790	Head Right and Old Warrant
Grover, Stephen	——	Oct. 3, 1786	Head Right
Gregg, Henry	——	Oct. 3, 1786	Head Right
Harper, John P.	1000	May 2, 1791	Head Right
Hall, William	100	Feb. 7, 1784	Head Right
Howington, William	85	Apr. 4, 1781	Part Head Right
Hightower, Thomas	550	Jan. 20, 1784	Head Right
Hilley, Thomas	——	Sept. 5, 1781	Part Head Right

	Acres	Date Granted	Reason
Hunter, Samuel	150	Apr. 4, 1791	Head Right
Hartsfield, Godfrey	300	Feb. 2, 1782	Lieu Old Warrant
Hodge, John	200	Mar. 2, 1789	Head Right
Henderson, John	200	Sept. 5, 1791	Head Right
Hendricks, Hillary	81	May 7, 1787	Part Head Right
Hendricks, Sarah	131	May 7, 1787	Part Head Right
Hunt, Richardson	300	Sept. 5, 1791	Head Right
Higginbotham, Jacob	**400**	Feb. 2, 1791	Head Right
Hambleton, Isiah	—	Aug. 5, 1791	Head Right
Ishaw, Edward	400	Feb. 2, 1791	Head Right
Johnson, William	60	June 7, 1790	Head Right
Kain, Richard	60	Sept. 7, 1789	Head Right
Karr, Walter	200	Sept. 3, 1787	Head Right
King, Thomas	200	Jan. 2, 1791	Head Right
Lamb, John	100	Aug. 1, 1786	Head Right
Long, Nicholas	800	Sept. 5, 1791	Old Warrant
Long, Joseph	200	Apr. 1, 1787	Head Right
McConnell, Josiah	100	1796	Head Right
McConnell, Joseph	200	Jan. 4, 1796	Head Right
McDonald, Hugh	650	Aug. 6, 1792	Head Right
McDonald, Hugh	450	Feb. 7, 1791	Head Right
McDonald, Hugh	1000	Apr. 25, 1794	Renewed
McDonald, John W.	200	Apr. 3, 1787	Renewed
McDonald, John W.	100	Dec. 3, 1787	Head Right
McKinsey, John	250	Apr. 2, 1787	Renewed
McRight, Matthew	—	Oct. 3, 1786	Head Right
Maxwell, James	300	Oct. 1, 1791	Head Right
Maxwell, Thomas	350	Oct. —, 1795	Head Right
Norris, William	100	Oct. 5, 1795	Head Right
Pope, Leroy	1000	June 4, 1794	Head Right
Pickens, Joshua	200	Apr. 8, 1784	Head Right
Pollard, John	50	May 7, 1792	Head Right
Robartson, John	200	June 6, 1785	Head Right
Ross, Drury	200	Sept. 5, 1791	Head Right
Ryal, John	200	June 7, 1790	Head Right
Smith, William	200	June 2, 1788	Head Right
Stinchcomb, Absolom	25	Sept. 15, 1791	Head Right
Selman, Thomas	150	Feb. 11, 1792	Head Right
Spurlock, James	50	May 2, 1791	Head Right
Taylor, John	—	Aug. —, 1797	Head Right
Thornton, Thomas	305	Aug. —, 1787	Old Warrant of William Shaw
Tidwell, William	200	Mar. —, 1797	Head Right
Underwood, Joshua	200	Mar. —, 1797	Head Right
Wyche, George	—	Oct. —, 1795	Head Right
Wyche, Peter	—	Feb. —, 1792	Head Right
Whitney, John M.	—	Oct. —, 1795	Head Right

It will be noted that a number of warrants were dated prior to the creation of Elbert County in 1790. Such warrants were filed in Wilkes County and after the creation of Elbert all warrants appertaining to lands located in the new county were transferred to it. It is, of course, a fact that little care has been taken of these documents and in consequence many hundreds of them have in the course of almost 150 years been lost and destroyed.

CENSUS OF ELBERT COUNTY—1800-1930

Elbert County (Including Towns)	District 189	Elberton City
1800—10,094	No census	No census
1810—12,156	No census	No census
1820—11,788	No census	No census
1830—12,354	No census	No census
1840—11,125	No census	No census
1850—12,959	No census	No census
(Of this number there were 3,374 white males, 3,306 white females, 6 free negro males, 10 free negro females, 6,267 slaves		
1860—10,433	No census	No census
1870— 9,249	1,512	No census
1880—12,957	1,508	927
1890—15,376	2,244	1,572
1900—19,729	4,841	3,834
1910—24,125	7,800	6,483
1920—23,905	7,276	6,475
1930—18,485	5,730	4,650

AGGREGATE TAXABLE VALUE OF ELBERT COUNTY PROPERTY BI-ANNUALLY—1894-1928 INCLUSIVE

Year	Value	Year	Value	Year	Value
1894	$2,005,173	1906	$2,755,891	1918	$4,683,281
1896	2,090,025	1908	3,002,485	1920	6,014,551
1898	2,190,736	1910	3,225,877	1922	5,369,515
1900	2,247,845	1912	3,554,783	1924	Digest missing
1902	1,118,176	1914	4,167,004	1926	4,972,054
1904	2,412,722	1916	4,042,750	1928	5,188,134

ELBERT COUNTY REVOLUTIONARY SOLDIERS AND THEIR WIDOWS
(Partial List)

Alston, Gilly
Adams, James
Adams, Thomas
Alexander, Isaac
Allen, William
Algood, Spencer
Allgood, John
Allen, Agnes
Beck, Sarah (widow of John Beck)
Bell, Elizabeth (widow of Joseph Bell)
Bond, Nathan
Bramblett, Elizabeth
Bray, Patience
Brown, Benjamin
Brown, James
Brumfield, Ann C.
Burch, Elizabeth
Burton, Thomas
Butler, Patrick
Cade, Druey

Carter, James
Carter, Elizabeth (widow of Thomas A. Clark.)
Cabiness, Henry
Cash, John
Chisholm, Ann
Clark, Larkin
Clark, Rebecca (widow of Christopher Clark Sr.)
Colbert, Thomas
Cook, John
Cook, Mary (widow of Benjamin Cook)
Cook, Thomas
Cook, Theodosius
Coulston, Mariam
Colson, Benjamin
Cunningham, William
Daniel, John Sr.
David, John

Davis, Nancy
Deadwyler, Alice (widow of Joseph Deadwyler)
Dennard, John
Derrecott, Rebecca
Dilliard, James
Eagin, John
Eavenson, Eli
Enlo, John
Evans, Elizabeth
Evans, Rhoday
Fitts, Mary
Ford, Mary
Flemming, Margaret
Gaines, Francis
Gaines, William
Ginn, Transylvania
Ginn, Sarah
Grag, Susannah
Gray, Susannah

Grissop, James Hailey, William
Hansard, Janet (widow of William Hansard)
Harmon, John Sr.
Harris, Rebecca
Harris, John Sr.
Hathcock, Oziah
Heard, Sarah (widow of Thomas Heard)
Heard, Elizabeth (widow of Colonel Stephen Heard)
Higginbotham, Jean
Higginbotham, Jacob
Highsmith, Milly (widow of James Highsmith)
Hilley, Thomas Sr.
Hinton, Peter
Horton, Elizabeth
Hudson, Elizabeth
Hudson, David
Hunt, James
Hunt, Moses
Hudson, Molly
Jack, Margaret (widow of Captain Patrick Jack)
Johnston, Mary
Jones, Fanny
Jourdain, Fountain
Kelly, William
Kerlin, Elizabeth
Key, William Bibb
King, Thomas

LeGrand, John W.
Lockhart, James
Lowreymore, Sarah
McCurry, Angus
McGuire, Anderson
Mann, Judith (widow of James Mann Sr.)
Maupin, Jesse
Maxwell, John
Maxwell, Thomas Sr.
Mills, Moses
Murry, Nancy
Naish, Frances
Nunnelee, James F.
Newberry, Nancy
Oliver, Dyonsius
Oliver, Peter
Oliver, Jane
Owens, Barsahba (widow of John Owens)
Parks, Mary
Pledger, Thomas
Pulliam, Robert
Redwine, Jacob
Reed, Sarah
Richardson, Amos
Riley, James
Roberts, Joseph Sr.
Royal, Elizabeth (widow of James Royal)
Rucker, John
Rucker, William
Rumsey, Richard
Sandidge, Claiborne
Satterwhite, Elizabeth (widow of Francis Satterwhite)

Shackleford, Edmond
Saxton, Elizabeth
Seals, Elizabeth
Skaggs, Tabitha
Smether, Gabriel
Stowers, Lewis Sr.
Staples, Frances (widow of David Staples)
Tate, Elizabeth (widow of Enos Tate Sr.)
Tatum, Jesse
Teasley, Sarah (widow of David Staples)
Teasley, Silas
Terrell, Levisa
Terrell, Joseph
Thornton, Dozier Sr.
Tucker, Robert
Tucker, Godfrey
Underwood, Wyneford
Upshaw, John
Vacray (Vickery), Joseph
Wansley, John
Ward, William
Ward, Jane
Wheeler, Thomas Sr.
Wilkins, Nancy
Wilhite, Lewis
White, William Sr.
White, John M.
Wilkins, Nancy
Wilkins, John
Willis, Milley
Yoes, Catherine

REVOLUTIONARY OFFICERS OF ELBERT COUNTY

(This list does not purport to give the names of all Revolutionary officers who resided in Elbert County, but only those of which the author has official record).

General George Mathews, General Samuel Blackburn, Colonel Stephen Heard, Colonel Samuel Colson, Colonel George Wyche, Colonel Holman Freeman, Colonel Jacob Higginbotham, Lieutenant Colonel William Alston, Major Barnard Heard, Captain Patrick Jack of Mecklenburg Declaration of Independence fame, Captain William Barnett, Captain Drury Cade, Lieutenant Thomas Fortson.

PARTIAL MUSTER ROLL OF CONFEDERATE SOLDIERS FROM ELBERT COUNTY

COMPANY C, 15TH GEORGIA REGIMENT OF INFANTRY VOLUNTEERS

Colonel William M. McIntosh.
Lieutenant Colonel William T. Millican (Franklin County).
Major Peter J. Shannon.

MARTIN, L. H. O.—Captain, July 15, 1861. Resigned, February 21, 1862. Later commissioned on staff of General Robert Toombs.

HEARD, ROBERT M.—First Lieutenant, July 15, 1861. Promoted to Captain, May 21, 1862. Wounded, 1862. Resigned, July 11, 1862.
BOURNE, P. B.—Second Lieutenant, July 15, 1861. Resigned July 11, 1862.
LOFTON, J. H. Jr.—Second Lieutenant, July 15, 1861. Resigned October 30, 1861.
BROWN, JOHN M.—First Sergeant, July 15, 1861. Wounded at Fussell's Mill, Virginia, August 16, 1864.
McCARTY, JOHN T.—Second Sergeant, July 15, 1861. Transferred, 1862.
LOFTON, BEDFORD H.—Third Sergeant, July 15, 1861. Promoted to Ordinance Sergeant, May 17, 1862.
HUDSON, DAVID—Fourth Sergeant, July 15, 1861. Promoted to First Sergeant, May 14, 1862. Wounded at Garnett's Farm, Virginia, June 27, 1862. Promoted to Captain, September 30, 1863. Surrendered at Appomattox Court House, Virginia, April, 1865.
ALEXANDER, D. B.—First Corporal, July 15, 1861. Transferred to Company F.
MARCUS, MADISON J.—Second Corporal, July 15, 1861.
TATE, EDMUND B.—Third Corporal, July 15, 1862. Promoted to Second Sergeant, June, 1862. Promoted to First Sergeant, 1864. Wounded.
HUDSON, JOHN S.—Fourth Corporal, July 15, 1861. Discharged, 1861.
BARR, GEORGE J.—Fifth Corporal, July 15, 1861. Discharged, 1861.
ALMOND, WILLIAM W.—Private, August 27, 1861.
ALLGOOD, ELIJAH—Private, August 27, 1861. Wounded at Sharpsburg, Maryland, September 7, 1862. Mortally wounded at Wilderness, Virginia, May 6, 1864.
ANDERSON, J. L.—Private, July 15, 1861. Surrendered at Appomattox.
ALMOND, T. F.—Private, July 15, 1861. Discharged, June 25, 1862.
AYERS, T. J.—Private, May 10, 1862. Died, May 17, 1862.
ALEXANDER, H. C.—Private, March 4, 1862. Transferred, May 21, 1864.
BRAWNER, J. R.—Private, June 12, 1864.
BULLARD, G. R.—Private, June 15, 1861. Transferred to Company "I," 15th Georgia. Elected First Corporal, June, 1862.
BARR, G. J.—Private, April 26, 1862.
BAILEY, F. O.—Private, October 24, 1861. Transferred to Company "F," 15th Georgia, May 15, 1862.
BLACKWELL, L. I.—Private, June 15, 1861.
BRADFORD, NATHANIEL M.—Private, July 15, 1861. Appointed Third Corporal, July 15, 1861. Killed in action at Sharpsburg, Maryland, 1862.
BRADFORD, DANIEL W.—Private, July 15, 1861. Transferred to Company "F," 15th Georgia, March 4, 1862.
BLACK, THOS. J.—Private, July 15, 1861. Deserted, February 23, 1864.
BOWERS, THOMAS J.—Private, July 15, 1861.
BUFFINGTON, JOHN H.—Private, July 15, 1861. Killed, May 9, 1863.
BURROUGHS, JOHN E.—Private, July 15, 1861.
BREWER, JOHN M.—Private, July 15, 1861. Discharged, November 1, 1861, by reason of furnishing a substitute.
BRITT, N.—Private, February 25, 1862. Transferred to Band, April, 1862.
BULLARD, W. H.—Private, February 27, 1862. Surrendered at Appomattox.
BULLARD, G. T.—Private, March 4, 1862. Died, May 15, 1862.
BROWN, T. J.—Private, February 27, 1862. Discharged May 15, 1862.
BELL, G. S.—Private, March 1, 1862. Discharged, November 1, 1862.
BELL, W. L.—Private, March 16, 1862. Captured at Gettysburg, Penn.
BROWN, L. M.—Private, March 4, 1862. Died, June 7, 1862.
BUTLER, E. A.—Private, March 4, 1862. Died, June 13, 1862.
CARPENTER, THOS. J.—Private, July 15, 1861. Transferred to Company "F," 15th Georgia Regiiment, May 15, 1862.
CHANDLER, HOWARD M.—Private, July 15, 1861. Wounded, June 27, 1862, at Garnett's Farm, Virginia. Died, July 2, 1862, Richmond, Va.

CAUTHRON, JOHN G.—Private, July 15, 1861.
CRAWLEY, T. J.—Private, July 15, 1861. Discharged, 1861.
COSBY, JOHN M.—Private, July 15, 1861.
COSBY, DAVID—Private, July 15, 1861. Surrendered at Appomattox.
COSBY, J. H.—Private, July 15, 1861. Wounded at Sharpsburg, Maryland, September 17, 1862. Surrendered at Appomattox.
COSBY, N. B.—Private, March 4, 1862. Surrendered at Appomattox.
CLARK, G. W.—Private, February 27, 1862. Died, May 25, 1862.
CUMMING, J. G.—Private, July 15, 1861. Wounded.
CLARK, J. R.—Private, February 27, 1862. Died, May 25, 1862.
COLSON, S. D.—Private, July 15, 1861. Discharged, March 15, 1862.
CLARK, W. T.—Private, February 27, 1862. Promoted to Second Corporal. Surrendered at Appomattox.
CLARK, W. B.—Private, March 1, 1862. Appointed Third Sergeant, 1862. Died, November 5, 1862, at Winchester, Virginia.
CALDWELL, EDWARD—Private, July 15, 1861. Surrendered at Appomattox.
CALDWELL, HENRY—Private, July 15, 1861. Surrendered at Appomattox.
CALDWELL, A. V.—Private, August 29, 1862. Surrendered at Appomattox.
CADE, J. R.—Private, March 4, 1862. Surrendered at Appomattox.
DEERBURG, CHARLES—Private, July 15, 1861. Transferred to Company "F," 15th Georgia Regiment.
DAVIS, MARK—Private, 1862. Died, March, 1863.
DENNARD, JOHN A.—Private, July 15, 1865. Captured at Gettysburg.
DENNARD, THOMAS G.—Private, July 15, 1861. Died, November 7, 1861.
DAVID, JAMES W.—Private, August 27, 1861. Died, August 13, 1862.
DYE, B. F.—Private, March 4, 1862. Died, April 23, 1862.
DYE, J. R.—Private, March 27, 1864. Surrendered at Appomattox.
EAVES, JAMES A.—Private, July 16, 1862. Transferred to Company "F," 15th Georgia Regiment.
EAVES, JOEL—Private, July 15, 1861.
FRANKLIN, HARWELL—Private, July 15, 1861.
FRANKLIN, SAMUEL—Private, July 15, 1861. Appointed Third Sergeant, June, 1862. Junior Second Lieutenant, July 24, 1862. Captured at Gettysburg, July 2, 1863.
FORTSON, RICHARD E.—Private, July 15, 1861. Discharged, August, 1862.
FRANKLIN, MANUEL—Private, July 15, 1861. Surrendered at Appomattox.
GOTHARD, HENRY C.—Private, July 15, 1861. Wounded at Fredericksburg, December 13, 1862. Captured at Gettysburg, July 2, 1863.
HARRIS, JEPTHA A.—Private, July 15, 1861. Died, March 28, 1862.
HUDSON, WILLIAM D.—Private, July 15, 1865. Promoted to Fourth Sergeant, October, 1862. Captured at Gettysburg, July 2, 1863.
HUBBARD, JOHN M.—Private, July 15, 1861.
HUBBARD, WILLIAM D.—Private, July 15, 1861. Discharged, December, 1861.
HULNER, JOHN—Private, July 15, 1861. Discharged, December 6, 1861.
HARMON, F. C.—Private, February 26, 1862. Died of wounds, March, 1862.
HULME, JOHN D.—Private, July 15, 1861.
HUDSON, J. S.—Private, February 27, 1862. Appointed Fourth Sergeant, August, 1862. Killed at Sharpsburg, Maryland, September 17, 1862.
HUDSON, Z. J.—Private, July 15, 1861. Died September 18, 1861.
HUDSON, J. M.—Private, March 2, 1862. Promoted to Second Sergeant.
HUDSON, J. C.—Private, March 4, 1862. Died, July 8, 1862.
HUBBARD, T. P.—Private, March 4, 1862. Died, July 2, 1862.
HOLBROOK, P. C.—Private, March 4, 1864.
HEARD, M. L.—Private, March 15, 1861. Surrendered at Appomattox.
JOHNSON, ROBERT H.—Private, July 15, 1861. Captured at Gettysburg.
JOHNSON, T. B.—Private, March 9, 1863.

KINNEBREW, EDWARD—Private, July 15, 1861. Fourth Sergeant.
KNIGHT, MARCUS A.—Private, July 15, 1861. Transferred to Company "F," 15th Georgia Regiment.
KERLIN, D. S.—Private, April 22, 1862. Wounded, May 10, 1864.
KIRKLAND, J. H.—Private, July 15, 1861. Died, November 8, 1862.
KINNEBREW, W. H.—Private, April 22, 1862.
KINNEBREW, E. N.—Private, July 15, 1861. Wounded, May 12, 1864.
LOVINGOOD, GEO. W.—Private, July 15, 1861. Wounded at Throughfair Gap, Virginia, August, 1862.
MOON, WILLIAM H.—Private, July 17, 1862.
MOON, J. M.—Private, July 15, 1861. Surrendered at Appomattox.
MURRAH, BENJAMIN—Private, July 15, 1861. Transferred to Company "F."
MURRAH, JOHN W.—Private, July 15, 1861. Surrendered at Appomattox. **Appointed Fourth Sergeant. Promoted** to Second Lieutenant. Killed, June, 1863.
MOORE, J. W.—Private, July 15, 1861.
MAYLEY, W. D.—Private, September 10, 1862. Captured, July 2, 1863.
McLANAHAN, J. W.—Private, March 4, 1862. Surrendered at Appomattox.
NASH, J. C.—Private, March 8, 1862. Died, July 6, 1862.
NASH, J. B.—Private, March 4, 1862. Killed, July 2, 1863.
NASH, H. H.—Private, March 29, 1864.
NORMAN, J. L.—Private, July 15, 1861. Surrendered at Appomattox.
PULLIAM, FRANCIS M.—Private, July 1, 1861—Transferred to Company "I."
PEGG, L. M.—Private, July 11, 1861. Discharged, July 25, 1862.
PICKENS, JOHN—Private, November 21, 1861.
ROBERTS, EDWARD M.—Private, July 15, 1861. Surrendered at Appomattox.
ROSE, A. J.—Private, March 4, 1862.
RUFF, MARTIN—Private, July 15, 1861. Surrendered at Appomattox.
RUFF, JAMES C.—Private, December 1, 1864. Deserted, February 20, 1865.
SMITH, W. T.—Private, June 26, 1864. Surrendered at Appomattox.
SMITH, T. B.—Private, August 27, 1862. Captured, July 2, 1863.
SIMPSON, THOMAS—Private, March 4, 1862.
SEIDEL, CHARLES W.—Private, July 15, 1861. Captured, July 2, 1863.
STRIBLEY, JAMES M.—Private. Died, December 21, 1864.
SIMPSON, LEONARD R.—Private, July 15, 1861. Died, June 4, 1863.
SMITH, JAMES W.—Private, July 15, 1861. Surrendered at Appomattox.
STAY, JAMES T.—Private, July 18, 1863. Mortally wounded, May 31, 1864.
STOVALL, GEORGE M.—Private, July 15, 1861.
SNELLINGS, GEO. W.—Private, July 15, 1861. Discharged, December, 1861.
SNELLINGS, WILLIAM H.—Private, August 27, 1861.
SORROW, McKINZEY—Private, July 15, 1861.
SORROW, STINSON P.—Private, July 15, 1861. Died, November 27, 1861.
SORRELLS, TERRELL T.—Private, March 9, 1863. Died of wounds, July 8, 1864.
STOVALL, J. H.—Private, July 15, 1861.
SLAY, G. F.—Private, March 4, 1862
SNELLINGS, P. P.—Private, March 4, 1862. Wounded, July 1, 1862.
TATE, ENOS—Private, July 15, 1861. Mortally wounded, July 2, 1863.
TATE, JASPER S.—Private, July 15, 1861. Promoted to Fourth Corporal.
TAYLOR, WILLIAM T.—Private, July 15, 1861.
TURMAN, GEORGE E.—Private, July 15, 1861.
TURMAN, THOMAS M.—Private, July 15, 1861.
THOMAS, REMSON—Private, March 1, 1862.
TATE, W. T.—Private, —— 25, 1862. Captured July 2, 1863. Died in Fort Delaware Prison, September 20, 1863.
TATE, J. S.—Private, March 3, 1863.

VAUGHAN, PETER D.—Private, July 15, 1861.
WILLIS, T. B. F.—Private, July 15, 1861.
WILLIS, RICHARD M.—Private, July 15, 1861. Lost right leg at North Anna, Virginia, May 26, 1864.
WILKINS, JUDAS L.—Private, July 15, 1861.
WILKINS, F. M.—Private, March 27, 1862. Wounded, July 1, 1862.
WHEELER, D. M.—Private, March 4, 1862. Wounded, July 1, 1862.
WILLIS, W. J.—Private, July 15, 1861. First Lieutenant, May 21, 1862. Promoted to Captain, July 11, 1862.

COMPANY "F," 15TH GEORGIA REGIMENT

BURCH, JOHN C.—Captain, July 15, 1861. Killed in action, June 27, 1862.
CLARK, LARKIN L.—First Lieutenant, July 15, 1861. Resigned, August, 1862.
CRAFT, JOHN F.—Second Lieutenant, July 15, 1861. Appointed A. C. S., 1861.
EDWARDS, EMORY P.—Second Lieutenant, July 15, 1861. Wounded, June 27, 1862. Promoted to Captain, July 24, 1862. Resigned, March 15, 1863
BURCH, JAMES J.—First Sergeant, July 15, 1861. Promoted Second Lieutenant, August 28, 1862. Promoted to Captain, April, 1863 Surrendered at Appomattox.
BLACKWELL, D. R.—Second Sergeant, July 15, 1861 Discharged, January 18, 1862, by furnishing Allen Haverel as substitute
HULME, EASTON A.—Third Sergeant, July 15, 1863. Wounded, 1862 Captured, 1863.
GAINES, LINDSEY A.—Fourth Sergeant, July 15, 1861. Promoted to First Sergeant, July, 1862. Promoted to First Lieutenant, 1863.
HUNT, SION S. W.—First Corporal, July 15, 1861. Mortally wounded, 1862.
GAINES, JAMES H.—Second Corporal, July 15, 1861. Died of wounds, 1864.
WHITE, WILLIAM B.—Third Corporal, July 15, 1861. Mortally wounded, 1862.
NELMS, VANDIVER C.—Fourth Corporal, July 15, 1861. Discharged, 1861.
ALEXANDER, GAINES T.—Private, July 15, 1861.
ALEXANDER, GEORGE W.—Private, July 15, 1861.
ALEXANDER, H. C.—Private, July 15, 1861. Discharged, 1862.
ALEXANDER, D. B.—Private, July 15, 1861. Wounded, July, 1863.
ALEXANDER, J. H.—Private, July 15, 1861. Died of wounds, 1864.
ASBELL, JAMES—Private, July 15, 1861.
ASBELL, WILLIAM F.—Private, March 4, 1862.
ALMOND, W. U.—Private, July 15, 1861. Wounded, July 1863.
BROADWELL, JOHN M.—Private, July 15, 1861.
BALCHIN, THOMAS—Private, July 15, 1861.
BROWN, SAMUEL F.—Private, July 15, 1861. Mortally wounded, September, 1862.
BUTLER, WILLIAM P.—Private, July 15, 1861.
BUTLER, MARTIN T.—Private, July 15, 1861.
BUTLER, ROBERT—Private, March 4, 1862. Mortally wounded, June 27, 1862.
BOND, WILLIAM—Private, March 4, 1862.
BAILEY, F. O.—Private, July 15, 1861. Transferred to Company "C."
BURROUGHS, JOHN E.—Private, July 15, 1861.
BRADFORD, D. W.—Private, July 15, 1861.
BRADFORD, J. B.—Private, July 15, 1861.
CRAFT, DANIEL—Private, July 15, 1861.
CAMPBELL, JAMES C.—Private, July 15, 1861. Transferred to 38th Georgia Regiment.
CRAWFORD, BENJAMIN S.—Private, July 15, 1861.
COLLINS, RICHARD—Private, July 15, 1861. Discharged, 1862.
CRAWFORD, JAMES C.—Private, March 4, 1862. Died, April, 1862.

CRAFT, WILLIAM A.—Private, March 2, 1862.
CRAFT, J. E.—Private, March 4, 1862. Died, July 1, 1862.
CARPENTER, THOMAS J.—Private, July 15, 1862.—Transferred to Company "A."
DAVID, PETER—Private, July 15, 1862. Mortally wounded, 1862.
DANIEL, JAMES W.—Private, July 15, 1861. Died, November, 1862.
DANIEL, WILLIAM J.—Private, July 15, 1861. Killed, June 27, 1862.
DENBURG, CHARLES—Private, July 15, 1861. Killed, September, 1863.
DICKERSON, C. Y.—Private, July 15, 1861.
EDWARDS, JAMES A.—Private, July 15, 1861. Promoted to Junior Second Lieutenant, August 4, 1862.
EAVES, J. A.—Private, July 15, 1861.
GULLEY, JAMES M.—Private, July 15, 1861.
GUIN, MIDDLETON G.—Private, July 15, 1861. Deserted, August, 1862.
GALLOWAY, RICHARD B.—Private, July 15, 1861.
GLOER, JOHN S.—Private, July 15, 1861.
GLOER, ISAAC D.—Private, July 15, 1861.
GRAHAM, W. P.—Private, July 15, 1861.
HALL, WILLIAM S.—Private, July 15, 1861. Promoted to Second Sergeant, 1862. Transferred to 38th Georgia Regiment, January, 1863.
HIGGINBOTHAM, NELSON R.—Private, July 15, 1861.
HOWARD, ALLEN—Private, January 18, 1862. Substitute for D. R. Blackwell.
HULME, G. W.—Private, March 4, 1862.
HULME, EUSTIS—Private.
HULME, L. H.—Private.
HULME, JOHN D.—Private, May 28, 1862.
HADDEN, C. C.—Private, July 15, 1861.
HUNT, HARRISON—Private.
HAMMOND, W. H.—Private, July 15, 1861. Deserted, February 20, 1865.
IVEY, J. N.—Private, July 15, 1861. Died, May 4, 1862.
JONES, JAMES W. Jr.—Private, July 15, 1861. Promoted, Fourth Sergeant.
JONES, MARTIN—Private, May 18, 1863.
JENKINS, ELIAS—Private.
KING, RUFUS—Private.
LUNSFORD, WILLIAM P.—Private, July 15, 1861. Wounded, July 1, 1862.
MURRAH, BENJAMIN—Private, July 15, 1861. Transferred from Company "C."
McCARTY, JOHN T.—Private, July 15, 1861.
McDANNIE, ELLERT—Private.
MOORE, W. M.—Private, October 16, 1861. Captured, January 18, 1864.
MOON, JUD—Private.
NELMS, DAVID L.—Private, July 15, 1861. Mortally wounded, June, 1862.
NELMS, D. VANDIM—Private.
NICHOLS, GEORGE T.—Private, July 15, 1861. Lost arm at Fort Horsman.
OLIVER, JOHN A.—Private, July 15 1862.
PAGE, JOHN O.—Private, July 15, 1861. Died, June, 1862.
PEARSON, G. W.—Private, July 15, 1862.
PARNELL, ABRAM—Private.
ROEBUCK, ROBERT C.—Private, July 15, 1862. Discharged for reason of furnishing Alexander M. Stratton as substitute.
ROUZEE, THEODORE F.—Private, July 15, 1862. Promoted to Second Sergtant.
ROBERT, ED—Private.
SMITH, FRANKLIN—Private, July 15, 1862.
SCARBOROUGH, FRED D.—Private, July 15, 1861. Wounded, June 27, 1862
SCARBOROUGH, WILLIAM A.—Private, July 15, 1861. Captured, July 2, 1863.
STOVALL, GEORGE M.—Private, July 15, 1861. Transferred to Company "C." Wounded, May 6, 1864. Died, May 29, 1864. Promoted to Second Sergeant.

STEADMAN, LEVI—Private. Died, 1862.
SMITH, J. H.—Private, July 15, 1862. Killed, August 16, 1864.
THOMASON, MATTHEW D.—Private, July 15, 1861. Died, October, 1861.
TERRY, JAMES J.—Private, July 15, 1861. Died, October 29, 1862.
TERRY, W. T.—Private, August 30, 1861.
TERRY, JOHN W.—Private, March 4, 1862.
TAYLOR, WILLIAM T.—Private July 15, 1861. Transferred to Company "C."
TAYLOR, Z. B.—Private, March 4, 1862. Wounded, July 1, 1862.
TAYLOR, J. H. C.—Private, March 4, 1862. Transferred from Company "I."
TAYLOR, J. M.—Private, March 4, 1862. Took oath of allegiance.
TURMAN, THOMAS T.—Private, March 4, 1862.
VASSAR, GEORGE L.—Private, July 15, 1862.
WILEY, SYLVANUS G.—Private January 5, 1862.
WHITE, ARCHIBALD L.—Private, July 15, 1861. Promoted to First Corporal.
WALSEMAN, WILLIAM—Private, July 15, 1861. Wounded, September 17, 1862.
WILKINS, J. T. M.—Private, July 15, 1861. Killed, September 19, 1863.

COMPANY "I," 15TH GEORGIA REGIMENT

SMITH, JOSEPH T.—Captain, July 15, 1861. Promoted to Major, December, 23, 1861. Promoted to Lieutenant Colonel.
CHANNON, PETER J.—First Lieutenant, July 15, 1861. Promoted to Adjutant, February 9, 1862. Promoted to Major, August 1, 1862.
CLARK, W. J.—Second Lieutenant, July 15, 1861. Died, October, 1861.
MATTOX, WILLIAM H.—Junior Second Lieutenant, July 15, 1861. Second Lieutenant, October, 1861. Captain, December, 1861. Resigned, April 9, 1862.
SMITH, FRANCIS A.—First Sergeant, July 15, 1861. Wounded, August 30, 1862. Second Lieutenant, 1863.
MARCUS, MADISON A.—Second Sergeant, July 15, 1862. First Lieutenant, 1863. Captain, August, 1863.
NORMAN, James J.—Third Sergeant, July 15, 1863. First Lieutenant, 1863. Killed, Fort Harrison, Virginia, September 29, 1864.
HOLLINGSWORTH, W. J.—Fourth Sergeant, July 15, 1861. First Sergeant, April 4, 1863. Died at Elmira, New York, prison.
HESTER, THOMAS J.—First Corporal, July 15, 1861. Second Lieutenant, 1862. Resigned, March 1, 1863.
MATTOX, NATHAN M.—Second Corporal, June 15, 1861. Second Sergeant, May 14, 1862. Ordinance Sergeant, July 1, 1863. Wounded, July 2, 1862.
CLEVELAND, REUBEN W.—Third Corporal, July 15, 1861. Fourth Sergeant, May, 1862. Wounded at Sharpsburg, Maryland, September 17, 1862. Third Sergeant, April 4, 1863. Wounded, July 2, 1863. Wounded, May 6, 1864. Surrendered at Appomattox.
ADAMS, ASHBURN G.—Fourth Corporal, July 15, 1861. Died, March 18, 1862.
ADAMS, JOHN D.—Private, July 15, 1861. Fourth Sergeant.
ADAMS, WILLIAM H.—Private, February 8, 1864.
ADAMS, RICHARD C.—Private, March 9, 1863.
ARNOLD, JULIUS B. D.—Private, July 15, 1861. Captured, July 2, 1863.
ALEXANDER, GUILFORD—Second Lieutenant, 1864.
BROWN, A. W.—Private, July 15, 1861.
BROWN, WILLIAM H.—Private, July 15, 1861. **Wounded.**
BROWN, SOLOMON W.—Private, July 15, 1861.
BROWN, ANDREW F.—Private, February 28, 1862. Wounded.
BROWN, MARTIN R.—Private, July 15, 1861.
BOND, JOHN B.—Private, February 28, 1862. Died after capture.
BRIGGS, THOMAS D.—Private, July 15, 1861.
BOOTH, JAMES C.—Private, July 15, 1861.
BUTLER, WILLIAM S.—Private, July 15, 1861.

BUFFINGTON, JEPTHA R.—Private, July 15, 1861.
BUFFINGTON, WILLIAM R.—Private, November 30, 1861. Substitute for W. K. Bond.
BULLARD, R. T.—Private, July 15, 1861.
CLEVELAND, DANIEL E.—Private, July 15, 1861. Courier, 1863.
CLARK, WILLIAM T.—Private, July 15, 1861.
COKER, BURGESS—Private, July 15, 1861.
CLEVELAND, WILLIAM L.—Private, February 22, 1862. Died, October, 1862.
DEADWYLER, JOSEPH L.—Private, July 15, 1861. Fourth Sergeant.
DICKERSON, JAMES E.—Private, July 15, 1861. Died of wounds, 1863.
DICKERSON, CHARLES Y.—Private, July 15, 1861. Wounded, July 1, 1862.
FORTSON, ELIJAH R.—Private, July 15, 1861.
FORTSON, MOSES E.—Private, July 15, 1861.
FORD, JORDAN R.—Private, July 15, 1861.
FRANKLIN, HENRY—Private, July 15, 1861.
FRAYLEY, LAFAYETTE—Private, July 15, 1861.
FORTSON, JOHN W.—Private, February 22, 1862.
FORTSON, ABNER—Private, March 4, 1862.
FRANKLIN, ABRAHAM—Private, March 9, 1862. Substitute for Z. H. C. Mattox.
FORTSON, D. A.—Private, May 14, 1862.
FORTSON, JOHN B.—Private, February 28, 1862. Surrendered at Appomattox.
FORTSON, WILLIAM W.—Private, —— 24, 1864.
FAULKNER, ISAAC N.—Private, March 4, 1862.
GAINES, J. A.—Private, July 15, 1861. Captain, May, 1862. Killed, July, 1863.
GAINES, THOMAS S.—Private, July 15, 1861. Wounded.
GAINES, JAMES A.—Private, July 15, 1861. Mortally wounded, June 27, 1862.
GAINES, I. J.—Private, July 15, 1861. Surrendered at Appomattox.
GAINES, FRANCIS—Private, —— 28, 1862.
GAINES, PETER C.—Private, March 4, 1862.
GAULDIN, WILLIAM D.—Private, July 15, 1861.
HARBIN, JOHN W.—Private, July 15, 1861. Wounded.
HAMMOND, WILLIAM H.—Private, July 15, 1861.
HADDON, CHALMERS—Private, July 15, 1861.
HOLLINGSWORTH, WARREN T.—Private July 15, 1861.
HIGGINBOTHAM, ELI—Private, March 4, 1862.
JONES, JOHN H.—Private, July 15, 1861. Wounded, July 1, 1862.
JAMES, ALVIN A.—Privatt, July 15, 1861.
KING, RUFUS—Private, March 4, 1862. Captured, May, 1864.
KING, WILLIAM B.—Private, September 2, 1862. Deserted.
KING, JOHN M.—Private, March 20, 1863.
LOEHR, GEORGE—Private, July 15, 1861.
LUMPKIN, SAMUEL J.—Private, August 7, 1862. Deserted.
MARCUS, M. J.—Private, July 15, 1861.
McDANIEL, ELBERT C.—Private, September 10, 1862.
MOON, WILLIAM—Private, July 15, 1861.
MOON, JOHN S.—Private, July 15, 1861.
MATTOX, Z. H. C.—Private, July 15, 1861. Discharged by furnishing substitute.
MATTOX, HOSEA B.—Private, July 15, 1861. Wounded and captured, July 2, 1863.
MOBLEY, ISAAC M.—Private, July 15, 1861.
MASON, ALFRED—Private, July 15, 1861. Wounded.
McCLELLAN, T. T.—Private, July 15, 1861. Transferred to S. C.
MAILEY, MARTIN V.—Private, July 15, 1861. Twice wounded.
MATHEWS, GEORGE B.—Private, July 15, 1861. Died, November 3, 1864.

MAILEY, J. M.—Private, July 15, 1861. Died, July, 1862.
NORMAN, ELIJAH B.—Private, August 29, 1862. Died, 1863.
PEARSONS, GEORGE W.—Private, July 15, 1861.
PERRYMAN, J. A.—Private, July 15, 1861. Deserted.
PULLIAM, JOHN—Private, July 15, 1861.
PATTERSON, WILEY W.—Private, July 15, 1861. Died, November, 1861.
PULLIAM, MATTHEW—Private, March 4, 1864.
PLEDGER, WILLIAM—Private, March 4, 1862.
PULLIAM, FRANCIS M.—Private, March 14, 1862. Wounded.
PULLIAM, NATHAN—Private, March 26, 1863.
ROBERTS, WILLIAM H.—Private, July 15, 1861.
SMITH, W. P.—Private, July 15, 1861.
SMITH, H. G.—Private, July 15, 1861.
SMITH, G. C.—Private, July 15, 1861. Died, April, 1864.
SEYMOUR, MARSHALL—Private, March 4, 1862. Transferred to 38th Georgia.
THORNTON, MALLORY J. Private, July 15, 1861. Captured, January 22, 1864.
TREADWELL, TERRY—Private, July 15, 1861. Wounded, September, 1862.
TENANT, HENRY A.—Private, July 15, 1861. Captured, July 2, 1863.
TENANT, O. T.—Private, July 15, 1861. Deserted February, 1865.
TENANT, W. C.—Private, July 15, 1861. Surrendered at Appomattox.
TEASLEY, ALFRED J.—Private, June 15, 1862. Second Lieutenant.
TAYLOR, CONNOR H.—Private, March 1, 1862.
TAYLOR, J. J.—Private, 1862. Died, 1862.
TAYLOR, W. C.—Private, April 15, 1864.
TAYLOR, J. H. C.—Private, March 4, 1862.
WHITE, TINSLEY R.—Private, July 15, 1861. Wounded, June 27, 1862.
WEBB, JOHN C.—Private, July 15, 1861. Wounded.
WANSLEY, WILLIAM J.—Private, July 15, 1861.
WEBB, MARTIN—Private, July 15, 1861. Discharged, May, 1862.
WILLIAMS, WILLIAM—Private, July 15, 1861. Drum Major, December, 1862.
WILLIAMS, GEORGE T.—Private, February 28, 1862.
WEBB, ANDREW J.—Private, September 15, 1862.
WEBB, MARTIN—Private.
WEBB, R. A.—Private, July 15, 1861. Captured, 1864.

37TH GEORGIA INFANTRY REGIMENT

EBERHARDT, GEORGE—Captain, March 4, 1862. Resigned, June 27, 1862.
BAILEY, AUGUSTUS—First Lieutenant, March 4, 1862. Resigned, March 19, 1863.
TURNER, THOMAS M.—Second Lieutenant, March 4, 1862. Resigned, February, 1863.
SANDERS, JAMES A.—Junior Second Lieutenant, March 4, 1862. Captain, June, 1863.
BAILEY, E. P.—First Sergeant, March 4, 1862.
BAILEY, N. L.—Second Sergeant, March 4, 1862.
GAINES, W. M.—Third Sergeant, March 4, 1862.
JONES, THOMAS—Fourth Sergeant, March 4, 1862.
HERNDON, F. A.—First Corporal, March 4, 1862.
ROBERTS, W. J.—Second Corporal, March 4, 1862. Deserted, 1864.
KING, W. H.—Third Corporal, March 4, 1862.
BURDEN, J. A.—Fourth Corporal, March 4, 1862.

ALMOND, JAMES M.—Private, March 4, 1862.
ANDERSON, JOHN H.—Private, March 4, 1863.
ADAMS, R. C.—Private, March 4, 1862.
ADAMS, J. L.—Private, March 4, 1862.

ADAMS, R. E.—Private, March 4, 1862.
ADAMS, M. B.—Private, March 4, 1862.
ADAMS, W. M.—Private, March 4, 1862.
ADAMS, D. L.—Private, September 12, 1863.
ALLGOOD, L. J.—Private, —— 12, 1864.
ALLGOOD, JOHN W.—Private, August 14, 1863.
ABNER, JOHN—Private, March 4, 1862.
ALEXANDER, ISAAC E.—Private, March 4, 1862.
ALEXANDER, W. H.—Private, March 4, 1863.
ALEXANDER, GAINES T.—Private, March 4, 1862.
ALEXANDER, G. W.—Private, March 4, 1862.
ANDERSON, ZEDEKIAH—Private, March 4, 1862. Deserted, 1864.
BOOTH, ANDREW W.—Private, March 4, 1862.
BAILEY, J. M.—Private, April 8, 1863.
BAILEY, E. P.—Private.
BANKS, CARSON—Private, January 8, 1864.
BAILEY, GRIFFIN—Private, May 10, 1862.
BELL, HENRY B.—Private, March 4, 1862.
BROOKS, THOMAS H.—Private, 1862.
BELL, JAMES E., Dr.—Private, March 4, 1862.
BROWN, HARRIS H.—Private May 10, 1862.
BROWN, GEORGE W.—Private, May 10, 1862.
BRIDGES, S. A.—Private, 1863.
BRUCE, PERRY S. F.—Private, March 4, 1862.
BAILEY, L. L.—Private, May 10, 1862.
BAILEY, J. R.—Private, May 4, 1862.
BURCH, THOMAS C.—Private, March 4, 1862.
BRADFORD, B. W.—Private, March 4, 1862. Wounded, 1863.
BAKER, L. A.—Private, March 4, 1862.
BROWN, G. G.—Private, May 10, 1862.
BROWN, J. S.—Private, March 4, 1863.
BURDEN, JAMES A.—Private, March 4, 1862.
BROWN, THOMAS J.—Private, January 8, 1864.
BURDEN, THOMAS—Private, March 4, 1862.
BURDEN, W. J.—Private, March 4, 1862. Died, December 7, 1863.
COLVARD, THOMAS—Private, 1864. Died, August 1, 1864.
COKER, JAMES—Private, March 4, 1864.
COKER, B. F.—Private, March 4, 1864. Deserted, 1864.
COLVARD, BENJAMIN—Private, March 4, 1862.
CONNELL, G. H.—Private, October 14, 1863.
CUNNINGHAM, L. J.—Private, March 4, 1862.
COKER, HENRY E.—Private, March 4, 1862. Deserted, 1864.
COKER, JOHN—Private, March 4, 1862.
DYE, WASHINGTON—Private, March 4, 1862.
DYE, THOMPSON H.—Private, March 4, 1862.
DYE, JOSEPH B.—Private, March 4, 1862. Killed, July 4, 1863.
DUDLEY, C. P.—Private, March 4, 1862.
DANIEL, D. F.—Private, March 4, 1862.
DENNARD, WILLIAM—Private, March 4, 1862.
DEADWYLER, JAMES S.—Private, March 4, 1862. Died of wounds, July, 1864.
EBERHARDT, GEORGE—Private, May 10, 1862. Second Lieutenant, June, 1863.
EBERHARDT, J. G., Dr.—Private, May 10, 1862.
EVANS, WILLIAM—Private, May 10, 1862.
FLEMING, JAMES—Private, May 10, 1862.
FLEMING, W. D.—Private, March 4, 1862.
FORTSON, HENRY A.—Private, March 4, 1862. Wounded.
GAULDING, JOHN R.—Private, March 4, 1862. Lost right arm, June, 1864.
GALBRETH, MANANSAS—Private, March 4, 1862.

GLAZE, A. N.—Private, March 4, 1862.
GREENWAY, G. W.—Private, March 4, 1862.
GAINES, PETER C.—Private.
GAINES, HIRAM S.—Private, March 4, 1862.
GAINES, WILLIAM—Private, March 4, 1862.
GRAY, W. J.—Private, March 4, 1862.
GUNTER, J. N.—Private, May 10, 1862.
HALL, B. P.—Private, 1864.
HALL, JEREMIAH—Private, March 4, 1863. Killed, 1864.
HALL, J. N.—Private, June 21, 1863.
HALL, W. A.—Private, February 27, 1864.
HAHN, JOHN D.—Private, 1863.
HERNDON, FRANCIS—Corporal, March 4, 1862. Killed, 1864.
HENDRICKS, J. L.—Private, March 4, 1862.
HENDRICKS, A. C.—Private, March 4, 1862.
HARMON, J. R.—Private, March 4, 1862.
HARDEN, THOMAS W.—Private, March 4, 1862.
HARDEN, N. H.—Private, March 4, 1862.
HOLMES, JACKSON—Private, March 4, 1862.
HEARD, JAMES L.—Private, March 4, 1862. Later Lieutenant Colonel, 3rd Regiment, Carswell's Brigade.
HARRIS, DAVID E.—Private, March 4, 1862. Died, July, 1862.
HARPER, FERDINAND—Private, March 4, 1862.
HAMMOND, A. E.—Private, March 4, 1862. Wounded, July 22, 1864.
HULME, JOSEPH M.—Private, March 4, 1862.
HUNT, W. H.—Private, March 4, 1862. Died in service.
JOHNSON, THOMAS—Private, May 10, 1862.
JOHNSON, ENOS—Private, March 4, 1862.
JONES, NATHAN—Private, May 10, 1862.
JONES, WILLIAM J.—Private, December 16, 1862.
JONES, GATES—Private, March 4, 1862.
JONES, THOMPSON S.—Private, March 4, 1862.
KELLEY, JOHN S.—Private, March 4, 1862.
KELLEY, JAMES S.—Private, March 6, 1862.
KENT, A. J.—Private, March 4, 1862. Deserted.
McMULLAN, G. W.—Private, March 4, 1862.
McMULLAN, JAMES L.—Private, March 4, 1864.
MIMMS, JOHN G.—Private, March 4, 1862.
MOBLEY, M. D.—Private, March 4, 1862.
MORRIS, RUFUS—Private, March 4, 1862.
NASH, G. T.—Private, March 4, 1862.
NASH, J. T.—Private, March 4, 1862. Died, June 3, 1864.
OGLESBY, D. P.—Private, May 10, 1862. Second Lieutenant, December, 1862. First Lieutenant, June 27, 1863.
OSLEY, JESSE—Private, March 4, 1862. Wounded and captured, 1863.
PRATHER, GEORGE T.—Private, March 4, 1862. Killed at Chickamauga.
PRATHER, J. W.—Private, March 4, 1862.
PARRISH, A. A.—Private, March 4, 1862.
PARTAIN, BENJAMIN—Private, March 4, 1862.
PHILLIPS, A. C.—Private, March 4, 1862. Wounded.
PHILLIPS, J. B.—Private, March 4, 1863.
ROUSEY, EDMOND—Private, March 4, 1862.
RAY, CHARLES A.—Private, March 4, 1862.
RICKS, D. L.—Private, May 10, 1862.
RUCKER, J. T.—Private, May 10, 1862.
RUFF, WILLIAM P.—Private, March 4, 1862. Died, June 22, 1862.
SPURLOCK, A. S.—Private, March 4, 1862. Died, 1864.
SANDERS, WILLIAM—Private, March 4, 1862.
SAYER, J. D.—Private, 1864.
SEYMOUR, Z. G.—Private, March 4, 1862. Wounded, 1864.

SEAGRAVES, J. C.—Private, 1863.
SEYMOUR, ASA—Private, March 4, 1862.
SEYMOUR, CHARLES C.—Private, March 4, 1862.
SEYMOUR, WILEY G.—Private, March 4, 1862.
SIZEMORE, W. J.—Private.
SNELLINGS, J. S.—Private, March 4, 1862.
TURNER, J. W.—Private, May 10, 1863.
TURNER, JOHN WILLIAM—Private, March 4, 1862.
TURNER, WILLIAM P.—Private, March 4, 1862.
TATE, ENOS A.—Private, March 4, 1862.
THOMPSON, W. G.—Private, October 18, 1863.
THOMPSON, JOEL—Private, March 4, 1862.
WEBB, ABNER—Private, February 28, 1864.
WELLS, JAMES—Private, May 10, 1862.
WOODS, MIDDLETON—Private, March 4, 1862. Deserted.

CONFEDERATE SOLDIERS COMMANDS PARTIALLY UNKNOWN

ALMOND, JOHN B.
ADAMS, S. A.
ARNOLD, JOSEPH Y.
ARNOLD, McALPIN—15-year-old volunteer.
BLACK, STEPHEN H.
BOOTH, J. W.—38th Georgia Infantry.
BREWER, J. H.—Toombs Brigade.
BOND, A. J.—38th Georgia Infantry.
BROWN, BENJAMIN D.—7th Georgia Calvary.
BULLARD, J. W.—7th Georgia Calvary.
BROWN, J. D.—38th Georgia Infantry.
BRYANT, WILLIAM
BROWN, D. S.—38th Georgia Infantry.
CRAWFORD, FRANCIS M.
CHILDS, S. G.
CRAWFORD, JAMES C.
CARROUTH, J. A.—38th Georgia Infantry.
CAMPBELL, W. G.—38th Georgia Infantry.
DIXON, ANDREW
DIXON, ABRAM
DAVIS, THOMAS—7th Georgia Calvary.
DYE, T. B.—Toombs Brigade.
EBERHARDT, R. P.—Lieutenant-Colonel, 38th Georgia Infantry.
EAVENSON, JOHN W.—38th Georgia Infantry.
FORTSON, W. E.
FORTSON, D. A.—38th Georgia Infantry.
GINN, S. S.—38th Georgia Infantry.
GUEST, S. B.
GAINES, JOHN L.
HIGGINBOTHAM, E. B.—38th Georgia Infantry.
HAWKINS, J. W.—38th Georgia Infantry.
HAM, P. H.—Missouri Troops.
HUDGENS, JOHN C.
JONES, THOMAS A.—7th Georgia Calvary.
JAMES, JOHN D.—6th Georgia Infantry, Company "K."
JONES, A. V.
LOFTON, JOHN—Colonel, 6th Georgia Infantry. Killed in action.
MAXWELL, D. J.—Toombs Brigade.
McINTOSH, SINGLETON A.—7th Georgia Calvary.
McINTOSH, W. M., Jr.
MOORE, W. T.
MOORE, THOMAS
MATTHEWS, A. J.—38th Georgia Infantry.
MANN, E. J.—38th Georgia Infantry.
NORMAN, E. B.—Holcomb's Legion.
OGLESBY, ABDA—38th Georgia Infantry.
PARTAIN, L. B.
REESE, W. W.
SMITH, B. C.
SWIFT, THOMAS M.
SEYMOUR, J. G.—38th Georgia Infantry.
THORNTON, T. D.—38th Georgia Infantry.
THORNTON, W. M.—38th Georgia Infantry.
VAUGHAN, A. W.—38th Georgia Infantry.
WALL, BUDD C.—7th Georgia Calvary
WILHITE, JOHN L.

The foregoing list does not purport to include all soldiers of the Confederate States who served from Elbert County. An entire Company from Elbert and adjoining counties was inducted into the 38th Georgia Regiment of Volunteers, but the compiler has been unable to secure the muster roll.

THE DEAD IN THE WAR BETWEEN THE STATES FROM ELBERT COUNTY

COMMISSIONED OFFICERS

(With Rank, Command and Death Date)

WILLIAM M. McINTOSH—Colonel, Brevet Brigadier General, 15th Georgia Regiment. Died June 29, 1862.
JOHN T. LOFTON—Colonel, 6th Georgia Regiment. Died, 1864.
JOHN C. BURCH—Captain, 15th Georgia Regiment. Died, June 27, 1862.
JOHN C. THORNTON—Captain, 1st Georgia Regiment.
WILLIAM J. WILLIS—Captain, 15th Georgia Regiment. Died, September, 1863.
JAMES A. GAINES—Captain, 15th Georgia Regiment
MADISON A. MARCUS—Captain, 15th Georgia Regiment
WILLIAM J. CLARK—Lieutenant, 15th Georgia Regiment
JOHNS, MURRAH—Lieutenant, 15th Georgia Regiment
JAMES J. NORMAN—Lieutenant, 15th Georgia Regiment.
JOHN OGLESBY—Lieutenant, 38th Georgia Regiment.
J. G. VASSAR—Lieutenant, 15th Georgia Regiment.
WILLIAM B. RUCKER—Lieutenant, 15th Georgia Regiment.

NON-COMMISSIONED OFFICERS AND PRIVATES

(With Rank, Command and Death Date)

ADAMS, A. G.—Corporal, 15th Georgia Regiment. Died, March, 1862.
ADAMS, H—Private, 15th Georgia Regiment.
ADAMS, A. H.—Private, 38th Georgia Regiment.
ADAMS, HIRAM
ADAMS, L. M.—Private, 15th Georgia Regiment.
ALEXANDER, JAMES J.—Private, 37th Georgia Regiment.
ALEXANDER, J. H.—Private, 15th Georgia Regiment. Died, August, 1864.
ALLGOOD, JOHN W.—Private, 37th Georgia Regiment.
ALLGOOD, ELIJAH—Private, 15th Georgia Regiment.
ALMOND, JAMES W.—Private, 37th Georgia Regiment.
ALMOND, JAMES—Private, 38th Georgia Regiment.
ALMOND, ALFRED—Private, 7th Georgia Regiment.
ANDERSON, JAMES—Private, 15th Georgia Regiment.
ANDERSON, A. J.—38th Georgia Regiment.
ANDREWS, A. F.—Private, 7th Georgia Calvary.
ANDREWS, PARKS
ANDREWS, J. O.—Private, 38th Georgia Regiment.
ARNOLD, JULIUS B. D.—Private, 15th Georgia Regiment. Died, summer, 1863.
AYERS, THOMAS J.—Private, 15th Georgia Regiment.
BELL, H. B.—Private, 37th Georgia Regiment.
BOND, MARTIN—38th Georgia Regiment.
BOND, THOMAS—Private, 38th Georgia Regiment.
BOND, JOHN—Private, 15th Georgia Regiment.
BOND, WILLIAM—Private, 38th Georgia Regiment.
BOND, NELSON—Private, 38th Georgia Regiment.
BOND, EPPY—Private, 38th Georgia Regiment.

BROWN, LUTHER M.—Private, 15th Georgia Regiment.
BROWN, ASA—Private, 38th Georgia Regiment. Died, May, 1864.
BROWN, MIDDLETON—Private, 38th Georgia Regiment.
BROWN, MARION—38th Georgia Regiment.
BROWN, NOAH L.—Private, 37th Georgia Regiment.
BROWN, SAMUEL L.—Private, 15th Georgia Regiment.
BROWN, JESSE A.—Private, 38th Georgia Regiment.
BROWN, SAMUEL
BROWN, IRA—Private, 15th Georgia Regiment.
BROWN, B. T.—38th Georgia Regiment.
BOOTH, A. W.—Private, 37th Georgia Regiment.
BOOTH, JOHN R.—Private, 15th Georgia Regiment.
BOOTH, GABRILE—Private, 15th Georgia Regiment.
BENTLEY, McALPIN—38th Georgia Regiment.
BRADFORD, R.—Private, 37th Georgia Regiment.
BRADFORD, N. M.—Corporal, 15th Georgia Regiment. Died, 1862.
BLACK, JOHN W.—38th Georgia Regiment.
BELL, H. R.
BULLARD, GEORGE T.—Private, 15th Georgia Regiment.
BULLARD, JEPTHA R.—Private, 15th Georgia Regiment.
BUTLER, GEORGE—Private, 38th Georgia Regiment.
BUTLER, WILLIAM—Private, 15th Georgia Regiment.
BUTLER, ROBERT—Private, 15th Georgia Regiment.
BUTLER, NEWTON—Private, 15th Georgia Regiment. Died, June, 1862.
BUTLER, ROBERT—Private, 15th Georgia Regiment. Died, June, 1862.
BURDEN, JOHN H.—15th Georgia Regiment.
BURDEN, W. J.—Private, 37th Georgia Regiment.
BURDEN, WOODSON—Private, 37th Georgia Regiment.
BULLARD, GEORGE T.—15th Georgia Regiment.
BULLARD, JEPTHA R.—Private, 15th Georgia Regiment.
BUFFINGTON, JOHN H.—Private, 15th Georgia Regiment.
BUFFINGTON, WILLIAM R.—Private, 15th Georgia Regiment.
BRADSHAW, HENRY
BRUCE, JAMES—Private, 1st Reserves.
BREWER, CLEMENT
CHANDLER, H. M.—15th Georgia Regiment.
CAUTHREN, J. G.—Private, 15th Georgia Regiment.
CLARK, WILLIAM B. Jr.—15th Georgia Regiment.
CLARK, RICHARD—15th Georgia Regiment.
CLARK, GEORGE W.—15th Georgia Regiment.
COLVARD, GIBSON
COLVARD, JOHN—15th Georgia Regiment.
COLVARD, THOMAS—Private, 37th Georgia Regiment.
COLVARD, BENJAMIN
CHEEK, DAVID W.
CRAFT, JEFFERSON
CRAFT, LINDSEY—Private, 15th Georgia Regiment. Died, August, 1862.
CRAFT, DANIEL
CRAWFORD, COLUMBUS—15th Georgia Regiment. Died, April, 1862.
CRAWFORD, JAMES—Private, 15th Georgia Regiment. Died, 1862.
CLEVELAND, WILLIAM L.—38th Georgia Regiment.
CORROUTH, ASBURY—38th Georgia Regiment.
CROOK, JAMES—38th Georgia Regiment.
CASH, SEABORN—38th Georgia Regiment.
CHRISTIAN, RUSSELL—Morgan's Cavalry.
CARPENTER, THOMAS J.—Morgan's Cavalry.
CUNNINGHAM, T. C.—Private, 37th Georgia Regiment.
COKER, JOHN—Private, 37th Georgia Regiment.
CARLTON, H. C.—Private, 38th Georgia Regiment.
DEADWYLER, JOHN S.

DEARBURG, CHARLES—Private, 15th Georgia Regiment. Died, 1863.
DICKERSON, EDWARD—Private, 15th Georgia Regiment.
DENNARD, J. A. M.—Private, 15th Georgia Regiment.
DENNARD, THOMAS J.—Private, 15th Georgia Regiment.
DYE, FLEMING—Private, 15th Georgia Regiment.
DAVIS, JAMES—Private, 37th Georgia Regiment.
DICKERSON, E.—Private, 15th Georgia Regiment. Died, 1862.
DICKERSON, WILLIAM J.—Private, 15th Georgia Regiment.
DANIEL, W. J.—Private, 15th Georgia Regiment.
DYE, WILEY—Private, 38th Georgia Regiment.
DYE, THOMAS—Private, 38th Georgia Regiment.
DUNCAN, CHARLES—Private, 37th Georgia Regiment.
EAVES, JESSE—Private, 15th Georgia Regiment.
EAVES, JOEL—Private, 15th Georgia Regiment.
EAVENSON, THOMAS M.—38th Georgia Regiment.
EAVENSON, GEORGE A.—38th Georgia Regiment.
EBERHARDT, WILLIAM—38th Georgia Regiment.
FLEMING, JOHN R.—Private, 15th Georgia Regiment.
FLEMING, DAVID—Private, 15th Georgia Regiment.
FLEMING, JOHN R. Jr.—Private, 38th Georgia Regiment.
FORTSON, FRANCIS—7th Georgia Cavalry.
FORTSON, JESSE W.—38th Georgia Regiment.
FORTSON, WILLIAM T.—38th Georgia Regiment.
FORTSON, ABNER—Private, 15th Georgia Regiment.
FORTSON, W.—Private, 15th Georgia Regiment.
FLEMING, ROBERT—Private, 38th Georgia Regiment.
GAINES, JOHN L.
GAINES, WILLIAM—38th Georgia Regiment.
GAINES, ROBERT—38th Georgia Regiment.
GAINES, H. S.—37th Georgia Regiment. Died, 1863.
GAINES, THOMAS—Private, 15th Georgia Regiment.
GAINES, WILLIAM—7th Georgia Cavalry.
GINN, H.—Private, 38th Georgia Regiment.
GINN, ALFRED—Private, 38th Georgia Regiment.
HUNT, D.—Private, 15th Georgia Regiment. Died, 1862.
HUNT, B.—Private, 15th Georgia Regiment. Died, 1862.
HUNT, L. A.—Private, 15th Georgia Regiment. Died, 1862.
HUNT, H.—Private, 15th Georgia Regiment. Died, 1863.
HUNT, THOMAS—Private, 15th Georgia Regiment. Died, 1862.
HUNT, BEVERLY—Private, 15th Georgia Regiment. Died, 1862.
HUNT, JAMES J.—Private, 15th Georgia Regiment. Died, 1862.
HUNT, S. W. A.—Corporal, 15th Georgia Regiment. Died, June 27, 1862.
HOLLINGSWORTH, W. J.—Sergeant, 15th Georgia Regiment.
HARRIS, JEPTHA—Private, 15th Georgia Regiment.
HERNDON, FRANCIS A.—Private, 15th Georgia Regiment.
HERNDON, GEORGE M.—37th Georgia Regiment.
HAM, JOHN HENRY—38th Georgia Regiment.
HULME, WILLIAM—7th Georgia Cavalry.
HALL, SAVAGE—Private, 15th Georgia Regiment.
HALEY, JAMES M.—Private, 15th Georgia Regiment.
HALEY, GEORGE W.—Private, 15th Georgia Regiment.
HUBBARD, THOMAS—Private, 15th Georgia Regiment.
HUDSON, THOMAS J.—15th Georgia Regiment.
HUDSON, JOHN C.—Private, 15th Georgia Regiment.
HUDSON, JOHN S.—Sergeant, 15th Georgia Regiment. Died, 1862.
HARMON, F. C.—Private, 15th Georgia Regiment.
HARVARD, ALLEN—Private, 15th Georgia Regiment.
HANSARD, W. J.—38th Georgia Regiment.
HAMMOND, HENRY—Private, 38th Georgia Regiment.
HALL, J. C.—Private, 38th Georgia Regiment.

HALL, LINDSEY—Private, 38th Georgia Regiment.
HALL, BEVERLY—Private, 38th Georgia Regiment.
HENDRICKS, JOHN—Private, 38th Georgia Regiment.
HALL, PHILLIP—Private, 38th Georgia Regiment.
HENDRICKS, MARTIN—Private, 37th Georgia Regiment.
HEWELL, WILLIAM
HEWELL, HENRY
HERNDON, GEORGE—37th Georgia Regiment. Died, 1862.
HARRIS, DAVID—Private, 37th Georgia Regiment. Died, July, 1862.
HULME, JOSEPH P.—Private, 37th Georgia Regiment. July, 1862.
HENDRICKS, STEPHEN—Private, 37th Georgia Regiment.
HULME, JOHN—Private, 37th Georgia Regiment.
HARRIS, B. F.
HUTCHERSON, J.—Private, 38th Georgia Regiment.
JONES, GATES
JONES, WILLIAM—Private, 15th Georgia Regiment.
JOHNSON, JAMES
JOHNSON, JOEL
JONES, JOHN E. S.—Private, 38th Georgia Regiment.
JONES, MILTON—Private, 38th Georgia Regiment. Died, November, 1862.
JONES, THOMPSON S.—Private, 37th Georgia Regiment. May, 1862.
JONES, ENOS—Private, 37th, Georgia Regiment. Died, May, 1862.
KING, JOHN M.—Private, 15th Georgia Regiment.
MAXWELL, WILLIAM J.—Private, 38th Georgia Regiment.
MAXWELL, B. M.—38th Georgia Regiment.
MAXWELL, W. H.—Private, 38th Georgia Regiment.
MATHEWS, GEORGE B.—15th Georgia Regiment.
McLANAHAN, J. W.—Private, 7th Georgia Cavalry.
MOON, W. H.—Private, 15th Georgia Regiment.
MALEY, DAVIDSON—Private, 15th Georgia Regiment.
NASH, JAMES C.—Private, 15th Georgia Regiment.
NELMS, DAVID L.—15th Georgia Regiment. Died, July, 1862.
NELMS, J.—38th Georgia Regiment.
NELMS, J. H.—38th Georgia Regiment.
OGLESBY, THOMAS—37th Georgia Regiment. Died, July, 1862.
OGLESBY, JESSE—Private, 38th Georgia Regiment.
OZLEY, JESSE—Private, 38th Georgia Regiment.
PRATHER, JAMES—37th Georgia Regiment. Died, September, 1862.
PARTAIN, W. S.—Private, 37th Georgia Regiment. Died, October, 1863.
PARHAM, WILLIAM J.
PATTERSON, WILEY—Private, 15th Georgia Regiment. Died, May, 1862.
POWELL, JOSEPH—Private, 38th Georgia Regiment.
POWELL, JAMES—Private, 38th Georgia Regiment.
RUCKER, U.—38th Georgia Regiment.
ROUSEY, MITCHELL—38th Georgia Regiment.
SIMPSON, L. K.—15th Georgia Regiment.
SORROW, TERRELL T.—Private, 15th Georgia Regiment.
SLAY, THOMAS J.—Private, 15th Georgia Regiment.
SORROW, S. P.—Private, 15th Georgia Regiment.
SANDERS, JACOB—15th Georgia Regiment.
SANDERS, PETER—38th Georgia Regiment.
SEYMOUR, WILEY—Private, 37th Georgia Regiment.
SEYMOUR, A. C.—Private, 37th Georgia Regiment.
SEYMOUR, ALEXANDER—38th Georgia Regiment.
SEYMOUR, A. C.
STOVALL, GEORGE M.—15th Georgia Regiment.
SMITH, T. W.—Private, 15th Georgia Regiment. Died, May, 1862.
SMITH, R. P.—Private, 15th Georgia Regiment. Died, April, 1863.
TEASLEY, JAMES R.—3rd S. G.
THORNTON, B. F.—38th Georgia Regiment.

THOMASON, MACK
TEASLEY, J. H. H.—38th Georgia Regiment.
THORNTON, WILLIAM T.—38th Georgia Regiment.
THOMPSON, JERRY
TURNER, WILLIAM—37th Georgia Regiment. Died, October, 1863.
THORNTON, JESSE
WILSON, T. M.—7th Georgia Cavalry.
WILKINS, J. L. M.—Private, 15th Georgia Regiment.
WHITE, WILLIAM B.—Sergeant, 15th Georgia Regiment.
WHITE, A. L.—Corporal, 15th Georgia Regiment. Died, 1863.
WHITE, LUKE—Private, 15th Georgia Regiment.
WHITE, STEPHEN—Private, 38th Georgia Regiment.
VAUGHAN, ALEXANDER—Private, 15th Georgia Regiment.
VAUGHAN, PETER—Private, 15th Georgia Regiment.
VAUGHAN, I. H.—Private, 38th Georgia Regiment.
WILLIS, THOMAS A.—15th Georgia Regiment.
WILLIS, ROBERT M.—15th Georgia Regiment.
WILLIS, JAMES A.—15th Georgia Regiment.

While the foregoing list does not show all of the soldiers killed or who died from disease in the service of the Southern Confederacy the compiler believes that most of those who died in the service of their country are therein listed.

SOLDIERS OF THE WAR OF 1812 WHO PARTICIPATED IN GOLD LOTTERY OF 1832

Thompson, Gaines, Captain

Allgood, William Sr.	Christian, Elijah J.	Lunsford, Rollin
Allgood, William Jr.	Colvard, John S.	Mawbray, Thos. W. Sr.
Almond, Isaac	Denny, Edward A.	Nelms, William
Booth, John	Denny, Robert	Phelps, Thomas
Booth, Robert Sr.	Denny, David	Raines, Dabney
Booth, Gabriel	Dudley, Ignatius	Smith, Zachariah
Brawner, Middleton	Edwards, John	Smith, Benjamin
Burden, William	Faulkner, William	Smith, William S.
Butler, Haley	Haynes, Thomas	Stinchcomb, Levi
Bentley, Samuel	Hendrick, Whitehead	Scales, George
Burton, Thomas Sr.	Hendrick, Russell	Tucker, John M.
Campbell, William B.	King, William	Wilhite, Joseph Y.
Carter, George	Lawrimore, Samuel	Wade, John
Carter, Thomas	Lunsford, Russell	

OLD GRAVES IN ELBERT COUNTY, NEAR PEARL STATION

In memory of

JAMES CLARK

Who died in the 47th year of his age, October 26, 1826.

In memory of

WILLIAM A. CLARK

Who died in the 30th year of his age, November 7, 1843.

OLD WALL CEMETERY, ON PLANTATION OF JAMES McINTOSH, NEAR LONGSTREET

MRS. ANN WALL

Born in 1786. Departed this life, March 18, 1850.

MISS MARTHA HICKS WALL

Born January 5, 1800. Departed this life June 8, 1838.

GRAVEYARD NEAR BALCHIN'S STORE, IN PETERSBURG DISTRICT

Sacred to the memory of

MRS. JANE TATE

Who departed this life on the 26th, April, 1820, in her 77th year A. T.

VAN'S CREEK BAPTIST CHURCH, RUCKERSVILLE

JOSEPH RUCKER

Born January 5, 1788. Died August 27, 1864.

MARGARET RUCKER

Born December 1, 1792. Died September 5, 1864.

DILLARD HERNDON

Born Orange County, Virginia, April 22, 1795, and died in Elbert County, Georgia, July 14, 1873.

AT THE OLD HUNT PLACE, NEAR THE WESTERN CITY LIMITS OF ELBERTON

RICHARDSON HUNT

Born September 2, 1762. Died January 3, 1813.

RUCKERSVILLE METHODIST CHURCH

MRS. NANCY MURRY

Consort of John Murry. Born, 1756. Died, 1850. Aged 95 years.

Sacred to the memory of

PETER ALEXANDER

Born June 22, 1783. Died May 15, 1856.

A just man. A patriot in the service of his country, and a Christian in his daily walk and life, he has gone to his reward.

Sacred to the memory of

ELIZABETH ALEXANDER

Wife of Peter Alexander. Born February 6, 1796. Died December 19, 1852.

Praises on tombs are titles vainly spent;
Woman's good name is her best monument.

STINCHCOMB CHURCH

Hear lie the boddy of

MARTHA ANN KING

Died 10 September, 1826, in the 55 year of her age.

JOSEPH H. SEWELL

Born December 28, 1802. Died September 25th, 1884.

OLD DEADWYLER GRAVEYARD, ON ATHENS HIGHWAY
In memory of
HENRY R. DEADWYLER

Born March 25, 1814, and died December 17, 1851, in City of Savannah, while representing the County of Elbert in the General Assembly of Georgia. Erected by the State of Georgia

To the memory of Henry R. Deadwyler, who died a member of the Legislature from the County of Elbert, Anno Domini 1851.

PETERSBURG CEMETERY
In memory of
JANE WATKINS

Who died on the 21st day of December, 1798. Aged 70 years.

In memory of

Born February 12, 1766. Died April 6, 1841. Leaving a wife and five
JOHN WATKINS
children to deplore their irreparable loss.

Sacred to the memory of
JAMES POPE JR.

A native of the State of Delaware. Obit 4th December, 1808—Etat 35 years, who in attempting to visit his friends in this State after an absence of four years on the wilds of Louisiana, was overtaken by sickness on the way, which terminated in his death two days after he had reached the home of his brother, Alexander Pope, in Petersburg.

Sacred to the memory of
GEORGE PATTON

Of Woodbridge, N. J., who died June 1826, aged 86 years.

Sacred to the memory of
CATHERINE STOKES

Consort of Archibald Stokes and daughter of Col. James and Hannah Patto of Woodridge, N. J., who was born October 24, 1788, and died March 15, 1814.

GRAVEYARD ON PROPERTY OF MRS. S. S. BREWER, NEAR BREWER'S BRIDGE
THOS. DAVIS

Died March 26, 1828, age 50 years.

AMY DAVIS

Died September 20, 1825, age 52 years.

ELMHUST CEMETERY, ELBERTON
Sacred to the memory of
BENAJAH HOUSTON

Was born in the year 1790, and departed this life on the 1st day of February, 1835.

ELIZABETH BURCH

Consort of William S., born April 27, 1770, died July 3, 1855.

BENJAMIN BURCH

Was born November 21, 1801, died January 17, 1819. Aged 18 years.

BETTY HARDMAN

Born January 3, 1763, died October 16, 1849.

HEARDMONT CEMETERY

Sacred to the memory of

SINGLETON W. ALLEN

Born January 14, 1791, died June 6, 1853.
Truth, kindness and justice marked his character through life and his heart and hand were ever ready to relieve the wants of the friendless, the desolate and the afflicted.

"He that hath pity on the poor tendeth to the Lord. And that which he hath given will pay him again."

JUSTICES OF THE PEACE OF ELBERT COUNTY
1790—1805

Allen, William
Allen, Reuben
Alexander, John B.
Alston, James
Bell, James
Barnett, William
Banks, Ralph
Banks, James
Cook, Thomas
Cook, Francis
Carroll, John
Coleman, John
Caldwell, Harry
Cameron, James
Christian, Elijah
Cunningham, John
Daniel, Allen
Fortson, Thomas
Fergus, John
Goode, Edward

Gray, Hezekiah
Hodge, William
Haynes, Moses
Harper, John P.
Hightower, William
Hudson, J. O. A.
Hudson, David
Hunt, R.
Higginbotham, Samuel
Higginbotham, William
Jarratt, Archalus
Jeter, Barnett
Jones, Thomas
Lindsey, Reuben
Lewis, John
Leeper, Allen
Martin, James
McCleskey, James
McCune, William
McDonald, Hugh
McDonald, James

Moss, William
Nelson, Samuel
Pope, Leroy
Pace, Barnabas
Ragland, Evan
Rogers, James
Rucker, Joseph
Shields, Samuel
Scott, Thomas B.
Smith, B.
Staples, John
Stinchcomb, Absolom
Tait, James
Thompson, Robert
Wood, Middleton
Wood, Samuel
Wooten, Thomas
Worsham, Robert
Walker, J.
Watkins, Robert

JUDGES OF CITY COURT OF ELBERTON

1896-1908—P. P. Proffitt
1909-1910—W. D. Tutt.
1911-1916—George C. Grogan.
1917-1920—W. D. Tutt.
1921-1924—George C. Grogan.
1925—Worley A. Nall.
1926-1936—Raymonde Stapleton.

SOLICITORS OF CITY COURT OF ELBERTON

1896-1900—H. J. Brewer.
1901-1908—Thomas J. Brown.
1909-1910—Samuel L. Olive.
1911 —Howard P. Payne.
1925—Raymonde Stapleton.
1926-1936—Howard P. Payne.

COMMANDERS OF EDMUND B. TATE POST OF AMERICAN LEGION

Howard P. Payne	Drukell Jones	Bob Mize
Fred W. Auld	Webb Tatum	Howard P. Payne
Richard P. Adams	Joe Allen	Walter Whitehead
	Walter P. Smith	

MAYORS, COUNCILMEN AND CLERKS OF ELBERTON

1876—Mayor: J. S. Barnett; Councilmen: T. M. Swift Sr., S. L. McCarty, Robert M. Heard, R. F. Tate; Clerk: E. B. Tate Jr.
1877—Mayor: E. W. Bristol; Councilmen: John H. James, R. F. Tate, T. M. Swift Sr., — — Smith; Clerk: E. B. Tate Jr.
1878—Mayor: E. W. Bristol; Councilmen: J. A. Bentley, R. F. Tate, A. C. Matthews; Clerk: W. M. McIntosh Jr.
1879—Mayor: J. L. Heard; Councilmen: E. W. Bristol, J. T. McCarty, McAlpin Arnold; Clerk: W. M. McIntosh Jr.
1880—Mayor: B. A. Matthews; Councilmen: McAlpin Arnold, John P. Shannon, F. B. McMillan, T. M. Swift Sr.; Clerk: W. M. McIntosh Jr.
1881—Mayor: J. H. Jones; Councilmen: W. B. Henry, J. F. Auld, H K Gairdner, A. S. Oliver; Clerk: J. N. Worley.
1882—Mayor: J. I. Chandler; Councilmen: R. F. Tate, A. S. Oliver, J. L. Heard, J. T. McCarty, S. L. Carter; Clerk: J. N. Worley
1883—Mayor: I. G. Swift; Councilmen: J. L. Heard, Z. B. Taylor, E. A. Cason, D. P. Oglesby, S. L. Carter; Clerk: (?)
1884—Mayor: I. G. Swift; Councilmen: J. L. Heard, Z. B. Taylor, E. A. Cason, D. P. Oglesby, S. L. Carter; Clerk: (?)
1885—Mayor: I. G. Swift; Councilmen: L. H. Turner, A. S. Oliver, N. G. Long, T. M. Swift Sr., W. C. Smith; Clerk: George C. Grogan.
1886—Mayor: H. F. Chandler; Councilmen: L. H. Turner, A. S. Olvier, N. G. Long, W. C. Smith, T. M. Swift Sr.; Clerk: George C. Grogan.
1887—Mayor: George C. Grogan; Councilmen: D. P. Oglesby, J. C. Swearengin, T. M. Swift Sr., W. W. Reese, John P. Shannon; Clerk: (?)
1888—Mayor: George C. Grogan; Councilmen: James McIntosh, T. O. Tabor Sr., T. M. Swift Sr., R. M. Heard, W. B. Adams; Clerk: H. J. Brewer.
1889—Mayor: P. M. Hawes; Councilmen: E. A. Cason, I. C. Vanduzer, H. F. Chandler, W. O. Jones, S. N. Carpenter; Clerk: H. J. Brewer.
1890—Mayor: P. M. Hawes; Councilmen: P. M. Heard, R. F. Tate, W. M. Wilcox, D. H. Brown, S. H. Williams; Clerk: J. S. Andrews.
1891—Mayor: N. G. Long; Councilmen: W. B. Henry, R. F. Tate, S. H. Williams, P. M. Hawes, — — Herndon; Clerk: John H. Craig.
1892—Mayor: N. G. Long; Councilmen: D. P. Bell, P. M. Hawes, W. O. Jones, W. W. Adams; Clerk: W. B. Henry.
1893—Mayor: W. O. Jones; Councilmen: McAlpin Arnold, A. S. Oliver, S. S. Brewer, T. O. Tabor Sr., W. W. Adams; Clerk: W. B. Henry.
1894—Mayor: John C. Brown; Councilmen: T. O. Tabor Sr., D. P. Oglesby, A. S. Oliver, W. C. Pressley; Clerk: W. B. Henry.
1895—Mayor: T. O. Tabor Sr.; Councilmen: W. C. Pressley, B. B. Braswell, D. H. Brown, H. J. Brewer; Clerk: W. B. Henry.
1896—Mayor: T. O. Tabor Sr.; Councilmen: P. M. Hawes, W. C. Pressley, B. B. Braswell, D. H. Brown, H. J. Brewer; Clerk: W. B. Henry.
1897—Mayor: W. B. Adams; Councilmen: I. G. Swift, I. C. Vanduzer, W. C. Pressley, D. H. Brown, W. W. Adams; Clerk: W. B. Henry.
1898—Mayor: W. B. Adams; Councilmen: McAlpin Arnold, I. G. Swift, I. C. Vanduzer, John R. Mattox, D. H. Brown; Clerk: W. B. Henry.
1899—Mayor: W. B. Adams; Councilmen: I. C. Vanduzer, John R. Mattox, P. M. Hawes, Fred W. Auld, J. C. Swearengin; Clerk: E. A. Cason.
1900—Mayor: W. B. Adams; Councilmen: I. C. Vanduzer, W. T. Arnold, M. J. Brown, J. R. Mattox, J. A. Almond; Clerk: E. A. Cason.

1901—Mayor: Robert M. Heard; Councilmen: M. J. Brown, J. A. Almond, H. L. Cleveland, H. J. Brewer, W. T. Arnold; Clerk—E. A. Cason.
1902—Mayor: Robert M. Heard; Councilmen: W. T. Arnold, H. L. Cleveland, W. O. Jones, McAlpin Arnold, T. M. Swift Sr.; Clerk: E. A. Cason.
1903—Mayor: Robert N. Heard; Councilmen: E. W. Vest, J. G. Ginn, W. O. Jones, McAlpin Arnold, T. M. Swift Sr.; Clerk: (?)
1904—Mayor: Robert M. Heard; Councilmen: McAlpin Arnold, M. E. Maxwell, E. W. Vest, J. G. Ginn, W. O. Jones; Clerk: (?)
1905—Mayor: B. I. Thornton; Councilmen: R. L. Cauthen, McAlpin Arnold, W. O. Jones, M. E. Maxwell, J. R. Mattox; Clerk: W. F. Jones Sr.
1906—Mayor: B. I. Thornton; Councilmen: S. O. Hawes, I. G. Swift, W. J. Matthews, J. H. Blackwell, R. L. Cauthen; Clerk: W. F. Jones Sr.
1907—Mayor: J. R. Mattox; Councilmen: M. J. Brown, R. L. Cauthen, S. O. Hawes, W. J. Matthews, J. H. Blackwell; Clerk: W. F. Jones Sr.
1908—Mayor: J. R. Mattox; Councilmen: S. O. Hawes, J. H. Blackwell, M. J. Brown, R. L. Cauthen, H. B. Swearengin; Clerk: W. F. Jones Sr.
1909—Mayor: J. M. Wester; Councilmen: J. H. Blackwell, S. O. Hawes, H. B. Swearengin, M. J. Brown, R. L. Cauthen; Clerk: W. F. Jones Sr.
1910—Mayor: J. M. Wester; Councilmen: M. J. Brown, S. O. Hawes, Z. W. Copeland, J. R. Mattox, W. E. Wallis; Clerk: W. F. Jones Sr.
1911—Mayor: J. M. Wester; Councilmen: Z. W. Copeland, R. L. Cauthen, M. J. Brown, W. E. Wallis, J. R. Mattox; Clerk: W. F. Jones Sr.
1912—Mayor: J. M. Wester; Councilmen: R. L. Cauthen, J. R. Mattox, M. J. Brown, W. E. Wallis, Z. W. Copeland; Clerk: W. F. Jones Sr.
1913—Mayor: J. M. Wester; Councilmen: T. J. Hulme, J. G. Ginn, W. E. Wallis, J. R. Mattox, Z. W. Copeland; Clerk: W. F. Jones Sr.
1914—Mayor: J. M. Wester; Councilmen: R. L. Cauthen, S. O. Hawes, W. E. Wallis, T. J. Hulme, J. G. Ginn; Clerk: W. F. Jones Sr.
1915—Mayor: W. A. Nall; Councilmen: W. E. Wallis, J. G. Ginn, S. O. Hawes, J. E. Thornton, R. L. Cauthen; Clerk: W. F. Jones Sr.
1916—Mayor: W. A. Nall; Councilmen: P. R. Wilhite, S. O. Hawes, R. L. Cauthen, W. E. Wallis, J. G. Ginn; Clerk: W. F. Jones Sr.
1917—Mayor: W. A. Nall; Councilmen: J. G. Ginn, S. O. Hawes, J. E. Thornton, T. T. Thornton, P. R. Wilhite; Clerk: W. F. Jones Sr.
1918—Mayor: W. A. Nall; Councilmen: T. T. Thornton, P. R. Wilhite, J. E. Thornton, J. G. Ginn, H. E. Hawes; Clerk: W. F. Jones Sr.
1919—Mayor: W. A. Nall; Councilmen: J. W. Champion, George A. Gaines, P. R. Wilhite, T. T. Thornton, J. G. Ginn; Clerk: W. F. Jones Sr.
1920—Mayor: W. A. Nall; Councilmen: H. E. Hawes, T. T. Thornton, C. A. Arnold, George A. Gaines, J. W. Champion; Clerk: W. F. Jones Sr.
1921—Mayor: John T. Dennis Jr.; Councilmen: George A. Gaines, E. G. Nock, T. T. Thornton, H. E. Hawes, C. A. Arnold; Clerk: W. F. Jones Sr.
1922—Mayor: John T. Dennis Jr.; Councilmen: Fred Herndon, J. H. Grogan, C. A. Arnold, H. E. Hawes, T. T. Thornton; Clerk: W. F. Jones Sr.
1923—Mayor: John T. Dennis Jr.; Councilmen: D. V. Bailey, E. G. Nock, C. A. Arnold, Fred Herndon, J. H. Grogan; Clerk: W. F. Jones Sr.
1924—Mayor: John T. Dennis Jr.; Councilmen: Fred Herndon, R. H. Johnson, C. A. Arnold, E. G. Nock, D. V. Bailey; Clerk: W. F. Jones Sr.
1925—Mayor: T. T. Thornton; Councilmen: R. E. Hudgens, D. V. Bailey, C. A. Arnold, R. H. Johnson, Fred Herndon; Clerk: Albert Higginbotham, H. R. Bynum.
1926—Mayor: T. T. Thornton; Councilmen: R. H. Johnson, C. A. Arnold, T. M. McLanahan, D. V. Bailey, R. E. Hudgens; Clerk: H. R. Bynum.
1927—Mayor: T. T. Thornton; Councilmen: T. M. McLanahan, R. H. Johnson, Perry H. Smith, D. V. Bailey, R. E. Hudgens; Clerk: Miss L. Stillwell.

1928—Mayor: T. T. Thornton; Councilmen: D. V. Bailey, R. H. Johnson, Perry H. Smith, Mrs. Nella S. Paine, R. E. Hudgens; Clerk: Miss L. Stillwell.
1929—Mayor: A. S. Hawes; Councilmen: Mrs. Nella S. Paine, Perry H. Smith, R. H. Johnson, D. V. Bailey, R. E. Hudgens; Clerk: Miss L. S itllwell.
1930—Mayor: A. S. Hawes; Councilmen: H. J. Brown, R. H. Johnson, T. O. Tabor Jr. (successor to Perry H. Smith, deceased), R. E. Hudgens, D. V. Bailey; Clerk: Miss L. Stillwell.
1931—Mayor: A. S. Hawes; Councilmen: D. V. Bailey, R. E. Hudgens, R. H. Johnson, J. S. Asbury, T. O. Tabor Jr.; Clerk: Miss L. Stillwell.
1932—Mayor: A. S. Hawes; Councilmen: T. O. Tabor Jr., R. E. Hudgens, J. S. Asbury, D. V. Bailey, A. S. Johnson; Clerk: Miss L. Stillwell.
1933—Mayor: H. P. Hunter; Councilmen: A. S. Johnson, D. V. Bailey, J. S. Asbury, R. E. Hudgens, T. O. Tabor Jr.; Clerk: Miss L. Stillwell.
1934—Mayor: H. P. Hunter; Councilmen: A. S. Johnson, D. V. Bailey, J. S. Asbury, T. O. Tabor Jr., R. E. Hudgens; Clerk: Miss L. Stillwell.
1935—Mayor: H. P. Hunter; Councilmen: D. V. Bailey, J. S. Asbury, T. O. Tabor Jr., T. R. Stark, Joe Allen; Clerk: Miss L. Stillwell.
1936—Mayor: H. P. Hunter; Councilmen: Joe Allen, T. R. Stark, T. O. Tabor Jr., D. V. Bailey, E. Chandler Brown; Clerk: Miss L. Stillwell.

MEMBERS OF ELBERTON LIGHT INFANTRY MUSTERED INTO FEDERAL SERVICE, AUGUST 7, 1917

OFFICERS

Captain J. E. Kelly
First Lieutenant A. N. Drake
Second Lieutenant Carl L. Bailey
First Sergeant Marshall Adams
Sergeant Fred W. Auld
Sergeant Broadus W. Duncan
Sergeant James Lofton Jones
Sergeant James Wallace Kay
Corporal H. L. Simpson
Corporal Coy C. Partain
Corporal Hubert White
Corporal Rufus N. Hall
Corporal Hilliard C. Avery
Cook William Wansley
Cook Caron Almond
Artificer James Clark Mickle
Bugler Guy M. Sanders

PRIVATES

Thomas J. Almond
Weston C. Almond
Roy Bond
Edward K. Bradshaw
Obie S. Bridges
John W. Brown
George L. Burriss
Willie G. Boswell
David C. Brown
Louis H. Childs
Andrew A. Crawford
Albert A. Dutton
John C. Durham
Marion L. Gaines
Judson B. Grimes
John A. Greeson
Seth S. Hainey
Robert N. Hill
Charles A. Jones
Ernest T. Jones
Henry L. Lingold
J. D. Lock
Rufus Oglesby
H. V. Pleasants
O. E. Pulliam
J. T. Rayle
Marvin L. Rice
Guy W. Rucker
Hascal Smith
Jesse L. Smith
N. W. Snellings
Samuel S. Stalnaker
Ben I. Thornton
Richard A. Truitt
Clifford T. Turner
Sanford A. Turner
James H. Terry
James D. Vaughan
Coy C. Warren
George H. Ward
Fred C. Wansley
Wiley S. Willis
Harry E. Wyche
Robert Wright

A separate sanitary department of the Hospital Corps was temporarily attached to the Elberton Light Infantry composed of First Lieutenant, Benjamin B. Mattox; Sergeant, Edmond B. Grogan; Privates, William M. McIntosh III, Collie Wansley, M. C. Stalnaker, and John Phelps. This entire detachment served in France throughout the war.

Both organizations were camped to the rear of the present Elberton High School Building, on the school playground, and shortly entrained for permanent camp at Macon, Georgia.

EARLY FERRIES OF ELBERT COUNTY, OPERATING UNDER LEGISLATIVE ACTION

SAVANNAH RIVER		BROAD RIVER	
McDonald's	1812	Deadwyler's	1831
Tucker's	1817	Oliver's	1836
Bowman's	1817	Nelms'	1836
Petersburg	1818	Dudley's	1840
Allen's	1831	Nash's	1840

Cook's Ferry was in operation on Savannah River in 1795, but not by legislative action. This Ferry became known officially as Allen's Ferry in 1831 and is now called Cherokee Ferry. It was owned first by Mr. Cook; next by John Heard who sold the same to Reverend Daniel Tucker in 1798, and it was later purchased by Singleton W. Allen. From the Allen estate it went into the possession of William H. Mattox and is today owned by a large power company. Operation ceased during the year 1928.

ABSTRACT OF EARLY WILLS AND ADMINISTRATIONS

January 29, 1791—David Adams applied for Letters of Administration on James Adams estate, late of this county, deceased. Granted 2nd day of March, 1791.

February 22, 1791—John Ferrel applied for Letters of Administration on the estate of Lewis Davis, late of this county, deceased.

June 18, 1791—Stephen Fulghum applied for Letters of Administration on the estate of Martin Fulghum of the county aforesaid, deceased.

January 17, 1792—Samuel Watkins, Robert Thompson and Jesse Thompson made application for Letters of Administration on the estate of Oliver Thompson.

Will of Jacob Cleveland. Executed April 4, 1790. Recorded May 16, 1791. Value of estate: P., 352; S., 7; D., 10.
Provisions: All just debts to be paid. "Give to my wife house wherein I do now dwell with all furniture and the lands and the negro named Chain, Tom and Aaron, and all other tenements that lie about it, and if the above named wench named Chain have another child after this date I give it to my daughter, Elizabeth, during her life and then to her heirs, if any, and if she dies without any heirs then it shall fall to my two youngest sons, and to be equally divided between them, Reuben Cleveland and Daniel Cleveland and ITEM. I give to my son, Jeremiah Cleveland, a bond that I have on John Stagton."
Executors: Wife, Will Kidd and Jeremiah Cleveland. Witnesses: Reuben White and John White.

Will of Jasper Smith. Executed December 1, 1790. Recorded May 19, 1791. Value of estate: P., 213; S., 8; D., 0.
Provisions: To wife, Rebeckah, one negro wench named Lucy during her life and at her death to be equally divided among those children she had by me, and her son, Thos." Remainder of estate to go to wife for life and to children, share and share alike, upon her death. Daughters,

Betsy and Sally, and step-son, Thomas, given 15 pounds in property when they become of age or marry.

Executors: Wife, James Marks and Thomas B. Scott. Appraisers: Benjamin Rogers, Brazel Brawner and James Shepard.

Will of James Meredith. Executed January 13, 1791. Recorded May 19, 1791. Value of estate: P., 350.

Provisions: All just debts to be paid. "I give to my wife, Sarah, during her life one-fifth of my real estate and to my four youngest children, namely, Patty, Nancy, Molly and Sally or the survivant of them at her death and to their heirs all of my real estate saving to my said wife the use of one-fifth thereof during her life, as above mentioned." To daughter, Rebeckah, the account due by her deceased husband, Jasper Smith, and one negro named Sarah, loaned her husband in North Carolina.

Executors: Wife, William Moore of Rock Creek, in Wilkes County. Appraisers: Basil Brawner, William Hallen and James Tuttel. (Note: James Meredith was the first man to be executed in Elbert County).

Will of Benjamin Higginbotham. No execution date given. Recorded July 25, 1791. Value of estate: P., 464; S., 5; D., 9.

Provisions: Gives one slave each to daughter, Ann; sons, Caleb, William, Benjamin, Joseph, Francis. To wife, Elizabeth, four slaves, household goods, cattle, hogs, and all crops on hand for her life and at her death to be divided between children.

Executors: Wife; sons, William, Joseph and Francis. Witnesses: Joseph Williams, Drury Ledbetter and John Henley. Appraisers: William Mulvern, Nathan Bond and Robert Pulliam.

Will of James Easter. Executed May 19, 1791. Recorded February 14, 1792. Value of estate: P., 1171; S., 12; D., 3.

Provisions: To wife, land and four negroes. To daughter, Mary Ann, personal property. To daughter, Elizabeth, five shillings; and to son, William Thompson Easter, 350 acres of land. To son, Booker Burton Easter, 250 acres of land, one negro boy, two cows and calves and one feather bed. To daughter, Patty Aycock, and William Aycock (son-in-law), a tract of land and one negro wench with increase. To sons, Lewis and Champain, a tract of land and slaves. To daughter, Tabby Napier and Thomas Napier (son-in-law), a tract of land and one negro girl with increase. To daughter, Teres, a negro woman with increase, and two cows and calves. To daughters, Lottie, Sophia and Teres, land in Franklin County. To daughter, Marjary, five shillings.

Executors: Wife, Sarah Easter, William Thompson Easter, Richard Easter, William Thompson Sr., Robert Thompson, Benjamin Taliaferro. (The latter declining to serve). Witnesses: Phillip Wray, Wells Thompson, Stephen Ellington. Appraisers: None given.

Will of Joseph Williams. Executed September 13, 1792. Recorded October 15, 1792. Value of estate not given.

Provisions: To sons, John, Matthew, and grandson, Joseph, negroes. To son, Matthew, all household goods and stock.

Executors: John and Matthew Williams. Witnesses: W. Hatcher, William Sandhester and Jenny Freeman.

Will of John Farley Thompson. Executed September 3, 1792. Recorded February 5, 1793. Value of estate: P., 427; S., 9; D., 7.

Provisions: Property divided between children, John, Isham, Peter, Lewis, Sally, Milly, Mary and Tabby.

Executors: John Farley Thompson Jr., Lewis Thompson. Appraisers: Robert L. Tate, William Chisholm and Nathaniel Allen.

The estate of Reverend Jeremiah Walker, famous Baptist minister, was appraised by William Booker, David Hudson and William on February 3, 1793. The value of the estate was P., 800.

The estate of Samuel Crockett was appraised by William Banks, William McKenzee and Solomon McAlpin on June 2, 1793. Value: P., 180; S., 13; D., 4.

The estate of John Dudley was appraised on January 29, 1793, and the value shown was: P., 113; S., 14; D., 2.

The appraisal of the estate of James Cook filed for record October 17, 1792, shows a value of: P., 167; S., 12; D., 4. James Watson Cooke was appointed administrator.

The estate of Hugh Kinkade was appraised by Christopher Clark, William Walton and William Blake on January 20, 1790. The value shown was: P., 37; S., 1; D., 2.

David Adams applied for letters of administration, January 29, 1791, on the estate of James Adams. Letters granted March 2, 1791. Value of estate: P., 40; S., 6; D., ½.

John Ferrell applied for letters of administration, February 22, 1791, on the estate of Lewis Davis. Letters granted May 7, 1791. Value of estate: P., 20; S., 13; D., 4.

Aley Sutton and James McCluskey applied for letters of administration, June 16, 1791, on the estate of William Sutton. Letters granted July 22, 1792. Value of estate: P., 108; S., 0; D., 6.

Thomas Burton applied for letters of administration, October 4, 1791, on the estate of Bradock Vodan. Letters granted January 5, 1792.

Matthew Collier applied for letters of administration, December 15, 1791, on the estate of Hugh Kincade. Letters granted January 17, 1792. Value of estate: P., 37; S., 1; D., 2.

LAND LOTTERIES OF 1806, 1821, 1827, 1832

LOTTERY OF 1806

CAPTAIN THOMAS OLIVER'S DISTRICT

Name	Draws	Name	Draws
Allgood, John	2	Ferington, Aaron, deceased, orphans of	1
Burden, Archibald	2	Gatewood, Catherine, wid.	1
Burden, James	2	Greenwood, Beverly	2
Burgamy, Nathaniel	2	Greenwood, George	2
Burden, Edmond	1	Hunt, Richardson	2
Burden, Hannah, wid.	1	Hendricks, Abijah	2
Childres, Thomas	2	Higginbotham, Wm.	2
Christian, James	2	Hathcock, Oziah	2
Chrittington, Wm.	2	Higginbotham, Benj.	2
Christian, Jesse	2	Hendricks, Sarah, wid.	1
Chrittington, Henry	2	Higginbotham, Anna	1
Chrittington, Pryor	2	Higginbotham, Sarah	1
Chrittington, Henry	1	Higginbotham, Joseph	2
Chrittington, Robert	1	Hawthorn, Joseph	2
Coker, Abraham	2	Higginbotham, Francis	2
Coker, Malachi	2	Hathcock, William	2
Christian, Presley	2	Ham, Ambrose	2
Christian, William	2	Hathcock, Harbert	1
Christian, Charles	2	Harris, Jeptha V.	2
Carter, Thomas	2	Ham, John	2
Davis, Hickman	2	Hathcock, Harbert	1
Davis, Nancy	1	Higginbotham, Gabriel	2
Ellis, Ziller	1	Jorden, Redden	2
Fowler, Arthur	2		

	Draws		Draws
Jorden, James Sr.	2	Paten, Mary	1
James, Enoch	2	Paten, Margarette, wid.	1
King, William	2	Penn, William	1
Kannady, William M.	1	Page, Levil	1
Lawremore, Sarah, wid.	1	Rogers, Elisha	2
Lawremore, Nicholas, deceased, orphans of	1	Rowsey, John Sr.	2
		Ridgedale, Daisy	2
Lawremore, Sally	1	Rowsey, Edmond	2
Lawremore, Anna	1	Rowsey, Clary	2
Lawremore, Alex	1	Shepard, Robert	2
Lawremore, James	1	Shepard, Samuel	2
Lawremore, Samuel	1	Shepard, Peter	2
Lawless, John, deceased, orphans of	2	Shepard, Anna, wid.	1
		Shepard, Nancy	1
McCoy, William	2	Satterwhite, Nancy	1
Martin, John	1	Smith, John Sr.	2
McCoy, Reuben	2	Staples, John	2
Oliver, Dyonecious	2	Stephens, John, deceased, orphans of	1
Penn, Eliz. R.	1		
Penn, Fanney	1	Upshaw, John Sr.	2
Penn, Thomas	2	Upshaw, Sarah	1
Purkins, William	2	Upshaw, Catherine	1
Penn, Benjamin	2	Upshaw, Leroy	1
Penn, Phillip	2	Upshaw, John Jr.	2
Pledger, Sally	1	Varner, James	2
Purkins, Elizabeth	1	White, Joshua	2

We certify the foregoing statement for Captain Thomas Oliver's Company in Major Richardson Hunt's Battalion to be correct as far as we know or believe. Given under our hands as Commissioners for said Battalion, for the ensuing Land Lottery, this 26th of August, 1806.

(Signed) WILLIAM BANKS.
CHAS. CARTER.

CAPTAIN DUNSTON BLACKWELL'S DISTRICT

	Draws		Draws
Arnold, James Jr.	2	Blackwell, Banks	1
Anglin, James	2	Blackwell, Dunston	1
Adams, James Sr.	2	Blackwell, Ralph	1
Allen, Thomas	2	Blackwell, Sally N.	1
Brown, James N.	2	Blackwell, Jos., deceased, orphans of	1
Brown, Benjamin	2		
Burks, Robert	2	Banks, William	2
Beverly, Anthony	2	Clark, Francis, deceased, orphans of	1
Bramblett, Henry	2		
Bramblett, John	2	Carr, Samuel	2
Bramblett, Reuben	2	Clark, Williamson	2
Bailey, Julin	2	Carrel, Jessey	2
Bailey, Samuel	2	Christler, Julius	2
Bailey, James	2	Craft, John	2
Bond, Nathan Sr.	2	Carter, James	2
Bramblett, Margaret	1	Clement, Simon	2
Bramblett, Lott	1	Dudley, Nicholas	2
Brown, Margarett	1	Davis, Meredith	2
Bond, Nathan Jr.	2	Driver, Betsy, wid.	1
Bowers, William	2	Driver, Bird, deceased, orphans	1
Bailey, Elizabeth	1	Davis, Sarah	1
Bailey, Hezekiah	2	Dutton, James	2

	Draws		Draws
Eavenston, George	2	Magee, William Sr.	2
Eavenston, Susannah	1	Maxwell, Thomas Sr.	2
Eavenston, Eli	2	Newborn, Archabald	2
Easter, Champion	2	Nix, Joseph Sr.	2
Fannin, Laughlin	2	Norris, James	2
Faulkenberry, Jacob	2	Nelms, Jurden	2
Ford, Sarah, wid.	1	Nelms, Ann, wid.	1
Ford, John, deceased, orphans of	1	Nelms, Wm., deceased, orphans of	1
Fannin, Benjamin	2	Nelms, Polley	1
Fleming, Moses	2	Nelms, Penelepy	1
Fleming, John	1	Nix, Lewcy	1
Fortson, Benjamin	2	Patterson, John Sr.	2
Gaar, Lewis	2	Ponder, Abner	2
Gatewood, Eliz., wid.	1	Ponder, Jesse	2
Golden, Matthew	2	Powell, Honourrias	1
Gaar, Joel	2	Ponder, Ruben	1
Gaar, Adam	2	Ponder, Betsy	1
Gaines, William	2	Pulliam, Joseph	1
Gunn, Elisha	2	Rucker, Amzon	1
Ginn, Jesse	2	Robertson, William	1
Gaar, Michel, deceased, orphans of	1	Rucker, John Sr.	2
Hulme, William	2	Sandidge, Claiborn	2
Hall, Robert Sr.	2	Smith, John	2
Hall, Robert Jr.	2	Smith, Zachariah	2
Henderson, Simeon	2	Smith, David	2
Hunt, Nathaniel	1	Smith, Jesse	2
Hansard, Jane, wid.	1	Smith, Jemima, wid.	1
Hansard, William, deceased, orphans of	1	Smith, Benj., deceased, orphans of	1
Herndon, Edward	2	Stubbs, Peter	2
Higginbotham, John	1	Sullivant, Patsy	1
Higginbotham, Jacob Sr.	2	Thornton, Mark Sr.	2
Hilley, Thomas Jr.	2	Taylor, Benjamin	2
Higginbotham, James	2	Thornton, Dozier Sr.	2
Higginbotham, John S.	2	Thornton, Jeremiah	2
Henderson, James	2	Taylor, Benjamin	2
Hall, William	2	Teasley, James	2
Kettler, John	2	Teasley, Isom	2
Lions, John	2	Tomason, George	2
Meret, Towan	2	Teasley, William	2
Magee, William	2	Underwood, Ann, wid.	1
Maxwell, Thomas Jr.	2	Underwood, Joshua, deceased, orphans of	1
Maxwell, Joel	2	White, Henry	2
Moss, Ephraim	2	White, Daniel	2
Morrison, Peter	2	White, William	1
Murrah, Tabitha	1	Witt, Charles	2
Murrah, Nancy, wid.	1	Woodall, Joseph	2
Murrah, John, deceased, orphans of	1	Williamson, Betsy C.	1
Magee, Lewis	2	White, Thomas	1

We certify the foregoing sheets for Captain Dunston Blackwell's District in Major Richardson Hunt's Battalion to be correct as far as we know or believe. Given under our hands as Commissioners in said Battalion for the ensuing Land Lottery, this 26th day of August. 1806.

(Signed) WILLIAM BANKS.
CHAS. CARTER.

CAPTAIN GEORGE ROEBUCK'S DISTRICT

No certificates attached.

Name	Draws
Adams, William	2
Alexander, William	2
Allen, Ephraim	2
Boughtright, William Sr.	2
Boughtright, William Jr.	2
Cash, Nancy	1
Cash, Howard Sr.	2
Cunningham, John Sr.	2
Crump, Charles	2
Chipman, Joseph	2
Cash, John	2
Cash, James	2
Doss, Joel	2
Dutton, Thomas	2
Franklin, Polley	1
Franklin, David	2
Ferrell, Micajah	2
Franklin, Henry	2
Franklin, Sarah, wid.	1
Franklin, Edmond, orphans of	1
Franklin, Mary, wid.	1
Franklin, Philemon, orphans of	1
Franklin, Milly E.	1
Franklin, Sampson	1
Ferrell, Sampson	1
Ferrell, Wiley	1
Gaines, Francis	2
Gaines, Talefaria	2
Gully, Richard	2
Gaines, Richard S.	2
Gregg, Joanas, wid.	1
Gregg, Thomas, orphans of	1
Hulme, John	2
Hinton, Peter	2
Hailey, Ruben	1
Head, William	2
Humber, John	1
Hailey, William	2
Johnston, John	2
Jones, James	2
Jurden, John	2
Jinkins, Samuel	2
Jurden, Fountain	2
Jurden, James	2
Jurden, Margaret	1
King, Thomas	2
Lockhard, James	2
Lively, Charles	2
Lovell, Gabrile	2
McAlpin, Mary, wid.	1
McCune, Thomas	2
McCune, Jean, wid.	1
McCune, Wm., orphans by Jane McCune	1
McCune, Wm., orphans by Mary McCune	2
McGwing, John	2
McGuire, Anderson	2
Meanes, William	2
Meanes, Hugh	2
McGuire, Allegena	2
Patterson, John Sr.	2
Patterson, Alex	2
Patterson, Joseph	2
Prewitt, William	2
Pealer, Abner	2
Riley, James	2
Roebuck, Robert Jr.	1
Shiflett, Pickett	2
Smith, Richard	2
Shackleford, James	2
Turner, Martin, orphans of	1
Terrell, William	2
Taylor, William	2
Terrell, Jeremiah	2
Terrell, Mary	2
Underwood, William H.	2
Underwood, Joseph	2
Wheeler, Thomas	2
Wheeler, George	2
Wade, Ann, wid.	1
Wade, Joshua, orphans of	1
Warren, Jeremiah, orphans of	1

CAPTAIN ISAAC J. BARRETT'S DISTRICT

Name	Draws
Bennett, Moses	2
Bobo, Benjamin	2
Barrett, Isaac J.	2
Braden, William	2
Bennett, Joel	2
Brown, Daniel	1
Bobo, Lewis, orphans of	1
Cunningham, John Jr.	1
Crow, Samuel	2
Cauthin, John	2
Cauthin, Polley	1
Carter, Thos. Sr.	2
Childrus, Robert	2
Carter, Sarah	1
Carden, Robert	2
Cook, William	2
Dobbs, Josiah	2
Dobbs, Silus	2
Dunnyhoo, Cornelius	2
Dollar, Ambrus	2
Dollar, James	2
Dobbs, John	2

	Draws		Draws
Dobbs, Lucey, wid.	1	McGarrita, Gardner	2
Dobbs, Peter	2	Nail, Benjamin	2
Dobbs, Lot	2	Parks, Mary, wid.	1
Fitzjarreld, George Sr.	2	Pritchett, George	1
Gore, Lydia	1	Pritchett, Nicholas	2
Haynes, Moses Sr.	2	Rumsey, Thomas	2
Haynes, Stephen, orphans of	1	Rumsey, John	2
Harper, Edward	2	Rumsey, Fanny	1
Holms, Shadrack	2	Rumsey, Polly	1
Harper, Sarah	1	Rumsey, William	2
Holmes, Gideon Sr.	2	Rumsey, Henry	1
Howard, Nehemiah	2	Richardson, Amos	2
Hooker, Thomas Sr.	2	Richardson, Ann, wid.	1
Haynes, Moses Jr.	2	Scales, Thomas, deceased, orphans of	1
Holmes, Gideon Jr.	2	Sammons, Lewis	2
Howard, Joseph	2	Skelton, Reecy	2
Holmes, Richard	2	Smith, Ralph	2
Haynes, William	2	Smith, Betsy, wid.	1
Hooker, Thomas Jr.	2	Smith, Archer, deceased, orphans of	1
Holmes, Ezekiel	1	Scales, John Jr.	2
Hooker, William	2	Skelton, Jachariah	2
Hathcock, William, orphans of	1	Thompson, Samuel	1
Jarrall, Archabald	2	Tweedle, James	2
Kidd, Martin	2	Thompson, Solomon	2
Kees, Cornelous	2	Thompson, Nathan	2
Lovengood, Polly	1	Taylor, Elisha	2
Lovengood, Harmon W.	1	Thompson, Jesse	2
Mitchell, William	2	Thompson, Andrew	1
Mitchell, John	2	Williamson, John	2
Mitchell, Patrick	2	Willmath, William	2
Moor, Nancy	1	Ward, Mathias	2
Mitchell, Elizabeth	1	White, William	2
Megarity, Abner	1	Woodward, Thomas, deceased, orphans of	1
Moor, John, deceased, orphans of	1	No certificate attached.	
McDonald, John Sr.	2		
McMartin, Dunkin	2		
McMullan, John Sr.	2		

26th day of August, 1806.

CAPTAIN WILLIAM McGUIRE'S DISTRICT

	Draws		Draws
Ashworth, Benjamin	2	Dooly, William Jr.	2
Adderson, Thomas	2	Driver, William	1
Ashley, John	2	Dodd, Elizabeth	1
Ashworth, Joab	1	Dooly, Nancy	1
Ashworth, John	2	Faguson, Norman	2
Braden, Rachel	1	Foster, Worsham	1
Braden, Hannah, wid.	1	Gay, Ann, wid.	1
Brown, Polly	1	Gordon, Gilbert, orphans of	1
Brown, Andrew	2	Herndon, Iseral	2
Brown, James Sr.	2	Harper, Rhoderick	2
Brown, Roland	2	Hill, Jacob	2
Beedon, Ephraim	2	Harper, Henry	2
Braden, John	2	Harper, Thomas	2
Banks, John	2	Highsmith, James	2
Childs, John	2	Harcrow, Hugh	2
Dodd, William	2	Hunt, James	2
Dooly, William Sr.	2	Herndon, Thomas	2

	Draws		Draws
Hutchings, Zachariah	2	McGuire, William	2
Herndon, George, deceased, orphans of	2	Page, William	2
		Powell, Killis	2
James, Enoch Sr.	2	Powell, Francis Jr.	1
Johnson, Malcolm	2	Powell, Lanston	1
Johnson, Caty, wid.	1	Powell, Francis Sr.	2
Johnson, John, deceased, orphans of	1	Powell, William R.	2
		Parks, Abraham	2
James, Thomas	2	Powell, Lurany	1
Johnson, Angus	2	Rice, Robert	2
James, Angus	2	Roe, Susannah	1
James, Samuel	2	Skelton, John	2
Johnson, Archabald	2	Scales, John Sr.	2
Johnson, Rachael, wid.	1	Selfridge, Robert	2
King, Catherine, wid.	1	Stowers, Lewis	2
King, John	2	Sharyer, William	2
McMullin, Patrick	2	Sharyer, Thomas	1
McCurry, Angus	2	Scales, Thomas	1
McDonald, Roderick	2	Scales, Thomas	1
McDonald, Donald Sr.	2	Shiflett, Powell	1
McDonald, John	2	Sawyer, Robert	1
Magee, Ansell	2	Selfridge, Nancy	1
McDonald, Ronnald	2	Standerfer, Anderson	1
McCurry, John	2	Standeford, Benjamin	2
McDonald, Donald Jr.	2	Teasley, Silus	2
McCurry, Flora, wid.	1	Tyner, Richard Sr.	2
McCurry, Daniel, orphans of	1	Tyner, Richard Jr.	1
Montgomery, Elizabeth, wid.	1	White, Jenny	1

We certify the foregoing statement for Captain Wm. McGuire's Company in Major Richardson's Hunt's Battalion for ensuing Land Lottery.

(Signed) WILLIAM BANKS.
CHAS. CARTER.

The land given in this lottery was acquired from the Creek Indians and was situated in what is now Baldwin and Wilkinson Counties.

Persons entitled to draw were free white males, 21 years of age and upward, who were citizens of the United States and had been citizens of Georgia three years before the passage of the act, and who had paid taxes, were entitled to draw once. Every free white male, coming under the foregoing qualifications having a wife and legitimate child, or children, under the age of 21 years were entitled to two draws. All widows, coming under the citizenship qualifications, all free white females and all families of orphans were entitled to one draw. In the event the orphan, or orphans, father and mother were both deceased they were entitled to two draws pro- provided, however, said orphan, or orphans, did not draw a prize in the last land lottery.

No mention is made of military service being requisite to drawing and no special provision is made for the soldiers of any war.

LAND LOTTERY OF 1821

The land disposed of in this lottery was secured from the Creek and Cherokee Indians by treaty. This territory at the time of the survey comprised the five original counties of Dooly, Fayette, Henry, Houston, and Monroe. This territory has since been divided into 21 counties.

No mention is made of military service and no provision is made for the soldiers of any war.

MAJOR CHARLES W. CHRISTIAN'S BATTALION, NO. 152
CAPTAIN RUFUS CHRISTIAN'S DISTRICT, NO. 202

	Draws		Draws
Almand, John	2	Moon, Stephen	2
Beard, Robert	2	Moore, William	2
Beard, Samuel	1	Moon, John	2
Bradley, Ann, wid.	1	Nix, Edward	1
Bradley, Robt. C., orphans of	1	Oglesby, Lindsey	1
Booth, Nancy, wid.	1	Oliver, James	2
Boothe, Nathaniel, orphans of	1	Parham, Southern	1
Boothe, Prudence	1	Parham, Sarah, wid.	1
Chambless, James E.	1	Ridgeway, Bazel	1
Christian, Ira	1	Ridgeway, James	2
Chappell, Thomas B.	2	Webb, Margaret, wid.	1
Deadwyler, Joseph	1	Webb, Clairborn, orphans of	1
David, Jacob W.	2	Webb, Clabourn	1
Deadwyler, Martin	2	Wells, William	2
Eadwards, John	2	Wilhite, John R.	1
Falkner, John	2	Webb, Archer	1
Johnson, James	1	White, Sally, wid.	1
Jones, Micajah	2	White, Anderson	2
Kerlin, Elizabeth	1	Wood, Francis	1
Kerlin, Samuel	1	White, Nicholas, orphans of	1
King, James	2	Woods, Bennett	1
Lesuer, Samuel Sr.	2	Unis, Samuel	1
Lesuer, Mede	1	Upshaw, William	2

CAPTAIN JAMES HANNA'S DISTRICT

	Draws		Draws
Booth, Joel	1	Ham, Reuben, orphans of	1
Dudley, John T.	2	Handley, Jarrett Sr., orphans of	1
Dudley, James L.	1	Handley, Drury B. P.	1
Denny, Robert	2	Jordan, Rachel, wid.	2
Davis, William	1	LeGrand, John N.	1
Dudley, Jarrott	1	Largent, Jesse, orphans of	1
Dudley, John D.	2	Moon, Sarah, wid.	1
Elder, William	1	McCommack, John	2
Falk, Thomas	1	Nelms, William	2
Hendrick, Whitehead	1	Nelmes, Jonathan	2
Hanna, James Jr.	1	Nix, Samuel	2
Hendrick, Brantley	1	Rains, Dabney	2
Hendrick, James	1	Ruff, Stephen	2
Hendrick, Milam	1	Ruff, Allen	1
Hendrick, Eli	1	Robbards, John	1
Ham, Jenny, wid.	1	Penn, Phillip	2

	Draws		Draws
Quinn, Matthew	2	Skinner, Clary, wid.	1
Seemore, Zachariah	2	Skinner, George M.	2
Story, Lucy, wid.	1	Tucker, Robert	1

CAPTAIN JOHN MERRITT'S DISTRICT

	Draws		Draws
Baskin, Robert	2	Horton, Elizabeth	1
Bray, David	2	Horton, Walker	1
Ballenger, John Jr.	2	Hagan, Richard, orphan of	1
Ballard, Jesse	2	Jordan, Matthew	2
Brown, Abraham	2	LeGrand, Jesse	1
Brown, Henry	2	LeGrand, William	1
Ballenger, David	2	Merritt, John	1
Blackwell, Sarah, wid.	1	Magarity, Kindred	2
Bray, John	2	Meritt, Torren	2
Burnett, Jeremiah	2	Nix, Lucy, wid.	1
Brantlet, Henry	2	Page, William	2
Brantlet, Lott	1	Patterson, Rebecca, wid.	1
Bates, George	2	Parker, Benjamin B.	1
Cheek, Burgess	2	Rice, Leonard	2
Carr, David	2	Spears, Salian, wid.	1
Cheek, William	2	Spears, Joshua, orphans of	1
Clark, Edward	2	Spears, Shadrack	1
Carr, John	1	Smith, Nathaniel	1
Coker, John	1	Smith, Fulden	1
David, Humphrey	1	Steel, Robert	1
Duncan, Nathaniel	1	White, Eppy	2
Duncan, Henry	1	Winn, Benjamin	2
Davis, Thomas L.	1	Wallis, Thomas	2
Gates, James	2	White, Martin	2
Ginn, Jesse	2	Vines, Sarah, wid.	1
Gentry, Wiatt	2	Vines, Isaac, orphans of	1
Harbin, Sally, wid.	1	Vines, John	1
Harbin, William, orphans of	1	Vines, Parnal	1
Hendrick, Jesse	2	Vines, James	1
Head, Jabes B.	2		

CAPTAIN BENJAMIN PENN'S DISTRICT

	Draws		Draws
Andrew, Benjamin Jr.	2	Harmon, John Sr.	2
Allgood, John	1	Hicks, David	2
Bond, William	2	Hendrick, Abijah's orphans	1
Brawner, Joel	2	Hicks, Samuel	1
Coleman, Jesse	2	Hicks, Frederick	2
Carter, George	2	Jordan, William	2
Chambers, John	2	King, John	1
Chambers, William S.	2	King, Ambrose B.	1
Christian, William P.	2	McCoy, Nancy	1
Christian, Elijah D.	1	McCoy, William's orphan	1
Christian, Elisha	2	Mann, William H.	2
Christian, James G.	1	Mann, William	2
Christian, Elijah W.	1	Mann, James W.	1
Christian, James Sr.	2	Pledger, Isaac M.	1
Critendon, Juda, wid.	1	Penn, William	2
Ford, Joseph	1	Pucket, James	2
Fitts, William H.	2	Peler, Benjamin	2

	Draws		Draws
Pledger, Lemuel	2	Scales, George	2
Pruitt, William	1	Stephens, Fereby, wid.	1
Pruitt, Sunsannah, wid.	1	Shepherd, Nathan	2
Pledger, Joseph P.	1	Shepherd, Nathaniel	1
Pruitt, David	2	Shepherd, Richard H.	1
Pledger, Thomas Jr.	2	Stinchcomb, Nathaniel	1
Peeler, Abner	2	Statham, John	1
Richards, Rachel, wid.	1	Statham, William	2
Richards, Reuben's orphans	1	Thompson, Gaines	1
Stinchcomb, Levi	2	Turman, Seaborn	2
Standerford, Tilman	1	Roberts, Jesse	2
Shepherd, Samuel	1		

CAPTAN LEROY UPSHAW'S DISTRICT

	Draws		Draws
Akins, Absolom's orphans	1	Inskeep, George	1
Andrew, Charles	1	King, Jacob W.	2
Brown, Reben	2	King, William Sr.	2
Brown, Edward	2	Maxwell, Simeon	2
Burns, William	2	Mason, Joseph P.	1
Carter, Robert M.	2	Oliver, Thomas Sr.	2
Cook, Fenton	1	Pledger, John S.	Illegible
Cook, William, orphans of	2	Rowsey, Edmond	1
Chandler, Washington	1	Ragland, Evan	1
Depriest, James A.	1	Stodghill, Willis	1
Dailey, Samuel C.	2	Skinner, Morris	2
David, Isaac	1	Skinner, Archer, orphan of	1
Ellington, Stephen, orphans of	1	Smith, Thomas	1
Fortson, Richard	2	Turman, Samuel	1
Fortson, William	2	Thornton, Thomas A.	2
Fortson, Thomas Sr.	2	Tait, William	2
Green, Castoe	1	Verdel, John A.	2
Griffin, Margaret, wid.	1	Weston, Job	1
Griffin, Joseph, orphans of	1	Wilhite, Lewis	2
Gibbs, William	2	Wilhite, Joseph G.	2
Hickman, Walter	2	Wood, James L.	1
Hendricks, William	2	Wilhite, John B.	2
Hall, Thomas	1	Winkfield, John Y.	1
Hall, Samuel	1	Williams, John	1
Hall, John	1		

GEORGIA, Elbert County.

We, James D. Jarratt and Samuel Bentley, appointed by the Honorable, the Inferior Court of the State and County aforesaid to take a return of the amount of draws claimed in the Land Lottery contemplated and authorized by an Act of the General Assembly of said State passed at an extra session thereof, assented to the 15th day of May, 1821, by persons residing in the 142nd Battalion Georgia Militia in said State and County, do hereby certify the foregoing is a correct list and return of the same.

Given under our hands this 13th of July, 1821.

(Signed) SAMUEL BENTLEY.
JAMES D. JARRATT.

LAND LOTTERY OF 1827

The lands disposed of in this lottery were ceded at Indian Springs on February 12, 1825, and embraced the five original counties of Carroll, Coweta, Lee, Muscogee, and Troup.

Persons eligible for participation were Revolutionary soldiers, widows of Revolutionary soldiers, white males over the age of 18 years who had resided in Georgia for more than three years, soldiers of the War of 1812, soldiers of the Indian wars and persons who had not taken part in previous lotteries.

KEY

h. of f.	Head of famliy.
s.	Single.
id.	Idiot.
f. a.	Minor whose father had been absent three years from State.
h. a.	Woman whose husband had been absent three years.
orphs.	Orphans.
wid.	Widow.
w. r. s.	Widow of Revolutionary soldier.
r. s.	Revolutionary soldier.

MAJOR THOMAS ALLEN'S BATTALION
CAPTAIN TATE'S DISTRICT

Name	Draws	Name	Draws
Burton, Thomas, r. s.	2	Hudson, John H., h. of f.	2
Beville, Thomas, h. of f.	2	Colbert, Susannah, w. r. s.	1
Miller, Jedidah S., h. of f.	2	Fleming, Margaret, w. r. s.	1
Watkins, Henry M., s.	1	Chisenhall, Dilany, h. of f.	2
Tate, Zimri W., s.	1	Cunningham, William, r. s.	1
Tate, Thomas J., s.	1	Hudson, David B., h. of f.	2
Hamilton, Elisha, s.	1	Burton, Nicholas, s.	1
Evans, Elizabeth, w. & w. r. s.	2	Rich, John, orphs. of	1
Tate, Elizabeth, w. r. s.	1	Cunningham, Minter, orphs. of	1
Tate, Elam, s.	1	Coleman, James, h. of f.	2
Tate, Enos Minor, s.	1	Coleman, Abraham, s.	1
Urquhart, John A., s.	1	Banks, John, s.	1
Dickson, Blackman, s.	1	Speed, Wade, s.	1
Tate, Isaac M., s	1	Tate, Thomas, orphs. of	2
Burton, Girman, s.	1	Tate, Jessey C., s.	1
Burton, Paten, s.	1	Saxton, Eliz. M., w. r. s.	1
Barron, Britton B., s.	1	Burton, Nelson B., h. of f.	2
Roan, John, h. of f.	2	Rich, Richmond, s.	1
Dickson, Samuel, orphs. of	1	Rembert, Samuel H., s.	1

CAPTAIN BELL'S DISTRICT

Name	Draws	Name	Draws
Clark, Samuel, s.	1	Clark, wid. & w. r. s.	2
Naish, Frances, wid.	1	Turman, Robert G., s.	1
Williams, Matthew J., orph. of	1	Cook, Jesse M., s.	1
Snellings, Rebecka, w. r. s.	1	Cook, Joshua, orphs. of	1
Cook, John, r. s.	2	Carter, Nathis, orphs. of	1
Jones, Jensey, orph. of	1	Moon, William, s.	1
Cook, Mary, wid. & w. r. s.	2	Clark, Christopher H., s.	1
Jack, Margaret, wid. & w. r. s.	2	Kemp, David V., h. of f.	2

	Draws		Draws
Bell, David, s.	1	Childers, William, s.	2
Martin, Nathaniel, s.	1	Bell, Joseph, orph. of	1
Martain, Henry, s.	1	Cook, Smith Jr., s.	1
Dye, Jane, wid.	1	Allgood, Mary, wid.	1
Dye, Thompson orphs. of	1	Allgood, Peter, orphs. of	1
Williams, John, h. of f.	2	Barr, Robert S., h. of f.	2
Key, William B., r. s.	1	Mobley, William, s.	2
Perrian, John, s.	1	Allgood, John, r. s.	1
Wodley, Temporine, wid.	2	Bullard, Ann, wid. & w. r. s.	2
Wodley, John, orphs. of	2	Burton, Joseph, s.	1
Key, Thomas J., s.	1	Jones, Jesse, s.	1
Bell, James, h. of f.	2	Cook, Beverly C., s.	1
Taylor, Nathias, orphs. of	1	Moon, Elizabeth, wid.	1
Naish, Frances, w. r. s.	1	Clark, James O., h. of f.	2
Williams, Frances E., wid.	1	Cook, Theodosius	2
Tinsley, William D., s.	1	Burton, Richard, orph. of	1
Royster, Robert, s.	1	Dye, Brown, orphs. of	2
Anderson, Ann, h. a.	1	Mobley, Francis, wid.	1
Cook, Daniel, s.	1	Hudson, David, r. s.	2
Brown, Aaron, h. of f.	2	Clark, Christopher, orphs. of	1
Cook, Joshua, s.	1	Taylor, Rebecca, wid.	1
Brewer, Hundley J., s.	1	Taylor, John C., orph. of	1
Rich, John, h. of f.	2	Cook, Thomas, r. s.	2
Maupin, Jesse, r. s.	2	Moon, Jesse, orphs. of	1
Turman, Mary, wid.	1	Snellings, Samuel, h. of f.	2
Good, John M., s.	1	Burton, Mary, wid.	1
Clark, Jachariah, orphs. of	1	Dye, Mary, wid. & w. r. s.	2
Davis, William C., h. of f.	2	Bell, Elizabeth, w. r. s.	1
Edward, Sarah P., wid.	1	Mobley, Isaac, orphs. of	1
Carter, Elizabeth, w. r. s.	2	Hudson, William, h. of f.	2
Cannada, Elizabeth, orph. of	1	Oliver, Berrien, h. of f.	2
Cape, Merian, h. of f.	1	Oliver, Peter, r. s.	2
Cook, Samuel, h. of f.	2	Cook, Theodocius, r. s.	2
Hubbard, Vincent, h. of f.	2		

CAPTAIN BUTLER'S DISTRICT

	Draws		Draws
Martin, Rebecca, wid.	1	Dennard, John, citizen	2
Head, William, orphs. of	1	Thrilkill, John W., s.	1
Butler, David C., h. of f.	2	White, John H., s.	1
Hardy, Mary, orph. of	1	Campbell, Daniel, h. of f.	2
Rousey, Forester, h. of f.	2	Cook, Lewis, h. of f.	2
White, Thomas J., s.	1	Christian, John M., s.	1
Hall, Seales, s.	1	Rodgers, Isham G., h. of f.	2
Wyche, William H., s.	1	Wright, Warren, s.	1
Wyche, Joshua C., s.	1	Wright, Charles, h. of f.	2
Stephens, Henry H., h. of f.	2	Algood, Spencer, r. s.	2
Hall, Thomas S., s.	1	Brawner, Simuel, h. of f.	2
Allgood, William, h. of f.	2	Kerlin, Elizabeth, wid. & w. r. s.	2
Webb, Abner, h. of f.	2	Allman, Usry, orphs. of	2
Butler, Patrick, r. s.	2	Rodgers, John W., h. of f.	2
Brown, James N., r. s.	2	Thrilkill, Wm. H., h. of f.	2
Hardy, Jetha, minors of f. a.	2	Brown, Asa A., h. of f.	2
Glenn, Mitchell, s.	1	Adams, George, s.	1
Thrilkill, Willis, h. of f.	2	Bragg, Mary, wid.	1
Allmand, Sarah, wid.	1	Dennis, Stephen, orphs. of	1
Dennard, John, r. s.	2	Dillard, James, citizen & r. s.	2

	Draws		Draws
Taylor, William, h. of f.	2	Dillard, Isaac, s.	1
Kerlin, Samuel, s.	1	Butler, John, h. of f.	2
Kennebrew, Edwin, s.	1	Snellings, John, h. of f.	2
Christian, Samuel, s.	1	Kerlin, William, orphs. of	1
Golden, Alexander Sr., h. of f.	2	Brawner, Asa, s.	1
Golden, Alex, orphs. of	1	Butler, Peter D., s.	1
Wilkins, John, r. s.	2	Brawner, William M., s.	1
Bowen, Horatius C., h. of f.	2	Brawner, John W., s.	1
Fortson, Thomas, h. of f.	2	Brawner, Joseph W., s.	1
Dillard, Nehemiah V., s.	1		

CAPTAIN TUCKER'S DISTRICT

	Draws		Draws
Brewer, Horatio, orphs. of	2	Davis, Thomas F., s.	1
Brewer, Susan, wid.	1	Gholston, Charles T., s.	1
Hudson, Charles, minors of f. a.	2	Terrell, Joseph, r. s.	2
Nunnelee, James F., r. s.	2	Davis, Nany, w. r. s.	1
Tate, Sarah, wid.	1	Seales, Elizabeth, wid. & w. r. s.	2
Tate, John, orphs. of	2	Bray, Bannister R., h. of f.	2
Davis, Absolom, orphs. of	1	Lane, John A., s.	1
Edwards, Robert L., h. of f.	2	Johnson, James, s.	1
Jones, Fanny, wid. & w. r. s.	2	Foster, William, h. of f.	2
Middleton, Robert, orphs. of	1	Tatum, Jesse, r. s.	2
Terrell, Jowel, s.	1	Wall, Bud C., s.	1
Terrell, Timothy, s.	1	Childs, Lewis G., s.	1
Tate, Enos Sr., r. s.	2	Hudson, William, h. of f.	2
McGehee, Thomas G., s.	1	Staton, John, h. of f.	2
Tucker, Godfrey, r. s.	2	Johnson, Susan, wid.	1
Jones, Edmond, h. of f.	2	Johnson, Phillip, orphs. of	2
Hudson, Richard D., s.	1	Owens, Barshaba, wid.	1
Whiteman, William, h. of f.	2	Owens, Barshaba, w. r. s.	1
Johnson, John H., s.	1	Hudson, Elizabeth, wid. & w. r. s.	2
Martin, Beverly, h. of f.	2	Owens, James S., s.	1
Hudson, Lucy, h. a.	1	Arnold, William, s.	1
Childs, John, citizen & r. s.	4	Smith, Wells, h. of f.	2
Jones, Samuel, s.	1	Collins, Samuel, h. of f.	2
Brewer, Edmond H., h. of f.	2	Rose, Sarah, wid.	1
Wall, Cade, s.	1		

CAPTAIN ALLSTON'S DISTRICT

	Draws		Draws
Chandler, Mordecai, s.	1	Beck, Sary, wid. & w. r. s.	2
Oliver, Nancy, wid.	1	Lewis, Jeptha, s.	1
Oliver, Caleb, orphs. of	2	Heard, Eliz., wid. & w. r. s.	2
Jones, William H., h. of f.	2	Jeter, Barnett Jr., s.	1
Statham, Augustus D., s.	1	Keys, John D., s.	1
Arnold, John, s.	1	White, Reuben, orphs. of	2
Rucker, Zachariah, h. of f.	2	Banks, William, orphs. of	2
Grag, Sussannah, w. r. s.	2	Rosser, Jeptha, h. of f.	2
Clark, Larkin, r. s.	2	Bourne, Henry, s.	1
Banks, William R., s.	1	Clark, William D., s.	1
Rucker, James, s.	1	Banks, Richard, s.	1
Rucker, Milly, wid.	1	Arnold, William, s.	1
Rucker, John, orphs. of	1	Cleveland, Jacob M., s.	1
Gillespie, Geo. J., h. of f.	2	Alston, Gilley, w. r. s.	1
Howard, Lucy, h. a.	1	Alexander, Elam, s.	1

	Draws		Draws
Cleveland, Early, s.	1	Allen, Thomas, h. of f.	2
Aiken, Johnson, s.	1	Niash, Jeremiah, h. of f.	2
Fortson, Tavner, h. of f.	2	Harper, Bedford, h. of f.	2
Banks, Ann, wid.	1	Henderson, John, orphs. of	1
Banks, Henry, h. of f.	2	Nellums, Wm., s.	1
Lyons, Thomas, s.	1	Ramsey, B., h. of f.	2
Perryman, William G., h. of f.	2	Alexander, Willis, h. of f.	2
Nix, John, s.	1	Arnold, Wm., orphs. of	1
Henderson, James B., s.	1	Whitt, Mary, wid.	1
Jones, Marshall, s.	1	White, David, orphs. of	2

GEORGIA, Elbert County.

This is to certify that we have made a true list of the names for a draw or draws in the approaching Land Lottery in the above State and County and Major Allen's Battalion.

This, 1st day of October, 1825.

(Signed) WILLIAM JONES.
BANISTER R. BRAY.
Receivers.

MAJOR DAVID DOBBS' BATTALION

CAPTAIN HARTON'S DISTRICT

	Draws		Draws
Mills, Moses, r. s.	2	Wallis, Rhody, wid.	1
Higginbotham, Jacob, r. s.	2	Dodd, William, orphs. of	2
Thornton, Benj., h. of f.	2	Maxwell, Thomas Sr., r. s.	2
Moulding, Thomas, h. of f.	2	Maxwell, John, r. s.	2
Thornton, Elizabeth, wid.	1	Hunt, James, r. s.	2
Thornton, Reuben, orphs. of	1	Dickerson, John, h. of f.	2
Bond, Nathan, r. s.	2	Lunsford, William, h. of f.	2
Haircrow, Ezekiel, s.	2	Mewborn, Thomas, h. of f.	2
Haircrow, Hugh, s.	1	Hilley, Thomas Sr., r. s.	2
Ginn, Transvania, wid.	1	Hilley, Thomas Jr., s.	1
Ginn, Transvania, w. r. s.	1	Johnson, Angus, s.	1
Maxwell, Jesey, s.	1	Teasley, Sarah, wid. & w. r. s.	2
Maxwell, Martin, s.	1	Burden, Hannah, wid.	1
Maxwell, Thomas, s.	1	Thornton, Daniel, s.	1
Maxwell, Wm. Jr., s.	1	Sandidge, Claiborne, r. s.	2
Teasley, John, s.	1	McCurry, Lauchlin Jr., s.	1
Teasley, Levi, orphs. of	1	McCurry, Lauchlin Sr., h. of f.	2
Adams, Nicholas N., s.	1	Pulliam, Robert, r. s.	2
Adams, Calvin M., h. of f.	2	Tibis, Thomas, h. of f.	2
Adams William, h. of f.	2	Teasley, Isham, h. of f.	2
Adams, Lawrence M., s.	1	Thornton, Elsey B., s.	1
Ashworth, Elisha, h. of f.	2	Murry, Nancy, wid. & w. r. s.	2
McCurry, Katherine, wid.	1	Thornton, Thomas, orphs. of	5
Nelms, Joshua B., h. of f.	2	Adams, Thomas, r. s.	2
Underwood, Ann, wid. & w. r. s.	2	Adams, James Sr., r. s.	2
Ginn, Thomas, h. of f.	2	Runnals, Williams, s.	1
Ginn, William, s.	1	Cabennis, Henry, r. s.	2

CAPTAIN CARPENTER'S DISTRICT

	Draws		Draws
Wooldridge, Thos., h. of f.	2	Skelton, John, s.	1
Rumsey, Richard, h. of f.	2	Vacray, Jos., h. of f. & r. s.	2
Rimsey, Richard, r. s.	2	Coulston, Mariam, wid. & w. r. s.	2

	Draws		Draws
Watson, Thomas, h. of f.	2	Harper, William G., s.	1
Chrisler, Benj., h. of f.	2	Ashworth, Noah, s.	1
Tiner, William, s.	1	Rucker, William, r. s.	2
Tiner, Cabel, s.	1	Teasley, Silas, r. s.	2
Dutton, William, s.	1	Shiflet, James, s.	1
Hickman, Martha, wid.	1	Shiflet, Picket, s.	1
Hickman, Walker, orphs. of	1	Johnson, Lindsey, s.	1
Scales, William, s.	1	Johnson, Neal, s.	1
Richardson, Amos, r. s.	2	Johnson, Alexander, s.	1
Bryan, Sarah, wid.	1	Totman, Rebecca, wid.	1
Pritchett, Delpha, wid.	1	Hill, Ealum, s.	1
Pritchet, Nicholas, orphs. of	1	Stowers, Lewis Sr., r. s.	2
Pritchet, Nicholas, orph. of	1	Skelton, Jabez, h. of f.	2
Brown, Rolen, s.	1	Adams, Robert, h. of f.	2
Dutton, Thomas, h. of f.	2	Jones, Simeon, orphs. of	1
Carpenter, Joshua S., h. of f.	2	Macgehee, Jesse, s.	1
Ashworth, John, h. of f.	2	Macgehee, John, s.	1
Ray, James H., s.	1	Adams, Solomon, s.	1
Bobo, Lewis, s.	1	Dooley, Allen D., h. of f.	2
Hickman, William, s.	1	Johnson, John, s.	1
Tiner, Tolison, h. of f.	2	Johnson, Daniel, s	1
McMullan, Daniel, h. of f.	2	Jones, Jos, h. of f	2
Sittin, William, h. of f.	2	Jones, Rebecca, wid.	1
Teasley, Bebeverly A., s.	1	Hickman, Thomas S., s	1
McCurley, Moses, h. of f.	2	Thompson, Jesse, h. of f.	2
Stowers, Jeremiah, s.	1	Scales, Joel, h. of f.	2
Saddlar, James R., h. of f.	2	Macgehee, Jonathan, s.	1
Wright, Gabriel, orphs. of	1	Skelton, Richmond, h. of f.	2
Fain, Charles, s.	1	Crump, Pleasant D., h. of f.	2
Pritchett, Thomas, h. of f.	2	Healing or Keeling, Thos., s.	1
Jones, Simeon, orphs. of	1	McGuire, Thomas M., s.	1
Lovingood, Samuel, s.	1	Powell, Francis Sr., h. of f.	2
Hutarson, Samuel, s.	1	Highsmith, Milly, wid.	1
Highsmith, John, h. of f.	2	Highsmith, Milly, w. r. s.	1
Highsmith, Thomas, h. of f.	2		

CAPTAIN DOBBS' DISTRICT

	Draws		Draws
Self, Frances, wid.	1	Tiller, William L., h. of f.	2
Self, Samuel L., orphs. of	1	Smith, Archibald, h. of f.	2
Prothro, James, h. of f.	2	Alexander, Isaac, r. s.	2
Sullivan, William H., h. of f.	2	McGarity, Willson, s.	1
Bradley, Robert C., orphs. of	1	White, William Sr., r. s.	2
McCurry, Angus Sr., r. s.	2	White, Jesse, h. of f.	2
Sanders, Calvin P., h. of f.	2	Couch, Sarah, wid.	2
Sanders, Lewis M., h. of f.	2	Coulston, Nancy, h. a.	1
Neal, Linsey, s.	1	Skelton, Martin, h. of f.	2
Vaughters, Linsey, s.	1	McMullan, Willis, s.	1
Vaughters, Russell, orphs. of	1	Scales, Thomas, h. of f.	2
Boatwright, Daniel, h. of f.	2	Rhodes, Hannah, wid.	1
Prothro, Joshua, h. of f.	2	Rhodes, John W., orphs. of Moses R. Rhodes	1
Prothro, Nathaniel, orphs. of	2	McCurry, John, s.	1
Prothro, Zilpha, wid.	1	Gill, Elizabeth, orphs. of Robert Gill	1
Enlo, John, h. of f. & r. s.	4	White, Tabitha, h. a.	1
McDonald, Angus	1	Minors, of John W. White, f. a.	2
Furgerson, John, s.	1	McDonald, Margaret, wid.	1
Kelley, Wm., h. of f. & r. s.	4	McDonald, John, orphs. of	1
Dobbs, Louisanna, wid.	1	Fowler, Rachel, wid.	1
Dobbs, Silas, orphs. of Josiah Dobbs	1		
Childers, Jesse C., h. of f.	2		

Name	Draws
Fowler, James, orph.	1
Salmon, Jeremiah, s.	1
Vickery, James, h. of f.	2
Furgerson, Daniel, s.	2
Neal, Chriswell, s.	1
McDonald, Donald, s.	1
Keeling, Leonard W., s.	1
Gardner, Nancy, minor of Elijah Gardner, r. a.	1
Saddler, Wm. B., h. of f.	2
Williamson, Walker, h. of f.	2
Fain, John, h. of f.	2
Fain, John, s.	1
Dobbs, Josiah, s.	1
Haynes, Moses G., s.	1
Dean, John, h. of f.	2
Carder, Moses, s.	1
Haynes, Moses Jr., h. of f.	2
Park, Mary, w. r. s.	1
Fain, Robert, s.	1
Fain, Epperson, s.	1

CAPTAIN DUNN'S DISTRICT

Name	Draws
Underwood, Joseph, h. of f.	2
Hailey, William, r. s.	2
Hailey, Thomas, minor f. a.	1
Jourdain, Fountain, r. s.	2
Jourdain, John S., s.	2
Gaines, Francis, r. s.	2
Hinton, James S., s.	1
Craft, John Jr., s.	1
Roberson, Samuel, s.	1
Head, Benjamin, s.	1
Means, Jacob, h. of f.	2
Means, Elizabeth, wid.	1
Means, Wm., orphs. of	2
Crawford, Lucy, wid.	1
Johnston, Mary, wid. & w. r. s.	2
Talor, Wm. Jr., s.	1
Chapman, David, h. of f.	2
Hunt, Henry, orphs. of	1
Davis, John, r. s.	2
Craft, William, s.	1
Wright, Isaac, h. of f.	2
Lockhart, James, r. s.	2
Cook, David, h. of f.	1
Preuitt, Jacob G., s.	1
Dunn, Joseph, s.	1
Ham, Reuben, orphs. of	2
Smether, Gabriel, h of f.	2
Smether, Gabriel, r. s.	2
Strickland, Joseph, h of f.	2
Terrell, Levisa, wid. & w. r. s.	2
King, Zuriah, h. of f.	2
Yoes, Katherine, wid. & w. r. s.	2
Snoe, Eli, h. of f.	2
Allen, Reuben, h. of f.	2
Underwood, Wyneford, wid.	1
Underwood, Wyneford, w. r. s.	1
McGure, Anderson, r. s.	2
Grissop, James, r. s.	2
Prather, William M., s.	1
Craft, Washington, h. of f.	2
Harris, John Sr., r. s.	2
Craft, John Sr., h. of f.	2
Craft, Samuel, h. of f.	2
Hinton, John L., s.	1
Hinton, Peter Jr., s.	1
Shiflet, Joseph, s.	1
King, Thomas, s. & r. s.	3
Turner, Thomas, h. of f.	2
Tailer, John, orphs. of	2
Buffington, Joseph, orph. of	2
Hinton, Peter, r. s.	2
Allen, Edmond, h. of f.	2
Champman, Frederick, s.	1
Crawford, Oliver, s.	1
Ganes, Henry S., s.	1
Preuit, Joshua, s.	1
Preuit, John, h. of f.	2
Jourdain, Isaac, h. of f.	2
Skaggs, Tabitha, wid. & w. r. s.	2
Alexander, Mary, wid.	1
Bell, John, orphs. of	1
Dodds, William, s.	1
Jourdain, John Jr., s.	1
Buffington, William, s.	1
Hinton, Robert, s.	1
Alexander, George C., s.	1
Taylor, Jesse W., h. of f.	2
Teasley, Benajah S., h. of f.	2
Harris, John Jr., h. of f.	2
Harris, Ezekiel, s.	1
Bowman, Willis W., s.	1
Gaines, Sarah, wid.	1
Ganes, Levingston W., orph. of	1
Hunt, George, h. of f.	2
Hunt, Moses, r. s.	2
Tailer, Elizabeth, wid.	1
Tailer, John, s.	1
Smith, Robert, h. of f.	2
Cash, John, r. s.	2
Terrell, Robert W., s.	1
Faubes, Henry, h. of f.	2
Hunt, John S., h. of f.	2
Hunt, Joel, s.	1
Terry, Thomas, s.	1
Riley, James, r. s.	2
Harper, John S., s.	1
Saddler, John F., s.	1
Powell, William R., h. of f.	2

	Draws		Draws
Daniel, John Jr., s.	1	& r. s.	4
Davis, James, s.	1	Mabry, Thomas W., h. of f.	2
Rowzee, John, s.	1	Cunningham, John Sr., h. of f.	2
Daniel, John Sr., r. s.	2	Buffington, Ann, wid.	1
Word (Ward), Wm. Sr., h. of f.			

CAPTAIN BLACKWELL'S DISTRICT

	Draws		Draws
Cunningham, Joseph, h. of f.	2	Word (Ward), Sarah, wid.	1
Rucker, John, h. of f. & r. s.	3	Word, Richards, orphs. of	2
Banks, Lemuel, s.	1	Carter, Lucy, wid.	1
Anderson, Thomas, s.	1	Carter, Thomas P., s.	1
Brown, Dozier T., h. of f.	2	Carter, Chas. N. B., orph. of	1
Alexander, William, h. of f.	2	Carter, Robert M., s.	1
James, William, s.	1	Carter, John J., s.	1
Henderson, Richard S., s.	1	Carter, Elizabeth, w. r. s.	1
Ganes (Gaines), Wm., h. of f. & r. s.	4	Hansard, Janet, w. r. s.	1
		Rodlander, William B., s.	1
Wansley, Reuben, h. of f.	2	Dickerson, William B., s.	1
Wansley, John, s.	1	Dickerson, Robert W., s.	1
David, Susannar, wid.	1	Henderson, Simeon Jr., s.	1
Thornton, Dozier Sr., r. s.	2		

MARRIAGE RECORD OF ELBERT COUNTY—BOOK "H" REBOUND INTO BOOK "L-F"

Groom, Bride and Date		Page
Ansley, Jesse and Betsy Rose	Sept. 30, 1807	28
Almond, Ezra and Sally Brown	Aug. 22, 1807	28
Burton, Blackman and Jinsey Saxon	Mar. 30, 1806	28
Booth, Gabriel and Betsy Stinchcomb	July 26, 1806	55
Bird, Daniel and Sarah Oliver	Dec. 26, 1806	28
Bullard, Tapley and Anna Bell	June 29, 1807	28
Berry, Robert and Mary Fincher	Dec. 17, 1807	42
Bevill, Thomas and Elizabeth Cunningham	Nov. 26, 1807	44
Bragg, William S. and Polly Rogers	Feb. 24, 1808	54
Bullard, Jesse G. and Judah Clark	Sept. 9, 1807	55
Bevers, Ansley and Susanna Donahoo	Jan. 14, 1808	55
Butler, Peter and Hannah Snellings	Jan. 21, 1808	133
Bevers, Allen and Elizabeth Braden	June 19, 1807	57
Butler, Christopher and Mahal Cole	Jan. 8, 1809	133
Brown, Benjamin and Ann Griffith	Dec. 22, 1808	151
Brown, Hardie and Delilah Lowry	Jan. 5, 1809	151
Cape, Lewis and Elizabeth Coker	Dec. 18, 1806	28
Coursey, Daniel and Catty Burton	June 26, 1806	28
Christian, Isaac and Milly White	Feb. 12, 1807	28
Christian, Chas. W. and Nancy Ruff	June 6, 1807	39
Childs, Benjamin and Catherine Irons	Oct. 22, 1807	42
Crittenden, Henry P. and Kizzia Fitts	Oct. 10, 1807	42
Cole, Samuel and Charlotte Harper	Dec. 12, 1807	45
Clay, Simeon and Mary Lockhart	Feb. 21, 1808	55
Crider, David and Parmelia Bond	Oct. 22, 1807	55
Cranshaw, Cornelius and Milly Parham	Dec. 27, 1807	97
Cash, Moses and Nancy Hudson	Sept. 6, 1808	111
Cash, Howard and Susanna Scales	Nov. 21, 1808	151
Crawford, William and Peggy Holbrook	Mar. 9, 1809	151
Crock, Robert and Martha Walker	—— 20, 1809	151

Groom, Bride and Date		Page
Davis, Shadrack and Betsy Stephens	July 20, 1806	28
Davis, Edward and Frances Ragland	Feb. 19, 1807	28
Davis, William and Sally Dickson	June 15, 1807	55
Dean, Frederick and Sally Bray	Jan. 8, 1807	42
Denay, David and Polly Ruff	Dec. 2, 1807	55
Dobbs, David and Dosha Walters	Nov. 4, 1807	58
Dye, Randolph and Elizabeth Bell	Jan. 9, 1808	44
Ellington, Garland and Catherine Garrett	Sept. 25, 1806	28
Etchison, William and Tabitha Hayes	Nov. 15, 1808	151
Ewin, James D. and Mary E. McClary	Nov. 9, 1809	151
Ewing, William D. and Rebecca Ewing	Oct. 11, 1808	63
Evans, Robert and Mahala Granger	Feb. 12, 1807	28
Faulkner, Peter and Nancy Cook	Oct. 31, 1807	55
Ferrell, John and Peggy McCune	Oct. 1, 1807	55
Ferrenton, Edward F. and Elizabeth Robertson	Feb. 25, 1808	55
Ford, John and Jinsey Head	Jan. 1, 1808	133
Gilmer, Francis and Patsy Barnett	Jan. 28, 1808	45
Groves, Samuel and Rachel Forgus	July 14, 1808	63
Hall, Taliaferro and Sarah Clark	June 16, 1808	110
Hailey, Reuben and Sally Wood	Aug. 13, 1807	38
Hailey, Martin and Betsy Jennings	Mar. 3, 1808	151
Haley, John and Polly Underwood	Jan. 5, 1809	151
Harris, Stephen and Sarah H. Watkins	Jan. 19, 1808	44
Harris, John and Joannah Gragg	Jan. 22, 1809	151
Hartchcock, Debton and Polly Jones	Oct. 26, 1806	28
Horton, William and Jane Crawford	Oct. 9, 1809	110
Henderson, Joseph and Frances Johnston	June 6, 1808	110
Hubbard, Richard and Patsey Jones	Jan. 22, 1807	28
James, Samuel and Ruth Hendon	June 6, 1806	151
Jones, Asa and Martha Butler	June 10, 1808	63
Langdon, John and Jane Ellington	Nov. 11, 1806	28
Love, James K. and Jane Rucker	Apr. 25, 1807	38
Lowrymore, Andrew and Sally Bentley	Oct. 14, 1808	63
Martin, Cluff and Martha Vaughan	Sept. 8, 1808	110
Martin, Ewel and Nancy Vaughan	Sept. 8, 1808	110
Mauchelt, Samuel and Mary Eastridge	Mar. 27, 1806	28
Maxwell, Elijah and Betsy Jordan	Oct. 13, 1808	110
Morgan, John and Nancy Towns	Dec. 20, 1807	44
McMartin, Duncan and Catherine McCurry	Aug. 8, 1806	58
McMullan, Neal and Polly Thornton	Aug. 1, 1807	39
Oliver, William and Frances Ragland	Dec. 27, 1807	42
Orr, Barrett and Betsy Hendricks	Sept. 24, 1807	55
Osler, William and Sally Butler	Jan. 26, 1809	133
Page, Dempsey and Margaret Ashworth	Mar. 20, 1806	55
Parham, Dixon and Elizabeth Hicks	Mar. 8, 1807	55
Powell, Losten and Sally McKinney	Aug. 28, 1806	58
Power, David and Susannah Moon	Oct. 15, 1807	55
Pritchet, George and Eliz. Mitchell	July 26, 1807	55
Ragland, Evans and Sally Evans	May 21, 1806	28
Roberts, Wiliam and Polly Lunceford	May 11, 1807	55
Rowsey, Foster and Polly Dennard	Dec. 15, 1808	97
Rucker, Willis and Milly Alexander	Oct. 29, 1807	45
Sale, Dudley and Nancy Hatcher	Nov. 1, 1807	42
Saxon, Lewis and Sally Spencer	Jan. 14, 1806	28
Scales, Aaron and Ann Harbin	Nov. 29, 1808	97
Sherrod, Benjamin and Eliza H. Watkins	Jan. 1, 1808	44
Smith, Valentine and Catherine Upshaw	Dec. 23, 1806	38
Smith, Leonard and Charlotte Lane	Dec. 29, 1807	45
Stinchcomb, Levi and Polly Ridgway	July 27, 1806	28

Groom, Bride and Date		Page
Stubblefield, William and Catey Brown	Feb. 23, 1809	151
Tate, Enos and Mary J. Tait	Aug. 26, 1806	35
Tait, Caleb and Polly Middleton	Dec. 25, 1806	35
Talliaferro, Benj. and Martha Watkins	Oct. 15, 1807	44
Tait, Waddy and Eliza E. Thompson	Jan. 4, 1808	44
Tatom, Thomas and Sarah Davis	Oct. 6, 1808	110
Thompson, Allen C. and Charlotte Thompson	Mar. 3, 1808	133
Turman, Jacob and Polly Brewer	Oct. 15, 1807	42
Vaughan, Alex and Elizabeth David	Aug. 20, 1807	55
Vawter, Richard and Cynthey McGuire	Nov. 11, 1806	57
Vincent, Pleasant and Susan Edwards	Jan. 14, 1808	63
Vineyard, George and Patience Bassile	Mar. 9, 1807	28
Walker, Robert and Sally Colt	Aug. 8, 1808	151
Ward, Abner and Frances Kidd	Dec. 24, 1807	47
Warren, Harrison and Susannah Gaines	Oct. 20, 1808	151
Watkins, William Jr. and Ruth Pope	May 15, 1806	45
Webb, Burrell and Sarah Booth	Oct. 18, 1806	39
Wheeler, Benjamin and Patsy Dutton	Sept. 3, 1808	151
White, Joseph and Avarilla Harper	Aug. 28, 1806	28
White, Martin and Patsy White	Feb. 11, 1807	28
White, John and Marshaba Gunter	June —, 1803	42
Wiley, George and Milly David	Feb. 4, 1808	63
Willis, Samuel and Piety Skinner	Jan. 8, 1807	28
Winn, John and Jane Childs	Nov. 10, 1808	133
Witcher, Benjamin and Frances McLeroy	Sept. 10, 1807	55
Woods, William and Martha N. Middleton	Sept. 16, 1807	38
Woodward, Henry and Betsy Figgs	Aug. 24, 1806	28
Worrell, Richard and Lucy Hammond	May 8, 1806	28
Wynn, George and Polly Ingraham	Dec. 30, 1807	111

(Note: No records previous to 1803 can be located).

MARRIAGES, 1809-1812, IN BOOK OF MIXED RECORDS OFFICE OF ORDINARY OF ELBERT COUNTY

Groom, Bride and Date		Page
Alston, John and Charity Tait	Oct. 4, 1810	118
Ashworth, Joab and Nancy Teasley	June 4, 1809	251
Bailey, William and Amely Reily	Sept. 9, 1811	251
Baker, George and Polly Brown	June 13, 1811	242
Banks, James Jr. and Milly Jones	Sept. 11, 1810	98
Barnett, Thomas N. and Margaret Micou	Sept. 23, 1811	251
Bentley, William A. and Charlotte C. Nunnelee	Jan. 23, 1812	315
Bibb, John D. and Mary Oliver	Feb. 6, 1812	335
Blackwell, Jospeh and Elizabeth McGehee	Mar. 3, 1812	335
Bond, Gabriel and Clary Rowsey	Mar. 9, 1809	1
Booth, John and Ann Faulkner	Dec. 11, 1810	251
Bradley, Drury and Sally Ridgway	Sept. 9, 1809	2
Bradley, Robert C. and Anna Deadwyler	Dec. 11, 1810	196
Brawner, Russell and Sally Tidwell	Aug. 10, 1809	2
Brawner, Bazel and Nancy Campbell	Sept. 27, 1810	78
Bray, David and Lucy Hall	Apr. 4, 1810	66
Brewer, William and Anny Bates	Oct. 12, 1810	136
Brown, Reuben and Dosha McMullan	June 6, 1810	136
Brown, Jesse and Lucy Staples	Jan. 17, 1811	137
Brown, John and Polly Statham	Dec. 12, 1811	339
Burdon, Edward and Sally White	Dec. 22, 1811	307
Cabaniss, Henry and Nancy Crittenden	Feb. 10, 1810	66
Capel, Brittain and Sarah Terrell	May 25, 1809	1

Groom, Bride and Date		Page
Carlton, Stephen and Susannah Childs	May 3, 1810	75
Carter, George and Martha Higginbotham	July 15, 1812	355
Casey, Stephen and Sally Anthony	Oct. 31, 1811	307
Cawhon, James and Jane Millican	July 9, 1810	141
Cheatham, Stephen and Clarysa Higginbotham	Apr. 5, 1810	66
Childs, John and Elizabeth Thornton	Oct. 17, 1811	251
Childress, Robert and Sarah Carter	Aug. 8, 1809	76
Chisholm, Wm. Jr. and Eliza L. Easter	May 13, 1810	79
Chisholm, Andrew C. and Ann W. King	June 8, 1811	197
Clark, Micajah and Tabitha Raglin	June 17, 1808	66
Coker, Larkin and Ann Bray	Nov. 15, 1810	98
Colliday, William and Tabitha Downer	Sept. 30, 1810	196
Collins, Willis and Phebe Martin	Dec. 2, 1810	188
Cook, Francis Jr. and Ann Swet	Nov. 12, 1809	2
Cook, Benjamin and Jane England	Apr. 30, 1810	42
Cook, James and Rhoda Faulkner	Aug. 15, 1807	76
Cook, Benjamin and Elizabeth Hudson	Nov. 8, 1810	98
Cook, John and Polly Alexander	Feb. 25, 1810	116
Colly, Zachariah and Eliza D. Saunders	Apr. 20, 1809	1
Crawford, John and Henrietta Hailey	Feb. 25, 1810	76
Cunningham, Franklin and Nancy Daniel	Dec. 26, 1811	307
Davis, Benjamin and Patsy Wanslow	May 10, 1810	76
Davis, Richard and Phebe Franklin	Feb. 14, 1811	196
Deadwyler, Martin and Rebecca Wilhite	Aug. 7, 1809	2
Denny, Edward and Barbary Staples	June 30, 1812	355
Denton, James and Silvey Pollard	Feb. 20, 1810	26
Dobbs, John and Jane Haynes	Sept. 14, 1810	197
Dobbs, James and Sarah Thomason	Sept. 6, 1810	110
Dollar, Ambrose and Sally Skelton	Mar. 28, 1811	188
Dunlap, Joseph and Mary Whitman	Dec. 18, 1811	307
Dye, Brown and Polly Martin	Apr. 23, 1809	1
Dye, William and Elizabeth Bullard	Aug. 22, 1811	251
Easter, Booker B. and Catherine Yumans	May 21, 1809	2
Evans, Henry and Martha Whitney	Dec. 16, 1811	196
Freeman, Fleming and Martha Bibb	Apr. 16, 1812	335
Fitts, John and Jennie DePriest	Nov. 12, 1809	22
Flaherty, Thomas and Milly Grace	Feb. 15, 1810	26
Foster, John S. and Martha Jones	Nov. 26, 1809	2
Gaar, William and Lucy Rucker	May 20, 1810	76
Gaar, John and Polly Blair	Jan. 23, 1812	261
Garner, Richard S. and Anna Alexander	May 10, 1811	111
Gandy, Uriah and Polly Means	Mar. 20, 1811	196
Garner, William and Franky Pulliam	Jan. 27, 1808	1
Garner, John and Nancy Head	Feb. 14, 1811	196
Glover, Richard and Elizabeth Glover	Sept. 21, 1811	307
Gray, William and Peggy Bevers	Dec. 24, 1811	261
Grimes, Thomas M. and Anney Power	June 15, 1809	1
Ham, Reuben and Jane Jordan	Jan. 6, 1809	2
Hales, Wiley and Jane Buchannon	Mar. 15, 1810	66
Hamilton, James and Nancy Rucker	July 30, 1812	325
Harper, Roderick and Susanna Selfridge	Feb. 10, 1806	251
Hardy, Jethro and Polly Dennard	Feb. 10, 1810	13
Head, James and Patsy Richardson	Dec. 25, 1810	141
Head, William and Sally Hall	Dec. 4, 1811	296
Henderson, George and Penina Woolridge	Aug. 2, 1810	76
Hendricks, Sylvan and Nancy Bailey	Dec. 2, 1810	76
Hicks, William and Polly Phelps	Nov. 23, 1809	2
Higginbotham, William G. and Polly Eveston	Sept. 26, 1808	1
Higginbotham, Bartley G. and Tabitha Oliver	Jan. 11, 1811	196

Groom, Bride and Date		Page
Higginbotham, Benj. C. and Polly Lollis	Jan. 2, 1812	325
Hightower, William and Mary Higginbotham	Oct. 3, 1811	251
Hilley, William and Patsy McGuire	May 30, 1812	325
Holloway, John and Martha Bryan	June 5, 1808	22
Hoopwell, Thomas and Harriet Clements	Dec. 20, 1811	266
Hudson, Boukes and Elizabeth Burton	Sept. 15, 1809	1
Hudson, Charles and Lucy McGehee	Oct. 30, 1811	266
Hulsey, John and Polly Johnston	Feb. 2, 1809	196
Human, Jesse and Sally Wood	June 19, 1810	178
Jenkins, Joshua and Milly Ellet	Apr. 19, 1810	75
Johnston, William and Sarah Grizzle	Nov. 17, 1802	2
Jones, Standley and Ezza Alexander	Jan. 3, 1811	195
Jordan, James and Beda White	Nov. 26, 1807	77
Jordan, James and Tabitha Murrah	Mar. 16, 1809	136
Kelly, William and Sarah Allen	Jan. 4, 1810	136
Key, James and Rebecca Grizzle	Oct. 17, 1811	296
Luce, Freeborn and Elizabeth Irons	Sept. 1, 1809	1
McCane, William D. and Nancy Childs	Feb. 23, 1810	79
McMullin, Charles and Nancy Breadin	Jan. 26, 1809	137
McMullin, Lewis and Frances Stowers	June 28, 1808	251
McMullin, Jeremiah and Sarah Harper	Feb. 8, 1811	196
McMullen, William and Elizabeth Maxwell	Sept. 3, 1812	372
Magesryth, Gardner and Susannah McGure	Mar. 5, 1810	76
Mann, Asa and Betsy White	Jan. 24, 1810	76
Middleton, Robert and Betsy C. Williamson	Nov. 11, 1810	110
Mann, Henry and Sally Haley	June 26, 1809	116
Moon, John and Tabitha Staples	Aug. 15, 1811	251
Moore, Lobard and Winey Sanders	Aug. 17, 1809	1
Morris, James and Lucy Parham	Sept. 8, 1811	251
Morgan, William and Lucy Karr	Nov. 9, 1809	66
Moss, Abram and Betsy Smith	Oct. 5, 1809	26
Nelums, Nathaniel and Rebema Carpenter	Mar. 3, 1809	196
Nix, Jeremiah and Fanny Webb	Oct. 25, 1810	178
Nix, Joseph and Sally Coleman	Mar. 10, 1811	188
Nunnelee, James F. and Jincy Naish	Sept. 28, 1810	251
Oliver, John Major and Susan Watkins	Feb. 19, 1811	116
Pledger, Samuel and Hetty Sheperd	Sept. 29, 1809	2
Plunket, Reuben and Patsy Taylor	July 6, 1812	355
Porterfield, James and Tabitha Bond	Sept. 6, 1808	1
Posey, Humphrey and Milly Key	Jan. 3, 1811	110
Pulliam, Joseph and Betsy Bonds	Feb. 18, 1808	1
Pulliam, Matthew and Eannah Eavenson	Jan. 19, 1809	2
Rice, William and Sally Brown	Jan. 13, 1812	339
Rice, Robert and Anny Pace	Nov. 16, 1809	178
Richardson, William and Betsy Harrison	Oct. 29, 1809	58
Roberts, James W. and Polly Ledbetter	June 28, 1812	355
Roebuck, Robert Jr. and Franky White	May 27, 1810	99
Rucker, Barton and Betsy Brown	Nov. 10, 1809	2
Rucker, Azmond and Nancy Harper	Feb. 4, 1810	26
Satterwhite, James and Milly Wiche	July 26, 1810	251
Scales, Joel and Fanny Cash	Jan. 3, 1811	196
Shoemaker, Jeremiah and Nancy Deadwiler	Aug. 31, 1809	2
Shoemaker, Talton and Belender Booth	Dec. 22, 1811	307
Sims, Edward and Sally Banks	July 11, 1811	251
Skelton, Jonathan and Elizabeth Cox	July 17, 1810	78
Smith, Joseph and Nancy Morrow	Aug. 24, 1809	2
Smith, John and Zele Hill	Feb. 2, 1809	2
Spears, Mercer and Elizabeth Dodds	Apr. 19, 1810	75
Spencer, Octavius and Patsy Ann Gray	Nov. 26, 1810	197

Groom, Bride and Date		Page
Spencer, William and Dama Gross	Feb. 28, 1811	196
Standifer, Andrew and Elizabeth James	Apr. 12, 1809	26
Stamps, Britton and Polly Sanders	Dec. 19, 1810	251
Steedley, William and Patsy Ballinger	Sept. 16, 1810	99
Story, William and Polly Dean	Aug. 18, 1808	26
Tait, Zimri and Susanna Tait	Oct. 28, 1809	1
Tait, James M. and Jane Watkins	July 10, 1810	77
Thornton, Reuben Jr. and Anna Crisler	Aug. 23, 1810	77
Thurman, John and Theney Irons	Dec. 11, 1810	196
Tiner, Thomas B. and Polly Crump	Mar. 5, 1811	111
Teasley, Joshua and Polly Chrisler	Mar. 4, 1812	315
Underwood, Ezekiel and Elizabeth Wheeler	May 1, 1812	355
Wade, John B. and Milly Hilley	Jan. 22, 1811	196
Walker, John Wm. and Matilda Pope	Jan. 30, 1810	26
Walker, George C. and Milly Childers	Dec. 1, 1809	53
Wanslow, Thomas and Jemima Means	Apr. 15, 1810	134
Wheeler, Henry and Polly Underwood	Mar. 18, 1810	75
White, John and Elizabeth Jones	Jan. 5, 1809	76
White, James E. and Janey Brown	July 10, 1811	196
White, Stephen and Rebecca Pulliam	Dec. 6, 1808	339
Whitman, William and Sarah Colson	May 28, 1812	325
Williamson, Basil and Mary Skelton	July 28, 1811	251
Woodley, John and Tempy Bullard	Mar. 5, 1808	1
Wootan, James and Rachel Ruthcerford	Oct. 5, 1809	1
Worrell, Ransom and Elender Harper	Nov. 3, 1811	251

MARRIAGES, 1812-1816, WILL BOOK "K," MIXED RECORDS

Groom, Bride and Date		Page
Alexander, Peter and Betsy A. Banks	Dec. 24, 1812	10
Alexander, Allen and Sarah M. Thompson	Feb. 5, 1815	309
Allgood, Samuel and Fanny Naish	Nov. 10, 1814	163
Allgood, James Y. and Prudeece Turman	July 12, 1815	164
Aycock, Milton and Susan E. Aycock	Oct. 25, 1815	294
Bell, Mayfield and Nancy Arnold	Nov. 1, 1812	10
Bird, John and Martha B. Tyner	Feb. 7, 1812	33
Birds, Billions and Charity Tyner	Feb. 5, 1815	309
Berry, Elijah and Sarah Rich	Feb. 8, 1811	32
Blake, James and Susannah F. Horn	Oct. 28, 1813	187
Boughtright, Daniel and Elizabeth Carpenter	Dec. 15, 1813	178
Braswell, William B. and Polly Pollard	Oct. 26, 1812	32
Brown, Jacob and Mary S. Higginbotham	July 15, 1813	161
Burton, John Jr. and Elizabeth G. Pate	Nov. 25, 1813	162
Burden, Henry and Sarah Burden	Aug. 20, 1815	308
Butler, Daniel and Martha Naish	Sept. 29, 1814	167
Butler, Haley and Nancy J. Ward	Dec. 7, 1815	215
Butler, George and Polly Deprest	Apr. 13, 1815	309
Byrd, Edward and Mahala Pate	May 5, 1816	311
Cabiness, Henry and Sally Booker	Feb. 4, 1816	310
Caldwell, Matthew T. and Eliza M. Jones	Dec. 22, 1814	162
Cape, Brinkley and Jenny Braswell	Nov. 7, 1812	32
Casey, Ephriam and Rebecca Anthony	Dec. 21, 1816	210
Carter, Robert and Patsy S. Wall	Oct. 15, 1815	308
Chambers, John and Elizabeth Sheperd	Dec. 29, 1814	164
Childs, John and Elizabeth Rucker	Dec. 20, 1812	10
Childers, Osborn and Malinda Burton	June 28, 1815	309
Clark, James and Mary Alston	Apr. 8, 1813	161
Colbert, William and Martha Clark	Jan. 24, 1813	161

Groom, Bride and Date		Page
Colley, Edward and Martha White	Sept. 7, 1813	179
Craft, David and Elizabeth Elliott	Dec. 3, 1812	10
Crittenden, Elijah and Elizabeth Greenwood	Sept. 11, 1814	164
Cook, John and Gilly Colbert	Jan. 16, 1816	310
Cunningham, Menter and Polly Cunningham	Oct. 18, 1815	312
Davis, Thomas W. and Polly H. Banks	Dec. 24, 1812	10
Denny, Thomas and Polly Hanna	Sept. 1, 1814	163
Denny, Robert and Mititia Staples	Feb. 2, 1815	309
Dickerson, John and Elizabeth Thornton	Dec. 29, 1812	32
Dudley, William and Clemontyne Butler	May 20, 1813	162
Durratt, Marshall and Nancy K. Lindsey	Jan. 21, 1811	162
Earp, Westley and Morin Alexander	Sept. 8, 1814	193
Elliott, John and Elizabeth Agee	Oct. 30, 1814	163
Fields, Samuel and Milly Hill	July 29, 1813	161
Fortson, John and Sarah Moore	Mar. 17, 1815	162
Fortson, James and Elizabeth Lewis	Dec. 16, 1814	163
Franklin, Job and Hannah Wheeler	Oct. 19, 1815	199
Gaines, John and Elizabeth Hearndon	Dec. 25, 1814	163
Gaines, Levingston and Sarah Johnson	Oct. 25, 1815	265
Ginn, Sherwood and Susannah Tomason	Jan. 12, 1815	164
Glover, John and Elizabeth Y. Alston	Sept. 6, 1816	310
Gober, John and Elizabeth Bramblett	Dec. 15, 1813	179
Gully, John and Mary Ann H. Decker	July 29, 1813	162
Gully, William and Franky P. Taylor	Oct. 26, 1815	243
Gunter, John and Rebecca Bell	Dec. 31, 1812	32
Gunter, James and Rebecca Anderson	Dec. 13, 1813	162
Grider, Jacob and Frances Wilkins	Jan. 12, 1815	309
Hale, Henry and Levity Royal	Mar. 5, 1816	310
Harben, John and Sophia Hendry	Nov. 14, 1814	161
Harris, Richmond and Rachel Tait	Sept. 18, 1813	162
Heard, George W. and Sarah Carter	Apr. 20, 1813	132
Hearndon, Charles M. and Sarah Whitman	Feb. 1, 1816	310
Hearndon, James and Sarah Thornton	Mar. 30, 1814	163
Hendrick, John and Rebecca Adams	July 13, 1815	310
Henrey, Benjamin and Nancy W. Beck	Aug. 11, 1816	311
Hickman, Walker and Rebecca Harris	Sept. 27, 1816	312
Higginbotham, William and Susannah Bonds	Dec. 29, 1814	163
Higginbotham, Larkin and Polly Howard	June 12, 1815	164
Hill, Lewis and Nancy Anthony	Mar. 2, 1815	309
Hilley, Richard and Elizabeth Dillard	Apr. 20, 1813	308
Hudson, George and Ann Samuel	Jan. 9, 1816	279
Hunt, Henry and Nancy Craft	July 20, 1815	212
Irons, McKinney and Synthia Brewer	Oct. 21, 1816	312
Jarratt, Archelus and Frances C. M. Brewer	Nov. 2, 1815	243
Johnston, Solomon and Ann Campbell	Dec. 28, 1815	243
Jennings, John and Elizabeth Childs	Mar. 26, 1814	162
Johnston, Thomas and Peggy C. Gaines	Jan. 18, 1815	311
Jones, Wiley W. and Charlotte Jones	Dec. 1, 1814	164
Jones, Lewis and Patcy Jones	Mar. 2, 1815	311
Kidd, Webb and Rebecca Allen	Dec. 1, 1814	164
Kidd, Jacob W. and Mary A. Hackney	Sept. 5, 1815	309
King, William and Sarah Coleman	Sept. 8, 1815	310
Lovingood, Harmon and Martha Bell	Dec. 22, 1814	164
McCoy, William and Nancy Sheperd	Mar. 18, 1816	310
McGehee, Hugh and Sarah S. White	Sept. 29, 1814	164
McGuire, William D. and Jane Wimmes	Dec. 1, 1813	178
Maso, William and Fannay Penn	Nov. 14, 1814	210
Matthews, Phillip and Elizabeth Clark	Feb. 8, 1815	2
Mercer, John and Sally Kee	Sept. 1, 1812	33

Groom, Bride and Date		Page
Mills, James and Nancy McMullan	Sept. 24, 1812	2
Mills, William and Nancy Brown	Dec. 12, 1815	203
Milligan, James and Mary Smithwick	Aug. 10, 1815	310
Mitchum, John and Surreny Childs	Feb. 13, 1815	163
Moore, Joel and Sally Brady	Nov. 5, 1812	8
Moore, Henry and Polly L. Lewis	Jan. 9, 1815	164
Morgan, Isham and Mary Rich	—— ——, 1816	310
Mullin, William and Susannah Brewer	Sept. 3, 1815	309
Naish, Abraham and Polly Butler	Oct. 13, 1814	164
Northern, John and Molly Bedinfield	Mar. 13, 1813	33
Oliver, Thomas W. and Frances Roebuck	Dec. 21, 1815	199
Oliver, John and Lucey Penn	Apr. 7, 1816	311
Owens, George and Margarett Childs	Feb. 23, 1816	311
Pace, Bazil and Claricy Sheperd	Sept. 28, 1815	310
Peyton, William and Polly McCormac	Feb. 11, 1816	311
Phipps, Lewis and Patsy Faulkner	Dec. 22, 1812	32
Phillips, Williamson and Betsey Coleman	Mar. 20, 1814	163
Pledger, Thomas and Nancy Ford	Mar. 2, 1814	309
Powell, Francis and Nancy Dooly	Dec. 12, 1813	167
Rich, James and Polly Gaines	Feb. 25, 1813	33
Riddle, Anderson and Sarah Y. Tate	Feb. 21, 1815	309
Ridgway, Thomas and Elizabeth Irvin Morgan	May 14, 1812	162
Roberts, Jesse C. and Susannah Coker	Oct. 13, 1816	312
Rose, Amos and Catherine Brown	Dec. 4, 1814	164
Royal, John Jr. and Martha H. Brewer	Dec. 1, 1814	163
Rumsey, Benjamin and Nancy Tompskins	Aug. 11, 1816	311
Scales, George and Polly Pledger	Oct. 5, 1815	294
Simmons, Dudley and Elizabeth Spears	Sept. 1, 1813	161
Skinner, George M. and Polly Henry	Feb. 28, 1816	311
Smith, James and Deborah Adams	Jan. 18, 1816	310
Smith, Green W. and Margarett A. Cook	Feb. 22, 1816	311
Smithwick, Edmond and Piety Willis	May 2, 1816	310
Snow, Joel and Gilley Patterson	Nov. 23, 1815	212
Spencer, Griffith and Elizabeth Owens	Sept. 30, 1813	162
Stinson, Samuel and Nancy Gulley	Sept. 24, 1816	310
Stone, William and Sarah Colbert	Oct. 27, 1812	32
Stowers, Benjamin and Ann Roebuck	Oct. 14, 1813	172
Stowers, Lewis and Harriet Roebuck	Oct. 12, 1815	308
Sullivan, John and Mima Booker	Apr. 15, 1814	163
Tait, David and Frances Tait	Nov. 21, 1816	312
Tate, James and Maria S. Verdell	Jan. 14, 1813	33
Tate, Enos C. and Nancy M. Callister	Nov. 22, 1815	162
Taylor, Hugh and Mehetable C. Sayre	Nov. 20, 1813	162
Thompson, William and Sarah Ragland	Mar. 3, 1814	191
Thompson, Drury and Jane Thompson	Jan. 24, 1816	311
Thomason, Arnold and Elizabeth Shackleford	Apr. 23, 1816	311
Thurman, John and Theany Irons	July 20, 1814	164
Upshaw, Leroy and Prudence T. Richardson	May 14, 1814	163
Walker, James and Margaret Poelston	Mar. 16, 1816	311
Wall, Burgess and Martha Carter	Oct. 6, 1815	309
Wallis, Jesse C. and Sally Stone	Sept. 14, 1813	161
Wansley, John and Sally Greenway	Mar. 14, 1813	33
White, Nicholas and Sally Pollard	Oct. 25, 1812	2
White, John and Margaret Harbin	Dec. 15, 1814	164
White, Eppy and Catherine Herndon	May 11, 1815	308
Woods, Joseph and Polly Campbell	Jan. 3, 1815	164

MARRIAGE RECORD, 1816-1824, WILL BOOK "L" OF MIXED RECORDS

Groom, Bride and Date		Page
Adams, James B. and Polly Haley	Apr. 10, 1817	111
Adams, William and Sarah Head	Jan. 11, 1819	296
Adams, Richard and Milly Murry	Dec. 30, 1819	350
Adams, John and Elizabeth Pledger	Feb. 7, 1821	477
Adams, John and Nancy Davis	Feb. 27, 1823	484
Aiken, William E. and Sarah K. Mann	Jan. 8, 1824	486
Alexander, Edmond and Catherine Alexander	Dec. 6, 1816	21
Alexander, Modeci and Judy M. Shackleford	Aug. 7, 1817	193
Alexander, Willis and Sarah C. Banks	Mar. 15, 1820	475
Alexander, William G. and Juliann Patterson	Mar. 16, 1824	487
Allen, John W. and Elizabeth McMullan	Aug. 6, 1818	304
Allen, Samuel and Pheba Rhodland	Nov. 25, 1819	435
Allen, Rugen and Patsy Rhodelander	July 17, 1821	478
Allen, Joseph and Charlotte Hendry	Mar. 11, 1824	488
Algood, William and Jincy Wright	Jan. 2, 1817	69
Algood, John and Jane Algood	Jan. 17, 1822	481
Algood, Asa and Sarah Wilkins	May 20, 1824	487
Algood, John and Mary Algood	Sept. 13, 1824	489
Almon, John and Mary V. Dillard	Jan. 20, 1820	435
Allmond, Isaac and Elizabeth Fortson	Dec. 20, 1821	477
Alston, William H. and Elizabeth Rucker	Jan. 25, 1820	476
Andrew, Burley and Caty Stinchcomb	Jan. 15, 1818	193
Andrew, Benjamin and Lucy Tate	Dec. 18, 1817	217
Anderson, James and Bathashe Hightower	Dec. 10, 1818	231
Anderson, James and Elizabeth Mobley	Dec. 24, 1818	230
Anderson, Thomas G. and Elizabeth Smith	Jan. 1, 1823	479
Arnett, John Adams and Mary Chandler	Mar. 18, 1824	489
Banks, Ralph Jr. and Elizabeth Maxwell	Dec. 22, 1818	261
Banks, Willis and Mary W. Oliver	Oct. 3, 1819	261
Banks, Thomas A. and Mary J. Chipman	Jan. 3, 1821	469
Banks, John H. and Sarah B. Clark	July 4, 1821	478
Banks, Willis and Mary Gray	Sept. 3, 1822	479
Barr, Robert S. and Nancy Perrin	Jan. 20, 1822	481
Barron, John and Polly Wright	Sept. 7, 1817	193
Barron, Barnabas and Polly Dooley	Feb. 17, 1820	476
Ball, Henry M. and Susan Tate	Aug. 2, 1821	478
Beard, John P. and Elizabeth O. Pledger	Feb. 5, 1818	193
Beck, John Jr. and Willie M. Bowman	Apr. 21, 1824	487
Bell, William and Elizabeth Thornton	Feb. 6, 1817	112
Bell, James and Susan Key	Jan. 22, 1819	297
Bell, Joseph and Mary Key	July 13, 1823	482
Beck, William A. and Ann Welch	May 30, 1820	475
Berreman, John and Sucky Bragg	Apr. 6, 1817	111
Black, Mathew J. and Mary Deadwyler	May 10, 1821	477
Bolton, William and Sarah Nunnelee	Dec. 7, 1819	423
Bolton, Isaac N. and Rachel Gibbs	Mar. 2, 1823	482
Booth, Joel and Patsy Elder	Jan. 20, 1822	481
Bowen, William U. and Ann A. Banks	Apr. 26, 1820	476
Bond, John and Catherine Bond	Jan. 24, 1821	477
Brawner, Joel and Betsy King	Dec. 9, 1816	52
Brawner, Simeon and Mrs. Susannah Webb	Nov. 10, 1824	486
Brawner, Henry P. and Cherry Barnes	Dec. 10, 1815	297
Brawner, James M. and Elizabeth Allman	Dec. 14, 1819	349
Brawner, Tilmon and Sarah B. Higginbotham	Aug. 13, 1822	480
Brantley, Joseph M. and Nancy J. Dooly	Mar. 18, 1823	482
Breeding, Ansel and Frances Davis	Sept. 4, 1815	4
Brewer, Horatio G. and Susannah Davis	Nov. 27, 1817	216

Groom, Bride and Date		Page
Brewer, Edmund H. and Lucy F. Carter	May 7, 1823	483
Brown, Daniel and Betsy Folley	Dec. 5, 1816	52
Brown, Aron and Elizabeth Cook	Mar. 21, 1819	297
Brown, Demsey and Martha Raines	Jan. 11, 1820	476
Brown, Asa and Maria W. Oliver	Nov. 1, 1821	478
Brown, Adam and Nancy Harbin	May 25, 1823	483
Brown, Benjamin and Mrs. Prudence Richardson	Apr. 3, 1823	485
Brown, James L. and Dicey Skelton	Aug. 22, 1819	399
Bryant, Mason and Catherine Raine	Dec. 5, 1816	50
Bryant, Moses and Nancy Ginn	Jan. 19, 1817	95
Bryant, William and Lucy D. Christler	Oct. 21, 1823	485
Bruce, Walter and Polly David	Sept. 24, 1822	480
Burton, Alanson and Jane Curry	Jan. 15, 1818	193
Burton, Richard and Mary Snellings	Dec. 24, 1818	219
Butler, James and Elizabeth Hansard	Dec. 16, 1823	483
Butler, Patrick Jr. and Jane Hansard	Jan. 16, 1823	484
Cade, Bedford and Mrs. Agnes Wilkins	Nov. 5, 1823	484
Callaway, Jeptha and Mary McGehee	Feb. 27, 1817	85
Campbell, William and Sally Dillard	Oct. 25, 1820	474
Carter, John and Sarah Ausley	Sept. 20, 1820	474
Carter, Thomas P. and Lucy Hudson	Dec. 22, 1818	231
Cash, Reuben and Elizabeth Buffington	Dec. 10, 1818	296
Cash, Moses and Nancy Hunt	July 6, 1824	489
Cason, Edmond and Sophia M. Turner	May 4, 1820	423
Chambers, William S. and Sarah Shepard	Nov. 18, 1819	396
Chambers, Joseph F. and Frances A. Stinchcomb	Aug. 29, 1822	480
Childs, John and Sarah Alexander	Feb. 15, 1820	476
Childers, Holman and Martha Colbert	Feb. 24, 1819	297
Childers, John S. and Permelia Burton	Jan. 4, 1821	474
Childers, Jesse C. and Peggy Ferguson	Nov. 21, 1822	474
Chisenhall, Debany and Nancy Cunningham	Apr. 3, 1821	476
Cheek, William and Cynthia Coker	Sept. 13, 1821	476
Christian, Elijah J. and Rebecca Coleman	Jan. 16, 1821	476
Christian, Elijah W. and Mary Christian	Dec. 19, 1823	484
Christler, Benjamin and Sarah McGehee	Dec. 11, 1824	488
Christler, Wesley and Anna Teasley	Oct. 28, 1824	488
Clark, William B. and Judith C. Rucker	Jan. 22, 1822	481
Clark, James O. and Margaret Clark	Mar. 29, 1821	476
Clark, Edward and Rhodey Davis	Dec. 9, 1819	327
Cloud, Samuel G. and Elizabeth A. Cox	Jan. 9, 1816	32
Cook, Samuel and Ann Williams	Jan. 18, 1817	103
Cook, Thomas S. and Nancy Patterson	Dec. 22, 1818	261
Cook, John and Gilly Colbert	Jan. 16, 1816	
Cook, Fenton and Emaly Schofield	Jan. 10, 1819	296
Cook, Franklin and Sarah Anderson	Sept. 21, 1823	483
Cook, Lewis and Nancy Cook	Jan. 16, 1824	487
Cook, Theodocius and Nancy Wood	Jan. 15, 1824	487
Coker, John and Nancy Ballenger	Feb. 19, 1824	486
Coker, Asa and Mrs. Polly Ann Ballinger	Oct. 12, 1820	475
Craft, Anderson and Lucy Alexander	Feb. 4, 1819	343
Craft, Washington and Polly Daniel	Dec. 26, 1820	446
Craft, John and Elizabeth Daniel	Jan. 28, 1821	477
Craft, Samuel and Lear H. Dunn	May 23, 1822	479
Craft, John and Agatha Crump	Aug. 1, 1822	479
Crump, Robert and Milly Cason	Nov. 5, 1818	306
Cunningham, John A. and Sarah Daniel	Apr. 13, 1823	485
Corry, John S. and Elizabeth J. Carter	Nov. 26, 1822	479
Dailey, Samuel C. and Milly T. Oliver	Feb. 14, 1822	481
Daniel, James and Peggy Means	Dec. 23, 1817	190

Groom, Bride and Date		Page
Daniel, David and Frances Means	——— —, 1822	479
David, Jacob W. and Peggy Allman	Jan. 2, 1817	14
David, Maraset and Elizabeth David	May 2, 1819	320
David, James and Nancy Henry	Dec. 9, 1818	320
David, Isaac and Patsy Sartain	July 3, 1823	482
Davis, William C. and Mary Burton	May 4, 1820	475
Davis, James and Louisa Hudson	July 31, 1823	482
Davis, Absolom T. and Martha Underwood	Oct. 27, 1825	488
Dean, George and Mary Ann Anthony	Mar. 30, 1820	476
Dennard, Isaac and Edne Harris	Jan. 3, 1821	476
Decker, Young A. and Nancy Cnapman	Sept. 8, 1822	480
Dennard, John and Mary Ann Allman	July 21, 1819	400
Depriest, James A. and Judith Booth	Jan. 7, 1819	296
Dobbs, David and Elizabeth McMullan	Apr. 28, 1819	297
Dobbs, Jesse and Mary Prothro	Aug. 31, 1824	489
Dobbs, James and Winny Burden	Oct. 12, 1820	474
Dollars, Henry and Polly Slef	Sept. 1, 1819	327
Dooly, Benett and Suckey Rice	Dec. 5, 1816	40
Dooly, Adam D. and Letty M. Brantley	Apr. 22, 1824	490
Doss, Hamlet and Alphia F. O. Crump	Jan. 3, 1817	46
Downer, Joseph and Elcy Waters	Aug. 29, 1819	399
Downer, John and Elizabeth Butler	July 6, 1823	482
Downer, William H. and Elener Bell	Dec. 7, 1823	484
Drake, Meredith and Della Wolen	Aug. 14, 1823	483
Dutton, Henry and Elizabeth Couch	Aug. 22, 1819,	328
Dudley, Ignatius and Sally Horton	Dec. 26, 1819	379
Dupuy, William L. and Frances T. Moore	Oct. 29, 1818	217
Duncan, Henry and Mary Vines	Dec. 23, 1823	485
Edwards, Isaac O. and Mary Clark	Oct. 24, 1816	79
Edwards, Isaac O. and Frances Wyche	Nov. 7, 1824	488
Elliott, Thomas C. and Sally Key	Dec. 28, 1819	400
Fannin, Lauchlin and Susannah Downer	Jan. 27, 1820	476
Farrar, Thomas J. and Martha Royster	Nov. 2, 1824	488
Faulk, Thomas and Louranie Largent	Jan. 11, 1822	481
Felts, Walker and Ann P. Christian	Jan. 8, 1824	486
Ferguson, William and Fanny Karr	July 9, 1821	478
Fitts, William H.T. and Mary M. Christian	May 16, 1820	475
Flemming, Benjamin and Frances Hudson	Sept. 18, 1821	477
Ford, Elisha and Elizabeth Deadwyler	June 11, 1818	193
Fortson, Easton and Tabitha Haley	Dec. 26, 1819	378
Fortson, William and Eliza Lane	Aug. 10, 1820	474
Fortson, Thomas and Mira Kennebrew	Feb. 9, 1821	476
Fortson, William T. and Sarah H. Shackleford	Nov. 22, 1821	478
Fortson, Tavnah and Catherine D. Tate	Dec. 2, 1824	488
Fortson, Richard and Polly Cunningham	Dec. 25, 1823	485
Freeman, Henry and Pamelia Cook	Jan. 11, 1820	476
Foster, James M. and Nancy White	May 12, 1822	480
Gaines, Ralph and Elizabeth M. Turner	Jan. 3, 1822	478
Gaines, James H. and Ann B. Henderson	May 2, 1822	481
Gaines, George and Polly Craft	Jan. 7, 1823	482
Gartman, Daniel and Susannah Pledger	Sept. 26, 1816	85
Ginn, Wiley and Sintha Henry	Jan. 24, 1823	480
Ginn, Elisha and Charity Runnels	Sept. 9, 1823	483
Ginn, Isaac and Martha Burden	June 17, 1824	489
Ginn, Jesse and Sarah Brown	Aug. 8, 1824	489
Gibson, Samuel and Dosha Franklin	Aug. 9, 1820	475
Goode, James J. and Martha Clark	Dec. 8, 1818	217
Goss, Horatio J. and Ann Bradley	Sept. 18, 1823	484
Greenway, John W. and Lucy Hulme	Dec. 9, 1822	487

Groom, Bride and Date		Page
Grinway, Elisha and Sally Hale	June 8, 1818	193
Grice, Demsey and Caty Williams	June 23, 1824	489
Grizzle, John P. and Jane Key	Oct. 20, 1820	436
Gully, Volintine and Elizabeth P. King	Jan. 8, 1818	193
Glover, William and Milley Alexander	Jan. 4, 1816	4
Ham, Gideon and Elizabeth Terrell	Apr. 18, 1820	474
Hamilton, Robert and Louisa McGehee	Jan. 24, 1822	480
Hammond, Herbert and Elizabeth Rich	May 7, 1821	477
Hanley, Jarratt and Polly Coker	Dec. 23, 1818	291
Harbin, William and Elizabeth Kennedy	Dec. 18, 1817	190
Harmon, George W. and Susan Carpenter	Mar. 4, 1821	476
Harris, John L. and Catherine W. King	May 7, 1817	100
Harris, John and Mary J. Shackleford	Dec. 6, 1820	469
Harris, Jonathan and Rachel W. Fortson	Oct. 17, 1823	483
Harper, William W. and Lucy Allen	Nov. 4, 1817	175
Harper, Caselton and Polly Adams	Jan. 7, 1819	261
Harrison, John B. and Elizabeth Burton	Jan. 6, 1823	479
Harper, Bedford and Gilly Y. Banks	Mar. 6, 1823	485
Hardeman, Charles and Mrs. Betty Cook	Oct. 3, 1820	474
Haynes, Waller G. and Polly W. Harper	Dec. 29, 1818	231
Hausley, Nedeygate and Sarah Davis	Feb. 2, 1817	100
Harcrow, Samuel and Alphia Ginn	Sept. 21, 1817	135
Head, Benjamin and Rebecca Terrell	Apr. 22, 1817	89
Head, James B. and Elizabeth Allen	Jan. 7, 1821	477
Hearndon, Edward and Nancy Brown	Aug. 17, 1820	474
Henderson, Simeon and Biddy Heard	Mar. 6, 1817	112
Henry, William and Sucey Skinner	Mar. 20, 1817	106
Henry, John and Polly Skinner	Jan. 25, 1818	306
Henry, William P. and Sarah L. Beck	June 7, 1821	478
Hicks, Wyatt and Melinda Phelps	Feb. 8, 1824	486
Highsmith, Thomas and Elizabeth Parks	Aug. 12, 1824	489
Horton, John and Winny Teasley	Aug. 21, 1817	133
Hilley, Francis and Mary R. Oliver	Feb. 24, 1820	476
Holeyness, McKinney and Susannah V. Nunnelee	Jan. 22, 1823	482
Holdbrook, Flemmon and Aggy Clark	Nov. 6, 1817	297
Holtzclaw, Silas and Rosannah Stone	Feb. 4, 1819	296
Howell, Samuel and Sally Brown	Mar. 22, 1821	476
Huddleston, William and Sarah C. Rice	Nov. 13, 1817	154
Hubbard, John and Ann F. Nunnelee	Dec. 17, 1818	296
Hudson, David and Matilda Oliver	Sept. 9, 1817	190
Hubbard, Vinson and Sarah Dye	July 12, 1821	478
Hudson, John H. and Martha Snellings	Dec. 19, 1924	487
Hudson, David and Lucinda Jones	Feb. 8, 1824	486
Hudson, William and Mary Ann Oliver	June 13, 1824	488
Hunt, George and Elizabeth Adams	Oct. 3, 1822	480
Hunt, Sion and Priscilla Thornton	July 31, 1823	484
Hunt, James and Mary W. Haynes	Dec. 18, 1823	485
Jack, James and Ann Gray	Oct. 27, 1822	479
Johnston, James and Jane Gains	Dec. 12, 1816	479
Johnston, John and Nancy Powell	Jan. 20, 1820	476
Johnston, James and Ann F. Oglesby	Aug. 15, 1822	480
Johnston, Daniel M. and Nancy Highsmith	Aug. 14, 1823	483
Johnston, Lindsey and Sarah Oglesby	Aug. 24, 1823	484
Jones, Hiram and Settey Jones	Mar. 19, 1818	193
Jones, Thomas and Hitty Pathro	Oct. 29, 1818	262
Jones, Davis and Rhody Jones	Dec. 31, 1820	463
Jones, Macajah and Genoa Tate	July 18, 1820	475
Jones, Garland and Winny Shackleford	Dec. 7, 1820	476
Jones, Simeon and Rebecca Banks	Sept. 6, 1821	478

Groom, Bride and Date		Page
Jones, Joseph and Lucy Banks	Feb. 26, 1822	480
Jones, Standley and Frances Rucker	July 24, 1823	483
Jones, Edmond and Keziah Jones	Nov. 10, 1824	486
Jones, John and Nancy Hambleton	Dec. 29, 1818	291
Kemp, David V. and Nancy Butler	Dec. 25, 1823	484
Kennedy, William J. C. and Elizabeth Cason	Jan. 24, 1822	481
Kerlin, David and Icy Kennebrew	Mar. 23, 1824	486
King, John and Matilda Bond	Dec. 12, 1822	479
King, William Jr. and Sukey King	Oct. 3, 1822	480
Klugh, Pascoll D. and Martha N. Tate	June 8, 1821	478
Landers, John and Lotty Meret	Mar. 30, 1817	297
Lawrimore, Andrew and Margaret Kerlin	Dec. 22, 1820	473
Lewis, James H. and Elizabeth H. Kidd	Dec. 3, 1820	474
Lipford, H. F. M. M. and Frances A. Tate	May 20, 1819	297
Loftis, William and Catharine King	Feb. 10, 1824	487
Lofton, James and Lucinda A. Howard	Dec. 22, 1824	488
Logan, John and Matilda Craft	Jan. 2, 1823	485
Lunsford, James and Polly White	Sept. 18, 1817	169
Lunsford, George and Winney White	Jan. 16, 1818	193
Lunsford, James and Honor Eaves	Mar. 17, 1822	480
Lunsford, William and Amelia Teasley	Aug. 28, 1823	483
McConnic, John and Rosannah Prewit	Jan. 17, 1819	297
McCune, James A. and Ruth Ferrell	Mar. 20, 1817	116
McCurley, Moses and Susannah Stowers	Feb. 5, 1824	487
McCurry, Lauchlin and Polly Penn	Jan. 21, 1819	296
McDonald, Alex and Martha P. Hudson	Mar. 22, 1821	477
McGarity, John and Ann Burnett	Oct. 14, 1824	489
McGehee, William and Eliza Watkins	May 22, 1817	133
McGuire, John S. and Susannah A. Clark	Aug. 26, 1824	490
McMullan, Thomas and Sally Gaines	Jan. 12, 1815	4
McMullan, Daniel and Sally Wilson	Sept. 16, 1822	480
McMullan, Fielding and Polly Dollar	Mar. 3, 1822	482
McMullan, Sinclair and Crissa Richardson	Jan. 11, 1824	486
Mann, John and Polly Harper	Dec. 26, 1816	52
Mann, Abner L. and Diana Crittenden	Oct. 14, 1816	69
Mann, William H. and Fanny Hearndon	Jan. 6, 1820	476
Mann, John R. and Rebecca Bentley	Feb. 17, 1821	477
Mann, James and Esther Lewis	Apr. 7, 1822	481
Mann, Stephen A. and Malinda Oliver	July 8, 1824	489
Manning, Robert H. and Louisiana Thompson	Jan. 30, 1822	482
Mann, William H. and Dicey Bentley	Sept. 27, 1817	169
Martin, Jesse and Elizabeth Bentley	Feb. 26, 1824	487
Mason, Allen and Bathena Brannan	Nov. 24, 1819	349
Maxwell, William and Susannah Owens	Mar. 20, 1821	476
Maxwell, Simeon and Elizabeth Fortson	Dec. 9, 1819	353
Maxwell, Ruben and Elizabeth Thornton	Dec. 13, 1821	478
Means, Alexander and Judith Cridenton	Oct. 22, 1822	479
Meanes, Samuel and Sarah Elliott	Sept. 15, 1817	193
Merrell, Joshua and Betsy C. Williamson	Dec. 30, 1818	287
Mewborn, Thomas and Frances Burden	Oct. 26, 1824	489
Middleton, John and Elizabeth P. Tait	June 26, 1817	133
Milton, William and Caty Baskins	Dec. 3, 1817	134
Molden, Thomas and Nancy Cristler	Feb. 20, 1824	486
Miller, Jedediah and Elizabeth C. Edwards	June 17, 1819	353
Moon, Jacob and Anny Staples	Nov. 28, 1816	46
Moon, Stephen and Fanny Phelps	Jan. 20, 1820	475
Moon, James B. and Mary Davis	Aug. 2, 1821	477
Moon, Jesse and Mary Phelps	Oct. 28, 1823	484
Morgan, William C. and Lucindey Oglesby	Mar. 30, 1819	297

Groom, Bride and Date		Page
Moore, Elijah and Sarah White	Dec. 10, 1819	379
Morris, John W. and Anny Allgood	Feb. 6, 1817	85
Moss, Beverly and Lucy Lewis	Dec. 18, 1823	483
Moss, Martin and Nancy Fannen	Nov. 20, 1823	484
Moss, William and Dosha Underwood	Feb. 20, 1823	484
Morgan, Thomas and Lucy Colbert	Feb. 5, 1824	486
Napier, John W. S. and Mary J. Jones	Aug. v, 1824	488
Nash, George B. and Nancy Butler	Aug. 28, 1817	193
Nelmes, John and Mary Underwood	July 23, 1818	306
Nelmes, Jesse and Alis Duncan	Jan. 10, 1822	482
Nelmes, Joshua B. and Nancy Wheeler	Aug. 19, 1823	483
Nelson, William and Grace A. Adams	July 6, 1824	489
New, Samuel and Nancy Dudley	Oct. 5, 1820	474
Nix, William S. and Polly Smith	Mar. 2, 1820	476
Norman, Elijah B. and Polly S. Higginbotham	Apr. 3, 1821	476
Nunnelee, John and Martha Thompson	Jan. 9, 1817	103
Nunnelee, Howell and Malinda Morgan	Feb. 4, 1818	193
Nunnelee, Simeon and Martha Terrell	May 24, 1819	384
Nunnely, William and Mariah O. Tittle	Apr. 24, 1817	89
Oglesby, Robert C. and Zeriah G. Wilhite	Dec. 25, 1823	485
Ozburn, Pleasant and Letty Wood	Jan. 16, 1820	475
Page, Watson D. and Margarett Denna	Jan. 1, 1824	485
Parker, John D. and Nancy Merret	Oct. 23, 1819	314
Patterson, Henry and Elizabeth Cook	June 7, 1818	193
Patterson, Thomas and Nancy Hendry	May 31, 1821	478
Patterson, Robert H. and Martha Moore	Dec. 5, 1824	488
Patterson, James and Mary Jones	Aug. 17, 1824	489
Pealor, Benjamin and Elitha Ginn	Mar. 15, 1819	297
Pealor, Abney and Elvey Allgood	Apr. 10, 1819	297
Pealor, Abner and Betsy Akens	Dec. 30, 1819	350
Penn, Thomas H. and Polly Burden	Jan. 18, 1821	477
Perrin, Bannister and Nancy Carter	Dec. 2, 1824	487
Pledger, Johnston and Nancy Oglesby	July 6, 1820	475
Pledger, Westley and Sarah Oglesby	Jan. 18, 1821	476
Pledger, Joseph P. and Frances P. Chambers	Jan. 3, 1822	482
Pledger, Isaac M. and Polly Ginn	Oct. 21, 1822	482
Prothro, Joshua and Lucy Dobbs	Jan. 4, 1823	485
Presley, Charles and Mildred Kerlin	Dec. 21, 1819	343
Prewit, John and Letha Craft	Dec. 23, 1819	400
Price, Matthew and Sally Skinner	May 12, 1824	490
Pulliam, William and Permelia Turman	Jan. 29, 1824	487
Ramsey, David B. and Polly Brown	Sept. 19, 1820	474
Ready, Peter and Sally Dooly	July 1, 1817	304
Redwine, Lewis and Mary Merret	Jan. 14, 1817	297
Reed, William P. and Harriet Allen	July 22, 1824	486
Rembert, Andrew and Margaret M. Sayre	Feb. 12, 1819	297
Rice, Jesse and Webby Dooly	Sept. 3, 1818	304
Rice, Richard and Eliza White	Jan. 1, 1823	482
Richards, Ruben and Rachel Bond	Nov. 12, 1819	2
Roan, John and Jane Davis	Dec. 19, 1821	476
Roberts, Jesse and Tabitha Ruff	May 9, 1821	477
Roberts, Joseph and Polly Folk	Jan. 1, 1822	481
Rodgers, John and Jane Dennard	Mar. 20, 1883	485
Roan, John and Frances Tate	Apr. 15, 1824	486
Rose, Pleasant and Sarah Hubbard	Oct. 17, 1819	405
Rose, Thomas G. and Sarah Christian	Mar. 11, 1824	486
Runnels, Meredith and Milly Powel	Apr. 26, 1821	476
Runnels, Berry and Crissy Powel	Mar. 15, 1822	481
Runnels, William and Sarah Bobo	June 6, 1824	489

Groom, Bride and Date		Page
Ruff, Shadrack and Patsy Penn	Nov. 17, 1822	479
Saddler, James R. and Pressilla Jones	Jan. 8, 1824	487
Saggs, Henry M. and Polly Gregg	May 9, 1820	475
Sanders, Thomas and Isabel Totman	Sept. 16, 1819	397
Sanders, Benjamin and Nancy White	July 15, 1824	489
Sartain, James and Bethana Burnett	Nov. 18, 1824	488
Saxton, John M. and Elizabeth Burton	Dec. 31, 1817	217
Schelds, Thomas E. and Matilda Bailey	Mar. 27, 1823	483
Self, Sinclair and Nancy James	Feb. 24, 1820	476
Sheat, Burgess and Milsy Coker	Nov. 19, 1818	219
Shell, George and Sarah L. Hearne	Dec. 19, 1815	297
Shelman, John and Unity Phillips	Aug. 3, 1818	193
Shephard, Richard and Judea J. Mann	Dec. 27, 1820	457
Sheperd, Nathan and Betsy Bently	Nov. 30, 1820	474
Shorter, Eli S. and Sophia H. Watkins	June 18, 1817	133
Simmons, John and Mary B. Harrison	May 25, 1817	190
Skinner, Morris and Sally Hendrick	Aug. 12, 1819	349
Skelton, Jabez and Julia Davis	Feb. 14, 1823	485
Snow, Eli and Elizabeth Gully	Jan. 22, 1824	490
Smith, David and Selah David	May 15, 1817	86
Smith, John M. and Nancy L. Suttles	Nov. 27, 1810	2
Smith, Thomas A. and Elizabeth Hullum	Nov. 28, 1820	473
Smith, Westley and Averilla Royal	Apr. 18, 1820	475
Smith, Charles and Martha T. Blenn	Jan. 20, 1820	476
Smith, Henry and Rachel Pemelton	Mar. 1, 1821	476
Smith, Archibald and Levina McMullan	Jan. 24, 1822	481
Smith, William A. and Rebecca Anderson	Feb. 1, 1824	487
Smith, Joseph and Mary Ann Harris	Dec. 30, 1824	488
Smith, Samuel and Mary Dobbs	Oct. 17, 1824	489
Smithey, Isaac and Polly Terrell	Nov. 25, 1819	406
Statham, John Jr. and Nancy Hicks	Jan. 5, 1823	482
Stephens, Thomas and Patsy Lesuer	May 11, 1823	485
Stephens, Henry H. and Martha Oglesby	Oct. 7, 1824	487
Steelman, William H. and Elizabeth T. Underwood	July 8, 1824	488
Stricklin, Joseph and Sarah Davis	July 14, 1819	386
Standerford, Bailey and Betsy Hales	Apr. 23, 1810	2
Tate, Zimri and Martha Owens	May 14, 1817	89
Tate, William and Sarah Upshaw	Nov. 4, 1819	314
Tate, James and Mary S. Brown	July 27, 1819	396
Tate, Edmond B. and Mahala Fortson	Oct. 16, 1823	484
Taylor, Jesse and Phereby Decker	Nov. 14, 1822	479
Taylor, John and Rebecca Snellings	Jan. 7, 1821	477
Teasley, Levi and Elizabeth Horton	Nov. 27, 1817	190
Teasley, James S. and Mary A. Hansard	Oct. 17, 1822	479
Teasley, Benager and Lucy Haley	Oct. 31, 1822	482
Thomas, Evans and Polly Moore	Jan. 11, 1821	477
Thompson, Joel and Betsy Smith	Nov. 3, 1816	21
Thomason, John and Martha Gaines	Nov. 4, 1817	405
Thornton, Benjamin and Nancy Payne	Sept. 16, 1819	397
Thornton, Evans and Morening Adams	Oct. 23, 1817	171
Thornton, Jeremiah and Frances Colbert	Oct. 28, 1819	397
Thornton, Thomas A. and Polly Willis	Oct. 5, 1820	474
Thornton, Thomas A. and Sarah Fortson	Oct. 23, 1823	484
Thornton, John and Frances Adams	Oct. 23, 1823	484
Therikeld, Oliver and Mariah Cook	Nov. 18, 1824	488
Toles, Suddeth and Nancy A. Nolan	Aug. 3, 1820	474
Tucker, Robert and Martha Staples	Dec. 16, 1824	488
Turman, Abner T. and Martha Jones	Dec. 9, 1822	479
Turner, Thomas and Ann Gregg	Dec. 23, 1819	378

Groom, Bride and Date		Page
Tyner, Tollison and Jane Totman	Aug. 28, 1820	423
Underwood, Jarratt and Nellie Moss	Jan. 1, 1818	327
Unis, Samuel and Sarah Jorden	July 5, 1824	486
Upshaw, John and Tabitra Lawlis	Apr. 2, 1818	193
Upshaw, Richard and Rebecca Elder	Feb. 27, 1820	475
Upshaw, George and Elizabeth Tate	Jan. 4, 1820	476
Upshaw, Huston and Rhoda Oglesby	Aug. 3, 1823	484
Vaughan, Murphy and Sarah Ann Tate	Dec. 21, 1823	484
Virdell, John A. and Sally C. Williamson	Jan. 21, 1819	297
Wallis, Burrell and Rhoda Dickenson	Dec. 12, 1816	52
Ward, John B. and Rebecca Coulson	July 1, 1823	483
Ward, Walter H. and Jane Gray	Jan. 23, 1823	485
Warren, Jeremiah S. and Elizabeth Thornton	Oct. 14, 1823	485
Webb, Wiley and Betsy Morris	Nov. 9, 1816	79
Webb, Milton P. and Letitia Deadwyler	Nov. 16, 1820	475
Webb, Abner and Nancy Deadwyler	Nov. 9, 1824	486
Welborn, Burkett and Nancy Pace	Sept. 16, 1818	261
West, William and Elizabeth P. Wood	July 30, 1823	483
White, John M. and Elizabeth Harper	Dec. 26, 1816	52
White, Asa and Agnes Moore	Dec. 26, 1816	79
White, James and Lucy Cash	Oct. 25, 1821	478
White, Martin and Ann Burden	Feb. 27, 1823	485
Wheeler, Thomas B. and Judith Bates	July 24, 1822	480
Wheeler, Leroy and Sarah Wheeler	Oct. 8, 1818	304
Wilhite, Joseph and Nancy F. Wilhite	Dec. 19, 1820	463
Wilhite, John B. and Elizabeth P. Wilhite	Aug. 17, 1820	474
Williams, John and Keziah Cook	Jan. 3, 1822	481
Willis, Thomas F. and Milly Clark	Nov. 7, 1822	479
Willis, John and Fanny Sartain	Feb. 20, 1820	475
Woods, John and Tabitha Ridgway	Mar. 27, 1817	116
Woolridge, Thomas and Nancy Banks	Feb. 13, 1822	481
Young, John and Ann Cook	May 1, 1823	483

MARRIAGES, 1825-1829, WILL BOOK "N," OLD NUMBER

Groom, Bride and Date		Page
Ashworth, Noah and Nancy C. Lockhart	Aug. 6, 1827	409
Adams, Lawrence M. and Nancy H. Hunt	Nov. 14, 1826	409
Adams, Abner and Betsy A. Fortson	July 20, 1826	410
Adams, George and Jemima Anderson	Apr. 8, 1828	415
Alexander, Elam and Lucy Terry	Dec. 8, 1825	411
Akin, Johnson and Charity A. Banks	Oct. 28, 1828	416
Allgood, John and Nancy Burden	Dec. 27, 1825	411
Allen, Thomas J. and Elizabeth White	Jan. 26, 1826	411
Allen, Edmond B. and Sarah Ashworth	Jan. 12, 1826	411
Almond, Simeon and Mary Fortson	Nov. 21, 1826	409
Alston, James J. Y. and Mary A. R. Chambers	Apr. 12, 1827	413
Arnold, William and Nancy Woodly	Sept. 3, 1826	410
Arnold, John and Mary W. Hudson	Dec. 15, 1825	410
Anthony, William A. and Milly Hightower	Nov. 15, 1827	413
Bailey, Hezekiah and Sally Gaines	Jan. 12, 1826	411
Banks, Henry and Judith Oliver	Feb. 8, 1826	169
Banks, John and Sarah Watkins	Feb. 14, 1828	415
Barnes, John and Martha C. Stodghill	Sept. 6, 1827	415
Bell, Jonathan and Sarah Bell	Aug. 17, 1828	415
Bentley, Hiram and Levicy Bentley	Mar. 31, 1828	415
Benedict, Eli and Selah Smith	Dec. 18, 1828	416
Blair, Middleton and Peggy Wallis	Oct. 19, 1826	412

Groom, Bride and Date		Page
Black, John W. and Betsy Ham	Mar. 4, 1828	414
Bond, Daniel and Claricey Bond	Feb. 19, 1825	227
Bond, Willis and Leah Carpenter	Mar. 13, 1825	408
Booth, Victor E. and Elizabeth Parham	Dec. 20, 1827	414
Bray, Maston H. and Elizabeth Faulkner	Apr. 17, 1828	415
Brown, James and Sarah Alexander	Nov. 15, 1827	413
Bryant, William and Sarah Teasley	Dec. 31, 1820	408
Burch, Benjamin and Mary Ann Cook	Mar. 20, 1828	414
Burden, Archibald and Lydia Fortenberry	Jan. 1, 1826	411
Burton, Nicholas and Eliza F. Nunnelee	Apr. 20, 1828	416
Bailey, Henry S. and Lucy Patterson	Nov. 22, 1827	413
Campbell, Daniel and Ann C. E. P. Wright	Mar. 31, 1825	408
Campbell, Obediah and Elizabeth Edwards	Jan. 24, 1828	414
Carlisle, James W. and Mazy Pace	Mar. 26, 1826	410
Carpenter, Joshua S. and Mary W. Bond	Apr. 3, 1825	408
Canning, John and Elizabeth Moore	Oct. 9, 1825	408
Chandler, Mordeci and Elizabeth Banks	Feb. 26, 1828	414
Childers, William B. and Nancy L. Hudson	Aug. 6, 1826	409
Childers, Seaborn and Permelia Rich	June 28, 1827	413
Christian, Charles W. and Mary Maxwell	Jan. 18, 1827	412
Clark, Zachariah H. and Elizabeth Mattox	Jan. 10, 1828	414
Clark, James and Permelia T. Wilbern	Aug. 25, 1828	415
Coker, Newell and Catherine Cunningham	Oct. 27, 1825	409
Cook, Issachar and Nancy Wood	Jan. 28, 1827	412
Cook, Beverly C. and Martha Tate	May 3, 1827	412
Cook, William T. O. and Nancy T. Ridgway	Sept. 16, 1828	415
Craft, John Jr. and Ann Gaines	Oct. 23, 1828	416
Cunningham, Joseph and Polly Robertson	May 13, 1825	201
David, Samuel and Harriet Threlkeld	May 25, 1826	410
Davis, Vatchel and Malinda O. Kelly	Jan. 23, 1827	412
Davis, James and Frances Terrell	Jan. 18, 1827	412
Davis, Joseph and Susannah Wall	Nov. 4, 1827	416
Deadwyler, Joseph P. and Martha P. Webb	Nov. 8, 1825	409
Dean, Alvin and Eliza F. White	Jan. 3, 1826	411
Dickerson, Robert P. and Martha Henderson	July 20, 1826	409
Dobbs, Asa and Frances McMullan	Oct. 18, 1826	409
Dooly, William W. and Mary Brantley	July 5, 1827	413
Dooly, Thomas and Mary Brooks	July 26, 1825	408
Dobbs, Silas and Nancy Mires	Oct. 4, 1827	413
Edmondson, James and Rebecca Jones	Mar. 15, 1826	409
Edmondson, Samuel and Eliza Perryman	June 1, 1827	412
Edwards, William H. and Elizabeth Burton	Dec. 23, 1828	416
Etchieson, Allen and Sarah M. Ragan	Jan. 20, 1826	411
Everson, Willis and Frances Higginbotham	Dec. 9, 1827	414
Fortson, Tavnah W. and Elizabeth D. Tate	Sept. 13, 1827	413
Forrester, Jesse and Mary White	Sept. 26, 1826	409
Foster, William and Judah Parrot	Jan. 31, 1827	411
Franklin, Wiley and Elizabeth Dutton	Jan. 22, 1828	414
Gaar, William and Keziah Davis	Oct. 25, 1827	413
Garey, Van D. and Elizabeth Dooley	Feb. 9, 1826	411
Ginn, Joshua and Nancy Statham	Nov. 3, 1826	408
Glenn, Simeon G. and Jane Ann Carden	Sept. 25, 1828	416
Golding, Wm. Barnett and Eveline Adams	Oct. 9, 1828	415
Grant, Gregory and Lucinda H. Davis	Oct. 25, 1827	413
Griffin, William W. and Elenor W. Smith	Dec. 18, 1827	414
Gunter Jesse and Susan Butler	Nov. 10, 1825	409
Hall, John and Maria Turman	Apr. 12, 1827	412
Hall, Simeon and Lucy Stinchcomb	July 29, 1828	415
Hall, Thomas and Nancy Laremore	Oct. 14, 1828	416

Groom, Bride and Date		Page
Hammond, Alfred and Louisa Hudson	Jan. 24, 1826	411
Harmon, Frederick and Rhody Carpenter	Apr. 4, 1825	
Hardeman, Joel and Elizabeth B. Upshaw	Dec. 5, 1825	408
Heard, Thomas J. and Nancy P. Middleton	Apr. 1, 1828	415
Hearne, Thomas and Frances E. Williams	June 3, 1828	415
Henderson, Simeon and Sarah D. Lewis	July 20, 1828	415
Hendricks, Levi and Cloey Coker	June 3, 1825	408
Hendricks, Milum and Julia Ann Eaves	Aug. 17, 1826	410
Hendrick, James J. and Cissale Kelly	July 5, 1827	413
Handy, Joseph J. L. and Rebecca Martin	Sept. 28, 1826	409
Harcrow, Hugh and Sarah Powell	July 11, 1827	413
Harris, Tryon and Sarah Alexander	Oct. 29, 1825	411
Herring, William A. and Mary S. White	Jan. 11, 1825	104
Hickman, Thomas J. and Mary McCurry	Aug. 23, 1827	413
Higginbotham, John G. and Sally Thornton	Oct. 25, 1827	413
Hill, Abram and Bitha Coker	Jan. 22, 1828	414
Hilley, Thomas and Claray G. Higginbotham	May 13, 1828	415
Hinton, John L. and Elizabeth Hulme	Sept. 10, 1828	415
Horton, Walker and Malinda Colbert	Feb. 28, 1828	415
Hubbard, Woodson and Mary Dye	Jan. 20, 1825	408
Hudson, Richard D. and Mary W. Burton	Jan. 13, 1828	414
Hudson, Lewellen W. and Eliza D. Jarratt	Oct. 22, 1828	416
Hulme, William and Nancy Ann Oliver	Oct. 8, 1826	409
Hunt, John S. and Mary Gaines	July 14, 1825	285
Hutchenson, Moses and Nancy J. Brantley	July 14, 1828	285
Jackson, William and Ann F. McGehee	Dec. 13, 1825	408
Jarratt, James D. and Sarah Heard	Jan. 18, 1825	29
Johnston, James and Ann Prothro	Aug. 26, 1825	408
Johnston, Thomas and Mildred A. Roebuck	May 4, 1826	410
Jones, Jordan and Lucy Nix	Jan. 27, 1825	227
Jones, Samuel G. and Elizabeth A. Edwards	Jan. 21, 1826	409
Jones, Dewy H. and Sophia Akin	Mar. 22, 1827	412
Jones, James W. and Delina Foster	Oct. 30, 1828	416
Kirby, Willis and Babary Jentry	July 19, 1827	413
Koochagey, Samuel and Martha Carter	Feb. 10, 1825	29
LeGrand, John W. and Lucinda Christian	Aug. 8, 1827	413
Lewis, Jeptha and Frances R. Harris	Oct. 13, 1825	408
Lunsford, Rolen and Patsey Roberts	Jan. 5, 1826	411
Mannen, William and Sarah Deadwyler	Apr. 21, 1825	169
Mannen, Seaborn and Lucy Newborn	Sept. 28, 1826	409
Mannen, William and Mary Ford	Dec. 4, 1827	413
Martin, James S. and Rebecca Wright	Apr. 11, 1825	407
Martin, Henry and Permelia Nash	Apr. 6, 1828	415
Martin, James B. and Lucy Powell	June 19, 1828	415
Mattox, Nathan and Lucy Key	Feb. 19, 1826	410
Maxwell, Benson and Elizabeth B. Johnson	July 25, 1826	410
Merrewether, Chas. S. and Mildred Banks	Dec. 1, 1827	414
Moon, William H. and Susan Moon	Oct. 20, 1825	408
Moore, John N. and Martha Vaughan	Mar. 6, 1828	414
Morgan, Kindred and Sarah T. Mann	Dec. 20, 1827	414
McCallister, Richard and Phebe Powell	July 14, 1828	415
McCoy, Thomas and Lucy Brawner	Feb. 21, 1826	410
McCurry, John and Nancy P. Goss	Aug. 31, 1825	408
McGuire, Thomas M. and Elizabeth Skelton	Mar. 27, 1828	415
Nash, Henry E. and Mary Jones	Jan. 5, 1826	411
Nelms, James M. and Susan Moss	Nov. 18, 1825	411
Nelms, Wiley and Polly Gay	May 12, 1826	409
Nuckols, Nathaniel and Susannah Thornton	Nov. 13, 1826	409
Oglesby, James and Sarah Booth	Mar. 6, 1826	412

Groom, Bride and Date		Page
Oliver, Jaxson and Polly Maxwell	Feb. 14, 1826	410
Oliver, Thomas W. and Elizabeth Ann Oliver	June 6, 1826	410
Oliver, Shelton and Martha B. Williams	Sept. 9, 1828	415
Pace, Dreadzil and Charlotty Sandridge	Oct. 4, 1825	408
Page, John and Emelia Akin	Oct. 26, 1826	409
Palmore, Thomas N. and Catherine Denna	Feb. 14, 1827	412
Patterson, William and Sarah Clark	Aug. 20, 1826	409
Pealer, Joseph and Sarah Allgood	Nov. 29, 1827	414
Penn, Edmond T. and Katherine McCurry	Sept. 4, 1828	415
Perrin, John and Lucinda Nash	Oct. 19, 1826	409
Perryman, William J. and Lucinda Head	Sept. 30, 1823	411
Prather, James and Elizabeth Rowze	May 3, 1825	270
Prather, William M. and Nancy Rowsey	Nov. 17, 1825	411
Prewit, Joshua and Elizabeth Means	Dec. 21, 1826	412
Pritchet, John and Mary Farmer	Nov. 13, 1818	408
Prothro, William and Mittey Powell	Nov. 29, 1827	414
Raines, John W. and Lucinda Hicks	Dec. 18, 1828	416
Rhodelander, Peter and Sally Howell	Oct. 28, 1825	411
Rice, Aaron and Lettey Ballenger	Feb. 6, 1827	412
Ridgway, Samuel and Charlotte Brawner	Sept. 20, 1825	408
Roebuck, John W. and Martha D. Brown	Dec. 30, 1828	416
Rosser, Jeptha and Sarah N. Harris	Oct. 6, 1825	411
Rowsey, John and Martha S. Warren	Jan. 3, 1828	414
Rucker, Lemuel and Priscilla Teasley	Aug. 11, 1825	408
Saxon, Drury T. and Elizabeth Coleman	Jan. 3, 1827	412
Scales, William and Ann R. Higginbotham	Dec. 16, 1828	416
Self, Samuel E. and Milly Ashworth	Mar. 13, 1827	413
Sewell, Joseph and Polley C. Stinchcomb	Nov. 1, 1827	413
Shackleford, Henry and Martha Lewis	May 29, 1828	415
Shelton, John and Mariah Sullivan	Jan. 8, 1828	414
Shackleford, Joseph H. and Ann Thornton	Dec. 22, 1825	411
Shiflett, Pickett and Sarah Ann Henderson	Jan. 23, 1828	414
Tate, Jacob M. and Anna A. Keys	June 7, 1827	413
Taylor, Willis W. and Cathrine Hall	Nov. 14, 1825	411
Teasley, Thomas J. and Martha W. Teasley	Dec. 20, 1827	414
Teasley, Beverally A. and Elizabeth Eavenson	Feb. 15, 1828	414
Thompson, Jesse and Permelia McGuire	Jan. 13, 1820	408
Thompson, Jeffrey and Tabitha Clark	Jan. 25, 1826	410
Thornton, Daniel and Lucy C. Bradley	Oct. 3, 1826	409
Thornton, William and Nancy J. Shackleford	July 20, 1826	410
Thornton, Elzey B. and Nancy Harper	Apr. 13, 1826	410
Tinsley, Thomas C. and Martha M. Harris	Apr. 7, 1826	410
Tinsley, Thomas D. and Sarah D. Edwards	Jan. 3, 1828	414
Tucker, Ethal Jr. and Nancy Davis	May 17, 1825	270
Tucker, Stephen H. and Mary Akin	Jan. 16, 1827	412
Tucker, John M. and Lucinda Tucker	Jan. 13, 1827	412
Turman, Samuel and Polly Fortson	Dec. 20, 1827	414
Tyner, Richard Je and Elizabeth Harman	May 31, 1821	408
Webb, Fortunatus and Lenna Almond	Nov. 22, 1826	409
Webb, Walton P. and Susannah Deadwyler	Nov. 13, 1827	413
White, John M. and Milly Satterwhite	Dec. 19, 1826	409
Wilkens, Clement and Mary Moon	July 20, 1826	410
Wilson, James and Fanny Prickett	Sept. 23, 1819	408
Wilson, George and Susan Cook	Jan. 13, 1828	414
Williams, Thomas J. and Hannah Cook	July 27, 1826	410
Wimbish, Alex F. and Elizabeth P. Higginbotham	Dec. 18, 1828	416

MARRIAGES, 1829-1831, WILL BOOK "N," MIXED RECORDS

Groom, Bride and Date		Page
Adams, Nicholas N. and Drucilla Hunt	Dec. 2, 1829	220
Adams, Hiram G. and Mary A. Williams	Dec. 3, 1829	221
Alexander, George and Elizabeth Cash	Sept. 9, 1830	222
Allen, William and Jincey Fannin	Dec. 9, 1829	220
Almond, William M. and Mary Thornton	Jan. 6, 1831	351
Almond, John and Mrs. Mary Johnson	Nov. 8, 1829	220
Andrew, Charles and Martha Christian	Jan. 6, 1830	221
Bailey, Wesley S. and Harriet E. Morrison	Feb. 1, 1831	351
Barr, George I. and Rachel W. Willis	Dec. 15, 1829	219
Bell, David and Elizabeth Snellings	Jan. 6, 1829	218
Bell, James Jr. and Martha Ousley	Sept. 13, 1829	219
Bentley, Jesse and Baba Moon	Feb. 16, 1830	221
Blackwell, James M. and Irena Coker	Dec. 26, 1831	352
Blackwell, Banks and Mrs. Elizabeth Clark	June 28, 1831	352
Bobo, Sampson and Elizabeth Bobo	Sept. 4, 1828	218
Bobo, Lewis and Mrs. Letty Dooly	July 7, 1829	219
Bond, John W. and Lucy Harris	Sept. 15, 1829	220
Booth, William S. and Lucy Parham	Feb. 12, 1829	218
Booth, Joseph and Jincey Hicks	Dec. 15, 1829	220
Boler, Bennett and Nancy Harris	Nov. 20, 1830	222
Brock, James L. and Nancy Johnson	Dec. 23, 1828	218
Brown, Wiley B. and Sarah Clark	Dec. 13, 1827	218
Brown, Elbert and Elizabeth Herndon	July 28, 1829	219
Brown, Julian N. and Mrs. Catherine Alexander	Dec. 6, 1829	221
Brown, John and Martha Eaves	Apr. 1, 1830	222
Bullard, Thomas B. and Elizabeth P. Gunter	July 1, 1829	219
Burch, James J. and Mary Eades	May 4, 1830	221
Burden, Micajah and Sarah Pulliam	Sept. 14, 1830	222
Cade, Drury B. and Julia A. Edwards	May 4, 1830	222
Calloway, Lawrence and Sarah Eaves	Jan. 7, 1829	219
Christian, Elijah L. and Elizabeth Edwards	Oct. 28, 1828	218
Christian, Thomas J. and Mary J. Christian	June 10, 1829	220
Clark, William D. and Jane E. Hearne	Sept. 6, 1830	222
Clayton, George R. and Ann R. Harris	Oct. 7, 1830	222
Cleveland, James M. and Penina Haley	Dec. 20, 1827	218
Couch, Elijah W. and Nancy Allen	June 8, 1830	222
Cook, Joseph and Adeline Threlkeld	Aug. 2, 1830	222
Crawford, Thomas and Martha A. Banks	July 7, 1829	219
Crawford, Oliver and Barbara Cook	July 24, 1830	222
Collins, John W. and Pheba L. Hudson	June 7, 1831	332
Cox, William B. and Rhoda Allen	Nov. 9, 1830	351
Davis, Thomas F. and Matilda Brown	Aug. 20, 1829	219
Davis, Isaac N. and Mrs. Eliz. Ann Oliver	Oct. 15, 1829	220
Dobbs, Elijah and Cyrena A. Smith	Dec. 12, 1830	222
Dobbs, Josiah and Elizabeth Prothro	Nov. 18, 1830	353
Eaves, William and Peggy A. Maxwell	Apr. 29, 1829	229
Eavenson, Thomas and Sarah Thornton	Dec. 9, 1830	222
Fortson, Easton and Susan Ham	Feb. 10, 1831	351
Gaar, William and Sarah Craft	Dec. 30, 1830	351
Gaar, George and Mary Rucker	Mar. 10, 1814	352
Gaines, Francis and Didema Haley	Dec. 17, 1829	220
Gay, James and Eliza Hendrick	Apr. 2, 1830	222
Ginn, William and Nancy Dodds	Nov. 24, 1828	218
Goss, Benjamin and Sarah C. Roebuck	June 3, 1830	352
Gray, Reece and Mary Jane Pratt	Sept. 10, 1829	219
Griffin, Robert T. and Mary Patterson	Nov. 2, 1830	222
Hall, William and Orpha Nelms	Feb. 20, 1829	219

Groom, Bride and Date		Page
Harmon, John S. and Nancy A. Ford	Apr. 28, 1831	352
Hawthorne, William S. and Martha W. Davis	Dec. 3, 1829	220
Henry, Daniel N. and Caroline Edmondson	Mar. 20, 1827	218
Henry, Alexander and Keziah Mason	Jan. 7, 1829	218
Holmes, James and Nancy Adams	Oct. 18, 1829	220
Housley, John and Mrs. Frances Cook	Feb. 24, 1829	218
Houston, Alex P. and Mrs. Martha Deadwyler	Dec. 8, 1829	220
Hubbard, Benson and Mrs. Susan Gunter	Dec. 28, 1830	351
James, William and Elizabeth Henderson	Jan. 11, 1829	221
Jarratt, James D. and Jane H. Jack	July 7, 1829	219
Johnson, Larkin and Mrs. Milly Rucker	July 19, 1827	219
Johnson, Bedford and Harriet Brawner	Dec. 9, 1829	220
Johnson, Larkin and Mrs. Jane Martin	Mar. 11, 1830	221
Johnson, Neal and Katherine McCurry	Jan. 21, 1831	352
Jones, William B. and Mandy S. Rucker	July 24, 1829	219
Jones, Lewis R. and Elizabeth K. Dye	Sept. 29, 1829	220
Jordan, Stephen W. and Elizabeth Burden	Mar. 4, 1830	221
Kelly, Barnabas and Margaret M. Scales	Dec. 30, 1828	218
Kelly, Thomas O. and Eliz. L. Sandridge	Dec. 8, 1829	220
Kennebrew, Edwin and Elizabeth Horton	Sept. 15, 1829	219
Lee, Robert W. and Finetty Kennebrew	Sept. 22, 1830	222
Lewis, Jeremiah and Rhoda Hansard	Dec. 30, 1829	220
McAllester, Alex and Sarah Brown	Jan. 14, 1830	221
McGuire, Frederick S. and Martha Goolsby	July 7, 1831	352
McKerley, George and Nancy McMullan	May 12, 1831	353
McStowers, Jeremiah and Mary Neal	May 7, 1829	219
Maley, Johnston and Mrs. Eliz. L. Roebuck	Jan. 9, 1831	351
Malden, Flemming and Eliza Hickman	Feb. 18, 1830	221
Masters, Levi and Mary McCurry	Jan. 13, 1829	218
Maxwell, William T. and Sarah Horton	Sept. 28, 1830	352
Maxwell, Thomas J. and Ann B. Adams	May 31, 1831	352
Mitchell, Isaac G. and Mary Dudley	Jan. 15, 1829	218
Morris, Garrett and Mary Keys	Dec. 30, 1829	220
Nelms, Nathaniel H. and Ann Cash	Dec. 23, 1830	222
Nix, James and Sophia Rich	Jan. 2, 1830	221
Oglesby, William and Plyne Wiley	May 21, 1830	221
Oliver, Florence M. and Hannah K. Banks	Sept. 15, 1829	220
Parham, Isham and Polly Booth	Nov. 15, 1828	218
Parham, Harrison and Polly Colvard	Dec. 27, 1829	220
Patterson, Wiley and Emeline E. Edwards	May 1, 1830	221
Perce, Jacob and Mary Downs	May 27, 1830	221
Pritchett, Nicholas and Polly Shiflett	Mar. 18, 1830	353
Powell, Tinsley and Eliza Shiflett	May 17, 1831	352
Rich, Richmond and Frances W. Dye	Sept. 23, 1829	220
Richardson, James V. and Milly Bobo	Feb. 11, 1830	221
Rowell, Joshua W. and Elizabeth Tucker	Sept. 23, 1831	352
Rush, Lewis B. and Hanna Bobo	Jan. 20, 1831	352
Sandridge, James W. and Mary Pulliam	Feb. 23, 1830	221
Shackleford, Allen and Elizabeth Maxwell	Oct. 14, 1830	222
Shackleford, John H. and Sarah Hansard	Apr. 12, 1831	352
Shepherd, Thomas J. and Mary A. Henderson	Dec. 31, 1830	351
Shockley, James H. and Sarah E. Henderson	Mar. 26, 1831	352
Smith, Fielding and Lucy Davis	Nov. 11, 1824	218
Smith, Lindsay and Rhoda Bell	Sept. 6, 1829	219
Smith, Redick and Martha H. Glynn	Feb. 24, 1831	352
Smith, Drury and Susannah Harbins	Dec. 7, 1830	284
Sneed, Terrell and Sarah D. Raymond	Feb. 22, 1829	219
Steel, Robert and Sarah Rice	Jan. 3, 1828	218
Tatum, Jesse and Rowsau Sarah	Apr. 9, 1829	219

Groom, Bride and Date		Page
Taylor, Tavnah and Sarow Craft	Jan. 12, 1831	351
Teasley, John A. and Betsy C. Haley	Dec. 18, 1828	218
Thomason, John and Mary Jenkins	Dec. 22, 1830	222
Thornton, William D. and Sarah W. Cleveland	Jan. 27, 1829	221
Upshaw, Middleton C. and Eliz. H. Rucker	Feb. 2, 1830	221
Upshaw, Leroy and Mrs. Catherine Ellington	Nov. 18, 1830	222
Vines, Joseph and Mary McGarity	Mar. 22, 1829	219
Vineyard, Joseph and Susannah Christian	Mar. 28, 1830	221
Walters, Abraham and Margaret Salmons	Dec. 13, 1827	218
Ware, Francis and Lucy Hines	Dec. 26, 1829	220
Wall, Budd C. and Martha W. Nunnelee	Aug. 19, 1830	222
Ward, Jeptha H. and Mary Terry	Jan. 15, 1829	221
Webb, Urbin A. and Mrs. Sarah Lauramore	Jan. 21, 1829	218
Webb, Elijah W. and Ann B. Deadwyler	Dec. 24, 1829	220
Wheeler, Isaac and Sally Underwood	Aug. 6, 1829	219
White, Nathaniel H. and Mrs. Martha Pace	Jan. 28, 1829	219
White, Martin and Martha N. Burton	Dec. 6, 1830	351
Wiley, William S. and Katherine Morris	Mar. 7, 1830	221
Williams, Nathan and Polly Ballinger	Mar. 21, 1829	219
Williford, Reuben S. and Mary Bowers	Dec. 21, 1830	352

MARRIAGES, RECORD BOOK 1830-1838

Groom, Bride and Date		Page
Abney, Wiley and Elender Haley	Apr. 19, 1832	201
Adams, William H. and Nancy Cheek	Oct. 3, 1833	408
Adams, John M. and Agnes M. Hulme	Oct. 7, 1834	499
Alexander, Fleming A. and Ann Jones	Oct. 7, 1831	199
Alexander, Robert B. and Sarah L. Ward	Nov. 6, 1834	499
Almond, John W. and Mildred Gibbs	Sept. 7, 1831	199
Almond, James and Amanda N. M. Fortson	Oct. 20, 1831	199
Almond, Micajah and Eliza Cleveland	Oct. 3, 1833	408
Arnold, Wilton J. and Edna Ann Bell	Jan. 14, 1834	408
Asher, Thomas J. and Moriah L. Housley	Dec. 11, 1832	201
Ashworth, John S. and Julia Ann E. Gaar	Jan. 15, 1835	500
Bailey, James B. and Susan M. Foster	Dec. 13, 1832	201
Bailey, John M. and Harriet Dunn	Dec. 18, 1834	499
Banks, William R. and Eliz. Bowman	Apr. 3, 1832	200
Banks, Lemuel and Louisa A. Tate	Dec. 24, 1833	408
Barnes, Barnabas and Milly McMullan	Aug. 7, 1834	500
Bell, Asmond and Sarah Ann Arnold	Sept. 6, 1831	199
Bell, Lucious J. M. and Sarah Ann Cheek	July 3, 1834	500
Bentley, John E. and Adaline A. Arnold	Sept. 16, 1832	201
Black, Thomas and Hannah Rucker	Sept. 25, 1832	326
Bobo, Benjamin and Mary Bray	Sept. 15, 1831	199
Bond, Henry W. and Sarah Caroline Floyd	Aug. 29, 1834	326
Bonds, Isham R. and Nancy L. Harris	Nov. 12, 1832	201
Bowen, Samuel and Nancy Freeman	Mar. 17, 1835	500
Bourne, Henry and Mrs. Mary Heard	Feb. 20, 1833	326
Brawner, James and Jemima W. Smith	Mar. 26, 1833	326
Brown, Thomas H. and Sarah D. Edwards	Mar. 28, 1833	326
Brown, Edward and Eliz. Herndon	Dec. 28, 1831	199
Brown, William H. and Eliza Maxwell	Sept. 12, 1833	408
Burden, Nelson and Nancy Ginn	Dec. 19, 1833	408
Burton, Thomas and Ann Brown	July 18, 1833	326
Burnet, Pleasant and Martha Henry	Oct. 13, 1831	200
Butler, George S. and Katherine Booth	Feb. 17, 1830	498
Butler, Wiley W. and Malinda Jones	Dec. 19, 1834	499
Bryson, James and Eliza Banks	June 28, 1833	326

Groom, Bride and Date		Page
Carlton, Henry A. and Elizabeth Rice	Oct. 25, 1832	201
Carter, Lesley G. and Mary Gaulden	Dec. 25, 1831	199
Cheek, William F. and Elizabeth Cape	Sept. 25, 1831	199
Christian, Lindsey and Prudence S. Webb	Nov. 8, 1832	201
Christian, Elijah L. and Mary J. Fitts	Apr. 9, 1832	498
Christian, John M. and Amelia A. Key	May 30, 1833	499
Christian, Drury and Sarah Stinchcomb	Mar. 5, 1834	499
Clark, James and Flora McCurry	Dec. 6, 1832	201
Clark, Bolen B. and Sophia Snellings	Feb. 21, 1833	499
Cleveland, John W. and Matilda Alexander	Dec. 28, 1831	199
Cleveland, Peter and Merial K. Rowzee	Mar. 28, 1833	326
Cleveland, Daniel and Harriet McGarity	Oct. 9, 1833	499
Coker, John and Martha Hathcock	Apr. 28, 1833	499
Cosby, Henry H. and Lucinda Clark	June 10, 1834	500
Cox, Arus and Leah Boatright	June 24, 1833	326
Crawford, William H. and Sarah Ann Dooly	Aug. 20, 1832	200
Crawford, Richard C. and Elizabeth A. White	Sept. 27, 1832	201
Crawford, Leroy and Elizabeth A. Dooly	Dec. 13, 1832	201
Cristler, Abel and Ann Maxwell	Mar. 4, 1834	500
Daniel, John and Averilla Fanning	Apr. 14, 1833	327
Dennard, Mitchell and Nancy Hanson	May 19, 1833	327
Durrett, Richard J. D. and Martha E. Rucker	Jan. 8, 1833	327
Edwards, John and Margaret S. Clark	Aug. 22, 1833	327
Evans, Jachariah and Mrs. Lucy Manning	Oct. 30, 1833	408
Farmer, Josiah and Elizabeth White	Apr. 26, 1833	327
Faulkner, William and Mrs. Sarah Nanon	Dec. 2, 1833	498
Flemming, Moses C. and Permelia Flanningham	Nov. 15, 1831	199
Flemming, Moses T. and Theodicia Jones	June 20, 1833	327
Flemming, David C. and Averilla Cunningham	Aug. 27, 1833	327
Fortson, Richard and Nancy Ham	Nov. 8, 1832	199
Fowler, Robert and Sarah McGarity	Dec. 31, 1833	408
Gaines, Strawter and Merial Ann Ward	Nov. 27, 1834	499
Gaulding, Richard and Mary Mattox	Dec. 16, 1834	499
Glasco, William and Elizabeth Turner	Sept. 2, 1834	499
Gray, Absolom and Rhoda Rousey	Oct. 21, 1834	499
Griswell, John and Jenny King	Oct. 12, 1831	199
Hall, Henry and Mrs. Elizabeth Arnold	Oct. 2, 1831	199
Hall, Fenton and Lucinda D. Shepard	Sept. 26, 1833	408
Ham, Willis R. and Elizabeth Dickey	Feb. 25, 1834	499
Hammond, Ferney and Teresa Deadwyler	Oct. 6, 1831	199
Hammond, Amos W. and Eliza C. Hudson	Jan. 22, 1833	327
Hansard, James A. and Phebe Hardy	Aug. 23, 1833	327
Harper, John Sr., and Polly Mitchell	Sept. 7, 1831	199
Harper, Elijah and Martha Eavenson	Oct. 29, 1833	199
Harris, James S. and Sarah Means	Dec. 3, 1833	408
Harcrow, David and Joice Powell	July 20, 1834	499
Haynes, Charles W. and Flora McCurry	Dec. 15, 1833	408
Hendrick, Barnett and Mary Nelmes	Jan. 22, 1832	300
Herndon, Benjamin and Mahulda Almond	Nov. 27, 1834	499
Higginbotham, John S. and Sally Lawrimore	Mar. 30, 1834	500
Hill, Josiah W. and Sarah McGehee	Sept. 22, 1831	199
Hudson, John R. and Martha E. Banks	Jan. 17, 1833	327
Hunt, Hullum and Harriet C. Ward	Mar. 8, 1832	201
Hunt, Willis and Priscilla T. Teasley	Nov. 7, 1833	408
Jenkins, James and Furlishe Warren	Jan. 26, 1832	200
Johnson, James and Milly Butler	Dec. 22, 1831	199
Johnson, William A. and Jane Tate	Dec. 29, 1831	200
Johnson, Nathan and Sarah Gaines	Feb. 9, 1832	200
Jones, William and Lucy Ann Brown	Sept. 27, 1831	199

Groom, Bride and Date		Page
Jones, Arthur Jr., and Mary Dye	Nov. 6, 1833	498
Jones, Willis S. and Sarah T. Dye	Oct. 30, 1834	499
Keys, John D. and Martha R. Teasley	Aug. 28, 1832	201
King, Francis W. and Sarah T. Smith	Jan. 8, 1832	200
Kilgore, William M. and Ann Alexander	July 7, 1833	327
Kirbee, Lewis and Frances E. King	Nov. 20, 1832	201
Lovingood, John and Priscilla Watson	Feb. 21, 1833	327
McCurry, Lauchlin and Eliza Brown	Feb. 14, 1832	200
McCurry, Daniel E. and Elizabeth Ashworth	June 26, 1832	200
McDonald, Donald and Mary M. Johnson	Dec. 8, 1831	200
McGehee, Jesse and Susannah King	May 3, 1832	200
Mann, Asa and Milly T. Oliver	Sept. 6, 1832	201
Mann, Robert B. and Lucy Higginbotham	July 27, 1833	408
Mantooth, Robert and Elizabeth Butler	Oct. 22, 1833	408
Matthews, William and Jane Cook	Dec. 23, 1834	499
Mattox, John W. and Mrs. Caroline Whitlow	Dec. 31, 1833	408
Mattox, Henry P. and Sophia Nunnelee	Oct. 1, 1833	499
Maxwell, Martin and Julia Ann Upshaw	Jan. 29, 1835	500
Marbury, Thomas W. and Mary Ann Booth	June 20, 1832	200
Medford, Dempsey and Rebecca Dodds	Sept. 18, 1833	408
Moore, Jere E. and Juley Ann Colson	Feb. 14, 1832	200
Moore, William J. and Elizabeth Booth	Sept. 20, 1832	201
Moseley, Joseph and Sarah Cook	Dec. 24, 1833	499
Moore, John S. and Sophia Colson	Dec. 18, 1832	201
Moss, Christopher C. and Ann Nelms	July 22, 1834	500
Myers, William and Sarah Highsmith	Feb. 21, 1833	327
Nash, Hudson J. and Mrs. Maria Nunnelee	Dec. 21, 1831	498
Nelms, William T. and Elizabeth Banks	Aug. 2, 1832	200
Nelms, William B. and Eliz. Patterson	Dec. 20, 1832	327
Nelms, William R. and Ann J. Lewis	June 9, 1833	327
Oliver, Winston and Elizabeth Brawner	Oct. 18, 1832	201
Oliver, James O. and Charity A. Chambers	Dec. 24, 1833	408
Oliver, Florence M. and Sarah A. H. Glenn	Mar. 13, 1834	500
Osley, David and Elizabeth Nix	Oct. 2, 1831	99
Parham, George W. and Alcey W. Webb	Sept. 22, 1834	500
Penn, James B. and Nancy Burton	Nov. 14, 1831	199
Penn, Benjamin J. and Harriett Penn	Dec. 3, 1834	500
Peeler, Allen and Elizabeth Ann Coker	Mar. 28, 1833	499
Perryman, Albert G. and Sarah Allgood	Dec. 24, 1833	409
Prather, Josiah and Jane Ann Wall	Jan. 29, 1832	200
Prewit, Willis and Hester Lewis	Oct. 25, 1832	201
Ragain, John and Nancy M. Brawner	Nov. 7, 1833	408
Raines, Josiah and Sarah Denna	Apr. 5, 1832	493
Reynolds, James H. and Penina J. Wheeler	Nov. 16, 1832	201
Richardson, James and Mary E. Clark	Feb. 7, 1832	327
Richardson, Willis and Drucilla E. Gaines	Feb. 28, 1833	327
Ridgway, John T. and Sarah L. Colvard	Nov. 27, 1834	500
Roberts, John and Sarah Faulk	Jan. 19, 1832	200
Salmons, Wiley and Elizabeth Chrisley	Oct. 27, 1831	200
Saxon, Drury T. and Elizabeth Bennett	Dec. 25, 1831	200
Scott, Samuel N. and Mary M. Dillard	Dec. 27, 1832	409
Semore, John W. and Nancy Christian	Jan. 20, 1835	500
Shackleford, Starling M. and Frances Higginbotham	July 16, 1833	327
Shackleford, Asa C. and Mary Christian	Jan. 21, 1834	409
Sheerer, Alex and Claricy Marbury	May 31, 1832	201
Shiflett, John and Polly Anderson	Mar. 4, 1832	200
Smith, William W. and Sarah J. Penn	May 20, 1831	200
Smith, Thomas A. and Winney Penn	Sept. 15, 1833	409
Smith, Samuel W. and Catharine Swindle	Dec. 26, 1833	409

Groom, Bride and Date		Page
Stedey, James P. and Amanda W. Kelly	Aug. 18, 1831	199
Stovall, Thomas and Lucinda W. Key	Dec. 16, 1833	499
Stribling, Simpson and Sarah Bates	Mar. 6, 1834	500
Tabor, Briton C. and Lidey Horton	Apr. 9, 1832	200
Tailor, William T. and Martha Means	Dec. 14, 1831	200
Teasley, Isham and Mary Maxwell	Dec. 6, 1833	327
Terrell, William B. and Eliza White	Mar. 20, 1834	500
Thornton, Reuben and Emilia Cleveland	July 28, 1831	199
Thornton, Memory and Polly Higginbotham	Feb. 9, 1832	200
Thornton, Eppy and Mary C. Higginbotham	Dec. 6, 1833	327
Thornton, Dozier Jr., and Jane M. Fortson	Sept. 25, 1834	499
Tibbis, Joseph C. and Matilda Fowler	May 4, 1834	499
Vassar, William C. and Mary W. Edwards	Dec. 30, 1832	498
Walker, Benjamin and Lucy Kerlin	Dec. 13, 1831	199
Walsh, Robert and Nancy E. Davis	Apr. 10, 1833	498
Ward, Nisbit L. and Tabitha Haley	Dec. 19, 1833	409
Ward, William W. and Nancy T. Greenway	Jan. 9, 1834	409
Wanslow, Wiley T. and Martha L. Cleveland	Dec. 20, 1831	201
Wanslow, Fleming and Becky Patterson	Dec. 13, 1832	201
Webb, John B. and Nancy Christian	July 30, 1833	409
White, David O. and Catherine E. Rucker	May 6, 1834	500
White, William Jr., and Rachel Eavenson	Sept. 11, 1834	500
White, Wm. Bowling and Mildred Rucker	Jan. 8, 1833	327
Wiley, Hugh A. and Moddy W. Sullivan	Feb. 22, 1833	327
Williamson, Stephen and Polly Reynolds	Mar. 4, 1831	199
Williamson, Walker and Betsy Farmer	May 2, 1833	327
Wilson, Stephen and Feanetty Threlkeld	Feb. 28, 1832	200

MARRIAGES, 1836-1850

Groom, Bride and Date		Page
Adams, Moses and Louisa Ann Willis	July 15, 1841	114
Adams, Thomas B. and Lucy E. Warren	Sept. 30, 1841	119
Adams, Thomas J. and Elizabeth Alexander	Dec. 21, 1841	121
Adams, Elbert B. and Emira E. James	Sept. 14, 1843	160
Adams, Lawrence M. and Lucy H. Teasley	Sept. 28, 1843	161
Adams, Winston and Nancy Haley	May 11, 1844	163
Adams, William Joseph and Mary Rodgers	Dec. 10, 1844	169
Adams, Richard C. Jr., and Mary J. Dickerson	Apr. ...., 1846	194
Adams, Moses F. Jr., and Lucy E. Teasley	Dec. 2, 1847	232
Adams, William R. and Elizabeth A. Teasley	Nov. 16, 1848	232
Adams, John D. and Flora Reynolds	Aug. 20, 1850	283
Adams, James B. and Sarena I. Hansard	June 1, 1851	313
Adams, James W. and Frances A. Crawford	Oct. 4, 1849	331
Alexander, George and Catherine Hall	Jan. 22, 1835	1
Alexander, Elijah and Savannah Wilhite	Oct. 27, 1836	20
Alexander, Thomas R. and Lucinda M. Clark	Dec. 20, 1838	59
Alexander, William H. and Sarah A. Terrell	Nov. 24, 1842	132
Alexander, Thomas J. and Sarah Jones	Dec. 13, 1842	133
Alexander, Gaines T. and Margaret Rucker	Aug. 24, 1843	140
Alexander, William and Sophia Cason	Dec. 26, 1843	161
Alexander, Wiley T. and Willey E. Butler	Feb. 2, 1846	185
Alexander, William B. and Willy M. Beck	Mar. 15, 1846	195
Algood, James F. and Susan W. Roberts	Jan. 3, 1839	52
Algood, Levi and Mary Ann Downer	Aug. 18, 1842	123
Algood, Levi S. and Louisa Downer	Aug. 19, 1847	218
Algood, Peter and Nancy Jones	Aug. 17, 1848	234
Algood, James W. and Mary Pickerel	Jan. 20, 1850	266
Allen, Samuel and Martha Clark	Nov. 1, 1835	2

Groom, Bride and Date		Page
Allen, James and Mary A. Haynes	Jan. 7, 1837	26
Allen, William D. and Elizabeth Chapman	May 29, 1841	110
Allen, William D. and Mary Shiflett	Feb. 7, 1850	264
Allen, Gerrard Jr., and Isabella Blackwell	Oct. 31, 1850	269
Almond, Jones R. and Synthia Jones	Sept. 24, 1835	1
Anderson, John H. and Martha B. Tibbetts	May 5, 1842	125
Anderson, Alfred and Sarah Oglesby	Nov. 17, 1842	131
Andrew, Gideon B. and Ann W. Nix	May 11, 1836	14
Andrew, William and Eliza Bond	Nov. 6, 1838	47
Andrew, Charles H. and Lucy A. Andrew	May 26, 1843	142
Andrew, Charles and Mary Ann Rice	Nov. 19, 1843	148
Andrew, John B. and Harriet Burton	Feb. 24, 1850	269
Argrove, Leven and Anna Larrimore	Oct. 18, 1838	52
Arnold, Joseph Y. and Sarah K. Thornton	Oct. 5, 1841	116
Arnold, Charles Wesley and Mary E. Banks	Aug. 27, 1843	145
Ashworth, Elijah and Melinda Steedman	Aug. 6, 1835	1
Ashworth, Benjamin and Nancy Steedman	Sept. 21, 1841	120
Ashworth, John and Mary Greenway	Dec. 12, 1844	177
Attaway, William F. and Priscilla Brown	Jan. 15, 1846	187
Bailey, Dilliard J. and Nancy Crawford	Jan. 15, 1839	61
Banks, James J. Jr., and Lucy Maxwell	Feb. 15, 1838	42
Banks, William C. and Rebecca E. Hunt	Sept. 8, 1842	129
Baird, Robert E. and Mary Scales	Jan. 23, 1840	84
Barron, William and Elizabeth Hilly	Jan. 16, 1841	103
Barron, Barnabas and Lucy Crawford	Dec. 29, 1847	220
Barton, Joseph and Mildred Adams	May 14, 1850	267
Barron, Rufus and Lettie Hilly	June 13, 1841	114
Bell, Enoch and Mary B. Snellings	Dec. 22, 1836	19
Bell, James W. and Martha White	Aug. 25, 1840	107
Bell, William and Elizabeth Pendleton	Oct. 31, 1841	116
Bell, Thomas and Louisa A. Truman	Aug. 10, 1843	145
Beggs, Andrew J. and Lucy Shiflett	Nov. 14, 1850	286
Beasley, William W. Y. and Mary E. Duncan	Nov. 28, 1850	275
Bennett, Richard H. and Martha Strickland	Dec. 27, 1838	46
Berrett, William M. and Ann E. Hilly	May 4, 1837	27
Berryman, Charles T. and Elizabeth Ray	Oct. 14, 1840	99
Berryman, Robert N. and Sarah C. Bowers	Aug. 9, 1849	253
Black, Thomas and Drucilla Bowie	Aug. 20, 1851	286
Blair, Thomas F. and Mary Andrew	Sept. 3, 1830	282
Black, James J. and Mildred E. Clark	Nov. 7, 1844	166
Bobo, Thomas M. and Louisa H. C. Crump	Apr. 4, 1843	158
Bond, Willis and Sarah Ann Loftis	Dec. 20, 1842	133
Bond, Richard and Milly Gaines	Jan. 4, 1844	152
Bond, Francis K. and Susan H. Black	Dec. 4, 1845	199
Bond, Thomas J. and Martha Higginbotham	Dec. 1, 1846	212
Bond, Martin and Elizabeth Christian	Aug. 6, 1835	3
Bond, Moses W. and Rossie Means	Nov. 15, 1835	3
Bond, Eppy and Sarah Butler	Aug. 10, 1837	26
Bond, William and Arminda Christian	Mar. 28, 1839	67
Bone, Asa S. and Caroline Haley	Dec. 31, 1845	187
Bobo, Chaney and Elizabeth Powell	Oct. 17, 1847	218
Booth, Andrew J. and Martha Ann Booth	Jan. 22, 1848	226
Booth, Nathaniel and Martha Colvard	Jan. 9, 1838	46
Booth, Andrew W. and Mrs. Eliza Taylor	Jan. 11, 1844	153
Booth, John R. and Elizabeth K. Tucker	Apr. 1, 1847	210
Booth, Washington A. and Elizabeth J. Davis	Jan. 2, 1849	241
Bowman, Briggs and Jane S. Prather	Mar. 25, 1841	108
Bowman, Thomas J. and Sarah Ann Blackwell	Apr. 8, 1841	109
Bowers, William and Lettie E. Haynes	Dec. 21, 1837	40

Groom, Bride and Date		Page
Bowers, Asa and Sarah E. Brown	Mar. 30, 1843	156
Bradford, James M. and Rebecca Hudson	Dec. 27, 1849	264
Bradley, Jeptha W. and Mary E. Saddler	Jan. 1, 1846	195
Bradshaw, Henry C. and Sarah E. Campbell	Mar. 29, 1849	248
Brawner, Joseph and Elizabeth Snellings	Dec. 24, 1835	4
Brawner, Joseph Jr., and Mrs. Elizabeth B. Hardman	Feb. 23, 1836	11
Brawner, Jesse M. and Elizabeth Gaulding	Aug. 6, 1835	32
Brawner, John F. and Lucy Ann Brawner	Oct. 31, 1837	35
Brawner, Jeptha F. and Martha Jones	Dec. 15, 1836	19
Brawner, John W. and Lucy B. Gaulding	Nov. 29, 1835	27
Brewer, Benjamin J. and Mary Cox	June 21, 1840	92
Broadwell, John M. and Nancy Turner	Dec. 19, 1843	150
Brown, Benjamin Jr., and Millie L. Crawford	Dec. 24, 1835	3
Brown, Rolan and Mary J. Hughes	Nov. 17, 1835	3
Brown, Edmond G. and Lettie Duncan	Mar. 24, 1836	13
Brown, Robert W. and Elizabeth A. Maxwell	Oct. 6, 1836	19
Brown, George W. and Elmira Herndon	Sept. 28, 1837	30
Brown, Roland J. and Elizabeth A. Teasley	Aug. 8, 1839	73
Brown, Andrew J. and Sarah Ann Rucker	Sept. 12, 1839	75
Brown, James E. and Nancy McCurry	Dec. 12, 1839	83
Brown, John W. and Martha Ann Gaines	Aug. 6, 1840	96
Brown, Berry and Martha M. Carlton	Sept. 19, 1841	119
Brown, Morgan M. and Julia F. O. Crump	Oct. 3, 1842	130
Brown, Dillard H. and Lettie E. Bowers	Jan. 8, 1843	138
Brown, John M. and Eliza S. Adams	Oct. 3, 1843	163
Brown, David S. and Frances A. Tucker	Mar. 6, 1845	165
Brown, Obed M. and Eletha Skelton	Nov. 3, 1844	168
Brown, Elbert J. and Sarah McCurry	Mar. 27, 1845	176
Brown, Henry T. and Frances M. Means	Nov. 12, 1846	205
Brown, John M. and Mary E. Means	Dec. 15, 1846	207
Brown, John A. and Margaret J. Herndon	Feb. 23, 1849	249
Brown, Francis M. and Drucilla Roberts	Dec. 20, 1849	254
Brown, William A. D. and Sophia C. Crump	Dec. 25, 1849	260
Brown, Asa C. and Priscilla E. Thornton	Jan. 23, 1851	277
Brown, Jesse L. and Mary E. Craft	Nov. 13, 1850	279
Burden, James and Jane Seals	Apr. 28, 1836	3
Burden, Woodson and Elizabeth Jordan	Jan. 9, 1842	121
Burden, Gaines W. and Mary Crump	Jan. 13, 1842	126
Burden, John N. and Delilah Ginn	Sept. 8, 1842	129
Burden, William and Sarah Ann Winn	Sept. 12, 1844	168
Burden, Job W. and Frances E. Cobb	Dec. 11, 1845	193
Bullard, William G. and Milly Wyche	Oct. 19, 1837	31
Burnett, John and Elizabeth McGarity	Feb. 8, 1838	46
Burton, Peter W. and Pulutha J. Gaulding	Dec. 15, 1840	102
Burton, John H. and Mary E. Nash	Nov. 12, 1839	77
Burton, John and Mrs. Frances Mantz	Dec. 25, 1842	135
Burton, Augustus T. and Nancy Colson	Apr. 29, 1845	175
Burton, Thomas and Susan McCoy	Apr. 25, 1850	269
Butler, James F. and Nancy Dye	Aug. 11, 1841	113
Butler, Joel and Eliza F. Ward	Sept. 9, 1841	118
Butler, David and Narcissa Tibbetts	Dec. 18, 1842	135
Butler, Isaac N. and Mary A. Fowler	Aug. 17, 1848	236
Butler, Isaac N. and Martha Andrew	July 4, 1850	271
Butler, Lentine and Margaret Brownlee	Dec. 20, 1848	237
Cade, Guilford and Sarah A. H. Stark	Mar. 22, 1838	44
Cade, James M. and Susan A. Nunnelee	Nov. 15, 1838	48
Caldwell, Henry and Permelia Jones	Oct. 25, 1842	141
Campbell, James C. and Sarah Higginbotham	Feb. 23, 1843	139
Campbell, William D. and Jane Dilliard	Oct. ___, 1839	151

Groom, Bride and Date		Page
Campbell, Francis A. and Rachel J. Kerlin	Sept. 19, 1844	166
Campbell, James C. and Jereshia Higginbotham	Dec. 1, 1846	213
Campbell, William G. and Elizabeth Kerlin	Apr. 27, 1848	230
Cantrell, Moses L. and Nancy Williford	Feb. 28, 1836	10
Carlton, Henry and Mary T. Burch	May 16, 138	74
Carlton, William R. and Sophia Brown	Sept. 12, 1839	74
Carlton, John M. and Elizabeth Winn	July 4, 1840	93
Carlton, Stephen S. and Sarah McGarity	Nov. 10, 1842	134
Carlton, Will S. and Sarah Duncan	Aug. 8, 1843	147
Carter, Charles N. B. and Eugenia Beck	May 5, 1838	45
Carter, Thomas S. and Matilda Harmon	Feb. 21, 1839	61
Carter, Lemarquis and Frances McCurry	Sept. 2, 1841	136
Carter, Macajah and Mrs. Mourning Earps	Jan. 22, 1850	272
Cash, Reuben and Pheletia W. Taylor	Feb. 11, 1836	20
Cash, James G. and Martha Wanslow	Jan. 21, 1847	203
Cason, Thomas J. and Lucy Teasley	Dec. 3, 1846	215
Cason, James M. and Malinda Maxwell	Mar. 2, 1848	227
Calhoun, Francis A. and Louisa V. Jones	July 28, 1842	124
Carithers, Hugh M. and Sarah P. Burton	Dec. 21, 1848	247
Charping, Richard L. and Martha A. Kilgore	July 11, 1847	210
Childers, Eldridge and Martha N. Gray	Feb. 11, 1848	228
Chislom, Patrick and Martha A. Smith	Dec. 5, 1837	35
Chrisler, Joseph and Penelope Sayre	Nov. 7, 1839	95
Chapman, Daniel and Elizabeth Shiflett	Oct. 30, 1844	83
Chapman, Elijah and Matilda C. Crawford	Oct. 10, 1845	87
Christian, Franklin and Frances Moon	Feb. 25, 1836	11
Christian, Ira and Elizabeth Mabry	Aug. 3, 1837	27
Christian, William I. and Elizabeth Scales	Apr. 20, 1837	35
Christian, Jesse G. and Ann Maxwell	Mar. 25, 1841	109
Christian, George W. and Elizabeth Payton	Jan. 5, 1842	127
Charping, John M. and Sarah Griffin	Sept. 3, 1846	202
Cheek, David W. and Flora Clark	Oct. 10, 1847	224
Clark, Larkin and Matilda McMullan	Oct. 1, 1844	171
Clark, Larkin Jr., and Sarah Dooly	Jan. 10, 1837	20
Clark, James A. and Frances M. Williams	Sept. 20, 1838	48
Clark, Thomas E. and Elizabeth Downer	Aug. 28, 1839	74
Clark, John M. and Judith R. Ginn	Feb. 14, 1843	144
Cleveland, Weston and Emily Johnston	Oct. 20, 1848	230
Cleveland, Irby B. and Piety Adams	July 9, 1840	96
Cleveland, Peter and Mary Frances White	May 10, 1838	88
Coker, Washington and Canzady Patrick	Sept. 28, 1843	156
Cole, Henry W. and Frances E. Prather	May 21, 1846	193
Colson, William W. and Elizabeth Adams	Aug. 25, 1835	4
Colvard, John W. and Lucy Ann Almond	Mar. 15, 1838	43
Colvard, Joseph A. and Frances M. Brown	Apr. 6, 1848	230
Comer, Milton C. and Ann Allen	Apr. 20, 1839	229
Conwell, James A. and Sarah D. Mann	Dec. 19, 1843	150
Colvard, Joseph A. and Lucy Ann Booth	Sept. 24, 1840	98
Corry, John S. and Ann Daniel Carter	Dec. 26, 1839	81
Cowen, Archie W. and Mary Sayer	Aug. 19, 1849	258
Cox, Thomas M. and Nancy Elliott	Aug. 11, 1850	273
Cook, William J. and Martha A. F. Campbell	Aug. 17, 1848	237
Craft, John M. and Nancy Gaines	Jan. 9, 1844	163
Craft, Thomas M. and Amanda A. Taylor	Sept. 12, 1847	220
Craft, John W. and Martha Ann Craft	Nov. 29, 1847	256
Crawford, Elisha and Eliza Christian	Dec. 28, 1837	40
Crawford, William B. and Nancy M. Ward	Sept. 26, 1844	182
Crawford, Benjamin S. and Katherine Turner	Feb. 23, 1847	221
Crider, Richard L. D. and Drucilla A. Hanley	Sept. 30, 1847	228

Groom, Bride and Date		Page
Crittenden, John S. and Evalina Driver	Dec. 27, 1835	4
Crittenden, Henry W. and Eliza C. Tyler	Jan. 17, 1839	50
Crittenden, William M. and Julia Ann Chapman	Feb. 22, 1842	137
Crittenden, Robert M. and Jane E. Burton	Nov. 2, 1843	164
Crocker, Lemuel and Jane White	Feb. 28, 1839	67
Crittenden, Thomas J. and Sarah Ann Rice	Dec. 5, 1850	274
Crum, John and Mrs. Jane McAfee	July 14, 1846	193
Crump, Robert and Nancy Tyner	Jan. 16, 1846	192
Cunningham, Joseph and Keziah Jones	Nov. 11, 1844	167
Cunningham, James S. and Matilda C. Hunt	Dec. 22, 1846	202
Daniel, Allen and Mary Cash	Nov. 23, 1838	53
Daniel, John Jr., and Eliza Alexander	Mar. 15, 1840	90
David, William W. and Milly Vaughan	Sept. 18, 1835	5
David, Henry A. and Elizabeth Oglesby	Dec. 27, 1838	62
Davis, John W. and Sarah Hunt	Apr. 30, 1840	94
Davis, William and Elizabeth Ham	Feb. 20, 1842	127
Davis, William T. and Susan A. Hulme	Dec. 28, 1843	153
Davis, Thomas S. and Emily E. Lovingood	June 12, 1845	177
Davis, William C. and Milly A. Rice	Sept. 18, 1845	184
Davis, Absolom S. and Frances Ozley	Sept. 20, 1847	218
Deadwyler, Joseph P. and Alice A. M. Webb	Sept. 19, 1841	118
Deadwyler, John T. and Permelia Ann Hall	Feb. 15, 1844	157
Deadwyler, Valentine H. and Harriett A. Wilhight	Apr. 16, 1846	194
Dennard, Jeptha and Ann Dye	Nov. 4, 1849	252
Denny, William and Emely Stinchcomb	June 13, 1846	194
Denny, John A. and Temperance Russell	Oct. 7, 1845	198
Dickerson, John T. and Phobe Nelms	May 23, 1837	33
Dickerson, Gaines T. and Clancy Dickerson	Aug. 18, 1840	105
Dickerson, Burrell and Lucy Dickerson	May 1, 1849	259
Dillashaw, Andrew and Viney Hendricks	Dec. 21, 1848	242
Dooley, Barney J. and Nancy McCurry	Oct. 4, 1836	21
Dooley, Barnabas J. and Priscilla Banks	Nov. 4, 1838	55
Dooley, Hamilton and Mary Banks	Jan. 16, 1842	117
Doneley, Frances E. and Mrs. Emily M. Burbank	Apr. 26, 1849	249
Dockins, Lewis and Elizabeth McAllister	Mar. 4, 1840	89
Downer, Joseph and Mary Threlkeld	Mar. 22, 1838	43
Downer, Thomas and Nancy Wilkins	Oct. 28, 1841	126
Downer, John H. and Antoinette Smith	Apr. 18, 1850	270
Duncan, John Jr., and Nancy Brown	Jan. 17, 1837	21
Duncan, Pearson and Sarah Vaughan	Oct. 29, 1837	36
Duncan, Moses and Eliazbeth Dooley	Oct. 31, 1841	117
Duncan, Asa and Flora Ann Johnson	Feb. 1, 1844	152
Duncan, Oliver M. and Sarah Brown	Feb. 8, 1844	156
Duncan, William R. and Sarah Ann Ford	Dec. 23, 1848	238
Dudley, Pickney and Martha Thompson	Sept. 30, 1845	188
Dye, Thompson B. and Martha Brewer	Dec. 12, 1838	65
Dye, Joseph and Nancy A. Nash	May 10, 1840	92
Dye, Thomas and Matilda Pressley	Sept. 1, 1841	112
Dye, Thomas W. and Emily Hubbard	Dec. 7, 1842	132
Dye, Martin H. and Elizabeth J. McKinley	Feb. 18, 1845	188
Dye, John and Sarah Ozley	Dec. 11, 1845	188
Dye, George J. and Elizabeth F. Butler	May 11, 1848	243
Dyer, John and Julia Ann Jones	Feb. 11, 1847	205
Dyer, Elias S. and Sarah Ann Powell	July 5, 1849	257
Dyer, William and Amea Powell	Aug. 19, 1849	259
Eavenson, George and Sarah S. Thornton	Aug. 1, 1839	71
Eberhardt, Jacob and Lettie Webb	Dec. 10, 1843	145
Eberhardt, James G. and Priscilla J. Brawner	Dec. 21, 1848	244
Edwards, Joseph T. and Caroline T. Clark	Dec. 10, 1835	5

Groom, Bride and Date		Page
Edwards, Felix G. and Eliza A. Cade	Dec. 28, 1835	5
Edwards, John F. and Sarah E. A. Rich	Oct. 10, 1838	56
Edwards, Jackson J. and Elizabeth Gaulding	Aug. 28, 1840	98
Edwards, William H. and Hannah N. Salmons	Sept. 28, 1840	146
Edwards, Robert M. and Eliza J. Brown	Nov. 17, 1840	110
Edwards, Jonathan and Jane Shaw	Dec. 27, 1847	220
Ellington, Rice and Martha Cook	Aug. 27, 1839	73
Elliot, Andel M. and Damarius Thornton	Dec. 23, 1849	266
Fain, Charles and Mary Johnson	Dec. 14, 1834	6
Farmer, Jesse and Elizabeth Ward	Jan. 1, 1837	21
Farmer, Caswell and Mary Fain	Dec. 23, 1845	197
Faulkner, Asa E. and Antionette Oglesby	Oct. 25, 1838	55
Fitts, Tandy and Seiser Ann Edwards	Aug. 22, 1838	46
Fleming, Mathew L. and Permelia Fleming	Oct. 19, 1837	30
Fleming, Moses T. and Mrs. Frances Thornton	Oct. 12, 1837	40
Fleming, Thomas M. and Ann Cunningham	Dec. 30, 1841	121
Fleming, David R. and Drucilla A. Teasley	Dec. 22, 1846	201
Ford, Elisha and Matilda Carter	Feb. 26, 1846	193
Fortson, Benjamin G. and Martha A. Mills	Oct. 8, 1839	78
Fortson, Benjamin and Martha Ham	Mar. 13, 1844	164
Fortson, Benjamin and Barbary H. Cook	Sept. 29, 1840	100
Fortson, Edwin K. and Mary L. Mills	Dec. 7, 1845	190
Fountain, Edwin K. and Lockey Davis	Mar. 4, 1841	110
Fowler, Martin G. and Permelia A. Pulliam	Aug. 8, 1848	236
Freeman, Samuel and Virginia White	Sept. 22, 1837	30
Gaines, Robert T. and Agga Crump	Jan. 6, 1842	126
Gaines, James B. and Elizabeth Barron	Aug. 13, 1844	174
Gaines, James B. and Frances Johnson	Dec. 28, 1845	188
Gaines, Henry W. and Mary Daniel	Feb. 7, 1850	260
Gaines, William M. and Sarah Craft	Feb. 1, 1851	280
Galloway, William and Jane Cleveland	Dec. 1, 1842	132
Galloway, Cornelius and Mahulda Jones	July 25, 1843	141
Galloway, Michael and Mary F. Cleveland	Oct. 5, 1846	208
Galloway, Levi C. and Louisa Powell	Sept. 16, 1847	221
Gardner, James T. and Sarah C. Gibbs	May 12, 1849	250
Gaulding, William and Margaret Ham	Feb. 19, 1839	62
Ginn, Middleton and Emily Brown	Aug. 24, 1837	30
Ginn, Andrew B. and Sarah Peeler	Mar. 24, 1845	178
Ginn, William E. and Rebecca Mewborn	Nov. 30, 1848	238
Ginn, Moses and Elizabeth Brown	Apr. 15, 1849	249
Glenn, William and Mary H. Smith	Oct. 6, 1847	224
Glover, John F. and Margaret Brown	Feb. 19, 1850	271
Goss, Benjamin and Flora Gordon	Jan. 28, 1840	87
Goss, William R. and Priscilla Eavenson	Aug. 6, 1841	112
Goss, Isham and Mary Gordon	Mar. 5, 1840	89
Goss, Horatio J. and Sarah F. Warren	Dec. 21, 1843	146
Gober, John and Milly Bramblett	Oct. 21, 1846	207
Goolsby, William J. A. and Elizabeth K. Adams	Dec. 13, 1849	259
Graham, William and Elizabeth Vaughan	Jan. 21, 1841	104
Gray, John F. and Mrs. Mildred Allen	Oct. 26, 1848	234
Greenway, John H. and Louisanna Ward	Dec. 8, 1836	22
Greenway, John H. and Nancy C. Mann	Feb. 9, 1840	89
Griffin, Andrew J. and Sarah Sharpton	Oct. 22, 1844	169
Gunter, John W. and Elizabeth Downer	Nov. 30, 1839	76
Gunter, James and Ruth Brownlee	Dec. 22, 1844	167
Gunter, Elijah B. and Mary Ann Davis	May 11, 1843	181
Gunter, James N. and Mary Wheelis	Sept. 23, 1848	230
Haley, William R. and Sarah Ann Gaines	Feb. 7, 1839	67
Hailey, Willis and Rachel Taylor	Nov. 23, 1846	201

Groom, Bride and Date		Page
Hailey, Reuben T. and Milly A. Greenway	Feb. 9, 1847	208
Hall, Robert and Olivia Lovingood	Jan. 29, 1839	66
Hall, Asa and Martha Ozley	Jan. 7, 1845	165
Hall, John and Mahulda Stinchcomb	Jan. 20, 1848	236
Hall, Asa and Martha Adams	June 26, 1849	251
Hall, James C. and Mary A. Loftis	June 25, 1850	281
Hall, Samuel and Caroline Roberts	June 11, 1844	160
Ham, Thomas C. and Sarah Sewell	Dec. 20, 1849	267
Hansard, Loranzey I. and Matilda Smith	Jan. 28, 1834	6
Hansard, William P. and Lucinda Hardy	Dec. 15, 1836	18
Hansard, Eliah and Milly Hansard	Mar. 5, 1840	95
Hansard, John and Jane Tyner	Aug. 18, 1840	97
Hancock, John and Susan Peeler	Aug. 6, 1843	147
Haslett, William and Elizabeth Willis	May 18, 1845	175
Harris, William T. and Rachel M. Tait	Dec. 26, 1848	241
Harris, Robert L. and Elizabeth Upshaw	Dec. 2, 1840	103
Haynes, James and Cassa Ann Threlkeld	Dec. 24, 1835	6
Haynes, Asa J. and Elizabeth Clark	Dec. 6, 1838	57
Haynes, Benjamin F. and Sarah Burns	Feb. 6, 1846	198
Harmon, James C. and Malinda Stone	Nov. 1, 1849	258
Harper, William H. and Mary McDonald	Aug. 31, 1837	29
Hathcock, William R. and Elizabeth Seamore	Apr. 21, 1839	68
Heard, Benjamin W. and Martha Oliver	Jan. 5, 1848	227
Henry, James M. and Lucinda Shoemaker	Jan. 3, 1836	7
Henry, William B. and Martha E. Wall	Dec. 19, 1850	274
Heaton, Emezirah and Martha Richardson	Nov. 15, 1848	243
Hendricks, Lindsey and Cornelia Hinton	Nov. 12, 1844	167
Herndon, William T. and Catherine E. Hulme	Nov. 30, 1848	242
Herndon, Thomas J. and Sarah Ann Terrell	Oct. 20, 1842	151
Hester, Robert and Cornelia Jones	Nov. 24, 1836	18
Herndon, Michael and Elizabeth Cook	Dec. 17, 1840	102
Henderson, William J. and Eliza A. Patterson	Nov. 7, 1839	79
Herring, James and Mrs. A. E. McCurry	Jan. 7, 1847	209
Hickman, Middleton and Mary E. Jones	Dec. 17, 1839	82
Hickman, James M. and Martha Banks	June 6, 1843	142
Highsmith, John C. and Sarah L. Brown	Aug. 26, 1847	219
Highsmith, Thomas E. and Mary Ann Thornton	Nov. 19, 1846	200
Higginbotham, Benjamin and Frances E. Cook	Dec. 13, 1849	255
Higginbotham, Eli and Martha Algood	Sept. 19, 1850	284
Higginbotham, William and Eliza Tyner	May 16, 1841	114
Higginbotham, Daniel and Minerva Christian	Oct. 5, 1842	130
Hill, Dennet R. and Louisa Nelms	Jan. 5, 1844	155
Hill, Richard and Elizabeth Saddler	Feb. 10, 1848	242
Hill, James and Lucy Ann Smith	June 1, 1837	36
Hill, William Y. and Frances G. Nelms	Feb. 4, 1841	104
Hill, Whitman and Sarah Ann Verdel	June 6, 1843	142
Higginbotham, Benjamin and Mary Ann Tyner	Sept. 13, 1843	149
Hilly, Thomas M. and Mary E. Smith	June 22, 1848	229
Hilly, William and Rebecca Brown	Aug. 9, 1838	57
Holmes, James and Matilda Jenkins	May 13, 1838	45
Holmes, Willis and Harriet White	Nov. 4, 1838	54
Holmes, Gideon and Eliza Stone	Aug. 17, 1841	117
Hoff, Henry P. and Elizabeth Fortson	Aug. 9, 1847	211
Horton, Jeremiah T. and Ann P. Christian	Apr. 13, 1837	34
Horton, Jesse and Keziah Christian	Aug. 8, 1844	171
Horton, Stephen and Elizabeth E. Burns	Jan. 3, 1847	213
Howard, Jared and Eliza Cooper	Jan. 9, 1842	137
Hudson, David and Mary M. Willis	July 1, 1847	211
Hopper, Jonathan and Delilah Dye	Feb. 28, 1839	64

Groom, Bride and Date		Page
Hunt, James L. and Milly Richardson	Mar. 6, 1846	196
Hunt, William and Dosha Shiflett	Oct. 3, 1839	106
Hunt, Hullum and Harriet Farmer	Mar. 10, 1842	128
Hulme, Thomas and Elizabeth Loftis	May 16, 1844	167
Hulme, Henry B. and Sarah F. Hall	Dec. 29, 1850	282
Hulme, George W. and Mary A. Mann	Apr. 7, 1836	15
Huff, Henry P. and Elmira Adams	Jan. 26, 1843	138
James, William E. and Martha Gaines	Sept. 18, 1844	168
James, Thomas E. and Katherine M. Adams	Nov. 13, 1844	181
James, Isaac R. and Lucy E. Adams	Dec. 12, 1850	276
Jenkins, Joseph and Sarah Wanslow	Nov. 26, 1838	49
Johnson, Angus and Susan Winn	Jan. 8, 1836	10
Johnson, William and Frances Moore	Aug. 2, 1837	39
Johnson, James and Mary Moore	Dec. 19, 1839	80
Johnson, John H. and Mary Ann Ginn	Nov. 24, 1842	134
Johnson, Malcolm A. and Phronacy H. Teasley	Apr. 10, 1845	177
Johnson, Neal and Maria Skelton	Jan. 11, 1846	192
Johnston, Nathan and Mrs. Susan Brewer	Sept. 22, 1839	93
Johnston, Elijah W. and Sarah Hearn	Apr. 17, 1852	316
Jones, Thomas and Sarah Morgan	Dec. 7, 1848	239
Jones, Drury and Sarah A. P. Kelly	Oct. 13, 1836	33
Jones, Solomon S. and Mary M. Sadler	Sept. 21, 1837	44
Jones, Thomas and Harriet Jones	Sept. 6, 1838	55
Jones, William S. and Lucy Ann Davis	Feb. 26, 1839	66
Jones, Wiley and Elizabeth Alexander	Feb. 27, 1842	126
Jones, James W. and Mildred White	Oct. 25, 1842	134
Jones, John H. and Samantha L. Hammond	Dec. 19, 1843	155
Jones, John and Susan Dye	Apr. 18, 1844	164
Jones, Arthur and Martha Dye	Mar. 25, 1845	178
Jones, Franklin and Mary Ann Bradshaw	Feb. 9, 1846	185
Jones, Wiley and Milly B. Alexander	Nov. 16, 1847	223
Jones, James S. and Susan M. Barr	July 6, 1848	231
Jones, Edwin and Cornelia Blackwell	Nov. 2, 1848	232
Jones, Thomas and Sarah E. A. Morgan	Dec. 7, 1848	239
Jones, Edmond and Eliza Foster	July 1, 1850	270
Jones, Robert F. and Sarah Sayres	Mar. 30, 1851	294
Jordan, James N. and Mary Lunsford	Mar. 23, 1841	107
Jordan, William and Milly Hilly	May 16, 1847	216
Kennebrew, Jasper and Lucy Ann Mills	Sept. 15, 1836	15
Kirby, William and Rebecca Pulliam	June 29, 1836	16
Kirkpatrick, William and Clerisee Threlkeld	Nov. 10, 1836	22
Kelly, James and Susannah Jones	Dec. 23, 1836	22
Kirkpatrick, William and Candada Struten	Feb. 23, 1838	44
Kirkpatrick, John and Liddy Hall	Dec. 16, 1837	38
Kirbee, James M. and Lucy King	May 15, 1838	47
Key, Joel M. and Nancy Terrell	Aug. 8, 1839	72
King, Zuriah and Sarah Terry	Sept. 25, 1842	129
King, James H. and Rachel Ares	Oct. 1, 1843	161
King, Robert A. and Hester Ann Scales	Sept. 30, 1847	215
King, William L. and Nancy Adams	Dec. 29, 1849	267
Kelly, James and Elizabeth Bradford	Oct. 29, 1846	205
Kendley, Jackson and Mary A. McDonald	Jan. 9, 1848	227
Kerbee, Mannon S. and Harrada M. Gully	Oct. 22, 1848	233
Kelly, John and Nancy Terry	June ___, 1849	257
Landham, William and Permelia Pryor	Feb. 24, 1846	203
Lard, Albert and Nancy Smith	Jan. 25, 1851	291
Leekroy, Luke and Tabatha Holmes	Nov. 12, 1848	233
Loftis, William F. and Elizabeth S. Hall	Dec. 19, 1850	278
Lowery, Frederick D. and Olevia Rucker	Dec. 15, 1836	23

Groom, Bride and Date		Page
McAllister, Thomas and Mary Ann Ford	Oct. 11, 1840	100
McCalla, George R. and Mary Jane Allen	Nov. 21, 1849	255
McCollester, John and Easter Brownlee	Jan. 7, 1849	245
McCoy, Jackson and Martha Lunsford	Dec. 22, 1836	17
McCord, George and Virginia Gibbs	Oct. 23, 1845	189
McCurry, John G. and Rachel S. Brown	Jan. 29, 1842	128
McCurry, Alexander and Nancy Roberts	Mar. 14, 1850	271
McCurley, William and Milly Shiflett	Nov. 22, 1849	262
McDougle, John and Milly Vickery	Dec. 16, 1836	65
McGee, Elias and Elizabeth Gaines	Jan. 12, 1847	208
McGehee, John and Lucy C. Thornton	Oct. 2, 1845	184
McGehee, William and Emily P. Thornton	Nov. 13, 1845	185
McGuire, David W. and Ann Skelton	Jan. 25, 1835	12
McIntosh, William M. and Maria Louisa Allen	Jan. 27, 1842	122
McMillan, Robert and Ruth Ann Banks	Feb. 10, 1836	16
McMullan, Washington and Agatha Gaines	Oct. 22, 1840	103
McMullan, Thomas and Permelia Cash	June 11, 1849	106
McMullan, Neal and Milly A. Banks	June 4, 1843	141
McMullan, Marion and Judith M. Stowers	Aug. 14, 1845	179
McMullan, William and A. E. Thornton	July 1, 1849	256
McMullan, Patrick and Elizabeth Haley	July 20, 1839	71
Maley, Sidney and Arena Deadwyler	Nov. 26, 1845	7
Martin, Richard and Rosey Fleming	Mar. , 1837	28
Martin, George H. and Louisa M. P. Lovingood	Dec. 24, 1839	80
Martin, Luther H. O. and Sarah E. Heard	Dec. 17, 1846	204
Martin, Martin and Rachel Bush	Oct. 6, 1847	217
Mann, Henry H. and Susannah Conwell	Dec. 26, 1847	225
Mann, Edward J. and Katherine L. Gaines	Feb. 15, 1844	181
Marks, Joseph and Rebecca Deadwyler	Feb. 1, 1844	157
Mason, Daniel and Elizabeth M. Nelms	Oct. 3, 1837	33
Mason, John and Elizabeth Rookes	June 11, 1840	97
Mason, Silas and Martha Jane White	June 5, 1842	124
Maxwell, Benjamin and Nancy M. Christian	Feb. 13, 1837	41
Maxwell, Jesse and Katherine Johnson	Aug. 8, 1844	158
Maxwell, Elijah and Martha E. Teasley	Jan. ..., 1851	275
Matthews, Doctor N. and Rachel A. Fortson	Feb. 6, 1844	155
Mathews, Samuel and Elizabeth Trader	May 13, 1849	250
Maxwell, William and Serepta Rucker	Jan. 26, 1837	18
Mattox, William and Urena M. Bell	Aug. 15, 1837	29
Merritt, John and Nancy Bowers	June 2, 1844	159
Mewborn, William A. and Avereller Moss	Sept. 15, 1845	172
Mewborn, John and Harriet Lunsford	Feb. 9, 1837	17
Middleton, James and Sarah A. Cook	Dec. 6, 1844	173
Mills, Moses E. and Mary A. Rucker	Dec. 12, 1843	146
Mize, William and Levincey Williams	Nov. 3, 1850	275
Mobley, Middleton and Nancy Cox	Dec. 18, 1836	17
Moon, James B. and Charlotte Butler	Dec. 3, 1835	7
Moon, Charles G. and Mellisee E. Booth	Aug. 1, 1838	54
Moon, Calvin and Nancy Colvard	Nov. 16, 1843	149
Moon, John B. and Mary S. Butler	Jan. 9, 1845	166
Moon, Jacob D. and Sarah White	Dec. 3, 1846	206
Moon, Joel and Sarah Ann Hewell	Dec. 16, 1847	223
Moon, Jesse and Martha White	Dec. 7, 1847	244
Moss, Benson and Clary Mewborn	May 30, 1844	159
Nash, James and Sarah Gunter	May 8, 1836	15
Nash, Junius B. and Sarah Johnson	Jan. 29, 1850	261
Neal, Christopher and Milly Craft	Nov. 30, 1848	243
Nelms, William T. and Mary M. Sewell	Nov. 27, 1844	170
Nelms, William B. and Martha Ann Salmons	June 4, 1844	158

Groom, Bride and Date		Page
Nelms, James M. and Frances Denny	May 16, 1837	37
Norman, James Henry and Elizabeth Beggs	Sept. 5, 1839	111
Norman, Jeptha W. and Sarah A. Norman	Dec. 18, 1842	133
Nunnelee, James F. Jr., and Rachel D. McKindley	Dec. 1, 1836	23
O'Briant, Thomas and Martha L. Wansley	Oct. 4, 1837	31
Oglesby, Rufus and Mary Eavenson	Jan. 9, 1838	41
Oglesby, Shaler and Sarah Key	Dec. 11, 1838	58
Oglesby, Drury Jr., and Cynthia Henderson	Sept. 26, 1839	76
Oglesby, John P. and Permelia Ann Deadwyler	Sept. 17, 1846	202
Oglesby, John and Margaret Eberhardt	Dec. 23, 1850	304
Olds, Daniel and Mary E. Black	Dec. 25, 1850	268
Oliver, Robert R. and Sarah Ann Whitman	Nov. 9, 1837	37
Oliver, Christopher and Laura Reed	Oct. 1, 1839	78
Oliver, James S. and Sarah Ann White	Nov. .. , 1839	78
Oliver, John A. and Susan R. Nash	Oct. 26, 1842	131
Owens, Seaborn and Mary L. Tate	Dec. 20, 1849	253
Ozley, Larkin and Martha Ann Jones	Oct. 3, 1837	39
Ozeley, Thomas and Mary Dye	Sept. 11, 1845	180
Page, William and Mary Hunt	Nov. 28, 1836	23
Page, John S. and Mary Ann Atttaway	Oct. 3, 1843	150
Page, Watson D. and Mary Roberts	May ..., 1840	152
Parks, Leroy and Mary C. Andrews	Oct. 29, 1835	8
Parks, Lindsey and Henry (?) Highsmith	Dec. 15, 1842	135
Parker, Rev. Benjamin and Jane Tyler	Nov. 15, 1848	240
Parham, James I. and Jane Booth	July 30, 1842	138
Parrott, Gibson and Sophia Jones	Dec. 28, 1845	189
Patterson, Weston and Elizabeth A. Wansley	Dec. 21, 1837	39
Patterson, Benjamin G. and Louisa A. F. M. Manning	July 10, 1845	176
Payton, Archibald and Matilda Threlkeld	Jan. 12, 1849	245
Penn, James and Jane E. Ham	Oct. 2, 1839	62
Perrin, Mathias and Edna M. A. Saxon	Dec. 3, 1840	115
Peyton, Henry D. and Elminee E. Tucker	Nov. 25, 1841	120
Phelps, Thomas Jr., and Elizabeth Ann Stinchcomb	Dec. 24, 1846	206
Phillips, Nelson and Mary O. Nix	June 20, 1843	148
Pickeral, William and Elizabeth Landrum	Oct. 30, 1845	204
Phillips, James and Dolly Lowrimore	Sept. 12, 1838	50
Pledger, William and Irena E. Ford	Jan. 7, 1847	212
Powell, Upson and Mary Dooley	Jan. 12, 1843	137
Power, William D. and Virginia Caroline Tucker	Nov. 17, 1844	170
Prather, William E. and Julia Ann Smith	Jan. 23, 1840	86
Prather, James and Mrs. Elizabeth McMullan	Jan. 24, 1839	140
Pratt, William and Margaret Jones	May 24, 1838	45
Prewit, Jacob and Lucinda Daniel	Mar. 16, 1849	239
Poss, Dr N and Jane J. Stephens	Sept. 3, 1846	206
Price, Washington and Dythia Briant	Nov. 20, 1838	50
Pritchett, James Monroe and Nancy Pritchett	Feb. 9, 1845	196
Pritchett, William M. and Milly Chapman	Aug. 8, 1848	234
Pulliam, Willis and Mary Ann Tucker	Oct. 2, 1839	73
Pulliam, George and Eliza M. Forrester	Apr. 11, 1843	143
Pulliam, George and Martha Bell	Dec. 12, 1844	173
Pulliam, Matthew E. and Ruth C. Harris	Dec. 31, 1846	215
Pulliam, Robert J. and Susannah Harman	——— ..., 1848	235
Ramsey, John and Susan James	May 21, 1850	269
Ray, Thomas J. Jr. and Mary A. F. Skelton	Aug. 1, 1844	172
Ray, William R. and Dicey Brown	Mar. 2, 1848	226
Rayle, Wyatt and Elizabeth Turman	Dec. 25, 1845	189
Reagan, William M. and Elizabeth F. Lowrimore	Dec. 15, 1835	8
Reed, Joseph D. and Elizabeth Smith	Sept. 18, 1846	203
Reynolds, Freeman and Elizabeth E. Andrew	Oct. 15, 1840	101

Groom, Bride and Date		Page
Reynolds, Samuel and Serepta Tyner	Jan. 20, 1849	248
Rice, Walton and Malinda T. Horton	Jan. 10, 1839	59
Rice, Robert and Elizabeth Ann Denny	Apr. 29, 1841	111
Rice, Wiley and Susan Brown	Dec. 29, 1843	136
Rice, William and Sarah Henry	Dec. 23, 1843	154
Rice, Richard M. and Royster E. Harper	Apr. 22, 1849	247
Richardson, James V. and Elizabeth McMullan	Nov. 24, 1836	24
Richardson, John C. and Milly Brown	Jan. 2, 1845	173
Ridgway, Abdah and Mary C. Stinchcomb	Dec. 17, 1839	77
Roberts, Hugh and Mary Algood	Apr. 11, 1837	28
Roberts, Francis S. and Emily Algood	Dec. 28, 1837	39
Roberts, Olive and Caroline Harman	Jan. 10, 1839	51
Roberts, John and Susan A. D. Roberts	Sept. 23, 1844	170
Robertson, William and Susan Holmes	Feb. 19, 1838	82
Robertson, Samuel and Elizabeth A. F. McMullan	May 25, 1835	12
Roebuck, Eppy W. and Melissee C. Carter	Dec. 6, 1838	58
Roebuck, William and Ann E. Goss	June 6, 1841	113
Roebuck, Robert C. C. and Mary F. Craft	June 6, 1850	281
Rogers, William R. and Barbara Kerlin	Dec. 2, 1847	222
Roney, Thomas and Mrs. Joanah L. Kelly	Jan. 12, 1836	10
Roper, James and Martha Patterson	Oct. 18, 1849	254
Royster, William and Harriet C. Baker	Feb. 16, 1836	14
Rouzee, Thomas and Louisa Cleveland	Dec. 1, 1837	38
Rousey, Edward and Mary Ann Jones	Dec. 25, 1849	252
Rucker, Tinsley and Sarah Elizabeth Harris	Dec. 24, 1834	47
Rucker, Peter and Mary Haley	July 4, 1838	69
Rucker, Alexander and Mary E. Hall	Dec. 21, 1848	240
Rumsey, Archibald and Sarah Jenkins	Oct. 7, 1838	50
Russum, Jesse and Margaret J. Brown	Dec. 9, 1847	225
Saxon, Lewis and Maria Threlkeld	Sept. 22, 1847	225
Saxon, John Yancey and Julia A. E. Ward	Sept. 6, 1844	159
Sanders, George and Elizabeth T. Pledger	Sept. 22, 1846	213
Sanders, Briggs and Nancy K. Crittenden	Dec. 20, 1845	197
Sanders, James M. and Amanda E. Andrews	Sept. 22, 1844	172
Sanders, Henry and Sarah H. Tucker	Feb. 27, 1842	122
Sanders, David M. and Mahulda Booth	Sept. 19, 1841	118
Sanders, James A. and Margaret A. Turman	Nov. 23, 1848	239
Sayre, David W. and Susan A. Nelms	May 26, 1839	68
Sartain, Calvin and Sarah Burnett	Dec. 17, 1840	101
Sayer, John T. and Martha E. James	Aug. 23, 1844	162
Scroggins, James and Elizabeth Sheppard	July 31, 1851	289
Settles, William M. and Lucinda Oglesby	June 7, 1849	251
Seamore, Mason and Julia Ann Brown	Sept. 21, 1849	256
Seymore, Jesse and Louisa Thompson	Jan. 9, 1840	84
Seals, John and Priscialla B. Nelms	Dec. 17, 1835	9
Shields, John F. and Elizabeth F. Tucker	Dec. 29, 1836	24
Shields, John W. and Ann E. Cleveland	Dec. 1, 1848	241
Shaw, Edward and Mary M. Christian	Oct. 10, 1837	38
Shaw, Andrew J. and Mary Ann Booth	Feb. 22, 1848	226
Shaw, Craton and Narcissa Thompson	Mar. 22, 1849	266
Shackleford, Thomas J. and Martha Wall	Feb. 8, 1842	127
Shackleford, John and Martha Oglesby	June 11, 1844	169
Shiflet, Lewis B. and Elizabeth Powell	Feb. 8, 1838	43
Shiflet, Marion and Mary Richardson	Nov. 17, 1842	135
Shiflet, Powell and Martha S. Watson	Feb. 6, 1850	264
Skelton, Littleton and Nancy Highsmith	Dec. 13, 1838	58
Skelton, Wesley and Mary Ann Walters	Oct. 4, 1849	254
Slay, Parker and Sarah Nash	——, 1832	151
Sloan, John B. and Mary Lucilla Houston	Sept. 2, 1847	210

Groom, Bride and Date		Page
Smith, Franklin and St. Abegale Smith	Apr. 11, 1847	219
Smith, Julius P. and Mary M. Smith	Dec. 23, 1847	222
Smith, James D. and Elizabeth Shaw	Nov. 17, 1851	279
Smith, David S. and Sarah Parham	Nov. 7, 1841	119
Smith, Caleb J. and Elizabeth Christian	Nov. 16, 1841	120
Smith, Singleton and Sarah T. Cunningham	Sept. 3, 1843	140
Smith, Jacob B. and Frances Penn	Aug. 10, 1837	36
Smith, Isham and Mary A. M. Phipps	Oct. 25, 1838	56
Smith, Zion and Mary Ann Rooks	Jan. 29, 1839	63
Smith, Singleton and Mary Ashworth	Nov. 22, 1838	60
Smith, Larkin and Roan Evelina Cunningham	Oct. 24, 1839	75
Smith, John Sr., and Agatha Allen	Nov. 8, 1840	101
Smith, Asa and Sealey Duncan	Jan. 26, 1841	104
Smith, George and Martha Ann Palmore	Feb. 17, 1841	105
Smith, John and Phebe McAllister	Mar. 9, 1840	106
Smith, John M. and Malinda Ford	July 15, 1840	113
Snellings, Richard W. and Elizabeth F. Nunnelee	Aug. 8, 1839	72
Snellings, Peter P. and Frances Booth	Jan. 22, 1840	85
Sorrow, Samuel and Gilly Ozeley	Apr. 22, 1841	115
Sprague, John and Sarah P. Dickey	Mar. 18, 1840	90
Spencer, Abraham and Sarah C. Saxon	Sept. 1, 1846	202
Stephenson, William and Sarah C. McCurry	Jan. 6, 1848	229
Stephenson, John and Sarah Ann Pugh	Feb. 11, 1838	42
Stone, James A. and Sarah V. Ward	Jan. 31, 1837	28
Stone, William A. and Martha E. Tate	Aug. 17, 1843	147
Stone, George and Louisa D. Gunter	Oct. 28, 1847	217
Stodghill, Joel and Martha A. Moss	July 30, 1840	94
Stufle, David and Mary Parks	July 7, 1839	70
Standford, Samuel and Eliza James	Feb. 4, 1840	85
Steadman, Thomas and Elizabeth Greenway	Feb. 25, 1840	86
Stinchcomb, James T. and Lucy Craft	Dec. 13, 1849	253
Stocks, William and Louisa Asbell	Feb. 11, 1851	276
Strickland, James E. and Rachel E. White	May 8, 1851	288
Steedman, James and Milly Greenway	Jan. 4, 1849	245
Stephens, Thomas J. and Julia Ann Moore	Jan. 29, 1850	262
Stowers, Francis G. and Mary Elizabeth Gaines	Dec. 30, 1849	88
Stowers, Thomas and Malissa Ann McCurley	Dec. 9, 1841	125
Stowers, Lewis M. and Katherine Dooly	Dec. 21, 1843	153
Stark, Samuel C. Jr. and Mary Adeline Brewer	May 18, 1843	154
Summers, William and Martha Wallace	Mar. 20, 1845	190
Sullivan, Kelly and Nancy Alexander	Apr. 14, 1846	198
Smith, James M. and Mary M. Nelms	Dec. 21, 1848	240
Sorrow, McKinzie and Sarah A. E. Gunter	Feb. 7, 1844	162
Taylor, Barden R. and Mary Ann Bowman	Nov. 13, 1837	34
Taylor, Robert P. and Sarah M. Nunnelee	Nov. 17, 1839	83
Taylor, John W. and Elizabeth Blackwell	Mar. 9, 1841	108
Taylor, James and Susannah E. Beck	June 25, 1841	115
Taylor, Samuel D. and Eliza Davis	Oct. 13, 1842	131
Taylor, John B. and Sarah A. Dye	Dec. 8, 1842	143
Taylor, Tavner W. and Martha Craft	Sept. 28, 1845	183
Taylor, William E. and Martha E. Cleveland	Sept. 5, 1848	232
Tate, Uriah O. and Rebecca Clark	July 2, 1846	198
Tate, William J. and Elizabeth Pickerell	Aug. 14, 1845	203
Tate, James, and Mary C. Edwards	Sept. 17, 1839	73
Terry, John and Sarah Caroline Greenway	May 18, 1837	26
Terrell, John W. and Matilda Haley	Oct. 2, 1846	201
Teasley, Alfred H. and Sarah Ann Craft	Jan. 9, 1840	87
Teasley, Osburn G. and Lucy A. Crawford	Nov. 18, 1841	116
Teasley, James R. and Mary B. F. Norman	May 1, 1845	175

Groom, Bride and Date		Page
Teasley, Thomas J. and Nancy Mewborn	Apr. 14, 1844	160
Teasley, James and Mary E. Alexander	Jan. 22, 1846	186
Teasley, William A. and Drucilla Adams	Aug. 12, 1846	195
Teasley, John E. and Drucilla Ann Teasley	Dec. 16, 1847	219
Teasley, William H. and Jane Ann Wanslow	Jan. 11, 1849	246
Thornton, Benjamin Sr., and Rebecca Upshaw	Feb. 20, 1836	9
Thornton, John M. and Elizabeth E. Ward	Mar. 23, 1837	34
Thornton, Eppy W. and Margaret C. Adams	Jan. 18, 1842	122
Thornton, Fleming P. and Harriet F. Adams	Oct. 3, 1842	130
Thornton, William E. and Elizabeth E. Thornton	Mar. 4, 1843	143
Thornton, Thomas S. and Lucy Pulliam	Nov. 2, 1843	162
Thornton, Benjamin C. and Telicia E. Gaines	Nov. 17, 1846	200
Thornton, William T. and Lucinda A. Almond	Nov. 2, 1847	223
Thornton, Richard and Martha Ann Pressley	Feb. 8, 1849	246
Threlkeld, William and Lucinda Penn	Oct. 7, 1840	99
Threlkeld, Willis and Mrs. Mary Duncan	Mar. 8, 1849	248
Thompson, Reese and Martha Ann Burden	May 14, 1850	272
Thomas, Jet and Eliza S. Oliver	Dec. 29, 1836	24
Thomason, William G. and Sarah Riley	Oct. 12, 1845	190
Thomason, Hiram W. and Sarah Turner	Dec. 24, 1846	207
Thomason, Matthew D. and Frances Craft	Mar. 2, 1847	231
Timmons, John B. and Caroline Bailey	May 27, 1843	144
Treadwell, Terry and Susan Elmira Gunter	Jan. 7, 1846	184
Turner, Thomas M. and Sarah Gaines	Apr. 2, 1846	200
Turner, John and Mary Jane Hall	Jan. 2, 1848	226
Turner, James B. and Frances Terry	Dec. 16, 1847	207
Turner, James A. and Sarah J. Edwards	Jan. 8, 1846	186
Tucker, John J. and Amanda R. Tucker	Jan. 23, 1851	278
Tucker, William and Nancy Edwards	Apr. 16, 1839	69
Tucker, John and Elizabeth Eaves	Oct. 3, 1843	149
Tyner, William and Mary Ann Dickerson	Aug. 7, 1845	179
Tyner, John H. and Susan A. Dickerson	Dec. 14, 1848	246
Upshaw, John and Ann Maxwell	Mar. 10, 1836	13
Vail, Amos L. and Sarah O. A. Henry	Feb. 16, 1843	139
Vawter, Lindsey and Mary Hulme	Jan. 7, 1844	154
Vaughan, Jacob D. and Martha J. Hewell	Dec. 16, 1847	222
Vernon, Robert and Sarah Richardson	Aug. 7, 1845	196
Verdell, Dunstan B. and Prudence A. E. C. Hearn	July 8, 1847	210
Vickery, James and Mary Powell	July 19, 1849	257
Wall, Jesse and Lenah B. Stone	Nov. 13, 1835	9
Ward, William G. and Elizabeth Colson	Nov. 12, 1837	37
Ward, George M. and Susan M. McMullan	Dec. 21, 1848	244
Watson, Jonathan and Martha L. Neal	Aug. 8, 1838	53
Warsing, Henry and Lydia W. White	Aug. 22, 1842	124
Wanslow, Reuben and Emily Cobb	Dec. 15, 1843	165
Wanslow, Reuben R. and Martha Ann Houston	Jan. 19, 1847	209
Watt, Joseph and Mary T. Alexander	Oct. 5, 1846	214
Wallace, Jesse G. and Sarah J. Allgood	Oct. 19, 1848	235
Ward, Robert M. and Mary T. E. McMullan	Oct. 3, 1844	182
Wells, Samuel and Maria Scales	Jan. 5, 1836	12
Webb, Claborn and Mary Oglesby	Oct. 7, 1841	123
Willis, David C. and Martha A. Dobbs	Apr. 17, 1845	176
Willis, James M. and Melissa Jones	Oct. 18, 1838	48
Wilson, James and Mary Threlkeld	Nov. 13, 1836	25
Winn, Gustavus and Nancy Burden	Sept. 9, 1836	25
Winn, Benjamin F. and Nancy Burnes	Feb. 3, 1848	237
Winn, Alfred S. and Elizabeth Haynes	Dec. 21, 1848	238
White, Benjamin and Ann H. Adams	Feb. 28, 1839	60
White, Thomas H. and Martha McMullan	Mar. 19, 1840	91

Groom, Bride and Date		Page
White, James and Prudence Hinton	Dec. 27, 1842	139
White, John and Naomi Welch	Apr. 28, 1843	144
White, Edward R. and Martha Roberts	Jan. 8, 1846	191
White, William B. Jr., and Mary M. Brown	Dec. 18, 1845	192
White, William and Elizabeth Gunter	Sept. 9, 1847	217
Whitman, Jesse and Lucinda Kelley	Dec. 7, 1848	233
Wilhight, Phillip A. and Cora L. Hilley	Feb. 22, 1848	228
Wilhight, Calvin F. and Mary Ann Worrill	Sept. 2, 1841	112
Williford, Samuel W. and Sarah McMullan	Nov. 17, 1840	109
Whitlow, William M. and Susannah E. Carleton	Nov. 5, 1846	214
Wheelis, David and Sarah E. Moor	Oct. 3, 1847	216
Woods, Thomas and Julia Ann Turner	Oct. 31, 1839	81
Woods, Middleton and Angeline Ruff	Dec. 25, 1846	212
Worrill, Thomas C. and Mary A. E. S. Christian	Oct. 23, 1850	268

MISCELLANEOUS MARRIAGES—NOT OF RECORD IN ELBERT COUNTY AUTHENTIC

Alston, William and Charity Alston, 1774; in Halifax County, North Carolina.
Banks, Ralph and Rachel Jones, Nov. 27, 1788; in Wilkes County, Georgia.
Barnett, William and Mary Meriwether, 1783; in Richmond County, Georgia.
Christian, Turner and Anne Payne, 1778.
Cleveland, Jacob and Milly White, 1749; in Prince William County, Virginia.
Clark, Christopher and Milicent Terrell, 1757; in Virginia.
Darden, George and Martha Burch, 1759; in Virginia.
Fortson, Thomas and Rachel Winn, 1775; in Caroline County, Virginia.
Fortson, Benjamin and Sally Head, 1790.
Hailey, William and Mary Turman, Oct. 10, 1779.
Heard, Stephen and Elizabeth Darden, Aug. 25, 1785; in Wilkes County, Georgia.
Hudson, Booker and Elizabeth Burton, 1786.
Hunt, James Jr., and Jemima Carter, Nov. 11, 1790; in Wilkes County, Georgia.
Key, William Bibb and Mourning Clark, Aug. 17, 1782.
Maxwell, Thomas Jr., and Mary Pemberton, 1761; in Virginia.
Teasley, John III and Lucy Hunt, 1776.
Thornton, Dozier Sr. and Lucy Hill, 1777; in Goochland County, Virginia.
Webb, Clairborn and Margaret Deadwyler, 1783.
All of the above were residents of Elbert County.

FEMALE MARRIAGE INDEX

Bride, Groom and Date	
Adams, Rebecca and John Hendricks	July 13, 1815
Adams, Deborah and James Smith	Jan. 18, 1816
Adams, Polly and Castleton B. Harper	Jan. 7, 1819
Adams, Elizabeth and George Hunt	Oct. 3, 1822
Adams, Grace A. and William Nelson	July 6, 1824
Adams, Mourning and Evans Thornton	Oct. 23, 1817
Adams, Frances and John Thornton	Oct. 23, 1823
Adams, Nancy and James Holmes	Oct. 18, 1829
Adams, Ann B. and Thomas J. Maxwell	May 31, 1831
Adams, Mildred and Joseph Barton	May 14, 1850
Adams, Eliza S. and John M. Brown	Oct. 3, 1843
Adams, Elizabeth and William W. Colson	Aug. 25, 1835
Adams, Elizabeth K. and William J. A. Goolsby	Dec. 13, 1849
Adams, Martha and Asa Hall	June 26, 1849
Adams, Elmira and Henry P. Huff	Jan. 26, 1843

Bride, Groom and Date

Bride and Groom	Date
Adams, Katherine M. and Thomas H. James	Nov. 13, 1944
Adams, Nancy and William L. King	Dec. 29, 1849
Adams, Drucilla and William E. Teasley	Aug. 12, 1846
Adams, Margaret and Eppy W. Thornton	Jan. 18, 1842
Adams, Harriet F. and Fleming P. Thornton	Oct. 3, 1842
Adams, Eveline and William Barnett Golding	Oct. 9, 1828
Agee, Elizabeth and John Elliott	Oct. 30, 1814
Akin, Emelia and John Page	Oct. 26, 1826
Akin, Mary and Stephen H. Tucker	Jan. 16, 1827
Alexander, Milly and Willis Rucker	Oct. 29, 1807
Alexander, Polly and John Cook	Feb. 25, 1810
Alexander, Ann and Richard S. Gaines	Mar. 10, 1811
Alexander, Ezza and Standley Jones	Jan. 3, 1811
Alexander, Catherine and Edmond Alexander	Dec. 6, 1816
Alexander, Morin and Westley Earps	Sept. 18, 1814
Alexander, Sarah and John Childs	Feb. 15, 1820
Alexander, Lucy and Anderson Craft	Feb. 4, 1819
Alexander, Milly and William Glover	Jan. 4, 1816
Alexander, Eliza and John Daniel Jr.	Mar. 15, 1840
Alexander, Milly B. and Wiley Jones	Nov. 16, 1847
Alexander, Catherine, Mrs. and Julian K. Brown	Dec. 6, 1829
Alexander, Elizabeth and Thomas J. Adams	Dec. 21, 1841
Alexander, Nancy and Kelly Sullivan	Apr. 14, 1846
Alexander, Mary E. and James Teasley	Jan. 22, 1846
Alexander, Mary T. and Joseph Watt	Oct. 5, 1846
Alexander, Sarah and Tryon Harris	Oct. 25, 1825
Allen, Sarah and William Kelly	Jan. 4, 1810
Allen, Rebecca and Webb Kidd	Dec. 1, 1814
Allen, Lucy and William W. Harper	Nov. 4, 1817
Allen, Elizabeth and James B. Head	Jan. 7, 1821
Allen, Harriet and William P. Reed	July 22, 1824
Allen, Ann and Milton C. Comer	Apr. 30, 1839
Allen, Mildred, Mrs. and John F. Gray	Oct. 26, 1848
Allen, Mary Jane and George R. McCalla	Nov. 21, 1849
Allen, Maria Louisa and William M. McIntosh	Jan. 27, 1842
Allen, Agatha and John Smith Sr.	Nov. 8, 1840
Allen, Nancy and Elijah W. Couch	June 8, 1830
Aycock, Susan E. and Milton Aycock	Oct. 25, 1815
Allgood, Jane and John Allgood	Jan. 17, 1822
Allgood, Mary and John Allgood	Sept. 13, 1824
Allgood, Anny and John W. Morris	Feb. 6, 1817
Allgood, Elvey and Abner Pealer	Apr. 10, 1819
Allgood, Nancy and John Ozeley	Mar. 26, 1840
Allgood, Mary and Hugh Roberts	Apr. 11, 1837
Allgood, Emily and Francis S. Roberts	Dec. 28, 1837
Allgood, Sarah and Joseph Pealer	Nov. 29, 1827
Allgood, Sarah J. and Jesse G. Wallace	Oct. 19, 1848
Allman, Elizabeth and James W. Brawner	Dec. 14, 1819
Allman, Peggy and Jacob W. Davis	Jan. 2, 1817
Allman, Mary Ann and John Dennard	July 21, 1819
Almond, Lucy Ann and John W. Colvard	Mar. 15, 1838
Almond, Lenna and Fortunatus Webb	Nov. 26, 1826
Almond, Mahulda and Benjamin Herndon	Nov. 27, 1834
Almond, Lucinda A. and William T. Thornton	Nov. 2, 1847
Alston, Mary and James Clark	Apr. 8, 1813
Anderson, Rebecca and James Gunter	Dec. 13, 1813
Anderson, Sarah and Franklin Cook	Sept. 21, 1823
Anderson, Rebecca and William A. Smith	Feb. 1, 1824

Bride, Groom and Date

Bride and Groom	Date
Anderson, Jemima and George Adams	April 8, 1828
Anderson, Polly and John Shiflett	March 4, 1832
Andrew, Mary and Thomas F. Blair	Sept. 3, 1850
Andrew, Martha and Isaac N. Butler	July 7, 1850
Andrew, Elizabeth E. and Freeman Reynolds	Oct. 15, 1840
Andrew, Lucy A. and Charles H. Andrew	May 26, 1843
Andrews, Mary O. and Leroy Parks	Oct. 29, 1835
Andrews, Amanda E. and James H. Sanders	Sept. 22, 1844
Anthony, Sally and Stephen Casey	Oct. 31, 1811
Anthony, Nancy and Lewis Hill	March 2, 1815
Anthony, Mary Ann and George Deane	March 30, 1820
Arnold, Nancy and Mayfield Bell	Nov. 1, 1812
Arnold, Sarah Ann and Asmond Bell	Sept. 6, 1831
Arnold, Adeline A. and John E. Bentley	Sept. 16, 1832
Arnold, Elizabeth, Mrs. and Henry Hall	Oct. 2, 1831
Asbell, Louisa and William Stocks	Feb. 11, 1851
Ashworth, Sarah and Edmond B. Allen	Jan. 12, 1826
Ashworth, Milly and Samuel E. Self	March 13, 1827
Attaway, Mary S. and John S. Page	Oct. 3, 1843
Bailey, Caroline and John B. Timmons	May 27, 1843
Bailey, Nancy and Sylvan Hendricks	Dec. 4, 1810
Bailey, Matilda and Thomas E. Schelds	March 27, 1823
Baker, Harriet C. and William Royster	Feb. 16, 1836
Ballinger, Polly and Nathan Williams	March 21, 1829
Ballinger, Nancy and John Coker	Feb. 19, 1824
Ballinger, Patsy and William Steedly	Sept. 16, 1810
Ballinger, Lettie and Aaron Rice	Feb. 6, 1827
Banks, Sally and Edward Sims	July 11, 1811
Banks, Betsy A. and Peter Alexander	Dec. 24, 1812
Banks, Polly H. and Thomas W. Davis	Dec. 24, 1812
Banks, Lucy and Joseph H. Jones	Feb. 26, 1822
Banks, Rebecca and Simeon Jones	Sept. 6, 1821
Banks, Nancy and Thomas Woolridge	Feb. 13, 1822
Banks, Sarah C. and Willis Alexander	March 15, 1820
Banks, Anna and William U. Bowen	April 26, 1820
Banks, Gilly M. and Bedford Harper	March 6, 1823
Banks, Martha and James M. Hickman	June 6, 1843
Banks, Milly and Neal McMullan	June 4, 1843
Banks, Mary and Hamilton Dooly	Jan. 16, 1842
Banks, Priscilla and Barnabas J. Dooly	Nov. 4, 1838
Banks, Eliza and James Bryson	June 28, 1833
Banks, Martha E. and John R. Hudson	Jan. 17, 1833
Banks, Elizabeth and William T. Nelms	Aug. 2, 1832
Banks, Mary E. and Charles Wesley Arnold	Aug. 27, 1843
Banks, Charity A. and Johnson Aiken	Oct. 28, 1828
Banks, Elizabeth and Mordecai Chandler	Feb. 26, 1828
Banks, Mildred and Charles S. Merrewether	Dec. 1, 1827
Banks, Martha and Thomas Crawford	July 7, 1829
Banks, Hannah K. and Florence M. Oliver	Sept. 15, 1829
Barnes, Cherry and Henry P. Brawner	Dec. 10, 1815
Barnett, Patsy and Francis Gilmer	Jan. 28, 1808
Barr, Susan M. and James S. Jones	July 6, 1848
Barron, Elizabeth and James B. Gaines	Aug. 13, 1844
Barton, Sarah P. and Hugh M. Carithers	Dec. 21, 1848
Bassile, Patience and George Vineyard	March 9, 1807
Baskins, Caty and William Milton	Dec. 3, 1817
Bates, Anny and William Brewer	Oct. 12, 1810
Bates, Judith and Thomas B. Wheeler	July 24, 1822

Bride, Groom and Date		
Bates, Sarah and Simpson Stribling	March	6, 1834
Beck, Willy M. and William B. Alexander	March	15, 1846
Beck, Eugenia and Charles N. B. Carter	May	5, 1838
Beck, Susannah E. and James Taylor	June	25, 1841
Beck, Nancy W. and Benjamin Henry	Dec.	31, 1812
Beggs, Elizabeth and John Henry Norman	Sept.	9, 1839
Bell, Edna Ann and Wilton J. Arnold	Jan.	14, 1834
Bell, Sarah and Jonathan Bell	Aug.	17, 1828
Bell, Urina M. and William Mattox	Aug.	15, 1837
Bell, Martha and Harmon Lovingood	Dec.	22, 1814
Bell, Rebecca and John Gunter	Dec.	31, 1812
Bell, Anna and Tapley Bullard	June	29, 1807
Bell, Elener and William M. Downer	Dec.	7, 1823
Bell, Martha and George Pulliam	Dec.	12, 1844
Bell, Rhoda and Lindsey Smith	Sept.	6, 1829
Bell, Elizabeth and Randolph Dye	Jan.	9, 1808
Bennett, Elizabeth and Drury T. Saxon	Dec.	25, 1831
Bentley, Betsy and Nathan Sheperd	Nov.	30, 1820
Bentley, Levicy and Hiram Bentley	March	31, 1831
Bentley, Rebecca and John R. Mann	Feb.	17, 1821
Bentley, Dicey and William H. Mann	Sept.	27, 1817
Bentley, Sally and Andrew Lowrymore	Oct.	14, 1808
Bevers, Polly and William Gray	Dec	24, 1811
Bibb, Martha and Fleming Freeman	Apr.	16, 1812
Bibb, Sally S. and William Barnett	Mar.	21, 1807
Black, Mary E. and Daniel Oldss	Dec.	25, 1850
Black, Susan H. and Francis K. Bond	Dec.	4, 1845
Blackwell, Isabella and Gerrard Allen Jr.	Oct.	31, 1850
Blackwell, Martha Ann and Thomas J. Bowman	Apr.	8, 1841
Blackwell, Cornelia and Edwin Jones	Nov.	2, 1848
Blackwell, Elizabeth and John M. Taylor	Mar.	9, 1841
Blackwell, Eliza and William B. White	Dec.	18, 1845
Blair, Polly and John Gaar	Jan.	23, 1812
Boatright, Leah and Arus Cox	Jan.	24, 1833
Bobo, Elizabeth and Samuel Bobo	Sept.	4, 1828
Bobo, Milly and James V. Richardson	Feb.	11, 1830
Bobo, Hannah and Lewis B. Rush	Jan.	20, 1831
Bobo, Sarah and William Runnells	June	6, 1824
Booker, Mima and John Sullivan	Apr.	15, 1814
Booker, Sally and Henry Cabiness	Feb.	14, 1816
Bond, Matilda and John King	Dec.	25, 1823
Bond, Rachel and Reuben Richardson	Nov.	12, 1819
Bond, Catherine and John Bond	Jan.	24, 1821
Bond, Tabitha and James Porterfield	Sept.	6, 1808
Bond, Permelia and David Crider	Oct.	22, 1807
Bond, Eliza and William Andrew	Nov.	6, 1838
Bond, Claricey and Daniel Bond	Feb.	9, 1825
Bond, Mary W. and John S. Carpenter	Apr.	3, 1825
Bonds, Susannah and William Higginbotham	Dec.	29, 1814
Bonds, Betsy and Joseph Pulliam	Feb.	18, 1808
Booth, Elizabeth and William J. Moore	Sept.	20, 1832
Booth, Benelder and Talton Shoemaker	Dec.	22, 1811
Booth, Jane and James I. Parham	July	30, 1842
Booth, Mahulda and David M. Sanders	Sept.	19, 1841
Booth, Martha Ann and Andrew J. Shaw	Feb.	22, 1848
Booth, Frances and Peter P. Snellings	Jan.	22, 1840
Booth, Lucy Ann and Joseph A. Colvard	Sept.	24, 1840
Booth, Judith and James A. DePriest	Jan.	7, 1819

Bride, Groom and Date

Booth, Polly and Isham Parham ....Nov. 15, 1828
Booth, Mary Ann and Thomas W. Marbury ....June 20, 1832
Booth, Milassee and Charles G. Moon ....Aug. 1, 1838
Booth, Sarah and Burrell Webb ....Oct. 18, 1806
Booth, Susan and James Oglesby ....Mar. 16, 1826
Bowers, Sarah P. and Robert N. Berryman ....Aug. 9, 1849
Bowers, Mary and Reuben S. Williford ....Dec. 21, 1830
Bowers, Nancy and John Merritt ....June 2, 1844
Bowers, Lettie E. and Dilliard H. Brown ....Jan. 8, 1843
Bowie, Drucilla and Thomas Black ....Aug. 20, 1851
Bowman, Willie M. and John Beck Jr. ....Apr. 21, 1824
Bowman, Mary Ann and Barden R. Taylor ....Nov. 13, 1837
Bowman, Eliz. and William R. Banks ....Apr. 3, 1832
Bragg, Suckey and John Berryman ....Apr. 6, 1817
Brannan, Bethenda and Allen Mason ....Nov. 24, 1819
Brantley, Nancy J. and Moses Hutchenson ....July 14, 1828
Brantley, Mary and Thomas Dooley ....July 26, 1825
Brantley, Letty M. and Adams D. Dooley ....Apr. 22, 1824
Brawner, Charlotte and Samuel Ridgway ....Sept. 20, 1824
Brawner, Harriet and Bedford Johnson ....Dec. 9, 1829
Brawner, Elizabeth and Winston Oliver ....Oct. 18, 1832
Brawner, Nancy M. and John Raigen ....Nov. 7, 1833
Brawner, Lucy Ann and John F. Brawner ....Oct. 31, 1837
Bradley, Lucy and Daniel Thornton ....Oct. 3, 1822
Bradley, Ann and Horatio J. Goss ....Sept. 18, 1823
Bray, Mary and Benjamin Bobo ....Sept. 15, 1831
Bray, Sally and Frederick Dean ....Jan. 8, 1807
Bray, Ann and Larkin Coker ....Nov. 15, 1810
Bradshaw, Mary Ann and Franklin Jones ....Feb. 9, 1846
Bradford, Elizabeth and James Kelly ....Oct. 29, 1846
Bramblett, Milly and John Gober ....Oct. 21, 1846
Bramblett, Eliz. and John Gober ....Dec. 15, 1813
Braden, Elizabeth and Allen Bevers ....June 19, 1807
Braswell, Jenny and Brickley Cape ....Nov. 7, 1812
Brady, Sally and Joel Moore ....Nov. 5, 1812
Breadin, Nancy and Charles McMullin ....Jan. 26, 1809
Brewer, Martha H. and John Royal Jr. ....Dec. 1, 1814
Brewer, Mary Adeline and Samuel C. Stark Jr. ....May 18, 1843
Brewer, Frances C. M. and Archelus Jarrett ....Nov. 12, 1815
Brewer, Synthia and McKinley Irons ....Oct. 21, 1816
Brewer, Polly and Jacob Turman ....Oct. 15, 1807
Brewer, Susannah and William Mullin ....Sept. 3, 1815
Brewer, Martha and Thompson B. Dye ....Dec. 12, 1838
Brewer, Susan, Mrs. and Nathan Jones ....Sept. 22, 1839
Briant, Dythia and Washington Price ....Nov. 20, 1838
Brooks, Mary and Thomas Dooly ....July 5, 1827
Brownlee, Margaret and Lentine Butler ....Dec. 27, 1848
Brownlee, Ruth and James Gunter ....Dec. 22, 1844
Brownlee, Easter and John McAllister ....Jan. 7, 1849
Brown, Sally and William Rice ....Jan. 30, 1812
Brown, Betsy and Barton Rucker ....Nov. 10, 1809
Brown, Janey and James E. White ....July 10, 1811
Brown, Sally and Ezra Almond ....Aug. 22, 1807
Brown, Catey and William Stubblefield ....Feb. 23, 1809
Brown, Polly and George Baker ....June 13, 1811
Brown, Nancy and William Mills ....Dec. 12, 1815
Brown, Catherine and Amos Rose ....Dec. 4, 1814
Brown, Sarah and Jesse Ginn ....Aug. 8, 1824

Bride, Groom and Date
Brown, Nancy and Edward Hearndon ....Aug. 17, 1820
Brown, Sally and Samuel Howell ....Mar. 22, 1821
Brown, Polly and David B. Ramsey ....Sept. 19, 1820
Brown, Mary S. and James Tate ....July 27, 1819
Brown, Ann and Thomas Burton ....July 18, 1833
Brown, Lucy Ann and William Jones ....Sept. 27, 1831
Brown, Elizabeth and Lauchlin McCurry ....Feb. 14, 1832
Brown, Priscilla and William F. Attaway ....Jan. 15, 1846
Brown, Martha D. and John W. Roebuck ....Dec. 30, 1828
Brown, Matilda and Thomas F. Davis ....Aug. 20, 1829
Brown, Sarah and Alex McAllister ....Jan. 14, 1830
Brown, Sarah E. and Asa Bowers ....Mar. 30, 1843
Brown, Frances M. and Joseph A. Colvard ....Apr. 6, 1848
Brown, Nancy and John Duncan Jr. ....Jan. 17, 1837
Brown, Sarah and Oliver M. Duncan ....Feb. 8, 1844
Brown, Eliza J. and Robert M. Edwards ....Nov. 14, 1840
Brown, Elizabeth and Moses Ginn ....Apr. 15, 1849
Brown, Emily and Middleton Ginn ....Aug. 24, 1837
Brown, Margaret and John F. Glover ....Feb. 19, 1850
Brown, Nancy and John M. Haynes ....June 10, 1841
Brown, Sarah C. and John C. Highsmith ....Aug. 26, 1847
Brown, Rebecca and William Hilley ....Aug. 9, 1838
Brown, Rachel S. and John G. McCurry ....Jan. 29, 1842
Brown, Dicey and William R. Ray ....Mar. 2, 1848
Brown, Julia Ann and Mason Seamore ....Sept. 21, 1849
Brown, Mary M. and William B. White Jr. ....Dec. 18, 1845
Brown, Susan and Wiley Rice ....Dec. 29, 1843
Brown, Milly and John C. Richardson ....Jan. 2, 1845
Bryan, Martha and John Halloway ....June 5, 1808
Butler, Milly and James Johnson ....Dec. 22, 1831
Butler, Sarah and Eppy Bond ....Aug. 10, 1837
Butler, Susan and Jesse Gunter ....Nov. 10, 1825
Butler, Sally and William Osler ....Jan. 26, 1809
Butler, Clementyne and William Dudley ....May 20, 1813
Butler, Nancy and David V. Kemp ....Dec. 25, 1823
Butler, Nancy and George B. Nash ....Aug. 28, 1817
Butler, Charlotte and James B. Moon ....Dec. 3, 1835
Butler, Mary S. and John B. Moon ....Jan. 9, 1845
Butler, Elizabeth F. and George J. Dye ....May 11, 1848
Butler, Elizabeth and John Downer ....July 6, 1823
Butler, Elizabeth and Robert Mantooth ....Oct. 22, 1833
Burton, Milinda and Osburn Childers ....June 28, 1815
Burton, Nancy and James B. Penn ....Nov. 4, 1831
Burton, Harriet and John B. Andrew ....Feb. 24, 1850
Burton, Martha N. and Martin White ....Dec. 6, 1830
Burton, Elizabeth and William H. Edwards ....Dec. 23, 1828
Burton, May W. and Richard H. Hudson ....Jan. 13, 1828
Burton, Elizabeth and Boukes Hudson ....Sept. 15, 1809
Burton, Caty and Daniel Coursey ....Jan. 26, 1806
Burton, Jane E. and Robert M. Crittenden ....Nov. 2, 1843
Burton, Elizabeth and John M. Saxon ....Dec. 31, 1817
Burton, Permelia and John S. Childers ....Jan. 4, 1821
Burton, Mary and William C. Davis ....May 4, 1820
Burton, Elizabeth and John B. Harrison ....Jan. 5, 1823
Burden, Martha and Isaac Ginn ....June 17, 1824
Burden, Winney and James Dodds ....Oct. 12, 1820
Burden, Frances and Thomas Mewborn ....Oct. 26, 1824
Burden, Polly and Thomas H. Penn ....Jan. 18, 1821

Bride, Groom and Date

Burden, Ann and Martin White .... Feb. 27, 1823
Burden, Martha Ann and Reese Thompson .... Mar. 14, 1850
Burden, Nancy and John Allgood .... Dec. 27, 1825
Burden, Elizabeth and Stephen W. Jordan .... Mar. 4, 1830
Burden, Nancy and Gustavus Winn .... Sept. 9, 1836
Burden, Sarah and Henry Burden .... Aug. 20, 1815
Burnett, Sarah and Calvin Sartain .... Dec. 17, 1840
Burnes, Nancy and Benjamin F. Winn .... Mar. 3, 1848
Burnes, Sarah and Benjamin Haynes .... Feb. 6, 1846
Burnes, Elizabeth E. and Stephen Horton .... Jan. 3, 1847
Buchannon, Jane and Wiley Hales .... Mar. 15, 1810
Bullard, Tempy and John Woodley .... Mar. 5, 1808
Bullard, Elizabeth and William Dye .... Aug. 22, 1811
Burch, Mary T. and Henry Carlton .... May 16, 1839
Burbanks, Emily M., Mrs. and Francis E. Doneley .... Apr. 26, 1849
Buffington, Elizabeth and Ruben Cash .... Dec. 10, 1818
Burnett, Bethana and James Sartain .... Nov. 18, 1824
Cade, Eliza A. and Felix G. Edwards .... Dec. 28, 1835
Callister, Nancy M. and Enos C. Tate .... Nov. 22, 1815
Campbell, Sarah E. and Henry C. Bradshaw .... Mar. 29, 1849
Campbell, Martha A. F. and William J. Cook .... Aug. 17, 1848
Campbell, Nancy and Bazel Brawner .... Sept. 27, 1810
Campbell, Ann and Solomon Johnston .... Dec. 28, 1815
Campbell, Polly and Joseph Woods .... Jan. 3, 1815
Cape, Elizabeth and William F. Cheek .... Sept. 25, 1831
Carden, Jane Ann and Simeon G. Glenn .... Sept. 25, 1828
Carleton, Susannah and William W. Whitlow .... Nov. 5, 1846
Carleton, Martha M. and Berry Brown Jr. .... Dec. 24, 1835
Carpenter, Leah and Willis Bond .... Mar. 13, 1825
Carpenter, Rhoda and Frederick Harmon .... Apr. 4, 1825
Carpenter, Susan and George W. Harmon .... Mar. 4, 1821
Carpenter, Rebema and Nathaniel Nelums .... Mar. 3, 1809
Carpenter, Eliz. and Daniel Boughtright .... Dec. 15, 1813
Cash, Fanny and Joel Scales .... Mar. 3, 1811
Cash, Lucy and James White .... Oct. 20, 1821
Cash, Elizabeth and George Alexander .... Sept. 9, 1830
Cash, Ann and Nathaniel H. Nelms .... Dec. 23, 1830
Cash, Mary and Allen Daniel .... Nov. 23, 1838
Cason, Parmelia and Thomas McMullan .... June 11, 1840
Cason, Milly and Robert Crump .... Nov. 5, 1818
Cason, Elizabeth and William J. C. Kennedy .... Jan. 24, 1822
Carter, Sophia and William Alexander .... Dec. 26, 1843
Carter, Sarah and George W. Heard .... Apr. 20, 1813
Carter, Lucy F. and Edmund H. Brewer .... May 7, 1823
Carter, Elizabeth J. and John S. Corry .... Nov. 25, 1822
Carter, Martha and Samuel Koochagey .... Feb. 10, 1825
Carter, Nancy and Bannister Perrin .... Feb. 2, 1824
Carter, Melissee and Eppy W. Roebuck .... Dec. 6, 1838
Carter, Ann Daniel and John S. Corry .... Dec. 26, 1839
Carter, Matilda and Elisha Ford .... Feb. 26, 1846
Carter, Sarah and Robert Childrers .... Aug. 9, 1809
Carter, Martha and Burgess Wall .... Oct. 6, 1815
Chambers, Mary A. R. and James J. Y. Alston .... Apr. 12, 1827
Chambers, Frances P. and Joseph P. Pledger .... Jan. 3, 1822
Chapman, Nancy and Young A. Decker .... Sept. 8, 1822
Chapman, Milly and William M. Pritchett .... Aug. 8, 1848
Chapman, Elizabeth and William D. Allen .... May 25, 1841
Chapman, Julia Ann and William M. Crittenden .... Feb. 22, 1842

Bride, Groom and Date

Bride and Groom	Date
Chamber, Charity A. and James O. Oliver	Dec. 24, 1833
Chandler, Mary and John Adams Arnett	Mar. 18, 1824
Cheek, Nancy and William H. Adams	Oct. 3, 1833
Cheek, Sarah Ann and Lucious J. M. Bell	July 3, 1834
Childs, Elizabeth and John Jennings	Feb. 20, 1814
Childs, Surreny and John Mitchum	Feb. 13, 1815
Childs, Margaret and George Owens	Feb. 23, 1816
Childs, Jane and John Winn	Nov. 10, 1808
Childs, Susannah and Stephen Carlton	May 3, 1810
Childs, Nancy and William D. McCane	Feb. 23, 1810
Childers, Milly and George C. Walker	Dec. 1, 1809
Chipman, Mary J. and Thomas A. Banks	Jan. 3, 1821
Christian, Mary and Elijah J. Christian	Dec. 19, 1823
Christian, Ann P. and Walker Felts	Jan. 8, 1824
Christian, Mary and William H. T. Fitts	May 16, 1820
Christian, Lucinda and John W. LeGrand	Aug. 8, 1827
Christian, Sarah and Thomas G. Rose	Mar. 11, 1824
Christian, Mary M. and Edward Shaw	Oct. 10, 1837
Christian, Elizabeth and Caleb J. Smith	Nov. 16, 1814
Christian, Mary A. E. and Thomas C. Worrill	Oct. 23, 1850
Christian, Martha and Charles Andrew	Jan. 5, 1830
Christian, Mary J. and Thomas J. Christian	June 10, 1829
Christian, Nancy M. and Benjamin Maxwell	Feb. 13, 1839
Christian, Kezieh and Jesse Horton	Aug. 8, 1844
Christian, Ann P. and Jeremiah T. Horton	Apr. 17, 1839
Christian, Elizabeth and Martin Bond	Aug. 6, 1835
Christian, Armanda and William Bond	Mar. 28, 1839
Christian, Eliza and Elijah Crawford	Dec. 28, 1837
Christian, Minerva and Daniel Higginbotham	Oct. 5, 1842
Chrisley, Elizabeth and Wiley Salmons	Oct. 27, 1831
Christler, Lucy D. and William Bryant	Oct. 21, 1823
Christler, Nancy and Thomas Morgan	Feb. 5, 1824
Clark, Margaret and James O. Clark	Mar. 29, 1821
Clark, Mary and Isaac Edwards	Oct. 24, 1816
Clark, Milly and Thomas F. Willis	Nov. 7, 1822
Clark, Sarah and William Patterson	Aug. 20, 1826
Clark, Tabitha and Jeffry Thompson	Jan. 25, 1826
Clark, Martha and James J. Goode	Dec. 8, 1818
Clark, Aggy and Flemmon Holbrook	Nov. 6, 1817
Clark, Susannah A. and John S. McGire	Aug. 26, 1824
Clark, Rebecca and Uriah O. Tate	July 2, 1846
Clark, Elizabeth, Mrs. and Banks Blackwell	June 28, 1831
Clark, Sarah and Wiley B. Brown	Dec. 13, 1827
Clark, Lucinda and Henry H. Cosby	June 10, 1834
Clark, Margaret S. and John F. Edwards	Aug. 22, 1833
Clark, Mary E. and James Richardson	Feb. 7, 1833
Clark, Lucinda M. and Thomas Alexander	Dec. 20, 1838
Clark, Martha and Samuel Allen	Nov. 1, 1835
Clark, Mildred E. and James J. Black	Nov. 7, 1844
Clark, Flora and David W. Cheek	Oct. 10, 1847
Clark, Caroline T. and Joseph T. Edwards	Dec. 10, 1835
Clark, Elizabeth and Asa J. Haynes	Dec. 6, 1838
Clark, Judah and Jesse G. Ballard	Sept. 9, 1807
Clark, Sarah and Talliaferro Hall	June 16, 1808
Clark, Martha and William Colbert	Jan. 24, 1813
Clark, Elizabeth and Phillip Matthews	Feb. 8, 1815
Clark, Sarah B. and John H. Banks	July 4, 1821
Cleveland, Louisa and Thomas Rouzee	Dec. 1, 1837

Bride, Groom and Date

Name	Date
Cleveland, Ann E. and John W. Shields	Dec. 1, 1848
Cleveland, Martha E. and William E. Taylor	Sept. 9, 1848
Cleveland, Sarah W. and William D. Thornton	Dec. 27, 1829
Cleveland, Eliza and Micajah Almond	Oct. 3, 1833
Cleveland, Emelia and Reuben Thornton	July 28, 1838
Cleveland, Martha L. and Wiley J. Wanslow	Dec. 20, 1832
Cleveland, Jane and William Galloway	Dec. 1, 1842
Cleveland, Mary F. and Michael Galloway	Oct. 5, 1846
Cobb, Frances E. and Job W. Burden	Dec. 11, 1845
Cobb, Emily and Reuben Wanslow	Oct. 15, 1843
Coker, Polly and Jarratt Hanley	Dec. 23, 1818
Coker, Elizabeth and Lewis Cape	Dec. 18, 1806
Coker, Eliz. Ann and Allen Peeler	Mar. 28, 1833
Coker, Irenia and James M. Blackwell	Dec. 26, 1831
Coker, Susannah and Jesse C. Roberts	Oct. 13, 1816
Coker, Sinthia and William Cheek	Sept. 13, 1821
Coker, Milsy and Burges Sheats	Nov. 19, 1818
Coker, Cloey and Levi Hendricks	June 3, 1825
Coker, Bitha and Abraham Hill	Jan. 22, 1828
Colbert, Martha and Holman Childers	Feb. 24, 1819
Colbert, Melinda and Walker Horton	Feb. 28, 1828
Colbert, Lucy and Thomas Morgan	Feb. 5, 1824
Colbert, Gilly and John Cook	Jan. 16, 1816
Colbert, Sarah and William Stone	Oct. 27, 1812
Colson, Elizabeth and William G. Ward	Nov. 12, 1837
Colson, Juley Ann and Jere E. Moore	Feb. 14, 1832
Colson, Sophia and John S. Moore	Dec. 18, 1832
Colson, Nancy and Augustus T. Burton	Apr. 29, 1845
Colson, Sarah and William Whitman	May 28, 1812
Coleman, Rebecca and Elijah J. Christian	Jan. 16, 1821
Coleman, Betsy and James Dudley	Dec. 26, 1822
Coleman, Elizabeth and Drury T. Saxon	Jan. 3, 1827
Coleman, Sarah and William King	Sept. 8, 1815
Coleman, Betsy and William Phillips	Mar. 20, 1814
Cole, Mahala and Christopher Butler	Jan. 8, 1809
Cole, Sally and Robert Walker	Aug. 8, 1808
Colman, Sally and Joseph Nix	Mar. 10, 1811
Conwill, Susannah and Henry H. Mann	Dec. 26, 1847
Cook, Elizabeth and Aaron Brown	Mar. 21, 1819
Cook, Nancy and Lewis Cook	Nov. 16, 1824
Cook, Hannah and Thomas J. Williams	July 27, 1826
Cook, Mariah and Oliver Threlkeld	Nov. 18, 1824
Cook, Keziah and John William	Jan. 3, 1822
Cook, Ann and John Young	May 1, 1823
Cook, Mary Ann and Benjamin Burch	May 20, 1838
Cook, Susan and George Wilson	Jan. 13, 1828
Cook, Pamelia and Henry Freeman	Jan. 11, 1820
Cook, Elizabeth and Henry Patterson	June 6, 1818
Cook, Sarah and Joseph Moseley	Dec. 24, 1833
Cook, Barbary and Oliver Crawford	June 24, 1830
Cook, Frances, Mrs. and John Housley	Feb. 24, 1829
Cook, Jane and William Matthews	Dec. 23, 1834
Cook, Martha and Rice Ellington	Aug. 27, 1839
Cook, Barbery H. and Benjamin Fortson	Sept. 29, 1840
Cook, Elizabeth and Michael Herndon	Dec. 17, 1840
Cook, Frances E. and Benjamin Higginbotham	Dec. 13, 1849
Cook, Sarah A. and James Middleton	Dec. 6, 1844
Cook, Margaret and Green W. Smith	Feb. 22, 1816

Bride, Groom and Date

Cook, Nancy and Peter Faulkner	Oct. 31, 1807
Cook, Betsy, Mrs. and Charles Hardeman	Oct. 3, 1820
Cooper, Eliza and Jared Howard	Jan. 9, 1842
Colvard, Sarah L. and John T. Ridgway	Nov. 27, 1834
Colvard, Polly and Harrison Parham	Dec. 27, 1829
Colvard, Martha and Nathaniel Booth	Jan. 9, 1838
Colvard, Nancy and Calvin Moon	Nov. 16, 1843
Couch, Elizabeth and Calvin Moon	Nov. 16, 1843
Coulson, Rebecca and Henry Dutton	Aug. 22, 1819
Cox, Elizabeth and Samuel G. Cloud	Jan. 9, 1816
Cox, Elizabeth A. and Jonathan Skelton	July 17, 1810
Cox, Mary and Benjamin J. Brewer	June 21, 1840
Cox, Nancy and Middleton Mobley	Dec. 18, 1836
Craft, Nancy and Henry Hunt	July 25, 1815
Craft, Polly and George Gaines	Jan. 7, 1823
Craft, Matilda and John Logan	Feb. 2, 1823
Craft, Letha and John Prewit	Dec. 23, 1819
Craft, Susan and William Gaar	Dec. 30, 1830
Craft, Mary and Robert C. C. Roebuck	June 6, 1850
Craft, Sarow and Tavner Taylor	June 12, 1831
Craft, Lucy and James T. Stinchcomb	Dec. 13, 1849
Craft, Martha and Tavner W. Taylor	Sept. 28, 1845
Craft, Sarah Ann and Alfred H. Teasley	Jan. 9, 1840
Craft, Frances and Matthew D. Rhomason	Mar. 2, 1847
Craft, Sarah and William M. Gaines	Feb. 1, 1851
Craft, Milly and Christopher Neal	Nov. 30, 1848
Craft, Mary E. and Jesse L. Brown	Nov. 13, 1850
Craft, Martha Ann and John W. Craft	Nov. 29, 1848
Crawford, Milly L. and Benjamin Brown Jr.	Dec. 24, 1835
Crawford, Matilda C. and Elijah Chapman	Oct. 10, 1845
Crawford, Lucy A. and Osburn G. Teasley	Nov. 18, 1841
Crawford, Frances A. and James W. Adams	Oct. 4, 1849
Crawford, Nancy and Dilliard J. Bailey	Jan. 5, 1839
Crawford, Lucy and Barnabas Barron	Dec. 29, 1847
Crawford, Jane and William Horton	Oct. 9, 1809
Cridenton, Judith and Alexander Means	Aug. 22, 1822
Crittenden, Diana and Abner L. Mann	Aug. 14, 1816
Crittenden, Nancy and Henry Cabiness	Feb. 10, 1810
Crittenden, Nancy K. and James M. Sanders	Dec. 20, 1845
Crisler, Anna and Reuben Thornton Jr.	Aug. 23, 1810
Crump, Polly and Thomas B. Tiner	Mar. 5, 1811
Crump, Aggy and Robert T. Gaines Jr.	Jan. 6, 1842
Crump, Julia F. O. and Morgan M. Brown	Oct. 3, 1842
Crump, Sophia C. and William A. D. Brown	Dec. 25, 1849
Crump, Mary and Gaines W. Burden	Jan. 13, 1842
Crump, Louisa H. C. and Thomas M. Bobo	Apr. 4, 1843
Crump, Agatha and John Craft	Aug. 1, 1822
Crump, Alphia F. O. and Hamilton Doss	Jan. 3, 1817
Cunningham, Polly and Richard Franklin	Dec. 25, 1823
Cunningham, Polly and Menter Cunningham	Oct. 18, 1815
Cunningham, Catherine and Newell Coller	Oct. 22, 1825
Cunningham, Nancy and Debany Chisenhall	Apr. 3, 1821
Cunningham, Averilla and David C. Flemming	Aug. 27, 1833
Cunningham, Sarah T. and Singleton Smith	Sept. 3, 1843
Cunningham, Rosa Evelina and Larkin Smith	Oct. 24, 1939
Cunningham, Anna and Thomas M. Fleming	Dec. 30, 1841
Cunningham, Elizabeth and Thomas Bevill	Nov. 26, 1807
Curry, Jane and Alason Burton	Jan. 15, 1818
Davis, Frances and Ancel Breeding	Sept. 14, 1815

Bride and Groom.

Davis, Eliza and Samuel D. Taylor
Davis, Jane and John Roan
Davis, Julia and Jebez Skelton
Davis, Lockey and Edwin Fountain
Davis, Lucy and Fielding Smith
Davis, Lucy Ann and William S. Jones
Davis, Martha W. and William Hawthorne
Davis, Mary and James B. Moon
Davis, Mary Ann and Elijah B. Gunter
Davis, Nancy and Ethal Tucker Jr.
Davis, Nancy E. and Robert Walsh
Davis, Nancy and John Adams
Davis, Polly and Walter Bruce
Davis, Rhoda and Edward Clark
Davis, Sarah and Newdegate Hausley
Davis, Sarah and Thomas Tatom
Davis, Sarah and Joseph Schackleford
Davis, Susannah and Horatio G. Brewer
Daniel, Elizabeth and John Craft
Daniel, Nancy and Franklin Cunningham
Daniel, Polly and Washington Craft
Daniel, Sarah and John A. Cunningham
David, Elizabeth and Maraset David
David, Elizabeth and Alex Vaughan
David, Lucinda and Jacob Prewit
David, Mary and Henry W. Gaines
David, Milly and George Wiley
David, Selah and David Smith
Deadwyler, Arena and Sidney Maley
Deadwyler, Rebecca and Joseph Marks
Deadwyler, Permelia and John P. Oglesby
Deadwyler, Teresa and Furney Hammond
Deadwyler, Anna and Robert C. Bradley
Deadwyler, Ann B. and Elijah W. Webb
Deadwyler, Martha, Mrs. and Alex. P. Houston
Deadwyler, Letitia and Milton P. Webb
Deadwyler, Nancy and Abner Webb
Deadwyler, Eliz. and Elisha Ford

Bride, Groom and Date

Dean, Polly and William Story ....Aug. 18, 1809
Decker, Mary Ann H. and John Gully ....July 29, 1813
Decker, Phereby and Jesse Taylor ....Nov. 14, 1822
Denna, Sarah and Josiah Raines ....Apr. 5, 1832
Danna, Margaret and Watson D. Page ....Nov. 1, 1824
Denna, Catherine and Thomas N. Palmour ....Feb. 14, 1827
Dennard, Polly and Jethro Hardy ....Feb. 10, 1810
Dennard, Jane and John Rodgers ....Mar. 20, 1823
Dennard, Polly and Foster Rowsey ....Dec. 18, 1808
Denny, Frances and James M. Nelms ....May 16, 1837
Denny, Elizabeth Ann and Robert Rice ....Apr. 29, 1841
DePriest, Polly and George Butler ....Apr. 13, 1815
DePriest, Jenny and John Fitts ....Nov. 2, 1809
Dickerson, Mary J. and Richard C. Adams ....Apr. —, 1846
Dickerson, Clancy and Gaines T. Dickerson ....Aug. 18, 1840
Dickerson, Lucy and Barnwell Dickerson ....May 1, 1849
Dickerson, Mary Ann and William Tyner ....Aug. 7, 1845
Dickerson, Susan A. and John H. Tyner ....Dec. 14, 1848

Bride, Groom and Date

Bride, Groom	Date
Dickson, Sally and William Davis	June 15, 1807
Dickey, Elizabeth and William R. Ham	Feb. 25, 1834
Dickey, Sarah P. and John Sprague	Mar. 18, 1840
Dilliard, Elizabeth and Richard Hilly	Apr. 20, 1813
Dilliard, Mary V. and John Allman	Jan. 20, 1820
Dilliard, Mary M. and Samuel N. Scott	Dec. 27, 1832
Dilliard, Sally and William Campbell	Oct. 25, 1830
Dilliard, Jane and William D. Campbell	Oct. —, 1839
Dobbs, Martha A. and David C. Willis	Apr. 17, 1845
Dobbs, Mary and Samuel Smith	Oct. 17, 1824
Dobbs, Lucy and Joshua Prothro	Jan. 4, 1823
Dollar, Polly and Fielding McMullan	Mar. 3, 1822
Dodds, Elizabeth and Mercer Spears	Apr. 19, 1810
Dooly, Nancy and Francis Powell	Dec. 12, 1813
Dooly, Polly and Barnabas Barron	Feb. 17, 1820
Dooly, Nancy J. and Joseph M. Brantley	Mar. 18, 1823
Dooly, Sarah and Larkin Clark Jr.	Jan. 10, 1837
Dooly, Sally and Peter Ready	July 1, 1817
Dooly, Webby and Jesse Rice	Sept. 3, 1818
Dooly, Elizabeth and Moses Duncan	Oct. 31, 1841
Dooly, Katherine and Lewis M. Stowers	Dec. 21, 1843
Dooly, Eliz. and Van D. Garey	Feb. 9, 1826
Dooly, Letty, Mrs. and Lewis Bobo	July 7, 1829
Dooley, Sarah Ann and William H. Crawford	Aug. 20, 1832
Dooley, Elizabeth and Leroy R. Crawford	Dec. 13, 1832
Dooley, Mary and Upson Powell	Jan. 12, 1843
Downer, Tabitha and William Colliday	Sept. 30, 1810
Downer, Mary Ann and Levi Algood	Aug. 14, 1842
Downer, Louisa and Levi S. Algood	Aug. 19, 1847
Downer, Elizabeth and Thomas E. Clark	Aug. 28, 1839
Downer, Elizabeth and John M. Gunter	Nov. 30, 1839
Downs, Mary and Jacob Perce	Mar. 27, 1830
Driver, Evelina and John S. Crittenden	Dec. 27, 1835
Dudley, Mary and Isaac G. Mitchell	Jan. 15, 1829
Dudley, Nancy and Samuel New	Oct. 5, 1820
Duncan, Sealey and Asa Smith	Jan. 26, 1841
Duncan, Mary, Mrs. and Willis Threlkeld	Mar. 8, 1849
Duncan, Mary E. and William W. Y. Beasley	Nov. 20, 1850
Duncan, Letty and Edmond G. Brown	Mar. 24, 1836
Duncan, Sarah and Will S. Carlton	Aug. 8, 1843
Duncan, Alis and Jesse Nelms	Jan. 10, 1822
Dunn, Harriet and John M. Bailey	Dec. 18, 1834
Dunn, Lear H. and Samuel Craft	May 23, 1822
Dutton, Patsy and Benjamin Wheeler	Sept. 3, 1838
Dye, Mary and Arthur Jones	Nov. 6, 1833
Dye, Sarah T. and William S. Jones	Oct. 30, 1834
Dye, Nancy and James F. Butler	Aug. 11, 1841
Dye, Ann and Jeptha Dennard	Nov. 4, 1849
Dye, Sarah and Vinson Hubbard	July 12, 1821
Dye, Mary and Woodson Hubbard	Jan. 20, 1825
Dye, Elizabeth K. and Lewis R. Jones	Sept. 29, 1829
Dye, Frances W. and Richmond Rich	Sept. 23, 1829
Dye, Sarah A. and John B. Taylor	Dec. 8, 1842
Dye, Mary and Thomas Ozeley	Sept. 11, 1845
Dye, Mary A. E. and Thomas J. Nash	Sept. 2, 1842
Dye, Martha and Arthur Jones	Mar. 25, 1845
Dye, Susan and John Jones	Apr. 18, 1844
Dye, Delilah and Jonathan Hooper	Feb. 28, 1839

Bride, Groom and Date

Eades, Martha and James J. Burch	Mar.	4, 1830
Earps, Mourning and Macajah Carter	Jan.	22, 1850
Easter, Eliza L. and Wm. Chisholm Jr.	May	13, 1810
Eastridge, Mary and Samuel Mauchelt	Mar.	27, 1806
Eavenson, Hannah and Matthew Pulliam	Jan.	19, 1809
Eavenson, Elizabeth and Beverly A. Teasley	Feb.	15, 1828
Eavenson, Priscilla and William R. Goss	Aug.	6, 1841
Eavenson, Mary and Rufus Oglesby	Jan.	9, 1838
Eaves, Elizabeth and John Tucker	Oct.	3, 1843
Eaves, Sarah and Lawrence Calloway	Jan.	7, 1829
Eaves, Julia Ann and Milum Hendricks	Aug.	17, 1826
Eaves, Martha and John Brown	Apr.	1, 1830
Eaves, Honor and James Lunsford	Mar.	3, 1806
Eberhardt, Margaret and John Oglesby	Dec.	23, 1850
Edwards, Sieser Ann and Tandy Fitts	Aug.	22, 1838
Edwards, Mary C. and James Tate	Sept.	17, 1839
Edwards, Sarah J. and James A. Turner	Jan.	8, 1846
Edwards, Nancy and William Tucker	Apr.	16, 1839
Edwards, Susan and Pleasant Vincent	Jan.	14, 1808
Edwards, Eliza C. and Jedediah Miller	June	17, 1819
Edwards, Elizabeth and Obediah Campbell	Jan.	24, 1828
Edwards, Sarah B. and William D. Tinsley	Jan.	3, 1828
Edwards, Julia A. and Drury B. Cade	May	4, 1830
Edwards, Elizabeth and Elijah J. Christian	Oct.	28, 1828
Edwards, Sarah D. and Thomas H. Brown	Mar.	28, 1833
Edmondson, Caroline and Daniel N. Henry	Mar.	20, 1827
Elder, Patsy and Joel Booth	Jan.	20, 1822
Elder, Rebecca and Richard Upshaw	Feb.	27, 1820
Ellett, Milly and Joshua Jenkins	Apr.	19, 1810
Ellington, Jane and John Langdon	Nov.	11, 1806
Elliott, Elizabeth and David Craft	Dec.	3, 1812
Elliott, Sarah and Samuel Meanes	Sept.	15, 1817
Elliott, Nancy and Thomas M. Cox	Aug.	11, 1850
England, Jane and Benjamin Cook	Apr.	30, 1810
Evans, Sally and Evans Ragland	May	21, 1826
Eveston, Polly and Wm. G. Higginbotham	Sept.	26, 1808
Ewing, Rebecca and James D. Ewing	Oct.	18, 1808
Earps, Mourning and Macajah Carter	Jan.	22, 1850
Fannen, Nancy and Martin Moss	Nov.	20, 1823
Fannin, Jincy and William Allen	Dec.	9, 1829
Farmer, Betsy and Walker Williamson	May	2, 1833
Faulk, Sarah and John Roberts	Jan.	19, 1832
Faulkner, Ann and John Booth	Dec.	11, 1810
Faulkner, Elizabeth and Masten H. Bray	Apr.	17, 1828
Faulkner, Patsey and Lewis Phipps	Dec.	22, 1812
Ferguson, Peggy and Jesse C. Childers	Nov.	21, 1822
Figgs, Betsy and Henry Woodward	Aug.	24, 1806
Fincher, Mary and Robert Berry	Dec.	11, 1807
Fitts, Keziah and Henry P. Crittenden	Oct.	10, 1807
Fitts, Mary J. and Elijah J. Christian	Apr.	9, 1832
Flanningham, Permelia and Moses C. Fleming	Nov.	15, 1831
Fleming, Permelia and Mathew L. Fleming	Oct.	9, 1837
Fleming, Rosey and Richard Martin	Mar.	—, 1837
Floyd, Sarah Caroline and Henry W. Bobo	Aug.	29, 1833
Folk, Polly and Joseph Roberts	Jan.	1, 1822
Folley, Betsy and Daniel Brown	Dec.	5, 1816
Ford, Nancy and Thomas Pledger	Mar.	2, 1814
Ford, Mary and William Mannen	Dec.	4, 1827

Bride, Groom and Date

Ford, Nancy A. and John S. Harmon .... Apr. 28, 1831
Ford, Sarah Ann and William R. Duncan .... Dec. 23, 1848
Ford, Malinda and John M. Smith .... July 15, 1840
Ford, Mary Ann and Thomas McAllister .... Oct. 11, 1840
Ford, Irena E. and William Pledger .... Jan. 7, 1847
Forgus, Rachel and Samuel Grover .... July 14, 1808
Fortenberry, Lydia and Archibald Burton .... Jan. 1, 1826
Fortson, Elizabeth and Isaac Almond .... Dec. 20, 1821
Fortson, Rachel W. and Jonathan Harris .... Oct. 17, 1823
Fortson, Elizabeth and Simeon Maxwell .... Dec. 9, 1819
Fortson, Elizabeth and Henry P. Hoff .... Aug. 9, 1847
Fortson, Mahala and Edmond B. Tate .... Oct. 16, 1823
Fortson, Sarah and Thomas A. Thornton .... Oct. 27, 1823
Fortson, Polley and Samuel Turman .... Dec. 20, 1827
Fortson, Amanda N. M. and James Almond .... Oct. 20, 1831
Fortson, Jane M. and Dozier Thornton Jr. .... Sept. 25, 1834
Fortson, Rachel A. and Dr. N. Matthews .... Feb. 6, 1844
Fortson, Betsy and Abner Adams .... July 20, 1826
Foster, Delina and James W. Jones .... Oct. 30, 1828
Foster, Susan and James B. Bailey .... Dec. 13, 1832
Fowler, Matilda and Joseph C. Tibbs .... May 5, 1834
Fowler, Mary A. and Isaac N. Butler.. Aug. 17, 1848
Franklin, Dosha and Samuel Gibson .... Aug. 9, 1820
Franklin, Phebe and Richard Davis .... Feb. 14, 1811
Freeman, Nancy and Samuel Bowen .... Mar. 15, 1835
Gaines, Susannah H. and Harrison Warren .... Oct. 20, 1808
Gaines, Peggy and Thomas Johnston .... Jan. 18, 1816
Gaines, Sally and Thomas McMullan .... Dec. 15, 1815
Gaines, Martha and John Thomason .... Nov. 4, 1817
Gaines, Sally and Hezekiah Bailey .... Jan. 12, 1826
Gaines, Ann and John Craft Jr. .... Oct. 23, 1828
Gaines, Mary and John S. Hunt .... July 14, 1825
Gaines, Sarah and Nathan Johnson .... Feb. 9, 1832
Gaines, Drucilla and Willis Richardson .... Feb. 28, 1833
Gaines, Milly and Richard Bond .... Jan. 4, 1844
Gaines, Martha Ann and John W. Brown .... Aug. 6, 1840
Gaines, Nancy and John M. Craft .... Jan. 9, 1844
Gaines, Sarah Ann and William R. Haley .... Feb. 7, 1839
Gaines, Martha and William E. James .... Sept. 18, 1844
Gaines, Elizabeth and Elias McGee .... Jan. 12, 1847
Gaines, Agatha and Washington McMullan .... Oct. 22, 1840
Gaines, Katherine L. and Edwin J. Mann .... Feb. 15, 1844
Gaines, Mary Elizabeth and Francis G. Stowers .... Dec. 20, 1839
Gaines, Sarah and Thomas M. Turner .... Apr. 2, 1846
Gains, Jane and James Johnston .... Dec. 12, 1816
Garrett, Catherine and Garland Ellington .... Sept. 25, 1806
Gaulding, Elizabeth and Jesse M. Brawner .... Aug. 6, 1835
Gaulding, Pulutha J. and Peter W. Burton .... Dec. 15, 1840
Gaulding, Elizabeth and Jackson J. Edwards .... Aug. 28, 1840
Gaulden, Mary and Lesley G. Carter .... Dec. 25, 1831
Gay, Polly and Wiley Nelums .... May 12, 1826
Gibbs, Mildred and John W. Almond .... Sept. 7, 1831
Gibbs, Rachel and Isaac N. Bolton .... Mar. 2, 1823
Gibbs, Sarah C. and James T. Gardner .... May 12, 1849
Gibbs, Virginia and George McCord .... Oct. 23, 1845
Ginn, Nancy and Moses Bryant .... Jan. 19, 1817
Ginn, Alphia and Samuel Harcrow .... Sept. 21, 1817
Ginn, Elitha and Benjamin Pealor .... Mar. 18, 1819

Bride, Groom and Date

Bride, Groom	Date
Ginn, Polly and Isaac N. Pledger	Oct. 21, 1822
Ginn, Nancy and Nelson Burden	Dec. 19, 1833
Ginn, Delilah and John W. Burden	Sept. 8, 1842
Ginn, Judith R. and John M. Clark	Feb. 14, 1843
Ginn, Mary Ann and Charles Smith	Jan. 20, 1820
Glenn, Martha H. and Redick Smith	Feb. 24, 1831
Glynn, Martha T. and Charles Smith	Jan. 20, 1820
Goss, Nancy P. and John McCurry	Aug. 31, 1825
Goss, Ann E. and William Roebuck	June 6, 1841
Gordon, Flora and Benjamin Goss	Jan. 28, 1840
Gordon, Mary and Isham Goss	Mar. 5, 1840
Grace, Milly and Thomas Falherty	Dec. 2, 1809
Granger, Mahaha and Robert Evans	Feb. 17, 1807
Gragg, Jeannah and John Harris	Jan. 22, 1809
Gray, Jane and Walter H. Ward	Dec. 23, 1803
Gray, Martha N. and Elbridge Childers	Feb. 11, 1848
Gray, Patsy Ann and Octavious Spencer	Nov. 26, 1810
Gray, Ann and James Jack	Oct. 27, 1822
Gregg, Polly and Henry M. Saggs	May 9, 1820
Greenway, Sarah Caroline and John Terry	May 18, 1837
Greenway, Sally and John Wansley	Mar. 14, 1813
Greenway, Nancy T. and William W. Ward	Jan. 9, 1834
Greenway, Mary and John Ashworth	Dec. 12, 1834
Greenway, Milley and James Steedman	Jan. 4, 1839
Greenway, Milly A. and Reuben T. Hailey	Feb. 9, 1847
Greenway, Harriet and James Reynolds	Apr. 14, 1844
Greenway, Elizabeth and Thomas Steadman	Feb. 25, 1840
Greenwood, Eliz. and Elijah Crittenden	Nov. 14, 1814
Griffin, Sarah and James Charping	Sept. 3, 1846
Griffith, Ann and Benjamin Brown	Dec. 22, 1808
Grizzle, Rebecca and James Key	Oct. 17, 1810
Grizzle, Sarah and William Johnston	Nov. 17, 1802
Gross, Dama and William Spencer	Feb. 28, 1811
Gully, Nancy and Samuel Stinson	Sept. 24, 1816
Gulley, Elizabeth and Eli Snow	Jan. 22, 1824
Gulley, Harrada M. and Mannon J. Kerbee	Oct. 22, 1848
Gunter, Susan, Mrs. and Benson Hubbard	Dec. 28, 1830
Gunter, Bershaba and John White	June —, 1803
Gunter, Sarah and James Nash	May 8, 1836
Gunter, Louisa D. and George Stone	Oct. 28, 1847
Gunter, Sarah A. E. and Francis G. Stowers	Dec. 30, 1839
Gunter, Elizabeth and William White	Sept. 9, 1847
Hackney, Mary A. and Jacob W. Kidd	Sept. 5, 1815
Haines, Jane and John Dobbs	Sept. 14, 1810
Hale, Sally and Elisha Grinway	June 8, 1818
Hales, Betsy and Bailey Standeford	Apr. 23, 1810
Hailey, Elender and Wiley Abney	Apr. 19, 1832
Hailey, Tabathia and Nisbet L. Ward	Dec. 19, 1833
Haley, Elizabeth and Patrick McMullan	July 19, 1839
Haley, Mary and Peter Rucker	July 4, 1838
Haley, Matilda and John W. Terrell	Oct. 2, 1846
Haley, Caroline and Asa S. Bond	Dec. 31, 1845
Haley, Betsy and John A. Teasley	Dec. 18, 1828
Haley, Diadem and Frances Gaines	Dec. 17, 1829
Haley, Polly and James B. Adams	April 10, 1817
Haley, Tabitha and Easton Fortson	Dec. 26, 1819
Haley, Henrietta and John Crawford	Feb. 28, 1810
Haley, Nancy and Winston Adams	May 11, 1844

Bride, Groom and Date		
Haley, Sally and Henry Mann	June	26, 1809
Haley, Lucy and Benager Teasley	Oct.	31, 1822
Hall, Liddy and John Kirkpatrick	Dec.	16, 1837
Hall, Elizabeth and William F. Loftis	Dec.	19, 1850
Hall, Mary E. and Alexander Rucker	Dec.	21, 1848
Hall, Mary Jane and John Turner	Jan.	2, 1848
Hall, Permelia Ann and John T. Deadwyler	Feb.	15, 1844
Hall, Sarah F. and Henry B. Hulme	Dec.	29, 1850
Hall, Catherine and George Alexander	Jan.	22, 1835
Hall, Catherine and William W. Taylor	Nov.	14, 1825
Hall, Lucy and David Bray	Apr.	4, 1810
Hall, Sally and William Head	Dec.	4, 1811
Ham, Betsy and Betsy Ham	Mar.	4, 1828
Ham, Jane E. and James Penn	Oct.	2, 1839
Ham, Elizabeth and William Davis	Feb.	20, 1842
Ham, Martha and Benjamin Fortson	Mar.	13, 1844
Ham, Margaret and William Gaulding	Feb.	19, 1839
Ham, Nancy and Richard Fortson	Feb.	8, 1832
Ham, Susan and Easton Fortson	Feb.	10, 1831
Hambleton, Nancy and John Hones	Dec.	29, 1818
Hammond, Lucy and Richard Worrell	May	8, 1806
Hanna, Polly and Thomas Denny	Sept.	1, 1814
Hanley, Drucilla A. and Richard L. D. Crider	Sept.	30, 1847
Hansard, Milly and Eliah Hansard	Mar.	5, 1840
Hansard, Serena I. and James B. Adams	June	1, 1851
Hansard, Sarah and John Shackleford	Apr.	12, 1831
Hansard, Rhoda and Jeremiah Lewis	Dec.	30, 1829
Hansard, Elizabeth and James Butler	Dec.	16, 1823
Hansard, Jane and Patrick Butler Jr.	Jan.	16, 1823
Hansard, Mary A. and James S. Teasley	Oct.	17, 1822
Hanson, Nancy and Mitchell Dennard	May	19, 1833
Harbin, Ann and Aaron Scales	Nov.	19, 1808
Harbin, Margaret and John White	Dec.	14, 1815
Harbins, Nancy and Adam Brown	May	23, 1823
Harbin, Susannah and Drury Smith	Dec.	7, 1830
Hardman, Elizabeth, Mrs. and Joseph Brawner Jr.	Feb.	23, 1836
Hardy, Lucinda and William P. Hansard	Dec.	15, 1836
Hardy, Phobe and James A. Hansard	Aug.	23, 1833
Harman, Caroline and Oliver Roberts	Jan.	10, 1839
Harman, Susannah and Robert J. Pulliam		, 1848
Harman, Matilda and Thomas S. Carter	Feb.	21, 1839
Harman, Elizabeth and Richard Tyner Jr.	May	31, 1821
Harper, Royster E. and Richard M. Rice	Apr.	22, 1849
Harper, Nancy and Elzey B. Thornton	Apr.	13, 1826
Harper, Polly W. and Waller E. Haynes	Dec.	29, 1819
Harper, Elender and Ramson Worrell	Nov.	3, 1811
Harper, Nancy and Azmond Rucker	Feb.	4, 1810
Harper, Averilla and Joseph White	Aug.	28, 1806
Harper, Sarah and Jeremiah McMullan	Feb.	8, 1811
Harper, Polly and John Mann	Dec.	26, 1816
Harper, Elizabeth and John M. White	Dec.	26, 1816
Harris, Ruth C. and Matthew E. Pulliam	Dec.	13, 1846
Harris, Nancy and Isham R. Bonds	Nov.	12, 1832
Harris, Sarah N. and Jeptha Rosser	Oct.	6, 1825
Harris, Lucy and John M. Bond	Sept.	15, 1829
Harris, Nancy and Bennett Boler	Nov.	20, 1830
Harris, Ann R. and George R. Clayton	Oct.	7, 1830
Harris, Rebecca and Walker Hickman	Sept.	27, 1816

Bride, Groom and Date

Bride and Groom	Date
Harris, Edne and Isaac Dennard	Mar. 3, 1821
Harris, Mary Ann and Joseph Smith	Dec. 30, 1824
Harris, Frances R. and Jeptha Lewis	Sept. 30, 1823
Harrison, Betsy and William Richardson	Oct. 29, 1809
Hatcher, Nancy and Dudley Sale	Nov. 1, 1807
Hathcock, Martha and John Coker	Apr. 28, 1833
Hayes, Mary A. and James Allen	Jan. 7, 1837
Hayes, Tabitha and William Etichison	Nov. 5, 1808
Haynes, Elizabeth and Alfred S. Winn	Dec. 21, 1848
Haynes, Lettie E. and William Bowers	Dec. 21, 1837
Head, Jincy and John Ford	Jan. 1, 1808
Head, Sarah and William Adams	Jan. 11, 1819
Head, Nancy and John Garner	Feb. 14, 1811
Head, Lucinda and William J. Perryman	Sept. 30, 1823
Heard, Mary, Mrs. and Henry Bourne	Feb. 20, 1833
Heard, Sarah E. and Luther H. O. Martin	Dec. 17, 1846
Heard, Biddy and Simeon Henderson	Mar. 6, 1817
Heard, Sarah and James D. Jarrett	Jan. 18, 1825
Hearndon, Fanny and William H. Mann	Jan. 6, 1820
Hearndon, Elizabeth and John Gaines	Dec. 24, 1814
Hearndon, Catherine and Eppy White	May 11, 1815
Hearn, Prudence A. E. C. and Dunstan B. Verdell	July 8, 1847
Hearn, Sarah and Elijah W. Johnston	Aug. 17, 1852
Hearne, Sarah L. and George Shell	Dec. 19, 1815
Hearne, Jane E. and William D. Clark	Sept. 6, 1836
Henderson, Martha and Robert P. Dickerson	July 20, 1826
Henderson, Elizabeth and William James	Jan. 11, 1829
Henderson, Mary A. and Thomas J. Shepheard	Dec. 31, 1830
Henderson, Sarah E. and James H. Shockley	Mar. 26, 1831
Henderson, Cynthia and Drury Oglesby Jr.	Sept. 26, 1839
Henderson, Ann B. and James H. Gaines	May 2, 1822
Henderson, Sarah Ann and Pickett Shiflett	Jan. 23, 1828
Hendon, Ruth and Samuel James	June 6, 1806
Hendrick, Viney and Andrew Dillashaw	Dec. 21, 1848
Hendrick, Sally and Morris Skinner	Apr. 12, 1819
Hendrick, Eliza and Janus Gay	Apr. 2, 1830
Hendricks, Betsy and Barrett Orr	Sept. 24, 1807
Herndon, Elmira and George W. Brown	Sept. 28, 1837
Herndon, Margaret and John A. Brown	Feb. 23, 1849
Herndon, Eliz. and Elbert Brown	July 28, 1829
Hendry, Charlotte and Joseph Allen	Mar. 11, 1824
Hendry, Sophia and John Harbin	Nov. 17, 1814
Hendry, Nancy and Thomas Patterson	May 21, 1821
Henry, Polly and George M. Skinner	Feb. 28, 1816
Henry, Nancy and James David	Sept. 9, 1819
Henry, Sinthia and Wiley Ginn	Jan. 24, 1823
Henry, Sarah A. O. and Amos L. Vail	Feb. 16, 1843
Henry, Sarah and William Rice	Dec. 23, 1843
Henry, Martha and Pleasant Burnett	Oct. 3, 1831
Hewell, Sarah Ann and Joel Moon	Dec. 16, 1847
Hewell, Martha J. and Jacob D. Vanghan	Dec. 16, 1847
Hickman, Eliza and Fleming Malden	Feb. 18, 1830
Hicks, Elizabeth and Dixon Parham	Mar. 8, 1807
Hicks, Nancy and John Statham Jr.	Jan. 5, 1823
Hicks, Luncinda and John W. Raines	Dec. 18, 1828
Hicks, Jincy and Joseph G. Booth	Dec. 15, 1829
Higginbotham, Mary C. and Eppy Thornton	June 6, 1833
Higginbotham, Polly and Memory Thornton	Feb. 9, 1832

Bride, Groom and Date

Higginbotham, Frances and Starling M. Shackleford...........July 16, 1833
Higginbotham, Lucy and Robert B. Mann ....July 27, 1833
Higginbotham, Elizabeth P. and Alex F. Wimbish ....Dec. 18, 1828
Higginbotham, Ann R. and William Scales ....Dec. 16, 1828
Higginbotham, Clary G. and Thomas Hilley ....May 13, 1828
Higginbotham, Frances and Willis Eavenson ....Dec. 9, 1827
Higginbotham, Polly S. and Elijah B. Norman ....Apr. 3, 1821
Higginbotham, Mary and William Hightower ....Oct. 3, 1811
Higginbotham, Clarysa and Stephen Cheatham ....Apr. 5, 1810
Higginbotham, Martha and George Carter ....July 15, 1812
Higginbotham, Sarah and James C. Campbell ....Feb. 23, 1843
Higginbotham, Jerushia and James C. Campbell ....Dec. 1, 1846
Higginbotham, Martha and Thomas J. Bond ....Dec. 1, 1846
Higginbotham, Sarah and Tilmon Brawner ....Aug. 13, 1822
Highsmith, Henry (?) and Lindsey Parks ....Dec. 15, 1842
Highsmith, Nancy and Littleton Skelton ....Dec. 13, 1838
Highsmith, Nancy and Daniel M. Johnston ....Aug. 14, 1823
Highsmith, Sarah and William Myers ....Feb. 21, 1833
Hightower, Milly and William A. Anthony ....Nov. 15, 1827
Hightower, Bathashe and Janus Anderson ....Dec. 10, 1818
Hill, Milly and Sampel Fields ....July 29, 1813
Hill, Milly and William Jordan ....May 16, 1847
Hill, St. Abegail and Franklin Smith ....Apr. 11, 1847
Hill, Zele and John Smith ....Feb. 2, 1809
Hilley, Lettie and Rufus Barron ....June 13, 1841
Hilley, Ann E. and William E. Berrett ....May 4, 1837
Hilley, Elizabeth and William Barron ....Jan. 16, 1841
Hilley, Milly and John B. Wade ....Jan. 22, 1811
Hilley, Cora L. and Phillip A. Wilhight ....Feb. 22, 1848
Hinton, Cornelia and Lindsay Hendricks ....Nov. 12, 1844
Hinton, Prudence and James White ....Dec. 27, 1842
Holbrook, Peggy and William Crawford ....May 9, 1809
Holmes, Tabatha and Luke Leekroy ....Nov. 12, 1848
Holmes, Susan and William Robertson ....Feb. 19, 1838
Holton, Sally and Ignatius Dudley ....Dec. 26, 1819
Horn, Susannah and James Blake ....Oct. 28, 1813
Horton, Elizabeth and Edwin Kennebrew ....Sept. 15, 1829
Horton, Sarah and William T. Maxwell ....Sept. 29, 1830
Horton, Elizabeth and Levi Teasley ....Nov. 27, 1817
Horton, Lidey and Britton C. Tabor ....Apr. 9, 1832
Housley, Moriah L. and Thomas J. Asher ....Dec. 11, 1832
Houston, Mary Lucilla and John B. Sloan ....Sept. 2, 1847
Houston, Martha Ann and Rueben R. Wanslow ....Jan. 19, 1847
Howard, Lucinda A. and James Lofton ....Dec. 22, 1824
Howard, Polly and Larkin Higginbotham ....Jan. 15, 1815
Howell, Sarah and Peter Rhodelander ....Oct. 28, 1825
Hubbard, Sarah and Pleasant Rose ....Oct. 17, 1819
Hubbard, Emily and Thomas W. Dye ....Dec. 7, 1842
Hudson, Phebe L. and John W. Collins ....June 7, 1831
Hudson, Eliza C. and Amos W. Hammond ....Jan. 22, 1833
Hudson, Nancy and Moses Cash ....Sept. 6, 1808
Hudson, Elizabeth and Benjamin Cook ....Nov. 8, 1810
Hudson, Louisa E. and James Davis ....July 31, 1823
Hudson, Frances and Benjamin Flemming ....Sept. 18, 1821
Hudson, Martha P. and Alex McDonald ....Mar. 22, 1821
Hudson, Mary W. and John Arnold ....Dec. 15, 1825
Hudson, Nancy L. and William B. Childers ....Aug. 6, 1826
Hudson, Louisa and Alfred Hammond ....Jan. 24, 1826

Bride, Groom and Date

Hudson, Rebecca and James M. Bradford .... Dec. 27, 1849
Hughes, Mary J. and Roland Brown .... Nov. 17, 1835
Hulme, Susan A. and William T. Davis .... Dec. 28, 1843
Hulme, Catherine E. and William T. Herndon .... Nov. 30, 1848
Hulme, Mary and Lindsey Vawter .... Jan. 7, 1844
Hulme, Lucy and John W. Greenway .... Dec. 9, 1824
Hulme, Elizabeth and John L. Hinton .... Sept. 10, 1828
Hullum, Elizabeth and Thomas A. Smith .... Nov. 28, 1820
Hunt, Matilda C. and James S. Cunningham .... Dec. 22, 1846
Hunt, Sarah and John W. Davis .... Apr. 30, 1840
Hunt, Drucilla and Nicholas N. Adams .... Dec. 2, 1829
Hunt, Rebecca E. and William C. Banks .... Sept. 8, 1842
Hunt, Mary and William Page .... Nov. 28, 1836
Hunt, Nancy and Moses Cash .... July 6, 1824
Hunt, Nancy H. and Lawrence M. Adams .... Nev. 14, 1826
Ingraham, Polly and George Wynn .... Dec. 30, 1807
Irons, Catherine and Benjamin Childs .... Oct. 22, 1807
Irons, Elizabeth and Freeborn Luce .... Sept. 1, 1809
Irons, Theny and John Thurman .... Dec. 11, 1810
Irons, Theny and John Thurmond .... July 20, 1814

(Theney Irons and John Thurman or John Thurmond seem to have been twice married. First marriage record appearing in "Mixed Record Book 1809" at page 196 and second in "Will Book K" at page 164, office Ordinary of Elbert County).

Bride, Groom and Date

Jack, Jane H. and James D. Jarratt .... July 7, 1829
James, Elizabeth and Andrew Standifer .... Apr. 12, 1809
James, Nancy and Sinclair Self .... Feb. 24, 1820
James, Theodicia and Moses T. Flemming .... June 20, 1833
James, Emira and Elbert B. Adams .... Sept. 14, 1843
James, Eliza and Samuel Stanford .... Feb. 4, 1840
James, Susan and John Ramsey .... May 21, 1840
James, Martha E. and John T. Sayer .... Aug. 23, 1844
Jarratt, Eliza D. and Lewellen W. Hudson .... Oct. 22, 1828
Jenkins, Mary and John Thomason .... Dec. 22, 1830
Jenkins, Matilda and James Holmes .... May 13, 1838
Jenkins, Sarah and Archibald Rumsey .... Oct. 7, 1838
Jenkins, Betsy and Martin Hailey .... Mar. 3, 1808
Jones, Polly and Debton Harthcock .... Oct. 26, 1806
Jones, Patsey and Richard Hubbard .... Jan. 22, 1807
Jones, Milly and James Banks Jr. .... Sept. 23, 1811
Jones, Martha and John S. Foster .... Nov. 26, 1809
Jones, Elizabeth and John White .... Jan. 5, 1809
Jones, Eliza M. and Matthew T. Caldwell .... Dec. 22, 1814
Jones, Charlotte and Wiley W. Jones .... Dec. 1, 1814
Jones, Patcey and Lewis Jones .... Mar. 2, 1815
Jones, Lucinda and David Hudson .... Feb. 8, 1824
Jones, Settey and Heiram Jones .... Mar. 19, 1818
Jones, Rhoda and Davis Jones .... Dec. 31, 1820
Jones, Keziah and Edmond Jones .... Nov. 10, 1824
Jones, Mary J. and John W. S. Napier .... Aug. 3, 1824
Jones, Mary and James Patterson .... Aug. 17, 1824
Jones, Pressilla and James R. Saddler .... Jan. 8, 1824
Jones, Mellissa and James M. Willis .... Oct. 18, 1838
Jones, Martha and Abner T. Turman .... Dec. 9, 1822
Jones, Rebecca and James Edmondson .... Mar. 15, 1826

Bride, Groom and Date
Jones, Mary and Henry E. Nash ....Jan. 5, 1826
Jones, Ann and Fleming A. Alexander ....Oct. 7, 1831
Jones, Mahulda and Wiley W. Butler ....Dec. 19, 1834
Jones, Sarah and Thomas J. Alexander ....Dec. 14, 1842
Jones, Nancy and Peter Algood ....Aug. 17, 1848
Jones, Synthia and John R. Almond ....Sept. 24, 1835
Jones, Martha and Jeptha F. Brawner ....Dec. 15, 1836
Jones, Permelia and Henry Caldwell ....Oct. 22, 1842
Jones, Louisa V. and Francis A. Calhoun ....July 28, 1842
Jones, Keziah and Joseph Cunningham ....Nov. 11, 1844
Jones, Julia Ann and John Dyer ....Feb. 11, 1847
Jones, Mahulda and Cornelius Galloway ....July 25, 1843
Jones, Cernelia and Robert Hester ....Nov. 24, 1836
Jones, Mary E. and Middleton Hickman ....Dec. 17, 1839
Jones, Harriet and Thomas Jones ....Sept. 6, 1838
Jones, Susannah and James Kelley ....Dec. 23, 1836
Jones, Martha Ann and Larkin Ozley ....May 24, 1838
Jones, Sephia and Gibson Parrott ....Dec. 25, 1849
Jones, Margaret and William Pratt ....July 25, 1836
Jones, Mary Ann and Edward Rousey ....Nov. 8, 1829
Johnson, Eliz. B. and Benson Maxwell ....Dec. 23, 1828
Johnson, Ann, Mrs. and John Almond ....Dec. 8, 1831
Johnson, Nancy and James L. Brock ....Oct. 25, 1815
Johnson, Mary M. and Donald McDonald ....Feb. 1, 1844
Johnson, Sarah and Levingston Gaines ....Dec. 14, 1834
Johnson, Flora Ann and Asa Duncann ....Aug. 8, 1844
Johnson, Mary and Charles Fain ....Dec. 29, 1850
Johnson, Catherine and Jesse Maxwell ....Oct. 20, 1848
Johnson, Sarah and Junius B. Nash ....Dec. 28, 1845
Johnston, Emily and Weston Cleveland ....Feb. 2, 1809
Johnston, Frances and James B. Gaines ....June 6, 1808
Johnston, Polly and John Hulsey ....June 9, 1842
Johnston, Frances and Joseph Henderson ....June 6, 1809
Jordan, Elizabeth and Woodson Burden ....Jan. 9, 1842
Jordan, Jane and Reuben Ham ....Jan. 6, 1809
Jordan, Betsy and Elijah Maxwell ....Oct. 13, 1808
Jorden, Sarah and Samuel Unis ....July 5, 1824
Karr, Fanny and William Furguson ....July 9, 1821
Karr, Lucy and William Morgan ....Nov. 9, 1809
Kee, Sally and John Mercer ....Sept. 1, 1812
Kelly, Lucinda and Jesse Whitman ....Dec. 7, 1848
Kelly, Johan L., Mrs. and Thomas Roney ....Jan. 12, 1836
Kelly, Sarah A. P. and Drury Jones ....Oct. 13, 1836
Kelly, Amanda M. and James P. Stedey ....Aug. 18, 1831
Kelly, Cissale and James J. Hendricks ....July 5, 1837
Kennebrew, Mira and Thomas Fortson ....Feb. 9, 1821
Kennebrew, Icey and David Kerlin ....Mar. 23, 1824
Kennebrew, Finetty and Robert W. Lee ....Sept. 22, 1830
Kennedy, Elizabeth and William Harbin ....Dec. 18, 1817
Kerlin, Margaret and Andrew Larimore ....Dec. 22, 1820
Kerlin, Mildred and Charles Pressley ....Dec. 21, 1819
Kerlin, Barbara and William R. Rogers ....Dec. 2, 1847
Key, Milly and Humphrey Posey ....Jan. 3, 1811
Key, Susan and James Bell ....Jan. 22, 1819
Key, Mary and Joseph Bell ....July 13, 1823
Key, Jane and John P. Grizzle ....Oct. 20, 1820
Key, Lucy and Nathan Mattox ....Feb. 19, 1826
Key, Amiela A. and John M. Christian ....May 30, 1833

Bride, Groom and Date

Key, Lucinda W. and Thomas Stovall	Dec. 17, 1833
Key, Sarah and Shaler Oglesby	Dec. 11, 1838
Keys, Mary and Garrett Morris	Dec. 30, 1829
Keys, Anna A. and Jacob W. Tate	June 7, 1827
Kidd, Elizabeth H. and James H. Lewis	Dec. 3, 1820
King, Betsy and Joel Brawner	Dec. 9, 1816
King, Elizabeth P. and Volintine Gully	Jan. 8, 1818
King, Catherine W. and John L. Harris	May 7, 1817
King, Sukey and William King Jr.	Oct. 3, 1822
King, Catherine and William Loftis	Feb. 10, 1824
King, Jenny and John Griswell	Oct. 12, 1831
King, Frances E. and Lewis Kerbee	Nov. 20, 1832
King, Susannah and Jesse McGehee	May 3, 1832
King, Lucy and James M. Kerbee	May 15, 1838
Kirlin, Lucy and Benjamin Walker	Dec. 18, 1831
Lain, Charlotte and Leonard Smith	Dec. 29, 1837
Landham, Elizabeth and William Pickeral	Oct. 30, 1845
Lane, Eliza and William Fortson	Aug. 10, 1820
Laremore, Nancy and Thomas Hall	Oct. 14, 1828
Largent, Louranie and Thomas Faulk	Jan. 11, 1822
Lawlin, Tabitha and John Upshaw	Apr. 2, 1818
Ledbetter, Polly and James W. Roberts	June 28, 1812
Leseur, Patsy and Thomas Stephens	Mar. 11, 1823
Lewis, Elizabeth and James Fortson	Dec. 16, 1814
Lewis, Polly L. and Henry Moore	Jan. 9, 1815
Lewis, Esther and James Mann	Apr. 7, 1822
Lewis, Lucy and Bevery Moss	Dec. 18, 1823
Lewis, Sarah D. and Simeon Henderson	July 20, 1828
Lewis, Martha and Henry Shackleford	May 29, 1828
Lewis, Ann J. and William P. Nelms	June 9, 1833
Lewis, Hester and Willis Prewit	Oct. 25, 1832
Lindsay, Nancy K. and Marshall Durratt	Jan. 21, 1811
Lockhart, Mary and Simeon Clay	Feb. 21, 1808
Loftis, Mary A. and James C. Hall	June 25, 1850
Loftis, Sarah Ann and Willis Bond	Dec. 20, 1842
Loftis, Elizabeth and Thomas Hulme	May 16, 1844
Lollis, Polly and Benj. C. Higginbotham	Jan. 2, 1812
Lovingood, Emily E. and Thomas S. Davis	June 12, 1845
Lovingood, Olivia and Robert Hall	Jan. 29, 1839
Lovingood, Louisa M. P. and George H. Martin	Dec. 24, 1839
Lowrimore, Dolly and James Phillips	Sept. 12, 1838
Lowrimore, Elizabeth F. and William M. Reagan	Dec. 16, 1835
Lowry, Delilah and Hardie Brown	Jan. 5, 1809
Lunceford, Polly and William Roberts	May 11, 1807
Lunsford, Martha and Jackson McCoy	Dec. 22, 1836
Lunsford, Mary and James N. Jordan	May 23, 1841
Lunsford, Harriet and John Mewborn	Feb. 9, 1837
McAfee, Jane and John Crum	Aug. 14, 1846
McAllister, Elizabeth and Lewis Dockins	Mar. 4, 1840
McAllister, Phobe and John Smith	Mar. 9, 1840
McClary, Mary E. and James D. Ewin	Nov. 9, 1809
McCormac, Polly and William Peyton	Feb. 11, 1816
McCoy, Susan and Thomas Burton	Apr. 25, 1850
McCune, Peggy and John Ferrell	Oct. 1, 1807
McCurley, Melissa Ann and Thomas Stwrs	Dec. 9, 1841
McCurry, Katherine and Duncan McMartin	Mar. 8, 1806
McCurry, Nancy and Barney J. Dooley	Oct. 4, 1836
McCurry, Katherine and Edmond T. Penn	Sept. 4, 1828

Bride, Groom and Date

McCurry, Mary and Thomas J. Hickman ....Aug. 23, 1827
McCurry, ——— and Neal Johnson ....Jan. 21, 1831
McCurry, Mary and Levi Masters ....Jan. 3, 1829
McCurry, Flora and James Clark ....Dec. 6, 1832
McCurry, Flora and Charles W. Haynes ....Dec. 15, 1833
McCurry, Nancy and James E. Brown ....Dec. 12, 1839
McCurry, Sarah and Elbert J. Brown ....Mar. 27, 1846
McCurry, Frances and Lemarquis Carter ....Sept. 2, 1841
McCurry, Mary A. E. and James Herring ....Jan. 7, 1847
McCurry, Sarah C. and William Stephenson ....Jan. 6, 1848
McDonald, Mary and William H. Harper ....Aug. 31, 1837
McDonald, Mary A. and Jackson Kendley ....Jan. 9, 1848
McGarity, Mary and Joseph Vines ....Mar. 22, 1829
McGarity, Harriet and Daniel Cleveland ....Oct. 9, 1834
McGarity, Sarah and Robert Fowler ....Dec. 31, 1833
McGarity, Elizabeth and John Burnett ....Feb. 8, 1838
McGarity, Sarah and Stephen S. Carlton ....Nov. 10, 1842
McGehee, Elizabeth and Joseph Blackwell ....Mar. 3, 1812
McGehee, Lucy and Charles Hudson ....Oct. 30, 1811
McGehee, Mary and Jeptha Calloway ....Feb. 27, 1817
McGehee, Sarah and Benjamin Christler ....Dec. 11, 1824
McGehee, Louise Y. and Robert Hamilton ....Jan. 24, 1822
McGehee, Ann F. and William Jackson ....Dec. 13, 1825
McGehee, Sarah and Josiah W. Hill ....Sept. 22, 1831
McGuire, Cynthey and Richard Vawter ....Nov. 11, 1806
McGurire, Patsy and William Hilley ....May 30, 1812
McGuire, Susannah and Gardner Magesryth ....Mar. 5, 1810
McGuire, Permelia and Jesse Thompson ....Jan. 13, 1820
McKindley, Rachel D. and James Franklin Nunnelle Jr.....Dec. 1, 1836
McKinley, Elizabeth and Martin B. Dye ....Feb. 18, 1845
McKinney, Sally and Losten Powell ....Aug. 28, 1806
McLeroy, Frances and Benjamin Witcher ....Sept. 10, 1807
McMillan, Martha and Thomas H. White ....Mar. 19, 1840
McMillan, Matilda and Larkin Clark ....Oct. 1, 1844
McMullan, Sarah and Samuel W. Williford ....Nov. 17, 1840
McMullan, Mary T. E. and Robert M. Ward ....Oct. 3, 1844
McMullan, Susan and George M. Ward ....Dec. 21, 1848
McMullan, Elizabeth and James V. Richardson ....Oct. 24, 1836
McMullan, Elizabeth A. F. and Samuel Robertson ....May 25, 1835
McMullan, Elizabeth, Mrs. and James Prather ....Jan. 24, 1839
McMullan, Lavina and Moses Adams ....May 5, 1850
McMullan, Milly and Barnabas Barron ....Aug. 7, 1834
McMullan, Nancy and George McKerley ....May 12, 1831
McMullan, Levina and Archibald Smith ....Jan. 24, 1822
McMullan, Frances and Asa Dobbs ....Oct. 18, 1826
McMullan, Elizabeth and David Dobbs ....Apr. 29, 1819
McMullan, Elizabeth and John W. Allen ....Aug. 6, 1818
McMullan, Nancy and James Mills ....Sept. 24, 1812
McMullan, Elizabeth and Jesse Martin ....Feb. 26, 1824
McMullan, Dosha and Reuben Brown ....June 6, 1810
Mabry, Elizabeth and Ira Christian ....Aug. 3, 1837
Mann, Sarah K. and William E. Aiken ....Jan. 8, 1824
Mann, Sarah T. and Kindred Morgan ....Dec. 20, 1827
Mann, Judea J. and Richard Shepard ....Dec. 27, 1820
Mann, Sarah D. and James A. Conwell ....Dec. 19, 1843
Mann, Mary A. and George W. Hulme ....Apr. 7, 1836
Mann, Nancy C. and John H. Greenway ....Feb. 9, 1840
Manning, Lucy, Mrs. and Jachariah Evans ....Oct. 30, 1833

Bride, Groom and Date

Mantz, Frances, Mrs. and John Burton	Dec.	25, 1842
Marbury, Claricy and Alex Shearer	May	31, 1832
Martin, Phebe and Willis Collins	Dec.	2, 1810
Martin, Polly and Brown Dye	Apr.	23, 1809
Martin, Rebecca Joseph and J. L. Handy	Sept.	28, 1826
Martin, Jane, Mrs. and Larkin Johnson	Mar.	11, 1830
Mason, Jane and Joel Seymour	May	19, 1836
Mattox, Elizabeth and Zachariah H. Clark	Jan.	10, 1828
Mattox, Mary and Richard Gaulding	Dec.	16, 1834
Maxwell, Elizabeth and William McMullan	Sept.	3, 1812
Maxwell, Elizabeth and Ralph Banks Jr.	Dec.	22, 1818
Maxwell, Mary and Charles W. Christian	Jan.	18, 1827
Maxwell, Polly and Jaxson Oliver	June	6, 1826
Maxwell, Peggy A. and William Eaves	Apr.	29, 1829
Maxwell, Elizabeth and Allen Shackleford	Oct.	14, 1830
Maxwell, Malinda and James M. Cason	Mar.	2, 1848
Maxwell, Eliza and William H. Brown	Sept.	12, 1833
Maxwell, Ann and Abel Christler	Mar.	4, 1834
Maxwell, Mary and Isham Teasley	Dec.	6, 1833
Maxwell, Lucy and James J. Banks Jr.	Feb.	15, 1838
Maxwell, Elizabeth A. and Robert W. Brown	Oct.	6, 1836
Maxwell, Ann and Jesse G. Christian	Mar.	25, 1841
Maxwell, Ann and John Upshaw	Mar.	10, 1836
Means, Polly and Uriah Gandy	Mar.	20, 1811
Means, Jemima and Thomas Wanslow	Apr.	15, 1810
Means, Peggy and James Daniel	Dec.	23, 1817
Means, Frances and David Daniel		, 1812
Means, Elizabeth and Joshua Prewit	Dec.	2, 1826
Means, Martha and William T. Taylor	Dec.	14, 1831
Means, Sarah and James S. Harris	Dec.	3, 1833
Means, Rossie and Moses W. Bond	Nov.	15, 1835
Means, Frances R. and Henry T. Brown	Nov.	12, 1846
Means, Mary E. and John M. Brown	Dec.	15, 1846
Meret, Lotty and John Landers	Mar.	30, 1817
Merrett, Mary and Lewis Redwine	Jan.	14, 1817
Mewborn, Nancy and Thomas J. Teasley	Apr.	14, 1844
Mewborn, Clary and Benson Moss	May	30, 1844
Mewborn, Rebecca and William E. Ginn	Nov.	30, 1848
Micou, Margaret and Thomas N. Barrett	Sept.	23, 1811
Middleton, Polly and Caleb Tait	Dec.	25, 1806
Middleton, Martha N. and Middleton Woods	Sept.	16, 1807
Middleton, Nancy and Thomas J. Heard	Apr.	1, 1828
Milligan, Jane and John Cawhorn	July	9, 1810
Milligan, Polly Ann, Mrs. and Asa Coker	Oct.	12, 1820
Mills, Martha A and Benjamin G. Fortson	Oct.	8, 1839
Mills, Mary L. and Edwin K. Fortson	Dec.	7, 1845
Mills, Lucy Ann and Jasper Kennebrew	Sept.	15, 1836
Mires, Nancy and Silus Dobbs	Oct.	4, 1827
Mitchell, Elizabeth and George Pritchett	July	26, 1807
Mitchell, Polly and John Harper Sr.	Sept.	7, 1831
Mobley, Elizabeth and James Anderson	Dec.	24, 1818
Morgan, Sarah A. E. and Thomas Jones	Dec.	7, 1848
Morgan, Elizabeth Irvin and Thomas Ridgway	May	14, 1812
Morgan, Malinda and Howell Nunnelee	Feb.	4, 1818
Morris, Betsy and Wiley Webb	Nov.	9, 1816
Morris, Katherine and William S. Wiley	Mar.	7, 1830
Moss, Maetha A. and Joel Stogdhill	July	30, 1840
Moss, Susan and James M. Nelms	Nov.	18, 1825

Bride, Groom and Date

Moss, Nellie and Jarratt Underwood	Jan. 1, 1818
Morrison, Harriet E. and Wesley S. Bailey	Feb. 1, 1831
Morrow, Nancy and Joseph Smith	Aug. 24, 1809
Moon, Sarah, Mrs. and William Faulkner	Dec. 2, 1833
Moon, Baba and Jesse Bently	Feb. 16, 1830
Moon, Mary and Clement Wilkins	July 20, 1826
Moon, Susannah and David Power	Oct. 15, 1807
Moor, Sarah E. and David Wheelis	Oct. 3, 1847
Moore, Frances and William Johnson	Aug. 2, 1847
Moore, Mary and James Johnson	Dec. 19, 1839
Moore, Julia Ann and Thomas S. Stephens	Jan. 29, 1850
Moore, Martha and Robert H. Patterson	Dec. 5, 1824
Moore, Polly and Evan Thomas	Jan. 8, 1821
Moore, Agnes and Asa White	Dec. 26, 1816
Moore, Elizabeth and John Canning	Oct. 9, 1825
Moore, Frances and William Dupuy	Oct. 29, 1819
Murrah, Tabitha and James Sorrow	Mar. 16, 1809
Murry, Milly and Richard Adams	Dec. 30, 1819
Naish, Jincy and James F. Nunnelee	Sept. 28, 1810
Naish, Fanny and Samuel Allgood	Nov. 10, 1814
Naish, Martha and Daniel Butler	Sept. 29, 1814
Nash, Permelia and Henry Martin	Apr. 6, 1828
Nash, Sarah and Parker Slay	——, 1832
Nash, Nancy A. and Joseph B. Dye	May 10, 1840
Nash, Susan R. and John A. Oliver	Oct. 26, 1847
Nash, Permelia and Henry Martin	Apr. 6, 1828
Neal, Martha L. and Jonathan Watson	Aug. 8, 1838
Nelmes, Mary M. and James M. Smith	Dec. 21, 1842
Nelms, Phobe and John T. Dickerson	May 23, 1837
Nelms, Frances C. and William Y. Hill	Feb. 4, 1841
Nelms, Elizabeth M. and Daniel Mason	Oct. 3, 1837
Nelms, Susan A. and David W. Sayre	May 26, 1839
Nelms, Priscilla B. and John Seals	Dec. 17, 1835
Nelms, Mary and Barnett Hendricks	Jan. 22, 1832
Nelms, Orpha and William Hall	Feb. 20, 1829
Nix, Sally and John Nix	Jan. 15, 1811
Nix, Ann W. and Gideon B. Andrews	May 11, 1836
Nix, Mary O. and Nelson Phillips	June 30, 1843
Nolan, Nancy A. and Suddeth Toles	Aug. 3, 1820
Norman, Sarah A. and Jeptha W. Norman	Dec. 18, 1842
Norman, Mary B. F. and James R. Teasley	May 1, 1845
Nunnelee, Charlotte C. and William A. Bentley	Jan. 23, 1812
Nunnelee, Sarah and William Bolton	Dec. 7, 1819
Nunnelee, Susannah W. and McKinney Holyness	Jan. 22, 1823
Nunnelee, Ann F. and John Hubbard	Dec. 17, 1818
Nunnelee, Sophia and Henry P. Mattox	Oct. 1, 1833
Nunnelee, Maria, Mrs. and Hudson J. Nash	Dec. 22, 1831
Nunnelee, Sara M. and Robert P. Taylor	Nov. 17, 1839
Nunnelle, Susan A. and James M. Cole	Nov. 15, 1838
Oglesby, Rhoda and Hutson Upshaw	Aug. 3, 1823
Oglesby, Martha and Henry W. Stephens	Oct. 7, 1824
Oglesby, Sarah and Westley Pledger	Jan. 18, 1821
Oglesby, Ann F. and James Johnston	Aug. 15, 1822
Oglesby, Sarah and Lindsay Johnston	Aug. 24, 1823
Oglesby, Lucindey and William C. Morgan	Mar. 30, 1819
Oglesby, Nancy and Johnston Pledger	July 6, 1820
Oglesby, Sarah and Alfred Anderson	Nov. 17, 1842
Oglesby, Antionette and Asa E. Faulkner	Oct. 25, 1838

Bride, Groom and Date
Oglesby, Lucinda and William M. Settles .... June 7, 1849
Oglesby, Martha and John Shackleford .... June 11, 1844
Oglesby, Mary and Claborn Webb .... Oct. 7, 1841
Oliver, Sarah and Daniel Bird .... Dec. 26, 1806
Oliver, Milly T. and Asa Mann .... Sept. 6, 1832
Oliver, Elizabeth Ann, Mrs. and Isaac N. Davis .... Oct. 15, 1829
Oliver, Nancy Ann and William Hulme .... Oct. 8, 1826
Oliver, Judith and Henry Banks .... Feb. 8, 1825
Oliver, Malinda and Stephen A. Mann .... July 8, 1824
Oliver, Mary Ann and William Hudson .... June 13, 1824
Oliver, Mary and John D. Bibb .... Feb. 6, 1812
Oliver, Tabitha and Bartley C. Higginbotham .... Jan. 11, 1811
Oliver, Mary W. and Willis Banks .... Oct. 3, 1819
Oliver, Eliza S. and Jet Thomas .... Dec. 29, 1836
Oliver, Mariah W. and Asa Brown .... Nov. 1, 1821
Oliver, Milly T. and Samuel C. Dailey .... Feb. 14, 1822
Oliver, Mary R. and Francis Hilley .... Feb. 24, 1820
Oliver, Martha and Benjamin W. Heard .... Jan. 5, 1848
Oliver, Martha and David Hudson .... Sept. 19, 1817
Ousley, Martha and James Bell Jr. .... Sept. 13, 1829
Owen, Elizabeth and Griffith Spencer .... Sept. 30, 1813
Owens, Susannah and William Maxwell .... Dec. 9, 1819
Owens, Martha and Zimri Tate .... May 14, 1817
Ozeley, Gilly and Samuel Sorrow .... Apr. 22, 1841
Ozley, Frances and Absolom S. Davis .... Sept. 20, 1847
Ozley, Sarah and John Dye .... Dec. 11, 1845
Ozley, Martha and Asa Hall .... Jan. 7, 1845
Pace, Anny and Robert Rice .... Nov. 6, 1809
Pace, Nancy and Burkett Wellborn .... Sept. 16, 1818
Palmore, Martha Ann and George Smith .... Feb. 19, 1841
Parham, Lucy and William S. Booth .... Feb. 12, 1829
Parham, Sarah and David S. Smith .... Nov. 7, 1841
Parham, Lucy and James Morris .... Sept. 8, 1811
Parks, Mary and David Stufle .... July 7, 1838
Parks, Elizabeth and Thomas Highsmith .... Aug. 12, 1824
Parrott, Juda and William Foster .... Jan. 31, 1826
Pate, Elizabeth and John Burton .... Nov. 25, 1813
Pate, Mahala and Edward Byrd .... May 5, 1816
Pathro, Hetty and Thomas Jones .... Oct. 29, 1810
Patrick, Cazady and Washington Coker .... Feb. 28, 1843
Patterson, Lucy and Henry S. Bailey .... Nov. 22, 1827
Patterson, Mary and Robert T. Griffith .... Nov. 12, 1830
Patterson, Elizabeth and William B. Nelms .... Dec. 20, 1832
Patterson, Becky and Fleming Wanslow .... Dec. 13, 1832
Patterson, Eliza A. and William J. Henderson .... Nov. 7, 1839
Patterson, Martha and James Roper .... Oct. 18, 1849
Patterson, Gilley and Joel Snow .... Nov. 25, 1815
Patterson, Juliana and William G. Alexander .... Mar. 16, 1824
Patterson, Nancy and Thomas S. Cook .... Dec. 22, 1818
Payne, Nancy and Benjamin Thornton .... Sept. 16, 1819
Payton, Elizabeth and George W. Christian .... Jan. 5, 1842
Peeler, Sarah and Andrew B. Ginn .... Mar. 24, 1845
Peeler, Susan and John Hancock .... Aug. 6, 1843
Pemelton, Rachel and Henry Smith .... Mar. 1, 1821
Pendleton, Elizabeth and William Bell .... Oct. 31, 1841
Penn, Harriet and Benjamin J. Penn .... Dec. 3, 1834
Penn, Sarah J. and William W. Smith .... May 26, 1831
Penn, Winney and Thomas A. Smith .... Sept. 15, 1833

Bride, Groom and Date
Penn, Frances and Jacob B. Smith .... Aug. 10, 1839
Penn, Lucinda and William Threlkeld .... Oct. 7, 1840
Penn, Lucey and John Oliver .... Apr. 17, 1816
Penn, Polly and Lachlan McCurry .... Jan. 21, 1819
Perkin, Nancy and Robert S. Barr .... Jan. 20, 1822
Perryman, Eliza and Samuel Edmondson .... Jan. 1, 1827
Phelps, Polly and William Hicks .... Nov. 23, 1809
Phelps, Malinda and Wyatt Hicks .... Feb. 8, 1824
Phelps, Fanny and Stephen Moon .... Jan. 20, 1820
Phelps, Mary and Jesse Moon .... Oct. 23, 1823
Phillips, Unity and John Shelman .... Aug. 3, 1818
Phipps, Mary A. H. and Isham Smith .... Oct. 25, 1838
Pickeral, Mary and James W. Allgood .... Jan. 20, 1850
Pickerall, Elizabeth and William J. Tate .... Apr. 15, 1845
Pledger, Elizabeth T. and George Sanders .... Sept. 22, 1846
Pledger, Polly and George Scales .... Oct. 5, 1815
Pledger, Elizabeth and John Adams .... Feb. 7, 1821
Pledger, Eliza O. and John P. Beard .... Feb. 5, 1818
Pledger, Susannah and Daniel Gartman .... Sept. 26, 1816
Poelston, Margaret and James Walker .... Mar. 16, 1816
Pollard, Silvey and James Denton .... Feb. 20, 1810
Pollard, Polly and William B. Braswell .... Oct. 26, 1812
Pollard, Sally and Nicholas White .... Oct. 25, 1812
Powel, Mitty and Merideth Runnels .... Apr. 26, 1821
Powel, Creasy and Berry Runnels .... Mar. 15, 1822
Powell, Nancy and John Johnston .... Jan. 20, 1820
Powell, Sarah Ann and Elias J. Dyer .... July 5, 1849
Powell, Elizabeth and Chaney Bobo .... Oct. 17, 1847
Powell, Sarah and Hugh Harcrow .... July 20, 1834
Powell, Lucy and James B. Martin .... June 19, 1828
Powell, Phobe and Richard McAlister .... July 14, 1828
Powell, Mitty and William Prothro .... Nov. 29, 1827
Powell, Joicee and David Harcrow .... July 20, 1834
Powell, Amea and William Dyer .... Aug. 19, 1849
Powell, Louisa and Levi C. Galloway .... Sept. 16, 1847
Powell, Elizabeth and Lewis B. Shiflett .... Feb. 8, 1838
Powell, Mary and James Vickery .... July 19, 1849
Power, Anney and Reuben Ham .... June 15, 1809
Pope, Matilda and John Wm. Walker .... Jan. 30, 1810
Prather, Jane S. and Briggs Bowman .... Mar. 25, 1841
Prather, Frances E. and Henry W. Cole .... May 21, 1846
Pratt, Mary Jane and Reece Gray .... Sept. 10, 1829
Pressley, Martha Ann and Richard Thornton .... Feb. 8, 1849
Pressley, Matilda and Thomas Dye .... Sept. 1, 1841
Prewit, Rosannah and John McConnic .... Jan. 17, 1819
Prickett, Fanny and John M. White .... Dec. 19, 1826
Prothro, Mary and Jesse Dobbs .... Aug. 31, 1824
Prothro, Ann and James Johnston .... Aug. 26, 1825
Prothro, Elizabeth and Josiah Dobbs .... Nov. 18, 1830
Pryor, Permelia and William Landrum .... Feb. 24, 1846
Pugh, Sarah Ann and John Stephenson .... Feb. 11, 1838
Pulliam, Rebecca and William Kerbee .... June 29, 1836
Pulliam, Lucy and Thomas S. Thornton .... Nov. 2, 1843
Pulliam, Sarah and Micajah Burden .... Sept. 14, 1830
Pulliam, Mary and John W. Sandridge .... Feb. 23, 1830
Pulliam, Franky and William Garner .... Jan. 27, 1808
Pulliam, Rebecca and Stephen White .... June 6, 1808
Ragland, Frances and Edward Davis .... Feb. 19, 1807

Bride, Groom and Date

Name	Date
Ragland, Frances and William Oliver	Dec. 27, 1807
Ragland, Sarah and William Thompson	Mar. 3, 1814
Raglin, Tabitha and Micajah Clark	July 17, 1808
Raines, Catherine and Mason Bryant	Dec. 5, 1816
Raines, Martha and Demsey Brown	Jan. 11, 1820
Ray, Elizabeth and Charles T. Berryman	Oct. 14, 1840
Raymond, Sarah D. and Terrell Speed	Feb. 22, 1829
Reed, Reily Laura and Christopher Oliver	Oct. 1, 1839
Reily, Amely and William Bailey	June 3, 1811
Reynolds, Polly and Stephen Williamson	Mar. 4, 1831
Reynolds, Flora and John D. Adams	Aug. 20, 1850
Rhodland, Phobe and Samuel Allen	Nov. 25, 1819
Rhodlander, Patsy and Rugen Allen	July 17, 1821
Rice, Suckey and Bennett Dooly	Dec. 5, 1816
Rice, Sarah C. and William Huddleston	Nov. 13, 1817
Rice, Sarah and Robert Steel	Jan. 3, 1828
Rice, Elizabeth and Henry A. Carlton	Oct. 25, 1832
Rice, Mary Ann and Charles Andrew	Nov. 19, 1843
Rice, Sarah Ann and Thomas J. Crittenden	Dec. 5, 1850
Rich, Sarah A. E. and John F. Edwards	Oct. 11, 1838
Rich, Elizabeth and Herbert Hammond	May 7, 1821
Rich, Sophia and James Nix	Jan. 2, 1830
Rich, Sarah and Elijah Berry	Feb. 8, 1811
Rich, Mary and Isham Morgan	1816
Richardson, Crissa and Sinclair McMullan	Jan. 11, 1824
Richardson, Sarah and Robert Vernon	Aug. 7, 1845
Richardson, Martha and Emeziah Heaton	Nov. 15, 1848
Richardson, Milly and James L. Hunt	Mar. 6, 1846
Richardson, Mary and Mann Shiflett	Nov. 17, 1842
Richardson, Prudence, Mrs. and Benjamin Brown	Apr. 3, 1823
Richardson, Patsy and James Head	Dec. 25, 1810
Richardson, Prudence T. and Leroy Upshaw	May 14, 1814
Ridgway, Tabitha and John Woods	Mar. 27, 1817
Ridgway, Nancy T. and William T. O. Cook	Sept. 16, 1828
Ridgway, Polly and Levi Stinchcomb	July 27, 1806
Ridgway, Sally and Drury Bradley	Sept. 9, 1809
Riley, Sarah and William G. Thomason	Oct. 12, 1845
Roberts, Mary and Thomas Dodds	May 7, 1822
Roberts, Patsy and Rolan Lunsford	Jan. 5, 1826
Roberts, Martha and Edward R. White	Jan. 8, 1846
Roberts, Susan A. D. and John Rubens	Sept. 23, 1844
Roberts, Mary and Watson D. Page	May, — 1840
Roberts, Nancy and Alexander McCurry	May 14, 1850
Roberts, Susan W. and James F. Algood	Jan. 8, 1839
Roberts, Drucilla and Francis M. Brown	Dec. 20, 1849
Roberts, Milly A. and William C. David	Sept. 18, 1845
Roberts, Caroline and Samuel Ham	July 11, 1844
Robertson, Elizabeth and Edward F. Ferrington	Feb. 25, 1808
Rodgers, Mary and William Joseph Adams	Dec. 10, 1844
Roebuck, Frances and Thomas W. Oliver	Dec. 21, 1815
Roebuck, Ann and Benjamin Stowers	Oct. 14, 1813
Roebuck, Harriet and Lewis Stowers	Oct. 14, 1813
Roebuck, Eliza L., Mrs. and Johnston Maley	Jan. 9, 1831
Roebuck, Sarah C. and Benjamin Goss	June 3, 1830
Roebuck, Mildred and Thomas Johnston	May 4, 1826
Rogers, Polly and William S. Bragg	Feb. 24, 1808
Rooks, Elizabeth and John Mason	June 11, 1840
Rose, Betsy and Jesse Ansley	Sept. 30, 1807

Bride, Groom and Date

Rouze, Elizabeth and James Prather ....May 3, 1825
Rowsey, Clary and Gabriel Booth ....May 9, 1809
Rowsey, Nancy and William M. Prather ....Nov. 17, 1825
Rowsey, Rhoda and Absolom Gray ....Oct. 21, 1834
Rowzee, Merial K. and Peter Cleveland ....Mar. 28, 1833
Rowsau, Sarah and Jesse Tatum ....Apr. 9, 1829
Royal, Levity and Henry Hale ....Mar. 5, 1816
Royal, Averilla and Wesley Smith ....Apr. 18, 1820
Royster, Martha and Thomas J. Farrar ....Nov. 2, 1824
Rucker, Catherine and David O. White ....May 6, 1834
Rucker, Mildred and Wm. Bowling White ....Jan. 8, 1833
Rucker, Margaret and Gaines T. Alexander ....Aug. 24, 1843
Rucker, Sarah Ann and Andrew Brown ....Sept. 19, 1839
Rucker, Olivia and Frederick D. Lowry ....Dec. 15, 1836
Rucker, Serepta and William Maxwell ....Jan. 26, 1837
Rucker, Mary A. and Moses E. Mills ....Dec. 12, 1843
Rucker, Jane and James K. Love ....Apr. 25, 1808
Rucker, Lucy and William Gaar ....May 20, 1810
Rucker, Nancy and James Hamilton ....July 30, 1812
Rucker, Elizabeth and John Childs ....Dec. 20, 1812
Rucker, Elizabeth and William H. Alston ....Jan. 25, 1820
Rucker, Judith and William B. Clark ....Jan. 22, 1822
Rucker, Frances and Standley Jones ....July 24, 1823
Rucker, Mary and George Gaar ....Mar. 10, 1814
Rucker, Milly, Mrs. and Larkin Johnston ....July 19, 1827
Rucker, Manda B. and Willis B. Jones ....July 24, 1829
Rucker, Elizabeth H. and Middleton C. Upshaw .....Feb. 2, 1830
Rucker, Hannah and Thomas Black ....Sept. 25, 1832
Rucker, Martha E. and Richard J. D. Durrett ....Jan. 8, 1833
Ruff, Nancy and Charles W. Christian ....June 6, 1807
Ruff, Polly and David Denay ....Dec. 2, 1807
Ruff, Tabitha and Jesse Roberts ....May 9, 1821
Runnells, Charity and Elisha Ginn ....Sept. 9, 1823
Russell, Temperence and John A. Denny ....Oct. 7, 1845
Saddler, Mary M. and Solomon S. Jones ....Sept. 21, 1837
Saddler, Mary E. and Jeptha W. Bradley ....Jan. 1, 1846
Saddler, Elizabeth and Richard S. Hall ....Feb. 10, 1848
Salmons, Margaret and Abraham Walters ....Dec. 13, 1827
Salmons, Hannah N. and William H. Edwards ....Sept. 28, 1843
Samuel, Ann and George Hudson ....Jan. 9, 1816
Sanders, Winey and Lobard Moore ....Aug. 17, 1809
Sanders, Polly and Britton Stamps ....Dec. 19, 1810
Sandridge, Elizabeth L. and Thomas O. Kelley ......Dec. 8, 1829
Sandridge, Charity and Dreadzil Pace ....Oct. 4, 1825
Sartain, Fanny and John Wilson ....Feb. 20, 1820
Sartain, Patsy and Isaac Davis ....July 3, 1823
Satterwhite, Milley and John M. White ....Dec. 19, 1826
Saunders, Eliza D. and Zachariah Colly ....Mar. 20, 1809
Saxon, Jincey and Blackman Burton ....Mar. 30, 1806
Saxon, Sarah C. and Abraham Spencer ....Sept. 1, 1846
Saxon, Edna M. A. and Mathias Perrin ....Dec. 3, 1840
Sayer, Mary and Archie W. Cowen ....Aug. 19, 1849
Sayre, Margaret M. and Andrew Rembert ....Feb. 12, 1819
Sayre, Mahetable C. and Hugh Taylor ....Nov. 30, 1813
Sayre, Sarah and Robert F. Jones ....Mar. 30, 1851
Scales, Hester Ann and Robert A. King ....Sept. 30, 1847
Scales, Mariah and Samuel Wells ....Jan. 5, 1836
Scales, Susannah and Howard Cash ....Nov. 21, 1808

Bride, Groom and Date

Bride and Groom	Date
Scales, Margaret M. and Barnabas Kelly	Dec. 30, 1828
Scales, Mary and Robert E. Biard	Jan. 23, 1840
Scales, Elizabeth and William I. Christian	Apr. 20, 1839
Shackleford, Judey M. and Mordeci Alexander	Aug. 7, 1817
Schofield, Emaly and Fenton Cook	Jan. 10, 1819
Seamore, Elizabeth and William R. Hathcock	Apr. 21, 1839
Self, Polly and Henry Dollar	Sept. 1, 1817
Selfridge, Susanna and Roderick Harper	Feb. 10, 1806
Sewell, Sarah and Thomas C. Ham	Dec. 20, 1849
Sewell, Mary M. and William T. Nelms	June 4, 1844
Shackleford, Elizabeth and Arnold Thomason	Oct. 27, 1844
Shackleford, Mary J. and John Harris	Dec. 6, 1820
Shackleford, Winney and Garland Jones	Dec. 7, 1820
Shackleford, Sarah H. and William T. Fortson	Nov. 22, 1821
Shackleford, Nancy J. and William Thornton	July 20, 1826
Sharpton, Sarah and Andrew J. Griffin	Oct. 27, 1844
Shepard, Lucinda D. and Fenton Hall	Sept. 26, 1833
Shepard, Nancy and William McCoy	Mar. 18, 1816
Shepard, Sarah and William S. Chambers	Nov. 18, 1819
Shepard, Claricy and Bazel Pace	Sept. 28, 1815
Sheperd, Elizabeth and John Chambers	Dec. 29, 1814
Sheppard, Hetty and Samuel Pledger	Sept. 28, 1809
Sheppard, Elizabeth and James Scroggins	July 31, 1851
Shaw, Elizabeth and James D. Smith	Nov. 17, 1851
Shiflett, Eliza and Tinsley Powell	Mar. 17, 1831
Shiflett, Mary and William D. Allen	Feb. 2, 1850
Shiflett, Dosha and William Hunt	Oct. 3, 1839
Shiflett, Milly and William McCurley	Nov. 22, 1849
Shiflett, Polly and Nicholas Pritchett	Mar. 18, 1830
Shiflett, Lucy and Andrew J. Beggs	Nov. 14, 1850
Shiflett, Elizabeth and Daniel Chapman	Oct. 30, 1844
Shoemaker, Lucinda and James M. Henry	Jan. 3, 1836
Skelton, Mary and Basil Williamson	July 28, 1811
Skelton, Elithia and Obed M. Brown	Nov. 3, 1844
Skelton, Dicey and James L. Brown	Aug. 22, 1819
Skelton, Elizabeth and Thomas M. McGuire	Mar. 27, 1828
Skelton, Sally and Ambrose Dollar	Mar. 28, 1811
Skelton, Maria and Neal Johnson	Jan. 11, 1846
Skelton, Ann and David W. McGuire	Dec. 25, 1835
Skelton, Mary A. F. and Thomas J. Ray Jr.	Aug. 1, 1844
Skinner, Sucey and William Henry	Mar. 20, 1817
Skinner, Polly and John Henry	Dec. 25, 1818
Skinner, Sally and Matthew Price	May 12, 1824
Skinner, Piety and Samuel Willis	Jan. 8, 1807
Smith, Cyrena A. and Elijah Dobbs	Dec. 12, 1830
Smith, Jemima W. and James Brawner	Mar. 26, 1833
Smith, Sarah T. and Francis W. Key	Jan. 8, 1832
Smith, Mary E. and Thomas M. Hilly	June 2, 1848
Smith, Nancy and Albert Lord	Jan. 25, 1851
Smith, Selah and Eli Benedict	Dec. 18, 1828
Smith, Polly and William S. Nix	Mar. 2, 1820
Smith, Betsy and Joel Thomas	Nov. 3, 1816
Smith, Julia Ann and William E. Prather	Jan. 23, 1840
Smith, Elizabeth and Joseph D. Reed	Sept. 18, 1846
Smith, Mary M. and Julius P. Smith	Dec. 23, 1847
Smith, Betsy and Abraham Moss	Oct. 5, 1809
Smith, Elizabeth and Thomas G. Anderson	Jan. 1, 1826
Smith, Martha and Patrick Chislom	Dec. 5, 1837

Bride, Groom and Date

Smith, Antoinette and John H. Downer ....Apr. 18, 1850
Smith, Mary H. and William Glenn ....Oct. 6, 1847
Smith, Matilda and Loranzey I. Hansard ....Jan. 28, 1834
Smith, Lucy Ann and James Hill ....June 1, 1837
Smithwick, Mary and James Milligan ....Aug. 10, 1815
Snellings, Hannah and Peter Butler ....Jan. 21, 1808
Snellings, Mary and Richard Burton ....Dec. 24, 1818
Snellings, Martha and John H. Hudson ....Dec. 19, 1824
Snellings, Rebecca and John Taylor ....Jan. 7, 1821
Snellings, Elizabeth and David Bell ....Jan. 6, 1829
Snellings, Sophia and Bolen B. Clark ....Feb. 21, 1833
Snellings, Mary B. and Enoch Bell ....Dec. 22, 1836
Snellings, Elizabeth and Joseph Brawner ....Dec. 24, 1835
Spears, Elizabeth and Dudley Simmons ....Sept. 1, 1813
Spencer, Sally and Lewis Saxon ....Jan. 14, 1806
Staples, Malitia and Robert Denny ....Feb. 2, 1815
Staples, Lucy and Jesse Brown ....Jan. 17, 1811
Staples, Barbara and Edward Denny ....June 30, 1812
Staples, Tabitha and John Moon ....Aug. 15, 1811
Staples, Anny and Jacob Moon ....Nov. 28, 1816
Staples, Martha and Robert Tucker ....Dec. 6, 1824
Stark, Sarah A. N. and Guilford Cade ....Mar. 22, 1838
Statham, Polly and John Brown ....Dec. 12, 1811
Statham, Nancy and Joshua Ginn ....Nov. 3, 1825
Steedman, Melina and Elijah Ashworth ....Aug. 6, 1835
Steedman, Nancy and John Ashworth ....Sept. 21, 1841
Stephens, Jane J. and Dr. N. Poss ....Sept. 3, 1846
Stephens, Betsy and Shadrack Davis ....July 20, 1806
Stinchcomb, Caty and Burley Andrew ....Jan. 15, 1818
Stinchcomb, Mahulda and John Hall ....Jan. 20, 1848
Stinchcomb, Elizabeth Ann and Thomas Phelps Jr. ....Dec. 24, 1846
Stinchcomb, Mary C. and Abdah Ridgway ....Dec. 17, 1839
Stinchcomb, Betsy and Gabriel Booth ....July 26, 1806
Stinchcomb, Polly C. and Joseph Sewell ....Nov. 1, 1827
Stinchcomb, Lucy and Simeon Hall ....July 29, 1828
Stinchcomb, Frances R. and Joseph S. Chambers ....Aug. 22, 1822
Stodghill, Martha C. and John Barnes ....Sept. 6, 1827
Stone, Rosanna H. and Silas Holtzclaw ....Mar. 22, 1821
Stone, Malinda and James C. Harmon ....Nov. 1, 1849
Stone, Sally and Jesse C. Wallis ....Sept. 14, 1813
Stone, Lenah B. and Jesse Wall ....Nov. 13, 1835
Stone, Eliza and Gideon Holmes ....Aug. 17, 1841
Stowers, Judith M. and Marion McMullan ....Aug. 14, 1845
Stowers, Frances and Lewis McMullan ....Jan. 28, 1808
Stowers, Susannah and Moses McCurley ....Feb. 5, 1824
Strickland, Martha and Richard H. Bennett ....Dec. 27, 1838
Struten, Canadada and William Kirkpatrick ....Feb. 23, 1838
Sullivan, Moddy W. and Hugh A. Wiley ....Feb. 22, 1833
Sullivan, Mariah and John Shelton ....Jan. 8, 1828
Suttles, Nancy L. and John M. Smith ....Nov. 27, 1810
Swet, Anna and Francis Cook Jr. ....Nov. 12, 1809
Swindle, Catherine and Samuel W. Smith ....Dec. 26, 1833
Tait, Elizabeth P. and John Middleton ....June 27, 1816
Tait, Mary J. and Enos Tait ....Aug. 26, 1806
Tait, Charity and John Alston ....Oct. 4, 1810
Tait, Susannah and Zimri Tate ....Oct. 28, 1809
Tait, Rachel and Richmond Harris ....Sept. 18, 1813
Tait, Frances and David Tait ....Nov. 21, 1816

Bride, Groom and Date

Tait, Rachel M. and William T. Harris	Dec. 26, 1848
Tate, Louisa A. and Lemuel Baker	Dec. 24, 1833
Tate, Jane and William A. Johnson	Dec. 29, 1831
Tate, Mary L. and Seaborn Owens	Dec. 20, 1849
Tate, Sarah Y. and Anderson Riddle	Feb. 21, 1815
Tate, Lucy and Benjamin Andrew	Dec. 18, 1817
Tate, Susan and Henry M. Ball	Aug. 2, 1821
Tate, Martha E. and William A. Stone	Aug. 17, 1843
Tate, Elizabeth D. and Tavnah W. Fortson	Dec. 20, 1821
Tate, Martha and Beverly C. Cook	May 3, 1827
Tate, Sarah Ann and Murphy Vaughan	Dec. 21, 1823
Tate, Catherine D. and Tavnah Fortson	Dec. 2, 1824
Tate, Genoa and Macajah Jones	July 17, 1820
Tate, Martha W. and Pascoil D. Klugh	June 8, 1821
Tate, Frances A. and H. F. M. M. Lipford	May 20, 1819
Tate, Frances and John Roan	Apr. 15, 1824
Tate, Elizabeth and George Upshaw	Jan. 4, 1820
Taylor, Patsy and Ruben Plunkett	July 6, 1812
Taylor, Franky and William Gully	Oct. 26, 1815
Taylor, Rachel and Willis Hailey	Nov. 23, 1846
Taylor, Amanda and Thomas M. Craft	Sept. 12, 1847
Taylor, Eliza, Mrs. and Andrew W. Booth	Nov. 11, 1844
Taylor, Phelitia and Reuben Cash	Feb. 11, 1836
Teasley, Anna and Westley Christler	Oct. 28, 1824
Teasley, Winney and John Horton	Aug. 21, 1817
Teasley, Amela and William Lunsford	Aug. 28, 1823
Teasley, Sarah and William Bryant	Dec. 31, 1820
Teasley, Priscilla and Lemuel Rucker	Aug. 11, 1825
Teasley, Martha W. and Thomas J. Teasley	Dec. 20, 1827
Teasley, Drucilla Ann and John E. Teasley	Dec. 16, 1847
Teasley, Nancy and Joab Ashworth	June 4, 1809
Teasley, Martha E. and Elijah Maxwell	Jan. —, 1851
Teasley, Priscilla T. and Willis Hunt	Nov. 7, 1833
Teasley, Martha R. and John D. Keys	Aug. 28, 1832
Teasley, Lucy H. and Lawrence M. Adams	Sept. 28, 1843
Teasley, Lucy E. and Moses F. Adams Jr.	Dec. 2, 1847
Teasley, Elizabeth A. and Roland J. Brown	Aug. 8, 1839
Teasley, Lucy and Thomas J. Cason	Dec. 3, 1846
Teasley, Drucilla A. and David R. Fleming	Dec. 22, 1844
Teasley, Phronacy H. and Malcolm H. Johnson	Apr. 10, 1845
Terrell, Polly and Isaac Smithy	Nov. 25, 1819
Terrell, Frances and James Davis	Jan. 18, 1827
Terrell, Elizabeth and Gideon Ham	Apr. 18, 1820
Terrell, Rebecca and Benjamin Head	Apr. 22, 1817
Terrell, Martha and Simeon Nunnelee	May 24, 1819
Terrell, Sarah and Brittain Capel	May 25, 1809
Terrell, Sarah Ann and Thomas J. Herndon	Oct. 20, 1842
Terrell, Nancy and Joel M. Key	Aug. 8, 1839
Terrell, Sarah A. and William H. Alexander	Nov. 24, 1842
Terry, Mary and Jeptha H. Ward	Jan. 15, 1829
Terry, Sarah and Zuriah King	Sept. 25, 1842
Terry, Nancy and John Kelly	June —, 1849
Terry, Frances and John B. Turner	Dec. 16, 1847
Terry, Lucy and Elam Alexander	Dec. 8, 1825
Thompson, Louisiana and Robert H. Manning	Jan. 30, 1822
Thompson, Louisa and Jesse Seymour	Jan. 9, 1840
Thompson, Narcissa and Craton Shaw	Mar. 22, 1849
Thompson, Sarah M. and Allen Alexander	Feb. 5, 1815

Bride, Groom and Date

Name	Date
Thompson, Jane and Drury Thompson	Jan. 26, 1816
Thompson, Eliza E. and Waddy Tait	Jan. 4, 1808
Thompson, Charlotte and Allen C. Thompson	Mar. 3, 1808
Thompson, Martha and Pickney Dudley	Sept. 30, 1845
Thompson, Martha and John Nunnelle	Jan. 9, 1817
Thomason, Sarah and James Dobbs	Sept. 6, 1810
Thornton, Mary and William M. Allmand	Jan. 6, 1831
Thornton, Sarah and Thomas Eavenson	Dec. 9, 1830
Thornton, Sarah K. and Joseph Y. Arnold	Oct. 5, 1841
Thornton, Priscilla E. and Asa C. Brown	Jan. 23, 1851
Thornton, Sarah S. and George Eavenson	Aug. 1, 1839
Thornton, Damarius and Andel M. Elliott	Dec. 23, 1849
Thornton, Frances, Mrs. and Moses T. Fleming	Dec. 12, 1837
Thornton, Mary Ann and Thomas E. Highsmith	Dec. 19, 1846
Thornton, Lucy C. and John McGehee	Oct. 2, 1845
Thornton, Emily P. and William McGehee	Nov. 13, 1845
Thornton, A. E. and William McMullan	July 1, 1849
Thornton, Polly and Neal McMullan	Aug. 1, 1807
Thornton, Elizabeth and John Childs	Oct. 17, 1811
Thornton, Elizabeth and John Dickerson	Dec. 29, 1812
Thornton, Sarah and James Hearndon	Mar. 30, 1814
Thornton, Elizabeth and William Bell	Feb. 6, 1817
Thornton, Elizabeth E. and William E. Thornton	Mar. 4, 1843
Thornton, Sally and John G. Higginbotham	Oct. 25, 1827
Thornton, Susannah and Nathaniel Nuckles	Oct. 13, 1826
Thornton, Priscilla and Sion Hunt	July 31, 1823
Thornton, Elizabeth and Reuben Maxwell	Dec. 13, 1821
Thornton, Elizabeth and Jeremiah S. Warren	Oct. 14, 1823
Thornton, Ann and Joseph S. Shackleford	Dec. 22, 1825
Threlkeld, Adeline and Joseph Cook	Aug. 2, 1830
Threlkeld, Feanelty and Stephen Wilson	Feb. 28, 1832
Threlkeld, Mary and Joseph Downer	Mar. 22, 1838
Threlkeld, Harriet and Samuel Davis	Mar. 25, 1826
Threlkeld, Mary and James Wilson	Nov. 13, 1831
Threlkeld, Casa Ann and James Haynes	Dec. 24, 1835
Threlkeld, Clarissa and William Kirkpatrick	Nov. 10, 1836
Threlkeld, Matilda and Archibald Payton	Nov. 12, 1849
Threlkeld, Maria and Lewis Saxon	Sept. 22, 1847
Tibbitts, Martha B. and John W. Anderson	May 5, 1842
Tibbitts, Narcissa and David Butler	Dec. 17, 1842
Tidwell, Sally and Russell Brawner	Aug. 10, 1809
Tiner, Charity and Billions Bird	Feb. 5, 1815
Tittle, Mariah O. and William Nunnelee	Apr. 24, 1817
Towns, Nancy and John Morgan	Dec. 20, 1807
Tomason, Susannah and Sherwood Ginn	Jan. 12, 1815
Tompkins, Nancy and Benjamin Rumsey	Aug. 11, 1816
Totman, Isabel and Thomas Sanders	Sept. 16, 1819
Totman, Jane and Tollison Tyner	Aug. 28, 1820
Trader, Elizabeth and Samuel Mathews	Mar. 13, 1849
Turman, Permelia and William Pulliam	Jan. 29, 1824
Turman, Mariah and John Hall	Apr. 12, 1827
Turman, Elizabeth and Wyatt Rayle	Dec. 25, 1845
Turman, Margaret A. and John A. Sanders	Nov. 23, 1848
Turman, Prudence and James M. Allgood	Feb. 7, 1813
Turman, Louisa A. and Thomas Bell	Aug. 10, 1843
Turner, Nancy and John M. Bradwell	Dec. 19, 1843
Turner, Sophia A. and Edmond Cason	May 4, 1820
Turner, Elizabeth M. and Ralph Gaines	Jan. 3, 1822

Bride, Groom and Date		
Turner, Sarah and Hiram H. Thomason	Dec.	24, 1846
Turner, Julia Ann and Thomas Wood	Oct.	31, 1839
Turner, Katherine and Benjamin S. Crawford	Feb.	23, 1847
Tyler, Jane and Benjamin Parker	Nov.	15, 1848
Tyler, Eliza C. and Henry M. Crittenden	Jan.	17, 1839
Tyner, Martha B. and John Bird	Feb.	7, 1813
Tyner, Nancy and Robert Crump	Jan.	16, 1846
Tyner, Jane and John Hansard	Aug.	10, 1840
Tyner, Eliza and William Higginbotham	May	16, 1841
Tyner, Mary Ann and Benjamin Higginbotham	Sept.	13, 1843
Tyner, Serepta and Samuel Reynolds	Jan.	20, 1849
Tucker, Mary Ann and Willis Pulliam	Oct.	2, 1839
Tucker, Lucinda and John M. Tucker	Jan.	13, 1827
Tucker, Sarah H. and Henry Sanders	Feb.	27, 1842
Tucker, Martha H. and John B. Maxwell	Aug.	6, 1843
Tucker, Elminee and Henry B. Peyton	Nov.	25, 1840
Tucker, Vanania Caroline and William D. Power	Nov.	17, 1844
Tucker, Elizabeth and Joshua F. Rowell	Sept.	23, 1831
Tucker, Elizabeth and John R. Booth	Apr.	8, 1847
Tucker, Frances A. and David S. Brown	Mar.	6, 1845
Tucker, Elizabeth F. and John F. Shields	Dec.	29, 1836
Tucker, Amanda R. and John J. Tucker	June	23, 1851
Underwood, Polly and John Haley	Jan.	5, 1809
Underwood, Polly and Henry Wheeler	Mar.	18, 1810
Underwood, Martha and Absolom T. Davis	Oct.	27, 1824
Underwood, Dosha and William Moss	Feb.	20, 1823
Uderwood, Mary and John Nelmes	July	23, 1818
Underwood, Sally and Isaac Wheeler	Aug.	6, 1829
Vaughan, Martha and Cluf Martin	Sept.	18, 1808
Vaughan, Nancy and Ewel Martin	Sept.	18, 1808
Vaughan, Martha and John H. ?	Mar.	6, 1828
Vaughan, Mitty and William M. David	Sept.	18, 1835
Vaughan, Sarah and Pearson Duncan	Oct.	29, 1837
Vaughan, Elizabeth and William Graham	Jan.	21, 1841
Verdell, Maria S. and James Tate	Nov.	14, 1813
Verdell, Sarah Ann and Whitman Hill	June	6, 1843
Vickery, Milly and John McDougal	Dec.	16, 1836
Vines, Mary and Henry Duncan	Dec.	23, 1823
Walker, Martha and Robert Crock	———	20, 1809
Wall, Patsy S. and Robert Carter	Oct.	15, 1815
Wall, Susannah and Joseph Davis	Nov.	4, 1828
Wall, Jane Ann and Josiah Prather	Jan.	29, 1832
Wall, Martha E. and T. J. Shackleford	Feb.	8, 1842
Wall, Martha and William B. Henry	Dec.	19, 1850
Wallace, Martha and William Summer	Mar.	20, 1845
Wallis, Peggy and Middleton Blair	Oct.	19, 1826
Walters, Mary Ann and Wesley Skelton	Oct.	4, 1849
Walters, Dosha and David Dobbs	Nov.	4, 1807
Wansley, Martha L. and Thos. O'Brient	Oct.	4, 1837
Wansley, Elizabeth A. and Weston Patterson	Dec.	21, 1837
Wanslow, Martha and James G. Cash	Jan.	21, 1847
Wanslow, Sarah and Joseph Jenkins	Nov.	26, 1838
Wanslow, Patsy and Benjamin Davis	May	10, 1810
Wanslow, Jane Ann and Wm. H. Teasley	Nov.	11, 1849
Waters, Elcy and Joseph Downer	Aug.	29, 1819
Warren, Martha S. and John Rowsey	Jan.	3, 1828
Warren, Furlishie and James Jenkins	Jan.	26, 1832
Warren, Lucy E. and Thomas B. Adams	Sept.	30, 1841

Bride, Groom and Date
Warren, Sarah F. and Horatio J. Goss ....Dec. 21, 1843
Ward, Elizabeth E. and Jno. M. Thornton ....Mar. 23, 1837
Ward, Nancy J. and Haley Butler ....Dec. 7, 1815
Ward, Sarah L. and Robt. L. Alexander ....Dec. 6, 1834
Ward, Harriet C. and Hullum Hunt ....Mar. 8, 1832
Ward, Merial Ann and Strawter Gaines ....Nov. 24, 1834
Ward, Eliza F. and Joel Butler ....Sept. 9, 1841
Ward, Nancy M. and Wm. B. Crawford ....Sept. 26, 1844
Ward, Elizabeth and Jesse Farmer ....Jan. 1, 1837
Ward, Julia A. E. and John Yancy Saxon ....Sept. 6, 1844
Ward, Sarah V. and James A. Stone ....Sept. 30, 1837
Watkins, Sarah H. and Stephen W. Harris ....Jan. 8, 1808
Watkins, Elizabeth and Benjamin Sherrod ....Jan. 1, 1808
Watkins, Martha and Benj. Talliferro ....Oct. 15, 1807
Watkins, Susan and Major John Oliver ....Feb. 19, 1811
Watkins, Jane and James M. Tait ....Oct. 28, 1809
Watkins, Eliza and William McGehee ....May 22, 1817
Watkins, Sophia and Elis S. Shorter ....June 6, 1817
Watkins, Sarah and John Banks ....Feb. 14, 1828
Watson, Priscilla and John Lovingood ....Feb. 21, 1833
Watson, Martha S. and Powell Shiflett ....Feb. 6, 1850
Webb, Fanny and Jeremiah Nix ....Oct. 25, 1810
Webb, Susannah, Mrs. and Simeon Brawner ....Nov. 10, 1824
Webb, Prudence S. and Lindsey Christian ....Nov. 18, 1834
Webb, Alcey W. and George W. Parham ....Sept. 22, 1834
Webb, Alice A. M. and Joseph P. Deadwyler ....Sept. 19, 1841
Welch, Lucy and Larkin Clark ....Dec. 25, 1810
Welch, Ann and William A. Beck ....May 30, 1820
Welch, Naomi and John White ....Apr. 28, 1848
Wheeler, Elizabeth and Ezekiel Underwood ....May 1, 1812
Wheeler, Hannah and Job Franklin ....Oct. 19, 1815
Wheeler, Polly and Pleasant Davis ....Sept. 17, 1820
Wheeler, Nancy and Joshua B. Nelms ....Aug. 19, 1823
Wheeler, Penina J. and James H. Reynolds ....Nov. 8, 1832
Wheeler, Sarah and Leroy Wheeler ....Oct. 8, 1818
Wheeler, Hannah and Job Franklin ....Oct. 19, 1815
Wheeler, Polly and Pleasant Davis ....Sept. 17, 1820
Wheelis, Mary and James N. Gunter ....Sept. 23, 1848
White, Milly and Isaac Christian ....Feb. 17, 1807
White, Patsy and Martin White ....Feb. 11, 1807
White, Sally and Edward Burdon ....Dec. 22, 1811
White, Beda and James Jordan ....Nov. 26, 1807
White, Betsy and Asa Mann ....Jan. 24, 1810
White, Franky and Robert Roebuck Jr. ....May 27, 1810
White, Martha and Edward Colley ....Sept. 9, 1813
White, Sarah and Hugh McGehee ....Sept. 28, 1814
White, Nancy and James M. Foster ....May 12, 1832
White, Polly and James Lunsford ....Sept. 18, 1817
White, Winney and George Lunsford ....Jan. 16, 1818
White, Sarah and Elijah Moore ....Dec. 10, 1819
White, Eliza and Richard Rice ....Nov. 1, 1823
White, Nancy and Benjamin Sanders ....July 15, 1824
White, Eliza F. and Alvin Dean ....Jan. 3, 1826
White, Mary and Jesse Forrester ....Sept. 26, 1826
White, Mary and William A. Herring ....Jan. 11, 1825
White, Martha and James W. Bell ....Aug. 25, 1840
White, Eliza and William B. Terrell ....Mar. 30, 1834
White, Elizabeth and Thomas J. Allen ....Jan. 26, 1826
White, Elizabeth and Richard C. Crawford ....Sept. 27, 1832
White, Elizabeth and Josiah Farmer ....Apr. 26, 1843

Bride, Groom and Date

Bride and Groom	Date
White, Mary Frances and Peter Cleveland	May 10, 1838
White, Lydia W. and Henry Warsing	Aug. 22, 1842
White, Sarah and Joel Mann	Dec. 3, 1846
White, Margaret Jane and Silas Mason	June 5, 1842
White, Jane and Lemuel Crocker	Feb. 28, 1838
White, Virginia and Samuel Freeman	Sept. 23, 1837
White, Harriet and Willis Holmes	Nov. 4, 1838
White, Mildred and James W. Jones	Oct. 25, 1842
White, Martha and Jesse Moon	Dec. 7, 1847
White, Sarah Ann and James S. Oliver	Nov. —, 1839
White, Rachel and James E. Strickland	May 8, 1851
Whitman, Mary and Joseph Dunlap	Dec. 18, 1811
Whitman, Sarah and Charles M. Hearndon	Feb. 1, 1816
Whitman, Sarah Ann and Robert R. Oliver	Nov. 9, 1837
Whitney, Martha and Henry Evans	Dec. 16, 1811
Whitlow, Capline, Mrs. and John W. Mattox	Dec. 31, 1833
Wiche, Milly and James Satterwhite	July 26, 1810
Wilhight, Harriet A. and Valentine H. Deadwyler	Apr. 16, 1846
Wilhite, Rebecca and Martin Deadwyler	Aug. 7, 1809
Wilhite, Zeriah G. and Robert C. Oglesby	Dec. 25, 1823
Wilhite, Nancy F. and Joseph W. Wilhite	Dec. 19, 1820
Wilhite, Savannah and Elijah Alexander	Oct. 27, 1836
Wilhite, Elizabeth and John B. Wilhite	Aug. 17, 1820
Wilkins, Frances and Jacob Grider	Jan. 12, 1815
Wilkins, Agnes, Mrs. and Bedford Cade	Nov. 15, 1823
Wilkins, Nancy and Thomas Downer	Oct. 28, 1841
Williams, Levincey and William Mize	Nov. 3, 1850
Williams, Frances M. and James A. Clark	Sept. 20, 1838
Williams, Caty and Demsey Grice	June 23, 1824
Williams, Mary A. and Hiram Adams	Dec. 3, 1829
Williams, Frances E. and Thomas Hearne	June 3, 1828
Williams, Ann E. and Samuel Cook	Jan. 18, 1817
Williams, Martha B. and Shelton Oliver	Sept. 8, 1828
Williamson, Sally C. and John A. Verdell	Jan. 21, 1819
Williamson, Betsy C. and Robert Middleton	Nov. 11, 1810
Williamson, Betsy B. and Joshua Merrell	Dec. 30, 1818
Williford, Nancy and Moses L. Cantrell	Feb. 28, 1836
Willis, Piety and Edmond Smithwick	May 2, 1816
Willis, Louisa Ann and Moses Adams	July 18, 1841
Willis, Polly and Thomas A. Thornton	Oct. 5, 1820
Willis, Rachel and George I. Barr	Dec. 15, 1820
Willis, Elizabeth and William Haslett	May 18, 1845
Willis, Mary M. and David Hudson	July 1, 1847
Wilson, Sally and Daniel McMullan	Sept. 16, 1822
Wimmes, Jane and William McGuire	Dec. 1, 1813
Winn, Sarah Ann and William Burden	Sept. 12, 1844
Winn, Elizabeth and John M. Carlton	July 4, 1840
Worrill, Mary Ann and Calvin F. Wilhite	Sept. 2, 1841
Wood, Sally and Reuben Hailey	Aug. 13, 1807
Wood, Sally and Jesse Human	June 19, 1810
Wood, Nancy and Theodocius Cook	Jan. 15, 1824
Wood, Elizabeth and William West	July 30, 1823
Wood, Nancy and Issachar Cook	Jan. 28, 1827
Woodly, Nancy and William Arnold	Sept. 3, 1826
Woolridge, Penina and George Henders	Aug. 2, 1810
Wright, Rebecca and James S. Martin	Apr. 11, 1825
Wright, Ann C. E. P. and Daniel Campbell	Mar. 31, 1825
Wright, Jincy and William Algood	Jan. 2, 1817
Wright, Polly and John Barron	Sept. 7, 1817
Wyche, Frances and Isaac O. Edwards	Nov. 7, 1824
Wyche, Milly and William G. Bullard	Sept. 17, 1837

SUPPLEMENT *of* GENERAL INFORMATION

By

Stephen Heard Chapter
Daughters of the American Revolution

MARY HILL ARNOLD (Mrs. C. A.)
Regent

ELBERTON RESTS ON ACRES OF DIAMONDS

SOME time ago Mr. J. E. Tate of Middleton, was informed by his son "Ned," that his teacher had given the children in his class instructions to write an essay on "Elberton." The son requested help. Without a moment's reflection Mr. Tate said: "Well, son, get your pencil and write what I give out to you as follows:

"And the rain descended, and the floods came, and the winds blew and beat upon that house, and it fell not, for it was founded upon a rock."

"Elberton is built upon a rock, which is called Blue Granite, found only in one other section of the United States. Time is the essence of all things. Silk and cotton mills may come and go, and other industries from time to time flourish like the green bay tree, but the foundation upon which our lasting prosperity rests, and upon which a city is gradually being built, is the foundation upon which Elberton is built, for has not this Blue Diamond already attracted the canny Scot and the music-loving Italian, both valuable additions to the citizenship of any community? The polished surface of Blue Granite withstands the ravages of time, and as time rolls away into the future, our city will continue to attract citizens from all climes on account of the foundation upon which it is built."

ELBERTON

"The Granite Center of the South"

Population, 7,500 within 1½ mile radius.
Average temperature, 62.2°, with 273 clear days annually.
Elevation 670 feet. Average rainfall, 54 inches.
Two railroads: Seaboard Airline Railway and Southern Railway.
Three motor truck lines.
Three hotels.
Excellent schools and churches.
One cotton mill, Mr. Byron Miller, Superintendent.
One silk mill, the first in the South, Mr. John Cook, Superintendent.
One textile novelties factory.
One bakery.
Three machine shops.
Three wholesale grocery companies.
Twnty-two wholesale manufacturers of granite memorials, granite for buildings, and for sculptural works.
Two granite machinery supply houses.
Three bonded cotton warehouses.
One ice and cold storage plant.
Municipal electric and water plants.
Municipal swimming pool.
Municipal athletic field, flood lights.
Municipal airport.
Municipal park, beautifully landscaped, and containing ten acres of natural forest.
Rotary, Kiwanis, and Pilot Clubs.
American Legion Home.
Boy Scouts Hut, with public tennis courts adjoining.
Two banks.
One theatre.
One golf course.
One semi-weekly newspaper.
Three paved highway outlets, with four more under construction.
One public produce and poultry market.
One cottonseed oil mill.
Eight wholesale gas and oil firms.
Two hospitals.
Two laundries.
Two woodworking plants.
$5,000 Livestock auction sales barn.
$50,000 new theatre.
Security Loan Co., Mr. Z. C. Hayes, President.

CONGRESSMAN PAUL BROWN

Hon. Paul Brown has been a prominent citizen and attorney of Elberton since 1920. Graduate University of Georgia (Law School). Member of Alpha Tau Omega fraternity. He served as county attorney of Elbert County for five years. He was a delegate to the Democratic National Convention in 1932.

Before moving to Elberton Mr. Brown was Mayor of Lexington for four years, and he represented Oglethorpe County in the General Assembly of Georgia in 1907-08.

Mr. Brown was elected as Representative in Congress from the Tenth District of Georgia in July, 1933, and has served with distinction in that body ever since. He has been on some of the most important committees of the House and is now one of the ranking members of the Banking and Currency Committee.

JUDGE CLARK EDWARDS, JR.

Judge Clark Edwards, Jr., born August 14, 1897, Dewy Rose, Elbert County, Georgia, son of Larkin Clark Edwards, Sr., October 5, 1861, teacher 1889-1894; Justice of the Peace 1890-1908; Ordinary of Elbert County 1908 until death January 6, 1921; and Olive Charlotte Edwards, daughter of Robert White, Confederate Soldier. Grandson of Emory Parks Edwards, Lawyer, Solicitor, Judge, Legislator, and Captain in Civil War; and Georgia Willis.

Judge Edwards succeeded his father as Ordinary, age 23, serving without opposition until elected Judge Superior Courts, Northern Circuit, 1938. Educated at Elberton High School and office Judge W. D. Tutt, Elberton Attorney. Admitted to bar 1918. Married Jewette Hester Webb 1918; children, Dorothy, Clark III (deceased), Charlotte, Carolyn, Charles Emory, Jacqueline, James Clark. Mrs. Harry Bell, Olive, Emory White, Eulalia (deceased), sisters and brothers.

JOHN JUDSON BROWN

Son of Ira M. Brown and Susan Campbell Brown was born on January 12, 1867.

Married Captora Teresa Ginn, daughter of Middleton and Irene Roberts Ginn.

Father of five children; four living:
(1) Pearl Brown married Carl Teasley
(children) (1) Edgar, (2) Harold Teasley
(2) James Polk Brown married Leonia Mewbourne
(children) (1) Marjorie Polk, (2) John Franklin Brown
(3) Kyle Brown (deceased), no children
(4) Sylvester Brown married Leotis Pulliam
(children) (1) Sylvester Brown Jr.

(5) Walter Johnson Brown married Georgia Watson Lee, granddaughter of the late Senator Thomas E. Watson
(children) (1) Thomas Watson Brown.

J. J. Brown spent his early life in upper Elbert County, engaged in farming and the mercantile business. He always took an active part in agricultural development by working as a Liberal for farm legislation and the betterment of agriculture.

He was a member of the old Grange Organization, Farmers' Alliance and was state president of the Farmers Union. He was elected state Commissioner of Agriculture in 1916, an office which he held for 12 years, being the only state house official ever to be elected from Elbert County.

Since his retirement from public life, he has been engaged in farming and as agronomist and game technician for the Federal Government.

LIST OF OFFICIALS—CITY OF ELBERTON

1935
Mayor—H. P. Hunter.
Councilmen—J. S. Asbury, Joe Allen, T. R. Starke, D. V. Bailey, T. O. Tabor, Jr.
Clerk and Treasurer—Miss Lilly Stilwell.
City Attorney—W. D. Tutt.
Assistant Clerk and Treasurer—Mrs. E. W. Mashburn.

1936
Mayor—H. P. Hunter.
Councilmen—Joe Allen, D. V. Bailey, E. C. Brown, T. R. Starke, T. O. Tabor, Jr.
Clerk and Treasurer—Miss Lilly Stilwell.
City Attorney—P. S. Hawes.
Assistant Clerk and Treasurer—Mrs. E. W. Mashburn.
Chief of Police—C. W. Johnson.
Librarian—Mrs. Pauline Brewer Brown.

1937
Mayor—J. S. Asbury.
Councilmen—D. C. Auld, D. V. Bailey, E. C. Brown, C. E. Ray, T. O. Tabor, Jr.
Clerk and Treasurer—D. J. Thornton and C. L. Smith.
City Attorney—P. S. Hawes.
Assistant Clerk and Treasurer—Mrs. E. W. Mashburn.
Chief of Police—C. W. Johnson.
Librarian—Mrs. Pauline Brewer Brown.

1938
Mayor—J. S. Asbury.
Councilmen—David C. Auld, D. V. Bailey, Thos. N. Colley, R. H. Johnson, T. O. Tabor, Jr.
Clerk and Treasurer—C. L. Smith.
City Attorney—J. T. Sisk.
Assistant Clerk and Treasurer—Mrs. E. W. Mashburn.
Chief of Police—C. W. Johnson.
Librarian—Mrs. Pauline Brewer Brown.

1939

Mayor—J. S. Asbury.
Councilmen—David C. Auld, D. V. Bailey, Thos. N. Colley, R. H. Johnson, T. O. Tabor, Jr.
Clerk and Treasurer—C. L. Smith.
City Attorney—Raymonde Stapleton.
Assistant Clerk and Treasurer—Mrs. E. W. Mashburn.
Chief of Police—C. W. Johnson.
Librarian—Mrs. Pauline Brewer Brown.

1940

Mayor—J. S. Asbury.
Councilmen—David C. Auld, D. V. Bailey, Thos. N. Colley, E. O. Coogler, T. O. Tabor, Jr.
Clerk and Treasurer—C. L. Smith.
City Attorney—Raymonde Stapleton.
Assistant Clerk and Treasurer—Mrs. E. W. Mashburn.
Chief of Police—C. W. Johnson.
Librarian—Mrs. Pauline Brewer Brown.

COUNTY OFFICERS

County Attorney—Tate Conyers.
Senator, Elbert, Hart and Madison Counties—T. F. Kelley.
Representative from Elbert County—W. H. Thornton.
Ordinary of Elbert County—C. B. Thornton.
Sheriff of Elbert County—J. A. Starke.
Home Demonstration Agent—Miss Lula Peek.
County Agent—Webb Tatum.
Clerk of Superior Court—W. A. Rucker.
Tax Commissioner—Frank Harper.
Judge, City Court—W. D. Tutt.
Solicitor, City Court—Peyton S. Hawes.
County Commissioner—S. B. Seymour.

CITY BOARD OF EDUCATION

Carter A. Arnold, Chairman; John A. Logan, Co-Chairman; Herbert H. Wilcox, Secretary; Fred W. Auld, Frank S. Fortson.
Superintendent of Elberton Public Schools—R. E. Hood.
Central High School Principal—R. E. Lee.
Stilwell Primary School Principal—Miss Edna Rogers.
Stevens Primary School Principal—Miss Zora Carlton.
Central High School P.-T. A. President—Mrs. T. M. Martin.
Stilwell Primary School P.-T. A. President—Mrs. Jack Smith.
Stevens Primary School P.-T. A. President—Mrs. Tom Crawford.
Commercial Department (Central High School)—Mrs. D. N. Thompson.
Librarian, Central High School—Mrs. Vesta Turnell.

Elberton is to have a twelve-grade school system. The board of education has voted unanimously for this change after consulting nationally known experts on education. The new grade will be worked into the system as rapidly as practicable and feasible.

ELBERT COUNTY SCHOOLS

The schools of Elbert County, exclusive of the City System of Elberton, are serving the purpose of educating the youth in a great way. There are fifteen white schools in Elbert County, with an enrollment of 2,200 pupils, 25 per cent of these are in high school. These high school pupils are given four years of training in Vocational Guidance and advice in the selection of a Vocation. Ten of these schools operate nine months per year. The others hold for eight months. The Board of Education of Elbert County own and operate twenty-four school buses which transport at least 1,800 pupils to these schools.

There are thirty-five Negro schools in Elbert County with an enrollment of 1,500 pupils. About 10 per cent of these are in high school. These operate for seven months per year.

This 2nd day of December, 1939.

(Signed) MARY HANSARD,
Supt., Elbert County Schools.

ELBERTON CHAMBER OF COMMERCE

The first commercial organization in Elberton was formed early in the Twentieth Century, and was called the Board of Trade. It was succeeded in 1924 by the Elberton Chamber of Commerce, which has functioned continuously since July 4, 1924, when a judgment granting the charter was signed by Hon. W. L. Hodges, Judge of the Superior Court of Elbert County.

The petitioners in alphabetical order were J. Y. Arnold, W. E. Bates, Z. W. Copeland, Z. C. Hayes, Fred Herndon, H. P. Hunter, D. D. Mercer, R. Stapleton, T. O. Tabor, Jr., and H. L. Wiggs. This list was unanimously chosen as the first Board of Directors. The youngest Director, J. Y. Arnold, was made President.

Throughout its fifteen years of activity, the Elberton Chamber of Commerce has been instrumental in bringing to the City and County many industries which added materially to local payrolls. It has been untiring in its efforts to increase the income of the farmers throughout this section, and there exists a most friendly feeling between the Chambber and the rural citizens.

Officers and Directors for 1939: Ben I. Sutton, President; F. S. Fortson, Treasurer; G. C. Grogan, Secretary; Dave Cohn, J. H. Cook, W. E. Fortson, J. A. Logan, W. B. Minter, H. B. Payne, H. G. Thornton, J. S. Wingo. (M. B. Asbury President, 1940).

ELBERT COUNTY JUNIOR CHAMBER OF COMMERCE

The object of a Junior Chamber of Commerce is primarily to promote the welfare of the community in which it is located. The Junior Chambers of Commerce in Georgia banded together under the name of "The Georgia Junior Chamber of Commerce" and have made the State their community; therefore, each new local Junior Chamber of Commerce is promoting the welfare of the State as well as the local community—so with this in mind, the Atlanta Junior Chamber of Commerce came to Elberton in 1934 and organized The Elbert County Junior Chamber of Commerce.

Since that time, besides cooperating whole-heartedly with The Georgia Junior Chamber of Commerce, the Elbert County Jaycees have done much to make Elberton and Elbert County better places in which to live, and also have given as much favorable publicity of the City and its resources as possible. A few of the many Jaycees sponsored projects are: the building of the city's tennis courts, half-holidays during the summer months for the business houses of Elberton, annual 'Clean-up, Paint-up" Week, published envelopes to be used by the business firms of Elberton advertising its industries. And this year gave "Elberton, The Granite Center of the South" nationwide publicity through an advertisement put on the back cover of the State Jaycee publication, *The Georgia Builder*, which was distributed to the delegates at the U. S. Junior Chamber of Commerce Convention in Tulsa, Oklahoma.

The presidents of the Elbert County Junior Chamber of Commerce are listed in order of their period of service: C. R. McLanahan, J. Cleve Allen, Young Smith, William D. Fortson, and Louis Patz. The other officers serving with Mr. Patz for 1939 are: First Vice-President, J. E. Johnson, Jr.; Second Vice-President, R. E. Lee, Jr.; Treasurer, J. M. Cleveland; Secretary, C. E. Teasley, Jr.

SOUTHERN MARBLE AND GRANITE CREDIT SERVICE

An organization known as the Southern Marble and Granite Credit Service was established in November, 1938, by the leading granite and marble concerns of the Elberton and the Southern area, with the purpose of keeping a more accurate check on delinquent accounts within the industry.

Mrs. J. R. Farmer, of Elberton, who for years had been connected with the granite industry, was placed in charge of this service.

WHOLESALE GRANITE MANUFACTURERS AND QUARRIES OF THE ELBERTON DISTRICT—1939

Allen Granite Company—J. Cleve Allen, President.
American Granite Quarries—W. H. Allen, President.
Beaver Dam Granite Company—C. O. Yarbrough, Manager.
Brockington Granite Sales Company—R. C. Brockington, Manager.
Canales Granite Company—J. Ganales, Owner.
Central Granite Company—G. Giannoni, Owner and Manager.
Comolli Granite Company—C. Comolli, President.
J. B. Coogler Granite Company—Manufacturer.
T. T. Coogler Quarries.
Dixie Granite Company—J. E. Hammond and O. Minervini, Partners and Owners.
Elberton City Quarries—John Weiblen, Owner.
Elberton Granite Company—Manufacturers.
Elberton Granite Industries—J. J. McLanahan, President and General Manager.
Empire Granite Company—Dobbs Smith, Vice-President; H. H. Stoner, Secretary-Treasurer.
Georgia Granite Company—Julian D'Amico, General Manager.
Haley & Krick—Quarriers.
Harmony Blue Granite Company—T. G. McGarity, Secretary-Treasurer.
Herbert Hedquist—Quarrier.
Ideal Granite Company—O. P. Scales, Owner.
Highpoint Granite Company—Clarence R. McLanahan, Owner.
M. W. Kantala—Quarrier.
Liberty Granite Company—A. Parker Hunt, Owner.
Lincoln Granite Company—Walton Y. Harris, Sales Manager.
D. D. Mercer, Sr.—Manufacturer.
Modern Granite Company—C. M. Mattox, C. J. Helton, and Mrs. Omer Bond, Owners.
National Granite Company of Georgia—J. A. Logan, President.
North Georgia Granite Company—Manufacturers.
Oglesby Granite Quarries—J. M. Thornton, Sales Manager.
Piedmont Granite Quarries—Julian D. Amico, General Manager.
Premier Granite Company—Manufacturers.
Puritan Granite Quarries—F. Borzynski and Jimmie McDonald, Owners.
Quick Service Granite Company—Joel Hunt, T. J. Hendrix and C. O. Reagin, Partners.
Southeastern Granite Company—J. Frank Bailey, Owner.
Southern Quarrying Company—C. R. Deadwyler, Sales Manager.
Sterling Granite Company—Julius P. McLanahan and James T. McLanahan, Owners.
Victory Granite Company—G. Bondi and S. Fernandez, Owners.

ELBERTON COCA-COLA PLANT

In 1927 the Coca-Cola Company made available to all the bottlers of Coca-Cola plans and specifications for different sizes of modern plants in which to bottle Coca-Cola.

The Elberton Coca-Cola Bottling Co. has the distinction of being first to build a plant according to these specifications.

Mr. H. J. Miller has been president of this plant for more than ten years. Since 1934 Mr. B. C. Beard, Jr., has been Vice-President and local manager.

ELBERTON OIL MILLS

Among Elberton Industries we have one of the oldest and best Oil Mills in the State. The Mill being chartered as the Elberton Oil Mills in 1888, was a three press institution at the time, and by its upright dealings and conscientious management has been in seasonal operation every year since it was started, and has grown to an eight press Mill at present. As well as being a great help to its many patrons, it has helped its many employees throughout its fifty-two years of operations, and both State, County and Municipal Governments have benefitted by the large amount of taxes paid, and has largely contributed to the railway success of the town.

The officals and employees who guide the extensive operations of this Coproration are P. D. McCarley, President, John T. Dennis, Jr., Vice-President and Manager, Homer C. Mickel Agent and Superintendent of Construction, and E. W. Vest, Superintendent. It is a notable fact that all of these have been connected with the Elberton Oil Mills for more than forty years.

THE AMERICAN LEGION, ELBERTON, GEORGIA
EDMUND BREWER TATE POST No. 14

The Edmund Brewer Tate Post of the American Legion was chartered August 29, 1919, having only a few members at the time of chartering. The Post received its name in honor of First Lieutenant Edmund Brewer Tate, who was killed in action in France on the last day of fighting. The following Commanders and Adjutants have served the Post since its beginning to date, 1939-1940:

Year	Commander	Adjutant
1919	Howard B. Payne	Robert Wright
1920	Howard B. Payne	Robert Wright
1921	Fred W. Auld	Clarke Edwards, Jr.
1922	Fred W. Auld	Clarke Edwards, Jr.
1923	Fred W. Auld	Clarke Edwards, Jr.
1924	D. K. Jones	Richard P. Adams
1925	Tom H. Cooley	H. S. Hunter

1926	Walter P. Smith	Tom A. Tinman
1927	J. S. Asbury	A. N. Drake
1928	Chas. A. Johnson	Joe Allen
1929	Webb Tatum	Warren Crick
1930	Robert W. Mize	Warren Crick
1931	Howard B. Payne	David C. Auld
1932	Walter E. Whitehead	David C. Auld
1933	Walter E. Whitehead	David C. Auld
1934	Walter E. Whitehead	David C. Auld
1935	Walter E. Whitehead	David C. Auld
1936	Walter E. Whitehead	David C. Auld
1937	C. A. Dunbar	David C. Auld
1938	C. A. Dunbar	David C. Auld
1939	Joe Allen	David C. Auld
1940	Joe Allen	David C. Auld

Edmund Brewer Tate was the second son of Mr. O. E. Tate and Carrie Hudson Tate, both being native citizens of Elbert County. The present membership of the Post is 155, as compared with 40 charter members.

The Post owns a Club House, which is located in the City Park, and is dedicated to the service of the community. The Post seeks to carry out in its activities in peace time the service for which they are honored by being eligible for membership in the American Legion, by serving their country in time of war.

THE AMERICAN LEGION AUXILIARY

The American Legion Auxiliary, Unit 14, Edmund Brewer Tate Post, of Elberton, Georgia, was organized in December, 1936. Mrs. C. N. Brannon was the first president; Mrs. Charles Johnson, second President. The officers for the year 1940 are: Mrs. Felix Borzynski, President; Mrs. T. M. Martin, First Vice-President; Mrs. Verner Auld, Second Vice-President; Mrs. H. J. Price, Secretary; Mrs. O. P. Cochran, Treasurer.

They have assisted the Post in all of their activities, among them: Reforestation, Rehabilitation, Memorial Service, Child Welfare, Hospital Services, and the building of the American Legion Home in Elberton. The Auxiliary and Post have jointly sponsored the Elberton Children's Band.

THE SERVICE STAR LEGION

The Service Star Legion, the second to organize in the State, was organized in Elberton on September 8, 1921, at the home of Mrs. H. A. Payne, with 15 charter members and officers as follows:

Mrs. Ora Tate	President
Mrs. W. C. Mattox	First Vice-President
Mrs. Fannie Adams	Second Vice-President

Mrs. George Grogan..Third Vice-President
Mrs. W. A. Rucker...Treasurer
Mrs. M. L. Stevens...Correspondoing Secretary
Mrs. H. B. Payne..Recording Secretary
Mrs. W. F. Jones..Historian
Mrs. B. I. Thornton..Publicity Chairman

OFFICERS FOR 1939-1940

Mrs. Clark Edwards..President
Mrs. T. M. Martin...Vice-President
Mrs. Clark Mattox..Corresponding Secretary
Mrs. W. A. Rucker..Recording Secretary
Mrs. L. D. Hewell..Treasurer

On November 11, 1938, a handsome monument was erected at the Service Star Legion Memorial Park by the Chapter, honoring the men who served in the World War from Elbert County.

HISTORY OF JEFFERSON DAVIS CHAPTER, U. D. C.

Jefferson Davis Chapter, United Daughters of the Confederacy, was organized in 1899, with Mrs. Louise Jones Heard, president. The following were charter members: Mesdames Annie Brewer Warren, Julia Cade Hawes, Annie Burney Smith, Susan Heard Swift, Bessie Hines Little, Louise Jones Heard, Mary McIntosh Brown, Jessie McIntosh Hawes, Georgia Heard Johnson, Mattie Wright Tate, Alice Oglesby Brewer, Gussie Oglesby Jones, Lavonia Jones Gairdner, Misses Lucia Brewer, Azalee Herndon, May Tate, Nora Jones, Rebecca Tate, Roberta Heard, Julia Hines and Fannie Hawes.

The Chapter was organized to care for the graves of the deceased veterans of the War Between the States and to pay honor to those who returned home alive. It has been said that more men from Elbert County surrendered at Appamattox Court House than from any other county in all the Confederate States. Three companies were formed from the County, one under Capt. L. H. O. Martin, called "The Fireside Guards;" one under Capt. J. C. Burch, called "The Bowman Volunteers," and a third under Major W. M. McIntosh, joining with others from surrounding counties to form the 15th Georgia Regiment of Volunteers, commanded by Colonel Thomas W. Thomas and Lieutenant-Colonel Linton Stevens.

The graves of all Veterans in the local cemetery have been marked with Iron Crosses and Government Markers have been placed at more than thirty unmarked graves.

In 1898, the Chapter erected a monument of a Confederate soldier in the U. D. C. Park on the public square, honoring all the soldiers from the county. Crosses of Honor have been bestowed upon all Confederate veterans and many Crosses of Military Service have been bestowed upon their descendants who served a united country in the World War, the Spanish-American War and the War of the Phillipine Insurrection.

In 1922, during the presidency of Mrs. Nona Burris, a Children of the Confederacy Chapter was organized with 44 charter members. Mrs. C. F. Herndon was the first Leader, followed by Mrs. J. T. Dennis, Mrs. Harry S. Bell, Mrs. Boyce Grier, Mrs. Grover Cleveland and Mrs. Milton Fortson, Assistants. The Chapter was named for Mrs. Louise Jones Heard, the organizer of the U. D. C. and mother of Mrs. Dennis. Under Mrs. Bell's leadership, more than 80 members were added and the State Convention was entertained.

Presidents serving the U. D. C. Chapter after the Organizing President, Mrs. Heard, who served for ten years, have been Mesdames E. B. Tate, Harry L. Cleveland, Nona Burris, W. F. Jones, L. D. Hewell, S. S. Brewer, W. A. Rucker and Miss Mary Lizzie Wright.

The Chapter membership at present is 53, with the following officers: Mrs. W. A. Rucker, President; Miss Mary Lizzie Wright, First Vice-President; Mrs. Clark Edwards, Jr., Second Vice-President; Mrs. M. F. Folsom, Recording Secretary; Mrs. D. J. Thornton, Corresponding Secretary; Miss Sarah Anne Wright, Treasurer, with Mrs. J. E. Webb, Assistant; Miss Nora Jones, Historian, with Mrs. Lon Rice, assistant; Mrs. Grover Cleveland, Registrar; Mrs. H. S. Bell, Auditor; Mrs. L. D. Hewell, Recorder of Crosses, and Miss Ada Almond, Custodian of Scrap Book.

There is only one surviving Veteran in the county at present, Mr. J. H. Fleming, who is hale and hearty for his many years.

HISTORY OF ELBERTON W. C. T. U.

The Elberton Woman's Christian Temperance Union, an organization of Christian women banded together for the protection of the home, the abolition of the liquor traffic and the triumph of Christ's Golden Rule, was organized in 1906, with seven charter members, and Mrs. Dudley Sheppard, Organizing President. Of these, only Mrs. Sue Haslett and Mrs. W. M. Wilcox remain members today.

The motto is all inclusive, "For God and Home and Every Land." The World's W. C. T. U. is organized in fifty-two countries. The badge, "the little white ribbon bow," is symbolic of peace and purity. Noon-tide is the trysting time, when every white ribboner is asked to lift her heart to God in prayer for His work and the workers.

The Union has always stood for everything good and uplifting and is often called "Organized Mother Love."

Mrs. Sheppard served very capable and efficiently as President until her death in 1937, when Miss Mary Lizzie Wright was elected President. Others serving with her are: Miss Gladys Sheppard, Vice-President; Mrs. Sue Haslett, Vice-President from Methodist Church; Mrs. W. M. Wilcox, from Presbyterian Church, and Mrs. N. L. Johnson, from Baptist Church; Mrs. A. R. Cheek, Treasurer; Mrs. J. Hood Fortson, Recording Secretary; Mrs. J. E. Asbury, Corresponding Secretary, and Mrs. A. W. Haslett, Leader of L. T. L. The Union sponsored the organization of a Loyal Temperance Legion recently with sixteen charter members, and the President is Mary Eleanor Haslett. The membership of the Union at present is 48, and nine honorary members. During the year, Mrs. Sheppard's name was placed on the Memorial Roll and the present President was made a Life member by the Union. Other Life members are Mrs. A. R. Cheek, Mrs. N. D. Taylor, (Mrs. Z. W.) Edna Arnold Copeland, Miss Sara Anne Wright, and Mrs. Mary E. Wright is a Memorial member.

ROTARY CLUB OF ELBERTON

"Service Above Self."   *"He Profits Most Who Serves Best."*

The Rotary Club of Elberton, the 964th member of Rotary International, was presented with its charter on the night of July 5, 1921. Presentation was made to Herman P. Hunter, the first President, by W. R. C. Smith, of Atlanta, Georgia, acting in the capacity of District Governor John Turner, of Tampa, Florida. (Governor Turner was at that time Governor of the Eighth District of Rotary International and he was in Europe doing extension work.)

Charter members: Herman P. Hunter, Zack W. Copeland, Raymonde S. Stapleton, James Y. Arnold, William T. Arnold, Julian T. Brown, Paul Brown, John T. Dennis, Fred Herndon, Travis O. Tabor, Jr., Herbert L. Wiggs, John P. Heard, Parks E. Heard, Ernest G. Nock, Matthew B. Pitts, Boyce M. Grier, Paschel C. Maxwell, James E. Hall, Charlie Herndon.

The Athens Rotary Club sponsored the Elberton Club, and their President, Abit Nix, delivered the Charter Night inspirational address.

Since organization, the Club has had the leadership of the following Presidents: Herman P. Hunter, Zack W. Copeland, Travis O. Tabor, Jr., Boyce Grier, Raymonde S. Stapleton, John T. Dennis, Howard B. Payne, Hal S. Jaudon, Fred Herndon, Chandler Brown, Tom N. Gaines, Paul Brown, Henry T. Brookshire, Corwin Robertson, Walter E. Whitehead, John Cook, Clyde Teasley, Peyton S. Hawes, J. Cleve Allen.

Present officers are: W. Byron Minter, President; George M. Johnson, Secretary-Treasurer; and Burton C. Beard, Jr., Sergeant-at-Arms.

Present membership: Cleve Allen, granite monumental manufacturer; Stewart Asbury, refined oil products, wholesale; Jack Beard, carbonated beverages, bottling; Bill Bowers, furniture retailing; Chandler Brown, merchant, department store; Tom Coggins, monumental distributor; Lucas Carpenter, dry cleaning; Zack Copeland, wholesale groceries; Gradus Christian, newspaper publishing; John Dennis, cotton oil milling; Haley Denny, master barber; Joe Hanna, Jr., wholesale electric representative; Peyton Hawes, civil law; Wilber Hoover, associate, monumental dealer; Ralph Hood, education; Fred Herndon, building supplies, retail; Lat Heard, motion pictures; Charles Johnson, dentist; George Johnson, retail hardware; Walton Johnson, pediatrice; Angus Lee, railway transportation; John Logan, granite quarrying; Lester Lunsford, granite machinery and supplies; Byron Minter, cotton manufacturing; P. C. Maxwell, fire insurance; Tom Maxwell, funeral directing; Frank Martin, cotton marketing; Glenn McGarity, monumental dealer; Boozer Payne, corporation law; Ike Reid, retail drugs; Hoke Shirley, Christianity, Protestantism; Furman Smith, banking; T. O. Tabor, Jr., grain, feed, etc., retail; Norman Thompson, surgeon; Tom Thornton, retail groceries; Mark C. Weersing, associate Christianity, Protestantism; Henry Wise, ice and coal, retail; Allison Rowe, cotton warehousing; Walter Whitehead, farmer; Joe Wingo, automobile retailing; Clinton Sanders, electrical equipment, retail; J. S. Asbury, wholesale, gas and oil.

Club Motto: *"Service above self. He profits most who serves best."*

Club Aim: Through fellowship and understanding to make our vocations better, improve our personal relations, our community, our state, our nation, and the world at large.

KIWANIS CLUB

The Elberton Kiwanis Club was organized June 5, 1925, and its charter was presented by Lieutenant-Governor W. W. Munday, of Cedartown, August 27, 1925. There were 33 charter members.

The first officers were: Thos. H. Cooley, President; D. C. Hudson, Vice-President; F. S. Fortson, Secretary and Treasurer; Clark Edwards, Jr., Trustee. The first Board of Directors was composed of Z. B. Rogers, J. C. Styles, J. S. Asbury, G. P. Ransom, J. A. Metcalf, W. J. Coppedge, and H. J. Price.

Officers for 1940 are Sam Patz, President; Lloyd Mewbourne, Vice-President; Z. B. Rogers, Secretary; Leon Landau, Treasurer, and the Board of Directors is composed of Judge Clark Edwards, Jr, Joe Allen, Dobbs Smith, John Ralph Rice, Webb Tatum, Lewis Wallis, and Frank S. Fortson.

Past Presidents have been Thos. H. Cooley, D. C. Hudson, J. S. Asbury, J. M. Cleveland, Joe Allen, L. D. Hewell, Z. B. Rogers,

Rev. H. R. Boswell, Clark Edwards, Jr., Frank S. Fortson, Joe Wingo, and Retiring President, Rev. B. Frank Pim.

Among outstanding accomplishments of the Club are furnishing and placing a $700 road marker at the highway junction just out of Athens; getting out a Homecoming edition of *The Elberton Star* in May, 1938; sponsoring the planting of dogwood and crepe myrtle over the city, and supporting an under-privileged two-year old orphan child in a good rural home. The Club is interested in all matters affecting the progress and welfare of the community.

THE ELBERTON PILOT CLUB—PILOT INTERNATIONAL

On Friday, April 5, 1935, at 8 o'clock the Pilot Club of Athens, Georgia, entertained fifteen business women of Elberton at dinner at the Samuel Elbert Hotel, hoping to interest these women in forming a Pilot Club here. The purpose of this meeting was to acquaint the business women of Elberton with the purpose and ideals of Pilot International, which is patterned along similar lines of the men's civic organizations, such as Rotary and Kiwanis membership being confined to two women representatives from each profession or business. Membership in the Pilot Club is by invitation only and those women are selected because of outstanding prominence in their profession or business. The chief objective of the Club is civic welfare.

The Elberton Pilot Club was presented her charter May 17, 1935. Anna Patchen was the first President of the Club, and the charter members were:

Ima Birdsong	Ruby Brock	Mary Brown
Maggie Brown	Mamie Carithers	Louree Deadwyler
Marigene Funsten	Ruth Haley	Flora Hall
Norma Hawes	Emma Hunter	Lady Byrd Jones
Gene Knight	Violet Miller	Nella Paine
Anna Patchen	Sara Patz	Ruth Seymour

The Presidents of the Elberton Pilot Club are: Anna Patchen, 1935; Norma Hawes, 1936-38; Mary Brown, 1938-40.

The present enrollment of the Club is:

Ruby Brock	Mary Brown	Maggie Brown
Mamie Carithers	Louree Deadwyler	Lillian Echols
Olive Edwards	Gladys Fambrough	Flora Hall
Norma Hawes	Nina Hunt	Helen Jones
Jean McGinty	Ruth McMullan	Ruth McMullan
Lois McMullan	Edna Oglesby	Anna Patchen
Kathryn Rainey	Virginia Rainey	Ruth Seymour
Julia Webb	Anne Rucker	Emily Gary

THE ELBERTON GARDEN CLUB

The Elberton Garden Club was organized June 8, 1938, under the leadership of Mr. Roy Bowden, horticulturist of the University of Georgia, Mesdames W. D. Hooper, E. D. Pusey, President of the Athens Ladies Garden Club, and Miss Nina Scudder, of Athens.

The purpose of the Club is to encourage the love, study and culture of flowers along with Landscape Gardening.

The officers of the Club:

Mrs. Sam Combs..President
Mrs. John S. Jenkins..Vice-President
Mrs. H. B. Payne...Recording Secretary
Mrs. P. C. Maxwell...Treasurer
Mrs. Harris Bailey..Corresponding Secretary
Mrs. Tom Colley..Parliamentarian
Mrs. Fred Herndon..Auditor

The membership is forty-one.

The Club's project is to beautify the historical spring, located in the heart of the city.

GEORGIA SOROSIS CLUB

Georgia Sorosis Club of Elberton, the oldest federated club of the State, was organized July 2, 1892, at "Rosehill," the home of Mrs. E. B. Heard. This Club was patterned after the Sorosis Club of New York, and organized by five ladies, Mrs. S. A. Bowman, Mrs. Omer Harper, Mrs. E. B. Heard, Mrs. A. S. Oliver, all of Elberton, and Mrs. G. C. Thomas, of Athens.

In July, 1893, Georgia Sorisis joined the General Federation, and in November, 1896, two of her members, Mrs. E. B. Heard and Mrs. A. Omer Harper, were present and very active in the organization of the State Federation in Atlanta.

In 1912 a renewal of the charter was made by Col. Jule Brewer, and in 1932 a second renewal was made by Judge Raymonde Stapleton.

The different members who have served as Presidents from the beginning are as follows: Mrs. S. A. Bowman, Mrs. A. O. Harper, Mrs. H. W. Williams, Mrs. A. S. Oliver, Mrs. J. M. Wester, Mrs. A. S. Oliver, Mrs. H. J. Brewer, Mrs. F. L. Bartow, Mrs. M. L. Stevens, Mrs. C. J. Almond, Mrs. E. A. Cason, Mrs. J. M. Wester, Mrs. E. B. Heard, Mrs. A. S. Oliver, Mrs. W. D. Tutt, Mrs. A. S. Simmons, Mrs. C. J. Almond, Mrs. J. M. Wester, Mrs. Raymonde Stapleton, Mrs. C. F. Herndon, Mrs. Carter Arnold, Mrs. H. B. Payne, and Mrs. C. F. Herndon.

The officers at present are:

Mrs. C. F. Herndon..President
Mrs. Fred Herndon..First Vice-President
Mrs. A. S. Simmons..Second Vice-President

Mrs. Raymonde Stapleton..................................Recording Secretary
Mrs. Carter Arnold...Corresponding Secretary
Mrs. Perry Smith...Treasurer
Miss Jessie Champion ....Press Reporter
Mrs. B. F. Pim...Auditor
Mrs. H. B. Payne
Mrs. C. J. Almond
Mrs. T. N. Colley } ....Chairman of Board
Mrs. Pauline Brown

With this band of women, Georgia Sorosis is today among the most outstanding and active of the Clubs of the Federation. It reviews its life of forty-eight years with a measure of satisfaction in the results achieved. The Club occupies a place in the State all its own and its hopes and aims are that it may prove worthy of the traditions of the past and equal to the responsibilities of the future.

THE CIVIC LEAGUE OF ELBERTON

The Civic League of Elberton was organized and federated in 1908.
Past President: Mrs. A. O. Harper, Mrs. E. B. Tate, Mrs. Harry
  Hawes, Mrs. R. E. Hudgens, Miss Nora Jones.
The Woman's Club was the outgrowth of the Civic League, and was federated in 1929.
Past Presidents: Miss Nora Jones, Mrs. T. O. Tabor, Jr., Mrs. W.
  H. Paine, Mrs. G. C. Robertson, Mrs. J. H. Miller, Mrs. W. A.
  Johnson, Mrs. C. F. Cummings.

1939-40 OFFICERS

Mrs. Johnson Webb...President
Mrs. Tom Swift...First Vice-President
Mrs. McWhorter Thornton..................................Second Vice-President
Mrs. Bob Drennan...Secretary
Miss Mary Richardson..Treasurer
Mrs. George Gaines...Parliamentarian
Mrs. Zach McLanahan...Auditor

MARKERS PLACED BY STEPHEN HEARD CHAPTER, D. A. R.

(See 1st Section of History for early data of D. A. R.)

Assisted in placing Granite Marker (boulder), valued at $400.00, at Van's Creek Baptist Church in Ruckersville, eight miles from Elberton, in Elbert County, in 1935.

Bronze Tablet let in chimney of Nancy Hart Cabin, valued at $60.00, 12 miles from Elberton, in Elbert County.

A Memorial to Nancy Morgan Hart (granite boulder) placed on Elberton High School grounds, valued at $300.00.

Pink Granite Marker on old Court House site in City Park, Elberton, valued at $30.00.

Cherokee Indian Trail, granite marker, valued at $30.00, 15 miles from Elberton in Elbert County.

A field stone column, valued at $35.00, holding a bronze tablet furnished by the Government and executed by the students of Technological School, Atlanta, Ga., marker placed near Nancy Hart Spring, directing to the historic spot, 15 miles from Elberton in Elbert County.

Granite Marker placed on Petersburg Road, Georgia's oldest highway. Marker valued at $300.00. (Near the old Verdell home.)

A beautiful eight-foot electric flag on the dome of the Court House, presented to the City of Elberton and Elbert County, on Flag Day, June 14, 1917.

Granite Marker, in 1929, valued at $125.00 on Nancy Hart Highway.

Two corner stones of Elbert County granite were donated to Tamassee School for use in new building.

A FEW OF THE GRAVES MARKED BY STEPHEN HEARD CHAPTER, D. A. R.

James Adams—buried at Coldwater Church.
Thomas Adams—near Brewer's Mill.
Turner Christian—near Dewey Rose.
Thomas Carter—near Electric Light plant, family burial ground.
George Snellings—Fortsonia.
Capt. James C. Cunningham—near Rockbranch Church.
John Rucker—Ruckersville.
Benjamin Brown—Ruckersville.
Capt. Jacob Higginbotham—near Centerville School.
David Clark—See Mrs. Rosa Willis Reeves.
Christopher Clark—See Mrs. Ora Tate.
Lieut.-Col. William Alston—Ruckersville Methodist Church.
Dionysious Oliver—old Stinchcomb Church.
James Gaines—See Mrs. S. P. Rampley.
John Daniel—old Rock Branch Church.
Moses Hunt—See family of Hunts.
David Hudson—near Fortsonia—See Kellys in neighborhood.
William Rucker—Old Williams' place in Elbert County.
William Haley—To be placed.
John Duncan—near Bowman.
Andrew Brown—near Bowman.
John Norman—To be placed.
Joseph Deadwyler—See Vail Deadwyler.

The Chapter received the State prize offered by Edna Arnold Copeland for marking the greatest number of graves.

The Chapter also received the Daniel Silver Trophy, State prize, for the greatest number of Historical papers sent in.

Publishing the Elbert County History is its greatest accomplishment.

HOME SITE OF NANCY HART

Before the Revolutionary War there came to settle in the backwoods of Northeast Georgia (now known as Elbert County, Georgia), Nancy Morgan Hart, Benjamin (her husband), and their eight children.

The spot where the Harts built their cabin was known as the Broad River Settlement, near a romantic stream called Wahatche Creek (War Woman). The cabin stood on a steep hill, thickly wooded with pines and oaks that extended down to the water's edge, and had the appearances of belonging to nature nearly as much as did Nancy Hart, the "War Woman." The Nancy Hart home site was deeded to the State D. A. R. by the owners, Stephen Heard Chapter and the Nancy Hart Chapter, D. A. R.

Location of Nancy Hart's grave was made public by Edna Arnold Copeland. The location is at Henderson County, Kentucky, old Hart burial ground, about nine miles from Henderson, Kentucky). See sketch of Nancy Hart in another part of History.

THE ELBERTON STAR

By B. I. Thornton, Sr.

The Elberton Star for more than half a century has been the outstanding newspaper of Elberton, and of this section of the famous Piedmont section of Northeast Georgia. Larry Gantt, famous newspaper founder and editor of earlier days, founded it in September, 1888. Next year Gantt returned to Athens and repurchased *The Athens Banner* from Mark Cooper Pope, to whom he had previously sold, leaving *The Star* in the hands of his son, Jesse T. Gantt, who afterwards became Secretary of State of South Carolina. The management of *The Star* then fell into the hands of Schevenel and Ferd Williams, of Athens, who in turn were succeeded by Ira C. VanDuzer, with James L. Harper associate editor. Later Chas. M. Morcock bought half interest in the paper. Dr. N. G. Long then bought out VanDuzer, and Long and Morcock conducted the paper for some time. Col. W. D. Tutt, Sr., bought out Long and Morcock and edited and published *The Star* for several years, selling out to W. L. Skelton, native of Walhalla, South Carolina, but coming to Elberton from Atlanta. For more than a quarter of a century Skelton edited and published *The Star*. In his old age he sold half interest to Gradus T. Christian, who has been manager for more than 15 years, and who after Mr. Skelton's death, became sole owner and manager. Under Mr. Christian's administration the paper has been greatly improved in every respect, the printing plant has been greatly improved and enlarged, and as high class printing work is turned out as can be produced in any plant in the country.

The first press on which *The Star* was printed was a rebuilt flatbed press formerly used by *The Atlanta Journal*. Larry Gantt brought with him a Negro boy, Jim Short, as janitor and man-of-all-work. He could not read or write. Jim remained with *The Star* as long as he lived, and before he died knew the name and record of every baseball player of the major and minor leagues of America, and died leaving two farms, two houses and lots and many thousands of dollars in bank, having attained a good practical education while working at *The Star* office.

ELBERTON AIR LINE RAILWAY

By B. I. Thornton Sr.

The Elberton Air Line Railway, running from Elberton to Toccoa, was completed in November, 1878. It runs on a perfect watershed for 50 miles. It was a narrow-gauge railroad for the first 25 to 30 years. Until grading work was completed Dr. Dave Mathews was president, and through his efforts, largely, its construction was assured. Farmers along the route contributed rights-of-way gladly, and many of them subscribed to stock in varying amounts from $100 to $500. Elberton voters authorized $50,000 worth of stock in the enterprise. Major J. H. Jones became president after the grading work was completed. Lavonia was named in honor of Major Jones' wife. Bowman was named in honor of Thos. J. Bowman, prominent local capitalist of Elberton who generously contributed to building the road. The Elberton Air Line tapped the Richmond and Danville Railroad at Toccoa, now known as the Southern Railway. Prominent among the engineering crew of this railroad was Patrick Calhoun, relative of John C. Calhoun, to whose efforts and skill was largely due the worming of the railroad from mountain peak to mountain peak between Lula and Toccoa. Calhoun was afterwards a candidate for United States Senator against General John B Gordon before the General Assembly of Georgia, and Elbert's representative, Henry Heard, cast his vote for him.

GENEALOGICAL SECTION

ADAMS

The following chart shows intermarriages with the following families:

Almond — Amos — Attaway — Allen — Appleby — Arnold — Bynum — Bridwell — Bacon — Baber — Brewster — Bryan — Black — Brown — Bond — Brewer — Bradford — Bailey — Bush — Benson — Bray — Boswell — Burton — Burnett — Beggs — Cook — Clark — Coggins — Coleman — Cordell — Cheek — Cunningham — Crawford — Carlton — Cleveland — Colson — Charles — Dellis — Dobbs — Davis — Dudley — Durham — Dickerson — Deadwyler — Daird — Estes — Edwards — Eavenson — Fleming — Fortson — Ford — Goolsby — Gloer — Gary — Giles — Gaines — Hilliard — Haynes — Harmon — Harris — Hagood — Hall — Hunt — Herndon — Higginbotham — Hulme — Hailey — Holt — Hanner — Ingram — Johnson — Jordan — James — King — Kidd — Leard — Lewis — Lee — Leaser — Mewbourn — Matthews — Maxwell — McGee — McMullan — McCurry — McClure — McKay — McCalla — Mason — Majure — Mattox — Massey — Moore — Oglesby — Owens — Ooghee — Powers — Phelps — Pledger — Powell — Pierce — Pierson — Peek — Perryman — Payne — Roberts — Rucker — Rogers — Smith — Seawright — Scattergood — Swearingen — Scott — Snow — Souther — Seymour — Skelton — Seals — Stamps — Starr — Thornton — Tiller — Teasley — Tucker — Vickery — Wansley — Williams — Warren — Wilson — Ward — Winn — Willis — West — Webb — Young — Zachery.

(Note: Numbers represent generations, as: (1) first generation, (2) second generation, (3) third generation, etc.)

1—Robert Adams, d. 1740; m. Mourning Lewis.
  2—James Adams, m. Cecily Ford, 1751.
    3—James Adams Jr., R. S., b. October 18, 1753; d. 1835; m. June 19, 1772, Jane Cunningham, b. about 1756.
      4—William Adams, m. (1) March 20, 1797, Catherine Mansfield, and (2) Sarah Head.
        5—Rhoda Adams.
        5—Osburn Adams.
        5—William Adams Jr., m. October 3, 1833, Nancy Cheek.
        5—Frances Adams, m. October 23, 1823, John Thornton.
          6—William Thornton, C. S., d. January 29, 1863; m. 1852, Lucinda Almond, b. October 29, 1831. (See Thornton line).
          6—Sarah Thornton, b. August 5, 1824; d. December 16, 1863; m. August 1, 1839, George W. Eavenson; b. February 23, 1817; d. July 16, 1898. (See Thornton line).
        5—James Adams, m. Mary A. Hunt.
          6—Serepta A. Adams.
          6—Harriet F. Adams, m. Fleming Thornton (See Thornton line).
          6—William R. Adams, m. Elizabeth Teasley.
          6—Moses H. Adams, m. Lavina McMullan.
          6—Louise C. Adams, m. William Goolsby.
        5—Lawrence Adams, m. (1) Nancy Hunt, (2) Lucy Teasley.
          6—(By second wife) Emily Adams, m. 1867, Marion Gaines.
          6—Drucilla Adams, m. 1869, Marion Gaines.
          6—Beverly Allen Adams.
        5—Ann R. Adams, b. October 4, 1814, d. May 12, 1886; m. May 31, 1831, Thomas Maxwell, b. May 31, 1804; d. March 5, 1869.
          6—Mary Elizabeth Maxwell, m. (1) John Mize, (2) Charles Sorrells.

6—William Hayden Maxwell, m. (1) Harriet Almond, (2) Amelia Oglesby.
6—Frances Jane Maxwell, d. unmarried.
6—Martin Maxwell, m. Catherine Teasley.
6—Jackson Oliver Maxwell, m. Caroline Fleming.
6—Sarah Catherine Maxwell, m. (1) William B. Rucker, (2) Roland J. Brown.
7—Reverend Thomas Rucker, m. Fanny Thornton. (See Thornton line).
7—William A. Rucker, Clerk, Superior Court of Elbert County, m. Annie Bailey.
8—Thomas Rucker, Deputy Clerk, Superior Court of Elbert County, m. Margaret Bond.
8—Albert Rucker.
8—Annie Rucker.
8—Mack Rucker.
7—Lou M. Brown, m. Essie McCurry.
8—Clyde Brown.
8—Thomas Brown.
8—Benson Brown.
8—Katherine Brown.
8—Mary Brown.
8—Lonnie Brown.
8—Neal Brown.
7—Lon C. Brown, Postmaster of Elberton, m. Miss Yow.
8—Monget Brown.
8—Helen Brown.
7—Cran O. Brown, m. Eunice Allen.
8—Roland Brown.
8—Joseph S. Brown.
6—Chandler Maxwell, m. Mary Hester Brown.
6—Julia Ann Maxwell, m. William Benson Jefferson Norman.
7—Martin Norman.
7—Sarah Quillie Norman.
7—Mary Annie Norman.
7—Georgia Irene Norman, m. Bartow Mason.
7—Frances Emma Norman.
7—James William Norman.
6—Louisa Maxwell, m. Calvin Tucker Bond.
6—John Matt Maxwell, m. Emma Davis.
6—Thomas J. Maxwell, d. unmarried.
6—Amanda P. Maxwell, m. Elbert Gordon Brown.
6—Benson Mansfield Maxwell, m. Eula Beatrice Eavenson.
7—Mozelle Maxwell, m. Lonnie A. Teasley.
8—Margarette Teasley.
7—Paschal Chandler Maxwell, m. Eshter Pierce.
8—Jane Maxwell.
7—Willis Benson Maxwell, m. Mary Elizabeth Benson.
7—Annie Lou Maxwell.
7—Juia Maxwell.
5—Madison Adams, m. Melitta Hulme.
5—Jane Adams, m. James Hunt.
5—Fleming Adams.
5—Thomas Adams, m. (1) Miss Warren, (2) Miss Skelton.
5—Elbert Adams, m. Elizabeth James.
5—Katherine Adams, m. Thomas Jones.
5—Margaret Adams, m. Eppy Thornton.
5—Adeline Adams, m. John King.
5—Lucy Adams, m. Richard James.

4—Samuel Adams, b. February 1, 1784, d. November 6, 1861; m. 1803, Martha Ann Thornton, b. 1789, d. 1860.
5—Charlotte Adams, m. Abraham Evans.
5—Sandford Adams, m. Lou ———.
5—Elizabeth Jane Adams, m. (1) Mr. Colson, (2) Williamson Rogers.
5—Merial Caroline Adams, b. July 14, 1826, d. October 8, 1893; m. December 31, 1845 (the widower of her eldest sister, Elizabeth Jane) Williamson Rogers, b. July 15, 1817, d. 1890. (See Thornton line).
5—Thompson Adams, m. Frances Witherspoon.
5—Jeremiah Adams, b. May 15, 1823; d. May 15, 1860; m. Miss Witherspoon.
5—Alfred N. Adams, M. D., b. July 17, 1831; d. December 13, 1906; m. Mary Lamb.
5—Joe Adams, m. Miss Mary Witherspoon.
5—Eldredge Adams, m. Amanda Alldredge.
5—James Adams.
4—Jane Adams, m. Isham Teasley, d. 1829.
5—Benager Teasley, b. February 27, 1802; d. November 1, 1836; m, October 31, 1822, Lucy Hailey, b. September 21, 1804; d. January 1, 1859.
6—Elizabeth Ann Teasley, b. November 18, 1823, d. March 13, 1869, m. June 30, 1839, Roland J. Brown, b. March 11, 1816, d. August 1, 1894.
7—Benager Teasley Brown, C. S., b. 1841; d. 1862.
7—John A. Brown, b. June 1843; m. Phronie Teasley.
7—Isham Hailey Brown, b. May 24, 1846; m. (1) Eliza Teasley, (2) Sarah Ann Eliza Hailey, b. November 30, 1847, d. March 4, 1913.
8—(By second wife) J. A. Brown, b. June 18, 1866; m. Nora Harris.
8—Elizabeth Brown, b. February 27, 1868; m. J. J. Gaines.
8—Sarah Brown, b. November 23, 1869, m. James T. Giles.
8—Jerome Brown, b. August 1, 1874; m. Ruby Peek.
8—Laura Brown, b. September 3, 1878; m. R. L. Norman.
8—Isham Brown, b. August 25, 1880; m. Ruby Peek.
8—Mary Brown, b. May 18, 1882; m. L. M. Hanner.
8—Claud Brown, b. July 27, 1884; m. M. L. Nevers.
8—Bessie Brown, b. June 27, 1887; m. H. W. McMillan.
8—Henry Brown, m. Bonnie Jean Majure.
8—Clois C. Brown, m. Nellie Charles.
7—Laura Cornelia Brown, b. August 10, 1850; m. September 2, 1869, Henry F. Hailey, b. September 23, 1845, d. March, 1920.
8—Dr. W. I. Hailey, b. June 20, 1870; m. February 1894, Mertis E. Snow.
9—John Henry Hailey, m. Addie Kidd.
9—Rucker Marion Hailey.
9—William Howard Hailey, m. Helen McClure.
9—Isham Brown Hailey, m. Grace Allen.
9—Joel S. Hailey, d. 1929 unmarried.
9—Frank Elmo Hailey, m. Lula Boswell.
9—Lamar Rankin Hailey, m. Katherine McKay.
9—Hugh Edward Hailey.
8—Ten additional children whose names are unavailable to the compiler.
6—Martha Jane Teasley, b. October 4, 1835; d. 1907; m. September 1853, William M. Dobbs, d. 1904.
7—Georgia A. Dobb, b. 1855; d. 1880.

7—Mary Ophelia Dobbs, b. 1857; m. William Alfred Teasley, d. 1908.
7—James E. Dobbs, Clerk of the Superior Court of Cobb County, Georgia.
7—Emma Dobbs, b. 1859; d. 1919; m. 1885, Thomas W. Scott.
7—William Oscar Dobbs, b. 1864; d. 1905; m. 1890, Irene Whipple, b. 1866.
6—John Easton Teasley, b. December 4, 1827; d. September 24, 1904; m. (1) December 16, 1847, Drucilla Ann Allen Teasley, b. November 11, 1827; d. November 25, 1880; (2) March 1, 1881, Martha A. Burden, b. October 26, 1841; d. July 20, 1889. (3) Mary F. Hulme.
7—(By first wife) Mary Elizabeth Ann Teasley, b. January 17, 1851; d. July 7, 1902; m. November 23, 1867, William Isham Brown, b. March 6, 1849.
8—Drucilla Ione Brown, b. January 23, 1873; m. March 13, 1889, Thomas R. Estes, b. December 12, 1866.
8—Fanny P. Brown, b. April 8, 1875; m. November 1891, James F. Brown.
8—Lettie G. Brown, b. April 4, 1877; m. (1) George E. Brown, b. 1872; d. 1910; (2) Charles Vickery.
8—Mary O. Brown, b. 1883; d. 1884.
8—William W. Brown, m. (1) Lula Herndon; (2) Cathie Maxwell.
9—(By first wife) Clyde Brown, m. Lois Seymour.
9—Easton Brown, m. Katie Lou Oglesby.
9—Mary Brown, m. Luther Goolsby, b. November 27, 1895.
9—Ford Brown, m. Vera Roberts.
9—William W. Brown Jr.
9—George I. Brown.
9—(By second wife) Virginia Brown.
9—Rachel Brown.
8—Nancy Ann Brown, b. 1887; m. Gordon Clark.
7—Isham Jefferson Teasley, b. July 22, 1852; m. April 27, 1871, Amanda J. Brown, b. September 1, 1851; d. April 2, 1902.
8—John Easton Teasley, b. 1872, d. 1898.
8—William E. Teasley, b. 1874, d. 1895.
8—Dr. Benager Columbus Teasley, M. D., b. January 26, 1876; m. December 10, 1901, Effie G. Adams, b. November 22, 1881.
9—Harvey Eugene Teasley, b. September 29, 1902.
9—Gerald Haynes Teasley, b. June 30, 1907.
9—Benager Columbus Teasley Jr., b. March 13, 1913.
8—Hailey Isham Teasley, b. 1877, d. 1898.
8—Lucy Ann Teasley, b. 1881, d. 1907.
8—Sally E. Teasley, b. June 12, 1888.
8—Drucilla C. Teasley, b. August 20, 1892, d. 1913; m. E. L. Bacon.
8—George Allen Teasley, b. March 25, 1883; m. Ellie Coggins.
7—Benager Pierce Teasley, b. August 9, 1854; d. September 29, 1914; m. November 25, 1875, Lettie Rice, b. June 13, 1861.
8—William Alfred Teasley, b. December 22, 1877; m. November 7, 1900, Alice L. Adams, b. April 17, 1879.
8—Oscar Lee Teasley, b. October 12, 1881; d. February 1, 1919; m. December 27, 1908, Miss Gloer, b. September 18, 1886.
8—Edgar Carl Teasley, b. April 4, 1885; m. December 25, 1910, Pearl W. Brown, b. March 19, 1888.
8—Clyde E. Teasley, insurance agent, b. August 7, 1889; m. November 12, 1912, Leila Sue Cordell, b. January 1, 1893.
8—Ruth Teasley, b. August 29, 1892; m. November 15, 1915, Dr. Walton A. Johnson, M. D., b. March 3, 1892.
8—Benager Pierce Teasley Jr., b. September 15, 1896.
8—John Easton Teasley, b. December 16, 1904.

7—John Easton Cone Teasley, b. May 1, 1856; m. (1) December 13, 1837, Sarah Margarette Brown, b. December 7, 1860, d. July 11, 1904; (2) Mrs. Ann Cunningham nee Johnson.
8—(By first wife) Sallie I. Teasley, b. July 24, 1879; m. December 25, 1900, L. L. Gurley, b. January 28, 1871.
8—Lonnie A. Teasley, b. September 27, 1882; d. February 14, 1912; m. Mozelle Maxwell.
8—Drucilla Elizabeth Teasley, b. March 9, 1885; m. December 12, 1906, John Thompson Williams, b. December 25, 1878.
8—Inez C. Teasley, b. August 29, 1893; m. March 19, 1913, Jesse L. Massey, b. November 9, 1885.
7—James William Alfred Teasley, b. April 8, 1859; m. (1) May 5, 1881, Eddie M. Burden, b. January 3, 1864; d. March 16, 1903; (2) October 23, 1903, Lois Maxwell b. October 22, 1874; d. November 25, 1911; (3) Emmie Jordan, b. 1883.
7—Ida Ione Teasley, b. June 10, 1868; d. September 25, 1901; m. December 10, 1887, Allen Turner Jones, b. April 28, 1867; d. January 6, 1914.
7—B. A. L. Teasley, b. 1862, d. 1864.
6—James A. Teasley, b. October 20, 1825; m. Lucy Alexander.
6—Isham Hailey Teasley.
6—Benager Teasley.
5—John Adams Teasley, b. January 8, 1804; d. January 11, 1853, m. December 18, 1828, Elizabeth Carroll Hailey, b. November 24, 1806, d. February 14, 1853.
6—Isham Asbury Teasley, m. (1) Hattie Saddler; (2) Georgia Cox.
6—Mary Jane Teasley, b. October 4, 1835; m. 1852, Reuben Benjamin Thornton.
6—Catherine Teasley, m. 1854, Martin Eavenson.
6—Lucy Teasley, b. September 21, 1837; m. Thomas J. Eavenson.
6—Eliza Teasley, b. September 15, 1838; m. March 11, 1888, Martin Mewbourn.
6—John H. H. Teasley, C. S., Lieutenant; d. 1862.
6—William Hailey Teasley, b. October 24, 1830; d. March 11, 1907; m. January 11, 1849, Jane Ann Wansley, b. May 26, 1834; d. October 2, 1877.
5—Jency Adams Teasley, b. August 6, 1806.
5—Isham Hailey Teasley Jr., b. July 12, 1807; d. November 12, 1883; m. Mary Maxwell, b. December 31, 1818; d. July 22, 1851.
6—William Alfred Teasley, b. September 16, 1833; d. 1908; m. (1) January 1, 1856, Jane Baber, b. February 20, 1837; d. September 25, 1892; (2) Ophelia Dobbs Durham.
6—John I. Teasley, b. April 19, 1848; d. September 18, 1922; m. September 25, 1875, Lou Skelton, b. June 22, 1843; d. May 1900.
6—Jane Teasley, m. December 8, 1852, Norman Camp.
6—Mary Teasley, b. January 15, 1842; m. Dr. A. J. Brewster.
6—Rinnie Teasley, b. December 14, 1843; m. W. T. Berlin, b. 1839.
5—Osburn G. Teasley, b. November 10, 1817; d. August 1864; m. November 18, 1841, Lucy Ann Crawford, b. September 3, 1824; d. 1867.
6—William Isham Teasley, b. Nov. 13, 1842; d. July 12, 1908; m. March 12, 1862, Lucy A. Crawford, b. Sept. 1848; d. 1915.
6—Lucy J. Teasley, b. 1844; d. 1846.
6—John Alfred Teasley, b. July 28, 1836; m. Dec. 10, 1867, Telitia Aggie Turner, b. Oct. 8, 1850.
6—James A. Teasley, b. May 28, 1848; d. Nov. 8, 1878; m. July 14, 1867, Mary D. McGee.
6—Benager P. Teasley, b. 1853, d. 1907; m. Sarah Beggs.

6—Sarah Luella Teasley, b. Nov. 6, 1857, d. July 2, 1888; m. Jan. 25, 1878, F. Marion Hailey, b. Oct. 10, 1852.
6—Cora A. Teasley, b. May 5, 1850; d. Jan. 15, 1911; m. Alfred M. Adams.
5—Alfred Hunt Teasley, b. Aug. 14, 1819; d. Feb. 18, 1878; m. (1) Sarah Ann Craft, b March 9, 1821, d. April 14, 1864; (2) Dec. 26, 1866, Laura Elizabeth Hagood.
4—Ann T. Adams, m. Hiram Gaines, Sept. 26, 1792, Fluvannah County, Virginia.
5—James H. Gaines.
5—William Shanklin Gaines.
5—Margaret C. Gaines, m. Thomas Johnston.
5—Jency Gaines.
4—Elizabeth Adams, m. John Seals.
4—John C. Adams, m. Miss Dickerson, 1833.
3—Thomas Adams, R. S., b. 1758; d. 1836; m. Oct. 4, 1786, Sarah Ford.
4—Elizabeth Adams, b. July 13, 1787; m. Anthony Perryman.
4—Thomas F. Adams, b. June 5, 1791; m. (1) Widow Crawford; (2) Miss Jenkins.
4—James B. Adams, b. March 25, 1795; m. April 10, 1817, Polly Hailey.
4—Mourning Adams, b. Feb. 18, 1793; m. Oct. 23, 1817, Evans Thornton.
4—Calvin Adams, b. March 9, 1797; m. Miss Key.
4—Richard Adams, b. June 24, 1798; m. (1) Dec. 30, 1819; (2) Widow Tucker.
4—Abner Adams, b. March 6, 1800; m. July 20, 1826, Betsy Fortson.
5—William H. H. "Sheriff Bill" Adams, C. S. Sheriff of Elbert County, m. Eliza Teasley.
6—Fortson Adams, m. Leila Carpenter.
6—Richard Adams, d. unmarried.
6—Mittie Adams, m. John Cleveland.
7—Leroy Cleveland, m. Miss Smith.
7—Woodfin Cleveland, m. Miss Higginbotham.
6—Leila Adams, m. Reverend D. C. Brown.
6—Arthur Adams, m. Katie Parks.
6—Beuna Adams, d. unmarried.
6—Emma Adams, m. (1) Archie Parks; (2) W. J. Pearce.
6—William Adams, d. unmarried.
6—May Adams, m. Carl Neese.
6—Ernest Adams
5—Richard Adams, C. S., member Georgia House of Representatives, 1886-1887, m. Antoinette Cleveland.
6—Elizabeth Adams, m. George J. Hall.
7—James E. Hall, m. Lillian Deadwyler.
8—Willie Elizabeth Hall, m. L. A. Moore.
8—James E. Hall Jr.
7—William Hall, m. Miss Bryan.
7—Lila Hall, m. Henry Seegars.
7—Annie Hall, m. Mr. Cooper.
7—Sarah Hall, m. Ben Neal Smith.
6—Mamie Adams, d. unmarried.
6—Bud Adams, d. unmarried.
6—E. L. Adams, County Commissioner of Elbert County 1919-1920, d. unmarried.
6—Willis B. Adams, b. May 13, 1861; d. Feb. 11, 1913, Militia Captain, member Georgia House of Representatives, Mayor of

Elberton, Chairman Elberton School Board; m. 1895, Susan McCalla, b. Sept. 19, 1861; d. Dec. 23, 1923.
7—Willis Sue Adams, m. June 1918, H. R. Bynum, b. 1892.
6—Addie Adams, m. James Carpenter.
7—Lucile Carpenter, m. Jack Hailey, Sheriff of Elbert County. No issue.
7—Thomas Carpenter.
7—Lucas Carpenter, m. Sally Mann.
7—Helene Carpenter.
7—Ivan Carpenter.
6—Ida Adams.
6—Reese Adams, m. Dr. C. P. Ward, druggist.
7—Robert Ward.
4—John Adams, b. May 30, 1801; m. Feb. 27, 1823, Nancy Davis.
5—Thomas J. Adams, C. S., b. Dec. 1823; d. 1866; m. 1841, Elizabeth Alexander, b. 1824, d. 1909.
6—William Adams, b. 1845; d. 1930; m. Elizabeth Stamps.
7—Alice Adams, m. Charles Leard.
7—Fanny Adams, m. Ryan Hilliard.
7—Laura Adams, m. Lee Payne.
7—Nancy Adams, m. Mr. Coleman.
7—Oscar J. Adams, m. Miss Starr.
7—Genobe Adams.
7—Wesley Adams, m. Miss Pulliam.
6—Henry J. Adams, b. 1848; m. 1869 Mary (?)
7—Annie Adams.
7—Sally Adams.
7—Thomas Adams.
7—Newton Adams.
7—Minnie Adams.
7—Mitta Adams.
7—Stella Adams.
7—Augustus Adams.
7—James Adams.
7—Lula Adams.
7—Maud Adams.
7—Aetna Adams.
6—Thomas L. Adams, b. Dec. 25, 1850; d. July 1906; m. 1876, Louise Genobia Haynes, b. Feb. 23, 1859.
7—Delray Adams, Past Grand Matron of Georgia Eastern Star.
7—Aetna Adams, b. March 13, 1880; m. Oct. 13, 1901, William H. Arnold, b. 1881.
8—Louise Arnold, b. Aug. 15, 1902; m. 1919, Max Bridwell.
7—Royal Adams.
7—Effie G. Adams, b. Nov. 22, 1881; m. Dec. 10, 1901, Dr. Benager Columbus Teasley, M. D., b. Jan. 26, 1876.
7—Eldo Haynes Adams, b. March 16, 1883.
7—Valdis Adams.
6—Peter Adams, b. 1852; m. 1873, Lou Scoggins.
7—Onie Adams, m. Frank Collins.
7—Ambus Adams, m. Minnie Davis.
7—Gertrude Adams, m. Henry Dudley.
7—John Adams.
7—Lizzie Adams.
7—Marcus Adams.
7—Lou Adams, m. Grover Moore.
7—Laura May Adams.
7—Bessie Adams.
7—Claud Adams, m. Miss Harris.
7—Elmer Adams.

6—Houston Adams S 1880, Sally Williams.
7—Viola Adams.
7—Thomas Adams.
7—Walter Adams.
7—Mamie Adams.
6—Milly L. Adams, m. 1882, Warren Smith.
7—Ada Smith.
7—George Smith.
7—Dozier Smith.
7—Thomas Smith.
6—Julia Ann Adams, m. Stephen Carlton.
7—Annie Carlton.
7—William Carlton.
7—Robert Carlton.
7—Joseph Carlton.
7—Corrie Carlton.
5—Reverend John D. Adams, C. S., m. Aug. 20, 1850, Flora Reynolds.
6—Sally Adams, m. Marion Harmon.
6—Milliard F. Adams, m. Sarah Cordell.
6—Mary Adams, m. John Harmon.
6—Emma Adams, m. William Reed.
6—Lula Adams.
6—Laura Adams, m. Cullen Ward.
6—Addie Adams, m. A. F. Westmoreland, d. 1935.
6—Corrie Adams, m. (1) McMullin; (2) Cordell.
6—James Adams.
5—Richard Adams, C. S., m. Mary Dickerson.
6—Mary Adams.
6—Lula Adams.
6—Lenora Adams, m. David Higginbotham.
6—Lee Adams, m. Jones.

ALLEN

The following chart shows intermarriages with the following families:
Ackers — Algood — Alford — Adams — Arnold — Archer — Allston — Andrews — Alexander — Abercrombie — Bell — Bynum — Brown — Blackwell — Beck — Burriss — Barnett — Bates — Bacon — Benson — Bowers — Beacham — Bullard — Bradford — Cleveland — Carpenter — Carter — Chandler — Caldwell — Cash — Cosner — Comer — Clark — Coggins — Dickson — Douglas — Dockery — Deadwyler — DuBose — Downer — Dodd — Davis — Dye — Eavenson — Estes — Athridge — Fisher — Fleming — Gaines — Green — Goolsby — Gunter — Gray — Gloer — Gurley — Helton — Hudson — Hearne — Hawes — Heard — Hall — Hammond — Hill — Harris — Howard — Higginbotham — Hunt — Hairston — Haynes — Hedquist — Harding — Hulme — Jordan — Jones — Johnson — Kilpatrick — Kelly — Keys — Kennedy — LeConte — Lindsey — Long — Lee — Mattox — Moore — McCurry — McIntosh — Marburg — McCullough — Mitchell — Maxwell — Massey — Mewbourn — McGarity — McLanahan — Martin — Morrison — Neese — Norman — Nash — Nichols — Oglesby — Owens — Perrien — Page — Parks — Pearce — Porter — Pierce — Purdue — Pressley — Quillian — Rice — Rhodes —

Roberts — Scott — Shumate — Snellings — Skelton — Starke — Stone — Stovall — Stewart — Stelling — Speed — Smith — Stephens — Seymour — Scarborough — Stanford — Sullivan — Stevens — Tinsley — Teasley — Thornton — Vickery — Veronee — Wyche — Wainwright — Williams — Wansley — Warren — Wickliffe — White — Wayble — Walthour — Wood.

(Note: Numbers represent generations, as: (1) first generation, (2) second generation, (3) third generation, etc.)

1—William Allen, R. S., Captain, Elbert County Militia 1790, b. 1756; d. 1826; m. (1) Unknown; (2) Nancy Walthall; (3) Sarah Keys.
  2—(By first wife) Martha Allen, b. 1779; m. Zachariah Smith, R. S., b. about 1761, postmaster of Elberton.
    3—Singleton Smith, m. Sarah Cunningham.
    3—Lindsey Smith, m. Sept. 9, 1829, Rhoda Bell, daughter of Thomas Bell and Elizabeth Key.
      4—Thomas Smith, m. Cynthia Gunter.
        5—Samuel Smith, m. Betty Bradford.
          6—Cynthia Smith, m. John A. Stark, Sheriff of Elbert County.
          6—Henry Smith, m. Eva Brown.
          6—Duncan Smith, m. Lizzie Thornton.
          6—Annie Smith, m. Jan. 5, 1913, G. Carswell Hulme.
            7—Elizabeth Hulme.
            7—Tinsley Hulme.
          6—Mary Smith, m. Jan. 26, 1916, W. P. Stone Jr.
          6—Ethel Smith, m. Howard Thornton.
          6—Otis Smith, m. Miss Fortson.
          6—Ruby Smith, m. Mr. Dye.
        5—William Allen "Buddy" Smith, m. Belle Kelly.
          6—Thomas W. Smith.
          6—Beverly Allen Smith, m. March 5, 1920, Marie Edwards.
        5—Charles "Boy" Smith, m. Hattie Kelly.
          6—Leverette H. Smith, County Commissioner of Elbert County, 1921-1922, m. Aug. 18, 1909, Lula May Smith.
            7—Shirley Smith.
            7—Forrest Smith.
          6—Taylor B. Smith, b. Oct. 19, 1891; m. Jessie Smith.
            7—Seigler Smith, b. June 12, 1917.
            7—Joseph O. Smith, b. Nov. 9, 1925.
          6—William Oscar Smith, clerk, Elbert County Commissioner, 1921-1922.
        5—Rhoda Smith, m. Dec. 6, 1894, David C. Downer, warden of Elbert County, 1921-1922.
          6—George Downer, m. Jan. 24, 1918, Mattie Gunter.
        5—Bennie Smith, d. unmarried.
        5—O. H. Smith, County Commissioner of Elbert County, 1925-1936, killed in automobile accident 1936; m. Bessie McLanahan.
          6—Frances Smith.
      4—Lindsey Smith, m. Miss Morrison.
      4—Martha Smith, m. Julius P. Smith.
        5—John Smith.
        5—Nettie Smith.
        5—Corrie Smith, b. Sept. 1, 1856; d. 1931; m. George T. Dye, b. Jan. 6, 1851; d. 1936.
          6—Sammie Dye, m. Wootie Scott.
            7—Martha Dye, b. Dec. 14, 1896; m. Henry Bell.

8—Frances Bell, b. 1912.
8—Hubert Bell, b. 1914.
8—H. A. Bell, b. 1916.
8—Ward Bell, b. 1918.
8—Jones Bell.
8—Catherine Bell.
7—Matthew Dye, m. Genobe Adams.
8—Jim Starr Dye, b. 1924.
7—Frank Dye.
7—James Dye.
7—Julia Dye, m. Cecil Davis.
8—Martha Davis, b. May 1931.
6—Poppy Dye, b. Aug. 30, 1875; m. Sept. 29, 1897, Jeptha B. Hammond, b. Sept. 24, 1875.
7—George Hammond, b. Dec. 30, 1898; m. Sept. 6, 1918, Annie May Shumate.
8—Hazel Hammond.
8—Minnie Pope Hammond.
7—Mozelle Hammond, b. Sept. 21, 1900; m. 1918, Robert "Bob" Mize, S. W. W., Commander Edmund Brewer Tate Post American Legion.
8—Robert Mize Jr.
8—Hammond Mize.
7—Louise Hammond, b. Nov. 13, 1902; m. Hopkins Atkinson.
8—Lee Atkinson.
7—Jeptha B. Hammond Jr., b. 1904; m. Oct. 22, 1927, Willie Lyle.
7—Archie Pope Hammond, b. Oct. 3, 1911; m. Jan. 31, 1931, Lois Gaines.
6—Mary Dye, b. Nov. 24, 1877; m. Nov. 15, 1895, Grogan Perrin.
7—Lois Perrin, b. Oct. 21, 1896, m. M. Flowers.
7—George Perrin, b. Sept. 15, 1899; m. Roselle Thornton.
7—Thomas Perrin, b. Jan. 10, 1901.
7—Carl Perrin, b. 1903.
7—Julian Perrin, b. 1908.
7—Fred Perrin, b. 1914.
7—Forrest Perrin, b. Oct. 11, 1918.
7—Margaret Perrin, b. Oct. 21, 1920.
6—Ida Dye.
6—Lucy Ann Dye.
5—Annie Smith, m. Kit Bullard.
5—Ida Smith, m. Thomas J. McLanahan; d. 1932.
6—John J. McLanahan, b. 1880; m. Clara Rhodes.
7—Julian McLanahan, m. 1932, Ruth Ackers.
7—James McLanahan.
7—Clarence McLanahan, lawyer.
6—William McLanahan, m. Sarah Wyche.
6—Annie McLanahan.
6—Benjamin McLanahan.
6—Asbury McLanahan, killed in automobile accident, 1934; m. Annie Lou Nash.
7—Edward McLanahan drowned 1934.
7—Thomas McLanahan.
7—Benard McLanahan.
5—William Smith, m. Julia DuBose.
5—Lucy Smith, m. Andrew Wansley.
6—Belle Wansley, m. E. K. Beacham.
7—Edward Beacham.
7—Herman Beacham.
7—Marion Beacham.

7—Wilma Beacham.
7—James Beacham.
6—Colley Wansley, b. Nov. 24, 1890. S. W. W.
6—T. Quinn Wansley, b. June 4, 1894; m. Fanny M. Maxwell.
6—D. C. Wansley, S. W. W., m. Ruby Hailey.
7—William Wansley.
6—Augustus Wansley, m. Lanier Cleveland.
7—Augustus Wansley Jr.
6—Jack Wansley, m. Minnie Harding.
7—Jack Wansley Jr.
6—Thelma Wansley.
6—Ida Ruth Wansley.
5—Minnie Smith, m. Charles Jordan.
4—Antoinette Smith, m. John H. Downer.
4—Elizabeth Smith, m. Luther G. Smith.
5—Willie Smith.
5—Tommie Smith.
5—Ida Smith.
5—Robert Smith, m. Betty Algood.
5—Fanny Smith, m. George Clark.
5—Emma Smith, m. Jeptha McLanahan.
6—Alice McLanahan.
6—Luther McLanahan.
6—May McLanahan.
6—George McLanahan.
6—Graham McLanahan.
6—Belle McLanahan.
5—Lindsey Smith, m. Lula Bell.
4—Frances Smith, m. (1) Thomas Bullard; (2) George W. Snellings, C. S.
5—Tommy Bullard, m. D. C. Smith.
6—Julian Smith, m. Beatrice Norman.
6—Evelina Smith, m. Henry Caldwell.
6—C. T. Smith, m. Minnie Snellings.
6—Martha Smith, m. Warren Dixon.
5—Mattie Snellings, m. William Downer.
5—Rose Snellings, m. George Caldwell.
5—Oscar Snellings, m. Betty Owens.
5—Walter Snellings.
5—Cynthia Snellings, m. George Dixon.
6—Adeline Dixon.
6—Henry Dixon.
6—Clyde Dixon.
2—Elizabeth Allen, b. 1780; m. Daniel Thornton; d. 1846.
3—William D. Thornton, m. Jan. 27, 1829, Sarah Cleveland.
3—Elizabeth Thornton, m. Feb. 6, 1817, William Bell.
2—Drucilla Allen, b. March 1, 1782; d. July 4, 1847; m. James Teasley, b. March 1779; d. Feb. 10, 1849.
3—Beverly Allen Teasley, b. July 6, 1806; d. April 9, 1862; m. Feb. 15, 1828, Elizabeth Eavenson, b. June 22, 1810; d. Jan. 13, 1891.
4—Lucy Teasley, b. Dec. 12, 1828; m. 1846, Thomas Cason.
5—Allen Cason and other issue.
4—Alfred J. Teasley, b. Dec. 6, 1830; m. Sept. 30, 1851, Martha Frances Cleveland.
4—Elizabeth Ann Teasley, b. 1832; d. 1848; m. William R. Adams.
4—Priscilla Jane Teasley, b. July 24, 1834; d. May 23, 1896; m. Sept. 4, 1851, Benjamin Calloway Thornton, b. Dec. 13, 1827; d. Oct. 30, 1881.
5—Thomas A. Thornton, b. July 31, 1852; m. Georgia Carter.

5—Sarah Thornton, b. Jan. 1, 1854; d. April 5, 1924; m. D. C. Alford.
5—James Thornton, b. Sept. 5, 1857; d. March 14, 1921; m. Sarah Speed.
5—Janie Thornton, d. infancy.
5—Cornelia Thornton, d. infancy.
5—Amanda Thornton, b. Nov. 27, 1864; m. George Page.
5—John Thornton, d. unmarried.
5—Rebecca Thornton, d. infancy.
5—Jessie Thornton, b. April 4, 1871; m. Dec. 23, 1891, J. H. Skelton, member Georgia House of Representatives from Hart County, member Georgia Senate, lawyer.
5—McAlpin Thornton, b. Oct. 3, 1873.
5—Dunstan Thornton, b. July 2, 1876.
5—Annie Thornton, b. June 28, 1878; m. J. P. Cash.
4—Mary Frances Adeline Teasley, b. July 25, 1836; m. Mr. Adams.
4—Drucilla Catherine Teasley, b. Aug. 12, 1838; m. Martin Maxwell.
4—Phronie Teasley, b. June 3, 1843; m. 1865, John A. Brown.
4—Martha M. Teasley, b. 1841; d. 1843.
4—Eliza Emily Teasley, b. May 18, 1847; d. Nov. 1, 1864; m. May 3, 1864, Isham Hailey Brown, C. S., b. May 24, 1846.
3—James Riley Teasley, m. Mary B. F. Norman.
4—Jane Teasley, m. J. William Thornton.
5—Luther Thornton, m. Ida Herndon.
6—Seal Thornton.
6—Eula Lee Thornton.
6—Marion Thornton
6—Roselle Thornton.
6—Reba Thornton.
6—Bertha Thornton.
6—Susan Thornton.
6—Joel Thornton.
6—James Thornton.
5—James Thornton, m. Lucy Gaines. No issue.
5—Dr. Henry Thornton, M. D., m. Sarah Ward.
6—Pelham Ward Thornton, m. Ruth Hunt.
6—William Thornton.
6—Alston Thornton.
6—Jewell Thornton, m. Benson Brown.
5—Ida Thornton, m. Lindsey Hall.
6—James Hal.
6—Melvin Hall.
6—Sarah Hall.
6—Condal Hall.
6—William Hall.
6—Lucy Jim Hall.
5—Melvin Thornton, d. unmarried.
4—Lucy Ellen Teasley, m. Reuben Carter.
5—Thomas Carter.
5—Mack Carter.
5—James Carter.
5—Riley Carter and other issue.
3—Lucy H. Teasley, m. Lawrence Adams.
4—Emily Adams, m. Marion Gaines.
4—Drucilla Adams.
4—Beverly Adams.
3—Priscilla Teasley, m. Nov. 7, 1833, Willis Hunt; d. 1872.
4—Lucy Ann Drucilla Hunt, b. March 29, 1836.

4—B. A. T. Teasley Hunt, b. Aug. 12, 1839.
4—T. J. M. Hunt, b. July 16, 1841.
4—S. T. W. Hunt, b. June 28, 1843.
4—Judge M. B. Hunt, b. May 18, 1845.
4—William S. A. Hunt, b. April 5, 1848; m. Frances Cunningham.
5—John Hunt, m. Elizabeth "Lizzie" Gaines.
5—Looney H. Hunt, merchant, b. Feb. 2, 1881; m. Annie G. Gaines.
6—Annie Lee Hunt, b. April 1902; m. L. L. Stovall, merchant, clerk Commissioner of Elbert County, member Elbert County Tax Board.
6—Willie Hunt, merchant, b. Nov. 23, 1903; m. June 27, 1921, Ruth Maxwell, b. Oct. 6, 1902.
6—Parker Hunt, b. Aug. 3, 1906, granite shed operator, m. March 25, 1929, Grovia Dockery, b. Sept. 19, 1903.
6—Joel Hunt.
6—L. H. Hunt Jr.
6—James Hunt.
5—Evey Hunt, m. John Reynolds.
4—Laura C. P. Hunt, b. Aug. 10, 1850.
4—Berry M. T. Hunt, b. 1852.
4—Mary M. Hunt, b. Oct. 13, 1854.
3—Phronie Teasley, m. Malcolm Johnson.
4—Beverly Allen Johnson, m. Annie White.
4—Dr. Alexander S. Johnson, M. D., m. Ida Deadwyler.
5—Dr. Walton A. Johnson, M. D., b. March 3, 1892; m. 1915, Ruth Teasley, b. Aug. 29, 1892.
6—Wenona Johnson, d. infancy.
6—Phyllis Johnson, b. 1919.
5—Henry M. Johnson, d. infancy.
5—Harry Lee Johnson, b. 1887; d. 1914.
5—Lyndon Pope Johnson, b. Dec. 15, 1889.
5—Hoke S. Johnson, b. Jan. 1897.
5—Evelyn Johnson, b. March 10, 1900; m. John H. Green, b. 1900, Superintendent Elberton Public Schools.
6—Walton Green.
6—Harold Green.
5—Ida Johnson, b. Aug. 10, 1903.
4—John Johnson, m. Miss Bowers.
4—Sarah Johnson, m. Dec. 16, 1863, Walton Rice.
5—Mary E. Rice, b. 1870; d. 1931; m. 1893, R. D. Harris.
6—Lucy Harris.
6—Guy Harris.
6—William Harris.
6—Lessie Harris.
6—Quilla Harris.
6—Phillip R. Harris.
6—Ruby Harris.
6—Charles Harris.
6—Fred Harris.
5—Kate Rice, b. Oct. 1, 1872; m. Austin Fleming.
5—Sarah Rice, b. Nov. 28, 1874; m. Dec. 23, 1894, C. P. Hairston, member Elbert County Bond Commission, member Elbert County Tax Board.
6—Julius Hairston, b. 1895.
6—Horace Hairston, b. 1898.
6—Clara Hairston, b. 1905.
5—Lettie Rice, b. Jan. 27, 1877; m. Dec. 17, 1902, R. Dozier Harris.
6—Mauline Harris.
6—Eva Harris.

6—R. Dozier Harris Jr.
6—William P. Harris.
6—Rupert G. Harris.
5—Leonard Rice, b. Oct. 14, 1879; m. 1906, Bessie Lee Stevens.
6—John W. Rice.
6—Sarah Rice.
6—Grace Louise Rice.
5—Ida Rice, b. April 30, 1886; m. Dec. 3, 1905, William C. McGarity.
6—Thomas G. McGarity.
6—Katie Lou McGarity.
6—Mildred Lee McGarity.
6—William C. McGarity Jr.
6—Leonard A. McGarity.
6—Betty Jo McGarity.
5—N. A. Rice, b. 1885, d. 1887.
4—Katie Johnson, m. James Elbert Brown.
4—Patsy Johnson, m. Mallory Haynes.
3—Drucilla Ann Allen Teasley, b. Nov. 10, 1827; d. Nov. 25, 1880; m. Dec. 10, 1847, John Easton Teasley, b. Dec. 4, 1827; d. Sept. 5, 1904.
4—Mary Ann Elizabeth Teasley, b. Jan. 15, 1851; d. July 1902; m. Nov. 23, 1868, William Isham Brown, b. May 6, 1849.
5—Drucilla Ione Brown, b. Jan. 23, 1873; m. March 13, 1889, Thomas R. Estes, b. Dec. 12, 1866.
6—Mary Ethel Estes, b. Dec. 18, 1889; m. Dec. 5, 1910, Rev. D. C. William, Baptist Minister.
6—Letitia Gertrude Estes, b. May 15, 1892; m. March 4, 1918, Henry A. Jordan.
6—William L. Estes, b. May 15, 1892.
6—Lizzie K. Estes, b. June 6, 1896.
6—Annie V. Estes, b. Nov. 20, 1897.
6—James R. Estes, b. June 21, 1899, S. W. W., d. June 28, 1918, when Transport "Westover" was torpedoed by German submarine.
6—Thomas R. Estes Jr., b. Jan. 23, 1904.
6—Fannie S. Estes, b. Oct. 5, 1905.
6—Joel C. Estes, b. Aug. 25, 1908.
6—Dorothy Estes, b. Sept. 16, 1912.
5—Fannie Pierce Brown, b. April 8, 1875; m. Nov. 1891, James F. Brown.
6—William Howard Brown, b. 1892; m. Lois Cook.
7—Harold Brown.
7—Francis Brown.
7—Claudine Brown.
6—Mary E. Brown, b. 1896; d. 1901.
6—Isham T. Brown, b. 1903.
6—Joel Brown, b. 1908.
5—Lettie G. Brown, b. April 4, 1877; m. (1) George E. Brown, b. 1872; d. 1910; (2) Charles Vickery.
6—Mattie L. Brown, b. 1896; m. J. Carl Mattox.
6—Eugene Brown, b. 1898; m. 1920, Frances Harris.
6—Margaret Brown, b. 1908.
6—Charles Vickery Jr., b. 1919.
5—Mary O. Brown, d. infancy.
5—William Watkins Brown, m. (1) Lula Herndon; (2) Cathie Maxwell.
6—(By first wife) Ford Brown, m. Vera Roberts.
7—Rebecca Brown.

7—Robert Brown.
6—Clyde Brown, m. Lois Seymour.
7—Clyde Brown Jr.
6—Easton Brown, m. Katie Lou Oglesby.
6—Mary Brown, m. Luther Goolsby, b. 1895, postmaster, Carlton, Georgia, merchant, S. W. W.
7—Mary Carolyn Goolsby, b. 1935.
6—William Watkins Brown Jr.
6—George Brown.
6—(By second wife) Rachel Brown.
6—Virginia Brown.
5—Nancy Ann Brown, b. 1887; m. Gordon Clark.
6—Aubrey Clark.
6—Fritz Clark.
4—Isham Jefferson Teasley, b. July 25, 1852; m. April 27, 1871, Amonda J. Brown, b. Sept. 1, 1851; d. April 2, 1902.
5—John E. Teasley, b. April 2, 1872; d. Aug. 1898.
5—William E. Teasley, b. 1874; d. 1895.
5—Dr. Benager Columbus Teasley, M. D., b. Jan. 26, 1876; m. Dec. 10, 1901, Effie G. Adams, b. Nov. 22, 1881.
6—Harvey E. Teasley, b. Sept. 29, 1902.
6—Gerald H. Teasley, b. June 30, 1907.
6—Benager Columbus Teasley Jr., b. March 13, 1913
5—Hailey I. Teasley, b. 1877; d. 1898.
5—Lucy Ann Teasley, b. 1881; d. 1907.
5—Sally A. Teasley, b. June 12, 1888.
5—Drucilla C. Teasley, b. Aug. 20, 1892; d. July 4, 1913; m. E. L. Bacon.
4—Benager Pierce Teasley, b. Aug. 9, 1854; d. September 29, 1914; m. Nov. 25, 1875, Lettie Rice, b. June 13, 1861.
5—William Alfred Teasley, b. Dec. 22, 1877; m. Nov. 7, 1900, Alice L. Adams, b. April 17, 1879.
6—Alice Lucile Teasley, b. Feb. 1, 1903; m. 1925, Joe Wicliffe.
7—Alice Wickliffe, b. 1926.
7—Josephine Wickliffe, b. Aug. 1, 1928.
7—Winell Wickliffe, b. Aug. 1, 1928.
6—Thelma Teasley, b. April 26, 1905.
6—Wilton Alfred Teasley, b. 1909; d. 1919.
5—Oscar Lee Teasley, b. Oct. 12, 1881; d. Feb. 1, 1919; m. Dec. 22, 1908, Jewel Gloer, b. Sept. 1886.
6—Charlotte B. Teasley, b. Aug. 2, 1910.
6—Mildred Teasley, b. Jan. 25, 1917.
5—Edgar C. Teasley, b. April 4, 1885; m. Dec. 25, 1910, Pearl Willow Brown, b. March 19, 1888.
6—Edgar N. Teasley, b. Oct. 7, 1912.
6—Harold Teasley, b. Aug. 7, 1914.
5—Clyde E. Teasley, insurance broker, b. Aug. 7, 1889; m. Nov. 12, 1912, Leila Sue Cordell, b. Jan. 1, 1893.
6—Clyde E. Teasley Jr., b. July 8, 1914.
6—Benjamin Cordell Teasley, b. Dec. 5, 1918.
5—Ruth Teasley, b. Aug. 29, 1892; m. Nov. 15, 1915, Dr. Walton A. Johnson, M. D., b. March 3, 1892.
6—Winona Johnson, b. 1916, d. 1918.
6—Phyllis Johnson, b. Sept. 22, 1919.
5—Benager Pierce Teasley Jr., b. Sept. 15, 1896; m. Aug. 1934, Ona Howard.
5—John E. Teasley, b. Dec. 16, 1904.
4—John Easton Cone Teasley, b. May 11, 1856; m. (1) Dec. 13, 1877, Sarah M. Brown, b. Dec. 7, 1860; d. June 11, 1904; (2) Sept. 5, 1905, Mrs. C. Ann Cunningham nee Johnson.

5—(By first wife) Sally I. Teasley, b. July 25, 1879; m. Dec. 25, 1900, L. L. Gurley, b. Jan. 28, 1871.
6—Easton W. Gurley, b. April 6, 1902.
6—Hoyt L. Gurley, b. December 24, 1904.
6—Sarah T. Gurley, b. May 10, 1906.
5—Lonnie A. Teasley, b. Sept. 27, 1882; d. Feb. 14, 1912; m. Nov. 9, 1910, Mozelle Maxwell.
6—Margarette Teasley.
5—Drucilla Elizabeth Teasley, b. March 9, 1885; m. Dec. 12, 1906, John Thompson Williams, b. Dec. 25, 1878.
6—Anna E. Williams, b. June 16, 1908.
6—John T. Williams, b. Feb. 25, 1914.
5—Inez C. Teasley, b. Aug. 29, 1893; m. March 19, 1913, Jesse L. Massey.
6—Joel W. Massey, b. Aug. 3, 1916.
3—Patsy Martha Teasley, m. Thomas Jefferson Teasley.
4—James Teasley, m. Martha Clark.
4—William A. Teasley, m. Lucy Jane Adams.
4—Eliza Teasley, m. William H. H. Adams, C. S., Sheriff of Elbert County.
4—Phronie Teasley, m. Jefferson Brown.
3—Jefferson Teasley, m. Nancy Mewbourn.
4—Martin Teasley, m. Lucy Brown.
4—Harrison Teasley, m. Sally Chandler.
4—Thomas J. Teasley, m. Miss Olbon.
4—Mindy Teasley, m. William Eavenson.
5—Eula E. Eavenson, m. Zary Maxwell.
6—Mozelle Teasley, m. Nov. 9, 1910, Lonnie A. Teasley, d. 1912.
7—Margarette Teasley.
6—Paschal Chandler Maxwell, bank teller, m. Esther Pierce.
7—Jane Maxwell.
6—Willis Benson Maxwell, m. Mary Elizabeth Benson.
6—Mary Lou Maxwell.
6—Julia Maxwell.
2—Daughter of William Alen, m. Mr. Lindsey.
3—William Allen Lindsey.
2—Beverly Allen, member Georgia House of Representatives, member Georgia Senate, delegate to anti-tariff convntion, Justice of the Inferior Court of Elbert County; m. Mildred Beck. No issue.
2—Ann Allen, m. Mr. Hammond.
2—(By second wife) Singleton Walthall Allen, b. Jan. 1, 1791; d. June 6, 1853; m. Jane Lanier Heard, b. March 23, 1797, daughter of Governor Stephen Heard and Elizabeth Darden. (Singleton Walthall Allen served in the Georgia House of Repsentatives and in the Georgia Senate).
3—Elizabeth Allen, m. George Williams.
4—Rebecca Wiliams, m. DuBose Hill.
5—Janie Hill, m. Benjamin H. Hill.
6—Janie Hill.
4—George Wiliams, C. S., d. unmarried.
4—William Williams, m. Jessie Arnold.
5—William McIntosh Williams.
4—Janie Williams, m. John Burriss.
5—Dilliard Burriss.
3—Ann Allen, m. Dr. Milton Comer.
4—Janie Comer, m. 1874, Samuel Barnett, C. S., Captain, b. Aug. 16, 1841; d. Nov. 26, 1898.
5—Comer Barnett, mayor of Washington, Georgia, b. May 11, 1878; d., March 13, 1938; m., June 19, 1901, Corneill Bounds b. Feb. 14, 1880.

6—Lillis Barnett, b. March 25, 1911.
4—Bevelle Comer, m. Dr. Hampton. No issue.
4—Annie Comer, b. 1849; d. 1928, unmarried.
3—Susan Allen, m. Young L. G. Harris, member Georgia House of Representatives, member Georgia Senate, donor of Harris-Allen Library of Elberton, president Southern Mutual Insurance Company of Athens, Georgia. No issue.
3—Maria Louisa Allen, b. Aug. 10, 1824; d. Aug. 1885; m. Jan. 27, 1842, William McPherson McIntosh, C. S., Colonel and Brevet Brigadier-General, killed in action June 1862, lawyer, planter, member Georgia House of Representatives, member Georgia Senate, electo state-at-large for Beckinridge 1860.
4—Singleton Allen McIntosh, C. S., b. Feb. 19, 1845; d. Nov. 17, 1908; m. Mary Eliza Cade.
5—Sarah Howell McIntosh, b. Dec. 29, 1867; m. S. J. Zeigler.
6—Samuel Zeigler, S. W. W., naval officer, m. Fanny Marburg.
7—Howell Zeigler.
6—Howell Zeigler, m. George Lee Dickson, S. W. W., Major, U. S. Army retired.
7—Howell Rees Dickson.
7—George Lee Dickson Jr.
5—William McPherson McIntosh, b. 1870; d. 1930 unmarried.
5—Guilford "Guy" McIntosh, b. July 6, 1873; m. Sept. 14, 1918, Addie Tinsley.
6—Mary McIntosh, b. Sept. 3, 1921.
6—William Kenneth McIntosh, b. Nov. 10, 1922.
6—Louise McIntosh, b. Nov. 1923.
5—Victoria Augusta McIntosh, b. March 1875; m. Joseph Allston.
6—Joseph Allston Jr., m. Lillis McCullough.
7—Joseph Allston III.
6—Mary Allston.
5—Mary Louise McIntosh, b. Aug. 10, 1877; m. Henry M. Long.
6—Mary Louise Long, d. infancy.
4—William McPherson McIntosh Jr., C. S., m. Helen Dean.
5—William McPherson McIntosh III.
4—Anna Cassandra McIntosh, b. March 5, 1849; m. Dec. 11, 1866, Budd Clay Wall, C. S., mayor of North Augusta, South Carolina, merchant.
5—Martha Louise Wall, b. April 6, 1868; m. Thomas Andrews. No issue.
5—James Singleton Wall, b. Jan. 1, 1873; m. Rose Douglas. No issue.
5—McPherson Wall, d. infancy.
5—William Clay Wall, d. infancy.
5—Bevel McIntosh Wall, b. June 30, 1875; m. Mary Stewart.
6—Margaret Wall.
6—Bevel Clay Wall, m. 1929, Virginia Alexander.
7—Bevel Carles Wall, b. July 22, 1930.
5—Jessie McIntosh Wall, b. Dec. 20, 1878; m. John D. Stelling.
6—Sterling Stelling, b. Feb. 14, 1900; m. Eula Mitchell. No issue.
6—Dr. Richard Stelling, b. May 14, 1901.
6—Martha McIntosh Stelling, b. Dec. 14, 1903; m. June 1930, Dr. Charles McCord Kilpatrick, M. D.
6—Howard Cree Stelling, b. Sept. 1906; m. Helen Wainwright, international swimming star.
6—Budd Clay Wall Stelling, b. Feb. 1909.
5—Harry Wall, m. (1) Maryland Randall, divorced; (2) Hattie Smith. No issue.
4—Jessie McIntosh, d. infancy.

4—Maria Louise McIntosh, b. March 15, 1851; d. May 7, 1894; m. Feb. 2, 1869, Guilford Cade Jr.
5—Julia May Cade, b. Dec. 30, 1871; m. Nov. 23, 1892, Dr. Albert Sidney Hawes, M. D., member Georgia House of Representatives, mayor of Elberton, merchant, planter, b. Nov. 14, 1864; d. Nov. 1936.
6—Guilford Moseley Hawes, b. July 24, 1894; m. 1913, Onie Lee, b. 1893.
6—Mary Lee Hawes, b. Sept. 14, 1917.
6—Robert Hawes, d. infancy.
6—Julia Ann Hawes, b. Feb. 25, 1925.
6—Albert Lee Hawes, architect, b. Feb. 11, 1901; m. Bertha Bates of New York, who died without issue.
6—Peyton Samuel Hawes, b. Sept. 4, 1903, member Georgia House of Representatves, city attorney of Elberton, solicitor City Court of Elberton; m. 1933, Virginia Smith.
5—Guilford Cade III, b. June 9, 1875; m. Dec. 4, 1904, Jane Kennedy.
6—Malvina "Mally" Cade, b. Sept. 9, 1905; m. Milo Abercrombie; d. 1931.
7—Milo Abercrombie Jr., b. 1931.
6—Guilford Cade IV, b. April 18, 1911.
5—Annie Lee Cade, b. Feb. 21, 1878; m. Feb. 24, 1903, Dr. Robert Franklin Moore, M. D. and dentist, b. Jan. 30, 1871; d. 1923.
6—Alan Moore, b. Nov. 25, 1905; d. 1923.
6—Guilford McIntosh Moore, b. Sept. 27, 1908; m. Miss Mauldin of South Carolina.
4—Mary Bevelle McIntosh, b. June 1856; d. June 1926; m. 1895, John Chandler Brown, b. 1857; d. 1917, mayor of Elberton, merchant, planter. No issue.
4—James McIntosh, b. Sept. 1, 1857, sheriff of Elbert County, County Commissioner of Elbert County, member City Council of Elberton, member Tax Board, City of Elberton; m. Oct. 1882, Mary Jane Arnold, b. Sept. 3, 1859.
5—Sarah Louise McIntosh, b. July 29, 1883; m. Feb. 24, 1903, A. F. Archer. No issue.
5—William McPherson McIntosh, d. infancy.
5—Jessie McIntosh, d. infancy.
5—Mary James McIntosh, d. infancy.
5—John Hawes McIntosh, b. Nov. 26, 1895, historian of Elbert County, County Attorney of Elbert County, Assistant Secretary Georgia Senate; m. June 19, 1918, Fay Ann White, b. Oct. 21, 1900. Divorced 1937.
6—Mary Louise McIntosh, b. July 16, 1920.
6—Elizabeth "Betty" Arnold Penn McIntosh, b. March 15, 1923.
5—McAlpin McIntosh, b. 1897; d. 1899.
4—Jessie McIntosh, b. 1859; m. Peyton M. Hawes, member Georgia House of Representatves, member Georgia Senate, Militia Captain, president Elberton Loan & Savings Bank, president Elbert County Bank, trustee Georgia School for the Deaf. No issue.
3—Gerrard Allen, m. Oct. 31, 1850, Isabella Blackwell.
4—Gerrard Allen Jr., m. Adeliade Stanford.
5—Singleton Allen, m. May Wood.
6—Gerrard Allen, m. Sadie Ethridge.
5—Hattie Allen, m. Charles Whitmire.
6—Charles Whitmire Jr.
6—Harriet Whitmire.
6—Annie Bevelle Whitmire.

6—Martha Whitmire.
3—Mary Allen, m. George McCalla.
4—Isaac McCalla, m. Raymond Speed.
5—Leila McCalla, m. Mr. Linder.
6—Alice Linder, m. J. P. Sullivan.
7—J. P. Sullivan Jr.
5—Mack McCalla, m. Ella Nichols.
6—Mack McCalla Jr.
6—Elmira McCalla.
5—John McCalla, m. Parniče Brown. No issue.
4—Jennie McCalla, m. Joseph Speed.
5—Florence Speed, m. A. A. McCurry.
6—Speed McCurry.
6—A. A. McCurry Jr.
6—Jennie May McCurry.
6—Horace McCurry.
6—Althea McCurry.
6—Joseph McCurry.
4—John W. McCalla, County Commissioner of Elbert County, merchant, planter, m. Mitta Allen.
5—Olivia McCalla, m. Perry H. Smith, merchant, member City Council of Elberton.
6—Ethel Smith, m. Mr. LeConte.
5—Annie McCalla, m. J. H. Purdue, lawyer of Birmingham, Ala.
6—Frances Purdue.
6—Mary Olivia Purdue.
6—J. H. Purdue Jr.
5—J. Earl McCalla, m. Catherine "Kate" Stephens.
6—John McCalla.
6—Catherine McCalla.
6—J. Earl McCalla Jr.
6—David McCalla.
4—Ida McCalla, m. (1) Frank Cleveland; (2) Bedford Heard
5—Andrew B. Cleveland, m. Agnes Hall.
6—Frank Cleveland, m. Cleo Smith.
7—Agnes Cleveland.
6—Lanier Cleveland, m. Augustus Warren.
7—Augustus Wansley Jr.
6—Elizabeth Cleveland, m. Frank Veronee.
6—Helen Cleveland.
6—McCalla Cleveland.
6—Andrew B. Cleveland Jr.
5—Jessie Cleveland, m. Jesse Warren.
6—Hilda Warren.
6—Jeremiah Warren.
5—Sarah Heard, m. Frank Hammond.
6—Frank Hammond Jr.
6—Mildred Hammond.
5—M. E. Heard, m. Allen Pressley.
5—Erskin Heard, m. Lottie Seymour.
6—Martha Heard.
6—Bedford Heard.
6—Emma Heard.
6—Mattie Heard.
6—Hazel Heard.
5—Bevelle Heard, m. Thomas Wayble.
6—Bevelle Wayble.
5—Caroline Heard, m. Guy Quillian.

4—Susan McCalla, b. Sep. 19, 1861; d. Dec. 23, 1923; m. 1895, Willis B. Adams, b. May 13, 1861; d. Feb. 11, 1913, member Georgia House of Representatives, mayor of Elberton, chairman Elbert School Board, Militia Captain, merchant, planter.
5—Willis Sue Adams, b. July 20, 1896; m. June 1918, H. R. Bynum.
6—Susan Margaret Bynum, b. May 9, 1919.
4—Dr. Lawrence "Larry" McCalla, M. D., m. Hettie Hearne.
5—Dr. Lawrence McCalla Jr., M. D., m. Mildred Cosner.
6—Lawrence McCalla III.
6—Mary McCalla.
4—Mary "May" McCalla, m. George Gaines. No issue.
3—Theodore Allen, d. unmarried.
3—Rebecca Allen, m. William H. Mattox, C. S. Captain, member Georgia House of Representatives, member Georgia Senate, delegate to Constitutional Convention 1877, merchant, planter.
4—Lena Mattox, m. Jeptha Jones.
5—Reba Jones, m. George W. Gray, member Board of Registrars of Elbert County, merchant, planter.
6—George W. Gray Jr.
6—Page Gray.
5—Allen Jones, m. Annie Lou Snellings. No issue.
5—H. P. M. Jones, m. August 20, 1911, Mary Wall.
6—H. P. M. Jones Jr.
6—Martha Jones.
6—Rebecca Jones.
6—Thomas Jones.
5—Annie Sue Jones.
5—Callie May Jones, b. 1891; m. April 19, 1909, Albert R. Hudson, b. 1878.
6—Albert Hudson, b. 1910; m. Elizabeth Bell.
6—Clark Hudson, b. 1912.
6—Francis Hudson, b. 1915.
6—Mack Hudson, b. 1917.
6—David Hudson, b. 1919.
6—Carroll Hudson, b. 1922.
4—Singleton Mattox, m. Annie Jones.
5—Jessie Mattox.
4—Clark McIntosh Mattox, m. Sarah Jones.
5—Clark McIntosh Mattox Jr., b. Jan. 29, 1903; m. Dec. 25, 1925, Annie Bertha Helton.
5—Jeptha Mattox, m. Louise Scarborough.
6—John Clark Mattox.
6—Jeptha Mattox Jr.
4—Susan Mattox, d. unmarried.
4—Annie Mattox, d. unmarried.
4—Carroll Mattox, m. Charles Fisher.
5—Mamie Fisher.
4—Janie Mattox, m. Raymond Gaines; d. 1934. No issue.
2—(By third wife) Major Thomas Allen.

ALLGOOD

(Note: Numbers represent generations, as: (1) first generation, (2) second generation, (3) third generation, etc.)

1—William Allgood, of Elbert County, Georgia, 1785 (formerly of Virginia) married Mary Hudson. He fought in the War of 1812 (Shown in records as William Allgood, Sr.)
  2—Sarah Allgood, b. 1805, m. Jacob Hogue.
  2—Rebecca Allgood, b. 1807, m. Rev. Willis Matthews.
  2—Nancy Allgood, b. 1809.
  2—John Young Allgood, b. 1811; m. (1) Anna Sophia Lyle; (2) Cynthia McMillan, nee Brewer.
  2—Mary W. Allgood, b. 1813, m. Rev. William Smith.
  2—Rev. William Allgood Jr., b. 1816, m. Eliza Christian.
  2—Nathan Allgood, b. 1819.
  2—Peter Patrick (or Patrick H.) Allgood, m. Emily Brice.
  2—Sarah Allgood, b. 1805, Elbert County, Georgia; m. Jacob Hogue, b. 1800.
  3—Mary Hogue, b. Draketown, Ga.; m. Samuel Sewell.
  3—Martha Katerine (Kate) Hogue; never married; d. Ida, La.
  3—William Taylor Hogue, m. (1) Mary ———; (2) Mattie Jane Fox.
  3—Eliza Hogue, m. James D. Little.
    Eliza and Amanda Hogue were twins; James D. and John O. Little were brothers.
  3—Amanda Hogue, m. John O. Little.
  3—Bailey D. Hogue (or Jacob B. Hogue).
  3—James Hogue, b. 1836; m. Nancy Caroline McClung.
  3—Ellen Hogue, m. Dr. Robert B. Hutcheson.
  3—Sallie Hogue, m. LaFayette Peacock.
  3—Jonathan Patrick Hogue, b. about 1847; m. Lydia Jane Yates.
  3—Jonathan Patrick Hogue, b. about 1847, Draketown; m. Lydia Jane Yates.
  4—Frank Erastus Hogue, b. 1872; m. Vida Smith.
  4—Joseph Jacob Hogue, b. 1874; m. Fannie Thomas.
  4—Annie Laura Hogue, d. in childhood.
  4—Sallie Ellen Hogue, b. 1878; m. Robins Pinkney Yates.
  4—Ben D. Hogue, b. 1879; m. Connie Ethel Easter.
  4—Maud Hogue, died when a baby.
  4—Mary Rush Hogue, b. 1883; m. (1) Watha Brewer; (2) Lee Nabors.
  4—Eva Bell Hogue, b. 1885; never married; died at age of 20.
  4—Willia Eugene Hogue, b. 1888; m. Katie Pillow.
  4—Sallie Ellen Hogue, b. 1879; m. 1895, Robins Pinkney Yates.
  5—Duard Bryan Yates, b. 1896; m. Lula Smith.
  5—Adlai Robin Yates, b. 1900; m. Gladys Mae Collins.
  5—Lydia Grace Yates, b. 1903; m. Robert Paschal Odom.
  5—Della Pearl Yates, b. 1905; d. at 10 months.
  5—Ennis Emmet Yates, b. 1906; d. 1912, age 6.
  5—Frank Ivans Yates, b. 1910; m. Rebecca ———.
  5—Boyce Odell Yates, b. 1913, in U. S. Army.
  5—Sallie Ellen Yates, b. 1916; d. at birth.

William Allgood, Senior, enlisted in Elberton, Elbert County, Georgia, November 21, 1814, served as private in Captain Gaines Thompson's Company of Georgia Militia and was discharged May 6, 1815, at Fort Hawkins when the Company was discharged. He received no written certificate of discharge and no battle was referred to. He stated that another William Allgood served in the same Company, but did not say they were related.

November 6, 1850, William Allgood, Senior, applied for bounty land which was due him on account of his service in the War of 1812. He was then a resident of Paulding County, Georgia. On that application he was granted eighty acres of bounty land on Warrant No. 3875, under the Act of September 28, 1850. He applied March 24, 1855, for additional bounty land which was due on account of above-noted service. He was then aged seventy years and a resident of Paulding County, Georgia. On that application he was granted eighty acres of bounty land on Warrant No. 26823, under the Act of March 3, 1855. He made his last application before John Y. Allgood, Justice of the Peace of Paulding County, Georgia, and John Hutcheson, aged sixty years, James A. Reeves, aged forty-one years, and Marcus A. Bell witnessed his signature. No relationship between any of these persons is shown.

The data which follows was obtained from the papers on file in Revolutionary War claim for pension, S. 41408, based upon service of William Algood in the Revolutionary War.

William Algood enlisted in Virginia, the place not shown, November 11, 1776, for three years in Captain Isaac Hicks' Company, Colonel Screven's Georgia Regiment, marched directly to Savannah, Georgia, for service in that state, and sometime in May, 1777, was placed in Captain Clem Nash's Company of light infantry, was in the siege of Sunbury under Major Lane, where he (Algood) was taken prisoner when the Fort surrendered, marched to Savannah, was transferred to the Whitley prison ship where he remained nine months, five days, and made his escape during the siege of Savannah and continued in the Army until the "retreat" to Charleston, when he was discharged by General McIntosh. He served subsequently in Captain Michael Rudolph's Company, Colonel Lee's Legion, length of this service eighteen months, and was discharged in Salisbury. He was in the attack on Georgetown on the Pee Dee, taking of Scotch Lake Fort on the Santee near Nelson's Ferry, Friday's Ferry, Mott's Hill, Galphin's Fort, Siege of Ninety-Six, Augusta, and in the Battle of Eutaw Springs.

He was allowed pension on his application executed February 13, 1828, at which time he was aged sixty-seven years and a resident of Surry County, North Carolina.

In 1828, his wife and four daughters were living with him; their names are not given and no other family data are found in the papers in this claim.

In order to obtain date of last payment of pension, the name of person paid and possibly the date of death of William Algood, you

should write to the Comptroller-General, General Accounting Office, Records Division, this city, and cite the following data:
    William Algood
    Certificate No. 19879
    Issued March 1, 1828
    Rate, $8.00 per month
    Commenced February 13, 1828
    Acts March 18, 1818 and May 1, 1820
    North Carolina Agency.
    From Veterans Adms., Washington, D. C.

Data furnished by Adlai Robin Yates, Bogalusa, La.

March 18, 1851, William Allgood, Junior, applied for bounty land which was due him for his service in the War of 1812. He was then (1851) aged sixty-three years and a resident of Elbert County, Georgia. On this application, he was granted Warrant No. 51419 for 80 acres of bounty land; the warrant was issued June 11, 1853, under the Act of September 28, 1850. He died June 5, 1853, prior to date of issuance of warrant, in Elbert County, Georgia.

William Allgood, Junior, was not survived by a widow, his wife having died one year prior to his death. Her name and the date and place of their marriage are not shown. He was survived by two minor children, Sarah Ann Allgood, born June 19, 1835, and Lindsay Allgood, born November 11, 1837.

June 22, 1855, one John H. Smith of Elberton, Georgia, aged twenty-six years, applied as next friend of the two minor children named above, for bounty land which was due them on account of their father's service in the War of 1812. Their father having died prior to issuance of his bounty land warrant, said warrant was returned to the Government and Warrant No. 35924 for 160 acres of bounty land was issued in behalf of his two minor children, under Act of March 3, 1855. They were then residents of Elbert County, Georgia.

James Johnson, aged fifty-one, and Miley Johnson, aged forty-four years, stated in 1855 that they had known William Allgood, Junior, and his family for more than fifteen years. No relationship of these two persons and John H. Smith to the soldier's family is shown, and there are no further family data on file than that given above.

John Allgood or Algood was born May 12, 1751, in Richmond County, Virginia, between the Potomac and the Rappahannock Rivers. The names of his parents are not shown in the pepars in the pension claim.

While residing in Mecklenburg County, Virginia, John Allgood enlisted and served as a private with the Virginia Troops, as follows: From November 15, 1778, ten days in Capt. William Lewins' Company; from October 1, 1879, fourteen or fifteen days under Capt. William Pinter and carried provisions to Petersburg, Va.; from

January 1, 1781, three months and four days in Capt. Asa Oliver's Company, Col. Flemming's Regiment and was in a small skirmish at Portsmouth, Va.; from August 10, 1781, two months and fourteen days in Capt. Killies Jeffries' Company under Colonels Lew Burrell and Williams.

In 1788, he moved to Elbert County, Georgia, and in 1826, to Walton County, Georgia.

ALSTON

The following chart shows intermarriages with the following families:
Allen — Anthony — Arnold — Asbury — Atherton — Banks —Barnes — Blackwell — Burges — Cain — Chambers — Chancey — Clark — Collins — Cooper — Copeland — Cotton — Crowell — Daniel — De 'Graffendeidt — Dudley — Estes — Fisher — Gantt — Goodloe — Green — Groves — Harris — Hamlin — Harvey — Hill — Hinton — Hodges — Holt — Hunter — Hynes — Jaudon — Johnson — Kearney — Lillington — Montford — Moody — Moore — Mickle — Nuckles — Potts — Pickett — Palmer — Randolph — Rucker — Sanders — Sales — Saunders — Scruggs — Speed — Tate — Taylor — Temple — Thomas — Thompson — Thornton — Vaughan — Walker — Wallace — Whitmel — Wilcox — Williams — Wilson — Woods — Worley — Wright — Yancey.

ALSTON of ODELL
BEDFORDSHIRE
CREATED BARONET JUNE 13, 1642.

Saxham Hall, in Newton, was anciently the seat of the Alstons for many years. We find them mentioned so early as Edward the First reign, when William Alston of Stisted, in Essex, for want of warranty of Brockseroft, in Stisted, did grant and confirm to John de Carpenter of Naylinghurst, so much of his better land in Stisted, except his mansion house there. In Edward the 3rds time, Hugh Alston bore for Arms azure ten stars of 4-3-21, which was long before coat armor was granted by patent. The same coat of arms is used by the Georgia, North Carolina and South Carolina families.

Alston purchased "Odell" from Chitwood in 1640. The Castle Odell has nearly a century ago passed by purchase to the Alstons ancient family of Saxon origin. Alston was the Saxon Lord of Stanford in Norfolk before the Conquest.

Reference: Kimber and Johnson, *Baronetage of England* 1771, Vol. I, p. 457. Bloomfield list of Norfolk, Vol. I, p. 540.

See "Royal Ancestry of Lieut.-Col. William Alston," By Edna Arnold Copeland (Mrs. Z. W.), 1935.

(Note: Numbers represent generations, as: (1) first generation, (2) second generation, (3) third generation, etc.)

1—John Alston, b. about 1652; d. 1704 (son of John Alston of the Inner Temple and of Parvenham Co., Bedfordshire, Eng., b. 1610; d. 1687, and Dorothy Temple, b. 1612; m. Odell Jan. 4, 1634, daughter of Sir John Temple, Knight); m. Ann Wallis, b. about 1654 (daugh-

ter of John Wallis, b. 1567, d. 1622, English Grammarian and Logician, Mathematician and member of Royal Society.
2—John Alston Jr., m. Mary Clark.
3—Joseph John Alston, m. (1) Elizabeth Chancey; (2) Euphan Wilson.
4—(By first wife) John Alston, m. Ann Hunt Macon.
5—Colonel Joseph John Alston, m. Esther Wright.
6—John Alston, m. Betty Wilcox.
7—William Alston.
7—Joseph Alston.
7—Esther Alston.
7—Sarah Alston.
6—Joseph Alston, m. Louisa Thomas.
7—Sarah Alston.
6—Nancy Alston, m. (1) Mr. Hill; (2) Dr. Goodloe.
7—Ann Hill.
7—Cornelia Goodloe.
7—Horwell Goodloe.
5—Gideon Alston, m. Frances Atherton.
6—Elizabeth Alston, b. 1790; d. 1833.
6—John Alston, m. Dorothy Crowell.
7—Benjamin Alston.
7—Miriam Alston.
7—Francis Alston.
7—John Alston.
7—Gideon Alston.
7—Thomas Alston, m. Margaret T. Montford.
6—Dorothy Alston.
6—Gideon Alston, b. 1795; d. 1828.
6—Temperance Alston.
6—Mary Ann Alston.
6—Arabella Alston, b. 1803; d. 1864.
6—Amerylis Alston.
6—Jesse Alston.
6—Matilda Alston, b. 1810; d. 1837.
6—Dolly Alston.
5—William Alston, m. (1) Patty Moore; (2) Sally Potts.
6—Charles Alston.
6—Leonidas Alston.
6—Missouri Alston.
6—Edgar Alston.
5—Robert W. Alston, b. 1781; m. Harriet Green.
6—William Alston.
6—Daniel Alston.
6—Willis Alston.
6—Augustus Alston.
6—Henrietta Alston.
6—Robert Alston.
6—Ann Alston.
6—Gideon Alston.
6—Caroline Alston.
6—Angelica Alston, m. Colonel J. L. Cooper.
7—Robert Cooper.
7—Ann G. Cooper.
7—J. L. Cooper Jr.
7—Martha Cooper.
7—Sophia Cooper.
6—Sarah Alston.
6—Philoclea Alston, m. Governor D. S. Walker, of Florida.
7—Phillip Walker.

7—David Walker.
7—Florida Walker.
7—Augustus Walker.
6—Florida Alston, m. Colonel Hugh Fisher.
5—Priscilla Alston.
5—Ann Alston.
4—Colonel Philip Alston, m. Mary Drew Temple.
5—John Alston—wife's name unknown.
6—Samuel Alston.
6—Mary Alston.
6—James Alston.
6—John A. Alston.
5—James Alston, m. Mary Wilcox.
6—John Wilcox Alston.
6—James Alston Jr.
6—Rebecca Alston.
6—Elizabeth Alston.
6—Philip Alston.
6—Margaret Alston.
6—Ann Alston.
6—Willis Alston.
6—Drew Alston.
6—Henry Alston.
5—Philip Alston—wife's name unknown.
6—Philip Alston III.
6—James Alston.
6—John Alston.
5—Drew Alston.
5—Mary Alston, b. 1784; d. 1841; m. William Harris.
6—William Harris Jr.
6—Mary Harris.
6—Sarah Harris, m. Albert J. Pickett.
7—William R. Pickett, m. Mary L. Holt.
8—Mary Pickett.
8—Sarah Pickett.
8—Albert Pickett.
7—Mary Pickett.
7—Martha Pickett, m. Colonel M. L. Woods.
8—Albert Woods.
8—Corinna Woods.
8—Martha Woods.
7—Mary Pickett, m. Bishop S. W. Harris.
7—Sarah Pickett, m. R. C. Randolph.
7—Joseph Pickett.
7—Albert J. Pickett Jr.
7—Allston Pickett.
7—John Pickett.
4—Martha Alston, m. Mr. Merony.
4—William Alston, m. Sarah Yeargin.
4—(By second wife) Henry Alston, m. Sarah Hill.
4—Colonel William Alston, m. Elizabeth Wright.
5—Joseph J. Alston, m. Margaret Thomas.
5—James Alston, m. Temperance Thomas.
5—Henry Alston, m. Miss Long.
5—Thomas Alston, m. Miss Chambliss.
5—Fanny Alston, m. Robert M. Hamlin.
5—Jane Alston, m. Littleberry Wilcox.
5—Joseph J. "General Jack" Alston, m. Margaret B. Thomas.
6—Dr. William Alston.
6—Dr. James W. Alston.

6—Annie L. Alston.
6—Bessie Alston.
6—Dr. Kemp Alston.
6—Colonel Thomas Alston.
6—Blake Alston.
6—Major Willis Alston.
6—Sally N. Alston, m. Marion Sanders.
7—Elizabeth Sanders.
7—Margaret Sanders.
7—William A. Sanders.
7—Mary Sanders.
7—Epsy Sanders.
7—Helen Sanders.
7—Eunice Sanders.
7—Clara Sanders.
7—Marion Sanders.
7—Sarah Sanders.
7—Pauline Sanders.
7—James Sanders.
7—Clo Sanders.
7—Betty Sanders.
4—Mary Alston, m. William Palmer.
4—Joseph J. Chatham "Jack" Alston, m. Martha Kearney.
5—Joseph J. Alston Jr.
5—Elizabeth Alston.
5—Margaret Alston, m. Carney Cotton.
5—Martha Alston.
5—Nathaniel Alston.
5—Emily Alston.
5—Gideon Alston.
5—Robert Alston, m. Ann Alston.
5—Phillip Alston.
5—John Alston, m. (1) Permelia De Graffenreidt; (2) Decimus Palmer.
3—Solomon Alston, m. Ann Hinton, M. 1729.
4—Mary Alston.
4—Solomon Alston Jr., m. Sarah ———.
5—Lemuel J. Alston, m. Elizabeth Williams.
6—Lemuel J. Alston Jr.
6—James Alston.
6—William D. Alston, m. Mary Burges.
7—Sarah Alston.
7—Mary Alston.
7—William Alston.
7—Lemuel Alston.
7—Laura Alston.
7—Cornelia Alston.
7—Thomas Alston.
7—Ann D. Alston.
7—Joseph J. Alston.
7—Emma Alston.
7—Alfred Alston.
5—Henry Alston, m. Sarah Hill.
6—William Alston.
6—Fanny Alston.
6—Thomas Alston.
4—Lieutenant-Colonel William Alston, R. S., b. December 25, 1736; d. 1810; m. 1774, Charity Alston, b. 1738 (Cousin).
5—James Alston, m. Catherine Hamilton.

5—Philip H. Alston, m. Mrs. Woolfolk (nee Winn).
5—William H. Alston, m. Elizabeth Rucker.
5—Solomon Alston.
5—George Alston.
5—Elizabeth Alston, m. Thompson.
5—Christian Alston.
5—Sally Alston, m. Thos. Chambers.
5—Nancy Alston, m. J. M. Tate.
5—Mary Alston, m. Lt. James Clark.
4—John Alston, m. Elizabeth Hynes.
5—William A. Alston.
5—Philip Alston.
5—Ann Alston.
5—Solomon Alston.
5—Lucretia Alston.
4—Charity Alston, m. James Jones.
4—Ann Alston, m. Jesse Hunter.
4—Rachel Alston, m. Inman Jones.
4—Sarah Alston, m. Mr. Morgan.
3—Philip Alston, m. Winfred Whitmel.
4—William Alston, b. 1747; d. 1795.
4—Philip Alston, b. 1749.
4—Mary Alston, b. 1751.
4—Elizabeth Alston, b. 1753.
4—James Alston, b. 1754; d. 1805.
4—Thomas Alston, b. 1755.
4—Martha Alston, b. 1757.
4—Henry Alston, b. 1760.
4—Philips Alston, b. 1762.
4—Winfred Alston, b. 1764.
3—James Alston, m. Christian Lillington.
4—John Alston—wife's name unknown.
5—John Alston Jr.
5—George Alston.
5—Philip Alston.
5—Lemuel Alston.
5—Alfred Alston.
5—Mary Alston.
5—Martha Alston.
5—Sarah Alston.
5—Absolom Alston.
5—Christian Alston, m. Solomon Jones.
4—Mary Alston.
4—Charity Alston, m. Lieut. Col. William Alston, R. S.
5—James Alston, m. Catherine Hamilton.
5—William H. Alston, m. Jan. 25, 1820, Elizabeth Rucker.
5—Solomon Alston.
5—George Alston.
5—Elizabeth Alston, m. Mr. Thompson.
5—Christian Alston.
5—Mary Alston, m. Lieut. James Clark, of Orange County, Va.
6—Charity Clark m. John Tennat.
6—Charity Clark, m. Samuel Hill.
7—Laura Hill, m. W. H. Lockwood.
7—Robert Hill, m. Mary Moore.
7—Ella Hill, m. Dr. Dula.
7—Preston Hill.
7—William H. Hill.
7—James Hill.

6—Catherine Clark, m. Charles H. Allen.
7—Eliza Allen.
7—Dora Allen.
7—Mary Allen.
7—William Allen.
7—Edward Allen.
7—Eugene Allen.
6—William Clark.
6—James D. Clark.
6—Laura Clark, m. Henry M. Mood.
7—Catherine Mood, m. Mr. Stubbs.
7—Dr. Julius Mood (Father of Julia Peterkin, famous South Carolina author).
7—Lulah Mood.
7—Sally Mood.
7—Preston Mood.
6—Sarah Clark, m. John Wilcox.
7—William Wilcox.
7—James C. Wilcox.
7—Henry Wilcox.
7—Edward Wilcox.
7—Phillip Wilcox.
6—Mary Louisa Clark, m. Nov. 12, 1846, James M. Carter, C. S. His last service in the War was bringing the pontoon boats from Abbeville County, South Carolina, to Petersburg Ferry, on Savannah River, for President Davis and his Cabinet to cross on their way to Washington, Ga.; member Georgia Senate 1859-60, officer in C. W.
7—Annie E. Carter, b. Nov. 25, 1848; d. July 29, 1899; m. May 5, 1875, McAlpin Arnold, C. S., banker, city councilman of Elberton, merchant, planter, b. Nov. 1, 1847; d. Aug. 23, 1912.
8—Sarah Louise Arnold, m. Dec. 16, 1900, Henry Scudder Jaudon, Civil Engineer, b. July 20, 1871; d. Aug. 22, 1930.
9—Carter Jaudon, b. July 25, 1906; m. April 26, 1927, Marshall K. Hunter, b. Oct. 26, 1901, banker.
10—Jaudon Hunter II, Oct. 1933.
9—Mayson Jaudon, b. Jan. 12, 1909, (cotton factor), m. 1933, Betsy Grogan.
10—Henry Jaudon, b. Nov. 23, 1934.
10—Arnold Starke Jaudon, b. Oct. 29, 1939.
8—Julius Arnold, b. Aug. 19, 1878; d. 1906.
8—Edna Arnold, Genealogist (Fellow I. A. G.), m. Nov. 26, 1901, Z. W. Copeland, wholesale distributor, President Chamber of Commerce, city Councilman of Elberton, graduate of Law, Mercer University, Macon, Ga., b. Feb. 2, 1880.
9—Edna May Copeland, b. June 3, 1909, m. E. H. Christie (Associated with Hinde & Dauch Paper Mfg., St. Louis Mo.).
10—Ann Christie, b. April 18, 1937.
8—Carter Alston Arnold, wholesale distributor, Mayor Pro-tem of Elberton, Chairman Board of Education, Chairman Board of Stewards First Methodist Church, graduate, Cornell University, Ithaca, N. Y. (Civil Engineering), b. Aug. 7, 1886, m. Jan. 9, 1919, Mary Hill (S. C.).
9—Mary Ann Arnold, b. Oct. 22, 1922.
9—McAlpin Hill Arnold, b. March 28, 1924.
7—Georgia Carter, m. T. A. Thornton.
8—Mamie Thornton, m. T. D. Johnson.
8—Other issue.
7—James Carter, m. Miss Estes.
8—Copeland Carter.

8—McAlpin Carter.
8—Nora Carter, m. J. S. Asbury.
9—James Asbury.
8—Other issue.
7—Kate Carter, m. Mr. Stubbs.
7—Florence Carter, m. Ella Speed (S. C.) issue.
7—Leola Carter, m. H. C. Mickel, contractor.
8—Carey Mickel, m. Elizabeth Worley, World War Veteran.
8—Clark Mickel (Granite manufacturer), m. Reba Vaughan (World War Veteran).
9—Buck Mickel.
8—Homozelle Mickel, m. Charlie Daniel, graduate, The Citadel, First Lieutenant, World War, President of Daniel Construction Co. (South Carolina).
7—Captain Yancey Carter, m. Miss Sanders.
5—Sallie Alston, m. Thomas Chambers.
5—Nancy Alston, m. J. M. Tate.
6—Charity Tate, m. John Alston.
4—Sarah Alston, m. (1) Sir Thomas Dudley; (2) William Cain.
4—James Alston, m. Gilly Yancey.
5—Nathaniel Alston, b. 1775; d. 1852.
5—Charity Alston, b. 1777; d. 1828; m. James Banks.
5—Sarah Alston, b. 1779; d. 1861; m. Joseph Groves.
6—James A. Groves, b. Sept. 29, 1798.
6—John J. Groves, m. Mary L. Harvey.
6—Elizabeth Groves.
6—Rignol S. Groves.
6—Martha Groves.
6—Sylvanus Groves, b. 1822.
6—Frances E. Groves, m. Thomas W. Gantt.
7—Richard G. Gantt, b. 1837; d. 1894; m. Margaret G. Sales, b. April 7, 1842.
8—Dr. H. A. Gantt.
8—Emma N. Gantt.
8—Richard G. Gantt.
8—Martha Gantt.
8—Drayon Gantt.
7—Sarah Gantt.
7—Elizabeth Gantt, m. Llellyn Blackwell.
8—Elizabeth Blackwell, m. Thomas T. Hodges.
9—Sarah Hodges.
7—Thomas L. "Larry" Gantt, newspaper editor and columnist, m. Anna Johnson.
8—Jesse T. Gantt, Secretary of State (South Carolina).
8—Robert Gantt, attorney.
8—Yancey Gantt, editor.
8—Mark Gantt.
8—Helen Gantt.
5—Martha Alston, b. 1781; d. 1854.
5—John Alston, b. 1783; d. 1835; m. Oct. 4, 1810, Charity Tate.
5—Hannah Alston, m. James J. Banks.
3—Sarah Alston, m. Thomas Kearney.
3—Martha Alston, m. Lemuel Wilson.
3—Charity Alston, m. John Dawson.
4—Charity Dawson, b. 1756; m. Samuel Williams.
5—William Williams.
5—Elizabeth Williams, m. William Alston.
5—John Williams, m. Elizabeth Taylor.
5—Lewis Williams, m. Priscilla Kearney.
5—Charity Williams.

5—Samuel Williams, m. Mary Thompson.
5—Sarah Williams, m. Samuel Alston.
5—Joseph J. Williams, m. Mary Collins.
5—Mary Williams, m. Jeptha Barnes.
6—Charity Barnes, m. Col. Whitmell Hill Anthony.
7—James Anthony.
7—Mary Anthony.
7—Whitmell Anthony.
7—Henrietta Anthony.
4—Elizabeth Dawson.
4—John Dawson, b. 1759; m. Elizabeth B. Atherton.
The Alston and Temple lines are traced without an unbroken link through Alfred The Great to Harderick, the first known Saxon King, B. C. 90.
(See papers of Edna Arnold Copeland, member of Descendant of Most Noble Order of K. G.)
See Nat. No. D. A. R. No. 49019.
See Alstons and Allstons of N. C. and S. C. by J. A. Groves, Md.

ARNOLD

The following chart shows intermarriages with the following families:
Adams — Archer — Almond — Agee — Ashworth — Andrews — Aycock — Barnwell — Bentley — Bertam — Birch — Black — Bond — Bowden — Brown — Browning — Bryan — Calloway — Carey — Carter — Clark — Cleckler — Copeland — Corrouth — Day — Dixon — Duncan — Edwards — Evans — Frazier — Goolsby — Grant — Grogan — Grimes — Guest — Gunn — Hall — Hawkes — Heindel — Herndon — Hill — Horne — Hulsey — Hunter — Hutto — Ivey — Jaudon — Johnson — Kelly — Kittle — Krutes — Lamber — Lewis — Lunsford — Mahoney — Mealor — Miller — Mitchell — Molote — Moon — Moore — McConnell — McEwen — McGinty — McIntosh — McKeen — Newsome — Oglivie — Patton — Peppers — Pope — Poss — Poole — Power — Reid — Revier — Roberts — Sayer — Scudder — Sears — Sherrer — Shirley — Smith — Sturdivant — Strozier — Suttles — Thornton — Tiller — Tough — Turner — Wall — Watson — Webb — Wiggins — White — Wilhite— Williams — Wilson — Worley.

BASIS OF ARNOLD GENEALOGY

1—Ynir 1100—King of Gwentland m. Nesta, daughter of Justin, King of Glamorgan. 2—Meiric, King of Gwentland m. Eleanor of the House of Trevor. 3—Ynir Vichar, King of Gwentland m. Gladice, daughter of the Lord of Ystradyr. 4—Carador, King of Gwentland m. Nesta, daughter of Sir Roderick De Gros. 5—Dyewall, Lord of Gwent m. Joyce, daughter of Hamlet, son of Sir Druce, Duke of Balladon, France. 6—Systal, Lord of Upper Gwent m. Annest, daughter of Sir Peter Russell, Lord of Kentchinch in Herefore. 7—Arthur M. Jane, daughter of Lein, Lord of Cantrosblyn. 8—Merric M. Annest, daughter of Craddock. 9—Gwillin M. Jane, daughter of Ivon, Lord of Lighs—Tabyvont. 10—Arnholt M. Janet, daughter of Phillip Fleming Esquire. 11—Arnholt II, m. Sibyl, daughter of Madoc. 12—Roger Arnold, m. Joan, daughter of Sir Thomas Gammage. 13—Thomas Arnold, m. Agnes, daughter of Sir Richard Warnstead. 14—Richard Arnold, m. Emmate, daughter of Pierce Young. 15—Richard Arnold II, wife unknown. 16—Thomas Arnold, m. Alice Gulley. 17—William Arnold, b. 1578, wife unknown. He came to Massachusetts in 1635 and was associated with Roger Williams in the founding of Providence, Rhode Island.

ELBERT COUNTY ARNOLD FAMILY

(Note: Numbers represent generations, as: (1) first generation, (2) second generation, (3) third generation, etc.)

1—Solomon Arnold, b. 1758, Lunenburg County, Va., R. S., m. (Mollie) Mary Gurley, married in Warren County, North Carolina. (John Arnold signed marriage bond).
2—Davis Arnold, mathematician, m. Elizabeth McClain Wilhite.
3—Adeline Ann Arnold, m. John Edward Bentley.
4—Lucinda Bentley, d. unmarried.
4—John Davis Bentley, m. Middie Wilhite.
5—Edward Bentley, b. March 22, 1859; m. Celia Frazier.
6—Mamie Bentley.
6—Ruth Bentley.
5—William Bentley, m. Hilla Miller.
5—John Oscar Bentley, m. Ann Carey.
4—Joseph A. J. Bentley, m. Fanny Almond. No issue.
4—Adeline Bentley, m. Henry Kelly. No issue.
4—Martha C. Bentley, d. Jan. 5, 1904; m. Oct. 12, 1865, John Wall.
5—McAlpin Wall.
5—Arthur Wall.
5—Kenneth Wall.
5—Leslie Wall.
5—Hillie Wall.
5—Abbie Wall.
4—Robertus Bentley, b. 1843; d. 1871; m. Mollie Evans.
5—McAlpin Bentley, m. Miss Strozier.
5—Georgia Bentley.
4—William Chandler Bentley, b. Jan. 7, 1848; d. Nov. 27, 1900; m. Feb. 4, 1869, Demarius Lunsford.
5—William Bentley, b. June 16, 1870; m. Dec. 18, 1895, Bertie Shirley.
6—Herbert Bentley.
6—Lena Bentley.
6—"Shorty" Bentley.
6—Martha Bentley.
6—Paul Bentley.
6—Phillip Bentley.
6—Marie Bentley.
6—Allen Bentley.
6—Maggie Bentley.
6—Una Bentley.
5—Dozier Bentley, b. Aug. 24, 1874; m. Dec. 7, 1897, Ada Mae Clark.
6—Enoch Bentley.
6—William Bentley.
6—Fred Bentley.
5—Itis Bentley, b. Sept. 13, 1875; m. Jan. 10, 1895, Samuel E. Gunn.
6—Alvada Gunn.
6—Fortson Gunn.
6—Esther Gunn.

6—Samuel Gunn.
6—Helen Gunn.
6—Doris Gunn.
6—Grace Gunn.
—Nellie Bentley, b. July 20, 1880; d. July 29, 1918; m. Aug. 22, 1908, George Duncan.
6—Madeline Duncan.
6—Bentley Duncan.
5—Julius Bentley, b. Dec. 1, 1883; m. Feb. 2, 1908, Cassie Carter.
6—Inez Bentley.
6—Marvin Bentley.
6—William Bentley.
6—James Bentley.
6—Joseph Bentley.
5—Maggie Belle Bentley, b. May 27, 1887; m. 1902, William Newsome.
6—Robert Newsome.
6—Raymond Newsome.
6—Gladys Newsome.
6—Elmore Newsome.
6—Archie Newsome.
6—Julian Newsome.
5—Ada Bentley, b. Jan. 27, 1890; m. Dec. 31, 1916, Clarence Agee.
4—Thaddeus Bentley, b. March 29, 1850; d. April 3, 1916; m. Sept. 27, 1887, Anna E. Revier, b. Nov. 24, 1849; d. Dec. 16, 1918.
5—Pearl Bentley, b. Aug. 10, 1878; m. Dec. 8, 1908, E. C. Moore.
5—Daisy H. Bentley, b. Nov. 6, 1879; m. Dec. 15, 1905, W. J. Strudivant.
6—Elton B. Sturdivant, b. Sept. 24, 1906; m. Regina Sherrer.
4—Ava Priscilla Bentley, b. Sept. 18, 1852; d. April 21, 1920; m. Henry A. Poss, b. Feb. 28, 1850; d. Feb. 26, 1918.
5—Clara Emma Poss, b. Dec. 20, 1872; m. Feb. 14, 1894, John Lewbannon Adams, b. May 26, 1867.
6—Eunice C. Adams, b. Dec. 29, 1894.
6—Tressie Adams, b. Dec. 29, 1896; m. Jan. 12, 1918, W. K. Hawes, b. April 12, 1891.
7—Dorothy Hawkes, b. Nov. 12, 1919.
7—Martha Hawkes, b. June 11, 1922.
6—Lillian "Lillie" Adams, b. Aug. 24, 1899; m. Jan. 25, 1920, Alex Saye, b. Nov. 27, 1897.
7—Harold Saye.
6—Horace Adams, d. unmarried.
6—Floyd Adams, b. Oct. 24, 1904; m. Oct. 26, 1926, Louise Ivey, b. May 20, 1903.
7—Barbara Adams, b. Oct. 26, 1927.
7—Floyd Adams Jr., b. Oct. 4, 1930.
6—Hiram Adams, b. 1906; m. Oct. 23, 1923, May Bell Wilson, b. Sept. 7, 1907.
7—Robert Adams.
5—Katie Jewell Poss, b. Aug. 14, 1878; m. Nov. 18, 1906, James Pope.
6—Ava Pope, b. Sept. 9, 1907; m. Jan. 5, 1930, Guy Patton, b. Sept. 27, 1909.
6—Katie R. Pope, b. Sept. 9, 1912.
6—Howard Pope, b. Aug. 24, 1914.
6—Forrest Pope.
5—Claud E. Pope, b. Aug. 28, 1880; d. Sept. 5, 1922; m. July 17, 1906, Mrs. Dora Kittle.
6—Allen D. Poss, b. March 15, 1908.
6—Claud Poss, d. unmarried.

5—Jessie M. Poss, b. June 5, 1882; m. (1) Nov. 24, 1904, Nicholas Krutes; (2) Dec. 25, 1916, Charles T. Lambert.
6—Ruth Krutes, b. Oct. 25, 1908.
6—Kathleen Krutes.
6—Charles Lambert, b. 1918.
6—Frances Lambert.
6—Joseph Lambert.
5—Joseph Poss, m. Ruby Mealor.
5—Adeline Poss, b. Sept. 5, 1887.
3—McAlpin Arnold, member Georgia House of Representatives from Elbert County, 1846-1847, lawyer; d. unmarried.
3—Joseph Y. Arnold, C. S., b. June 11, 1817; d. Jan. 31, 1895; m. Oct. 5, 1841, Sarah Kindred Thornton, b. Feb. 14, 1826; d. Aug. 4, 1912.
4—Elizabeth "Betty" Arnold, b. Oct. 23, 1845; d. Aug. 25, 1905; m. Aug. 4, 1861, John L. Wilhite, C. S., b. Nov. 12, 1830; d. Dec. 7, 1912.
5—Anna Wilhite, b. 1862; d. 1931; m. B. B. Grimes.
6—Maud Grimes, m. Dr. R. Molote.
7—Infant daughter died 1918.
7—R. Molote Jr. m. (?)
8—R. Molote III.
6—Elizabeth Grimes, m. (1) Raymond Bertram; (2) Mr. Barnwell.
7—(By first wife) Anita Bertram.
5—James Wilhite, b. 1864; d. 1911; m. Daisy Watson.
6—Edwin Wilhite.
6—James Wilhite.
6—Victor Wilhite.
6—Alice Wilhite, m. William McKeen.
7—William McKeen Jr.
6—Dorothy Wilhite.
5—Mattie Wilhite, m. Mr. Wiggins. No living issue.
5—Floyd Wilhite, b. 1872; d. 1898; m. 1890, Ferdinand Williams.
6—Hoyt Williams, b. 1892.
5—Minnie Wilhite, m. (1) Eugene Brown; (2) J. W. Manuel. No issue.
5—Joe Tom Wilhite, b. 1878; d. 1921.
5—May Wilhite, m. William Penn White, d. 1926, Mayor of Augusta, Ga. No issue.
5—Lyndon Wilhite.
5—Gordon Wilhite.
5—Janna Wilhite, b. Dec. 15, 1882; m. 1907, Ralph O. Bowden, banker of Hampton, S. C.
6—R. O. Bowden Jr., b. 1910.
6—John Lewis Bowden, b. 1912.
4—Julius B. D. Arnold, C. S., died in U. S. prison during the War Between the States. Unmarried.
4—McAlpin Arnold, b. Nov. 1, 1847; d. Aug. 23, 1912; banker, merchant, planter; m. May 5, 1875, Annie Carter, b. Nov. 25, 1848; d. July 29, 1899.
5—Sarah Louise Arnold, b. Feb. 27, 1876, m. Dec. 6, 1900, Henry Scudder Jaudon, Educated at Hollins College, Roanoke, Va. H. S. Jaudon was graduate of Lehigh University, Bethlehem, Pa., elected associate member of the American Society of Civil Engineers, Past President Rotary Club, b. July 20, 1871; d. Aug. 22, 1930.

6—Carter Jaudon, b. July 25, 1906, educated at Mary Baldwin, Va.; m. April 26, 1927, Marshall K. Hunter, banker, b. Oct. 26, 1901.
7—Jaudon Hunter, b. Oct. 1933.
6—Mayson Jaudon, cotton factor, educated at Emory College, b. Jan. 12, 1909; m. Betsy Grogan.
7—Henry Jaudon, b. Nov. 23, 1934.
7—Arnold Starke Jaudon, b. Oct. 29, 1939.
7—Julius Y. Arnold, b. Aug. 9, 1878; d. 1906. Educated at Technological College, Atlanta, Ga.
5—Edna Arnold, Genealogist (Fellow Institute of American Geneology, graduate of Private Seminary, education completed at Wesleyan, Macon, Ga.; m. Nov. 26, 1901, Z. W. Copeland, lawyer, Mercer University, City Councilman of Elberton, wholesale distributor, b. Feb. 3, 1880.
6—Edna May Copeland, graduate Converse College, Spartanburg, S. C., b. Jan. 3, 1909; m. Edward H. Christie, associated with Hinde & Dauch Paper Mfg. Co., of St. Louis, Mo..
7—Ann Christie, b. April 18, 1937.
5—Carter Alston Arnold, civil engineer, graduate of Cornell University, Ithaca, N. Y., wholesale distributor, b. Aug. 7, 1886; m. Jan. 8, 1919, Mary Hill, (S. C.) Regent, D. A. R., 1938-39, Educated at Converse College, Spartanburg, S. C.
6—Mary Ann Arnold, b. Oct. 26, 1922.
6—McAlpin Hill Arnold, appointed Page in Congress, 1939, by Con. Paul Brown, b. March 28, 1924.
4—Saluda Arnold, m. Stephen Black, C. S., planter.
5—McAlpin Black.
5—Emma Black.
5—J. W. Black, m. 1901, Cora McEwen.
5—Birdie Black, m. Mr. Birch. No issue.
5—Sarah Black, educator, master's degree, University of Georgia, m. Thomas Mitchell, wholesale distributor. No issue.
5—Leonidas Black, m. Daisy Roberts.
6—Caroline Black.
6—Leonidas Black Jr. Other issue.
5—Harry Black, d. unmarried.
5—Annie Black, m. Thomas Calloway, wholesale distributor. No issue.
5—Mary George Black, m. Mr. Heindel. No issue.
4—Sarah Arnold, m. Joseph N. Worley, Judge Superior Court, Northern Circuit, City Attorney of Elberton, County Commissioner of Elbert County, Clerk and Treasurer of Elberton.
5—Arnold Worley, attorney, b. March 2, 1880; m. (1) Edith Williams; (2) Miss Peppers.
6—(By first wife) Nellie Worley.
5—Elizabeth Worley, m. Oct. 26, 1903, Arthur McGinty, b. Oct. 11, 1880; d. July 1935.
6—Joseph McGinty, attorney, b. Aug. 14, 1904; m. Jean Grier.
7—Joseph McGinty Jr.
6—Luther McGinty, b. April 11, 1906.
5—Carter Worley, b. Oct. 12, 1883; m. Minnie Andrews.
6—Carter Worley Jr.
4—Georgia Arnold, b. Feb. 11, 1858; m. Nov. 1878, Luther Goolsby, merchant, planter, b. Sept. 24, 1855; d. Aug. 2, 1895.
5—Mary Goolsby, b. Jan. 16, 1881; d. May 8, 1908; m. March 18, 1903, Joseph Turner.
6—Henrietta Turner, m. Jack Edwards. No issue.
5—Ernest Goolsby, b. July 3, 1883; m. Dec. 23, 1912, Nell Lewis.
6—Mary Nell Goolsby, b. July 15, 1917.

6—Ernest Goolsby Jr., b. April 2, 1922.
5—Charles Goolsby, b. May 4, 1885.
5—Irene Goolsby, b. Feb. 8, 1889; m. June 5, 1907, F. D. Smith, banker, President Elberton Chamber of Commerce.
6—F. D. Smith Jr., Granite manufacturer, b. Aug. 2, 1908; m. Frances Yates.
6—Henry Luther Smith, b. Dec. 9, 1909; m. 1932, Elizabeth Bond.
7—Priscilla Bond Smith, b. March 13, 1933.
7—Elizabeth Ann Smith.
5—Sarah Goolsby, b. Feb. 15, 1894; m. Jan. 24, 1922, Dr. Isaac Reid, b. July 27, 1889, druggist, 2nd Lieut. World War, first honor graduate University of Georgia (Pharmacy).
6—Mary Arnold Reid, b. Feb. 19, 1928.
5—Luther Goolsby Jr., soldier World War, Postmaster at Carlton, Ga., b. Nov. 27, 1895; m. Mary Brown.
6—Mary Carolyn Goolsby.
4—Mary Jane Arnold, b. Sept. 1, 1859; m. Oct. 18, 1882, James McIntosh, b. Sept. 23, 1857, Sheriff of Elbert County, County Commissioner of Elbert County, Tax Assessor City of Elberton, City Councilman of Elberton.
5—Sarah Louise McIntosh, b. July 29, 1883; m. Feb. 24, 1902, Arthur F. Archer. No issue.
5—William McPherson McIntosh, d. infancy.
5—Jessie McIntosh, d. infancy.
5—Mary James McIntosh, d. infancy.
5—John H. McIntosh, lawyer, historian, b. Nov. 26, 1895; m. June 19, 1918, Fay Ann White, b. Oct. 21, 1900.
6—Mary Louise McIntosh, b. July 16, 1920.
6—Elizabeth Arnold Penn McIntosh, b. March 15, 1923.
5—McAlpin McIntosh, b. Nov. 26, 1897; d. 1899.
4—William T. Arnold, retired merchant, b. March 24, 1867; m. Dec. 5, 1888, Eddie Herndon, b. Dec. 25, 1870.
5—George Clifton Arnold, b. Sept. 9, 1889; d. unmarried.
5—William Herman Arnold, contractor, Palm Beach, Fla., b. Aug. 26, 1897; m. June 25, 1918, Catherine Cleckler, b. Oct. 23, 1898.
6—Beth Arnold, b. May 11, 1919.
6—Catherine "Kitty" Arnold, b. April 24, 1924.
5—James Arnold, contractor, Palm Beach, Fla., b. Sept. 14, 1899; m. April 21, 1921, Kathleen Grogan, b. Dec. 27, 1898.
6—James "Jimmy" Arnold Jr., b. Oct. 11, 1924.
4—Lofton Arnold, d. unmarried.
3—Medicus Franklin Arnold, b. June 13, 1827; d. Feb. 13, 1908; m. April 8, 1849, Martha Ann Webb.
4—Laura McClain Arnold, b. May 20, 1850; d. Sept. 20, 1927; m. June 10, 1868, Abram Dixon, C. S.
5—Anna Icylona Dixon, b. July 10, 1869; m. Dec. 24, 1885, William B. Moon.
5—Lola J. Dixon, b. 1872; m. William A. Reagan. No issue.
5—Minnie Lee Dixon, b. 1874; m. G. Thomas Moon.
5—Georgia Ola Dixon, m. Dec. 2, 1899, Thomas Moon.
5—Mary Elizabeth Dixon, m. Fletcher Whitehead.
5—Mattie Dixon, m. Lonnie Wall.
6—Era Wall.
6—Sybyl Wall.
6—Lonnie Wall Jr.
4—Adeline Eloid Arnold, b. July 21, 1851; d. April 4, 1918; m. Fletcher Edwards.
5—Alice Edwards.
5—Joseph Edwards, b. Nov. 25, 1872; d. June 21, 1928; m. March 18, 1907, Mrs. Evelyn Browning.

6—Robert B. Edwards, b. Jan. 11, 1908.
6—Bertha Edwards, b. 1909.
6—George Edwards, b. Sept. 28, 1913.
6—Louise Edwards, b. Feb. 24, 1916.
6—Inez Edwards, b. Dec. 30, 1917.
6—Ruby Edwards, b. Jan. 2, 1920.
5—J. Asbury Edwards, m. Annie Hutto.
6—Fletcher Edwards.
6—Emory Edwards, m. Miss Ashworth.
6—Annie May Edwards, m. Lloyd Suttles.
6—Daisy Edwards.
6—Sarah Edwards.
6—J. Asbury Edwards Jr.
6—William Edwards.
6—Arthur Edwards.
6—Azalee Edwards.
5—Robert Edwards.
5—Lizzie Edwards.
5—Lucy Edwards.
5—Mattie Edwards.
5—Sam Edwards.
5—Essie Edwards.
5—Eddie Edwards.
4—Alice Elizabeth Arnold, b. May 2, 1854; d. 1910; m. 1874, Reid Day.
5—Augustus Day.
5—Medicus Day.
5—Sarah Day.
5—Frances Day.
5—Lum Day.
5—Ossie Day.
5—Stella Day.
4—Edwin Davis James Arnold, b. July 6, 1855; d. Feb. 15, 1932; m. Aug. 18, 1880, Clemmie Webb.
5—Mattie Maud Arnold, b. Aug. 30, 1881; m. April 1906, William C. Tiller.
5—James Olin Arnold, b. Aug. 17, 1884; m. 1905, Mary Johnson.
5—Eva Jessie Arnold, b. June 16, 1887; m. Feb. 1908, T. Vandiver Hilley.
5—Olera Arnold, b. June 25, 1890; m. May 1922, John L. Brown.
5—Noel Webb Arnold, b. Dec. 24, 1892; m. June 1922, Ivah Raiford.
5—Allene Arnold, b. May 2, 1896; m. July 1922, Walker Bryan.
4—Annie Lou Arnold, b. Oct. 4, 1857; m. (1) 1878, Colman Guest; (2) Oscar H. Corrouth.
5—Mamie Jessie Guest, b. May 10, 1880; m. James Moore.
5—Vesta Eufaula Guest, b. Aug. 11, 1881; m. Clifford Matthews.
5—Arnold Elbert Corrouth, b. Aug. 31, 1895; m. July 1928, Eddie Davis.
4—May Lavonia Arnold, b. May 25, 1859; d. Sept. 17, 1928; m. May 19, 1882, James W. Guest.
5—Madge Guest, m. Spurgeon Wilson.
5—Walter Arnold Guest, m. Ollie Love Grant.
5—Clara Belle Guest, m. William Russell Scudder.
4—Zorah Frances Arnold, b. April 8, 1862; m. John T. Mahoney.
5—Marvin Mahoney.
5—Nellie Lou Mahoney.
5—Eddie Frank Mahoney.
5—L. Elizabeth Mahoney.
5—Hoyt Mahoney.

4—Usilla Lee Arnold, b. Nov. 17, 1865; m. Nov. 20, 1887, John Oglivie.
5—Jessie Oglivie, b. Feb. 25, 1890; m. Oct. 30, 1906, Marion Horne.
5—Julius Oglivie, b. 1892; m. 1920, Addie Belle Yon.
5—Garrie Oglive, b. Jan. 1895; m. June 1926, Sarah Hall.
5—Grace Oglivie, b. Dec. 6, 1897; m. June 14, 1919, William Hulsey.
4—Samuel Franklin Arnold, b. Dec. 10, 1869; d. unmarried.
4—Jessie E. Arnold, b. March 22, 1871; m. Jan. 2, 1900, Goss Power.
5—Mary Ruth Power, m. Dec. 22, 1928, Hugh Tough.
5—Martha Naomi Power, m. June 7, 1922, Grady Turner.
5—James Huett Power, m. 1927, Thelma Smith.
4—Willie Aufaula Arnold, b. July 31, 1873; m. November 25, 1909, James Ossie McConnell.
5—Martha Frances McConnell.
3—Boyd Arnold, b. 1819; m. Sarah (Sallie) Evelyn Sayer.
4—Sebrel Arnold, b. Sept. 25, 1843, C. S.
4—Ann Elizzie, b. Jan. 2, 1845; m. John S. Poole, Nov. 6, 1870.
4—Mary Emma, b. Oct. 27, 1847; m. R. J. Matthews.
4—Helen Alvera, b. March 26, 1850; m. James Aycock.
4—Georgia Savannah, b March 26, 1852; m. William Williamson.
4—D. B. Callaway, b. July 24, 1854; m. Sallie Bobo (Sarah Frances Bobo).

Note: Carswell Garvin Aycock (President C. G. Aycock Realty Co., Atlanta, Ga.) furnished the following data: Davis Arnold and Elizabeth McClain (Wilhite) Arnold had children: Sebrel, Joe, Mc., John Boyd, Medicus, and Adeline. Sallie Evelyn (Sayer) Arnold had four brothers and one sister: Ichabod Sayer, David Sayer, John Sayer, James Sayer, and Ann Sayer.
See National No. 49019 (D. A. R.) Washington, D. C.

BANKS

The following chart shows intermarriages with the following families: Adams — Allen — Allston — Arnold — Blackwell — Bloodworth — Bowman — Butts — Chandler — Chipman — Cleveland — Clark — Conyers — Cosby — Davis — Day — Dean — Dockery — Dorough — Ethridge — Fitzgerald — Ford — Frazer — Gump — Harper — Hammond — Harvey — Heard — Hodges — Horton — James — Jeter — Jones — Kay — Landrum — Long — Maxwell — Moon — Moss — Murray — McCalla — McGehee — McLain — Oliver — Payne — Peacock — Peurifoy — Pierce — Pretty — Pressley — Price — Pritchard — Quillian — Seymour — Sims — Skidmore — Stephens — Sondidge — Stanford — Tate — Thomas — Turner — Watkins — Wayble — Webb — White — Whitmire — Wood — Wright — Yarborough — Young.

(Note: Numbers represent generations, as: (1) first generation, (2) second generation, (3) third generation, etc.)

1—Thomas Banks, of North Carolina, d. June 28, 1789; m. (1) Sarah Chandler; (2) Betty White; (3) Susannah Pretty.
2—(By first wife) Richard Banks, b. Aug. 23, 1744.
2—Thomas Banks, b. Nov. 27, 1747.

2—Sally C. Banks, b. June 4, 1748; m. Joseph Blackwell.
3—Dunstan Blackwell.
3—Banks Blackwell, m. June 28, 1831, Mrs. Elizabeth Clark.
3—Ralph Blackwell, d. 1853.
3—Joseph Blackwell Jr., d. 1857; m. March 3, 1812, Elizabeth McGehee.
4—Sarah Ann Blackwell, m. April 8, 1841, Thomas J. Bowman.
4—Eliza Blackwell, m. Aug. 2, 1845, William B. White.
4—Cornelia Blackwell, m. Nov. 2, 1848, Edwin A. Jones.
5—Robert Jones.
5—Edwin Jones.
4—James Y. Blackwell.
4—Samuel D. Blackwell.
4—Thomas P. Blackwell.
4—Mary E. Blackwell.
4—Claudia Blackwell.
4—William M. Blackwell.
4—George L. Blackwell.
4—Llewyllen Blackwell, m. (1) Elizabeth Gantt; (2) Widow Cosby.
5—(By first wife) Elizabeth Blackwell, m. Thomas Hodges.
6—Sarah Hodges; d. unmarried.
3—Parks Blackwell, m. Elizabeth Murray.
4—James P. Blackwell.
4—J. L. Blackwell.
4—Isabella Blackwell, m. (1) Gerrard Allen; (2) William Clark; (3) John James.
5—(By first husband) Gerrard Allen Jr., m. Adeliade Stanford.
6—Singleton W. Allen, m. May Wood.
7—Gerrard Allen, m. Saide Ethridge.
6—Hattie Allen, m. Charles Whitmire.
7—Charles Whitmire Jr.
7—Harriet Whitmire.
7—Annie Bevelle Whitmire.
7—Martha Whitmire.
5—(By second husband) Elizabeth Clark, m. Mr. Carr.
5—William Parks Clark, Lieutenant Spanish-American War.; d. unmarried.
5—Overton Clark.
5—Fanny Clark, m. W. W. Adams.
6—Clark Adams.
6—Raymond Adams.
6—Marshall Adams.
6—Murray Adams.
6—Richard Adams.
6—Samuel Adams.
6—Lewis Adams.
6—Freeman Adams.
5—Josie Clark.
5—(By third husband) Belle James, m. Ben H. Kay.
6—Herbert Kay.
6—Elizabeth Kay, m. Harris Landrum.
6—Wallace Kay, m. Mary McLain.
6—Katherine Kay, m. Ralph Pierce.
6—Ralph Kay.
5—Julia James, m. Mr. Day.
6—Douglas Day and other issue.
4—Mary Frances Blackwell, d. 1858; m. 1852, Thomas W. Thomas, Judge Superior Court, Northern Circuit of Georgia, son of William Thomas and Nancy Wright.

5—Cora Thomas, m. Asbury Tate.
6—May Tate.
6—Rebecca Tate, m. Benjamin Conyers.
7—Benjamin Conyers Jr.
7—Tate Conyers.
7—Christian "Chris" Conyers.
6—Zimri Tate.
2—(By second wife) Ralph Banks, R. S., J. P. Elbert County 1795, b. Oct. 27, 1757; d. Aug. 24, 1824; m. Nov. 27, 1788, Rachel Jones, b. about 1770.
3—Thomas Banks, b. Dec. 19, 1789; m. Jan. 3, 1821, Mary Chipman, b. about 1800.
4—Mary Lou Banks, b. 1822; m. John Stephens.
4—Elbert Banks, b. 1824; m. Fanny Peurifoy.
5—Thomas Banks, m. Eppy Bloodworth.
5—George Banks, m. Fanny Rudisell.
6—Elbert Banks.
6—John Banks.
5—Mary Banks, m. William Ford.
5—John Banks, m. Alice White.
4—Ralph Banks, m. (1) Miss Pritchard; (2) Miss Davis; (3) Miss Stephens.
5—(By first wife) Thomas Banks.
5—Pike Banks.
5—Kate Banks.
5—Ralph Banks Jr.
5—John Banks.
4—Richard Banks, m. (1) Fanny Green; (2) Rebecca Horton.
5—(By first wife) Mary E. Banks, m. Benjamin Turner.
5—William A. Banks, m. Fanny White.
6—James Banks.
6—Vallie Banks.
6—Lula Banks.
6—Oliver Banks.
6—Benjamin Banks.
6—Mattie Banks.
5—(By second wife) Lucy Banks, m. Henry Price.
5—Richard Banks Jr.
5—Elbert Banks.
3—James J. Banks, b. April 5, 1792; m. Hannah Allston.
4—Jasper Banks.
4—Jabez Banks, m. Jane Harvey.
5—William Banks.
5—Sarah Banks.
5—Loula Banks.
5—Newton Banks.
5—James J. Banks, m. Lee Frazer.
6—Frazer Banks.
6—James J. Banks Jr., m. Feb. 15, 1838, Lucy Maxwell.
3—Sallie Banks, m. Edwards Sims.
3—Dr. Richard Banks, for whom Banks County, Georgia, was named, m. Martha Butts.
4—James Banks.
4—Philocea Banks.
4—Dunstan Banks.
4—Susan Banks.
3—Ralph Banks Jr., m. Dec. 22, 1818, Elizabeth Maxwell; d. Jan. 13, 1840.
4—Russell Banks, m. Jane Yarborough.

4—Mary Banks, m. Memory Gump.
4—Jane Banks, m. Fleming Moss.
4—Rachel Banks, m. Augustus Moss.
4—Marion Banks, m. Martha Ressler.
3—John Banks, b. Sept. 10, 1799; m. Feb. 14, 1828, Sarah Watkins.
4—John T. Banks.
4—Willis Banks, Captain C. S. A.
4—George Banks, member Georgia Convention of Secession, m. (1) Susan Mitchell; (2) Dolly Jeter.
5—(By first wife) John Banks.
5—Mattie Banks.
5—Sallie Banks.
5—Lizzie Banks.
5—Eugenia Banks.
5—George Banks Jr.
5—Maymie Banks.
5—(By second wife) Dolly Banks.
4—Daniel Banks.
4—Edward Banks.
4—Susan Banks.
4—Gilmer Banks.
4—Richard Banks, Lieut., C. S. A.
4—Elbert A. Banks.
4—Sarah Banks, m. Edward Young.
4—Josephine Banks, m. G. J. Peacock.
5—Sallie Peacock.
5—Elberta Peacock.
5—James P. Peacock.
5—John B. Peacock.
4—Mary Priscilla Banks.
3—Dunstan Banks, m. Lucretia Webb.
4—Martha Banks.
4—Henrietta Banks.
4—Robert Banks.
4—Lucretia Banks.
4—Julia Banks.
3—Priscilla Banks, m. Moses Butts.
3—Henry Banks, m. Feb. 8, 1825, Judith Oliver.
4—Sarah Banks, m. Henry Scales.
4—Lucy Banks, m. Thomas Wilkinson.
3—Lemuel Banks, b. May 22, 1806; m. Dec. 24, 1833, Louisa Tate.
4—Lemuel Banks Jr.
4—Ralph Banks.
4—George Banks, m. Susan Love.
5—Lemuel Banks, m. Lillian Fitzgerald.
5—William L. Banks, m. Lucy Hatsell.
6—Hatsell Banks.
6—King Banks.
6—David Banks.
5—George Banks.
5—David Banks.
4—Charles Banks.
4—Mary Banks, m. Jordan Payne.
4—Richard Banks, m. (1) Betsy Campbell; (2) Ida Campbell.
5—(By first wife) Richard M. Banks.
5—George Banks.
5—Nicholas Banks.
5—(By second wife) Harry Banks.
5—Charles Banks.

4—Henry Banks, m. Sally Dockery.
5—Henry Banks Jr.
5—Love Banks.
2—James Banks, m. Charity Allston.
3—James Banks Jr., m. May 20, 1821, Millie Oliver.
4—William C. Banks.
3—Nathaniel Banks, m. Caroline Hughes.
4—Mary Banks, m. August 27, 1843, Charles Wesley Arnold.
3—Caroline Banks, m. William Arnold.
3—Gilly Y. Banks, m. March 6, 1823, Bedford Harper.
4—William J. Harper, m. Fanny Dorough.
5—Richard Harper.
5—Anna Harper.
5—William Harper, m. Genevieve Dean.
5—Thomas Harper, m. Mattie Moon.
5—Elizabeth "Lizzie" Harper.
5—Sarah "Sally" Harper.
5—Allston Harper.
4—Charity Harper.
4—Martha Harper, m. G. Erskin Heard.
5—Bedford Harper, m. Ida Cleveland nee McCalla.
6—M. E. Heard, m. Allen Pressley.
6—Erskin Heard, m. Lottie Seymour.
7—Martha Heard.
7—Bedford Heard.
7—Emma Heard.
7—Mattie Heard.
7—Hazel Heard.
6—Sarah Heard, m. Frank Hammond.
7—Frank Hammond Jr.
7—Mildred Hammond.
6—Bevelle Heard, m. Thomas Wayble.
7—Bevelle Wayble.
6—Caroline Heard, m. Guy Quillian.
5—Thomas J. Heard, m. Willie Sondidge.
5—Emma Heard, m. Dr. N. G. Long. No issue.
3—Thomas Banks, m. Miss Arnold.
3—Hannah Banks, m. Sept. 15, 1829, Florence Oliver.
4—James Oliver, Major, C. S. A.
3—Frances Banks, m. Sidney Skidmore.
3—Martha Banks, m. July 7, 1829, Thomas Crawford.
4—Elizabeth Crawford, m. Mr. Reese.
3—Emily Banks, m. Mr. Dorrough.
2—Dunstan Banks.
2—William Banks.
2—John Banks.
2—(By third wife) Thomas Banks.

BARNETT

Shortly before the Revolution Nathaniel "Nat" Barnett, with his family and a number of relatives, moved from Virginia to Georgia. They settled in Wilkes County but soon removed to Elbert County.

When War was declared William and Joel Barnett, brothers, returned to Amherst County, Virginia, and enlisted in the American Army. They were sons of Nathaniel Barnett and his wife Susannah Crawford. William received the rank of Captain and served under Marquis de' LaFayette and after the War returned to Georgia in 1784. He was President of the Georgia Senate; a member of Congress, and was also a delegate to the Constitutional Convention of Georgia in 1798.

Nathaniel Barnett remained in Georgia during the Revolution taking an active part against the Tories in upper Georgia and was captured by them, not being released until 1781. He died at the age of 93 in the year 1820.

The following chart shows intermarriages with the following families:
Arnett — Atwood — Atchley — Baldwin — Bracy — Bradford — Brain — Brightwell — Bryne — Bussey — Burke — Chowing — Clegg — Collier — Crawford — Dansby — DeGroot — Dewoody — Emerson — Fletcher — Frazier — Gatling — Gillespie — Gilmer — Gould — Green — Graves — Goolsby — Haskins — Hendricks — Holland — Hudson — Hughes — Lampkin — Marks — Martin — Mathews — May — Meriwether — Micou — Miller — Milstead — Mosely — McGehee — McLean — Nobles — Patterson — Pettigrew — Phillips — Poindexter — Price — Reeves — Rogers — Ross — Russell — Sanders — Schull — Sloss — Smith — Sorrells — Stewart — Taliaferro — Thomas — Thompson — Timberlake — Vance — Walpole — White — Willey — Williams.

(Note: Numbers represent generations, as: (1) first generation, (2) second generation, (3) third generation, etc.)

1—Nathaniel Barnett, b. 1727; d. 1820; m. Susannah Crawford, b. 1729.
    2—David Barnett, b. 1749.
    2—Peter Barnett, b. 1750.
    2—Nancy Barnett, m. Joel Crawford.
    2—Joel Barnett, b. 1762; m. Ann or Elizabeth Crawford and Mildred Meriwether, b. 1772; d. 1852.
    2—William Barnett, b. 1761; d. 1815; m. (1) Mary Meriwether; (2) Mrs. Sally Bibb nee Wyatt. No issue.
        3—Martha J. Barnett, m. Francis M. Gilmer, b. July 27, 1785.
        3—Thomas Meriwether Barnett, m. Margaret Micou.
        3—Mary B. Barnett, d. 1809; m. David Taliaferro.
        3—Lucy Barnett, d. 1798; m. George Mathews.
        3—Frances Barnett, m. Isaac Ross.

3—Nathaniel Barnett Jr., b. 1784; m. Mary "Polly" Hudson, b. 1796; d. 1831 in New Edinburg, Arkansas.
4—David Barnett, b. 1817; d. unmarried.
4—May Elizabeth Barnett, b. 1818; d. unmarried.
4—Louisa A. Barnett, b. 1820; d. unmarried.
4—Susan Barnett, b. 1826.
4—Frances L. Barnett, b. 1822; m. Judge Josiah Gould.
5—James Nathaniel Gould, m. (1) Belle Holland; (2) Beulah Holland.
4—Martha Valeria Barnett, b. 1830; m. Dr. Thomas Crowing.
4—Nicholas Barnett, b. 1828; m. (1) Elizabeth Hudson; (2) Olive Mathews; (3) Sallie Mathews.
5—(By first wife) Mary Elizabeth Barnett, b. 1858; m. W. S. Amis.
5—(By second wife) Sydney O. Barnett, b. 1862; d. 1905; m. 1886, Sally Virginia Rogers, b. 1864; d. 1914.
5—William Eugene Barnett, b. 1864; m. Katherine Williams.
4—Mary Meriwether Barnett, b. 1815; d. 1848; m. 1829, John Harvie Marks II.
5—Rebecca Mathews Marks, b. 1831; d. 1913; m. 1851, Judge Theodoric Finley Sorrells, b. 1821; d. 1900.
6—William Samuel Sorrells, m. (1) Frances L. Patterson. No issue. (2) Mrs. W. T. Milstead. No issue.
6—Theodoric Finley Sorrells Jr., m. Mollie Walpole. No issue.
6—Mary Magdaline Sorrells, b. 1854; m. William Lawrence Dewoody.
7—Marion Louise Dewoody, b. 1876; m. 1903, Clarence W. Pettigrew.
7—Rebecca Dewoody, b. 1877; m. 1901, Earl W. Phillips.
8—William Wardon Phillips, m. Helen Bradford.
8—Earl Taylor Phillips.
7—Martha Alma Dewoody, m. 1911, Newton Edward Brightwell.
8—Bewton Edward Brightwell Jr.
7—Emma Virginia Dewoody, b. 1881; m. 1920, Joe Sloss.
8—Mary Elizabeth Sloss.
8—Virginia Antoinette Sloss.
7—Florence Antoinette Dewoody, b. 1883; m. John W. Briley.
7—William Lawrence Dewoody Jr., d. unmarried.
7—Sorrells Dewoody, b. 1887; m. (1) Mary Kate Riley; (2) Marguerite Smith.
8—(By first wife) T. Sorrells Dewoody Jr., b. 1916.
7—Margaret Coman Dewoody, b. 1891; m. 1919, H. E. Miller.
8—Marian Coman Miller, b. 1922.
7—James Valliant Dewoody, d. unmarried.
7—Mildred and Edith Dewoody, twins, d. infancy.
7—John Marshall Dewoody, d. infancy.
6—Emma Virginia Sorrells, b. 1867; d. 1900; m. Thomas E. Gillespie.
7—John Finley Gillespie, m. Kate Wilson.
8—John Finley Gillespie Jr.
8—Lula Worsham Gillespie.
8—Ben Evan Gillespie.
8—Mary Virginia Gillespie.
8—Frances Gillespie.
7—Frances Gillespie, m. Clarence H. Collier, Troup, Texas.
8—Charles H. Collier Jr.
8—Thomas Gillespie Collier.
7—James Harvey Gillespie, m. Elizabeth Thompson.
8—James Harvey Gillespie Jr.
8—Jack Lee Gillespie, d. 1930.

8—Mildred Gillespie.
6—Walter Barnett Sorrells, m. Mary Iva Fletcher.
7—John Harvie Sorrells, m. Ruth Arnett.
7—Emma Virginia Sorrells, m. Theodore M. Green.
8—Dorothy Green.
8—Marjorie Green.
7—Mary Iva Sorrells, m. Augustus W. Willey.
7—Walter Barnett Sorrells Jr., m. Porta McLean.
8—Walter Barnett Sorrells III.
5—Frank Marks, b. 1831; m. Ellen Dansby.
6—Georgia Marks, b. 1856; m. John Bussey.
7—Samuel Bussey, m. Ellen Price.
7—James Bussey, m. Emma Price.
7—Thomas Bussey.
6—Hattie Marks, b. 1860; m. 1878, A. H. Reeves.
7—Orrie Reeves, m. Oscar Gatling.
7—Pearl Reeves, m. Claud Clegg.
7—Frank Reeves, m. Fay Scull. No issue.
7—Ellie Reeves.
7—Sannie Reeves, m. W. R. Stitch.
6—Ellie Marks.
6—Thomas Marks.
6—Frank Harvie Marks.
5—William Marks, m. Margaret Frazier.
6—Ida Marks, m. 1888, Larkin A. Mosely.
7—Margaret Mosely.
7—Ruth Mosely.
7—Marks Mosely.
7—William D. Mosely.
7—Ralph Mosely.
6—Margaret Marks, m. W. D. Atwood.
6—Willie Marks, m. Dr. O. J. Vance.
6—Mary Marks.
5—Amelia Meriwether Marks, m. (1) Thomas Dansby; (2) Voluntine Meriwether McGehee.
6—(By first husband) Thomas Dansby Jr., m. Lillian Thomas.
6—(By second husband) Barbara Cosby McGehee, m. 1896, Postelle Russell.
7—Jean Russell, m. Malcolm Sanders.
8—Jean Sanders.
8—Emily Moss Sanders.
7—Emily Russell, m. Captain William May.
7—James Meriwether Russell.
6—Mary McGehee, m. 1898, James White, b. 1867; d. 1902; (2) A. W. Nobles.
7—Bertha White.
7—James White Jr.
7—(By second husband) Lillian Nobles.
7—Elsie Nobles.
6—Madison Tate McGehee, m. Nancy Spencer, Abilene, Texas.
7—Thomas McGehee.
7—William Spencer McGehee.
6—Voluntine Meriwether McGehee, b. Oct. 14, 1876; d. May 1930; m. Oct. 1896, MeKendree Atchley.
7—Cornelia Atchley, d. infancy.
7—Robert McGehee Atchley, m. Clyde Williams.
7—Oliver Atchley, m. Merle Martin.
7—Mary Valuntine Atchley, b. Jan. 14, 1916.

5—Martha Harvey Marks, b. 1841; m. James Madison Hudson, b. 1842; d. 1925.
6—Charles Edward Hudson, m. Edith Frazier.
6—Mary Hudson, m. J. Lorraine De Groot.
6—James Harvey Hudson, m. Annibel Bracy.
6—Walter Cole Hudson, m. Nellie Ray Brain.
6—Lucy Hudson, m. Louise Vance.
4—William D. Barnett, b. 1824; d. 1882; m. 1849, Lydia G. Hughes.
5—Addie Valeria Barnett, m. George Clark Atwood.
5—William Hughes Barnett, m. Eleanor Tomkins Marks.
5—Fanny May Barnett, m. Dr. Jack Chowing.
5—Charles Caldwell Barnett, b. 1856; m. Betty Graves.
4—Martha Valeria Barnett, m. 1845, Dr. Thomas W. Chowing, b. 1814.
5—Dr. John Chowing, b. 1846; d. 1882; m. 1870, Martha Barnett.
5—Dr. Nathaniel Chowing, b. 1856; d. 1901; m. 1893, Deborah Marks.
6—Frank Chowing, Little Rock, Ark.
6—Montine Chowing.
6—Eleanor Chowing.
5—Thomas Chowing, b. 1847; d. 1866; m. Lucy Haskins.
5—Fanny Chowing, m. Edward Emerson.
2—Joel Barnett, b. 1762; d. 1851; m. Mildred Meriwether, b. 1772; d. 1852.
3—Elizabeth Barnett, b. 1793; m. 1809, Joseph H. Ponder.
3—Charles Barnett, b. 1800; d. 1890; m. 1824, Eliza Gresham.
4—Eleanor Barnett, b. 1828; m. Nicholas J. Gilmer.
5—Susan Josephine Gilmer, b. 1847; m. 1867, W. P. Timberlake.
6—Mary Eleanor Timberlake and other issue.
4—Martha J. Barnett, b. 1831; d. 1862; m. 1848, W. R. Poindexter.
4—Margaret Barnett, b. 1836; m. 1858, A. W. Lampkin.
4—Nathaniel Barnett, C. S.
3—Frank Barnett, b. 1802; d. 1856; m. Sarah G. Ponder.
4—Mary Jane Barnett, m. 1816, Dr. John T. Gilmer; d. 1865.
4—Martha Barnett, m. Benjamin J. Baldwin.
4—Cordelia Barnett, m. Frank Mathews.
4—Susie Barnett, m. George Meriwether.
4—Nicholas Barnett, b. 1836; m. (1) Mary Meriwether; (2) 1886, Mrs. Zara Jones Campbell, b. 1843; d. 1905.
4—Luckie Barnett, m. William George Meriwether.
4—Joel Barnett, m. Ruth Micou.
3—Nathaniel Barnett, b. 1805; m. (1) Eliza Goolsby; (2) Mrs. Lucy Hendricks Byrne; (3) Mary Hendricks.
3—Mary Barnett, m. William H. Smith of Mississippi.
3—Rebecca Barnett, b. 1810; m. Michael Johnson.
3—Emily Barnett, b. 1815; m. (1) Craven W. Totten; (2) Wiley V. Stewart.
3—Susan Crawford Barnett, b. 1798; m. (1) John Gresham; (2) John Gilmer, d. 1874.
3—Lucy Ann Barnett, b. 1818; m. Virgil Burke.
3—Martha Johnson Barnett, b. 1796; m. 1820, Hinton Crawford.

BLACKWELL

The following chart shows intermarriages with the following families: Adams — Allen — Banks — Bowman — Carr — Carlton — Carroll — Clark — Clinton — Conyers — Davis — Day — Dennis — Ethridge — Gantt — Hammond — Harbin — Harper — Hearne — Heard — Hodges — James — Jones — Johnson — Kay — Landrum — Langston — Latimer — Little — Long — Lynch — Marshall — Martin — Matthews — Middleton — Murray — McCalla — McLain — Pressley — Pierce — Pharr — Quillian — Seymour — Sondidge — Swift — Tate — Thomas — Thornton — Wayble — Whitmire — Williams — Wright.

(Note: Numbers represent generations, as: (1) first generation, (2) second generation, (3) third generation, etc.)

1—Joseph Blackwell, R. S., d. 1806; m. Sarah "Sally" Banks; b. June 4, 1748, daughter of Thomas Banks and Sarah Chandler.
  2—Dunstan Blackwell.
  2—Banks Blackwell, m. June 28, 1831, Mrs. Elizabeth Clark.
  2—Ralph Banks, d. 1853.
  2—Joseph Blackwell Jr., d. 1857; m. March 3, 1812, Elizabeth McGehee.
    3—Sarah Ann Blackwell, m. April 8, 1841, Thomas J. Bowman.
    3—Eliza Blackwell, m. Aug. 2, 1845, William B. White, C. S.
    3—Cornelia Blackwell, m. Nov. 2, 1848, Edwin A. Jones.
      4—Robert Jones.
      4—Edwin A. Jones Jr.
    3—James Y. Blackwell.
    3—Samuel D. Blackwell.
    3—Thomas P. Blackwell.
    3—Mary E. Blackwell.
    3—Claudia Blackwell.
    3—William M. Blackwell.
    3—George L. Blackwell.
    3—Llewyllen Blackwell, m. (1) Elizabeth Gantt; (2) Widow Cosby.
      4—(By first wife) Elizabeth Blackwell, m. Thomas Hodges.
        5—Sarah Hodges, d. unmarried.
  2—Parks Blackwell, m. Elizabeth Murray.
    3—James P. Blackwell.
    3—J. L. Blackwell.
    3—Isabella Blackwell, m. (1) Gerrard Allen; (2) William Clark, C. S.; (3) John James, C. S.
      4—Gerrard Allen Jr., m. Adelaide Stanford.
        5—Singleton W. Allen, m. May Wood.
          6—Gerrard Allen, m. Sadie Ethridge.
        5—Hattie Allen, m. Charles Whitmire.
          6—Charles Whitmire Jr.
          6—Harriet Whitmire.
          6—Annie Bevelle Whitmire.
          6—Martha Whitmire.
      4—William Parks Clark, Lieutenant Spanish-American War, d. unmarried.
      4—Overton Clark.
      4—Fanny Clark, m. W. W. Adams, City Councilman of Elberton.
        5—Clark Adams.
        5—Raymond Adams.

5—Marshall Adams, S. W. W.
5—Murray Adams.
5—Richard Adams, S. W. W.
5—Samuel Adams.
5—Lewis Adams.
5—Freeman Adams, m. Frances Thornton.
6—Priscilla Adams.
4—Elizabeth Clark, m. Mr. Carr.
4—Josie Clark.
4—Belle James, m. Benjamin H. Kay.
5—Herbert Kay.
5—Elizabeth Kay, m. J. Harris Landrum, editor Elbert County News.
5—Wallace Kay, S. W. W., m. Mary McLain.
5—Katherine Kay, m. Ralph Pierce.
5—Ralph Kay.
4—Julia James, m. Mr. Day.
5—Douglas Day and other issue.
3—Mary Frances Blackwell, d. 1858; m. 1852, Thomas W. Thomas, Judge Superior Courts Northern Circuit of Georgia, served short time as Colonel 15th Georgia Regiment Infantry Volunteers, son of William Thomas and Nancy Wright.
4—Cora Thomas, m. Asbury Tate.
5—May Tate.
5—Rebecca Tate, m. Benjamin Conyers, lawyer of Atlanta.
6—Benjamin Conyers Jr., county attorney of Elbert County, appointed 1937.
6—Tate Conyers.
6—Chris Conyers.
5—Zimri Tate.
2—Betsy C. Blackwell, m. (1) Mr. Williamson; (2) Nov. 11, 1810, Robert Middleton.
3—Sally Chandler Williamson, m. Jan. 21, 1819, John A. Verdell.
4—Dr. Dunstan Verdell, m. Prudence Hearne.
5—Clarence Verdell, Methodist Minister.
5—Dunstan Verdell Jr.
5—Thomas Verdell, civil engineer, U. S. Deputy Marshal.
5—Mattie Verdell.
5—Catherine Verdell.
5—Rosa Verdell.
4—Ann Verdell.
4—Adeline Verdell.
4—Martha Verdell.
4—Mary Verdell, m. Dr. Langston.
5—John Langston, Superintendent Elberton Public Schools, author Langston's Poems, Supt. Sylvania, Georgia, Public Schools.
5—Ada Langston, m. Mr. Marshall.
3—Betsy Williamson.
3—Robert Middleton Jr.
3—James Lawrence Middleton.
3—John Middleton.
3—Nancy Middleton, m. Thomas J. Heard.
4—Jane Ann Heard, m. Dr. David Matthews. No issue.
4—Sarah Heard, m. L. H. O. Martin, C. S.
5—Sarah Martin.
5—L. H. O. Martin Jr., member Georgia House of Representatives, m. Rossie Harper.
4—James Lawrence Heard, C. S., m. Melissa Harper.
5—Mary Heard, m. Thomas Carlton, Baptist evangelist.

5—William H. Heard, m. Kathleen Carroll.
6—Margaret Heard.
6—Carroll Heard.
6—James Lawrence Heard.
6—Janie Heard.
6—Sarah Heard.
6—William Heard.
6—Martin Heard.
6—Joseph Heard.
5—Nancy Heard, m. Phil W. Davis, member Georgia House of Representatives, member Georgia Senate, Baptist minister, lawyer.
6—Melissa Davis, m. Fred Lynch. No issue.
6—Phil W. Davis Jr., lawyer; m. Cecile Little.
5—Oliver M. Heard, m. Victor Harbin.
5—Janie Heard, m. Dr. Fred Clinton. No issue.
4—Robert M. Heard, Captain C. S. A., member Georgia House of Representatives, Mayor of Elberton; m. Louisa Jones.
5—John T. Heard, d. unmarried.
5—Vohammie Heard, m. Marcus A. Pharr.
6—Marcus A. Pharr Jr.
6—Robert Pharr.
6—Camilla Pharr.
6—Mitta Pharr.
6—Louise Pharr.
5—Luther Martin Heard, President Citizens Bank of Elberton, m. Mamie Lattimer.
6—Luther Martin Heard Jr.
6—Lattimer Heard.
6—Robert Heard.
5—Georgia Heard, m. Dr. J. E. Johnson.
6—Dr. J. E. Johnson Jr.
5—Carroll Heard. Unmarried.
5—Roberta Heard, m. John T. Dennis, Captain State Militia, Mayor of Elberton. No issue.
5—Parks E. Heard. Unmarried.
4—Erskin Heard, m. (1) Martha Harper; (2) Caroline Calhoun.
5—(By first wife) Thomas J. Heard, m. Willie Sondidge.
5—Bedford Heard, m. Ida Cleveland nee McCalla.
6—M. E. Heard, m. Allen Pressley.
6—Sarah Heard, m. Frank Hammond.
6—Erskin Heard, m. Lottie Seymour.
6—Bevelle Heard, m. Thomas Wayble.
6—Caroline Heard, m. Guy Quillian.
5—Emma Heard, m. Dr. N. G. Long, member Georgia House of Representatives, Georgia State Senator. No issue.
5—(By second wife) George E. Heard. Unmarried.
4—William Henry Heard, m. Jennie Harper.
5—Harper Heard.
5—Thomas Parks Heard, d. unmarried.
5—Rebecca Heard, m. Frank Wright. No issue.
4—Eugene Heard, C. S., m. Sarah Harper.
5—Susan Heard, d. 1934; m. J. Y. Swift. No issue.

BREWER

The following chart shows intermarriages with the following families:
Allen — Arnold — Auld — Bagwell — Baker — Bennett — Bigham — Bowen — Brown — Bruce — Bunn — Butler — Carey — Carpenter — Carter — Childs — Cleveland — Curtis — Davis — Deadwyler — Dixon — Dugar — Dye — Easter — Freeman — Foreman — Fortson — Fox — Gaines — Godshall — Graham — Grogan — Harper — Harris — Haygood — Hill — Hitchcock — Horton — Irons — Jones — Jordan — LaHatte — Lyons — Manley — Mattox — Maxwell — Morris — McKinley — McLanahan — Moore — Newton — Oglesby — Phillips — Pruitt — Russell — Sanders — Schuler — Simmons — Sledge — Smith — Stevens — Stooks — Start — Stone — Summerson — Swearingen — Talliaferro — Tate — Tillman — Vaughan — Womack — Warren — Wooten — Worrell — Wright.

(Note: Numbers represent generations, as: (1) first generation, (2) second generation, (3) third generation, etc.)

1—Edmund Brewer, m. Sarah Easter.
   2—Daughter, m. Robert Gaines.
   2—Daughter, m. Reuben Curtis.
   2—Daughter, m. Thomas Brown.
   2—Elisham Brewer.
   2—William B. Brewer, b. about 1770; m. about 1793, Charlotte Easter, b. 1777; d. 1857.
     3—Hopkins R. Brewer, b. 1794; m. Miss McKinley. No issue.
     3—Cynthia Brewer, b. 1796; m. Oct. 21, 1816, McKinley Irons.
     3—Edmund H. Brewer, b. 1797; m. May 7, 1823, Lucy Farris Carter, b. Sept. 7, 1806; d. Dec. 24, 1857.
       4—Adeline Brewer, b March 9, 1824; d. Nov. 13, 1911; m. May 18, 1843, Samuel Stark Jr., b. March 13, 1818; d. May 9, 1901.
         5—Mary Stark, b. Nov. 5, 1847; d. May 19, 1921; m. Jan. 20, 1869, Thomas W. Hill.
           6—Sally May Hill.
           6—Thomas W. Hill Jr., m. Mrs. Jennie Phillips nee Sledge.
           6—Samuel Hill.
           6—Adeline Hill, m. Carroll Summerson.
           6—Nan Hill, m. (1) Laurens Foreman; (2) Louis Godshall.
           6—Irene Hill.
           6—Welborn Hill, m. Jessie Sledge.
              7—Mary Hill.
              7—Dorothy Hill.
           6—Maud Hill.
           6—Ruby Hill.
         5—Sarah, b. Sept. 11, 1849; d. Jan. 27, 1928; m. Jan. 8, 1868, Benjamin R. Tillman, C. S., Governor of South Carolina, United States Senator.
           6—Adeline Tillman, d. unmarried.
           6—Benjamin R. Tillman Jr., m. Lucy Dugar, granddaughter of Governor Pickens of South Carolina.
              7—Douschka Tillman, God-daughter of Nicholas, Czar of Russia, who attended her christening.
              7—Sarah Tillman.

6—Molana Tillman, m. Charles Moore.
7—Benjamin Moore.
7—Minnie Moore.
6—Henry Tillman, m. Mary Fox.
7—Mary Tillman.
7—Adeline Tillman.
7—Sarah Tillman.
7—Benjamin R. Tillman.
6—Sophia Tillman, m. Henry Hughes.
7—Elizabeth Hughes.
7—Adeline Hughes.
7—Sarah Hughes.
6—Sally May Tillman, m. John Schuler.
7—John Schuler Jr.
7—Harry Schuler.
5—Edmund Brewer Stark, b. Oct. 19, 1852; d. May 10, 1915; m. Oct. 15, 1872, Julia Baker.
6—Samuel Stark, d. unmarried.
6—Julia Stark, m. Dec. 16, 1896, A. H. Womack.
7—Maud Womack.
7—Edmund Womack.
7—Lyons Womack.
7—A. H. Womack Jr.
6—Mary Stark, m. A. B. Jones.
7—Louise Jones.
6—Sarah Louise Stark, m. (1) H. E. Russell; (2) J. L. Smith.
7—Essie Russell.
7—Earl Russell.
7—Julia Russell.
6—Brewer Stark, m. Alice Newton.
7—Nell Stark.
7—Harriet Stark.
6—Ruth Stark, m. Jan. 17, 1904, C. B. Haygood.
7—Catherine Haygood.
7—Albert Haygood.
6—John A. Stark, Sheriff of Elbert County, 1937-1940, m. Cynthia Smith. No issue.
6—Thomas R. Stark, member City Concil of Elberton, b. Feb. 15, 1890; m. 1912, Elizabeth Auld, b. 1895.
7—Julia Stark, b. March 1914.
5—Mary Adeline Stark, b. July 24, 1859; m. March 26, 1879, George C. Grogan, Judge City Court of Elberton, Captain Elberton Light Infantry, attorney for Elbert County Bond Commission, county attorney of Elbert County, b. April 5, 1857; d. Dec. 15, 1925.
6—Stark Grogan, head statistician U. S. Census Bureau, b. Feb. 14, 1880; m. Oct. 3, 1900, Ailene Harper.
7—Stark Grogan Jr.
6—George C. Grogan Jr., b. Nov. 16, 1881; m. Nov. 16, 1904, Louise Phillips.
7—Phillip Grogan.
7—George C. Grogan III.
6—Sarah Grogan, b. Aug. 21, 1884; m. Feb. 3, 1904, Henry D. Jordan.
7—Ralph Jordan.
7—Henry D. Jordan Jr., m. Addie Sanders.
8—Lovett Jordan.
8—Sarah Adeline Jordan.
6—Henry Grogan, b. May 7, 1888; m. Jan. 20, 1907, Clyde McLanahan.

7—George Albert Grogan.
7—Betsy Grogan, m. Mayson Jaudon.
8—Henry Jaudon.
8—Arnold Starke Jaudon.
6—May Bruce Grogan, b. Aug. 24, 1894; m. June 6, 1916, James Hagood Bruce.
7—Virginia Bruce.
7—James McDuffie Bruce.
6—Edmund Brewer Grogan, b. Sept. 11, 1896; m. Dec. 23, 1922, Bernice Lyons.
7—Jeanne Grogan.
7—Carroll Grogan.
6—Kathleen Bruce Grogan, b. Dec. 27, 1898; m. April 21, 1921, James Y. Arnold, b. 1899.
7—James Y. "Jimmy" Arnold Jr.
4—William Thomas Brewer, m. Malinda Talliferro.
5—Rose Brewer.
5—Nicholas Brewer.
5—Benjamin Brewer.
5—Lucy Brewer.
5—Thomas Brewer.
4—Hopkins Brewer, b. Sept. 30, 1829; m. Oct. 23, 1851, Amanda Carpenter.
5—Lucy Brewer, d. 1937; m. J. C. Swearingen.
6—H. Brewer Swearingen, member City Council of Elberton; m. Lottie Morris.
7—Dorothy Swearingen.
6—Allie Sue Swearingen, m. June 7, 1900, B. F. Bennett.
7—Louise Bennett.
7—B. F. Bennett Jr.
6—J. C. Swearingen Jr.
6—L. H. Swearingen, b. 1892; d. 1933; unmarried. S. W. W.
5—James E. Brewer, tax collector of Elbert County; d. 1935; m. Fanny Freeman.
6—Marion Brewer, m. Nov. 8, 1900, A. S. Simmons.
6—John Brewer.
6—Pauline Brewer, m. April 20, 1905, John Brown.
7—John Brown Jr.
5—Mary "Mollie" Brewer, m. L. H. Turner. No issue.
5—Thomas Brewer, m. Miss Oglesby.
6—James T. Brewer, m. Oct. 10, 1901, Florence Smith.
7—Janice Brewer.
7—Eva Brewer.
7—Ralph Brewer.
7—Mary Brewer.
6—Pearl Brewer, m. June 29, 1905, T. V. Bagwell.
7—Thomas Bagwell; d. unmarried.
7—Virginia Bagwell.
7—Jack Bagwell.
6—Luther Brewer.
6—Ruby Brewer.
5—Samuel Stark Brewer, m. (1) Annie LaHatte; (2) Miss Warren.
6—(By first wife) Albert T. Brewer, m. Valeria Allen.
7—Elizabeth Brewer.
6—Samuel Stark Brewer Jr. Unmarried.
5—Charles H. Brewer, m. Jane Pruitt.
6—Charles H. Brewer Jr.
6—Mabel Brewer.
6—Claud Brewer, m. Josie Earl Worrell.

6—Irene Brewer, m. Dec. 7, 1921, Hugh Cleveland.
6—Thelma Brewer, m. Robert Bass.
7—Robert Bass Jr.
6—Pauline Brewer, m. Wilton Auld.
6—Hoke Brewer.
4—John M. Brewer, C. S., b. Nov. 13, 1843; m. April 29, 1859, Mary Lofton.
5—Mary Brewer, m. Dec. 23, 1884, Thomas S. Jones, Marshal of Elberton.
6—Brewer B. Jones, m. Sept. 27, 1908, Beulah Oglesby.
7—Brewer B. Jones Jr.
6—Mary Jones, m. Hollis Graham.
6—Nona Jones, m. Homer Hitchcock.
6—Thomas S. Jones Jr., m. Lillian Stook.
6—James Lofton Jones, m. James Smith.
6—Claud Jones.
5—Annie Brewer, m. June 18, 1891, J. M. Warren.
6—Mary Warren.
6—Annie Warren.
5—Julian Brewer, solicitor City Court of Elberton, m. Oct. 29, 1886, Alice Oglesby.
6—Marguerite Brewer, m. Horace H. Maley.
7—Mary Alice Manley.
7—Marguerite "Rita" Manley.
6—Herbert Brewer, d. unmarried.
6—Julian Brewer Jr.
2—John Brewer, d. unmarried.
2—Patsy Brewer, m. Robert Tate.
3—Betsy Tate.
3—Edmund B. Tate, m. Oct. 6, 1823, Mahala Fortson, b. April 3, 1806; d. June 6, 1882.
4—Anne Tate, m. Dec. 26, 1848, Thomas Harris.
4—Mary Tate, m. Mr. Stone.
4—Edmund B. Tate Jr., C. S., County Commissioner of Elbert County, m. (1) Miss Matthews; (2) Mattie Wright.
5—(By first marriage) Ora E. Tate, m. Oct. 16, 1889, Carrie May Hudson, b. Oct. 3, 1871.
6—Eugene Tate, S. W. W.
6—Brewer Tate, b. 1895, killed in action during World War, Lieutenant. Elberton Post of the American Legion named in his honor.
6—Ora E. Tate Jr.
6—Samuel Tate.
6—Maurice Tate.
6—Clark Tate.
6—Duncan Tate.
6—Carrie Sophia Tate.
6—Corrie Jane Tate and four other children.
5—Dr. Albert Tate, d. unmarried.
5—Carrie Tate, m. Rev. Bigham. No issue.
5—(By second wife) J. Wright Tate.
5—Emmae Tate, m. John Horton of Belton, South Carolina.
4—Tustin Tate, C. S., m. Fanny Herndon.
5—James Tate, m. Lade Maxwell.
6—Phillip Tate.
5—Belle Tate, m. Richard "Dick" Deadwyler.
6—Carnival Deadwyler, m. Fanny Freeman.
7—Ralph Allen Deadwyler.
6—Fanny Emma Deadwyler, m. Morrison Dixon.

6—James Tustin Deadwyler.
4—Robert Tate, C. S., m. Ellen Wooten.
5—Enos Tate, m. Nettie Bowen.
5—Alice "Allie" Tate, m. Feb. 25, 1886, Marquis Lee Stevens, of North Carolina.
6—Robert Tate Stevens, Lieutenant, Air Service, U. S. Army, during World War; m. Gladys Bunn.
5—Mary Tate, m. Nov. 23, 1887, John R. Mattox, City Councilman of Elberton, Mayor of Elberton, Chairman of Board of Tax Assessors of Elbert County.
6—Robert Tate Mattox, d. unmarried.
6—Ellen Mattox, m. Robert Carey.
7—John R. Carey.
6—Elizabeth Mattox.
6—John R. Mattox Jr., m. Ruth Vaughan.
7—Dorothy Mattox.
7—John C. Mattox.
7—Mary Alice Mattox.
7—Harold T. Mattox.
6—Alice Mattox.
2—Gates Brewer, d. 1827; m. Nov. 27, 1817, Susan Davis.
3—Frances Brewer, m. Sept. 30, 1824, William Butler.
4—Susan Butler.
4—Penelope Butler.
4—Mila Butler.
4—Martha Butler.
4—Fanny Butler.
4—Mary Butler.
3—Sarah Ann Brewer, m. Oct. 30, 1834, William Jones.
3—Martha Brewer, m. Dec. 25, 1838, Thompson Dye.
3—Mary Brewer, m. Lewis Childs.

BROWN

The following chart shows intermarriages with the following families: Arnold — Charles — Cunningham — Davis — Gaines — Ginn — Giles — Harbin — Hailey — Harris — Herndon — Johnson — Majure — Mewbourn — McMillan — Nevers — Norman — Parks — Peek — Rucker — Skelton — Talmadge — Teasley — Thornton — Warren.

(Note: Numbers represent generations, as: (1) first generation, (2) second generation, (3) third generation, etc.)

1—Andrew Brown, R. S., m. 1793, Margaret Adams.
  2—William Brown, b. May 4, 1794; m. Joannah Harbin.
  2—Hiram Brown, b. Feb. 14, 1797; m. Sarah Harbin.
  2—James L. Brown, b. Feb. 14, 1799; m. Deen Skelton.
  2—Adams Brown, b. Nov. 18, 1801; m. Nancy Harbin.
  2—Henry Brown, b. 1803; m. Miss McGee.
  2—Sarah Brown, b. Jan. 1, 1805; m. Jesse Ginn.
  2—Wiley Brown, b. 1807; m. Sarah Clark.
    3—Andrew Brown, m. Sept. 12, 1839; m. Sarah Rucker.
      4—Jefferson Brown, m. Miss Teasley.

4—Andrew Rucker Brown, m. Martha Thornton.
5—George Brown, d. unmarried.
5—Thomas J. Brown, Solicitor Superior Courts, Northern Circuit of Georgia; d. unmarried.
5—Birch Brown, m. Essie Brown.
6—Martha Brown.
6—Ralph Brown.
6—Mary M. Brown.
5—Leila Brown, m. John Gaines.
6—Dr. Thomas R. Gaines, m. Lucile Talmadge.
5—Paul Brown, member U. S. House of Representatives, 10th Georgia District, member Georgia House of Representatives from Oglethorpe County, County Attorney of Elbert County; m. Frances Arnold.
6—Robert "Bobby" Brown.
6—Rosalyn Brown.
5—Heber Brown, m. Hattie Parks.
6—Pauline Brown.
6—Thornton Brown.
6—Parks Brown.
6—Irene Brown.
4—Elzie Brown, m. Frances Cunningham.
5—Jackson Brown.
5—Dorris Brown, Tax Collector of Madison County, Georgia.
5—Sarah Brown.
5—Samantha Brown.
5—Glenn Brown and other issue.
4—Columbus Brown, m. Samantha Cunningham.
5—Otis Brown.
5—Rucker Brown, Sheriff of Hart County, Georgia.
5—Susie Brown.
5—A. Britt Brown, Sheriff of Hart County, Georgia.
4—Jackson Brown, m. Miss Johnson.
4—Leasie Brown, m. (1) Mr. Teasley; (2) James Skelton of South Carolina.
4—Elizabeth Brown, m. Elias Jenkins.
5—Sarah Jenkins, m. Oscar Herndon.
5—Drucilla Jenkins, m. John Gaines.
5—Dr. J. C. Jenkins.
5—Dr. J. I. Jenkins.
5—Mary Jenkins, m. Joseph Johnson.
5—Harriet Jenkins.
4—Fanny Brown, m. John Glenn.
5—Jack Glenn.
5—Easton Glenn.
5—John B. Glenn.
5—Sarah Glenn.
5—Fanny Glenn.
4—Louisa Brown, m. Columbus Glenn.
5—James Glenn.
5—Columbus Glenn Jr.
5—Lillian Glenn and other issue.
4—Cassie Brown, m. George E. Herndon.
5—Elzie Herndon.
5—Lee Herndon.
5—Lula Herndon, m. W. W. Brown.
5—Susie Herndon, m. Fred Mewbourn.
5—Sarah Herndon, m. Mark Warren.
5—Flora Herndon.
5—Clara Herndon.

5—William Herndon.
5—Isham Herndon.
5—Paul Herndon.
4—Felicia Brown, m. W. T. Johnson.
5—Rapheal "Rafe" Johnson.
5—W. T. Johnson Jr., and other issue.
2—Martha Brown, b. April 15, 1809; m. Moses Davis.
2—Emily Brown, m. Sept. 24, 1837, Middleton Ginn.
2—Roland J. Brown, m. (1) Elizabeth Teasley; (2) Mrs. Sarah Rucker nee Maxwell.
3—(By second wife) John A. Brown.
3—Benajah Brown.
3—Isham H. Brown, b. May 24, 1846; m. (1) Eliza Teasley, b. 1846; d. 1864; (2) Sept. 14, 1865, Sarah Hailey; d. 1913.
4—(By second wife) J. A. Brown, b. June 18, 1866; m. Nora Harris.
4—Elizabeth Brown, b. Feb. 27, 1868; m. J. J. Gaines.
4—Sarah Brown, b. Nov. 23, 1869; m. James T. Giles.
4—Jerome Brown, b. Aug. 1, 1874; m. Ruby Peek.
4—Mary Brown, b. May 18, 1882; m. L. M. Hanner.
4—Laura Brown, b. Sept. 3, 1878; m. R. L. Norman.
4—Isham Brown, b. Aug. 25, 1880; m. Coral Peek.
4—Claud Brown, b. July 27, 1884; m. Lealand Nevers.
4—Bessie Brown, b. June 27, 1887; m. H. W. McMillan.
4—Henry Brown, m. Bonnie Jean Majure.
4—Clois C. Brown, b. Feb. 28, 1894, S. W. W.; m. Nellie Charles.
5—Clois C. Brown Jr.
5—James "Jimmy" Brown.
3—Laura Brown, m. Mr. Hailey.
3—Lou M. Brown, m. Essie McCurry.
4—Clyde Brown.
4—Thomas Brown.
4—Benson Brown.
4—Katherine Brown.
4—Mary Brown.
4—Lonnie Brown.
4—Neal Brown.
3—Lon C. Brown, Postmaster of Elberton.
3—Cran O. Brown, cashier Bank of Elberton.

BUTLER

(Note: Numbers represent generations, as: (1) first generation, (2) second generation, (3) third generation, etc.)

1—Zachariah Butler was Revolutionary Soldier from Virginia. Came to Elbert County to get land granted by United States for services as soldier in war. Buried in Elbert County about 1838. Married Mary Edwards. Buried in Elbert County.
  2—James, born June 5, 1758. Revolutionary Soldier, came to Elbert County but in late years moved to Mississippi, where he died.
  2—Patrick, Revolutionary Soldier, came to Elbert County from Virginia. Lived over 80 years. Died in Elbert County about 1838, married Elizabeth Fannin. They came to Georgia after the war with one son.
  2—Nathan, Revolutionary Soldier. Not known where he died.
  2—Nancy, married John Snellings.
    3—John, married Miss Hubbard. Lived in Elbert County.

3—David, married Miss Sarah King in Elbert County, June 22, 1819.
3—Peter Patrick, b. March 1789, in Elbert County. Died in 1851 in Elbert County. Married Hannah Snellings, Elbert County. She was born Oct. 1788; died Jan. 1839. They were married Jan. 21, 1808.
4—Peter Patrick Butler.
5—George—married Miss Booth first, later married Miss Mary Richards. He died in Wilkes County.
5—Patrick—married second cousin Patsy Butler. Moved to Louisana.
5—William—died at age of 16 years.
5—Simeon—went to Louisana and married.
5—Samuel—went to Louisana and married twice.
5—Charlotte—married James Moon in Elbert County.
5—Elizabeth—married Jackson Dye May 8, 1848. Born Jan. 6, 1822. Died Nov. 14, 1921. Jackson Dye born April 16, 1815; died Sept. 20, 1875.
5—Rebecca—died at age of 19 years.
5—Mary—married John Bonar Moon.
5—Isaac Newton—moved to Louisiana and married.
5—Lucy—died at age of 11 years.
1—George Snellings came from Virginia, was Revolutionary Soldier. Settled in Elbert County. Married Rebecca Hudson in Virginia and brought her to Elbert County.
2—John—Born in Virginia, came to Georgia and married Nancy Butler. Died in Elbert County.
2—Samuel—Born in Virginia, married Elizabeth Burton. Died in Elbert County.
2—Elizabeth—Born in Virginia, married as an old maid to Joseph Brawner.
2—Hannah—Born in Virginia, married Peter Patrick Butler in Jan. 1808.
2—Mary—Born and died in Elbert County. Married Richard Hudson.
2—Martha—Married John Hudson and later moved to Alabama.

ZACHARIAH BUTLER

Zachariah Butler was born in Ireland. He came to America before the Revolutionary War. He lived in Hanover County, Virginia. Private in Andersons' Company, Nelson's Regiment, Virginia Troops. Land grant—headright for self, two in family. Book B, page 194, Wilkes County, Georgia. Died in Elbert County, Georgia, in 1838. Married Mary Edwards.

PATRICK BUTLER

Patrick Butler was son of Zachariah Butler. He was born in Hanover County, Virginia, March 1, 1760. Served 15 months in Virginia Troops. Land grant—headright for self and four in family, on Wahatchee Creek, Wilkes County records, Book B, page 189. Living in Mecklenburg County, Virginia, in time of Revolution. Died in Elbert County, Georgia, in 1838. In 1781, he served under Captain Brown, was discharged and sent home after the Battle of

Guilford Court House. He was in the Battle of Camden, also. He applied for pension January 21, 1833. His residence was Elbert County, Georgia, the last payment being made 1838-39. In the Virginia State Library is a list of Revolutionary Soldiers of Virginia (Supplement), page 54, is found: *Patrick Butler* S. of W-1833-Pen-3-Georgia 36.

In a list of Georgia Revolutionary Soldiers, including Continentals, 3rd Report D. A. R., page 372, his name is found (Vol. 9, page 227), the following information is found (In Pierce's Register, 17th Report, D. A. R. Senate (Doc.): His wife was Elizabeth Noble of Amelia County, Virginia. John Butler, son of Patrick Butler, was born in 1782, died November 11th, 1831—married Elizabeth Hubbard—born 1788—died 1806. Mary Butler, daughter of John Butler, married George A. Broach in 1840.

JONES BROACH

Jones Broach was born in North Carolina. He served in the Revolution as Private in Captain Moores' Company from Caswell County, North Carolina. Commanded by Lieut-Col. Archibald Lytle. He was paid for service of six months, five days, from May 22, 1778-December 1, 1778. (From C. H. Bridges, Major General, the Adjutant General, Washington, D. C.)

George Broach, son of Jones Broach, born 1780; died 1862.

George A. Broach, son of George Broach, born Sept. 1, 1811; died December 11, 1831. Married Mary Butler in 1840.

CADE

The following chart shows intermarriages with the following families:
Abercrombie — Allston — Abney — Bates — Bryant — Colley — Dickson — Edwards — Frazier — Hawes — Heard — Hillingsworth — Kennedy — Lee — Long — Lyle — Moore — Mauldin — Marburg — Morange — Matthews — McNeil — McIntosh — McCullough — Nunnelee — Pope — Porter — Partlow — Rogers — Smith — Stark — Slaughter — Saffold — Tinsley — Thomas — Walton — Zeigler.

(Note: Numbers represent generations, as: (1) first generation, (2) second generation, (3) third generation, etc.)
1—Captain Drury Cade, R. S., m. Winifred Pope.
  2—Robert Cade, m. Diana Wade.
    3—Drury B. "Captain Tom" Cade, m. Julia Edwards.
      4—Sarah Cade, m. Thomas W. Thomas, C. S., Judge of the Superior Court. No issue.
      4—Drury Cade, m. Miss Partlow.
        5—Bessie Cade, m. (1) William Heard; (2) Mr. Frazier.

5—Sarah Cade, m. Mr. Mathews.
5—John Cade, m. Miss McNeil.
5—Robert Cade.
4—Guilford Cade, m. Mary Thomas.
5—Boykin Cade.
5—Daisy Cade, m. Mr. Colley.
5—Benjamin Cade, m. Annie McNeil.
6—Julia Cade, m. Mr. Abney.
6—Annie Cade.
6—Mary Cade.
5—Thomas Cade, m. Miss Lyle.
3—William Cade, m. Julia Smith nee Walton.
3—James Cade, m. Nov. 15, 1838, Susan Nunnelee.
3—Matilda Cade, m. Mr. Saffold, of Alabama.
3—Eliza Cade, m. Dec. 28, 1835, Felix Edwards.
4—Sarah E. Edwards.
4—Tallulah Edwards.
4—Adonia Edwards.
4—Ella Julia Edwards.
3—Guilford Cade, m. March 22, 1838, Sarah Howell Stark.
4—Samuel Robert Cade, m. Sarah Slaughter.
5—William G. Cade, d. unmarried.
5—Walter Cade, m. Miss Hollingsworth.
6—Sarah Louise Cade.
6—Wooder Cade, m. Patrick Porter.
6—Roy Cade.
5—Samuel Cade, m. Mary Slaughter.
6—Sarah Cade.
6—Jane Cade.
5—Albert Cade, m. Miss Morange.
6—Thelma Cade.
5—Rennie Cade.
5—Clifford Cade.
4—Mary Eliza Cade, m. Singleton A. McIntosh, C. S.
5—Sarah Howell McIntosh, b. Dec. 29, 1867; m. S. J. Zeigler.
6—Samuel Zeigler, S. W. W., U. S. Naval Officer, m. Fanny Marburg.
7—Howell Zeigler.
6—Howell "Polar" Zeigler, m. George Lee Dickson, Major U. S. A.
7—Howell Rees Dickson.
7—George Lee Dickson Jr.
5—William McPherson McIntosh, b. 1870; d. 1930, unmarried.
5—Guilford "Guy" McIntosh, b. July 6, 1872; m. Addie Tinsley.
6—Mary McIntosh, b. 1921.
6—William Kenneth McIntosh, b. 1922.
6—Louise McIntosh, b. 1923.
5—Victoria Augusta McIntosh, b. March 1875; m. Joseph Allston.
6—Joseph Allston Jr., m. Lillis McCullough.
7—Joseph Allston III.
6—Mary Allston.
5—Mary Louise McIntosh, b. Aug. 10, 1877; m. Henry M. Long.
6—Mary Louise Long, d infancy.
4—Victoria Cade, m. Augustus Lee.
5—Mamie Lee, m. Major Bryant of New Jersey.
6—John Bryant.
6—Lewis Lee Bryant.
5—Sarah Lee, m. Z. B. Rogers, City Attorney of Elberton, County Attorney of Elbert County, member Georgia House of Representatives, vice-president Georgia Bar Association, Chairman Board of Education of Elberton.

6—Lee Rogers.
6—William Rogers.
6—Mary Rogers.
5—Augustus Lee Jr., m. Margaret Smith. No issue.
4—Guilford Cade Jr., m. Mary Louisa McIntosh.
5—Julia May Cade, m. Dr. A. S. Hawes, member Georgia House of Representatives, Mayor of Elberton; b. 1863; d. 1936.
6—Guilford Moseley Hawes, m. Onie Lee.
7—Mary Lee Hawes.
7—Robert Hawes, d. infancy.
7—Julia Ann Hawes.
6—Albert Lee Hawes, m. Bertha Bates. No issue.
6—Peyton Samuel Hawes, City Attorney of Elberton, member Georgia House of Representatives, Solicitor City Court of Elberton; m. Virginia Smith.
5—Guilford Cade III, m. Jane Kennedy.
6—Malvina "Mally" Cade, m. Milo Abercrombie.
7—Milo Abercrombie Jr.
6—Guilford Cade IV.
5—Annie Lee Cade, m. Dr. R. F. Moore.
6—Alan Moore.
6—Robert Moore, d. infancy.
6—Guilford McIntosh Moore, m. Miss Mauldin.

CARPENTER

The following chart shows intermarriages with the following families:
Adams — Alexander — Allen — Auld — Bagwell — Barnett — Bennett — Bond — Brown — Brewer — Bass — Gaines — Hailey — Hawes — Herndon — Lee — Lofton — Mann — Mattox — Morris — Oglesby — Pruitt — Rouse — Simmons — Smith — Stroud — Swearengin — Tribble — Turner — Wall Williams — Worrell — Wray.

(Note: Numbers represent generations, as: (1) first generation, (2) second generation, (3) third generation, etc.)

1—Joshua Carpenter, m. Leah Smith.
  2—Joshua Carpenter Jr., m. April 2, 1825, Mary Bond.
  2—James Carpenter, m. Harriet Eliza Barrett, daughter of Isaac Barrett and Mary (?) Howard and granddaughter of N. Barrett and Mary James.
    3—Amanda Carpenter, m. Oct. 25, 1851, James Hopkins Brewer, b. Sept. 30, 1829.
      4—Lucy Brewer, d. 1937; m. James C. Swearingen.
        5—H. Brewer Swearingen, member City Council of Elberton, m. Lottie Morris.
          6—Dorothy Swearingen.
        5—Allie May Swearingen, m. June 7, 1900, B. F. Bennett.
          6—Louise Bennett.
          6—B. F. Bennett Jr.
        5—J. C. Swearingen Jr.
        5—Luther H. Swoaringen, S. W. W., d. 1933 unmarried.
      4—James E. Brewer, Tax Collector of Elbert County; d. 1935; m. Fanny Freeman.
        5—Marion Brewer, m. A. S. Simmons.
        5—John Brewer.
        5—Pauline Brewer, m. John Brown.

6—John Brown Jr.
4—Mary Brewer, m. L. H. Turner. No issue.
4—Irene Brewer, unmarried.
4—Addie Brewer, unmarried.
4—Thomas Brewer, m. Miss Oglesby.
5—James T. Brewer, m. Oct. 10, 1901, Florence Smith.
6—Janice Brewer.
6—Eva Brewer.
6—Ralph Brewer.
6—Mary Brewer.
5—Pearl Brewer, m. June 29, 1905, T. V. Bagwell.
6—Thomas Bagwell, b. 1907; d. unmarried.
6—Virginia Bagwell.
6—Jack Bagwell.
5—Luther Brewer.
5—Ruby Brewer, registered nurse.
4—Samuel Stark Brewer, m. (1) Annie LaHatte; (2) Miss Warren.
5—Albert T. Brewer, m. Valeria Allen.
6—Elizabeth Brewer.
5—Samuel Stark Brewer Jr., unmarried.
4—Charles H. Brewer, m. Jane Pruitt.
5—Charles H. Brewer Jr.
5—Mabel Brewer.
5—Claud Brewer, m. Josie Worrell.
5—Irene Brewer, m. Dec. 7, 1921, Hugh Cleveland.
5—Thelma Brewer, m. Robert Bass.
6—Robert Bass Jr.
5—Pauline Brewer, m. Wilton Auld.
5—Hoke Brewer.
3—William Hilliard Carpenter, C. S., m. (1) Fanny Wall; (2) Helen Drewry.
4—(By first wife) Willie Carpenter, m. Lindsey Gaines.
5—Raymond Gaines, m. Janie Mattox.
5—Underwood Gaines.
5—Helen Gaines, m. Armand Alexander.
5—Lindsey Gaines Jr.
5—Rosa Gaines, m. Mr. Webb.
6—Rosa Mary Webb.
4—Leila Carpenter, m. Frotson Adams.
4—(By second wife) Minor Carpenter, m. Jan. 28, 1901, A. F. Smith.
5—Matilde Smith, m. Fred Herndon, member City Council of Elberton, contractor.
6—Virginia and Marjorie Smith, twins.
5—Margaret Smith, m. Augustus Lee Jr. No issue.
5—Mary Helen Smith, m. Fred Herndon (widower of elder sister).
6—Minor Herndon.
5—A. F. Smith Jr., m. Ellen Wray.
5—Minor Ruth Smith, m. C. L. Shockley.
5—Virginia Smith, m. 1933, Peyton S. Hawes, attorney.
4—James Thomas Carpenter, m. Nov. 11, 1893, Addie Adams.
5—Lucile Carpenter, m. Jack Haley, Sheriff of Elbert County. No issue.
5—James Thomas Carpenter Jr., m. Olga Rouse.
5—L. A. Carpenter, m. Sally Mann.
6—L. A. Carpenter Jr.
6—James Chandler Carpenter.
5—Helen Carpenter.
5—Ivan Carpenter.

4—Nicholas Albert Carpenter, m. (1) Nora Tribble; (2) Leila Stroud.
5—(By first wife) Frances Myrtle Carpenter.
5—(By second wife) Nicholas Drewry Carpenter.
5—Mary Helen Carpenter.
4—Cleora Carpenter, m. Mr. Bond.
5—Willie Bond and other issue.
3—Ophelia Carpenter, m. James Lofton, C. S.
3—Thomas Napoleon Carpenter, C. S.; d. unmarried.
3—Laura Carpenter, m. Mr. Williams.
4—Ed Williams and other issue.
4—Eddie Carpenter.

CARTER AND FAMILY

David Carter was born in East New Jersey in 1758; married Mehitable Cobb.

His services in assisting in the establishment of American Independence during the War of the Revolution were as follows:

Fall of 1774, three months under Colonel Morgan in Virginia; June, 1775, one month; Spring, 1778, four months under Colonel Cleveland in North Carolina; June, 1780, one month.

In 1780, Rifle Company under General Rutherford. In 1780 he was taken prisoner at Battle of Camden and imprisoned on Prison Ships Concord, King George, and Fidelity, at Charleston until Aug., 1781. November, 1781, one month under Colonel Isaacs; December, 1781, two months. He died in Hart County in 1850.

Micajah Carter, son of David Carter, was born in Pentleton District, South Carolina, in 1787. He married Nancy Goolsby (daughter of William Goolsby, Revolutionary Soldier).

James M. Carter, son of Micajah Carter and Nancy Goolsby Carter, was born February 11, 1822, near the Savannah River, in tht portion of Hart County that was taken from Franklin County. The old home is still standing.

In 1846 James M. Carter married Louisa Clark, of Abbeville County, South Carolina, (later moved to Elbert County). Her mother, Mary Alston Clark, was a first cousin of Governor Alston, who married Theodosia, daughter of Aaron Burr. She was related to five Governors of that State.

James M. Carter was a leading citizen and a large planter. He represented his District (Elbert County) in the Senate, and before the War Between the States owned a large body of land on the Savannah River, including the site of the Memorial Bridge on the Calhoun Highway. It is a pleasing incident that James Carter's great granddaughter, Edna May Copeland, should be given an important part in the ceremonies opening the Memorial Bridge.

James M. Carter was among the first to build and operate a line of boats to carry freight and cotton from the now dead town of Andersonville to Augusta.

He served during the War as an officer in the Confederate Army in Toombs' Regiment to the end of the struggle, and was in charge of the pontoon corps that threw a bridge across the Savannah River when Jefferson Davis and his Cabinet crossed the River on their way from Abbeville, S. C., to Washington, Ga. (landing at Petersburg Ferry in Elbert County).

See Veterans Administration, Washington, D. C. David Carter, Soldier No. 16335.

CARTER

The following chart shows intermarriages with the following families: Allen — Arnold — Auld — Baker — Bagwell — Bass — Beck — Bennett — Brewer — Brown — Bruce — Clayton — Cleveland — Corry — Dugar — Fannin — Farris — Foreman — Ford — Fox — Freeman — Godshall — Graham — Grogan — Hagood — Harper — Harris — Heard — Hill — Higginbotham — Hitchcock — Hudson — Hughes — Hunt — Jaudon — Jones — Jordan — Koockogey — LaHatte — Lyons — Manley — Moore — Morris — McAlpin — McKinley — McLanahan — Newton — Oglesby — Phillips — Pruitt — Rucker — Russell — Saddler — Sanders — Schuler — Stark — Simmons — Stubbs — Stinchcomb — Summerson — Swearengin — Talliaferro — Tillman — Turner — Warren — Wimbish — Womack — Worrill.

Thomas A. Carter came to Georgia from Virginia with a number of other Virginians to receive land grants from the Government in payment for their services as soldiers during the Revolutionary War. They became prominent and splendid citizens of the section of Georgia that is now Elbert County. Thomas A. Carter received as his quota land grants three miles north of Elberton, the County seat of Elbert County. His land grants were on and adjacent to Beaverdam Creek near the present Electric Plant.

(Note: Numbers represent generations, as: (1) first generation, (2) second generation, (3) third generation, etc.)

1—Thomas A. Carter, R. S., m. (1) Miss Farris; (2) Elizabeth Stubbs.
  2—(By first wife) James Carter, d. 1837; m. Lucy Martin.
    3—John Carter, m. Elizabeth (?).
      4—Elector F. Carter.
      4—Lucy Ann Elizabeth Carter.
    3—Sarah Carter, m. April 20, 1813, Dr. George Washington Heard, son of Governor Stephen Heard.
      4—Stephen Heard, m. Miss Fannin.
        5—Phillip Heard, m. Miss Tillman.
    3—Robert Carter.
    3—Charles Carter.

3—Patsy Carter, m. Feb. 10, 1825, Mr. Koockogey.
3—Betsy Carter, m. John Corry.
4—Sarah Corry, m. Mr. Saddler.
4—Robert Corry, m. Miss Gaines.
3—Ann Daniel Carter, m. Dec. 26, 1839, John Corry.
2—Robert Carter.
2—Thomas S. Carter, d. July 20, 1843; fought at New Orleans in War of 1812; m. (1) Dec. 15, 1805, Mary Smith; (2) Feb. 21, 1839, Matilda Harmon.
3—(By first wife) Lucy Farris Carter, b. Sept. 7, 1806; d. Dec. 24, 1857; m. May 7, 1823, Edmund H. Brewer, b. about 1802; d. March 16, 1851.
4—Adeline Brewer, b. March 9, 1824; d. Nov. 3, 1911; m. May 18, 1843, Samuel C. Stark Jr., b. March 13, 1818; d. May 9, 1901.
5—Mary Stark, b. Nov. 5, 1847; d. May 19, 1921; m. Jan. 20, 1869, Thomas W. Hill.
6—Sallie May Hill.
6—Thomas W. Hill Jr., m. Mrs. Jennie Phillips nee Sledge.
6—Samuel Hill.
6—Adeline Hill, m. Carroll Summerson.
6—Nan Hill, m. (1) Laurens Foreman; (2) Louis Godshall.
6—Irene Hill.
6—Wellborn Hill, m. Jessie Sledge.
7—Mary Hill.
7—Dorothy Hill.
6—Maud Hill, m. Robert Willis.
6—Ruby Hill.
5—Sarah Stark, b. Sept. 11, 1849; d. Jan. 27, 1928; m. Jan. 8, 1868, Benjamin R. Tillman, Governor of South Carolina, United States Senator.
6—Adeline Tillman, d. unmarried.
6—Benjamin R. Tillman Jr., m. Lucy Dugar.
7—Douschka Tillman.
6—Sarah Tillman.
6—Molana Tillman, m. Charles Moore.
7—Benjamin Moore.
7—Minnie Moore.
6—Henry Tillman, m. Mary Fox.
7—Mary Tillman.
7—Adeline Tillman.
7—Sarah Tillman.
7—Benjamin R. Tillman.
6—Sallie May Tillman, m. John Schuler.
7—John Schuler Jr.
7—Harry Schuler.
6—Sophia Tillman, m. Henry Hughes.
7—Elizabeth Hughes.
7—Adeline Hughes.
7—Sarah Hughes.
5—Edmund Brewer Stark, b. Oct. 19, 1852; d. May 10, 1915; m. Oct. 15, 1872, Julia Baker.
6—Samuel Stark, d. unmarried.
6—Mary Stark, m. A. B. Jones.
7—Louise Jones.
6—Julia Stark, m. A. H. Womack.
7—Maud Womack.
7—Edmund Womack.
7—Lyons Womack.

7—A. H. Womack Jr.
6—Sarah Louise Stark, m. (1) Mr. Russell; (2) J. L. Smith.
7—Essie Russell.
7—Earl Russell.
7—Julia Russell.
6—Brewer Stark, m. Alice Newton.
7—Nell Stark.
7—Harriet Stark.
6—Ruth Stark, m. Jan. 1904, C. B. Hagood.
7—Catherine Hagood.
7—Albert Hagood.
6—John A. Stark, Sheriff of Elbert County 1936-1940; m. Cynthia Smith. No issue.
6—Thomas R. Stark, City Councilman of Elberton; b. Feb. 15, 1890; m. 1912, Elizabeth Auld, b. 1895.
7—Julia Stark, b. March 1914.
5—Mary Adeline Stark, b. July 24, 1859; m. March 26, 1879, George C. Grogan, b. April 5, 1857; d. Dec. 15, 1925; Judge City Court of Elberton, Captain Elberton Light Infantry, Clerk City of Elberton, Attorney for Elbert County Bond Commission, City Attorney of Elberton.
6—Stark Grogan, b. Feb. 14, 1880; m. Oct. 3, 1900, Allene Harper.
7—Stark Grogan Jr.
6—George C. Grogan Jr., b. Nov. 16, 1881; m. Nov. 16, 1904, Louise Phillips of Oklahoma.
7—Phillips Grogan.
7—George C. Grogan III.
6—Sarah Grogan, b. Aug. 21, 1884; m. Feb. 3, 1904, Henry D. Jordan of South Carolina.
7—Ralph Jordan.
7—Henry D. Jordan Jr., m. Addie Sanders.
8—Lovett Jordan.
8—Sarah Adeline Jordan.
6—Henry Grogan, b. May 7, 1888; m. 1907, Clyde McLanahan.
7—George Albert Grogan.
7—Betsy Grogan, m. Mayson Jaudon.
8—Henry Jaudon.
6—May Grogan, b. Aug. 24, 1894; m. June 6, 1916, James Hagood Bruce.
7—Virginia Bruce.
7—James McDuffie Bruce.
6—Edmund B. Grogan, b Sept. 11, 1896; m. Dec. 23, 1922, Bernice Lyons.
7—Jeanee Grogan.
7—Carroll Grogan.
6—Kathleen Grogan, b. Dec. 27, 1898; m. April 21, 1921, James Arnold, b. Sept. 14, 1899.
7—James "Jimmy" Arnold Jr.
4—William Thomas Brewer, m. Malinda Talliaferro.
5—Rose Brewer.
5—Nicholas Brewer.
5—Benjamin Brewer.
5—Lucy Brewer.
5—Thomas Brewer.
4—J. Hopkins Brewer, b. Sept. 30, 1829; m. Oct. 23, 1851, Amanda Carpenter.
5—Lucy Brewer, d. 1937; m. J. C. Swearingen.
6—Brewer Swearingen, City Councilman of Elberton; m. Lottie Morris of Tennessee.
7—Dorothy Swearingen.

6—Allie Sue Swearingen, m. June 1900, B. F. Bennett.
7—Louise Bennett.
7—B. F. Bennett Jr.
6—J. C. Swearingen Jr.
6—L. H. Swearingen, S. W. W., b. 1892; d. 1933 unmarried.
5—James E. Brewer, Tax Collector of Elbert County; m. Fanny Freeman.
6—Marion Brewer, m. A. S. Simmons.
7—Son died in infancy.
6—Pauline Brewer, m. John Brown.
7—John Brown Jr.
6—John Brewer.
5—Mary Brewer, m. L. H. Turner. No issue.
5—Addie Brewer.
5—Irene Brewer.
5—Thomas Brewer, m. Miss Oglesby.
6—James T. Brewer, m. Oct. 10, 1901, Florence Smith.
7—Janice Brewer.
7—Eva Brewer.
7—Ralph Brewer.
7—Mary Brewer.
6—Pearl Brewer, m. T. V. Bagwell.
7—Thomas Bagwell, d. unmarried.
7—Virginia Bagwell.
7—Jack Bagwell.
6—Luther Brewer.
6—Ruby Brewer, registered nurse.
5—Stark Brewer, m. (1) Annie LaHatte; (2) Miss Warren.
6—(By first wife) Albert T. Brewer, m. Valeria Allen.
7—Elizabeth Brewer.
6—Stark Brewer Jr., unmarried.
5—Charles H. Brewer, m. Jane Pruitt.
6—Charles H. Brewer Jr.
6—Mabel Brewer, m. Mr. Higginbotham.
6—Claud Brewer, m. Jessie Worrill.
6—Irene Brewer, m. Dec. 1921, Hugh Cleveland.
6—Pauline Brewer, m. Wilton Auld.
6—Thelma Brewer, m. Robert Bass.
7—Robert Bass Jr.
6—Hoke Brewer.
4—John M. Brewer, C. S., b. Nov. 13, 1834; m. April 29, 1859, Mary Lofton.
5—Mary Brewer, m. Dec. 23, 1884, Thomas S. Jones.
6—Brewer B. Jones, m. Sept. 27, 1908, Beulah Oglesby.
7—Brewer B. Jones Jr.
6—Mary Jones, m. Hollis Graham.
6—Nona Jones, m. Homer Hitchcock.
6—Thomas S. Jones Jr., m. Lillian Stook.
6—James Lofton Jones, m. James Smith.
6—Claud Jones.
5—Annie Brewer, m. June 18, 1891, J. M. Warren.
6—Mary Warren, m. Earl Clayton.
6—Annie Warren.
5—Julian Brewer, Solicitor of City Court of Elberton; m. Oct. 29, 1886, Alice Oglesby.
6—Herbert Brewer, d. unmarried.
6—Marguerite Brewer, m. Horace H. Manley.
7—Mary Alice Manley.
7—Marguerite "Rita" Manley.
6—Julian Brewer Jr.

3—(By second wife) Sarah Carter.
3—Farris Carter.
2—Nancy M. Carter, m. Richardson Hunt.
3—Sally Hunt, m. Jeptha Harris, member of Georgia House of Representatives, and member Georgia Senate 1825.
4—Jeptha Harris Jr.
4—James Harris.
4—Eugene Harris.
4—Elijah Harris.
4—Sally Harris, m. Tinsley Rucker.
5—Tinsley W. Rucker, member U. S. Congress; m. Miss Cobb.
6—Lamar Rucker and other issue.
5—Jeptha H. Ruckerr, Postmaster Athens, Georgia.
5—Sarah Rucker.
5—Margaret Rucker, m. Mr. McAlpin.
5—Georgia Rucker, m. Mr. Ford.
3—James Hunt.
3—Elijah Hunt.
2—Frances Carter, m. Mr. Wimbish.
3—James Wimbish, m. Miss McKinley.
3—Farris Wimbish, m. Miss Stinchcomb.
2—Charles Carter, Militia Captain, 1809.
2—George W. Carter, m. Martha Higginbotham.
2—(By second wife) Thomas P. Carter, m. 1818, Lucy Hudson.
3—Charles Carter, m. May 5, 1838, Eugenia Beck.

CHRISTIAN

The following chart shows intermarriages with the following families:
Payne — Maxwell — Seymour — Phelps — Tabor — Brewer — Brown — Thornton — Auld — Asbury — Vaughan — Eaves — Cooper — Williford — Murray — Evans — Walters — Davis — Coyne — Johnson — Ruff.

(Note: Numbers represent generations, as: (1) first generation, (2) second generation, (3) third generation, etc.)

1—Thomas Christian came to America previous to 1687.
  2—Charles Christian. Wife unknown.
    3—Charles Christian Jr., d. 1784, will of record in Goochland County, Virginia. Wife unknown.
      4—William Christian.
      4—Walter Christian.
      4—George Christian.
      4—Charles Christian III.
      4—John Christian.
      4—Elijah Christian.
      4—Turner Christian, R. S., b. 1750; m. 1778, Anne Payne, b. 1753.
        5—Charles Woodson Christian, m. Nancy Ruff.
        5—William Payne Christian, b. 1781; m. 1807, Sarah Maxwell, b. Jan. 4, 1786; d. May 29, 1838.
          6—Jackson Christian.
          6—Nancy Turner Christian, b. Sept. 1, 1811; d. 1880; m. 1834, John Warren Seymour, b. 1810; d. 1880.
            7—Minnie Seymour.
            7—Martin Seymour.

7—Kezia Blake Seymour.
7—Ardesia Seymour.
7—Sarah Seymour.
7—Charles Marion Seymour, m. Jan. 7, 1867, Locky Ann Phelps.
8—Dora Penelope Seymour, m. Charles H. Allen.
9—Zelma Allen, m. T. O. Tabor Jr.
10—T. O. Tabor III, attended University of Georgia, student at Naval Academy, Annapolis.
9—Valeria Allen, m. Albert T. Brewer.
10—Elizabeth Brewer.
9—Gladys Allen, m. Herman J. Brown, member City Council of Elberton.
10—Allen Brown.
9—Hughie Allen, m. Harry G. Thornton, member Staff of Governor of Georgia 1931-32, president First National Bank of Elberton. wholesale grocer.
10—Harry Allen Thornton, b. 1823.
10—Earl Thornton.
9—Charles Seymour Allen, m. Janie Auld.
10—Charles Seymour Allen Jr.
9—Sarah Elizabeth "Beth" Allen, m. Maurice Asbury.
10—Allen Asbury.
10—Ed Asbury.
7—Marshall Seymour.
6—Jesse G. Christian, m. March 25, 1841, Ann Maxwell.
7—Elizabeth M. B. Christian, b. Feb. 1, 1842; m. William Brown.
8—George Brown.
8—Lucy Brown.
8—Sally Brown.
7—Ira Jackson Christian, b. June 25, 1844; m. (?)
8—Vandiver Christian.
8—Mamie Christian.
8—Lizzie Christian.
8—Tommie Christian.
8—Lou Charles Christian.
8—Howard Christian.
7—Sarah Ann Josephine Christian, b. Sept. 5, 1845; m. Jacob Vaughan.
8—William "Billy" Vaughan.
7—Mary Frances Christian, b. May 13, 1847; m. William Vaughan.
8—Nealie Vaughan.
8—Betsy Vaughan.
8—Sarah F. Vaughan.
8—George Vaughan.
7—Joseph Marion Christian, b. June 23, 1849; m. Martha Brown.
8—Lens Christian.
8—Rossie Christian.
8—Ace Christian.
8—Clarence Christian.
8—Morris Christian.
7—John Thomas Christian, b. Dec. 14, 1850; m. Betty Brown.
8—Daisy Christian.
8—Ossie Christian, m. Frank K. Eaves.
9—"Boots" Eaves.
9—Walter Eaves.
9—Frank K. Eaves Jr.
9—Other issue.
8—Ollie Christian.
8—Johnny Christian.

7—Martha Permelia Christian, b. Jan. 1, 1853; m. James Vaughan.
8—Vaughnie Vaughan.
8—Jessie Vaughan.
8—Luke Vaughan.
8—May Vaughan.
8—Homer Vaughan.
8—Ronnie Vaughan.
7—William Cornelius Christian "Cousin Billy,' b. Jan. 1, 1853 (twin); m. Mary Cooper.
8—Arles Christian, m. Aubrey Christian.
9—Carmen Christian.
8—Arva Christian, m. Robert Williford.
9—Robert Williford Jr.
9—William Williford.
8—Nolley Christian, m. Thomas Murray.
8—Savias Christian, m. Josephine Evans.
9—Robert Christian.
9—Betty Christian.
9—Nancy Christian.
9—Joe Ann Christian.
9—Marylyn Christian.
8—Gradus Christian, editor Elberton Star, member Elberton School Board; m. Florie Walters.
9—Mary Jean Christian.
9—Evelyn Christian.
9—Gradus Christian Jr.
9—Helen Christian.
8—Vesta Christian, m. J. Porter Davis.
9—Mary Christian Davis.
9—Cornelius Davis.
8—Mary Christian, Executive Secretary-Treasurer Georgia Baptist Woman's Missionary Union.
8—Evelyn Christian, m. William Coyne.
8—Cornelius Christian.
8—James Christian.
7—Jesse G. Christian, d. unmarried.
7—Charles W. Christian, m. Nealie Johnson.
8—William "Billy" Christian.
8—Sterlie Christian.
8—Boyd Christian.
6—Charles Woodson Christian, m. Jan. 18, 1827, Mary Walton Maxwell, b. Feb. 8, 1811.
7—William P. Christian, b. Dec. 15, 1828.
7—Charles Woodson Christian Jr., b. Dec. 3, 1830.
6—Mel Christian.

BIBLE RECORDS

Records copied from the old family Bible of the late Judge William Tusten Vanduzer. The present owner of the Bible is Mr. Nicholas Oglesby (past postmaster of Elberton and grandson of Judge Vanduzer).

Marriages:

Ira Christian, born in 1801, and Martha Ann Lesuer were married Feb. 7, 1826.

Ira Christian and Elizabeth H. Marbrey were married Aug. 22, 1837. (He died Dec. 27, 1857). The said Ira Christian was married four times.

James C. Chrsitian (blotted not clear) and Sulenea M. Smith were married Oct. 3, 1839.

BIRTHS

Edna Ann Christian, daughter of Ira and Martha Ann Christian, was born November 24, 1826.
Camilia Zeree Christian was born July 23, 1828.
Sarah Helen Christian was born November 12, 1838.
Althea (Vernon) Christian was born December 8, 1845. (Third wife of Ira Christian.
Shelby Christian was born December 25, 1840.
Robert E. Christian was born October 28, 1842.
Robert Bryan Christian was born March 15, 1770, died June 16, 1844; aged 74 years. Edna Lesueur, wife of Robert B. Christian, was born April 16, 1772; died July 4, 1852; aged 80 years.

DEATHS

Shelby T. Christian, son of James C. Christian and Suleanea M. Christian, died December 5, 1841.
Martha Ann Christian, wife of Ira Christian, died October 17, 1831, about 11 o'clock A. M., Monday, aged 31 years, 11 months, and 19 days.

Judge William Tusten Vanduzer was born in New York State, removed to Petersburg, Elbert County, when a lad of 19 years of age, later settling in Elberton where he practiced law. He was attorney for the Southern branch railway from Elberton to Toccoa; died 1881.

Alex Lesuer owned 300 acres of land, including Watkins Island, which he sold to a member of the Calhoun family. This spot is near the Memorial Bridge in Elbert County.

We find that Wm. T. Vanduzer was the Administrator of the estate of Ira Christian. (Copied by D. A. R.)

Additional data furnished by Roselyn (Reid) Carlisle (Mrs. E. F.), Griffin, Ga.:

Ira Christian's fourth wife was Permelia Amanda Fryer, born in Pike County, Georgia, December 6, 1824; died August 1906.

CHILDREN

Mary, born 1849; died at three months.
Robert Zachariah, born -850.
Alice Gertrude Christian, born December 8, 1852.
Ira Christian Jr., born 1855.
Bryant Lewis Christian, born 1857.

Robert Bryant Christian and Edna Leseuer (mentioned elsewhere) were the parents of Ira Christian.

Ira Christian (who died December 27, 1857) lived only nine years after his marriage to Permelia Amanda Fryer (4th wife). In 1848, she gave up the house that was built for her as a bride and Judge William Tusten Vanduzer (who had married her oldest step- daughter, Edna Ann Christian), purchased it and it has descended to Judge Vanduzer's grandchildren (the Oglesbys). This lovely old house is of the true Colonial architecture and was built in the year 1848. A picture of this house was sent (with other pictures of Elbert County's Colonial type houses) to Continental Hall, Washington, D. C.

CLARK OR CLARKE

The following chart shows intermarriages with the following families:

—Adams — Anderson — Anthony — Arnold — Beall — Bell — Blackwell — Bowen — Bolling — Bridges — Buis — Candler — Carroway — Carter — Chappell — Cheadle — Cooper — Daley — Davis — Dearing — Doane — Eberhardt — Elliott — Few — Flemming — Goff — Gilmer — Glenn — Goodwin — Grant — Green — Grizzle — Ham — Hayes — Hearne — Henderson — Hood — Jackson — Johnson — Jordan — Kimsey — Kroner — Martin — Matthews — Mealor — Menza — Meriwether — Moore — Moorman — Morris — Munger — Myrick — McGehee — Parrish — Posey — Rainey — Reynolds — Roberts — Rowland — Schoeller — Scroggins — Settles — Simpson — Slaughter — Smith — Spencer — Stirkley — Stone — Swift — Talbot — Tate — Terrell — Watts — Way — Weaver — Webb — White — Williams — Wyche.

The name Clark, Clarke, Clerk, Clerke or Clarkston is of ancient Origin, having been known in Britian years before the Norman Conquest. In the Domesday Book it was spelled Clericus and Le Clerk in the One Hundred Roll, compiled during the reign of Edward I. The name originally meant a learned person or one who could read and write. The family is of Anglo-Saxon origin and became connected by marriage with the nobleman Joseph of Arimathea. The Clarks were closely related to the Gordon family of Scotland.

(Note: Numbers represent generations, as: (1) first generation, (2) second generation, (3) third generation, etc.)

1. Edward Clark came from England to Virginia at the time of the first settlement of Jamestown.
2. Christopher Clark, born in Virginia in the year 1698, died 1754; married Penelope (?). Many historians agree that she was Penelope Bolling, a direct descendant of the Indian Princess, Pocahontas, through Colonel Robert Bolling, who married Jean Rolfe, granddaughter of the Princess. The name "Bolling" appears in latter generations which gives credit to the fact.

3—Edward Clark, a Quaker.
3—Bolling Clark, a Quaker.
3—Micajah Clark, b. 1718; d. 1754; m. Judith Adams, b. 1716, Q. V.
3—Elizabeth Clark, b. Feb. 15, 1722; m. 1741, Joseph Anthony Sr., R. S., b 1713.
4—Sarah Anthony, b. 1742; m. Thomas Cooper Sr.
4—Christopher Anthony, b. 1744; m. (1) Judith Moorman; (2) Mary Jordan, daughter of Samuel Jordan and Hannah Bates.
4—Elizabeth Anthony, b. 1746; m. 1761, William Candler.

5—Mary Candler, m. Ignatus Few.
5—Henry Candler, b. 1762.
5—Falby Candler.
5—William Candler Jr., d. unmarried.
5—Charles Candler.
5—Elizabeth Candler.
5—John Candler, d. without issue.
5—Amelia Candler.
5—Joseph Candler.
5—Mark Anthony Candler.
5—Daniel Candler, b. 1779; d. 1816; m. 1799, Sarah Slaughter.
6—William Candler, m. 1824, Martha Moore.
6—Elizabeth Anthony Candler, b. March 3, 1803; d. 1872; m. 1820, Owen H. Myrick; b. 1801; d. 1830.
7—Martha Myrick, b. 1822; m. 1845, Isaac Scroggins.
7—William Love Myrick, b. 1824; m. 1850, Martha Goff.
7—Daniel Jackson Myrick, b. 1826; d. 1909; m. 1850, Mary Adeline (?), b, Feb. 10, 1825; d. Sept. 1904.
8—Minnie Margaret Elizabeth Myrick, b. April 29, 1854; m. April 29, 1877, Henry Schoeller.
9—Minnie May Schoeller, b. March 11, 1878; m. June 2, 1898; m. G. A. Weaver Jr.
9—Annie Wright Schoeller, b. Oct. 1, 1881; m. (1) Marvin H. Neese.
10—Maisie Neese, b. 1902; m. W. M. Lester.
10—Myrick Schoeller, b. April 9, 1884; m. Ina Vivian Stirkley.
10—Myrick Schoeller Jr., b. Aug. 17, 1909.
7—ISSUE OF ELIZABETH ANTHONY CANDLER AND OWEN MYRICK.
7—Sarah Adeline Myrick, b. 1828; m. 1852, James Henderson.
7—Richard Myrick.
6—ISSUE OF DANIEL CANDLER AND SARAH SLAUGHTER.
6—John Kingston Candler, b. 1802; m. Caroline Smith.
6—Frances Emily Candler, b. 1806; m. Wilson Simpson.
6—Samuel Charles Candler, b. 1809; m. Martha Beall.
6—Daniel Candler, m. Nancy Mathews.
6—Ezekiel Slaughter Candler, b. 1815; m. Jane Williams.
4—ISSUE OF JOSEPH ANTHONY AND ELIZABETH CLARK CONTINUED.
4—Penelope Anthony, b. 1748; m. James Johnson.
4—Joseph Anthony Jr., b. 1850; m. first cousin, Betty Clark, a daughter of Micajah Clark Sr. Joseph Anthony Jr. was R. S.
4—James Anthony, b. 1752; m. Nancy Tate.
5—Sarah Anthony, m. Thomas Anderson.
5—Joseph Anthony, m. Mary Anderson.
5—Henry Anthony.
5—James Anthony Jr., m. (1) Lucinda Menza; (2) Miss Mealler; (3) A widow whose name is unknown.
5—Elizabeth Anthony, m. M. Buis.
5—Nancy Tate Anthony, m. Mr. Grant.
5—Charles Anthony, d. unmarried.
5—Edward Anthony, d unmarried.
5—Milton Anthony, m. Nancy Goodwin.
5—Mary Anthony, m. Green Talbot.
4—Mary Anthony, b. 1755; m. Josiah Carter.
4—Charles Anthony, b. 1757.
4—Micajah Anthony, m. Miss Tate.
4—Agnes Anthony, b. 1761.
4—Rachel Anthony, b. 1763; m. James Lane.

4—Winifred Anthony, b. 1765; m. William Carter.
4—Mark Anthony, b. 1767; m. Miss Tate.
4—Bolling Anthony, b. 1768; m. Nancy Stone.
4—Judith Anthony, b. 1769; m. Mr. Green.
3—Sarah Clark (daughter of Christopher Clark), b. 1716; m. 1733, Charles Lynch, b. 1698.
4—John Lynch.
4—Charles Lynch Jr., R. S.
4—Penelope Lynch, b. 1734; m. 1750, Robert Adams, b. 1733; d. 1789, R. S.
5—Elizabeth Adams, b. 1765; d. 1834; m. 1783, Ensign James Dearing, R. S., b. July 3, 1750; d. 1811 in Campbell County, Virginia.
6—Captain William Smith Dearing, b. 1790; d. June 12, 1876; m. Mary Terry Harrison.
7—Virginia Dearing, b. July 3, 1823; d. 1908; m. 1850, Hugh Lawson White Hill, b. 1813; d. 1883.
8—Sue Hill, b. 1853; d. 1917; m. 1874, John Myers, b. 1848.
9—Flora Myers, m. L. S. Gillentine.
3—Rachel Clark (daughter of Christopher Clark), m. Thomas Moorman.
3—Agnes Clark (daughter of Christopher Clark), m. Benjamin Johnson.
3—MICAJAH CLARK SR., SON OF CHRISTOPHER CLARK CONTINUED, m. Judith Adams.
4—Christopher Clark, b. April 20, 1737; d. 1803; m. 1757, Millicent Terrell, b. June 7, 1741, daughter of David Terrell and Agatha Chiles, Q. V.
4—Robert Clark, b. 1738; m. Susan Henderson and migrated to Kentucky in 1799.
4—Judith Clark, m. Samuel Moorman.
4—William Clark, m. Judith Cheadle.
4—Micajah Clark Jr., m. Mildred Martin.
4—John Clark, m. Mary Moore.
4—Penelope Clark, m. Rueben Rowland.
4—Bolling Clark, m. Elizabeth Cheadle.
4—James Clark, m. Lucy Cheadle.
4—Betty Clark, m. James Anthony.
4—Christopher Clark, son of Micajah Carter continued, m. Millicent Terrell.
5—Micajah Clark, b. Feb. 25, 1758; m. Penelope Gatewood.
6—Amelia Clark, m. Nicholas Meriwether Gilmer, son of John Gilmer and Mildred Meriwether.
6—Daughter, m. David Gilmer.
5—Christopher Clark Jr., b. Jan. 6, 1760; d. Sept. 19, 1819; m. Oct. 17, 1799, Rebecca Davis, b. April 1780; d. Dec. 6, 1857, daughter of William Davis, R. S., and Mary Chisholm.
6—Samuel Clark, b. Oct. 10, 1800.
6—Margaret Ann Clark, b. Feb. 21, 1803; m. James Opher Clark.
7—Micajah Clark, m. (1) Miss Parrish; (2) Elmira Munger of Texas.
7—Christopher Clark III, m. (1) Elvira Nail; (2) Hannah Anderson.
7—Mary Penelope Clark, b. Sept. 16, 1828; m. June 1848, George S. Turner.
7—Rebecca Davis Clark, b. Nov. 24, 1830; m. 1849, V. H. Glass; (2) Robert Chappell.
7—Margaret Chisholm Clark.
7—Amanda Malvina Clark, m. (1) James Blackwell; (2) Thomas Fisher; (3) Mr. Young.

6—William Davis Clark, son of Christopher Clark Jr., b. Feb. 14, 1805; m. 1830, Jane Elizabeth Hearne.
7—Rebecca Elizabeth, b. Aug. 24, 1831; m. Nov. 28, 1850, George Thomas Snellings, b. Dec. 10, 1827; d. Jan. 24, 1862.
8—William Garvin Snellings, b. 1853; d. 1869.
8—George Burton Snellings, b. July 13, 1850; m. Feb. 18, 1883, Mary Wynn Snellings.
8—Jane Elizabeth Hearne Snellings, b. April 6, 1857; d. Nov. 1895; m. Nov. 28, 1876, William J. Snellings, C. S., b. Sept. 4, 1846; d. Feb. 27, 1927.
9—Rebecca Snellings.
9—Elizabeth Snellings.
9—Willie Snellings, m. J. B. Morris.
9—Thomas Snellings.
9—Irene Hearne Snellings.
8—Richard Thomas Snellings, b. 1859; d. 1869.
7—Rebecca Elizabeth Snellings, (Continued), m. (2) Jan. 1870, William Duncan Hudson.
9—Charlie Hudson, b. Oct. 3, 1871.
9—Callie Rebecca Hudson, b. Oct. 3, 1871.
9—Carrie May Hudson, b. Oct. 3, 1871; m. Oct. 16, 1889, Ora Eugene Tate.
10—Eugene Tate.
10—Brewer Tate, Lieutenant in World War, killed in action.
10—Samuel Tate.
10—Ora Eugene Tate Jr.
10—Maurice Tate.
10—Clark Tate.
10—Duncan Tate.
10—Carrie Sophia Tate.
10—Corrie Jane Tate and four other children.
7—George Thomas Davis Clark, b. Jan. 1834; m. Mary E. Bell, b. Dec. 10, 1827; d. Jan. 1862.
7—William Brockington Clark, b. Jan. 1838; m. Dec. 1860, Rhodie Bell.
6—Christopher Hull Clark (son of Christopher Clark Jr.), b. 1807; d. 1848.
6—Thomas Jefferson Clark, b. March 1809; m. (1) 1837, Sarah Bowen; (2) June 1854, Elizabeth Jane Hood.
7—Martha Bowen Clark (by first wife).
7—Christopher Clark, b. 1842 (by first wife).
7—(By second wife) Margaret Ann Clark, b. July 11, 1855.
7—Samuel Hood Clark, b. July 24, 1857.
7—Rebecca Dacis Clark, b. March 22, 1861.
7—Thomas Jefferson Clark Jr., b. Sept. 29, 1868.
6—George Washington Clark, b. Jan. 25, 1811; d. Nov. 1826.
6—Mary Clark, b. Dec. 1813; m. Feb. 1830, Thomas Burge.
5—David Clark (son of Christopher Clark Sr., and Millicent Terrell), b. April 8, 1762; d. Dec. 9, 1834; m. 1794, Mary Ann Clark, b. 1775; d. 1840. He was R. S.
5—Mourning Clark, b. Aug. 12, 1764; d. 1840; m. Aug. 17, 1782, William Bibb Key, R. S., b. Oct. 2, 1759; d. Dec. 7, 1836.
6—Chiles Terrell Key, b. Jan. 30, 1784; d. 1859; m. 1805, Mary Ann Clark.
6—Martha Key, b. Nov. 5, 1786; m. Nicholas Goode.
6—James Key, b. July 14, 1788; m. Oct. 17, 1818, Rebecca Grizzle.
6—Milly Key, b. July 20, 1790; m. Jan. 3, 1811, Humphrey Posey.
6—Nancy Key, b. July 20, 1790; m. Simeon Glenn.
6—Elizabeth Key, b. June 1, 1792; m. Thomas Bell.

6—Margaret Key, b. Jan. 18, 1794; m. Thomas Goode.
6—Keturah Key, b. Oct. 25, 1795; m. James Ham.
6—Mary Key, b. Sept. 3, 1797; m. July 13, 1823, Joseph Bell.
6—Susan Key, b. April 24, 1799; m. Jan. 22, 1819, James Bell Jr.
6—Henry Key, d. unmarried.
6—Jane Key, b. March 26, 1801; m. Oct. 20, 1820, John Grizzle.
6—⸺⸺, b. March 9, 1803; m. Dec. 28, 1819, Thomas Elliott.
6—Thomas Key, b. Jan. 4, 1805.
6—Lucy Key, b. June 26, 1807; d. 1895; m. Feb. 18, 1826, Nathan Mattox, b. Nov. 2, 1807; d. Jan. 9, 1862.
7—Sarah Mourning Mattox, b. Jan. 22, 1827; d. Dec. 27, 1905; m. July 1842, John Wynn Eberhardt, b. Oct. 18, 1822; d. Dec. 19, 1886.
8—Nathan Eberhardt, C. S., killed in action, b. July 1, 1843.
8—Jacob Eberhardt, C. S., b. Nov. 16, 1848; d. 1917 unmarried.
8—George Eberhardt, b. 1850; d. infancy.
8—John Eberhardt, b. Jan. Jan. 14, 1852; m. Lillian Mattox.
8—Lizzie Eberhardt, b. 1858; d. 1902; m. 1887, George Rush. No living issue.
8—Mary Eberhardt, b. Aug. 10, 1860; d. 1936; m. Feb. 10, 1892, J. W. Wright.
9—Sarah Ann Wright.
9—Mary Lizzie Wright.
7—Martha Key Mattox.
7—Christopher Mattox.
7—Frank Mattox, m. Mary Anna (?).
8—Georgia Mattox, m. J. N. Jackson.
9—Lizzie Jackson.
9—Kate Jackson, m. John T. Rainey.
9—Daughter unmarried.
9 ⸺⸺ Jackson, m. Jep. E. Webb.
8—John Mattox, m. Alice Webb.
8—N. F. Mattox, m. Katie Smith.
9—Nannie Mattox, m. Mack Watts.
10—Minnie Lee Watts.
10—Walton Watts.
10—Mary L. Watts.
10—Katie Watts.
10—Opal Watts.
10—Ruby Watts.
10—Frances Watts.
10—Hastings Watts.
9—William Mattox, m. Kathryn Fleming.
10—G. W. J. Mattox.
10—Sarah Frances Mattox.
9—Lucy Mattox, m. J. D. Carroway.
10—Molly Lou Carroway.
10—William Carroway.
9—Samuel Mattox.
9—Mary Mattox, m. W. H. Fleming.
10—Lawrence Fleming.
10—Paul Brown Fleming.
10—J. Henry Fleming.
9—Raymond Mattox, d. 1916.
9—Katherine Mattox, m. Henry Kimsey.
8—Sol Mattox.
8—Teedie Mattox.
8—Bill Mattox.
8—Minnie Mattox, m. Cal Bridges.
8—Texas Mattox.

8—Myrtle Mattox, m. Bob Roberts.
7—Lucy Mattox.
7—Nathan M. Mattox, C. S., m. ―――――.
8—Benjamin Bibb Mattox, Lieutenant Medical Corps, World War, m. Florence Settles.
9—Susan Mattox.
8—E. D. Mattox.
7—Thomas Jefferson Mattox.
5—Judith Clark, b. Oct. 22, 1766; m. Peter Wyche.
6—Abigail Wyche, m. Zachariah Clark.
7—Zachariah Clark Jr., m. Elizabeth Mattox.
8—Mary Elizabeth Clark, b. 1832; m. Elijah Johnson.
9—Zachariah Clark Johnson, b. 1849; d. 1850.
8—Lula Clark, m. Mr. Arnold.
8—Zachariah Clark III, b. 1839; d. 1840.
8—Susan Anna Clark, b. Feb. 5, 1837; d. 1914; m. (1) Mr. Landrum; (2) Howard A. Hayes, b. July 19, 1830; d. Sept. 3, 1898.
9—Martha Louise Hayes, b. April 24, 1864; m. Frank H. Kroner, b. April 4, 1851.
10—Susan Kathleen Kroner, b. Jan. 18, 1890; m. June 1915, Robert Doane.
10—H. A. C. Kroner, b. 1892; m. Hilda Way.
10—Louise Kroner, b. Oct. 1904.
9—William Hayes, b. 1866; m. Minnie Reynolds.
9—Zachariah Clark Hayes, president Elberton Loan and Savings Bank, b. 1869; m. (1) Mamie Swift; (2) April 27, 1916, Elizabeth Fortson.
10—(By first wife) Thomas Swift Hayes, m. Florence Bryan.
10—Zachariah Clark Hayes Jr., Methodist Minister, m. Sarah Thompson.
10—(By second wife) Hanson Hayes.
5—Rachel Clark, b. Oct. 8, 1768, m. (1) John Bowen; (2) John Daley.
5—Agatha Clark, b. Aug. 28, 1770; m. George Wyche.
5—Mary Clark, b. Oct. 1772; m. Thomas Winfrey Oliver. No issue.
5—Samuel Clark, b. 1774; d. 1779.
5—Joshua Clark, b. July 7, 1777.
5—Mildred Clark, b. March 4, 1779; m. 1794, Shelton White.
6—Christopher Clark White.
6—Sarah White, m. Hugh McGehee.
6—Mildred Terrell White, b. March 21, 1801; m. 1816, Simeon Oliver.
7—Asa Thompson Oliver, b. 1819.
7—Shelton Oliver.
7—Lawrence Mansfield Oliver, b. 1821.
7—Simeon Oliver, b. 1825.
7—Mildred Oliver, b. 1827.
7—Sarah Oliver, b. 1828.
7—Lucy Oliver, b. 1830.
7—Prudence Oliver, b. 1832.
7—John Thomas Oliver, b. 1834.
7—David Terrell Oliver, b. 1836.
7—Elizabeth Oliver, b. 1839.
7—Elbert Oliver, b. 1841.
7—Georgia Oliver, b. 1844.
7—James Shelton Oliver, b. 1817; d. 1882.
6—Thomas White.
6—John White.
6—Mary White.
6—David White.

6—Shelton White.
6—Chiles Terrell White.
6—William White.
5—Chiles Terrell Clark, b. Sept. 3, 1781.
5—Susan Clark, b. March 5, 1783; m. Oct. 27, 1796, Rev. Florence McCarthy Oliver, b. 1775.
6—Samuel Oliver, b. 1799; m. 1826, Mildred Spencer.
6—Mary Melissa Oliver, b. 1801.
6—Thomas Winfrey Oliver, b. 1804; d. 1827.
6—Mildred Terrell Oliver, b. 1807; d. 1892.
6—Florence McCarthy Oliver Jr., b. 1809.
6—James Oliver, b. 1811.
6—Dr. John Alfred Oliver, b. 1813.
6—Susan Rebecca Oliver, b. 1816.
6—Rev. Christopher Dionsysius Oliver, b. 1819; d. 1892 in Alabama.
5—Lucy Clark, b. April 19, 1786; m. James Oliver.
6—Shelton Oliver.
6—Mary Winfrey Oliver.
6—Mildred Oliver.
6—Judith Oliver.
6—James Oliver Jr.
6—Washington Oliver.
6—Alfred Oliver.
6—Eliza Oliver.
6—Francis Oliver.
6—Lucinda Oliver.
6—Martha Oliver.

JOSEPH CLARK AND LARKIN CLARK

Joseph Clark, son of William Clark Sr. and Martha (Foster) Clark, was born in Orange County, Virginia, April 12, 1752, m. (1) Jan. 24, 1774, Ann Haynes, b. Feb. 21, 1758, daughter of Jasper Haynes and Elizabeth (Sparks) Clark, m. (2) Catherine Cannady, Jan. 12, 1812. No children by last marriage.

Children of Joseph Clark and (1st) wife, Ann Haynes:

Frances Clark, b. Feb. 13, 1775 (without issue).

Martha E. Clark, b. May 17, 1777, m. Reuben Clark (Madison County, Virginia), son of her uncle, William Clark, Dec. 17, 1801.

Larkin Clark, b. Oct. 27, 1778 (lived at one time in Morgan County, Georgia), m. Rebecca Bell, Jan. 30, 1797.

James Clark, b. 1779; d. 1826 (moved from Orange County, Virginia, to Abbeville County, S. C., later to Elbert County, Ga., where he died and is buried), m. Mary Alston 1831, b. 1781; d. 1871 (daughter of Rev. Sol., Lt.-Col. William Alston.

Mary Clark, b. Nov. 21, 1782; m. Col. Barnard Heard, of Georgia.

Ann Powell Clark, b. Nov. 2, 1784; m. Adjutant General John C. Easter, of Elbert County, Georgia.

Elizabeth H. Clark, b. Oct. 7, 1786; m. Col. Thomas White, of Jones County, Georgia.

Tabitha Clark, b. Feb. 5, 1796; m. Cuthbert Reese, of Jones County, Georgia.

Eunice Henrietta Clark, b. Jan. 9, 1798; m. Solomon H. McIntire, of Madison County, Georgia.

William David Clark, b. Oct. 13, 1793; m. Jane Mary Eliason, March 16, 1825. (See Nat. No. D. A. R. 101706).

Sarah Taylor Clark, b. Nov. 3, 1788; m. Lewis Shirler, of Louise County, Virginia.

Bathesda Sampson Clark, b. Sept. 10, 1791, unmarried.

Revolutionary Services of Joseph Clark:
He served in Captain William Murray's and Captain Eddin's Company, 1st Artillery Regiment, Continental Troops, commanded by Col. Chas. Harrison, enlisted Jan. 9, 1777, discharged Jan. 10, 1780.
(See Nat. No. D. A. R. of Edna Arnold Copeland (Mrs. Z. W.) No. 49019).

The year 1784, Joseph, Larkin and George Clark (sons of William Clark Sr.), Thomas Wells and his wife, Mary, daughter of John and Mary (Towles) Clark—the said John was son of William Clark by first wife, Ann (Christopher) James, the members of the Anthony Foster family, the family of Henry Shorter and others, came to the settlement on the Savannah River (now known as Elbert County, Georgia). (Elbert was taken from Wilkes County in 1790), founded by Benjamin Taliaferro in 1784. Joseph Clark returned to Orange County, Virginia, leaving several of his children in Georgia.

Joseph Clark's will was made Sept. 28, 1836, and proved in Orange County, Virginia. By his will dated Oct. 20, 1787 (Book C, Page 342), William Clark Sr., "old and infirm," left his land to son, Joseph, personal estate to sons, Robert, George, Ambrose and Larkin, and daughters, Ann Griffin, Lucy Beck, and Sarah Clark; sons, Reuben and Joseph, Executors.

From the decree in Boughan et. al. vs. Beckam et. al, the Chancery suit (1820) dividing the property of Ambrose and from family records, it appears that William Sr.'s children were born in the following order:

By (1) wife, Ann James:

James Clark, b. 1737; d. 1789; m. Mary Marston. His will is recorded at Culpeper County, Virginia (Book C, Page 342), June 2, 1789. (James Clark referred to as Captain).

William Clark, b. 1739; d. 1815; m. Sarah, b. 1738, daughter of Thomas Wharton and his wife, Jane Sparks, who was Stokeley Towles' second wife.

John Clark, b. Feb. 19, 1741; m. Mary (daughter of Stokeley and Jane Towles), Nov. 4, 1765. He was the John "of Clark's Mountain," for whom the mountain was named. He was born on the mountain and died in that neighborhood Oct. 28, 1831.

Reuben Clark, m. Methesda Sampson, of Culpeper County, Virginia. (See will of his brother, Ambrose, Madison County, Virginia, made June 10, 1807, proved Oct. 28, 1814. Names of Reuben's children given.)

Ann Clark, m. Zachariah Griffin.

Lucy Clark, m. Andrew Beck. (Ambrose Clark's will mentions their children as sharing in his estate.)

Children of William Clark, Sr., and second wife, Martha Foster:

Joseph Clark, b. April 12, 1752; d. Feb. 5, 1839; m. (1) Jan. 24, 1774, Ann, b. Feb. 21, 1758, daughter of Jasper Haynes and his wife, Elizabeth (Sparks) Clark. (Names of their children given elsewhere.) No children by second marriage (Catherine Cannady).

Robert Clark (usually known as "The Robin"), m. Joanna Jones, Nov.

8, 1791, by whom he had one daughter, Jaqueline, who married William T. Berry. (Papers on file with Robert Clark's claim for pension as a Revolutionary Soldier show him so very old and infirm that memory of the facts of his service had failed. A witness testified that in 1854 he was believed to be more than 100 years old and had an enviable reputation for uprightness and truth. Robert Clark d. 1855 in Orange County, Virginia, 101 years old).

Larkin Clark (Rev. Sol.), b. Oct. 7, 1760, Orange County, Virginia; m. Mrs. Lucy Simpson Welsh, of Baltimore, Maryland. He died in Elbert County, Georgia, where his will dated Feb. 5, 1841, was proved Jan. 2, 1843; wife, Lucy, son, James A. Clark, and Robert McMillan, Executors, leaving a large estate to his wife, daughter, Martha Goode, son, Larkin L. Clark, a minor, son, James A. Clark, and the latter's wife, Frances M. William, daughter, Caroline, wife of Joseph Edwards, and daughter, Mary Richardson. Larkin Clark died in Ruckersville, Elbert County, Georgia, Sept. 1848. His place of residence during the Revolutionary War was Orange County, Virginia. He drew two lots in Elbert County, Georgia, land lottery draw in 1825-1827.

Children:
William Clark, married Miss Trippe.
Ann Clark married (1) William Beck.
Martha Clark married Robert Goode.
Sara Clark married John Banks.
Mary Clark married Richardson.
Margaret Clark married (2nd wife) Fletcher Edwards.
James A. Clark married Frances M. William.
Caroline Clark married Joseph Edwards.

Ambrose Clark, m. Mary Thomas, Nov. 1, 1797, had one daughter Martha, who married William Davis and died without issue. (See deed of heirs of Ambrose's brother, Reuben, to Joseph Hume, dated April 15, 1819. The suit of Chancery of Broughan et al, vs. Beckam et al as stated, arose over the partition of his plantation and personal estate.) Ambrose Clark's marriage to Mary Thomas is recorded in 1797, Orange County, Virginia.

George Clark, married Leanna Reddish Oct. 20, 1798, in Madison County, Virginia. (Jeremiah Reddish in his will dated Aug. 12, proved Sept. 28, 1812, left property to "Cousins George Jr., and James Jr.," sons of George Clark Sr.). From the memorandum in possession of Dr. Taliaferro Clark, it appears that George Clark Sr. had four children, but the names of the other two are unknown. George Clark Sr. was living in Elbert County, Georgia, in 1820.

Sarah Clark married Elisha W. Beckman (whose first wife was Caroline, thought to be a sister of Nathaniel Welsh). Sarah was alive in 1820; she was about 50 years of age when she married Elisha W. Beckman, Sept. 7, 1813.

For references, See Nat. Soc. D. A. R. No. 204417.
Pauline Edwards Bell (Mrs. H. S.).

(The Clarks of Orange County, Virginia, were all descended from William Clark, the youngest son of Edward Clark and Ann Christopher).

The belief that William Clark, called "Senior" to distinguish him from the multitude bearing that name, and Christopher Clark, of Louisa County, Virginia, were kinsmen is widespread among their descendants, as well as the belief that both were of the same family as George Rogers Clark. The writer's father shared the belief and quoted as authorities his grandfathers, Henry Clark (1773-1865) and John Newman (1782-1869) who knew contemporary members of what they termed the Bedford Clarks, as well as General George Rogers Clark and his brother William.

Ref.: "TOWLES AND CLARK FAMILIES," by Wm. B. Newman, of Washington, D. C., which appears in Tyler's *Quarterly Historical and Genealogical Magazine*, Vol. XIII, No. 1, July 1931.

There is extant a letter from George Rogers Clark, (the hero of Old Vincennes) to Governor Randolph, referring to William Marston Clark as "my cousin." William Marston Clark was a son of James (son of William and Ann James), and his wife Mary Marston. This is proof that the William Clark family was closely related to the family of General George Rogers Clark.

There can be seen a facsimile of the signature of General William Clark (brother of George Rogers Clark), and he signs himself "William Clark, Junior." It must have been because of William Clark (his uncle) who was called "William Senior." This was a custom in those days. Patrick Henry signed himself "Junior" because of his uncle Rev. Patrick Henry.

CLEVELAND

The following chart shows intermarriages with the following families:
Abney — Adams — Alford — Alexander — Almond — Amos — Anderson — Bailey — Beall — Bell — Benson — Black — Brewer — Brownlee — Bryan — Bryant — Burgiss — Bynum — Campbell — Carpenter — Chandler — Clark — Coffee — Cox — Craft — Cooper — Deadwyler — Doolittle — Ethridge — Facing — Fortson — Gaston — Gay — Gilbert — Ginn — Glenn — Green — Hailey — Hall — Helton — Herring — Higginbotham — Hulme — Hollingsworth — James — Kidd — Lyle — Lyons — Mann — Martin — Moore — McAllister — McCann — McCurry — McGarity — Pressley — Quillian — Rousey — Rucker — Rumble — Saddler — Sanders — Scott — Seaggs — Shannon — Skelton — Seegars — Smith — Snellings — Teasley — Terrell — Thornton — Veronee — Vickery — Wansley — Wanslow — Ward — Warren — West — White — Whiteside.

(Note: Numbers represent generations, as: (1) first generation, (2) second generation, (3) third generation, etc.)

1—Alexander Cleveland, b. 1617, wife unknown, came to Prince William County, Virginia, from England.
    2—Alexander Cleveland Jr., b. 1659; d. 1770; m. Mildred Pressley, b. 1667; d. 1770. (The unusual ages reached by these persons is authenicated by official records).
        3—John Cleveland, b. 1695; m. Martha Coffee.
            4—John Cleveland Jr., b. 1730; m. Martha McCann, d. 1809.

5—John Cleveland III, m. Comfort Gilbert.
6—Reuben Cleveland, m. Mary Bryant.
7—John Cleveland, m. Mary Skelton.
7—Cornelius Cleveland, m. Melvina Sanders.
6—Gilbert Cleveland.
6—Ullysses Cleveland.
6—Benjamin Cleveland.
6—William Cleveland.
6—John Cleveland IV.
6—Neal Cleveland.
6—Polly Cleveland.
6—Phobe Cleveland.
6—Nellie Cleveland.
5—Neal Cleveland.
5—Cornelius Cleveland.
5—William Cleveland.
5—Fanny Cleveland.
5—Elizabeth Cleveland.
5—Larkin Cleveland.
5—Benjamin Cleveland.
4—Mary Cleveland.
4—Benjamin Cleveland.
4—Robert Cleveland, d. 1774.
4—Jeremiah Cleveland.
4—Larkin Cleveland, b. 1749.
3—Alexander Cleveland III, b. 1696; d. 1774; m. Margaret Doolittle.
3—Jeremiah Cleveland, b. 1701, wife unknown.
4—Reuben Cleveland, m. Elizabeth (?).
5—John Cleveland.
5—Cynthia Cleveland.
5—Rhoda Cleveland.
4—Jacob Cleveland, R. S., b. 1729; d. 1791; m. Milly White, b. 1739; d. 1806; daughter of Revolutionary Colonel Jeremiah White and Miss Martin who was daughter of Absolom Martin of Maryland.
5—Jeremiah Cleveland, m. (1) Nancy Clark; (2) Nancy Smith.
6—James Cleveland, wife unknown.
7—Sevier Cleveland.
7—Rebecca Cleveland.
6—John Cleveland, m. Rachel Scott.
7—Helen Cleveland.
6—Sillette Cleveland.
6—Helen Cleveland.
6—Jefferson Cleveland.
5—Rice Cleveland.
5—Wyatt Cleveland.
5—William Cleveland, m. Mary Seaggs.
6—Absolom Cleveland.
6—Mary Cleveland.
6—Mildred Cleveland.
6—Elizabeth Cleveland.
6—Martha Cleveland.
6—Washington Cleveland.
5—Martha Cleveland.
5—Mary Cleveland.
5—John Cleveland, b. 1772; d. 1840; m. Rhoda Kidd.
6—Martha Cleveland.
6—Sarah Cleveland, m. Daniel Thornton.
7—Martha Thornton.

- 7—Elmira Thornton.
- 7—Priscilla Thornton.
- 7—Helen Thornton.
- 6—Jacob Mimms Cleveland, b. 1798; m. Permelia Rucker.
- 7—Willis Cleveland.
- 7—Elizabeth Cleveland.
- 7—Andrew J. Cleveland, C. S., m. Mildred Bailey.
- 8—Paul Cleveland.
- 8—Jule M. Cleveland, m. Miss West.
- 9—Caroline Cleveland.
- 7—Antoinette Cleveland, m. R. E. Adams, C. S., member Georgia House of Representatives.
- 8—Elizabeth Adams, m. George J. Hall.
- 9—James E. Hall, b. Jan. 1, 1885; m. July 1906, Lillian Deadwyler.
- 10—Willie Elizabeth Hall, m. L. A. Moore.
- 10—James E. Hall Jr.
- 9—William Hall, m. Miss Bryan.
- 9—Lila Hall, m. Henry Seegars.
- 9—Annie Hall, m. Mr. Cooper.
- 9—Sarah Hall, m. Benjamin Neal Smith.
- 8—Mamie Adams, d. unmarried.
- 8—Willis B. Adams, b. May 13, 1861; d. Feb. 11, 1913, member Georgia House of Representatives, Chairman Elberton Board of Education, Militia Captain, Director of U. S. Census, 8th Georgia Congressional District; m. Susan McCalla, b. Sept. 19, 1861; d. Dec. 23, 1923.
- 9—Willis Sue Adams, b. July 20, 1896; m. June 2, 1918, H. R. Bynum, b. Feb. 27, 1892.
- 10—Susan Margaret Bynum, b. May 9, 1919.
- 8—E. L. Adams, d. unmarried. County Commissioner of Elbert County 1919-1920.
- 8—Bud Adams, d. unmarried.
- 8—Addie Adams, m. Nov. 11, 1893, James T. Carpenter.
- 9—Lucile Carpenter, m. Jack Haley, Sheriff of Elbert County. No issue.
- 9—Thomas Carpenter, m. Olga Rouse.
- 9—L. A. Carpenter, m. Sallie Mann.
- 10—L. A. Carpenter Jr.
- 10—James Carepnter.
- 9—Helen Carpenter.
- 9—Ivan Carpenter.
- 8—Ida Adams. Unmarried.
- 8—Reese Adams, m. Dr. Charles P. Ward.
- 9—Robert Ward.
- 6—Sarah Cleveland, m. William D. Thornton.
- 6—John Cleveland.
- 6—Martha Cleveland, m. Wiley "Tandy" Wansley.
- 7—Jane Ann Wansley, b. May 26, 1834; d. Oct. 2, 1877; m. June 11, 1849, William Haley Teasley, b. Oct. 24, 1830; d. May 11, 1907.
- 8—Martha E. Teasley, b. Dec. 5, 1849.
- 8—John Wiley Teasley, b. Aug. 7, 1851; m. Nov. 18, 1874, Lenora R. McAllister, b. Dec. 10, 1856; d. Fed. 18, 1904.
- 9—Paul Reid Teasley.
- 9—Mary Hamilton Teasley, b. Feb. 25, 1880; m. March 29, 1905, Clarence Gay, b. July 25, 1878.
- 9—Sumpter Ophelia Teasley, b. June 18, 1882; m. June 4, 1902, Benjamin C. Alford, b. March 26, 1882.

10—Elmer Guy Alford, b. June 22, 1903.
10—Sarah L. Alford, b. Oct. 31, 1906.
10—Benjamin Alford.
9—William DeWitte Teasley, b. Oct. 11, 1885.
9—Bessie Teasley, d. June 29, 1913; m. Jan. 1913, Norton Gaston.
9—Lucia Teasley, b. April 1890; m. May 13, 1918, William Slade.
9—Lois Teasley, b. Aug. 22, 1892.
9—Floyd Teasley, b. April 1894; m. June 1918, Iantha Wood.
8—Andrew J. Teasley, b. June 7, 1855; d. July 1923; m. Feb. 17, 1880, Georgia Ann Fortson.
9—Bertha Teasley, m. James W. Cooper.
8—Thomas William Teasley, b. Sept. 17, 1853; d. Sept. 12, 1911; m. Feb. 1879, Elizabeth Saddler.
9—Lloyd Teasley, b. Nov. 6, 1879; m. Nov. 22, 1905, Grace Benson.
9—Carl Teasley, b. March 22, 1884.
9—Ralph Teasley, b. July 14, 1886; m. July 14, 1920, Frances Green.
9—Mary Lillie Teasley, b. March 26, 1889; m. June 15, 1916, William B. McCurry, b. March 23, 1889.
10—Elizabeth Saddler McCurry, b. Nov. 30, 1919.
9—Charles Teasley, b. June 24, 1892; m. March 24, 1923, Mrs Anna Smith nee Boyd.
8—Mattie Teasley, d. 1892; m. Cicero Alexander.
8—Samantha Teasley, b. 1859; d. 1916; m. Thomas A. Alexander.
8—Mary C. Teasley, d. Jan. 15, 1918; m. (1) Willis S. Gaines; (2) Joseph Vickery.
8—I. H. H. Teasley, b. 1863; d. 1890.
8—James H. Teasley, b. 1866; d. 1905.
8—Amos L. Teasley, b. May 26, 1869; m. Jan. 25, 1902, Ethel Linder; d. March 5, 1904.
8—Minnie Teasley, b. Dec. 31, 1871; d. Dec. 29, 1900; m. Nov. 15, 1893, Martin J. Abney.
8—Gertrude Teasley, b. Nov. 1876; d. 1893.
6—Ivory Cleveland.
6—Frank Cleveland, m. Ida McCalla.
7—Andrew B. Cleveland, m. Nov. 19, 1900, Agnes Hall.
8—Frank Cleveland, m. Cleo Smith.
9—Agnes Cleveland.
8—Lanier Cleveland, m. Augustus Wansley, S. W. W.
9—Augustus Wansley Jr.
8—Elizabeth Cleveland, m. Frank Veronee.
8—Helen Cleveland.
8—McCalla Cleveland.
8—Andrew B. Cleveland Jr.
7—Jessie Cleveland, m. Jesse Warren.
8—Hilda Warren.
8—Jeremiah Warren.
6—James M. Cleveland.
5—Jacob Cleveland, m. Martha Lyons.
6—Olin Cleveland.
6—Benjamin Cleveland.
6—Allen Cleveland, m. Rebecca Anderson.
7—Elizabeth Cleveland.
7—Jane Cleveland.
7—Allen Cleveland Jr.
7—Henry Cleveland.
7—Ann Cleveland.
7—James Cleveland, m. Martha Beall.
8—Claud Cleveland.
8—Loyd Cleveland.

8—Marie Cleveland.
8—Albert Cleveland.
8—Esther Cleveland.
5—Reuben Cleveland, b. 1776; d. 1851; m. Mary Alexander, b. 1784; d. 1855.
6—Peter Cleveland, m. (1) March 28, 1833, Amelia K. Rousey; (2) Mary Frances White.
7—Mary Cleveland, m. Alfred Teasley.
8—W. E. Teasley.
8—Eliza Teasley.
8—Mary Teasley.
8—B. A. Teasley.
8—Sarah Teasley.
8—Peter Teasley.
8—Frances Teasley.
8—Alfred Teasley Jr.
8—Thomas Teasley.
8—Minnie Teasley.
8—Alice Teasley.
7—William L. Cleveland, m. Mary Hailey.
7—Reuben Weston Cleveland, C. S., b. March 14, 1843; d. 1935; m. (1) Oct. 12, 1859, Mary A. V. Fortson, b. 1842; d. 1892; (2) India F. Wansley.
8—(By first wife) Georgia Cleveland, b. 1860; m. L. A. Clark, Warden of Elbert County, b. 1854.
9—Nora Clark, m. Joseph Bond.
10—Roy Bond, m. Miss Snellings.
10—Omer Bond, m. Miss Helton.
10—Harris Bond.
9—Otis Clark, m. Vesta Higginbotham.
10—Edna Clark.
10—Raymond Clark.
9—Cleveland Clark, m. Callie Craft.
9—Daughter, m. Mr. Barnes.
10—Malcolm Barnes.
9—Blandina Clark, m. Raymond Cox.
9—Mary Clark, m. William G. Cleveland.
9—Other issue. Names unavailable.
8—Ed Cleveland, m. Nov. 28, 1909, Ella Vickery.
8—Mary Cleveland, m. J. W. Lyle.
9—Coy Lyle.
9—Russell Lyle.
8—William Weston Cleveland, m. Miss Hulme.
9—Ruth Cleveland, m. George Attaway.
9—Pearl Cleveland.
9—Grace Cleveland, m. Crate Herring.
8—Jesse Cleveland, m. Nov. 30, 1899, Carrie Thornton.
9—Arthur Cleveland, m. Sept. 21, 1925, Jessie Brownlee.
10—Geraldine Cleveland, b. Aug. 17, 1927.
10—Dorothy Cleveland, b. July 31, 1929.
10—Jesse P. Cleveland, b. Feb. 10, 1932.
9—Myrtis Cleveland, m. June 15, 1919, R. H. Almond; d. 1936.
10—Virginia Almond, m. 1936, Joe Deadwyler.
10—Alice Almond.
10—Susie Almond.
10—R. H. Almond Jr.
9—Sarah Cleveland, m. G. W. Ginn.
9—Ruby Cleveland, m. Jack Facing.
10—Juanita Facing.

8—(By second wife) Hugh Cleveland, m. Irene Brewer.
8—Mark Cleveland, b. 1897.
8—Harry Cleveland, b. 1899; m. Janie Wallis.
7—Daniel Early Cleveland, C. S., m. (1) Clara Glenn; (2) Sarah Glenn (sisters).
8—Augustus Cleveland.
8—Clara Cleveland.
8—Bessie Cleveland.
8—Harry Cleveland, m. Cleta Quillian.
9—Jack Cleveland.
9—Harry Cleveland Jr.
8—Peter Cleveland.
8—Glenn Cleveland, m. Theodore Rumble, Superintendent Elberton Public Schools.
8—William G. Cleveland, m. Dec. 15, 1914, Mary Clark.
7—Peter Washington Cleveland, m. Cora Turner.
8—Janie Cleveland, m. Dr. A. C. Smith.
9—Mary Smith, m. Dr. J. W. Amos.
10—Mary Gay Amos.
9—Benjamin Smith.
9—McRae Smith.
8—William Cleveland, m. Ava Chandler.
8—George W. Cleveland.
8—Grover Cleveland, d. 1932, Superintendent Elberton Light and Water Department; m. Nathleen Thornton.
9—Jane Cleveland.
7—Eliza Cleveland, m. Dixon Warren.
7—Louisa Cleveland, m. B. T. Almond.
7—Alexander S. Cleveland.
7—Clara E. Cleveland, m. J. W. (J. W. Lyle subsequently married Mary Cleveland, niece of Clara E. Cleveland).
6—Amelia Cleveland, m. Reuben Thornton.
7—Mary Thornton.
7—William Thornton.
7—Ann F. Thornton.
7—Reuben Thornton.
7—Amelia Thornton.
6—Thomas F. Cleveland, m. Sarah Shannon.
6—LeRoy Cleveland, m. Samantha Rouzee.
7—Lila Cleveland, m. L. G. Adams.
7—John Cleveland, m. Mittie Adams.
8—Woodfin Cleveland, m. Cleora Higginbotham.
8—LeRoy Cleveland, m. 1910, Nora Smith.
7—Mary Cleveland, m. James Burriss.
7—Virginia Cleveland, m. (1) J. W. Gantt; (2) Reverend James N. Wall, Methodist Minister, County School Superintendent of Elbert County, member Georgia House of Representatives. No issue.
6—Daniel Cleveland, m. Harriet McGarity.
6—Eliza Cleveland, m. Micajah Almond, b. 1810; d. 1883.
7—Mary Ann Almond, m. Delancy Fortson.
7—Louisa Almond, m. (1) John W. Black; (2) John Ethridge.
8—Lola Black, m. Frank C. Thornton.
9—Norma Thornton, m. Enoch Bell.
10—Lorene Bell.
10—Ralph Bell.
9—Nathleen Thornton, m. Grover Cleveland.
10—Jane Cleveland.
9—Carmen Thornton, m. Wade A. Thornton.
10—Edward Thornton.

9—Grace Thornton, m. Emory Adams.
7—Sarah Almond, m. Reuben Campbell.
6—Louisa Cleveland, m. Thomas Rouzee.
6—William Cleveland, m. L. A. M. Terrell.
7—Robert Cleveland, m. Cassie James.
7—Roy Cleveland, m. Miss Gingles.
7—Cade Cleveland, m. Amie Burriss.
7—Paul Cleveland, m. Emma Ward.
7—William Cleveland.
7—Mamie Cleveland.
6—Mary L. Cleveland, m. Joseph Alexander.
7—William Alexander, m. Ruby Brown.
7—John Alexander, m. Emma Ward.
8—J. B. Alexander.
8—William Alexander.
8—Frank Alexander.
8—Louise Alexander.
8—Harvey Alexander.
8—Robert Alexander.
8—Cleveland Alexander.
8—Hugh Alexander.
6—Weston Cleveland, m. Sarah Emily Johnston, b. March 1830.
7—Mary E. Cleveland, b. 1851; m. John Hollingsworth.
8—Mary Hollingsworth.
8—Elizabeth Hollingsworth.
8—Ada Hollingsworth.
7—Thomas Cleveland, m. Fanny L. White.
7—William H. Cleveland.
7—Harriet Cleveland.
7—Louisa Cleveland.
7—Viola Cleveland.
7—James Cleveland.
7—Eppy Cleveland.
7—Newton Cleveland.
7—George W. Cleveland.
5—Daniel Cleveland, b. 1778; d. 1852; m. Oct. 9, 1834, Miss McGarity.
5—Elizabeth Cleveland, m. Nathan Wanslow.
3—Micajah Cleveland, b. 1704.
3—Elizabeth Cleveland, m. James Coffee.
4—Elizabeth Coffee, m. Robert Whiteside, b. 1740.
5—Jonathan Whiteside, b. 1776; d. 1860; m. Thankful Anderson, b. 1775; d. 1859.
3—William Cleveland, b. 1719; d. 1798.

CRAWFORD

(Note: Numbers represent generations, as: (1) first generation, (2) second generation, (3) third generation, etc.)

1—James L. Crawford, b. June 7, 1809; m. Nov. 30, 1831, Mourning Gaines, b. July 3, 1810.
  2—Sarah Harriet Crawford, b. Oct. 17, 1832.
  2—Mary Jane Crawford, b. Jan. 17, 1835.
  2—William Asburn Crawford, b. July 17, 1837.
  2—James Columbus Crawford, b. April 21, 1841; d. unmarried.
  2—Nancy Catherine Crawford, b. Aug. 3, 1843.

 2—Francis Marion Crawford, b. May 19, 1846; m. Mary Lucinda Freeman.
 3—Holman Strauder Crawford, m. Mrs. Ophelia Gaines.
 4—Holman Crawford.
 3—Francis Paul Crawford, m. Carrie Eavenson.
 4—Mary Crawford.
 4—Janice Crawford.
 4—Frances Crawford
 3—Ollie Crawford, m. Thomas Conwell.
 4—Tommie Conwell.
 4—Frank Conwell.
 3—Eunice Crawford, m. Howell Thomas.
 4—Crawford Thomas.
 4—Joseph Thomas.
 4—Ralph Thomas.
 2—Tyrissa Emily Crawford, b. July 22, 1850; m. George McMullan.
 NOTE: The compiler has been unable to secure further data regarding this family. There are a number of Crawfords in Elbert County, but are unable to give information.

GEORGE BARRETT CONWELL AND FAMILY

George Barrett Conwell was born in Gaines District, Elbert County, October 12, 1848. His parents were James A. Conwell and Sallie Dupree Mann Conwell.

The Conwell side of this union originally came from Virginia—two Conwell brothers, the first stock in this country, having come from England in the early sixteen hundreds—one brother eventually setting forth north to seek his fortune and the other south.

The Dupree and Mann families came to Georgia from Alabama. James A. Conwell died in a few years after his marriage to Sallie Dupree Mann, leaving her with four young sons to support.

But she having inherited the ingenuity, industriousness and courage of her pioneering family, with her own added indomitable will succeeded in rearing her sons to be successful and highly respected men of the county, and she, herself, until her death at the age of 92, was a great credit to all that is fine in womanhood, ever living according to her own beliefs and ideals, regardless of what others believed.

George, the second son, in 1877 married Sallie Violetta Hall, of Pike District, Elbert County.

Her parents were James C. Hall and Mary Loftis Hall. James C. was the only son of John P. and Maria Turman Hall. He died in some dozen years after his marriage.

Shortly after the outbreak of the Civil War he organized a company to fight in the South's cause, and was soon sent to Virginia where the battle was raging thickest, first as Lieutenant and soon afterwards promoted to Captain. In a few months he was stricken down with typhoid fever and died at Lynchburg, Virginia, leaving in addition to his wife, five small children and his crippled mother.

His wife, Mary, was one of the great unsung heroines of that terrible period in the South, and upwards through the years proved to be a woman of most unusual business and managerial ability.

When she was notified that her husband had died and that his remains would be shipped to Athens, 40 miles away and the nearest railroad station, she immediately rose to the situation. All men of the community, except the old and decrepid, had gone to war, there was no one but herself to meet her husband's remains and bring them home. She at once made ready and set out on the hazardous and heart-breaking trip, apprehensively leaving her five small children, the youngest but a few months old and feeding at her breast, with her incapacitated mother-in-law and two faithful negro servants The old carriage driver accompanied her in a wagon, filled with straw to ease the body over the rough roads, she, herself, traveling on horseback.

There was a wait of some ten days in Athens before the body arrived—all trains in that period were running off schedules and were loaded with war dead. It was a slow trip back home and each step taken was with increasing anxiety for her little ones. On her arrival she found her wee baby dangerously ill from unnatural feeding and the rest of the children, save Sally, in bed with measles.

But she was not dismayed. She again rose to the occasion, brought her children safely through their illnesses and immediately set to work, finding ways and means to carry on the farm and support her family. Eventually she not only made the farm yield plentifully and to spare, but as her children reached maturity she was able to give to each of them substantial (for those times) lands and monies to start in life for themselves.

The old Hall homestead, a half mile from what is now known as Goss, was built in 1811 and has been occupied and owned by succeeding generations until today. Nearby is the family burial ground, where most of the old stock and many of the younger, also sons-in-laws, are buried.

George Barrett Conwell and Sally Violetta Hall Conwell after their marriage settled on a part of the old Hall plantation and built a home near what later became a station when the Eastern Airline Railway (now the Southern) was built

George engaged in farming at first and soon opened up a mercantile store. In a comparatively few years he had bought much larger acreage and enlarged his mercantile business. Success came to him at every hand and turn until he had built a little empire, so to speak, of his own, and which had great influence upon shaping the economic life and development of the community. For a number of years, and all at the same time, he was engaged in farming on a large scale, merchandising, buying and selling cotton, rock quarrying, and carrying on other activities closely allied with farming, and all to such an extent that the village of Goss became the most active center in the county other than Elberton. The Southern railroad having given him the privilege of naming the station, he named it Goss in honor of a friend.

He was very ambitious for his children and the children of the community. Rural schools in Elbert County, those days, were kept open only five months in the year, but that the community might have the benefit of a nine months' school, he, himself, paid teachers' salaries for the other four months.

In his ambitions and activities, his wife, Sally Violetta, was ever his right-hand bower. She was a woman of exceptional intelligence, rare tact and winning personality. Much of her husband's success, he, himself, freely admitted, was due to those qualities in her and her judgment.

Seven children were born to this union: James (who died in infancy), Sallie May, John, Ruby, George Jr., Norma, and Chessie.

Sallie May when but little out of her teens became a pioneer (at least for this section) in publication work, and rose to recognition in that field in Atlanta, New Orleans, and Buffalo, and later in publicity work in New York City. She married Robert Jerome Dean, of Buffalo, at that time art director of the old Uncle Remus' Magazine, in Atlanta, and he was recognized for his unusual illustrations and magazine covers. Since that time he has had a very notable career as cartoonist on New Orleans and Buffalo newspapers, and as a widely syndicated writer and artist of the old *New York Herald*, on to executive editor and publisher of the old *Morning Telegraph* of New York City.

For the last sixteen years Mr. and Mrs. Dean have been residents of Dutchess County, New York, near Poughkeepsie, where they have both become among the most active and prominent citizens in civic and economic affairs, as well as the art life of the county, having recently accomplished the feat of obtaining greatly lowered taxes for the county. Mr. Dean is also now an etcher and painter of note, his etchings, particularly, obtaining recognition for their originality and ideality of subjects as well as for superior technique.

John A. also inherited the adventurous spirit of the old original Conwell stock, and at an early age went to the far west, where he has been engaged mostly in lumber up and down the Pacific Coast. He is a veteran of the World War, having served in France almost the full extent of the war with the 23rd Engineers. He was gassed in the Argonne.

Ruby, educated at LeGrange Female College, LeGrange, Ga., married Fred W. Brock, formerly of Honea Path, S. C. The Brock family is one of the oldest, most prominent and highly respected families in South Carolina, the various members of that large family engaged in banking, manufacturing, mercantiling and farming. Fred is now a successful merchant in Elberton and since his coming there some thirty years ago has won the highest respect of the town and county for his integrity and uncommon common sense. Mrs. Brock is associated with him in business.

George, Jr., noted for his happy disposition and consideration for others, after he grew up became associated in business with his father at Goss and after the latter's death in 1912 carried on until the estate was settled. He then went to Buffalo and went into the grocery business, but in less than two years he enlisted for the World War, in the 6th U. S. Marines—later was transferred to the 96th Company, Second Division.

He served in France beginning in June 1918, and on in Germany after the Armistice with the Army of Occupation. In January 1919, he was stricken for the second time with influenza after "Over There," and died March 3, 1919, at Coblenz, a few days before his Company embarked for home. A little more than a year later his remains were shipped to his family and were buried with honors in the old Hall burial ground.

Norma, after teaching in the schools of Elberton and elsewhere, attended the Savage School of Physical Training, in New York City, and shortly after graduation married Oliver Richmond Foss, then of Port Chester, N. Y., and formerly of Boston. Mr. Foss is superintendent of the American Felt Company's largest mill, located near Greenwich, Conn. In his field he is recognized as most exceptional and is highly rated among manufacturers in both Canada and America because of his peculiar ingeniousness in constantly developing new felts to meet the requirements of ever changing modern manufacturing.

The Fosses now live near Greenwich, Conn., and are prominently identified with the social as well as business life of that section. They have two children, Sallie Conwell Foss and Oliver Richmond Foss, Jr., who, respectively, attend Greenwich Academy and Brunswick School for Boys.

Chessie also attended the Savage School of Physical Education, in New York City, and after graduation taught in colleges in Pennsylvania, Connecticut and in Pelham, New York, schools. She married William A. Rowan, Jr., of Pelham, the son of William A. Rowan, once Grand Master Mason of New York State, and, until he died a few years ago, vice-president of the country-wide known J. S. Stewart Construction Company.

William A., Jr., held a responsible position with one of the subsidiary organizations of the great Hearst organization, and had great promise, even for these drastic times, but his career came to an end on November 15, 1938, when he suddenly died in his office in New York City from congestion of the viscera.

DARDEN

(Note: Numbers represent generations, as (1) first generation, (2) second generation, (3) third generation, etc.)

1—Stephen Darden settled in Nansemond County, Virginia in 1640.
  2—Captain John Darden, R. S., m. Miss Dandridge, sister of Martha Washington.
    3—John Darden Jr., R. S., b. 1734.
    3—Jacob Darden, R. S., m. Mary Hilliard.
      4—Ziephia Darden, m. Joshua Roundtree.
      4—Cynthia Darden, m. Needham Bryant.
      4—Jacob Darden Jr., d. unmarried.
    3—William Darden, b. 1736; m. Mary Dekle.
      4—Dennis Darden, m. Phobe Dilliard.
      4—Ellis Darden, m. Mary Barwick.
      4—Simeon Darden, m. Eliza Barwick.
      4—Lucinda Darden, m. Manning Roundtree.
      4—Ebernezer Darden, m. (1) Roxie Roundtree, and (2) Mrs. Ly-Lythia Boatwright Nee Bryant.
      4—Mary Darden, m. James Dilliard.
    3—Stephen Darden, b. 1737.
    3—George Darden R. S., b. 1739, received land grants in Wilkes County, Georgia for war services; m. about 1759, Martha Burch, b. 1741, daughter of Richard Burch.
      4—George Darden Jr., b. 1760.
      4—Richard Darden, b. 1763.
      4—Elizabeth Darden, b. 1765; d. 1848; m. Governor Stephen Heard R. S., b. 1740, d. 1815.
        5—Barnard Carroll Heard, b. March 12, 1787; m. Polly Hutson.
          6—Boliver Heard.
          6—Stephen Heard.
          6—John Heard, m. Elizabeth Williamson.
        5—Martha Burch Heard, b. Oct. 10, 1788; d. Dec. 7, 1824; m. about 1805, Bartlett Tucker, b. 1784.
          6—Stephen Heard Tucker, m. Jan. 16, 1827, Mary Aiken, daughter of Thomas Aiken.
          6—Elizabeth Tucker, m. (1) Mr. Upshaw, (2) Dec. 2, 1840, Robert Harris.
            7—(By first wife), daughter m. Mr. Harris.
            7—Robert Harris Jr.
            7—(By second wife) Alva Harris.
            7—Clarence P. Harris, m. Eva Wakefield.
              8—Alice Pope Harris, m. Frank Asbury Jr.
                9—Frank Asbury III.
            7—James Harris.
            7—Walton Harris.
          6—Sarah Tucker, m. Jan. 27, 1842, Henry Sanders. No issue.
        5—Bridget Carroll Heard, b. June 17, 1795, m. (1) March 6, 1817, Simeon Henderson and (2), Elbert H. Thompson.
          6—William Henderson, b. 1796.
          6—Daughter Thompson, m. Mr. Riddle.
          6—Daughter Thompson, m. Mr. Jones.
        5—Dr. George Washington Heard, member Georgia Legislature, b. June 17, 1791; m. April 20, 1815, Sarah Carter, daughter of Thomas A. Carter R. S.
          6—Stephen Heard, m. Mary Aiken.
            7—Phillip Heard, m. Miss Tillman.
        5—John Adams Heard, b. March 17, 1793; d. 1838, solicitor general Western Circuit of Georgia. Unmarried.

5—Jane Lanier Heard, b. March 23, 1797; m. Singleton Walthall Allen, b. Jan. 14, 1791; d. June 6, 1853, member Georgia House of Representatives—member Georgia State Senate.
6—Elizabeth Allen, m. George Williams.
7—George Williams C. S., d. unmarried.
7—William Williams, m. Jessie Arnold.
8—William McIntosh Williams.
7—Janie Williams, m. John Burriss.
8—Dillard Herndon Burriss.
6—George Allen, d. unmarried.
6—Theodore Allen, d. unmarried.
6—Ann Allen, m. April 30, 1839, Dr. Milton Comer.
7—Janie Comer, m. 1874, Samuel Barnett, Captain C. S. A., b. Aug. 16, 1841; d. Nov. 26, 1898.
8—Comer Barnett, b. May 11, 1878; m. June 19, 1901, Cornell Bounds, b. Feb. 14, 1880.
9—Lillis Barnett, b. March 25, 1911.
7—Bevelle Comer, m. Dr. Hampton. No issue.
7—Annie Comer, b. 1849; d. 1928. Unmarried.
6—Susan Allen, m. Young L. G. Harris, founder of Young-Harris College, president Southern Mutual Insurance Company, member Georgia House of Representatives, member Georgia State Senate. No issue.
6—Maria Louisa Allen, b. Aug. 10, 1824; m. Jan. 27, 1842, William McPherson McIntosh, b. Feb. 14, 1815, d. June 1862. Colonel 15th Georgia Regiment Infantry Volunteers C. S. A. Mortally wounded in the action at Garnett's Farm, Virginia, member Georgia House of Representatives, member Georgia State Senate, elector state-at-large for Beckenridge in 1860, planter, lawyer.
7—Singleton Allen McIntosh C. S., b. Feb. 19, 1845; d. Nov. 17, 1908; m. Feb. 1867, Mary Eliza Cade.
8—Sarah Howell McIntosh, b. Dec. 29, 1867; m. S. J. Zeigler.
9—Samuel Ziegler, U. S. naval officer, m. Fanny Marburg.
10—Howell Zeigler.
9—Howell "Polar" Zeigler, m. George Dickson, major U. S. Army, retired.
10—Howell Rees Dickson.
10—George Dickson Jr.
8—William McPherson McIntosh, b. 1870, d. 1930, unmarried.
8—Victoria Augusta McIntosh, b. March 1875, m. Joseph Allston of South Carolina.
9—Joseph Allston Jr., m. Lillis McCollough.
10—Joseph Allston III.
9—Mary Allston.
8—Mary Louise McIntosh, b. Aug. 10, 1877; m. 1903, Henry M. Long.
9—Mary Louise Long, d. infancy.
8—Guilford "Guy" McIntosh, b. July 6, 1872; m. Sept. 14, 1918, Addie Tinsley.
9—Mary McIntosh, b. Sept. 3, 1921.
9—William Kenneth McIntosh. b. Nov. 10, 1922.
9—Louise McIntosh, b. Nov. 1923.
7—Anna Cassandra McIntosh, b. March 5, 1849; m. Dec. 11, 1866, Budd Clay Wall C. S., b. April 1847; d. Jan. 1930.
8—Martha Louise McIntosh, b. April 6, 1868; m. Thomas B. Andrews. No issue.
8—McPherson Wall, d. infancy.
8—William Clay Wall, d. infancy.

8—James Singleton Wall, b. Jan. 1, 1873; m. Rose Douglas. No issue.
8—Bevel William McIntosh Wall, b. June 30, 1875; m. Mary Stewart.
9—Margaret Wall.
9—Bevel Clay Wall, m. Virginia Alexander.
10—Bevel Charles Wall, b. July 22, 1930.
8—Jessie McIntosh Wall, b. Dec. 20, 1878; m. 1899, John D. Stelling.
9—Sterling Stelling, b. Feb. 14, 1900; m. Eula Mitchell. No issue.
9—Richard Nunnelee Stelling, b. May 14, 1901.
9—Martha McIntosh Stelling, b. Dec. 14, 1903; m. June 1930, Dr. Charles McCord Kilpatrick.
9—Howard Cree Stelling, b. Sept. 1906, Lieutenant U. S. Air Corp; m. Helen Wainwright.
9—Budd Clay Wall Stelling, b. Feb. 1909.
8—Harry Hall, m. (1) Maryland Randall and (2) Hattie Smith. No issue.
7—Maria Louise McIntosh, b. March 15, 1851; d. May 7, 1894; m. Feb. 2, 1869, Guilford Cade Jr.
8—Julia May Cade, b. Dec. 30, 1871; m. Nov. 23, 1892, Dr. Albert Sidney Hawes, b. Nov. 14, 1863; d. Nov. 19, 1936; Mayor, City Elberton, member Georgia House of Representatives.
9—Guilford Mosely Hawes, b. July 24, 1894; m. 1913, Onie Lee, b. 1893.
10—Mary Lee Hawes, b. Sept. 14, 1917.
10—Robert Hawes, d. infancy.
10—Julia Ann Hawes, b. Feb. 25, 1925.
9—Albert Lee Hawes, b. Feb. 11, 1901; m. Bertha Bates who died without issue.
9—Peyton S. Hawes, b. Sept. 4, 1903; City Attorney of Elberton, member Georgia House of Representatives 1931-1932, m. 1933, Virginia Smith.
8—Guilford Cade III, b. June 9, 1875; m. Dec. 4, 1904, Jane Kennedy.
9—Malivna Cade, b. Sept. 1905; m. Dec. 1929, Milo Abercrombie. killed in automobile accident, 1931.
10—Milo Abercrombie Jr.
8—Annie Lee Cade, b. Feb. 21, 1878; m. Feb. 24, 1903, Dr. Robert Franklin Moore, b. Jan. 30, 1871, d. 1923.
9—Alan Moore, b. Nov. 25, 1905, d. 1933.
9—Frank Moore, d. infancy.
9—Guilford McIntosh Moore, b. Sept. 1908; m. Miss Mauldin.
7—Ada McIntosh, d. infancy.
7—Jessie McIntosh, d. infancy.
7—Mary Bevelle McIntosh, b. June 1856; d. June 11, 1926; m. 1895, John C. Brown, Mayor of Elberton, merchant. No issue.
7—James McIntosh, b. Sept. 23, 1857, Sheriff of Elbert County, City Councilman of Elberton, County Commissioner of Elbert County, Tax Assessor of Elberton, m. Oct. 18, 1882, Mary Jane Arnold, b. Sept. 1, 1859, daughter of Joseph Y. Arnold and Sarah K. Thornton.
8—Sarah Louise McIntosh, b. July 29, 1883, m. Feb. 24, 1903, A. F. Archer. No issue.
8—William McIntosh, d. infancy.
8—Jessie McIntosh, d. infancy.
8—Mary James McIntosh, d. infancy.
8—John Hawes McIntosh, b. Nov. 26, 1895; m. June 19, 1918, Fay Ann White, b. Oct. 21, 1900. Divorced 1937.
9—Mary Louise McIntosh, b. July 16, 1920.

9—Elizabeth Arnold Penn McIntosh, b. March 15, 1923.
8—McAlpin McIntosh, b. Nov. 26, 1897; d. 1899.
7—Jessie McIntosh, b. 1859; m. Peyton M. Hawes, militia captain, member Georgia House of Representatives, member Georgia State Senate, president Elberton Loan and Savings Bank, president Elbert County Bank, merchant, planter. No issue.
6—Mary Allen, m. Nov. 21, 1859, George McCalla.
7—Isaac McCalla, m. Raymond Speed.
8—Mack McCalla, m. Ella Nichols.
9—Mack McCalla Jr.
9—Elmira McCalla.
8—Leila McCalla, m. Mr. Linder.
9—Alice Linder, m. J. P. Sullivan, of Anderson, S. C.
10—J. P. Sullivan Jr.
8—John McCalla, m. Parnice Brown. No issue.
7—John W. McCalla, county commissioner of Elbert County, m. Mitta Allen.
8—Olivia McCalla, m. Perry H. Smith, city councilman of Elberton, merchant.
9—Ethel Smith, m. Mr. Le Conte.
8—Annie McCalla, m. Oct. 20, 1909, J. H. Purdue, of Alabama.
9—Frances Purdue.
9—Mary Olivia Purdue.
9—J. H. Purdue Jr.
8—J. Earl McCalla, m. Katherine Stephens.
9—John McCalla.
9—Katherine McCalla.
9—J. Earl McCalla Jr.
9—David McCalla.
7—Ida McCalla, m. (1) Frank Cleveland and (2) Aug. 31, 1887, Bedford Heard.
8—Andrew Cleveland, m. Nov. 19, 1900, Agnes Hall.
9—Frank Cleveland, m. Miss Smith.
10—Agnes Cleveland.
9—Lanier Cleveland, m. Augustus Wansley.
10—Augustus Wansley Jr.
9—McCalla Cleveland.
9—Helen Cleveland.
9—Elizabeth Cleveland, m. Frank Veronee.
9—Andrew B. Cleveland Jr.
8—Jessie Cleveland, m. Jesse Warren.
9—Hilda Warren.
9—Jeremiah Warren.
8—M. E. Heard, m. Sept. 14, 1904, Allen Pressley.
8—Erskin Heard, m. Lottie Seymour.
9—Martha Heard.
9—Bedford Heard.
9—Emma Heard.
9—Mattie Heard.
9—Hazel Heard.
8—Sarah Heard, m. June 9, 1912, Frank Hammond.
9—Frank Hammond Jr.
9—Mildred Hammond.
8—Bevelle Heard, m. Feb. 20, 1917, Thomas Wayble.
9—Bevelle Wayble.
8—Caroline Heard, m. Guy Quillian.
7—Jennie McCalla, m. Joseph Speed.
8—Florence Speed, m. A. A. McCurry, Georgia State Senator, 30th District, lawyer.
9—Speed McCurry.

9—A. A. McCurry Jr., m. Bee Porter.
9—Jennie May McCurry.
9—Horace McCurry.
9—Althea McCurry.
9—Joseph McCurry.
7—Susan McCalla, b. Sept. 19, 1861; d. Dec. 23, 1923; m. Willis B. Adams, b. May 13, 1861, d. Feb. 11, 1913. Captain Elberton Light Infantry, member Georgia House of Representatives 1905-06-07-08, member City Council of Elberton, Mayor of Elberton, Chairman Elberton Board of Education, merchant.
8—Willis Sue Adams, b. July 20, 1896, m. June 2, 1918, H. R. Bynum, b. Feb. 27, 1892. Clerk and Treasurer City of Elberton.
9—Susan Margaret Bynum, b. May 9, 1919.
7—Mary "May" McCalla, m. George Gaines. No issue.
7—Dr. Lawrence "Larry" McCalla, m. Hettie Hearne.
8—Dr. Lawrence McCalla Jr., m. Mildred Cosner of Greenville, S. C.
9—Lawrence McCalla III.
6—Rebecca Allen, m. William H. Mattox. Captain C. S. A. Member Georgia House of Representatives, member Georgia State Senate, delegate to Georgia Constitutional Convention of 1877, planter, merchant.
7—Lena "Lady" Mattox, m. Jeptha Jones.
8—Reba Jones, m. June 27, 1909, George W. Gray, member Elbert County Board of Registrars, merchant, planter.
9—George W. Gray Jr.
9—Page Gray.
8—Allen Jones.
8—Annie Jones.
8—Henry P. Mattox Jones, m. Aug. 20, 1911, Mary Wall.
9—Henry P. Mattox Jones Jr.
9—Martha Jones.
9—Rebecca Jones.
9—Thomas Jones.
8—Callie May Jones, b. 1891; m. Apr. 19, 1909, Albert R. Hudson.
9—Albert R. Hudson Jr., b. 1910; m. 1930, Elizabeth Bell.
9—Clark Hudson, b. 1912.
9—Francis Hudson, b. 1915.
9—Mack Hudson, b. 1917.
9—David Hudson, b. 1919.
9—Carroll Mattox Hudson, b. 1922.
7—Singleton Mattox, m. Aug. 17, 1887, Annie Jones.
8—Jesse Mattox.
7—Allen Mattox.
7—Clark McIntosh Mattox, m. Sarah Jones.
8—Clark McIntosh Mattox Jr., m. Miss Helton.
8—Jeptha Mattox.
7—Susan Mattox, died unmarried.
7—Annie Maddox, d. unmarried.
7—Carroll Mattox, m. Charles Fisher, St. Louis, Mo.
8—Mamie Fisher.
7—Janie Mattox, m. Raymond Gaines.
6—Gerard Allen, m. Oct. 30, 1850, Isabella Blackwell.
7—Gerard Allen Jr., m. Adelaide Stanford.
8—Singleton W. Allen, m. May Wood.
9—Gerard Allen, m. Sadie Ethridge.
8—Hattie Allen, m. Charles Whitmire, Atlanta, Ga.
9—Charles Whitmire Jr.
9—Harriet Whitmire.
9—Annie Bevelle Whitmire.
9—Martha Whitmire.

5—Permelia Heard, b. 1799; d. 1816.
5—Sarah J. Heard, d. Aug. 16, 1825; m. Jan. 18, 1825, Jas. D. Jarrett.
5—Thomas Jefferson Heard, b. 1801; d. 1876; m. (1) Nancy Middleton and (2) Miss Arnold. (Children by Nancy Middleton.)
6—Sarah Heard, m. 1846, L. H. O. Martin, Col. on Staff on Gen. Rbt. Tombs, member of Ga. Legislature, Elbert County, Delegate to Ga. Secession Convention.
7—L. H. O. Martin Jr., member of Ga. Legislature, m. Rossie Harper.
7—Sarah Martin, d. unmarried.
6—James Lawrence Heard, Major Confederate Army, member Ga. Legislature, first Mayor of Elberton, m. Mary Melissa Harper.
7—Mary Heard, b. 1858; d. 1929; m. Thomas Carleton, D. D., State Baptist Evangelist, Oklahoma; Judge City Court Elberton.
8—Thomas Carleton Jr., Pharmecist.
7—William Harper Heard, b. 1860; d. 1919; m. Nov. 14, 1889, Kathleen Carroll.
8—Margaret Melissa Heard, m. Charles Louis Dohme, 1929.
8—Kathleen Carroll Heard, m. W. E. Adams, U. S. Army, 1920.
9—Robert Carroll Adams, b. 1924.
8—James Lawrence Heard, m. Eva Underwood, 1914.
9—Margaret Melissa Heard, m. Charles A. Winans, 1937.
9—Eva Kathleen Heard, b. 1917.
9—J. Lawrence Heard III, b. 1918; d. 1921.
9—Betsy Meredith Heard, b. 1923.
8—Jane Clinton Heard, m. William N. Hallman, World War Vet., 1922.
9—William Hallman Jr., b. 1923.
9—Helen Meredith Hallman, b. 1925.
8—Luther Martin Heard, U. S. Navy World War.
8—Sarah Heard, m. Smith Wise, World War Vet., 1920.
9—Dorothy Heard Wise, b. 1921.
8—William Harper Heard, m. Vivian Burnett, 1925.
9—Donald Tate Heard, b. 1926.
8—Joseph Day Heard, b. 1908; m. Frances Weber, 1939.
7—Nancy Heard, b. 1865; d. 1935; m. Phil W. Davis, Baptist minister, Judge, member Ga. Legislature.
8—Melissa Heard Davis, m. Fred B. Lynch, 1927.
8—Phil W. Davis, lawyer, m. Cecile Little, 1921.
9—Cecile Little Davis, b. 1922.
7—Oliver McDonald Heard, d. 1924; m. Victor Nardin, 1899.
8—Lucie Evelyn Heard, m. Arthur Lanham Jr., 1930.
9—Mary Lanham, b. 1935.
9—Arthur Lanham Jr., b. 1937.
8—Mary Melissa Heard.
8—Victor Nardin Heard, m. Mildred Z. Harbuck, 1931.
9—Nardin McDonald Heard, b. 1933.
9—Victor Marion Heard, b. 1937.
7—Jane Carroll Heard, m. Fred S. Clinton, M. D., Tulsa, Oklahoma.
6—Robert Middleton Heard, Captain C. S. A., member Georgia House of Representatives, Mayor of Elberton, m. April 19, 1864, Louisa Jones, b. April 24, 1846; d. September 23, 1910.
7—John T. Heard, d. 1932. Merchant, banker.
7—Carroll Heard.
7—Vohammie Heard, m. Marcus A. Pharr.
8—Marcus Pharr, lieutenant World War. Accidentally killed, 1918.
9—Marcus A. Pharr Jr.
8—Robert H. Pharr, m. Hallie Smith.
9—Robert Heard Pharr Jr.

8—Camilla Pharr, m. G. D. Barnett.
9—Aurelius Barnett.
9—Camilla Barnett.
9—Ida Barnett.
9—Vohammie Barnett.
8—Mitta Pharr, m. S. A. Fields, Nov. 25, 1926.
9—S. A. Fields Jr., b. Dec. 25, 1932.
8—Vohammie Pharr, m. J. M. Carr.
9—J. M. Carr Jr.
9—Robert Carr.
9—Mitta Carr.
8—Louise Pharr, m. H. C. Sparks.
9—Lavonia Sparks.
9—H. C. Sparks Jr.
7—Luther Martin Heard, president Citizens Brank of Elberton, m. Mamie Lattimer, daughter of United States Senator Lattimer of South Carolina.
8—Luther Martin Heard Jr., m. Miriam Dean.
9—Miriam Heard.
9—Ann Heard.
8—Lattimer Heard.
8—Robert Heard.
7—Georgia Heard, m. Nov. 29, 1898, Dr. J. E. Johnson, a native of Hall County, Georgia.
8—J. E. Johnson Jr., M. D., m. Marie Williams; m. (2) Nell Steed.
9—J. E. Johnson III.
7—Roberta Heard, m. John T. Dennis Jr., Mayor of Elberton. No issue.
7—Parks E. Heard, unmarried, d. Oct. 1938.
6—Erskin Heard, m. (1) Nov. 26, 1855 and (2) Caroline Calhoun.
7—Bedford Heard, m. Ida Cleveland Nee McCalla.
8—M. E. Heard, m. Allen Pressley.
8—Erskin Heard, m. 1911, Lottie Seymour.
7—Jefferson Heard, m. Willie Sondidge.
8—Mattie C. Heard.
8—Eugene Heard, M. D.
9—Martha Heard.
9—Bedford Heard.
9—Emma Heard.
9—Mattie Heard.
9—Hazel Heard.
8—Sarah Heard, m. June 9, 1912, Frank Hammond.
9—Frank Hammond Jr.
9—Mildred Hammond.
8—Bevelle Heard, m. Thomas Wayble.
9—Bevelle Wayble.
8—Caroline Heard, m. Guy Quillian.
7—Emma Heard m. Dr. N. G. Long. No issue.
7—(By second wife) George E. Heard. No issue.
6—William Henry Heard, m. Oct. 29, 1873, Jennie Harper.
7—Thomas Parks Heard, d. unmarried.
7—Harper Heard.
7—Rebecca Heard, m. Frank Wright. No issue.
6—Eugene B. Heard, b. 1847, d. March 31, 1934; C. S. m. Sarah Harper, founder of Seaboard Air Line Traveling Library.
7—Susan Heard, d. April 1934; m. J. Y. Swift. No issue.
4—David Darden.
4—Mary Jane Darden, m. (1) Mr. Williamson and (2) Mr. Wynn.
5—Henrietta (?) m. Mr. Wilkinson.
6—Joseph Wilkinson m. (?).

7—E. B. Wilkinson m. Laura Fortson.
6—Annie (?).
6—Florida (?).
5—Samuel Wynn, m. Miss Moss.
6—Samuel Wynn Jr.
6—Mary Wynn, m. (1) Wilberfore Daniel and (2) F. P. Pope.
5—John Wynn.
4—Richard Darden.
4—Buckner Darden.
4—Washington Darden.

JOSEPH DEADWYLER, THE REVOLUTIONARY PATRIOT

Martin Deadwyler, a native of Germany, emigrated to this country about 1750 and settled in North Carolina where he lived until 1786, when he and his family migrated to Wilkes (now Elbert) County, Georgia where they settled.

The first record we find of Martin Deadwyler in Georgia is on 11th September, 1786, when he sells land in Wilkes County to William Langham adjoining D. Coleman and Henry Coats. In 1790 we find his name among those subject to pay taxes in Capt. Black's Company, Wilkes County. Others mentioned were Joseph Deadwyler, Christopher Deadwyler and John Duncan.

Martin Deadwyler died in Elbert County, in the summer of 1809 as will appear from his will. His children: Joseph Deadwyler married Alice Duncan; Eve Deadwyler; Nancy Deadwyler married in Elbert County 31st August, 1809, Jeremiah Shoemake; Frances Deadwyler married Isaac Mobley; Anna Deadwyler married Abel Howell; Barbara Deadwyler married Barrett Ford. It is believed that Christopher Deadwyler was a son although he didn't share in the estate.

Joseph Deadwyler, the founder of the Deadwyler family of Elbert County, was a son of Martin Deadywler. He was born in North Carolina about 1760 and died on his farm near Doves Creek in Elbert County about 1830. He married Alice Duncan, a daughter of John Duncan, a Revolutionary Soldier who settled in Elbert County after the war.

Joseph Deadwyler served as a soldier in the Revolutionary War from North Carolina. He drew in the Land Lottery of 1827 as a Revolutionary Soldier and in the Lottery of 1838 his widow, Alice Deadwyler, received recompence as a widow of a Revolutionary Soldier. They were residents of Deadwyler's District, Elbert County where they took a prominent part in the early development of the county. The characteristics of the Deadwyler Family has been thrift and good business judgement.

The children of Joseph and Alice Duncan Deadwyler were:

1. Martin Deadwyler born in Wilkes (now Elbert) County, Georgia, 8th February, 1788; died 8th September 1866; married in Elbert County, Georgia, 7th August, 1809—Sarah Rebecca Wilhite, born in Elbert County, Georgia, 10th May, 1791; died 8th January,

1844 and buried beside her husband in the Deadwyler Cemetery, seven miles from Elberton near Sweet City in Elbert County. She was the daughter of Philip Wilhite who was of French lineage. He was born in North Carolina and died in Elbert County.

2. Anna Deadwyler, born in Wilkes (now Elbert) County, 22nd May, 1790; died in Hart County, Georgia, 3rd November, 1860; married first in Elbert County, 11th December, 1810, Robert C. Bradley, born in Virginia about 1780 and died about 1822 at the age of 42. She married second in Elbert County 18th September, 1823, Rev. Horatio James Goss, born in Virginia, 10th October, 1788; died in Elbert County ———.

3. Joseph P. Deadwyler, married in Elbert County, 8th November, 1825 Martha P. Webb, daughter of Claibon Webb Jr., of Elbert County. She married second in Elbert County 8th December, 1829, Alex P. Houston.

4. Asa Deadwyler born in Elbert County 12th February, 1808; died in Madison County, Georgia, 1st April, 1881; married first in Madison County, 17th December, 1834, Margaret Eberhart, daughter of Geo. Eberhart of Madison County.

5. Arena Deadwyler, born in Elbert County, 17th August, 1810; died 22nd September, 1881; married Sidney Mailey, born 1813; died 2nd October, 1893 and buried beside his wife in the Deadwyler Cemetery. Sidney Mailey was the son of John Mailey of Virginia.

6. John G. Deadwyler, born in Elbert County, 25th December, 1815; died 16th February, 1875 and buried in the Deadwler Cemetery. Never married.

7. Elizabeth Deadwyler married in Elbert County, 11th June, 1818, Elisha Ford.

8. Letitia (Letty) Deadwyler married in Elbert County, Georgia, 16th Novmeber, 1820, Milton Pope Webb, died 1826 as will appear from his will recorded in Elbert County, Georgia.

9. Mary (Polly) Deadwyler married in Elbert County, 10th May, 1821, Mathew J. Black.

10. Nancy Deadwyler married in Elbert County, 9th November, 1824, Abner Webb, son of Claiborn Webb Jr.

—Compiled by Laura Lee Saterfield (Geneologist) Hartwell, Ga.

THE DuBOSE FAMILY

(1) Andrew DuBose, the first of this family to come to America from France, was the son of Peter DuBose, born in France. The said Peter DuBose was the son of Isaac DuBose, born in Dieppe, Normandy, France, and his wife, Susanne Cillandeau, emigrated in 1689, married in France. Andrew DuBose assisted in establishing American Independence while acting in the capacity of Captain in Benton's Regiment in South Carolina. The children of Andrew DuBose were: Benjamin, Hugh, Herbert, Joshua and Samuel.

(2) Benjamin DuBose, son of Andrew DuBose, born about 1742, and Rebecca DuBose, born about 1745, were married in 1769.

1-2 (3) Joshua Wilson DuBose was the son of Benjamin DuBose, born about 1770, died 1851, and his first wife, Susanna Campbell, born about 1778, and died 1870. Benjamin DuBose and Susanna Campbell were married in 1799. (Ref. — "History of the Old Cheraw's", Page 407, book to be found in Carneigie Library, of Atlanta, Ga.)

Captain Joshua Wilson DuBose and his wife, Frances Hughes DuBose, lived in lower Elbert County and the following were children of Joshua DuBose and his wife, Frances DuBose: Mary DuBose Edwards, Rebecca DuBose Bell, Eugenia DuBose DeWitt, Sallie DuBose Olds, Eliza DuBose, Benjamin DuBose, John DuBose; Joel Herbert DuBose, Jefferson Davis DuBose, all deceased; and Julia DuBose Smith, wife of William Thomas Smith, of Elbert County, Georgia, deceased, and Victoria Letitia Rembert DuBose Fambrough, wife of Leonidas Gaines Fambrough, of Green County, Georgia, deceased. Julia Smith and Victoria Fambrough now reside in Elbert County.

Captain Joshua Wilson DuBose, pioneer, and head of the DuBose family in Elbert County, Georgia, was born in Darlington, C. H. South Carolina, January 1, 1814. On his father's side he was of French Huguenot, and on his mother's side, Scotch. The family name was originally written "du Bosc," being changed to "DuBose" after his ancestor, Isaac du Bosc came to America. The earliest mention of the name dates back to the year 1066, when William du Bosc sailed with William the Conqueror from the Port of Dives, France, to the conquest of Britain, and was knighted by the Conqueror. The family coat-of-arms may still be seen emblazoned in the original colors on the walls of the ancient hostelry of the Conqueror.

Early in the year 1836 Joshua Wilson DuBose volunteered for service in the Florida Indian Seminole War, in which his rank was Ensign. Some years later we find Joshua Wilson DuBose Captain of a military company at Elberton, Georgia.

At the outbreak of the War of Secession, Captain DuBose's two sons-in-law, James A. Edwards and Dr. James E. Bell, volunteered and served throughout the four-year period of the War. The former rose to the rank of Lieutenant, and the latter to that of Surgeon. Captain DuBose's son, Benjamin (later Dr. DuBose), volunteered early in 1864, and served to the close of the War. Captain DuBose himself, though over 50, went with the State militia to the defense of Atlanta, but his infant son, Jefferson Davis, becoming dangerously ill, the Captain was called back home and was not present at the fall of the city.

Julia DuBose Smith now lives in the little village of Huguenot, the original home of Joshua Wilson DuBose, her father. It is generally understood that Huguenot received its name from Joel Herbert DuBose, years ago when a Post Office was established there, which has long since been abolished.

Victoria DuBose Fambrough lives on the Southern outskirts of Elberton, on the Mattox Bridge Road, where she and her husband, Leonidas Gaines Fambrough, lived most of their 61 years of married life. Nine of their ten children are now living, most of them in Elbert County.

—(Gladys Fambrough)

EBERHARDT

The following chart shows intermarriages with the following families:
Arnold — Ash — Bagwell — Bishop — Brawner — Brewer — Bryant — Calloway — Carmichael — Carter — Cater — Chandler — Christian — Cole — Cox — Cunningham — Davenport — Deadwyler — Drake — Fortson — Gantt — Gorman — Gilbert — Goolsby — Griffith — Hall — Hawes — Herndon — Herring — Hitt — Hogan — Hollis — Hunt — Jones — Kison — Lumpkin — Manley — Mann — Marshall — Martin — Maxwell — Mattox — Moncrief — Mollay — Moore — McElreath — McGill — McCurley — Oglesby — Patton — Pettigrew — Roberts — Rush — Rylee — Saunders — Seymour — Smith — Steadman — Stephenson — Strickland — Taylor — Tidwell — Vickers — Waldrop — Winn — Woodrum — Wright — Wynn.

(Note: Numbers represent generations, as: (1) first generation, (2) second generation, (3) third generation, etc.)

1—Jacob Eberhardt, d. Elbert County, Jan. 1811; m. (?).
    2—Jacob Eberhardt Jr., R. S., d. 1848.
    2—David Eberhardt, S. W., 1812 m. Susannah Griffith.
    2—Christena Eberhardt, m. Mr. McElrath.
    2—Catherine Eberhardt, m. Mr. Patton.
    2—George Eberhardt, S. W., 1812 d. Jan. 1848; m. Margaret Patton.
        3—Robert Eberhardt, b. Aug. 31, 1803; d. Sept. 19, 1873; m. July 27, 1826, Jane Griffith, b. Dec. 29, 1807; d. June 21, 1857. (2) m. Mrs. Elizabeth L. Thornton, widow of Reuben.
            4—James Griffith Eberhardt, b. Oct. 20, 1827; d. March 23, 1907; m. (1) Priscilla Jane Brawner, b. Dec. 29, 1831; d. May 16, 1875, and (2) Mrs. Sidney Tiller Davenport, b. 1839; d. 1902.
                5—(By first wife) Sarah Wilimina Eberhardt, b. July 15, 1855; d. March 4, 1924; m. Dec. 9, 1875, Asa P. Deadwyler, b. July 4, 1852; killed in automobile and train accident 1919, member Georgia House of Representatives.
                    6—Margaret Lee Deadwyler, m. George Lee Herndon. No issue.
                    6—Lillian Eberhardt Deadwyler, m. James E. Hall.
                        7—Willie Elizabeth Hall, m. Lowery Moore.
                        7—James E. Hall Jr., m. Miss Seymour.
                    6—Luke Deadwyler, m. Frances Herring. No issue.
                5—Amarintha J. Eberhardt, b. Nov. 18, 1849; d. Dec. 28, 1930, m. John Deadwyler.
                    6—Mamie L. Deadwyler, m. E. S. Rylee.
                    6—Janie P. Deadwyler, m. M. L. Calloway.
                    6—Nuna Blance Deadwyler, m. E. C. Calloway.
                    6—Thomas Joseph Deadwyler, m. Mabel Waldrop.

4—Margaret Eberhardt, b. Oec. 5, 1829; m. John Oglesby.
5—George Oglesby, m. Katie Martin.
6—John P. Oglesby, m. Margaret Bryan.
7—Maggie Lee Oglesby, m. Mr. McCurley.
6—Alexander Oglesby.
6—William Oglesby, m. Mamie Fortson.
7—Katie Lou Oglesby, m. Easton Brown.
6—Jannie Oglesby, m. Walter C. Jones.
7—Geneva Jones.
7—Helen Jones.
7—Jenelle Jones.
6—Elizabeth Oglesby, m. Frank Steadman.
6—Clarence Oglesby, m. (1) Ethel Arnold and (2) Edna May Paul.
7—(By first wife) Margaret Oglesby.
7—Carrie Kate Oglesby.
7—George Oglesby.
7—C. D. Oglesby.
7—Arnold Oglesby.
7—Virginia Oglesby.
4—George Eberhart, b. May 18, 1832, C. S., d. 1893; m. 1856, Helen Christian, b. 1838; d. Oct. 27, 1897.
5—Robert Eberhardt.
5—George Eberhardt.
5—Thomas Eberhart.
5—Ira Eberhardt.
5—Laura Eberhardt, m. J. H. McGill.
6—George McGill.
6—Helen McGill.
6—Clara McGill.
6—Lucile McGill.
6—William McGill.
6—Harry McGill.
5—F. Shilon Eberhardt.
5—J. Walter Eberhardt, m. Nelle Cater.
6—Lillian Eberhardt.
6—William Eberhardt.
6—Helene Eberhardt.
6—George Eberhardt.
5—Edwin Eberhardt.
5—Alexander Eberhardt.
5—Halbert Eberhardt.
4—Robert Patton Eberhardt, lieutenant-colonel, C. S. A., b. Oct. 13, 1834; d. Jan. 17, 1907; m. Sept. 26, 1861, Emma Priscilla Hunt, b. April 9, 1846; d. April 4, 1907.
5—Leila Hilliard Eberhardt, b. 1862, d. 1864.
5—John Lee Eberhardt, b. Nov. 26, 1864.
5—Thomas L. Eberhardt, b. June 29, 1866; m. (1) Eliza Marshall, and (2) Harriet Rebecca Saunders.
6—(By first wife) Maud Marshall Eberhardt, b. April 26, 1891.
6—(By second wife) Harriet Rebecca Eberhardt, b. 1909.
5—Elizabeth Helen Eberhardt, b. Nov. 25, 1869; d. Aug. 25, 1918; m. May 17, 1887, David E. Moncrief.
6—Herbert R. Moncrief, b. July 3, 1889; m. 1908, Lillian Hollis.
7—Mary Elizabeth Moncrief.
6—David E. Moncrief Jr., b. Sept. 5, 1891; m. 1917, Margaret Mollay.
7—David B. Moncrief.
5—Robert W. Eberhardt, b. Dec. 5, 1871; m. Oct. 5, 1893, Florence Pelligrini.
6—Dora Eberhardt.

6—Robert W. Eberhardt Jr., m. Elizabeth Cater.
6—Ruth Eberhardt.
6—John Eberhardt.
6—William Eberhardt.
5—Jane Leeper (Jennie) Eberhardt, b. Aug. 11, 1873; m. Feb. 15, 1909, Charles Fox Cole.
6—Emma Loula Cole.
5—Augusta Louise Eberhardt, b. Sept. 11, 1876.
5—James Frank Eberhardt, b. March 16, 1879.
5—Harry Lawrence Eberhardt, b. July 3, 1882; m. 1914, Grace Bishop.
6—Henry Joyce Eberhardt.
4—Sarah Frances Eberhardt, b. Jan. 23, 1837; m. Thomas Oglesby.
5—Thomas Griffith Oglesby, b. Oct. 17, 1859; m. Ada Lumpkin.
6—Lucy Lumpkin Oglesby.
5—Emma Jane Oglesby, b. Sept. 28, 1857; m. April 1, 1880, Thomas Brewer.
6—James Thomas Brewer, m. Florence Smith.
7—Thomas Griffith Brewer.
7—Janice Brewer.
7—Eva Brewer, m. Floyd Taylor.
7—Ralph Brewer.
7—Mary Brewer.
6—Pearl Brewer, m. T. V. Bagwell.
7—Thomas Bagwell, d. unmarried.
7—Virginia Bagwell.
7—Jack Bagwell.
6—Luther Turner Brewer, d. 1916; m. Bernice Vickers.
7—Thomas Brewer.
6—Ruby Brewer, registered nurse.
6—Sally Jane Brewer, d. March 20, 1887.
4—Mary Malinda Eberhardt, b. May 10, 1841; m. Abda Oglesby, C. S., justice of the peace.
5—Lola Jane Oglesby, m. Peyton McMullan. No issue.
5—Thomas Oglesby.
5—Leila Oglesby, m. James Chandler, sheriff of Elbert County.
6—Bertha Chandler, m. Leroy Mann.
6—Marie Chandler, m. A. N. Drake, Captain U. S. Army in American Expeditionary Forces World War, Major Georgia National Guard.
7—Mildred Drake.
6—Carswell Chandler.
5—Robert Eberhardt Oglesby, m. Azalee Herndon, d. 1937.
6—Robert Eberhardt "Bobby" Oglesby Jr.
5—Margaret Oglesby, m. D. B. Maxwell. No issue.
5—Elise Oglesby, m. Dr. Hitt.
3—Samuel Eberhardt.
3—Catherine Eberhardt, m. Mr. Gholston.
3—Margaret Eberhardt, m. Asa Deadwyler.
4—George Deadwyler, m. Mary Strickland.
5—Eula Deadwyler, m. W. C. Ash.
5—Harriet Deadwyler, m. C. E. Moore.
5—Pauline Deadwyler, m. J. D. Cox.
5—Asa Van Deadwyler, m. Lena Tidwell.
6—May Lillie Deadwyler, m. W. T. Cunningham.
7—W. T. Cunningham Jr.
7—Kathryn Cunningham.
7—Virginia Cunningham.
6—Kate D. Deadwyler.
6—Madeline Deadwyler.

6—Emily Jane Deadwyler, m. K. A. Stephenson.
5—George E. Deadwyler Jr., m. Lucile Kison.
5—M. P. Deadwyler, m. Rose Gorham.
5—John G. Deadwyler.
5—T. W. Deadwyler.
5—A. P. Deadwyler.
5—Mary P. Deadwyler.
4—Mary Ann Deadwyler, m. Miles Calloway.
5—Maggie Calloway.
5—Ida Calloway.
5—Willie Calloway, m. Larry Gantt. No issue.
4—Margaret Deadwyler, m. Drury P. Oglesby, C. S. Lieutenant.
5—Tommie Oglesby, m. Dr. B. A. Henry.
6—Louise Henry.
6—Marguerite Henry.
5—Alice Oglesby, m. H. J. Brewer, solicitor City Court of Elberton.
6—Herbert Brewer, d. unmarried.
6—Marguerite Brewer, m. H. H. Manley.
7—Mary Alice Manley.
7—Marguerite "Rita" Manley.
6—Julian Brewer.
5—Gussie Oglesby, m. William Fitzpatrick Jones, lieutenant-colonel Georgia National Guard, first captain and organizer Elberton Light Infantry, teacher, poet, author of Elberton County Men in World War, d. 1936.
5—Addie Oglesby, m. S. A. Hawes.
6—William Fitzpatrick Jones Jr., S. W. W. lieutenant, first lieutenant Georgia National Guard.
6—Drukell Jones, S. W. W., member Georgia House of Representatives.
6—Gussie Jones.
6—Adeline Jones.
6—Mozelle Jones.
6—John G. Jones, drowned 1931, unmarried.
3—Francis Eberhardt.
3—Elizabeth Eberhardt, m. John Winn.
3—Asinith (Cinnie) Eberhardt, m. James Griffith, b. Dec. 28, 1805.
3—George Eberhardt Jr., m. Sarah Adeline Griffith, b. Sept. 25, 1814.
3—Polly Eberhardt, m. Mr. Gilbert.
4—George Gilbert.
4—Isacc Gilbert.
4—James Gilbert.
3—Jacob Eberhardt, b. Aug. 23, 1797; d. Dec. 21, 1862; m. April 21, 1820, Elizabeth Winn, b. Oct. 27, 1802; d. May 3, 1843.
4—John Winn Eberhardt, b. Oct. 18, 1822; d. Dec. 19, 1886; m. 1842, Sarah Mourning Mattox, b. Jan. 22, 1827; d. Dec. 27, 1905.
5—Nathan Mattox Eberhardt, b. July 1, 1843; C. S., killed in action during War Between the States.
5—Jacob Eberhardt, C. S., b. Nov. 16, 1848; d. Aug. 1917, unmarried.
5—Mary Eberhardt, b. Aug. 10, 1860, m. 1890, J. W. Wright.
6—Sarah Ann Wright.
6—Mary Lizzie Wright.
5—William Harrison Eberhardt, b. Sept. 3, 1868; m. Lell Smith.
4—Margaret "Peggy" Eberhardt, b. Dec. 15, 1824; m. Mr. Griffith.
5—Jacob Griffith.
5—George Griffith.
5—Margaret Griffith.

5—Mattie Griffith.
4—William Eberhardt, b. Dec. 2, 1826; d. Dec. 1857.
4—George Eberhardt, b. Sept. 18, 1828; d. May 14, 1864, C. S.
4—Henry Eberhardt, b. 1830; d. 1834.
4—Mary Eberhardt, b. 1832; d. 1834.
4—Adeline Eberhardt, b. Jan. 5, 1834; d. 1935; m. Dr. Milton Pope Deadwyler. No issue.
4—Edward Eberhardt, b. Nov. 25, 1835.
4—Isaac Eberhardt, C. S., b. May 23, 1837; d. Dec. 22, 1863.
4—Harrison Eberhardt, C. S., b. Nov. 4, 1838, killed in action during War Between the States.
4—Jacob Eberhardt, C. S., b. Jan. 5, 1841; d. Jan. 23, 1910; m. Elizabeth Goolsby.
5—Harry Eberhardt, m. (1) Miss Power and (2) Beuna Fortson.
6—(By first wife) Clyde Eberhardt.
6—(By second wife) Jacob Eberhardt, S. W. W., lieutenant in American Expeditionary Forces, postmaster Carlton, Georgia.
6—Edward Harrison "Bill" Eberhardt, m. Margaret Hambrick.
5—Dr. L. P. Eberhardt, city physician of Elberton, county physician of Elbert County, m. (1) Agnes Hogan and (2) Willie Roberts.
6—(By first wife) Jacob Pope Eberhardt, M. D., m. Miss Woodruff.
5—Hamilton "Ham" Eberhardt m. Sarah Etta Huff.
5—Mattie Eberhardt, m. L. D. Mattox.
6—Elizabeth Jane Mattox, president Georgia Division Children of the Confederacy.
5—Elizabeth "Lizzie" Eberhardt, m. Mr. Carmichael.

EAVENSON

From the best information we have been able to gather, the name was derived first from EVAN-second, EVANS-third, EVANSON-fourth. EAVENSON (the latter two meaning the son of Evans.)

The Elbert County branch of EAVENSONS are descended from Ralph Eavenson of Wales, Great Britain (from his family Bible.)

The fifth generation, ELI, being the first to come to Georgia, during the 18th century; it has been handed down that he, his wife, son George and two daughters came from Virginia in a covered wagon, crossing the James river on ice. He was in the Revolutionary war, and the War of 1812. Was a saddlemaker and died in Elberton; buried near the old courthouse where Brown Brothers store now stands. His only son, George, had three sons, Willis, Thomas, and George. Willis was deacon in Vans Creek church, 1829, served as deacon till his death 1871, in Miss. He prayed God would give him one of his grandsons to preach; this prayer was answered three-fold in the persons of Joel Sturdivant, George Boon in Texas, and Ira Dennis, a missionary in Kaifeng, Honon China, all Baptist preachers. George II, who m. (1) Sarah Thornton (2) Frances Hunt, was a Methodist; farmer; was in Mexican War; served in Cherokee Disturbance in Capt. Bowman's Co., 1st Ga. Militia; was Confederate Soldier, Co. E., 4th Ga. Regt. Died 7-16-1898, buried Concord, Ga. Will recorded in Ordinary's' office, Elberton, Ga. In

"Eavenson-Strickland and Allied Families" we find his descendants as follows: 21 children, 96 grandchildren, 203 great grandchildren, 88 great-great grandchildren, 1 great-great-great grandchild. Most of these were born and raised in Elbert County, Georgia and lived on the farm, making good citizens, of a domestic, and docile dispositions, and family devotions, preferring these to the limelight. He had four sons in the Confederate Army: John William, Willis Jefferson, Thomas and George III, all in the 38th Ga. Regiment.

John Wm. m. (1) Lucy Brown, (2) Josephine Oglesby, died at the age of 95½. Served in the Army under Capt. John Thornton, in Jackson's Division, with General Robert E. Lee, Commander. In first and second battles of Manassas, was wounded in 2nd Fredericksburg fight, and disabled for field services; later was Capt. of Cavalry, helped hold Atlanta, and surrended at Macon, April 1865. Democrat, Methodist, farmer and merchant. Steward nearly forty years. Thomas was wounded in the War Between the States and died within 3 days. GeorgeIII died before reaching home from the War Between the States. Willis Jefferson was also Methodist (as was most of the Eavensons) m. (1) Arminda Teasley, (2) Emma Adams. Reached home from War Between the States safe, and raised a large family in Elbert County.

Among the thirteen Eavensons in the World War, six of them were descendants of (the 2nd) George Eavenson, and many others of his descendants were in the World War from maternal side, and not bearing the names of EAVENSON. His descendants are too numerous to mention in this limited space. They have moved into many of the states, and found in Paris and China.

Sexta Eavenson Strickland

(Note: Author of sketch: organ official, Geneologist, author of Allegiance to the Georgia Flag, and Historical Compilations.)

FORTSON

The following chart shows intermarriages with the following families:

Allen — Adams — Almond — Anderson — Ashworth — Arnold —Bunn — Brock — Bolton — Bryan — Brewer — Blanchard — Bond — Brownlee — Barnes — Bell — Brown — Black — Belknap — Boyd — Barksdale — Boyst — Baker — Barrow — Bellamy — Bridges — Butler — Broach — Barr — Bailey — Carpenter — Clark — Cole — Cooper — Carithers — Craft — Cox — Cook — Campbell — Carlton — Deadwyler — Doolittle — Eberhardt — Eiland — Edwards — Frye — Fitzpatrick — Gaines — Griffin — Green — Gabbett — Galloway — Gill — Goolsby — Ham — Harrison — Heard — Hudson — Hill — Hayes — Hightower — Harris — Hunt — Higginbotham — Horton — Hall — Hailey —Herndon — Hambrick — Irvin — Johnson — Keaton — King — Lombard — Landrum — Lane —Lyle — LeGear — Looney — McCrary — McCalla — McKenzie — McLanahan — Martin — Mashburn — Meaders — Menefree — Maxwell — Mealing — Mann — Moore — Mattox — Murray — Matthews — Neal — Nelson — Norman — O'Kelly — Oglesby — Oglivie — Orr — Orrison — Prewit — Phinizy — Peabody — Prettyman — Power — Palner — Rice — Reeves — Rich — Rouse — Smith — Stevens — Seegars — Snellings — Schreader — Seymour — Simms — Schmitzman — Sturgis — Stephens — Teasley — Turnell — Tate —Thornton —Travis — Turner — Toombs — Tompkins — Truitt — Taylor — Thigpen — Thrasher — Verner — Wester — Wall — White — Wright — Wooten — Ward — Wilkinson — Wilson — Willingham — Walton — Welborn — Wimberly — Walker — Webb — Willis — Walters — Yount.

Fortson Lineage from
THOMAS FORTSON

THOMAS FORTSON, SR.: (1) born abt. 1716, nothing is known of his birth or from whence he came; died in Caroline County, Va., in 1742; married abt. 1739, Mrs. Elizabeth (Winn?) Richards, widow of Ralph Richards; born abt. 1718; died in 1800, in either Spottsylvania or Orange Count, Va. They had two sons:
Children:
1. William Fortson: born abt. 1740.
2. Thomas Fortson, Jr.: of whom further.
(Ref.: Will Book 1741-1746, Caroline Co., Va., p. 158. Deed Book M, p. 218, Spottsville Co., Va., and Will Book F, same county, p. 163.)

THOMAS FORTSON, JR. (2): born May 1, 1742, in Caroline County, Va.; died Feb. 15, 1824, in Elbert County, Ga., age 81 yrs.; married abt. 1764, in Va., Caroline Co., Rachel Wynn, bort abt. 1744-46; died   , in Elbert Co., Ga., before her husband, she is not mentioned in his will. Daughter of Benjamin and Ann Winn, of Caroline Co., Va. (Records found certify her parentage almost positively as the above.)

Thomas Fortson moved to Elbert County, Ga., in 1792, with his wife and some of his children, where he bought land on Beaverdam Creek.

In Scott's History of Orange County, Va., we find that he was appointed a Lieutenant in the Revolutionary War, in 1780, page 262.

From "Public Claims of Orange County, Va.," he furnished supplies for Revolutionary Soldiers.

Thomas Fortson furnished 415 pounds of beef for the use of the Revolutionary Soldiers Oct. 18, 1781. Certification by Benj. Winslow, Dep. Clerk of Orange County.

May 28, 1784, Thomas Fortson furnished 490 pounds of Indian Meal to the Albermarle Barracks.

Dec. 6, 1780, John Thomas certified to Joseph Hawkins A. C. P. that Thomas Fortson furnished 400 pounds of beef for the Army.

(This can be used for his services for D. A. R. purposes.)

In 1782, Thomas Fortson lived in Orange County, Virginia, with a family of 8 whites and 6 servants.

In 1785, Thomas Fortson lived in above county, with a family of 9 whites. He is listed by Zach'y Burnley, in the first census of Virginia.

Thomas and Rachel (Wynn or Winn) Fortson had 6 children, all born in Caroline County, Va.

Children:
1. Benjamin Fortson: of whom further.
2. Elizabeth Fortson: b. 1767; m. Dr. William Gibbs.
3. William Fortson: b. abt. 1770.
4. Jesse Fortson: 1783-1827.
5. Millie (Mildred) Fortson: m. John Willis.
6. Richard Fortson: b. Feb. 6, 1778; d. Nov. 2, 1836.

BENJAMIN FORTSON (3): born in 1765; died in 1823; married (first) Dec. 28, 1790, in Va., Sally Head Heard; married (second) in 1797, Elizabeth Gains, daughter of a wealthy Va. planter. She inherited one sixth interest in a 3,000 acre tract of land situated in the state of Kentucky. He served in the War of 1812. He moved to Elbert County, Georgia. Elizabeth Gains Fortson died in 1846.

Children by 1st wife:
1. James Fortson: b. Dec. 22, 1791.
2. John Fortson: b. Feb. 12, 1794; d. Dec. 6, 1860.

Children by 2nd. wife, Elizabeth Gains:
3. Easton Fortson: of whom further.
4. Sarah (Sallie) Fortson: b. Mar. 30, 1800.
5. Thomas Fortson: b. Feb. 2, 1802.
6. Maud (Nancy) Fortson: b.   ; d. while a girl.
7. Mahaleth Fortson: b. Apr. 30, 1806; d. Jan. 6, 1882.
8. Rachel Fortson: b. May 15, 1808.
9. Elizabeth A. Fortson: b. Nov. 1, 1810; d. May 26, 1839.
10. Richard Fortson: b. Jan. 2, 1813.
11. Benjamin G. Fortson: b. July 6, 1815.
12. Amanda M. Fortson: b. Aug. 19, 1817; d. Aug. 6, 1898.

(Ref.: Family Data.)

EASTON FORTSON (4): born June 4, 1798; died July 19, 1851, age 53; married (first) Dec. 26, 1819, in Elbert Co., Ga. TABITHA (Tabby) HALEY, born in 1801; died in 1828, age 27; daughter of Wm. Haley (b. Aug. 27, 1784), of the historic Haley family. (He served in Revolutionary War from Mechlenburg Co., Va. He was born in Delaware and died in Georgia, Nov. 1830. Her mother was Mary Turman, of Virginia (b. 1744; d. 1838; m. 1779.)

Hanna says, "Hayleys were in Amaugh and Antrim Counties, Ireland, and placed there by James 1, purposely to form a Protestant settlement in Romas Catholic Ireland, and thus infuse a more progressive spirit among the people, which was successful, and the north of Ireland today is the center of Irish endeavor."

O'Hart says, he has traced the Haleys back through the Irish

Kings, to King Milenus, to the Spanish Prince who conquered Ireland in the remote ages, and that the name, HAYLEY, is purely old English. Irish being called Hibernium because they came from the Hibernium Peninsular. He gives the name of several Irish soldiers who fought in the Spanish Wars in 1700. Don Francisco and Don Guillermo Haley (O'Hart says) fought in the Spanish Wars in 1700.

Bontell's Hand Book of English Heraldry says, that the Coat-of-Arms are the Lion and Boers heads, which show kingly origin. He says in English Rolls of Arms the Lion is the only animal that is found in Blason with the sole addition of the Boers head, and the Haley Arms has both. Bontell says, this shows a fine and exceedingly old Blason, being one of the most ancient.

The pioneer of the Haley Family of America was JAMES HALEY, the father of WILLIAM HALEY, Revolutionary Soldier, from whom the children of Easton and Tabitha (Haley) Fortson descended.

Easton Fortson married (second) Feb. 10, 1831, SUSAN HAM, born Nov. 12, 1803; died Aug. 17, 1866.

Easton Fortson was a learned man and one of the foremost men of this section of the state. He was a large land and slave holder and successful business man. He took an interest in the advancement of his country and was a moving spirit in all laudable enterprises. Brave and fearless, he was of great service to the early settlers in the Indian War.

Children: by first marriage:
1. Haley Fortson: b. May 28, 1821; d. Aug. 11, 1898.
2. Benjamin Fortson: b. Oct. 31, 1823; d. Mar. 7, 1896.
3. Thomas Jefferson Fortson: of whom further.
4. George Green Fortson: b. May 9, 1828; d. July 5, 1912.

Children by second marriage:
5. Elizabeth Ann Fortson: b. Feb. 15, 1833; d. June 3, 1883.
6. John Easton Fortson: b. Mar. 17, 1835; d. unmarried.
7. Stephen Ham Fortson: b. Oct. 19, 1836; d. April 13, 1916.

THOMAS JEFFERSON FORTSON (5): son of Easton and Tabitha (Haley) Fortson, was born Oct. 9, 1825, at Elbert Co., Ga.; died April 10, 1881, in Elbert Co., Ga., buried in City Cemetery in Elberton, Ga.; married April 21, 1851, at Elbert Co., Ga., SUSAN REBECCA SNELLING, born July 10, 1830, at Elbert Co., Ga.; died Jan. 19, 1908, age 77 yrs., buried in City Cemetery, Elberton, Ga.; daughter of Samuel and Elizabeth Neil (Burton) Snelling, and granddaughter of George Snelling, a Revolutionary Soldier. They were Virginians, later making their home in Georgia. Sam'l Snelling was a true "Southern Gentleman" and a large land and slave holder.

The name SNELLING is of Anglo Saxon origin, meaning quick, active, bold, brave, and is variously written—Snelling, Snelline, Snellinge, Snellen. It was in use before the Norman Conquest, in the early part of the 6th century, about 1700. It is found in the Dooms Day Book, 1085-86. This was a statistical survey of that part of England then under the sway of William the Conqderor. The word Dooms, at that time, meaning Judgement, etc., as applied to the proper owning of land estates. The crest is a demi-eagle displayed argent. (—Information given in Heraldic Journal 2 1886-10 1.) (Genealogical Dictionary — Savaga—Lib. (4) 137.) (Strongs Genealogy, page 631.) All the above to be found in the Virginia State Library.) The German branch as well as the Holland family spell the name as Snellincks. One of this name, Jan Snellincks (1544-1638) being a celebrated Dutch painter.

The English family. The most ancient Charitable bequest to the poor of Guilford, Eng. was made by Joann Snellinge, daughter of William Snellinge Esq. of Guilford, Eng. She married John Austin Esq. of Shelford. (Burk's Com. of Great Britain, Vol. 1, p. 465. Ralph Snellinge, Esq. of Oxford, m. Althea, daughter of Sir Edward Drake, Bart of Bendall, in 1671 (Burk.) Mary Snellinge m. William Martin, Jan. 19, 1699. Recording as living in the parish of Compton (Surrey Register Charter House Chapel). Erasmus Snellinge of London, applied to the Virginia Company for certain settlements in Virginia, under date of June 26, 1623. (Record of Virginia Colony, Vol. 1.)

The American Family. The Parish Register of Christ Church, Barbadoes Island, under date of Jan. 7, 1678, records the baptism of John, infant son of Robt. and Anne Snelling. Robert Snelling's name also occurs in the tax list.

The Virginia Family. John Snellinge with Major Broomfield, was awarded eleven hundred acres of land by Samuel Mathews, Esq., for transportation of 22 persons to the colony in 1651. (Land Office, Vol. 4, p. 169.)

1. William Snelling, mentioned as being granted land in Gloucester Co., Oct. 11, 1659. On his death he left this land to his son, Alexander.

2. Alexander (L.) Snelling (son of William) deed land by his father on April 7, 1670. Land being in Gloucester Co. (Land Office, Vol. 6, p. 515.) He had son, Aquilla (1) and 2 daughters. Sara (m. Dec. 30, 1708) and Priscilla (m. Wm. Tigwell, April 30, 1708. Christ Church Records.) Samuel Snelling is a lineal descendant of the Snelling family.

Thomas Jefferson Fortson was a Confederate Soldier of Elbert Co., Ga. He was a Lieutenant in Company H, of 3rd Georgia Volunteers, commanded by Capt. Clark H. Matton. He was wounded in the head in the Battle at Honey-Hill. Company H belonged to Toombs Regiment.

Seven children were born to Thomas Jefferson and Susan Rebecca (Snelling) Fortson.

Children:
1. Mary Elizabeth Fortson: b. 1854-1935, of whom further.
2. Georgia Ann Fortson: b.
3. Son born asleep: b.
4. Susan Rebecca Fortson: b.
5. Thomas Samuel Fortson: b. July 20, 1863; d. Nov. 7, 1911.
6. Gertrude Fortson: b.
7. Vester Fortson: b.

(Ref.: Family data.)

Lucile Mathews Herndon (Mrs. H.), Genealogist

GOOLSBY

Wood's History of Albermarle Co., p. 211, the following account of the GOOLSBY family is given: "Thomas Goolsby was one of the earliest settlers of Albemarle Co., Va. He located there in 1732, thirteen years before the county was organized. He took out a Crown Grant for 1,200 acres on the James River, (this location would suggest that it was in that part of Fluvanna or Goochland Co. that became Albermarle later). In 1745 he sold 500 acres to S. Shelton on the tributaries of the James River, called Holman's & Goolsby Creeks. The first deed of record was destroyed by the depredations of the British Army. Thos. Goolsby died in 1774. He married twice. The name of his first wife is not recorded. His second wife was Lucy Bryant. Wood's does not mention her parents. The issue by the Bryant marriage were: William; Thomas; Susan, Mrs. Childress; Ann, Mrs. Nowlin; Lucy, Mrs. Saunders; Elizabeth.

Wm. Goolsby owned lands on the headwaters of the Hardware River in Albemarle. He died in 1819. His children were: William; (Wm. Goolsby Jr. settled in Georgia. See David Carter); Tabitha, wife of Jos. Harlan; Tarlton, who married MILDRED, daughter of THOS. WALKER; Sarah, who married a Mr. Thurmon; Susan, Mrs. Davis; Fleming; Jane, who married Mr. S. Harlan; Arthur; Mary, Mrs. Sam Richardson; Nancy, Mrs. Phillips.

Chas., James and John Goolsby were all three in Army of the Revolution and were in the 9th Va. Charles was a non-commission officer. He and James were prisoners at Germantown, Penn. All three died in the service of their country. They were beyond doubt sons of Thos. Goolsby, Sr., as William was stated to have been their heir.

Benj. Harrison of "Wakefield," Surry Co., Va., married 23 Aug., 1739, Susannah, daughter of Hon. Cole Digges. Their 4th child was Nathaniel, b. 24 Aug. 1744. A sister of his was Ludwell (or Eliz. Ludwell) who was "born on a Tuesday about ½ hour after 11 in the evening, decrease of the moon. Baptised by the Rev. Mr. Finney, 31 Dec., 1754.

Wm. Goosley or Goolsby (the le is printed in places as b) married Ludwell Harrison, daughter of Benjamin Harrison (of the

Presidential Harrison's), 16 Jan., 1773. They had: Anne, dy; George, b. 5 May, 1780; Lucy, b. 30 March, 1782; Frances, b. 29 Dec., 1783, baptized by the Rev. Mr. Andrews; Sarah Cary, b. 5 Feb., 1790, bapt. by the Rev. Mr. Shield; Anne, b. 15 Sept., 1794; Cary, b. 21 Aug., 1797, dy; Susan, b. 29 Aug., 1799; Aug. 22nd. "My d'r son George Goosley (Goosby evidently meant) was lost on his way to Charleston, 1806. On Dec. 31, 1809, died my beloved husband, Wm. Goosby, of York Co., Va."

These notes were taken from the family bible of Wm. Goosby. This book was "presented to Jas. Brown McCaw, M. D., eldest son of Anne Ludwell Brown who married Dr. Wm. R. McCaw, eldest grandson of Frances Goosby, wife of James Brown, Jr., g-g-son of Ludwell Harrison, wife of Wm. Goosby, of York Co., g-g-g-son of Benj. Harrison, Esq., of "Wakefield," by his g-aunt Susan Campbell, child of Ludwell Harrison."

Further confirmation, see v. 7, Wm. & Mary, 1st Series, pp. 39-40.

In the U. S. Census, 1780-1790, the first that has been published, note the following:

James Goolsbey had a family of 4 in Amherst Co.; Martha, 3.; Wm. Sr. family of 8; 1 residence and 4 other bldgs; Thomas, family of 6, 1 residence and 5 other bldgs.

Arms—Azure, a cross patonce Argent.

—Compiled by D. A. R.

HAILEY OR HALEY

The following chart shows intermarriages with the following families:
Abney — Adams — Allen — Anderson — Black — Bolton — Brock — Brown — Cash — Clark — Cleveland — Cloud — Cole — Cooper — Covan — Fortson — Frye — Gaines — Greenway — Gray — Ham — Hanson — Haroway — Hayes — Herndon — Hood — Harkness — Johnston — Jones — Kidd — Lindsey — Mashburn — Matthews — Maxwell — Murray — McClure — McEwen — McMullan — Prather — Rucker — Sheland — Smith — Snellings — Snow — Taylor — Teasley — Terrell — Tinsley — Turman — Turnell — Underwood — Wall — Wester — Ward — Yoles.

(Note: Numbers represent generations, as: (1) first generation, (2) second generation, (3) third generation, etc)

   1—James Hailey came to America, 1712 and settled in Delaware. Will probated in Wilmington, Delaware, m. Ann Elnora Cloud.
      2—Mary Hailey, m. William Haraway.
      2—Isham Hailey.
      2—William Hailey, R. S., d. Nov. 24, 1830; m. Oct. 10, 1779, Mary Truman, b. Oct. 15, 1744, d. Aug. 19, 1838.
         3—James Hailey, b. 1780; m. Miss Johnston.
         3—Reuben Hailey, m. (1) Sarah Ward and (2) Mary Yoles.
            4—(By first wife) William Rabun Hailey, m. Sarah Ann Gaines.

5—James, C. S., b. 1840, d. 1861.
5—George Hailey, b. 1843.
5—H. F. Hailey, b. Sept. 25, 1845, d. Feb. 18, 1920; m. 1869, Laura Cornelia Brown.
5—A. C. Hailey.
5—Sally Hailey.
5—Nancy Hailey.
4—Reuben Hailey, m. Milly Ann Greenway.
4—Christine Hailey, m. Mr. Teasley.
4—Mattie Hailey, m. Mr. Lindsay.
4—Eleanor Hailey, b. Nov. 25, 1816; m. Mr. Abney.
4—Nancy Hailey, d., unmarried.
4—(By second wife) Willis Hailey, m. Mary Taylor.
5—Frank Hailey.
5—John W. Hailey.
5—S. N. Hailey, sheriff of Elbert County 1909-1916, d. 1916; m.
6—Marvin Hailey.
6—Jack Hailey, sheriff of Elbert County, m. Lucile Carpenter. No issue.
6—Ruth Hailey.
6—Joe Hailey.
6—Idell Hailey, m. I. V. Hulme.
5—George W. Hailey and other issue.
4—Other children by second marriage whose names are unavailable.
3—John Hailey, d. March 25, 1857; m. Jan. 5, 1809, Polly Underwood, d. March 10, 1856.
4—Penia Hailey, b. July 10, 1810; m. Dec. 20, 1827, James Madison Cleveland, b. May 14, 1808.
4—Hattie Hailey, m. Lins Ward.
4—Diadem Hailey, b. 1813; m. Frank Gaines.
4—Polly Hailey, b. 1814; m. Peter Rucker.
4—Malinda Hailey, b. 1816; m. John Terrell.
4—Betsy Hailey, b. 1818; m. Patrick McMullan.
4—Nancy Hailey, m. Winton Adams.
3—Thomas Hailey, d. unmarried.
3—William Hailey, d. unmarried.
3—Tabitha Hailey, m. Dec. 25, 1819, Easton Fortson, b. June 4, 1798, d. July 19, 1851.
4—Benjamin Fortson, m. (1) Martha Ham and (2) Mary Jones.
5—Sarah Fortson, m. William Murray.
5—Thomas Fortson, m. Adele Jones.
5—Benjamin Fortson Jr., m. Marie Covan.
4—Hailey Fortson, b. May 24, 1821, d. Aug. 11, 1898; m. (1) Jan. 13, 1842, Elizabeth Hanson, b. June 22, 1819, d. Jan. 25, 1853, (2) Elizabeth Prather, b. March 17, 1829, d. July 20, 1871, and (3) Alice L. McEwen, b. April 13, 1851, d. Aug. 13, 1883.
5—(By first wife) John Hanson Fortson, d. infancy.
5—William W. Fortson, b. March 2, 1843.
5—Easton L. Fortson, b. May 2, 1844.
5—Eleanor A. Fortson, b. May 25, 1848; m. Reverend James N. Wall, Methodist minister, member Georgia House of Representatives, county school commissioner of Elbert County.
6—Elizabeth Wall, m. James Rucker.
6—William Wall, m. (1) Miss Parrot and (2) Mrs. Black.
6—Walter Wall.
6—James Wall.
6—Anna C. Wall.
6—George Wall, m. Leo Maxwell.
7—John Wall.

7—James Wall.
7—Mary Eleanor Wall.
6—Sarah Wall.
6—Lonstreet Wall, m. Miss Frierson.
6—Lula Wall.
6—Janie Wall.
6—Harry Wall.
5—George T. Fortson, b. Aug. 1, 1850, d. May 19, 1918; m. Tallulah Hill Sheland.
6—Elizabeth Fortson, m. Z. C. Hayes, president of Elberton Loan and Savings Bank.
7—Hanson Hayes.
6—Pauline Fortson.
6—Lovic Fortson.
6—Ellie Fortson.
6—W. H. Fortson.
5—Milliard F. Fortson, b. April 13, 1852; m. Elizabeth Gray.
5—(By second wife) Elizabeth M. Fortson, b. 1855, d. 1858.
5—Stephen Fortson, d. infancy.
5—Mary Nancy Fortson, b. March 22, 1859; m. James Harkness.
5—Robert E. Fortson, b. Nov. 17, 1860.
5—Lillie L. Fortson, b. March 3, 1863.
5—(By third wife) Mary M. Fortson, b. April 14, 1876.
5—Eugene B. Fortson, b. Jan. 21, 1878.
5—Albert S. Fortson, b. Nov. 29, 1879.
5—Lucien Fortson, b. 1881, d. 1883.
5—Alice L. Fortson, b. Oct. 3, 1883.
4—Thomas Jefferson Fortson, b. Oct. 9, 1825, d. April 10, 1881; m. April 21, 1851, Susan Rebecca Snellings, b. July 10, 1830, d. Jan. 19, 1908.
5—Mary Elizabeth Fortson, m. Nov. 21, 1872, James Edward Herndon, d. March 6, 1906.
6—George Lee Herndon, b. Jan. 19, 1874; m. April 25, 1905, Margaret Deadwyler. No issue.
6—Charles Fortson Herndon, druggist, member board of education of Elberton; m. April 3, 1908, Annie Mashburn.
7—Elizabeth Herndon, d. infancy.
7—Charles Fortson Herndon Jr.
7—Annie Josephine Herndon.
7—John Edward Herndon.
7—Dorothy Herndon.
6—Marvin S. Herndon, b. June 18, 1878; m. Nov. 4, 1909, Clara Taylor.
7—James Edward Herndon.
7—Sarah Elizabeth Herndon.
7—Helen Herndon.
6—Harry H. Herndon, b. November 23, 1881, d. Dec 29, 1928; m. Dec. 14, 1905, Lucile Matthews.
7—Thelma Herndon.
6—Julian Herndon, b. Feb. 5, 1887; m. Jane Ann Hood.
7—Julian Herndon Jr.
6—Fred Herndon, contractor, member city council of Elberton, b.Sept. 16, 1890; m. (1) April 23, 1913, Matilde Smith and (2) May 15, 1922, Mary Helen Smith, sister of deceased wife.
7—(By first wife) Marjorie Herndon and Virginia Herndon. Twins.
—(By second wife) Minor Herndon.
5—Georgia Ann Fortson, m. Feb. 17, 1880, Andrew J. Teasley, d. July 22, 1923.
6—Bertha Thomas Teasley, m. March 2, 1907, J. W. Cooper, d. 1929.

7—Corinne Cooper, m. March 1926, Carl Cole.
8—Helen Cole, b. June 12, 1927.
8—Rosalyn Cole, b. May 29, 1928.
5—Susie Rebecca Fortson, m. (1) Dec. 9, 1891, George Michael Herndon, d. April 17, 1893 and (2) J. M. Wester, mayor of Elberton, railroad official.
6—(By first husband). Infant died.
6—(By second husband). Thomas Fortson Wester, b. June 10, 1905; m. Jan. 20, 1937, Mary Maxwell.
7—Susan Wester, b. 1938.
7—Thomas Fortson Wester Jr., B. 1939.
5—Vesta Fortson, m. Jan. 9, 1900, Joseph Henry Turnell, d. 1914.
6—Vesta Fortson Turnell, m. Oct. 4, 1921, John Lee Wester.
7—Vesta Fortson Wester and Jacquelyn Wester. Twins, b. April 15, 1925.
7—John Lee Wester Jr., b. Oct. 9, 1927.
5—Thomas Samuel Fortson, d. 1911, unmarried.
5—Gertrude Fortson. Unmarried.
4—George Green Fortson, b. May 9, 1828, d. July 15, 1912; m. April 9, 1852, Louisa S. Wall, b. Jan. 26, 1836, d. July 17, 1893.
5—Wilton G. Fortson, b. Oct. 3, 1853, d. Feb. 1927; m. Mary Barksdale nee Clark. No issue.
5—Martha Wall Fortson, b. Sept. 9, 1856, d. Aug. 1903; m. Dec. 1876, James Murray.
5—Lawrence B. Fortson, b. 1853, d. 1880.
5—George Hailey Fortson, captain Spanish-American War, lawyer, killed in action March 27, 1896, b. Oct. 19, 1860; m. Minnie Frye.
5—Louisa Elizabeth Fortson, b. 1863, d. 1880.
5—Francis B. Fortson, member Elbert County Board of Education, planter, merchant; m. Alice Brock.
5—Fannie Fortson, d. unmarried.
5—Sallie A. Fortson, b. May 13, 1872; m. Nov. 6, 1898, Claud D. Bolton.
5—Minnie Nunnelee Fortson, b. June 19, 1875; m. Oct. 31, 1895, Albert Anderson, d. 1932. No issue.
3—Ritta Hailey, m. Mr. Adams.
3—Mary Hailey, m. Mr. Adams.
3—Betsy Hailey, m. Mr. Cash.
3—Betsy (?) Hailey, m. Beverly Teasley.
3—Lucy Hailey, b. Sept. 21, 1804, d. Jan. 1, 1859; m. Oct. 31, 1822, Benager Teasley, b. Feb. 27, 1802, d. Nov. 1, 1836.
4—Elizabeth Ann Teasley, b. November 18, 1823, d. March 13, 1869; m. June 30, 1839, Roland J. Brown, b. March 11, 1816, d. Aug. 1, 1894.
5—Benager Teasley Brown, C. S., b. 1841, d. 1862.
5—John A. Brown, C. S., b. 1843; m. Phronie Teasley.
5—Isham Hailey Brown, C. S., b. May 24, 1846; m. (1) Emily Eliza Teasley. No issue. m. (2) Ann Eliza Hailey, b. Nov. 30, 1847, d. 1914.
5—Laura Cornelia Brown, b. Aug. 10, 1850; m. Sept. 2, 1869, Henry F. Hailey, son of William Rabun Hailey and Sarah Ann Gaines.)
6—Dr. W. I. Hailey, b. June 20, 1870; m. Feb. 1894, Mertis Snow.
7—John Henry Hailey, b. 1895; m. Addie Kidd.
7—Rucker Marion Hailey.
7—Dr. William Howard Hailey, m. Helen McClure.
7—Isham Brown Hailey, m. Grace Allen.
7—Joel S. Hailey, d. 1929.

7—Frank Elmore Hailey.
7—Lamar Rankin Hailey.
7—Dr. Hugh Rankin Hailey.
6—Ten additional children whose names are unavailable.

CARLTON AND HALL

Daniel Milton Carlton, son of Thomas Carlton and Ruth Burch Carlton, was born in Wilkes County, N. C., Sept. 28, 1823. He married Mary Louise Steele. They came to Elbert county, Ga., to make their home in 1849. They settled two and one half miles east of Elberton, where he lived until he died July 31, 1894. To this union was born four children, namely: Anne, Thomas C., Sallie, and James M. During the Civil War he served in Co. H., 3rd Reg., Ga. Militia. In 1863 his wife died, and he obtained a furlough to go home and be with his motherless children. In May, 1864, he married Nancy Brown, granddaughter of the Revolutionary Soldier, Benjamin Brown, and daughter of Elbert Brown and Mary McCurry Brown. After he married he returned to the war and remained until it closed. He fought in the battle of Atlanta, Jonesboro, and other battles. He was one of the most progressive farmers of his day in Elbert County. He was always trying to help his community. He contributed largely to the building of the Elberton Airline Railroad. which was built from Toccoa to Elberton in 1878. He also gave the right of way to the Seaboard R. R. through his plantation. He was a member of the Falling Creek Baptist Church, but realized the town of Elberton needed a Baptist Church, so he gave time and money to help build the first Baptist Church in Elberton.

There were ten children born to him and his last wife as follows: the first died in infancy, Elbert, John B., Benjamin Harvey, Mary, Welborn Chaudoin, Lela, Pope, Charlie C., and Zora.

Anne married B. T. Herndon. Sallie married Thomas F. Willis. Thomas C. graduated at the University of Ga. in 1875. He married Mary, daughter of Mr. and Mrs. J. Lawrence Heard. He taught school and practiced law for a few years and then entered the Baptist ministry, and was pastor of churches at Newnan, Ga., Slater, Mo., St. Louis, Mo., and Oklahoma City.

James M. graduated at the Medical College in Augusta, Ga., and practiced medicine in Mount Carmel, S. C. He married Minnie, daughter of Mr. an dMrs. Thomas C. Burch.

Elbert and Pope died when boys in their teens.

John B. completed a course in telegraphy and went to south Ga. to work, where he married ELLA BELL MORRISON, and went into the turpentine business.

Benjamin Harvey graduated at the Medical College in Augusta, Ga., and practiced medicine for forty years in Donalds, S. C. He married Annie Lou Tufts.

Mary taught school in Elbert Co. for a number of years, then married J. M. German and went to Wilkes Co., N. C. to live.

Welborn Chaudoin graduated at Mercer University, and received his Master's degree from the State University, at Athens. Among the schools W. C. taught are: Bessie Tift College, A. & M. at Cochran, Piedmont at Waycross, Brenau, at Gainesville, Cox College, College Park. He is now teaching in Marsh's Business College, Atlanta. He married Florence Grace.

Charlie C. graduated at Mercer University and has taught in the public schools of Ga. and Tenn He married Lessie Cofer.

Lela first married Rev. H. M. Adams of Wilkes Co., Ga. After his death she married George J. Hall. To this union was born George Milton Hall, who attended Erskine College and Emory University.

Zora is teaching in the Elberton Public Schools, where she has taught for twenty four years. She is the Principal of Stevens school.

George J. Hall was the grandson of John P. Hall and Maria Turman Hall, and the son of James C. Hall and Mary Loftis Hall. James C. was First Lieutenant in the Civil War, and died for the Confederate cause in Lynchburg, Va., in 1862. His other children are: Emma, who married Asa Maley. They went to Elk City, Okla., where they died.

Louise Catherine (Lutie) married Asa C. Fortson. They lived in Elbert Co. until Asa died. After that Louise went to Atlanta where she lived the remainder of her life.

John W. went to Oklahoma, married and died there.

Sara married George B. Conwell. They lived and died in Elbert County.

George J. first married Lizzie, daughter of Mr. and Mrs. R. E. Adams. To this union was born James E., John Will, Lila, Annie, and Sara.

George J.'s second wife was Mrs. Lela Adams, daughter of Mr and Mrs. D. M. Carlton. George Milton Hall was born to this union

George J. Hall died July 5, 1931.

HAMMOND

(Note: Numbers represent generations, as: (1) first generation, (2) second generation, (3) third generation, etc)

1—Job Hammond, m. 1645, d. 1718; m. Elizabeth (?).
  2—Job Hammond Jr., b. 1667; m. Amandine (?).
    3—Thomas Hammond, m. Mary Heath.
    3—Susannah Hammond.
    3—Elizabeth Hammond.
    3—Mary Mammond.
    3—Amandine Hammond.
    3—Samuel Hammond, b. 1722, R. S. Captain, m. Mary Jenkins.
      4—Job Hammond, R. S., b. 1750, d. 1822; m. Lucy Howard, daughter of John Howard, b. 1700, d. 1765 and Lucy Davis. Granddaughter of Cornelius Howard, b. 1664, d. 1716 and Mary Hammond who was the daughter of Thomas Hammond and Mary eaH hG.t reat granddaughter of Cornelius Howard Sr., b. 1630, d. 1680; great-great granddaughter of Matthew Howard, b. 1600, d. 1650.
        5—Job Hammond Jr., grandfather of Nathaniel Hammond, M. C.
        5—William Hammond.
        5—Dudley Hammond.
        5—Samuel Jenkins Hammond.
        5—John Hammond.
        5—Lucy Hammond, m. May 8, 1806, Richard Worrell.
        5—Elizabeth Hammond.
        5—Herbert Hammond, m. Jan. 7, 1821, Elizabeth Rich.
        5—Major Alfred Hammond, m. Jan. 24, 1826, Louisa Hudson, b. 1808, d. 1833, daughter of Nathaniel Hudson, R. S., b. 1750 and Mary Carroll, who was the daughter of John Carroll, b. 1760, d. 1820.
          6—William Hammond, m. Miss Blount.
          6—Lavonia Hammond, b. March 13, 1827, d. Dec. 27, 1909; m. Dec. 9, 1843, John Henry Jones, b. Oct. 11, 1816, d. Sept. 23, 1899.
            7—Thomas Jones, C. S., b. 1844, d. 1923, postmaster of Elberton. Unmarried.
            7—Louisa Jones, b. April 24, 1846, d. Sept. 23, 1910; m. April 19, 1864, Robert M. Heard, C. S. Captain, mayor of Elberton, member Georgia House of Representatives.
              8—John T. Heard, merchant, d. 1932, unmarried.
              8—Carroll Heard, unmarried.
              8—Vohammie Heard, m. Marcus A. Pharr.
                9—Marcus A. Pharr Jr., S. W. W. Lieutenant, killed accidentally in 1918. Unmarried.
                9—Robert Pharr.
                9—Camilla Pharr, m. G. D. Barnett.
                  10—Aurelius Barnett.
                  10—Camilla Barnett.
                  10—Ida Barnett.
                  10—Vohammie Barnett.
                9—Mittie Pharr.
                9—Louise Pharr, m. H. C. Sparks.
                  10—Louise Sparks.
                  10—H. C. Sparks Jr.
                9—Vohammie Pharr, m. J. C. Carr.
                  10—J. C. Carr Jr.

Luther Martin Heard, president Citizens Bank of Elberton, m. Mamie Lattimer, daughter of United States Senator Lattimer of South Carolina.

9—Luther Martin Heard Jr.
9—Latimer Heard.
9—Robert Heard.
8—Georgia Heard, m. Dr. J. E. Johnson.
9—J. E. Johnson Jr., m. Marie Williams.
10—J. E. Johnson III.
8—Parks E. Heard. Unmarried.
8—Roberta Heard, m. John T. Dennis Jr. Mayor of Elberton. No issue.
7—Ida Jones, b. Feb. 19, 1848, d. 1931; m. Feb. 1, 1870, James J. Burch, C. S. Captain, ordinary of Elbert ounty, member Georgia House of Representatives.
8—Irene Burch, m. James Balchin. No issue.
8—Janet Burch, m. Samuel Shiver.
9—Samuel Shiver Jr., Professor of German. Emory College.
8—William J. Burch, m. Mrs. ———.
8—Hammond Burch, m. (1) Charles Shipman and (2) Jack Flemming.
9—(By first husband) Charles Shipman Jr.
9—(By second husband) Jack Flemming Jr.
7—Georgia Jones.
7—Mary Jones, b. Oct. 10, 1851; m. 1874, T. J. Blackwell.
8—Jones Blackwell.
8—Banks Blackwell.
8—Fred Blackwell.
8—Daisy Blackwell, m. Dr. W. T. Shannon.
8—Wenona Blackwell, m. 1911, Thomas Hewlett.
7—Lavonia Jones, b. Feb. 12, 1854; m. Harry K. Gairdner.
8—Jamie Gairdner. Unmarried.
7—Lenora Jones. Unmarried.
7—William Oscar Jones, mayor of Elberton, member city council of Elberton, chairman Elberton Board of Education, president Bank of Elberton, b. Sept. 11, 1861, d. 1931; m. Jan. 25, 1893, Molly Gairdner.
8—Margaret Jones, d. unmarried.
8—William Oscar Jones Jr., d. infancy.
8—Margaret Jones, m. Thomas Colley.
9—William Colley.
9—Thomas Colley Jr.
8—John Henry Jones, m. Lois McKnight.
9—William Oscar Jones, b. 1931.
8—Mitta Byrd Jones.
8—Mamie Jones.
4—Raleigh Hammond.
4—Samuel Hammond.
4—Charlotte Hammond.
3—Jarvis Hammond.
3—Job Hammond III.

WILLIAM HANSARD

The Hansford or Hansard family trace their name to the Hanse League formed in London during the thirteenth century for the protection and control of the trade of England and the continent. For several centuries the family of this name has been scribes to the King, the position being handed down from father to son or one generation to the next.

From the best information it is altogether probable that the

Hansfords of this line came by way of Thomas Hansford of Bacon's Rebellion. (The family name is spelled both ways, Hansford or Hansard.)

Col. John Hansford—wife Elizabeth (who later married Edward Lockey.) His will made in York County, Virginia in 1654, probated 1661.

Capt. Charles Hansford was a brother of Col. Thomas Hansford of Bacon's Rebellion who has been called the first native martyr of American Liberty.

Capt. William Hansford, born in York Co., Va., lived in Spotsylvania County, Va. Will made in Culpepper Co., Va. in 1750, probated in 1754. His wife, Sarah Sallis, widow of Alex Donephen, daughter of Samuel Sallis. In the will of this Capt. William Hansford he mentions a daughter who m. Nicholas Porter. Sons: William Sallis who married Lucy   and died in Culpepper Co., Va., 1764; Charles whose will was made in Orange Co., Va., 1761; and a son, John. Also daughter, Ann, who m. Thomas Finnell and a grandson, Benonni (who evidently was a son of John) was born in Virginia. His first child, Charles P. Hansford, was born in Virginia in 1776. Benonni or Benjamin was commissioned Lieut. in Va. Militia 1777 and 1778. His wife was Grace   . He lived in Va. until 1790 when he moved to Wilkes County, Georgia. He drew a land grant in the Creek Indian lottery in 1802. William Hansford (oldest son of Capt. William of York Co., Va.) and born in 1774, and died in Elbert County, Georgia. Will made in 1790, probated in 1798 in Elberton, Georgia. In this will is mentioned sons: William, Jessie, Brown, John, and Thomas Scott. Daughters mentioned but not named; one granddaughter, Chancey Hansard. He and James Moss (for whom Moss 196 Militia District is named) drilled the militia in this district. William Hansard, son of William Hansard, born in Elbert County, Georgia, 1768. Married   Fannin of Elbert County, Ga., daughter of Benjamin Fannin. This William Hansard was killed by being thrown from a spirited horse. He had two sons; James and William Patrick. Six daughters, Polly, who never married; Sallie, m. John H. Shackleford and moved to Alabama; Janet, m. Patrick Butler Jr.; Elizabeth, m. James Butler; Amie, m. James Faulkner; Nancy, m. Michael Dennard. James Hansford, son of said William Hansard, m. Phoebie Hardee; their children are: William, Marion, Jim, Asa, Mary, Jethro, Ben, Sarah, Martha, Eliza, and Joel.

His other son, William Patrick, m. Lucinda Hardee; their children are: Mary Jane who m. Singleton Johnson; William James was killed on battle field in Va. during the Civil War. Jeptha Riley who served for four years in the Civil War m. Mary Frances White.

Patrick Henry, who also served in Civil War, m. Louanna Thornton first, then Viletta Hall; Sarah Lucinda m. Crunly Adams. Susan Leanna died in childhood. Eugenia m. W. H. H. Walton. Mildred

m. William S. Hall. Martha Alvera m. Milford Adams. Elizabeth died in childhood. Georgianna Stephens m. William Dennard.

The children of Jeptha Riley and Mary Frances White are: Henry Sigman, Robert White, Mary Ann, Tallie Hassie, Sarah Frances, Eliza, Eugenia Elmira, Eunice Lois, Sam Jones and James Riley, all born and reared in Elbert County, Georgia.

The children of Patrick Henry Hansard are: sons, Simeon Hall, Patrick and Jeptha. Daughters are Serepta and Ida.

Jeptha Riley Hansard is buried in the cemetery at Harmony Baptist Church in Elbert County, Georgia.

Patrick Henry Hansard is buried in Alabama.

FAMILY OF MOSES HAYNES, SENIOR

Moses Haynes Sr. was a pioneer settler of Elbert County, Georgia. He came there from South Carolina about 1790 or a little earlier. He settled in the upper part of the county on land bounty containing one thousand acres which he received as a Revolutionary soldier. On this land was located a large spring known as Big Holly Springs. Nearby was built in 1796 a church, which was called Holly Springs Baptist Church. Moses Haynes gave the land on which the church was built. It was first located about one-half mile from the present site. In 1836, his son, Thomas Haynes, who came into possession of the land containing the Big Holly Springs, gave three acres, including the spring, to the church in lieu of the three acres given by his father, Moses, and sold them five acres more.

Moses Haynes was one of the first grand jurors of Elbert County and served as Justice of the Peace for a number of years. He was a native of Culpepper County, Virginia, and left there prior to 1790. He lived for a while in South Carolina, where he was a member of Padgett's Creek Baptist Church. He was the son of Jasper Haynes, whose will in Culpepper County, Virginia, names the following children: Joseph Haynes, Jasper Haynes, Mary Haynes, James Haynes, Ann Haynes, and William Haynes. This will was written in June 1779, and recorded Jan. 21, 1782.

The will of Moses Haynes Sr. was written on Dec. 18, 1828, and was recorded on May 4, 1829. The following children were named in this will: Stephen, William, Moses, Thomas, Nancy, Elizabeth Keeling, Mary Ellen (Polly), Sara Cardin, and grandchildren, Moses Cardin and Jane Glenn.

The will of Lettie Duncan Haynes, widow of Thomas Haynes, was written in 1855, in Elbert County, and was recorded on Aug. 9, 1855. She names the following children: Sarah G., William D., Thomas J., I Haynes, Benjamin F., Mary Ellen, wife of Marion Allen, Moses M., Asa J., James W., Lettie Bowers, wife of William Bowers; she also mentions her grandchildren, Thomas J. Bowers, Lettie and Elizabeth Winn, daughters of Wm. D. Haynes, and Marion Haynes and Lettie Haynes, children of Moses M. Haynes, Sarah and Lettie Haynes, daughters of James W. Haynes.

Asa J. Haynes was the executor of his mother's, Lettie Duncan Haynes, estate. He was Justice of the Peace of Elbert County for a number of years. He had the following children: William Harrison, James, Columbus, Beecher, Bartow, Lettie Vickery, Sara McCurry, Laura Hendrick, Mary Rice, and Louise Genobia Adams. Thomas Haynes had two children who were not mentioned in their mother's, Lettie Duncan Haynes, will. They were Henry Haynes and Millege Haynes. All of the Haynes family were Baptists and a goodly number of them were members of the Holly Springs Baptist Church, which was the gift of their Revolutionary ancestor, Moses Haynes Sr.

The last of the older set of Haynes, Mrs. Louise Genobia Adams, has just passed away, on Nov. 10, 1939. She still lived on part of the original land bounty granted to Moses Haynes Sr. She leaves the following children: Miss Del Rey Adams, of Bowman, Ga.; Mrs. Wm. Howard Arnold, of Atlanta; Mrs. B. C. Teasley, of Hartwell, Ga., and Mr. Eldo Haynes Adams, of Atlanta. She was eighty years of age.

Moses Haynes was buried at Holly Springs Baptist Church. His grave has been marked by John Benson Chapter, D. A. R.

HEARD

The following chart shows intermarriages with the following families: Abercrombie — Adams — Aiken — Alford — Allen — Alexander — Allston — Archer — Arnold — Asbury — Austin — Babb — Banks — Barker — Barnett — Bates — Beatty — Blackwell — Bland — Bledsoe — Boyd — Boyer — Beall — Bozeman — Brady — Bounds — Bryan — Bradley — Brown — Burris — Butt — Burnett — Bynum — Cade — Calhoun — Calloway — Campbell — Carlton — Carroll — Carter — Carr — Chisholm — Clinton — Chunn — Clark — Cleveland — Comer — Coffee — Cook — Cooper — Crook — Crouch — Darden — Davie — Davis — Dean — Dennis — Dickson — Dixon — Dohme — Douglas — Downs — Duggar — Edwards — Elder — Elliott — Ethridge — Evans — Faulkner — Fielding — Fields — Fisher — Foster — Fox — Gaines — Germany — Gilham — Glass — Gray — Gorby — Grier — Hall — Hammond — Hankins — Harris — Harmon — Hawes — Helton — Hearne — Heggie — Hightower — Hill — Holman — Hudson — Hull — Hunter — Isham — Jarrett — Jones — Kendricks — Kilpatrick — Lane — Lanier — Lattimer — Lee — Lide — Linder — Little — Logan — Long — Lumpkin — Lyle — Lyons — Martin — Mattox — Malatte — Maddox —Middleton— Moore — Morrow — Mulligan — McCalla — McCurry — McDonald — McGruder — McIntosh — McLendon — Napier — Nelms — Nichols — Pantecost — Peeples — Pharr — Porter — Powell — Prescott — Pressley — Prince — Pleasants — Pryor — Purdue — Quillian — Quinn — Rainey — Reeves — Reid — Rice — Richards — Riddle — Roberson — Robbins — Robers — Royal — Seymour — Sill — Smith — Sondidge —

Spierman — Speed — Stanford — Standifer — Staton — Stewart — Stephens — Still — Stelling — Sullivan — Suffold — Swift — Tailor — Thomas — Thompson — Tinsley — Townsend — Tucker — Tate — Underwood — Upshaw — Vass — Wansley — Warren — Watt — Wayble — Walker — Walthall — Webster — Wellborn — Whatley — White — Whitehead — Whitaker — Wilfrey — Wilkinson — Williams — Wilkes — Wilcox — Wise — Williamson — Woodson — Wood — Wright.

(Note: Numbers represent generations, as: (1) first generation, (2) second generation, (3) third generation, etc.)

1—John Heard, Earl of Tyrone, came to America with his family in 1718, m. Margaret McDonald, a lineal descendant of the "Great O'Neil." John Heard was forced to leave Ireland almost overnight due to an altercation in which he attacked a Roman Catholic priest with a pitch fork growing out of an attempt by the churchman to collect from him a greater amount than his regular tithe.
  2—Stephen Heard, d. Oct. 29, 1774, in Pittsylvania County, Virginia; m. Mary Faulkner, daughter of Sir Thomas Faulkner, of Wales.
    3—Thomas Heard, b. 1742, m. Elizabeth Fitzpatrick, b. 1750.
      4—Catherine Heard, m. Isacc Stocks, (2) Mr. Watts.
        5—Thomas Stocks, m. Cynthia Coffee.
        5—Elizabeth Stocks, m. Mr. Bledsoe.
        5—John Stocks.
        5—Ellen Watts, m. Mr. Hightower.
        5—Joseph Watts.
        5—Atherine Watts, m. (1) Mr. Kelly and (2) Mr. Elliott.
      4—Abram Heard, b. 1769, d. 1822; m. Nancy Coffee.
        5—Franklin Coffee Heard, m. (?).
          6—James Abram Heard, m. Ann C. Hunter.
            7—Franklin Heard.
            7—James Heard.
            7—Martha Heard.
            7—Altona Heard.
            7—Thompson Heard.
            7—Ann Eliza Heard.
          6—George Heard, d. unmarried.
          6—Julia Munger Heard, m. James Elder.
            7—Ruth Elder.
          6—Ann Bozeman Heard, m. Carey Butt.
            7—Clara Butt.
            7—Julia Butt.
            7—Elder Butt.
            7—Fannie Butt.
            7—Mary Butt.
            7—Cary Butt Jr.
          6—James Faulkner Heard, d. unmarried.
          6—Franklin Heard Jr., d. unmarried.
          6—Eliza Longstreet Heard, m. Douglas Vass.
          6—Mary Morgan Heard, m. Thomas Lyons.
            7—Ann Butts Lyons.
        5—Julia Smith Heard, m. Seaborn Suffold.
          6—Ann Heard Suffold, m. Nathaniel Green Foster, M. C.
          6—Thomas Peter Suffold, m. (1) Mary Thomas and (2) Sallie Reid.
            7—Mary Suffold.
            7—William Suffold.
            7—Ann Suffold.
            7—Seaborn Suffold.
          6—Isham Suffold, m. Louisa Prescott.

7—Julia Prescott.
6—Seaborn Jones Suffold, m. Maggie Malette.
7—Ann Coffee Suffold.
5—Thomas Peter Heard, d. unmarried.
5—Abram Augustus Heard, m. Nancy McGruder.
6—Antionette Heard.
6—Virginia Heard, m. Dr. Foster.
5—Minerva Ann Heard, m. Pryor Lee.
6—Abram Heard Lee.
6—Mannie Coffee Lee.
6—Julia Smith Lee.
6—Cynthia Ellen Lee.
5—John Joseph Heard, b. 1809; m. (1) Cynthia Ann Beatty and (2) Mrs. Ann T. Wilkins.
6—Susan Ann Heard, m. 1857 Dr. Hunter.
7—Edward Hunter.
7—John Hunter.
7—Cynthia Hunter.
7—Fannie Hunter.
6—Julia Maria Heard, m. Reverend Joseph Barker.
7—Annie Lowe Barker.
6—Cunthia Heard.
6—Sarah Eliza Heard.
6—Franklin Coffee Heard.
6—Lucy Hammond Heard.
5—George Felix Heard, m. (1) Emily Smith Tailor and (2) Mary Ann Webster.
6—George Smith Heard.
6—Franklin Heard.
5—Joshua Heard, b. 1817, m. Mary M. Robers.
6—Mary Ann Heard.
6—Caroline Heard.
6—Nancy Coffee Heard.
6—Lillian Heard.
6—Minerva Heard.
6—Louisa Heard.
6—Elizabeth Heard.
4—Mary Heard, b. 1770; m. Caleb Cook.
5—Thomas Cook.
5—Elizabeth Cook, m. Mr. Webster.
5—Sarah Cook, m. Mr. Gordon.
5—John James Wesley Cook.
5—Gales Cook.
5—Polly Cook, m. Mr. McLendon.
5—Rebecca Cook, m. Mr. Still.
5—Nancy Cook, m. Mr. Kendrick.
5—Patsy Cook, m. Mr. Spierman.
5—Drucilla Cook, d. unmarried.
4—Joseph Heard, b. 1773, d. 1848; married three times but names of wives unknown to compiler. All are buried ten miles west of Madison, Morgan County, Georgia, on Little River.
5—Elizabeth Thornbury Heard, b. 1798, d. 1847; m. Dec. 1815, Obediah Martin Berge Fielding, d. 1857.
5—Susan Heard, m. Henry Boyd.
5—Catherine Heard, m. Turman Walthall.
6—Joseph Walthall.
6—Thomas Walthall.
6—Turman Walthall Jr., m. Miss Rice.
6—Felix Walthall.
6—Louisa Walthall, m. Colonel James R. Lyon.

5—Olive Heard, m. Peeples Lee.
6—Augusta Heard Lee.
6—William Peeples Lee, m. Caroline Hendricks.
6—Woodson Lee.
6—Ann E. Lee.
6—Susan Lee, m. Lounds Hendricks.
5—Mary Heard, m. John Durden.
6—Mary Durden.
5—Nancy Heard, m. Henry Sill.
5—Fitz Herbert Heard, m. Emily Davis.
4—Thomas Heard, b. 1775, d. 1810; m. (?).
5—Wyatt Heard.
5—George Heard.
5—Thomas Heard Jr.
5—Amelia Heard.
5—Mary Heard, m. Mr. Wallock.
4—Elizabeth Heard, m. (1) Mr. Peeples and (2) Mr. Whidby.
5—Thomas (?).
5—Elizabeth (?).
5—Teal (?).
5—Tabitha (?), m. Mr. Lanier.
5—Minerva (?), m. Mr. Glass.
5—Amanda (?), m. Mr. Trimble.
4—Sallie Heard, m. Wilson Whatley.
5—Seaborn Whatley.
5—Wilson O. B. Whatley, m. Elizabeth Lumpkin, daughter of Governor Lumpkin of Georgia.
5—George C. Whatley, C. S., killed in action.
5—Tabitha Whatley.
5—Elizabeth Whatley, m. Thomas A. Chisholm.
5—Sarah Whatley, m. Mr. Crook.
5—Mary Whatley, m. Mr. Crook.
5—Antionette Whatley, m. Andrew J. Prior.
4—Woodson Heard, b. 1782; m. (?).
5—Suphoemane Heard, m. Mr. Hunter.
5—Almira Heard.
5—Cordelia Heard.
5—Joseph Columbus Heard.
5—Thomas Heard.
5—Nathan Gustavus Heard.
5—Selina Heard.
5—Sabrina Heard.
5—Francis Heard.
5—Woodson Heard Jr.
(Woodson Heard Sr. was the maternal grandson of Joseph Fitzpatrick, son of William Fitzpatrick and Mary Perrin Woodson, who ancestry is charter below:
Dr. John (1) Woodson, immigrant 1619, wife Sarah. John Woodson wife's name unknown. John (3) Woodson wife, Mary Tucker. Benjamin Woodson, d. 1777.
Mary Tucker's parents were: Samuel Tucker, ship captain, immigrant, wife Jane Larcome who married second John Pleasants.
Benjamin (4) Woodson married Frances (3) Napier. Her line follows:
Dr. (1) Patrick Napier, immigrant, married Elizabeth Booth. Her father was Robert Booth and a member of House of Burgesses of King William County, Virginia and later of Henrico County, Virginia. He married Mary Perrin and had Frances (3) Napier. Mary Perrin's line follows: Richard (1) Perrin, immi-

grant, wife's name unknown. Richard (2) Perrin Jr., m. Catherine Royall. They had Mary (3) Perrin who married Captain Robert (2) Napier. Catherine Royall's parents were: Joseph Royall and Catherine Banks. She married second Henry Isham of Henrico County, Virginia.

Benjamin (4) Woodson and Frances (3) Napier were parents of Mary (5) Perrin Woodson).
4—George Heard, b. 1785, d. 1858; m. Martha Coffee.
5—Martha Faulkner Heard, m. Colonel Beall.
6—Martha Beall.
6—Catherine Beall.
6—Julia Beall.
6—Egbert Beall.
5—Peter Abram Heard, m. Mary Alford.
5—Dr. Thomas Henry Heard, m. Posey Alford.
4—Faulkner Heard, b. 1787, d. 1830; m. Mary Roberson.
5—Thomas Heard.
5—Adeline Heard, m. Mr. Eavans.
5—Martha Heard.
5—George Heard.
5—Marion Heard.
3—John Heard, b. 1744, wife unknown.
4—James Heard.
4—Elizabeth Heard, m. Mr. Edwards.
4—John Heard Jr.
4—Susan Heard, m. Mr. Babb.
4—Sarah Heard.
3—Stephen Heard, member Georgia House of Representatives 1795, m. (1) unknown and (2) unknown.
4—(By first wife) George Heard.
4—Elizabeth Heard, m. Mr. Downs.
4—Lucy Heard, m. Mr. Clark.
4—(By second wife) six children who lived in Mississippi.
3—George Heard, m. (1) unknown and (2) unknown.
4—George Heard Jr.
4—Mary Heard, m. Mr. Dixon.
4—Nancy Heard, m. Mr. Rainey.
3—Jesse Heard, d. 1803, R. S., lieutenant Pittsylvania County, Virginia Minute Men, captain, member Georgia House of Representatives from Wilkes County, Georgia, m. 1794, Judith Wilkinson, daughter of "Silver Fist" Wilkinson so called by virtue of the fact that he had lost a hand and caused a new one of silver to be made.
4—Stephen Heard. No record of descendants.
4—Lucy Heard, b. 1789, m. William Harmon.
4—Sarah Heard, m. Stephen Martin.
4—Jesse Heard, secretary of state of Mississippi.
4—Judith Heard, m. Wyatt Smith.
4—Jesse Faulkner Heard, b. June 19, 1785, d. Sept. 6, 1832; m. March 5, 1809, Caroline Wilkinson, b. Jan. 1, 1792, d. March 8, 1880.
5—Judith Heard, m. (1) Abner Wellborn and (2) R. R. Winfry. No issue.
5—Jesse Heard. No living descendants.
5—John W. Heard, m. (1) Lidia Willis nee Calloway and (2) Sarah Lane.
5—Francis S. Heard, m. (1) Mary Caroline Wilkinson and (2) Mary Campbell.
6 (By first wife) Marion W. Heard, m. Miss Davie.
6—Emma Heard, m. (1) Mr. Hearne and (2) Mr. Lyle.

6—Jesse F. Heard.
6—Caroline Jane Heard, b. June 24, 1854, d. Oct. 14, 1916; m. Dec. 24, 1874, Augustus S. Quinn, b. May 1, 1849, d. Oct. 3, 1901.
7—Ella Quinn, b. Dec. 1, 1876, m. John C. Williams.
8—Mary Ella Williams.
8—Ware B. Williams.
7—Francis Quinn, d. without issue.
7—Willis Quinn, m. Helen Cooper.
7—Sarah E. Quinn, m. Edgar L. Smith.
7—William D. Quinn.
7—Augustus S. Quinn Jr., m. Nona Hill.
8—Statham Quinn.
8—Nona C. Quinn.
7—Hinton Quinn, b. Dec. 24, 1888.
7—John Quinn, b. Sept. 23, 1890; m. June 3, 1927, Bessie Whitaker.
8—John Quinn Jr.
5—William Heard, C. S., Colonel, b. April 14, 1818, d. June 10, 1870; m. Aug. 6, 1854, Sarah E. Whitehead, b. Aug. 8, 1883, d. Jan. 1, 1894.
6—N. M. Heard.
6—Jesse F. Heard.
6—Mary Heard.
6—John W. Heard, b. March 7, 1860, captain 3rd U. S. Cavalry, 1891, brigadier-general W. W., m. Mildred J. Townsend.
7—Jack W. Heard, S. W. W., major, b. March 6, 1887.
7—Ann Heard, b. Oct. 3, 1890.
7—Marguerite Heard, b. May 11, 1893.
7—Ralph T. Heard, b. Aug. 15, 1897.
7—Jesse Heard, d. unmarried.
5—Ann W. Heard, b. Dec. 25, 1819, d. 1872; m. Aug. 2, 1842, Nicholas W. Bradley, son of Dr. John A. Bradley, who was born 1773.
6—Richard Barley, C. S., d. Nov. 2, 1861.
6—Benjamin Bradley, m. Mattie Hankins.
6—William Heard Bradley, b. Sept. 22, 1849, d. March 17, 1890; m. Aug. 12, 1877, Luella Wolfe, b. Aug. 13, 1861.
7—Ann Pearl Bradley, b. Feb. 16, 1880, m. June 1897, Guy E. Wood.
8—Dorothy Pearl Wood, m. William David Lide.
9—William D. Lide Jr.
9—Dorothy A. Lide.
9—Thomas E. Lide Jr.
8—Preston B. Wood.
8—Joanna Wood.
8—Charlotte Wood.
7—William Ellis Bradley, m. Margaret Wilkes.
6—Mary Bradley, m. James M. Hull.
7—Florence Dexter Hull, m. Mr. Burnes.
7—Nicholas B. Hull.
7—James W. Hull.
7—Joseph M. Hull.
7—Mary E. Hull.
6—Ann Bradley, m. (1) Mr. Ellis and (2) Mr. Hall.
5—Benjamin W. Heard, C. S., b. Sept. 2, 1821, d. May 13, 1893. brigadier-general Georgia militia; m. (1) Martha Oliver and (2) Victoria Bradley; (3) Miss Blakely.
6—Ann Heard, m. (1) Dr. Mulligan and (2) P. T. Calloway.
6—Willis W. Heard.
6—Jesse F. Heard.

NOTE: Compiler does not have data as who the mothers of the above were.

5—Caroline W. Heard, b. June 28, 1823, d. 1863; m. Dr. N. M. Riddle.
6—Ida Riddle, b. June 25, 1855, d. Sept. 1, 1903; m. Sept. 1, 1875, Daniel L. Morgan, d. March 1901.
7—Lloyd Morgan, m. Elsie Bradford.
7—Ida Morgan, b. 1885, m. Dec. 10, 1910, Llewellyn Duggar, d. Jan. 10, 1931.
8—Lloyd L. Duggar, b. 1913.
8—Mary Duggar, b. 1919.
8—Helen Duggar, b. 1922.
6—Addie Riddle, m. Samuel Tate.
7—Caroline Tate.
7—Watkins Tate.
6—Archie Riddle, m. Louise Gorby.
5—Eliza J. Heard, m. Reverend Willis Wooten.
5—Stephen Heard, m. Mary Etta Simmons.
5—Caroline Heard, m. W. W. Richards.
6—Stephen Richards.
6—Willis W. Richards.
6—Lila Richards.
6—Lucile Richards.
5—Faulkner Heard, m. Lodiska Bryan.
6—Jesse F. Heard.
6—Bryan Heard, m. Stella Chunn.
5—Henrietta W. Heard, b. April 4, 1830, m. J. F. Heggie.
6—Alice Heggie.
6—Jesse F. Heggie.
6—James F. Heggie Jr.
6—Augusta Heggie, m. Mr. Pantecost.
6—Ophelia Heggie, m. Benjamin Wooten.
4—Elizabeth Heard, m. John Stanton.
4—Susan Heard, m. (1) Thomas Beatty and (2) Dr. Robbons.
5—Thomas Beatty Jr.
5—Henry Beatty.
5—Cynthia Beatty.
5—Julia Beatty, m. Lindsey C. Warren.
4—Mary Heard, m. Robert Grier, b. June 4, 1786, d. Oct. 28, 1823.
5—Isaac Grier.
5—Robert A. Grier, m. Mildred J. Fitzpatrick, daughter of Colonel Fitzpatrick, of Georgia.
6—Robert F. Grier, d. unmarried.
6—Mary M. Grier, m. F. C. Fox.
3—Susan Heard, m. Israel Standifer, U. S. congressman from Tennessee.
3—Mary Heard.
3—Anne Heard, m. Peter Gilham.
4—Charles Gilham.
4—Sallie Gilham, m. Mr. Morrow.
4—Mary H. Gilham, m. Mr. Rieves.
4—Nancy Gilham, m. Mr. Prince.
4—Patsy Gilham, m. Mr. Nelms.
4—Elizabeth Gilham, m. Mr. Morrow.
2—Charles Heard, m. Margaret Brady.
2—James Heard.
2—Jesse Heard.
2—John Heard Jr., d. 1789; m. Bridget Carroll.
3—Barnard Heard, R. S. major, m. Miss Germany.
3—John Heard III, m. Elizabeth (?).

3—Daughter Heard, m. Joseph Staton.
3—Daughter Heard, m. Mr. Austin.
3—Stephen Heard, R. S. colonel, colonial captain under Washington, governor of Georgia 1781, president Executive Council, commissioner to view the Tennessee lands, lawyer, civil engineer, planter, b. 1740 (in Virginia), d. Nov. 13, 1815; m. (1) Miss Germany and (2) Elizabeth Darden, b. 1765, d. June 5, 1848.
4—(By second wife) Barnard Carroll Heard, b. March 12, 1787, m. Polly Hutson.
5—Boliver Heard, d. unmarried.
5—Stephen Heard, d. unmarried.
5—John Heard, m. Elizabeth Williamson.
4—Martha Burch Heard, b. Oct. 10, 1788, d. Dec. 7, 1824; m. about 1805, Bartlett Tucker, b. 1784.
5—Martha Tucker, b. 1807, m. John Maxwell, C. S. No issue.
5—Stephen Heard Tucker, m. Jan. 16, 1827, Mary Aiken, daughter of Thomas Aiken.
5—Elizabeth Tucker, m. (1) Mr. Upshaw and (2), Dec. 2, 1840, Robert Harris.
6—(By first husband) Daughter Upshaw, m. Mr. Harris.
6—(By second husband) Robert Harris Jr.
6—Alva Harris.
6—Clarence Harris, m. Eva Wakefield.
7—Alice Pope Harris, m. Frank Asbury Jr.
8—Frank Asbury III.
7—James Harris.
7—Walton Harris.
5—Sarah Tucker, m. Jan. 27, 1842, Henry Sanders. No issue.
4—Bridget Carroll Heard, b. June 17, 1795, m. (1) March 6, 1817, Simeon Henderson and (2) Elbert H. Thompson.
5—William Henderson.
5—Daughter Thompson, m. Mr. Riddle.
5—Daughter Thompson, m. Mr. Jones.
4—Dr. George Washington Heard, member Georgia House of Representatives, b. June 17, 1791; m. April 20, 1815, Sarah Carter, daughter of Thomas A. Carter.
5—Stephen Heard, m. Miss Aiken.
6—Phillip Heard, m. Miss Tillman.
4—John Adams Heard, b. March 17, 1793, d. 1838, solicitor general Western Circuit of Georgia, d. unmarried.
4—Jane Lanier Heard, b. March 23, 1797; m. Singleton Walthall Allen, b. Jan. 14, 1791, d. June 6, 1853, member Georgia House of Representatives 1828-29-31, Georgia state senator 1845-46, planter.
5—Elizabeth Allen, m. George Williams of Athens, Georgia.
6—Rebecca Allen Williams, m. DuBose Hill.
7—Janie Hill, m. Benjamin H. Hill.
6—George Williams, C. S., d. unmarried.
6—William Williams, m. Jessie Arnold.
7—William McIntosh Williams.
6—Janie Williams, m. John Burriss.
7—Dilliard Herndon Burris.
5—George Allen, d. unmarried.
5—Theodore Allen, d. unmarried.
5—Ann Allen, m. April 30, 1839, Dr. Milton Comer.
6—Janie Comer, m. 1874, Samuel Barnett, C. S. captain, b. Aug. 16, 1841, d. Nov. 26, 1898.
7—Comer Barnett, b. May 11, 1878, m. June 19, 1901, Corneille Bounds, b. Feb. 14, 1880.

8—Lillis Barnett, b. March 25, 1911.
6—Bevelle Comer, m. Dr. Hampton. No issue.
6—Anne Comer, b. 1849, d. 1928, unmarried.
5—Susan Allen, m. Young L. G. Harris, founder of Young-Harris College, president Southern Mutual Fire Insurance Company, member Georgia House of Representatives from Elbert County, member Georgia Senate from Elbert County. No issue.
5—Maria Louisa Allen, b. Aug. 10,1824, d. Aug. 1885; m. Jan. 27, 1842, William McPherson McIntosh, b. Feb. 14, 1815, d. June 1862. Colonel 15th Georgia Regiment Infantry Volunteers, C. S. A. Mortally wounded in action at Garnett's Farm, Virginia, brevet brigadier-general for gallantry in action, member Georgia House of Representatives, member Georgia State Senate, elector state-at-large (Georgia) for Breckenridge 1860, lawyer, planter.
6—Singleton Allen McIntosh, C. S., b. Feb., 19, 1845, d. Nov. 17, 1908; m. February 1867, Mary Eliza Cade.
7—Sarah Howell McIntosh, b. Dec. 29, 1867; m. S. J. Zeigler.
8—Samuel Zeigler, S. W. W., U. S. naval officer, m. Fanny Marburg.
9—Howell Zeigler.
8—Howell "Polar" Zeigler, m. George Dickson, major U. S. Army, retired.
9—Howell Rees Dickson.
9—George Dickson Jr.
7—William McPherson McIntosh, b. 1870, d. 1930, unmarried.
7—William Guilford "Guy" McIntosh, b. July 6, 1872, m. Sept. 14, 1918, Addie Tinsley.
8—Mary McIntosh, b. Sept. 3, 1921.
8—William Kenneth McIntosh, b. Nov. 10, 1922.
8—Louise McIntosh, b. Nov. 1923.
7—Victoria Augusta McIntosh, b. March 1875, m. Joseph Allston, of South Carolina.
8—Joseph Allston Jr., m. Lillis McCullough.
9—Joseph Allston III.
8—Mary Allston.
7—Mary Louise McIntosh, b. Aug. 10, 1877, m. 1903, Henry M. Long of Kentucky.
8—Mary Louise Long, d. infancy.
6—William McPherson McIntosh Jr., b. Feb. 28, 1847, C. S., m. Nellie Dean of Auburn, N. Y.
7—William McPherson McIntosh III, S. W. W.
6—Anna Cassandra McIntosh, b. March 5, 1849, m. Dec. 11, 1866, Budd Clay Wall, C. S., merchant, mayor of North Augusta, South Carolina, b. April 24, 1847, d. 1930.
7—Martha Louise Wall, b. April 6, 1868, m. Thomas B. Andrews. No issue.
7—McPherson Wall, d. infancy.
7—William Clay Wall, d. infancy.
7—James Singleton Wall, b. Jan. 1, 1873, m. Rose Douglas. No issue.
7—Bevel William Wall, b. June 20, 1875, m. Mary Stewart.
8—Margaret Wall.
8—Bevel Clay Wall, m. 1929, Virginia Alexander.
9—Bevel Charles Wall, b. July 22, 1930.
7—Jessie McIntosh Wall, b. Dec. 20, 1878, m. John D. Stelling.
8—Sterling McIntosh Stelling, b. Feb. 14, 1900, m. Eula Mitchell. No issue.
8—Richard Nunnelee Stelling, b. May 14, 1901, physician.

8—Martha McIntosh Stelling, b. Dec. 14, 1903, m. June 1930, Dr. Charles McCord Kilpatrick.
8—Howard Cree Stelling, b. Sept. 1906, lieutenant U. S. Air Corps, m. Helen Wainwright, famous swimming champion.
8—Budd Clay Wall Stelling, b. Feb. 1909.
7—Harry Wall, m. (1) Maryland Randall, daughter of James R. Randall, author of "Maryland, My Maryland," and (2) Nell Smith. No issue.
6—Maria Louise McIntosh, b. March 15, 1851, d. May 7, 1894, m. Feb. 2, 1869, Guildford Cade Jr.
7—Julia May Cade, b. Dec. 30, 1871, m. Nov. 23, 1892, Dr. Albert Sidney Hawes, b. Nov. 14, 1863, d. Nov. 1936, member Georgia House of Representatives 1926-27, mayor of Elberton 1929-30-31-32, merchant, planter.
8—Guilford Mosely Hawes, b. July 24, 1894, m. March 26, 1913, Onie Lee of Cullman, Alabama, b. 1893.
9—Mary Lee Hawes, b. Sept. 14, 1917.
9—Julia Ann Hawes, b. Feb. 25, 1925.
9—Robert Hawes, d. infancy.
8—Albert Lee Hawes, b. Feb. 11, 1901, m. Bertha Bates, d. 1932. No issue.
8—Peyton Samuel Hawes, b. Sept. 4, 1903, member Georgia House of Representatives 1931-32, city attorney of Elberton, lawyer, m. 1933, Virginia Smith, daughter of A. F. Smith and Minor Carpenter.
7—Guilford Cade III, b. June 9, 1875, m. Dec. 4, 1904, Jane Kennedy.
8—Malvina "Mally" Cade, b. Sept. 1905, m. Dec. 1929, Milo Abercrombie, d. 1931.
9—Milo Abercrombie Jr.
8—Guilford Cade IV, b. April 1911.
7—Annie Lee Cade, b. Feb. 21, 1878, m. Feb. 24, 1903, Dr. Robert Franklin Moore, b. Jan. 31, 1870, d. 1923.
8—Alan Moore, b. Nov. 1905, d. 1933.
8—Frank Moore, d. infancy.
8—Guilford McIntosh Moore, b. Sept. 1908.
6—Ada McIntosh, d. infancy.
6—Jessie McIntosh, d. infancy.
6—Mary Bevelle McIntosh, b. 1856, d. June 1926, m. 1895, John C. Brown, merchant, mayor of Elberton, b. 1857, d. 1917. No issue.
6—James McIntosh, b. Sept. 23, 1857, sheriff of Elbert County, county commissioner of Elbert County, city councilman of Elberton, tax assessor of Elberton; m. Oct. 18, 1882, Mary Jane Arnold, b. Sept. 1, 1859, daughter of Joseph Y. Arnold, C. S., and Sarah K. Thornton.
7—Sarah Louise McIntosh, b. July 29, 1883, m. Feb. 23, 1903, Arthur F. Archer, educator of Kentucky. No issue.
7—William McIntosh, d. infancy.
7—Jessie McIntosh, d. infancy.
7—Mary James McIntosh, d. infancy.
7—John Hawes McIntosh, b. Nov. 26, 1895, county attorney of Elbert County, official historian of Elbert County, compiler city code of Elberton, assistant secretary Georgia Senate 1931-32, secretary Elbert County tax assessors; m. June 19, 1918, divorced March 1937, Fay White, b. Oct. 21, 1900.
8—Mary Louise McIntosh, b. July 16, 1920.
8—Elizabeth Arnold Penn McIntosh, b. March 15, 1923.
7—McAlpin McIntosh, b. Nov. 26, 1897, d. 1899.
6—Jessie McIntosh, b. 1859, m. Peyton M. Hawes, member Georgia

House of Representatives, member Georgia Senate, captain Elberton Light Infantry, president Elberton Loan and Savings Bank, president Elbert County Bank, planter. No issue.
5—Mary Allen, m. Nov. 21, 1849, George McCalla of South Carolina.
6—Isaac McCalla, m. Raymond Speed.
7—Mack McCalla, m. Ella Nichols.
8—Mack McCalla Jr.
8—Elmira McCalla.
7—Leila McCalla, m. Mr. Linder of Hart County, Geeorgia.
8—Alice Linder, m. J. P. Sullivan of South Carolina.
9—J. P. Sullivan Jr.
7—John McCalla, m. Parnice Brown. No issue.
6—John W. McCalla, county commissioner of Elbert County, merchant, planter, m. Mitta Allen.
7—Annie McCalla, m. Oct. 20, 1909, J. H. Purdue of Birmingham, Alabama.
8—Frances Purdue.
8—Mary Olivia Purdue.
8—J. H. Purdue Jr.
7—Olivia McCalla, m. Perry H. Smith, city councilman of Elberton, merchant.
8—Ethel Smith, m. Mr. LeConte.
7—J. Earl McCalla, m. Katherine Stephens of Hart County, Georgia.
8—John McCalla.
8—Katherine McCalla.
8—J. Earl McCalla Jr.
8—David McCalla.
6—Ida McCalla, m. (1) Frank Cleveland and (2) Aug. 31, 1887, Bedford Heard.
7—Andrew B. Cleveland, m. Nov. 19, 1900, m. Agnes Hall.
8—Frank Cleveland, m. Miss Smith.
9—Agnes Cleveland.
8—Elizabeth Cleveland, m. Frank Veronee.
8—Lanier Cleveland, m. Augusta Wansley.
9—Augusta Wansley Jr.
8—McCalla Cleveland.
8—Helen Cleveland.
8—Andrew B. Cleveland Jr.
7—Jessie Cleveland, m. Jesse Warren.
8—Jeremiah Warren.
8—Hilda Warren.
7—M. E. Heard, m. Sept. 14, 1904, Allen Pressley.
7—Erskin Heard, m. May 5, 1911, Lottie Seymour.
8—Martha Heard.
8—Bedford Heard.
8—Emma Heard.
8—Mattie Heard.
8—Hazel Heard.
7—Sarah Heard, m. June 9, 1912, Frank Hammond.
8—Frank Hammond Jr.
8—Mildred Hammond.
7—Bevelle Heard, m. Feb. 20, 1917, Thomas Wayble.
8—Bevelle Wayble.
7—Caroline Heard, m. Guy Quillian.
6—Jennie McCalla, m. Joseph Speed.
7—Florence Speed, m. A. A. McCurry, Georgia State Senator, 30th district.
8—Speed McCurry.

8—A. A. McCurry Jr., m. B. Porter.
8—Jennie May McCurry.
8—Horace McCurry.
8—Althea McCurry.
8—Joseph McCurry.
6—Susan McCalla, b. Sept. 19, 1861, d. Dec. 23, 1903; m. 1895, Willis B. Adams, b. May 13, 1861, d. Feb. 11, 1913, captain Elberton Light Infantry, mayor of Elberton, chairman Elberton Board of Education, member Georgia House of Representatives 1905-06-07-08, member city council of Elberton.
7—Willis Sue Adams, b. July 20, 1896; m. June 2, 1918, H. R. Bynum, S. W. W., Clerk and treasurer of Elberton, b. Feb. 27, 1892.
8—Susan Margaret Bynum, b. May 9, 1919.
6—Mary McCalla, m. George Gaines. No issue.
6—Dr. Lawrence McCalla, m. Hettie Hearne.
7—Lawrence McCalla Jr., m. Mildred Cosner.
8—Lawrencce McCalla III.
5—Rebecca Allen, m. William H. Mattox, C. S. captain, member Georgia House of Representatives, member Georgia Senate, delegate to Georgia Constitutional Convention of 1877, planter, merchant.
6—Lena Mattox, m. Jeptha Jones.
7—Reba Jones, m. June 27, 1909, George W. Gray, justice of the peace, member Elbert County Board of Registrars.
8—George W. Gray Jr.
8—Page Gray.
7—Allen Jones.
7—Annie Jones.
7—Henry P. Mattox Jones, m. Aug. 20, 1911, Mary Wall.
8—Henry P. Mattox Jones Jr.
8—Martha Jones.
8—Rebecca Jones.
8—Thomas Jones.
7—Callie May Jones, b. 1891, m. April 19, 1909, Albert R. Hudson, b. 1878.
8—Albert S. Hudson Jr., b. 1910, m. 1930, Elizabeth Bell.
8—Clark Hudson, b. 1912.
8—Francis Hudson, b. 1915.
8—Mack Hudson, b. 1919.
8—David Hudson, b. 1919.
8—Carroll Mattox Hudson, b. 1922.
6—Singleton Mattox, m. Aug. 17, 1887, Annie Jones.
7—Jessie Mattox.
6—Allen Mattox.
6—Clark McIntosh Mattox, m. Sarah Jones.
7—Clark McIntosh Mattox Jr., m. Miss Helton.
7—Jeptha Mattox.
6—Susan Mattox.
6—Annie Mattox, d. unmarried.
6—Carroll Mattox, m. Charles Fisher.
7—Mamie Fisher.
6—Janie Mattox, m. Raymond Gaines. No issue.
5—Gerrard Allen, m. Oct. 31, 1850, Isabella Blackwell.
6—Gerrard Allen Jr., m. Adeliade Stanford.
7—Singleton W. Allen, m. May Wood.
8—Gerard Allen, m. Sadie Ethridge.
7—Hattie Allen, m. Charles Whitmire of Atlanta, Ga.
8—Charles Whitemire Jr.
8—Harriet Whitmire.
8—Annie Bevelle Whitmire.

8—Martha Whitmire.
4—Permelia Heard, b. 1799, d. 1817.
4—Sarah J. Heard, d. Aug. 16, 1825, m. Jan. 18, 1825, Jas. D. Jarret.
4—Thomas Jefferson Heard, b. Ang. 21, 1801, d. May 4, 1876, member Georgia Legislature, Elberton, lawyer, planter; m. (1) Nancy Middleton and (2) Miss Arnold.
(Children by first wife).
5—Sarah Heard, m. Dec. 11, 1846, L. H. O. Martin, Col. on Staff of Gen. Robert Toombs, member of Georgia Legislature, delegate to Georgia Secession Convention.
6—Sarah Martin, d. unmarried.
6—Col. L. H. O. Martin Jr., member of Georgia Legislature, m. Rossie Harper.
5—James Lawrence Heard, b. 1832, d. 1922, Major in Confederate Army, first mayor of Elberton, member of Georgia Legislature, second president of first railroad into Elberton; m. Mary Melissa Harper, d. 1915.
6—Mary Heard, b. 1858, d. 1929; m. 1881, Thomas Carleton, D. D., Baptist State Evangelist, Okla., minister,, lawyer, judge city court of Elberton; d. 1928.
7—Thomas Carleton Jr., pharmacist, b. 1882.
7—Lawrence Heard Carleton, M. D., b. Jan. 1891; m. Ruth.
6—William Harper Heard, b. 1860, d. 1919; m. Kathleen Carroll, b. 1866.
7—Margaret Melissa Heard, m. 1929, Charles Louis Dohme, d. 1935.
7—Kathleen Carroll Heard, m. 1920, W. E. Adams.
8—Robert Carroll Adams, b. 1924.
7—James Lawrence Heard, m. Eva Underwood, 1914, d. 1925.
8—Margaret Melissa Heard, b. 1915, m. Charles Winans, Feb. 1937.
8—Eva Kathleen Heard, b. 1917.
8—Betsy Meredith Heard, b. 1923.
8—J. L. Heard III, b. 1918, d. 1921.
7—Jane Clinton Heard, m. William N. Hallman, 1922.
8—William Hallman Jr., b. 1923.
8—Helen Meredith Hallman, b. 1925.
7—Luther Martin Heard.
7—Sarah Carroll Heard, m. 1920, Smith H. Wise.
8—Dorothy Heard Wise, b. 1921.
7—William Harper Heard Jr., m. Vivian Burnett, 1925
8—Donald Tate Heard, b. 1926.
7—Joseph Day Heard, m. April 15, 1939, Frances Weber.
6—Nancy Middleton Heard, m. Phil W. Davis, lawyer, judge, Baptist minister, member of Georgia Legislature from Elbert and Oglethorpe counties.
7—Melissa Heard Davis, m. 1927, Fred B. Lynch, d. 1935.
7—Phil W. Davis Jr., lawyer, m. Cecile Little, 1921.
8—Cecile Little Davis, b. 1922.
6—Oliver McDonald Heard, d. 1924, m. Victor Nardin, 1899.
7—Lucie Evelyn Heard. m. Arthur Lanham Jr., 1930.
8—Mary Ann Lanham, b. 1935.
8—Arthur Lanham Jr., b. 1937.
7—Jane C. Heard, m. Fred S. Clinton, M. D., 1895.
7—Mary Melissa Heard.
7—Victor Nardin Heard, m. Mildred Z. Harbuck, 1931.
8—Nardin McDonald Heard, b. 1933.
8—Victor Marion Heard, b. 1937.
5—Robert Middleton Heard, Capt. Confederate Army, Mayor of Elberton, lawyer, member Georgia Legislature; m. 1864, Louisa Jones.

6—John T. Heard, d. 1932; merchant, banker, unmarried.
6—Vohammie Heard, d. Aug. 1930; m. Marcus Pharr, 1888.
7—Robert Pharr, m. Hallie Smith.
8—Robert Pharr Jr.
8—Marcus Pharr Jr.
7—Marcus Pharr Jr., d. 1918, Lieut. World War.
7—Camilla Pharr, m. G. D. Barnett.
8—Aurelius Barnett.
8—Ida Hill Barnett.
8—Vohammie Barnett.
8—Camilla Barnett.
7—Mitta Pharr, m. S. A. Fields.
8—Sherman Fields.
7—Vohammie Pharr, m. J. M. Carr.
8—J. M. Carr Jr.
8—Robert Carr.
8—Mitta Carr.
7—Louise Pharr, m. H. C. Sparks.
8—Lavonia Sparks.
8—H. C. Sparks Jr.
6—Carroll Heard. Unmarried.
6—Luther Martin Heard, d. Jan. 1917, banker, m. June 15, 1904, Mamie Lattimer, daughter of United States Senator Lattimer, of South Carolina.
7—Luther Martin Heard Jr., m. Miriam Dean.
8—Miriam Heard.
8—Ann Heard.
7—Lattimer Heard.
7—Robert Heard.
6—Georgia Heard, m. Dr. J. E. Johnson.
7—J. E. Williams Jr., m. Marie Williams.
8—J. E. Johnson III, m. (2) Nell Steed.
6—Roberta Heard, m. John T. Dennis Jr., mayor of Elberton, captain Elberton Light Infantry. No issue.
6—Parks E. Heard. Unmarried, d. Oct. 1938.
5—Erskin Heard, m. (1) Nov. 26, 1855, Martha Harper and (2) Caroline Calhoun.
6—(By first wife) Bedford Harper, m. Ida Cleveland nee McCalla.
7—M. E. Heard, m. Allen Pressley.
7—Erskin Heard, m. 1911, Lottie Seymour.
8—Martha Heard.
8—Bedford Heard.
8—Emma Heard.
8—Mattie Heard.
8—Hazel Heard.
7—Sarah Heard, m. June 9, 1912, Frank Hammond.
8—Frank Hammond Jr.
8—Mildred Hammond.
7—Bevelle Heard, m. Thomas Wayble.
8—Bevelle Wayble.
7—Caroline Heard, m. 1917, Guy Quillian.
6—Thomas J. Heard, m. Willie Sondidge.
7—Mattie Carrie Heard.
7—Eugene Heard, M. D.
6—Rebecca Heard, m. Frank Wright, d. without issue.
6—(By second marriage) George E. Heard. Unmarried.
5—William Henry Heard, m. Oct. 29, 1873, Jennie Harper.
6—Harper Heard.
6—Thomas Park Heard, d. unmarried.
6—Rebecca Heard, m. Frank Wright. D. without issue.

5—Eugene B. Heard, C. S., b. 1847, d. March 31, 1934; m. Sallie Harper, founder of Seaboard Air Line Traveling Library, co-founder of Georgia Woman's Club.
6—Sue Heard, d. March 1934; m. April 25, 1895, James Y. Swift.
2—George Heard.
2—Thomas Heard, m. Polly MacDonald.
3—Deville Heard.
3—James Heard.
3—Charles Heard, m. Jennie Logan.
4—Stephen Heard, m. Delilah Wilcox.
4—George Heard, m. Sarah Wright.
4—Charles MacDonald Heard, m. Sarah Moore.
5—John W. Heard, m. Hannah Crouch.
5—James M. Heard, m. Inez Bozeman.
5—Charles H. Heard, m. Isabella Walker.
6—Samuel Heard, d. without issue.
6—George W. Heard, d. without issue.
6—Charles E. Heard, d. without issue.
6—Silas Wright Heard, m. Anna Harris.
7—Isabella Heard, m. Charles Bland.
8—Isabella Bland.
8—Harriet C. Bland.
8—Catherine M. Bland.
7—Virginia Heard, m. C. G. Gist.
8—Virginia Gist.
7—G. T. H. Heard, m. Gabrielle Boyer.
5—Mary Heard, m. J. J. Powell.
5—Elizabeth Heard, m. Anderson Goudy.

FAMILY RECORD FROM BIBLE OF WILLIAM P. HENRY PUBLISHED IN 1818

1—William P. Henry was born February 4, 1796 in Virginia, on June 17th, 1821. Married to Sarah Lucy Beck, who was born on April 3, 1803. He died March 18, 1833 in Forsyth, Georgia. Sarah Lucy Beck Henry died February 4th, 1881.

"In Forsyth on the 18th of March, 1833, died Wm. P. Henry, Esq., Clerk of the Superior Court of Monroe County, Georgia. A kind and indulgent father, an affectionate husband, and a sincere friend; his loss will long be felt by the community in which he lived. His amiable qualities and social disposition had endeared him to all with whom he was acquainted. Few men have lived more beloved, none have died more regretted. If the line of the poet be true to none could it be more appropriately applied than to the subject of this sketch, 'An honest man is the noblest work of God.' "

2—John P. Henry was born June 12, 1822; died October 27, 1822.

2—William Benson Henry was born March 24, 1825; on December 19th, 1850, married Martha Elizabeth Wall, who was born March 27, 1834.

2—Sarah Ann Ofelia Henry was born April 19th, 1827; on February 16, 1843 was married to Amos L. Vail.

2—Beverly Allen Henry was born February 20th, 1829; married Mary Hamilton Lewis, October 14, 1852.

2—Benjamin Cabaniss Henry, born November 4, 1830, married R. Dankins August 15, 1860.

2—Captain William Benson Henry was born in Forsyth, Ga. in 1825 and moved to Elbert County at the age of 8 years, after the death of his father, William P. Henry, and was a resident of Elbert County until his death in 1918. His boyhood was spent on the farm until he entered college at Emory, Oxford, Ga. On account of the death of his uncle, Beverly Allen, he was recalled home a few months before his graduation. He united with the Methodist Church while at Oxford and later joined the First Methodist Church in Elberton, was a faithful member until his death. He was secretary and treasurer of the Sunday School for 50 years and was up to his death in 1918. In 1853 he was engaged in farming and mercantile business at Longstreet, Elbert County, and also kept Post Office in his store in an old safe which is now owned by his daughters. The mail was carried by horseback from Carnesville to Augusta twice a week and the only subscribers to a weekly paper in the county were Mr. B. C. Wall and Col. Heard, and the paper was the Augusta Chronicle. He was a Confederate soldier and was stationed in Atlanta just before the city was taken by Sherman. Several letters are still in the possession of his children written at that time.

HERNDON FAMILY GENEALOGY

Among the names inscribed on the roll of Battle Abbey as having come with William the Conqueror into Britian in 1066 is the name of the first member of this family that we have record of. In 1193 a member of the family journeyed with Richard III. to the Holy Land, for his escutcheon is carved on a stone gateway in the city of Rhodes. A modification of these Arms—Argent, a heron volant azure, between three escallops sable—is also found in stained glass in Lincoln Chapel London.

The first Herndon in America, of whom we have authentic record, is William, who patented lands in New Kent County, Virginia, in Feb. 1674. He married in 1677, Catherine Digges, daughter of Edward Digges, Colonial Governor of Virginia 1656-1658. Through this Digges connection the Herndon family is eligible to many of the Patriotic Societies, among them:

The Society of Daughters of the Barons of Runnemede—ancestor, Edward Digges.

The Society of Colonial Governors—ancestor, Edward Digges.

The Society of Daughters of the Crown—ancestor, Edward Digges to Alfred the Great.

The Society of Founders and Patriots—ancestors, Edward Digges.

The Society of Scions and Cavaliers—ancestor, Edward Digges, son of Sir Dudley Digges.

The Society of The First Families of Virginia—ancestor, Sir Dudley Digges, father of Edward Digges, whose daughter, Catherine, married William Herndon.

Reference of the above is found—Virginia Historical Magazine, Vol. 9, pp. 318, 319; William and Mary Quarterly, Vol. 1, pp. 87, 88, 140, 141; and in Herndon, Hunt and Allied Families, p. 55, by Nesbit and Wood.

The first member of the family, in America, that we have authentic record of is:

1—William Herndon, b. 1621, d. 1690; m. 1677, Catherine Digges, b. 1627, d. 1689.
  2—Edward Herndon, 1678-1745; m. 1698 Mary Waller, d. 1727.
    3—William Herndon, 1706-1783; m. Ann Drysdale, b. 1711, d. 1777.
      4—Edward Herndon, 1737-1831; m. 1762, Mary Gaines, b. 1742 d. 1829.

This Edward Herndon was the Revolutionary soldier. He was Captain in Colonel Francis Taylor's Regiment. His record is found in War Department, Washington, D. C., in Heitman's Historical Register of Officers of the Continental Army during the Revolution, p. 900, and in List of Revolutionary Soldiers, Virginia State Library, p. 215. His children were:

        5—William Herndon, b. 1764, m. Mary Rucker.
        5—Benjamin Herndon, b. 1765, m. Susan Ahart, of whom further.
        5—Elizabeth Herndon, b. 1766, m. ———— Pennell.
        5—Rachel Herndon, b. 1767, m. ———— Hawkins.
        5—Edward Herndon, b. 1768, m. Nancy Rucker.
        5—John Herndon, b. 1771, m.
        5—Mary Herndon, b. 1774, m. ———— Jackson.
        5—George Herndon, b. 1776, m. Franky Zachery.
        5—Nancy Herndon, b. 1780, m. ———— Jossum.
        5—Joel and Henry Herndon, b. 1782.
        5—Benjamin Herndon, 1765-1805; m. 1787, Susan Ahart, 1769-1835.
          6—Michael Herndon, 1788-1857; m. 1812, Sarah Seals, 1796-1837.
            7—Thomas Jefferson Herndon, 1823-1896; m. 1842, Sarah Ann Terrell, 1823-1906.
              8—George Michael Herndon, 1843-1862, died in Confederate Army.
              8—Sarah Elizabeth Herndon, b. 1845, d. 1912; m. Tom D. Thornton.
              8—Frances Herndon, b. 1847, d. 1913; m. J. S. Tate.
              8—Benjamin Thadeus Herndon, b. 1849; m. Sallie Carlton.
              8—James Edward Herndon, b. 1850, d. 1906; m. 1872, Mary Elizabeth Fortson, of whom further.
              8—Mary Louise Herndon, m. Isham H. Thornton.
              8—Thomas T. Herndon, m. Pelly Witcher.
              8—Georgia Herndon, m. Walter Stevens.
              8—Ida Herndon, m. Frank Howard.
              8—James Edward Herndon, b. 1850, d. 1906; m. 1872, Mary Elizabeth Fortson.
                9—George Lee Herndon, b. 1874; m. 1905, Margaret Deadwyler.
                9—Charles Fortson Herndon, b. 1876; m. 1908, Annie Mashburn.
                  10—Elizabeth Herndon, b. 1909, d. in infancy.
                  10—Dr. Charles Fortson Herndon Jr., b. 1911. (Dentist).
                  10—Annie Josephine Herndon, b. 1913, d. 1934; m. 1933, Walter Hodges.
                    11—Anne Hodges, b. 1934 d. in infancy.
                  10—John Edward Herndon, b. 1916, m. Mildred Drake.
                    11—Marian Ann Herndon, b. 1939.

10—Dorothy Herndon, b. 1925.
9—Marvin Samuel Herndon, b. 1878; m. 1909, Clara Taylor.
10—James Marvin Herndon, b. 1910; m. 1934, Frances Groover.
11—Frances Groover Herndon, b. 1936.
10—Sara Elizabeth Herndon, b. 1912; m. 1934, Ralph F. Lehman.
11—Sarah Joyce Lehman, b. 1935.
11—Ralph F. Lehman Jr., b. 1937.
10—Clara Helen Herndon, b. 1917; m. 1938, Gregg Wilson.
10—Marvin Samuel Herndon Jr., b. 1919.
9—Harry Herbert Herndon, b. 1881, d. 1928; m. 1905, Lucile Matthews.
10—Thelma Mathews Herndon, b. 1912, m. 1934, Dr. Norman W. Holman.
9—Julian Herndon, b. 1887; m. 1914, Jane Hood.
10—Julian Herndon Jr., b. 1928.
10—Lola Elizabeth Herndon, b. 1930.
9—Fred Herndon, b. 1890; m. (1) Mathilde Smith and (2) Mary Helen Smith.
10—Marjory and Virginia Herndon (1), b. 1914.
10—Minor Herndon (2), b. 1925.
6—Michael Herndon, b. 1788, d. 1857; m. 1812, Sarah Seals, b. 1796, d. 1837.
7—John S. Herndon, b. 1825, d. 1900; m. 1853, Susan Ann Elizabeth Brown, b. 1833, d. 1920.
8—George Elbert Herndon, b. 1855.
8—John Altheus Herndon, b. 1857, d. 1908; m. 1877, Mary Mildred Brown, 1860, of whom further.
8—Cornelia Herndon, b. 1860; m. Charlie McCurry.
8—Thomas Oscar Herndon, b. 1867; m. Sallie Jenkins.
8—Flora Herndon, b. 1869; m. James Brown.
8—Claudius Michael Herndon, b. 1871; m. Chloe Judd.
8—Clayton Milton Herndon, b. 1871; m. Bessie Webb.
8—Ida Herndon, b. 1875; m. Luther Thornton.
8—Eula Herndon, b. 1880; m. Joseph Rucker.
8—John A. Herndon, b. 1857, d. 1908; m. 1877, Mary Mildred Herndon.
9—Dr. Dallas Herndon, graduate of Auburn University, Auburn, Alabama, later holding chair of history at the University. Later did post-graduate work at Auburn, and received his doctor's degree from the University of Chicago. In 1911 was named Historian for State of Arkansas, and is located in Little Rock. He was appointed Secretary of Archives and History Department, of which he was the founder. He married Joyce Adkinson and had:
10—Dallas Edward Herndon.
9—Lois Herndon, m. Lon Fortson, and had:
10—Herndon Fortson.
10—Dallas Fortson.
9—Dr. Vandiver Herndon, pastor of First Baptist Church of Lake Charles, La., past president of the State Baptist Convention of Louisiana, Chairman of the Board of the State Baptist School, and member of the Board of the Southwestern Theological Seminary. He married Martha Collins and has:
10—Virginia Herndon.
10—John Herndon.
10—George Herndon.
8—Claudius Michael Herndon, b. 1871, m. Chloe Judd.
9—Claude Herndon, a portrait painter. He studied under the best masters in America and abroad. His home is Atlanta, Georgia, and he has done work at "The High Museum" there.

For reference—see National Society D. A. R., No. 302044
Thelma Herndon, Holman (Mrs. N. W.)
Herndon data compiled by Mrs. Harry Herndon, (Brunswick, Ga.)

HIGGINBOTHAM

(Note: Numbers represent generations, as: (1) first generation, (2) second generation, (3) third generation, etc.)
1—John Higginbotham, m. Frances Riley.
  2—Mose Higginbotham, m. (?).
    3—Joseph Higginbotham, b. 1790 in Amherst County, Virginia.
    3—Robert Higginbotham, d. 1826.
    3—William Higginbotham, d. 1832; m. Mary Shannon.
    3—Rachel Higginbotham.
    3—Charles Higginbotham.
    3—Frances Higginbotham, m. Joseph Higginbotham.
  2—John Higginbotham, R. S., m. 1767, Rachel Banks, daughter of Gerrard Banks and Ann Staunton.
    3—Thomas Higginbotham, b. 1769, d. 1835.
    3—James Higginbotham, b. 1770, d. 1835.
    3—John Higginbotham, b. 1722, d. 1822; m. Margaret Cahill.
    3—Ann Staunton Higginbotham, b. 1773; m. John Higginbotham.
    3—David Higginbotham, b. 1774.
    3—May Higginbotham, b. 1777.
    3—Jesse Higginbotham, b. 1779.
    3—Daniel Higginbotham, b. 1781.
    3—Tirzah Higginbotham, d. 1841.
    3—Frances Riley Higginbotham, b. 1785.
    3—Eugene Higginbotham, b. 1787.
    3—Reuben Higginbotham, b. 1789.
  2—Aaron Higginbotham, b. 1785, m. Clara Green.
    3—Colonel Samuel Higginbotham, R. S., m. Jane Satterwhite, daughter of John Satterwhite.
      4—John Higginbotham, m. Ann Staunton Higginbotham.
      4—Joseph Higginbotham.
      4—Viletta Higginbotham.
      4—Daughter Higginbotham, m. Stephen Cheatham.
      4—George Green Higginbotham.
      4—Bleckley Higginbotham.
      4—Daughter Higginbotham, m. William Fortson.
      4—Aaron Higginbotham.
  2—James Higginbotham, R. S., d. 1813; m. 1779, Rachel Campbell.
  2—Ann Higginbotham.
  2—Benjamin Higginbotham, d. 1800; m. Elizabeth Reid.
  2—Joseph Higginbotham.
  2—Rachel Higginbotham, d. 1761; m. William Morrison.
  2—Thomas Higginbotham. In 1776, according to the William and Mary Quarterly, the wife of Thomas Higginbotham and ten of his children were living.

HUDSON

The following chart shows intermarriages with the following families:
Adams — Almond — Amis — Andrews — Atkinson — Bailey — Banks — Barnett — Bell — Bennett — Blackburn — Bowen — Boyd — Bond — Bracey — Brain — Bullard — Cargill — Chapman — Cherry — Childs — Chowing — Cobb — Cosby — Crawford — Crook — Cupp — Danner — Davis — De Groot — Dinsmore — Dunning — Dye — Edwards — Fortson — Frazier — Fulk — Gillespie — Gould — Hall — Hammond — Harwell — Heard — Hogg — Holland — Howson — Hunney — Hunter —Inglet — Johnson — Jones — Juniel — Keister — Kelly — Kilpatrick — Kirkland —Lang — Marks — Matthews — Montgomery — Moore — Murphy — McDaniel — McDonnell — McGehee — McKamey — Neeley — Newman — Newsome — Oglesby — Oliver — Overstreet — Paradise — Parker — Pearson — Rayle — Rhodes — Rivers — Rius — Rortenberg — Ruse —Ryland — Samuel — Sallee — Sligh — Smallwood — Smart — Smith — Stokeley — Stuart — Taylor — Thornton — Titus — Treadwell — Urquhart — Vance — Van Brunt — Washburn —Waters — West — White — Wilkins — Wilmer — Williams — Williamson — Willis..

1—David Hudson, b. Dec. 6, 1762 in Prince Edward County, Virginia, d. subsequent to 1833, R. S., member Georgia House of Representatives 1810-1811, member Georgia Senate 1814-1815; m. Mary Cobb, b. 1765, d. 1831.
  2—Booker Hudson, d. 1831, m. Elizabeth Burton.
    3—Grandison Hudson.
    3—Augustus Hudson.
    3—Monroe Hudson, killed in Alabama.
    3—Robert Hudson, m. Mrs. (?) Bailey.
      4—Elizabeth Hudson, m. Charles Howsen.
        5—Garrett Howsen, m. Charlie May Boyd.
      4—William Hudson.
    3—Elizabeth Hudson, b. 1828, d. March 7, 1860; m. Nicholas Barnett, b. 1828.
      4—Mary Elizabeth Barnett, b. 1858, m. W. S. Amis.
    3—George Hudson.
    3—Amanda Hudson, b. 1813, m. (1) Daniel Frazier and (2) Henry Urquehart.
  2—David Hudson Jr., b. about 1790; m. Malinda Oliver.
  2—William Hudson, b. about 1792; m. June 13, 1824, Ann Oliver.
    3—Mary Hudson, m. Mr. Parker of Alabama.
    3—Elizabeth Hudson, m. David Edwards.
    3—David Newton Hudson, m. Mary Willis.
  2—Charles Hudson, b. about 1794; m. Oct. 30, 1811, Lucy McGehee.
    3—Marion Emmett Hudson, b. Feb. 22, 1812, d. March 11, 1862. m. Dec. 8, 1842, Emily V. Treadwell, b. 1827, d. Oct. 10, 1891.
    3—Lawrence B. Hudson, b. 1814, d. 1836, unmarried.
    3—James Asbury Hudson, b. Jan. 28, 1817, d. Sept. 16, 1902, m. (1) 1840, Nancy Gillespie, b. 1820, d. 1867, and (2) Mrs. Mary Ingram nee Warren.
      4—Lucy J. Hudson, b. 1840, d. 1887; m. March 26, 1861, Joel Hunter.
        5—Susie Belle Hunter, m. James Smith McDonnell, d. 1931.
          6—Hunter McDonnell, m. 1917, Castra Corsa.

6—James Smith McDonnell Jr.
6—Susie Belle McDonnell, m. 1925, Scott Hamilton.
5—Howard Hunter, m. Betty Dinsmore, d. 1915. No issue.
4—James Madison Hudson, b. 1842, d. 1925; m. 1865, Martha Harvie Marks, b. 1841.
5—Charles Edward Hudson, m. Edith Frazier.
5—Mary Hudson, m. J. Loraine De Groot.
5—James Harvey Hudson, m. Annibelle Bracey.
5—Walter Cole Hudson, m. Nellie Ray Brain.
4—William Lawrence Hudson, d. infancy.
4—Sarah Isabella Hudson, b. 1850, d. 1927; m. Feb. 8, 1872, Glenn Allen Hogg.
5—Frances Owen Hogg, b. 1876; m. 1902, Dr. Henry Clay Cupp.
6—Annabella Cupp, b. 1903; m. Ernest Keister.
6—Harvey Allen Cupp, b. 1905.
5—Harvey Hogg, b. 1879; m. 1906, Gussie Murphy.
6—Helen Hogg.
6—Lois Hogg.
5—Isabella Hogg, b. 1881; m. 1905, Mercer Sligh.
6—Virginia Sligh, b. 1912.
5—Grant Allen Hogg Jr., b. 1902.
4—Martha Virginia Hudson, b. 1852; m. 1882 John W. Crawford.
4—Mary Eliza (Ida) Hudson, b. 1845; m. 1867, Felix G. Smart.
5—Lutie Belle Smart, m. 1896, Lafayette Montgomery.
6—Catherine Montgomery, b. 1897; m. Adrian Williamson.
7—Adrian Williamson Jr.
7—Catherine Ann Williamson.
6—LaFayette Montgomery, b. 1899, d. 1915.
5—Corrie Lee Smart, m. Feb. 1898, John H. Bond.
6—John H. Bond Jr.
6—Anina Bond, b. 1908; m. Lieutenant John Williams.
7—John Williams Jr., b. 1931.
5—Felix Gillespie Smart, b. 1876, d. 1915; m. 1897, Ethel Van Valkenburg.
6—Felix Gillespie Smart Jr., m. 1920, Elize Moore.
7—Felix Gillespie Smart III, b. 1921.
7—Richard Lee Smart.
7—Elise Smart.
6—Mary Corinne Smart, m. 1922, Sebastine Ray West.
7—Sebastine Ray West Jr.
5—Martha William Smart, m. 1907, Hinton Harwell Furguson.
6—Hartwell Smart, b. 1916, d. 1922.
5—James Hudson Smart, m. Annie Oldham.
6—Annie Smart.
6—James Hudson Smart Jr.
4—Marion Alexander Hudson, b. 1855, m. Bessie Atkinson.
5—Virginia Hudson, m. 1910, Robert Ryland.
6—Marian Ryland.
6—Nancy Bess Ryland.
6—Robert Ryland Jr.
6—Martha Virginia Ryland.
5—James Hudson, m. 1912, Mary Fitzhugh Banks.
6—Jamie Hudson.
6—Virginia Hudson.
5—Rufus Hudson, d. 1920, m. Mary Lee Sallee.
5—Crawford Hudson, m. Miss Cargill.
5—Fred Hudson, m. 1921, Emma White.
5—Sarah Jane Hudson, m. Ralph James Dunning.
6—Ralph James Dunning Jr.
5—Bessie Hudson, b. 1898, d. 1911.

4—John Asbury Hudson, b. 1857, m. (1) Lula Holmes and (2) 1911, Mrs. Fannie C. Crawford, (3) Mrs. Fannie Culp.
5—(By first wife) Lillian Hudson, m. 1909, Edward Chambers.
5—Walter Cole Hudson, m. 1912, Mamie McKamey.
6—John A. Hudson.
4—Walter Cole Hudson, b. 1859, d. 1879.
3—Q. V. James Asbury Hudson, son of Charles Hudson and Lucy McGehee, m. (2) Mrs. Ingram nee Warren.
4—Frederick Mitchell Hudson, m. 1896, Nora B. Andrews.
5—Martha Hudson, b. 1899, m. 1918, Raleigh Williams Van Brunt.
6—Martha Hudson Van Brunt, b. April 15, 1919.
6—Roberta Van Brunt.
5—James Andrews Hudson, b. 1900, m. 1925, Bessie Blackburn.
6—Elizabeth Hudson, b. June 6, 1930.
5—Mary Warren Hudson, b. Oct. 3, 1907.
2—George Hudson, b. about 1797; m. Jan. 9, 1816, Ann Samuel.
3—Mary Ann Hudson, d. 1887, m. Judge James McDaniel, d. 1887.
4—Thomas McDaniel, b. 1841, d. 1864, C. S.
4—William McDaniel, C. S., b. 1842; m. Emma Juniel.
4—Mary McDaniel, b. 1844; m. J. W. Juniel, b. 1844.
5—James W. Juniel, m. Beulah Lindsay.
6—Lindsay Juniel.
6—Lois Juniel.
6—Morris Juniel.
5—M. E. Juniel.
5—Paul Juniel.
5—Edna Juniel, m. Giles Taylor.
6—Juniel Conger Taylor.
6—Mary Taylor.
6—Boyce Taylor.
6—Thomas Easton Taylor.
6—Warren Taylor.
6—Ruth Taylor.
6—Esther Taylor.
4—James McDaniel, b. 1846, m. Emma Washburn.
5—Maggie McDaniel.
4—Amanda McDaniel, b. 1847, m. Robert Neeley.
4—Lucy McDaniel, b. 1849, m. Mr. Overstreet.
5—Daughter Overstreet, m. Henry Childs.
5—Henry McDaniel Overstreet.
5—Lucy Amanda Overstreet.
5—Tommie Overstreet.
5—Ruth Overstreet.
5—Esther Overstreet.
4—Ann Boutwell McDaniel, b. 1852.
4—Margaret and Nathaniel McDaniel, twins, b. 1854.
4—Henry Clay McDaniel, m. Florence Cherry. No issue.
4—Lettie McDaniel, m. B. S. Washburn.
5—Katie Washburn.
5—Bailey Washburn.
5—Benjamin Washburn.
5—Mary Ethel Washburn.
5—Annie Washburn.
5—Henry Washburn.
5—Edwin Washburn.
5—Mary Washburn.
3—Richard Hudson, d. unmarried.
2—Madison Hudson, b. 1809, d. 1886, m. Eliza Terrell Clark, daughter of General Elijah Clark.
3—David Hudson, m. Mrs. Titus.
4—Madison Hudson.

4—David Hudson Jr.
3—John Christopher Hudson, m. Mildred Agatha Bullard.
4—Georgia Hudson, m. Robert Johnson.
4—Johnny Hudson.
3—Reverend James Madison Hudson, b. 1839; m. Mrs. Sarah A. Wilkins.
4—James T. Hudson, b. 1860; m. Theodosia Crook.
4—Mary Hudson, b. 1862.
4—Cora Hudson, m. 1884, H. B. Ross.
4—Fannie T. Hudson, b. 1868; m. 1887, O. B. Paradise.
5—Pauline Paradise.
4—May Hudson, b. May 10, 1870; m. 1890, Julian Paradise.
5—Harry Paradise, b. 1895.
5—Eula Paradise, b. 1896.
4—Sallie C. Hudson, b. 1871; m. 1897, Samuel C. Cosby.
4—Addie Hudson, b. 1873.
4—Alice Hudson, b. 1874, d. 1877.
4—Emma Hudson, b. 1877, m. George Hunney.
5—Paul Hunney.
5—Clark Hunney, b. 1903.
5—Rosa Hunney, b. 1906.
4—Kate Hudson, b. 1881; m. J. B. Lang.
5—Miller Lang, b. 1901.
5—Velma Lang, b. 1903.
4—Rose Hudson, m. L. J. Danner.
5—Vance Danner, b. 1908.
3—Samantha Lavonia Hudson, m. Thomas F. Almond.
3—Thomas Jefferson Hudson, C. S.
3—William Albert Clark Hudson, C. S., m. Frances Rayle.
4—Madison Wyatt Hudson.
4—Annie Hudson.
4—Albert Rayle Hudson, b. 1878; m. April 19, 1909, Callie May Jones, b. 1891.
5—Albert Hudson, b. 1910; m. Elizabeth Rayle.
5—Clark Hudson, b. 1912.
5—Francis Hudson, b. 1915.
5—Mack Hudson, b. 1917.
5—David Hudson, b. 1919.
5—Carroll Allen Hudson, b. 1922.
3—Elizabeth Ann Hudson, m. Thomas F. Willis, C. S.
4—William Willis.
4—Thomas Willis.
4—Carswell Willis
3—Stockton Cobb Hudson, C. S., m. Louisa Dye.
4—David Cobb Hudson, m. Emma Thornton. No issue.
4—Edward Hudson, d. unmarried.
4—William Oscar Hudson, m. June 11, 1902, Maud Jones.
5—Daisy Hudson.
5—Louise Hudson.
4—Stockton Calloway Hudson, d. unmarried.
4—Jessie Lou Hudson, m. William A. Jones.
5—Freddie Jones.
5—Harold Jones.
5—John Allen Jones.
5—Vesta Jones.
4—Bertha Hudson.
4—Emma Hudson.
4—Elizabeth May Hudson.
4—Vesta Irene Hudson.
4—Stockton Cobb Hudson Jr., m. Fanny G. Fortson. No issue.

3—Emma L. Hudson, m. J. W. Jones.
2—Martha Hudson, m. Alex McDonald.
2—Louise Edith Hudson, b. 1804, m. July 31, 1823, James Davis.
3—Elizabeth Davis, d. 1858; m. Frank Bowen.
4—Mollie Bowen.
4—Louise Bowen.
4—Passie Bowen.
3—William Hudson Davis, d. 1878; m. Sarah Ann Kilpatrick.
4—William Hudson Davis Jr., m. Marie Wilkins.
4—Hattie Davis, m. Mr. Wilmer.
4—Jessie Davis, m. Mr. Stokeley.
4—Ida Davis, m. J. A. Hall.
5—Jessie Hall.
5—J. A. Hall Jr..
5—Davis Hall.
3—James J. Davis, m. 1877, Mrs. Virginia Jones nee Inman.
4—Inman Jones Davis.
3—Anna T. Davis, m. 1858, William Benjamin Chapman.
4—Mollie Chapman, m. Robert Huie.
4—Reverend Joseph Davis Chapman.
4—Jessie Almeda Chapman.
4—John Courtney Chapman.
4—William Augustus Chapman.
3—Isacc Newton Davis.
3—Dr. David Davis, m. Mattie Heard.
4—Jefferson H. Davis.
4—Wade Davis.
4—Walter Davis.
3—Jesse Davis, C. S., killed in action.
2—Mary "Polly" Hudson, b. Jan. 11, 1796; m. Nathaniel Barnett.
3—David Barnett, b. 1817.
3—Martha Elizabeth Barnett, b. 1818.
3—Louise A. Barnett, b. 1820.
3—Susan Barnett, b. 1826.
3—Frances L. Barnett, m. Judge Josiah Gould.
4—James Nathaniel Gould, m. (1) Belle Holland, (2) Beulah Benton.
3—Martha Valeria Barnett, b. 1830; m. Dr. Thomas Chowing.
3—Nicholas Barnett, m. (1) Elizabeth Hudson, (2) Olive Matthews and (3) Sallie Matthews.
4—(By first wife) Mary Elizabeth Barnett, b. 1858; m. W. S. Amis.
4—(By second wife) Sydney O. Barnett, b. 1862, d. 1905; m. 1886, Sallie Virginia Rogers, b. 1864, d. 1914.
4—William Eugene Barnett, b. 1864; m. Catherine Williams.
4—Mary Meriwether Barnett, b. 1815, d. 1848; m. 1829, John Harvey Marks Jr.
3—Amanda Hudson, m. Daniel Frazier.
4—John Frazier.
4—James Frazier.
4—Catherine Frazier.
4—Margaret Frazier, b. 1841, d. 1913; m. 1868, William D. Marks.
3—David Newton Hudson, m. Mary Mildred Willis, d. 1908.
4—Martha Lavonis Hudson, m. Andrew Adams.
4—William Thomas Hudson, m. Sallie Rivers.
4—Georgia Mildred Hudson.
4—Sarah Ella Hudson.
4—Ada Hudson.
4—Mary Emma Hudson, m. Felix Edwards.
4—Laura Capitola Hudson, m. William Kirkland.

5—David Kirkland.
5—Richard Kirkland, m. Emma Ruis.
6—Mary Kirkland.
6—Alice Kirkland.
6—Arnold Kirkland.
5—Julia Kirkland.
5—Carrie Kirkland.
5—Irene Kirkland, m. John Kelly.
6—Laura Kelly.
6—Rose Kelly.
6—Lee Kelly.
6—John Kelly Jr.
5—Dora E. Kirkland, m. John Newman.
6—Claud Newman.
6—Bowdry Newman.
5—Charles Tate Kirkland, m. Martha Inglet.
6—Louise Kirkland.
6—Eva Kirkland.
6—Mary Kirkland.
5—Lizzie May Kirkland, m. Joseph Stewart.
6—Lizzie May Stewart.
6—Lena Stewart.
5—Ada D. Kirkland.
5—Minnie L. Kirkland.
4—David Albert Hudson.
4—Lula Virginia Hudson, m. Boldin Waters.
5—Sarah Hudson Waters, m. Thomas Smallwood.
5—Patrick Waters, m. Carrie Dent.
5—Emma Vernon Waters, m. Thomas Newsome.
5—Mary Frances Waters, m. Luther Johnson.
5—Mattie Lizzie Waters, m. William Reese.
5—Georgia Virginia Waters, m. Robert Reese.
5—Janie Waters, m. Benjamin Reese.
5—Ruth Lee Waters.
5—Mac Willis Waters.
5—Nina Waters.
5—David Daniel Waters.
4—Lillian Electra Hudson.
4—Robert Madison Hudson, m. Eva Rortenberg.
5—George Hudson.
5—Mildred Hudson.
5—Henry Hudson.
5—Edward Hudson.
5—Lillie V. Hudson.
5—Ernest Hudson.
5—David R. Hudson.
4—Samuel Wynn Hudson.
4—Elizabeth Hudson, m. Robert Murphy.
5—Allie Murphy.
5—Mary Lou Murphy.
5—David S. Murphy.
5—Leona V. Murphy.
3—David Hudson, m. Matilda Oliver.
4—William Hudson m. Miss Jones.
5—Henry Hudson.
5—William Hudson Jr.
3—Martha Hudson.
3—Mary Hudson, m. John Barnett.
4—Martha Barnett.
4—James Barnett.

4—Sarah Barnett.
4—John Barnett Jr.
3—Marion Emmett Hudson, m. Emily V. Treadwell.
4—James Rembert Hudson, d. 1888, m. 1869, Laura Elma Donelson.
5—Virginia Grace Hudson, b. 1870, m. Mr. Pearsons.
5—John Donelson Hudson, b. 1872.
5—Lena Rembert Hudson, b. 1873, d. 1874.
5—Marion Emmett Hudson, b. 1875.
5—Delia Waters Hudson, b. 1877.
5—R. L. Hudson, b. 1879, d. 1889.
5—James Rembert Hudson, b. 1882.
5—Charles Tolbert Hudson, b. 1885, d. 1917.
5—Benjamin W. Hudson.
5—**Elma Hudson.**
3—Emma L. Hudson, m. Dec. 7, 1868, Jackson M. Jones.
4—Sallie Jones, m. Barnard Smith.
5—Carl Smith, m. Dec. 25, 1910, Pauline Rhodes.
5—Lula May Smith, m. Leverette H. Smith.
6—Shirley Smith.
6—Forrest Smith.
5—Jack Smith.
4—Ida Jones, m. Nov. 16, 1888, m. James E. Hammond, county commissioner of Elbert County, member Elbert County Board of Tax Assessors, b. Feb. 10, 1868.
5—Jack Hammond, S. W. W.
5—Edward Hammond.
5—Walter Hammond.
5—Jessie Hammond.
5—Julia May Hammond.
5—Raymond Hammond.
5—Genora Hammond.
5—Lenora Hammond.
4—Walter C. Jones, m. Janna Oglesby.
5—Neva Jones.
5—Jenelle Jones.
5—Helen Jones.
4—Stockton Hudson Jones, m. Miss Jones.
4—Mary Jones, m. A. D. Jones.

HUNT

The following chart shows intermarriages with the following families:
Allen — Adams — Alford — Basford — Brown — Coon — Cole — Cristler — Cason — Cleveland — Carter — Cash — Cunningham — Clifton — Craft — Dodd — Dockery — De 'Georgis — Eberhardt — Edwards — Gaines — Gray — Gupton — Hewitt — Hood — Hunter — Johnson — Maxwell — Mewbourn — Moncrief — Molloy — McCrary — Norman — Nicholson — Parrent — Paxson — Page — Parker — Pelligrini — Reynolds — Redwine — Satterfield — Sanders — Stovall — Skelton — Speed — Sheron — Simpkins — Street — Shaw — Swift — Thornton — Teasley — Tyner — Vandiver — Whitehouse — Weakley.

(Note: Numbers represent generations, as: (1) first generation, (2) second generation, (3) third generation, etc.)
1—James Hunt Sr., b. July 24, 1732; will probated in Robertson County, Tennessee, Feb. term, 1805; m. Mary (?). Was soldier of Revolution.

2—Henry Hunt, b. Sept. 17, 1755.
2—Lucy Hunt, b. May 18, 1757, d. 1846; m. John Teasley III, b. 1755, d. April 1816. Was R. S.
3—John W. Teasley, b. Dec. 28, 1788, d. Oct. 20, 1852; m. Mary Hunter.
4—John W. Teasley Jr., m. Sarah Nicholson.
5—Louis Scott Teasley, b. Nov. 1, 1847; m. Oct. 16, 1873, Melvina Tennessee Teasley.
6—Leila Bell Teasley, b. July 21, 1874; m. James Bailey Basford, b. Oct. 2, 1867.
7—Walter Martin Basford, b. Feb. 21, 1901.
7—Mary B. Basford, b. Sept. 13, 1903.
7—Madalyn May Basford, b. Aug. 7, 1907.
6—Lucy Ann Teasley, b. Feb. 11, 1876; m. Nov. 18, 1896, George Edwin Shaw, b. March 3, 1873.
6—Mary Elizabeth Teasley, b. March 15, 1878; m. Feb. 12, 1902, Robert Hewitt, b. Jan. 20, 1872.
6—Walter Scott Teasley, b. Aug. 9, 1880.
6—Ethel May Teasley, b. Dec. 3, 1882; m. April 12, 1908, Thomas E. Weakley.
6—Ellen Earl Teasley, b. Jan. 7, 1885; m. March 10, 1912, Henry E. Simpkins, b. Aug. 7, 1884. .
3—Joshua Teasley, m. March 4, 1812, Polly Cristler.
3—George Teasley, b. 1782, m. Lucretia Sheron.
3—James Teasley, b. March, 1779, d. Feb. 10, 1849; m. Drucilla Allen, b. March 1, 1782, d. July 4, 1847.
4—Beverly Allen Teasley, b. July 6, 1806, d. April 9, 1862; m. Feb. 12, 1828, Elizabeth Eavenson, b. July 22, 1810, d. Jan. 13, 1891.
5—Lucy Teasley, b. Dec. 18, 1828; m. Dec. 1846, Thomas Cason.
6—Allen Cason and other issue.
5—Alfred J. Teasley, b. Dec. 6, 1830; m. Sept. 30, 1851, Martha Frances Cleveland.
5—Elizabeth Ann Teasley, b. July 3, 1832; m. Nov. 16, 1848, William R. Adams.
5—Priscilla Jane Teasley, b. July 24, 1834, d. May 23, 1896; m. Sept. 4, 1851, Benjamin Calloway Thornton, b. Dec. 13, 1827, d. Oct. 30, 1881.
6—Thomas A. Thornton, b. July 31, 1852, m. Georgia Carter.
6—Sarah Thornton, b. Jan. 1, 1854, d. April 5, 1924; m. D. C. Alford.
6—James Thornton, b. Sept. 5, 1857, d. March 14, 1921; m. Sarah Speed.
6—Janie Thornton, d. infancy.
6—Cornelia Thornton, d. infancy.
6—Amanda Thornton, b. Nov. 27, 1864; m. George Page.
6—John C. Thornton, b. 1866, d. 1899.
6—Rebecca Thornton, d. infancy.
6—Jessie Thornton, b. April 4, 1871; m. Dec. 23, 1891, James H. Skelton, lawyer, member Georgia House of Representatives, member Georgia Senate.
6—McAlpin Thornton, b. Oct. 3, 1873; m. Claire Dodd.
6—Dunstan Thornton, b. July 2, 1876.
6—Annie Thornton, b. June 24, 1878; m. J. P. Cash.
5—Mary F. A. Teasley, b. July 25, 1836; m. Mr. Adams.
5—Drucilla C. Teasley, b. Aug. 12, 1838; m. Martin Maxwell.
5—Martha M. Teasley, d. infancy.
5—Phronie Teasley, b. June 3, 1843; m. J. A. Brown.
5—Eliza E. Teasley, b. May 18, 1847; m. Nov. 11, 1864, Isham Hailey Brown, b. May 24, 1846.

4—James Riley Teasley, m. Mary B. F. Norman.
5—Jane Teasley, m. J. William Thornton.
5—Lucy E. Teasley, m. Reuben Carter.
4—Lucy H. Teasley, m. Lawrence Adams.
5—Emily Adams m. Marion Gaines.
5—Drucilla Adams.
5—Beverly Adams.
4—Priscilla Teasley, m. Nov. 7, 1843, Willis Hunt, d. 1872.
5—Lucy Ann Drucilla Hunt, b. March 29, 1836.
5—James W. H. Hunt, b. Oct. 29, 1837.
5—B. A. T. Hunt, b. April 12, 1839.
5—Judge M. B. Hunt.
5—T. J. M. Hunt
5—S. T. W. Hunt.
5—W. S. A. Hunt, b. April 5, 1848; m. Frances Cunningham.
6—John Hunt, m. Elizabeth Gaines.
6—Looney H. Hunt, merchant, justice of the peace, b. Feb. 2, 1881; m. June 5, 1900, Annie E. Gaines.
7—Annie Lee Hunt, b. April, 1902, m. Sept. 9, 1923, L. L. Stovall, merchant, member tax board of Elbert County.
7—Willie Hunt, merchant, b. November 23, 1903; m. June 27, 1921, Ruth Maxwell.
7—Parker Hunt, b. Aug. 3, 1906; m. Grovia Dockery, b. Sept. 9, 1903.
7—L. H. Hunt Jr.
7—Joel Hunt.
7—James Hunt.
6—Evey Hunt, m. John Reynolds.
4—Phronie Teasley, m. Malcolm Johnson.
4—Drucilla Ann Teasley, b. Nov. 10, 1827; m. Dec. 16, 1847, John Easton Teasley, b. Dec. 4, 1827, d. Sept. 5, 1904.
4—Jefferson Teasley, m. Nancy Mewbourn.
3—Aquilla Teasley, b. 1785; m. Adam Brown.
3—Priscilla Teasley, b. 1788, d. May 8, 1846; m. (1) Mr. Parker, and (2) Joshua Tyner.
3—Lucy Teasley, b. 1790, d. Nov. 4, 1846; m. Henry Hunter and removed to Illinois.
3—Peter Teasley, b. Nov. 30, 1793, m. Miss Clifton.
3—Thomas Teasley, b. Sept. 2, 1796; m. Miss Hunter.
3—Isham Teasley, m. Jane Adams.
(For Further TEASLEY Data See Chart of TEASLEY)
2—Mary Hunt, b. April 16, 1759.
2—Moses Hunt, b. June 18, 1760; m. Tamar Tyner.
2—James Hunt Jr., b. June 6, 1762, d. March 23, 1832; m. Nov. 11, 1790, Jemimah Carter, b. 1772, d. Jan. 7, 1869. (James Hunt Jr. received land grant in Elbert County for services in the American Revolution. Miss Laura Lee Satterfield of Hartwell, Georgia has established this line with **Daughters of the American Revolution No. 189685**).
3—Elizabeth Hunt, b. Oct. 21, 1791, d. March 23, 1844; m. Jesse Redwine.
3—Henry Hunt, b. Aug. 27, 1793; m. July 20, 1815, Nancy Craft.
3—Sion Hunt, b. 1798, d. Feb. 11, 1875; m. July 31, 1823, Priscilla Thornton, d. Aug. 16, 1846.
4—James J. Hunt, C. S., b. Dec. 21, 1830, d. July 25, 1863.
4—Mary Elizabeth Hunt, b. June 15, 1833.
4—Benjamin Thornton Hunt, C. S., b. Feb. 10, 1837, d. July 31, 1862.
4—Reuben Smith Hunt, C. S., b. April 8, 1838; m. Dec. 20, 1860, Mary Elizabeth McCrary.

5—Reuben Harrison Hunt, b. Feb. 2, 1862; m. May 3, 1894, Kate De 'Georgis.
6—Louise Hunt, b. Nov. 10, 1895; m. Nov. 10, 1917, Thomas G. Street.
7—Thomas G. Street Jr., b. Dec. 21, 1918.
7—Richard Street, b. Feb. 4, 1922.
7—Katherine Louise Street, b. Oct. 1, 1924.
7—Edward Street, b. Aug. 14, 1925.
5—Almeda Priscilla Hunt, b. Oct. 3, 1864.
5—Mary Ella Hunt, b. Aug. 18, 1866.
5—Jesse Dozier Hunt, b. Jan. 12, 1868, d. Aug. 23, 1899; m. May 28, 1891, Annie Bell Parrent.
6—Jessie Parrent Hunt, b. 1892, d. 1918.
6—Richadson Harrison Hunt, b. 1893, d. 1896.
6—Margaret Elizabeth Hunt, b. Oct. 19, 1895.
6—Robert Edwin Hunt, b. Jan. 20, 1898.
6—Ann Dozier Hunt, b. Feb. 7, 1900.
5—Fanny Jane Hunt, b. April 17, 1871.
5—Minnie Elizabeth Hunt, b. 1873, d. 1889.
5—Harriet Emma Hunt, b. March 31, 1877; m. Oct. 6, 1898, Charles Francis Hood.
6—Harriet Elizabeth Hood, b. Aug. 8, 1899; m. Oct. 8, 1919, Sim Allen Gray, d. April 1, 1925.
7—Harriet Jane Gray, b. Oct. 19, 1920.
7—Allen Hood Gray, b. 1923, d. 1928.
7—Sarah Evelyn Gray, b. Oct. 27, 1925.
6—Almeda Marie Hood, b. July 20, 1902.
6—Charles Francis Hood Jr., b. Aug 11, 1908.
5—Sion Madison Hunt, b. May 29, 1880; m. Joe Willie Swift.
5—Benjamin Fortson Hunt, b. Sept. 1, 1883; m. June 6, 1906, Agnes Paxson.
6—Mary Emily Hunt, b. Nov. 14, 1907, m. July 5, 1930, Alfred H. Allen.
6—Benjamin Paxson Hunt, b. Jan. 9, 1909.
6—Ella Katherine Hunt, b. Dec. 22, 1912.
4—T. W. Harrison Hunt, C. S., b. Jan. 18, 1841, d. July 7, 1862.
4—Dozier Calloway Hunt, C. S., b. Oct. 4, 1842, d. Oct. 14, 1864.
4—Daniel Crumley Hunt, C. S., b. Dec. 14, 1844.
4—Emma Priscilla Hunt, b. April 8, 1846, d. April 2, 1907; m. Sept. 26, 1861, Robert Patton Eberhardt, C. S. lieutenant-colonel b. Oct. 13, 1834, d. Jan. 17, 1907.
5—Leila Hilliard Eberhardt, b. 1862, d. 1864.
5—John Lee Eberhardt, b. Nov. 26, 1864.
5—Thomas Llellyn Eberhardt, b. June 29, 1866; m. (1) Eliza Marshall, and (2) Harriet Sanders.
6—(By first wife) Maud Marshall Eberhardt, b. 1891.
6—(By second wife) Harriet Rebecca Eberhardt.
5—Elizabeth Helen Eberhardt, b. Nov. 25, 1868, d. Aug. 25, 1918; m. David Edwin Moncrief.
6—Herbert Raymond Moncrief, b. July 3, 1889; m. 1908, Lillian Hollis.
7—Mary Elizabeth Moncrief.
6—David Edwin Moncrief Jr., b. Sept. 5, 1891; m. 1917, Margaret Malloy.
7—David Buckley Moncrief, b. Aug. 6, 1919.
5—Robert Wade Eberhardt, b. Dec. 5, 1871; m. Oct. 5, 1893, Florence Italia Pelligrini.
6—Dora Eberhardt.
6—Robert Wade Eberhardt Jr.
6—Ruth Eberhardt.

6—John William Eberhardt.
5—Jane Leeper Eberhardt, b. Aug. 11, 1873; m. Feb. 15, 1909, Charles Fox Cole.
6—Emma Lou Cole, b. Jan. 8, 1910.
5—Augusta Louise Eberhardt, b. Sept. 11, 1876.
5—Jim Frank Eberhardt, d. infancy.
5—Harry L. Eberhardt, b. July 3, 1882; m. John Grace Bishop.
6—Harry Joyce Eberhardt.
3—James Hunt III, b. Feb. 9, 1800, d. 1838.
3—Moses B. Hunt, b. Oct. 12, 1802.
3—Drucilla Hunt, b. March 18, 1806; m. Dec. 2, 1839, Nicholas N. Adams.
3—Willis Hunt, b. Dec. 3, 1810; m. Nov. 5, 1833, Priscilla Teasley.
4—Lucy Ann Drucilla Hunt, b. March 29, 1836.
4—James Willis Henry Hunt, b. Oct. 29, 1837.
4—Beverly Allen Teasley Hunt, b. Aug. 12, 1839.
4—Thomas Jefferson Monroe Hunt, b. July 16, 1841.
4—Singleton T. W. Hunt, b. June 28, 1843.
4—William Singleton Allen Hunt, b. April 5, 1848; m. Frances Cunningham.
5—John Hunt, m. Lizzie Gaines.
5—Evey Hunt, m. John Reynolds.
5—Looney H. Hunt, b. Feb. 2, 1881, merchant, justice of the peace; m. June 5, 1900, Annie E. Gaines.
6—Annie Lee Hunt, b. April 1902; m. Sept. 19, 1923, L. L. Stovall, merchant, member board of tax assessors of Elbert County.
6—Willie Hunt, b. Nov. 23, 1903; m. June 27, 1921, Ruth Maxwell, b. Oct. 6, 1902.
6—Parker Hunt, granite shed operator, b. Aug. 3, 1906; m. March 23, 1929, Grovia Dockery, b. Sept. 9, 1903.
6—L. H. Hunt Jr.
6—Joel Hunt.
6—James Hunt.
4—Laura Cordelia Drucilla Hunt, b. Aug. 10, 1850.
4—Mary Mildred Hunt, b. Oct. 13, 1854.
3—Richard Carter Hunt, b. June 29, 1813.
3—Mary Polly Hunt, b. Aug. 16, 1817, d. Aug. 15, 1863; m. Aug. 16, 1836, William "Buck" Page, b. Feb. 28, 1808, d. April 20, 1877.
4—Dr. William Henry Page, M. D., b. 1837, d. 1899.
4—James "Jim" R. Page, b. March 18, 1839, d. Feb. 25, 1865, in Elmira Prison, New York, having been captured by Union troops.
4—Drucilla Page, b. Aug. 6, 1840, d. May 31, 1909; m. J. W. Williams.
4—Mary Page, b. April 12, 1842, d. May 1912; m. Ira Edwards.
4—Martha L. Page, b. May 30, 1845, d. Jan. 31, 1920; m. Jan. 1, 1867, Henry W. Satterfield, b. April 11, 1842.
4—Early S. Page, b. March 8, 1853, d. July 1925.
4—Alice Hunt Page, b. Sept. 15, 1855, d. Aug. 1922; m. Robert Vandiver.
4—George J. Page, b. May 28, 1858.
2—Shadrack Hunt, b. April 11, 1764; m. Elizabeth Whitehouse.
2—Agnes Hunt, b. July 27, 1766; m. Mr. Coon.
2—William Hunt, b. Nov. 9, 1768
2—Matthew Hunt, b. April 26, 1771.
2—Sion Hunt, b. Sept. 30, 1773.
2—Judith Hunt, b. Aug. 9, 1777; m. Abner Gupton.
2—John Hunt, b. May 24, 1781.

JONES

The following chart shows intermarriages with the following families:
Blackwell — Barnett — Balchin — Burch — Caldwell — Carr — Colley — Darricotte — Dennis — Fields — Fleming — Foster — Gairdner — Hammond — Heard — Hester — Hewlett — Johnson — Lattimer — McKissett — Pharr — Shackleford — Shannon — Shipman — Shiver — Sparks — Statham — West — Williams — Wittock.

(Note: Numbers represent generations, as: (1) first generation, (2) second generation, (3) third generation, etc.)

1—John Jones, m. Annie Shackleford.
  2—Stephen Jones, m. Miss Caldwell.
  2—Allen Jones.
  2—Wiley Jones, m. Miss West.
  2—John Jones Jr., m. Miss Dickey.
  2—Patsy Jones, m. Nov. 26, 1809, John S. Foster.
  2—Eliza Jones, m. John Wingfield.
  2—Polly Jones, m. Mordeci Shackleford.
  2—Betsy Jones Jones, m. John White.
  2—Thomas Jones, b. 1781, d. 1840, sheriff of Elbert County; m. April 12, 1815, Eliza M. Darricotte, b. Nov. 27, 1796, d. 1857.
    3—Thomas Jones Jr.
    3—Oscar Jones, m. (1) Miss Hammond, (2) Miss Wittock.
    3—Edwin A. Jones, m. Jane Blackwell.
    3—Cornelia Jones, m. Robert Hester, member Georgia House of Representatives, lawyer.
      4—Thomas J. Hester, m. Anna Statham.
        5—Lamar Hester.
      4—Kate Hester, m. Mr. Robinson.
    3—John Henry Jones, b. Oct. 11, 1816, d. Sept. 23, 1899; m. Dec. 19, 1843, Lavonia Hammond, b. March 13, 1827, d. Dec. 27, 1909.
      4—Thomas Jones, C. S., postmaster of Elberton, b. 1844, d. 1923, unmarried.
      4—Louisa Jones, b. April 24, 1846, d. Sept. 23, 1910; m. April 19, 1864, Robert M. Heard, C. S. captain, mayor of Elberton, member Georgia House of Representatives.
        5—John T. Heard, d. 1932, unmarried.
        5—Carroll M. Heard.
        5—Vohammie Heard, m. Marcus A. Pharr.
          6—Marcus A. Pharr Jr., S. W. W., d. unmarried.
          6—Robert Pharr.
          6—Camilla Pharr, m. G. D. Barnett.
            7—Aurelius Barnett.
            7—Camilla Barnett.
            7—Ida Barnett.
            7—Vohammie Barnett.
          6—Mitta Pharr, m. S. A. Fields.
          6—Louise Pharr, m. H. C. Sparks.
            7—Louise Sparks.
            7—H. C. Sparks Jr.
          6—Vohammie Pharr, m. J. C. Carr.
            7—J. C. Carr Jr.
        5—Luther Martin Heard, president Citizens Bank of Elberton; m. Mamie Lattimer, daughter of U. S. Senator Lattimer of South Carolina.
          6—Luther Martin Heard Jr.
          6—Lattimer Heard.

6—Robert Heard.
5—Georgia Heard, m. Dr. J. E. Johnson.
6—J. E. Johnson Jr., m. Marie Williams.
7—J. E. Johnson III.
5—Roberta Heard, m. J. T. Dennis Jr. No issue.
5—Parks E. Heard.
4—Ida Jones, b. Feb. 19, 1848, d. 1931; m. Feb. 1, 1870, Captain James J. Burch, C. S., ordinary of Elbert County. member of Georgia House of Representatives, lawyer.
5—Irene Burch, m. James Balchin. No issue.
5—William J. Burch.
5—Hammond Burch, m. (1) Charles Shipman and (2) Jack Flemming.
6—Charles Shipman Jr.
6—Jack Flemming Jr.
4—Georgia Jones.
4—Mary C. Jones, b. Oct. 10, 1851; m. Jan. 28, 1874, Thomas J. Blackwell.
5—Jones Blackwell.
5—Daisy Blackwell, m. W. T. Shannon.
5—Fred Blackwell.
5—Banks Blackwell.
5—Wenona Blackwell, m. June 5, 1911, Thomas Hewlett.
4—Lavonia Gairdner, b. Feb. 12, 1854, d. 1935, m. Harry K. Gairdner.
5—Jamie Gairdner.
4—Lenora Jones.
4—William Oscar Jones, b. Sept. 11, 1861, d. 1931, mayor of Elberton, chairman Elberton Board of Education, president Bank of Elberton, president Elberton Cotton and Compress Company, president Elberton & Eastern Railroad, chairman board of stewards First Methodist Church of Elberton, merchant; m. Mollie Gardner of Columbus, Georgia.
5—Margaret Jones, d. unmarried.
5—William Oscar Jones Jr., d. infancy.
5—Martha "Polly" Jones, m. Thomas Colley.
6—William "Billy" Colley.
6—Thomas Colley Jr.
5—John Henry Jones, m. Lois McKissett.
6—William Oscar Jones, b. 1931.
5—Mitta Byrd "Ladybird" Jones.
5—Mamie Jones.

KEY

The following chart shows intermarriages with the following families:
Albright — Avera — Bagnell — Bailey — Bell — Bibb — Blaydes — Bonifay — Bowles — Boyd — Bradford — Brown —Calhoun — Cantrell — Carroll — Carroway — Chambers — Christian — Collier — Clark — Cottingham — Cyre — Daniel — Davenport — Deshe — Donaldson — Downer — Dye — Eberhardt — Edwards — Fitzgerald — Fleming — Ford — Fortson — Garrett — German — Glenn — Grimes — Grizzle — Gunter — Hadden — Halsey — Harmon — Henry — Hilsman — Holland — Hopkins — Hulme — Jackson — Johnson — Jones — Keith — Kilpatrick — Kelly — King — Kimsey — Lambert — Litcher — Little — Long — Mattox — Meriwether — Miller — Montgomery — Morgan — Moss — McCarthy — McDaniel — McLanahan — McWhorter — Oglesby — Osburn — Peek —

Perkins — Peterman — Pickens — Posey — Pritchett — Ramsaur — Ray — Reeves — Rush — Sandiford — Scott — Settles — Sewell — Shaw — Smith — Snyder — Stark — Stone — Stovall — Sutton — Talbot — Tandy — Taylor — Thornley — Thornton — Tiller — Tillman — Upshaw — Walker — Webb — Wells — White — Wilson — Wooly — Webb — Wright — Yeary.

The earliest records of this family are found in England. On the Fabric Roll of York appears the name of one John Key. Thomas Key, born 1540, died 1578, was sergeant porter to Queen Elizabeth. In the month of August, 1565 he secretly married Mary Grey. She was the daughter of Henry Grey and Frances Brandon and granddaughter of King Henry VII. One of her sisters was the famous Lady Jane Grey.
(Reference: Dictionary of National Biography volume 31.)

(Note: Numbers represent generations, as: (1) first generation, (2) second generation, (3) third generation, etc.)

1—John Key came to America with William Penn.
  2—John Key, b. 1682, d. 1767, m. Martha Tandy.
    3—Martin Key, b. 1715, d. 1791 in Albermarle County, Virginia; m. Nancy Ann Bibb, a daughter of William Bibb.
      4—John Key, d. prior to 1815; m. (?).
        5—Mary "Polly" Key, m. John C. Blades.
      4—Martin Key Jr.
      4—Tandy Key, b. Oct. 29, 1754, m. Mildred Perkins.
        5—Walter Key.
        5—Thomas Key.
        5—Martin Key, b. Oct. 16, 1780, S. W. 1812.
        5—Sallie Bibb Key, m. William Jones.
        5—Nancy Bibb Key, m. Captain Thomas German.
        5—Jesse Bibb Key, m. Mary Bailey.
        5—Daniel Key.
        5—Patsy Key, m. Elijah Brown.
      4—Walter Key.
      4—Joshua Key.
      4—William Bibb Key, R. S., b. Oct. 2, 1759, d. Dec. 7, 1836; m. Aug. 17, 1782, Mourning Clark, b. Aug. 12, 1764, d. 1840.
        5—Chiles Terrell Key, b. Jan. 30, 1784, d. March 4, 1846; m. 1805, Mary Ann Clark, b. about 1787.
          6—Thomas Jefferson Key, b. Aug. 28, 1806; m. Martha Little.
            7—James Key, d. 1866.
            7—Mary Ann Key, m. E. W. Fitzgerald.
            7—Robert Terrell Key, d. 1902.
            7—William Key, d. 1882.
            7—Clark Key, d. 1888.
          6—George Key, b. Jan. 24, 1808, d. 1883; m. (1) Adeline C. Stephens and (2) Marie Morgan.
            7—(By first wife) Thomas Terrell Key, b. Jan. 21, 1835, d. March 23, 1922; m. Jan. 5, 1858, Rhoda Carroll.
              8—George Oscar Key, b. 1858; m. Catherine Sewell.
                9—Alma Key, m. Ewing Avera.
                9—Armory Key.
                9—Blanche Key, m. Thomas Montgomery.
                9—Lottie Key, m. Walter Yeary.
                9—Oscar Key, S. W. W., killed in action 1918.
                9—Doris Key.
                9—King Key.
                9—Kathryn Key.
              8—William Duerrell Key, b. Oct. 26, 1860; m. 1880, Emma Albright.

9—Paul W. Key, m. Dora Snyder.
9—Fannie May Key, m. Robert Webb.
9—Earnest D. Key, m. (1) Ruby Kennedy and (2) Marie Morgan.
8—John Edgar Key, d. unmarried.
8—Mary Leola Key, d. infancy.
8—James Lee Key, b. 1867; m. Ella Tillman.
9—James Lee Key Jr., d. infancy.
9—Ruth Key.
8—Lola L. Key.
8—Maud Madeline Key, b. 1874; m. 1905, C. A. McDaniel.
9—Carroll Key McDaniel.
9—Martha McDaniel, m. Mr. Long.
9—Helen McDaniel, d. 1910.
8—Annie Irene Key, b. 1877, d. 1920; m. 1899, Alex Walker.
7—William Bibb Key, C. S., son of George Key, b. 1837, m. Fanny Meriwether.
8—Eva Key m. (1) Mr. Couch and (2) Mr. Peek.
6—Amelia Ann Key, daughter of Chiles Terrell Key, m. John Marshall Christian.
7—Tilda Christian.
7—Althea Christian, m. Dr. Hadden, C. S.
7—John Christian, m. Amanda Stovall.
8—Oscar Christian, d. infancy.
8—George M. Christian, d. infancy.
8—Charles J. Christian.
8—Beatrice Christian, m. L. C. Upshaw.
8—Jesse H. Christian, m. Daisy Osburn.
8—William Yancy Christian.
8—Lois Christian, m. Mr. Ramsaur.
6—Sarah Terrell Key, b. 1822, d. 1877; m. Shaler Hillyer Oglesby.
7—Junius G. Oglesby, b. Jan. 31, 1847, d. May 5, 1919; m. 1876, Eugenia Cottingham.
8—Junius G. Oglesby Jr., m. Susan Calhoun.
8—Eugenia Oglesby, m. R. F. Kilpatrick.
7—Martha Ellen Oglesby, d. infancy.
7—Ira Dancy Oglesby, b. Aug. 31, 1851, d. Dec. 11, 1919; m. 1872, Louise Miller.
8—Ira Dancey Oglesby Jr., S. W. W., b. Jan. 24, 1876; m. 1908, Anna McCarthy.
9—Anna Oglesby, b. 1909.
9—Ira Dancy Oglesby III, b. 1910.
8—Agnes Oglesby, b. 1874.
8—Hillyer M. Oglesby.
6—Joel Martin Key, b. Feb. 18, 1813; m. Aug. 8, 1839, Nancy Wellborn Terrell.
7—John W. Key, d. 1920, m. Kitty Keith.
7—Terrell Key, m. Milly Goode, d. 1923.
6—Lucinda Key, b. Jan. 24, 1817, d. 1865; m. 1833, Thomas Stovall.
7—Mollie Stovall.
7—George Terrell Stovall, b. 1838, d. 1924; m. (1) 1860, Mary Dunning Pickens and (2), 1889, Minnie De'She.
8—(By first wife) John Terrell Stovall, b. 1861, d. 1889; m. 1883, Stella Thompson.
9—Ouida Stovall, b. 1884.
9—Eva Clyde Stovall, b. 1886, m. 1908, Dr. Marion Scott.
9—Thomas F. Stovall, b. 1889.
9—(By second wife) Love Stovall, b. 1890; m. W. E. Ferrell.
9—John H. Stovall.
9—De'She Stovall.

9—Travis Stovall.
9—Frank Stovall.
6—John Key, C. S., killed in action.
6—Nancy E. Key, m. three times with no issue.
6—William Bibb Key.
5—Martha Key, daughter of William Bibb Key IV, b. Nov. 5, 1786, m. Nicholas Goode.
5—James Key, b. July 14, 1788, m. 1811, Rebecca Grizzle.
6—Eliza Amanda Key, b. Oct. 28, 1812; m. Matthew Boyd.
7—Joseph M. Boyd, m. Victoria Davenport.
8—Laura Boyd, m. Edwin Ford.
5—Milley Key, b. July 20, 1790; m. Jan. 3, 1811, Humphrey Posey.
5—Nancy Key, b. July 20, 1790; m. Simeon Glenn.
5—Elizabeth Key, b. Jan. 1, 1792, m. Thomas Bell.
6—Rhoda Bell, m. Sept. 6, 1829, Lindsey Smith.
7—Thomas B. Smith, m. Cynthia Gunter.
8—Samuel Smith, m. Betty Bradford.
9—Cynthia Smith, m. John A. Stark.
9—Henry Smith, m. Eva Brown.
9—Duncan Smith, m. Lizzie Thornton.
9—Annie Smith, m. Carswell Hulme.
10—Elizabeth Hulme.
10—Tinsley Hulme.
9—Mary Smith, m. W. P. Stone Jr.
10—Allen Stone.
9—Ethel Smith, m. Howard Thornton.
9—Otis Smith, m. Vera Fortson.
9—Ruby Smith, m. Floyd Dye.
8—Charles "Boy" Smith, m. Hattie Kelly.
9—Leverette H. Smith, m. Lula May Smith.
10—Shirley Smith.
10—Forrest Smith.
9—Taylor B. Smith, b. Oct. 19, 1891; m. Jessie Smith.
9—William Oscar Smith.
8—William Allen Smith, m. Belle Kelly.
9—Thomas W. Smith.
9—Beverly Allen Smith, m. March 30, 1920, Marie Edwards.
10—Holder Smith.
8—Rhoda Smith, m. David C. Downer.
9—George Downer, m. Jan. 1918, Mattie Gunter.
8—Bennie Smith, unmarried.
8—O. H. Smith, m. July 7, 1913, Bessie McLanahan.
9—Frances Smith.
6—Sarah Bell, b. May 12, 1808; m. 1828, Jonathan Bell.
7—James Bell.
7—Jonathan Bell Jr.
7—Rhoda Bell, m. (1) Henry Mattox and (2) Mannie Tiller.
7—Frances Bell.
7—Susan Bell, m. (1) Mr. Grimes and (2) Christopher Mattox.
7—Martha Bell, b. April 13, 1845, d. June 3, 1893; m. Christopher Mattox.
8—Juddie Mattox, m. Mr. Johnson.
8—Martha Mattox.
8—William Henry Mattox.
8—James Mattox.
8—Robert Mattox.
8—Fanny Mattox, m. 1896, R. O. B. Grimes.
8—Mourning Mattox.
8—Annie Mae Mattox, m. W. J. Grimes.
8—George W. Mattox.

8—John A. Mattox, m. Rossie Bell.
5—Margaret Key, b. Jan. 18, 1794; m. Thomas Goode.
6—Joseph Terrell Goode.
6—William Bibb Goode.
6—James Clark Goode.
6—John Martin Goode.
6—Martha Mildred Goode.
6—Joshua Marion Goode, m. Matilda Cyre.
6—Jabez Wootson Goode, m. Mary Wood, d. 1866.
7—Martha Elizabeth Goode.
7—Joseph Terrell Goode, b. 1850; m. 1873, Susan Pritchett.
8—Hollis L. Goode.
8—Luther L. Goode.
8—Claud Goode.
8—Lillie G. Goode.
8—Ella Shelton Goode.
8—Lula Sisk Goode.
8—Clara Goode.
7—Maud Jane Goode.
7—William Martin Goode.
7—James W. Goode, b. Feb. 17, 1863; m. Mary Bagnell.
8—Lillie L. Goode, m. W. A. Cantrell.
8—Paul L. Goode, m. Lula Sutton.
8—William W. Goode, m. Ree Chambless.
8—Watson T. Goode, m. Eva Shaw.
8—Wade H. Goode, m. Mattie Holland.
5—Keturah Key, b. Oct. 25, 1795; m. James Hamm.
5—Mary Key, b. Sept. 3, 1797; m. July 1823, Joseph Bell.
6—Thomas Alfred Bell, b. April 22, 1824, d. 1888; m. (1) Frances Reeves, b. 1828, d. 1850, and (2), 1850, Marian Jackson.
5—Henry Key, b. April 24, 1799, d. unmarried.
5—Susan Key, b. April 24, 1799; m. James Bell Jr., b. 1789.
6—Eugene M. Bell, b. Dec. 11, 1819.
6—Dabon M. Bell, b. Jan. 3, 1821, d. infancy.
6—Addison A. Bell, b. Jan. 26, 1823; m. (1) Miss McWhorter, and (2) Ida Hilsman.
7—(By second wife) Addsion Key Bell, b. July 3, 1861; m. (1) Miss Bowles, and (2) Mona L. Donaldson.
6—Jasper M. Bell, b. 1824, d. 1863, C. S.
6—Elisha J. Bell, d. infancy.
6—Marcus A. Bell, b. Feb. 3, 1828; m. Mary J. Halsey.
7—Pironia Bell, b. 1858.
7—Crelia Bell, b. 1864.
7—Ada Bibb Bell, b. 1873; m. Robert Cade Wilson.
6—Marianna Emiline Bell, m. (1) William S. Peterman, and (2) Spencer Taylor.
7—William Peterman, d. unmarried.
7—Addison Eugene Peterman, b. 1857; m. July 16, 1890, Mollie Bonify.
8—William Addison Peterman, b. 1891; m. Gertrude Wooly.
8—Cleveland Peterman, b. 1892, d. 1909.
8—Addison E. Peterman, b. June 22, 1894.
8—Marcus Peterman, b. July 25, 1897.
8—Lavonia Peterman, b. 1900; m. John Hamm.
8—Cyril Peterman, b. Feb. 9, 1903.
8—Mollie Peterman, b. March 4, 1906.
8—Margaret Peterman, b. Aug. 12, 1909.
7—Lavonia Bell Peterman, m. F. A. Bonifay.
8—Mae Bonifay.
8—Emmie Bonifay.

8—Gussie Bonifay.
7—Eugene Taylor, d. unmarried.
7—Mollie Taylor, m. Nov. 11, 1883, G. W. Sandiford.
8—Mattie E. Sandiford, b. Oct. 4, 1884; m. Dec. 12, 1906, J. E. Henderson.
8—Oreola Sandiford, b. Feb. 12, 1886.
8—Frank Bell and Hollis Sandiford, b. 1889, twins.
8—Margie Sandiford, b. Nov. 13, 1890; m. J. E. Swatman, (7 children.)
8—Annie Lillian Sandiford, b. Jan. 13, 1894; m. Robert King.
8—Addison Bell Sandiford, b. 1896.
8—Vivian L. Sandiford, b. August, 1897.
8—Herbert Hoover Sandiford, b. Sept. 5, 1900.
8—Pierpont Morgan Sandiford, b. 1903.
8—Hendon M. Sandiford, b. 1905.
6—Jedekiah Falrius Bell, b. Dec. 16, 1831.
6—Lycurgus M. Bell, b. Sept. 1, 1833.
6—Margenius A. Bell, b. Sept. 1, 1835.
6—James Eugene Bell, b. May 31, 1837.
6—Christopher Bell, b. 1840, d. infancy.
6—William Henry Bell, C. S., b. July 4, 1841, killed in action.
5—(Issue of William Bibb Key IV) Jane Key, b. March 26, 1801; m. 1920, John Grizzle.
5—Sarah Key, b. March 9, 1803; m. Dec. 28, 1819, Thomas Elliott.
5—Thomas Key, b. Jan. 4, 1805.
5—Lucy Key, b. June 26, 1807, d. 1895; m. Feb. 18, 1826, Nathan Mattox, b. Nov. 2, 1807, d. Jan. 9, 1862.
6—Sarah Mourning Mattox, b. Jan. 22, 1827, d. Dec. 27, 1905; m. July 1842, John Wynn Eberhardt, b. Oct. 18, 1822, d. Dec. 19, 1886.
7—Nathan Eberhardt, C. S., b. July 1, 1843, killed in action.
7—Jacob Eberhardt, C. S., b. Nov. 16, 1848, d. 1917, unmarried.
7—George Eberhardt, d. unmarried.
7—John L. Eberhardt, b. Jan. 1852, m. Lillian Mattox.
8—Robert Toombs Eberhardt.
7—Lizzie Eberhardt, b. 1858, d. 1902, no living issue.
7—Mary Eberhardt, b. Aug. 10, 1860, d. 1936; m. Feb. 10, 1892, J. W. Wright.
8—Sarah Ann Wright.
8—Mary Elizabeth Wright.
6—Martha Key Mattox.
6—Christopher Mattox.
6—Frank Mattox.
6—Lucy Mattox.
6—Nathan M. Mattox, C. S. M.
7—Dr. Benjamin Bibb Mattox, M. D., S. W. W. lieutenant; m. Florence Settles.
8—Susan Mattox.
7—E. D. Mattox.
6—Thomas Jefferson Mattox.
4—(Issue of Martin Key III) Henry B. Key, b. 1730, R. S.; m. Mary Clark.
5—Malinda Key, b. Oct. 11, 1755; m. James Lietcher.
5—John Key, b. March 20, 1757.
5—Henry Key Jr., b. April 11, 1759; m. (1) Elizabeth Garrett, and (2) Phobe Talbot.
6—(By first wife) Lucy Key.
6—Elizabeth Key.
6—John Key.

6—(By second wife) Henry Key III, b. 1794.
5—William Key, b. April 2, 1761.
5—Tandy Clark Key, b. May 19, 1763.
5—Mary Key, b. May 31, 1765.
5—Martha Key, b. March 7, 1768.
5—Elizabeth Key, b. April 11, 1773.
4—Jesse Key, m. Eliza T. Graves.
5—Albert J. Key, b. Feb. 14, 1818.
5—Robert J. Key, b. Feb. 14, 1818.
4—James Key, m. 1776, Mary "Polly" Daniel.
5—Beverly Key, b. 1805, d. 1843; m. Judith Browder.
5—Jefferson Key.
5—James Key, m. Lucy Hopkins.
5—Chesley Key, m. Narcissus Bailey.
5—Anne Key.
5—Judith Key, b. 1799; m. Reverend Jordan Lambert.
4—Walter Key.
4—Elizabeth Key, m. Mr. Daniel.
4—Martha Key, b. 1760, d. 1853; m. John White, b. Oct. 25, 1765, d. 1837.
5—Emma P. White.
5—Jesse Key White, m. Helen Thornley.
6—Aaron Thornley White, b. March 4, 1823.
6—John W. White, b. Oct. 25, 1825, d. Nov. 1867; m. 1857, Mary Ray.
6—Edmund Pendleton White, b. April 1827, d. 1895.
6—Katherine White, b. 1828, d. 1873.
6—Jessie Anne White, b. 1833, d. 1908.
5—William F. White, b. Sept. 12, 1800, d. July 17, 1854; m. Catherine Louise White.
6—Jesse White, b. 1834, d. 1843.
6—Charles W. White, b. 1836.
6—John Wesley White, b. 1838.
6—George A. White, b. 1840.
5—Anne White, b. 1798, d. 1830.
4—Thomas Key, b. 1750, d. 1821; m. (1) Frances Henry nee Garrett, and (2) Elizabeth Scott. He was R. S.
5—(By first wife) Robert Key, m. Martha Moss.
5—Elizabeth Key.
5—(By second wife) Catherine Key, m. 1807, James Scott.
5—Lucy Key, m. 1816, Edward Collier.
5—Joshua Key, b. 1786, d. 1862.
5—Mary Key.
5—Martha Key, d. prior to 1820; m. Mr. Garrett.

LANIER

The following chart shows intermarriages with the following families:
Abercrombie — Adams — Aiken — Allen — Allston — Archer — Arnold — Andrews — Barnett — Blackwell — Bounds — Brown — Burch — Burris — Cade — Calhoun — Carter — Cleveland — Comer — Darden — Dean — Dickson — Douglas — Flood — Gray — Gaines — Hampton — Harper — Harris — Hawes — Heard — Henderson — Hicks — Hill — Hutson — Jarrett — Jones — Kilpatrick — Lee — Linder — Long — Marburg — Martin — Mattox — Maxwell — Mitchell — Moore — McCalla — McIntosh — Nichols — Purdue — Smith — Speed — Stephens — Stelling — Stewart — Sullivan — Thompson — Tillman — Tinsley — Tucker — Upshaw — Wall — Washington — White — Williams — Williamson — Winston — Zeigler.

(Note: Numbers represent generations, as: (1) first generation, (2) second generation, (3) third generation, etc.)

1—John Lanier, will proven in London 1650; m. Eleanor (?).
  2—Elizabeth Lanier.
  2—John Lanier Jr., will proven in 1717; m. (?).
    3—Nicholas Lanier, m. (?).
      4—Thomas Lanier, b. 1722; m. Elizabeth Hicks.
        5—Robert B. Lanier, b. 1742.
        5—Molly Lanier, b. 1744.
        5—Sarah Lanier, b. 1748; m. (1) Colonel Joseph Willliams, and (2) Robert Williams.
        5—Betty Lanier, b. 1750; m. Colonel Joseph Winston.
        5—Caty Lanier, b. 1752.
        5—Patsy Lanier, b. 1754.
        5—Rebecca Lanier, m. 1757.
        5—Thomas Lanier, b. 1760.
        5—Susannah Lanier, b. 1763.
        5—Lewis Lanier, b. 1767.
        5—William Lanier, b. 1770.
    3—Robert Lanier.
    3—Sampson Lanier, b. about 1724; m. Elizabeth Washington, b. about 1728, daughter of Richard Washington and Elizabeth Jordan, and granddaughter of John Washington and Mrs. Blount nee Flood.
      4—John Lanier.
      4—Nicholas Lanier.
      4—Robert Lanier.
      4—Sampson Lanier Jr., m. (?).
        5—Priscilla Elizabeth Lanier, m. Richard Burch.
          6—Martha Burch, m. George Darden, grand nephew of Martha Washington. He was R. S.
            7—George Darden Jr., b. 1760, R. S.
            7—Richard Darden, b. 1763, R. S.
            7—Buckner Darden, b. 1767.
            7—Washington Darden, b. 1769.
            7—Elizabeth Darden, b. 1765, d. June 5, 1848; m. Stephen Heard, governor Georgia, colonial captain under George Washington, colonel in American Revolution, commissioner to view the Tennessee lands, planter, president of the Georgia Executive Council, b. 1740 in Virginia, d. Nov. 13, 1815, in Elbert County, Georgia.
              8—Barnard Carroll Heard, b. March 12, 1787; m. 1808, Polly Hutson, b. 1791.

9—Boliver Heard, b. 1809, d. unmarried.
9—Stephen Heard, b. 1810, d. unmarried.
9—John Heard, m. Elizabeth Williamson.
8—Martha Burch Heard, b. Oct. 10, 1788, d. Dec. 7, 1824; m. 1805, Bartlett Tucker, b. 1784.
9—Martha Tucker, b. 1807; m. John Maxwell. No issue.
9—Stephen Heard Tucker, m. Jan. 16, 1827, Mary Aiken, daughter of Thomas Aiken.
9—Elizabeth Tucker, m. (1) Mr. Upshaw, and (2) Robert Harris.
9—Sarah Tucker, m. 1842, Henry Sanders, C. S.
8—Bridget Carroll Heard, b. June 17, 1795; m. (1) Simeon Henderson, and (2) Elbert H. Thompson.
9—William Henderson, b. 1818.
9—Daughter Thompson, m. Mr. Riddle.
9—Daughter Thompson, m. Mr. Jones.
8—Dr. George Washington Heard, member Georgia House of Representatives 1824-27 inclusive, b. June 17, 1791; m. April 20, 1815, Sarah Carter, b. 1795, daughter of Thomas A. Carter, R. S.
9—Stephen Heard, m. Mary Aiken.
10—Phillip Heard, m. Miss Tillman.
8—John Adams Heard, b. March 17, 1793, d. 1838, solicitor general Western Circuit of Georgia. Unmarried.
8—Jane Lanier Heard, b. March 23, 1797; m. Singleton Walthall Allen, b. Jan. 14, 1791, d. June 6, 1853, member Georgia House of Representatives 1828-1831, member Georgia Senate 1845-46, planter.
9—Elizabeth Allen, m. George Williams.
10—Rebecca Williams, m. DuBose Hill.
11—Janie Hill, m. Benjamin H. Hill.
10—George Williams, C. S., d. unmarried.
10—William Williams, m. Jessie Arnold.
11—William McIntosh Williams.
10—Janie Williams, m. John Burriss.
11—Dilliard Burriss.
9—George Allen, d. unmarried.
9—Theodore Allen, d. unmarried.
9—Ann Allen, m. April 30, 1839, Dr. Milton Comer.
10—Janie Comer, m. Captain Samuel Barnett, C. S., b. Aug. 16, 1841, d. Nov. 26, 1898.
11—Comer Barnett, b. May 11, 1878; m. June 19, 1901, Corneil Bounds, b. Feb. 14, 1880.
12—Lillis Barnett, b. March 25, 1911.
10—Bevelle Comer, m. Dr. Hampton. No issue.
10—Ann Comer, b. 1849; d. 1928. Unmarried.
9—Susan Allen, m. Young L. G. Harris, founder of Young Harris College, Young Harris, Georgia, donor Harris-Allen Library, Elberton, Ga., president Southern Mutual Insurance Company of Athens, Georgia. No issue.
9—Maria Louisa Allen, b. Aug. 10, 1824, d. Aug. 8, 1884; m. Jan. 27, 1842, Colonel William McPherson McIntosh, C. S., brevet brigadier-general C. S. A., mortally wounded June 1862, member Georgia House of Representatives, member Georgia Senate, elector state-at-large for Breckenridge 1860, lawyer, planter.
10—Singleton Allen McIntosh, C. S., b. Feb. 19, 1845, d. Nov. 17, 1908; m. Feb. 1867, Mary Eliza Cade.
11—Sarah Howell McIntosh, b. Dec. 29, 1867; m. S. J. Zeigler.
12—Samuel Zeigler, S. W. W., officer United States Navy, graduate U. S. Naval Academy; m. Fanny Marburg.
13—Howell Zeigler.

12—Howell Zeigler, m. George Lee Dickson, major U. S. Army retired.
13—Howell Rees Dickson.
13—George Lee Dickson Jr.
11—William McPherson McIntosh, b. 1870, d. 1930, unmarried.
11—Guilford "Guy" McIntosh, b. July 6, 1872; m. 1918, Addie Tinsley.
12—Mary McIntosh.
12—William Kenneth McIntosh.
12—Louise McIntosh.
11—Victoria Augusta McIntosh, b. March 1875; m. Joseph Allston.
12—Joseph Allston Jr., m. Lilis McCullough.
13—Joseph Allston III.
12—Mary Allston.
11—Mary Louise McIntosh, b. Aug. 10, 1877; m. 1908, Henry M. Long.
12—Mary Louise Long, d. infancy.
10—William McPherson McIntosh Jr., m. Helen Dean.
11—William McPherson McIntosh Jr., S. W. W.
10—Annie Cassandra McIntosh, b. March 5, 1849; m. Dec. 11, 1866, Budd Clay Wall, C. S., mayor of North Augusta, South Carolina, merchant.
11—Martha Louise Wall, m. Thomas Andrews. No issue.
11—McPherson McIntosh, d. infancy.
11—William Clay Wall, d. infancy.
11—James Singleton Wall, m. Rose Douglas. No issue.
11—Bevel William McIntosh Wall, b. June 20, 1875; m. Mary Stewart.
12—Margaret Wall.
12—Bevel Clay Wall, m. Virginia Alexander.
13—Bevel Charles Wall, b. July 1930.
11—Jessie McIntosh Wall, b. Dec. 20, 1878; m. John D. Stelling.
12—Sterling Stelling, b. Feb. 14, 1900; m. Eula Mitchell. No issue.
12—Martha McIntosh Stelling, m. Charles McCord Kilpatrick
12—Richard Stelling.
12—Cree Stelling.
12—Budd Clay Stelling.
11—Harry Wall, m. (1) Maryland Randall, and (2) Hattie Smith. No issue.
10—Maria Louise McIntosh, b. March 15, 1851, d. May 7, 1894; m. Feb. 2, 1869, Guilford Cade Jr.
11—Julia May Cade, b. Dec. 30, 1871; m. Nov. 23, 1892, Dr. Albert Sidney Hawes, b. Nov. 14, 1863, d. Nov. 19, 1936; mayor of Elberton, member Georgia House of Representatives, merchant, physician, planter.
12—Guilford Moseley Hawes, m. Onie Lee.
13—Mary Lee Hawes.
13—Robert Hawes, d. infancy.
13—Julia Ann Hawes.
12—Albert Lee Hawes, m. Bertha Bates, d. 1932. No issue.
12—Peyton Samuel Hawes, member Georgia House of Representatives, city attorney of Elberton; m. Virginia Smith.
11—Annie Lee Cade, b. Feb. 21, 1878; m. Feb. 24, 1903, Dr. Robert Franklin Moore, b. 1871, d. 1923.
12—Franklin Cade Moore, d. infancy.
12—Alan Moore.
12—Guilford McIntosh Moore, m. Miss Mauldin of South Carolina.
10—Mary Bevelle McIntosh, b. June 1856, d. June 1926; m. 1895, John Chandler Brown, mayor of Elberton, merchant. No issue.

10—James McIntosh, b. Sept. 1, 1857; m. Oct. 1882, Mary Jane Arnold, b. Sept. 23, 1859.
11—Sarah Louise McIntosh, b. July 1883; m. Feb. 24, 1903, A. F. Archer. No issue.
11—William McPherson McIntosh, d. infancy.
11—Jessie McIntosh, d. infancy.
11—Mary James McIntosh, d. infancy.
11—John Hawes McIntosh, b. Nov. 26, 1895; m. June 19, 1918, Fay Ann White, b. Oct. 21, 1900. Divorced 1937.
12—Mary Louise McIntosh, b. July 16, 1900.
12—Elizabeth Arnold Penn McIntosh, b. March 15, 1923.
11—McAlpin McIntosh, b. Nov. 26, 1897, d. 1899.
10—Jessie McIntosh, b. 1859; m. Peyton M. Hawes, member Georgia House of Representatives, member Georgia State Senate, president Elberton Loan and Saving Bank, president Elbert County Bank, captain Georgia militia, merchant, planter. No issue.
9—Mary Allen, b. 1825; m. 1849, George McCalla of Abbeville County, South Carolina.
10—Isacc McCalla, m. Raymond Speed.
11—Mack McCalla, m. Ella Nichols.
12—Mack McCalla Jr.
12—Elmira McCalla.
11—Leila McCalla, m. Mr. Linder.
12—Alice Linder, m. J. P. Sullivan of Anderson, South Carolina.
13—J. P. Sullivan Jr.
11—John McCalla, m. Parnice Brown. No issue.
10—John W. McCalla, county commissioner of Elbert County, merchant, planter; m. Mitta Allen.
11—Annie McCalla, m. J. H. Purdue.
12—Frances Purdue.
12—Mary Olivia Purdue.
12—J. H. Purdue Jr.
11—Olivia McCalla, m. Perry H. Smith, member city council of Elberton, merchant.
12—Ethel Smith, m. Mr. Le Conte.
11—J. Earl McCalla, m. Katherine Stephens of Hart County, Georgia.
12—John McCalla.
12—Katherine McCalla.
12—J. Earl McCalla Jr.
12—David McCalla.
10—Ida McCalla, m. (1) Frank Cleveland and (2) Bedford Heard.
11—Andrew B. Cleveland, m. Nov. 19, 1900, Agnes Hall.
12—Frank Cleveland, m. Miss Smith.
12—Elizabeth Cleveland, m. Frank Veronee.
12—Lanier Cleveland, m. Augustus Wansley.
13—Augustus Wansley Jr.
12—Helen Cleveland.
12—McCalla Cleveland.
12—Helen Cleveland.
11—Jessie Cleveland, m. Jesse Warren.
12—Jeremiah Warren.
12—Hilda Warren.
11—M. E. Heard, m. Allen Pressley.
11—Erskin Heard, m. Lottie Seymour.
11—Sarah Heard, m. Frank Hammond.
11—Bevelle Heard, m. Thomas Wayble.
11—Caroline Heard, m. Guy Quillian.
10—Jennie McCalla, m. Joseph Speed.

11—Florence Speed, m. A. A. McCurry.
10—Susan McCalla, m. Willis B. Adams, mayor of Elberton, member Georgia House of Representatives.
10—Mary McCalla, m. George Gaines. No issue.
10—Lawrence "Larry" McCalla, m. Hettie Hearne.
9—Rebecca Allen, m. William H. Mattox, C. S.
10—Lena Mattox, m. Jeptha Jones.
10—Singleton Mattox, m. Annie Jones.
10—Clark Mattox, m. Sarah Jones.
10—Carroll Mattox, m. Charles Fisher.
10—Janie Mattox, m. Raymond Gaines.
9—Gerrard Allen, m. Isabella Blackwell.
8—Permelia Heard, d. unmarried.
8—Sarah J. Heard, m. James D. Jarrett.
8—Thomas J. Heard, b. 1801, d. 1875; m. (1) Nancy Middleton, and (2) Miss Arnold.
9—(By first wife) Sarah Heard, m. L. H. O. Martin Sr., C. S.
9—James L. Heard, C. S., m. Melissa Harper.
9—Robert M. Heard, C. S., m. Louisa Jones.
9—Erskin Heard, m. (1) Martha Harper and (2) Caroline Calhoun.
9—William Henry Heard, m. Jennie Harper.
9—Eugene B. Heard, b. 1847, d. 1934; m. Sally Harper.
6—Other issue but data unavailable.

LE GRAND

(Note: Numbers represent generations, as: (1) first generation, (2) second generation, (3) third generation, etc.)

1—Peter Legrand, justice of the peace, Prince Edward County, Virginia, 1766-1782, representative of the assembly 1768; m. Jane Maidlan Michaux, daughter of Abraham Michaux and Susanna Rochelte.
2—John LeGrand, estate appraised 1784; m. Betty Chandler.
3—John LeGrand Jr., R. S., m. (1) April 19, 1779 in Halifax County, Virginia, Virginia Betty Zounger, and (2), 1827, Lucinda Christian.
4—(By first wife) Sally Le Grand, m. Jan. 25, 1805, John Seamster.
4—Nancy Le Grand, m. Sept. 25, 1795, Samuel Bentley.
4—Susannah Le Grand, m. 1807, Zachariah Seymour. Susannah Le Grand was b. 1785, d. 1846.
5—John Warren Seymour, b. 1810, d. 1880; m. 1834, Nancy Christian.
6—Martin Seymour married and had issue.
6—Hop Seymour married and had issue.
6—Charles Marion Seymour, m. Locky Ann Phelps.
7—Dora Penelope Seymour, m. Charles Harrison Allen.
8—Zelma Allen, m. T. O. Tabor Jr.
9—T. O. Tabor III.
8—Valeria Allen, m. Albert T. Brewer.
9—Elizabeth Brewer.
8—Gladys Allen, m. Herman Brown.
9—Allen Brown.
8—Huie Allen, m. Harry G. Thornton.
9—Harry Allen Thornton.
9—Earl Thornton.
8—Charles Allen, m. Janie Auld.
9—Charles Allen Jr.
8—Beth Allen, m. Maurice Asbury.

9—Beverly Asbury.

John Warren Seymour is the ancestor of many Elbert County citizens but the compiler has been unable to secure cooperation for authenic data.

Zachariah Seymour is the ancestor of practically all Elbert County persons of the name.

MARKS

James Marks, son of Hastings Marks whose will was dated 1761 in the records of Virginia and grandson of John Marks and Elizabeth Hastings of Suffolk, England, who came to America shortly after the year 1680 and settled in Albermarle County, Virginia, was born in Albermarle 1745 and married Elizabeth Harvey on November 14, 1771. James Marks died in Elbert County, Georgia, 1816.

James Marks and his wife, Elizabeth Harvey, were the parents of John Harvey Marks, born in 1773, married 1793, Susan Tompkins. The son of John Harvey Marks, John Henry Marks Jr., born 1807, died 1870, married Mary Meriwether Barnett. (2) Mary Marks married Nicholas Johnson. (3) Nicholas Meriwether Marks married Ann Paul Matthews. (4) Martha Gaines Marks married Reverend Guerry. (5) Samuel Winston Marks died unmarried.

John Harvey Marks and his wife, Susan Tompkins, were the parents of the following named children:

>Hastings Marks, m. Civility McCou.
>Mary Marks, m. John Runno Cargile.
>Nicholas Marks, m. Rebecca Wright.
>Amelia Marks, m. David Meriwether.
>John Marks, m. Mary Meriwether Barnett.
>James Marks, d. unmarried.

John Harvey Marks Jr. moved from Elbert County to a site near the present city of Montgomery, Alabama, at which place a number of his children were born. In 1834, before the State of Arkansas was admitted to the Union, he sold his holdings in the Alabama country for the sum of $17,000.00 and invested the whole of it in Arkansas lands. This investment made him the sole owner of three entire counties of the present time: Union, Cleveland and Bradley.

MATHEWS FAMILY

The first Mathews in Georgia was James, born in Virginia in 1755—and was a Revolutionary Soldier. While he was quite young his father, Moses Mathews, moved to South Carolina, near Charleston. Here James lived until 1785 when he came to Wilkes County, Georgia.

His father and mother were members of "High Church," but at the age of seventeen James united with the Baptist Church. He was ordained in 1785 and was closely associated with Silas and Jesse Mercer, Sanders Walker, Abraham Marshall, Edmund Botsford and others in establishing the Baptist Church in Georgia. There were only three Baptist Churches in Georgia, before the Revolution, and two were established during the Revolution, but the Church grew rapidly. In his early evangelical ministry, James had been instrumental in "gathering and constituting" the Church at Hebron in Elbert County, later serving as a pastoral supply of this Church. Most of his work was in Burke and Wilkes counties, and records of his ministry and sketches of his life can be found in

History of Georgia Baptist Association, by Jesse Mercer.

Georgia Baptists: Historical and Biographical, by J. H. Campbell.

Reminiscences of Georgia Baptists, by Rev. S. C. Hillyer, D. D.

James Mathews had three brothers that were ministers, and two of his sons were preachers—James Mathews Jr., and Philip Mathews.

Philip Mathews was converted 1827, united with Falling Creek Church, Elbert County, and was soon chosen pastor of that Church which pastorate he held until his removal to Meriwether County in the year 1851. He was also pastor of Bethel Church, Elbert County, Georgia. He aspired to no civil office, was Moderator of the Sarepta Association and Trustee of Mercer University.

Record of service and life may be found in—

History of the Baptist Denomination in Georgia, compiled for the Christian Idex.

Philip Mathews married in the year 1814, Miss Elizabeth Clark, daughter of David Clark, formerly of Virginia, and a Revolutionary Soldier. He moved to Elbert County, Georgia, and settled on a plantation in the Flatwood and was the father of Dr. Albert Clark Mathews, Dr. Judson Mathews, Dr. David Mathews and Colonel James Davant Mathews, all mentioned elsewhere in this volume.

MATHEWS LINEAGE

(Note: Numbers represent generations, as: (1) first generation, (2) second generation, (3) third generation, etc.)

1—Samuel Mathews, b. 1592, d. 1660, was sent to Virginia by King James I. in 1622. He was one of the Commissioners to examine the condition in 1623. Found it so much to his liking that he remained in the Colony. Was a member of the Colonial Council from 1624 to 1644. Was elected Governor of the Colony of Virginia in 1657 and held office until his death March 13, 1660. Married first Frances (Mary?) Hinton, daughter of Sir Thomas Hinton. She was the mother of his two sons, Samuel and Francis. His second wife was the widow of Abraham Piersy. His plantation home "Denbigh" is on the James river, twelve miles north of Newport News, Va.

2—Samuel Mathews, Lieutenant Colonel in 1655 and a member of the Colonial Council. In 1652 he was a member of the Assembly from Warwick Co., Va. He had one son John.

3—John Mathews, m. 1683, Elizabeth, only daughter of Michael Tavenor of York County. They had:

4—Samuel Mathews, a Captain of the Virginia Militia, also a representative from Virginia in the first Continental Congress, m. Elizabeth Broxton and had: Elizabeth, Mary John and Baldwin Mathews. His will is on file in Richmond, Va., dated 1718.

5—Mary Mathews married her cousin, Isaac Mathews. He died in S. C. in 1769. They had one son, Moses.

6—Moses Mathews, b. 1725 in Halifax County, Va., married Sarah Findley, 1748. Moved from Virginia to South Carolina. He had a gun-shop in which he repaired and manufactured guns for General Sumter's command during the Revolution. He was a Revolutionary patriot and had a land-grant of several hundred acres in what is now Lincoln Co., Ga. His will is on file in Lincoln Co. He died 1806. They had: James, Philip, Moses, Sarah Polly, Jesse and William Mathews.

7—James Mathews, born in Virginiia Oct. 15, 1755, was brought to South Carolina by his parents when a few years of age. He married in 1783, Miss Rebecca Carleton, daughter of Robert Carleton, and moved to Wilkes Co., Ga., in 1785. He was a Revolutionary Soldier. Children were: James, Elizabeth, Jacob, Philip, William, and Abraham.

8—Philip Mathews, b. 1792, d. 1858, was a Baptist Minister. He married in 1814, Elizabeth Clark, daughter of David Clark, Revolutionary Soldier. They had:

9—Mary Adeline Mathews, 1816.
9—Rebecca Ann Mathews, 1818.
9—Albert Clark Mathews, 1820.
9—Martha Rachael Mathews, 1824.
9—Emily Mathews, 1825.
9—Millicent Elizabeth Mathews, 1822.
9—James Davant Mathews, 1827.
9—Ann Hazeltine Mathews, 1829.
9—John Philip Mathews, 1831.
9—David Alfred Mathews, 1833.
9—Adoniram Judson Mathews, 1835.
9—George Boardman Mathews, 1837.
9—William Carey Mathews, 1839.
9—Sarah Ellen Mathews, 1841.
9—Oscar Pearce Mathews, 1843.

The eight sons of Philip Mathews were in active service in the War Between the States 1861-1865. John Philip, Boardman, Carey and Pearce lost their lives. The four who returned, Albert, James, Judson and David Mathews, were all professional and useful men.

9—Dr. Albert Clark Mathews, b. 1820, d. 1887, was educated at Mercer University and University Hospital, Augusta, Ga. He was a prominent physician and a philanthropist. He married (1) Sophia Frances Wootten, 1828-1880, and had:

10—Mary Elizabeth Mathews, b. 1846; m. Tinsley Rucker White.
11—Corra White, b. 1869; m. Lundy Harris, and was a writer both nationally and internationally known and read. She first began writing for the Independent Magazine in 1899, and contributed to The American Magazine in 1905-09. The first, and perhaps best of the twenty-four books she wrote, was "The Circuit Rider's Wife." She served as a war correspondent abroad during the World War. Many book reviews, short stories for leading magazines, and her "Candle-lit Column" in the Atlanta Journal were among her other literary achievements. She died Feb., 1935.
12—Faith Harris, m. Harry Leach.

11—Hope White, m. Al Harris.
12—John, Al, Fred and Walter Harris.
11—Albert White.
10—Ella Gertrude Mathews, b. 1849; m. 1866, E. B. Tate.
11—Ora Eugene Tate, b. 1867; m. Carrie Hudson.
12—Ella Rebecca Tate, b. 1890.
12—Jean Hudson Tate, b. 1892; m. 1938, Blanche Simpson.
12—Edmund Brewer Tate, b. 1895, d. 1918 in the Argonne while in active service in France in the World War. He was First Lieutenant 82nd Divisiion.
12—Ora Eugene Tate Jr., b. 1897, d. 1937; m. 1924, Blanche Simpson.
13—Emma Louise Tate, b. 1931.
13—Ora Eugene Tate III, b. 1933.
12—Samuel Enos Tate, b. 1900; m. 1919, Eva Belle Dye.
13—Mary Brewer Tate, b. 1920.
12—Maurice Tate, b. 1902; m. 1928, Helen Purser.
13—Jacqueline Tate, b. 1930.
12—Carrie Sophia Tate, b. 1904.
12—Albert Clark Tate, b. 1906; m. 1934, Minnie Belle Wofford.
13—Albert Clark Tate Jr., b. 1938.
12—Robert Duncan Tate, b. 1908; m. 1930, Mary Frances Almond.
13—Alice Sophia Tate, b. 1935.
12—Corra Jane Tate, b. 1910, m. 1932, Raymond Miller.
13—Carolyn Jane Miller, b. 1933.
13—Cleveland Miller, b., 1938.
12—Peter Martel Tate, b. 1913, m. 1934, Mattie Chapman.
13—William Brewer Tate, b. 1935.
12—Jefferson Davis Tate, b. 1916.
12—George Richard Tate, b. 1917, m. 1939, Edna Lyle.
11—Sophia Tate, b. 1872, d. 1894; m. 1893, Ernest Bigham.
12—Edmund Brewer Bigham, b. 1894, d. 1896.
11—Dr. Albert Mathews Tate, b. 1875, d. 1904.
10—Ora Eugene Mathews, b. 1851, d. young.
10—Corra May Mathews, b. 1854, d. young.
10—William Judson Mathews, b. 1856, d. in Texas.
10—George Byron Mathews, b. 1859, d. in Texas.
10—Albert Wootten Mathews, b. 1861, d. 1935; m. 1893, Sallie Goss.
11—Sophia Mathews, d. infancy.
11—Albert Goss Mathews, b. 1896; m. 1918, Cynthia Stevens. He was Captain in World War.
12—Carl Stevens Mathews, b. 1924.
11—Dr. Paul Wootten Mathews, b. 1898; m. 1924, Jewel Pope. Dr. Mathews, a prominent physician, Urology his specialty, is located at Dallas, Texas.
12—Eva Marie Mathews, b. 1925.
12—Paul Wootten Mathews, Jr., b. 1927.
11—George William Mathews, b. 1900; m. (1) Ola May Daniel and (2) Elsie J. Fleming.
12—Sarah Goss Mathews, b. 1923.
12—George William Mathews Jr., b. 1932.
11—Philip Mathews, died young.
10—Sophia Blanche Mathews, b. 1865, d. 1905; m. Will Maxwell.
11—Janie Maxwell, b. 1886, m. 1909, J. D. Springer.
12—J. D. Springer Jr., b. 1910; m. 1938, Mary Yolm.
12—Maxwell Springer, b. 1912; m. 1931, Bertha Liech.
13—Maxine Dolorice Springer, b. 1935.
12—Joseph C. Springer, b. 1915; m. 1937, Elizabeth Bowers.
13—Betty Jo Springer, b. 1938.

12—Albert Springer, b. ———.
11—Evelyn Maxwell, b. 1890, m. Roy Long.
12—Carolyn Long, m. E. Sullivan Kirk.
12—Miriam Long, m. Guy Biggs.
13—Guy Biggs Jr., b. 1936.
10—Vesta Pearce Mathews, 1869-1937; m. 1888, Dr. A. S. J. Stovall.
11—Alberta Stovall, b. 1889; m. 1910, George Arthur Booth.
12—Alberta Booth, b. 1915, m. 1937, Charles Hight.
12—Arthur Booth Jr., b. 1913; m. 1935, Catherine Carson.
12—George Byron Booth, b. 1931.
11—Nell Stovall, b. 1891, m. 1919, Albert D. Willie.
12—Winifred Willie, b. 1921.
11—Pearce Mathews Stovall, b. 1894; m. 1937, Sue Purcell.
11—Ruth Stovall, b. 1897, died in infancy.
11—Captain Sidney Stovall, b. 1898; m. 1921, Christine Simpson. Captain Stovall graduated at West Point and served his foreign service in the Philippine Islands. He is Captain in U. S. Army.
12—Vesta Stovall, b. 1921.
11—Francis Stovall, b. 1902; m. 1930, Alberta Quillian.
12—Sylvia Stovall, b. 1931.
11—Byron Stovall, b. 1905; m. 1938, Mary Teasley.
9—Dr. Albert Clark Mathews, m. (2) Eliza Julia Wootten
10—Lucile Mathews, b. 1881, m. 1905, Harry Herbert Herndon
11—Thelma Mathews Herndon, b. 1912; m. 1934, Dr. Norman W Holman.
9—Colonel James Davant Mathews, b. 1827; graduate of Mercer University and later a trustee of the University. He was a lawyer, a member of the legislature, elected to Georgia State Convention 1865, was a member of the Constitutional Convention of 1877 which framed the present Constitution of Georgia. Was elected to Congress and received his commission of Colonel in the War 1861-65. He married Dorothy Chappell.
10—Gertrude Mathews, b. 1857, d. 1933; m. Dr. A. S. Oliver.
11—Dr. Alfred S. Oliver Jr., m. Frances Laybold.
Dr. Oliver, a prominent Psychiatrist, former head of State Hospital of Washington State, and now with State Hospital of California.
11—Eleanor Oliver.
11—James Oliver, died young.
11—Thurmond Oliver.
11—Stanley Oliver, m. 1932, Sue Mathews.
12—Sue Oliver, b. 1937.
11—Maude Oliver.
11—Frank Oliver.
9—Dr. David Alfred Mathews, b. 1833, was a devout Christian and a physician. He was largely instrumental in getting the railroad from Elberton to Toccoa which was completed in Nov., 1878, and was the first president. The road was graded during his incumbency. He married Beatrice Hill of South Carolina.
9—Dr. Judson Mathews, b. 1835, a prominent physician. In his early life was active in politics. He married Clorinda Elziabeth Thornton, b. 1835, d. 1916.
10—Dr. Boardman Mathews.
10—Dr. William Mathews.
10—Stanley Mathews.
REFERENCE:
William and Mary Quarterly, Vol. 6, pp. 91-92.
William and Mary Quarterly, Vol. 3, p. 173.

McCall's Roster of Soldiers and Patriots of the American Revolution Buried in Georgia. p. 125.
Data of Dr. James Christopher Mathews, genealogist and member of Virginia Historical Society.
Family Records and Wills.
Lucile Mathews Herndon (Mrs. H.) Genealogist.

MAXWELL

The following chart shows intermarriages with the following families:
Adams — Adair — Addy — Allen — Almond — Asbury — Auld — Baker — Baskin — Berlin — Benson — Blake — Blalock — Blake — Bond — Bowers — Boston — Booth — Bradford — Branch — Brown — Bryan — Busha — Burgin — Bush — Brewster — Camp — Cason — Cheek — Christian — Cordell — Colvard — Cole — Coyne — Crisler — Crow — Davis — Denny — Devore — Dickerson — Doster — Durham — Dunagin — Eavenson — Eaves — Edwards — Elesia — Erwin — Evans — Freeman — Fleming — Fortson — Foster — Fritsche — Gaines — Gary — Green — Greer — Ginn — Grimes — Gunnels — Hamm — Hawkins — Hayes — Hendricks — Hendrix — Herndon — Higginbotham — Horton — Hulme — Inman — Johnson — Jordan — Letson — Long — Lunsford — McMulian — McCurry — McClure — McCollum — McKinney — McAllister — MacKay — Mason — Mayfield — Manning — Mason — Matthews — Mitchell — Moore — Mullins — Mize — Moore — Mansel — Murray — Myers — Neal — Nelms — Norman — Odom — Oglesby — Orr — Owens — Pemberton — Pierce — Pullen — Quillian — Richardson — Robbins — Robertson — Rousey — Rucker — Sanders — Scattergood — Scott — Searcy — Seymour — Shortley — Skelton — Smith — Sorrels — Shackleford — Stapleton — Strickland — Stewart — Swearingen — Sullivan — Teasley — Thornton — Tribble — Turner — Upshaw — Vaughan — Wall — Walker — Walters — Warren — Winn — White — Williford — Willis — Wright — Young.

(Note: numbers represent generations, as: (1) first generation, (2) second generation, (3) third generation, etc.)
- —Thomas Maxwell, m. Kiziah Blake.
    2— Johannah Maxwell, b. Aug. 29, 1739.
    2— John Maxwell, b. June 8, 1740.
    2—Thomas Maxwell Jr., R. S., b. Sept. 8, 1742, d. Dec. 12, 1837; pioneer Baptist minister in Virginia and Georgia; m. 1761, Mary Pemberton, b. 1744, d. Dec. 18, 1827.
    3—John Maxwell, R. S., b. May 9, 1763, d. Oct. 5, 1840; m. either Miss Benson or Agnes Henry.
    4—Simeon Maxwell, b. June 24, 1793, d. Feb. 10, 1865; m. Dec. 9, 1819, Elizabeth Fortson, b. March 19, 1801, d. Nov. 22, 1865 in Green County, Alabama.
    5—John Maxwell.
    5—Augustus Emmett Maxwell, b. Sept. 21, 1820, d. 1902; railroad president, lawyer, state senator, member U. S. Congress. Lived in Florida.
    5—Alex Maxwell.
    5—Amanda Maxwell, m. Patrick William and settled in Louisanna.
    5—Mildred Maxwell, m. Mr. Foster and settled in Texas.
    5—Josephine Maxwell, d. unmarried.

5—Elvira Maxwell.
5—Drucilla Maxwell.
5—Damarius "Mace" Maxwell, m. Dr. Willis of Texas.
4—Reuben Maxwell, b. Nov. 4, 1795; m. Dec. 13, 1821, Elizabeth Thornton.
5—F. M. Maxwell, m. (?).
6—Frank Maxwell.
6—Sidney Maxwell.
5—Allen Maxwell.
5—William W. Maxwell.
5—Eugenia Maxwell.
5—Elizabeth Maxwell.
5—Susan Maxwell.
5—Jennie Maxwell.
5—Mary Maxwell.
4— Nancy Maxwell, b. Nov. 9, 1797, d. 1880; m. Arthur T. Camp. No issue.
4—Benson Maxwell, b. Dec. 11, 1799, d. Aug. 16, 1875; m. (1) Elizabeth B. Johnston and (2) Mrs. Leonard.
5—(By first wife) John Maxwell, b. Oct. 7, 1827, d. Aug. 20, 1892; m. Martha Stephens Greer.
5—Reverend Simeon Maxwell, b. Dec. 14, 1829, d. Dec. 14, 1896; m. Elizabeth Stinson.
5—Wilder Richard Maxwell, b. Aug. 1839, d. June 1900; m. 1865, Melissa Ann Williams.
5—Zack Maxwell, C. S., d. in War Between the States.
5—Elizabeth Maxwell, m. Walker Glenn Camp.
5—Lucinda Maxwell, m. Jack MacDonald, of California.
5—Mary Maxwell, m. John Robbins of Talbot County, Georgia.
5—Missouri Maxwell, b. July 15, 1848; m. William Searcy.
4—Clara Maxwell, b. Oct. 18, 1801.
4—Mary Maxwell, b. Dec. 31, 1803, d. July 22, 1851; m. Dec. 6, 1832, Isham Teasley.
5—William Alfred Teasley, b. Sept. 16, 1833; m. (1) Jane Baber, and (2) Mrs. Ophelia Dobbs Durham.
5—Jane Teasley, b. Aug. 15, 1836; m. Dec. 8, 1852, Norman Camp.
5—Mary Teasley, b. Jan. 15, 1842; m. A. J. Brewster.
5—Rennie Teasley, b. Dec. 14, 1843; m. W. T. Berlin.
5—John I. Teasley, b. April 14, 1848, d. Sept. 18, 1922; m. September 25, 1875, Lou Skelton, b. June 22, 1843, d. May 1920.
6—Olin Teasley, b. May 29, 1878, m. Leila Shortley.
6—Oliver Teasley.
6—Frank Teasley.
4—Elizabeth Maxwell, b. Sept. 12, 1807, d. 1865; m. Oct. 14, 1830, Allen Shackleford.
5—John Shackleford, b. 1831.
5—Asmond Shackleford, b. Nov. 9, 1843; m. 1853, Matilda Green.
4—William P. Maxwell, b. Dec. 28, 1810, d. Jan. 31, 1885; m. Jan. 26, 1837, Serepta Rucker.
5—Arthur C. Maxwell, m. March 3, 1885, Emily Florence Maxwell.
5—William "Billy" Maxwell.
5—Edward "Ed" Maxwell.
5—Martha Maxwell.
5—Edna Maxwell.
5—Frances Maxwell.
5—Samantha Maxwell.
5—Agnes Maxwell.
5—Sophia Maxwell.
5—Caroline Maxwell.
5—Roxie J. Maxwell.

5—William B. Maxwell.
5—John E. Maxwell.
5—Mary Mildred Maxwell, m. Singleton Allen Maxwell.
4—Ann Maxwell, b. Nov. 12, 1813; m. March 10, 1836, John I. Upshaw.
3—Kezia Maxwell, b. Jan. 11, 1766; m. Benson Henry.
3—Thomas J. Maxwell, b. Jan. 1, 1769, d. Dec. 12, 1825; lived in Mississippi; m. (?).
4—Jerry Maxwell.
4—Henry Maxwell.
4—Thomas Maxwell.
4—John Maxwell.
4—Daughter Maxwell, m. Benton Owens.
4—Daughter Maxwell, m. Anderson Ham.
3—James Maxwell, b. Sept. 12, 1770; m. Patsy (?).
3—Elijah Maxwell, b. May 1, 1773, d. Jan. 22, 1847; m. Oct. 13, 1808, Elizabeth "Betsy" Jordan.
4—Rebecca P. Maxwell, b. Aug. 27, 1809; m. Aug. 2, 1827, James Hendricks.
5—Francis M. Hendricks, b. Oct. 22, 1828.
5—Mary E. Hendricks, b. Nov. 11, 1830.
5—James I. Hendricks, b. April 12, 1832.
5—Charles W. Hendricks, b. Feb. 2, 1834.
5—Martha P. Hendricks, b. Feb. 12, 1836.
5—Cynthia A. Hendricks, b. Dec. 25, 1837.
5—Thomas Whitfield Hendricks, b. Jan. 17, 1840.
5—Elijah W. Hendricks, b. April 4, 1844.
5—Joseph W. Hendricks, b. 1846.
5—Stephen Lumpkin Hendricks, b. 1849.
5—Leora Emeline Hendricks, b. Dec. 5, 1851.
4—Mary Walton Maxwell, b. Feb. 9, 1811; m. Charles Woodson, Christian, member Georgia House of Representatives 1820-1821-1822-1823, member Georgia State Senate, 1839-1840, justice of Inferior Court of Elbert County 1837-1838-1839-1840-1841.
5—William P. Christian, b. Dec. 15, 1828.
5—Charles W. Christian, b. Dec. 3, 1830.
4—Eliza Blake Maxwell, b. March 14, 1813; m. Sept. 12, 1833, William H. "Billy" Brown.
5—Elizabeth Ardecy Brown, b. Sept. 22, 1834.
5—Joseph W. J. Brown.
4—Elizabeth "Betsy" Anderson Maxwell, b. June 27, 1815; m. Oct. 6, 1836, Robert "Bob" Brown.
5—Mary Ann Malesy Brown, b. June 4, 1837, Lewis Walker.
5—Elizabeth Rebecca Pemberton Brown, b. April 18, 1839.
5—Eliza Matilda Brown, b. Dec. 30, 1841.
5—Thomas Middleton Brown, b. Feb. 10, 1844.
5—Martha Jane Brown, b. April 11, 1846.
5—Sarah E. Brown, b. July 21, 1849.
5—Harford Ophelia Brown, b. April 29, 1854.
5—Frances Margaret Brown, b. Jan. 24, 1859.
5—William Brown, m. Miss Strickland.
4—Ann Maxwell, b. Dec. 25, 1816; m. March 25, 1841, Jesse G. Christian.
5—Elizabeth M. B. Christian, b. Feb. 1, 1842.
5—Ira Jackson Harbey Christian, b. June 24, 1844.
5—Sarah Ann Josephine Christian, b. Sept. 5, 1845.
5—Mary Frances Christian, b. May 13, 1847.
5—Josephus Marion Christian, b. June 23, 1849.
5—John Thomas Christian, b. Dec. 14, 1850.

5—Martha Permelia Christian, b. Jan. 1, 1853.
5—William Cornelius Christian, b. Jan. 1, 1853; m. Mary Cooper.
6—Arles Christian, m. Aubrey Christian.
7—Carmen Christian.
6—Arva Christian, m. Robert Williford.
7—Robert Williford.
7—William Williford.
6—Nolley Christian, m. Thomas Murray.
6—Gradius Christian, editor Elberton Star, m. Florie Walters.
7—Maryjean Christian.
7—Evelyn Christian.
7—Gradus Christian Jr.
7—Helen Christian.
6—Savius Christian, m. Josephine Evans.
7—Robert Christian.
7—Betty Christian.
7—Mary Christian.
7—Nancy Christian.
7—Joe Ann Christian.
7—Marylyn Christian.
6—Vesta Christian, m. J. Porter Davis, automobile dealer.
7—Mary Christian Davis.
7—Cornelius Davis.
7—Infant died.
6—Mary Christian, corresponding secretary-treasurer, Georgia Baptist Woman's Missionary Union.
6—Evelyn Christian, m. William Coyne.
6—Cornelius Christian.
6—James Christian.
5—Jesse G. Christian, b. July 10, 1855, d. unmarried.
5—Charles W. Christian, m. Sarah White.
6—John Christian.
6—Sarah "Sally" Christian, m. Wallace Mason.
4—Thomas Sly Maxwell, b. Jan. 24, 1819; m. Mrs. Harriet Sanders nee Bond.
4—Willis Maxwell, b. 1821, d. 1829.
4—Martha P. Maxwell, b. April 14, 1824; m. Jan. 30, 1850, Leroy Hamm.
5—George J. Hamm, m. June 22, 1879, Mary A. Scott.
5—Sarah E. Hamm, m. Oct. 18, 1881, Thomas J. Richardson.
5—Jane Hamm, m. Lou Cordell.
5—Charles Hamm, m. Samantha Vickery.
4—Josephus Maxwell, b. May 11, 1826, d. Jan. 16, 1892; m. (1) Jane McAllister, and (2) May 3, 1877, Leonora McAllister.
5—(By first wife) William Pressley Maxwell, m. May 22, 1884, Blanche Matthews.
6—William Byron Maxwell, d. unmarried.
6—Janie Maxwell, m. J. D. Springer.
7—J. D. Springer Jr.
7—William Maxwell Springer, m. Bertha Elesia.
7—Joe Clark Springer.
7—Alfred Wooten Springer.
6—Evelyn Willie Maxwell, m. Roy D. Long.
7—Blanche Carolyn Long.
7—Miriam Long.
5—Luther McAllister Maxwell, d. unmarried.
5—Elizabeth Madora Maxwell, m. Levingston Strougher Gaines.
6—Blanche Gaines, m. Nov. 25, 1832. Floyd Thornton. No issue.
6—Ora Baxter Gaines, m. (1) Priscilla Gaines, and (2) Sallie Stowers.

7—(By first wife) Joseph Maxwell Gaines, m. Mildred Dean.
7—George Levingston Gaines, m. Doris Freeman.
7—Sarah Elizabeth Gaines.
7—Ora Erskin Gaines.
7—Vandiver Brown Gaines.
7—Mary Ellen Gaines.
7—Blanche Ophelia Gaines.
7—Martha Joan Gaines.
6—Hope Gaines, m. Howell Parker Adams.
7—Alvin Wesley Adams.
7—James Edgar Adams.
7—Hubert Teaslet Adams.
7—Gaines Howell Adams.
7—Georgia Madora Adams.
7—Neil Wade Adams.
7—Charles Thurmond Adams.
7—Clyde Thomas Adams.
7—Janie Sue Adams.
6—Faith Gaines, m. George Benjamin Crawford.
7—Lillian Crawford.
7—Flora Crawford.
7—Kathryn Crawford.
7—Jenelle Crawford.
6—Ira Alexander Gaines, m. Ora A. Adams.
7—Byron Adams Gaines.
7—Winifred Alexander Gaines.
7—James Ira Gaines.
6—Leonora Gaines, m. Marion Vandiver Duncan.
7—Marion Vandiver Duncan Jr.
7—Mary Eleanor Duncan.
6—Carl Simmons Gaines, m. Maggie Davis.
5—Samantha Leonora Maxwell.
5—Milton Erskin (M. E.) Maxwell, b. 1873, d. Aug. 14, 1835, merchant, president First National Bank of Elberton; m. Harriet Esther Smith.
6—Thelma Maxwell, m. Charles A. Johnson, dentist.
7—Charles A. Johnson Jr.
5—John Walton Crawford Maxwell, d. unmarried.
4—Marshall Harford Maxwell, b. Jan. 8, 1829, d. July 19, 1862; m. Eliza Bond.
4—Elijah Zerah Upson Maxwell, b. May 22, 1831; m. (1) Martha Elizabeth Teasley, and (2) Martha A. Cunningham.
5—(By first wife) John Marshall Maxwell, b. Dec. 4, 1852.
5—Thomas Jefferson Maxwell, b. June 23, 1854.
5—Mary Elizabeth Maxwell, b. 1855.
3—William Maxwell, b. Dec. 22, 1775, d. Sept. 25, 1852; m. Jane Higginbotham, b. March 3, 1782, d. 1863, daughter of Jacob Higginbotham, R. S.
4—Elizabeth Maxwell, d. Jan. 13, 1840; m. Dec. 22, 1818, Ralph Banks Jr., son of Ralph Banks Sr., R. S., b. Oct. 27, 1857, d. Aug. 24, 1824; m. Nov. 27, 1788, Rachel Jones.
5—Russell Banks, m. Jane Yarbrough.
5—Mary Banks, m. Memory Gump.
5—Jane Banks, m. Fleming Moss.
5—Rachel Banks, m. Augustus Moss.
5—Marion Banks, m. Martha Ressler.
4—Lucy Maxwell, m. Feb. 15, 1838, James Banks.
5—Mary Maxwell Banks.
5—Lena Banks.
4—Mary Maxwell, m. Feb. 14, 1826, Jackson Oliver.

5—Reverend Dionysius Oliver, m. Mary Sanders.
6—Sarah Jane Oliver.
6—Dionysius Jackson Oliver.
6—Sanders Bartow Oliver.
6—Tallulah Lee Oliver.
6—George Pierce Oliver.
6—Adisa Ann Oliver, m. D. C. Miller.
6—Mary Elizabeth Oliver, m. Dr. Howell Quillian.
6—Thomas Brittain Oliver.
6—Roberta Estelle Oliver.
5—William Capers Oliver, m. Leila MacKay.
6—Dewitte Oliver.
6—Lovick Pierce Oliver.
6—Lenora Oliver.
6—Denver Oliver.
6—Atticus Oliver.
6—William Oliver.
6—Nettie Oliver.
6—Leila Oliver.
6—John Oliver.
5—Thomas Parks Oliver, m. (1) Arminda MacDonald, and (2) Fanny Barrett.
6—(By first wife) Mittie Beatrice Oliver.
6—James Jackson Oliver.
6—Victor Oliver.
6—Robert Lee Oliver.
6—(By second wife) Thomas Parks Oliver Jr.
5—Jane Ann Oliver, m. Charles Allison Lilly.
6—Egbert Lilly.
6—Annie Lilly.
6—Roberta Lilly, d. infancy.
6—Lucy Lilly.
6—Charles Lilly, d. infancy.
6—Lilly Lilly.
4—Ann Maxwell, m. March 4, 1834, Abraham Chrisler.
5—William "Billy" Chrisler, m. Frances Rainwater.
6—Willie Crisler, m. (1) Joseph Waters, and (2) Oscar Eason.
7—Ollie Waters.
6—Jynie Crisler, m. Mr. King.
6—Simeon Crisler.
6—Thomas Crisler, m. Amanda Manning.
7—Betty Crisler, m. Newton Rucker.
7—Ida Crisler, m. Ida Haygood.
7—Joe Crisler, m. Joseph Gillespie.
7—Flora Crisler, m. Oscar Gentry.
7—Simeon Crisler.
7—Isham Crisler, m. Miss King.
6—George Crisler.
6—Joe Crisler.
6—John Crisler.
6—Benjamin Franklin Crisler, m. (1) Mary Maxwell Teasley, and (2) Emma McClure.
7—Annie Lou Crisler.
7—Daisy Crisler, m. Mr. Mullins.
7—Roy Crisler.
7—Max Crisler.
6—Isham Teasley Crisler, m. Mary Manning.
7—Cora Crisler, m. John Tribble.
7—Maud Crisler.
6—Robert Crisler.

6—Jane Ann Crisler, m. E. V. McCollum.
7—William Franklin McCollum.
7—Robert Dodge McCollum, m. Ella Herndon.
8—Leon McCollum.
8—Lyle McCollum.
8—Leslie McCollum.
8—Lucile McCollum.
7—Charles Edgar McCollum.
7—Claud McCollum.
6—Mary Crisler, m. William H. Mansell.
6—Abe Crisler, m. Fanny Letson.
7—Otis Crisler.
7—Homer Crisler, m. Miss McKinney.
7—Cottie Crisler.
4—Jane Maxwell, m. Dr. Doster. No issue.
4—Sarah Maxwell, m. John Mize.
5—William S. Mize, m. (1) Lou MacKay, and (2) Ella Neal.
5—Thomas Mize, m. Americus Gunnells.
5—Frank Mize, m. Addie Neal.
5—Mat Mize, m. Lola Wright.
4—Martin Maxwell, m. Jan. 29, 1835, Julia Ann Upshaw.
5—James W. Maxwell.
5—Thomas B. Maxwell, m. Phobe (?).
6—Irene Maxwell, m. Murray L. Upshaw.
7—Lee Upshaw.
7—Murray L. Upshaw Jr.
6—Julia Maxwell.
6—Lula Maxwell.
6—Charlie Maxwell.
6—Ira Maxwell.
6—Martin Maxwell.
6—Earl Thomas Maxwell, m. Mary Blalock.
7—Mary Phobe Maxwell.
6—Izetta Maxwell.
5—John V. Maxwell.
4—Thomas Jackson Maxwell, b. May 31, 1804, d. March 3, 1869; m. May 31, 1831, Ann Banks Adams, b. Oct. 4, 1814, d. May 12, 1886.
5—Mary Elizabeth Maxwell, b. April 2, 1832, d. Aug. 22, 1919; m. (1) John Mize, and (2) Charles Sorrels. No issue.
5—William Haden Maxwell, b. Feb. 18, 1834, d. June 22, 1864; m. (1) Harriet Almond, and (2) Amelia Oglesby.
6—Thomas Maxwell, d. infancy.
6—Francis Calloway Maxwell, b. Aug. 20, 1859, d. June 13, 1932; m. Feb. 4, 1885, Cornelia Crow.
7—Harriet "Hattie" Maxwell, m. Budd C. Vaughan.
8—Louise Vaughan, m. Everette Fortson.
9—Jane Fortson.
7—Griffin Maxwell, d. unmarried.
7—Roy Maxwell, m. Belle Fortson.
8—La Nelle Maxwell.
8—Frances Fortson Maxwell.
8—Laura Belle Maxwell.
8—Mabel Joe Maxwell.
7—Floyce Maxwell, m. Clay Fortson.
8—Marion Fortson.
8—Weyman Fortson (twin).
8—Wilton Fortson (twin).
8—Leonard Fortson.
8—Eugenia Adel Fortson.

7—Mary Lou Maxwell, m. Clayton Burriss.
8—Edna Burriss.
8—Martha Helen Burriss.
7—Ophelia Maxwell.
7—Calloway Maxwell, m. Elmer Rousey.
8—Cornelius Jackson Rousey.
8—Betty Jane Rousey.
6—Mary Lucy Maxwell, d. infancy.
6—Harriet Catherine Maxwell, b. Sept. 19, 1862, d. Feb. 20, 1884, m. July 19, 1877, Robert Turner.
7—Carrie Turner (twin), m. O. E. Moore. No issue.
7—Corrie Turner (twin), m. Robert S. Bowers.
8—William Robert Bowers, m. Moody Brown.
9—William Robert Bowers Jr.
7—Willie Turner, m. George P. Gary.
8—Paul Turner Gary.
8—Marvin Lee Gary.
8—Effie Catherine Gary.
8—George W. Gary.
8—Robert Maxwell Gary.
8—Albert Alexander Gary.
8—Beverly Allen Gary.
5—Martin Maxwell, b. March 5, 1837, d. Aug. 29, 1862, killed in War Between the States; m. Dec. 16, 1858, Catherine Teasley
6—Thomas Allen Maxwell, b. Nov. 28, 1859; m. Dec. 22, 1881, Rachel Brown.
7—Mary Catherine Maxwell, m. Watkins W. Brown.
8—Rachel Maxwell Brown.
8—Virginia Walker Maxwell.
7—Elizabeth Maxwell.
7—Vandiver Maxwell, m. Mamie Bond.
8—Julius Bond Maxwell.
8—Thomas Calvin Maxwell.
7—Jim Frank Maxwell.
7—Lilla Maxwell, d. infancy.
7—Martin Maxwell, m. Allie May Maxwell.
8—Joseph Maxwell.
8—James Maxwell.
8—Parks Maxwell.
7—Lucile Maxwell, m. Mack Sanders.
8—Robert Griggs Sanders.
7—Hoyt Maxwell, m. Ada Lou Fleming.
8—Hoyt Chandler Maxwell.
8—Benjamin Martin Maxwell.
8—Hannah Maxwell.
8—Henry Alfred Maxwell.
8—Pat Rice Maxwell.
8—Winona Maxwell.
7—Imogene Maxwell, m. Nobel Vivian Moore.
8—Raymond Maxwell Moore.
6—Genie Maxwell, d. infancy.
6—Howell P. Maxwell, d. infancy.
6—Elizabeth Maxwell, b. Dec. 22, 1862, d. Nov. 22, 1925; m. Dec. 22, 1880, Leonard Stephens Brown.
7—Thomas Maxwell Brown, m. Susie Myers.
8—Theron Myers Brown.
7—Flora Elizabeth Brown, m. William Oscar Herndon.
8—Dorothy Herndon.
8—Maxwell Herndon.
8—Leonard Oscar Herndon.

7—Clay Leonard Brown, m. Azalee Herndon.
8—Clay Leonard Brown Jr.
8—Julia LeRose Brown.
8—Louis Kendall Brown.
8—Herman Gaines Brown.
8—Bonner Sue Brown.
7—Roy Lucian Brown, m. Mauline Bryan.
8—William Murray Brown.
5—Jackson Oliver Maxwell, b. March 6, 1839, d. Feb. 16, 1881; m. Dec. 13, 1859, Mary Caroline Fleming.
6—Fannie Eunice Maxwell, b. Sept. 8, 1861, d. Dec. 7, 1887; m. John Granville Thornton.
7—Atticus Granville Thornton, m. Evelyn Woods.
8—Atticus Granville Thornton Jr.
8—Emma Alexander Thornton.
7—Beatrice Eunice Thornton, m. Dr. Harrison Tilly Sterling.
8—Harrison Tilly Sterling Jr.
8—Beatrice Thornton Sterling, m. Frederick Fritsche.
9—Frederick Fritsche Jr.
8—George Archibald Sterling.
8—Harrison Thornton Sterling.
8—John Maxwell Sterling.
8—Charles Sterling.
7—Reuben Oliver Thornton.
6—Panola Amanda Maxwell, d. infancy.
6—Martha Elizabeth "Elzora" Maxwell, b. Dec. 13, 1867, d. Aug. 1, 1907; m. July 25, 1889, Cone Eppy Bond.
7—Thomas Oliver Bond, b. May 18, 1890, d. Sept. 12, 1907. Unmarried.
7—Vera Caroline Bond, m. Raymond Stapleton, judge city court of Elberton, solicitor city court of Elberton, secretary to Governor Nat E. Harris of Georgia, secretary 30th Georgia senatorial district.
8—Vera Caroline Stapleton.
8—Merian Jane Stapleton.
6—Thomas Martin Maxwell, m. Janie Hulme.
7—Mary Thomas Maxwell, principal Elberton High School.
6—Torrence Mansfield Maxwell, m. Willie Teasley.
6—Lois Maxwell, b. Oct. 22, 1873, d. Nov. 25, 1911; m. James William Alfred Teaasley.
7—Gladstone Inman Teasley, m. Gipsy Inman.
8—Gladstone Inman Teasley Jr.
7—Mary Drucilla Teasley.
7—Julia Teasley.
6—William Jefferson Maxwell.
6—Robert Oliver "Ollie" Maxwell.
6—Lea Maxwell, m. George Nunnelee Wall.
7—John Oliver Wall, post office clerk.
7—James Wall.
7—Mary Eleanor Wall.
5—Sarah Catherine Maxwell, b. Aug. 12, 1841, d. June 18, 1923; m. (1) Feb. 5, 1858, William B. Rucker, and (2) Dec. 15, 1871, Roland J. Brown.
6—Reverend Thomas Jackson Rucker, b. 1859; m. Frances Catherine Thornton.
7—William F. Rucker, d. unmarried.
7—Isham Goss Rucker, m. Mary Bush.
8—Helen Frances Rucker.
8—Mary Louise Rucker.
8—John Thornton Rucker.

8—Isham Goss Rucker Jr.
8—Robert Joseph Rucker.
8—James Federick Rucker.
7—Benjamin Smith Rucker, m. (1) Mamie Hawkins, and (2) Lizzie Scattergood.
8—(By first wife) Mamie Rucker, d. infancy.
8—(By second wife) Eleanor Scattergood Rucker.
8—Benjamin Smith Rucker Jr.
7—Thomas Joseph Rucker, m. Eula Herndon.
8—Fannie Sue Rucker.
8—Charles Ralph Rucker.
7—John McAlpin Rucker, m. Petra Swearingen.
8—Frances Louise Rucker.
8—Leah Ruth Rucker.
8—Myrtle Pope Rucker.
8—Thomas Monroe Rucker.
8—John McAlpin Rucker Jr.
7—Vera Myrtle Rucker, d. infancy.
7—James Rucker, m. Grace Cheek.
8—Evelyn Rucker.
7—Mary Della Rucker, d. infancy.
7—Sarah Harriet Rucker.
7—Fanny Ruth Rucker, m. J. Stokely Warren.
8—Ethlyn Warren.
8—Winona Warren.
7—Tomilene Rucker, d. infancy.
7—Nora Rucker, m. Phillip Bradford.
8—Martha Frances Bradford.
8—Phillip Bradford, Jr.
7—Myrtle Rucker, d. infancy.
7—Florence Rucker, m. C. H. Denny.
8—Sarah Denny.
8—John Henry Denny.
7—Alma Rucker, m. Fred Young.
8—Anna Rucker Young.
8—Thelma Jo Young.
7—Julius Thornton Rucker, m. Ida Johnson.
8—Julius Thornton Rucker Jr.
8—Charles Thomas Rucker.
7—Nina Catherine Rucker.
6—Samantha Rucker, d. infancy.
6—William A. Rucker, clerk superior court of Elbert county 1901-1936, elected 1937-1940; m. Annie Marvin Bailey.
7—William Albert Rucker, m. Caroline Green White.
8—Caroline Anne Rucker.
7—Thomas Bailey Rucker, m. Margaret Bond.
8—William Thomas Rucker, b. 1935.
7—Annie Marie Rucker.
7—Carl Maxwell Rucker.
7—Charles Hulme Rucker.
6—Lou Martin Brown, m. Essie McCurry.
7—Corinne Brown, d. unmarried.
7—Clyde McCurry Brown.
7—Thomas Jefferson Brown, m. Willie Boston.
7—Benson Chandler Brown, m. Jewel Thornton.
7—William Albert Brown, d. unmarried.
7—Sarah Kathryn Brown, m. Ellison Mitchell.
7—Mary Lou Brown, m. Olin Burgin.
7—Lonnie Maxwell Brown.
7—Neal Martin Brown.

7—Essie Mildred Brown, d. infancy.
6—Lonnie Chandler Brown, m. May Noami Allen.
7—Monget Gerald Brown.
7—Helen Sarah Brown.
7—Lonnie Chandler Brown Jr., d. infancy.
6—Cran Oliver Brown, b. May 18, 1880, d. Dec. 14, 1932; m. Eunice Allen.
7—Richard Roland Brown.
7—Joseph Sidney Brown.
7—Gene Crandall Brown.
5—Chandler Maxwell, C. S., b. Sept. 5, 1843, d. April 25, 1926; m. Dec. 5, 1865, Mary Hester Brown.
6—Sarah Burnettie Maxwell, b. Jan. 16, 1867; m. John William Turner.
7—Clifford Turner, S. W. W., b. Sept. 18, 1892, d. Jan. 12, 1930; m. Irene Mize nee Almond.
8—Betty Turner.
7—Mary Lucile Turner.
7—Jim Chandler Turner.
6—James Thomas Maxwell, m. Lillian Busha.
7—Sarah Hester Maxwell.
7—Martha Lillian Maxwell.
7—Barbara Maxwell.
5—Julia Ann Maxwell, b. Nov. 6, 1845, d. Nov. 2, 1921; m. Nov. 9, 1871, William Benson Jefferson Norman, b. June 28, 1849, d. Dec. 7, 1920.
6—Thomas Jefferson Norman, d. infancy.
6—Martin Maxwell Norman.
6—Sarah Quillie Norman.
6—Mary Annie Norman.
6—Georgia Irene Norman, b. July 18, 1880, d. Nov. 20, 1926; m. Dec. 28, 1910, Bartow Bee Mason.
6—Frances Emma Norman.
6—James William Norman, dean Teacher's College, University of Florida; m. Sarah Lucile Pullen.
7—Frances Elizabeth Norman.
7—James William Norman Jr.
7—Sarah Ann Norman.
5—Louisa Maxwell, b. July 31, 1847, d. May 31, 1910; m. Dec. 23, 1873, Calvin Tucker Bond, b. Jan. 5, 1845, d. Dec. 28, 1911.
6—Dr. Thomas Willis Bond, b. Sept. 28, 1874, d. June 19, 1930; m. Elizabeth "Lizzie" Carpenter.
7—Ethlyn Bond, d. infancy.
7—Thomas Bond, m. Jewette Smith.
7—Margaret Bond, m. 1934, Thomas Rucker.
8—William Thomas Rucker, b. 1935.
7—Elizabeth Bond, m. Henry Smith.
8—Priscilla Bond Smith, b. March 13, 1933.
8—Elizabeth Ann Smith, b. 1934.
7—Sarah Bond.
6—Reverend George Calvin Bond, Baptist minister, m. Cora Eavenson.
7—Bernice Bond, m. Young Swift Smith, newspaper employee.
8—Theresa Smith.
7—Alton Eavenson Bond.
7—Harold Tucker Bond.
7—Corella Bond.
7—George Calvin Bond Jr.
7—Louise Bond.
6—Addie Julia Bond, m. (1) Elzie Herndon, and (2) Daniel Hogshed.

7—George Calvin Hearndon, d. infancy.
7—Tommie Lee Herndon, d. infancy.
6—Mamie Bond, m. Vandiver Maxwell.
7—Julius Bond Maxwell.
7—Thomas Calvin Maxwell.
6—William Llewllyn Bond, m. (1) Lottie Garner, and (2) Mae Booth.
7—(By first wife) Haskell Bond.
7—(By second wife) Jack Bond.
5—John Mat Maxwell, b. Dec. 3, 1849, d. March 11, 1883; m. Emma Davis, b. 1850, d. Oct. 1935.
6—Reverend William Albert Maxwell, m. (1) Bessie Eavenson, and (2) Sarah Odom.
7—(By first wife) Mary Sue Maxwell, m. Grady Sidwell.
7—Louise Maxwell, m. Roy Hayes.
8—Betty Sue Hayes.
8—Jane Hayes.
7—Quillian Maxwell, m. Bernice Herndon.
6—Thomas Jefferson Maxwell, m. Sally Mize.
7—Ophelia Maxwell, m. Thomas Irwin Baskin.
7—Marvin Maxwell, m. Nell Erwin.
8—Carol Imogene Maxwell.
8—Barbara June Maxwell.
8—Alice Amelia Maxwell.
7—Ruth Maxwell, m. Doyle Neal.
7—Minnie Lou Maxwell, m. Hood Fortson.
8—Sarah Alice Fortson.
7—Bessie Maxwell, m. James Willis.
8—James Willard Willis.
7—Doris Maxwell.
6—George Maxwell, m. Emma Bond.
7—Pearl Maxwell, m. Bebbett Stewart.
7—Clyde Maxwell.
7—Clifford Maxwell, S. W. W., m. Dora Jordan.
7—Annie Sue Maxwell, m. Fred Grimes.
8—Wilfred Grimes.
8—Jimmy Grimes.
8—Ted Grimes (twin).
8—Ned Grimes (twin).
7—John Maxwell.
7—Lizzie May Maxwell, m. James Holmes.
7—Harold Maxwell, m. Emma Brown.
8—Marjorie Pearl Brown Maxwell.
7—George Elliott Maxwell.
7—Nelle Maxwell.
7—Fred Maxwell.
7—Mildred Maxwell.
6—Reverend Terry Harper Maxwell, m. Orlanda Addy.
7—John A. Maxwell, d. infancy.
7—Terry Harper Maxwell Jr., d. infancy.
6—Charles "Charlie" Maxwell, m. Lucy Higginbotham.
7—Alma Maxwell, m. Ben Scott.
8—Stanley Scott.
7—Clarence "Cuz" Maxwell.
7—Bertha Maxwell, m. Curtis Dickerson.
8—Helen Dickerson.
7—Sam Maxwell.
7—Harris Maxwell.
7—L. E. Maxwell.
7—Mary Maxwell.

7—Hugh Maxwell.
7—Olana Maxwell.
7—Joe Maxwell.
7—Elmer Maxwell.
7—Sarah Maxwell.
6—Anna Maxwell, d. unmarried.
5—Amanda Priscilla Maxwell, b. Sept. 8, 1855; m. Nov. 10, 1881, Elbert Gordon Brown.
6—George Sanford Brown, m. Alice Sullivan.
7—Mary Hortense Brown, m. Silas O. Robertson.
8—Mary June Robertson.
8—Bobbie Ann Robertson.
7—Elbert Gordon Brown, m. Nina Elizabeth Benton.
7—John McCrary Brown, m. Hilda Blake.
7—Charles Sullivan Brown.
7—Amanda Catherine Brown.
7—George Sanford Brown Jr.
6—James Maxwell Brown, m. Curtis Hendrix.
7—James Maxwell Brown Jr.
7—Marian Elbert Brown.
6—Ann Brown, m. James M. Payne.
6—Lena Brown, m. John Albert Beggs.
7—James Gordon Beggs.
7—Frances Beggs.
7—John Albert Beggs Jr.
6—Benjamin Franklin Brown, m. Felicia Attaway.
7—Billy Chandler Brown.
6—Ed Neal Brown, m. Ina Wright.
5—Benson Mansfield Maxwell, b. April 23, 1862; m. Feb. 5, 1890, Beatrice Eula Eavenson.
6—Mary Mozelle Maxwell, b. 1891; m. Lonnie Aticus Maxwell.
7—Margarette Teasley.
6—Paschal Chandler Maxwell, m. Esther Pierce.
7—Jane Maxwell.
6—Willis Benson Maxwell, m. Mary Elizabeth Benson.
6—Mary Lou Maxwell, interior decorator.
6—Julia Maxwell.
4—Benjamin Maxwell, m. Feb. 3, 1837, Nancy Christian.
5—Annie Maxwell.
5—Charles W. Maxwell, m. Tibatha Brown.
6—Larae Maxwell.
6—Ben Maxwell.
6—Robert Maxwell.
6—William Maxwell.
6—Pearlie Maxwell.
6—Minnie Maxwell.
6—Gordon Maxwell.
6—Asmond Maxwell.
5—William W. Maxwell, m. Sarah Vaughan.
6—John B. Maxwell.
6—B. B. Maxwell.
6—Dock Maxwell.
6—Worley Maxwell.
6—Pea Maxwell.
6—Nancy Maxwell.
5—Martin G. Maxwell, m. Lucy Dickerson.
6—Early Maxwell.
6—Alvin Maxwell.
6—Josie Maxwell.
5—John Maxwell.

6—Mary Maxwell.
6—Jack Maxwell.
6—Jasper Maxwell.
6—Lessie Maxwell.
6—Martin Maxwell.
5—John R. Maxwell, m. Rachel Horton.
6—Frank Maxwell.
6—Sally Maxwell.
6—Mattie Maxwell.
6—Bartow Maxwell.
6—Mark Maxwell.
6—Tom Maxwell.
6—Coil Maxwell.
6—Rona Maxwell.
6—Dock Maxwell.
6—Hetero Maxwell.
6—Emma Maxwell.
6—Alonzo Maxwell.
5—Thomas J. Maxwell, m. Laura Vaughan.
6—Lula Maxwell.
6—Sethie Maxwell.
6—Vonnie Maxwell.
6—Charles Maxwell.
6—Ben Maxwell.
6—Robert Maxwell.
6—Jim Maxwell.
6—Lizzie Maxwell.
6—Peyton Hawes Maxwell.
6—Yancey Maxwell.
6—Allie Maxwell.
5—James F. Maxwell, m. Senie Christian.
6—Essie Maxwell.
6—Nora Maxwell.
6—Leo Maxwell.
6—Callie Maxwell.
5—Doctor Brawner Maxwell, m. Maggie Oglesby. No issue.
5—Lula Maxwell, m. John M. Vaughan.
6—Jimmie Vaughan.
6—Betsy Vaughan.
6—Mamie Vaughan.
6—General Vaughan.
6—Cap Vaughan.
6—Rissie Vaughan.
6—Maggie Vaughan.
6—Foggie Vaughan.
6—McIntosh Vaughan.
5—Jacob Maxwell.
5—Mary Maxwell.
4—James Madison Maxwell, b. Nov. 16, 1814; d. Sept. 1864; m 1848, Mary "Polly" Tabor.
5—Ophelia Maxwell, m. Tarpley Quillian.
4—Jerry Maxwell, m. Betsy Orr.
5—Diza Jane Maxwell.
5—Amanda Maxwell, m. Alfred Phillips.
5—Nealie Maxwell, m. Jimmie Neal.
5—Ann Maxwell, m. Pink Mayfield.
5—Emily Florence Maxwell, m. Arthur C. Maxwell.
4—Riley Maxwell, m. Frances Mitchell.
5—Wiliam Maxwell.
5—Brantley Maxwell.

5—Mattie Maxwell, m. Jack Story.
5—Eugene Maxwell.
3—Jesse Maxwell, b. Dec. 11, 1780, migrated to Mississippi.
3—Joel Maxwell, b. Sept. 30, 1783; d. Aug. 23, 1863; m. Mary Brown.
4—William Tallent Maxwell, m. (1) Sarah Horton; (2) Elmira Winn.
5—Melinda Maxwell, m. Monroe Cason.
5—Mary Maxwell, m. Mr. Sanders.
5—Emily Maxwell, m. Gaines Brown.
5—Jane Maxwell.
5—Nancy Maxwell.
5—Martha Maxwell, m. Mr. Moss.
5—Matilda Maxwell, m. Malcolm Duncan.
5—Elizabeth Maxwell.
5—Lettie Maxwell, m. Jasper Jordan.
5—Lucinda Maxwell, m. Wess Colvard.
5—Singleton Allen Maxwell, m. Mary Mildred Maxwell.
6—Singleton Allen Maxwell Jr.
5—John Maxwell, m. Miss Sanders.
5—Jesse Maxwell, m. Eliza Eavenson.
5—Joel Maxwell, C. S., killed in action.
4—Jesse Maxwell, b. Oct. 16, 1806; d. June 10, 1895; m. Aug. 8, 1844, Katie Johnson.
5—Daniel Johnson Maxwell, m. June 8, 1869, Amanda Eavenson.
6—George Maxwell, deputy sheriff of Elbert County; m. Alice Parks.
7—Elmer Maxwell, m. Ione Thornton.
8—Elmer Maxwell Jr.
7—Allie Mae Maxwell and other issue.
6—Augustus Maxwell, m. Mamie Gaines.
6—Eustace Maxwell.
6—Andrew Maxwell, m. Essie Mewbourn.
6—Kate Maxwell, m. Dr. Sam Bowie, optician. No issue.
6—Addie Maxwell, m. Thomas Eavenson.
6—Belle Maxwell, m. Ben Jordan.
6—Josephine Maxwell.
6—Edwin Maxwell, d. unmarried.
6—Artemus Maxwell, m. Sarah V. Norman.
6—Simeon Maxwell, m. Essie Bond.
5—Sarah Ann Maxwell, m. Milton Barrett Adams.
6—Lucy Adams, m. Austin Mewbourn.
7—Ethel Lucile Mewbourn, m. Paul Herndon.
7—Julia E. Mewbourn.
7—Sam Johnson Mewbourn.
6—Irvin Adams, m. Howell Mewbourn.
7—Lois Mewbourn, m. Julian Eavenson.
8—Marjorie Eavenson.
8—Winifred Eavenson.
8—Julian Eavenson Jr.
7—Olivia Mewbourn, m. Clyde Cole.
7—Vivian Mewbourn, m. Melvin Nelms.
7—Clarence Mewbourn.
7—Grace Mewbourn, m. Hoke Ginn.
7—Jack Mewbourn.
7—Gene Mewbourn.
7—Katherine Mewbourn.
6—Jesse Adams, m. Meanda Mewbourn.
7—Mabel Adams, m. Vernon Auld.
7—Flora Adams, d. unmarried.

6—Janie Adams.
6—Dewitte Adams, m. (1) Ruby Adair; (2) Lily Branch.
4—John B. Maxwell, m. (1) Martha Burch Tucker, granddaughter of Governor Stephen Heard; (2) Jane Gaines Crawford. No issue.
4—Washington Maxwell.
4—Robert Maxwell.
4—Allen Maxwell, m. (1) Mary Edwards; (2) Miss Hendricks.
4—Sarah E. Maxwell, m. March 29, 1855, Tinsley Ginn.
4—Elizabeth Maxwell, m. William Hutchinson. No issue.
4—Peggy A. Maxwell, m. April 9, 1829, William E. Eaves.
3—Sarah Maxwell, b. Jan. 4, 1786; d. May 29, 1838; m. 1807, William Payne Christian.
4—Jackson Christian.
4—Nancy Turner Christian, b. Sept. 1, 1811; d. 1880; m. 1834, John Warren Seymour.
5—Minnie Seymour.
5—Martin Seymour.
5—Kezia Blake Seymour.
5—Ardesia Seymour.
5—Sarah "Sally" Seymour.
5—Charles Marion Seymour, C. S., m. Jan. 7, 1867, Locky Ann Phelps.
6—Dora Penelope Seymour, m. Charles H. Allen, planter.
7—Zelma Allen, Regent Stephen Heard Chapter, Daughters of the American Revolution, President 10th Georgia District Woman's Club, m., T. O. Tabor Jr.
8—T. O. Tabor III.
7—Gladys Allen, m. Herman J. Brown.
8—Allen Brown.
7—Valeria Allen, m. Albert T. Brewer.
8—Elizabeth Brewer.
7—Huie Allen, m. Harry G. Thornton.
8—Harry Allen Thornotn.
8—Earl Thornton.
7—Charles H. Allen Jr., m. Janie Auld.
8—Charles H. Allen III.
7—Beth Allen, m. Maurice Asbury.
8—Beverly Allen Asbury.
8—Ed Asbury.
5—Marshall Seymour, C. S.
4—Jesse G. Christian, m. March 25, 1841, Ann Maxwell.
5—Elizabeth M. B. Christian, b. Feb. 1, 1842; m. William Brown.
6—George Brown.
6—Lucy Brown.
6—Sally Brown.
5—Ira Jackson Christian, b. June 25, 1844; m. Lou Booth.
6—Vandiver Christian.
6—Mamie Christian.
6—Lizzie Christian.
6—Tommie Christian.
6—Lou Charles Christian.
6—Corry Christian.
6—Howard Christian.
5—Sarah Ann Josephine Christian, b. Sept. 5, 1845; m. Jacob Vaughan.
6—William Vaughan.
5—Mary Frances Chrsitian, b. May 13, 1847; m. William Vaughan.
6—Nealie Vaughan.
6—Betsy Vanghan.

6—Sarah F. Vaughan.
6—George Vaughan.
5—Josephus Marion Christian, b. June 23, 1849; m. Martha Brown.
6—Lens Christian.
6—Rossie Christian.
6—Ace Christian.
6—Clarence Christian.
6—Morris Christian.
5—John Thomas Christian, b. Dec. 14, 1850; m. Lettie Brown.
6—Daisy Christian.
6—Ossie Christian, m. Frank K. Eaves.
7—Boots Eaves.
7—Walter Eaves, policeman, and other issue.
6—Ollie Christian.
6—Johnny Christian.
5—Martha Permelia Christian, b. Jan. 1, 1853; m. James Vaughan.
6—Vaughnie Vaughan.
6—Jessie Vaughan.
6—Luke Vaughan.
6—May Vaughan.
6—Homer Vaughan.
6—Ronnie Vaughan.
5—William Cornelius Christian, b. Jan. 1, 1853; m. Mary Cooper.
6—Arles Christian, m. Aubrey Christian.
7—Carmen Christian.
6—Arva Christian, m. Robert Williford.
7—Robert Williford Jr.
7—William Williford.
6—Nolley Christian, m. Thomas Murray.
6—Savias Christian, m. Josephine Evans.
7—Robert Christian.
7—Betty Christian.
7—Mary Christian.
7—Nancy Christian.
7—Joe Ann Christian.
7—Marylyn Christian.
6—Gradus Christian, m. Florie Walters.
7—Mary Jean Christian.
7—Evelyn Christian.
7—Gradus Christian Jr.
7—Helen Christian.
6—Vesta Christian, m. J. Porter Davis.
7—Mary Christian Davis.
7—Cornelius Davis.
7—Infant died
6—Mary Christian.
6—Evelyn Christian, m. William Coyne.
6—Cornelius Christian.
6—James Christian.
5—Jesse G. Christian, d. unmarried.
5—Charles W. Christian, m. Nealie Johnson.
6—Billy Christian.
6—Sterlie Christian.
6—Boyd Christian.
6—Lawrence Christian.
4—Charles Woodson Christian, m. Jan. 18, 1827, Mary Walton Maxwell, b. Feb. 8, 1811.
5—William P. Christian, b. Dec. 25, 1828.
5—Charles Woodson Christian Jr., b. Dec. 3, 1830.
4—Mel Christian.

3—Jeremiah Maxwell, b. July 14, 1789.
3—Elizabeth Maxwell, b. Sept. 25, 1791, d. Jan. 29, 1862; m. Sept. 3, 1812, William McMullan.
4—Sarah McMullan, b. Feb. 20, 1815, m. 1840, Samuel W. Williford.
4—Mary "Polly" McMullan, b. June 20, 1830; m. 1835, Joseph R. Hull.
4—Kezia McMullan, b. May 23, 1817, d. 1868.
4—Jesse Pemberton McMullan, b. 1820, d. 1879; m. 1859, America Dunagin.
4—Elizabeth Ann McMullan, b. May 17, 1823, d. 1907; m. Samuel W. Williford (widower of deceased sister.)
4—William Marion McMullan, b. 1825, d. 1920; m. 1859, Medline Dunagin.
5—William Jesse McMullan, m. Jan. 1889, Sarah J. Freeman.
4—Thomas J. McMullan, b. Aug. 9, 1830, d. Aug. 1879.

McINTOSH OR MACKINTOSH

The following chart shows intermarriages with the following families:
Abercrombie — Archer — Alexander — Andrews — Allston — Allen — Arnold — Annard — Baillie — Barclay — Bates — Brown — Campbell — Cuthburt — Cade — D'Montgomery — D'Sandylands — Dallas — Davidson — Dunbar — Douglas — Dean — Ennis — Fraser — Falconer — Forbes — Gilpatrick — Grant — Gordon — Grahme — Graham — Harie — Holland — Hawes — Hillary — Kennedy — Kilpatrick — Kekewich — Lockhart — Lindsay — Long — Lee — McLeod — McAllister — McCollough — MacDonald — MacKenzie — MacLean — MacCoy — MacPherson — MacAngus — Munro — Marburg — Menzies — Offutt — Oglivie — Robertson — Rose — Richards — Reade — Royal — Swinton — Stelling — St. Martin — Sterling — Thomson — Tinsley — Wainwright — White — Zeigler.

(Note: Numbers represent generations, as: (1) first generation, (2) second generation, (3) third generation, etc.)

1—Duncan MacDuff 1st Earl of Fife, nephew and avenger of King Duncan.
2—Defagon MacDuff, 2nd Earl of Fife.
3—Constantine MacDuff, 3rd Earl of Fife.
4—Gilmicheal McDuff, 4th Earl of Fife.
5—Dundan MacDuff, 5th Earl of Fife.
6—Shaw I, Commander of Scotland's armies; d. 1179; m. Giles D'Montgomery.
7—Shaw II, m. Mary D'Sandylands, daughter of Sir Harry.
8—William, m. Beatrix Learmonth.
9—Shaw III, d. 1265; m. Helen Campbell, daughter of Thane of Calder.
10—Shaw Ferquhard Mackintoich, m. Mona MacDonald, daughter of Angus of Isla.
11—Angus Mackintosh, b. 1268; d. 1345; m. Eva Gilpatrick, a lineal descendant of Feradach (610-680), King of Dalradia, Tribe of Lorn.
12—William Mackintosh, d. 1368, Chief of Clan Chattan, m. (1) Florence Calder; (2) Margaret McLeod.
13—(By first wife) Lachlan Mackintosh, m. Agnes Fraser.
14—Ferquhard Mackintosh.

13—(By second wife) Malcolm Mackintosh, m. Mona MacDonald.
14—Duncan Mackintosh, m. Flora MacDonald.
15—Ferquhard Mackintosh.
14—Lachlan Mackintosh, m. Catherine Grant.
15—William Mackintosh.
15—Lachlan "Beg" Mackintosh, m. Jean Gordon.
16—William Mackintosh, m. Margaret Oglivie.
17—Lachlan Mackintosh, m. Agnes Mackenzie.
18—Angus Mackintosh, d. 1593; m. April 1586, Jean Campbell, daughter of 5th Earl of Argyll.
19—Sir Lachlan Mackintosh, d. 1620; m. Anna Grant.
20—William Mackintosh, d. 1660; m. Margaret Grahme.
21—Lachlan Mackintosh, d. 1704; m. Margaret Lindsey.
22—Lachlan Mackintosh, d. 1731.
20—Lachlan Mackintosh of Kinrara, m. Isabel Graham.
21—Son died infancy.
21—Margaret Mackintosh, m. Hector MacKenzie.
21—Isabel Mackintosh, m. William MacPherson.
20—Angus Mackintosh of Daviot, m. (1) Jean Gordon; (2) Marjorie Robertson.
21—(By first wife) No descendants.
21—(By second wife) Isabel Mackintosh, m. Alexander Rose.
21—Lachlin Mackintosh, m. Anna Mackenzie.
22—William Mackintosh, d. 1740.
22—Aeneas Mackintosh, d. 1770.
22—Alexander Mackintosh, m. Miss Davidson.
23—Sir Aeneas Mackintosh.
21—Alexander Mackintosh, m. Ann Fraser.
22—Duncan Mackintosh of Castle Leathers, m. Agnes Dallas.
23—Alexander Mackintosh.
23—Angus Mackintosh, m. Archangle St. Martin.
24—Alexander Mackintosh, d. 1861; m. Charlotte McLeod.
25—Alexander Aeneas Mackintosh.
25—Alfred Donald Mackintosh, m. Harriet Richards.
26—Angus Alexander Mackintosh, b. 1885.
24—Aeneas Mackintosh of Daviot, m. Louisa F. S. McLeod.
25—Alexander Mackintosh.
25—Duncan Mackintosh.
25—Mary Marion Mackintosh, m. C. G. Kekewich.
25—Charlotte Eva Mackintosh, m. William Sterling.
25—Alexander Graham Mackintosh, m. Robert C. G. Campbbell.
18—William Macintosh, 1st of Borlom, d. 1630; m. Elizabeth Ennis.
19—Lachlan Mackintosh, m. Helen Gordon.
20—William Mackintosh, m. Mary Baillie.
21—William Mackintosh, "The Brigadier," m. Mary Reade.
22—Lachlan Mackintosh, m. Elizabeth Harie of New England.
23—Elizabeth Mackintosh, m. Isaac Royal of Boston.
24—Mary Mackintosh Royal.
24—Elizabeth Royal.
23—Mary Mackintosh.
22—Shaw Mackintosh, d. 1770; m. Jean Menzies.
23—Edward Mackintosh.
23—Helen Mackintosh.
23—Winwood Mackintosh, m. John Forbes.
24—James Forbes.
22—Winwood Mackintosh, m. Roderick MacKenzie.
22—Forbesia Maria Mackintosh.
22—Helen Macintosh, m. Jonathan Thomson.
21—Major John Mackintosh, m. Magdalen MacKenzie.

21—Captain Duncan Mackintosh, m. Elizabeth Mackintosh.
22—William Mackintosh, m. 1723, Janet MacLean.
23—Alexander Mackintosh also married a Janet MacLean.
24—Lieutenant Aeneas Mackintosh.
24—Marjorie Mackintosh, m. Alexander Frazer.
25—Charles-Frazer Mackintosh (in reality Charles Frazer who took the sir name of Mackintosh), m. Evilina Holland.
21—Joseph Mackintosh, m. Magdalen Mackintosh.
21—Alexander Mackintosh, m. Catherine Annard.
22—William Mackintosh and other issue.
21—Lydia Mackintosh, m. Patrick Grant.
21—Janet Mackintosh, m. Ludovic Gordon.
21—Lachlan Mackintosh, b. 1665; m. Mary Lockhart.
22—John "Mor" Mackintosh, b. March 1700; m. 1725, Marjory Fraser and settled in Georgia 1736.
23—William Mackintosh, b. Jan. 27, 1726; d. 1796; m. Jane MacCoy.
24—John Mackintosh, R. S., Lieutenant-Colonel, m. Sarah Swinton.
25—Major William Jackson Mackintosh, m. Mary Hillary.
26—Rev. William Hillary Mackintosh.
26—Maria Mackintosh, the writer.
26—Four other children.
23—Lachlan Mackintosh, R. S. General.
20—John Mackintosh, m. Margaret MacPherson.
19—Angus Mackintosh, m. Elspeth Mackintosh.
19—William Mackintosh, m. (1) Margaret Dunbar; (2) Widow Grant.
19—Jean Mackintosh, m. Ronald MacDonald.
19—Marjorie Mackintosh, m. Allen MacDonald.
18—Malcolm Mackintosh, m. (1) Janet MacAngus; (2) Christian Munro.
18—John Mackintosh, d. 1634; m. Catherine McKay.
18—Allan Mackintosh, m. (1) Elizabeth Rose; (2) Lillis Falconer; (3) Euphemia Campbell.
18—Duncan Mackintosh, m. (1) Beatrix Mackintosh; (2) Miss Dunbar.
19—(By first wife) William Mackintosh, m. Catherine McAllister.
20—Lachlan Mackintosh, m. Elspeth Mackintosh.
20—John Mackintosh.
20—William Mackintosh.
20—James Mackintosh.
19—(By second wife) Duncan Mackintosh (and other issue).
18—Lachlan Mackintosh, d. 1637 (founder of Corribrough branch); m. Jean MacPherson.
19—Angus Mackintosh.
19—William Mackintosh, d. 1674; m. Beatrix Mackintosh of Kyllachy.
20—Emelia Mackintosh, m. James Mackintosh.
20—Lachlan Mackintosh, d. 1726; wife's name unknown.
21—William Mackintosh, m. Katherine Mackintosh.
22—Lachlan Mackintosh, m. Christian Robertson.
23—William Mackintosh.
19—Janet Mackintosh, m. Colin Campbell.
19—Four other daughters, but names unavailable.
14—Alan Mackintosh, d. 1476; m. (1) Janet Fraser, daughter of Fraser Lord of Lovat; (2) Miss Forbes.
15—(By first wife) Lachlan Mackintosh.
15—William "Mor" Mackintosh, wife's name unknown.
16—John Mackintosh, m. Helen Rose.
16—Donald Mackintosh, tutor to 16th Chief of Clan Chattan, m. Catherine Rose.

17—John Mackintosh.
17—Angus Mackintosh, m. (1) Miss Dunbar, daughter of Mark Dunbar of Durris; (2) Agnes MacKenzie; (3) Marjorie Falconer.
18—(By first wife) Lachlan Mackintosh, 1st of Kyllachy, d. 1630; m. Miss Barclay, daughter of Barclay of Gartley.
19—Kenneth Mackintosh, m. Miss Cuthbut.
20—Lieutenant John Mackintosh, m. (1) Elspeth MacPherson; (2) Miss Mackintosh (ancestress of Sir James).
21—(By first wife) James Mackintosh, m. Emelia Mackintosh, descendant of the 7th son of the 16th Chief of Clan Chattan.
22—John Mackintosh, m. Isabella MacPherson.
23—James Mackintosh, came to United States in 1790; m. Dec. 23, 1795, Cassandra Offutt.
24—Jessie Mackintosh, m. Thomas Peter Randolph.
25—Richard Randolph, m. Miss Hacksell. No issue.
25—Jessie Randolph, m. Dr. Whaley.
25—Louise Randolph, m. Dr. John Bond, M. D.
26—Maria Bond.
26—Sarah Bond.
26—Nannie Bond, m. Dr. Hardy, M. D.
25—Edmund Randolph.
25—Isabella Randolph, m. Miles Henry Nash.
24—Isabella Mackintosh, d. unmarried.
24—William Archibald Mackintosh, d. unmarried.
24—John Mackintosh, d. unmarried.
24—Ossian Kenneth Mackintosh, d. unmarried in California during the famous gold rush.
24—James Mackintosh Jr., d. unmarried.
24—Angus Mackintosh, d. unmarried.
24—Ann Mackintosh, m. Dr. Wesley P. Arnold.
25—William MacPherson Arnold.
25—Ann Arnold.
25—Jessie Arnold, m. (1) William Williams; (2) Mr. Poole.
26—William Mackintosh Williams.
24—William MacPherson Mackintosh (who began the spelling of the name "McIntosh"), b. Feb. 14, 1815; d. June 1862, C. S., Colonel, 15th Georgia Regiment, Brevet Brigadier-General for gallantry in action, member Georgia House of Representatives, member Georgia Senate, elector state-at-large for Breckenridge 1860, lawyer, planter; m. Jan. 27, 1842, Maria Louisa Allen, b. Aug. 8, 1814; d. Aug. 1885.
25—Singleton Allen McIntosh, C. S., b. Feb. 19, 1845; d. Nov. 17, 1908; m. Feb. 1867, Mary Eliza Cade.
26—Sarah Howell McIntosh, b. Dec. 29, 1867; m. S. J. Zeigler.
27—Samuel Zeigler, S. W. W., U. S. Naval officer, m. Fanny Marburg.
28—Howell Zeigler.
27—Howell "Polar" Zeigler, m. George Lee Dickson, Major, U. S. A.
28—Howell Rees Dickson.
28—George Lee Dickson Jr.
26—William McPherson McIntosh, b 1870; d. 1930, unmarried.
26—Guilford "Guy" McIntosh, b. July 6, 1872; m. Sept. 14, 1918, Addie Tinsley.
27—Mary McIntosh, b. Sept. 3, 1921.
27—William Kenneth McIntosh, b. Nov. 10, 1922.
27—Louise McIntosh, b. Nov. 1923.
26—Victoria Augusta McIntosh, b. March 1875; m. Joseph Allston.
27—Joseph Allston Jr., m. Lillis McCullough.
28—Joseph Allston III.
27—Mary Allston.

26—Mary Louise McIntosh, b. Aug. 10, 1877; m. 1903, Henry M. Long.
27—Mary Louise Long, d. infancy.
25—William McPherson McIntosh Jr., C. S., b. Feb. 28, 1847; m. Helen Dean of Auburn, New York.
26—William McPherson Mackintosh III, S. W. W.
25—Anna Cassandra McIntosh, b. March 5, 1849; m. Dec. 11, 1866, Budd Clay Wall, C. S., b. April 24, 1847; d. 1930, Mayor of North Augusta, South Carolina, merchant.
26—Martha Louise Wall, b. April 6, 1868; m. Thomas B. Andrews. No issue.
26—McPherson McIntosh Wall, d. infancy.
26—William Clay Wall, d. infancy.
26—James Singleton Wall, b. Jan. 1, 1873; m. Rose Douglas. No issue.
26—Bevel William McIntosh Wall, b. June 20, 1875; m. Mary Stewart.
27—Margaret Wall, b. 1903.
27—Bevel Clay Wall, m. 1929, Virginia Alexander.
28—Bevel Charles Wall, b. July 22, 1930.
26—Jessie Wall, b. Dec. 20, 1878; m. John D. Stelling.
27—Sterling Stelling, b. Feb. 14, 1900; m. Eula Mitchell. No issue.
27—Martha McIntosh Stelling, b. Dec. 14, 1903; m. June 1930, Dr. Charles McCord Kilpatrick.
27—Dr. Richard Nunnelee Stelling, M. D., b. May 19, 1901.
27—Howard Cree Stelling, b. Sept. 1906, Lieutenant U. S. Air Corps, m. Helen Wainwright, nationally known swimming champion.
27—Budd Clay Wall Stelling, b. Feb. 1909.
26—Harry Wall, m. (1) Maryland Randall (divorced); (2) Hattie Smith. No issue.
25—Maria Louise McIntosh, b. March 15, 1851; d. May 7, 1894; m. Feb. 2, 1869, Guilford Cade Jr.
26—Julia May Cade, b. Dec. 30, 1871; m. Nov. 23, 1892, Dr. Albert Sidney Hawes, M. D., member Georgia House of Representatives, Mayor of Elberton, b. Nov. 14, 1863; d. Nov. 1936.
27—Guilford Moseley Hawes, b. July 24, 1894; m. March 26, 1913, Onie Lee of Cullman, Alabama, b. 1893.
28—Mary Lee Hawes, b. Sept. 14, 1917.
28—Robert Hawes, d. infancy.
28—Julia Ann Hawes, b. Feb. 27, 1925.
27—Albert Lee Hawes, b. Feb. 11, 1901; m. Bertha Bates; d. 1932. No issue.
27—Peyton Samuel Hawes, b. Sept. 4, 1903, member Georgia House of Representatives, City Attorney of Elberton, Solicitor City Court of Elberton; m. 1932, Virginia Smith.
26—Gulford Cade III, b. June 9, 1875; m. Dec. 4, 1904, Jane Kennedy.
27—Malvina "Mally" Cade, b. Sept. 9, 1905; m. Dec. 1929, Milo Abercrombie, killed in automobile accident 1931.
28—Milo Abercrombie Jr., b. 1931.
27—Guilford Cade IV, b. April 18, 1911.
25—Mary Bevelle McIntosh, b. June 1856; d. June 1936; m. 1895, John C. Brown, b. 1857; d. 1917, Mayor of Elberton, merchant. No issue.
25—James McIntosh, b. Sept. 1, 1857, sheriff of Elbert County, County Commissioner of Elbert County, member City Council of Elberton, member Tax Board City of Elberton, m. Oct. 18, 1882, Mary Jane Arnold, b. Sept. 23, 1859.
26—Sarah Louise McIntosh, b. July 29, 1883; m. Feb. 24, 1903, A. F. Archer. No issue.

26—Jessie McIntosh, d. infancy.
26—Mary James McIntosh, d. infancy.
26—John Hawes McIntosh, b. Nov. 26, 1895, historian of Elbert County, Secretary Tax Board of Elbert County, Chairman Board of Registrars of Elbert County, County Attorney of Elbert County, Assistant Secretary Georgia Senate; m. June 19, 1918, Fay Ann White, b. Oct. 21, 1900. Divorced 1937.
27—Mary Louise McIntosh, b. July 16, 1920.
27—Elizabeth Arnold Penn McIntosh, b. March 15, 1903.
26—McAlpin McIntosh, b. Nov. 26, 1897; d. 1899.
25—Jessie McIntosh, b. 1859; m. Peyton M. Hawes, member Georgia House of Representatives, member Georgia Senate, Militia Captain, bank president. No issue.
23—Angus Mackintosh.
23—Marjorie Mackintosh.
23—Ann Mackintosh.

McMILLAN

(Note: Numbers represent generations, as: (1) first generation, (2) second generation, (3) third generation, etc.)

1—Robert McMillan, b. Jan. 7, 1805, in County Antrim, Ireland; d. May 6, 1868; m. Ruth Ann Banks, Feb. 4, 1833. She died Dec. 22, 1867. Robert McMillan was naturalized in Elbert County, Georgia, Sept. 1833. State Senator from Elbert County and Colonel of 24th Georgia Regiment in the War Between the States.
2—Robert Emmett McMillan, b. Nov. 20, 1835; d. March 26, 1890, served as Major in the War Between the States.
2—James Curran McMillan, b. April 6, 1838; d. June 29, 1859.
2—Henry Gratton McMillan, b. Feb. 28, 1840, C. S. Captain, member Georgia House of Representatives 1872-1873, defeated Ben Hill for U. S. Representative in 1874, but died Jan. 14, 1875, before taking office; m. Julia Wales Erwin.
3—Georgia Erwin McMillan, b. Sept. 26, 1870; m. Dec. 23, 1902, John T. Pittard.
3—Robert McMillan, Mayor of Clarkesville, Georgia, 1898-1899, served with Y. M. C. A. Overseas during World War, Solicitor-General Northeastern Judicial Circuit of Georgia Jan. 1, 1911 to Jan. 1, 1919, and from Jan. 1, 1923 to date (1937); b. Jan. 7, 1872; m. Nov. 5, 1895, Dessa Sherman, b. July 27, 1873; d. June 22, 1930.
4—Garnett Sherman McMillan, S. W. W., Lieutenant, b. Nov. 13, 1896; d. March 4, 1928.
4—Julia Erwin McMillan, b. July 16, 1899; m. Feb. 29, 1931, Lloyd B. Peffer.
4—Robert McMillan Jr., b. July 25, 1901; m. Aug. 17, 1925, Samuel Ramsey.
5—Robert McMillan III, b. May 28, 1826.
4—Sherman McMillan, b. July 19, 1904; m. June 28, 1925, J. Thomas Askew, professor at University of Georgia.
4—Mary Ellen McMillan, b. Oct. 10, 1907.
2—Emma McMillan, b. Jan. 2, 1845, d. Jan. 17, 1862.
2—George McMillan, b. April 3, 1847; d. May 28, 1868.
2—William McMillan, b. June 27, 1850; d. 1851.
2—William Henry McMillan, b. Jan. 24, 1852; d. April 2, 1909.
2—Charles Banks McMillan, b. Feb. 15, 1855; d. Dec. 14, 1887.

Robert McMillan was admitted to the Bar in Elberton and then later removed to Clarkesville, Georgia. Four generations of the family have been engaged in the practice of law at Clarkesville: 1—Robert; 2—Garnett; 3—Robert; 4—Robert Sherman.

MIDDLETON

The following chart shows intermarriages with the following families: Adams — Arnold — Barnett — Blackwell — Burnett — Calhoun — Caldwell — Clinton — Carlton — Carr — Carroll — Davis — Dennis — Dohme — Fields — Hammond — Hardin — Harper — Heard — Hill — Holman — Johnson — Jones — Lattimer — Little — Lynch — Martin — McCalla — Nunnelee — Patterson — Pharr — Pressley — Quillian — Seymour — Sondidge — Sparks — Swift — Tate — Underwood — Wayble — White — Williams — Williamson — Wise — Woods — Wright.

(Note: Numbers represent generations, as: (1) first generation, (2) second generation, (3) third generation, etc.)

1—John Middleton came from North Ireland, 1712, to Lancaster County, Pennsylvania, m. Margaret Patterson.
2—John Middleton Jr., m. Martha Caldwell.
3—John Middleton III, m. Jan. 26, 1817, Elizabeth P. Tate.
3—Robert Middleton, m. (1) Patsy Nunnelee; (2) Nov. 11, 1810, Betsy C. Williamson nee Blackwell.
4—(By second wife) Robert Middleton Jr.
4—John Middleton.
4—Nancy Middleton, m. Thomas Jefferson Heard, b. Aug. 21, 1801; d. May 4, 1876, member Georgia House of Representatives from Elbert County 1833-1834, served as intendent of Elberton.
5—Sarah Heard, m. Dec. 11, 1846; m. L. H. O. Martin, C. S., Colonel on Staff of General Robert Toombs, member Georgia House of Representatives, delegate from Elbert County to Secession Convention.
6—Sarah Martin, d. unmarried.
6—L. H. O. Martin Jr., member Georgia House of Representatives; m. Rossie Harper. No issue.
5—James Lawrence Heard, C. S., mayor of Elberton, member Georgia House of Representatives 1873-1874; m. Melissa Harper.
6—Mary Heard, b. 1858; d. 1929; m. 1881, Rev. Thomas Carlton, Baptist evangelist, lawyer, Judge City Court of Elberton.
7—Thomas Carlton Jr.
7—Son Carlton.
6—William H. Heard, b. 1860; d. 1919; m. Nov. 14, 1889, Kathleen "Katie" Carroll, b. 1869, a direct descendant of William Merideth, a Revolutionary officer.
7—Margaret Heard, b. 1890; m. 1929, Dr. C. L. Dohme, a member of the firm of Sharpe & Dohme. No issue.
7—Kathleen Carroll Heard, b. 1892; m. 1920, W. E. Adams.
8—Robert Carroll Adams, b. 1924.
7—James Lawrence Heard, b. 1894; m. 1914, Eva Underwood; d. 1925.
8—Margaret Heard, b. 1915.
8—Eva Heard, b. 1917.
8—James Lawrence Heard Jr., b. 1918; d. 1921.
8—Betsy Heard, b. 1923.
7—Janie Heard, b. 1896; m. 1922, William Holman Jr.
8—William Heard III.
7—Martin Heard.
7—Sarah Heard, b. 1900; m. Smith Wise.
8—Dorothy Wise, b. 1921.
7—William Heard, m. Vivian Burnett.
8—Donald Tate Heard.

7—Joseph Heard.
6—Nancy Heard, m. Phillip W. Davis, Baptist minister, lawyer, member Georgia House of Representatives from Elbert County 1873-1874, member Georgia House of Representatives from Oglethorpe County, Georgia.
7—Melissa Davis, m. Fred Lynch. No issue.
7—Phillip W. Davis Jr., lawyer, m. Cecile Little of Franklin County, Georgia.
6—Oliver McDonald Heard, m. Victor Hardin.
6—Janie Heard, m. April 15, 1897, Fred Clinton, physician of Tulsa, Oklahoma. No issue.
5—Robert Middleton Heard, C. S., Captain, member Georgia House of Representatives, Mayor of Elberton, lawyer; m. April 19, 1864, Louisa Jones, b. April 26, 1846; d. Sept. 23, 1910, active in work of U. D. C.
6—John T. Heard, merchant, banker, president Elberton Chamber of Commerce; d. 1932, unmarried.
6—Vohammie Heard, m. Marcus Pharr.
7—Marcus Pharr Jr., S. W. W.; d. 1918.
7—Robert Pharr.
7—Camilla Pharr, m. G. D. Barnett.
8—Aurelius Barnett.
8—Camilla Barnett.
8—Ida Barnett.
8—Vohammie Barnett.
7—Mitta Pharr, m. S. A. Fields.
7—Vohammie Pharr, m. J. C. Carr.
8—J. C. Carr Jr.
7—Louise Pharr, m. H. C. Sparks.
8—H. C. Sparks Jr.
6—Luther Martin Heard, president Citizens Bank of Elberton; m. Mamie Lattimer, daughter of United States Senator Lattimer of South Carolina.
7—Luther Martin Heard Jr.
7—Lattimer Heard.
7—Robert Heard.
6—Georgia Heard, m. Dr. J. E. Johnson.
7—Dr. J. E. Johnson Jr., m. Marie Williams, divorced 1936.
8—Joseph Johnson III.
6—Roberta Heard, m. John T. Dennis Jr., Mayor of Elberton, Captain State Militia. No issue.
6—Carroll Heard.
6—Parks E. Heard.
5—Erskin Heard, m. (1) Nov. 26, 1855, Martha Harper; (2) Caroline Calhoun.
6—(By first wife) Bedford Heard, m. Ida Cleveland nee McCalla.
7—M. E. Heard, m. Allen Pressley.
7—Sarah Heard, m. June 9, 1912, Frank Hammond.
8—Frank Hammond Jr.
8—Mildred Hammond.
7—Erskin Heard, m. 1911, Lottie Seymour.
8—Martha Heard.
8—Bedford Heard.
8—Emma Heard.
8—Mattie Heard.
8—Hazel Heard.
7—Bevelle Heard, m. Thomas Wayble.
8—Bevelle Wayble.
7—Caroline Heard, m. Guy Quillian.
6—Emma Heard, m. Dr. N. G. Long. No issue.

6—(By second wife) George E. Heard, unmarried.
5—William Henry Heard, m. Jennie Harper.
6—Thomas Parks Heard, d. unmarried.
6—Harper Heard.
6—Rebecca Heard, m. Frank Wright. No issue
5—Eugene B. Heard, C. S., m. Sally Harper.
6—Sue Heard, m. J. Y. Swift.
3—James Middleton.
3—Samuel Middleton.
2—Andrew Middleton, d. 1749; m. Annabel White.
2—Ainsworth Middleton, d. 1793.
2—Elizabeth Middleton, m. Captain Robert Woods, R. S.; d. 1811 in Franklin County, Virginia; he came from North Ireland with brothers, George and John.
3—Middleton Woods, first Clerk of the Elbert County Superior Court.
3—Hugh Woods, m. (?).
4—William W. Woods.
3—Josiah Woods, m. Sarah Cotton Hill.

OLIVERS

Dionysius Oliver was one of the most enterprising of the early settlers of Georgia. He was a pioneer realtor. "No other early settler caught the vision of the possibilities of tobacco culture and the consequent prosperity." He was born in Petersburg, Virginia, in 1735, the son of Thomas Oliver and Mary McCarthy. In 1758 he married Mary Ann Winfrey, daughter of Valentine Winfrey, of Chesterfield County, Virginia.

Before 1779 they moved through South Carolina to Wilkes County, Georgia. In August of that year he was a member of the grand jury in the Court of Oyer and Terminer held in the home of Jacob McClendon Sr., by order of the executive council of Augusta, for the purpose of trying nine Tories, who were hanged a few days later. In 1784 Dionysius Oliver gave bond to keep a ferry "at the Fork of the Broad and Savannah Rivers where Thomas Carter formerly had a ferry." He sold this ferry to his son John in 1787.

The first tax digest of Wilkes County extant, 1785, shows him as living in Captain Ragsland's District, owning 5,000 acres of land. His sons, Peter and John, were also slave and land-owners in that district. The legislature passed an Act February 3, 1786, authorizing Dionysius Oliver to build a warehouse on his land in the Forks of the Broad and Savannah Rivers for the inspection and storage of tobacco. This warehouse was the nucleus of the town later called Petersburg in honor of his old home in Virginia..

Dionysius Oliver served as Captain of a privateer during the Revolution, was with General Lincoln at the Battle of Kettle Creek, Wilkes County. He was captured and imprisoned by the British and in later years described the hardships endured. He died in 1818, at his home place in Elbert County, and was buried near

"Stenchcomb Meeting House." His first wife, Mary Ann Winfrey, died in 1802. There were ten children of this union: Peter, John, James, Dionysius Jr., Thomas Winfrey, William, Eleanor, McCarthy, Martha, and Frances. (1) Peter, born 1763, married his cousin, Betty, daughter of Francis Oliver, whom he met on a visit to Virginia. His only son, Dionysius, moved with his children to Mississippi. (2) John, born 1765, married Frances Thompson, daughter of William Thompson and Mary Wells. Their two daughters, Prudence and Sally, attended the Moravian School in Bethlehem, Pa., in 1803. Frances died in 1808, and John died in 1816. John, like his father was an enterprising planter. (3) James, born 1767, was also a large planter in Elbert County. His first wife was Mary Thompson, sister of his brother, John's wife. They had one child, Simeon, who moved to Mississippi. By his second wife, Lucy, daughter of Christopher Clark, there were eleven children. (4) Dionysius Jr., born 1768, married his cousin, Frances, daughter of Francis Oliver, of Virginia, and sister of his brother Peter's wife. They live in Edgefield County, South Carolina. (5) Thomas Winfrey married Mary, another daughter of Christopher Clark. He owned a tavern in Elberton and was buried in the yard. (6) William Oliver, born 1778, married first, Barbara Tait; second, Frances Ragland. He fought in the Creek Indian Wars, and was in the battle of the Canoes in 1818. (7) Eleanor Oliver married John Goss and died after the birth of her first child. (8) Martha Oliver, born 1773, married Thomas Hancock, of Edgefield, S. C., and had four daughters. (9) Rev. Florence McCarthy Oliver, born 1775, a Methodist Wesleyan minister, married Susanna, daughter of Christopher Clark, sister of the wives of his brothers, Thomas and James. He moved with his family to Chambers County, Alabama, in 1840. (10) Frances Oliver married William T. Cook of Virginia.

After the death of his first wife, Dionysius Oliver Sr. married Jane Jackson of South Carolina. They had one child, Jackson, who married Polly Maxwell; died in Banks County, 1869.

James Oliver, third son of Dionysius Sr., was a large planter of Elbert County. By his second wife, Lucy Clark, he had the following children:

Shelton Oliver, of Lexington, m. Martha Williams.
Mary Winfrey Oliver, m. Willis Banks.
Mildred, m. (1) James Banks; (2) Charles Meriwether.
Judith, m. (1) Henry Banks; (2) William Moore.
James, died young.
Washington, died young.
Alfred Oliver (1816-1882), of Elbert County, was a large planter, and lived fifteen miles up the County from Petersburg, at the old family home. He married Sallie Pharr (1836-1860), of Newton County. Issue: Dr. Alfred Shelton Oliver (1857-1934), who married Gertrude Mathews, daughter of Col. James D. Mathews. (Mentioned above under Mathews family).
Eliza Oliver, m. Jett Thomas.
Francis Oliver, died young.

Lucinda m. Edmund Taylor, lived in Elgin, Arkansas.
Martha, m. Gen. Benjamin Heard, of Wilkes County, died without issue.
NOTE: For more detailed history of the Oliver family in Georgia, Alabama, and Mississippi, see "Early Settlers," Saunders.

RICE

The following chart shows intermarriages with the following families: Adams — Allen — Anthony — Bagwell — Ballenger — Berryman — Bowers — Bowden — Brambleton — Brown — Burden — Bussey — Cordell — Crawford — Crittenden — Deen — Dickinson — Eaves — Fleming — Franks — Gaines — Ginn — Glenn — Gloer — Griffin — Hairston — Hardin — Harris — Hewell — Hollock — Howard — Kellis — King — Lee — Madden — Matthews — Moss — McGarity — Nix — Paulk — Ray — Reinel — Roberts — Roundtree — Smith — Stevens — Suddeth — Teasley — Thomas — Turner — Vieregee — Verner — Wellborn — Whitten — Wickliffe — Yost.

Among the pioneers and early settlers of Elbert county the name Rice appears quite often. Doubtless, these are descendants of three lines of Rices,' the Pedigree of which comes continuously from the Saxon Prince Egbert 802-839 which is unbroken down to Deacon Edmond Rice, born in England, 1594, and came with eight children to Massachusetts in 1638.

This sketch, in which Deacon Edmond Rice appears as a descendant, is the only Pedigree that space will allow us to include in this book.

Following this Pedigree, verbatim, the following quotation (omitting quotation marks) is given: as an introduction to the Rice Sketch.

Record of the Rice family of England as abstracted from various authentic sources including an illuminated pedigree of the Family of Rice, in the possession of Lord Dynevor, drawn and attested in the year 1600, by Ralph Brooks, York Herald, and continued to the present time by Dr. Charles Elmer Rice, Alliance, Ohio, in his book entitled "By the Name of Rice," published in 1911.

Authorities for the line of Rice generations given in the next 34 paragraphs of this sketch are:

Collins Peerage of England, 1812, Vol. 1, p. 50-81.

Burke's Peerage, 1914.

County Genealogies, Pedigrees of Buckinghamshire Families, William Berry, 1837.

"BY THE NAME OF RICE" in 1911, by Dr. Charles Elmer Rice, Alliance, Ohio.

GENERATIONS:

1. Coel Codevog, King of the Britons.
2. Ason, (and daughter of Helena, Mother of Constantine the Great).
3. Mierchion Gul., grandson of King Codevog.
4. Gynvarch Oer ap-Mierchion Gil. (had three sons).

5. Vryan Reged, (also spelled Uryan Rheged and Urien Rheged), by by birth a Combre Briton, who in the 6th century was Prince of North Briton, but was expelled by the Saxons, and fled to Wales, married Margaret La-Faye, daughter of Gerlois, Duke of Cornwall, and was Prince of Rheged in Wales, Lord of Kidwelly, Carunllon, and Iskennen in South Wales. He built the Castle Garrey in Carmanthenshire.
6. Pafgen, (also spelled Pasgen) ....Lord of Kidwelly
7. Mori, (also spelled Mott) ....Lord of Kidwelly
8. Lairch, (also spelled Larch) ....Lord of Kidwelly
9. Rhyne ....Lord of Kidwelly
10. Cecil, (also spelled Cecilt) ....Lord of Kidwelly
11. Gurwared ....Lord of Kidwelly
12. Kynbatwey (also spelled Kynbatwye) ....Lord ofKidwelly
13. Liarch (also spelled Licarch) ....Lord of Kidwelly
14. Enyion (also spelled Eyenion) ....Lord of Kidwelly
15. Granway (also spelled Gronway) ....Lord of Kidwelly
16. Voed (in Burke's Peerage of 1914, called Rice of Iskennen) married Margaret, daughter of co-heir of Griffith of Kidds, Lord of Gwaynav.
17. Elidir ap-Rhye of Iskennen, Esquire, married Gladis (also spelled Gwadlys) daughter of Phillip, son of Bah.
18. Sir Elidir Dhu, Knight of the Holy Sepulchre, married Cicily, daughter of Siscilte ap-Hyn.
19. Phillip ap-Elidir Fitszuryan, married Gladis (also spelled Gwadlys), daughter of Davis Uras.
20. Dwyllian Nicholas (in Burke's Peerage, 1914, called Nicholas ap-Phillip Fitszuryan), married Joan, daughter of Llewellin Veythes.
21. Griffith ap-Nicholas, was slain at Wakesfield, on the dise of York.
22. Thomas ap-Griffith Fitz Uryan, married Elizabeth, daughter of Sir John Griffith of Abermarlais.
23. Sir Rhys ap-Thomas Fitz-Uryan, made a Knoght Banneret, by Henry VII, Knight of the Garter in the 21' year of the same reign (1506). He married (1) Eve, daughter and heir of Henry ap-Gwlliam, (2) Jvan, daughter of Thomas Matthew and widow of Thomas Stradling.
24. Sir Griffith Rice, made Knight of Bath at the marriage of Prince Arthur, Nov. 14, 1501; married Katherine, daughter of Sir John St. John, and by her had two daughters and a son.
Note: Connect here with Generation 14 in Pedigree "B."
25. Rice ap-Griffith Fitz-Uryan, married Katherine, daughter of Thomas Howard, (See pedigree of Howard family) Duke of Norfolk, and by her had issue a son and daughter Agnes and—
Griffith ap-Rice, born 1500, beheaded by Henry VIII, from whom the present Lord Dynevor is descended and
26. Wm. Rice, brother of above Griffith ap-Rice, called Wm. of Boemer, of Bucks — or Buckinghamshire. Granted arms in 1555 (born 1522) and was the grandfather of Deacon Edmund Rice.
27. Thomas Rice, son of Wm. of Boemer, and father of Deacon Edmund and of Robert Rice (Twins).
28. Edmund Rice and Robert Rice, born 1594.
Edmund came to Massachusetts in 1638.
Robert Rice came in 1631.
29. Edmund Rice, born in England, 1594, came with 8 children to Massachusetts in 1638. One child died in route, and 3 others were born in Massachusetts. His wife was Tamazin Hosner. She died at Sudbury, Mass., June 13, 1654. Later Deacon Edmund married Mercy Brigham (May 1, 1665) and by her had 2 daughters—Ruth and Ann Rice. Edmund Rice died in Marlboro, Mass, May 3, 1663.
30. Thomas Rice, 3rd son of Deacon Edmund Rice, was born in Buckinghamshire, England, in 1622. He married Mary King and resided

at Sudbury, Mass. There were 14 children. Thomas Rice died November 16, 1681.
31. Thomas Rice, 2nd son of Thomas (30) was born in Sudbury, Mass., June 30th, 1654, married Anne Rice, his cousin, and resided at Marlboro, Mass. She died in 1687. There were 13 children. Thomas died aged 94.
32. Charles Rice, fourth child of above, was born July 7, 1684, married Rachel Wheeler, April 26, 1711. There were 10 children. We do not have the date of death.
33. Elijah Rice, 5th child of Charles and Rachel Rice, was born June 26, 1719, married Sarah Shattuck, May 24, 1744. Resided at Westboro, Mass., where she died Nov., 1761. There were 12 children—six by his first wife and six by the second (Prudence Hardy). Elijah died April 19, 1785.
34. Leonard, 5th child of Elijah and Sarah Rice, was born in 1758—died in Georgia, 1842; he married Sarah Kellis (Duncan). There were 8 children. Leonard Rice "went South" at a very early age, as did several of his brothers. He was a Revolutionary soldier.

The remains of this Revolutionary soldier, Leonard Rice, are now resting in the Holly Springs cemetery, two miles from Bowman, Georgia; the location of this is properly marked by a granite slab. This Leonard Rice and his wife Sarah Kellis (Duncan), were the parents of 8 children, the youngest of whom was Aaron Rice—the subject of the book referred to in the opening of this sketch—and through whom all the geneology from Egbert, the Saxon Prince, 802, and Aaron Rice's descendants are shown in full in the following sections of this family record.

AARON RICE

Aaron Rice, 4th and youngest son of Leonard Rice (34) was born 1805 and died 1884. He married Lettie Ballinger, born 1807 and died 1855. In this family there were seven (7) sons and four (4) daughters.
    Leonard W., b. Dec. 2, 1827.
    Polly, b. 1829.
    William, b. May 16, 1831.
    Sarah, b. 1833.
    Walton, b. May 3, 1836.
    Newton, b. 1838. Killed in Battle (Confederate Army)
    Elizabeth, b. 1840.
    Hulda, b. 1842.
    Martin, b. 1845. Died in Service (Confederate Army).
    Elbert, b. 1847. Died in Service (Confederate Army).
    Peter, b. 1850.
I.—Leonard W. Rice, b. Dec. 2, 1827, d. July 29, 1905; m. March 28, 1867. Susan Hart, b. Feb. 26, 1849; d. Nov. 17, 18(?).
  1- –William P. Rice, b. April 15, 1870; m. Dec. 12, 1894, Julia Deen. No issue.
  1—Edgar Aaron Rice, b. Feb. 7, 1872, d. Sept. 26, 1915; m. Dec. 9, 1900, Alice Franks. No living issue.
  1—Lula Rice, b. Nov. 16, 1874, d. Dec. 7, 1925; m. July 12, 1897, H. R. Griffin, d. May 12, 1931.
  2—L. Arvin Griffin, b. July 26, 1899; m. Nov., 1923, Lana May Vieregee.
  3—Patsy Ruth Griffin, b. 1926.
  3—Weldon Arnold Griffin, b. March 23, 1933.
  1—Betty Rice, b. Nov. 1, 1876, d. July 4, 1888.
  1—L. Walton Rice, b. March 9, 1880; m. April 22, 1906, May Hardin.
  2—Martha Rice, b. June 29, 1909.

2—Mary Rice, b. Nov. 4, 1914.
2—L. Walton Rice Jr., b. Dec. 13, 1919.
1—Lettie Rice, b. Oct. 5, 1882; m. June 5, 1900, L. S. Whitten, d. 1922.
2—Jack Whitten, b. Nov. 6, 1905.
2—Grace Whitten, b. Feb. 18, 1908; m. Oct. 24, 1924, Larry Johnson.
3—Grace Kathryn Johnson, b. Aug. 6, 1926.
2—Billie Fern Whitten, b. Jan. 10, 1914; m. Feb. 21, 1935, H. H. Reimel.
II.—William Jasper Rice, b. May 16, 1831, d. April 16, 1920; m. Jan. 12, 1860, Martha Elizabeth Landers, b. Jan. 8, 1834, d. Oct. 29, 1913.
  1—Lettie Rice, b. June 13, 1861; m. Nov. 25, 1875, Benager Pierce Teasley, b. Aug. 9, 1854, d. Sept. 1914.
    2—William Alfred Teasley, b. Dec. 22, 1877; m. Nov. 7, 1900, Alice Lucile Adams, b. April 17, 1879.
      3—Lucile Teasley, b. Feb. 1, 1903; m. 1925, Joe Wickliffe.
        4—Alice Wickliffe, b. 1926.
        4—Josephine Wickliffe, b. 1928.
        4—Winell Wickliffe, b. 1928.
      3—Thelma Teasley, b. April 26, 1905.
      3—Wilton Teasley, b. 1908, d. 1908.
    2—Oscar Lee Teasley, b. Oct. 12, 1881, d. Feb. 1, 1919; m. Dec. 22, 1908, Jewell Gloer, b. Sept. 18, 1886.
      3—Charlotte Teasley, b. Aug. 2, 1910.
      3—Mildred Teasley, b. Jan. 25, 1917.
    2—Edgar Carl Teasley, b. April 4, 1885, m. Dec. 25, 1910, Pearl W. Brown, b. March 19, 1888.
      3—Edgar William Teasley, b. Oct. 7, 1912.
      3—Harold Teasley, b. Aug. 7, 1914.
    2—Clyde E. Teasley, insurance, b. Aug. 7, 1889; m. Nov. 12, 1912, Liela Cordell, b. Jan. 1, 1893.
      3—Clyde E. Teasley Jr., July 8, 1914.
      3—Benjamin Cordell "Billy" Teasley, b. Dec. 25, 1919.
    2—Ruth Teasley, b. Aug. 29, 1892; m. Nov. 17, 1915, Dr. Walton Johnson, physician, b. March 3, 1892.
      3—Winona Johnson, b. 1916, d. 1918.
      3—Phyllis Johnson, b. Sept. 22, 1919.
    2—B. P. Teasley Jr., b. Sept. 15, 1896; m. Aug. 23, 1934, Ona Howard.
    2—John Easton Teasley, b. Dec. 16, 1904; m. Sept. 11, 1933, Margaret E. Yost.
  1—Peter V. Rice, b. March 29, 1869, Assistant Secretary of Agriculture of Georgia, Secretary Elberton Chamber of Commerce; m. Jan. 19, 1890, Laura Helen Hewell.
    2—Howard Claucus Rice, b. July 18, 1891; m. Nov. 16, 1916, Ommye Paulk.
      3—Howard Glaucus Rice Jr., b. Aug. 28, 1917.
      3—Peter Jacob Rice, b. Oct. 2, 1919.
      3—Ommye Rice, b. April 26, 1929.
      3—William Rice, b. Sept. 13, 1930.
    2—Herbert Spencer Rice, b. Aug. 25, 1893; m. Dec. 27, 1923, Marion Allen.
      3—Marion Spencer Rice, b. Dec. 1924; d. infancy.
III.—Sarah Ann Rice, b. Aug. 12, 1832; d. Dec. 25, 1912; m. about 1851, Thomas J. Crittenden.
  1—Elijah Marion Crittenden, b. May 3, 1852; m. Dec. 23, 1875, Elizabeth Harriet Burden; d. April 14, 1912.

2—Lillian Ann Crittenden, b. Oct. 11, 1876; m. Dec. 21, 1893, John Wofford McGarity; d. 1915.
3—Ethel McGarity, b. 1894; d. 1895.
3—Floyce McGarity, b. Oct. 16, 1896; m. March 5, 1918, Arthur W. Ray.
4—John Arthur Ray, b. April 6, 1919.
3—Lois McGarity, b. June 8, 1902; m. June 1928, C. B. Wellborn.
3—Grace McGarity, b. 1905; d. 1924.
2—Nancy Josephine Crittenden, b. Jan. 10, 1881; m. Feb. 14, 1904, Earl James Rice.
3—Lillian Rice, b. Jan. 26, 1905.
3—Frances Elizabeth Rice, b. Aug. 19, 1906.
3—Thelma Rice, b. Dec. 21, 1908.
3—Howard James Rice, b. May 14, 1911.
1—William L. Crittenden, b. Dec. 24, 1860; d. Dec. 14, 1933; m. 1878, Melitia Smith.
2—Delia Crittenden, b. 1880.
2—Felia Crittenden, b. 1882; m. Feb. 6, 1902, C. Q. Dickinson.
3—Covie Dickinson, b. Aug. 26, 1905; m. 1925, Ruth Thomas.
4—Leroy Dickinson, b. 1930.
4—Winston Dickinson, b. 1932.
2—Thomas M. Crittenden, b. 1884; m. 1907, Emma Bagwell.
3—Ruth Crittenden.
3—Belle Crittenden.
2—J. Ervin Crittenden, m. 1918, Lula Moss.
IV—K. Walton Rice, b. May 3, 1836; d. April 8, 1891; m. Dec. 16, 1863, Sarah Drucilla Johnson.
1—Mary Elizabeth Rice, b. Oct. 24, 1870; d. Nov. 17, 1931; m. Feb. 19, 1893, Robert D. Harris.
2—Lucile Harris, b. Nov. 25, 1893; d. Dec. 20, 1932; m. July 1916, Willford Kieffer McGarity.
3—Robert Lewis McGarity, b. July 22, 1917.
3—Hugh Harris McGarity, b. May 27, 1919.
3—Willford S. McGarity, b. Nov. 13, 1924.
2—Guy Harris, b. March 7, 1895; m. July 31, 1921, Jane Glenn.
3—Annie Frances Harris, b. Jan. 23, 1926.
2—William Howard Harris, b. Dec. 2, 1896; m. May 4, 1918, Lois Turner.
3—William Howard Harris Jr., b. Feb. 27, 1920.
3—Mary Catherine Harris, b. Oct. 24, 1925.
3—Hugh Wallis Harris, b. March 31, 1933.
2—Lessie Harris, b. Sept. 18, 1898; m. Dec. 26, 1919, Hugh Matthews.
3—Robert Calvin Matthews, b. Sept. 13, 1920.
2—Quilla Harris, b. Aug. 27, 1900; m. June 5, 1921, Walter Glenn.
3—Radford Maxwell Glenn, b. Aug. 31, 1931.
2—Phillip Rice Harris, b. Jan. 17, 1903; m. Dec. 25, 1924, Gertrude Smith.
3—Isabella L. Harris, b. Sept. 3, 1927.
2—Ruby Arlee Harris, b. April 20, 1908; m. Dec. 24, 1932, Joseph B. Suddeth.
3—Kenneth Lamar Suddeth, b. Dec. 6, 1933.
1—Kate Mahulda Rice, b. Oct. 1, 1872; m. June 6, 1928, H. Austin Fleming. No issue.
1—Sarah Margaret Rice, b. Nov. 28, 1874; m. Dec. 23, 1894, Clayton P. Hairston, member Elbert County Bond Commission, member Elbert County Board of Tax Assessors.
2—Julius C. Hairston, b. Dec. 7, 1895; m. Dec. 19, 1914, Sallie May Brown.
3—Kenneth Hairston, b. Nov. 5, 1927.

2—Horace G. Hairston, b. Aug. 5, 1898; m. Nov. 27, 1921, Florence Gaines.
3—James C. Hairston, b. April 1, 1923.
2—Clara T. Hairston, b. Aug. 28, 1905; m. Feb. 12, 1928, Fred Roundtree.
3—Winifred Roundtree, b. Aug 5, 1930.
1—Lettie Phronissie Rice, b. Jan. 27, 1877; m. Dec. 17, 1902, R. D. Harris, merchant.
2—Mauline Harris, b. Nov. 8, 1903.
2—Eva Drucilla Harris, b. Sept. 9, 1905; m. June 1, 1922, Earl W. Bussey.
3—Eva Anita Bussey, b. Sept. 4, 1931.
2—R. D. Harris Jr., b. May 20, 1908; m. Sept. 24, 1930, Doris Gunn.
2—William Curtis Harris, b. July 10, 1910; m. Oct. 3, 1929, Lucile Anthony.
3—Sarah Caroline Harris, b. June 13, 1930.
3—William Curtis Harris Jr., b. 1932; d. 1932.
2—Rupert G. Harris, b. Feb. 23, 1913; m. Dec. 12, 1933, Lillian Madden.
3—Peggy Ann Harris.
1—Leonard Alexander Rice, b. Oct. 14, 1879; m. Feb. 22, 1906, Bessie Lee Stevens.
2—John Walton Rice, b. Oct. 15, 1908.
2—Sarah Rice, b. 1911; d. 1913.
2—Grace Louise Rice, b. Dec. 26, 1916.
1—Newton Allen Rice, b. 1882; d. 1887.
1—Ida Rice, b. April 30, 1886; m. Dec. 3, 1905, William C. McGarity.
2—Thomas Glenn McGarity, b. Nov. 4, 1906; m. July 23, 1929, Hattie Lee Eaves.
3—Thomas Glenn McGarity Jr., b. Jan. 31, 1934.
2—Katie Lou McGarity, b. May 15, 1911.
2—Mildred L. McGarity, b. July 5, 1915.
2—William C. McGarity Jr., b. June 14, 1919.
2—Leonard A. McGarity, b. Aug. 13, 1922.
2—Betty Jo McGarity, b. June 11, 1930.
V—Mary Elizabeth Rice, b. July 26, 1840; m. Dec. 28, 1857, John H. Bowers.
1—William F. Bowers, b. May 27, 1864; m. 1885, Ella King.
1—Aaron Newton Bowers, b. Aug. 15; m. (1) Dec. 20, 1893, Mattie Bond, d. Aug. 5, 1921; (2) Agnes Crawford, d. Dec. 23, 1931.
2—(By first wife) Esther Bowers, b. July 8, 1896; m. July 7, 1921, John E. Verner.
3—Martha Verner, b. Sept. 4, 1929.
2—Lucile Bowers, b. Feb. 8, 1898.
2—Hilda C. Bowers, b. Sept. 19, 1899.
2—Polly Ruth Bowers, b. Sept. 11, 1903; m. Aug. 8, 1931, Harry DuBignon Parker.
2—Elizabeth Bowers, b. Nov. 2, 1905; m. Oct. 3, 1926, Roy L. Bowden.
3—Elizabeth Bowden, b. Dec. 27, 1930.
3—Roy L. Bowden Jr., b. Feb. 2, 1933.
2—John H. Bowers, b. June 23, 1907; m. Aug. 31, 1934, Gertrude Brambleton.
2—Winifred Bowers, b. May 6, 1912.
2—Aaron Newton Bowers Jr., b. July 3, 1914.
2—(By second wife) Alexander Cree Bowers, b. Aug. 27, 1925.
2—Sophia Jean Bowers, b. Sept. 1, 1927.

1—John Martin Bowers, b. May 1, 1877; d. June 24, 1907; m. May 25, 1900, Bernice Berryman.
2—Leonard H. Bowers, b. June 16, 1901; m. Feb. 16, 1929, Ruby Edna Lee.
3—Fay Bowers, b. Sept. 13, 1930.
2—Alton Parker Bowers, b. Dec. 7, 1904; m. March 27, 1922, Achia Ada Nix.
3—Jeanne Bowers, b. Aug. 19, 1933.
2—Bill Bowers, b. Oct. 27, 1907; m. Sept. 10, 1932, Eloine Ann Hallock.
VI—Peter V. Rice, b. Sept. 27, 1850; m. Dec. 23, 1873, Artie Burden, b. July 15, 1847; d. Feb. 22, 1932.
1—Aaron Rice, b. May 11, 1876; m. Dec. 27, 1900, Bessie Roberts, d. Aug. 27, 1903.
1—Morgan Rice, b. Sept. 30, 1880; m. Nov. 11, 1913, Blythe Thomas.

Those desiring additional information concerning any of these descendants, such as addresses, etc., should write to Peter V. Rice Jr., Elberton, Georgia. (Author and publisher of booklet entitled, "Aaron Rice—1805-1886) or Mrs. Lettie Harris, Bowman, Georgia.

STARK

The following chart shows intermarriages with the following families: Abercrombie — Allston — Arnold — Auld — Baker — Bates — Brewer — Bruce — Bryant — Cade — Dickson — Dugar — Foreman — Fox — Godshall — Gower — Grogan — Harper — Hawes — Hill — Hollingsworth — Hughes — Jaudon — Jones — Jordan — Kennedy — Lee — Long — Madden — Marburg — Martin — Mickle — Moore — Morange — McCoy — McCullough — McIntosh — McLanahan — Newton — Phillips — Porter — Rogers — Russell — Sanders — Schuler — Slaughter — Sledge — Smith — Summerson — Tinsley — Tillman — Turnipseed — William — Womack — Zeigler.

(Note: Numbers represent generations, as: (1) first generation, (2) second generation, (3) third generation, etc.)

1—William Stark, R. S. (Had brother Reuben, R. S.).
  2—Samuel Stark, m. Ann Mickle.
    3—Abram Stark, m. Mary (?).
      4—Bascom Stark.
      4—Jacob Stark.
      4—Lula Stark.
      4—Oscar Stark.
    3—Thomas Stark, m. Miss Turnipseed.
      4—Samuel Stark.
    3—William Stark, m. (?).
      4—William Stark Jr.
      4—Samuel Stark.
    3—Samuel Stark Jr., b. March 31, 1818; d. May 9, 1901; m. May 18, 1843, Adeline Brewer, b. March 9, 1824; d. Nov. 3, 1911.
      4—Mary Stark, b. Nov. 5, 1847; d. May 19, 1921; m. Jan. 20, 1869, Thomas W. Hill.
        5—Sally May Hill.
        5—Thomas W. Hill Jr., m. Mrs. Jessie Phillips nee Sledge.
        5—Samuel Hill.
        5—Addie Hill, m. Carroll Summerson.
        5—Nan Hill, m. (1) Laurens Foreman; (2) Louis Godshall.

5—Irene Hill.
5—Wellborn Hill, m. Jessie Sledge.
6—Mary Hill.
6—Dorothy Hill, m. 1937, Thomas Dallas Champion.
5—Ruby Hill.
5—Maud Hill.
4—Sarah "Sally" Stark, b. Sept. 11, 1849; d. Jan. 27, 1928; m. Jan. 28, 1868, Benjamin R. Tillman, Governor of South Carolina, United States Senator from South Carolina.
5—Adeline Tillman, d. unmarried.
5—Benjamin R. Tillman Jr., m. Lucy Dugar, granddaughter of Governor Pickens of South Carolina.
6—Douschka Tillman.
6—Sarah Tillman.
5—Molana Tillman, m. Charles Moore.
6—Benjamin Moore.
6—Minnie Moore.
5—Henry Tillman, lawyer, m. Mary Fox.
6—Mary Tillman.
6—Adeline Tillman.
6—Sarah Tillman.
6—Benjamin R. Tillman.
5—Sophia Tillman, m. Henry Hughes.
6—Elizabeth Hughes.
6—Adeline Hughes.
6—Sarah Hughes.
5—Sally May Tillman, m. John Schuler.
6—John Schuler Jr.
6—Harry Schuler.
4—Edmund Brewer Stark, b. Oct. 19, 1852; d. May 10, 1915; m. Oct. 15, 1872, Julia Baker.
5—Samuel Stark, d. unmarried.
5—Mary Stark, m. A. B. Jones.
6—Louise Jones.
5—Julia Stark, m. A. H. Womack.
6—Maud Womack.
6—Edmund Womack.
6—Lyons Womack.
6—A. H. Womack Jr.
5—Sarah Louise Stark, m. (1) H. E. Russell; (2) J. L. Smith.
6—Essie Russell.
6—Earl Russell.
6—Julia Russell.
5—Brewer Stark, m. Alice Newton.
6—Nell Stark.
6—Harriet Stark.
5—John A. Stark, Sheriff of Elbert County, 1936-1940; m. Cynthia Smith. No issue.
5—Thomas R. Stark, druggist, b. Feb. 15, 1890; m. 1912, Elizabeth Auld.
6—Julia Stark, b. March 1914.
4—Mary Adeline Stark, b. July 24, 1859; m. March 26, 1879, George C. Grogan, b. April 5, 1857; d. 1925, lawyer, Judge City Court of Elberton, City Attorney of Elberton, Attorney for Elbert County Bond Commission, Exhaulted Ruler B. P. O. E. 1100, County Attorney of Elbert County.
5—Stark Grogan, b. Feb. 14, 1880; m. Oct. 3, 1900, Ailene Harper.
6—Samuel Stark Grogan.
5—George C. Grogan Jr., b. March 16, 1881; m. Nov. 16, 1904, Louise Phillips of Oklahoma.

6—Phillips Grogan.
6—George C. Grogan III.
5—Sarah Grogan, b. Aug. 21, 1884; m. February 3, 1904, Henry D. Jordan of South Carolina.
6—Ralph Jordan.
6—Henry D. Jordan Jr., m. Addie Sanders.
7—Lovett Jordan.
7—Sarah Adeline Jordan.
5—Henry Grogan, b. May 7, 1888; m. Jan. 20, 1907, Clyde McLanahan.
6—George Albert Grogan.
6—Betsy Grogan, m. 1933, Mayson Jaudon.
7—Henry Jaudon, b. 1934.
5—May Grogan, b. Aug. 24, 1894; m. June 6, 1916, James Haygood Bruce of South Carolina.
6—Virginia Bruce.
6—James McDuffie Bruce.
5—Edmund Brewer Grogan, b. Sept. 11, 1896; m. Dec. 23, 1922, Bernice Lyons.
6—Jeanne Grogan.
6—Carroll Grogan.
5—Kathleen Bruce Grogan, b. Dec. 27, 1898; m. April 21, 1921, James Arnold, contractor.
6—James Arnold Jr.
3—Daughter Stark, m. (1) Dr. McCoy; (2) Campbell Martin.
4—Flora McCoy.
4—Luther Martin.
4—John Martin.
4—Thomas Martin.
4—Stark Martin.
4—Jane Martin.
4—Campbell Martin Jr.
4—William Martin.
4—Mary Martin.
4—Sarah Martin, m. Mr. Gower.
3—Sarah Howell Stark, m. Guilford Cade.
4—Samuel Robert Cade, m. Sarah Slaughter.
5—William Cade, d. unmarried.
5—Walter Cade, m. Miss Hollingsworth.
6—Sarah Louise Cade.
6—Wooder Cade, m. Patric Porter.
6—Roy Cade.
5—Samuel Cade, m. Mary Slaughter.
6—Sarah Cade.
6—Jane Cade.
5—Albert Cade, m. Miss Morange.
6—Thelma Cade and other issue.
5—Rennie Cade, d. unmarried.
5—Clifford Cade.
4—Mary Eliza Cade, m. Singleton A. McIntosh, C. S.
5—Howell McIntosh, m. S. J. Zeigler.
6—Samuel Zeigler, m. Fanny Marburg.
7—Howell Zeigler.
6—Howell "Polar" Zeigler, m. George Lee Dickson, S. W. W., Major U. S. A., retired.
7—Howell Dickson.
7—George Lee Dickson Jr.
5—William M. McIntosh, b. 1870; d. 1930, unmarried.
5—Victoria Augusta McIntosh, m. Joseph Allston.
6—Joseph Allston Jr., m. Lillis McCullough.

7—Joseph Allston III.
6—Mary Allston.
5—Guilford "Guy" McIntosh, m. Addie Tinsley.
6—William Kenneth McIntosh.
6—Mary McIntosh.
6—Louise McIntosh.
5—Mary Louise McIntosh, m. Henry M. Long.
6—Mary Louise Long, d. infancy.
4—Victoria Cade, m. Augustus Lee.
5—Mamie Lee, m. Major Bryant of New Jersey.
6—John Bryant.
6—Lewis Lee Bryant.
5—Sarah Lee, m. Z. B. Rogers, member Georgia House of Representatives, County Attorney of Elbert County, City Attorney of Elberton.
6—Lee Rogers.
6—William Rogers.
6—Mary Rogers.
5—Augustus Lee Jr., m. Margaret Smith. No issue.
4—Guilford Cade Jr., m. Louisa McIntosh.
5—Julia May Cade, m. Dr. Albert Sidney Hawes, member Georgia House of Representatives, Mayor of Elberton.
6—Guilford M. Hawes, m. Onie Lee.
7—Mary Lee Hawes.
7—Robert Hawes, d. infancy.
7—Julia Ann Hawes.
6—Albert Lee Hawes, m. Bertha Bates.
6—Peyton S. Hawes, lawyer, member Georgia House of Representatives, City Attorney of Elberton, Solicitor City Court of Elberton, m. Virginia Smith.
5—Guilford Cade III, m. Jane Kennedy.
6—Malvina Cade, m. Milo Abercrombie.
7—Milo Abercrombie Jr.
6—Guilford Cade IV.
5—Annie Lee Cade, m. Dr. Robert Franklin Moore.
6—Alan Moore.
6—Frank Moore, d. infancy.
6—Guilford McIntosh Moore, m. Miss Madden.

SWIFT

Flower Swift, of Maryland, son of Flower Swift, of England, married Elizabeth Wilson. Tradition says that while returning to England to claim property he was lost at sea.

His son, David Flower Swift, whose Revolutionary record is on file in Raleigh, North Carolina, was living in North Carolina at the time of the Revolution and later moved to Franklin County, Georgia, where he built his home on the banks of the Tugalo River about five miles from Toccoa.

William, son of David Flower Swift, was a resident of Morgan County, Georgia, and was a planter.

His son, William Augustin Swift, moved to Elbert County, Georgia. He married Nancy Keller, of Abbeville County, South Carolina, on February 1, 1842. He was a merchant and about 1840 he was one of the trustees of the First Methodist Church of Elberton.

At the time of his death, the house in Elberton, known as the Oliver House, was being built for his occupancy. This house, situated on a wooded hill on the east side of McIntosh Street, is of a type of architecture that was popular in Louisiana and is very similar to the "Hermitage" in Savannah, Georgia. It is a three-storied building with tall square columns supporting the roof. The first story is of granite and beautiful curved stairs of stone, on the outside, leading up to a second-story porch, are a distinguishing feature of the building.

The children of William A. Swift and Nancy Keller Swift were: Thomas Madison, John Keller, Will, and Isaac Glasgow. John and Will never married.

Thomas, John, and Isaac built the Swift Cotton Mill, which was the first cotton mill to be built in Elberton.

Thomas married Elizabeth Young, of Abbeville, South Carolina. Throughout her life she took an active part in the work of the First Methodist Church. Thomas was prominent in politics and in the business life of Elberton.

The children of this union were: Mamie, Jim, Will, Pearl, and Thomas. Mamie married Z. C. Hayes; Jim married Sue Heard; Pearl married T. J. Halliburton; and Thomas married Eugenia Christian. Will was never married.

Isaac Glasgow married Bessie Thurmond, of Athens, Georgia. Her mother was Elizabeth Long, a sister of Crawford W. Long, the discoverer of anesthesia, to whose memory the Government has erected a beautiful monument at Danielsville, Georgia, the place of his birth. He later moved to Jefferson, Georgia, where the discovery of anesthesia was made. His statue stands in the Hall of Fame.

Isaac Glasgow Swift was one of Elberton's leading business men and financiers. He was one of the organizers of the Elberton Loan and Savings Bank, of which he was cashier for a number of years. His associates described him as a man of the highest integrity, with an extraordinarily active mind, and with an unassuming zeal for civic righteousness that gained him friends among all classes of citizens.

The children of Isaac Glasgow Swift and Bessie Thurmond Swift were: Elizabeth, Thurmond, and Sara. Elizabeth married William Duncan Tutt; Thurmond married Bessie Hall Wilson; and Sara married Julian C. Willson.

At the time of this writing, December, 1939, the Swifts in Elbert County are: Jim Swift, Tom Swift, and Pearl Halliburton Swift, children of Thomas Madison Swift; and Elizabeth Swift Tutt, daughter of Isaac Glasgow Swift.

THORNTON

The following chart shows intermarriages with the following families:
Adair — Adams — Agnew — Aldridge — Alford — Allen — Almond — Amos — Archer — Andrews — Appleby — Arnold — Ashworth — Attaway — Balchin — Bell — Bertram — Benson — Bentley — Bishop — Black — Blanchard — Bothwell — Boyd — Bradford — Bradberry — Brawner — Brogdon — Brewer — Brown — Burton — Bush — Bray — Bowden — Calloway — Carpenter — Carter — Cash — Cauthen — Carithers — Campbell — Cheek — Childs — Clinkscales — Clark — Comer — Cleckler — Cleveland — Cole — Cox — Cobb — Cordell — Craft — Crawford — Cunningham — Daird — Dellis — Denny — Dickerson — Dodd — Dozier — Duncan — Dye — Eavenson — Eberhardt — Edwards — Evans — Fleming — Fortson — Gaines — Gary — Gillison — Goss — Goolsby — Greenway — Grimes — Grogan — Hailey — Hall — Ham — Hamilton — Hansard — Harper — Hemphill — Higginbotham — Heindel — Herndon — Hopkins — Hughes — Holt — Hudson — Hulme — Hunt — Hunter — Ingram — Jackson — Jaudon — Johnson — Jones — Keeler — Leazer — Lee — Lewis — Logan — Lunsford — McCarty — McEwen — McGarrin — McGee — McGinty — McIntosh — McKagen — McKeen — McLanahan — McMullan — Malote — Manuel — Martin — Matthews — Maxwell — Meadow — Milford — Molloy — Moncrief — Mitchell — Mewbourn — Montgomery — Moore — Murray — Norman — Nuckles — Oglesby — Owens — Ooghee — Page — Parks — Payne — Pierce — Powers — Powell — Pierson — Pulliam — Rayle — Reid — Rice — Rich — Richardson — Roberts — Rogers — Sanders — Scattergood — Seawright — Seymour — Sewell — Seay — Sisk — Siler — Slaton — Smith — Snellings — Skelton — Speed — Spratlin — Souther — Sterans — Strickland — Stoddard — Steele — Talmadge — Tate — Taylor — Teasley — Thornton — Thompson — Tiller — Todd — Turner — Upshaw — Vickery — Ward — Warren — Wansley — Waters — White — Wilson — Winn — West — Worley — Wray — Whitfield — West — Wilhite — Watson — Williams — Wiggins — Willis — Wallis — Wall — Williamson — Warren — Yates — Young — Zackery.

(Note: Numbers represent generations, as: (1) first generation, (2) second generation, (3) third generation, etc.)

1—Mark Thornton, planter, married Susannah Dozier, daughter of Leonard Dozier, in Lunenburg County, Virginia. Among their children were:
  2—Reuben Thornton, d. 1810, Elbert County; m. Elizabeth Allen.
  2—Dozier Thornton, R. S. and Baptist Minister, b. April 4, 1755, in Virginia (Lunenburg Co.); d. Sept. 1843, in Georgia; m. Lucy Hill of North Coralina first, and second marriage to Mrs. Jane Pulliam, April 1826.
    3—Jeremiah Thornton, b. Oct. 2, 1777; d. Nov. 26, 1848; m. Elizabeth Allen, daughter of Rev. Nathaniel Allen, Methodist minister, 1798.
      4—Dr. Hudson Allen, b. July 14, 1800; d. April 16, 1859; m. Elizabeth Ragan; d. 1837.
      4—Major Dozier Thornton, b. Oct. 24, 1801; d. June 10, 1860; m. Anne Caroline Early, b. 1801; d. Jan. 26, 1861.

4—Major Nathaniel M. Thornton, b. Oct. 6, 1806; d. March 23, 1889; m. Arimenta H. Kidd, b. April 17, 1817; d. Nov. 28, 1882.
4—Louisiana Hawkins Thornton, b. Dec. 2, 1809; d. Jan. 11, 1868; m. Nov. 13, 1826, Nathaniel Nuckalls, b. Nov. 26, 1800; d. Sept. 24, 1868.
3—Benjamin Thornton, planter, b. 1779; m. 1796, Sarah Upshaw and second marriage Rebecca Upshaw, Jan. 21, 1836. No issue.
4—Reuben Thornton, b. 1797; d. Aug. 30, 1855; m. June 18, 1837, Elizabeth Lane Jackson, b. Jan. 12, 1813; d. April 17, 1893.
4—Thomas Thornton, b. 1798, migrated to Mississippi—no date.
4—Priscilla Thornton, b. 1800; m. July 31, 1823, Sion Hunt, b. Feb. 1, 1798; d. Feb. 11, 1875.
5—Emma Priscilla Hunt, b. May 8, 1846; d. May 2, 1907; m. Sept. 26, 1861, Robert Patton Eberhart, b. Oct. 13, 1834; d. Jan. 17, 1907.
4—Benjamin Thornton Jr., b. Aug. 15, 1801, Baptist minister, member Georgia House of Representatives 1851-1852; m. Sept. 16, 1819, Nancy Payne, b. 1804; d. 1850.
5—Sarah Kindred Thornton, b. Feb. 14, 1826; d. Aug. 4, 1912; m. Oct. 5, 1841, Joseph Y. Arnold, Confederate Soldier, planter, b. June 11, 1817; d. Jan. 31, 1895.
6—Elizabeth Arnold, b. Oct. 23, 1845; d. Aug. 25, 1905; m. Aug. 4, 1861, John L. Wilhite, C. S., Treasurer of Elbert County, b. Nov. 12, 1838; d. Dec. 7, 1912.
6—McAlpin Arnold, C. S., merchant, banker, planter, member City Council of Elberton, director Seaboard Air Line Railroad, b. Nov. 1, 1847; d. Aug. 23, 1912; m. May 5, 1875, Anne Carter, b. Nov. 25, 1848; d. July 29, 1899.
7—Sarah Louise Arnold, m. Dec. 6, 1900, Henry S. Jaudon, civil engineer; d. Aug. 22, 1929.
7—Julius Arnold, d. Jan. 21, 1906, unmarried.
7—Edna Arnold, Genealogist, Fellow I. A. G., m. Z. W. Copeland, wholesale distributor, Superintendent Baptist Sunday School 25 years, member City Council, Past President Chamber of Commerce, Past President Rotary Club.
7—Carter Alston Arnold, member City Council, Civil Engineer, graduate Cornell University, Ithica. N. Y., Chairman Board of Education; m. Mary Hill, Jan. 8, 1919.
6—Julius B. D. Arnold, C. S.; died in U. S. Army Prison during Civil War. Unmarried.
6—Saluda Arnold, b. 1847; d. Nov. 27, 1920; m. Stephen H. Black, C. S.
7—McAlpin Black.
7—Emma Black, died unmarried.
7—James Wm. "Coon" Black, d. March 11, 1934; m. 1901, Cora McEwen.
7—Birdie Black, m. Mr. Birch.
7—Sarah Black, m. Thos. Mitchell.
7—Lonnie Black, m. Daisy Roberts.
7—Harry Black, d. unmarried.
7—Annie Black, m. Thos. Calloway.
7—Mary George Black, designer, m. Mr. Heindel.
6—Sarah Arnold, b. 1857; d. May 17, 1894; m. Joseph N. Worley, Judge Superior Court, City Attorney, County Attorney of Elbert County, Clerk of Elberton, County Commissioner of Elbert County, member Georgia House of Representatives, Chairman Elbert County Democratic Committee, b. 1854; d. 1935.
7—Arnold Worley, lawyer, m. (1) Edith Wilton; (2) Miss Peppers.

7—Elizabeth Worley, m. Arthur McGinty, Oct. 6, 1903; d. July 1935.
7—Carter Worley, S. W. W., m. Minnie Andrews.
6—Georgia Arnold, b. Feb. 11, 1858; m. 1878, Luther Goolsby; d. 1895.
7—Mary Goolsby, d. May 8, 1908; m. May 18, 1903. Joseph Turner.
7—Ernest Goolsby, m. 1912, Nell Lewis.
7—Charles Goolsby, b. May 4, 1885.
7—Irene Goolsby, m. June 5, 1907, F. D. Smith, banker.
7—Sarah Goolsby, m. Jan. 24, 1922, Dr. Isaac Reid, druggist, 2nd Lieut. in World War, first honor graduate University of Georgia (Pharmacy).
7—Luther Goolsby, S. W. W., Postmaster at Carlton Georgia; m. Mary Brown.
6—Mary Jane Arnold, b. Sept. 23, 1859; m. Oct. 18, 1882, James McIntosh, b. 1857, Sheriff, County Commissioner of Elbert County, member Tax Board of Elberton and City Council.
7—Sarah Louise McIntosh, m. Feb. 23, 1903, A. F. Archer.
7—William McIntosh, d. infancy.
7—Jessie McIntosh, d. infancy.
7—Mary James McIntosh, d. infancy.
7—John Hawes McIntosh, County Attorney Elbert County, Compiler City Code, Elberton, Assistant Secretary Georgia Senate, Historian Elbert County, Assistant Circuit Court Clerk, Tulsa, Okla.; b. Nov. 26, 1895; m. June 19, 1918, Fay Anne White.
7—McAlpin McIntosh, d. 1899.
6—Joseph Arnold, d. unmarried.
6—William T. Arnold, merchant, b. March 24, 1867; m. Dec. 5, 1888, Eddie Herndon, b. Dec. 26, 1870.
7—George Clifton Arnold, b. 1889; d. 1912, unmarried.
7—William Herman Arnold, contractor and builder, b. Aug. 26, 1897; m. June 1918, Catherine Cleckler, b. Oct. 23, 1898.
7—James Arnold, contractor and builder, b. Sept. 14, 1899; m. April 21, 1921, Kathleen Grogan, b. Dec. 27, 1898.
6—Lofton Arnold, d. unmarried.
5—Fleming Thornton, planter, m. Oct. 3, 1842, Harriet F. Adams; d. June 16, 1902.
6—Mary Thornton, m. Dec. 28, 1865, Dr. B. C. Smith, C. S.
7—Alice Smith, m. R. T. Gaines. No issue.
7—A. F. Smith, contractor and builder, m. Jan. 28, 1891, minor carpenter.
8—Matilde Smith, m. April 23, 1913, Fred Herndon, member City Council of Elberton, contractor and builder.
8—Margaret Smith, m. Augustus Lee. No issue.
8—Mary Helen Smith, m. Fred Herndon, widower of elder sister.
8—Minor Ruth Smith.
8—A. F. Smith Jr., m. Ellen Wray.
8—Virginia Smith, M. 1933, Peyton S. Hawes, member Georgia House of Representatives, City Attorney of Elberton, Solicitor City Court of Elberton.
7—George Smith, m. Fanny Eavenson.
7—Charles H. Smith, Clerk and Treasurer of Elberton, m. Sudie Powell.
7—Dr. Amos C. Smith, M.D., m. Oct. 24, 1906, Janie Cleveland.
7—Ada Smith, m. Lawrence Gaines.
7—Florence Smith, m. James Thomas Brewer.
7—Albert P. Smith, m. Mary McGee.
7—Parker B. Smith, m. Julia Wilson.
7—Benjamin Smith, m. Elizabeth Marr nee Heffernan.

7—Luna Smith, m. James Cunningham.
7—Ruth Smith m. W. H. Seawright.
7—Leonard Smith, d. unmarried.
7—Lillie Smith, m. Julian Attaway.
7—Olin Smith, m. Martha Sparks.
7—Harvey Smith.
6—William Thornton, m. Jane Teasley.
7—Luther Thornton, m. Ida Herndon.
7—James Thornton, m. Lucy Gaines. No issue.
7—Dr. Henry Thornton, M. D., m. April 17, 1894, Sarah Ward.
7—Ida Thornton, m. Lindsey Hall.
7—Melvin Thornton, d. unmarried.
6—John Thornton.
6—Fanny Thornton, m. Rev. Thomas Rucker, Baptist minister.
7—Joseph Rucker, m. Eula Herndon.
7—Benjamin Rucker, m. Elizabeth Scattergood.
7—McAlpin Rucker, m. Petra Swearingen.
7—James Rucker, m. Grace Cheek.
7—Hattie Rucker.
7—Ruth Rucker, m. Oct. 16, 1912, Stokeley Warren.
7—Nona Rucker, m. Oct. 19, 1920, Phillip Bradford.
7—Florence Rucker, m. 1920, C. H. Denny.
7—Alma Rucker, m. Hoyle Winn.
7—Thelma Rucker, m. Fred Young.
7—Julius Rucker, m. Ida Johnson.
7—Catherine Rucker.
7—Isham Rucker, m. Mary Bush.
5—William E. Thornton, b. 1824; d. Oct. 1911; m. (1) March 4, 1843, Elizabeth E. Thornton; (2) Widow Oglesby.
6—J. F. Thornton.
6————— Thornton, m. William Greenway.
6—John Thornton, d. Feb. 22, 1918; m. Nov. 6, 1868, Sallie C. Bond.
7—Benjamin E. Thornton, m. (1) Lila Thornton; (2) Miss Ashworth.
7—Cone B. Thornton, Ordinary of Elbert County; m. Nov. 28, 1905, Mary Phelps.
7—Carrie Thornton, m. Nov. 30, 1899, Jesse Cleveland.
7—Anna Thornton, m. Alex Snellings.
7—Floyd Thornton, m. Nov. 25, 1932, Blanche Gaines; d. 1936.
7—Rowe Thornton.
7—Ida Thornton, m. Otis Hughes.
7—Grady Thornton, d. 1935, unmarried.
6—Arcola Thornton, m. Nov. 1888, T. J. Gaines.
6—W. W. Thornton, m. Carrie Gaines.
6—Priscilla Thornton, m. Berry Ficquett.
6—Willie Thornton, m. Feb. 1894, W. T. Teasley; d. 1932.
7—Paul Teasley, b. 1895; m. Lillian Teasley.
7—Delrey Teasley, m. Virgil Sheppard, S. W. W.
7—Vera Teasley, m. Lee Martin.
7—Hettie Teasley, m. Isaac Ward.
5—Mary Ann Thornton, m. (1) Nov. 9, 1846, Thomas E. Highsmith; (2) Mr. Siler.
5—Benjamin Calloway Thornton, b. Dec. 13, 1827; d. Oct. 30, 1881; m. (1) Melissa Gaines; (2) Priscilla Teasley, b. July 24, 1834; d. May 23, 1896.
6—(By first wife) Frank B. Thornton, b. 1848; d. 1888; m. Julia Waters.
7—Robert C. Thornton, m. Helen Linder.
7—Emma Thornton, m. Mr. Sequefield.

6—(By second wife) Thomas A. Thornton, b. July 31, 1852; m. Georgia Carter.
7—Mamie Thornton, m. T. D. Johnson.
7—George Thornton, m. Anna Moon.
7—J. C. Thornton, m. Alice Adams.
7—Joseph A. Thornton, m. Iviland Barksdale.
6—Sarah Thornton, b. Jan. 1, 1854; d. April 5, 1924; m. D. C. Alford.
7—Benjamin C. Alford, m. Sumter Teasley.
7—Addie Alford, m. L. L. Stapleton.
7—Clio Alford, d. 1911; m. George S. Clark.
7—Mack Alford, m. Sarah Vernon.
6—Dozier Thornton, b. Oct. 10, 1855; d. July 30, 1909; m. Susan Gillison.
7—Marion C. Thornton, m. Ora Julian.
7—Edna Thornton, m. Louie Morris, editor of the Hartwell (Ga.) Sun.
7—Almond Thornton, m. Juan Chandler.
6—James Thornton, b. Sept. 5, 1857; d. March 14, 1921; m. Sarah Speed.
7—Nina Thornton, m. George S. Clark.
7—Kathleen Thornton, m. J. C. Kidd.
7—James Thornton Jr., m. Emily Minter.
6—Janie Thornton, d. unmarried.
6—Cornelia Thornton, d. infancy.
6—Amanda Thornton, b. Nov. 27, 1864; d. 1935; m. March 2, 1881, George Page.
6—John C. Thornton, b. 1866; d. 1899.
6—Rebecca Thornton, d. infancy.
6—Jessie Thornton, b. April 20, 1871; m. Dec. 23, 1891, James C. Skelton, lawyer, member Georgia House of Representatives, member Georgia State Senate.
7—Emmett Skelton, S. W. W., lawyer.
7—James Skelton, lawyer, member Georgia House of Representatives; m. Bess Boyd.
7—Wilma Skelton, m. W. G. Brown.
7—Ralph Skelton, m. Louise Dye.
7—Annie Skelton, m. E. B. McGarin.
7—Parke Skelton, m. Montine Alford.
7—Hugh Skelton.
7—Carey Skelton.
7—Marion Skelton.
6—McAlpin Thornton, m. Claire Dodd.
7—Preston Thornton.
7—Joseph Thornton.
7—John Thornton.
7—Kelsie Thornton.
6—Dunstan Thornton, b. July 1876; m. Lola Skelton.
7—Frances Thornton, m. Freeman Adams.
7—Annie Ruth Thornton, m. Dallas Fortson.
6—Annie Ruth Thornton, b. June 24, 1878; m. J. P. Cash.
5—Thomas Thornton, m. Nov. 2, 1843, Lucy Pulliam.
6—Calloway Thornton, m. Lizzie Adams.
7—Thomas Thornton, m. 1891, Mattie Hulme.
7—James C. Thornton, Sheriff of Elbert County; m. Dec. 22, 1892, Hattie Crook.
7—Lucy Thornton, m. Dec. 1, 1896, J. B. Gaines.
7—George Thornton, U. S. Mail Carrier, m. Jan. 28, 1900, Annie Parks.
6—Priscilla Thornton, m. Obie McCurry.

7—A. A. McCurry, Georgia State Senator, lawyer, m. Lizzie May Speed.
7—Lucy McCurry, m. Thomas Higginbotham.
7—Mary McCurry, m. Dr. James Jenkins, M. D.
7—George McCurry.
7—Daniel Lee McCurry.
7—Robbie May McCurry.
6—Nancy Thornton, d. unmarried.
6—Benjamin Thornton, d. 1936; m. Fanny Brown.
7—J. Early Thornton, wholesale grocer, m. Dec. 22, 1896, Julia Willis.
8—Harry G. Thornton, wholesale grocer, president First National Bank, b. 1897; m. Huie Allen.
7—Wiley T. Thornton, stock dealer, b. March 12, 1873; m. 1904, Lucy Adams.
7—Luna Thornton, m. Isham Cordell.
7—Corra Thornton, m. Thomas Fleming.
7—Emma Thornton, m. Linton Agnew.
7—Frank Thornton, stock dealer, unmarried.
7—Elbert Thornton.
7—Grace Thornton, m. Garrett Wallis.
7—Ira Thornton, m. Aug. 15, 1915, Vesta Maxwell.
7—Nannie Belle Thornton, m. Walter Bothwell.
6—Martha Thornton, m. Andrew Rucker Brown.
7—George Brown.
7—Thomas J. Brown, Solicitor General Northern Circuit of Georgia; d. 1917, unmarried.
7—Birch Brown, m. Essie Brown.
7—Leila Brown, m. John Gaines.
7—Paul Brown, lawyer, member Georgia House of Representatives from Oglethorpe County, Georgia, member U. S. House of Representatives, m. Frances Arnold.
7—Heber Brown, m. Dec. 16, 1902, Hattie Parks.
6—Mathew "Mat" Thornton, d. 1930; m. Mary Cobb.
7—Priscilla Thornton, m. J. C. Reid.
7—Lois Thornton, m. Mr. McConnell.
7—Exil Thornton.
7—Fred Thornton, m. 1917, Mozelle Cauthen. No issue.
7—James Thornton, m. Flossie Duncan.
7—Flossie Thornton.
7—Fanny Ruth Thornton.
7—Donald Thornton.
7—Mary Thornton.
7—Marjorie Thornton.
7—L. C. Thornton.
6—Allen Thornton, m. Miss Norman. No issue.
5—Asa Thornton, m. Dec. 1, 1857, Dorcas Almond.
6—Laura Lofton Thornton, m. R. E. Bradberry.
6—John Thomas Thornton.
6—George Henry Thornton.
6—Francis Calloway Thornton.
6—Asa Stovall Thornton.
6—James Benjamin Thornton.
6—Rufus R. Thornton.
5—Priscilla Thornton, m. Jan. 23, 1851, Asa Brown, C. S., killed in action.
6—Sarah Brown, m. Charles P. Taylor; d. 1932.
7—Jessie Taylor, m. Rae Steele.
7—Maud Taylor, m. M. Brogdon.
7—Howell Taylor.

7—John C. Taylor, S. W. W., d. 1927, unmarried.
6—John C. Brown, b. 1857; d. 1917, Mayor of Elberton, merchant, planter; m. 1895, Mary Bevelle McIntosh, b. June 1856; d. June 1926. No issue.
6—Rachel Brown, m. Robert "Bob" Rayle.
7—Roy Rayle.
7—Mamie Rayle.
7—Susie Rayle, m. Mr. Spratlin.
6—Dillard H. Brown, merchant, planter; m. Nov. 7, 1888, Jessie Brawner.
7—Florence Brown, m. April 26, 1913, Dr. D. N. Thompson, M. D.
7—Herman J. Brown, insurance, member City Council of Elberton, m. (1) Gladys Allen; (2) Kate Sutton.
7—Ruth Brown, m. Thomas Dozier Seymour.
6—Mallory J. Brown, b. 1862; d. July 14, 1934, merchant, planter, member City Council of Elberton; m. (1) Maud McCarty; (2) Louise Clinton.
7—(By first wife) Maud Brown, m. 1913, William Adams.
7—Edgar Chandler Brown, merchant, member City Council of Elberton; m. (1) Zelma Stark; (2) Louise Wray.
7—Julian Thomas Brown, insurance, m. Kathleen Meadow.
7—Louise Brown, d. 1936; m. (1) George Mattox, S. W. W., Lieut.; (2) Jack Stoddard, Adjutant-General of Georgia.
5—John C. Thornton, C. S., b. Dec. 23, 1832; d. Oct. 19, 1864; m. Oct. 1857, Georgia Ann Hickman, b. Oct. 1, 1843; d. April 10, 1908.
6—Sarah Thornton, b. Jan. 25, 1860; m. May 13, 1888, E. H. Vickery, b. Nov. 18, 1859; d. Aug. 11, 1923.
7—Leila Vickery, Educational Work, m. July 15, 1919, R. L. Rice, b. June 13, 1882.
6—James Thornton, b. 1858; d. 1874.
6—John C. Thornton Jr., b. 1862; d. 1917.
6—Leila Thornton, b. July 9, 1864; m. Dec. 16, 1891, J. F. L. Bond, member Georgia Senate, b. Jan. 23, 1862; d. Feb. 24, 1916.
7—Jewell Bond, b. Sept. 8, 1892; m. Dec. 8, 1917, John T. Murray, b. Nov. 28, 1882.
7—Hamilton Bond, b. June 23, 1894; m. Sept. 7, 1927, Enola May Moore, b. Jan. 29, 1896.
5—Mallory J. Thornton, C. S., b. 1840; m. Nov. 7, 1865, Olivia Sewell.
6—Joseph Thornton, b. July 20, 1866; m. Sept. 18, 1887, Alice Bowman, b. April 19, 1866.
7—Lee Thornton, m. Mima Bone.
7—James Thornton, m. Mary Todd.
7—Olivia Thornton, m. Nov. 16, 1914, Orrs Clinkscales.
7—Alice Thornton, m. Thomas Wall.
7—Sarah Thornton, m. May 1916, Frank Taylor.
7—Grace Thornton.
7—Lois Thornton.
7—B. I. Thornton, m. Helen Griffith.
7—Josephine Thornton, m. J. T. Sisk, lawyer, member Georgia House of Representatives, member Georgia Senate.
7—Thomas Thornton.
7—Louise Thornton.
7—Mary Sue Thornton.
6—B. I. Thornton, newspaper editor, b. Oct. 13, 1868; m. June 27, 1906, Susan Williamson.
7—B. I. Thornton Jr., b. March 31, 1907; m. 1931, Cornelia Turner.
7—Thomas Thornton, b. 1908; m. Frances Yarbrough.
7—Susan Thornton, b. Jan. 16, 1916.

7—Rachel Thornton, b. May 25, 1927.
6—Olivia Thornton, m. Nov. 1898, Thomas S. Milford.
7—L. J. Milford.
7—Thelma Milford.
7—Thomas Milford.
7—Olivia Milford.
6—Majorie Thornton, m. Dec. 12, 1896, Eppy Anderson.
7—Elizabeth Anderson.
7—Mallory Anderson.
7—Margaret Anderson.
7—Mary Anderson.
7—Edna Anderson.
7—E. T. Anderson.
6—Harvey Thornton, d. unmarried.
6—Susie Thornton.
6—Mallory Thornton Jr.
6—Timothy Thornton, editor.
4—John Thornton, m. Frances Adams.
5—William Thornton, C. S., d. Jan. 28, 1863, from wounds; m. Lucinda Almond, daughter of William Almond and Mary Thornton.
6—Mary Thornton, m. Joseph Wright.
6—Burgess Thornton, b. 1849; d. 1902; m. Jan. 6, 1868, Emma Almond.
6—John William Thornton, m. Elizabeth Tiller.
6—Josie Thornton, m. Tug Fortson.
6—Frank Thornton, m. Ella Warren.
6—Amos Thornton, m. Dec. 17, 1884, Ella Black.
6—Webb Thornton, m. Ella Thornton. No issue.
5—Sarah Thornton, b. Aug. 5, 1824; d. Dec. 16, 1863; m. Aug. 1, 1839, George W. Eavenson, b. Feb. 23, 1817; d. July 16, 1898.
6—John W. Eavenson, C. S., m. Jane Oglesby.
6—Willis Jefferson Eavenson, m. Oct. 17, 1865, (1) Mary Arminda Teasley; (2) Emily Adams.
7—(By first wife) Harper Eavenson, m. Ida Turner.
7—William Allen Eavenson, m. Roxie Adams.
7—Eula Beatrice Eavenson, m. Benson Mansfield Maxwell.
7—Bessie Eavenson, m. William Albert Maxwell.
7—Fanny Eavenson, m. George H. Smith.
7—Carrie Eavenson, m. F. Paul Crawford.
7—Cora Eavenson, m. Rev. George C. Bond, Baptist minister.
4—Daniel Thornton, m. Oct. 3, 1826, Lucy Bradley, b. Oct. 11, 1811; d. Dec. 1848.
4—Mary Thornton, m. William Almond.
5—Lucinda Almond, m. William Thornton, C. S.; d. Jan. 28, 1863.
6—Mary Thornton, m. Joseph Wright.
7—Mattie Thornton, m. E. A. Ooghee.
5—Angeline Almond, m. Mr. Gulley.
5—Fanny Almond, m. (1) Mr. Bentley; (2) Mr. Moore. No issue.
5—Benjamin Almond, m. Louisa Cleveland. No issue.
4—Dozier Thornton, m. Sept. 25, 1834, Jane Fortson.
5—Thomas Thornton, m. Jan. 24, 1868, S. A. E. Herndon.
6—Gussie Thornton, m. Dec. 19, 1888, Dr. S. B. Adair, Dentist.
5—Henry Thornton, m. Feb. 14, 1873, Sarah Hill.
6—William Thornton, m. Missie Childs.
6—Benjamin Thornton, m. Miss Goolsby.
6—May Thornton, m. Edward Childs.
6—Georgia Thornton, m. Lester Bell.
6—Fortson Thornton, m. Corinne Balchin.
6—James Thornton, m. Lula Adams.

6—Laurie Thornton.
6—Estelle Thornton.
5—William Thornton, C. S., Treasurer of Elbert County; m. Lucinda Jones.
6—Julia Thornton, m. Omer Seymour.
7—Thomas Dozier Seymour, m. Ruth Brown.
7—William Seymour.
7—Grace Seymour.
7—Sarah Seymour, m. James Hall.
7—Dorothy Seymour.
6—Thomas T. Thornton, Mayor of Elberton, merchant, m. Feb. 11, 1903, Janie Carithers.
7—Mary Pope Thornton.
7—James Thornton.
7—Thomas Thornton.
6—Dozier J. Thornton, b. Dec. 23, 1877, merchant, Clerk of County Commissioner of Elbert County, Clerk and Treasurer of Elberton; m. Nov. 4, 1903, Clyde Arnold.
7—Arnoldina Thornton.
7—McWhorter Thornton, m. 1931, Lucy Johnson.
6—Emma Thornton, m. David C. Hudson, merchant. No issue.
6—Willie T. Thornton, cotton broker, m. Willie Rich.
5—Calvin Thornton, m. May 24, 1864, Eugenia Almond.
6—Ida Thornton, m. I. J. Goolsby. No issue.
6—Janie Thornton, m. 1914, William Anderson. No issue.
6—Fanny Thornton, m. 1885, Lucius Fortson.
6—James Thornton, m. Miss Fortson.
6—Charles Thornton.
6—Frank Thornton, m. Carlotta White.
5—Isham Thornton, m. Lou Herndon.
6—Elma Thornton, m. 1903, Herbert Whitehead.
6—Harold Thornton, m. April 11, 1906.
6—Dan Thornton, m. Miss Wilkinson.
6—Howard Thornton, m. Feb. 4, 1917, Ethel Smith.
6—Ione Thornton, m. Oct. 21, 1914, Joe L. Lunsford.
6—Lester Thornton, m. Chanaler Stevens.
5—Joseph B. Thornton, m. Elizabeth Fortson.
6—Jesse Thornton, d. unmarried.
6—Eula Thornton, m. David Cliatt.
6—Oscar Thornton, m. Nov. 17, 1910, Tommie Tate.
6—L. M. Thornton, m. Hallie Ham.
6—Birdie Thornton, m. Oct. 20, 1910, John W. McLanahan.
6—Connard Thornton, m. Icie Campbell.
6—Pearl Thornton, m. James Blanchard.
5—Frank C. Thornton, m. Lola Black.
6—Norma Thornton, m. Enoch Bell.
6—Nathleen Thornton, m. Oct. 25, 1910, Grover Cleveland, Past Superintendent City Water and Lights Department.
6—Carmen Thornton, m. Aug. 23, 1914, Wade A. Thornton.
6—Grace Thornton, d. 1934; m. Emory Adams.
4—Elizabeth Thornton, m. John Dickerson.
5—William H. Dickerson, b. Dec. 25, 1839; d. March 22, 1920; m. Susan Sewell.
6—Lula Dickerson, b. Nov. 3, 1870; m. Oct. 4, 1892, Thomas R. Maxwell, furniture merchant.
6—Mary Dickerson, b. June 27, 1872; m. 1890, Robert E. Lee.
6—Emma Dickerson, m. Herbert A. Taylor.
6—Weyman Dickerson, b. May 14, 1882; m. Nov. 23, 1906, Mary J. McNeill.

6—Elizabeth Dickerson, b. Sept. 15, 1873; m. March 1, 1893, C. D. Strickland.
6—Joseph Dickerson, b. Oct. 10, 1879; m. Oct. 28, 1914, Helen Rogers.
6—Myrtle Dickerson, b. June 19, 1884; m. Nov. 17, 1907, Bertram Maxwell.
4—Polly Thornton, m. Neal McMullan, Aug. 1, 1807.
4—Sarah Thornton, b. 1814; d. March 7, 1862; m. Aug. 25, 1828, Dr. John Green Higginbotham, b. March 1807; d. 1893.
5—Benjamin Higginbotham, b. July 6, 1830; d. Jan. 7, 1864; m. Frances Cook.
6—Mary J. Higginbotham.
6—Martha Higginbotham.
6—William Higginbotham.
6—John C. Higginbotham.
6—Thomas B. Higginbotham.
5—John Higginbotham.
5—Jane Higginbotham.
5—Mary Higginbotham.
5—Elijah Benjamin Higginbotham, C. S., b. Dec. 16, 1838; m. Dec. 7, 1859, Fannie Carter.
6—John Mat Higginbotham, m. Laura Eavenson.
6—Reuben Higginbotham, m. Georgia Ann Slaton.
7—T. B. Higginbotham.
7—James E. Higginbotham, m. Dec. 26, 1906, Maggie Cleveland.
6—Ada Higginbotham, m. Grogan Adams.
6—George Higginbotham, m. Jeanie Hansard.
6—Sarah Higginbotham, m. Earl Eavenson.
6—Alice Higginbotham.
6—Albert Higginbotham.
5—Dozier Higginbotham.
5—Pressley Higginbotham.
5—William Green Higginbotham.
5—Reuben Higginbotham, m. Maggie Slaton.
5—Jeptha Higginbotham, m. (1) Virginia Norman; (2) Lennie Harper.
3—Reuben Thornton, b. 1783; d. 1863; m. (1) Katherine Richardson; (2) Elizabeth Waters, b. 1790.
4—(By first wife) Walker Thornton, b. 1803.
4—Elizabeth Thornton, b. Aug. 4, 1809.
4—Martha Thornton, b. May 23, 1812.
4—Jeremiah Thornton, b. 1814; d. 1853.
4—Caroline Thornton, d. 1862.
4—Reuben Thornton Jr., b. 1825; d. 1911.
4—Robert Dozier Thornton, b. 1829; m. Eliza Seay (2nd wife).
4—Jonathan Thornton.
4—Catherine Thornton.
5—Elizabeth Thornton, m. Fletcher Comer.
5—Edward Thornton.
5—Carrie Thornton, m. Mr. Smith.
3—Dozier Thornton Jr., m. Elizabeth ―――――――.
3—Priscilla Thornton.
3—Evans Thornton, m. Mourning Adams, b. Oct. 23, 1817.
3—Martha Ann Thornton, b. 1789; d. 1860; m. 1803, Samuel Adams, b. Feb. 1, 1784; d. Nov. 6, 1861.
4—Charlotte Adams, m. Mr. Evans.
4—Sandford Adams.
4—Thompson Adams.
4—Elizabeth Jane Adams, m. (1) Aug. 1835, William W. Colson; (2) Williamson Rogers.

5—Elizabeth Jane Rogers, m. Charles T. Owen.
4—Merial Caroline Adams, b. July 4, 1826; d. Oct. 8, 1893; m. Dec. 31, 1845 (the widower of her elder sister, Elizabeth Jane) Williamson Rogers, b. July 15, 1817; d. 1882.
5—Reverend William Samuel Rogers, Baptist minister, b. Nov. 18, 1846; d. July 19, 1901; m. July 5, 1870, Mary Edna Gary, b. June 24, 1848; d. Aug. 4, 1931.
6—Alpha Rogers.
6—Z. B. Rogers, attorney, member Georgia House of Representatives, author Barrett-Rogers Bill, City Attorney of Elberton, County Attorney of Elbert County, Vice-President Georgia Bar Association, Chairman School Board of Elberton; m. (1) Lula Zachry; (2) Sarah Lee.
6—William S. Rogers, attorney, 33rd degree Mason, member Oklahoma Legislature; m. Ruth Young. No issue.
6—Daisy Rogers, m. Marshall Pierson.
6—Gary Rogers, m. Leila Fretwell.
6—Caroline Rogers.
6—Edna Rogers, Principal Stilwell Grammar School of Elberton.
6—Davis Rogers, d. infancy.
6—Marshall Rogers, d. infancy.
5—Martha Rogers, b. Dec. 7, 1848; m. A. M. Appleby, b. May 1841.
5—Robert Dozier Rogers, m. (1) Miss Ingram; (2) Lizzie Lowther.
5—Mary Ann Rogers, b. March 25, 1853; m. (1) G. K. Willis; (2) Thomas Bray.
5—Laura Adeline Rogers, m. (1) Thomas Ingram; (2) John A. Powell; (3) W. L. Ingram.
5—Thomas Williamson Rogers, b. July 10, 1857; m. Nannie Hailey.
5—Caroline Idella Rogers, b. Sept. 1, 1863; m. Nov. 20, 1883, Jacob W. Leazer, b. Jan. 20, 1862.
4—Jeremiah Adams, m. Miss Witherspoon.
4—Alfred Adams, m. Mary J. Lamb.
4—Marion Adams.
4—James Adams.
4—Eldridge Adams, m. Amanda Aldridge.
4—Joseph Adams, m. Mary Witherspoon.
4—Ann Adams, m. (1) Charles Smith; (2) John Logan.
3—Elizabeth Thornton, m. Reuben Maxwell, b. Nov. 4, 1795.
4—F. M. Maxwell.
4—Allen Maxwell.
4—William W. Maxwell.
4—Eugenia Maxwell.
4—Elizabeth Maxwell.
4—Susan Maxwell.
4—Jennie Maxwell.
4—Mary Maxwell.
3—Sandford Thornton.
3—Lucy Thornton, m. Oct. 14, 1823, Jeremiah S. Warren, Justice of the Inferior Court of Elbert County.
3—Jonathan Thornton, m. Martha ————.
4—Jeremiah Thornton.
4—Sanford Thornton.
4—George Thornton.
4—Mary Thornton.
3—Greene H. Thornton, b. 1796 in Kentucky; m. Rhoda ————, b, 1807 in Elbert County.
4—Euphemia Thornton, b. 1830.
4—Greene G. Thornton, b. 1836.
4—Blackstone R. Thornton, b. 1834.
4—Rhoda B. Thornton, b. 1840; m. (1) Edmund Cartledge, b. 1835; (2) Captain Cameron McKinnon.

WALL

The following chart shows intermarriages with the following families:
Adams — Alexander — Allen — Andrews — Asbury — Brawner — Carter — Carpenter — Cleveland — Douglas — Fortson — Frierson — Gaines — Geiger — Goodrich — Hammond — Henry — Kilpatrick — Mattox — Maxwell — McIntosh — Nunnelee — Oglesby — Pace — Parrott — Randall — Reynolds — Roan — Rucker — Sloan — Smith — Stelling — Stewart — Webb.

(Note: Numbers represent generations, as: (1) first generation, (2) second generation, (3) third generation, etc.)

1—Willis Wall, m. Nancy Pace, b. 1768; d. 1850, daughter of Barnard Pace.
  2—Martha Wall, d. unmarried.
  2—Cade Wall, d. unmarried.
  2—Budd Cade Wall, m. (1) Aug. 19, 1830, Martha W. Nunnelee; (2) Mrs. Gray nee Sloan.
    3—(By first wife) William D. Wall, d. unmarried.
    3—Elizabeth Wall, m. Captain William B. Henry, C. S.
      4—Charles Henry.
      4—Budd Henry.
      4—Sarah "Sally' Henry.
      4—Beverly Allen Henry, m. Tommie Oglesby.
        5—Louise Henry.
        5—Marguerite Henry.
      4—Fanny Henry.
      4—Lee Henry, m. Hallie Goodrich.
        5—Dr. C. G. Henry.
        5—Elizabeth Henry.
        5—Lucy Henry.
        5—W. B. Henry.
        5—Lee Henry Jr.
        5—Daughter Henry.
      4—Martha Henry, m. J. E. Asbury.
        5—Stewart Asbury, member City Council of Elberton, Mayor of Elberton, S. W. W., m. (1) Nora Carter; (2) Aileen Gaines.
          6—(By first wife) James Asbury.
          6—(By second wife) Gene Asbury.
        5—Maurice Asbury, m. Beth Allen.
          6—Allen Asbury.
        5—Sarah Frances Asbury, m. Mr. Geiger.
        5—Emm Asbury.
      4—Coralee Henry, m. J. E. Asbury, widower of elder sister.
    3—Louisa Wall, m. George G. Fortson.
      4—Wilton G. Fortson.
      4—Martha Wall Fortson.
      4—Lawrence B. Fortson.
      4—George Hailey Fortson.
      4—Louisa Elizabeth Fortson.
      4—Francis B. Fortson.
      4—Fannie M. Fortson.
      4—Sallie A. Fortson.
      4—Minnie Nunnelee Fortson.
    3—Mary Frances Wall, m. William Carpenter.
      4—Martha Carpenter.
      4—Willie Carpenter, m. L. A. Gaines.
        5—Raymond Gaines, m. Janie Mattox. No issue.

5—Helen Gaines, m. Armond Alexander.
5—Underwood Gaines.
5—L. A. Gaines Jr.
5—Rosa Gaines, m. Mr. Webb.
6—Rosemary Webb.
3—Sarah Wall, m. William Brawner.
4—Whitlock Brawner.
4—Budd Brawner.
4—Hugh Brawner, m. Catie Reynolds.
5—Walter Brawner.
5—Sarah Brawner.
3—Budd Clay Wall, C. S., m. Annie Cassandra McIntosh.
4—Martha Wall, m. Thomas B. Andrews. No issue.
4—James Wall, m. Rose Douglas. No issue.
4—Bevell Wall, m. Mary Stewart.
4—Jessie Wall, m. John D. Stelling.
4—Harry Wall, m. (1) Maryland Randall; (2) Hattie Smith.
3—James N. Wall, Methodist minister, member Georgia House of Representatives, School Commissioner of Elbert County; m. (1) Ella Fortson; (2) Mrs. Virginia Cleveland Gantt.
4—Elizabeth Wall, m. James Rucker.
4—William Wall, m. (1) Miss Parrott; (2) Mrs. Black.
4—James Wall.
4—Anna C. Wall.
4—George Wall, m. Leo Maxwell.
5—John Wall.
5—James Wall.
5—Mary Eleanor Wall.
4—Sarah Wall.
4—Longstreet Wall, m. Rebecca Frierson.
4—Lula Wall.
4—Janie Wall.
4—Harry Wall.
3—Annie Wall.
3—Laura Wall.
3—(By second wife) Thomas Wall, m. Georgia Hammond.
3—Mattie Wall, m. Dr. B. F. Smith.
4—Winnie May Smith.
4—Bert Moody Smith.
4—Mary Smith.
4—Frank Smith.
4—Bryant Smith.
4—Dorothy Smith.
3—Fanny Wall.
3—Edward Wall.
3—Florence Wall.
3—Daughter Wall.

WALTHALL

The following chart shows intermarriages with the following families: Abercrombie — Allen — Arnold — Allston — Andrews — Alexander — Archer — Adams — Bell — Barnett — Blackwell — Bates — Bynum — Brown — Cade — Comer — Cleveland — Cosner — Dean — Dickson — Douglas — Ethridge — Fisher — Gray — Gaines — Gates — Heard — Hill — Harris — Hawes — Hall — Hammond — Hearne — Helton — Hudson — Jones — Kilpatrick — Kennedy — Lee — Long — Linder — Mattox — Marburg — Mitchell — Moore — McCullough — McCalla — McIntosh — McCurry — Morris — Nichols — Porter — Purdue — Pressley — Quillian — Scarborough — Snellings — Seymour — Stephens — Speed — Sullivan — Stanford — Smith — Stelling — Stewart — Tinsley — Veronee — Wayble — Warren — Wansley — Williams — Wainwright — Wood — Whitmire.

(Note: Numbers represent generations, as: (1) first generation, (2) second generation, (3) third generation, etc.)

1—William Walthall, d. 1683; m. Ann Morris, d. 1695.
  2—Richard Walthall, d. 1715; m. Mary (?).
    3—Gerrard Walthall, m. Elizabeth (?).
      4—Gerrard Walthall Jr., m. Jane Gates of Virginia.
        5—Edward Walthall.
        5—John Walthall.
        5—Nancy Walthall, m. Captain William Allen, R. S., member Georgia House of Representatives.
          6—Singleton Walthall Allen, planter, member Georgia House of Representatives, Georgia State Senator; b. Jan. 14, 1791; d. June 6, 1853; m. Jane Lanier Heard, b. March 23, 1797.
            7—Elizabeth Allen, m. George Williams.
              8—Rebecca Williams, m. DuBose Hill.
                9—Janie Hill, m. Benjamin H. Hill.
                  10—Janie Hill.
              8—George Williams, C. S., d. unmarried.
              8—William Williams, m. Jessie Arnold.
                9—William McIntosh Williams.
              8—Janie Williams, m. John Burriss.
                9—Dilliard Burriss.
            7—Ann Allen, m. April 30, 1839, Dr. Milton Comer, M. D.
              8—Janie Comer, m. 1874, Captain Samuel Barnett, C. S., Judge County Court of Elbert County, b. Aug. 16, 1841; d. Nov. 26, 1898.
                9—Comer Barnett, Mayor of Washington, Georgia, b. May 11, 1878; m. June 19, 1901, Cornell Bounds, b. Feb. 14, 1880.
                  10—Lillis Barnett, b. March 25, 1911.
              8—Bevelle Comer, m. Dr. Hampton. No issue.
              8—Janie Comer, b. 1849; d. 1928, unmarried.
            7—Susan Allen, m. Young L. G. Harris, founder of Young Harris College, President of Southern Mutual Insurance Company, member Georgia House of Representatives, member Georgia Senate. No issue.
            7—Maria Louisa Allen, b. Aug. 10, 1824; d. 1885; m. Jan. 27, 1847, Colonel William McPherson McIntosh, b. Feb. 14, 1815; d. June 1862, C. S., Brevet Brigadier-General C. S. A. for gallantry in action, lawyer, planter, member Georgia House of Representatives 1847-1848, member Georgia Senate 1855-1856, elector State-at-Large for Breckenridge 1860.

8—Singleton Allen McIntosh, C. S., b. Feb. 19, 1845; d. Nov. 17, 1908; m. Feb. 1867, Mary Eliza Cade.
9—Sarah Howell McIntosh, b. Dec. 29, 1867; m. S. J. Zeigler.
10—Samuel Zeigler, S. W. W., U. S. Naval Officer; m. Fanny Marburg.
11—Howell Zeigler.
10—Howell Zeigler, m. George Dickson, Major in U. S. Army.
11—Howell Rees Dickson.
11—George Lee Dickson Jr.
9—William McPherson McIntosh, b. 1870; d. 1930, unmarried.
9—Guilford "Guy" McIntosh, b. July 6, 1873; m. Sept. 14, 1918, Addie Tinsley.
10—Mary McIntosh, b. Sept. 3, 1921.
10—William Kenneth McIntosh, b. 1922.
10—Louise McIntosh, b. Nov. 1923.
9—Victoria Augusta McIntosh, b. March 1875; m. Joseph Allston of South Carolina.
10—Joseph Allston Jr., m. Lillis McCullough.
11—Joseph Allston III.
10—Mary Allston.
9—Mary Louise McIntosh, b. Aug. 10, 1877; m. 1903, Henry M. Long.
10—Mary Louise Long, d. infancy.
8—William McPherson McIntosh Jr., C. S., b. Feb. 28, 1847; m. Helen Dean.
9—William McPherson McIntosh III, S. W. W.
8—Anna Cassandra McIntosh, b. March 5, 1849; m. Dec. 11, 1866, Budd Clay Wall, C. S., Mayor of North Augusta, South Carolina.
9—Martha Louise Wall, b. April 6, 1868; m. Thomas B. Andrews. No issue.
9—James Singleton Wall, b. Jan. 1, 1873; m. Rose Douglas. No issue.
9—Bevel William McIntosh Wall, b. June 30, 1875; m. Mary Stewart.
10—Margaret Wall.
10—Bevel Clay Wall, m. 1929, Virginia Alexander.
11—Bevel Charles Wall, b. July 22, 1930.
9—Jessie McIntosh Wall, b. December 20, 1878; m. 1899, John D. Stelling.
10—Sterling McIntosh Stelling, b. Feb. 14, 1900; m. Eula Mitchell.
10—Dr. Richard Stelling, M. D., b. May 14, 1901.
10—Martha McIntosh Stelling, b. Dec. 14, 1903; m. June 1930, Dr. Charles McCord Kilpatrick, M. D.
10—Howard Cree Stelling, b. Sept. 1906, Lieutenant, U. S. Air Corps; m. Helen Wainwright.
10—Budd Clay Wall Stelling, b. Feb. 1909.
9—Harry Wall, m. (1) Mary Randall; (2) Hattie Smith. No issue.
8—Maria Louise McIntosh, b. March 15, 1851; d. May 7, 1894; m. Feb. 2, 1869, Guilford Cade Jr.
9—Julia May Cade, b. Dec. 30, 1871; m. Nov. 23, 1892, Dr. Albert Sidney Hawes, M. D., member Georgia House of Representatives, Mayor of Elberton; b. Nov. 14, 1864; d. Nov. 1936.
10—Guilford Moseley Hawes, b. July 24, 1894; m. March 26, 1913, Onie Lee, of Cullman, Alabama, b. 1893.
11—Mary Lee Hawes, b. Sept. 14, 1917.
11—Robert Hawes, d. infancy.
11—Julia Ann Hawes, b. Feb. 27, 1925.
10—Albert Lee Hawes, b. Feb. 11, 1901; m. Bertha Bates. No issue.
10—Peyton Samuel Hawes, b. Sept. 4, 1903, member Georgia House of Representatives, City Attorney of Elberton, Solicitor City Court of Elberton; m. 1933, Virginia Smith.

9—Guilford Cade III, b. June 9, 1875; m. Dec. 4, 1904, Jane Kennedy.
10—Malvina "Mallie" Cade, b. Sept. 9, 1905; m. Milo Abercrombie; d. 1931.
11—Milo Abercrombie Jr., b. 1931.
10—Guilford Cade IV, b. April 18, 1911.
9—Annie Lee Cade, b. Feb. 21, 1878; m. Feb. 24, 1903, Dr. Robert Franklin Moore, b. Jan. 30, 1871; d. 1923.
10—Alan Moore, b. Nov. 25, 1905; d. 1933.
10—Frank Moore, d. infancy.
10—Guilford McIntosh Moore, b. Sept. 27, 1908; m. Miss Mauldin.
8—Mary Bevelle McIntosh, b. June 1856; d. June 1926; m. 1895, John Chandler Brown, b. 1857; d. 1917, merchant, planter, mayor of Elberton. No issue.
8—James McIntosh, b. Sept. 1, 1857, Sheriff of Elbert County, County Commissioner of Elbert County, member City Council of Elberton, member Tax Board of Elberton; m. Oct. 18, 1882, Mary Jane Arnold, b. Sept. 23, 1859.
9—Sarah Louise McIntosh, b. July 29, 1883; m. Feb. 24, 1903, A. F. Archer. No issue.
9—Jessie McIntosh, d. infancy.
9—William McIntosh, d. infancy.
9—Mary James McIntosh, d. infancy.
9—John Hawes McIntosh, S. W. W., b. Nov. 26, 1895, Historian of Elbert County, Assistant Secretary of Georgia Senate; m. June 19, 1918, Fay Ann White, b. Oct. 21, 1900. Divorced 1937.
10—Mary Louise McIntosh, b. July 16, 1920.
10—Elizabeth "Betty" Arnold Penn McIntosh, b. March 15, 1923.
9—McAlpin McIntosh, b. 1897; d. 1899.
8—Jessie McIntosh, b. 1859; m. Peyton M. Hawes, member Georgia House of Representatives, member Georgia Senate, trustee Georgia School for Deaf and Dumb, Militia Captain, President Elberton Loan and Savings Bank, President Elbert County Bank, planter. No issue.
7—Gerrard Allen, m. Oct. 31, 1850, Isabella Blackwell.
8—Gerrard Allen Jr., m. Adelaide Stanford.
9—Singleton W. Allen, m. May Wood.
10—Gerrard Allen, m. Sadie Ethridge.
9—Hattie Allen, m. Charles Whitmire.
10—Charles Whitmire Jr.
10—Harriet Whitmire.
10—Annie Bevelle Whitmire.
10—Martha Whitmire.
7—Mary Allen, m. Nov. 21, 1849, George W. McCalla.
8—Isaac McCalla, m. Raymond Speed.
9—Leila McCalla, m. Mr. Linder.
10—Alice Linder, m. J. P. Sullivan.
11—J. P. Sullivan Jr.
9—Mack McCalla, m. Ella Nichols.
10—Mack McCalla Jr.
10—Elmira McCalla.
9—John McCalla, m. Parnice Brown. No issue.
8—Jennie McCalla, m. Joseph Speed.
9—Florence Speed, m. A. A. McCurry, lawyer, member Georgia Senate.
10—Speed McCurry.
10—A. A. McCurry Jr.
10—Horace McCurry.
10—Althea McCurry.
10—Joseph McCurry.

8—John W. McCalla, planter, County Commissioner of Elbert County, merchant, m. Mitta Allen.
9—Annie McCalla, m. J. H. Purdue, lawyer of Birmingham, Ala.
10—Frances Purdue.
10—Mary Olivia Purdue.
10—J. H. Purdue Jr.
9—Olivia McCalla, m. Perry H. Smith, merchant, member City Council of Elberton.
10—Ethel Smith, m. Mr. LeConte.
9—J. Earl McCalla, m. Catherine Stephens.
10—John McCalla.
10—Catherine McCalla.
10—J. Earl McCalla Jr.
10—David McCalla.
8—Ida McCalla, m. (1) Frank Cleveland; (2) Bedford Heard.
9—Andrew B. Cleveland, m. Agnes Hall.
10—Frank Cleveland, m. Cleo Smith.
11—Agnes Cleveland.
10—Lanier Cleveland, m. Augustus Wansley.
11—Augusta Wansley Jr.
10—Elizabeth Cleveland, m. Frank Veronee.
10—Helen Cleveland.
10—McCalla Cleveland.
10—Andrew B. Cleveland Jr.
9—Jessie Cleveland, m. Jesse Warren.
10—Hilda Warren.
10—Jeremiah Warren.
9—M. E. Heard, m. Allen Pressley.
9—Sarah Heard, m. Frank Hammond.
10—Mildred Hammond.
10—Frank Hammond Jr.
9—Erskin Heard, m. Lottie Seymour.
10—Martha Heard.
10—Bedford Heard.
10—Emma Heard
10—Mattie Heard.
10—Hazel Heard.
9—Bevelle Heard, m. Thomas Wayble.
10—Thomas Wayble Jr.
9—Caroline Heard, m. Guy Quillian.
8—Susan McCalla, b. Sept. 19, 1861; d. Dec. 23, 1923; m. 1895, Willis B. Adams, b. May 13, 1861; d. Feb. 11, 1913, member Georgia House of Representatives, Mayor of Elberton, Militia Captain, Chairman Board of Education of Elberton, merchant, planter.
9—Willis Sue Adams, b. July 20, 1895; m. June 2, 1918, H. R. Bynum, S. W. W., b. Feb. 27, 1892.
10—Susan Margaret Bynum, b. May 9, 1919.
8—Mary "May" McCalla, m. George Gaines. No issue.
8—Dr. Lawrence "Larry" McCalla, M. D., m. Hettie Hearne.
9—Lawrence McCalla Jr., m. Mildred Cosner.
10—Lawrence McCalla III.
7—Theodore Allen, d. unmarried.
7—Rebecca Allen, m. William H. Mattox, C. S., Captain, Georgia State Senator, member Georgia House of Representatives, member Georgia Constitutional Convention of 1877.
8—Lena Mattox, m. Jeptha Jones.
9—Reba Jones, m. George W. Gray, merchant, member Elbert County Board of Registrars.
10—George W. Gray Jr.

  10—Page Gray.
  9—Allen Jones, m. Annie Lou Snellings. No issue.
  9—Henry P. Mattox Jones, m. Aug. 20, 1911, Mary Wall.
   10—Henry P. Mattox Jones Jr.
   10—Martha Jones.
   10—Rebecca Jones.
   10—Thomas Jones.
  9—Annie Sue Jones.
  9—Callie May Jones, b. 1891; m. April 19, 1909, Albert R. Hudson, b. 1878.
   10—Albert Hudson, b. 1910; m. Elizabeth Bell.
   10—Clark Hudson, b. 1912.
   10—Francis Hudson, b. 1915.
   10—Mack Hudson, b. 1917.
   10—David Hudson, b. 1919.
   10—Carroll Allen Hudson, b. 1922.
 8—Singleton Mattox, m. Annie Jones.
  9—Jessie Mattox.
 8—Clark McIntosh Mattox, m. Sarah Jones.
  9—Clark McIntosh Mattox Jr., b. Jan. 29, 1903; m. Dec. 23, 1925, Annie Bertha Helton.
  9—Jeptha Mattox, m. Louise Scarborough.
   10—John Clark Mattox.
   10—Jeptha Mattox Jr.
 8—Susan Mattox, d. unmarried.
 8—Annie Mattox, d. unmarried.
 8—Carroll Mattox, m. Charles Fisher.
  9—Mamie Fisher.
 8—Janie Mattox, m. Raymond Gaines, d. 1934. No issue.

WEBB

(Note: Numbers represent generations, as: (1) first generation, (2) second generation, (3) third generation, etc.)

1—John Webb, m. Peggy (?).
 2—Clairborn Webb, R. S., b. 1760; d. 1813; m. between 1782 and 1785, Margaret Deadwyler, b. 1765; d. 1833, daughter of Martin Deadwyler, who settled in North Carolina in 1750, having come from Germany.
  3—Bridger Webb, b. 1790.
  3—Margaret Webb, b. 1792; m. Joseph Glenn, son of Simeon Glenn.
  3—William Webb, b. 1794, d. unmarried.
  3—Clairborn Webb Jr., d. unmarried.
  3—Pleasant Webb.
  3—Milton Pope Webb, d. 1826; m. 1820, Letitia Deadwyler.
   4—Clairborn Webb.
   4—Ann Mildred Webb.
  3—Patsy Webb, m. Mr. Hainey.
  3—Abner Webb, m. 1824, Nancy Deadwyler.
  3—Alice Ann Martha Webb, m. Joseph P. Deadwyler, b. Aug. 7, 1816; d. Oct. 27, 1906.
   4—A. M. Deadwyler, m. Tommie Norman.
    5—Alma Deadwyler, m. Homer Vaughan.
    5—Janie Deadwyler, m. G. M. Neal.
     6—Doyle Neal.
     6—Norman Neal.
     6—Milton Neal.

6—Mary Lou Neal.
6—Jenelle Neal.
4—M. P. Deadwyler, m. Miney Fortson.
5—Lucy Mildred Deadwyler, m. Martin Brown.
5—Joseph Deadwyler.
4—Thomas Deadwyler.
4—D. C. Deadwyler.
4—Nancy Deadwyler, m. William Anderson.
4—Margaret Deadwyler.
4—John P. Deadwyler, d. unmarried.
3—Evelina Webb, m. 1820, Mial Smith.
3—Elijah W. Webb, b. 1808; d. July 9, 1885; m. Dec. 24, 1829, Ann B. Deadwyler, b. 1812; d. 1892, daughter of Martin Deadwyler and Rebecca Wilhite and granddaughter of Joseph Deadwyler and Alice Duncan.
4—Milton Pope Webb, C. S., b. Nov. 7, 1848; d. April 9, 1923; m. Jan. 17, 1871, Mary C. Moore, b. Oct. 10, 1850; d. Nov. 20, 1896.
5—Edward C. Webb, b. Oct. 18, 1874; m. Nov. 20, 1896, Rosa Lee Ayers, b. Aug. 15, 1879.
6—Ora Bell Webb, m. Lonnie King.
7—Martha Florence King.
7—Elizabeth King.
6—Jewette Webb, m. Clark Edwards Jr., S. W. W., Ordinary of Elbert County, President of Elberton Chamber of Commerce, lawyer, service officer of Edmund Brewer Tate Post No. 14, American Legion.
7—Dorothy Edwards.
7—Clark Edwards, d. infancy.
7—Charlotte Edwards.
7—Caroline Edwards.
6—Pauline Webb, m. Joseph B. Davis.
7—Loyce Davis.
6—Norma Webb.
6—Julia Webb.
6—Johnson Webb.
6—Mary Pope Webb.

WILHITE

The compiler has made exhaustive research in connection with this family but has been unable to prepare a comprehensive chart. The following data may be of some assistance to the investigator:

The German family Wilhoit, Wilheit, Wilhoyt, Wilhite, was closely associated with the Virginia Colony as early as the year 1717. On September 28, 1728, one Michael Wilhoit patented 289 acres. His name appears in church records of 1733. In his will, proved June 26, 1746, he mentions his wife, Mary; sons: Tobias, Adams, John, Matthais, and Phillip. One daughter is mentioned, Eva Hold.

Tobias Wilhoit married Catherine (?), and died 1762. Issue: Michael died 1804, married Mary (?), leaving the following children: Elizabeth, Spicer, Gabriel, James, Michael, Agnes Coginhill, Frances Lucas, Ann Hawkins, Sarah Green, and Mary.

Conrad Wilhoit, son of Tobias, married Elizabeth Broyles.

Jesse Wilhoit, son of Tobias, married Mildred (?) and had the following named children: Simeon, Evans, Allen, born 1789, died 1863; Zachariah, born 1791, died 1835, married Judith Clore; Larkin; Margaret, who married a Mr. Garriot, and Lucy who married Mr. Lacy.

William Wilhoit, son of Tobias, married Shirley (?) and had the following children: Ann, who married Mr. Barrickman; Frances, born 1782, died 1830, married Elijah Clore; Lucy, born 1783, died 1855, married a Mr. Clore; Bathsheba, married Mr. McGehee; Thomas, born 1795, died 1836; Dicey, who married Mr. Yowell; Judah married Mr. Harbold; Zachariah married Osnam Harbold; Jane who married Mr. Kennedy, and Nelly who married Mr. Pinnell.

Mary, daughter of Tobias, married Mr. Broile.

Adam Wilhoit, second son of Michael and Mary, married Catherine Broyles. Their children were: George, who married in 1804, Sally Harvey; John married (1) Miss Smith, (2) Elizabeth Blankenbaker; Michael, Elizabeth, and Mary, who married Mr. Carpenter.

John Wilhoit, third son of Michael and Mary, married Margaret Weaver. Issue: John Jr.; Margaret married Mr. Gaar; Elizabeth married Mr. Gantt; Mary married Mr. Yager; Nicholas; Daniel; Christian married Mr. Yager; Susan married Mr. Fisher.

John Wilhoit Jr. married Mary Fishback and had Moses and Samuel *Wilhite*.

Mathias Wilhite, fourth son of Michael and Mary, married (1) Mary (?); (2) in 1772, Hannah. The children of Mathias and Mary were: Lewis, who died in 1783; Tobias, a soldier of the Revolution, born 1750, died 1839, married Mary Shirley, b. 1755, died 1844, and had the following issue: Nathaniel, Abram, Judith, Rhoda, Ann, Nancy, Mary, Catherine, Lewis, Mason, Martha, Pressley, Lucy and Elizabeth.

Phillip Wilhite, youngest son of Michael and Mary, married 1754, Rachel (?). He came to Elbert County bringing with him the following children: John, Gabriel, Phillip Jr., Meshal, Thomas and Philemon.

John purchased land in Elbert County in 1797; Gabriel in 1800; Phillip in 1802; Meshal in 1809, and Philemon in 1823.

The estate of Phillip Jr. was appraised in Elbert County in 1817 and the record of the estate shows that he left minor children.

In all probability the Elbert County Wilhites are descendants of Phillip Wilhite Jr.

Michael Wilhite, Orange County, Virginia, m. Mary, will recorded, he lists John, Adams, Matthias, Tobias, Eva and Phillip, the youngest. The said Phillip Wilhite married Rachel (?), and immigrated to Franklin County, North Carolina (at that time known as Granville County, N. C.), about 1758-61. The first record of land grant dated 1761; Phillip died there in 1801 and left a large family. His will lists the following: William, Phillip, Lewis, Ambrose, Rhoda, Rachel, Polly, Patty, John, Gabriel, Nancy, Sally, Young. Of the children, William died early in North Carolina. Phillip immigrated to Elbert

County, Georgia, and died there in 1816 or 1817. Lewis also immigrated to Elbert County, Georgia, and died 1830 (grave marked). Ambrose died in North Carolina in 1824. John immigrated to Georgia but later to Madison County, and died there in 1840. (No record of Gabriel). Young also immigrated to Elbert County, Georgia, probably died there about 1836. Of the above record you will see that Phillip, Lewis (b. 1755), John and Young Wilhite immigrated to Elbert County, Georgia. Lewis Wilhite's family record by Gaar shows:

Lewis, son of Phillip and Rachel —— Wilhite, married Mary (Sally Colverd), immigrated to Elbert County, Georgia, about 1800-1810; Revolutionary Soldier, according to Knight, in Roster of Revolutionary Soldiers.

Reference: W. E. Wilhite, Bowie, Texas.

W. C. Barrickman, 3912 Avenue, Georgia, Austin, Texas.

See page 155, Reprint Land Lottery 1827 of Georgia, by Martha Houston—Lewis Wilhite, Rev. Sol., No. 207—11 Dis.—5th Sec.

See Edna Arnold Copeland (Genealogist), Elberton, Georgia.

WILLIS

(Note: Numbers represent generations, as: (1) first generation, (2) second generation, (3) third generation, etc.)

1—John Willis, b. Caroline County, Virginia, came to Elbert County, Georgia, after the Revolutionary War to take up his land grants. In 1878, he married Mildren Fortson, daughter of Captain Thomas Jefferson Fortson. Was a contractor; built the first Academy in Elbert County. He was sheriff of Elbert County in 1822. He was administrator of the estate of Thos. Fortson. Died in 1824. His will is recorded in the Ordinary's Office in Elbert County.

2—Thomas F. Willis, son of John Willis, born 1800; died in 1873. Married Millie T. Clark. He was Justice of Old Inferior Court Elbert County. He was sheriff and member of Legislature at one time. Was a charter member of Falling Creek Church.

3—William J. Willis, b. 1826; died in Atlanta Hospital, Oct. 1863. Was wounded at Chickamauga and started home; he got no further than Atlanta and was taken with lock-jaw. He was a member of Company C, 15th Georgia Regiment.

3—James A. Willis died Sept. 1861, in Richmond, Virginia, Hospital.

3—John T. Willis.

3—Mary Mildred Willis, m. David Hudson, 1846.

3—Sarah Elizabeth Willis.

3—Lucy Ellen Willis, d. 1883.

3—Thomas F. Willis, b. 1841.

3—Richard M. Willis, b. April 22, 1843; d. May 25, 1900.

3—Richard Madison Willis was born near Indian Hill in Elbert County, Georgia, April 22, 1843. His father and mother, Thomas F. and Mildred Clark Willis, belonged to the best families of this section of the state. Soon after reaching his 16th birthday, he volunteered for service in the Confederate Army, leaving with the first companies on the 15th of July, 1861. He was a member of Company C, 15th Georgia Regiment, Benning's Brigade, Hood's Division, Longstreet's Corps. He was wounded at Malvern Hill by grapeshot, in the week's fighting around Richmond in 1862. He suffered greatly from this wound, but rejoined his comrades in arms as soon as the authorities would permit. Two years later he was wounded again in the fighting on North Anna River in Virginia, and lost a leg as a result of this wound.

Returning to his native home he faced the responsibilities of peaceful pursuits with the same determination and courage that had characterized his career as a soldier. He efficiently served his family and friends and neighbors and his county as Clerk of the Superior and City Courts for twenty years with modesty, honesty, efficiency and self-sacrificing fidelity, until summoned on May 25, 1900, to come up higher and bivouac with the dead "on fame's eternal camping ground." Some 15 years before the summons came, he united with the First Methodist Church of Elberton, and lived a consistent Christian life, and died as he had lived, in the service of Elbert County. The funeral services were conducted at the home by Revs. Sam R. Belk and H. W. Williams, pastors of the First Methodist and First Baptist churches of Elberton, and his body was laid to rest in Elmhurst Cemetery, with such worthy citizens as H. J. Brewer, James McIntosh, P. P. Proffitt, W. D. Tutt, McAlpin Arnold, and Abda Oglesby as active pallbearers.

On December 9, 1868, Richard Madison Willis was married to Lucy Glenn Broach. To this union were born ten children, seven daughters and three sons: 4—Minnie, 4—Mamie, 4—Julia, 4—Rosa, 4—Lucy, 4—Albert, 4—Ernest, 4—Charles, 4—Elizabeth, 4—Willie, and 4—Ethel.

4—Julia married J. Early Thornton. Unto them was born: 5—Harry G. Thornton. Harry married Hughie Allen, and to them were born 6—Harry Allen, and 6—Earl.

4—Rosa married James F. Reeves. Their children are: 5—Katherine, 5—Marion, 5—Mildred, 5—Mamie, 5—Ralph, and 5—Virginia.

5—Katherine Reeves married R. Hampton Johnson, and to them were born 6—R. H. Johnson Jr., 6—Katherine, and 6—Violet.

5—Marion Reeves married Dr. Fred M. Patterson, Greensboro, North Carolina.

5—Mildred Reeves married William T. Johnson Jr., Washington, Georgia. They have two sons, 6—William and 6—James.

5—Mamie Reeves married Charles Hardy Jr., Washington, Georgia. They have two daughters, 6—Rosemary and 6—Mildred.

5—Ralph Reeves married Mary Seymour. They have a daughter, 6—Mary Patricia.

5—Virginia Reeves married Larton P. Rampey. They have one daughter, 6—Virginia.

5—Katherine Johnson married Robert L. Drennan.

4—Lucy Willis married George Ligon O'Kelley. They have four children, two sons and two daughters: 5—Miriam, 5—Elizabeth, 5—Ligon Jr., and 5—Willis.

5—Miriam O'Kelley married Harold Fleeman.

5—Willis O'Kelley married Janie Telford.

4—Ethel Willis married Weyman Mashburn. One son, 5—Charles Willis Mashburn, was born to them.

5—Charles Mashburn married Maude Hammond, and a daughter, 6—Lucy Ethel was born to them.

WOOLRIDGE

William Woolridge, of Elbert County, was the son of John Woolridge of Chesterfield County, Virginia. He is mentioned in his father's will.

John Woolridge took up a land grant in Henrico County, Virginia, in the year 1725. He is the ancestor of the family of Virginia. His brothers were Thomas, Edward and William, who lived in Goochland County, Virginia.

William Woolridge was in Virginia as early as 1622. He served as an officer in several of the Colonial Wars.

The earliest records of the Woolridge family are found in Chestershire, England, where William of that name was living in the reign of Edward the Confessor.

This is an amorail bearing family and the names William, John, Thomas, and Edward have been used by successive generations from the founding to the present date.

William Woolridge, Sr., the father of Gibson Woolridge, came to Surrey County, North Carolina, from Chesterfield County, Virginia, in 1773 as deeds of record in the former county show. He served as a member of the grand jury of Surrey County as shown in Book 1775-1778, Index of Colonial and State Records, Vol. XXX, page 424. William Woolridge was appointed Captain of his district in 1778 and retained this position until his removal to Georgia. This William married Sarah Flournoy, a Hugenot, who came to Virginia in 1700.

Edmund Woolridge, a brother of William, Sr., married Mary Flourney, also a daughter of Francis.

The children of William Woolridge, Sr., were: Richard, William, Gibson, Thomas, Edward, Sarah, and Martha.

William Woolridge, Sr., was accompanied to Elbert County by his son, Gibson, and a son-in-law by the name of Hudspeth. They arrived in Georgia in the winter of 1783, as deed records in Book C-P 103 in office of Clerk of the Superior Court of Elbert County shows.

Gibson Woolridge served as Justice of the Peace in Surrey County, North Carolina, during 1782 and in the same capacity in Wilkes County, Georgia, in 1786 and 1794. He was a delegate to the Constitutional Convention of Georgia, held in 1798 from Lincoln County.

Gibson Woolridge married in 1775 Lucy Elizabeth Hudspeth, the daughter of Ralph Hudspeth.

The children of Major Gibson Woolridge were:

John Woolridge, Lieutenant-Colonel, Lincoln County, Georgia, Militia, 1797. He was born 1776 and died in Abbeville County, South Carolina, in 1817. He was the father of one son, William, and six daughters.

Thomas Woolridge, born 1778. In 1827 was in Pickens County, Alabama. Died in Texas.

Elizabeth Woolridge, born 1786; married Samuel Linton Jr., of Abbeville County, South Carolina.

Lucy Woolridge married Mr. Hudson, of Elbert County, Georgia.

Sarah Flourney Woolridge, born June 12, 1788, married Hudson M. Pitman in 1815, and had the following children: Susan, Mary, Rebecca, Fotunatus, Nancy Eliza and John B.

Robert Woolridge married (1) Elizabeth Kellum; (2) Susannah Ball.

Mary Ann Woolridge married Benjamin Murray, of Lincoln County, Georgia, and have many descendants.

Sarah Flourney Woolridge, daughter of William Woolridge, married David Hudspeth in Surrey County, North Carolina.

William Woolridge, second son of William and Sarah Flourney Woolridge, remained in North Carolina and was appointed to the staff of Robert Williams when he was Commissioner Governor of the Mississippi Territory. His son, John, was a Captain in the Mexican War.

Edward Woolridge, youngest son of William and Sarah Flourney Woolridge, remained in North Carolina and his name is found in the Census of 1790.

Thomas F. Woolridge, son of William and Sarah, married Cheriah Davis, a daughter of Absolom Davis, of Elbert County, Georgia.

WORLEY

The following chart shows intermarriages with the following families:
Arnold — Andrews — Auld — Ansel — Fosch — Greer — Gaines — Garrett — Hayney — Headley — Hall — Haslett — Harper — Holzapple — Jackson — Kimbrough — Keaton — Lovern — McDonald — McGinty — Mitcham — Matthews — Moore — Nall — Nelms — O'Kelly — Palmer — Pate — Peppers — Rice — Sheppard — Stewart — Stephenson — Thrasher — Williams

(Note: Numbers represent generations, as: (1) first generation, (2) second generation, (3) third generation, etc.)

1—Nathan Worley, m. Miss Moore.
   2—Joseph Worley, m. Miss Gaines.
      3—Rev. Ambrose G. Worley, Presiding Elder and Methodist minister, m. Elizabeth Baker Worley, daughter of Nathan Worley Jr. and Susan Holzapple, and granddaughter of Nathan Worley Sr. and Miss Moore.
         4—Joseph N. Worley, twice Judge of Superior Court of the Northern Circuit of Georgia, County Commissioner of Elbert County, City Attorney of Elberton, member Georgia House of Representatives, Chairman Elbert County Democratic Executive Committee, b. March 25, 1854; m. (1) Sarah Arnold, d. May 17, 1894; (2) Lucy Tibbs nee Jackson; (3) Addie Mixon nee Harper.
            5—(By first wife) Arnold Worley, lawyer, b. Nov. 11, 1880; m. (1) Edith Williams; (2) Miss Peppers.
               6—(By first wife) Nellie Worley.

5—Elizabeth Worley, m. Oct. 26, 1903, Arthur McGinty, b. Oct. 11, 1880; d. 1935.
6—Joseph McGinty, lawyer, b. July 14, 1904; m. Jean Greer.
7—Joseph McGinty Jr.
6—Luther McGinty, b. April 11, 1906.
5—Carter Worley, b. Oct. 12, 1883; m. Minnie Andrews.
6—Carter Worley Jr.
5—(By second wife) John Worley, d. unmarried.
4—Dr. Samuel G. Worley, M. D., m. Mary Pate.
5—Gaines Worley, m. Gertrude Ansel.
6—Ansel Worley.
5—John Worley, m. Eva Garrett.
6—Mary Worley.
5—Claud Worley.
5—Samuel G. Worley Jr., m. Lizzie Bell Pressley.
4—Susan Maria Worley, m. George Haslett, Tax Collector of Elbert County.
5—Eugenia Haslett, m. James C. Thrasher.
6—Haslett Thrasher.
6—Aseneth Thrasher.
6—Susan Thrasher.
5—William M. Haslett, d. unmarried.
5—Elizabeth "Bessie" Haslett, m. Oct. 14, 1908, James Newton Rice.
6—Frances Rice.
6—Elizabeth "Liddie" Rice.
5—Pauline Haslett, County Demonstration Agent of Columbia County, Georgia.
5—Worley Haslett, m. Eleanor Keaton.
6—Mary Eleanor Haslett.
5—Julia Haslett.
5—Sarah Haslett.
4—William L. Worley, m. Ella Nelms, d. 1936.
5—J. Ambrose Worley, m. Anna (?).
6—Katrina Worley.
6—Herman Worley.
5—Myra Worley, m. Mr. Stephenson.
5—Gaines Worley, m. June 28, 1908, Bessie Palmer.
5—Elbert Worley.
5—Dunnie Worley, m. Oct. 6, 1907, Lora Hall.
5—Laura Worley, m. Mr. O'Kelly.
5—Lonnie Worley, m. Miss Lovern.
4—Elizabeth Worley, m. (1) Mr. Nall; (2) Mr. Mitcham.
5—Worley Nall, lawyer, Mayor of Elberton, Judge of City Court
6—Elizabeth Matthews.
of Elberton, m. Jennie Rae Auld.
6—Jennie Rae Nall.
5—Janie Nall, m. Mr. Matthews.
5—Frank Nall.
5—Samuel Nall.
5—Sarah Nall.
4—George Worley, lawyer, m. Kate Headley.
5—May Worley, m. Mr. Sheppard.
5—Christine Worley.
5—Gladys Worley.
5—George Worley Jr., lawyer.
5—Buster Worley.
5—Katrina Worley.
4—Kate Worley, m. Edward E. Kimbrough.
5—Elizabeth Kimbrough, m. Mr. Fosch.

5—Edward E. Kimbrough Jr.
3—Kate Worley, m. Mr. Hayney.
3—Maria Worley, m. Mr. Stewart.
3—Mary Worley, m. Mr. McDonald.
3—William Worley.
2—Nathan Worley, m. Susan Holzapple.
3—Elizabeth Worley, m. Rev. Ambrose G. Worley.
4—Joseph N. Worley, m. Sarah Arnold.
4—Dr. Samuel G. Worley, m. Mary Pate.
4—Susan Maria Worley, m. George Haslett.
4—William L. Worley, m. Ella Nelms.
4—Elizabeth Worley, m. (1) Mr. Nall; (2) Mr. Mitcham.
4—George Worley, m. Kate Headley.
4—Kate Worley, m. Edward E. Kimbrough.

WYCHE

(Note: Numbers represent generations, as: (1) first generation, (2) second generation, (3) third generation, etc.)

1—Henry Wyche came from England to America in 1650.
    2—James Wyche.
    2—Henry Wyche.
    2—William Wyche.
    2—George Wyche.
    3—George Wyche Jr.
    3—Benjamin Wyche.
    3—Peter Wyche.
    4—George Wyche III.
    4—Henry Wyche.
    5—Peter Wyche.
    5—George Wyche, R. S.
    6—James Wyche.
    6—Joshua Wyche.
    6—George Wyche, b. 1811.
    7—Columbus Wyche.
    7—George Wyche.
    7—Albert Wyche.
    7—James Wyche.
    8—George Wyche.
    8—Alvin Wyche.
    7—Madison Wyche.
    8—Baker Wyche.
    8—George Wyche.
    8—Harry Wyche.
    7—Edward Wyche.
    8—Homer Wyche.
    8—Edward Wyche Jr.
    8—Albert Wyche.
    7—John Wyche.
    7—David Wyche.
    7—Christopher Wyche.

Only the male descendants of this line are shown due to inability to secure additional data.

NAME INDEX

The Elbert County Historical Society, Inc. started this project several years ago and their work was expanded and edited for this new publication. Note that the following pages are **not** included in the index:

- p. 183-202 - land warrants, Revolutionary soldiers, CSA units, 1812 soldiers
- p. 205 J P's
- p. 226-297 marriage records

Linda Aaron

ABBIT
William 73
ABBOT
William 74
ABERCROMBIE
J.S. 85
Milo 339, 381, 414
452, 512, 527, 544
-----Jr 381, 414
452, 512, 527, 544
ABERNATHEE
Jno 180
ABNEY
Eleanor 53
Martin J. 404
Mr. 380. 434
Wiley 53
ACKERMAN
Amos T. 76, 124, 125, 126, 128 176
ACKERS
Ruth 331
ADAIR
Ruby 506
S.B. 133, 536
ADAMAS
W.B. 173
ADAMS
A.L. 142
Abner 327
Addie 328, 329, 382, 403
Adeline 323
Aetna 328
Alfred 539
Alfred N. 324
Alfred M. 327
Alice 328
Alice Lucile 521
Alice L. 325
Alvin Wesley 495
Ambus 328
Andrew 466
Ann 67, 539
Ann Banks 497
Ann R. 322
Ann T. 327
Annie 328
Arthur 328
Augustus 328

Barbara 354
Bessie 141, 328
Beuna 327
Beverly 322, 333
Bud 327, 403
Burnice vii
Calvin M. 223, 327
Carl Turner 156
Charles Emory 155
Charles Thurmond 495
Charlotte 324, 538
Clark 360, 368
Clarence D. 156
Claud 328
Clyde Thomas 495
Corrie 329
Crunly 441
David 47, 100, 180, 209, 211
Delray 141, 162, 328
Dewitte 506
Dilliard 112
Drucilla 322, 333, 470
E.L. 157, 327, 403
Early 134
Effie G. 325, 328
Elbert 323
Eldo Haynes 328
Eldredge 324
Eliza Jane 324
Elizabeth 67, 327, 394, 403
---Jane 538
Elmer 328
E. Lucas 170, 174
Emma 327, 329, 427
Emily 322, 333, 470 536
Emory 407, 537
Ernest 327
Eunice 354
F.C. ,Mrs 67
F .L. 162. 168
Family of 101
Fannie {Mrs} 309
Fanny 328
Fleming 323
Flora 505
Floyd 354
--- Jr 354
Fortson 327, 382

Frances 536
Freeman 360, 369, 533
Gaines Howell 495
Genobe 328, 331
George.141, 221
Georgia Madora 495
Gertrude 327, 328
Grogan 538
H.A. 150, 168, 175
H.M. 438
Harper Wesley 154
Harriett F. 322, 531
Harvey 154
Henry J. 328
Hiram 354
Horace 354
Houston 329
Howell Parker 495
Hubert T 495
Ida 328, 403
J.B. 176
J.J. 174
James 180, 209, 211, 317, 322, 324, 328, 329, 539
--- Sr 223
James B. 327
James E. 327
Jane 324, 323, 470
Janie 506
---Sue 495
Jeremiah 324, 539
Jesse 505
Joe 324
John 328
---- C. 327
---- D. 177, 329
John Lewbannon 354
Joseph 539
Judith 392, 394
Julia Ann 329
Katherine 323
L.G. 406
Laura 328, 329
Laura May 328
Lawrence 322, 333 470
Lawrence M. 223
Lee 329
Leila 327

Lela {Mrs} 438
Lenora 329
Lewis 360, 369
Lillian 354
Lizzie 328, 438, 533
Lou 328
Louis Paul 154
Louise C. 322
Lucy 323, 534
Lucy Jane 337
Lula 328, 329, 536
M.B. 135
M.F. 169, 173
Mabel 505
Madison 323
Mamie 327, 329, 403
Marcus 328
Margaret 323, 375
Marion 539
Marshall 208, 360, 369
Mary 329
Maud 328
May 327
McDowell W. 151
Merial Cardine 324
------Caroline 539
Milford 442
Milliard F. 329
Milly L. 329
Milton Barett 505
Minnie 328
Mitta 328
Mittie 327, 329, 406
Moses H. 322
Mourning 327, 538
Mr. 333, 436, 469
Murray 360, 369
Nancy 53, 67, 328
Neil Wade 495
Newton 328
Nicholas N 223, 472
Onie 328
Ora A 495
Osburn 322
Oscar 328
Peter 328
Priscilla 369
R. C. 135
R. E. 170, 173, 403, 438
Raymond 360, 368

Reese 328, 403
Richard 327, 329, 360, 369
Richard C 101
-----E 167
---- P 308
Ritta 67
Rhoda 322
Robert 224, 322, 354, 394
Robert Carroll 417, 455, 514
Roxie 536
Royal 328
S J 144
Sally 328, 329
Samuel 13, 67, 324 360, 369, 538
Sanford 324, 538
Serepta A 322
Sheriff 124
Solomon 224
Susan McCalla, Mrs. 139
Stella 328
The Family 98, 101
T R 173
Thomas 223, 317, 327, 328, 329, 323
----F 327
----J 328
----L 328
Thompson 324, 538
Tinsley R 177
Tressie 354
Valdis 328
Viola 329
W B 172, 173, 206
----Mrs 139
W E 417, 455, 514
W H H 169
W J 145
W W 206, 360, 368
Walter 329
Wesley 328
Will, Mrs 138
William 223, 322, 327 328, 535
----D 167
----H 167, 168
----H H 327, 337
----R 322, 332, 469

Willis 133
----B 144, 327, 341 403, 416, 454, 485 545
----Sue 328, 341, 403 416, 454, 545
Winton 434
Wylie W 154
ADDERHOLD
David W 156
ADDISON
W P 141
ADDY Orlanda 502
ADKINSON
Joyce 460
AGEE, Clarence 354
AGNEW Linton 534
AHART Susan 459
AIKEN[S]/AKIN
Johnson 223
Mary 412, 450, 482
Miss 450
Thomas 48, 73, 412 450, 482
William 73, 181
ALBRIGHT
Emma 475
ALEXANDER
A 49
Anne 53
Armand 382, 541
Cicero 404
Cleveland 407
Clifton L 151
D B 122, 169
Dun 133
Elam 222
Elizabeth 53, 203, 328
Family 101
Frank 407
George 47, 65
----C 225
Harvey 407
Henry 141
Hugh 407
----H 152
Isaac 224
J B 407
James 67
John 407

Joseph 407
Judy 67
L H 121
Louise 407
Lucy 326
Mary 53, 138, 141,
   225, 405
Nancy 53
Peter 101, 103
Peter W 98, 203
Polly 65
Robert 53, 407
Sarah L 53
Thomas A 404
Virginia 338, 414, 451
   483, 512, 543
William 53, 226, 407
Willis 223
Worley 154

ALFORD
Addie 533
Bear 134
Benjamin 403-04
---C 533
Clio 533
D C 333, 469, 533
Elmer Guy 404
Geo 147
Mack 533
Mary 447
Montine 533
Posey 447
Sarah L 404

ALLDREDGE
Amanda 324, 539

ALLEN/ALEN
Alfred H 471
Allen 454
Ann 63, 337, 413, 450
   482, 542
Annie 454
B P 85, 92
Benjamin 18, 61
Beth 485, 506, 540
Beverly 34, 70-2, 74,
   99, 167-8, 172-2,
   337, 458
----nephew of 82-3
C S, Mrs 162
Charles 485
Charles H 350, 389

   506
-----Harrison 485
----- Jr 506
-----Seymour 389
-------Jr 389, 485
----- III 506
Cleve 6
Dora 350
Drucilla 64, 332,
   469
Edward 35, 350
Edmond 225
Eliza 350
Elizabeth 181, 332,
   337, 413, 450, 482
   529, 542
Eugene 350
Eunice 323, 501
Family 40, 42, 329
Fred Walton 151
George 41, 413, 450
   482
Geo P 143
Gerrard 339, 360, 368
   416, 454, 485, 360,
   368, 416, 454, 544
Gerrard Jr 339, 544
Gerrard W 103
Gladys 389, 485, 506
   535
Grace 324, 436
Hattie 139, 339, 360
   368, 416, 454, 544
Hudson 529
Hughie 389, 485, 550
Huie 506, 534
J P B 142
Jane Heard 41, 67
----------Mrs 122, 126
J Cleve 306-07, 312,
   313
Joe 17, 160, 208, 303
   309, 313
Joseph 63
Louis Eugene 151
Major 7
Maria Louisa 41, 337,
   413, 451, 482, 511
   542
Marion 521
Martha 330
Mary 340, 350, 415

   453, 484, 544
May Noami 501
Mitta 340, 415, 453
   484, 545
Mr 73
N 63
Nathaniel 69, 181
   210, 529
Rebecca 341, 416,
   454, 485, 545
Sarah Elizabeth 389
Singleton 103, 339
_____W 53, 167-8
   205, 209, 360, 368
   416, 454, 544
Singleton Walthall 41,
   71, 104, 337, 413,
   450, 482, 542
Susan 126, 338, 413,
   451, 482, 542
Theodore 41, 341,
   413, 450, 482, 545
Thomas 220, 223, 341
Valeria 373, 382, 387,
   389, 485, 506
W C, Mrs. 161-2
W H 307
William 16, 34, 39,
   47-9, 71, 74, 166,
   178-90, 330, 337,
   350, 542
William, Capt 87, 100
W Singleton 53
Zelma 138, 389, 485
   506

ALLGOOD/
ALGOOD
Betty 332
Family 342,
John 221, 344
John Y 343
____ Young 342
Lindsay 344
Mr 35
Mary 221
---- W 342
Nancy 342
Nathan 342
Peter 221
----Patrick 342
Rebecca 342
Sarah 342

----Ann 344
Spencer 221
William 221, 342, 343
   344
---- Jr 87, 342, 344-5
---- Sr 87, 343, 344

ALMAND/ ALLMAND/ ALLMAN
Isaac 87
Sarah 221
Usry 221

ALMOND
Alice 405
Angeline 536
Ann 53
Ada 311
B T 406
Benjamin 536
C J, Mrs 163, 315
  316
Caron 208
Dorcas 534
Elizabeth 53
Emma 536
Eugenia 537
Fanny 353, 536
G L 169
G L A 145
Geo Milton 156
Gholston Long 155
Harriet 323, 497
Irene 501
Isaac 54, 172
James 53
John 54
John B 134
J A 206, 207
J L 74
J P 73
Louisa 406
Lucinda 322
M J 53
Mary Ann 406
----Frances 489
Micajah 406
R H 405
----Jr 405
Robert E 136
Sarah 407
Susie 405,

Thomas F 465
---J 208
Virginia 405
Weston C 208
William 536
William M 54, 172

ALSON
Nathaniel 180

ALSTON/ ALLSTON
Absolom 349
Ann 346, 347,
  349
Alfred 349, 348-9
Amerylis 346
Ann 348
---D 348
Angelica 346
Annie L 348
Arabella 346
Augustus 346
Benjamin 346
Bessie 348
Blake 348
Capt 222
Caroline 346
Charity 43, 263, 348
  349, 351, 363
Charles 346
Christian 43, 349
Cornelia 348
Daniel 346
Dolly 346
Dorothy 346
Drew 347
Edgar 346
Elizabeth 43, 346, 347
  348, 349
Emily 348
Emma 348
Esther 346
Family 42, 43, 345,
  352
Fanny 347
Florida 347
Francis 346
George 43, 349
Gideon 346, 348
Gilley 222
Gov 383
Hannah 361, 351, 361

Henrietta 346
Henry 347-349
Hugh 345
James 43, 61, 65, 80
  167, 176, 347, 348
  3349, 351
James Sr 180
James W 347
Jane 347
Jesse 346
John 345, 346, 347-
  349, 351
---A 347
---Jr 346, 349
---Wilcox 347
Joseph 338, 346, 380,
  413, 451, 483, 511,
  526, 543
----J 347-8
----Jr 338, 348, 380,
  413, 451, 483, 526
  543
----III 338, 380, 413,
  451, 483, 511, 527
  543
Joseph John 346
Kemp 346
Laura 348
Lemuel 348-9
---T 348
------Jr 348
Leonidas 346
Lucretia 349
Margaret 347-8
Martha 347-349,
  351
Matilda 346
Mary 43, 338, 347-
  349, 380, 383,
  398, 413, 451, 483
  511, 527, 543
Mary Ann 346
Miriam 346
Missouri 346
Nancy 43, 346, 349
  351
Nathaniel 348, 351
Philip 347- 349
----H 43, 349
----III 347
Philoclea 346
Priscilla 347

Rachel 349
Rebecca 347
Robert 346, 349
Robert W 346
Sallie 351
Sally 43, 348-9
Samuel 347, 352
Sarah 346, 348-9, 351
Solomon 43, 349
----Jr 349
Temperance 346
Theodosia 383
Thomas 346, 347-9
William 34, 42, 43, 186, 263, 317, 345 346-9, 351, 398
William A 348-9
----D 348
----H 349
----Hinton 43
Willis 346-8
Winifred 349

AMBROSE 2, 64, 65

AMIS
W S 365, 462, 466

AMOS
J W 406
Mary Gay 406

AMY, 65, 103

ANDERSON
Albert 436
Ann 221
Billy 133
Company 378
E T 536
Edna 536
Elizabeth 54, 536
Ella 140
Eppy 536
Hannah 394
J E 173
J L 121
J T B 93, 133, 145
Joseph 169
----P 156
Mallory 536
Margaret 536
Mary 393, 536
Minnie Fortson, Mrs

viii, 140
Peggy 61
Rebecca 404
Sanford G 153
Thankful 407
Thomas 226, 393
--- L 153
W A 142
Walton L 153
W F 145
W Frank 154
W G 121
William 537, 547
William N 151

ANDREW
James A 92
---- O 177
----Osgood 70, 77-9
John 180, 181
Mrs. 78

ANDREWS
A B 157
Benjamin 24
Charles 140
Dorsey 154
J S 206
James A 168
Minnie 356, 531, 553
Nora B 464
Rev Mr 453
Thomas 338, 483
Thomas B 413, 451, 512, 541, 543

ANNARD
Catherine, 510

ANNIE, Miss 129

ANSEL Gertrude 553

ANTHONY
Agnes 393
Bolling 394
Charles 35, 393
Edward 393
Elizabeth 392-3
Henrietta 352
Henry 393
Henry 393
James 352, 393-4,
---Jr 393
Jospeh Jr 393
-----Sr 392-3
Judith 394

Lucile 523
Margaret 97
Mark L 40, 394
Mary 352-3
Micajah 393
Milton 393
Nancy Tate 393
Penelope 393
Rachel 393
Sarah 392-3
Whitmel 352
-----Hill 352
Winifred 394

APPLEBY, A M 539

ARCHER
A F 142, 339, 414 484, 512, 531, 544
---, Mrs 137-8, 162
Arthur F 357, 452
Louise McIntosh 140

ARCHIBALD....92

ARMAND
Joseph T 120

ARNET, Ruth 366

ARNOLD ...181
Adeline 359
Adeline Ann 54, 353
---Eloid 357
Alice Elizabeth 358
Ann 511
Ann Elizzie 359
Annie Lou 358
Beth 357
Boyd 359
Brother 58, 60
C A 162, 207
---, Mrs v
Carter A 160, 161, 304
---, Mrs 162, 315, 316
--- Alston 350, 356, 530
Catherine 357
Charles Wesley 363
Clyde 537
Dave 133
D B Calloway 359
Davis 54, 353, 359
Edna 138, 318, 350 356, 530

Edwin Davis J 358
Elizabeth 355, 530
---- McClain Wilhite
  54, 359
Ethel 423
Eva Jessie 358
Family 352-3
Frances 376, 534
George Clifton 357
  531
Georgia 356, 531
----Savannah 358
Helen Alvera 358
Hugh 134
J Y 305
James 59, 64, 357,
  386, 526, 531
----Jr 357, 373, 386
  526
---- Olin 358
---- Y 312, 373
Jane 63
Jessie 337, 413, 450
  482, 511, 542
---E 359
Joe 359
John 222, 353
---Boyd 359
Joseph 531
Joseph Y 93, 355, 414
  452, 530
---, Mrs 93
Julius 350, 530
---B D 355, 530
--- Y 356
Laura McClain 357
Lofton 357, 531
Mary Ann 350, 356
---- Emma 359
----Hill, Mrs v
----Jane 339, 357, 414
  452, 484, 512, 531,
  544
Mattie Maud 358
May Lavonia 358
Mc 359
McAlpin 133, 143,
  148, 206-7, 350,
  355, 530, 550
---A 127, 167, 176
---Hill 350, 356
Medicus 359

---Franklin 357
Miss 363, 417, 455
  485
Mr 16, 35, 397
Noel Webb 358
Olera 358
Polly 63
Quince L 136
Richard 353
Roger 352
Sallie Evelyn 359
Sally 64
Saluda 356, 530
Samuel Franklin 359
Sarah, 133, 356, 530
  552, 554
-----Louise 350, 355
  530
Sebrel 359
Solomon 353
Susan 52
Susannah 181
Thomas 353
Usilla Lee 359
W T 132, 206-07
Wesley P 91, 511
William 58-9, 65-6,
  179, 181, 222-3,
  353, 363
William, Brother 61-3
--- H 328
---Herman 357, 531
---Jr 52, 63, 65
---McPherson 511
---T 312, 357, 531
Willie Aufaula 359
Zorah Frances 358
ASBURY
Allen 389, 540
Beverly 486
Beverly Allen 506
Bishop 69
Ed 389, 506
Emm 540
Frank 412
---Jr 412, 450
---III 450
Frank 540
J C 141
J F 143, 146, 160
  540
---, Mrs. 163, 312

J S 160-1, 208, 303-4
  309, 313, 351
James 351, 540
M B 305
Maurice 389, 485, 506
  540
Nora Carter 140
Sarah Frances 540
Stuart/Stewart, 163
  313, 540
ASH/ASHE
General 2, 26
W C 424
ASHLEY
John 167
ASHWORTH
Benjamin 35
Elisha 223
John 224
Miss 358, 532
Noah 224
Thomas N 155
ASKEW Thomas 513
ASSEHOHOLAR
...90
ATCHISON
Henry Y 152
ATCHLEY
Cornelia 366
Mary Valentine 366
McKendree 366
Oliver 366
Robert 366
ATHERTON
Elizabeth B 352
Frances 346
ATKINS
James Verdel 154
William H 154
ATKINSON
Bessie 463
Hopkins 331
Lee 331
ATTAWAY
Felicia 503
Geo W 144, 405
Jesse 151
Julian 532
ATWOOD

W D 366
AULD
  D C 303
  David C 161, 303-04
    309
  Elizabeth 372, 386,
    525
  Family 129
  Fred 160, 162-3, 304
  ---Mrs 163
  --- W 133, 206, 208
    308
  George Clark 367
  Janie 389, 485, 506
  Jennie Rae 138, 553
  J F, sons 139, 206
  Josiah F 92
  Rachel A 128
  Verner 505
  Verner, Mrs 309
  W N 139
  Wilton 374, 382, 387
AUSTIN
  James 92
  John 431
AVERA Ewing 475
AVERY
  Hilliard C 207
AYCOCK
  Carswell Garvin 359
  James 30, 359
  Patty 209
  Richard Jr 30
  William 74, 210
AYERS
  Hansel O 154
  Joseph G 154
  R W 149
  Rosa Lee 547

B

BABB Mr 447
BABER, Jane 326
  492
BACON, E L 325
  336
BAGNELL Mary
  478

BAGWELL
  Emma 522
  Jack 373, 382, 387
    424
  Pearl Brewer, Mrs 149
  T V 373, 382, 387,
    424
  Thomas 373, 382, 387
    424
  Virginia 373, 382, 387
    424
BAILEY
  Annie 323
  ---Marvin 500
  Carl L 151, 208
  D V 150, 160-1, 207
    208, 303-04
  E E, Mrs 163
  Elbert O 136
  E P 134, 135
  Ezekiel 74
  Family 101
  F O 121, 135
  Harris, Mrs. 162, 315
  --- Zadock 151
  Hezekiah 46, 49
  J F 6
  J Frank 307
  Lev 134
  Mary 475
  Mildred 403
  Moses 73
  ---Mrs 462
  Narcissus 480
  Vernon, Mrs. 163
  William 16, 101
BAILLIE Mary 509
BAKER
  Annie Lowe 445
  Benjamin 47, 179
  Elias 179
  James 48
  John 49, 50, 73
  ---A 73
  Joseph 445
  Julia 372, 385, 525
  Leslie, Mrs ix
  Samuel 47
BALCHIN
  Corinne 536
  Inez 162

J J 162
James 440, 474
Joseph 84
BALDWIN
  Benjamin 367
BALL Susannah 552
BALLARD ... 41
  Nat A 175
BALLINGER
  Ettie 520
BANGUS, A 127
BANKS ...57
  Ann 223
  Benjamin 361
  Caroline 363
  Catherine 447
  Charles 362
  Daniel 362
  David 362
  Dolly 362
  Dunstan 361-3
  Edward 362
  Elbert 361
  ---A 362
  Emily 363
  Eugenia 362
  Family 98, 101, 359
  Frances 363
  Frazer 361
  George 361, 362
  ---Jr 362
  Gerrard 461
  Gilly 363
  Gilmer 362
  Hannah 363
  Harry 362
  Hatsell 362
  Henrietta 362
  Henry 141, 223, 362-3
    517
  ---Jr 363
  Jabez 361
  James 91, 166, 171,
    351, 361, 363, 517
  ---J 351, 361
  ---Jrs 363
  Jane 362, 495
  Jasper 361
  Jno 48
  John 30, 35, 98, 99
    167, 220, 361, 362

363, 400
---T 362
Josephine 362
Julia 363
Kate 361
King 362
Lemuel 226, 362
---Jr 362
Lizzie 362
Loula 361
Love 362
Lucretia 362
Lucy 361, 362
Lula 361
Marion 362
Martha 362-3
Mattie 361-2
Marion 495
Mary 362-3, 495
Mary E 361
---Fitzhugh 463
Mary Lou 361
---Priscilla 362
Maymie 362
Miles 35
Nathaniel 363
Newton 361
Nicholas 362
Oliver 361
Philocea 361
Pike 361
Priscilla 362
Rachel 362, 461, 495
Ralph 49, 171, 263,
 361-2, 495
---Jr 361, 495
Richard 69, 99, 222
 359, 361, 362
---Dr 9, 51, 98, 361
---M 362
---Jr 361
Robert 362
Russell 361, 495
Ruth Ann 513
Sally 360, 361
Sarah 361, 362, 368
Susan 361, 362
Thomas 359, 361, 363
 369
Vallie 361
William 55, 57, 211,
 212, 213, 216, 222

361, 363
---A 361
---C 363
---L 362
---R 222
Willis 362, 517

BARCLAY
Miss 511

BARKER ...63
William 49

BARKSDALE
Iviland 533
John H 153
Mary 436
T F 153

BARNES
Jeptha 352
Malcolm 403
Mary 54
Mr 405
Priscilla 54

BARNETT
Addie Valeria 367
Aurelius 418, 439,
 456, 473, 515
Camilla 418, 439, 456
 473, 515
Charles 367
---Caldwell 367
Comer 337, 413, 450,
 482, 542
Cordelia 367
David 364, 365, 466
Eleanor 367
Elizabeth 367, 466
Emily 367
Family 364
Fanny May 367
Frances 364-5
--- L 466
Frank 367
G D 418, 439, 456,
 473, 515
---, Mrs 138
Harriett Eliza 381
Ida 418, 439, 473
 515
---Hill 456
J S 206
James 467
Joel 364, 367

John 47, 467
---Jr 467
Leonard 48
Lillis 338, 413, 451
 482, 542
Louise A 466
Luckie 367
Lucy 364
Lucy Ann 367
Margaret 367
Martha 367, 466, 467
----J 364, 367
---Johnson 367
Martha Valeria 365,
 367, 466
Mary 367
---B 364
---Elizabeth 365, 466
---Jane 367
---Meriwether 365,
 466, 486
May Elizabeth 365
N 381
Nancy 364
Nathaniel 74, 364,
 365, 367, 466
Nelson 73
Nicholas 365, 367,
 462, 466
Peter 364
Rebecca 367
Samuel 141, 337, 413,
 450, 482, 542
Sarah 468
Susan 365, 466
---Crawford 347
Susie 367
Sydney O 365, 466
Tho Meriwether 364
Vohammie 418, 439
 456, 473, 515
William 35, 49, 50,
 71-4, 83, 166, 170
 177, 186, 263, 364
---D 367
---Eugene 365, 466
---Hughes 367
---R 141
---W 48

BARNWELL
Claud 144
---Hamon 151

H A 149
Mr 355
BARR
  George 172
  ---Mrs 93
  Robert S 221
BARRETT
  Fanny 496
  Henry M 167
  Isaac 381
  Isaac J 214
  J H M 167
  William 168, 171
BARRICKMAN
  Mr 548
  W C 549
BARRON
  Britton B 220
  Wiley 70, 90
BARTOW
  B Barrow 8
  Florence Long, Mrs
    139, 145, 315
BARTRAM
  William 6, 11, 12
BARWICK
  Eliza 412
  Mary 412
BASFORD
  James Bailey 469
  Madalyn May 469
  Mary B 469
  Walter Martin 469
BASKIN
  Tho Irwin 502
BASS
  Robert 374, 382, 387
  ---Jr 374, 382, 387
  ---, Mrs. 163
BATES
  Bertha 339, 381, 414
    452, 483, 512, 543
    527
  Claud 154
  Hannah 392
  John W 154
  Hannah 392
  John W 154
  Milton 156

W E 305
William B 120
BAXTER, J H 92
BEACHAM
  E K 331
  Edward 331
  Herman 331
  James 332
  Marion 331
  Wilma 332
BEALL
  Catherine 447
  Col 447
  Egbert 447
  Julia 447
  Martha 393, 404, 447
BEARD
  B C Jr [Jack] 308, 312
    313
BEASLEY
  Ambrose 16
  Ben F 152
  George 136
  J F 144
  James Sr 146
BEATTY
  Cynthia 449
  Cynthia Ann 445
  Henry 449
  Julia 449
  Thomas 449
  ---Jr 449
BECK
  John 64, 181
  Lucy 399
  Mildred 337
  Miss 105
  Sarah Lucy 457
  Sary 222
  William 400
  William A 167-8
    171
BECKMAN
  Caroline 400
  Elisha W 400
BECKY, 64
BECKENRIDGE
  Henry 115, 122
BEGGS,

Frances 503
Gordon 503
John Albert 503
---Jr 503
Sarah 326
BELK, S R 92, 133
  Samuel R 550
BELL
  Ada Bibb 478
  Addison A 478
  ---Key 478
  Arthur Roy 154
  B B 174
  Brother 64
  Capt 220
  Catherine 331
  Christopher 479
  Crelia 478
  D P 206
  Dabon M 478
  Darlina 141, 142
  David 221
  ---P 167
  Dr 133
  E W 156, 173
  Elisha J 478
  Elizabeth 178, 221,
    341, 416, 454, 546
  Enoch 406, 537
  Eugene M 478
  Frances 331, 477
  Geo N 151
  Guy T 152
  H A 331
  H S, Mrs 400
  Harry Sanders 151
  --------, Mrs 302, 311
  Henry 162, 330
  ---A 152
  Hubert 331
  J L 73
  James 35, 48, 177-8
    180, 221, 477
  ---Jr 395, 478
  ---Bynum 136, 144
  ---E 421
  ---Eugene 479
  Jasper M 478
  Jedekiah Falrius 479
  John 225
  Jonathan 447
  ---Jr 447

Jones 331
Joseph 93, 178, 221,
   395, 478
---Jr 67
Joseph Sr 53
Lester 536
Lorene 406
Lula 332
Lycurgus M 479
M A , Mrs 176
Marcus 133
---A 141-2, 173, 175
   343, 478
Margenias A 479
Marianna Emiline 478
Martha 477
Mary E 395
Pauline Edwards, Mrs
   v, 4, 5, 400
Pironia 478
Ralph 406
Rebecca, Mrs. 149,
   398, 421
Rhoda 330, 477
Rhodie 395
Rossie 478
Sarah 477
Sue 141
Susan 477
T K 153
Thomas 92, 330, 395
   477
---Alfred 478
---J 152
Ward 331
William 332
---Henry 479
BELLEW, John 152
BENNETT
  B F 373, 381, 387
  ---Jr 373, 381, 387
  H C 154
  Louise 373, 381, 387
  Martha 58
BENSON
  Grace 404
  Mary Elizabeth 323,
    503
  Miss 491
BENTLEY
  Ada 354

Adeline 353
Allen 353
Ava Priscilla 354
Daisy H 354
Dozier 353
Edward 353
Enoch 353
Fred 353
Georgia 353
Herbert 353
Inez 354
Itis 353
J A 206
James 354
John Davis 353
---Edward 353
---Oscar 353
Jospeh 354
--- A J 353
Julius 354
Lena 353
Lucinda 353
Maggie 353
---Belle 354
Mamie 353
Marie 353
Martha 353
Marvin 354
McAlpin 353
Mr 536
Nellie 354
Paul 353
Pearl 354
Phillip 353
Robertus 353
Ruth 353
Samuel 219, 485
Shorty 353
Thaddeus 354
Una 353
William 353, 354
---Chandler 353
BENTON
  Beulah 466
  Capt 420
  Nina Elizabeth 503
BERLIN
  W T 326, 400, 492
BERRY, Wm T 400
BERRYMAN
  Bernice 524

Fayette 155
Scott 176-7
BERTRAM
  Anita 355
  Raymond 355
BEVERLY, 181
BEVILLE
  Thomas 220
BIBB
  Nancy Ann 475
  Sally S 179, 181
  Thomas 38, 166
  W W 35, 39, 81
  William 166, 179, 475
  William Wyatt
    9, 38
BIGGS
  Guy 490
  ---Jr 490
BIGHAM
  Ernest 489
  Rev 374
BIRCH, Mr 356, 530
BIRDSONG
  Ima 314
BISHOP
  Grace 424
  John Grace 472
BLACK
  Annie 356, 530
  Birdie 356, 530
  Capt 419
  Caroline 356
  Coon 134
  ---Mrs 134
  Ella 536
  Emma 356, 530
  Harry 134, 356, 530
  Hester T 156
  J W 356
  James William 530
  John 30, 31
  ---W 406
  Leonidas 356
  ---Jr 356
  Lola 406, 537
  Lonnie 132, 530
  Mary George 356, 530
  Matthew J 54, 420
  McAlpin 356, 530,

530
Mrs 434, 541
Sarah 141-2, 356
530
Stephen 356
---H 530
William A 167
BLACKBURN
Bessie 464
Samuel 34, 35, 73,
168, 176, 186
BLACKE
John 74
BLACKWELL
Banks 360, 368, 440
474
Bernice 138
Betsy 369, 514
Capt 226
Claudia 360, 368
Cornelia 360, 368
Daisy 440, 474
Dunstan 368
Dunston 86, 212-3
360
Eliza 360, 368
Elizabeth 351, 360,
368
Family 42, 101, 368
Fred 440, 474
Geo L 360, 368
Isabella 339, 360,
368, 416, 454, 485
544
J H 145, 207
J L 360, 368
James 394
---P 360, 368
---Y 360, 368
Jane 473
Jeremiah 73
John 16, 46
Jones 440, 474
Joseph 35, 49, 74
167-8, 171, 360
368
---Jr 360, 368
L L 127
Llellyn 351, 360, 368
L Y N, Mrs 133, 138
139

Mary E 360, 368
___Frances 360, 369
Matthew 127
Nathaniel 125
Parks 360, 368
Paul 142
Ralph 360
Samuel 172
---D 360, 368
Sarah Ann 360, 368
T J 440
Thomas 127
---J 474
---P 360, 368
Wenona 440, 474
William M 360, 368
Zan 170, 173
BLADES, John C
475
BLAIR, Ruth vii
BLAKE
Hilda 503
Kiziah 491
William 211, 212
---Jr 74
---Sr 73
Womack 50, 74
BLAKELY
Miss 448
BLAKENBAKER
Elizabeth 548
BLALOCK
Mary 497
BLANCHARD
James 537
BLAND
Catherine M 457
Charles 457
Harriet C 457
Isabella 457
BLANKINSHIP
Womack 50, 74
BLARE
Letty 64
Thomas 64, 66
BLOODWORTH
Eppy 361
BLOUNT, Miss 439
Mrs 481

BOARDMAN
Brewer G 93, 133
BOATWRIGHT
Daniel 224
Lythia, Mrs 412
BOBO
Isom 152
Lewis 224
Sarah Frances 359
BOLES
Allen 152
John Beard 153
BOLLING
Penelope 392
Robert 392
BOLTON
Claude D 436
BOND[S]
A J 135
Addie Julia 501
Alton Eavenson 501
Anina 463
Benjamin E 156
Bernice 501
Calvin Tucker 323,
501
Charles 168
---N 176
Charlie Walker 156
Cone 140
---Eppy 499
Corella 501
Eliza 495
Elizabeth 357, 501
Emma 502
Eppy 172
Essie 505
Ethlyn 501
George C 536
---Calvin 501
------Jr 501
Hamilton 535
Harriett 494
Harris 405
Harrison Tucker 501
Haskell 502
Holcombe B 154
J F L 535
J W Sr 173
Jack 502

Jewel 535
John 511
John H 463
---Jr 463
Jospeh 405
Louise 501
M R 121
Mamie 498, 502
Margaret 323, 500, 501
Maria 511
Martin 35, 169
Mary 381
Mattie 523
Mr 382-3
Nannie 511
Nathan 223
Omer 6, 405
---, Mrs 307
Richard 73
Roy 208, 405
Sallie C 532
Sarah 511, 501
Thomas 501
Thomas C 152
---J Sr 143
---Oliver 499
---W 150, 174
---Willis 501
Tom 133
Vera Caroline 499
W H 135
William Llewllyn 502
Worley 306
BONDI, G 306
BONE
  Henry Clayton 158
  James Willie 155
  Mima 535
  William Andrew 156
BONIFAY
  Emmie 478
  F A 478
  Gussie 479
  Mae 478
  Mollie 478
BOOKER
  William 49, 211
BOON, Geo 426
BOOTH
  Alberta 490

Ann 54
Arthur L 154
---Jr 490
Asa Grady 154
Bud 141
D S 91, 168
David S 91
Elizabeth 446
Elmer Hoyt 154
Gabriel 87
Geo Arthur 490
---Byron 490
James E T 155
John 53, 87
J P 141
J W 135
Lou 506
Mae 502
Miss 378
Mrs 125
Robert Sr 87
Silas G 162
BORDER/S
  Alvin Orin 155
  Gilbert 73
  Thomas W 154
BORZYNSKI
  F 307
  Felix, Mrs 309
BOSTON Willie 500
BOSWELL
  Clifton 151
  H R 128, 314
  Lula 324
  Willie G 208
BOTHWELL
  Walter 534
BOTSFORD
  Edmund 486, 487
BOUNDS
  Corneill/Cornell 337
  413, 450, 482, 542
BOURNE
  Henry 91, 98, 222
BOWDEN
  Elizabeth 523
  Janna Wilhite vii
  John Lewis 355
  Robert 355
  -----Jr 355

Roy 315
---L 523
------Jr 523
BOWEN
  Charles Benson 155
  Frank 466
  Horatius C 222
  John 397
  Louise 466
  Mollie 466
  Nettie 375
  Passie 466
  Sarah 395
  William 35, 103, 168
  ---- B 172
BOWERS
  Aaron Newton 523
  ---Jr 523
  Alex Cree 523
  Alton Parker 524
  Bill 313, 524
  D T 175
  Elizabeth 523
  Esther 523
  Fay 524
  Hilda C 523
  Jean 523
  Jeanne 524
  John H 523
  ---Martin 524
  Leonard H 524
  Lucile 523
  Lucille Baker v
  Lucius Edwin 156
  Miss 334
  Polly 523
  Robert S 498
  Ruth 523
  Sophia 523
  T J 176
  Thomas 140
  William F 523
  ------ Robert 498
  -------------Jr 498
  Winifred 523
BOWIE Sam 505
BOWLES Miss 478
BOWMAN, ... 58
  Alice 535
  Capt 426
  F B iii

Luther W 152
S A, Mrs. 315
Tho J 319, 360, 368
Willis W 225
BOYD
Anna 404
Bess 533
Charlie May 462
Col 15, 16, 23
Henry 445
John 35, 48
Joseph M 477
Laura 477
Matthew 477
Mrs. 16
BOYER, Gabrielle 457
BOZEMAN
Inez 457
BRAC[E]Y
Annibel 367, 463
BRADBERRY
R E 534
BRADFORD
Betty 330, 477
D W 122
Elsie 449
Helen 365
Mary Frances 500
Phillip 500, 532
---Jr 500
Rose West 140
Tho Jefferson 140
BRADLEY
Ann 448
Ann Pearl 448
Benjamin 448
John A 448
Lucy 536
Mary 448
Nicholas W 448
Richard 448
Robert C 224, 420
Victoria 448
Wm Ellis 448
Wm Heard 448
BRADSHAW
Ed K 208
H D 153
Kenny 153

BRADY
D 74
Henry Lee 151
James 73
Margaret 449
BRAGG
Charles W 155
Mary 221
BRAIN
Nelle Ray 367, 463
BRAMBLETON
Gertrude 523
BRANCH
Lily 506
William 132
BRANNON
C N, Mrs 309
Peter vii
BRASWELL
B B 206
James M 135
BRAUNER
John 46
BRAWNER
Asa 222
Basil 210
Benjamin 3
Brazel 210
Budd 541
Cherry 54
Elizabeth 53
Henry P 53, 73
Hugh 541
James 176
---M 53
Jessie 74, 535
Joe 181
John 48
---W 222
Joseph 378
---W 222
Priscilla Jane 422
Sarah 541
Samuel 221
Walter 541
Whitlock 541
William 74, 180
---M 222
BRAY
Bannister R 222, 223

Sarah 54
Thomas 539
BRECKENRIDGE
... 108
BREWER
Addie 382, 387
Adeline 371, 385
Albert T 382, 387, 389, 485
---Thomas 151, 373
Alice Oglesby, Mrs 310
Annie 374, 387
Benjamin 373, 386
Charles H 156, 373, 382, 387
---Jrs 373, 382, 387
Claud 373, 382, 387
Cynthia 342, 371
E H 103
Edmo[u]nd 35, 53, 371
---H 222, 371, 385
Edna 141
Elisham 371
Elizabeth 373, 382, 387, 389, 485, 506
Eva 373, 382, 387, 424
Family 42, 84, 371
Frances 375
Gates 375
H J 134, 139, 145, 176, 205-07, 425, 550
----, Mrs 134, 315
Herbert 374, 387, 425
Hoke 374, 382, 387
Hopkins R 371, 373
Horatio 222
Hundley J 221
Irene 374, 382, 387, 406
J H 135
J Hop 134
James E 169, 173-5, 373, 381, 387
---Hopkins 167, 381, 386
--- T 373, 382, 387
---Thomas 424, 531
Janice 373, 382, 387

424
Jesse 74
John 133, 373-4, 381
John M 134, 169, 374
   387
Jule 315
Julian 374, 387, 425
-----Jr 374, 387
Leonard Stephens 498
Leroy C 154
Lucia 310
Lucy 373, 381, 386
---Carter 53
Lula Treadwell, Mrs
   v
Luther 373, 382, 387
---Turner 424
Mabel 373, 382, 387
Marguerite 138, 374,
   387, 425
Marion 373, 381, 387
Martha 375
Matthew 65
Mary 373-5, 382, 387
   424
Nicholas 373, 386
Pauline 373-4, 381-2,
   387
Pearl 373, 382, 387
   424
Patsy 374
Rachel Maxwell 498
Ralph 373, 382, 387
   424
Rose 373, 386
Ruby 373, 382, 424
S S 133, 139, 143,
   206
---, Mrs 161-3, 204,
   311
Sally Jane 424
Samuel Stark 151,
   373, 382
-----Jr 373, 382
Sarah Ann 375
Stark 387
---Jr 387
Susan 222
Thelma 373, 382, 387
Theron Myers 498
Tho 373, 382, 386
   387, 424

---Griffin 424
---Maxwell 498
Watha 342
Watkins W 498
William B 371
William Thomas 373,
   386
BREWSTER
A J 326, 492
C H 379
BRICE, Emily 342
BRIDGES
C H 379
Cal 396
Obie 208
BRIDGET...5
BRIDWELL
Max 328
BRIESTER...64
BRIGHT
George 91
BRIGHAM
Mercy 519
BRIGHTWELL
Brewton Edward Jr
   365
Newton Edward 365
BRILEY
John W 365
BRINSFIELD
J W 85
BRISBANE..27
BRISCO, L H 113
BRISTOL
E W 206
Eliza, Mrs 143
BROACH
George 379
---A 379
Jones 379
Lucy Glenn 550
BROADWELL
Mr 125
W C 152
BROCK
Alice 436
Carrie, Mrs 143
Fred W 410

Homer, Mrs 161-2
Mrs 411
Ruby Conwell, Mrs
   140, 314
BROCKINGTON
R C 307
BROGDON M 534
BROILE Mr 548
BROOKS
Dudley 181
Leo 154
Ralph 518
BROOKSHIRE
Henry T 93, 312
BROOMFIELD
Major 431
BROUGH
Whit O 152
BROUGHTON
Joseph 146
BROWN
A 35
A W 121
Aaron 221
A Britt 376
Adam 470
Adams 375
Albert M, Mrs 143
Allen 389, 485, 506
Ama[o]nda J 325, 336
Amanda Catherine
   503
Andrew 179, 317, 375
---Rucker 376, 534
Ann 63, 503
Anne Ludwell 433
Arthur Barton 153
Asa 534
--- A 221
B D 135, 153
Benager Teasely 324,
   436
Benajah 377
Benjamin 47, 53, 73
   317, 437
----Jr 67, 171
Benson 323, 333, 377
--- Chandler 500
Bessie 324, 377
Betty 389

Billy Chandler 503
Birch 376, 534
Bobby 376
Bonner Sue 499
Brooks 153
Capt 378
Cassie 376
Chandler 312
Charles Sullivan 503
Clay Leonard 499
------Jr 499
Clois C 324, 377
----- Jr 377
Clois Clifton 151
Claud 324, 377
Claudine 335
Clyde 323, 325, 336, 377
---Jr 336
---McMurry 500
Columbus 376
Corinne 500
Cran O 323, 377
---Oliver 501
D C 327
D H 206
David C 208
Dillard 67, 133, 163
---, Mrs 134
---H 145, 535
Dorris 376
Dozier 67, 226
Drucilla Ione 325, 335
E C 303
Easton 325, 336, 423
Ed Neal 503
Edgar Chandler 151, 208, 535
Elbert 437
Elbert Gordon 323, 503
Elijah 475
Eliza Matilda 493
Elizabeth 59, 163, 324 376, 377
Elizabeth Ardecy 493
Elizabeth Rebecca Pemberton 493
Elzie 376
Emily 377
Essie 376, 534
---Mildred 501

Eugene 335, 355
Eva 330, 477
Family 375
Fanny 534
Fanny P 325, 376
---Pierce 335
Felicia 377
Flora Elizabeth 498
Florence 138, 535
Ford 325, 335
Frances Arnold v
--- Margaret 493
Francis 48, 335
Frank Start 156
Franklin 302
Gaines 505
Gene Crandall 501
George 154, 336, 376, 389, 506, 534
---E 325, 335
---I 325
---Sandord 503
------Jr 503
---W 67
Glenn 376
H J 208
Harford Ophelia 493
Harold 334
Heber 376, 534
Helen 323
---Sarah 501
Henry 324, 375, 377
--- H 173
Herman 485
---Gaines 499
---J 151, 389, 506, 535
Hiram 375
Ira M 302
Irene 376
Isham 324, 377
---Hailey 324, 333, 436 469
---T 335
Isom G G 155
J A 67, 324, 377, 469
---, Mrs 67
J J 303
J R 135
Jackson 376
James 61, 63, 73, 377 460

---Elbert 335
---F 325, 335
---Jr 433
---L 375
---Maxwell 503
-----Jr 503
---N 221
---Polk 155, 302
---W 154
Jefferson 375
Jerome 324, 377
Jimmy 377
Jincy 179
Joe 134
Joel 335
John 47, 74, 133, 302, 373, 381, 387
---, Mrs. 133, 134
---A 324, 333, 377 436
---C 133-4, 148, 206 414, 452, 512, 535
---Chandler 339, 483 544
---D 140, 148
---Hilliard 153
---J 149
---Judson 302
---Jr 373, 382, 387
---L 358
---McCrary 503
---S 67
---W 208
---William 155
Johnson 168
Joseph S 323
---Sidney 501
---W J 493
Julia Le Rose 499
Julian 312
---Thomas 151, 535
Katherine 323, 377
Kyle 302
L 141
L C 176
L G 150
Laura 324, 377
---Cornelia 324 434, 436
Leasie 376
Leila 376, 534

Lena 503
Leonard Stephens 498
Lettie G 325, 335, 5-7
Lon C 323, 377
Lonnie 323, 377
---Chandler 501
-------Jr 501
---Maxwell 500
Lou 377
--- M 323
Lou Martin 500
Louis Kendall 499
Louisa 376
Louise 535
Lucy 389, 427, 506
M J 145, 206, 207
Maggie 314
Mallory J 535
Mamie, Mrs. 133
Margaret 335
Marian Elbert 503
Marjorie Polk 302
Martha 376, 377, 389
 507
---Jane 493
Martin 547
Mary 67, 314, 323,
 324, 325, 336, 357
 505, 531
---Ann Malesy 493
---E 335
---Hester 323, 501
---Hortense 503
---Lou 500
---M 376
---McCurry 437
---McIntosh 140
------, Mrs 310
---Mildred 460
---O 325, 335
Mattie L 335
Maud 138, 535
Milly 53
Monjet 323
---Gerald 501
Moody 498
Mr 35
Nancy 67, 437
----Ann 325
Neal 323, 377
---Martin 500
Otis 376

Parks 376
Parnice 340, 415, 453
 484, 544
Paul viii, 160, 162,
 166, 170, 177, 302
 356, 376, 534
---, Mrs v, 163
Pauline 376
---Brewer 163, 303
 304, 316
Pearl 302
---W 325, 521
Peter 45, 48
Rachel 325, 336, 535
Ralph 376
Rebecca 335
Richard Roland 501
Robert 69, 336, 376
 493
Roland 323, 499
Roland J 323, 377,
 436
Rolen 224
Rosalyn 376
Roy J 154
Roy Lucian 499
Ruby 407
Rucker 376
Russell D 67
Ruth 535, 537
Sallie May 522
Sally 389, 506
Samantha 376
Sarah 324, 375, 376
 377
Sarah E 493
---F 67
---Katherine 500
---Margarette 326
---M F 67
Susan A E 460
-----Campbell 302
Susie 376
Sylvester 155, 302
T E, Mrs 141
Theron Myers 498
Tho 323, 371, 377
---Clyde 154
---J 157, 176, 205,
 376, 534
---Jefferson 500
---Maxwell 498

---Middleton 493
---Watson 303
Thornton 376
Vandiver 141
Virginia 325
W G 533
W W 376
Walter Johnson 303
Wiley 375
William 35, 73, 179,
 375, 389, 493, 506
---A 111
---Albert 500
---H 493
---Howard 335
---Isham 325, 335
---Murray 499
---N 153
---W 325
---Jr 325
---Watkins 335
------Jr 336

BROWNER
 Henry 73
 John 74

BROWNING
 Evelyn 357

BROWNLEE
 Jessie 405
 W T 168, 174-5

BROWNSON
 Nathan 44

BROYLES
 Catherine 548
 Elizabeth 547

BRUCE
 Family 129
 James Hagood 373,
  386, 526
 ---McDuffie 386, 526
 Sophia G 128
 Virginia 373, 386, 526

BRUXE
 Albert 38

BRYAN
 Florence 397
 Jonathan 24
 Lodiska 449
 Margaret 423
 Mauline 499

Miss 327, 403
Sarah 224
Walker 358
BRYANT
 J P Stinson 181
 John 380
 Lewis Lee 380
 Lucy 432
 Lythia Boatwright 412
 Major 380
 Mary 402
 Morrison M 155
 Needham 412
BUCKNER
 J D 128
BUFFINGTON
 Ann 226
 Joseph 225
 Nancy 67
 W M 67
 William 67, 225
BUGG, Jacob 35, 48
BUIS, M 393
BUKLEY
 Jospeh 180
BULLARD
 Ann 221
 J W 135
 Kit 331
 Mildred Agatha 465
 Thomas 332
 ---H 151
 Tommy 332
 W H 121
BUNN
 Gladys 375
BURCH
 Benjamin 205
 Elizabeth 103, 205
 Family 101
 Hammond 138, 440, 474
 Irene 440, 474
 J C 310
 James 124, 127, 135, 138, 167, 212, 440, 474
 ---, Mrs 127; 161
 ---T 169, 173, 176

Janet 440
Janie 138
Jim 133
John C 110 111, 115 116, 176
Martha 263, 412, 481
Minnie 437
Richard 412, 481
Thom C, Mr & Mrs 437
William 74
---J 440, 474
---S 93, 179
BURDEN
 Artie 524
 Eddie M 326
 Elizabeth Harriet 521
 G 144
 Grover C 154
 Hannah 223
 J A 135
 J B 141
 James Hoyt 155
 ---T 136
 L L 152
 Martha A 325
 Mary 133
 Nathaniel G 158
 William 87
BURDETTE
 William H 156
BURDIN
 Archibald 73
BURGE[S]
 Mary 348
 Thomas 395
BURGIN Olin 500
BURK
 Robert 61
 Sarah 61
 Thomas 178
BURKE
 Brother 57
 Edmund iv
 Robert 168
 Thomas 45
 Virgil 367
BURNES
 D M 176

Mr 448
BURNETT
 B F 136
 Vivian 417, 455 514
BURNLEY
 Zach'y 429
BURNS
 Andrew 24
BURR
 Aaron 383
 Theodosia 383
BURRELL
 Lew 345
BURRISS
 Amie 407
 Clayton 498
 Dilliard 337, 482, 542
 ---Herndon 413, 450
 Edna 498
 George L 208
 James 406
 John 337, 413, 450 482, 542
 Martha Helen 498
 Nona 311
 ----Herndon 140
 William Dean 153
BURTON
 Archibald 46, 92, 180
 Bins 93
 E Walter 153
 Elizabeth 92, 263, 378 462
 ---Neil 430
 Homer Sr 163
 Jasper Homer 155
 Joseph 221
 Mary 221
 Nancy 53, 67
 Richard 221
 Robert 47
 Sanson 93
 Thomas 35, 46, 47, 49, 64, 65, 73, 180
BUSBY
 J P 155
BUSH Mary 499, 532
BUSHA Lillian 501

BUSSEY
  A W 161, 162, 169
    176
  Earl W 523
  Eva Anita 523
  Evelyn 163
  James 366
  John 366
  Samuel 366
  Thomas 366
BUTLER
  Capt 221
  Charlotte 378
  David C 221, 378
  Elizabeth 378
  Fanny 375
  George 378
  Girman 220
  Isaac Newton 378
  James 181, 377, 441
  ---Albert 155
  Jasper C 155
  John 222, 377, 379
  Lucy 378
  Martha 375
  Mary 375, 378-9
  Mila 375
  Nancy 377-8
  Nathan 377
  Nelson B 220
  Nicholas 220
  P B 54
  Paten 220
  Patrick 221, 377
    378, 379, 441
  ---Jr 441
  Patsy 378
  Penelope 375
  Peter D 222
  ---Patrick 378
  Rebecca 378
  Sally 181
  Sam Jones 154
  Samuel 378
  Simeon 378
  Susan 375
  Thomas 211, 220
  Weston A 155
  William 375, 378
  Zachariah 377, 378
BUTT/BUTTS

Carey 444
---Jr 444
Clara 444
Col. 115
Elder 444
Fannie 444
Julia 444
Martha 361
Mary 444
Moses 362
BYNUM
  H B 158
  H R 207, 328, 341,
    403, 416, 454, 545
  Henry R 151
  Susan Margaret 341,
    403, 416, 454, 545
  Willie Sue Adams
    , Mrs v
BYRD, H L 92

C

CABINESS
  Henry 54
CADE
  Albert 380, 526
  Annie 380
  --- Lee 339, 381
    414, 452, 483, 543
    544
  Benjamin 380
  Bessie 379
  Boykin 380
  Clifford 380, 526
  Daisy 380
  Drury 16, 35, 39,
    186, 379
  ---B 379
  Eliza 41, 380
  Family 42
  Guildford 103, 380,
    381, 414, 452, 526
  ----IV 339, 381, 452
    512, 544
  ----Jr 339, 452, 483
    512, 543
  ---III 339, 381, 414
    452, 512, 543-4
  James 380
  Jane 380, 526

John 380
Julia 380
---May 339, 381, 414
  452, 483, 512, 543
Malvina 339, 381,
  414, 452, 512, 543
  544
Mary 380
Mary Eliza 338, 380,
  413, 451, 482, 511
  526, 543
Matilda 380
Rennie 380, 526
Robert 379, 380
Roy 380, 526
Samuel 380, 526
---Robert 380, 526
Sarah 379, 380, 526
---Louise 380, 526
Thelma 380, 526
Thomas 380
Victoria 380, 527
Walter 380, 526
William 380, 526
---G 380
Wooder 380, 526
William 351
CAHILL Margaret
  461
CAIN
  William 351
CAINES
  William 35
CALDER Florence
  508
CALDWELL
  A W 121
  George 332
  Harry 48, 171
  Henry 47, 332
  Martha 514
  Miss 473
  Reid, Mrs 162
  W R 153
CALHOUN
  Caroline 370, 418
    456, 485, 515
  Family 42, 391
  John 178
  ---C 86, 319
  Patrick 319

Susan 476
CALLOWAY
  E C 422
  Francis 54
  Ida 141, 425
  Lidia 447
  M L 422
  Maggie 425
  Miles 425
  P T 448
  Thomas 356, 530
  Willie 425
CAMERON
  Family 12
CAMP
  Arthur T 492
  Norman 326, 492
  Walker Glenn 492
CAMPBELL
  Betwy 362
  Col 16, 23
  Colin 510
  Daniel 221
  Euphemia 510
  G M 54
  Gibson 93
  Helen 508
  Icie 537
  Ida 362
  J H 487
  James 35
  Jean 509
  Mary 141, 447
  Rachel 461
  Reuben 407
  Robert G C 509
  Susan 433
  Susanna 421
  William B 87
CAMRON
  James 74
CANALES
  J 307
  Jose 6
CANDLER
  Allen Daniel 101
  Amelia 393
  Charles 393
  Daniel 393
  ---Chandler 393

David 393
Elizabeth 393
---Anthony 393
Ezekiel Slaughter 393
Falby 393
Frances Emily 393
Harry 393
John 393
---Kingston 393
Joseph 393
Mary 393
Mark Anthony 393
Samuel Charles 393
William 392, 393
William J 393
CANNADA
  Elizabeth 221
CANNADY
  Catherine 398-99
CANTRELL
  W A 478
CAPE
  Merian 221
CAPERS
  Thomas 91
CAR, Sister 58
CARDEN
  Moses 442
CAREY
  Ann 353
  John A 103
  Robert 375
CARGILE
  John Runno 486
CARGILL
  Miss 463
CARITHERS
  Claud W 155
  Harold G 155
  Howell W 149
  James P 154
  Janie 537
  Mamie 314
  T J 173, 174
CARLAN B B 153
CARLETON
  Rebecca 488
  Robert 488
CARLISLE

E, Mrs 391
Roselyn Reid 391
CARLTON
  Anne 437
  Annie 329, 438
  Benjamin Harvey 437
  Charlie C 437, 438
  Corrie 329
  D M 438
  Daniel Milton 437
  Elbert 437
  Emma 438
  Geo J 438
  James E 438
  ---M 437
  John 438
  ---B 437
  ---W 438
  Joseph 329
  Keifer A 151
  Lawrence Heard 455
  Lela 437, 438
  Louise Catherine 438
  Mary 141, 437
  Pope 437
  Robert 329
  Ruth Burch 437
  Sallie 437, 459
  Sara 438
  Stephen 329
  Thomas 176, 417,
    437, 455, 514
  ---C 437
  ---Jr 417, 455, 514
  Welborn Chaudoin
    437, 438
  Will 438
  William F 136
  Zora 304, 437-8
CARMICHAEL
  Mr 424
CARNES Peter 177
CARPENTER
  Amanda 371, 373,
    381, 386
  Capt 223
  Cleora 383
  Eddie 383
  Elizabeth 501
  Family 42, 381
  Frances Myrtle 383

Helen 382, 403
Helene 328
Ivan 328, 382, 403
James 328, 381, 403
---, Mrs 162
---Chandler 382
---T 403
---Thomas 382
-------Jr 382
Joshua 381
---Jr 381
---S 224
L A 382, 403
-----Jr 382, 403
Laura 383
Leila 327, 382
Lucas 313, 328
Lucile 328, 382, 403
Martha 540
Mary Helen 383
Minor 382
Mr 548
Myrtle 162
Nicholas Albert 383
---Drewry 383
Ophelia 383
S N 123, 126, 206
---, Mrs 161
Thomas 35, 328, 403
---Napoleon 383
W H 143
William 35, 540
---Hilliard 382
Willie 382, 540

CARR
J C 439, 473, 515
---Jr 439, 515
J M 418, 456
---Jr 418, 456
John C 133
Mitta 418, 456
Mr 360, 369
Robert 418, 456

CARRINGTON
W A, Mrs 148

CARROLL
Bridget 449
Brother 58, 59, 60,
   61, 63
Charles 13
John 60, 61, 62, 63

66, 167, 171, 439
Kathleen 370, 417-8
455, 514
Mary 439

CARROWAY
J D 396
Mary Lou 396
William 396

CARSON
Catherine 490

CARSWELL
E R 93
Kate 142

CARTER
Ann Daniel 385
Anne 530
Annie E 350, 355
Betsy 385
Cassie 354
Charles 212, 213, 216
   384, 388
Charles N B 226
Copeland 350
David 383-84, 432
Elector F 384
Elizabeth 221, 226
Eugene D 136
Family 42
Fannie 538
Farris 388
Florence 351
Frances 388
George 533
George W 91, 388
Georgia 332, 350, 469
Lucy Farris 371
J W 176
James 333, 350, 384
---M 168, 350, 383
---Martin 156
Jemima 263
Jeremiah 470
John 226, 384
---C 91
Josiah 30, 393
Kate 351
Leola 351
Lucy 226
---Ann Elizabeth 384
---Farris 385
Mack 333

McAlpin 351
----Calvin 156
Micajah 383, 394
Nancy M 388
---Goolsby 383
Nathis 220
Nora 351, 540
Patsy 385
Randolph 35
Raymond C 156
Reuben 333, 470
Riley 333
Robert M 226
---384, 385
S L 206
Sam 133
Samuel L 127
Sarah 384, 388, 412
   450, 482
Thomas 49, 64, 73,
   177, 226, 317, 333
   516
---A 16, 35, 47-8, 50
   69, 92, 384, 412
   450, 482
---C 155
---Jr 74
---P 388
---S 385
William 394
Yancey 351

CARTLEDGE
Edmund 539

CASEY
John 74
---A 38
Thomas 38

CASH
Family 129
J Clarence 154
J P 469, 533
John 225
---P 143, 333
Lucy 63
Mary 101
Mr 436
Patsy 67
S R 121

CASON
Allen 132, 332, 469
E A 35, 60-62, 64

206-07
---, Mrs 315
Mary Jim 138
Monroe 505
Thomas 332, 469
CASTER
John C 398
CASWELL
Gov 26
CATER
Elizabeth 424
Nelle 423
CAUTHEN
JA 143
Mozelle 534
RL 143, 145, 206
CERSY
Sister 62
CERTAIN
James 74
CHAMBERS
Edward 464
Thomas 349, 351
CHAMBL[E]ISS
Miss 347
Ree 478
CHAMPION
JA 139
---Mrs 139
JW 207
Jesse 316
Thomas Dallas 525
CHANCEY
Eliz. 346
CHANDLER
Asa 54, 67, 93
----Mrs 67
Ava 406
Bertha 424
Betty 485
Carswell 424
Ezekial 153
HF 206
Hezekiah 73
JI 169, 206
James 424
Joel 181
Marie 424
Mordecai 206

Raymond E 152
Sally 337
Sarah 359, 368
TA 168
Thomas 141
CHANY 65
CHAPMAN
John Courtney 466
David 225
Jessie Almeda 466
Frederick 225
Jos Davis 466
Mattie 489
Mollie 466
William 48
----Augustus 466
----Benj 466
CHAPPELL
Dorothy 490
JB 91
John B 91
Robert 394
CHARITY 66
CHARLES
Nellie 324, 377
CHARLET 65
CHARLTON
Major 122
CHARPING
Augustus C 154
JO 154
WL 135
CHASTINE
Boyd C 152
George Guy 152
Thomas N 152
CHATTAN
Clan 508, 510-11
CHEADLE
Eliz 394
Judith 394
Lucy 394
CHEATHAM
Stephen 461
CHEEK
AM Jr. 154
AR, Mrs 312
Grace 500, 532
John Bynum 151

Nancy 322
CHERRY Florence 464
CHIEF-CHIEF 88
CHILDERS
Cassy 52
Holman 53, 67
James 63, 65
Jesse C 224
Nancy 63
Sarah 67
Sister 66
Wiley 64, 66
William 221
CHILDRESS
Mrs. Susan 432
CHILDS
Amy 63
Ben Tillamn 153
Benjamin 64, 65
Cassie 65
Catey 64
Brother 59, 65
Edward 536
Haley 52
Henry 464
Hugh 153
JB, Mrs 143
John 63, 64, 65, 222
John Frank 153
LS 143
Lewis 375
Lewis G 222
Lewis H 208
Lucy 63
Missie 536
Nancy 52, 64, 65
Nathan 64, 65, 66
----& wife 52, 58
Peggy 52, 64, 65
SG 150
Susannah 64
Willis 153
CHILES
Agatha 394
Alexander 35
John 74
CHINN Stella 449
CHIPMAN
Joseph 54, 64, 65, 66,

181
Mary 361
Nancy 64
CHISENHALL
Dilany 220
CHISHOLM
Mary 394
Thomas 446
William 210
CHOWING
Eleanor 367
Frank 367
Fanny 367
Jack 367
John 367
Montine 367
Nathaniel 367
Thomas 367, 466
-----W 367
CHRISLER
Abe 497
Abraham 496
Annie Lou 496
Benjamin Frank 496
Betty 496
Cottie 497
Cora 496
Daisy 496
Flora 496
George 496
Homer 497
Ida 496
Isham 496
---Teasley 496
Jane Ann 497
Joe 496
John 496
Jynie 496
Mary 497
Maud 496
Max 496
Otis 497
Robert 496
Roy 496
Simeon 496
Thomas 496
Willie 496
William 496
CHRISTER
Benjamin 224
CHRISTIAN

Ace 389, 507
Alice Gertrude 391
Althea 391, 476
Arless 390, 494, 507
Arva 390, 494, 507
Aubrey 390, 494, 507
Beatrice 476
Betty 390, 494, 507
Billy 507
Boyd 390, 507
Bryant Lewis 391
Camilla Zeree 391
Carmen 390, 494, 507
Clarence 389
Charles 388
Charles W 99, 167-8,
  172, 217, 390, 493,
  494, 507
------Jr. 388
------III 388
------J 476
Charles Woodson
  388, 390, 507
---------Jr. 390, 507
Clarence 507
Cornelius 390, 494
  507
Corry 506
Daisy 389, 507
Edna Ann 391
Elijah 87, 388
Eliza 342
Elizabeth MB 398
  493, 506
Eugenia 528
Evelyn 390, 494, 507
Floyd 163
GJ 54
GT 160, 162
Gabriel 91
George 388
-------M 476
Gradus T 313, 319,
  390, 494, 507
Gradus Jr. 390, 494
  507
Harbey 493
Helen 390, 423, 494
  507
Howard 389, 506
Ira 390, 391
Ira Jackson 389, 493

506
Jackson 388, 506
James 35, 390, 494
  507
James C 152, 391
Jesse G 389, 390, 493
  494, 506, 507
Jessett 476
Joe Ann 507
John 141, 388, 476,
  494
-------M 221
-------Marshall 476
------Thomas 389, 493
  507
Johnny 389, 507
Jo Ann 390, 494
Joseph Marion 389
Josephus Marion 493
  507
Lawrence 507
Lens 389, 507
Lizzie 389, 506
Lois 476
Lou Charles 389, 506
Lucinda 485
Luther M 67
Mamie 389, 506
Martha Ann 391
---Permelia 494, 507
Martin 388
Mary 390, 391, 494
  507
Mary Frances 389,
  493, 506
Mary Jean 390, 507
Mary Permelia 390
Marylyn 390, 494,
  507
Mel 390, 507
Minnie 388
Morris 389, 507
Nancy 390, 485, 494
  503, 507
Nancy Turner 388
  506
Nolley 390, 494, 507
Ollie 141, 389, 507
Oscar 476
Ossie 389, 507
Pressley 169
Robert 151, 390, 391

494, 507
\--------B 171, 391
\--------Bryant 391
\--------E 391
Rossie 389, 507
Rufus 217
Samuel 222
Sarah 494
Sarah Ann Josephine 389, 493, 506
Sarah Helen 391
Savias 390, 494, 507
Senie 504
Shelby 391
Shelby T 391
Sterlie 390, 507
Suleana 391
Thomas 67, 388
Tilda 476
Tommie 389, 506
Turner 263, 317, 388
Vandiver 389, 506
Vesta 390, 494, 507
WC 150
WJ 174
W. Cornelius 494
Walter 388
Washington 169
William 388, 390
\----Cornelius 390, 507
\--------H 151
\--------P 390, 493, 507
\--------Payne 388, 506
\--------Yancy 476

CHRISTIE
Ann 350, 356
EH 350
Edward H 356

CHRISTOPHER
Ann 399, 400

CILLANDEAU
Susanne 420

CLAMP
JJ 152

CLARK...74
Ada Mae 353
Agatha 397
Agnes 394
Amanda Malvina 394
Ambrose 399, 400
Amelia 394

Ann 399, 400
Ann Powell 398
Aubrey 336
Bathesda Sampson 398
Betty 394, 393
Billy Parks 133, 136, 138
Blandina 405
Bolling 392, 394
Capt 35
Caroline 400
Chiles Terrell 398
Christopher 35, 73, 166, 211, 220, 221, 263 /, 317, 392, 394, 395, 400, 517
\------Jr. 394, 395
\-----III 394
\----Hull 395
Cleveland 405
Col 15
David 73, 92, 317, 395, 487, 488
Ed 173
EV, Mrs 143, 175
Edna 405
Edward 73, 178, 392, 400
Elijah 464
Eliza Terrell 464
Elizabeth 360, 369, 392, 393 398, 487, 488
\---, Mrs 368
Elizabeth H 338
Eunice Henretta 398
Families 42, 129, 401
Fanny 360, 368
Frances 398
Fritz 336
General 75, 76
George 332, 399, 400
\-----Jr. 400
Geo Rogers 400, 401
\---S 533
\---Thomas Davis 395
\---Washington 395
Georgia 23
Gordon 325, 336
Henry 401
I B 156

J L 174
J O A 85
Jackhariah 221
Jacqueline 400
James 202, 349, 394, 398, 399, 401
\---A 400
\---Andrew 153
\---D 350
\---L 136, 149
\---Jr 400
\---O 221
\---Opher 394
John Gov. 99
\---394, 399
Joseph 181, 398, 399
Joshua 74, 167, 397
Josie 360, 369
Judith 394, 397
L A 405
Larkin 398, 399, 400
\---L 111, 167, 222, 400
Laura 350
Louisa 383
Lucy 398, 399, 517
Margaret 400
\---Ann 394, 395
\---Chisholm 394
Martha 337, 398, 400
\---Bowen 395
\---E 398
Mary 23, 346, 395 397, 398-400, 405 406, 436, 479
Mary Alston 383
\---Ann 395, 475
\---Elizabeth 397
\---Louisa 350
\---Penelope 394
Micajah 392-94
Mildred 397, 549
Millie T 549
Minnie 141
Moon 23
Mourning 263, 395, 475
Mr 447
Nancy 401
Nora 405
Ora Frank 153
Otis 144, 405

Overton 360, 368
Penelope 394
Rachel 394, 397
Raymond 405
Rebecca 86
---Elizabeth 395
---Dacis 395
---Davis 394
Reuben 398-400
Richard 90
Robert 394, 399, 400
Sam 169, 175
Samuel 73, 220, 394, 397
---Hood 395
Sara 400
Sarah 350, 375, 394, 399, 400
---Taylor 398
Susan 398
---Anna 397
Tabitha 398
Taliaferro 400
Tho Jefferson 395
---Jr. 395
W J iii
W T 121
Widow 220
William 350, 360, 368, 394, 398-401
William A 202
---Brickington 395
---D 222
---David 398
---Davis 395
---J 172
---Marston 401
---Sr 399
---Parks 360, 368
Zack 73
Zacharian III 397

CLARKE
Elijah 22

CLAUDUS
Harry 48

CLAY
A S 138
Henry 86

CLAYTON(S)
Earl 387

The 97

CLECKLER
Catherine 357, 531
R C 92, 147

CLEGG
Claud 366

CLEMONS
John W 136

CLERICI
Geovanni 151

CLEVELAND
Absolom 402
Agnes 340, 404, 415, 453, 545
Albert 405
Allen 404
---Jr 404
Alexander 401
---Jr 401
S 406
---III 402
Andrew 415
---B 340, 404, 453, 484, 545
---J 134, 138, 403
---Jr 340, 404, 415, 453, 545
Ann 404
Antionette 327, 403
Arthur 405
Augustus 406
Aurelia 406
Benjamin 402, 404
Bessie 406
Cade 407
Caroline 403
Clara 406
---E 406
Claud 404
Colonel 382
Cornelius 402
Cynthia 402
D E 135
Daniel 209, 406, 407
---Early 406
Dorothy 405
Early 222
E D 405
Eliza 406
Elizabeth 209, 340, 402-04, 407, 415,

453, 484
Eppy 407
Esther 405
Family 401
Fanny 402
Frank 340, 404, 415, 453, 484, 545
Georgia 405
Geo W 406, 407
Geraldine 405
Gilbert 402
Glenn 141, 406
Grace 405
Grady 156
Grover 406, 537
---, Mrs 311
---F 151
H H 143, 207
Harriet 407
Harry 406
---Jr 406
---L 139, 143
-----, Mrs 311
Hastings L 151
Helen 340, 402, 404, 415, 453, 484, 545
Henry 404
Hugh 156, 406, 374, 382, 387
Ida 363, 370, 418, 456, 515
Ivory 404
J M 306, 313
Jack 406
Jacob 65, 74, 180, 209, 263, 402, 404
---M 222
---Mimms 403
James 402, 404, 407
---M 53, 404
---Madison 434
---Roy 154
Jane 404, 406
Janie 406, 531
Jefferson 402
Jeremiah 209, 402
Jesse 405, 532
---P 136, 405
Jessie 340, 404, 415, 453, 484, 545
John 74, 327, 401, 402-03, 406

---IV 402
---Jr 401
---III 402
Jule M 160, 403
-------, Mrs 163
L 143
Lanier 332, 340, 404
  415, 453, 484, 545
Larkin 402
Leroy 327, 406
Lila 406
Louisa 406-07, 536
Loyd 404
Maggie 538
Mamie 407
Marie 405
Mark 406
Martha 402, 403
---Frances 332, 469
Mary 53, 67, 402
  405, 406
---E 407
---L 407
McCalla 340, 404,
  415, 453, 484, 545
Mell 154
Micajah 407
Mildred 402
Milly 63
Myrtis 405
Neal 402
Nellie 402
Newton 407
Olin 404
Paul 403, 407
---A 143
---J 154
Pearl 405
Peter 67, 172, 405
  406
Peter Washington
  406
Phoebe 402
Polly 402
R W 121, 163, 169
  173-75
Rebecca 402
Reuben 209, 402, 405
---Weston 405
Rhoda 64, 402
Rhody 65
Rice 402

Robert 402, 407
---C 154
Roy 407
Ruby 405
Ruth 405
Sarah 332, 402-03
  405
Sevier 402
Sillette 402
Sister 62, 65
T J 162
T P 128
Thomas 407
Thomas F 406
---J 142, 173, 175
Ullysses 402
Viola 407
Virginia 406, 541
Washington 402
Weston 407
William 402, 406-07
---G 151, 405-06
---H 407
---L 405
Weston 405
Willis 403
Woodfin 406
---A 153, 327
Wyatt 402
CLIATT David 537
CLIFTON Miss 470
CLINE
  Francis Xavier 151
CLINKSCALES
  Orrs 535
CLINTON
  Fred 370, 515
  ---S 417, 455
  Louise 535
CLORE
  Elijah 548
  Judith 548
  Mr 548
CLOUD
  Ann Elnora 433
  Ezekiel, 179
  Noah 47
CLYNCH. Gen 88
COATS, Henry 419
COBB

Edd 134
Howell 111
Mary 462, 534
Mehitable 382
Miss 388
Thomas R R 7
COCHRAN
  Geo Hugh 155
  O P, Mrs 309
COFER, Lessie 438
COFFEE
  Cynthia 444
  Elizabeth 407
  James 407
  John 178
  Martha 401, 447
  Nancy 444
COGGINS
  Ellie 325
  Tom 313
COGINHILL
  Agnes 547
COHEN, Joe 143
COHN, Dave 305
COKER, Isaac 74
COLBERT
  Ann 178
  James 73
  Nicodemus 178
  Philpot 178
  Richard 47
  Savannah 220
  Sally 52, 65
  Thomas 47, 52, 66-7
    178
  Zidy 66
COLE
  Carl 436
  Charles Fox 424, 472
  Clyde 505
  Emma Lou 424, 472
  Helen 436
  J E 147
  Paschal 64, 66
  Rosalyn 436
  William 149
COLEMAN
  Abraham 220
  D 419

Edna 181
J M 177, 179
J N 180
J P 177
James 37, 46, 179
220
John 181
Mr 328
Thomas 181
COLLEY
Mr 380
Thomas 440, 474
---, Mrs 316
---Jr 440
---N 303, 304
Tom, Mrs 163, 315
W J 85
William 440
COLLIER
Charles H Jr 365
Clarence H 365
Edward 480
Matthew 211
Thomas Gillespie 365
COLLINS
Frank 328
Fred 156
Gladys Mae 342
Martha 460
Mary 352
Samuel 222
Sarah 48
William 74
Zach 73
Zachariah 49
COLSON
Abram 73
Frances 53, 67
Mr 324
S D 135
Samuel 186
William W 538
COLVA[E]RD..180
Benjamin 111
Edmond 121
Gibson C 155
H H 135
Henry 121
Howard H 151
J T 172
John S 87

Mary 549
Wess 505
COLVIN
Wilbur 142
COMBS
Sam, Mrs 315
COMER
Ann 413, 451, 482
Bevelle 338, 413,
450, 482, 542
Fletcher 538
Janie 337 413, 451,
482, 542
Milton 337, 413,
450, 542
COMOLLI
C 307
John 6
CONE, William C 92
CONNER, James 67
Robert 91
CONNOLLEY
Thomas 180
CONWELL
Chessie 410
Daniel 67
Frank 408
Geo. B. 158, 438
-----Barnett 408,409
Geo. 408
----Jr. 410, 411
Geo. S. 154
James 410
James A. 408
James Guy 154
John 410
John A. 410
Norma 410, 411
Pierce 154
Ruby 410
Sallie May 410
Sallie Dupree Mann
408
Sally Violetta Hall
409, 410
Susan 67
Thomas 408
Tommie 408
CONYERS
Benj. 361,369

----Jr. 361, 369
Christian 361
Tate 170, 177, 304,
361, 369
COOGLER
Brothers 6
EO 304
JB 307
TT 307
COOK
Benjamin 49, 73, 169,
179
Beverly C 221
Caleb 445
Daniel 221
David 69, 225
Drucilla 445
Dudley 73
Elisha 181
Elizabeth 181, 445
Endosius 78
Farar 73
Frances 181, 538
Francis 48
Frank 64
Gales 445
George 73, 171, 176
JE 91
JH 305
James 46, 48, 176,
211
---Wesley 445
Jesse M. 220
John 13, 28, 73, 74,
220, 301, 312,
----James Wesley 445
-----H 160
----Mrs 163
Joshua 220, 221
Josiah 73
Lewis 221
Lois 335
Mary 49, 50, 220
Mr. 209
Nancy 445
Patsy 445
Polly 445
RW 176
Rebecca 445
Ruben 48, 73
Samuel 221
Sarah 445

Smith 74
------Jr. 221
Theodosius 221
Thomas 13, 24, 25, 29, 49, 73, 180, 221, 445
William 50, 73
William T 136, 181, 517

COOLEY
Thomas 313
Thomas Hayes 154, 308, 313

COON Mr 472

COOPEDGE
Corrine 436

COOPER
Ann G. 346
Coopedge
Corrinne 436
Helen 448
J L 346
J W 435
James W 404
John 141
Martha 346
Mary 390, 494, 507
Mr 327, 403
Robert 346
Sophia 346
Thomas Sr 392
W H 85, 92
W J 313
William A 136

COPELAND
Edna Arnold , Mrs v, vii, 4, 138, 140, 159, 161, 162, 163, 312, 318, 345, 352, 399
Edna May 161, 162, 350, 356, 383
ZW 207, 356, 530
Zack W 144, 145, 160, 305, 312, 313, 350

CORDELL
Actor 151
BR 141
Benjamin R 150, 168, 173
Isham 534

Leila Sue 325, 336
Liela 521
Lou 494
Moses F 156
Sarah 329
TJ 149
Thurmaond R 155

CORNELL
Henry G 155
Lewis Thomas 155

CORNWALLIS
General 20, 27, 28, 29
Lord 68

CORNWELL
George H 53
Corrouth

CORROUTH
Arnold Elbert 358
Oscar H 358

CORRY
John 385
Robert 385
Sarah 385

CORSA Castra 462

COSBY
Charles 47, 73
---S 178-9
D 74
David 35
Fortunatus 176
Henry 48
J C 121
J H 121
J P 178
James O 169
John H
N B 121, 135
R G 144
R L 144
Richard T 166
Richmond T 16, 35, 73, 81
Robert 47, 73, 169
Samuel C 465
Uncle Nap 134
Widow 360, 368

COSNER
Mildred 341, 416, 454 545

COTTER
John 74
W J 92, 147

COTTINGHAM
Eugenia 476

COTTON
Carney 348

COUCH
Mr 476
Sarah 224

COULSTON
Mariam 223
Nancy 224

COULTER
James 38
Richard 50

COVAN
Marie 434

COWARD
A 116

COWART
L G 85
Oscar J 152

COWDEN
Elizabeth 77
James 77

COX
Georgia 326
J D 424
Raymond 405

COYNE
William 389, 390, 494 507

COZENE
Mr 134

CRAFT
Anderson 167, 172
Arthur Lee 156
Callie 405
Clark Howell 153
Edgar Boyd 156
J W 111
John Jr 63, 225
-----Sr 63, 225
Molly 64
Nancy 470
Pleasant 67
Ralph R 154
Raymond Roy 151

Samuel 225
Sarah Ann 327
Thomas G C 155
W A 133
Washington 225
William 225
Willis 167
CRAIG
John H 206
CRANDALL
Smith 91
CRAWFORD
...74, 75, 76
Agnes 523
Andrew A 208
B S 122
Claud 174
Eunice 408
F M 156
F Paul 536
Fannie C, Mrs 464
Flora 495
Frances 408
Francis Marion 408
----Paul 408
Geo Benjamin 495
Geo C 154
---W 110
Gipson Grady 154
H S 142
Hilliard O 154
Hinton 367
Holmon 408
-----Strauder 408
James L 407
---Columbus 407
Jane Gaines 506
Janice 408
Jenelle 495
John W 463
Kathryn 495
Lillian 495
Lucy 225
---Ann 326
Mary 408
---Jane 407
Matilda 53
Nancy Catherine 407
--- M 53
Oliver 225
Ollie 408

R S 141
Sarah Harriet 407
Susannah 364
Thomas 363
'---B 149, 170, 173
Tom, Mrs 304
Tyrissa Emily 408
Widow 327
William Asburn 407
--- H 28, 74-76
CREIGH
John J 178
CRICK
Warren 309
CRISP
A B 147
Ben 152
CRISTLER
Polly 469
CRITTENDON
Belle 522
Delia 522
Elijah Marion 521
Felia 522
Henry 152
J Ervin 522
L L 153
Lillian Ann 522
Nancy Josephine 522
Ruth 522
Thomas 522
--- J 521
William L 522
CROCKETT
Robert 179
Samuel 179, 211
CROOK
Hattie 533
Mr 446
Robert 35, 66
Theodosia 465
CROSBY
John 47
CROUCH
Hannah 457
CROUDER
Brother 60, 62
F 61
Frederick 59, 63, 64

Milly 60
Robert 47
CROW
Cornelia 497
J P 35
Joseph 73
CROWDER
Frederick Jr 52, 65
---Sr 52, 65
John 49
CROWELL
Dorothy 346
CROWING
Thomas 365
CRUMLEY
William C 91
CRUMP
Pleasant D 224
CUFFY.. 117
CULLEN
David 47
CULLMAN
Onie Lee 512
CULP
Fannie, Mrs 464
CUMMINGS
C F, Mrs 316
Family 97
J B 115
CUNNINGHAM
Ann 326
C Ann 336
Elizabeth 179
Frances 334, 376, 470
472
J 179
James 532
--- C 317
Jane 53, 322
John 46, 48, 53, 70,
180, 181
John Sr 226
Jospeh 226
Kathryn 424
Martha A 495
Minter 220
R E 158
Samantha 376
Sarah 330

Virginia 424
W T 424
---Jr 424
William 220
CUPP
  Henry Clay 463
CURRY
  L W 74
CURTIS
  Reuben 371
CUTHBERT
  Miss 511
CYRE Matilda 478

D

DABNEY
  Austin 16
DADE
  Major 89
DAILEY
  Samuel 174
DALEY
  John 397
DALLAS
  Agnes 509
D'AMICO
  Julian 307
DANDRIDGE
  Miss 412
DANIEL
  Allen 81, 87, 91, 99
    100-101, 166, 167
  Charlie 351
  David 53
  Enos Roscoe 156
  Fleming 101
  Francis 53
  Henry Willie 153
  James C 101
  John O 101, 154, 317
  --- Jr 226
  ---Sr 226
  Lindsey 101
  Marion 101
  Mary 53
  Mr 480
  Ola May 489

Raphel 101
William 48, 73
DANLEY
  Uncle Jimmy 85
DANKINS
  R 458
DANNER
  L J 465
  Vance 465
DANNING
  Ralph James 463
  ----- Jr 463
DANSBURY
  Ellen 366
  Thomas 366
DARDEN
  Buckner 179, 419
    481
  Cynthia 412
  David 412
  Dennis 412
  Ebenezer 412
  Elizabeth 40, 263, 337
    412, 450, 481
  Ellis 412
  Family 40
  George 30, 31, 35,
    41, 179, 263, 412,
    481
  ----Jr 412, 481
  Henrietta 418
  Jacob 412
  ---Jr 412
  John 35, 39, 41, 178
    412
  ---Jr 412
  Lucinda 412
  Mary 412
  ---Jane 418
  Richard 412, 419, 481
  Simeon 412
  Stephen 412
  Washington 419, 481
  William 412
  Ziephia 412
DAVANT
  Col. 176
DAVENPORT
  Sidney Tiller, Mrs
    422

Victoria 477
DAVES
  J T 92
DAVID
  Mr 141
  Susannar 226
DAVIDSON
  Gen 27-29
  Miss 509
DAVIE[S]...27
  John 28
  Miss 447
DAVIS
  Absolom 222, 552
  Amy 204
  Anna T 466
  Benjamin 64
  C A 153
  Cecil 331
  Cecile Little 417
    455
  Cheriah 552
  Cornelia 494
  Cornelius 390, 507
  D 175
  D W 151
  David 466
  Dorsey 175
  Eddie 358
  Elizabeth 466
  Emily 446
  Emma 323, 502
  Geo A 152
  ---Byrum 151
  Hattie 466
  Ida 466
  Inman James 466
  Isaac 73, 167
  ---Newton 466
  J Porter 390, 494, 507
  Jacob V 54
  James 68, 226, 466
  ---J 466
  Jefferson 110, 152,
    310, 350, 384
  ----H 466
  Jenkins 24
  Jepthan 68
  Jesse 68, 466
  ---M 176
  Jessie 466

John 79, 225
Jonathan 68
Joseph 62
---B 547
Lewis 209, 211
Loyce 547
Lucy 439
Maggie 495
Margaret 54
Martha 331
Mary Christian 390,
  494, 507
Minnie 328
Melissa 370, 515
---Heard 417, 455
Miss 361
Moses 49, 377
Nancy 63, 328
Nang 222
Obe Walker 153
Peggy 67
Phil/Phillip W
  167, 168, 176
  370, 418, 455, 515
----Jr 370, 455, 515
Reuben 394
Ruth 97
Susan, Mrs 375, 432
Thomas 35, 204
---F 222
---S 134
Wade 466
Walter 466
William 68, 394, 400
---C 169, 221
---Hudson 466
-------Jr 466, 468
---Jr 68

DAWSON
  Charity 351
  Elizabeth 352
  John 351, 352

DAY
  Augustus 358
  Douglas 360, 369
  Frances 358
  Lum 358
  Medicus 358
  Mr 360, 369
  Ossie 358
  Sarah 358
  Stella 358

Reid 358

DEADWYLER
  A B 168
  A M 546
  A P 170, 173, 425
  Adeline, Mrs 133
  Alice 419
  Alma 546
  Ann P 547
  Anna 419, 420
  Arena 420
  Asa 420, 424
  ---P 422
  ---Van 424
  Barbara 419
  C R 307
  Carl 136
  Carnival 374
  Christopher 48, 419
  D C 547
  Elizabeth 425
  Emily Jane 425
  Eula 424
  Eve 419
  Fanny Emma 374
  Frances 419
  Geo 424
  ---E 425
  ---W 145
  Harriett 424
  Henry P 111
  ---R 167, 169, 204
  Ida 334
  J L 121, 127, 168
  James Tustin 375
  Janie P 422, 546
  Jesse 141
  Jim, Mrs 162
  Joe 73, 133, 177, 405
  John 422
  ---G 172, 420, 425
  --P 547
  Joseph 35, 53, 61, 317
    419, 547
  ---P 420, 546
  Kate D 424
  Letitia [Letty] 420,
    546
  Lillian 327, 403
  ---Eberhardt 422
  Louree 314
  Lucy 547

Luke 134, 222
M P 93, 174, 425
  547
---, Mrs 93
Madeline 424
Mamie L 422
Margaret 263, 425,
  435, 459, 546-7
---Lee 422
Martin 53, 169, 172,
  419, 546, 547
Mary 420
---Ann 425
---Lillie 424
---P 425
Mildred 547
Milton Pope 426
Nancy 419, 420, 546
  547
Nana Blanche 422
Otis 53
Pauline 424
Ralph Allen 374
Richard 374
T W 425
Thomas 547
Tho Joseph 422
Vail 163
---, Mrs 317
Womack C 151

DEAN
  Genevieve 363
  Helen 38, 483, 512,
    543
  John 225
  Mildred 495
  Miriam 418, 456
  Nellie 451
  Robert Jerome 410
  Samuel C 93

DEARING
  Albin 97
  James 394
  Virginia 394
  William Smith 394

DEEN Julia 520

DE GEORGIS
  Kate 471

DE
GRAFFENREIDT
  Permelia 348

DE GROTT
J Loraine 463
DEKLE
Mary 412
DENNARD
John 221
Michael 441
William 442
DENNIS
Ira 426
J T 311
John T 145, 312-3, 370
---Jr 160, 162, 207, 308, 418, 440, 456, 474, 515
---, Mrs 137, 139, 162
Robert Heard v, viii, 140
Stephen 221
DENNY
C H 500, 532
Collins 147
David 87
Ed A 87
H A 174
Haley 313
Ivy 155
J W 141
James Elijah 155
John Henry 500
Judge Haley 155
Robert 87
---T 154
Sarah 500
William 170, 173
DENT Carrie 467
DEPRIEST
John 44
DE'SHE Minnie 476
DEWITT
Eugenia DuBose 421
DEWOODY
Edith 365
Emma Virginia 365
Florence Antionette 365
James Valliant 365
John Marshall 365
Margaret Coman 365

Marion Louise 365
Martha Alma 365
Mildred 365
Rebecca 365
Sorreils 365
T. Sorrells Jr 365
William Lawrence 365
William Lawrence Jr 365
DICKERSON
Alvin 155
Curtis 502
Elizabeth 538
Emma 537
Floyd T 154
G W 162
Helen 502
John 223
---Early 154
---Henry 154
Joseph 538
Llewellyn T 155
Lucy 503
Lula 537
Mary 329
Miss 327
Myrtle 538
R M 176
Robert 169
---W 226
Weyman 537
William B 226
---H 537
DICKEY
J M 92
Miss 473
DICKINSON
C Q 522
Covie 522
G W, Mrs v
Leroy 522
Margaret Marsh, Mrs v
Onie B 154
T Gaines 155
Tommie 154
William A 154
William T 154
Winston 522
DICKSON

Blackman 220
George 413, 451
---Jr 338, 380, 413, 451, 483
---Lee 338, 380, 483, 511, 526, 543
-----Jr 511, 526, 543
Howell Rees 338, 380, 413, 451, 483, 511, 526, 543
Samuel 220
DIGGES
Catherine 458, 459
Cole 432
Dudley 458, 459
Edward 458, 459
Susannah 432
DILLARD
Isaac 222
James 222, 412
Nehemiah V 222
Phoebe 412
W B 92
DINSMORE Betty 463
'DIRTY-HEAD'
Uncle, 133
DIXON
Abram 357
Adeline 332
Andrew C 154
Anna Icylona 357
Clyde 332
George 332
Georgia Ola 357
Henry 332
J F 153
John Liddell 177
Lola J 357
Mary Elizabeth 357
Mattie 357
Minnie Lee 357
Morrison 374
Mr 447
Robert H 153
Warren 332
D'MONTGOM-ERY Giles 508
DOANE
Robert 397

DOBB/DOBBS
　Asa 7
　Capt 224
　David 169, 223
　Emma 325
　Georgia A 324
　James E 325
　Josiah 225
　Lousianna 224
　Mary Ophelia 325
　Molly 64
　Silas 224
　William M 324
　---Oscar 325
DOCK...133
DOCKERY
　Grovia 334, 470, 472
　Sally 363
DODD(S)
　Claire 469, 533
　William 223, 225
DOHME
　C L 514
　Charles Louis 417, 455
　Margaret Heard, Mrs v, vii
DONALDSON
　Mara 478
DONELSON
　Laura Elma 468
DONEPHEN
　Alex 441
DOOLITTLE
　Margaret 401, 402
DOOLY/ DOOLEY
　Allen D 224
　Col. 15, 75
　Family 11
　John M 75, 76
　William 103
DOROUGH
　Fanny 363
DORROUGH
　Mr 363
DOSTER Dr 497
DOUGHERTY
　Capt 125
DOUGLAS
　Ann 58
　Rose 338, 414, 451, 483, 512, 541, 543
　Thomas 180
DOVE
　William S 152
DOW
　Lorenzo 85
DOWDY
　S C 176
DOWER
　David C 330
　George 330
　P C 175
DOWNER
　David C 477
　Geo 477
　John H 332
　S M 149
　William 169, 332
DOWNS Mr 447
DOZIER
　Leonard 529
　Susannah 51, 529
DRAKE
　A N 144, 208, 309, 424
　Althea 431
　Edward 431
　Mildred 424, 459
DRENNAN
　Bob, Mrs 316
　D G 154
　Robert L 550
　S A 154
DREWRY
　Helen 382
DRIVER
　Alexander 156
　John Hilliard 156
DRYDEN
　C E 142
DRYSDALE
　Ann 459
D'SANDYLANDS
　Harry 508

Mary 508
DUBOSE
　Andrew 420, 421
　Benjamin 420, 421
　Eliza 421
　Eugenia 421
　Frances 421
　Herbert 420
　Hugh 420
　Isaac 420, 421
　J D 163
　Jefferson Davis 421
　Joel Herbert 421, 422
　John 421
　Joshua 420
　---Wilson 421
　Julia 331, 421
　Mary 421
　Peter 420
　Rebecca 421
　Rembert 421, 422
　Sallie 421
　Samuel 420
　Victoria Letitia 421
　William 421
DUCHINI
　Petro 151
DUDLEY
　Henry 328
　James 46, 74
　Janitius 87
　John 30, 211
　Thomas 351
　William 49, 73
DUGAR
　Lucy 385, 371, 525
DUGGAN, M L 175
DUGGAR
　Helen 449
　Llewellyn 449
　Lloyd L 449
　Mary 449
DULA, Dr 349
DUNAGIN
　America 508
DUNBAR
　C A 153, 309
　Margaret 510
　Mark 511
　Miss 510-11

W 85
DUNCAN
Alice 419, 547
Anna Auld, Mrs
  v
Asa 54
Bentley 354
Broadus W 208
Flossie 534
George 354
J H 133, 176
John 317, 419
---Martin 155
Lacey Jones 155
Madeline 354
Malcolm 505
Marcus G 155
Marion Vandiver 495
-------------Jr 495
Mary Eleanor 495
N 8
P 35
Sarah Kellis 520
William Asa 155
DUNN
Capt 225
Joseph 225
Waco 153
DUPPY
John D 121
DUPREE
Family 408
DUPRIEST
John 46
DURDEN
John 446
Mary 446
DURHAM
James Oscar 152
John C 208
Ophelia Dobbs 326, 492
T P 152
W E 152
DURRETT
R D 103
DUTTON
Nancy 67
DYE
Albert A 208

Beckman 80
Brown 221
Carey C 152
Clarence L 152
Edgar C 152
Eva Belle 489
Floyd 477
Frank 331
George T 330
---W, Mrs viii
Herbert J 152
Ida 331
J R 121
Jackson 378
James 331
Jane 221
Jim Starr 331
Julia 331
Louisa 465
Louise 533
Lucy Ann 331
Martha 330
Mary 331
Matthew 331
Mr 330
Obe D 152
Poppy 331
Sammie 330
T B 135
Thomas 224
Thompson 221, 375
William 224
DYNEVOR 518-19

E

EAKES
J F 145
R F 92
EARL
C E 174
EARLY
Anne Caroline 529
EASON
Oscar 496
Thomas 172
EASTER
Booker Burton 210
Champion 210
Charlotte 371

Connie Ethel 342
Elizabeth 209
James 29, 47, 84, 210
John C 398
Lettie 209
Lewis 64, 66, 209
Marjary 210
Mary 179, 180, 209
Mr 16
Reuben 166
Richard 209
Richmond 38, 48, 179
  180
Sarah 371
Sophia 210
Teres 209
William Thompson
  209
EATON
Grover C 155
William P 155
EAVANS Mr 447
EAVENSON
Amanda 505
Beatrice Eula 503
Bessie 502, 536
Carrie 408, 536
Cora 501, 536
Croley C 156
Earl 538
Eli 50, 74, 426
Eliza 505
Elizabeth 469
Eula Beatrice 536
Family 426
Fanny 531, 536
Geo 426
---II 426, 427
---III 426, 427
---W 322, 536
Harper 536
Icie 142
John M 135
---William 427
Julian W 156, 505
Laura 538
Martin 326
Ola 142
Paul Pascal 156
Ralph 426
Roscoe L 151

Thomas 426, 427, 505
Thomas J 326
W J 135
William Allen 536
Willis 426
---Jefferson 427, 536
EAVES
Alfred R 155
Arthur C 155
Boots 389, 507
Frank K 389, 507
Hattie Lee 523
Joseph 507
Mr 93
Walter 507
--- K Jr 389
William E 506
EBERHARDT
Adeline 426
Agnes, Mrs 34
Alexander 423
Ararintha J 422
Asinith 425
Augusta Louise 424, 471
Catherine 422, 424
Christena 422
Clyde 426
David 422
Dora 423
Edward 426
---Harrison 426
Edwin 423
Elizabeth 425, 426
---Helen 471
Family 422
Francis 425
F Shilon 423
Geo 396, 420, 422 423, 426, 479
---Jr 425
Gussie L 120
Halbert 423
Hamilton 426
Harriet Rebecca 423, 471
Harrison 426
Harry 426
---L 471
---Lawrence 424
---Joyce 471
Helene 423

Ira 423
Isaac 426
Jacob 396, 422, 425 426, 479
---Jr 422
---Pope 426
James Frank 424
---Griffith 422
Jane Leeper 424, 471
Jim Frank 471
John 396, 424
---L 479
---Le3 423, 471
---William 471
---Wynn 396, 425, 479
L P 133, 134, 150 426
Laura 423
Leila Hilliard 423, 471
Lillian 423
Lizzie 396
---Mary 479
Lonnie 155
Margaret 420, 423-25
Mary 396, 425-26
---Malinda 424
Mattie 426
Maud Marshall 423, 471
Nathan 396, 479
---Mattox 425
Polly 425
R P 108, 119, 120
Robert 422, 423
---Jr 471
---P 111, 119
---Patton 423, 471
---Toombs 479
---W 423, 424
---Wade 471
Ruth 424, 471
---Patton 530
Samuel 424
Sarah Frances 424
---Willmina 422
Thomas 423
---L 423
---Llellyn 471
William 337, 423-4, 426

---Harrison 425
ECHOLS
A D 85
Lillian 314
EDDIN
Capt 399
EDGECOMB
... 65
Edward
Sarah P 220
EDWARDS
Adonia 380
Alice 357
Annie May 358
Arthur 358
Azalee 358
Bertha 358
Caroline 400, 547
Carolyn 302
Charles Emory 302
Charlotte 302, 547
Clark 547
Clarke Jr 160-62, 170, 175-6, 302, 308, 313, 314, 547
---, Mrs v, 310, 311
---III 302
Daisy 357
David 462
Dorothy 302, 547
E P 124
Eddie 358
Ella Julia 380
Emory 358
Emory P 110, 125, 167, 176, 302
Essie 358
Eulalia 302
Family 42
Felix 380, 466
---G 40, 103
Fletcher 357-8, 400
George 358
Inez 358
Ira 472
Jack 356
J Asbury 358
-----Jr 358
Jacqueline 302
James A 421
---Clark 302

Jewette Webb, Mrs v
John 87
Joseph 357, 400
Julia 379
L C 134, 141, 149
   169, 174
Larkin Clark 302
Lizzie 358
Louise 358
Lucy 358
Marie 330, 477
Mary 377, 378, 506
Mary DuBose 421
Mattie 358
Mr 447
Olive Charllotte 302
   314
Robert 358
---B 358
---L 91, 222
Ruby 357
Sam 358
Sarah 357
---E 380
Tallulah 380
Walter W 153
William 357
---H 93, 172
---P 168
EDY... 63
ELBERT
  Samuel 1, 2, 3
ELDER
  James 444
  Ruth 444
ELESIA Bertha 494
ELIASON
  Jane Mary 398
ELIOT
  Andrew 74
ELKINS
  C B 162
ELLET, Mrs 19
ELLINGTON
  Stephen 210
ELLIOTT
  Mildred Henry viii
  Mr 444
  Thomas 396, 479
  William Preston 179

ELLIS
  H J 85
  John G 136
  Mr 447
  Reuben 69
EMANUEL
  David 81
EMERSON
  Edward 367
EMORY
  H C 85
ENLO
  John 224
ENNIS
  Elizabeth 509
  Leonard J 151
ERTZBERGER
  H K 142
ERWIN
  Julia Wales 513
  Nell 502
ESCO
  Lonze E 136
ESTES
  Annie V 335
  Dorothy 335
  Fannie S 335
  James R 335
  Joel C 335
  Letitia Gertrude 335
  Lizzie K 335
  Mary Ethel 335
  Miss 350
  Thomas R 325
  ---Jr 325
  William L 335
ESTILL, J M 172
ETHRIDGE
  John 406
  Sadie 33, 360, 416
    454, 544
EVANS...138
  Abraham 324
  Clement A 119, 138
  E A 154
  Elizabeth 220
  Fred Wilborn 151
  J E B 67
  ---, Mrs 67

  Josephine 390, 494,
    507
  Mary J 67
  Milton 67
  Mollie 353
  Mr 538
  Saide 360
  Rhoda 87
  Williams 35
  Willis Sr 67
EVERETTE...108
EVINS
  Hardin 178
  Nathan 47
EXCELL, E V 146

F

FACING
  Jack 405
  Juanita 405
FAGAN
  Eulis Littleton 151
FAGLESON
  George 151
FAIN
  Charles 224
  E W 153
  Epperson 225
  John 225
  Robert 225
FALCONER
  Lillis 510
  Marjorie 511
FAMBROUGH
  Gladys 314, 422
  Karl T 151
  Leonidas Gaines 421,
    422
  Victoria L R DuBose
    421, 422
FANNIN(G)
  Arbuler 179
  Benjamin 73, 179
  Charles 63
  Col. 29
  Elizabeth 377, 381
  Miss 384
  Jincy 63

Laughlin 49, 73
FARMER
  C J J 93
  J R, Mrs 306
  James, Mrs viii
  ---R 151
FARRIS
  Miss 384
FAUBES
  Henry 225
FAULKNER
  A E 67
  J N 121
  James 441
  Mary 444
FAUST
  W C 121
FELTON
  Rebecca Lamar 138
FENTON
  C W 128
FERGUS
  Family 12
  John 49, 177
FERNANDEZ
  S 307
FERRELL
  John 209, 211
  Tabitha 67
  W E 476
FEW, Ignatus 393
FICQUETT
  Berry 532
FIELDING
  Obediah 445
  M B 445
FIELDS
  J C 154
  John Sam 154
  S A 418, 456, 515
  ---Jr 418
  Sherman 456
FINDLEY Sarah 488
FINLEY
  Mr 79
FINNELL Tho 444
FINNEY
  Rev Mr 432

FISHBACK Mary 548
FISHER
  Charles 341, 416, 454
    485, 546
  Hugh 347
  Mamie 341, 454
  Mr 548
  Thomas 394
FITE, A W 147
FITZGERALD
  E W 362, 475
  Lillian 362
FITZPATRICK
  Col. 449
  Dock 155
  Elizabeth 444
  J C 154
  Joseph 446
  Mildred J 449
  William 446
FLEEMAN
  Evan Lonnie 155
  Harold 550
  James Ezra 155
  William O 155
FLEMING
  A M 153
  Ada Lou 498
  Austin 334
  Caroline 323
  Col 345
  Elsie J 489
  Guy Isom 156
  H Austin 522
  Jack 6, 163, 440
    474
  ---Jr 440, 474
  ---, Mrs 138
  J H 135, 311
  Julian D 151
  Kathryn 396
  Lawrence 396
  L Henry 396
  M G 141
  Margaret 220
  Mary Caroline 499
  Moses 49
  Oscar L 155
  Paul Brown 396

T E 174
Thomas 534
W G 154
W H 396
William S 152
FLETCHER
  Mary Iva 366
FLOOD
  James 50
  Mrs 481
FLORENCE
  William A 91
FLOURNOY
  Francis 551
  Sarah 551
FLOWERS
  M 331
FLYNT
  J J 175
FOLSOM
  M F, Mrs 311
FORBES
  John 509
  Miss 510
  Patrick 178
FORD
  Barrett 419
  Cecily 322
  Darcas 63
  Edwin 477
  Elisha 420
  Elizabeth 64
  Isaac 74
  Jinsey 67
  John 67, 181
  John, Brother 61-2
  Mary 67
  Mr 388
  Sarah 327
  Sister 61
  William 361
FOREMAN
  Laurens 371, 385, 524
FORKNER
  William 73
FORRESTER
  E J 145
FORSON
  Benjamin 74

William 74
FORSYTHE...70
  Gov 43
  John 71
  Robert 71, 73
FORTSON
  Addie Bowie v
  Albert S 435
  Alice L 435
  Amanda M 429
  Asa C 438
  Belle 497
  Benjamin 63, 263,
    429, 430, 434
  ---Jr 434
  ---G 429
  Betsy 327
  Beuna 426
  C S 153
  Charles H 148
  Clay 497
  D A 121, 135
  Dallas 533
  Delancy 406
  E K 121
  Easton 429, 430, 434
  ---L 434
  Eleanor A 434
  Elizabeth 63, 397, 429
    435, 491, 537
  ---A 429
  ---Ann 430
  ---M 435
  Ella 540
  Ellie v, 140, 435
  Ethel Wilkinson v
  Eugene B 435
  Eugenia Adel 497
  Everette 497
  F S 313
  ---, Mrs v
  Family 427
  Fannie 436
  ---M 540
  Fanny G 465
  Francis B 436, 540
  ---B Sr 149
  --- S Sr 162, 304, 305
    313, 314
  Frank 160
  Geo G 540
  Geo Green 136, 430,

    436
  Geo Hailey 136, 436
    540
  ---T 157, 435
  Georgia Ann 404,
    432, 435
  Gertrude 432, 436
  H A 169, 173
  H C 153
  Hailey 434
  Haley 430
  Henry A Jr 156
  Hood 502
  --- Mrs 312
  J B 121, 533
  James 429
  Jane 536
  Jefferson H 156
  Jesse 439
  John 429
  ---Easton 430
  ---Hanson 434
  Laura 419
  Lawrence B 436, 540
  Lee Anderson 151
  Leonard 497
  Lillie 435
  Louisa Elizabeth 436,
    540
  Lovic 435
  Lucien 435
  Lucius 537
  M E 121
  Mahala 374
  Mahaleth 429
  Mamie 423
  Marion 497
  Martha Wall 436, 540
  Mary, Mrs viii, 39,
    162
  ---A V 405
  ---Clark 140
  ---Elizabeth 432, 435
    459
  ---M 435
  ---Nancy 435
  Maud 429
  Mildred 429, 549
  Milliard F 435
  Miney 547
  Minnie Nunnelee 436
    540

  Milton, Mrs 311
  Miss 330, 537
  P E 153
  Pauline 435
  Rachel 429
  Richard 429
  Robert E 435
  Sallie A 436, 540
  Samuel, Mrs vii
  Sarah 429, 434
  ---Alice 502
  Stephen 435
  Stephen, Mrs 141
  ---Ham 430
  Susan Rebecca 432
  Susie Rebecca 436
  Tabitha 430
  Tavner 223
  Thomas 61, 63, 186
    222, 263, 429, 434
  ---Jefferson 430, 431,
    435, 549
  ---Jr 428
  ---Sr 428
  Thomas Samuel 432,
    436
  Tug 536
  Vera 477
  Vester 432, 436
  W E 121, 305
  ---Mrs, v
  W H 435
  Weymon 497
  William 91, 167, 171,
    428, 429, 461
  ---D 306
  ---W 434
  Wilton 497
  Wilton G 436, 540
FOSCH Mr 553
FOSS
  Oliver Richmond 411
  -----------Jr 411
  Sally Conwell 411
FOSTER
  Anthony 399
  Dr 445
  Henry E 152
  J E 173
  John S 473
  Julia 127

Martha 398, 399
Mr 491
Nath'l Green 444
Thomas 73
William 167, 222
FOWLER
  A R 128
  Family 129
  James 225
  Joseph 140
  Paul Silas 153
  Rachel 224
  W L 150
FOX
  F C 449
  F C, Mrs vii
  Mary 372, 385
  Mattie Jane 342
FRANK ...176
FRANKLIN
  James Benjamin 155
  Manuel 121
  Peter 154
FRANKS
  Alice 520
FRANKY... 64
FRASER
  Agnes 508
  Ann 509
  Janet 510
  Lord 510
  Marjory 510
FRAZER
  Alexander 510
  Charles 510
  Lee 361
FRAZIER
  B F 92, 138
  Celia 353
  Catherine 466
  Daniel 462, 466
  Edith 367, 463
  James 466
  John 466
  Margaret 366, 466
  Mr 379
FREE
  Oscar 155
FREEMAN

B F 152
Doris 495
Fanny 373, 374, 387
Holman 24, 31, 38,
  186
James 73, 180-81
Jenny 210
Luther Lee 151
Mary 38
---Lucinda 408
Sarah J 508
FRETWELL
  Leila 539
FRIERSON
  Family 129
  Miss 435
  Rebecca 541
  William 129
  ---C 153
FRITSCHE
  Frederick 499
  ----Jr 499
FRY/FRYE
  George 137
  Minnie 137, 436
FRYER
  Permelia Amanda 391
FULGHUM/
  FULGUM
  Elizabeth 48
  Martin 209
  Stephen 209
FUNSTEN
  Marigene 314
FURGESON/
  FURGERSON/
  FURGUSON
  Daniel 225
  Hinton Harwell 463
  John 224

G

GAAR/GAR
  Adam 74, 169
  Lewis 48, 70
  Nancy 63
GAINES
  Andrew 136

Ann 53
Annie E 470, 472
Annie G 334
Benjamin Franklin
  156
Blanche 142, 494
---Ophelia 494
Byron Adams 495
Carl Simmons 495
Carrie 532
Claud Ralph 153
Diadem 53
Elizabeth 429
--- L 53, 334
F 121
F M 141
F L M 141
Faith 495
Florence 523
Francis 170, 224
Frank 143, 434
Fred 154
George 53, 341, 416
  454, 485, 545
---, Mrs 316
---A, Mrs 162, 207
--- Levingston 495
Helen 382, 451
Henry 64, 181
Hiram 180
Hope 495
I A 154
I M 154
Ira Alexander 495
Isom S 156
J J 324, 377
J L 121
James 317
---H 176, 327
---Ira 495
Jency 327
Joseph Maxwell 495
John 376, 534
L A 154, 540
L H 121
Lawrence 531
Leonora 495
Levingston Strougher
  494
Lindsey 382
---Jr 382
Lizzie 482

Lois 331
Lucy 333, 532
Mamie 505
Margaret 327
Marion 322, 333, 470
---L 208
Martha Joan 495
Mary 53, 459
---Ellen 495
Melissa 532
Mourning 407
Miss 385, 552
O B 154
Ora Baxter 494
---Erskin 495
Ophelia, Mrs 408
Otis 154
P 121
Patsy 65
Paul 136
Peter C 134
Priscilla 494
R A 154, 156
R T 531
Raymond 341, 382, 416, 454, 485, 540 546
Robert 371
Rosa 382, 541
Sarah 225
---Ann 433, 436
---Elizabeth 495
Seth Milton 151
Sidney 134
T S 135, 169
T J 532
Thomas N 142, 157, 160, 162
Tom N 312
Underwood 382, 541
Vandiver Brown 495
W F 154
W I, Mrs 148
William 35, 180, 226
---Shanklin 327
Willis S 404
Winifred Alexander 495

GAIRDNER
H K, Mrs vi
---206
Harry K 127, 176, 440

474
---, Mrs 139, 149
Jamie 440, 474
Lavonia 474
Molly 440

GANALIS, J 307

GANES
Henry S 225
Levingston W 225

GANTT
Drayton 351
Elizabeth 351, 360, 368
Emma 351
Fred H 151
H A 351
Helen 351
J W 406
Jesse T 318, 351
Larry 318, 319, 351, 425
Mark 351
Martha 351
Mr 548
Richard G 351
Robert 351
Sarah 351
Thomas L 351
---W 351
Virginia 541
Yancy 351

GARDNER
Elijah 225
Nancy 225

GARNER
Lottie 502

GARNETT
Eva 553
James 116

GARRETT
Elizabeth 479
Mr 480

GARRIOT
Mr 548

GARRISON
David 91

GARY
Albert Alexander 498
Beverly Allen 498

Effie Catherine 498
Emily 314
Geo P 498
---W 498
Marvin Lee 498
Mary Edna 539
Paul Turner 498
Robert Maxwell 498

GASTON
Norton 404

GATES Jane 542

GATEWOOD
Henry 74
John 74
Larkin 35, 73
Penelope 394

GATLING
Oscar 366

GAY, Clarence 403

GEIGER Mr 540

GENERAL R S 510

GENTRY
B T H 152
E 175
Edward 152
John A 135
O O 152
Oscar 496

GEORGE
....104
Indian 104
King III 3, 10, 13
William 48

GERMAN
J M 437
Thomas 475

GERMANY
Miss 449, 450

GHOLSTON
Charles T 222
Mr 424

GIANNONI
G 307

GIBBONS
William 36

GIBBS
Thomas F 167
William 35, 59, 62,

429

GIBSON
Sylvanus 68

GILBERT
Comfort 402
George 425
Isaac 425
James 425
Mr 425
Thomas 52

GILBY, John H 151

GILES, James T
324, 377

GILHAM
Charles 449
Elizabeth 449
Mary H 449
Nancy 449
Patsy 449
Peter 449
Sallie 449

GILL
Elizabeth 224
John 35, 73
Robert 224

GILLENTINE
L S 394

GILLESPIE
Alvin 157-8
Ben Evan 365
Frances 365
Geo I 222
Jack Lee 365
James Harvey 365
----Jr 365
John Finley 365
-----Jr 365
Joseph 496
Luda Worsham 365
Mary Virginia 365
Mildred 366
Thomas E 365

GILLEYLEN
John 177

GILLISON
Susan 533

GILMAN
James 84

GILMER
David 394
John 367, 394
---T 80, 367
Nicholas J 367
---Meriwether 394
Susan Josephine 367

GILPATRICK
Eva 508

GINGLES
Miss 407
S H 154

GINN
Captora Teresa 302
Fanny, Mrs 148
G W 148, 405
Hoke 505
Irene Roberts 302
J G 176, 207
Jesse 375
John Gordon 152, 157
J Tom 174
Lonnie C 151
Middleton 302, 377
Pope Bentley 155
Sat White 155
Thomas 223
Tinsley 506
Transvania 223
William 223

GIST
C G 457
Virginia 457

GLASCOCK
William 24

GLASS
Mr 446
V H 394

GLENN
Clara 406
Columbus 376
---Jr 376
Easton 376
Edwin 179
Fanny 376
G R 172
Jack 376
James 376
Jane 522
John 179, 376
---B 376

Joseph 546
Lillian 376
M W 136
Maxwell 522
Mitchell 221
N T 85
P M 153
R R 141
Radford 522
Robert 127
Sarah 376, 406
Simeon 395, 477, 546
Walter 522

GLISSON
Fred W 92

GLOER
I D 135
Jewel 336, 521
Jospeh A 135
Miss 325

GLOVER
Benjamin 74
James 73
Sister 62

GODSHALL
Louis 371, 385, 524

GOFF
Martha 393

GOLDEN
Alex Sr 222

GOOD, John M 221

GOODE
Claud 478
Hollis L 478
Jabez Wootson 478
James Clark 478
John Martin 478
Joseph Terrell 478
---Marion 478
Lillie G 478
Luther L 478
Martha 400
Martha Elizabeth 478
--- Mildred 478
Milly 476
Nicholas 395
Paul L 478
Robert 400
Thomas 396, 478
Wade H 478

Watson T 478
William Bibb 478
---W 478
GOODLOE
Cornelia 346
Dr 346
Horwell 346
GOODRICH
Hallie 540
GOODWIN
Nancy 393
GOOLSBY
Ann 432, 433
Arthur 432
Cary 433
Charles 357, 432, 531
Eliza 367
Elizabeth 432, 426
Ernest 356, 357, 531
Family 432
Fleming 432
Frances 433
George 433
I J 537
Irene 357, 531
James 432, 433
Jane 432
John 432
Lucy 432, 433
Luther 325, 336, 356
  533
---Jr 357
Martha 433
Mary 356, 432, 531
---Carolyn 357
---Nell 356
Miss 536
Nancy 383, 432
Sarah 357, 432, 531
---Cary 433
Susan 432-33
Tabitha 432
Tarlton 432
Thomas 432, 433
William 322, 383, 432
  433
---Jr 432
GORBY Louise 449
GORDON..89, 138
Alex 181
Ambrose 181

Family 392
Helen 509
Jean 509
John B 319
Lord George 10, 12
Ludovic 510
Mr 445
GORHAM
Rose 425
GORMAN
William H 139
GOSS
Benjamin 54, 73, 177
Charles 74
Horatio J Jr 54, 177
---James 420
---Sr 54
Isham 93, 177
---H 54
John 517
Lucy 141
Mary 54, 67
Sallie 489
Williams R 54
GOUDY Anderson
457
GOULD
James Nathaniel 365
Judge Josiah 365, 466
GOWER Mr 526
GRACE
Florence 438
GRADY
James Lamar 151
GRAHAM
Hollis 374, 387
Isabel 509
GRANHAM
Ann 84
David 84
GRAHME
Margaret 509
GRANT
Anna 509
Catherine 509
Mr 393
Ollie Love 358
Patrick 510
President 126

Widow 510
GRATTON..77
GRAVES
Betty 367
Eliza T 480
GRAY
Allen Hood 471
Elizabeth 435
Geo W 341, 416, 454
  545
---Jr 341, 416, 454
  545
Harriet Jane 471
Hez'h 73, 171
Lindsey A 136
Mrs 540
Page 341, 416, 454,
  546
Sarah Evelyn 471
Sussannah 222
T L 135
GREEN
Burket 74
Clara 461
Dorothy 366
E W 28
Fanny 361
Frances 404
Geo William 151
Harold 334
Harriet 346
John H 142, 334
Marjorie 366
Matilda 492
Mr 394
Rebecca 67
Sarah 547
Theodore M 366
Walton 334
GREENE
B H 85
General 27
GREENWAY
Aurelia 142
Barney 136
Coy 134
Grover 154
Hugh A 154
Lindsey A 154
Lucy 67
Milly Ann 434

Sally 67
William 532
Willie L 154
GREENWOOD
John 47, 48, 180
Jno 73
Leonara, Mrs 78
GREER Jean 553
GREESON
H C 152
John A 208
GREGG
John 37
Thomas 30, 49
GRESHAM
Eliza 367
J B 85
John 367
GRIER
Boyce M 142, 312
---, Mrs 311
Isaac 449
Jean 356
Mary A 449
Robert 449
---A 449
---F 449
GRIFFES
J A 85
GRIFFETH
Robert 49
GRIFFIN
Ann 178, 399
H R 520
James 178
John 178
L Arvin 520
Patsy Ruth 520
Thomas 176
Weldon Arnold 520
Zachariah 399
GRIFFITH
Alfred 79
George 425
Helen 535
Jacob 425
James 425
Jane 422
Mattie 426
Margaret 425

Mr 425
Sarah Adeline 425
Susannah 422
GRIMES
B B 355
Bynum 133
Elizabeth 355
Fred 502
Jimmy 502
Judson B 208
Maud 355
Mr 477
Ned 502
Robert 477
Ted 502
W J 477
Winifred 502
GRINNELL
John 46
GRISSOP
James 225
GRIZZLE
John 396
Rebecca 395, 477
GROGAN
Adeline Starke, Mrs
  v, viii, 83, 140
Barnard 186
Betsy 350, 356, 373,
  386, 526
Carroll 373, 386, 526
Edmond B 208, 386
---Brewer 373, 526
G C 305
George, Mrs vi, 310
---Albert 373, 386,
  526
---C 133, 147, 150
  176, 205, 206
  372, 386
---Jr 372, 386
---L 525
------Jr 525
---III 372, 386
Harry 175
Henry 386, 526
J H 207
J L 206
Jeanne 373, 386, 526
J Henry 152
John Henry 85, 92,

133, 141
Kathleen 357, 531
--- Bruce 373, 526
Mary Bruce 373
May 386, 526
Mrs vi, 310
Phillips 372, 386, 526
Samuel Stark 525
Sarah 372, 386, 526
---Pope 140
Stark 372, 386, 525
---Jr 372, 386
William 147, 174
W Manley 150
GROOT
J Lorraine de 367
GROOVER
Francis 460
GROVES ...176
Elizabeth 351
Frances E 351
J A 352
James
Joseph 351
Martha 351
Rignol S 351
Rignual 38
Sylvanus 351
GUERRY
Dupont 172
Rev 486
GUESS
C N 175
GUEST
Clara Belle 358
Coleman 358
James W 358
Jesse James 154
Madge 358
Mamie Jessie 358
Sidney J 156
Vesta Eufaula 358
Walker Davis 153
Walter Arnold 358
GULLEY
B A 154
C E 154
J M 122
Mr 536
Thomas M 153

GUMP
  Memory 362, 495
GUNN
  Alvada 353
  Doris 354, 523
  Esther 353
  Fortson 353
  Grace 354
  Helen 354
  Samuel 354
  ---E 353
GUNNELLS
  Americus 497
GUNTER
  Cynthia 330, 477
  Mattie 330, 477
  Thomas G 156
GUPTON Abner 472
GURLEY
  Easton W 337
  Hoyt 337
  L L 326, 337
  Mary 353
  Sarah T 337
GWINNETT
  Button 1
GYE
  Williams 63

H

HABERSHAM
  Joseph 41, 44
HACKSELL
  Miss 511
HADDEN, C 122
  Dr 476
HAGOOD
  Albert 372, 386
  C B 386
  Catherine 372, 386
  Ida 496
  Laura Elizabeth 327
  Robert H 152
HAIG, Betsy 106
HAILEY
  A C 434
  Ann Eliza 436
  Betwy 434, 436

Christine 434
Diadem 434
Eleanor 434
Elizabeth Carroll 326
Family 433
F Marion 327
Frank 434
---Elmo 324
---Elmore 437
Geo 434
---W 434
H F 434
Hattie 434
Henry F 324, 436
Hugh Edward 324
---Rankin 437
Idell 434
Isham 433
---Brown 324, 436
Jack 328, 434
James 433, 434
Joe 434
Joel S 324, 436
John 434
---Henry 324, 436
---W 434
Lamar Rankin 324, 437
Lucy 324, 436
Malinda 434
Marvin 434
Mary 405, 433, 436
Mattie 434
Mr 377
Nancy 434
Nannie 539
Penia 434
Polly 327, 434
Reuben 433, 434
Ritta 436
Ruby 332
Rucker Marion 324, 436
Ruth 434
S N 434
Sally 434
Sarah 377
Sarah Ann Eliza 324
Tabitha 434
Thomas 225, 434
W I viii, 324, 436
William 35, 225, 263

   433, 434
---- Howard 324, 436
---Rabun 433, 436
Willis 434
HAINEY
  Mr 546
  Seth S 208
HAIRCROW
  Ezekiel 223
  Hugh 223
HAIRSTON
  C P 157, 161-2, 334
  Clara 334
  ---T 523
  Clayton P 522
  Horace 334
  ---G 523
  James C 523
  Julius C 155, 334, 522
  Kenneth 522
HALES
  James 177
  Milly 63, 65
  Minnie 52
  Winey 63, 65
  Winny 52
HALEY .307
  Don Francisco 430
  Don Guillerno 430
  Family 429
  Frederick P 154
  George 141
  ---Marion 151
  J S 170
  Jack 151, 169, 382
  James 430
  John S 176-7
  Mary 53
  Ruth 314
  S N 169, 173-4
  Tabitha 429, 430
  Tommye 142
  William 67, 317, 429, 439
HALL
  Agnes 340, 404, 415, 453, 484, 545
  Annie 327, 403
  Boston 155
  Coleman 155
  Condal 333

Davis 466
E Everett 156
Flora 314
Frank Dupree 151
Geo J 327, 403, 438
---Milton 438
Horace Carlton 154
Hugh Hamilton 152
J A 466
---Jr 466
J N, Mrs 148
J W 144
Jack 382
James 84, 333, 537
---C 408, 438
---E 312, 327, 403
422
-----Jr 327, 403, 422
---William 153
Jessie 466
John 155
---P 408, 438
---Spruell 153
---W 156
Lila 327, 403
Lindsey 333, 532
Lora 553
Lucy Jim 333
Mariah Turman 438
Mary 409
---Loftis 438
Melvin 333
Mr 448
Patrick H 154
---Hansard 158
Raymond G 154
Richard E 136
Rufus N 208
Sallie Violetta 408,
409, 410
Sarah 327, 333, 359
403
Seales 221
Thomas C 154
---S 221
Viletta 441
W E, Mrs 162
William 73, 180, 327
333, 403, 442
Willie Elizabeth 327,
403, 422
Worley 177

HALLEN
William 210
HALLIBURTON
T J 528
HALLMAN
Helen Meredith 417,
455
William N 417, 455
------ Jrs 417, 455
HALLOCK
Elaine Ann 524
HALSEY
Mary J 478
HAM/HAMM
Ambros 73
Anderson 493
Charles 494
Geo J 494
Gladys 141
Hallie 537
James 396, 478
John 478
Leroy 494
Martha 434
Policeman 133
Reuben 225
Samuel 172
Sarah E 494
Susan 430
HAMBRICK
Margaret 426
Marion E 136
HAMILTON
Catherine 348-9
Elisha 220
Scott 463
HAMLIN
Hanibal 108
Robert M 347
HAMMAN
Jacob 48
HAMMOND
A E 173
Alfred 91, 101, 103
Amandine 439
Arch J 154
Archie Pope 331
Benjamin F 152
Charlotte 440

Dudley 439
Elizabeth 439
Family 101
Frank 340, 363, 370,
415, 418, 453, 456
515, 545
Jr 340, 363, 415,
418, 453, 456, 484
515
G V 147
Genora 468
George 331
--- E 154
Georgia 541
Hazel 331
Herbert 439
J E 170, 173-5, 307
Jack 153
---Edward 468
James E 153, 161, 468
Jarvis 440
Jeptha 331
---B 331
Jessie 468
Job 439
---Jr 439
---III 440
John 439
Julia May 468
Lavonia 439, 473
Lenora 468
Leroy 494
Louise 331
Lucy 439
Major Alfred 439
Mary 439
Maude 550
Mildred 340, 363, 415
418, 453, 456, 515
545
Minnie Pope 331
Miss 473
Mozelle 331
Mr 337
Nathaniel 439
---J 98
Poppy Dye, Mrs viii
Raleigh 440
Raymond 468
S T 154
Samuel 439, 440
---Jenkins 439

Sasannah 439
Thomas 35, 439
W J 147
Walter 468
William 439
Zachery B 152
HAMPTON
 C J 54
 Dr 413, 542
HAMSHIRE...64
HANCOCK
 John 13
 Thomas 517
HANES
 John 64
HANIE
 Anthony 179
HANKINS
 Mattie 448
HANNA
 James 217
 Joe Jr 313
HANNER
 L M 324, 377
HANSFORD/
 HANSARD
 Annie 441
 Ann 441
 Asa 441
 Ben 441
 Benonni 441
 Brown 441
 Chancey 441
 Charles 441
 ---P 441
 Eliza 142, 442
 Elizabeth 441, 442
 Eugenia 441
 ---Elmira 442
 Eunice Lois 442
 Georgianna Stephens 442
 Grace 441
 Henry Sigman 442
 James 441
 ---Riley 442
 Janet 226, 441
 Jeanie 538
 Jeptha 442
 ---Riley 441, 442

Jessie 441
Jethro 441
Jim 441
Joel 441
John 441
Marion 441
Martha 441
---Alvera 442
Mary v, 134, 141, 142 162, 175, 176, 305 441
---Ann 442
---Jane 441
Mildred 441
Nancy 441
Patrick 442
---Henry 441, 442
Polly 441
Robert White 442
Sallie 441
Sam Jones 442
Sarah 441
---Frances 442
---Lucinda 441
Simeon Hall 442
Susan Leanna 441
Tallie Hassie 442
William 46, 48, 73, 440, 441
---James 441
---Patrick 441
---Sallis 441
HANSON
 Elizabeth 434
 William 69, 73
HARALSON
 Joseph E 136
HARAWAY
 William 433
HARBERT
 Michael C 152
HARBIN
 Joannah 375
 Nancy 375
 Sarah 375
 T B 92
 Tyre B 85
 Victor 370
HARBOLD
 Mr 548
 Osnam 548

HARBUCK
 Mildred Z 417, 455
HARDEE
 Lucinda 441
 Phoebie 441
HARDIN[G]
 Dr 158
 May 520
 Minnie 332
 Victor 515
HARDMAN
 Betty 205
HARDWICK
 Samuel 91
HARDY
 Charles Jr 550
 Dr 511
 Jeptha 221
 Mary 221
 Prudence 520
HARIE Elizabeth 509
HARKLEFORD
 John 69
HARKNESS
 James 435
HARLAN
 Jospeh 432
 ---Jr 432
HARMON
 John 329
 Marion 329
 Matilda 385
 William 447
HARPER
 A O, Mrs vi, 315, 316
 Addie 552
 Aileen 139, 386
 Ailene 372, 525
 Allston 363
 Anna 363
 Bedford 99, 103, 223, 363
 Charity 363
 Charter 74
 Edmond 180
 Elijah H 172
 Elizabeth 363
 Eugenia Long, Mrs

139
Family 42
Frank 304
Guy E 136
Henry 70
J P 73
James C 172
Jennie 370, 418, 456
   485, 516
John 35
---Frank vii, 141, 152
   169
---P 49, 180
---S 225
L A 174
Lennie 538
Leonard A 152
Martha 363, 370, 456,
   485, 515
Mary Melissa 417
   455
Melissa 485, 514
Omer, Mrs 315
R O 16
Richard 363
Rossie 369, 417, 455
   514
Sallie 457
Sally 485, 516
Sarah 363, 370, 418
T C, Mrs 149
Thomas 363
Welina 141
William 16, 363
---G 224
---J 363

HARRIS
Al 488, 489
Alice Pope 412, 450
Alva 412, 450
Anna 457
Annie Frances 522
C P 143, 176
Charles 334
Clarence 133, 412,
   450
---P 143
Compton Pierce 151
Cora White, Mrs 98,
   147-8
David E 111
Elijah 388

Eugene 388
Eva 334
---Drucilla 523
Ezekiel 225
Faith 488
Fanny 65
Frances 335
Fred 334, 488
Grady Cantrell 156
Guy 334, 522
Hubbard 181
Hugh Wallis 522
Isabella L 522
James 388, 412, 450
---C Jr 156
---Gordon 155
Jeptha V 100, 167-8
   176, 388
---Jr 388
John 67, 488
---Jr 225
Lawrence D 155
Lessie 334, 522
Lettie, Mrs 524
Lucy 334
Lundy 488
Mary 67, 347
---Catherine 522
Matthew 69
Mauline 334, 523
Miss 328
Mr 412, 450
Nat E 499
Nathan 82
Nora 324, 377
Peggy Ann 523
Phillip P 334
---Rice 522
Quilla 334
R D 334, 523
---Jr 523
R Dozier 334, 335
Robert 412, 450, 482
---D 522
---Jr 412
Ruby 334
---Arlee 522
Rupert G 335, 523
S A 92
S W 347
Sally 388
Sarah Caroline 523

Stephen W 176
Thomas 374
W J 175
Walter 489
Walton 412, 450, 488
---Y 307
William 334, 347
---A 152
---Bub 155
---Jr 347
---Curtis 523
---Howard 522
--------Jr 522
-----Jr 523
---P 335
Young L G 82, 113,
   167, 338, 413, 451
   482, 542
Young Y G 176
Zeke 133

HARRISON
Benjamin 432, 433
Charles 399
Elizabeth Ludwell
   432, 433
Ludwell [see Eliz.]
Mary Terry 394
Nathaniel 432
President 433
W B 175

HART
Benjamin 318
James L 318
Nancy Morgan 316,
   318
Susan 520

HARTON, Capt 223

HARVEY
Elizabeth 486
Jane 361
Mary L 351
Sally 548

HASKINS
Lucy 367

HASLETT
A W, Mrs 312
Elizabeth 553
Eugenia 553
Geo 169, 173-4, 553
   554
Julia 553

Mary Eleanor 553
Pauline 553
Sarah 53
Sue, Mrs 311-12
William 553
Worley 553
HASTINGS
Elizabeth 486
HATCHER
James
W 210
William 181
HATSELL
Lucy 362
HAWES
A S 168, 174-5, 208
   381
Albert Lee 339, 381,
   414, 452, 483,
   512, 527, 543
--- Sidney 339, 414,
   452, 483, 512, 543
Dorothy 354
Fannie 310
Guilford M 527
--- Moseley 339,
   381, 414, 452, 483
   512, 543
H E 207
Harry 316
Jessie McIntosh, Mrs
   310
Julia Ann 339, 381,
   414, 452, 483
   512, 527, 543
---Cade , Mrs 310
Mary Lee 339, 381,
   414, 452, 483, 512,
   527, 543
Norma Wright 176,
   314
P M 206
Peyton M 168, 172-3,
   304, 339, 415, 452,
   484, 513, 544
Peyton S 177, 304,
   312, 313, 382, 414
   527, 531
---Samuel 339, 381,
   452, 483, 512, 543
Robert 512, 527, 543

S A 425
S O 207
W K 354
HAWKES
Martha 354
HAWKINS
Ann 547
Joseph 428
Mamie 500
HAYES
Betty Sue 502
Hanson 397, 435
Howard A 397
Jane 502
Martha Louise 397
Rob 502
Thomas Swift 397
William 397
Z C 435, 528
---Jr 177, 301, 305
Zachariah Clark 397
Zachariah Clark Jr
   397
HAYGOOD
C B 372
HAYNES
Ann 398, 442
Asa J 442-3
Bartow 443
Beecher 443
Benjamin F 442
Columbus 443
Elizabeth 442
Henry 443
I 442
James 442-3
---W 442-3
Jasper 398, 399, 442
Joseph 442
Laura 443
Lettie 443
---Duncan 442-3
Louisa Genobia 328
   443
Mallory 335
Marion 442-3
Mary 442-3
---Ellen 442
Milledge 443
Moses 442-3
---G 225

---Jr 225
---M 442-3
---Sr 442-3
Nancy 42
Sara 442
Sarah 443
---G 442
Stephen 442
Thomas 442-3
---J 442
William 169, 442
---D 442
---Harrison 443
HAYNEY Mr 554
HEAD
Barbary 181
Benjamin 225
John S 180
Sally 263, 429
Sarah 322
William 178, 221
HEADLEY
Kate 553-4
HEARD
Abram 444
---Augustus 445
Adeline 447
Almira 446
Altona 444
Amelia 446
Ann 418, 448-9
---Bozeman 444
---Eliza 444
---W 448
Antionette 445
Barnard 398, 449, 481
---C 167, 180
---Carroll 412, 450,
   481
Bedford 340, 363, 370
   415, 418, 453, 456
   484, 515, 545
---Carroll 450
---Harper 456
Benjamin 518
Benjamin W 448
Betsy 514
Betsy Meredith 417
Bevelle 340, 363, 370
   414, 418, 453, 456
   484, 515, 545

Bolivar 412, 450, 482
Bridget Carroll 412,
 450, 482
Bryan 449
Caroline 340, 363,
 370, 415, 418, 445
 449, 453, 456, 484
 515, 545
---Jane 448
---W 449
Carroll 370, 417, 439,
 456, 515
---M 176, 473
Catherine 444-5
Charles 449, 457
---E 457
---H 457
---McDonald 457
Colonel 458
Cordelia 446
Cynthia 445
Deville 457
Donald Tate 417, 455
 514
E D, Mrs 315
Eliza J 449
---Longstreet 444
Elizabeth 179, 180,
 222, 445, 447, 449
 457
Elizabeth Thornburg
 445
Emma 340, 363, 370
 415, 418, 447, 453
 456, 515, 545
Erskin 340, 363, 370
 415, 418, 453, 456,
 484, 485, 515, 545
Eugene 370, 418, 456
---B 418, 457, 485
 516
Eva 514
Eva Kathleen 417,
 455
Faulkner 447, 449
Fitz Herbert 446
Francis 446
---S 447
Franklin 444, 445
---Coffee 444-5
---Jr 444
G T H 457

George 444, 446, 447
 457
---E 370, 418, 456
 516
---Felix 445
---Jr 447
---Smith 445
---W 167, 457
---Washington 384,
 412, 450, 482
Georgia 370, 418, 440
 456, 474, 515
Harper 370. 418, 456
 516
Hazel 340, 363, 415
 418, 453, 456, 515,
 545
Henrieetta W 449
Henry R E, Mrs 316
Isabella 457
J L III 455
J Lawrence III 417
Jack W 448
James 444, 447, 449
 457
James Abram 444
---Lawrence 369, 370,
 417, 455, 514
-----Jr 514
---Faulkner 444
---L 485
---M 457
Jane Ann 369
---C 455
---Carroll 417
---Clinton 417, 455
---Lanier 337, 412,
 482, 542
Janie 370, 514-5
Jefferson 418
Jesse 179, 447, 448-9
---F 448, 449
---Faulkner 447
J Lawrence, Mr 437
---, Mrs 437
John 180, 209, 412,
 444, 447, 450, 482
John A 167, 176
---Adams 412, 450,
 482
---Joseph 445
---Jr 179, 449

---P 312
---T 176, 370, 417
 439, 456, 473
 515
---III 449
---W 447, 448, 457
Joseph 370, 445, 515
---Columbus 446
---Day 417, 455
Joshua 445
Judith 447
Julia Marie 445
---Monger 444
---Smith 444
Kathleen Carroll 417
 455, 514
Lattimer 313, 370,
 418, 440, 456, 473
 515
Lillian 445
Louisa 445
Louise Jones, Mrs
 310, 311
Lucie Evelyn 417,
 455
Lucy 447
---Hammond 445
Luther Martin 370,
 417-8, 439, 455-6
 473, 515
---Jr 370, 418, 440
 456, 473, 515
M E 340, 363, 370
 415, 418, 453
 456, 484, 515, 545
Margaret 370, 514
---Melissa 417, 455
Marguerite 448
Marion 447
---W 447
Martha 340, 363, 415
 418, 444, 447, 453
 456 515, 545
Martha Burch 412,
 450, 482
---Faulkner 447
Martin 370, 514
Mary 369, 417, 437
 445-9, 455, 514
---Ann 445
---Melissa 417, 455,
 457

---Morgan 444
Mattie 340, 363, 415
　418, 453, 456-7
　466, 515, 545
---C 418
---Carrie 456
Minerva 445
Miriam 418, 456
N M 448
Nancy 370, 417, 446
　447, 515
---Coffee 445
---Middleton 455
Nardin McDonald
　417, 455
Nathan Gustavus 446
Olive 446
Oliver M 370
---McDonald 417, 455
　515
Parks E 312, 370, 418
　440, 456, 474, 515
Permelia 417, 455,
　485
Peter Abram 447
Phillip 384, 412,
　450, 482
Ralph T 448
Rebecca 370, 418,
　456, 516
Robert 370, 418, 440
　456, 474, 515
---M 167, 176, 206-07
　370, 439, 473, 485
---Middleton 417, 455
　515
Roberta 310, 370, 418
　440, 456, 474, 515
Sabrina 446
Sallie 446
Sally Head 429
Samuel 457
Sarah 340, 363, 369
　370, 415, 417-8, 447,
　453, 455-6, 484-5
　514, 515, 545
Sarah Carroll 455
---Eliza 445
---Head 429
---J 417, 455, 485
Selina 446
Silas Wright 457

Stephen 166, 176,
　178-9, 181, 186, 263
　337, 384, 412, 444,
　447, 449, 450, 457
　482, 506
Sue 457, 516, 528
Suphoemane 446
Susan 370, 418, 445
　447, 449
---Ann 445
Thomas 444, 447, 457
---Henry 446
---J 168, 172, 363,
　369-70, 456, 485
---Jefferson 417, 455,
　514
---Park 456
---Parks 370, 418, 516
---Peter 445
---W 167
---Wyatt 446
Thompson 444
Victor Marion 417,
　455
---Nardin 417, 455
Virginia 445, 457
Vohammie 370, 417,
　439, 456, 473, 515
W M H 370
William 370, 379, 448
　514
---H 514
---Harper 417, 455
-----Jr 455
---Henry 167, 174,
　370, 418, 456, 485
　516
---III 514
Willis W 448
Woodson 446
---Jr 446
HEARDS
Thomas J 176
HEARNE
Hettie 341, 416
　545
Jane Elizabeth 395
Mr 447
Prudence 369
HEATH, Mary 439
HEDQUIST

Herbert 307
HEFFERNAN
Elizabeth 531
HEINDEL
Mr 356, 530
HEGGIE
Alice 449
Augusta 449
J F 449
Jesse F 449
---Jr 449
Ophelia 449
HEINDEL Mr 530
HELTON
Annie Bertha 341,
　546
C J 307
Miss 405, 416, 454
HENDERSON
J E 479
James 393
---B 223
John 223
Richard S 226
Simeon 412, 450, 482
Simeon Jr 226
Susan 394
William 412, 450, 482
HENDRICKS
Caroline 446
Charles W 493
Cynthia A 493
Elijah W 493
Emeline 493
Francis M 493
James 493
---I 493
Joseph W 493
Leora 493
Lounds 446
Martha P 493
Mary 367
---E 493
Miss 506
Stephen Lumpkin 493
Thomas Whitfield 493
HENDRIX
Curtis 503
Miss 506
T J 307

HENLEY, John 210
HENRY
 Agnes 491
 B A 168, 425
 Benjamin Cabaniss 458
 Benson 493
 Beverly Allen 457, 540
 Bud 540
 C G 540
 Charles 540
 Cora Lee 540
 Elizabeth 540
 Ella M 176
 Fanny 540
 Frances 480
 John P 457
 Lee 540
 ---Jr 540
 Louise 425, 540
 Lucy 540
 Marguerite 425, 540
 Martha 540
 Patrick 401
 Sarah 540
 Sarah Ann Ofelia 457
 W B 206, 540
 William B 540
 William Benson 457-8
 ---P 457-8
HENSLEE, A H 175
HERBERT
 Isaac 181
HERNDON
 Annie 459
 Annie Josephine 435
 Azalee 310, 424, 499
 B T 437
 Benjamin 459
 ---Thadeus 459
 Bernice 502
 C F, Mrs 311, 315
 Charles Fortson 435, 459
 ---Jr 435, 459
 Charlie 312
 Clara 376
 ---Helen 460
 Claude 460
 Claudius 460
 Clayton Milton 460
 Cornelia 460
 Dallas 460
 ---Edward 460
 Dillard 171, 203
 Dorothy 435, 460, 498
 Eddie 357, 531
 Edward 459
 Elizabeth 435, 459
 Ella 497
 Elzie 376, 501
 Eula 500, 532
 Fanny 374
 Flora 376, 460
 Frances 459
 ---Groover 460
 Fred 207, 305, 312, 313, 382, 435, 460, 531, 531
 ---, Mrs 315
 George 459, 460
 ---Calvin 502
 ---E 376
 ---Elbert 460
 ---Lee 422, 435, 459
 ---Michael 436, 459
 Georgia 459
 Harry, Mrs 461
 ---H 435
 ---Herbert 490
 Helen 435
 Henry 459
 ---Herbert 460
 Ida 333, 459, 532
 ---Eula 460
 Isham 377
 James Edward 435, 459
 ---Marvin 460
 Joel 459
 John 178, 459, 460
 ---A 460
 ---Altheus 460
 ---Edward 435
 ---S 460
 Julian 435, 460
 ---Jr 435, 460
 Lee 376
 Leonard Oscar 498
 Lois 460
 Lola Elizabeth 460
 Lou 537
 Lucile Mathews 432
 Lula 325, 335, 376
 Marian Ann 459
 Marjorie 435, 460
 Marvin S 435
 ---Samuel 460
 -------Jr 460
 Mary 459
 ---Louise 459
 ---Mildred 460
 Maxwell 498
 Michael 459, 460
 Minor 460
 Nancy 459
 Oscar 376
 Paul 377, 505
 Rachel 459
 S A L 536
 Sarah 376
 ---Elizabeth 435, 459, 460
 Susie 376
 Thelma 435, 461
 ---Mathews 460
 Thomas Jefferson 459
 ---Matthews 490
 ---Oscar 460
 ---T 459
 Tommie Lee 502
 Vandiver 460
 Virginia 435, 460
 William 167, 377, 458, 459
 ---Oscar 498
HERRING
 Crate 405
 Frances 422
 William A 167
HESTER
 Kate 473
 Lamar 473
 Robert 167, 168, 172, 176, 473
 Thomas J 473
HEWELL
 L D 313
 ---, Mrs 310, 311
 Laura Helen 521
 Thomas J Jr 168, 175

HEWITT Robert 469
HEWLETT Tho 474
HICKMAN
  Georgia Ann 535
  Martha 224
  Thomas S 224
  Walker 224
  William 224
HICKS
  Isaac 343
HIGGINBOTH-
  AM
  Aaron 461
  Ada 538
  Ann 209, 461
  ---Staunton 461
  Albert 207, 538
  Alice 538
  Benjamin 209, 210,
    461, 538
  Bleckley 461
  Caleb 209
  Charles 461
  Cleora 406
  Daniel 461
  David 329, 461
  Dozier 538
  Elijah Benjamin 538
  Elizabeth 210
  Eugene 461
  Frances 461
  ---Riley 461
  Francis 209
  Geo 538
  Geo Green 461
  Jacob 186, 223, 317,
    495
  James 461
  ---J 538
  Jane 495, 538
  Jeptha 538
  Jesse 461
  John 461, 538
  ---C 538
  --- Green 538
  ---Matt 538
  Joseph 209, 461
  Lucy 502
  Martha 388, 538
  Mary 538
  ---J 538

  May 461
  Miss 327
  Mose 461
  Mr 387
  Pressley 538
  Rachel 461
  Reuben 171, 461
    538
  Robert 461
  Samuel 171, 461
  Sarah 538
  T B 538
  Thomas 461, 534
  ---B 538
  Tirzah 461
  Vesta 405
  Viletta 461
  William 169-70, 180
    209, 461, 538
  ---Green 538
HIGHSMITH
  John 294
  Milly 294
  Thomas 294
  ---E 532
HIGHT Charles 490
HIGHTOWER
  Mr 444
  Sarah 177
  Thomas 177
  William 181
HILL
  Addie 524
  Adeline 371, 385
  Ann 346
  Beatrice 490
  Ben 513
  Benjamin H 337, 450,
    542
  Dorothy 371, 385, 525
  DuBose 337, 450, 542
  Ealum 224
  Ella 349
  Hugh Lawson White
    394
  Irene 371, 385, 525
  James 349
  Janie 337, 542
  Laura 349
  Lucy 263, 529
  Mary 350, 356, 371,

    385, 525, 530
  Maud 371, 385, 525
  Mr 346
  Nan 371, 385, 524
  Nona 448
  Preston 349
  Robert 349
  ---N 208
  Ruby 371, 385, 525
  Sally May 371, 385
    524
  Samuel 349, 371, 385
    524
  Sarah 347-8, 536
  ---Cotton 516
  Sue 394
  T J 175
  Tho W 371, 385
    524
  ---Jr 371, 385, 524
  Welborn 371, 385,
    525
  William H 349
HILLEY
  Thomas Jr 223
  ---Sr 223
  T Vandiver 358
HILLIARD
  Mary 412
  Ryan 328
HILLIARY
  Mary 510
HILLYER
  S C 487
  Shaier 176
HILSMAN Ida 478
HINES Julia 310
HINTON
  Ann 348
  Frances 487
  James S 225
  John L 225
  Peter Jr 225
  Robert 225
  Thomas 487
HITCHCOCK
  Homer 374, 387
HITT, Dr 424
HOBBY
  William I 176, 178

HODGES
Anne 459
Sarah 351, 360
Thomas 360, 368
---L 351
W L 305
HOGAN, Agnes 426
HOGG
Frances Owen
Glenn Allen
Grant Allen
---Jr
Harvey
Helen
Isabella
HOGSHED
Daniel 501
HOGUE
Amanda 342
Annie Laura 342
Bailey D 342
Ben D 342
Eliza 342
Ellen 342
Eva Bell 342
Frances Erastus 342
Jacob 342
James 342
Jonathan Patrick 342
Joseph Jacob 342
Martha Katherine 342
Mary 342
---Rush 342
Maud 342
Sallie 342
---Ellen 342
William Taylor 342
Willia Eugene 342
HOLD Eva 547
HOLDER
John N 175
HOLLAND
Belle 365, 466
Beulah 365
Evilina 510
Mattie 478
HOLLIDAY
James 181
HOLLINGS-

WORTH
Ada 407
Elizabeth 407
John 407
Mary 407
Miss 380, 526
Samuel 181
HOLLIS
Lillian 423, 471
HOLMAN
N W, Mrs 461
Norman W 460, 490
William 514
---Jr 514
HOLMES
James 502
Lula 464
HOLT
Mary L 347
HOLZAPPLE
Susan 552, 554
HOOD
Almeda Marie 471
Charles Francis 471
Elizabeth Jane 395
Harriet Elizabeth 471
Jane 450
Jane Ann 435
R E 304
Ralph 313
HOOPER
W D, Mrs 315
HOOVER
Wilbur 313
HOPKINS Lucy 480
HORNE, Marion 359
HORTON
Rachel 504
Rebecca 361
Sarah 505
HOSNER
Tamazin 519
HOUSTON
Alex P 167, 420
Benajah 176, 204
Benjamin 168
HOWARD
Cornelius 439

---Sr 439
Frank 459
John 439
Julius 179, 181
Katherine 519
Lucy 222, 439
Matthew 439
Mary 381, 439
Ona 336, 521
Thomas 439, 519
HOWELL Abel 419
HOWSEN
Charles 462
HUBBARD
Elizabeth 379
Miss 377
Vincent 221
HUDDLESTON
Robert 177
HUDGENS
J C 170
R E 207, 208
---Mrs 316
HUDSON
Ada 466
Addie 465
Albert 341, 546
Albert Clark 465
--------Jr 416, 454
---R 341, 416, 546
---Rayle 465
---S 454
Alice 465
Amanda 462, 466
Annie 465
Asbury 462
Augustus 462
Benjamin W 468
Bertha 465
Bessie 463
Booker 263, 462
Callie Rebecca 395
Carrie 489
Carrie May 374, 395
Carroll 341
---Allen 465, 546
---Mattox 416, 454
Charles 222
---Edward 367, 463
---Frederick 464

---Marion 462
---Tolbert 468
Charlie 395
Clark 341, 416, 454, 546
Cora 465
Crawford 463
D C 313
Daisy 465
David 166-8, 171, 211, 221, 317, 341, 416, 454, 462, 464-5, 467, 546, 549
David Albert 467
---B 220
---D
---C 537
---Cobb 465
---Jr 462, 465
---Newton 462, 466
---R 467
Delia Waters 468
Edith 466
Edward 465, 467
Elizabeth 222, 365, 462, 464, 467
Elizabeth Ann 465-6
---May 465
Elma 468
Emma 465
---L 466, 468
Emmitt 462
Ernest 467
Fanniet 465
Francis 341, 416, 454, 465, 546
Fred 463
George 462, 464, 467
---Mildred 466
Georgia 465
Grandison 462
Henry 467
James 462, 463
---Andrews 464
---Asbury 464
---Harvey 367, 463
---Madison 465
---Marvin 460
---Rembert 468
---T 465
Jamie 463
Jessie Lou 465

John 220, 378
---A 464
---Asbury 464
---Christopher 465
---Donelson 468
Johnny 465
Kate 465
Laura Capitola 466
Lawrence B 462
Lena Rembert 468
Lillian 464
---Electra 467
Lillie V 467
Louisa 439
Louise 465
Lula Virginia 467
Lucy 367, 388
---J 462
Mack 341, 416, 454, 465, 546
Madison 464
Marion Alexander 463
---Emmett 468
Martha 464, 466-7
---Lavonis 466
---Virginia 463
Mary 342, 365, 367, 462-3, 465, 466-7
---Ann 464
---Elizabeth 463
---Emma 466
---Warren 464
May 465
Mildred 467
Mitchell 464
Monroe 462
Mr 552
Nathaniel 439
Q V 464
R L 468
Rebecca 378
Richard 222, 378, 464
Robert 462
---Madison 467
Rose 465
Rufus 463
Sallie C 465
Samantha Lavonia 465
Samuel Wynn 467
Sarah Ella 466
---Isabella 463

---Jane 463
Stockton Calloway 465
Stockton Cobb 465
-----Jr 465
Tho Jefferson 465
Vesta Irene 465
Virginia 463
---Grace 468
Walter Cole 367, 463
William 221-2, 462, 467
--- Albert 465
---Duncan 395
---Jr 467
---Lawrence 463
---Oscar 465
---Thomas 466
HUDSPETH
David 552
Lucy Elizabeth 551
Ralph 551
HUFF, Sarah Etta 426
HUGHES
Adeline 372, 385, 525
Caroline 363
Elizabeth 372, 385, 525
Frances 421
Henry 372, 385, 525
Lydia G 367
Otis 532
Sarah 372, 385, 525
HUIE Robert 466
HULL
Dexter 448
Florence 448
James M 448
---W 448
Joseph M 448
---R 508
Mary E 448
Nicholas B 448
HULME
Carswell 477
Elizabeth 330, 477
George 177
G Carswell 330
I V 434
Janie 499
John T 171, 172

Mary F 325
Mattie 533
Melitta 323
Miss 405
Tinsley 330, 477
HULSEY
  William 359
HUMAN...180
  Basil 178
HUME Joseph 400
HUNNEY
  Clark 465
  George 465
  Paul 465
  Rosa 465
HUNT
  Agnes 472
  Almeda Priscilla 471
  Ann Dozier 471
  Annie Lee 334, 470, 472
  A Parker 307, 334, 470, 472
  B A T 470
  B A T Teasley 334
  Benjamin Fortson 471
  ---Paxson 471
  ---Thornton 471
  Berry M T 334
  Beverly Allen Teasley 472
  Daniel Crumley 471
  Dozier Calloway 471
  Drucilla 472
  Ella Katherine 471
  Elijah 388
  Elizabeth 470
  Emma Priscilla 423, 471, 530
  Evy 334, 470, 472
  Fanny Jane 471
  Frances 426
  George 225
  Harriet Emma 471
  Henry 225, 469, 470
  Hollis 423
  James 223, 323, 334, 388, 470, 472
  ---J 470
  ---Jr 263, 470
  ---Sr 468

---III 472
---W H 470
---Willis Henry 472
Jesse Dozier 471
Jessie Parrent 471
Joel 225, 307, 334, 470, 472
John 334, 470, 472
---L 175
---S 225
---Sr 225
Judge M B 334
Judith 472
L H Jr 334, 470, 472
Laura C P 334
---Cordelia Priscilla 472
Looney H 334, 470, 472
Louise 471
Lucy 263, 469
---Ann Drucilla 333, 470, 472
M B 470
Margaret Elizabeth 471
Mary 468, 470
---A 322
---Elizabeth 470
Mary Ella 471
---Emily 471
---M 334
---Mildred 472
---Polly 472
Matthew 472
Minnie Elizabeth 471
Moses 225, 317, 470
---B 472
Nancy 322
Nina 314
Parker [see A Parker]
R 177, 179, 181
Reuben Harrison 471
---Smith 470
Richard 179, 212-3, 216
Richard Carter 472
---Harrison 471
Richardson 170-2, 203, 388
Robert Edwin 471
Ruth 333

S T W 334, 470
Sally 388
Shadrack 472
Singleton T W 472
Sion 470, 472, 530
---Madison 471
T J M 334, 470
Tho Jefferson Monroe 472
T W Harrison 471
W M S A 334
W S A 470
William 472
---Singleton Allen 472
Willie 334, 470
Willis 333, 470, 472
HUNTER
  A E 176
  Ann C 444
  Cynthia 445
  Dr 445
  Edward 445
  Emma 314
  Fannie 445
  H P 208, 303, 305
  H S 308
  Henry 470
  Herman P 312
  Howard 463
  Jaudon 350, 356
  Jesse 349
  Joel 462
  John 445
  Marshall K 350, 356
  Mary 469
  Miss 470
  Mr 446
  Susie Belle 462
HUTARSON
  Samuel 224
HUTCHERSON
  J M 176
HUTCHESON
  John 343
  Robert B 342
HUTCHINSON
  William 506
HUTSON
  Polly 412, 481
HUTTO

Annie 358
B B 173
HYNES
  Elizabeth 349

I

INGLET
  Martha 467
INGRAM
  Mary 462
  Miss 539
  Mrs 464
  Thomas 539
  W L 539
INMAN
  Col 24
  Gipsy 499
  Virginia 466
INSKEEP
  George 176
IRONS
  McKinley 371
IRVIN
  Family 129
  Isaiah T 136
  Lula Verner vi
  W H 160, 174
  ---Mrs v , vi
  ---Sr 133
ISAACS, Col 383
ISBELL...64
ISHAM
  Henry 447
ISRAEL
  Sidney 144
IVEY, Lt 115
  Louise 354
  Richard 69
IVINS, Geo 74

JACK...64, 65,133, 168, 186, 220
JACKSON...138
  Abraham 81
  Absolom 178
  Andrew 87

Eliza Lane 530
J N 396
Jane 517
Kate 396
Lizzie 396
Lucy 552
Marion 478
Stonewall 119, 427
JACOB...
JAMES...64-5
  Ann 399
  ---Christopher 399, 401
  Belle 360
  Cassie 407
  David R 169
  Elizabeth 323
  John 134, 360, 368
  ---D 135
  ---H 206
  Julia 360, 369
  Mary 381
  Richard 323
  William 226
JAMISON, S Y 145
JANE .. 63, 104
JARRE[A]T[T]
  Archalus 91, 100, 166 171
  Howell 181
  James D 219, 417 455, 484
  Louisa 455
JAUDON
  Arnold Starke 350, 356, 373
  Carter 350, 356
  H S , Mrs vi
  Hal S 312
  Henry 350, 356, 373 526
  ---S 530
  ---Scudder 350, 356 355-6
  Mayson 350, 356, 373 386, 526
  Sarah Louise Arnold, Mrs viii, 140
JAWBS F 128
JEFFREY...61

JEFFRIES
  Killies 345
  Thomas H 144
JENKINS
  Clinton 151
  Drucilla 376
  Elias 376
  Harriet 376
  J C 376
  J I 376
  J P 151
  James 534
  John 161
  ---S, Mrs 315
  Mary 376, 439
  Miss 327
  Sallie 460
  Sarah 376
JESSE...93
JETER
  Barnett 64, 171
  ---Jr 222
  Dolly 362
JIM...103
JOE..64-66, 93
JOHN...64
JOHNS, G A 175
JOHNSON
  ...108, 113
  A S 160-1, 208
  Aaron 35
  Albert Sidney 151
  Alexander 224
  ---S 334
  Angus 223
  Ann 326
  Anna 351
  Benjamin 394
  Beverly Allen 334
  C F 153
  C W 303-04
  Charles 160, 313
  ---A 155, 162, 309 495
  ---Jr 495
  ---, Mrs 309
  Clarence L 153
  Daniel 224
  Elijah 397
  Evelyn 334

Grace Kathryn 521
Geo M 312-13
Georgia Heard, Mrs
  139, 140, 310
Harry Lee 334
Henry M 334
---T 154
Hoke S 334
Ida 334, 500, 532
J E 150, 370, 418, 440
  456, 474, 515
--, Mrs 162
---Jr 306, 370, 418,
  440, 474, 515
---Sr 160
---III 418, 440,
  456, 474, 515
James 222, 344, 393
---W 152
John 171, 224, 334
---H 222
Jospeh 376
Katherine 550
Katie 335, 505
L G 85
Larry 521
Lindsey 224
Littleton 58, 60, 171
Luther 467
Lyndon Pope 155,
  334
Malcolm 334
Mark E 153, 172
Mary 358
Michael 367
Miley 344
Mr 477
N L, Mrs 312
Neal 224
Nealie 390
Nicholas 486
Obie B 153
Patsy 335
Phillip 222
Phyllis 334, 521
R H 160, 207-08,
  303, 304
---Jr 550
R Hampton 550
Rapheal 377
Robert 35
Sarah 53, 334

---Drucilla 522
Singleton 441
Susan 222
T 167
T D 350, 533
Violet 550
W A, Mrs 163, 316
W T 153, 377
---Jr 377
Walton 160, 313, 521
Walton A 155, 325,
  334, 336
Wenona 334, 336
William 550
William E 151
Williard S 136
---T Jr 550
Winona 521
Zachariah Clark 397

JOHNSTON
Elizabeth 63, 492
John 62, 166-7
Larkin 67
Littleton 62, 64-5
Mary 225
Miss 433
Phillip 63
Sarah Emily 407
Thomas 67, 167-8,
  172, 327
William 168-9

JONES
...120
A A 121
A B 372, 385, 525
A D 468
Aaron 178
Adele 434
Adeline 425
Allen 73, 179, 341
  416, 473, 546
---Turner 326
Annie 341, 416, 454
  485, 546
---Sue 341, 546
Betsy 473
Brewer B 151, 374,
  387
---Jr 374, 387
Callie May 341, 416,
  454, 465, 546
Carrol W 152

Charles A 208
Claud 374, 387
Cornelia 473
D K 308
D R 117
Drukell 151, 425
Dudley 85
Edmond 222
Edmund Brewer 158
Edwin A 360, 368,
  473
Eliza 473
Elizabeth 100
Ernest T 208
Family 101
Fanny 222
Freddie 465
Garland 67
Geneva 423
Georgia 440, 473
Grady 152
Gussie 425
Gussie Oglesby, Mrs
  310
H P M 153, 341
---Jr 341
Hailey 65
Haley 64
Harold 465
Helen 314, 423, 468
Henry 132
---P Mattox 416, 454
  546
-----Jr 416, 454, 546
Henry Martin 153
Ida 127, 468, 473
Inman 349
J H 92, 119, 133, 135
  206, 319
J W 121, 466
Jackson M 468
James 62, 65, 67, 91
  100, 349
---Loftin 208, 374,
  387
Jenelle 423, 468
Jensey 220
Jeptha 341, 416, 454
  485, 545
Jeptha B 141, 167
Jesse 221
Joanna 399

John 57, 63-4, 66, 101
  473
---Allen 465
---G 425
---Henry 157, 172,
  439, 440, 473
---Jr 473
Jones 473
Jordan 53
Joseph 224
Lady Bird 314
Lavonia 319
Lenora viii, 81, 139,
  140, 157, 440, 473
Lewis I 53, 67
Lonnie Daniel 155
Louisa 370, 417, 439,
  473, 485
Louise 372, 515
Lucinda 537
Luther Thomas 151
Mamie 440, 474
Margaret 148, 440,
  473
Marshall 223
Martha 341, 416, 454
  473, 546
Martha, Mrs 141
Mary 100, 374, 387,
  439, 440, 468
---C 473
Mattie, Mrs 141
Maud 465
Miss 467
Mitta Byrd 440, 474
Mr 329, 412, 450, 482
Mozelle 425
Nancy 65, 66
Neva 468
Nona 374, 387
Nora vi, 163, 310-11,
  316
Obediah 76-77, 168
Ora Hollins 152
Oscar 473
Ossie Thompson 152
Patsy 65, 473
Polly 65, 473
Rachel 263, 361, 495
Reba 341, 416, 454
  545
Rebecca 224, 341,

  416, 454, 546
Robert 360, 368
Sallie 468
Sally 63, 65
Samuel 222
Sarah 341, 416, 454
  485, 546
---Emily 407
Simeon 224
Solomon 53, 349
Standley 66
Stephens 473
Stockton Hudson 468
T A 135
T S Jr 144
Thomas 73, 81, 91,
  100, 133, 181, 323,
  341, 416, 439, 454
  473, 546
Tho A 119, 138, 176
---Jr 473
---S 374, 387
---Solomon 151
Tom 118
Vesta 465
Virginia 466
W F Jr 151
W F Sr 207
W J Sr 174
Walter C 423, 468
William 38, 167, 172
  223, 475
---A 465
---B 54, 152
---F 94, 162-3
---, Mrs 310, 311
---F Jr 160
---F Sr viii, 139, 168
---Fitzpatrick 156, 158
  425
---------Jr 425
---H 222
---Jr 67
---Oscar 473
----Jr 473
W G B 162, 174-5
Wiley 473
William 375
William H 154
---O 138, 144-5
---Oscar 440
------Jr 440

Willie 153
Winny 67
W O 143, 145, 161
  206, 207
JORDAN
Ben 505
Charles 332
Clyde C 155
Dora 502
Elizabeth 481, 493
Emmie 326
Harry 335
Henry D 372, 386
  526
---Jr 372, 386
Jasper 505
Leman 155
Lovett 372, 386, 526
Mary 392
Obedience 87
Ralph 372, 386, 526
Samuel 392
Sarah Adeline 372,
  386, 526
Wilton 152
JORDEN
Absolom 178
Jean 178
John 178
JOSSUM 459
JOURDAIN
Fountain 225
Isaac 225
John 225
---Jr 225
JUDD Chloe 460
JUDY...64
JULIA...104
JULIAN Ora 533
JUNIEL
Edna 464
Emma 464
J W 464
James W 464
Lindsay 464
Lois 464
M E 464
Morris 464
Paul 464

K

KAIN
Richard 178-80
Rosannah
Ruth
KANTALA
M W 307
KARR Samuel 87
KATE
Mammy 13, 22, 23
KAVANAUGH
Bishop 85
KAY
Ben 132
---H 360
Benjamin H 369
--- Herbert 151
Elizabeth 360, 369
Herbert 144, 360, 369
James Wallace 208
Katherine 360, 369
Ralph 360, 369
Wallace 360, 369
KEARNEY
Martha 348
Priscilla 351
Thomas 351
KEATON
Eleanor 553
KEELING
Elizabeth Haynes 442
Leonard 225
Thomas 224
KEISTER Ernest 463
KEITH Kitty 476
KEKEWICH
C G 509
KELLER Nancy 527-8
KELLIS Sarah 520
KELLUM
Elizabeth 552
Gip 155
KELLY
Belle 330
G W 67
Hattie 330, 477
Henry 353
J E 144, 158, 208
John 467
---Jr 467
---Thomas 154
Laura 467
Lee 467
Robert Walton 154
Rose 467
T F 168, 304
William 224
KEMP
David V 220
KENDRICK Mr 445
KENNEBREW
E 134
Edwin 222
Jasper 172
Tho L 151
W C 144
KENNEDY
Jane 339, 381, 414, 452, 512, 527, 548
Mr 548
Robert 167, 169, 171
Ruby 476
KERLIN
Elizabeth 54, 221
Jacob 54
James 53
Lucy 53
Samuel 222
William 222
KERR, J C 145
KESLER
Dennis H 156
KEY
Albert J 480
Alma 475
Amelia Ann 476
Anne 480
Annie Irene 476
Armary 475
Beverly 480
Blanche 475
Catherine 480
Chesley 480
Chiles Terrell 395, 475, 476
Clark 475
Daniel 475
Doris 475
Eliza Amanda 477
Elizabeth 330, 395, 477, 479, 480
Ernest D 476
Eva 476
Fannie May 476
George 475
Geo Oscar 475
Henry 396, 478
---B 479
---Jr 479
---III 480
James 395, 475, 477, 480
---Lee 476
------Jr 476
Jane 396, 479
Jefferson 480
Jesse 480
---Bibb 475
Joel Martin 476
John 475, 477, 479
---Edgar 476
---M 47
---W 476
Joshua 475, 480
Judith 480
Kathryn 475
Keturah 396, 478
King 475
Lola L 476
Lottie 475
Lucinda 476
Lucy 396, 479, 480
Malinda 479
Margaret 396, 478
Martha 395, 477, 480
Martin 475
---Jr 475
---III 479
Mary 396, 475, 478, 480
---Ann 475
---Leola 476
Maud Madeline 476
Milley 477
Milly 395
Miss 327
Nancy 395, 477
---Bibb 475

---E 477
Oscar 475
Patsy 475
Paul W 476
Robert 480
Robert J 480
---Terrell 475
Ruth 476
Sallie Bibb 475
Sarah Terrell 476, 479
Susan 396, 478
Tandy 475
---Clark 480
Terrell 476
Thomas 35, 396, 475
   479, 480
---J 221
---Jefferson 475
---Terrell 475
Walter 475, 480
William 35, 221, 475,
   480
---Bibb 263, 395, 475
   476 477
------lv 479
---Durrell 475
KEYS
  Agatha 67
  John 48
  ---D 222
  Sarah 330
  Thomas 178
KIDD/KID
  Addie 324, 436
  Armenta H 530
  Brother 62-3
  Elizabeth 65
  Franky 65
  J ?
  J C 533
  Martin 63, 66
  Rhoda 402
  Sister 62-3
  Webb 63, 65, 74
  Will 209
  William 63-4, 180
KILPATRICK
  Charles McCord 338,
    414, 452, 483, 512
    543
  R F 476

Sarah Ann 466
KIMBROUGH
  Edward E 553, 554
KIMSEY, Henry 396
KING
  Claud Johnson 155
  D W 148
  Elizabeth 547
  Ella 523
  Ezekiel 74
  John 35, 177, 323
  Lembard 74
  Lonnie 547
  Martha Ann 203
  Mary 519
  ---Florence 547
  Miss 496
  Mr 496
  Sarah 378
  Robert 479
  Thomas 67, 225
  Willie S 155
  Zuriah 225
KINGSTON...89
KINKADE
  Hugh 211
KINNEBREW
  W T 143
KIRK E Sullivan 490
KIRKLAND
  Ada D 467
  Alice 467
  Arnold 467
  Carrie 467
  Charles Tate 467
  David 467
  Dora E 467
  Eva 467
  Irene 467
  Julia 467
  Lizzie May 467
  Louise 467
  Mary 467
  Minnie L 467
  Richard 467
  William 466
KISON Lucille 425
KITTLE
  Dora, Mrs 354

KNIGHT
  Gene 314
  J W 85, 92
  Judge 77
  Marcus A 176
KNOX, Maggie 141
KOELING H W 128
KOOCKOGEY
  Mr 385
KORTEN
  August 163
KRICK...307
KRONER
  Frank H 397
  H A C 397
  Kathleen 397
  Louise 397
  Susan 397
KRUTES
  Kathleen 355
  Nicholas 355
  Ruth 355

L

LAFAYETTE
  Marquis de 68, 364
LAFITTE, Ed 134
  Jim 134
LaHATTE
  Annie 373, 382, 387
LAMAR
  A R 110
  James S 96, 97
  Joseph R 98
  ---Rucker 97, 138
  -------, Mrs 97
  Phillip Jr 97
  ---Sr 97
  Robert 97
  Zachariah 35-6
LAMB
  John Sr 47
  Mary 324
  ---J 539
LAMBERT
  Charles 355

---T 355
Frances 355
Jospeph 355
LAMPKIN
  A W 367
LANDAU Leon 313
LANDERS
  Mary Elizabeth 521
LANDRUM
  Harris 360, 369
  ----Jr 369
  Mr 397
LANE ...108
  James 393
  John A 222
  Major 343
  Robert 91
  Sarah 447
LANG
  J B 465
  Miller 465
  Velma 465
LANGHAM
  William 419
LANGSTON
  Ada 369
  Dr 369
  John 133, 369
  ---C 141, 142
  Jesse 67
  Patsy 67
LANHAM
  Arthur Jr 417, 455
  Mary 417
  ---Ann 455
LANIER
  Betty 481
  Caty 481
  Elizabeth 481
  John 481
  ---Jr 481
  Lewis 481
  Molly 481
  Mr 446
  Nicholas 481
  Patsy 481
  Priscilla Elizabeth 481
  Rebecca 481
  Robert 481
  ---B 481

  Sampson 481
  ---Jr 481
  Sarah 481
  Susannah 481
  Thomas 481
  William 481
LANTI, Enrico 151
LARCOME
  Jane 446
LATTIMER
  Mamie 370, 418, 439
  456, 473, 515
  Senator 456, 473, 515
LAWRENCE
  Lewis Irvin 154
  Robert de T 175
LAWTON, A R 119
  Capt 119
LAYBOLD
  Frances 490
LEACH Harry 488
LEARD, Charles 328
LEARMONTH
  Beatrix 508
LEAZER
  Jacob W 539
LeCONTE, Mr 330,
  415, 453, 484, 545
LEDBETTER
  Drury 210
LEE ...138
  Abram Head 445
  Angus 313
  Ann E 446
  Augusta 527
  --- Head 446
  Augustus 380, 531
  ---Jr 381, 382, 527
  Col 343
  Cynthia Ellen 445
  General 122
  Georgia Watson 303
  Julia Smith 445
  L O C 154
  Lester, Mrs v
  Mamie 527
  Mannie Coffee 445
  Mary Carithers v
  Minnie 380

  Onie 339, 381, 414
  483, 527, 543
  Peeples 446
  Pryor 445
  R E 304
  ---Jr 306
  Robert E 427, 537
  Ruby Edna 524
  Sarah 380, 527, 539
  Susan 446
  William Peeples 446
  Woodson 446
LEEK, John 25, 28
LEGS
  Catherine 59
LEGRAND[E]
  John 35, 485
  ---Jr 485
  Nancy 485
  Peter 485
  Sally 485
  Susannah 485
LEHMAN
  Ralph F 460
  ---Jr 460
  Sarah Joyce 460
LEM, Uncle 133
LEOHR
  George 138
  ---W 144
  James 158
  ---L 157
LEONARD
  Mrs 492
LESTER,
  William 393
LESUER/
    LESEUER
  Alex 391
  Edna 391
  Martha Ann 390
LETSON Fanny 497
LEVIN, William 344
LEWIS ...64
  Catey 67
  Catherine 67
  Elenor 67
  Hattie 67
  J R 85

Jeptha 222
Mary Hamilton 457
Mourning 322
Nell 356, 531
Phillip 64
Thomas 24
W F 85
LIDE
Dorothy A 448
Thomas E Jr 448
William David 448
------------Jr 448
LIETCHER
James 479
LILLINGTON
Christian 43, 349
LILLY Annie 496
Charles 496
---Allison 496
Egbert 496
Lilly 496
Roberta 496
LINCOLN ...108
General 26, 516
LINDER
Alice 340, 415, 453, 484
Ethel 404
Helen 532
Mr 340, 415, 453, 484, 544
LINDSEY
Beulah 464
John O 128
Margaret 509
Mr 337, 434
Richard 35
Reuben 35, 73, 80
R N 181
Robert 168
LINGOLD
Henry L 208
LIPHAM, M 181
LITCH
William 48, 168
LITTLE
Bessie Hines, Mrs 310
Cecile 370, 417, 455, 515

James D 342
John O 342
Kate 141
Martha 475
Robert 168
LOCK, J D 208
John D 158
LOCKEY
Edward 441
LOCKHART
James 225
Mary 510
Samuel 42
LOCKLIN
D V 135
LOCKWOOD
W H 349
LOFTIS, Mary 408, 438
LOFTON
B H 176
Family 98
J H 111
James 98, 120, 172, 176, 382
John T 120
Mary 374, 387
LOGAN
J A 305, 307
Jennie 457
John 313, 539
---A 304
---G 92
Q G 160
LONG
Blanche 494
Carolyn 490
Crawford W 528
Elizabeth 528
Emma Heard, Mrs 139
Henry M 338, 380, 413, 451, 483, 512, 527, 543
J M 145
Joseph 180
Mary Louise 380, 413, 451, 483, 512, 527
Miss 347
Miriam 490, 494

Mr 476
N G 6, 133, 138, 149, 168, 206, 318, 363, 370, 515
---, Mrs 139
Roy 490
---D 494
LONGSTREET
...138
Lou 114
LOVE Susan 362
LOVELADY
Thomas 47, 48, 74
LOVERN Miss 553
LOVINGOOD
...180
J W 121
Lester 153
Samuel 224
W L 152
LOWERY
Elisha 73
J L 74
Jas 73
John 74
LOWTHER
Lizzie 539
LOTHER Lizzie 539
LUCAS Frances 547
LUCY 65, 209
LUMPKIN
Ada 424
Elizabeth 446
Gov 446
LUNSFORD.. 51
A S 141, 146
Alexander S viii
Carswell J 154
Demarius 353
Henry Grady 156
Holcomb B 156
J S 176
James 87
Joe L 537
Lester 313
Rollin 87
Thomas S 156
William 223
LYDDA...63

LYLE
 Anna Sophia 342
 Coy 405
 Edna 489
 J W 405, 406
 L W 85
 Miss 380
 Mr 447
 Norvelle 141
 Russell 405
 Willie 331
LYMAN, Elihu 177
LYNCH
 Charles 394
 ---Jr 394
 Fred 370
 ---B 417, 455
 John 394
 Penelope 394
LYON, John 63
LYONS
 A B viii
 Bernice 373, 386
  526
 Castleton 64
 Martha 404
 Patsy 64, 65
 Thomas 223
LYTLE
 Archibald 379

M

MABRY
 James Walton 151
 Thomas W 226
MACCLEAN
 Janet 510
MACCOY Jane 510
MACDONALD
 Aley 466
 Allen 509
 Angus 508
 Arminda 496
 Jack 492
 Mona 508-09
 Polly 457
 Ronald 509
MACDUFF

 Constantine 508
 Duncan 508
 Dundan 508
 Gilmichael 508
MACGEHEE
 Jesse 224
 John 224
 Jonathan 224
MACKAY
 Leila 496
 Lou 497
MACKENZIE
 Agnes 509, 511
 Anna 509
 Hector 509
 Maydalen 509
 Roderick 509
MACKINTOSH
 Aeneas 509-10
 Alan 510
 Alexander 509-10
 ---Graham 509
 Alfred 509
 Allan 510
 Angus 509-11, 513
 Ann 511, 513
 Beatrix 510
 Charlotte Eva 509
 Charles Frazer 510
 Donald 510
 Duncan 509-10
 Edward 509
 Elizabeth 509-10
 Elspeth 510
 Emelia 510-11
 Ferquhard 509
 Forbesia Maria 509
 Helen 509
 Isabel 509
 Isabella 510
 James 510-11
 ---Jr 511
 Janet 510
 Jean 510
 Jessie 511
 John 509-11
 ---Mor 510
 Joseph 510
 Katherine 510
 Kenneth 511
 Lachlan 509-11

 Lydia 510
 Magdalen 510
 Malcolm 509-10
 Margaret 509
 Maria 510
 Marjorie 510, 513
 Mary 509
 ---Marion 509
 Miss 511
 Ossian Kenneth 511
 Shaw 509
 William 509-10
 ---Archibald 511
 ---Hillary 510
 ---Jackson 510
 ---Mor 510
 Winwood 509
MACPHERSON
 Elspeth 511
 Isabella 511
 Jean 510
 Mary 510
 William 509
MACON
 Ann Hunt 346
MADDEN
 Lillian 523
 Miss 527
MAHONEY
 Eddie Frank 358
 Hoyt 358
 John T 358
 L Elizabeth 358
 Marvin 358
 Nellie 358
MAJURE
 Bonnie Jean 324, 327
MALETTE
 Maggie 445
MALEY/MAILEY
 Asa 438
 Davidson 130
 Elizabeth 67
 Horace H 374
 John 420
 Marguerite 374
 Mary Alice 374
 Sidney 130, 420
MALLOY
 Margaret 471

MANLEY
  H H 425
  Horace H 151, 387
  ---, Mrs 138, 162
  Julian B 151
  Marguerite 387, 425
  Mary Alice 387, 425

MANLINE
  Franklin 47

MANN
  Elizabeth 67
  Family 408
  Henry 64
  Hewell, Mrs 162
  Holman 67
  Jane 64
  John 58, 61-2, 65-6 174
  John A 154
  Judith 59
  Leroy 424
  Lizzie 64
  P O 154
  Paul Grady 154
  Polly 63
  Robert 67
  Sallie 403
  Sally 328, 382
  ---Dupree 408
  Thomas Floyd 154

MANNING
  Amanda 496
  Mary 54, 496

MANSELL
  Wm H 497

MANSFIELD
  Catherine 322

MANUEL, J W 355

MARBURG
  Fanny 338, 380, 413 451, 482, 511, 526, 543

MARBURY/ MARBREY
  Elizabeth H 390
  Horatio 177

MARCUS
  Madison A 170
  Solomon 172

MARKS
  Amelia 486
  ---Meriwether 366
  Deborah 367
  Eleanor Tomkins 367
  Ellie 366
  Frank 366
  --Harvie 366
  Georgia 366
  Hastings 486
  Hattie 366
  Ida 366
  James 210, 486
  John 486
  ---Harvie 486
  -----Jr 486, 466
  -----III 365
  Margaret 366
  Martha Gaines 486
  ---Harvey 367, 463
  Mary 366, 486
  Nicholas 486
  ---Meriwether 486
  Rebecca Mathews 365
  Samuel Winston 486
  Thomas 366
  William 366
  ---D 466
  Willie 366

MARR Elizabeth 531

MARSHALL...369
  Abraham 486
  David 52
  Eliza 423, 471

MARSTON
  Mary B 399, 401

MARTIN ...64
  Aaron 151
  Absolom 402
  Beverly 222
  Campbell 526
  ---Jr 526
  Christopher 396
  David 73
  Frank 313, 396
  George 178
  Georgia 396
  Henry 221
  Jacob B 152
  James 25
  Jane 526

  John 74, 181, 526
  Katie 423
  L H O 369, 417, 455
  -----Jr 168, 172-3, 310, 369, 417, 455 514
  Lee 532
  Lucy 384
  Luther H O Sr 110-11, 121, 138, 167, 485 526
  Martha Key 396
  Mary 526
  Merle 366
  Mildred 394
  Miss 401
  Nathaniel 221
  Rebecca 221
  Robert Jr 180
  Sarah 369, 417, 455 514, 526
  ---Mourning 396
  Stark 526
  Stephen 447
  T M, Mrs 304, 309-10
  Thomas 47, 526
  William 53, 431, 526

MASCH
  Early V Lee 155

MASHBURN
  Annie 435, 459
  Charles Willis 550
  E W, Mrs 303-04
  Ethel, Mrs 161
  John H 92, 152
  Lucy Ethel 550
  Weyman 550
  Weyman, Mrs 138

MASON
  A 121
  Bartow 323
  ---Bee 501
  Charlie 155
  Earl 150
  Wallace 494

MASSEY
  Jesse L 326, 337

MATHEWS...34
  A C 206
  Abraham 488
  Adeniram Judson 488

Albert Clark 146, 487
 488. 490
Albert Goss 489
---Wootten 489
Alfred 490
Ann Hazeltine 488
---Paul 486
B A 206
Baldwin 488
Blanche 489
Boardman 490
Carl Stevens 489
Clifford 358
Corra May 489
Dave 319
David 486, 490
---Alfred 488
Ella Gertrude 489
Elizabeth 488
Emily 488
Eva Marie 489
Frank 367
General 34
George 29, 31, 186
---Boardman 488
---Byron
---William 489
---Jr 489
Gertrude 490, 517
Gov 32, 33, 34, 51, 71
 72, 166
Isaac 488
Jacob 488
James 486, 487, 488
---Christopher 491
---D 517
James Davant 486,
 488, 490
---Jr 487
Jesse 488
John 34, 486, 488
---Philip 488
Judson 486, 490
Lucile 432, 490
Martha 488
Mary 488
---Adeline 488
---Elizabeth 488
Millicent 488
Moses 486, 488
Mr 380
Nancy 393

Olive 365
Ora Eugene 489
Oscar Pearce 488
Paul Wootten 489
------Jr 489
Philip 487-89
Polly 488
Rachel 488
Rebecca Ann 488
Sallie 365
Samuel 431, 486, 488
Sarah 488
---Ellen 488
---Goss 489
Sophia 489
Stanley 490
---Sue 490
Vesta Pearce 146, 490
William 488, 490
---Carey 488
---Judson 489
Willie 153

MATTHEWS
A J 134-5
Albert W vii, 31
Blanche 494
David 369
Elizabeth 553
George 166, 176
Hugh 522
Judd 134
Lee Walton 156
Lewis 181
Lucile 435
Miss 374
Mr 553
Olive 466
R J 359
Robert Calvin 522
Sallie 466
W J 133, 147, 149
 158, 168, 207
Willis 342

MATTON
Clark H 431
Henry P 167

MATTOX
Alice 375
Allen 416, 454
Annie 341, 416, 454
 546

---Mae 477
Benjamin 35
---Bibb 151, 208, 397
 479
Bill 106, 114, 396
C M 6, 307
Carroll 341, 416 454,
 485, 546
Christopher 396, 477,
 479
Clark 133, 485
---, Mrs 310
---McIntosh 341, 416,
 454, 546
-------Jr 341, 416, 454
 546
Dorothy 375
E D 397, 479
Elizabeth 375, 397
---Jane 426
Ellen 375
Family 23, 40
Fanny 477
Frank 396, 479
G W J 396
G W R 153
George 535, 535
Geo W 477
---William 151, 158
Georgia 396
H B 121
H P 103
Harold T 375
Henry 476
James 477
Janie 341, 382, 416
 454, 485, 540, 546
J Carl 335
Jeptha 341, 416, 454
 546
---Jr 341, 546
Jessie 341, 416, 454
 546
John 396
---C 375
---Clark 341, 546
---Jr 375
---R 133, 143, 206-07
 375
Juddie 477
Katherine 396
L D 426

Lena 341, 454, 485, 545
Lillian 396, 479
Lucy 396, 397, 479
Martha 477
---Key 396, 479
Mary 396
---Alice 375
---Anna 396
---Tate, Mrs viii
Minnie 396
Mourning 477
Myrtle 397
N F 396
Nannie 396
Nathan 396, 479
---M 397, 479
O F 144
Raymond 396
Robert 477
---Tate 151, 375
Samuel 396
Sarah Frances 396
---Mourning 396, 425, 479
Singleton 341, 416, 454, 485, 546
Sol 396
Susan 341, 397, 416, 454, 479, 546
Teedie 396
Texas 396
Thomas Jefferson 397, 479
'Uncle Dirty Head' 139
W C , Mrs 309
William 396, 454
---H 105, 106, 133, 167, 168, 209, 341, 416, 485, 545
---Henry 477

MAULDIN
Henry H 152
J W 152
Miss 339, 381, 414, 544

MAUPIN Jesse 221
MAXEY Bennet 69
MAXFIELD
Clary 67

MAXWELL
Addie 505
Agnes 492
Alex 491
Alice Amelia 502
Allen 492, 506, 539
Allie 504
---Mae 498, 505
Alma 502
Alonzo 504
Alvin 503
Amanda 491
---P 323
---Priscilla 503
Andrew 505
Ann 389, 493, 503
Anna 503
Annie 503
Annie Lou vii
---Sue 502
Arthur C 504
Artimus 156, 505
Asmond 503
Asmond L 151
Augustus 505
Augustus Emmett 491
B B 503
Barbara 501
---Jane 502
Bartow 504
Belle 505
Ben 503, 504
Ben D 136
Benjamin 503
---Martin 598
Benson 492
---Mansfield 323, 503, 536
Bertha 502
Bertram 538
Bessie 502
Boyce L 155
Brantley 504
Buford 163
Callie 504
Calloway 598
Carol Imogene 502
Caroline 492
Cathie 325, 335
Chandler 323, 501
Charles 502, 504
Charles P 155

---W 503
Charlie 597
Clara 492
Clarence 502
Clifford 502
Clyde 502
Coil 504
D B 145, 424
D J 135
Damarius 492
Daniel Johnson 505
Diza Jane 504
Dock 503, 504
Doctor Brawner 504
Doris 502
Drucilla 492
Earl Thomas 597
Early 503
Edna 492
Edward 492
Edwin 505
Elijah 493
Eliza Blake 493
---Zerah Upson 495
Elizabeth 361, 492, 495, 498, 505, 506, 508, 539
---Allen 493
---Madora 494
Elmer 503, 505
Elvira 492
Emily 505
Emily Florence 492, 504
Emma 504
Essie 504
Eugene 505
Eugenia 492, 539
Eustace 505
Evelyn 490
---Willie 494
F A 492
F M 539
Fannie Eunice 499
Fanny M 332
Frances 492
---Calloway 497
---Fortson 497
---Jane 323
Frank 492, 504
Fred 503
Genie 498

George 502, 505
---Elliott 502
---T 173
Gordon 154, 503
Griffin 497
Hannah 502
Harriet 497
---Catherine 498
Harris 502
Henry 493
---Alfred 498
Herbert Elmer 151]
Hetero 544
Howell P 498
Hoyt 498
---Chandler 498
Hugh 503
Imogene 498
Ira 497
Irene 497
Izetta 497
J H 149
Jack 504
Jackson Oliver 323 499
Jacob 504
James 24, 493
---F 504
---Madison 504
---Thomas 501
---W 497
Jane 323, 497, 503, 505
Janie 489, 494
---Hulme, v
Jasper 504
Jennie 492, 539
Jeremiah 508
Jerry 493, 504
Jesey 223
Jesse 505
Jim 504
---Frank 498
Jim T, Mrs 162
Joe 503
Joel 505
Johannah 491
John 223, 491-3, 450 482, 498, 502, 503, 505
---A 502
---B 503, 506

---E 493
---Marshall 495
---Matt 323, 502
---R 504
---V 497
Joseph 498
Josephine 491, 505
Josephus 494
Josie 503
Joyce 497
Lucy 361, 495
Julia 497, 503
--- Ann 323, 501
Julius Bond 498, 502
Kate 505
L E 502
Kezia 493
Lade 374
LaNelle 497
Larae 503
Laura Belle 497
Leo 434, 499, 504, 541
Leonard V 156
Lessie 504
Lettie 505
Lilla 498
Lizzie 504
---May 502
Lois 326, 499
Lonnie Aticus 503
Louisa 323, 501
Louise 502
Lucile 498
Lucinda 492, 505
Lucy 361
Lula 497, 504
Luther McAllister 494
M E 143, 207, 495
Mabel Joe 497
Marjorie Pearl Brown 502
Mark 504
--- McCoil 154
Marshall Harford 495
Martha 492, 495
---Lillian 501
---P 494
Martin 223, 323 333, 469, 497, 498, 504
--- G 503
Marvin 502

Mary 436, 492, 495 502, 504, 505, 539
---Catherine 498
---Elizabeth 322, 495, 497
---Lou 498, 503
---Lucy 498
---Mildred 493, 505
---Mozelle 503
---Phoebe 497
---Sue 502
---Thomas 162, 499
---Walton 390, 493 507
Matilda 505
Mattie 504, 505
Melinda 505
Mildred 491, 502
Minnie Lou 502
Missouri 492
Mozelle 323, 326, 337
Nancy 492, 503, 505
Nealie 504
Nelle 502
Nora 504
Olana 503
Ophelia 498, 502, 504
P C 151
Panola 499
Parks 498
Paschel C 312, 313, 323
---Chandler 503
---, Mrs 315
Pat Rice 498
Pea 503
Pearl 502
Pearlie 503
Peggy A 506
Peyton Hawes 504
Polly 517
Quillian 502
R M 153
Rebecca P 493
Reuben 492, 539
Riley 504
Robert 503, 504, 506
Robert B 155
---Oliver 499
Rona 504
Roxie J 492
Roy 497

Ruth 334, 470, 502
Sally 504
Sam 502
Samantha 492, 495
Sarah 377, 388, 497
　　503, 506
---Ann 505
---Barnettie 501
---Catherine 323, 499
---E 506
---Hester 501
Sethie 504
Simeon 505
Singleton Allen 505
----Jr 505
Sidney 492
Simeon 156, 491-2
Singleton Allen 493
Sophia 492
Susan 492, 539
T M, Mrs v
Terry Harper 502
---Jr 502
Thelma 495
Thomas 51, 52, 223,
　　322, 491, 493, 497
---Allen 498
---B 497
---Calvin 498, 501
---J 323, 491, 493
　　504
---Jackson 497-8
---Jefferson 495
---Jett 502
---Jr 263
---Martin 499
---R 517
---Sr 223
---Sly 494
Tom 313, 504
---, Mrs 162
Torrence Mansfield
　　499
T Jesse, Mrs 149
Vandiver 498, 502
Vesta 534
Virginia Walker 498
Vonnie 504
Washington 506
Wilder Richard 492
Will 489
William 492, 495,
　　503, 504
---Albert 502, 536
---B 493
---Byron 494
---Haden 497
---Hayden 323
---Jeff 499
---Jr 223
---Pressley 494
---Tallent 505
---W 492, 503, 539
Willis 494
---Benton 503
Winona 498
Worley 503
Yancey 504
Zack 492

MAY, William 366

MAYFIELD
Pink 504

MCALLISTER
Catherine 510
Jane 494
Lenora R 403, 494
Matthew 176
Sue Wilhite 133

MCALPIN
Mr 388
Solomon 211

MCANGUS
Janet 510

MCCALL
Capt Hugh 16
H C 153
T 177

MCCALLA
Annie 138, 139, 340
　　415, 453, 484, 545
Catherine 340, 545
David 340, 415, 453
　　484, 545
Earl, Mrs 162
Elmira 340, 415, 453
　　484, 544
George 340, 415, 543,
　　453, 484
---W 544
Harry 484
Ida 340, 363, 370 404
　　418, 415, 453, 456
　　484, 515, 545
Isaac 340, 415, 453
　　484, 544
J Earl 340, 415, 453
　　484, 545
----Jr 340, 415, 453,
　　484, 545
Jennie 340, 415, 453
　　484, 544
John 340, 415, 453
　　484, 544, 545
---W 415, 453, 484
　　545
Katherine 415, 453,
　　484
Lawrence 341, 416,
　　454, 485, 545
---Jr 341, 416, 454
　　545
---III 341, 416, 454
　　545
Leila 340, 415, 453
　　484, 544
Mack 340, 415, 453
　　484, 544
---Jr 340, 415, 453,
　　484, 544
Mary 341, 416, 454
　　485, 545
Olivia 340, 415, 453
　　484, 545
Susan 328, 341, 403,
　　416, 454, 485, 545
T B 170

MCCALLAS
Family 42

MCCANN, Martha
　　401

MCCARTHY
Anna 476
Mary 516

MCCARTY
J T 110, 206
John T 128
Maud 535
S L 206

MCCAW
Jas Brown 433
William R 433

MCCLAIN
Elizabeth 54

MCCLENDON
Jacob Sr 516
MCCLESKEY
David 177
James 177
Mary 177
MCCLOUD...25
MCCLUNG
Nancy Caroline 342
MCCLURE
Emma 496
Helen 324, 436
MCCLUSKY
David 46, 48
James 4, 73, 211
MCCOLLUM
Charles Edgar 497
Claud 497
Dodge 497
E V 497
Lear 497
Leslie 497
Lucile 497
Lyle 497
Robert 497
William Franklin 497
MCCONNELL
James Ossie 359
Martha Frances 359
Mr 534
MCCORD Ira L 145
MCCOU
Civility 486
MCCOY
Dr 526
Flora 526
MCCRARY
Mary Elizabeth 470
MCCULLOUGH
Lillis 338, 380, 413 451, 483, 511, 526 543
MCCURLEY
Moses 224
Mr 423
W H 154
MCCURRY

A A 340, 415, 453 485, 534, 544
---Jr 340, 416, 454 534, 544
Althea 340, 416, 454 544
Angus Sr 224
Charlie 460
David 531
Dr 141
Duncan 167
Elizabeth Saddler 404
Essie 323, 377, 500
Florence 340
George 534
Horace 340, 416, 453 544
Jennie 340, 453
---May 416
John 224
---W 340
Joseph 340, 416, 453 544
Katherine 223
Lauchlin Jr 223
---Sr 223
Lillie 142
Lucy 534
Mary 534
May Lillie Teasley 140
Obie 533
Robbie May 534
Speed 340, 415, 445 544
William B 151, 404
MCDANIEL
Amanda 464
Ann Boatwell 464
C A 476
Carroll Key 476
Helen 476
Henry Clay 464
James 464
John 47
Lettie 464
Lucy 464
Maggie 464
Margaret 464
Martha 476
Mary 67, 464
Nathaniel 464

Thomas 464
William 464
MCDONALD
Angus 224
Charles 180
Donald 225
Hugh 46, 177
Jimmie 307
John 224
Margaret 224, 442
Mr 554
MCDONNELL
Hunter 462
James Smith 462
---Jr 462
Susie Belle 463
MCDOWELL
Family 12
Thomas 73
MCELRATH
Mr 422
MCEWEN
Alice L 434
Cora 356, 530
MCGARIN
E B 533
MCGARITY
Betty Jo 335, 523
Ethel 522
Florence 522
Floyce 522
Gardner 171
Glenn 313
Grace 522
Harriet 406
Hugh Harris 522
John Wofford 522
Katie Lou 335, 523
Leonard A 335, 523
Lois 522
Mildred L 523
Mildred Lee 335
Miss 407
Robert Lewis 522
T G 307
Thomas G 335
---Glenn 523
------Jr 523
William C 335, 523
-----Jr 523

---Kieffer 522
Wilford S 522
---Jr 335
Willson 224
MCGARY
Edward 47, 48
MCGEE
Dillard Elzie 153
Mary 531
Mary D 326
Miss 375
Samuel 35
Tho G 222
MCGEHEE
Barbara Cosby 366
Elizabeth 360, 368
Hugh 397
Lucy 462, 464
Mary 366
Madison Tate 366
Mr 548
Thomas 366
Voluntine Meriwether 366
William Spencer 366
MCGILL
Clara 423
George 423
Harry 423
Helen 423
J H 423
Lucile 423
William 423
MCGINTY
Arthur 356, 552, 553
Jean 314
Joseph 177, 356, 553
---Jr 356, 553
Luther 356, 553
MCGIRTH...16
Daniel 13
MCGOVERN
Hannah 66
MCGOWEN
Hannah 70, 181
James 67
John 70, 179, 180
MCGRAW

Julia 141
MCGRUDER..115
Nancy 445
MCGUIRE
James Alonzo 155
Thomas 224
William 215, 216
MCGURE
Anderson 225
MCINTIRE
Solomon H 398
MCINTOSH
Ada 414, 452
Angus 508
Anna Cassandra 41, 338, 413, 451, 483, 512, 543
Annie Cassandra 541
Elizabeth Arnold Penn 339, 357, 415, 452, 484, 512, 544
Family 40
General 343
Guilford 338, 380, 413, 483, 511, 527, 543
Howell 526
Jack 134
James viii, 134, 137-8, 146, 169-70, 172-5, 202, 206, 339, 357, 414, 452, 484, 512, 531, 544, 550
--- Mrs 134
---Hawes 484
Jessie 338, 339, 357, 414, 415, 452, 484, 513, 531, 544
John H 158, 162-3, 170, 176, 357
---H, Mrs 162
---Hawes 151, 339, 414, 452, 513, 531, 544
Lachlan 508
Lackland 13
Louisa 527
Louise 338, 380, 413, 451, 483, 527
Louke 511, 543
Maria Louise 483

512, 543
Martha Louise 413
Mary 338, 380, 413, 451, 483, 511, 527, 543
---Bevelle 339, 414, 452, 483, 512, 535, 544
---James 339, 357, 414, 452, 484, 513, 531, 544
---Jane Arnold viii
---Louise 142, 338-9, 357, 380-1, 413-4, 415, 451, 452, 483, 484, 512, 513, 527, 543, 544
McAlpin 339, 357, 414, 452, 484, 513, 531, 544
McPherson 483
'Monkey Bill' 133
Sarah Howell 338, 380, 413, 451, 482, 511, 543
---Louise 137-8, 339, 357, 414, 452, 484, 512, 531, 544
Sing 133
Singleton 117, 119
---A 380, 526
---Allen 41, 338, 413, 451, 482, 511, 543
Uncle Billy 133
Victoria Augusta 338, 380, 413, 451, 483, 511, 526, 543
William 310, 414, 452, 508, 531, 544
---Guilford 451
---Jr 176
---Kenneth 338, 380, 413, 451, 483, 511, 527, 543
---Jr 42, 127, 206, 338
---M 76, 103, 111-14, 138, 167-8, 176, 526
---III 208, 338
---McPherson 41, 82, 108, 115-17, 137, 338-9, 357, 380

413, 451, 482-4,
511, 542
-------Jr 451, 483, 512
543
-------III 451, 512,
543
MCIVER
 Andrew 74
MCKAMEY
 Mamie 464
MCKAY
 Catherine 510
 Family 12
 John 73
 Katherine 324
MCKEE
 Family 12
 John 73
 William 73
MCKEEN...180
 William 355
 ---Jr 355
MCKENZEE
 William 211
MCKIBBEN
 J W O 92
MCKINLEY
 Miss 371, 388
MCKINNEY
 Miss 497
MCKINNON
 Cameron 539
MCKISSETT
 Lois 474
MCKIVER
 Family 12
 John 73
MCKLUSKEY
 Family 12
 James 73
MCKNIGHT
 Emma 134
 Lois 440
MCLAIN
 Mary 360, 369
MCLANAHAN
 Alice 332
 Annie 141, 331

Asbury 331
Belle 332
Benard 331
Benjamin 331
Bessie 330, 477
C R 306
Charles 177
Clarence R 307, 331
Clyde 372, 386, 526
Edward 331
George 332
George H 143, 157
Graham 332
J J 6, 307
J W 121
James 53, 67, 331
---, Mrs 67
---P 307
Jeptha 332
John J 331
John W 151, 537
Julian 331
Julius P 307
Luther 332
Mary 53
May 332
T B 152
T J 174
T M 207
Thomas 331
---J 151, 331
Tinsley W 168
William 331
Zach, Mrs 316
MCLEAN
 Porta 366
MCLENDON
 Mr 445
MCLEOD
 Charlotte 509
 Louisa F S 509
 Mary 408
MCLESKEY
 F M 85
MCMILLAN
 Charles Banks 513
 Cynthia 342
 Emma 513
 F B 206
 Garnett Sherman 513
 George 513

Georgia Erwin 513
H W 324, 377
Henry Gratton 513
James Curran 513
Julia Erwin 513
Mary Ellen 513
Robert 176, 400, 513
---Emmett 513
---Jr 513
---III 513
---Sherman 513
Sherman 513
William 513
---Henry 513
MCMULLA[I]N
 ...329
 Daniel 224
 Elizabeth Ann 508
 Frank Alex 154
 George 408
 Guy F 153
 Jesse Pemberton 508
 Kezia 508
 Lavina 322
 Lois 314
 Mary 508
 Mr 329
 Neal 538
 Patrick 434
 Peyton 424
 Ruth 314
 Sarah 508
 T C 154
 Thomas J 508
 William 508
 ---Jesse 508
 ---Marion 508
 --- O 151
 Willis 224
MCNAMOR
 Lake R 85
MCNEIL
 Annie 380
 Mary 537
 Miss 380
MCRAE
 Oscar Brents 151
MCREE
 Ford 92
MEADOW
 David W 157, 173

Kathleen 535
MEALLER
 Miss 393
MEALOR
 Ruby 355
MEANS
 Elizabeth 53, 225
 Jacob 225
 Robert 46
 William 73, 225
MEEKS
 Middleton 52
MENZA
 Lucinda 393
MENZIES Jean 509
MERCER
 D D 6, 305
 ---Sr 307
 D H 6
 Jesse 486-7
 Samuel W 153
 Silas 486
 Will Tom 152
MEREDITH
 James 48, 210
 Molly 210
 Nancy 210
 Patty 210
 Rebeckah 210
 Sally 210
 Sarah 210
 William 514
MERIT/
 MERRITT
 ...73
 John 218
 W D 172
MERIWETHER
 Charles 517
 David 486
 Fanny 476
 George 367
 James 44
 Mary 72, 263, 367
 Mildred 367, 394
 William George 367
MERONY, Mr 347
METCALF ...97
 J A 313

W 313
MEWBORN/
 MEWBOURNE
 A J 173
 Austin 505
 Clarence 505
 Essie 505
 Ethel 505
 Fred 376
 Gene 505
 Grace 505
 Grady 152
 Howell 505
 Jack 505
 Julia E 505
 Katherine 505
 Leonia 302
 Lloyd R 151
 ---313
 Lois 505
 Lucile 505
 Martin 326
 Meanola 505
 Nancy 337, 470
 Olivia 505
 Sam Johnson 505
 Thomas 223
 Vivian 505

MICAWBER...34
MICKLE[EL]
 Buck 351
 Carey 351
 Clark 351
 H C 351
 Homer C 308
 Homozelle 351
 James Clark 208
MICO-MICO 88
MICOU, Ruth 367
MIDDLETON
 Family 42
 Hugh vii
 James Lawrence 369
 John 369
 Mr 58, 65
 Nancy 369, 417
 Robert 35, 42, 58, 65
 169, 222, 369
 ---Jr 369, 514

MILES
 Allen 148
 Mary Stuart 140
MILLEDGE
 Gov John 81
 Hiller 353
MILLER
 H E 365
 J H 308
 --- Mrs 316
 Jedidah 220
 Joseph 74
 Marian Coman 365
 Violet 314
MILLICAN
 John 35, 74
 William T 112, 116
MILLS
 Joseph E 152
 Keppinhappuck 67
 M E 176
 Moses 67, 168, 223
 W B 85
 William 172
 ---R 152
MILNER
 Robert W 128
MILSTEAD
 W T, Mrs 365
MINERVINI
 O 307
MINTER
 Bernice Ivey v
 Byron 301, 312-3
 W B 305
 ---, Mrs v
MITCHELL
 Eula 338, 414
 Kathleen 141
 Patrick 180
 Susan 362
 Thomas 356
MITCHER
 Frances Letcher 123
MIZE
 Carl H 153
 Frank 497
 Geo B 173-4
 Hammond 331

John 322, 497
---L 141
Martin 497
Mat 497
Robert 331
---Jr 331
Robert W 153, 309
Thomas 497
William S 497

MOBLEY
Francis 221
Isaac 221
William 221

MOGIN
Samuel 73

MOLLAY
Margaret 423

MOLOTE
R   355
---Jr 355
---III 355

MONACK, John 94

MONCRIEF
David B 423
---Buckley 471
---E Jr 423
Edwin 471
---Jr 471
Herbert Raymond 471
Mary Elizabeth 423, 471

MONROE
President 38
Theodore 141

MONTEQUE
Susan 54

MONTFORD
Margaret T 346

MONTGOMERY
Catherine 463
LaFayette 463
Mae 141
Samuel

MOOD
Catherine 350
Henry M 350
Julius 350
Lulah 350
Preston 350

Sally 350

MOON
Bohler 136
C H 155
Elizabeth 221
Geo Henry 152
Isaac Lee 152
J M 121
James 378
Jesse 221
John Bonar 378
Joseph Worley 155
Mattie 363
Omer F 155
Sanford N 155
Thomas 357
William 47, 49, 220
--- B 357
---David 155

MOOR
Robert 60
Sister 60

MOORE
A Coleman 156
Alan 339, 381, 414, 452, 483, 527
Annie Lee Cade 140
Benjamin 372, 385
C E 424
Charles 372
Clifton 154
Comers G 177
Coyle 154
E C 254
Ezra 156
Frank 414, 452, 527
Franklin Cade 483
Geo S 156
Grover 328
Guilford McIntosh 339, 381, 414, 452, 483, 527
Gussie 141
Herbert Thomas 155
Hoyt 156
J W 151
James 358
John 48, 53, 64-5
Judy 54
Joseph 48
L A 327, 403

Lewis 74
Louis 175
Lowery 422
Luke W 176
Martha 53, 393
Mary 349, 394
Minnie 372
Patsy 66
Patty 346
R [Brother] 64
R F 133-4, 143, 175 381
---, Mrs 134
Robert 38
---Franklin 339, 414, 452, 483, 527
Toliver P 156
Vicey 65
W Stark 56
W T 135
William 99, 167, 179 210

MOORMAN
Judith 392
Thomas 394
Samuel 394

MORANGE
Miss 380

MORCOCK
Charles M 318

MORGAN
Col 382
Daniel L 449
Elizabeth 52
F M 175
Ida 449
Lloyd 449
Martha 52
Mr 349
Nathan 52

MOROSON
Viletty 64-5

MORRIS
J B 395
John 48
Lottie 373, 381, 386
Sherid 53
William 73

MORRISON...73
Clary G 64

Ella Bell 437
J H 73
John 167, 171
Miss 330
Violetta 63
MORROW
 Gaines W 153
MORSE William 47
MORTON
 J B 128
 P C 128
 W W 128
MOSELEY
 Benjamin 72
 Edgar A 155
 Elijah 54, 68
 Henry 73
 Larkin A 366
 Lewis 73
 Margaret 366
 Marks 366
 Ralph 366
 Richard 91
 Robert 73
 ---Jr 73
 Ruth 366
 William 54
 ---D 366
MOSES
 John 69
MOSLEY
 Henry 178
 Robert 179
MOSS
 Augustus 362
 Con 63
 Elmer B 152
 Fleming 362
 Ham 149
 Holcomb Harper 151
 J A 145
 Luther Adams 154
 Miss 419
 Omer Goss 151
 Oscar J 152
 William 31, 35, 178
MOTES
 Wade Hampton 154
MOULDING
 Thomas 223

MOULTRIE Gen 26
MUCKELROY
 Avington 47
MULALLY F P 128
MULLINAX
 Geo H 154
MULVERN
 William 210
MUNDAY, J A 93
 W W 313
MUNDY
 James Elmer 153
 John B 153
MUNGER
 Elmira 394
MURDOCK
 Patrick 47
MURRAH, Ben 122
MURRAY
 Elizabeth 360, 368
 James 436
 Minnie Tunison
 Mrs 140
 Nancy, Mrs 203
 Thomas 390
 William 399, 434
MURRELL, John 95
 ...96
MURRY
 James 91
 Nancy 223
MYERS
 John 394
 Flora 394
 Robert Lonnie 151
MYRICK
 D J 85
 Daniel Jackson 393
 Martha 393
 Mary Adeline 393
 Minnie Margaret
  Elizabeth 393
 Owen H 393
 Richard 393
 Sarah Adeline 393
 William Love 393

N

NABORS
 Lee 342
NAIL
 Elvira 394
 Joseph 47, 49
NAISH
 Frances 220-1
NALL
 Frank 553
 Janie 553
 Jennie Rae 553
 Samuel 553
 Sarah 553
 W A 150, 207
 Worley A 151, 176
  205
 ---, Mrs 138
NAPIER
 Frances 446, 447
 Geo M 175
 Patrick 446
 Reni 35
 Robert 446
 Tabby 210
 Thomas 49, 210
NAPPER
 Thomas 74
NARDIN
 Victor 417, 455
NASH
 Annie Lou 152
 Clem 342
 Elbert Bell 152
 Henry A 155
 Homer D 152
 William E 152
NAYLOR...176
NEAL
 Addie 497
 Chriswell 225
 Doyle 502, 546
 Ella 497
 G M 546
 Jenelle 547
 Jimmie 504
 Linsey 224
 Mary Lou 547
 Milton 546
 Norman 546

NEELEY Robert 464
NEESE
  Carl 327
  Maisie 393
  Marvin H 393
NEILSON
  Samuel 46
NELLUMS
  William 223
NELMS
  Alex Gaines 154
  Arthur C 154
  David 180
  Ella 554, 554
  George W 154
  Gordon T 155
  James C 86
  Jane 84
  Joshua B 223
  L A 176
  Llewellyn 76
  Melvin 505
  Mr 91
  Uncle Johnny 134
  Unity 180
  W B 169
  William 87
NELSON
  Rgt 378
  Samuel 47, 179
NESBIT, R T 172
NEVERS
  Lealand 377
  M L 324
NEWMAN
  Bowdry 467
  Claud 467
  John 401, 467
NEWSOME
  Archie 354
  Elmore 354
  Gladys 354
  Julian 354
  Raymond 354
  Robert 354
  William 354
NEWTON
  Alice 372, 386, 525
  Frederick F 154

NIASH
  Jeremiah 223
NICHOLAS
  Czar 371
NICHOLS
  Ella 340, 415, 453
    484, 545
NICHOLSON
  Sarah 469
NIX
  Achia Ada 524
  Abit 312
  Elizabeth 52, 64-5
  George 64, 66
  John 223
  Lucy 63
  Sully 64
NOBLE
  Elizabeth 379
NOBLES
  Elsie 366
  Lillian 366
NOCK
  E G 207
  Ernest G 312
NORMAN
  Anglo Wesley 156
  Beatrice 332
  E B 103, 121, 135
    140
  England 152
  Frances Elizabeth 501
  Frances Emma 323,
    501
  Georgia Irene 323,
    501
  Henry P 134
  J L 121
  James William 323
    501
  ---Jr 501
  Jeptha P 156
  John 317
  Leila 141
  Martin 323
  ---Maxwell 501
  Mary Annie 323
    501
  ---B F 333, 470
  Miss 534

  Parks 157
  R L 324, 377
  Sarah Ann 501
  ---Quillie 501
  ---V 505
  Thomas Jefferson
    501
  Tommie 346
  Virginia 538
  William Benson
    Jefferson 323, 501
NORRELL
  H A 133
NORTON
  Robert L 152
NOWLIN
  Mrs Ann 432
NUCCLES
  Nathaniel 67
NUCKALLS
  Nathaniel 530
NUNNELEE..42 ,
  176
  James F 35, 48, 86
    222
  Martha W 540
  Patsy 514
  Susan 380
  Walter 49, 171

O

O'DIGNAIL
  Charles 24
ODOM
  Jacob 35, 73
  Robert Paschal 342
  Sarah 502
OFFUTT
  Cassandra 511
  William Johnson 178
OGILVIE
  Garrie 359
  Grace 359
  Jessie 359
  John 359
  Julius 359
  Margaret 509

OGLESBY
  Abda 133-4, 424
    550
  Addie 425
  Agnes 476
  Alexander 423
  Alice 374, 387, 425
  Amelia 323, 497
  Anna 476
  Arnold 423
  Beulah 374, 387
  C D 423
  Carrie Kate 423
  Charles 149
  Clarence 423
  ---T 156
  D P 133, 145, 206
  Drue Gibson 156
  Drudy 35
  Drury 425
  Edna 314
  Elise 139
  Elizabeth 54, 423
  Elsie 424
  Emma Jane 424
  Eugenia 476
  George 423
  Gussie 425
  Hillyer M 476
  Ira Dancy 476
    ---Jr 476
    ---III 476
  Jane 536
  Janna 468
  Jannie 423
  J Charles 156
  John 134, 422
    ---F 54
    ---, Mrs 134
    --- P 423
  Josephine 427
  Jumius G 476
  Katie Lou 325, 336
    423
  Leila 424
  Lola Jane 424
  Lucinda 54
  Lucy Lumpkin 424
  Maggie Lee 423
  Margaret 423-4
  Martha Ellen 476
  Mary 54
  Mattie 504
  Miss 373, 382, 387
  Nathaniel W 156
  Nicholas 390
  Nick 176
  R E 139
  ---, Mrs 139
  Robert Eberhardt 424
    ----Jr 424
  Rufus 208
  Thomas 179, 424
    ---B 54
    ---Griffith 424
    ---Sr 54
  Tommie 425, 540
  Virginia 423
  Widow 532
  William 53, 148, 423

OGLETHORPE
  James x, 1

O' KELLEY
  Elizabeth 550
  Ligon Jr 550
  Miriam 550
  Mr 553
  Willis 550

OLDHAM Annie
  463

OLDS, Sallie DuBose
  421

OLIVE
  Sam 133, 143
  Samuel L 176, 205

OLIVER
  A S 206, 345, 490
  --, Mrs 315
  ---Jr 490
  Adisa Ann 496
  Alfred 398, 517
    ---Shelton 517
  Ann 64
  Asa Thompson 397
  Atticus 496
  Berrien 221
  Betty 517
  Caleb 222
  Calop 65
  Christopher Dionysius
    398
  David Terrell 397
  Denver 496
  Dewitte 496
  Dionysius 16, 29, 35
    36, 39, 496, 516
    ---Jackson 496
    ---Jr 517
  Elbert 397
  Eleanor 140, 490, 517
  Eliza 517, 398
  Elizabeth 397
  Florence 363
    ---McCarty 398, 517
  Frances 180
  Francis 398, 517
  Frank 490
  George Pierce 496
  Georgia 397
  Henry S 67
  Jackson 495, 517
  James 87, 171, 363,
    398, 490, 517
    ---Jackson 496
    ---Jr 398
    --Shelton 397
  John 36, 37, 39, 48-9
    83, 91, 180, 496
    516, 517
    ---Alfred 398
    ---Thomas 397
  Judith 517
  Lawrence Mansfield
    397
  Leila 496
  Lenora 496
  Lovick Pierce 496
  Lucinda 398, 518
  Lucy 397
  Major 103
  Martha 398, 517, 518
  Mary Elizabeth 496
    ---Melissa 398
    ---Winfrey 517
    ---Winifred 398
  Matilda 467
  Maude 490
  McCarty 92
  Mildred 397-8, 517
    ---Terrell 398
  Millie 363
  Mittie Beatrice 496
  Nancy 222
  Nettie 496
  Peter 92, 221, 516-7

Prudence 397, 517
Robert Lee 496
Roberta Estelle 496
Sally 517
Samuel 398
---L 145
Sanders Bartow 496
Sarah 397
---Jane 496
Shelton 397-8, 517
Simon 167-8, 397
  517
Stanley 490
----M 151
Sue 490
Susan Rebecca 398
Thomas 35, 87, 91,
  167, 177, 211, 516
---Brittain 496
---Parks 496
------Jr 496
---Winfrey 397-8, 517
Thurmond 490
Tullulah Lee 496
Victor 496
Washington 398, 517
William 73, 496, 517
---Capers 496
OMATLA
  Charles 88-9
O'NEAL, Major 29
ONOPO, King 88
OOGHEE E A 536
ORR Betsy 504
  Daniel 179
ORRISON
  Henry 48
  J T 140
OSBURN Daisy 476
OSCEOLA
  88-90
OUTZ
  F M 153
  Lloyd H 153
  ---Mrs 162
OVERSTREET
  Esther 464
  Henry McDaniel 464
  Lucy Amanda 464
  Mr 464

Ruth 464
Tommie 464
OWENS
  Barshaba 222
  Benton 493
  Betty 332
  Charles T 539
  James S 222
  John Shannon 153

P

PACE
  B 178-80
  Barnabas 48-9, 73
  Barnard 540
  Nancy 540
PACELY
  John 29
PAGE
  Alice Hunt 472
  Drucilla 472
  Early 472
  George 333, 469, 533
  ---J 472
  James B 472
  Martha L 472
  Mary 472
  Polly 67
  W H 163
  ---, Mrs vi, 160, 162
    316
  William 472
  ---Henry 472
PAISLEY
  Col 25-6
PALMA
  Filiberton D 151
PALMER
  Bessie 553
  Decimus 348
  John 48
  Mitchell 158
  William 348
PANTECOST
  Mr 449
PARADISE
  Eula 465
  Harry 465

Julian 465
O B 465
Pauline 465
PARHAM
  Jasper E 155
  Joe Griff 154
  Lester G 155
  Omer S 156
  S 174
PARK
  Mary 225
  Orville A 157
PARKER
  Charles W 176
  ------, Mrs 157
  Earl Rogers 155
  Harry DuBignon 523
  Homer C 175
  J R 92
  Joshua 85
  Mr 470
PARKS
  Abram 167
  Ada 142
  Alice 505
  Annie 533
  Archie 327
  Clara 141
  H H 92
  Hattie 376, 534
  Katie 327
  Moss 69
  ---, Mrs 136
  William J 91
PARR
  Camilla 370
  Louise 370
  Marcus 417
  ---A 370, 417
  ---Jr 370, 417
  Mitta 370
  Robert 370
  ---H 417
  ---Heard 417
  ------Jr 417
PARRENT
  Annie Bell 471
PARRISH
  Miss 394
PARROTT

Ledfind 180
Miss 434, 541
PARSONS
Janie 160
PARTAIN
A R 154
Bartow Butler 154
Charles S 153
Coy C 108
Dillard K 154
J F 154
L B 135
W E 154
PARTEL
Carl A 156
PARTLOW
Miss 379
PATCHEN
Anna 314
PATE Mary 553-4
PATILLO
Geo H 92
L P 175
PATTEN
William 49
PATTERSON
----180
Arthur S 155
Elizabeth 68
F M, Mrs v
Frances L 365
Fred 550
George W 155
J S 167
Jesse 64, 66
John 57, 61-2
Marion Reeves, v
Mary 514
William 64, 91
PATTO
Hannah 204
James 204
PATTON
George 204
Guy 254, 354
James 47
Margaret 422
Mr 422
William 46

PATZ
Louis 306
Sara 314
Sam 160, 313
PAUL
Edna May 423
PAULK Ommye 521
PAXON Agnes 471
PAXTON
Robert 74
PAYNE
Ann 263, 388
Boozer 313
Family 129
H B 149, 157-8
162, 305
---, Mrs v, viii
140, 310, 316
Howard B 170, 176
308-09, 312
---, Mrs 162, 315
Howard P 205
James E 503
Jim 148
Jordan 362
Lee 141, 328
M T, Mrs 139
Nancy 67-8, 530
Thelma Wright
[see Mrs H B]
Turner, Mrs 141
PEACOCK
G J 362
Edna 139
Lafayette 342
PEARCE, W J 327
PEARSONS Mr 468
PEEK
Coral 377
Lula v, 160, 162, 304
Mr 476
Ruby 324, 377
PEEPLES Mr 446
PEFFER
Lloyd B 513
PEGG L M 176
PEGGY...65
PELLIGRINI

Florence 423, 471
PEMBERTON
Mary 263, 491
PENDLETON
Clarinda Huntington 97
William K 97
PENN
Benjamin 218
Thomas 46, 74
William 475
PENNELL...459
PEPPERS
C S 153
Clifton W 152
Lester H 152
Miss 356, 530, 532
PERKINS
Joshua 179
Mildred 475
PERRIAN
John 221
PERRIN
Carl 331
Fred 331
Forrest 331
George 331
Julian 331
Lois 331
Margaret 331
Mary 446-7
Richard 446
---Jr 447
Thomas 331
PERRY/PERY
James A 175
Thomas 63
William C 85
PERRYMAN
Anthony 327
William G 223
PERSONS
George W 91
PETERKIN
Julia 350
PETERMAN
Addison E 478
---Eugene 478
Cleveland 478

Cyril 478
Lavonia 478
---Bell 478
Marcus 478
Margaret 478
Mollie 478
William Addison 478
PETTIGREW
  Clarence W 365
  John 49
PEURIFOY
  Fanny 361
PEYTON
  John Henry 152
  Robert 35
PHARR
  Aurelius 473
  Camilla 138, 418, 439
    456, 473, 515
  G W 85
  Ida 473
  J F 128
  Louise 418, 439, 456
    515
  Marcus A 370, 417
    439, 456, 515
  ---Jr 417, 439, 456, 473
    515
  ---, Mrs 139
  Mitta 418, 456, 473
    515
  Mittie 439, 473
  Robert 439, 456, 473
    515
  ---Jr 456, 473
  ---H 417
  ---Heard 417
  Sallie 517
  Vohammie 439, 456,
    473, 515
  ---Heard 418
PHELPS
  Amos Lester 154
  James O 136
  John 208
  ---A B 154
  ---Gairdner 154
  Locky Ann 389, 506
  Lonnie William 154
  Mary 532
  Thomas 87

PHILLIPS
  Alfred 504
  Earl Taylor 365
  ---W 365
  Jennie 371, 385
  Jessie 524
  Louise 372, 386, 525
  Nancy, Mrs 432
  Sam Jones 155
PHILLIS...65
PHINIZY
  Ferdinand 180
PHOEBE...65
PICKENS
  Col 15-6
  Gov 371, 525
  John 66
  Mary Dunning 476
  S M 139
PICKETT
  Allston 347
  Albert J 347
  ---Jr 347
  Joseph 347
  Martha 347
  Mary 347
  Sarah 347
  William R 347
  John 347
PICKFORD
  H P 91
PIERCE
  Esther 323, 337, 503
  G F 85
  Lovic Jr 121
  Luther Clayton 154
  Ralph 360, 369,
  --- E 151
PIERSON
  Marshall 539
PIERSY
  Abraham 487
PILLOW, Katie 342
PIM, B F, Mrs 316
  B Frank 92, 314
PINNELL Mr 548
PINTER
  William 344

PITNER, J M 175
PITTARD
  John T 513
PITTMAN
  Hudson M 552
PITTS, Era 141
  Matthew B 312
PLEDGER, S L 121
PLEASANTS
  H V 208
  John 446
PLONK, Tho M 151
POCAHONTAS
  392
POINDEXTER
  W R 367
POLLARD
  Daby 68
  John 181
  Sibrey 66
PONDER
  Joseph H 367
  Sarah G 367
POOLE
  B B viii
  Charlie B 156
  John S 359
  Mr 511
POPE
  A 169
  Alexander 40, 204
  Allen D 354
  Archibald 176
  Ava 354
  Claud 354
  ---E 354
  F P 419
  Forrest 354
  Howard 354
  James 354
  ---Jr 204
  Jessie M 355
  Jewel 489
  Katie 354
  Leroy 35, 38-9
    171, 181
  Mark Cooper 318
  Nicholas 38
  Winifred 379

PORTER
 B 454
 Bee 416
 Nicholas 441
 Patrick 380, 526
 Samuel 178
 ---B 177
PORTERFIELD
 David 74, 178
POSEY
 John 176
 ---B 166
 Humphrey 395, 477
POSS
 Adeline 355
 Clara Emma 354
 Henry A 354
 Katie Jewell 354
 Joseph 355
POST
 Elieu 49
 Ella 141
 Frank 35
 Geo M 153
 Lewis 53
 Powell
 T H, Mrs 148
 W L 154
POTTS Sally 346
POWELL
 Francis 224
 John A 539
 Sudie 531
 William R 225
POWER
 Charles H 136
 Goss 359
 James Huett 359
 Martha Naomi 359
 Mary Ruth 359
 Miss 426
 William 89
POWERS
 Sarah 134
PRATHER
 Elizabeth 434
 William M 225
PRESCOTT
 Julia 445

Louisa 444
Louise 444
PRESSLEY...132
 Allen 340, 363, 370
  415, 418, 484, 515,
  545
 Lizzie Bell 553
 Lucy 53
 M H 139
 Mildred 401
 Thomas H 153
 W C 206
PRETTY
 Geo 35
 Susannah 359
PREUIT
 Jacob 225
 John 225
 Joshua 225
PREWIT
 Brother 59
 Jacob 58, 63, 73
 Nancy 59
 William 73
PRICE
 Ellen 366
 Emma 366
 H J 313
 ---, Mrs 309
 Henry 361
 P V 160
 Thomas 180
PRINCE
 Henry 153
 Hugo W 153
 Mr 449
PRIOR Andrew J 446
PRITCHETT
 Delpha 224
 Nicholas 224
 Susan 478
 Thomas 224
PROFFIT
 Nell 141
 P P 133, 176, 205
PROTHRO
 James 224
 Joshua 224
 Nathaniel 224
 Zilpha 224

PRUITT
 Jane 373, 382, 387
PULLEN
 Sarah Lucile 501
PULLIAM
 Jane 529
 Lucy 533
 Miss 328
 O E 208
 Robert 48, 210, 223
 Sylvester Brown Jr
  302
PULLMAN
 Robert 47
PULLOM, Mr 59
 William 61
PURCELL Sue 490
PURDUE
 Frances 340, 415, 484
  545
 J H 340, 415, 455
  484, 545
 ---Jr 340, 415, 453
  484, 545
 John, Mrs 138, 139
 Mary Olivia 340, 415,
  453, 484, 545
PUSEY, E D, Mrs
 315

Q

QUILLIAN
 Alberta 490
 Cleta 406
 George 141
 Guy 340, 363, 370
  415, 418, 453, 456
  484, 515, 545
 Guyton R 151
 Howell 496
 Tarpley 504
QUINN
 Augustus S 448
 ----Jr 448
 Ella 448
 Francis 448
 Hinton John 448
 ---Jr 448

John Jr 448
Nona C 448
Sarah E 448
William D 448
Willis 448

R

RACHEL 63, 65, 66
RAGAN Elizabeth 529
RAGLAND
  Evan 29, 35, 39, 46
    47-50, 170-1, 177-9
  Family 42
  Frances 517
  John R 37-8
RAGSDALE, B D 145
RAIFORD, Ivah 358
RAINES, Dabney 87
RAINEY
  J N 396
  Kathryn 314
  Mr 447
  Virginia 314
RAINWATER
  Frances 496
RAMMAGE
  Edd 128
  Tillman 151
RAMPEY
  Calvin P 136
  Larton P 550
  Virginia 550
RAMPLEY
  Geo Herndon 140
  S P, Mrs vi
RAMSAUR
  Mr 476
RAMSEY
  B 223
  G G 85
  Richard 223
  Samuel 513
  Woodfin 151
RANDALL
  James R 452

  Maryland 338, 414
    452, 483, 512, 541
    543
RANDOLPH
  Edmund 511
  Gov 401
  Isabella 511
  Jessie 511
  Louise 511
  Peter 511
  R C 347
  Richard 511
  Thomas 511
RANSOM, G P 313
RANSOME
  Lillie Gray 140
RAVOT
  Abraham 24
RAY
  Arthur W 522
  C E 303
  Claud 155
  J H 224
  J T 208
  James William 151
  Mary 480
RAYLE
  Elizabeth 465
  Frances 465
  James T 158
  Mamie 535
  Robert 535
  Roy 535
  Susie 535
READE
  Mary 509
READY, James 47
REAGAN
  William A 357
REAGIN, C O 307
REDD
  William 329
  ---J 151
REDDISH
  Jeremiah 400
  Leanna 400
REDWINE
  Jesse 470
REESE

  Benjamin 467
  Cuthbert 398
  John C 144
  Mr 363
  Robert 467
  W W 157, 206
  William 136, 467
REEVES
  A H 366
  Ellie 366
  Frances 478
  Frank 366
  James A 343
  ---F 550
  ---F, Mrs viii
  Katherine 550
  Mamie 550
  Marion 550
  Mary Patricia 550
  Mildred 550
  Orrie 366
  Pearl 366
  Ralph 550
  Rosa Willis v
  Sannie 366
  Virginia 550
REID
  Elizabeth 461
  Ike 313
  Isaac 357, 531
  J C 534
  Mary Arnold 357
  Sallie 444
  Sara Goolsby v
  W D 142
REIMER H H 521
REMBERT
  Samuel H 220
REMBERTS
  Family 42
RESSLER
  Martha 362, 495
REVIER, Anna E 354
REYNOLDS
  Catie 541
  Flora 329
  John 334, 470, 472
  Minnie 397
RHODES

Clara 331
Claud H 153
E C 147
Enoch C 152
Hannah 224
Henry C 152
John W 224
Moses R 224
Pauline 468
William Leon 153
RHYNE
Clarence Little 155
RICE
Aaron 520, 524
Ann 519
Anne 520
Asa 53
Betty 520
Charles 520
Charles Elmer 518
Claud 155
Earl James 522
Edgar Aaron 520
Edmnd 518, 519
Elbert 520
Elijah 520
Elizabeth 520, 553
Elizabeth Haslett v
Frances 553
Frances Elizabeth 522
Griffith 519
Grace Louise 335, 523
Herbert Spencer 521
Howard Claucus 521
---James 522
Hulda 520
Ida 335, 523
J H 153
J N 134, 150
James Newton 553
Jim 144
John W 335
---Walton 523
K Walton 522
Kate 334
---Muhulda 522
L 35
Leila Vickery v, 162
Leonard 73, 335, 520
---Alexander 523
---W 520
Lester Richard 153

Lettie 325, 334, 336
 521
---Phronissie 523
Lillian 522
Lon, Mrs 311
Lula 520
L Walton 520
---Jr 521
Marion Spencer 521
Martha 520
Martin 520
Marvin 158
---L 208
Mary 334, 521
--- Elizabeth 522,
 523
Miss 445
Morgan 155, 524
N L 335
Newton 520
---Allen 523
Ommye 521
P V Jr 162, 163
Peter 520
---Jacob 521
---V 521, 524
----- Jr 141, 173
Polly 520
R L 150, 170, 535
---, Mrs 162
Rachel 520
Robert 519
Ruth 519
Sarah 334, 335, 520
 523
---Ann 521
---Margaret 522
Thomas 519, 520
Walton 334, 520
William 519, 520, 521
--- C 152
---Jasper 521
---P 520
RICH
Elizabeth 439
James M 151
John 181, 220-1
Richmond 220
William H 93
Willie 537
RICHARDS
Elizabeth, Mrs 428

Harriet 509
Lila 449
Lucile 449
Ralph 428
Stephen 449
W W 449
Willis W 449
RICHARDSON
Amos 224
Katherine 538
Mary 316
---Clark 400
Sam 432
Thomas J 494
Walker 48
William M 49, 153
RICHERSON
Prudence 68
Richmond 104-05
RICHISON
Walter 66
RIDDLE
Addie 449
Archie 449
Ida 449
Mr 412, 482
N M 449
RIDGEWAY
Jim, Mrs 162
RIEVES Mr 449
RILEY
Frances 461
James 225
Jeptha 442
Mary Kate 365
RIVERS
E D 175
Sallie 466
W P 92
ROAN, E G 127
John 220
ROBBINS
J B 92
John 492
ROBBONS Dr 449
ROBERS Mary M
 445
ROBERSON
Mary 447

Samuel 225
ROBERT, R B 144
ROBERTS
  Bessie 524
  Bob 397
  Daisy 356, 530
  Esward 89
  James Griggs 151
  Jasper 151
  Jessie 138-9
  J O 144
  J W 92
  John W 154
  Milton 154
  Pressley B 172
  Vera 325, 335
  W H 144, 151
  Willie 426
ROBERTSON
  Bobbie Ann 503
  Christian 510
  Corwin 312
  G C, Mrs 316
  Mary June 503
  Marjorie 509
  Silas 503
  Thomas 151
ROBINS
  William 181
ROBINSON
  Emmie De 162
  G C 162
  John 133
  Mr 473
  William F 121
ROCHETTE
  Susanna 485
RODLANDER
  William R 226
ROEBUCK
  A H 127
  Eppy W 169
  George 214
  Judge 132
  M A 133
  Mary 132
  Milly 64
  Mr 65
  Mrs 493
  Polly 64

Robert 167
'Tiny' 133
William J 172
ROGERS
  Alpha vi, 140, 539
  Benjamin 210
  Caroline 539
  ---Idella 539
  Carrie 141
  Daisy 539
  Edna v, vi, viii, 140
    161-3, 304, 539
  Elizabeth Jane 539
  Elizabeth Jane
    Williamson 324
  Erastus 89
  Ezekiel Q 156
  Gary 539
  Helen 538
  Isham 221
  James 35
  J S 145
  John 221
  Laura Adeline 539
  Lee 381, 527
  Marshall 539
  Martha 539
  Mary 381, 527
  ---Ann 539
  Robert Dozier 539
  Sally Virginia 365
  Sara Lee vi, 140
  Thomas Williamson
    539
  William 381, 527
  William S 93, 539
  ---Samuel 539
  Williamson 324, 538
    539
  Z B viii, 22, 142, 145
    149, 160-3, 168, 170
    174-6, 313, 380, 527
    539
ROLFE, Jean 392
RORTENBERG
  Eva 467
ROSE
  Alexander 509
  Catherine 510
  Elizabeth 510
  Harry 133

Helen 510
Sarah 222
ROSENBAUM
  ..102
  Mrs 102
ROSS, Jesse 73
  Robert 48
ROSSAR/
  ROSSER
  Geo T 152
  Jeptha 222
  W A 152
  Zera M 155
ROUNDTREE
  Fred 523
  Joshua 412
  Manning 412
  Roxie 412
  Winifred 523
ROUSE
  Olga 382, 403
ROUSEY
  Abraham 154
  Amelia K 405
  Betty Jane 498
  Cornelius Jackson 498
  Edmund 73
  Elmer 498
  Forest 221
  John 73
  T F 135
  William E 155
ROUZEE
  F F 121
  Frank 68, 133
  Louisa 68
  Mark, Mrs 148
  Samantha 406
  Thomas 407
ROWAN
  William A 411
  --- Jr 411
ROWE
  Allison 313
ROWLAND
  Reuben 394
ROWZEE
  John 226
ROYAL[L]

Catherine 447
Elizabeth 509
Isaac 509
Joseph 447
Mary Mackintosh 509
ROYSTER
Robert 221
ROYSTON
Arthur W 151
J 151
RUCH
Jeptha 180
RUCKER
Albert 323
Alma 532
Anne 314
Annie 323
---Marie 500
Benjamin 532
---Smith 500
------Jr 500
Carl Maxwell 500
Caroline Anne 500
Catherine 59, 60, 181, 532
Charles Hulme 500
----Ralph 500
---Thomas 500
E L 167
Earl W 98
Elbert M 97-8
Eleanor Scattergood 500
Elizabeth 349
Evelyn 500
Fannie Sue 500
Florence 500, 532
Frances Louise 500
George 180
Georgia 388
Guy G viii, 162
---Pressley 153
---W 208
Harley W 153
Hattie 532
Helen Florence 499
Isham 532
---Goss 499
-----Jr 500
James 222, 434

500, 532, 540
---Frederick 500
---H 153
Jeptha 97
---H 388
John 46, 73, 96, 171, 222, 226, 317
---McAlpin 500
-------Jr 500
---Thornton 499
Joseph 41, 48-9, 64, 66, 91, 97-9, 102, 203, 460, 532
Julius 532
--- Thornton 500
------Jr 500
K E 175
K Earl 153
Lamar 388
Leah Ruth 500
Lucia H viii, 162-3
Mack 323
Mamie 500
Margaret 203, 388
Mary 97, 459
---Della 500
---Louise 499
McAlpin 532
Milly 222
Myrtle 500
---Pope 500
Nancy 459
Newton 496
Nina Catherine 500
Nona 532
Nora 500
Peggy 64
Permelia 403
Peter 96, 434
Robert Joseph 500
Ruth 532
Samantha 500
Sarah 375, 377, 388
---Harriet 500
Serepta 492
T J 54
Thelma 532
Thomas 323, 501, 532
---Bailey 500
---J 177
---Jackson 499
---Joseph 500

---Monroe 500
Tinsley 158, 177, 388
---W 97, 167, 176-7, 388
---White 98
Tomilene 500
Vera Myrtle 500
W A 168, 172-6, 304
---, Mrs 310-11
William 35, 224, 317
---A viii, 149, 150, 323, 500
---Albert 500
---B 323, 499
---F 400
---Thomas 500, 501
Willie Vickery vi
Zachariah 222
RUDDER
Col. 120
Luther Verdel 151
RUDISELL
Fanny 361
RUDOLPH
Michael 343
RUE, John Ralph 313
RUFF Martin 121
Nancy 388
RUIS Emma 467
RUMBLE
Theodore 142, 406
RUMSEY
Richard 222
RUNNALS
W M S 223
RUSH, Geo 396
RUSSELL
Earl 372, 386, 525
Emily 366
Essie 372, 386, 525
H E 372, 525
James Meriwether 366
Jean 366
Jonathan 48
Joseph M 47
Julia 372, 386, 525
Mr 386
Postelle 366
R B Jr 175

Tho Commander 179
RUTHERFORD
General 383
Griffith 25, 26, 28
RYAN
Barry 68
Betty 68
Elizabeth 68
RYLAND
Marian 463
Martha Virignia 463
Nancy Bess 463
Robert 463
---Jr 463
RYLEE
E S 422

S

SADDLE[A]R
Elizabeth 404
Hattie 326
James R 224
John F 225
Mr 385
William B 225
SAFFOLD, Mr 380
SALES
Margaret G 351
SALLEE
Mary Lee 463
SALLIS Samuel 441
Sarah 441
SALMON
Jeremiah 225
SAMPSON
Methesda 399
SAMUEL Ann 464
SANDERS
Addie 372, 386, 526
Betty 348
Calvin P 224
Clara 348
Cleo 348
Clinton 313
Elizabeth 348
Emily Moss 366
Epsy 348

Eunice 348
Guy M 175, 208
Harriett 471
---, Mrs 494
Helen 348
Henry 412, 450, 482
James 348
Jean 366
Lewis M 224
Mack 498
Malcolm 366
Margaret 348
Marion 348
Mary 348, 496
Melvina 402
Miss 351, 505
Mr 505
Pauline 348
Robert Griggs 498
SANDHESTER
William 210
SANDIFORD
Addison Bell 479
Annie Lillian 479
Frank Bell 479
G W 479
Hendon M 479
Herbert Hoover 479
Hollis 479
Margie 479
Mattie E 479
Oreola 479
Pierpont Morgan 479
Vivian L 479
SANDRIDGE
Clabourne 180, 223
Sarah 209
SATTERFIELD
Henry W 472
Laura Lee 420, 470
SATTERWHITE
Jane 461
John 461
SAUNDERS
Harriet Rebecca 423
Lucy, Mrs 432
SAXTON
Elizabeth M 220
SAYE
Alex 354

Harold 354
SAYER
Ann 359
David 359
Evelyn 359
Ichabod 359
James 359
John 359
SAYLORS
Michael, 178-80
SCALES
Henry 362
Joel 224
O P 307
Thomas 224
William 224
SCARBOROUGH
Louise 341, 546
SCATTERGOOD
Elizabeth 532
Lizzie 500
SCHOELLER
Annie Wright 393
Henry 393
Minnie May 393
Myrick 393
---Jr 393
SCHULER
Harry 372, 385, 525
John 372, 385
---Jr 372, 385, 525
SCOGGINS
Lou 328
SCOTT
Ben 502
Betsy 180
James 178, 480
Marion 476
Mary A 494
Rachel 402
Tho B 178-80, 210
---W 325
Wootie 330
SCREVEN, Col 343
SCROGGINS
Isaac 393
SCUDDER
Nina 315

William Russell 358
SCULL
  Fay 366
SEAGGS, Mary 402
SEALES
  Elizabeth 222
SEALS, John 327
  Sarah 459, 460
SEAMSTER
  John 485
SEARCY
  William 492
SEAWRIGHT
  W H 532
SEAY Eliza 538
SEEGARS
  Henry 327, 403
SELF
  Frances 224
  Samuel L 224
SEQUEFIELD
  Mr 532
SETTLES
  Florence 397, 479
SEWELL
  Catherine 475
  Henry 179
  Joseph 172
  ---H 203
  Olivia 535
  Samuel 179, 342
  Susan 537
SEYMOUR
  Ardesta 389, 506
  Charles Marion 389, 485, 506
  Dora Penelope 389, 485, 506
  Dorothy 537
  Geo Lowery 176
  Grace 537
  Hop 485
  J Luther 174
  John Warren 388, 485, 486, 506
  Kezia Blake 389, 506
  Lois 325, 336
  Lottie 340, 363, 370, 415, 418, 453, 456,

484, 515, 545
  Marshall 389
  Martin 388, 485, 506
  Mary 550
  Minnie 388, 506
  Miss 422
  Omer 537
  Ruth 314
  S B 304
  Sarah 389, 506, 537
  Thomas Dozier 535, 537
  William 537
  Zachariah 485, 486
SHACKELFORD
  ...176
  Allen 492
  Annie 473
  E 177
  John H 441
  Mordeci 473
SHANNON
  John P 206
  Mary 461
  Sarah 406
  W T 440, 474
SHARP
  Arberrilar 181
  William 179, 180
SHATTUCK
  Sarah 520
SHAW
  Eva 478
  Geo Edwin 469
SHEERER
  Regina 354
SHELAND
  Tallulah Hill 435
SHEP[P]ARD
  Dudley, Mrs 311
  Gladys 312
  James 210
  Mr 553
  Virgil 532
SHERMAN
  Dessa 513
SHERON Polly 469
SHIELD, Mr 433
SHIFLET

James 224
Joseph 225
Picket 224
SHIPMAN
  Charles 440, 474
  ---Jr 440, 474
SHIRLER
  Lewis 398
SHIRLEY
  Bertie 353
  Hoke 313
  Mary 548
SHIVER Samuel 440
SHOCKLEY
  C L 382
SHOE, Eli 225
SHOEMAKER
  Jeremiah 419
  Lindsey 180
SHORT, Jim 319
SHORTER
  Henry 399
SHORTLEY
  Leila 492
SHUMATE
  Annie May 331
SIDWELL
  Grady 502
SILER Mr 532
SILLI Henry 446
SIMMONS
  A S, Mrs 315
  ---373, 381, 387
  Mary Etta 449
SIMPKINS
  Henry E 469
SIMPSON
  Blanche 489
  Christine 490
  H L 208
  John 177
  Wilson 393
SIMS
  Edwards 361
SISK, J T 175-6, 303, 535
  T J 168

SITTIN
  William 224
SKAGGS
  Tabitha 225
SKELTON
  Annie 533
  Carey 533
  Deen 375
  Emmett 533
  Hugh 533
  J H 333
  Jabez 224
  James 376, 533
  ---C 533
  ---H 469
  John 223
  Lola 533
  Lou 326, 492
  Marion 533
  Martin 224
  Mary 402
  Miss 323
  Parke 533
  Ralph 533
  Richard 224
  W L 318-9
  Wilma 533
SKIDMORE
  Sidney 363
SLADE
  William 404
SLATON
  Georgia Ann 538
  John 222
  ---M 175
  Maggie 538
SLAUGHTER
  Mary 380, 526
  Sarah 380, 393, 526
SLEDGE
  Jennie 371, 385, 524, 525
  Mr 524
SLIGH Mercer 463
SLOAN Mrs 540
SLOSS
  Antionette 365
  Joe 365
  Mary Elizabeth 365

  Virginia 365
SMALLWOOD
  Thomas 467
SMART
  Annie 463
  Corrie Lee 463
  Elsie 463
  Felix G 463
  ---Jr 463
  Hartwell 463
  Hudson 463
  ---Jr 463
  ---III 463
  Lutie Bell 463
  Martha 463
  Mary Corinne 463
  Richard Lee 463
SMETHER
  Gabriel 225
SMITH
  A C 406
  A F 382, 452, 531
  ---Jr 382, 531
  A P 173
  Ada 329, 531
  Albert 531
  Anna, Mrs 404
  Annie 330-1, 477
  Annie Barney, Mrs 310
  Antionette 332
  Archibald 224
  B C 531
  B F 541
  Barnard 468
  Ben Neal 327
  Benjamin 168, 171, 406, 531
  ---Neal 403
  Bennie 330, 477
  Bert Moody 541
  Betsy 210
  Beverly Allen 330, 477
  Bryant 541
  C L 303-4
  C T 332
  Carl 468
  Caroline 393
  Charles 330, 477
  ---Emory 177

  ---H 539
  Cleo 340, 404, 545
  Corrie 330
  Cynthia 330, 372, 386, 477, 525
  D C 332
  Dobbs 307, 313
  Dorothy 541
  Dozier 329
  Duncan 330, 477
  Edgar L 448
  Elizabeth 332
  ---Ann 357
  Emma 332
  Ethel 300, 340, 415, 453, 477, 484, 537
  Eveline 332
  F D 357, 531
  ---Jr 357
  Fanny 332
  Florence 373, 382, 387, 424, 531
  Forrest 330, 468, 477
  Frances 330, 332, 477
  Frank 541
  Furman 313
  George 329, 531
  ---W 536
  Gertrude 522
  Hallie 417, 456
  Harriet Esther 495
  Harvey 532
  Hattie 338, 414, 483, 512, 541, 543
  Henry 330, 477, 501
  ---Luther 357
  Holder 477
  Ida 331, 332
  J L 372, 386, 525
  Jack, Mrs 304
  ---468
  James 176, 374, 387
  Jaspar 209
  Jesse L 208
  Jessie 330, 477
  Jewette 501
  John 330
  ---Andy 176
  ---H 344
  Joseph O 330
  ---T 172
  Julia 380

---DuBose 421
Julian 332
Julius P 330
Katie 396
L H 170
Leah 381
Lell 425
Leonard 532
Leverette H 174, 330, 468, 477
Lillie 532
Lindsay 330, 332, 477
Lucy 331
Lula 342
---May 330, 468, 477
Luna 532
Luther 332
Margaret 381-2, 527 531
Marguerite 365
Marjorie 382
Martha 330, 332
Mary 330, 385, 406 477, 541
---, Mrs 176
---Helen 382, 435 460, 531
Matilde 382, 435, 460 531
McRae 406
Melitia 522
Mial 547
Minnie 332
Minor Ruth 382, 531
Miss 327, 415, 453, 484
Mr 538
Nancy 402
Neil 452
Nettie 330
O E 177
O H 170, 175, 330 477
Olin 532
Otis 330, 477
Parker B 531
Perry H 207-08, 340 415, 453, 484, 545
---, Mrs 316
Priscilla Bond 357
Rebekah 209
Rhoda 330, 477

Robert 225, 332
Ruby 330, 477
Ruth 532
Sally 210
Samuel 330, 477
Seigler 330
Shirley 330, 468, 477
Singleton 330
Sulenea M 391
Taylor 330
---B 477
Thelma 359
Theresa 501
Thomas 209, 329, 330
---B 477
---W 330, 477
Tommie 332
Vida 342
Virginia 339, 381-2, 414, 452, 483, 512 527, 531, 543
W C 206
W C R 312
W J 169, 173-4
W O 170
W T 173
Walter P 309
Warren 329
Wells 222
William 331, 342
---Allen 330, 477
---H 367
---Oscar 330, 477
---Thomas 421
Willie 332
Winnie May 541
Wyatt 447
Young 306
---Swift 501
Zachariah 330
SNELLINCKS
Jan 431
SNELLINGS[E]
Alexander 431, 532
Anne 431
Annie Lou 341, 546
Aquilla 431
Cynthia 332
Elizabeth 378, 395
---Neil 430
Erasmus 431
Family 430

Geo 317, 378, 430
---Burton 395
---Thomas 395
Hannah 378
Irene Hearne 395
J E 173
Jane Elizabeth Hearne 395
Joann 431
John 222, 377-8, 431
Martha 378
Mary 378, 431
---Winn 395
Mattie 332
Minnie 332
Miss 405
N W 208
Oscar 332
Priscilla 431
Ralph 431
Rebecca 395
---Elizabeth 395
Rebecka 220
Richard Tho 395
Robert 431
Rose 332
Samuel 222, 378, 430-1
Sara 431
Susan Rebecca 430-1, 435
Thomas 395
Walter 332
William 431
---Garvin 395
---J 395
Willie 395
SNOW
Mertis E 324, 436
SNYDER Dora 476
SONDIDGE
Willie 363, 370, 418 456
SORRELLS
Charles 322, 497
EmmaVirginia 365, 366
John Harvie 366
Mary Iva 366
---Magdaline 365
Theodoric Finley 365

----Jr 365
Walter Barnett 366
---Jr 366
---III 366
SPALDING
James Theodore 177
SPARKS
Elizabeth 398-9
H C 418, 439,
  456 473, 515
---Jr 418, 439, 456
  473, 515
Jane 399
Lavonia 418, 456
Louise 439, 473
Martha 532
SPEAR/SPEER
W J 175
William 178
SPEED
Ella 351
Florence 415, 453,
  485
Joseph 340, 415, 453
  484
Lizzie May 534
Raymond 340, 415,
  453, 484, 533, 534,
  544
Sarah 333, 469, 533
Wade 220
SPENCER
Mildred 398
Nancy 366
SPIERMAN Mr 445
SPIVEY, James 178
John 209
SPRATLIN Mr 535
SPRINGER
Albert 490
Alfred Wooten 494
Betty Jo 489
J D 489, 494
---Jr 489, 494
Joe Clark 494
Joseph C 489
Maxine Dolorice 489
Maxwell 489
William Maxwell 494
STALNAKER

M C 208
Samuel S 208
STAMPS
Elizabeth 328
SANDIFER
Israel 449
STANFORD
Adeliade 339, 360
  368, 416, 454, 544
STANLEY
Hal M 175
STANTON
John 449
Joseph 450
STAPLETON
L L 533
Merian Jane 499
Mrs 315, 316
Raymonde 176, 205,
  304-05, 312, 315,
  499
Vera Caroline 499
STARK
Abram 524
Bascom 524
Brewer 372, 386, 525
E B 173
Edmund Brewer 372,
  385, 525
Harriet 372, 386, 525
J A 304
John A 330, 372, 386
  525
Julia 372, 385, 386
  525
Lula 524
Mary 371-2, 385, 524
  525
---Adeline 372, 386
  525
Nell 372, 386, 525
Oscar 524
Ruth 372, 386
Sally 525
Sam C Jr 385
Samuel 167, 372, 385
  534, 525
---Jr 371, 524
Sarah 371
---Louise 372, 386,

525
---Howell 380, 526
T R 208, 303
Thomas 524
Tho R 372, 386, 525
William 524
---Jr 524
Zelma 535
STARR
Christopher 180
Mary 180
Miss 328
STATHAM
Anna 473
Augustus D 222
STAUNTON
Ann 461
STEADMAN
Frank 423
STEED, Nell 418,
  456
STEELE
Mary Louise 437
Rae 534
STELLING
Bud Clay Wall 338,
  414, 452, 483, 512
  543
Cree 483
Howard Cree 338,
  414, 452, 512, 543
John D 338, 414, 451,
  483, 512, 541,
  543
Martha McIntosh 338,
  414, 452, 483, 512
  543
Richard 338, 483, 543
---Nunnelee 414, 451
  512,
Sterling 338, 414, 483
  512
---McInstosh 451, 543
STEPHENS
Catherine 221, 545
Henry H221
John 361
Katherine 415
STEPHENSON
K A 425

Mr 553
STERLING
  Beatrice T 499
  Charles 499
  George Archibald 499
  Harrison Thornton 499
  Harrison Tilly 499
  ---Jr 499
  John Maxwell 499
  William 509
STEVENS
  Bessie Lee 335, 523
  Chanaler 537
  Cynthia 489
  Linton 310
  M L, Mrs 310
  Marquis Lee 375
  O B 172
  Robert Tate 375
  Walter 459
STEWART
  Bebbett 502
  J S 411
  Jospeh 467
  Lena 467
  Lizzie May 467
  Mary 338, 414, 451 483, 512, 541, 543
  Mr 554
  Wiley V 367
STILL Mr 445
STILWELL
  L 207, 208
  Lilly 303
STINCHCOMB
  Miss 388
STINSON
  Elizabeth 492
STIRKLEY
  Ina Vivian 393
STITCH
  W R 366
ST JOHN John 519
  Katherine 519
ST MARTIN
  Archangle 509
STOCKS
  Elizabeth 444

Isaac 444
John 444
Thomas 444
STODDARD
  Jack 535
STOKES
  Archibald 204
  Catherine 204
STONE, Mr 374
  Nancy 394
  W P Jr 330, 477
STONER, H H 307
STOOK
  Lillian 374, 387
STORY Jack 505
STOVALL
  A S J 490
  Alberta 490
  Amanda 476
  Byron 490
  De'she 476
  Eva Clyde 476
  Francis 490
  Frank 477
  Geo Terrell 476
  John H 476
  ---Terrell 476
  L L 334, 472
  Love 476
  Mollie 476
  Nell 489
  Ouida 476
  Pearce Mathews 490
  Ruth 490
  Sidney 490
  Sylvia 489
  Thomas 476
  ---F 476
  Travis 477
  Vesta 490
STOWERS
  Jeremiah 224
  Lewis Sr 224
STREET
  Edward 471
  Katherine Louise 471
  Tho G 471
  ---Jr 471
STRICKLAND
  C D 538

J L 169, 173-4
Jacob 181
Joseph 225
Mary 424
Mel 169, 174-5
Rachel 175
Sexta Eavenson 427
STRONG
  Elijah 180
STROUD
  Leila 382
STROZIER
  Miss 353
STRUDIVANT
  Elton B 354
  Joel 426
  W J 354
STUBBS
  Elizabeth 384
  Mr 350, 351
STYLES
  J C 313
SUDDETH
  Joseph B 522
  Kenneth 522
  Lamar 522
SUFFOLD
  Ann 444
  ---Coffee 444
  ---Head 444
  Isham 444
  Mary 444
  Seaborn 444
  ---Jones 444
  Thomas Peter 444
SULLIVAN
  Alice 503
  J P 544
  J P 340, 415, 453
  ---Jr 340, 415, 453
  William H 224
SUMMERSON
  Carroll 371, 385, 524
SUTTLES
  Isaac 177
  Lloyd 358
SUTTON
  Aley 211
  B I 305

H B 207
Kate 535
Lula 478
William 211
SWATMAN
J E 479
SWEARENGIN
Allie May 381
---Sue 373, 387
Brewer 386
Dorothy 373, 381, 386
H Brewer 373, 381
J C 206, 373, 386
---Jr 373, 381, 387
James C 381
L H 373, 387
Luther H 381
Petra 500, 532
SWIFT
Bessie Thurmond 528
David Flower 527
Elizabeth 528
Flower 527
I G 206-07
Isaac Glasgow 528
J Y 370, 516
James Y 457
Jim 528
Joe Willie 471
John 180
---Keller 528
Mamie 397, 528
Nancy 528
Pearl 528
Sara 528
Susan Heard, Mrs 310
Thomas 528
Tho M 167, 176
---Madison 528
---Sr 206-07
Thurmond 528
Tom, Mrs 316
Will 528
William 527
---A 528
---Augustin 527
SWILLING
S B 170, 176-7
SWINTON
Sarah 510

T

TABOR
J E 144
Fannie Herndon vi, 140
Mary 504
T O 143
---Jr 152, 160-1, 208 303-05, 389, 485 506
---, Mrs v, vi, 316
--- Sr 133, 144, 170 206
--- III 389, 485, 506
Travis O 312, 313
Zelma Allen viii, 138, 172
TAFT
William Howard 97, 144
TAILER[OR]
Elizabeth 225
Emily Smith 445
John 225
TAIT
Barbara 517
Charles 35, 38-9, 69 74-6, 166
Hudson 179
James 48-50, 73, 170 171, 179
---M 167-8
Zimri 178, 179
TALBOT
Green 393
Phobe 479
TALIAFERRO
Benjamin 210
TALLET, John 69
TALLIFERRO
Benjamin 399
Malinda 373, 386
TALMADGE
Eugene 175
Lucile 376
TALOR
William Jr 225
TAMAR...63

TANDY Martha 475
TATE ...181
Albert 374
---Clark 489
------ Jr 489
---Mathews 489
Alice 375
---Sophia 489
Anne 374
Asbury 133, 361, 369
Babe 133
Belle 374
Betsy 374
Brewer 374, 395
Capt 220
Caroline 449
Carrie 374
Carrie Hudson vi, 309
---Sophia 374, 395, 489
Charity 351
Clark 162, 374, 395
Cora Thomas viii
Corra Jane 489
Corrie Jane 374, 395
Duncan 374, 395
E B 133-5, 143, 170 173, 489
--- Jr 168-9, 206
---, Mrs 133, 311, 316
Edmund B 374
----Jr 374
Edmund Brewer 152, 158, 308-09, 489 547
Elam 220
Elizabeth 220
---P 514
Ella Rebecca 489
Emerson 158
Emma 138
---Louise 489
Emmae 374
Enos 220, 222, 375
Eugene 374, 395
Geo Richard 489
Isaac M 220
J E viii, 6, 147
---, Mrs 300
J M 349, 351
J S 173, 459
J Wright 374

Jacqueline 489
James 39, 374
---M 102
Jane, Mrs 203
Jean Hudson 489
Jefferson Davis 489
Jessey C 220
John 222
Lewis 35
Louisa 362
Mae 162
Mary 374-5
---Brewer 489
Mattie Wright 139
  310
Maurice 374-5, 489
May 310, 361, 369
Miss 393, 394
Nancy 393
Ned 300
O E 309
Ora E 158, 374
---Eugene 395, 489
------ Jr 395, 489
---Jr 374
---, Mrs 158, 309
Pete Martel 489
Philip 374
R F 206
Rebecca 310, 361,
  369
Robert 167, 374-5
---Duncan 489
---L 210
Samuel 374, 395, 449
---Enos 489
Sarah 222
Sophia 489
Tho J 220
Tommie 437
Tustin 374
U O 85, 103, 167
Watkins 449
William 47
---Brewer 489
---H 73
Z A 170
Zimri 361, 369
---A 149
---W 220
TATUM
Jesse 222

Webb 160, 162, 304,
  309, 313
TAVENOR
Elizabeth 487
Michael 487
TAYLOR
A C 155
Boyce 464
Charles P 534
Charlie 133
Clara 435, 460
Edmund 518
Elizabeth 351
Esther 464
Eugene 479
F M 140
Floyd 424
Francis 459
Frank 535
Frank G 153, 535
Frazier Brown 155
Giles 464
Herbert A 537
Howell 534
J R 152
Jesse W 225
Jessie 534
John C 152, 221
  535
John Lee 154
Juniel Conger 464
Manda Ann 53
Marion 141
Martha 53
Mary 434, 464
Maud 534
Mollie 479
N O, Mrs 312
Nathias 221
Rebecca 221
Ruth 464
Spencer 478
Tho Easton 464
Warren 464
William 35, 222
Z B 206
TEASLEY
A J 121
Alfred 405
---J 332, 469
---Jr 405

---Hunt 327
Alice 405
---Lucile 336
Amos L 404
Andrew J 404, 435
Aquilla 470
Arminda 427
B P Jr 521
Benager 326, 436
---Columbus 325, 328
  336
---Jr 325, 336
---P 326
---Pierce 324, 336
  521
-----Jr 336
---S 225, 324
Benjamin Cordell 336
  521
Bessie 404
Bertha 404
---Thomas 435
Beverly 436
Beverly A 224
---Allen 332, 469
C E Jr 306
Carl 302, 404
Catherine 323, 326
  498
Charles 404
Charlotte 521
--- B 336
Clyde 312
Clyde, Mrs 163
---E 325, 336, 521
-----Jr 521
Cora A 327
Delrey 532
Drucilla Ann 470
---Allen 325
---C 325, 336, 469
---Catherine 333
---Elizabeth 326, 337
Earl 469
Early C 156
Edgar 302
---C 336
---Carl 325, 521
---N 336
---William 521
Eliza 324, 326-7,
  337, 377, 405

---E 469
---Emily 333
Elizabeth 322, 377
   495
---Ann 324, 332, 436
   469
Ellen 469
Emily Eliza 436
Erwin Clifton 154
Ethel May 469
Floyd 404
Frances 405
Frank 492
Geo 469
Geo Allen 325
Gerald H 336
--- Haynes 325
Gertrude 404
Gladstone Inman 499
---Jr 499
Hailey I 336
--- Isham 325
Harold 302, 336, 521
Harrison 337
Harvey E 336
--- Eugene 325
Hettie 532
I H H 404
Ida Ione 326
Inez C 326, 337
Isham 223, 324, 470
   492
---Asbury 326
---Hailey 326
---Jefferson 325, 336
J A 173
James 332, 337, 469
---A 326
---H 404
---Riley 333, 370
---William Alfred 326
-----499
Jane 326, 333, 470
   492, 532
Jefferson 337, 470
Jency Adams 326
John 47, 180, 223
---Adams 326
---Alfred 326
---Cone 326
---E 336
---Easton 325 335

   521
------Cone 336
---H H 326
---I 326, 492
---III 263, 469
---W 469
-----Jr 469
---Wiley 403
Joshua 469
Julia 499
Leila Bell 469
Levi 223
Lloyd 404
Lois 404
Lonnie A 326, 337
Louis Scott 469
Lucia 404
Lucy 322, 326, 332
   469, 470
---Ann 325, 336, 469
---E 470
---Ellen 333
---J 326
---H 333, 470
Margarette 323, 337
   503
Martha E 403
Martha M 333, 469
Martin 337
Martin T 156
Mary 162, 326, 405
   490, 492
---Ann Elizabeth 335
---Arminda 536
---C 404
---Drucilla 499
---Elizabeth 469
Mary F A 469
---Frances Adeline
   333
---Hamilton 403
---Jane 324, 326
---Maxwell 496
Mattie 404
May Lillie 140, 404
Melvina Tennessee
   469
Mildred 336, 521
Mindy 337
Minnie 404, 405
Miss 375
Mozelle 337

Mr 376, 434
Olin 492
Oliver 492
Omer Gip 155
Osburn G 326
Oscar Lee 325, 336
   521
Patsy Martha 337
Paul 532
--- Reid 403
Peter 403, 470
Phronie 324, 333,
   334, 337, 436, 469
Priscilla 333, 470, 472
---Jane 332, 469
Ralph 404
Rennie 492
Rinnie 326
Ruth 325, 334, 336
   521
Sallie I 326, 337
Sally A 336
--- E 325
Samantha 404
Sarah 223, 405
---Luella 327
Silas 224
Sumpter Ophelia 403
Sumper 533
Thelma 336, 521
Thomas 405, 470
---J 337
---Jefferson 337
---W 404
Vera 532
W A 162
W E 405
W T 532
Walter Scott 469
William 176, 177
---A 337
---Alfred 325, 326,
   336, 492, 521
---DeWitte 404
---E 325, 336
---Hailey 326, 403
---Isham 326
Wilton 521
Wilton Alfred 336
TELFAIR
Edward 44, 50
TELFORD

Janie 550
TEMPLE
Dorothy 345
John 345
Mary Drew 347
Odell 345
TEMPLETON
John 48
TENNAT, John 349
TERRELL
David 394
Dr 133
J M 172
James 180
---Olin 153
John 434
Joseph 222
Jowel 222
L A M 407
Levisa 225
Martha 53
Millicent 263, 394-5
Nancy Wellborn 476
Robert W 225
Sarah Ann 459
Timothy 222
William 53
TERRY
James H 208
John 53
Joseph 73
Polly 68
Susan 53
Thomas 225
THIGPEN, A M 92
THOMAS
A C 92
A O 127
Blythe 524
Cora 361, 369
Crawford 408
Fannie 342
G C, Mrs 315
Herbert A 524
J C 173
Jesse 170, 173
Jett 517
Joel 35, 46
John 428
Lillian 366

Louisa 346
Margaret 347
---B 347
Mary 380, 400, 444
Ruth 522
Temperance 347
Thomas W 82, 112, 129-31, 310, 360, 369, 379
William 48, 369
THOMASON
Grover G 152
John 53
---Henry 152
William Ira 155
Willis E 152
THOMPSON...349
Alexander 48
Asa 37, 99, 179
D N 144, 160, 535
---, Mrs 162, 304
Dallas M 152
daughters 482
Drury 47
Elbert H 412, 450, 482
Elizabeth 365
Frances 517
Gaines 87-89, 168, 342
Howell 408
Isham 35, 47, 49, 178 210
Jeremiah 59
Jesse 209, 224
John 47, 210
---Farley 210
J William 333
Joseph 408
L B 210
Lewis 210
Mary 210, 352, 517
Mildred 172
Milly 210
Norman 313
Oliver 209
P R 120
Peter 210
Ralph 408
Robert 37-8, 209-10
Sally 210
Sarah 397

Stella 476
Tabby 210
Tom 209
Wells 179, 210
Wiley 70, 82, 87-9 100, 166, 168
William 46, 49, 517
---L 224
---Sr 210
THOMSON
Jonathan 509
THORNLEY
Helen 480
THORNTON
A E 138
Alice 535
Allen 534
Almond 533
Alston 333
Amanda 333, 469 533
Amelia 406
Amos 536
Ann F 406
Anna 532
Annie 333, 469
---Ruth 533
Arcola 532
Arnoldina vi, 537
Asa 534
---Stovall 534
Atticus Granville 499
-----Jr 499
B 8
B C 53
B I, 6, 162, 207-08 535
---Jr 535
---Sr 319
---, Mrs 310
Beatrice Eunice 499
Benjamin 68, 223 326, 530, 534, 536
---C 68
---Callaway 332, 469 532
---E 532
---J 177
---Jr 54, 68, 167, 530
---Sr 68
Bertha 333

Birdie 537
Blackstone 539
Burgess 536
C B 304
C W 153
Calloway 149, 533
Calvin 537
Carmen 406, 539
Caroline 538
Carrie 405, 532, 538
Catherine 538
Charles 537
Clarinda E 490
Clyde Arnold vi
Cone B 532
Connard 537
Cornelia 333, 469, 533
Corra 534
D 59, 60-2, 64
D J 161, 304
---, Mrs 311
Dan 537
--- J 153
Daniel 65, 68, 73, 223 332, 402, 536
Donald 534
Dozier 35, 51-2, 54-5, 59, 62-3, 68, 170, 172, 181, 529, 533 536, 538
---J 537
----Sr 226, 263
Dunstan 333, 469, 533
Earl 389, 485, 506, 550
Edna 533
Edward 406, 538
Elbert 534
Elijah 68
Elizabeth 52, 62, 68, 181, 223, 332, 492 537, 538
---E 532
---L, Mrs 422
Ella 536
Elma 537
Elsey B 223
Elvira 403
Emma 465, 532, 534 537
---Alexander 499

Eppy 323
Eula 537
--- Lee 333
Euphemia 539
Evans 327, 538
Exil 534
Fanny 323. 532
---Ruth 534
Fleming 53, 322, 531
Flossie 534
Floyd 494, 532
Fortson 536
Frances 369, 533
---Calloway 534
---Catherine 499
Frank 537
--- B 532, 534, 536
--- C 406, 537
Fred 534
George 533
---Henry 534
Georgia 536
Grace 407, 534, 535
Grady 532
Greene G 539
---H 539
Gussie 536
H G 305
Harold 141, 175, 537
Harriet Adams 53
Harry Allen 389, 485 506, 550
---G 149, 160-1, 389, 485, 506, 534, 550
Harvey 536
Helen 403
Henry 333, 532, 536
Howard 141, 477, 537
I H 170, 173
Ida 333, 532, 537
Ione 505, 537
Ira 534
Ira A 152
Isham 537
--- H 459
J C 533
J C Jr 150
J E 207
J Early 534
J F 153, 532
J M 307

James 333, 469, 532 533-36, 537
---Benjamin 534
---C 533
---C Jr 149
---Jr 533
Jamie 153, 533
Janie 333, 469, 537
Jeremiah 63, 66, 171 529, 538
Jesse 537
Jessie 333, 469, 533
Jewell 333, 500
Jim 63
Joel 333
John 322, 333, 427 532, 533, 536
---C 469, 533, 535
---F 157
---Granville 499
---Thomas 534
---William 536
Jonathan 64, 538, 539
Joseph 533, 535
---A 533
---B 537
Josephine 535
Josie 536
Kathleen 533
Kelsie 533
L C 534
L J 153
L M 153, 537
Laura Lofton 534
Lee 156
Leila 535
Lester 537
Lila 532
Lizzie 330
Lois 534, 535
Louanna 441
Louise 535
Louisana Hawkins 530
Lucy 533, 539
--- Elizabeth 52
Luna 534
Luther 333, 460 532
M J 134
Mallory 535, 536
Mallory J 135

Mamie 350, 533
Marion 333
---C 533
Marjorie 534, 536
Mark 30, 31, 35, 51
 57, 62, 64, 177, 180
 529
Martha 68, 376, 402
 534, 538
---Ann 324, 538
Mary 63, 180, 352
 406, 531, 534, 536
---Ann 532
---Pope 537
---Sue 535
Mathew 534
Mattie 536
May 536
McAlpin 333, 469
 533
McWhorter 537
McWhorter, Mrs 316
Melvin 333, 532
Molly 179
Mourning 68
Nancy 534
Nannie Belle 534
Nathaniel M 530
Nathleen 406, 537
Nina 533
Norma 406, 537
O J 153
Ollie Benjamin 154
Olivia 535-6
Oscar 537
Prarl 537
Peggy 63
Pelham W 156
---Ward 333
Priscilla 403, 470
 530, 532, 533-4, 538
Priston 533
Rachel 536
Reba 333
Rebecca 333, 469,
 533
Reuben 63, 73, 223,
 406, 422, 529, 530
 538
---Benjamin 326
---Oliver 499
--- Rhoda B 539

Robert C 532
---Dozier 538
Roselle 331, 333
Rowe 532
Rufus R 534
Sally 68
Sanford 539
Sarah 63, 68, 322-3
 426, 469, 533, 534,
 536
---K 414, 452
---Kindred 355, 530
Seal 333
Susan 333, 535
Susie 536
T A 350
T O 135
T T 160, 207-08
Thomas 35, 57-8,
 178-9, 223, 530,
 533, 535, 536, 537
---A 54, 332, 469
 533
---T 143, 537
Timothy 536
Tom 313, 459
W H 304
W T 163
---, Mrs 162
W W 532
Wade 537
--- A 152, 406
Walker 538
Webb 536
Wiley 66
--- T 534
William 127, 135, 333
 406, 470, 532, 536
---D 332, 403
---E 532
Willie 532
--- T 152, 537
THRASHER
Aseneth 553
Haslett 553
James C 553
Susan 553
THRELKELD/
 THRILKILL
Arthur Paul 152
Jesse 152

John W 221
William H 221
Willis 221
THRIFT
Calloway 155
THURMON[D]
Besie 528
Mr 432
TIBBETTS
Rachel 68
TIBBS
Lucy 552
Thomas 68
TIBIS, Thomas 223
TIDWELL
Lena 424
TIGWELL
William 431
TILLER
Elizabeth 536
Mannie 477
Wm C 358
TILLMAN
Adeline 525
Benjamin R 525
---Jr 525
Douschka 525
Ella 476
Henry 525
May 525
Miss 412, 450
Molana 525
Sally May 525
Sarah 525
Sophia 525
TILLY, A A 85
John 92
Lt 115
TILLMAN
Adeline 372, 385
Benjamin R 138, 371
 372, 385
---R Jr 371, 385
Douschka 371, 385
Henry 372, 385
Mary 372, 385
Miss 384, 412, 482
Molana 372, 385
Sally May 372, 385

Sarah 371-2, 385
Sophia 372, 385
TIMBERLAKE
  Mary Eleanor 367
  W P 367
TIMMONS
  Bel 85
TINER
  Cabet 224
  Tolison 224
  William 224
TINMAN
  Tom A 309
TINSLEY
  Addie 338, 380, 413
    451, 483, 511, 527
    543
  Elizabeth 96
  William D 221
TITUS Mrs 464
TOBS, Arthur 74
TODD, Geo 153
  Mary 535
TOLBERT
  Sanuel 74
TOMASON
  Elizabeth 68
TOMPKINS
  Susan 486
TOOMBS
  Robert 115-16, 121,
    417
TOTMAN
  Rebecca 224
TOTTEN
  Craven W 367
TOUGH
  Hugh 359
TOWLES
  Family 401
  Mary 399
  Stokeley 399
TOWNSEND
  James C 135
  Joel 91
  Mildred J 448
TREADWELL
  Emily V 462, 468

TRENCHARD
  John A 172, 176
TRIBBLE
  John 496
  Nora 383
  Robert B 136
  Samuel 149
TRIMBLE
  Moses 178
  Mr 446
TRIPPE
  Albert L 153
  Miss 400
TRUITT
  Richard A 208
TRUMAN
  Mary 433
TUBMAN
  Mrs 97
TUCKER[S]...42
  Bartlett 412, 450, 482
  Capt 223
  Daniel 32, 35, 42, 209
  Elizabeth 53, 412, 450
    482
  Ethreal 35
  Godfrey 23
  John M 87
  Martha 450, 482
  Mary 446
  ---Burch 506
  Samuel 446
  Sarah 412, 450, 482
  Stephen Heard 412,
    450, 482
  Widow 327
TUFTS
  Annie Lou 437
TUN[N]ISON
  J E 156
  Nellie 149
TURMAN
  George 48, 181
  Joseph 73
  Leonard 73
  Mariah 408, 438
  Martin 47
  Mary 221, 263, 429
  Robert 47, 181

---G 220
Thomas 47
TURNBULL
  Joseph 178
TURNELL J H 133
  Jospeh Henry 436
  Vesta Fortson 149,
    436
  ---Mrs 304
TURNER
  A A 155
  Benjamin 361
  Betty 501
  Carrie 498
  Clifford 501
  --- Lee 155
  ---T 208
  Cora 406
  Cornelia 535
  Corrie 498
  D R 35
  E H 138
  Geo S 394
  Grady 359
  Henrietta 356
  Ida 536
  J M 152
  Jim Chandler 501
  John 312
  ---W 501
  Joseph 356, 531
  L H 133, 206, 382
    373, 387
  Lois 522
  Luther 92
  M C 141
  Mary Lucile 501
  Neil 152
  Nora 382
  Robert 498
  Sanford A 208
  Telitia Aggie 326
  Thomas 225
  Willie 498
TURNIPSEED
  Miss 524
TUTT
  Elizabeth Swift vi,
    viii, 162
  W D 134-5, 160, 170
    176-7, 205, 302-04

550
---Mrs 315
---Sr 318
William Duncan 528
TUTTELL
James 210
TUTTLE
James Jr 48
Joseph 74
Nicholass 180
TYLER
Col. 120
TYNER
Joshua 470
Mary 94
Noah 94
Richard 30-1, 35, 49
94
Samuel 30
Tamar 94, 470
TYSON J F 85

U

UNDERWOOD
Ann 223
Eva 417, 455, 514
Hezziah 64
Jane 59
John 63-4
Joseph 35, 49, 225
Joshua 57, 61
Lemuel 66
Polly 434
Sarah 63
William H H 98-9, 176
Wyneford 225
UPSHAW
Haston 54
James 171
John I 493
John Jr 171
Julia Ann 497
L C 476
Lee 497
Leroy 169, 219
Mr 412, 450, 482
Murray L 497
---Jr 497

Rebecca 530
Rody 54
Sarah 530
Willie 134
URQUHART
Henry 462
John A 220

V

VACRAY
Joseph 223
VAIL A L 176
Amos 91
---L 457
Lula 127
VAINYARD
John 46
VALKENBURG
Ethel von 463
VAN ALAN...74
David 52
Peter Lawrence 74-5
176
VAN BRUNT
Raleigh W 464
VAN BUREN
Martin, Mrs 74
VANDIVER
Robert 472
VAN DUZER
I C 173, 176, 206
Ira C 318
W T 176
William Tusten 390-1
VANCE
Louise 367
O J 366
VASS Douglas 444
VAUGHAN
A G 144
A W 135
Albert J 155
Alexander 53
Betsy 389, 504, 506
Budd C 497
Cap 504
Charles B 155
Elizabeth 53

Foggie 504
General 504
Geo 389, 507
Homer 390, 507, 546
J B 156
Jacob 389, 506
James 396, 507
James D 208
---Homer 154
Jessie 390, 507
Jimmie 504
John M 504
Louise 497
Luke 390, 507
Maggie 504
Mamie 504
May 507
McIntosh 504
Milly 54
Mary 390
Nealie 389, 506
Reba 357
Rissie 504
Ronnie 390, 507
Ruth 375
Sarah 503
Sarah F 389, 507
Vaughnie 390, 508
W C 152
W W 174
William 53, 389, 506
Willis 132
VAUGHTERS
Linsey 224
Russell 224

VERDEL
Adeline 143, 369
Ann 369
Catherine 369
Clarence 369
Dunstan 369
John A 369
Martha 369
Mattie 369
Rosa 369
Thomas 369
---H vii, 84, 134, 136
158
VERNER
John E 523

VERNON
  Richard 28-9
  Robert 28
  Sarah 533
VERONEE
  Frank 340, 404, 415
    453, 484, 545
VEST E W 207, 308
VICKERS
  Bernice 424
VICKERY
  Charles 325, 335
  Charles Jr 335
  Chuck 134
  E H 535
  Early 141
  Ella 405
  James 225
  Joseph 404
  Leila 535
  O A 101
  Samantha 494
  Sully Thornton vi
  William 141
  Willie 142
VIEREGEE
  Lana May 520
VINEYARD
  David 35, 74
  James 47
  John 48
VODAN
  Bradock 211

W

WADDELL
  Col 122
WADE Diana 379
WAINWRIGHT
  Helen 338, 414, 452
    512, 543
WAKEFIELD
  Eva 412, 450
WALDROP Mabel
    422
WALKER
  A 123

Alexander 476
Andrew 84
Archelus 180
Archibald 38, 46
Augustus 347
Curtis E 152
David 347
F H 144
Florida 347
George 49
Hannah 52, 65
Henry G 37
Isabella 457
J 48
James 179
---G 35, 39, 84
Jeremiah 30, 35, 39,
  47, 58-9, 171, 211
John William 38
Lewis 493
Lloyd Z 155
M 179
Memorable 38, 181
Mildred 432
Oliver R 144
Phillip 346
Robert 176
Sanders 486
Thomas 35, 432
William 31, 120, 211
---J 152
WALL
  Abbie 353
  Ann 202
  Anna C 434, 541
  Annie 541
  Annie McIntosh vii,
    42, 103
  Arthur 353
  B C 458
  Bevel 541
  Bevel Carles 338, 414
    451, 483
  ---Charles 512, 543
  ---Clay 338, 414, 451
    483, 512, 543
  ---McIntosh 338, 414
  ---William 451
  ---William McIntosh
    483, 512, 543
  Bridget 64
  Bud Cade 540

  --- Clay 41, 102, 222
    338, 413, 483, 512,
    541
  Burgess 68
  Cade 223, 540
  Cassie 141
  Edward 541
  Elizabeth 434, 540,
    541
  Era 357
  Fanny 382, 541
  Florence 541
  George 434
  ---Nunnelee 499
  Harry 338, 435, 452
    512, 541
  ---Amrose 153
  Hillie 353
  J N 131, 133
  James 434, 435, 499,
    541
  ---N 78, 168, 177
    406, 434, 541
  ---Singleton 338, 414,
    451, 483, 512, 543
  Janie 435, 541
  Jessie 512, 541
  Jessie McIntosh 338,
    414, 451, 483, 543
  John 353, 541
  ---Oliver 499
  Joseph 141, 158
  Kenneth 353
  Laura 541
  Leslie 353
  Longstreet 153, 435
    541
  Lonnie 357
  ---Jr 357
  Louisa 136
  ---S 436
  Louise 540
  Lula 435, 541
  Margaret 338, 414,
    451, 483, 512, 543
  Martha 540, 541
  Martha Hicks 203
  ---Louise 338, 451
    483, 512, 543
  Mary 341, 454, 416
    546
  ---Eleanor 435, 499,

541
---Elizabeth 457
---Frances 540
Mattie 541
McAlpin 353
McPherson 338, 413, 451
---McIntosh 512
Paul Walton 152
Sarah 141, 162, 435, 541
Sybyl 357
Thomas 153, 535, 541
Virginia Cleveland viii, 162
Walter 434
William 434, 541
William Clay 338, 413, 451, 483, 412
---D 540
Willis 540

WALLACE
Lewis E 152
Lloyd 152
Tracey 155
W G F 128

WALPOLE
Mollie 365

WALLER Mary 459

WALLIS
Ann 345
Garrett 534
Janie 406
John 346
Lewis 313
Rhody 223
W E 207

WALSEMAN
William 122

WALTERS
Florie 390, 494, 507
John 178

WALTHALL
Edward 35, 48, 178-9
Family 42
Felix 445
Gerrard 35, 176
James 48
Joseph 445
Louisa 445

Nancy 71, 179, 330
Singleton 71
Thomas 445
Turman 445
---Jr 445

WALTHAM
Edward 542
Gerrard 542
---Jr 542
John 542
Nancy 542
Richard 542
William 542

WALTON
George 47, 48
John 178
Josiah 48
Julia 380
Nancy 178
Newel 181
W H H 441
William 211

WANSLEY
Andrew 331
Augusta 453
---Jr 453
Augustus 332, 404, 404, 415, 484, 545
---Jr 332, 404, 415, 484, 545
Belle 331
Colley 332
Collie 208
D C 332
Fred 158
---C 208
---Cole 153
Gaines 136
Hattie 142
Ida Ruth 332
India F 405
Jack 332
---Jr 332
Jane Ann 326, 403
John 226
Paul R 153
Pierce Ashby 154
Reuben 226
T Q 152
Thelma 332
T Quinn 332

Walter S 153
Wiley 403
William 208, 332
William H 156

WANSLOW
Elizabeth 65
Milly 66
Nathan 407
Patsy 65

WARD
Albert Marion 153
C P 142, 328
Charles P 403
Cullen 329
E H 174
E J 175
Emma 407
G M 173
George 181
---H 208
---Henry 155
---M 173-4
Grover Ben 152
H B 176
Ike Swift 155
Isaac 532
Lins 434
R E 142
Robert 328, 403
---Martin 155
---P 143
Sarah 333, 433
Susan 532
Thomas Marion 156
William 35, 64

WARE
Edward 73
Roland 178
William 74

WARLICK
Frances Rice vi

WARREN
Annie 374, 387
---Brewer, Mrs 311
Augustus 340
---Jr 340
Charles A 153
Cora 142
Coy C 208
---Tinsley 153
D H 173

Dixon 406
Elizabeth 68
Ella 536
Ethlyn 500
Hilda 340, 404, 415
   453, 484, 545
J J 148
J M 374, 387
Jeremiah 539, 545
---- S 172
Jesse 340, 404, 415,
   453, 484, 545
---Jeremiah 340, 404,
   415, 453, 484
John 176
---M 68
Josie Earl 373
Lindsey C 449
Mark 376
Mary 374, 387, 462
Miss 323, 373, 382
   387
Mrs 464
Stokely 500, 532
T J 68
William H 68
Winona 500

WARWICK
Wiley 91

WASHBURN
Annie 64
B S 464
Bailey 464
Benjamin 464
Edwin 464
Emma 464
Henry 464
Katie 464
Mary 464
---Ethel 464

WASHINGTON
Elizabeth 464
George 6, 13
John 481
Martha 412, 481
Richard 481

WATERS
Boldin 467
David Daniel 467
Elizabeth 538
Emma Vernon 467

Georgia Virginia 467
Janie 467
Joseph 496
Julia 532
Mac Willis 467
Mary Frances 467
Mattie Lizzie 467
Nina 467
Patrick 467
Ruth Lee 467
Sarah Hudson 467

WATKINS
Garland T 38
George 181
Harry M 40
Henry M 220
Jane 204
John 40, 101, 204
---D 8, 35
J W G 85
Robert 38
---H 38, 168
Samuel 38, 209
Sarah 362
W T 85, 152

WATSON
Daisy 355
Lucile Turner vi
Sue 141
Thomas 224
---E 158, 303

WATT Mack 152

WATTS
Atherine 444
Ellen 444
Frances 396
George 48, 49, 180
Hastings 396
Katie 396
Joseph 444
Mack 396
Mary L 396
Minnie Lee 396
Mr 444
Opal 396
Ruby 396
Walton 396

WAY Hilda 397

WAYABLE
Bevelle 340, 363, 415
   418, 453. 456, 515

Thomas 340, 363, 370
   415, 418, 453, 456
   484, 515, 545
---Jr 545

WAYNE
Henry C 111, 113

WEAVER
G A Jr 393
Margaret 548

WEBB, A J 121
Abner 54, 221, 420
   546
Alexander 176
Alice 396
---Ann Martha 546
Andrew J 148
Ann Mildred 546
Austin 47
Bessie 460
Bridger 546
Charles 73
Clairborne 70, 263
   420, 546
---Jr 420, 546
Clemmie 358
Edward C 547
Elijah W 547
Evelina 547
Fortunatus 54
Geo W Jr 156
Grover C 156
Hoyt 156
J E , Mrs 311
J R O 152
Jep E 396
Jewette 547
--- Hester 302
John 93, 177, 546
---B 3
---H 152
Johnson 547
Johnson, Mrs 316
Julia viii, 314, 547
Lester Austin 155
Letty 54
Lina 53
Lincoln Morrison 156
Lucretia 362
M 121
M D 135
Mart 133

Margaret 546
Martha Ann 357
---P 420
Mary Pope 546
Milton Pope 420, 546, 547
Mr 382, 541
Mrs 541
Norma 547
Ola Jackson vi
Ora Belle 547
Patsy 546
Pauline 547
Perlina 54
Pleasant 546
Prudence 53
Richard 35
Robert 476
Rosa Mary 382
Rosemary 541
Roy 154
Thomas 35
William 31, 546
---P 156
WEBER
  Frances 417, 455
WEBSTER
  Mary Ann 445
  Mr 445
WEERSING
  Mark C 313
WEIBEN
  John 307
WELBORN/
  WELLBORN
  Abner 447
  C B 522
  Joseph 152
WELLS
  David 179
  Ezekiel 178
  George 24
  Jessie Lee 155
  Jim 153
  Mary 399, 517
  Thomas 399
WELSH
  Lucy Simpson 400
  Nathaniel 400
  Simpson 400

WESLEY Mr 69
WEST J C 54, 162
  Miss 403, 473
  Sebastine Ray 463
  ------- 463
WESTBROOK
  John 47
WESTER
  J M 139, 145, 147, 207, 436
  Jacquelyn 436
  Jim, Mrs 14, 315
  John Lee Jr 436
  John Winder 152
  Susan 436
  ---Fortson viii
  Thomas Fortson 436
  ---Jr 436
WESTMORELAD
  A F 168-9, 175-6, 329
WESTON Job 168
WHALEY
  Dr 511
  Elizabeth 446
  George C 446
  Mary 446
  Sarah 446
  Seaborn 446
  Tabitha 446
  William 181
  Wilson 446
  ---O B 446
WHARTON
  Sarah 399
  Thomas 399
WHEELER
  Pamima 68
  Rachel 520
  Sarah 61
WHEELIS
  D M 135
  Grady W 153
  Hugh F 153
  Reuben D 153
WHIDBY Mr 446
WHIPPLE
  Anne E 68
  Irene 325
WHITAKER

Bessie 448
C B, Mrs 152
WHITE A C 144
Aaron Thornley 480
Albert 489
Alice 361
Amy 65
Anne 480
Annabel 516
Annie 334
Bertha 366
Betty 359
Brother 58-9
C C 35, 54
Carlotta 537
Caroline Green 500
Catherine Louise 480
Charles W 480
Chiles Terrell 398
Christopher Clark 397
Cora 488
Daniel 49, 74
David 223
---S 167, 397
Edmund Pendleton 480
Elizabeth 68
Emma P 480, 463
Eppy 87
Fanny 361
----L 407
Fay 452
Fay Ann 339, 357, 414, 484, 513, 531, 544
Geo A 480
Geo Lee 163
Hannah 57-8
Henry 68, 69, 171
Hope 489
Hubert 208
James 366
---Jr 366
Jeremiah 401
Jesse 73, 181, 224, 480
---Key 480
Jessie Anne 480
Joe 64
John 30, 39, 52, 58, 60-65, 180, 209, 397, 480, 473

---H 68, 221
---W 224, 480
---Wesley 480
Jonas H 68
Katherine 480
Lollie 141
Luke 74
Mary 57-8, 68, 397
---Frances 405, 441-2
Mildred Terrell 397
Milly 52, 263, 401
Oliver 35, 39
Patson 65
Rachel 68
Rev, Mr 35
Reuben 58, 60-2, 64-66, 209, 222
Robert 302
Sam 65
Sarah 397, 494
Shelton 171, 397-8
Steven 141
T R 121
Tabitha 224
Thomas 35, 57, 63-5, 221, 397-8
Tinsley 148
---Rucker 488
William 98, 398
---B 103, 168, 360 368
---F 480
---Penn 355
---Sr 224

WHITEHEAD
Fletcher 357
Herbert 537
Sarah E 448
Walter E 309, 312-3

WHITEHOUSE
Elizabeth 472

WHITEMAN
William 222

WHITESIDE
C C Sr 157
Charles C 152
Jim 133-4
---, Mrs 134
Jonathan 407
Robert 407

WHITMAN

Clifton Gary 155
Verman 155

WHITMEL
Winifred 349

WHITMIRE
Annie Bevelle 339, 360, 368, 416, 454 544
Charles 339, 360 368, 416, 454, 544
---Jr 339, 360 368, 416, 454, 544
---, Mrs 139
Harriet 339, 360, 368, 416, 454, 544
Martha 340, 360 368, 416, 455
William B 155

WHITNEY
Bridget 180
Eli 39
John M 180

WHITT
Mary 223

WHITTEN
Billie Fern 521
Grace 521
Jack 521
L S 521

WICH
Peter 64-5

WICKLIFFE
Alice 521
Joe 336, 521
Josephine 521
Thomas R 152
Winell 521

WIGGS
H L 305
Herbert L 6, 312

WIGGINS
L G R 91
Mr 355

WILCOX
A M 146
Betty 346
C R 152
Delilah 457
Edward 350
George 177

---W 128
H H 152
Henry 350
Herbert, Mrs 138
---H 304
James C 350
John 350
Littleberry 347
Marion 129
Mary 347
Moses 74
Phillip 350
William 200, 350
---, Mrs 311, 312
---M, Mrs 138

WILDRED
Joseph Dred 46
W M 146

WILHITE ...76
Abram 548
Adams 547-8
Agnes 547
Alice 355
Allen 548
Ambrose 548-9
Ann 547-8
Anna 355
Bathsheba 548
Catherine 547-8
Christian 548
Conrad 547
Daniel 548
Dicey 548
Dorothy 355
Edwin 355
Elizabeth 547-8
---- McClain 353
Eva 547-8
Evans 548
Floyd 355
Frances 547-8
Gabriel 547-9
George 548
Gordon 355
Hannah 548
James 132, 355 547
Jane 548
Janna 355
Jesse 547
Joe Tom 355
John 547-9

---Jr 548
John L 173, 355, 530
Jospeh Y 87
Judah 548
Judith 548
Larkin 548
Lewis 548-9
Lucy 548
Lyndon 355
Margaret 548
Martha 548
Mason 548
Mary 547-9
Mathias 548
Matthais 547-8
Mattie 355
May 355
Meshal 548
Michael 547-8
Middle 353
Mildred 547
Minnie 355
Moses 548
Nancy 548
Nathaniel 548
Nelly 548
Nicholas 548
P R 207
Philemon 548
Phillip 547-9
Phillip A 172, 420
---Jr 548
Pressley 548
Rachel 548
Rhoda 548
Sally 548
Samuel 548
Sarah 547
Sarah Rebecca 419
Shirley 548
Simeon 548
Spicer 547
Susan 548
Terry 54
Thomas 548
Tobias 547-8
Victor 355
W E 549
William 548
Young 548-9
Zachariah 548

WILKES
John 49, 73
Margaret 448

WILKINS
Ann T, Mrs 445
John 49, 73, 222
Marie 466
Sarah A 465
Thomas 48, 73

WILKINSON
Annie 419
Caroline 447
E B 418
Florida 419
J J 145
Joseph 418
Judith 447
Mary Caroline 447
Miss 537
Mr 418
'Silver Fist' 447
Thomas 362

WILL Charles 561

WILLEN, William 48

WILLET
Hugh, Mrs 144

WILLEY
Augustus W 366

WILLIAM, D C 335
Frances M 400
Patrick 491

WILLIAMS
A W 85
Catherine 466
Charity 351
Clyde 366
Col. 345
Delila 48
Ed C 143
Edith 356, 552
Elizabeth 58, 60, 178, 348, 351
Ferd 318
Ferdinand 455
Frances E 221
Geo 413, 450, 482
H W 93, 133, 138
---, Mrs 315
Hoyt 355
Katherine 365

J E Jr 456
J W 472
Jane 393
Janie 413, 450, 482
John 210, 221, 351, 463
---C 448
---Jr 463
---Thompson 326, 337
Joseph 30, 74, 210-11, 481
---J 352
Lewis 351
Marie 456, 418, 440, 474
Mary 352
---Ella 448
Matthews J 39, 209, 220
Melissa Ann 492
Mr 383
Rebecca 482
---Allen 450
Robert 481
Roger 353
S H 206
Sally 329
Samuel 351-2
Sarah 352
Schevenel 318
Ware B 448
Wiley 172
William 351, 413, 450
---McIntosh 413, 450, 482

WILLIAMSON
Adrian 463
---Jr 463
Betsy 369
---C 514
Catherine Ann 463
Elizabeth 412, 450, 482
Mr 369
Sarah Chandler 369
Susan 535
Walker 225
William 359

WILLIE
Albert D 490
Winifred 490

WILLIFORD
Robert 390, 494, 507
--- Jr 390, 507
Samuel W 508
William 390, 494, 507

WILLINGHAM
Miss 134

WILLIS
Albert 550
Ben H viii
Carswell 465
Charles 550
David C 68
E Paul 156
Elizabeth 550
Ernest 550
Ethel 138, 550
Euphan 346
F K 539
Georgia 302
James 502
---A 549
--- Carswell 153
--- M 172
---Milton 156
---Willis 502
John 63, 65-6, 169, 429, 549
---T 549
Julia 534, 550
Lidia 447
Lizzie 139
Lucy 141, 550
---Ellen 549
Madison 550
Mamie 550
Mary 462
---Mildred 466, 549
Matt 133
Mildred 549
Milley 53
Minnie 550
Onie H 152
R M 168-9
Rachel 93
Richard 550
---M 549
---Madison 540
Robert 385

Rosa 550
Sarah Elizabeth 549
T B F 173
Thomas 465
---F 167, 172, 437, 465, 549
Wiley S 208
William 465
---J 549
Willie 550

WILLSON
Julian C 528

WILMER Mr 466

WILMOT, Tho 177

WILSON
Bessie Hall 528
Gregg 460
John 171, 175
---S 98
Joseph 180
Julia 531
Kate 365
Lemuel 351
Littleberry 180-1
Mary Bell 354
Milford Lonnie 155
Nellie, Mrs 141
Robert Cade 478
S L 128
Samuel C 156
Sarah 53, 97
Spurgeon 358
Whitfield 180-1
Woodrow, Pres 150

WILTON Edith 530

WIMBISH
Farris 388
James 388
Mr 388
Samuel 178

WINANS
Charles A 417, 455

WINFREY
Mary Ann 516-17
R R 447
Vzlentine 516

WINGFIELD
John 30, 73, 473

WINGO, J S 305
Joe 313, 314

WINN, Ann 428
Benjamin 428
D J 170
Elizabeth 425
Elmira 505
Guy Earl 155
Hoyle 532
John 425
P B 142
Rachel 263, 429

WINSLOW
Benjamin 428

WINSTON Jos 481

WINTER L P 85

WISE
Dorothy 514
Dorothy Heard 417, 455
Henry 313
Smith 514
--- H 417, 455

WITCHER
Pelly 459

WITHERSPOON
Frances 324
Mary 324, 539
Miss 324, 539

WITTOCK
Miss 473

WODLEY
John 221
Temporine 221

WOFFORD
Minnie Belle 489

WOLDRIDGE
Mrs 65
Thomas 60, 66
William 48

WOLFE Luella 448

WOMACK
A H 372, 385, 525
---Jr 386, 525
Edmund 385, 525
Lyons 385, 525
Maud 385, 525

WOOD[S]
Charlie M 155
Charlotte 448
Dorothy Pearl 448

Evelyn 499
George 516
Guy E viii, 448
Hugh 516
Iantha 404
James 35, 91, 167
Joanna 448
John 516
Josiah 516
Mary 360
May 339, 368, 416
454, 544
Middleton 35, 74
516
Preston B 448
Robert 516
Samuel 73
Thomas 35
William W 516
WOODALL
Charity 64
Fanny 64
John 30
Mary 65
WOODRUFF
Miss 426
WOOD[S]
Albert 347
Corinna 347
James 169, 171
M 179-80
M L 347
Martha 180, 347
Mary 478
Middleton 168, 176-7,
180
William 168-9, 171
WOODSON
Benjamin 446
Charles 493
Frances 447
John 446
Mary 446
Mary Perrin 446-7
Sarah 446
WOOLFOLK
Mrs 349
WOOLRIDGE
Edward 180, 551, 552
Elizabeth 552
Flourney 552

Gibson 551
John 551, 552
Lucy 552
Martha 551
Mary Ann 552
Richard 551
Sally 181
Sarah 181, 551, 552
Thomas 223, 551
---F 552
William 551, 552
WOOLY
Gertrude 478
WOOTEN
Benjamin 449
Ellen 375
Thomas 178
W L 92
Willis 449
WOOTTEN
Eliza Julia 490
Sophia Frances 488
WORD
Sarah 226
William Sr 263
WORLEY
Addie Harper, Mrs
viii
Ambrose G 552, 554
Ansel 553
Arnold 136, 356, 530
552
Buster 553
Carter 356, 531, 553
---Jr 356, 553
Christine 553
Claud 553
Dunnie 553
Elbert 553
Elizabeth 351, 531,
553-4
---Baker 552
Gaines 553
George 553, 554
---Jr 553
Gladys 553
Herman 553
J Ambrose 553
J N 206
John 553
Joseph N 146, 176,

356, 530, 552, 554
Kate 553-4
Laura 553
Lonnie 553
Maria 554
Mary 553-4
May 553
Mura 553
Nathan 552, 554
---Jr 552
---Sr 552
Nellie 356, 552
Samuel G 553, 554
---Jr 553
Susan Maria 553, 554
William 176, 554
---L 553, 554
WORRELL
Jessie 387
Josie 373, 382
Richard 439
WRAY
Ellen 382, 531
Louise 535
Phillip 210
W A 93
WRIGHT
Augustus R 119
Charles 221
Elizabeth 347
Esther 346
Frank 370, 418
456, 516
Gabriel 224
Ina 503
Isaac 225
J W 396, 425, 479
James 2, 10, 13
Janie Tate 140
Joseph 536
Lola 497
Mattie 374
Mary E, Mrs 312
---Elizabeth 479
---Lizzie vi, viii, 140
162, 311-12, 396
425
Nancy 360, 369
R O 308
Rebecca 486
Robert 308

---F 133, 152
---Jr 158
Sarah 457
--- Anne 311-12, 396, 425, 479
Thelma 140
Warren 221
William Thomas 360

WURSING
  Mark 128

WYCHE
  Abigail 397
  Albert 554
  Alvin 554
  Baker 554
  Benjamin 554
  Christopher 554
  Columbus 554
  David 554
  Edward 554
  ---Jr 554
  Family 129
  George 31, 35, 73, 186, 397, 554
  ---A 144
  ---Jr 554
  ---III 554
  Harry 554
  Harry E 208
  Henry 554
  Homer 554
  J M 176
  James 554
  John 554
  Joshua 554
  Joshua C 221
  Lula 397
  Madison 554
  Mary 397
  P M 35
  Peter 73, 181, 397, 554
  Sarah 331
  William 554

WYNN, John 419
  Mary 419
  Rachel 428-9
  Samuel 419
  ---Jr 419

Y

YAEGER Mr 548
YANCEY, Gilly 351
YARBOROUGH
  C O 307
  Frances 535
  Jane 495
  John 361
  ---F 92
YATES
  Adlai Robin 342, 344
  Boyce Odell 342
  Della Pearl 342
  Durand Bryan 342
  Ennis Emmet 342
  Frances 357
  Frank Ivans 342
  Lydia Grace 342
  ---Jane 342
  Robin Pinkney 342
  Sallie Ellen 342
YEARGIN
  John Benjamin 154
  ---Thomas 156
  Sarah 347
  Thomas H 153
YEARY Walter 475
YET, Brother 63
YOES, Katherine 225
YOLES, Mary 433
YOLM Mary 489
YON
  Addie Belle 359
YONG, Tong 152
YOST Margaret E 521
YOUNG
  Anna Rucker 500
  E C 162
  Edward 362
  Elizabeth 528
  Emmate 353
  F M 162
  ---Mr 394
  ---, Mrs 162
  Fred 500, 532
  Pierce 353
  Ruth 539
  Thelma Jo 500
  Willie P 155
YOW, Miss 323
YOWELL Mr 548

Z

ZACHERY
  Franky 459
  Lula 529
ZEIGLER
  Howell 338, 380, 413, 451, 482, 483, 511, 526, 543
  S J 338, 380, 413, 451, 482, 511, 526, 543
  Samuel 338, 380, 413, 451, 482, 511, 526, 543
ZOUNGER
  Virginia Betty 485

www.ingramcontent.com/pod-product-compliance
Lightning Source LLC
Chambersburg PA
CBHW020630300426
44112CB00007B/69